# The history of the world; a survey of a man's record

## Hans F. 1865-1929 Helmolt, James Bryce Bryce Viscount, 1838-

ned

# HISTORY OF THE WORLD

# THE
# HISTORY OF THE WORLD

## A SURVEY OF MAN'S RECORD

EDITED BY

## DR. H. F. HELMOLT

WITH AN INTRODUCTORY ESSAY BY THE
### Right Hon. JAMES BRYCE, D.C.L., LL.D., F.R.S.

*COMPLETE IN EIGHT VOLUMES*

VOLUME I

PRE-HISTORY — AMERICA AND THE PACIFIC OCEAN

*WITH PLATES AND MAPS*

## NEW YORK
### DODD, MEAD AND COMPANY
1902

University Press · John Wilson
and Son · Cambridge, U. S. A.

# PREFACE

WHEN, in 1894, the undersigned editor received from the Bibliographical Institute the commission to prepare an outline of the "History of the World," there was no longer room for doubt as to the spirit in which the problem must be solved if the undertaking were to be properly adapted to the encyclopædic form of publication. Familiarity with the anthropogeographical views enunciated by Friedrich Ratzel in the introduction to his "Völkerkunde" gave the editor reason to believe that an arrangement of the new "History of the World" differing from all previous works of the kind — one which would form a compilation of the *history of the whole human race* on the earth — was not simply permissible, but greatly needed. It followed as a matter of course that the assured results of palæontological research and also the development of so-called savage into half-civilised peoples must be examined. After mature consideration and conscientious examination of all other possible methods, that of *grouping from an ethnographical standpoint* was selected as the principle of arrangement least open to objection.

Ethnographical division having been decided upon, it was now necessary to find the right point at which to begin. On practical grounds we decided on America; and scientific considerations supported the choice. Ratzel says, in his introduction to the section on the races of Oceania ("Völkerkunde," 2d ed., Vol. I. p. 136): "However much we compare individual characteristics of peoples in similar stages of civilisation we find the inhabitants of America resemble most those who dwell westward from them. When we look at a map on Mercator's projection, showing the earth and its peoples, we find that the Americans occupy a position on the eastern wing, opposite to and most distant from those whose habitation is on the eastern edge of the dividing abyss of the Atlantic Ocean. As the eastern part of the Pacific-American territory of the Rocky Mountains, America is also the east of the inhabited earth." A new meaning is thereby given to the old proverb, *Ex oriente lux.* In order, however, to avoid being misunderstood, we consider it advantageous to specially emphasise the fact that we differ from the view that, on the ground of palæontological discoveries, the new world must be regarded as the home of the human race, because the traces of man in America extend back to a period much more remote than that of Egyptian civilisation. And, however instructive the study of American conditions may be, for the reason that in many respects they precede European developments, yet such considerations have for us their limitations. Practical knowledge is our guide, not an uncertain theory as to the origin of man. The following is the plan of the work:

Vol. I. Universal History. Early History. America. The Pacific Ocean.

" II. Oceania. Eastern Asia. The Indian Ocean.

" III. Western Asia. Africa.

" IV. The Mediterranean Nations.

Vol. V. Southeastern Europe. The Slavs.

" VI. Germans and Romans.

" VII. Western Europe until 1800.

" VIII. Western Europe in the Nineteenth Century. The Atlantic Ocean.

For the first time in a "History of the World" will the historical significance of the oceans that link and separate nations be fully dealt with.

In the first part of the introductory section the editor has sought 'to show that the application of a standard of relative values to all civilisations is arbitrary, and that the development of a tendency is unscientific. Teleology is the domain of the philosopher of history, not of the historian, or, in other words: not until a complete "History of the World" lies before one — and on that foundation — will it be necessary to form a new opinion of the march of events. Science was restrictive in the first place for this reason, and was supported later on purely practical grounds: it would have been regarded as impossible to unite thirty collaborators of mature experience and independent views on one subjective world-system. Just because, however, no space was accorded in the "History of the World" to teleological ideas and achievements, the relations of the editor with his collaborators became particularly lasting, in many respects pleasant, and even friendly and elevating. One of the most faithful, Edward Reichsgraf von Wilczek, was, on October 17, 1897, to our great sorrow, called away from the midst of his labours on the "History of the World," after having with great pleasure partially prepared two sections; the subjects were completed by Dr. Karl Weule. Our collaborators have experienced no pressure with respect to their comprehension of the march of events, and, on the other hand, not one has misused his personal freedom of thought to give to his own subjective view of the world the stamp of universal currency. It was also necessary, in the development of the different sections, to grant a certain freedom to all co-workers, if we wished to avoid sacrificing many-sided manhood to a mistaken idea of unity. It would be a monstrosity to set forth for all peoples a single system according to which all forms of civilisation had developed; it is absolutely impossible to dispose of the history of the Oceanians in this way, of that of the Romans also. But to bring to a victorious issue, within these wide limits, the fundamental idea of the whole undertaking, and not simply in externalities, — that was the task to which the editor has devoted most of his energies. Therefore we hope that when the work is completed the reader will say: It is a perfect whole.

In the illustration of the work we have abstained from inserting drawings in the text: for this purpose supplements (maps, and colored and black cuts) have been selected and executed with the greatest care. It is well known that even scientific works of the severest character are embellished by a moderate amount of artistic illustration consonant with the text, and accompanied by detailed explanatory matter that is intelligible to all. Imaginative compositions are excluded; we have confined ourselves to the reproduction of authentic portraits and views, contemporary prints and monuments. We are therefore convinced that the accompanying illustrations can only redound to the honour of the work.

In closing, we have to perform the pleasing duty of expressing our warmest thanks to the archives, libraries, and other collections which have placed their valuable treasures at our disposal, often for weeks and months, with a willingness too great for adequate acknowledgment, — as also to numerous friends whose names we must withhold. If our undertaking should prove, as we hope it may do, a pleasure and a gain of lasting effect to a greater reading public, no small share of thanks will be due to them. For the volume before us, Vol. I., our thanks are especially due to the administrations of the K. Öff. Bibliothek, the K. Kupfer-stichkabinett, and the K. Anthropologisch-ethnographisch Museum at Dresden, the Universitäts-Bibliothek and the Museum für Völkerkunde at Leipzig, the Bureau of Rolls, and Library in the Department of State at Washington, and the K. u. K. Hofbibliothek at Vienna.

THE EDITOR.

Leipzig, March, 1899.

# PREFATORY NOTE

THE publishers of Dr. Helmolt's "History of the World" for some years contemplated an undertaking on similar lines. The enormous accession of material since the history of the world was last written, the sudden contraction of the world, by which each part is practically in momentary touch with every other part, appeared to be facts which called for a new presentation of the world's history on lines different from those previously followed. The appearance of Dr. Helmolt's history, however, forestalled this intention, and the recognised excellence of that undertaking appeared to render an entirely independent work on the subject superfluous. It was therefore arranged to bring out an English and American adaptation of Dr. Helmolt's work, using the advice of experts in the rejection here and there of sections which did not seem quite adequate from the point of view of its new circle of readers.

They have been fortunate to find in Dr. Bryce an enthusiastic admirer of the monumental work which modern research and scholarship have created, and they feel confident that Mr. Bryce's eloquent exposition of the plan of the present work, and the whole philosophy of the world's history, will not merely be read for its own interest, but will win many readers and students for the work itself.

The work is offered as a companion to every encyclopædia, and still more as a picture of the development of mankind in the light of modern discovery, modern research, — modern study of evolution. The writers have been inspired by the one desire to find the truth and to present it as fully and freely as the natural limitations and prejudices, which even the most open-minded are heir to, permit. It is to be especially observed that this is not a political history of the world, such as has often been written, but rather a survey of Man's record, or a History of the Human Race.

This great work is published simultaneously in Germany, England, and the United States.

# CONTENTS

# ILLUSTRATIONS

## COLOURED PLATES

## WOOD ENGRAVINGS AND ETCHINGS

## COLOURED MAPS

# INTRODUCTORY ESSAY

BY

THE RIGHT HON. JAMES BRYCE, D.C.L., LL.D., F.R.S.

# INTRODUCTION

W HEN History, properly so called, has emerged from those tales of the feats of kings and heroes and those brief entries in the roll of a temple or a monastery in which we find the earliest records of the past, the idea of composing a narrative which shall not be confined to the fortunes of one nation soon presents itself. Herodotus — the first true historian, and a historian in his own line never yet surpassed — took for his subject the strife between Greeks and Barbarians which culminated in the Great Persian War of B.C. 480, .and worked into his book all he could ascertain regarding most of the great peoples of the world, — Babylonians and Egyptians, Persians and Scythians, as well as Greeks. Since his time many have essayed to write a Universal History ; and as knowledge grew, so the compass of these treatises increased till the outlying nations of the East were added to those of the Mediterranean and West European world which had formerly filled the whole canvas. None of these books, however, covered the field, or presented an adequate view of the annals of mankind as a whole. It was indeed impossible to do this, because the data were insufficient. Till some way down in the nineteenth century, that part of ancient history which was preserved in written documents could be based only upon the literature of Israel, upon such notices regarding Egypt, Assyria, Babylon, and Iran as had been preserved by Greek or Roman writers, and upon those writers themselves. It was only for some of the Greek cities, for the kingdoms of Alexander and his successors, and for the city and Empire of Rome, that fairly abundant materials were then available. Of the world outside Europe and Western Asia, whether ancient or modern, scarcely anything was known, scarcely anything even of the earlier annals of comparatively civilised peoples, such as those of India, China, and Japan, and still less of the rudimentary civilisations of Mexico and Peru. Nor indeed had most of the students who occupied themselves with the subject perceived how important a part in the general progress of mankind the more backward races have played, or how essential to a true History of the World is an account of the semi-civilised and even of the barbarous peoples. Thus it was not possible, until quite recent times, that the great enterprise of preparing such a history should be attempted on a plan or with materials suitable to its magnitude.

The last seventy or eighty years have seen a vast increase in our materials, with a corresponding widening of the conception of what a History of the World should be. Accordingly the time for trying to produce one upon a new plan and enlarged scale seems to have arrived ; not indeed that the years to come will not continue to add to the historian's resources, but that those resources have recently become so much ampler than they have ever been before that the moment may be deemed auspicious for a new departure.

The century which has just ended has been marked by three changes of the utmost consequence for the writing of history :

*First.* That century has enormously widened our knowledge of the times hitherto called prehistoric. The discovery of methods for deciphering the inscriptions found in Egypt and Western Asia, the excavations in Assyria and Egypt, in Continental Greece and in Crete, and to a lesser extent in North Africa also, in the course of which many inscriptions have been collected and fragments of ancient art examined, have given us a mass of knowledge regarding the nations who dwelt in these countries larger and more exact than was possessed by the writers of classical antiquity who lived comparatively near to those remote times. We possess materials for the study not only of the political history but of the ethnology, the languages, and the culture of the nations which were first civilised, incomparably better than were those at the disposal of the contemporaries of Vico or Gibbon or Herder. Similar results have followed as regards the Far East, from the opening up of Sanskrit literature, and of the records of China and Japan. To a lesser degree, the same thing has happened as regards the semi-civilised peoples of tropical America, both north and south of the Isthmus of Panama. And while long periods of time have thus been brought within the range of history, we have also learnt much more about the times that may still be called prehistoric. The investigations carried on in mounds and caves and tombs and lake-dwellings, the collection of early stone and bronze implements, and of human skulls and bones found along with those of other animals, have thrown a great deal of new light upon primitive man, his way of life and his migrations from one region to another. As history proper has been carried back many centuries beyond its former limit, so has our knowledge of prehistoric times been extended centuries above the furthest point to which history can now reach back. And this applies not only to the countries previously little explored, but to such well-known districts as Western Europe and the Atlantic coast of America.

*Secondly.* There has been during the nineteenth century a notable improvement in the critical method of handling historical materials. Much more pains have been taken to examine all available documents and records, to obtain a perfect text of each by a comparison of manuscripts or of early printed copies, and to study each by the aid of other contemporary matter. It is true that, with the exception of Egyptian papyri and some manuscripts unearthed in Oriental monasteries (besides those Indian, Chinese, and other Early Eastern sacred books to which I have already referred), not very much that is absolutely new has been brought to light. It is also true that a few of the most capable students in earlier days, in the ancient world as well as since the Renaissance, have fully seen the value of original authorities and have applied to them thoroughly critical methods. This is not a discovery of our own times. Still, it may be claimed that there was never before so great a zeal for collecting and investigating all possible kinds of original texts, nor so widely diffused a knowledge of the methods to be applied in turning them to account for the purposes of history. Both in Europe and in America an unprecedentedly large number of competent men have been employed upon researches of this kind, and the result of their labours on special topics has been to provide the writer who seeks to present a general view of history with materials not only larger but far fitter for his use than his predecessors ever enjoyed. Then with the improvement in critical apparatus, there has come a more cautious and exact habit of mind in the interpretation of facts.

*Thirdly.* The progress of the sciences of nature has powerfully influenced history, both by providing new data and by affecting the mental attitude of all reflective men. This has happened in several ways, among which the following may be noted:

Geographical exploration has made known nearly every part of the surface of the habitable globe. The great natural features of every country, its mountain ranges and rivers, its forests or deserts, have been ascertained. Its flora and fauna have been described, and thereby its capacity for supporting human life approximately calculated. The other physical conditions which govern the development of man, such as temperature, rainfall, and the direction of prevalent winds have been examined. Thus we have acquired a treasury of facts relating to the causes and conditions which help the growth of civilisation and mould it into diverse forms, conditions whose importance I shall presently discuss, when I come to consider the relation of man to his natural environment. Although a few penetrating minds had long ago seen how much the career of each nation must have been affected by physical phenomena, it is only in the last two generations that men have begun to study these phenomena in their relation to history, and to appreciate their influence in the formation of national types and in determining the movement of races over the earth's surface.

Not less remarkable has been the increase in our knowledge of the more remote and backward peoples. Nearly every one of these has now been visited by scientific travellers or missionaries, its language written down, its customs and religious rites, sometimes its folk lore also, recorded. Thus materials of the highest value have been secured, not only for completing our knowledge of mankind as a whole, but for comprehending in the early history of the now highly civilised peoples various facts which had previously remained obscure, but which became intelligible when compared with similar facts that can be studied in their actuality among tribes whom we find in the same stage to-day as were the ancestors of the civilised nations many centuries ago. The progress thus achieved in the science of man regarded as a part of nature has powerfully contributed to influence the study of human communities as they appear in history. The comparative method has become the basis for a truly scientific inquiry into the development of institutions, and the connection of religious beliefs and ceremonies with the first beginnings of institutions both social and political has been made clear by an accumulation of instances. Whether or no there be such a thing as a Science of History, — a question which, since it is mainly verbal, one need not stop to discuss, — there is such a thing as a scientific method applied to history; and the more familiar men have become with the methods of inquiry and canons of evidence used in physical investigations, so much the more have they tended to become exact and critical in historical investigations, and to examine the causes and the stages by and through which historical development is effected.

In noting this, I do not suggest that what is popularly called the "Doctrine of Evolution" should be deemed a thing borrowed by history from the sciences of nature. Most of what is true or helpful in that doctrine was known long ago, and applied long ago by historical and political thinkers. You can find it in Aristotle, perhaps before Aristotle. Even as regards the biological sciences, the notion of what we call evolution is ancient; and the merit of Darwin and other great modern naturalists has lain, not in enouncing the idea as a general theory, but in elucidating, illustrating, and demonstrating the processes by which evolution takes place. The influence of the natural sciences on history is rather to be traced in the efforts we now see to accumulate a vast mass of facts relating to the social, economic, and political life of man, for the sake of discovering general laws running through them and imparting to them order and unity. Although the most philosophic and diligent historians have always aimed at and striven for this, still the general diffusion of the method in our own time, and the greatly increased scale on which it is applied, together with the higher standard of accuracy which is exacted by the opinion of competent judges, may be in some measure ascribed to the example which those who work in the spheres of physics and biology and natural history have so effectively set.

Finally, the progress of Natural Science has in our time, by stimulating the production and exchange of commodities, drawn the different parts of the earth much nearer to one another, and thus brought nearly all its tribes and nations into relations with one another far closer and far more frequent than existed before. This has been done by the inventions that have given us steam and electricity as motive forces, making transport quicker and cheaper, and by the application of electricity to the transmission of words. No changes that have occurred in the past (except perhaps changes in the sphere of religion) are comparable in their importance as factors in history to those which have shortened the voyage from Western Europe to America to five and a half days, and made communication with Australia instantaneous. For the first time the human race, always essentially one, has begun to feel itself one, and civilised man has in every part of it become a contemporaneous observer of what passes in every other part.

The general result of these various changes has been that while the materials for writing a history of the world have been increased, the conception of what such a history should be has been at the same time both enlarged and defined. Its scope is wider; its lines are more clearly drawn. And these are some of the reasons which suggest that the time has arrived when a new History of the World may be attempted with a better prospect of overcoming the difficulties of the subject than the most diligent writers of the past enjoyed. The able and

learned Editor of the present work, and the eminently competent staff of con-
tributors who have joined him, are penetrated by the scientific spirit of the
age, which has enriched the historian with a profusion of new materials and
has trained him to a higher skill in the critical use of them. Each of
these volumes — indeed each of their chapters — will be found to illustrate the
advantages enjoyed by the scholar of to-day whereon I have already dwelt.

In the two introductory chapters so much has been said, and said so well,
regarding the nature of a Universal History, the conditions it ought to fulfil, the lines
on which it ought to proceed, that one who writes an Introduction to the English
translation finds his field already largely covered by the facts and reflections presented by Dr. Helmolt and Professor Ratzel. I will, however, set down some
thoughts which have occurred to me on the subject. It is a large subject, which
different minds may regard from different sides; and even where the remarks
that follow touch the same aspects of it as those which have been dealt with in
the introductory chapters that follow, there need be no waste of space or of the
reader's time in considering those aspects in the light of different illustrations, or
in a somewhat different order of sequence.

What do we mean by a Universal History? Briefly: a History which shall
(first) include all the races and tribes of man within its scope and (secondly) shall
bring all these races and tribes into a connection with one another such as to
display their annals as an organic whole. Universal History has to deal not only
with the great nations, but also with the small nations; not only with the civilised,
but also with the barbarous or savage peoples; not only with the times of movement and progress, but also with the times of silence and apparent stagnation.
Every fraction of humanity has contributed something to the common stock, and
has lived and laboured not for itself only, but for others also through the influence which it has perforce exercised on its neighbours. The only exceptions we
can imagine are the inhabitants of some remote isle, "far placed amid the melancholy main." Yet they too must have once formed part of a race dwelling in the
region whence they came, even if that race had died out in its old home before
civilised man set foot on such an oceanic isle in a later age. The world would have
been different, in however small a measure, had they never existed. As in the
realm of physical science, so in that of history, no fact is devoid of significance,
though the true significance may remain long unnoticed. The history of the backward races presents exceptional difficulties, because they have no written records
and often scarcely any oral traditions. Sometimes it reduces itself to a description
of their usages and state of life, their arts and their superstitions, at the time when
civilised observers first visited them. Yet that history is instructive, not only
because the phenomena observable among such races enlarge our knowledge, but
also because through the study of those which survive we are able to interpret
the scanty records we possess of the early condition of peoples now civilised, and
to go some way towards writing the history of what we have hitherto called
prehistoric man. Thus such tribes as the aborigines of Australia, the Fuegians of
Magellan's Straits, the Bushmen of South Africa, the Sakalavas of Madagascar, the

Lapps of Northern Europe, the Ainos of Japan, the numerous "hill-tribes" of India, will all come within the historian's ken. From each of them something may be learnt; and each of them has through its contact with its more advanced neighbours affected those neighbours themselves, sometimes in blood, sometimes through superstitious beliefs or rites, frequently borrowed by the higher races from the lower,[1] sometimes through the strife which has arisen between the savage and the more civilised man, whereby the institutions of the latter have been modified.

Obviously the historian cannot record everything. These lower races are comparatively unimportant. Their contributions to progress, their effect on the general march of events, have been but small. But they must not be wholly omitted from the picture, for without them it would have been different. One must never forget, in following the history of the great nations of antiquity, that they fought and thought and built up the fabric of their industry and art in the midst of a barbarous or savage population surrounding them on all sides, whence they drew the bulk of their slaves and some of their mercenary soldiers, and which sometimes avenged itself by sudden inroads, the fear of which kept the Greek cities, and at certain epochs even the power of Rome, watchful and anxious. So in modern times the savages among whom European colonies have been planted, or who have been transported as slaves to other colonies — sometimes (as in the case of Portugal in the fifteenth century) to Europe itself — or with whom Europeans have carried on trade, must not be omitted from a view of the causes which have determined the course of events in the civilised peoples.

To dwell on the part played by the small nations is less necessary, for even a superficial student must be struck by the fact that some of them have counted for more than the larger nations to whose annals a larger space is commonly allotted. The instance of Israel is enough, so far as the ancient world is concerned, to show how little the numbers of a people have to do with the influence it may exert. For the modern world, I will take the case of Iceland. The Icelanders are a people much smaller than even was Israel. They have never numbered more than about seventy thousand. They live in an isle so far remote, and so sundered from the rest of the world by an inhospitable ocean, that their relations both with Europe to which ethnologically, and with America to which geographically they belong, have been comparatively scanty. But their history from the first settlement of the island by Norwegian exiles in A.D. 874 to the extinction of the national republic in A.D. 1264 is full of interest and instruction, in some respects a perfectly unique history. And the literature which this handful of people produced is certainly the most striking primitive literature which any modern people has produced, superior in literary quality to that of the Continental Teutons, or to that of the Romance nations, or to that of the Finns or Slavs, or even to that of the Celts. Yet most histories of Europe pass by Iceland altogether, and few persons in Continental Europe (outside Scandinavia) know anything about the

---

[1] As the Norsemen learnt magic from the Lapps, and the Semites of Assyria from the Accadians.

inhabitants of this isle, who amid glaciers and volcanoes have maintained themselves at a high level of intelligence and culture for more than a thousand years.

The small peoples have no doubt been more potent in the spheres of intellect and emotion than in those of war, politics, or commerce. But the influences which belong to the sphere of creative intelligence, that is to say, of literature, philosophy, religion, and art, are just those which it is peculiarly the function of a History of the World to disengage and follow out in their far-reaching consequences. They pass beyond the limits of the country where they arose. They survive, it may be, the race that gave birth to them. They pass into new forms, and through these they work in new ways upon subsequent ages.

It is also the task of Universal History so to trace the march of humanity as to display the relation which each part of it bears to the others: to fit each race and tribe and nation into the main narrative. To do this, three things are needed, — a comprehensive knowledge, a power of selecting the salient and significant points, and a talent for arrangement. Of these three qualifications, the first is the least rare. Ours is an age of specialists; but the more a man buries himself in special studies, the more risk does he incur of losing his sense of the place which the object of his own study fills in the general scheme of things. The highly trained historian is generally able to draw from those who have worked in particular departments the data he needs; while the master of one single department may be unable to carry his vision over the whole horizon and see each part of the landscape in its relations to the rest. In other words, a History of the World ought to be an account of the human family as an organic whole, showing how each race and State has affected other races or States, what each has brought into the common stock, and how the interaction among them has stimulated some, depressed or extinguished others, turned the main current this way or that. Even when the annals of one particular country are concerned, it needs no small measure of skill in expression as well as of constructive art to trace their connection with those of other countries. To take a familiar example, he who writes the history of England must have his eye always alive to what is passing in France on one side, and in Scotland on the other, not to speak of countries less closely connected with England, such as Germany and Spain. He must let the reader feel in what way the events that were happening in France and Scotland affected men's minds, and through men's minds affected the progress of events in England. Yet he cannot allow himself constantly to interrupt his English narrative in order to tell what was passing beyond the Channel or across the Tweed. Obviously, this difficulty is much increased when the canvas is widened to include all Europe, and when the aim is to give the reader a just impression of the general tendencies of a whole age, such an age as for instance the sixteenth century, over that vast area. If for a History of the World the old plan be adopted, — that of telling the story of each nation separately, yet on lines generally similar, cross references and a copious use of chronological tables become helpful, for they enable the contemporaneity of events to be seen at a glance, and as the history of each nation is being written with a view to that of other nations, the tendencies which are at work in each can be explained and illustrated in a way which shows their parallelism, and which gives to the whole that unity of meaning and tendency which a Universal History must constantly endeavour to display.  The connection between the progress or decline of different peoples is best understood by setting forth the various forms which similar tendencies take in each.  To do this is a hard task when the historian is dealing with the ancient world or with the world outside Europe even in mediæval and post-mediæval times.  For the modern European nations it is easier, because ever since the spread of Christianity made these nations parts of one great ecclesiastical community, similar forces have been at work upon each of them, and every intellectual movement which has told upon one has more or less told upon the others also.

Such a History of the World may be written on more than one plan, and in the light of more than one general theory of human progress.  It might find the central line of human development in the increase of man's Knowledge, and in particular of his knowledge of Nature and his power of dealing with her.  Or that which we call Culture, the comprehensive unfolding and polishing of human faculty and of the power of intellectual creation and appreciation, might be taken as marking the most real and solid kind of progress, so that its growth would best represent the advance of Man from a savage to a highly civilised condition.  Or if the moral and political sphere were selected as that in which the onward march of Man as a social being, made to live in a community, could best be studied, the idea of Liberty might be made a pivot of the scheme; for in showing how the individual emerges from the family or the tribe, how first domestic and then also prædial slavery slowly disappears, how institutions are framed under which the will of one ruler or of a small group begins to be controlled, or replaced as a governing force, by the collective will of the members of the community, how the primordial rights of each human creature win their way to recognition, — in tracing out all these things the history of human society is practically written, and the significance of all political changes is made clear.

Another way, again, would be to take some concrete department of human activity, follow it down from its earliest to its latest stages, and group other departments round it.  Thus one author might take Religion, and in making the history of religion the main thread of his narrative might deal incidentally with the other phenomena which have influenced it or which it has influenced.  Or, similarly, another author might take Political Institutions, or perhaps Economic Conditions, *i. e.*, wealth, labour, capital, commerce, or again the fundamental Social Institutions, such as the family, and the relations of the ranks and classes in a community, and build up round one or other of these manifestations and embodiments of the creative energy of mankind the general story of man's movement from barbarism to civilisation.  Even Art, even mechanical inventions, might be similarly handled, for both of these stand in a significant relation to all the rest of the life of each nation and of the world at large.

Nevertheless, no one of these suggested lines on which a Universal History might be constructed would quite meet the expectations which the name Universal

History raises, because we have become accustomed to think of history as being primarily and pre-eminently a narrative of the growth and development of communities, nations, and States as organised political bodies, seeing that it is in their character as bodies so organised that they come into relation with other nations and States. It is therefore better to follow the familiar plan of dealing with the annals of each race and nation as a distinct entity, while endeavouring to show throughout the whole narrative the part which each fills in the general drama of human effort, conflict, and progress.

A Universal History may, however, while conforming to this established method, follow it out along a special line, which shall give prominence to some one leading idea or principle. Such a line or point of view has been found for the present work in the relation of Man to his Physical Environment, that is to say, to the geographical conditions which have always surrounded and always must surround him, conditions whose power and influence he has felt ever since he appeared upon the globe. This point of view is more comprehensive than any one of those above enumerated. Physical environment has told upon each and every one of the lines of human activity already enumerated that could be taken to form a central line for the writing of a history of mankind. It has influenced not only political institutions and economic phenomena, but also religion, and social institutions, and art, and inventions. No department of man's life has been independent of it, for it works upon man not only materially but also intellectually and morally.

As this is the idea which has governed the preparation of the present book, as it is constructed upon a Geographical rather than a purely Chronological plan (though of course each particular country and nation needs to be treated chronologically), some few pages may properly be devoted to a consideration of the way in which Geography determines History, or, in other words, to an examination of the relations of Nature, inorganic and organic, to Man.

Though we are accustomed to contrast Man with Nature, and to look upon the world outside ourselves as an Object to be studied by man the conscious and intelligent Subject, it is evident, and has been always recognised even by those thinkers who have most exalted the place Man holds in the Kosmos, that Man is also to be studied as a part of the physical Universe. He belongs to the realm of Nature in respect of his bodily constitution, which links him with other animals, and in certain respects with all the phenomena that lie within the sphere of biology. All creatures on our earth, since they have bodies formed from material constituents, are subject to the physical laws which govern matter; and the life of all is determined, so far as their bodies are concerned, by the physical conditions which foster or depress or destroy life. Plants need soil, moisture, sunshine, and certain constituents of the atmosphere. Their distribution over the earth's surface depends not only upon the greater or less extent to which these things, essential to their existence, are present, but also upon the configuration of the earth's surface (continents and oceans), upon the greater or less elevation above sea level of parts of it, upon such forces as winds and ocean currents (occasionally also upon volcanoes), upon the interposition of arid deserts between moister regions, or upon the flow of great rivers. The flora of each country is the resultant (until Man appears upon the scene) of these natural conditions.[1] Similarly animals depend upon these same conditions which regulate their distribution, partly directly, partly indirectly or mediately through the dependence of the animal for food upon the plants whose presence or absence these conditions have determined. It would seem that animals, being capable of moving from place to place, and thus of finding conditions suitable for their life, and to some extent of modifying their life to suit the nature around them, are somewhat more independent than plants are, though plants too possess powers of adapting themselves to climatic surroundings; and there are some, such for instance as our common brake-fern and the Grass of Parnassus, which seem able to thrive unmodified in very different parts of the globe.

The primary needs of man which he shares with the other animals are an atmosphere which he can breathe, a temperature which he can support, water which he can drink, and food. In respect of these he is as much the product of geographical conditions as are the other living creatures. Presently he superadds another need, that of clothing. It is a sign that he is becoming less dependent on external conditions, for by means of clothing he can make his own temperature and succeed in enduring a degree of cold, or changes from heat to cold, which might otherwise shorten his life. The discovery of fire carries him a long step further, for it not only puts him less at the mercy of low temperatures, but extends the range of his food supplies, and enables him, by procuring better tools and weapons, to obtain his food more easily. We need not pursue his upward course, at every stage of which he finds himself better and still better able to escape from the thraldom of Nature, and to turn to account the forces which she puts at his disposal. But although he becomes more and more independent, more and more master not only of himself, but of her, he is none the less always for many purposes the creature of the conditions with which she surrounds him. He always needs what she gives him. He must always have regard to the laws which he finds operating through her realm. He always finds it the easiest course to obey and to use rather than to attempt to resist her.

Here let us pause to notice a remarkable contrast between the earlier and the later stages of man's relations to Nature. In the earlier stages he lies helpless before her, and must take what she chooses to bestow, — food, shelter, materials for clothing, means of defence against the wild beasts who are in strength far more than a match for him. He depends upon her from necessity, and is better or worse off according as she is more or less generous. But in the later stages of his progress he has, by accumulating a store of knowledge, and by the development of his intelligence, energy, and self-confidence, raised himself out of his old difficulties. He no longer dreads the wild beasts. They, or such of them as remain, begin to dread him, for he is crafty, and can kill them at a distance. He erects dwellings which can withstand rain and tempest. He irrigates hitherto barren lands and raises abundant crops from them. When he has invented machinery,

---

[1] Some plants are also affected by the presence of certain animals, particularly insects and birds.

he produces in an hour clothing better than his hands could formerly have produced in a week. If at any given time he has not plenty of food, this happens only because he has allowed his species to multiply too fast. He is able to cross the sea against adverse winds and place himself in a more fertile soil or under more genial skies than those of his former home. As respects all the primary needs of his life, he has so subjected Nature to himself that he can make his life what he will. All this renders him independent. But he now also finds himself drawn into a new kind of dependence. For he has now come to take a new view of Nature. He perceives in her an enormous storehouse of wealth, by using which he can multiply his resources and gratify his always increasing desires to an extent practically unlimited. She provides forces, such as steam and electricity, which his knowledge enables him to employ for production and transport so as to spare his own physical strength, needed now not so much for effort as for the direction of the efforts of Nature. She has in the forest, and still more beneath her own surface in the form of minerals, the materials by which these forces can be set in motion ; and by using these forces he can with comparatively little trouble procure abundance of those materials. Thus his relation to Nature is changed. It was that of a servant, or indeed rather of a beggar, needing the bounty of a sovereign. It is now that of a master needing the labour of a servant, a servant infinitely stronger than the master, but absolutely obedient to the master, so long as the master uses the proper spell. Thus the connection of Man with Nature, changed though his attitude be, is really as close as ever, and far more complex. If his needs had remained what they were in his primitive days, let us say, in those palæolithic days which we can faintly adumbrate to ourselves by an observation of the Australian or Fuegian aborigines now, he would have sat comparatively lightly to Nature, getting easily what he wanted, and not caring to trouble her for more. But his needs, that is to say, his desires, both his physical appetites and his intellectual tastes, his ambitions and his fondness for comfort, things that were once luxuries having become necessaries, have so immeasurably expanded that since he asks much more from Nature he is obliged to study her more closely than ever. Thus he enters into a new sort of dependence upon her, because it is only by understanding her capacities and the means of using them that he can get from her what he wants. Primitive man was satisfied if he could find spots where the trees gave edible fruit, where the sun was not too hot nor the winds too cold, where the beasts easy of capture were abundant, and no tigers or pythons made the forest terrible. Civilised man has more complex problems to deal with and wider fields to search. The study of Nature is not only still essential to him, but really more essential than ever. His life and action are conditioned by her. His industry and his commerce are directed by her to certain spots. That which she has to give is still, directly or indirectly, the source of strife, and a frequent cause of war. As men fought long ago with flint-headed arrows for a spring of water or a cocoanut grove, so they fight to-day for mineral treasures imbedded in the soil. It is mainly by Nature that the movements of emigration and the rise of populous centres of industry are determined.

Though Nature still rules for many purposes and in many ways the course of human affairs, the respective value of her various gifts changes from age to age, as Man's knowledge and power of turning them to account have changed.  The things most prized by primitive man are not those which semi-civilised man chiefly prized, still less are they those most sought for now.  In primitive times the spots most attractive, because most favourable to human life, were those in which food could be most easily and safely obtained from fruit-bearing trees or by the chase, and where the climate was genial enough to make clothing and shelter needless, at least during the greater part of the year.  Later on, when the keeping of cattle and tillage has come into use, good pastures and a fertile soil in the valley of a river were the chief sources of material well-being.  Wild beasts were less terrible, because man was better armed ; but as human enemies were formidable, regions where hills and rocks facilitated defence by furnishing natural strongholds had their advantages.  Still later, forests came to be recognised as useful for fuel and for carpentry and shipbuilding.  Mineral deposits, usually found in hilly or mountainous districts, became pre-eminently important sources of wealth ; and rivers were valued as highways of commerce and as sources of motive power by the force of their currents.  To the Red Indians of the Ohio valley the places which were the most attractive camping-grounds were those whither the buffaloes came in vast herds to lick the rock salt exposed in the sides of the hills.  It is now not the salt-licks but the existence of immense deposits of coal and iron that have determined the growth of huge communities in those regions whence the Red man and the buffalo have both vanished.  England was once, as New Zealand is now, a great wool-growing and wool-exporting country, whereas she is to-day a country which spins and weaves far more wool than she produces.  So too the influence of the sea on Man has changed.  There was a time when towns were built upon heights some way off from the coast, because the sea was the broad highroad of pirates who swooped down upon and pillaged the dwellings of those who lived near it. Now that the sea is safe, trading cities spring up upon its margin, and sandy tracts worthless for agriculture have gained an unexpected value as health resorts or as places for playing games, places to which the inhabitants of inland districts flock in summer, as they do in England and Germany, or in winter, as they do on the Mediterranean coasts of France.  The Greeks, when they began to compete with the Phœnicians in maritime commerce, sought for small and sheltered inlets in which their tiny vessels could lie safely, — such inlets as Homer describes in the Odyssey,[1] or as the Old Port of Marseilles, a city originally a colony from the Ionian Phocæa.  Nowadays these pretty little rock harbours are useless for the huge ships which carry our trade.  The Old Port of Marseilles is abandoned to small coasters and fishing-boats and the ocean steamers lie in a new harbour which is protected, partly by outlying islands, partly by artificial works.

So too river valleys, though still important as highways of traffic, are important not so much in respect of water carriage as because they furnish the easiest lines along which railways can be constructed.  The two banks of the Rhine, each

---

[1] Odyss. ix. 136.

traversed by a railroad, carry far more traffic than the great stream itself carried a century ago; and the same remark applies to the Hudson. All these changes are due to the progress of invention, which may give us fresh changes in the future not less far-reaching than those which the past has seen. Mountainous regions with a heavy rainfall, such as Western Norway or the coast of the Pacific in Washington and British Columbia, may, by the abundance of water power which they supply, and which can be transmuted into electrical energy, become sources of previously unlooked-for wealth, especially if some cheap means can be devised of conveying electricity with less wastage in transmission than is at present incurred.[1] Should effective and easily applicable preventives against malarial fever be discovered, many districts now shunned, because dangerous to the life of white men, may become the homes of flourishing communities. The discovery of cinchona bark in the seventeenth century affected the course of events, because it provided a remedy against a disease that had previously baffled medical skill. If quinine had been at the disposal of the men of the Middle Ages, not only might the lives of many great men, as for instance of Dante, have been prolonged, but the Teutonic Emperors would have been partially relieved of one of the chief obstacles which prevented them from establishing permanent control over their Italian dominions. Rome and the papal power defended themselves against the hosts of the Franconian and Hohenstaufen sovereigns by the fevers of the Campagna more effectively than did the Roman people by their arms, and almost as effectively as did the Popes by their spiritual thunders.

Bearing in mind this principle, that the gifts of Nature to Man not only increase, but also vary in their form, in proportion and correspondence to Man's capacity to use them, and remembering also that Man is almost as much influenced by Nature when he has become her adroit master as when she was his stern mistress, we may now go on to examine more in detail the modes in which her influence has told and still tells upon him.

It has long been recognised that Nature must have been the principal factor in producing, that is to say, in differentiating, the various races of mankind as we find them differentiated when our records begin. How this happened is one of the darkest problems that history presents. By what steps and through what causes did the races of man acquire these diversities of physical and intellectual character which are now so marked and which seem so persistent? It has been suggested that some of these diversities may date back to a time when Man, as what is called a distinct species, had scarcely begun to exist. Assuming the Darwinian hypothesis of the development of Man out of some pithecoid form to be correct — and those who are not themselves scientific naturalists can of course do no more than provisionally accept the conclusions at which the vast majority of scientific naturalists have arrived — it is conceivable that there may have been unconnected developments of creatures from intermediate forms into definitely human forms in different regions, and that some of the most marked types of humanity may therefore have had their first rudimentary and germinal beginning before any specifically

---

[1] Within the last few years considerable progress in this direction has been made.

human type had made its appearance. This, however, is not the view of the great majority of naturalists. They appear to hold that the passage either from some anthropoid apes, or from some long since extinct common ancestor of man and the existing anthropoid apes, — this latter alternative representing what is now the dominant view — did not take place through several channels (so to speak), but through one only, and that there was a single specifically human type which subsequently diverged into the varieties we now see. If this be so, it is plain that climate and the conditions of life which depend upon climate, soil, and the presence of vegetables and of other animals besides Man, must have been the forces which moulded and developed those varieties. From a remote antiquity, everybody has connected the dark colour of all or nearly all the races inhabiting the torrid zone with the power of the sun; and the fairer skin of the races of the temperate and arctic zones with the comparative feebleness of his rays in those regions. This may be explained on Darwinian principles by supposing that the darker varieties were found more capable of supporting the fierce heat of the tropics. What explanation is to be given of the other characteristics of the negro and negroid races, of the usually frizzled hair, of the peculiar nose and jaw, and so forth, is a question for the naturalist rather than for the historian. Although climate and food may be the chief factors in differentiation, the nature of the process is, as indeed is the case with the species of animals generally, sometimes very obscure. Take an instance from three African races which, so far as we can tell, were formed under similar climatic conditions, — the Bushmen, the Hottentots, and the Bantu, the race which include those whom we call Kafirs. Their physical aspect and colour are different. Their size and the structure of their bodies are different. Their mental aptitudes are different; and one of the oddest points of difference is this, that whereas the Bushmen are the least advanced, intellectually, morally, and politically, of the three races as well as the physically weakest, they show a talent for drawing which is not possessed by the other two.

In this case there is of course a vast unknown fore-time during which we may imagine the Bantu race, probably originally formed in a region other than that which it now occupies, and under more favourable conditions for progress, to have become widely differentiated from those which are now the lower African races. We still know comparatively little about African ethnography. Let us therefore take another instance in which affinities of language give ground for believing that three races, whose differences are now marked, have diverged from a common stock. So far as language goes, the Celts, the Teutons, and the Slavs, all speaking Indo-European tongues, may be deemed to be all nearly connected in origin. They are marked by certain slight physical dissimilarities and by perhaps rather more palpable dissimilarities in their respective intellectual and emotional characters. But so far as our knowledge goes, all three have lived for an immensely long period in the colder parts of the temperate zone, under similar external conditions and following very much the same kind of pastoral and agricultural life. There is nothing in their environment which explains the divergences we perceive; so the origin of these divergences must apparently be sought either in admixture with other races or in some other historical causes which are, and will forever remain, in the darkness of a recordless past.

How race admixture works, and how it forms a new definite character out of diverse elements, is a subject which any one may find abundant materials for studying in the history of the last two thousand years. Nearly every modern European people has been so formed. The French, the Spaniards, and the English are all the products of a mixture, in different proportions, of at least three elements, — Iberian (to use a current name), Celts, and Teutons, though the Celtic element is probably comparatively small in Spain, and the Teutonic comparatively small both in Spain and in Central and Southern France. No small part of those who to-day speak German and deem themselves Germans must be of Slavonic stock. Those who to-day speak Russian are very largely of Finnish, to some small extent of Tatar, blood. The Italians probably spring from an even larger number of race-sources, without mentioning the vast number of slaves brought from the East and the North into Italy between B.C. 100 and A.D. 300. In the cases of Switzerland and Scotland the process of fusion is not yet complete. The Celto-Burgundian Swiss of Neuchâtel is still different from the Allemanian Swiss of Appenzell; as the Anglo-Celt of Fife is different from the Ibero-Celt of the Outer Hebrides. But in both these cases there is already a strong sense of national unity, and in another three hundred years there may have arisen a single type of character. An interesting and almost unique case is furnished by Iceland, where isolation under peculiar conditions of climate, food, and social life has created a somewhat different type both of body and of mental character from that of the Norwegians, although so far as blood goes the two peoples are identical, Iceland having been colonised from Western Norway a thousand years ago, and both Icelanders and Norwegians having remained practically unmixed with any other race [1] since the separation took place. But by far the most remarkable instance of race admixture is that furnished in our own time by the United States of North America, where a people of predominantly English stock (although there were in the end of last century a few descendants of Dutchmen, with Germans, Swedes, and Ulster Irishmen, in the country) has within the last sixty years received additions of many millions of Celts, of Germans and Scandinavians, and of various Slavonic races. At least a century must elapse before it can be seen how far this infusion of new blood will change the type of American character as it stood in 1840.

There are however two noteworthy differences between modern race fusions and those which belong to primitive times. One is that under modern conditions the influence of what may be called the social and political environment is probably very much greater than it was in early times. The American-born son of Irish parents is at forty years of age a very different creature from his cousin on the coast of Mayo. The other is that in modern times differences of colour retard or forbid the fusion of two races. So far as the Teutonic peoples are concerned, no

---

[1] Save that some slight Celtic infusion came to Iceland with those who migrated thither from the Norse settlements in Ireland, Northern Scotland, and the Hebrides.

one will intermarry with a negro; very few with a Hindu, a Chinaman, or a Malay. In the ancient world there was but little contact between white men and black or yellow ones, but the feeling of race aversion was apparently less strong than it is now, just as it was much less strong among the Spaniards and Portuguese in the sixteenth and seventeenth centuries than it is among Americans or Englishmen to-day.[1]

As Nature must have been the main agent in the formation of the various races of mankind from a common stock, so also Nature has been the chief cause of their movements from one part of the earth to another, these movements having been in their turn a potent influence in the admixture of the races. Some geographers have alleged climate, that is to say, the desire of those who inhabit an inclement region to enjoy a softer and warmer air, as a principal motive which has induced tribes of nations to transfer themselves from one region to another. It is no doubt true that the direction of migrations has almost always been either from the north towards the south or else along parallels of latitude, men rarely seeking for themselves conditions more severe than those under which they were born. But it is usually not so much the wish to escape cold that has been an effective motive as the wish to find more and better food, since this means an altogether easier life. Scarcity of the means of subsistence, which is of course most felt when population is increasing, has operated more frequently and powerfully than any other cause in bringing on displacements of the races of man over the globe. The movement of the primitive Aryans into India from the plateaux of West Central Asia, probably also the movement of the races which speak Dravidian languages from South Central Asia into Southern India, and probably also the mighty descent, in the fourth and fifth centuries A.D., of the Teutonic races from the lands between the Baltic and the Alps into the Roman Empire, had this origin. In more advanced states of society a like cause leads the surplus population of a civilised state to overflow into new lands, where there is more space or the soil is more fertile. Thus the inhabitants of Southwestern Scotland, partly, no doubt, at the suggestion of their rulers, crossed over into Ulster, where they occupied the best lands, driving the aboriginal Celts into the rougher and higher districts where their descendants remain in the glens of Antrim, and in the hilly parts of Down, Derry, and Tyrone. Thus the men of New England moved out to the West and settled in the Mississippi Valley, while the men of Virginia crossed the Alleghanies into Kentucky. Thus the English have colonised Canada and Australia and New Zealand and Natal. Thus the Russians have spread out from their ancient homes on the upper courses of the Dnieper and the Volga all over the vast steppes that stretch to the Black Sea and the Caucasus, as well as into the rich lands of Southwestern Siberia. Thus the surplus peasantry of Germany has gone not only to North America, but also to Southern Brazil and the shores of the Rio de la Plata.

In another form it is the excess of population over means of subsistence at home that has produced the remarkable outflow of the Chinese through the East-

---

[1] It is less strong even now among the so-called "Latin races;" and as regards the Anglo-Americans, it is much less strong towards the Red Indians than towards negroes.

ern Archipelago and across the Pacific into North America, and that has carried the Japanese to the Hawaiian Islands. And here we touch another cause of migration which is indirectly traceable to Nature; namely, the demand in some countries for more labour or cheaper labour than the inhabitants of the country are able or willing to supply. Sometimes this demand is attributable to climatic causes. The Spaniards and Portuguese and English in the New World were unfitted by their physical constitutions for out-of-door labour under a tropical sun. Hence they imported negroes during the sixteenth and two following centuries in such numbers that there are now about eight millions of coloured people in the United States alone, and possibly (though no accurate figures exist) as many more in the West Indies and South America. To a much smaller extent the same need for foreign labour has recently brought Indian coolies to the shores of the Caribbean Sea, and to the hottest parts of Natal, as it brings Polynesians to the sugar plantations of Northern Queensland.

Two other causes which have been potent in bringing about displacements and mixtures of population are the desire for conquest and plunder and the sentiment of religion. But these belong less to the sphere of Nature than to that of human passion and emotion, so that they scarcely fall within this part of our inquiry, the aim of which has been to show how Nature has determined history by inducing a shifting of races from place to place. From this shifting there has come the contact of diverse elements, with changes in each race due to the influence of the other, or perhaps the absorption of one in the other, or the development of something new out of both. In considering these race movements we have been led from the remote periods in which they began, and of which we know scarcely anything except from archæological and linguistic data, to periods within the range of authentic history. So we may go on to see how Nature has determined the spots in which the industry of the more advanced races should build up the earliest civilisations, and the lines along which commerce, a principal agent in the extension of civilisation, should proceed to link one race with another.

It was long since observed that the first homes of a dense population and a highly developed civilisation lay in fertile river valleys, such as those of the lower Nile, the Euphrates, the Tigris, the Ganges, the Yang-tse-kiang. All these are situate in the hotter parts of the temperate zone: all are regions of exceptional fertility. The soil, especially when tillage has become general, is the first source of wealth; and it is in the midst of a prosperous agricultural population that cities spring up where handicrafts and the arts arise and flourish. The basins of the Lower Nile and of the Lower Euphrates and Tigris are (as respects the West Asiatic and Mediterranean world), the fountain-heads of material, military, and artistic civilisation. From them it spreads over the adjacent countries and along the coasts of Europe and Africa. On the east, Egypt and Mesopotamia are cut off by the deserts of Arabia and Eastern Persia from the perhaps equally ancient civilisation of India, which again is cut off by lofty and savage mountains from the very ancient civilisation of China. Nature forbade intercourse between these far eastern regions and the West Asian peoples, while on the other hand Nature permitted Egypt Phœnicia, and Babylon to influence and become teachers of the peoples of Asia Minor and of the Greeks on both sides of the Ægean Sea. The isolation and consequent independent development of India and of China is one of the most salient and significant facts of history. It was not till the end of the fifteenth century, when the Portuguese reached the Malabar coast, that the Indian peoples began to come into the general movement of the world; for the expedition of Alexander the Great left hardly any permanent result, except upon Buddhist art, and the conquests of Mahmud of Ghazni opened no road to the East from the Mediterranean West. Nor did China, though visited by Italian travellers in the thirteenth century, by Portuguese traders and Jesuit missionaries in the sixteenth and seventeenth, come into effective contact with Europe till near our own time.

As the wastes of barren land formed an almost impassable eastern boundary to the West Asian civilisations, so on the west the expanse of sea brought Egypt and, to a less extent, Assyria through Phœnicia into touch with all the peoples who dwelt on the shores of the Mediterranean. The first agents in the diffusion of trade and the arts were the Phœnicians established at Tyre, Sidon, and Carthage. The next were the Greeks. For more than two thousand years, from B.C. 700 onwards, the Mediterranean is practically the centre of the history of the world, because it is the highway both of commerce and of war. For seven hundred years after the end of the second century B.C., that is to say, while the Roman Empire remained strong, it was also the highway of civil administration. The Saracen conquests of the seventh century cut off North Africa and Syria from Europe, checked transmarine commerce, and created afresh the old opposition of East and West in which a thousand years earlier Herodotus had found the main thread of World History. But it was not till after the discovery of America that the Mediterranean began to yield to the Atlantic its primacy as the area of sea power and sea-borne trade.

Bordered by far less fertile and climate-favoured countries, and closed to navigation during some months of winter, the Baltic has always held a place in history far below that of the Mediterranean. Yet it has determined the relations of the North European States and peoples. So the North Sea has at one time exposed Britain to attack from the Danish and Norwegian lords of the sea, and at other times protected her from powerful continental enemies. It may indeed be said that in surrounding Europe by the sea on three sides, Nature has drawn the main lines which the course of events on this smallest but most important of the Continents has had to follow.

Of the part which the great bodies of water have played, of the significance in the oceans of mighty currents like the Gulf Stream, the Polar Current, the Japan Current, the Mozambique Current, it would be impossible to speak within reasonable compass. But two remarks may be made before leaving this part of the subject. One is that Man's action in cutting through an isthmus may completely alter the conditions as given by Nature. The Suez Canal has of late years immensely enhanced the importance of the Mediterranean, already in some degree restored by the decay of Turkish power, by the industrial revival of Italy, and by the French conquests in North Africa. The cutting of a canal at Panama would change the relations of the seafaring and fleet-owning nations that are interested in the Atlantic and the Pacific. And the other remark is that the significance of a maritime discovery, however great at first, may become still greater with the lapse of time. Magellan, in his ever memorable voyage, not only penetrated to and crossed the Pacific, but discovered the Philippine Islands and claimed them for the monarch who had sent him forth. His appropriation of them for the Crown of Spain, to which during these three centuries and a half they have brought no benefit, has been the cause which has led the republic of the United States to depart from its traditional policy of holding to its own continent by taking them as a prize, a distant and unexpected prize, of conquest.

A few words may suffice as to what Nature has done towards the formation of nations and States by the configuration of the surface of the dry land,—that is to say, by mountain chains and by river valleys.

The only natural boundaries, besides seas, are mountains and deserts. Rivers, though convenient frontier lines for the politician or the geographer, are not natural boundaries, but rather unite than dissever those who dwell on their opposite banks. Thus the great natural boundaries in Asia have been the deserts of Eastern Persia, of Turkistan, and of Northern Arabia, with the long Himalayan chain and the savage ranges apparently parallel to the Irawadi River, which separate the easternmost corner of India and Burmah from Southwestern China. To a less extent the Altai and Thian Shan, and to a still smaller extent the Taurus in Eastern Asia Minor, have tended to divide peoples and States. The Caucasus, which fills the space between two great seas, has been at all times an extremely important factor in history, severing the nomad races of Scythia from the more civilised and settled inhabitants of the valleys of the Phasis and the Kura. Even to-day, when the Czar holds sway on both sides of this chain, it constitutes a strategic weakness in the position of Russia, and it helps to keep the Georgian races to the south of it from losing their national identity in the mass of Russian subjects. Without the Alps and the Pyrenees, the annals of Europe must have been entirely different. The Alps, even more than the Italian climate, proved too much for the Romano-Germanic Emperors of the Middle Ages who tried to rule both to the north and to the south of this wide mountain region. The Pyrenees have not only kept in existence the Basque people, but have repeatedly frustrated the attempts of monarchs to dominate both France and Spain. The mass of high moorland country which covers most of the space between the Solway Firth and the lower course of the Tweed has had something to do with the formation of a Scottish nation out of singularly diverse elements. The rugged mountains of Northern and Western Scotland, and the similar though less extensive hill country of Wales, have enabled Celtic races to retain their language and character in both these regions. On the other hand the vast open plains of Russia have allowed the Slavs of the districts which lie round Novgorod, Moscow, and Kiev to spread out among and Russify the Lithuanian and Finnish, to some extent also the Tatar, races, who originally held by far the larger part of that area. So too the Ural range, which, though long, is neither high nor difficult to pass, has opposed no serious obstacle to the overflow of population from Russia into Siberia. That in North America the Alleghanies have had a comparatively slight effect upon political history, although they did for a time arrest the march of colonisation, is due partly to the fact that they are a mass of comparatively low parallel ranges with fertile valleys between, partly to the already advanced civilisation of the Anglo-Americans of the Atlantic seaboard, who found no great difficulty in making their way across against the uncertain resistance of small and non-cohesive Indian tribes. A far more formidable natural barrier is formed between the Mississippi Valley and the Pacific slope by the Rocky Mountains, with the deserts of Arizona, Utah, Nevada, and Idaho. But the discovery of steam power has so much reduced the importance of this barrier that it does not seriously threaten the maintenance of a united American republic.

In one respect the New World presents a remarkable contrast to the Old. The earliest civilisations of the latter seem to have sprung up in fertile river valleys. Those of the former are found not on the banks of streams like the Nile or Euphrates, but on elevated plateaux, where the heat of a tropical sun is mitigated by height above sea level. It was in the lofty lake basin of Tezcuco and Mexico, and on the comparatively level ground which lies between the parallel ranges of the Peruvian and Bolivian Andes, that American races had reached their finest intellectual development, not in the far richer, but also hotter and less healthy, river valleys of Brazil, or (unless we are to except Yucatan) on the scorching shores of the Caribbean Sea. Nature was in those regions too strong for Man, and held him down in savagery.

In determining the courses of great rivers, Nature has determined the first highways of trade and fixed the sites of many cities. Nearly all the considerable towns founded more than three centuries ago owe their origin either to their possessing good havens on the seacoast, or to the natural strength of their position on a defensible hill, or to their standing close to a navigable river. Marseilles, Alexandria, New York, Rio de Janeiro, are instances of the first; Athens, Edinburgh, Prague, Moscow, of the second; Bordeaux, Cologne, New Orleans, Calcutta, of the third. Rome and London, Budapest and Lyons, combine the advantages of the second with those of the third. This function of rivers in directing the lines of commerce and the growth of centres of population has become much less important since the construction of railroads, yet population tends to stay where it has been first gathered, so that the fluviatile cities are likely to retain their preponderance. Thus the river is as important to the historian as is the mountain range or the sea.

From the physical features of a country it is an easy transition to the capacities of the soil. The character of the products of a region determines the numbers of its inhabitants and the kind of life they lead. A land of forests breeds hunters or lumber-men; a land of pasture, which is too rough or too arid or too sterile for tillage, supports shepherds or herdsmen probably more or less nomadic. Either kind of land supports inhabitants few in proportion to its area. Fertile and well-watered regions rear a denser, a more settled, and presumably a more civilised population. Norway and Tyrol, Tibet and Wyoming and the Orange Free State, can never become so densely peopled as Bengal or Illinois or Lombardy, yet the fisheries of its coast and the seafaring energy of its people have sensibly increased the population of Norway. Thus he who knows the climate and the productive capacity of the soil of any given country can calculate its prospects of prosperity. Political causes may, of course, intervene. Asia Minor and the Valley of the Euphrates, regions once populous and flourishing, are now thinly inhabited .and poverty-stricken because they are ruled by the Turks. But these cases are exceptional. Bengal and Lombardy and Egypt have supported large populations under all kinds of government. The products of each country tend moreover to establish definite relations between it and other countries, and do this all the more as population, commerce, and the arts advance. When England was a great wool-growing and wool-exporting country, her wool export brought her into close political connection with the wool-manufacturing Flemish towns. She is now a cotton-manufacturing country, needing cotton which she cannot grow at all, and consuming wheat which she does not grow in sufficient quantities. Hence she is in close commercial relations with the United States on one side, which give her most of her cotton and much of her wheat, and with India, from which she gets both these articles, and to which she exports a large part of her manufactured cotton goods. So Rome, because she needed the corn of Egypt, kept Egypt under a specially careful administration. The rest of her corn came from Sicily and North Africa, and the Vandal conquest of North Africa dealt a frightful blow to the declining Empire. In these cases the common interest of sellers and buyers makes for peace, but in other cases the competition of countries desiring to keep commerce to themselves occasions war. The Spanish and Dutch fought over the trade to India in the earlier part of the seventeenth century, when the Portuguese Indies belonged to Spain, as the English and French fought in the eighteenth. And a nation, especially an insular nation, whose arable soil is not large enough or fertile enough to provide all the food it needs, has a powerful inducement either to seek peace or else to be prepared for maritime war. If such a country does not grow enough corn or meat at home, she must have a navy strong enough to make sure that she will always be able to get these necessaries from abroad. Attica did not produce all the grain needed to feed the Athenians, so they depended on the corn ships which came down from the Euxine and were practically at the mercy of an enemy who could stop those ships.

Of another natural source of wealth, the fisheries on the coast of a country, no more need be said than that they have been a frequent source of quarrels and even of war. The recognition of the right of each State to the exclusive control and enjoyment of the sea for three miles off its shores has reduced but not entirely removed the causes of friction between the fishermen of different countries.

Until recently, the surface of the soil was a far more important source of wealth than was that which lies beneath the surface. There were iron mines among the Chalybes on the Asiatic coast of the Euxine in ancient times: there were silver mines here and there, the most famous those at Laurium, from which the Athenians drew large revenues, gold mines in Spain and Dacia, copper mines in Elba, tin mines in the southwest corner of Britain. But the number of persons employed in mining and the industries connected therewith was relatively small both in the ancient world and indeed down till the close of the eighteenth century. The immense development of coal mining and of iron working in connection therewith has now doubled, trebled, or quadrupled the population of large areas in Britain, Germany, France, Belgium and the United States, adding vastly to the wealth of these countries and stimulating in them the growth of many mechanical arts. This new population is quite different in character from the agricultural peasantry who in earlier days formed the principal substratum of society. Its appearance has changed the internal politics of these countries, disturbing the old balance of forces and accelerating the progress of democratic principles. Nor have minerals failed to affect the international relations of peoples and States. It was chiefly for the precious metals that the Spaniards explored the American Continent and conquered Mexico and Peru. It was for the sake of capturing the ships that brought those metals back to Europe that the English sea-rovers made their way to the American coasts and involved England in wars with Spain. It was the discovery in 1885 of extensive auriferous strata unexampled in the certainty of their yield that drew a swarm of foreign immigrants into the Transvaal, whence arose those difficulties between them and the Dutch inhabitants previously established there, which, coupled with the action of the wealthy owners of the mines, led at last to the war of 1899 between Britain and the two South African Republics.

The productive capacity of a country is, however, in one respect very different from those great physical features — such as temperature, rainfall, coast configuration, surface character, geological structure, and river system — which have been previously noted. Those features are permanent qualities which man can affect only to a limited extent, as when he reduces the rainfall a little by cutting down forests or increases it by replanting them, or as when he unites an isle, like that of Cadiz, to the mainland, cuts through an isthmus, like that of Corinth, or clears away the bar at a river mouth, as that of the Mississippi has been cleared. But the natural products of a country may be exhausted and even the productive capacity of its soil diminished. Constant tillage, especially if the same crop be raised and no manure added, will wear out the richest soils. This has already happened in parts of Western America. Still the earth is there; and with rest and artificial help it will recover its strength. But timber destroyed cannot always be induced to grow again, or at least not so as to equal the vigour of primæval forests. Wild animals once extirpated are gone forever. The buffalo and beaver of North America, the beautiful lynxes of South Africa and some of its large ruminants are irrecoverably lost for the purposes of human use, just as much as the Dinornis, though a few individuals may be kept alive as specimens. So too the mineral resources of a country are not only consumable but obviously irreplaceable. Already some of the smaller coalfields of Europe have been worked out.

while in others it has become necessary to sink much deeper shafts, at an increasing cost. There is not much tin left in Cornwall, not much gold in the gravel deposits of Northern California. The richest known goldfield of the world, that of the Transvaal Witwatersrand, can hardly last more than thirty or forty years. Thus in a few centuries the productive capacity of many regions may have become quite different from what it is now, with grave consequences to their inhabitants.

These are some of the ways in which Nature affects those economic, social, and political conditions of the life of Man the changes in which make up history. As we have seen, that which Nature gives to Man is always the same, in so far as Nature herself is always the same, — an expression which is more popular than accurate, for Nature herself, that is to say, not the laws of Nature, but the physical environment of Man on this planet — is in reality always changing. It is true that this environment changes so slowly that a thousand years may be too short a period in which man can note and record some forms of change — such for instance as that by which the temperature of Europe became colder during the approach of the glacial period and warmer during its recession, — while ten thousand years may be too short to note any diminution in the heat which the sun pours upon the earth or in the store of oxygen which the earth's atmosphere holds. But as we have also seen, the relation to Man of Nature's gifts differs from age to age as Man himself becomes different, and as his power of using these gifts increases, or his need of them becomes either less or greater. Every invention alters those relations. Water power became less relatively valuable when steam was applied to the generation of motive force. It has become more valuable with the new applications of electricity. With the discovery of mineral dyes, indigo and cochineal are now less wanted than they were. With the invention of the pneumatic tire for bicycles and carriages, caoutchouc is more wanted. Mountains have become, since the making of railways, less of an obstacle to trade than they were, and they have also become more available as health resorts. Political circumstances may interfere with the ordinary and normal action of natural phenomena. A race may be attracted to or driven into a region for which it is not physically suited, as Europeans have gone to the West Indies and negroes were once carried into New York and Pennsylvania. The course of trade which Nature prescribes between different countries may be hampered or stopped by protective tariffs. But in these cases Nature usually takes her eventual revenges. They are instances which show, not that Man can disregard her, but that when he does so, he does so to his own loss.

It would be easy to add further illustrations, but those already given are sufficient to indicate how multiform and pervading is the action upon Man of the physical environment, or, in other words, how in all countries and at all times Geography is the necessary foundation of History, so that neither the course of a nation's growth nor its relations with other nations can be grasped by one who has not come to understand the climate, surface, and products of the country wherein that nation dwells.

This conception of the relation of Geography to History is, as has been said, the leading idea of the present work, and has furnished the main lines which it follows. It deals with history in the light of physical environment. Its ground plan, so to speak, is primarily geographical and secondarily chronological. But there is one difficulty in the way of such a scheme and of the use of such a ground plan which cannot be passed over. That difficulty is suggested by the fact already noted, that hardly any considerable race, and possibly no great nation, now inhabits the particular part of the earth's surface on which it was dwelling when a History begins. Nearly every people has either migrated bodily from one region to another, or has received such large infusions of immigrants from other regions as to have become practically a new people. Hence it is rare to find any nation now living under the physical conditions which originally moulded its character or the character of some at least of its component elements. And hence it follows that when we study the qualities, aptitudes, and institutions of a nation in connection with the land it inhabits, we must always have regard not merely to the features of that land, but also to those of the land which was its earlier dwelling-place. Obviously, this brings a disturbing element into the study of the relations between Land and People, and makes the whole problem a far more complicated one than it appeared at first sight.

Where a people has migrated from a country whose physical conditions were similar to those under which its later life is spent, or where it had reached only a comparatively low stage of economic and political development before the migration, the difficulties arising from this source are not serious. The fact that the English came into Britain from the lands round the mouth of the Elbe is not very material to an inquiry into their relations to their new home, because climate and soil were similar, and the migrants were a rude warlike race. But when we come to the second migration of the English from Britain to North America, the case is altogether different. Groups of men from a people which had already become highly civilised, had formed a well-marked national character, and had created a body of peculiar institutions, planted themselves in a country the climate and physical features of which are widely diverse from those of Britain. If, for the sake of argument, we assume the Algonquin aborigines of Atlantic North America as they were in A.D. 1600 to have been the legitimate product of their physical environment, — I say "for the sake of argument" because it may be alleged that other forces than those of physical environment contributed to form them, — what greater contrast can be imagined than the contrast between the inhabitants of New England in this present year and the inhabitants of the same district three centuries earlier, as Nature and Nature alone had turned them out of her factory? Plainly therefore the history of the United States cannot, so far as Nature and geography are concerned, be written with regard solely, or even chiefly, to the conditions of North American nature. The physical environment in which the English immigrants found themselves on that continent has no doubt affected their material progress and the course of their politics during the three centuries that have elapsed since settlements were founded in Virginia and on Massachusetts Bay. But it is not to that environment but to earlier days, and especially to the twelve centuries during which their ancestors lived in England, that their character and institutions are to be traced. Thus the history of the American people begins in the forests of Germany, where the foundations of their polity were laid, is continued in England, where they set up kingdoms, embraced Christianity, became one nation, received an influx of Celtic, of Danish, and of Norman-French blood, formed for themselves that body of customs, laws, and institutions which they transplanted to the new soil of America, and most of which, though changed and always changing, they still retain. The same thing is true of the Spaniards (as also of the Portuguese) in Central and South America. The difference between the development of the Hispano-Americans and that of their English neighbours to the north is not wholly or even mainly due to the different physical conditions under which the two sets of colonists have lived. It is due to the different antecedent history of the two races. So a history of America must be a history not only of America, but of the Spaniards, Portuguese, French, and English — one ought in strictness to add, of the negroes also — before they crossed the Atlantic. The only true Americans, the only Americans for whom American Nature can be deemed answerable, are the aboriginal Red Men, whom we, perpetuating the mistake of Columbus, still call Indians.

This objection to the geographical scheme of history writing is no doubt serious when a historical treatise is confined to one particular country or continent, as in the instance I have taken, to the Continent of North America. It is, however, less formidable in a Universal History, such as the present treatise, because by referring to another volume of the series the reader will find what he needs to know regarding the history of the Spaniards, English, and French in those respective European homes where they had grown to be that which they were when, with religion, slaughter, and slavery in their train, they descended upon the shores of America. Accordingly the difficulty I have pointed out does not disparage the idea and plan of writing Universal History on a geographical basis. It merely indicates a caution needed in applying that plan, and a condition indispensable to its utility; — viz., the regard that must be had to the stage of progress at which a people has arrived when it is subjected to an environment different from that which had in the first instance helped to form its type.

We have now considered some of the ways in which a Universal History written with special reference to the physical phenomena of the earth as geographical science presents them may bring into strong relief one large and permanent set of influences which determine the progress or retrogression of each several branch of mankind. Upon the other principles which preside over and direct the composition of such a work not much need be said. They are of course in the main those which all competent historians will follow in writing the history of any particular people. But a Universal History, which endeavours to present in a short compass a record of the course of events in all regions and among all peoples, since none can safely be omitted, is specially exposed to two dangers. The one is that of becoming sketchy and viewy. When a large subject has to be dealt with on a small scale, it is natural to sum up in a few broad generalisations masses of facts which cannot be described or examined in detail. Broad generalisations are valuable, when they proceed from a thoroughly trained mind, — valuable, even if not completely verifiable, because they excite reflection. But it is seldom possible to make them exact. They necessarily omit most of the exceptions, and thus suggest a greater uniformity than exists.

The other danger is that of sacrificing brightness and charm of presentation. When an effort is made to avoid generalisations and to squeeze into the narrative as many facts as the space will admit, the narrative is apt to become dry, because compression involves the curtailment of the personal and dramatic element. These are the rocks between which every historian has to steer. If he has ample space, he does well to prefer the course of giving all the salient facts and leaving the reader to generalise for himself. If, however, his space is limited, as must needs be the lot of those who write a Universal History, the impossibility of going into minute detail makes generalisations inevitable, for it is through them that the result and significance of a multitude of minor facts must be conveyed in a condensed form. All the greater therefore becomes the need for care and sobriety in the forming and setting forth every summarising statement and general conclusion or judgment. Probably the soundest guiding principle and best safeguard against error, is to be found in shunning all preconceived hypotheses which seek to explain history by one set of causes or to read it in the light of one idea. The habit of magnifying a single factor, such as the social factor, or the economic, or the religious, has been a fertile source of weakness in historical writing, because it has made the presentation of events one-sided, and destroyed that balance and proportion which it is the highest merit of any historian to have attained. Theory and generalisation are the life-blood of history. They make it intelligible. They give it unity. They convey to us the instruction which it always contains, together with so much of practical guidance in the management of communities as history is capable of rendering. But they need to be applied with reserve, and not only with an impartial mind, but after a painstaking examination of all the facts, whether or no they seem to make for the particular theory stated, and of all the theories which any competent predecessor has propounded. For the historian, though he must keep himself from falling under the dominion of any one doctrine by which it is sought to connect and explain phenomena, must welcome all the light which any such doctrine can throw upon facts. Even if such a doctrine be imperfect, even if it be tainted by error, it may serve to indicate relations between facts, or to indicate the true importance of facts, which previous writers had failed to observe or had passed too lightly over. It is thus that History is always growing. It is for this reason that History always needs to be rewritten. History is a progressive science, not merely because new facts are constantly being discovered, not merely because the changes in the world give to old facts a new significance, but also because every truly penetrating and original mind sees in the old facts something which had not been seen before.

As is well observed by Dr. Helmolt in the Introductory Chapter of this volume, a Universal History is fitted to correct such defects as may be incident to that extreme specialism in historical writing which is now in fashion. The broad and concise treatment which a History of all times and peoples must adopt naturally leads to efforts to characterise the dominant features and tendency of an epoch or a movement, whether social, economic, or political. Yet even here there is a danger to be guarded against. No epoch, no movement, is so simple as it looks at first sight, or as one would gather from even the most honest contemporary writer. There is always an eddy at the side of the stream; and the stream itself is the resultant of a number of rivulets with different sources and whose waters, if the metaphor may be extended, are of different tints. Let any man study minutely a given epoch, such as that of the Reformation in Germany or that of the Revolutionary War in America, and he will be surprised to find how much more complex were the forces at work than he had at first supposed, and on how much smaller a number of persons than he had fancied the principal forces did in fact directly operate. Or let any one — for this is perhaps the best, if the most difficult, method of getting at the roots of this complexity — study thoroughly and dispassionately the phenomena of his own time. Let him observe how many movements go on simultaneously, sometimes accelerating, sometimes retarding one another, and mark how the more fully he understands this complex interlacing, so much the less confident do his predictions of the future become. He will then realise how hard it is to find simple explanations and to deliver exact statements regarding critical epochs in the past.

Nevertheless, the task of summarising and explaining is one to which the writer of a History of the World must address himself. If he has the disadvantage of limited space, he has the advantage of being able to assume the reader's knowledge of what has gone before, and to invite the reader's attention to what will come after. Thus he stands in a better position than does the writer who deals with one country or one epoch only for making each part of history illustrate other parts, for showing how similar social tendencies, similar proclivities of human nature, work similarly under varying conditions and are followed by similar, though never identical results. He is able to bring out the essential unity of history, expunging from the reader's mind the conventional and often misleading distinctions that are commonly drawn between the ancient, the mediæval, and the modern time. He can bring the contemporaneous course of events in different countries into a fruitful relation. And in the case of the present work, which dwells more especially on the geographical side of history, he can illustrate from each country in succession the influence of physical environment on the formation of races and the progress of nations, the principles which determine the action of such environment being everywhere similar, though the forms which that action takes are infinitely various.

Is there, it may be asked, any central thread in following which the unity of history most plainly appears? Is there any process in tracing which we can feel that we are floating down the main stream of the world's onward movement? If there be such a process, its study ought to help us to realise the unity of history by connecting the development of the numerous branches of the human family.

One such process has already been adverted to and illustrated. It is the gradual and constant increase in Man's power over Nature, whereby he is emancipated more and more from the conditions she imposes on his life, yet is brought into an always closer touch with her by the discovery of new methods of using her gifts. Two other such processes may be briefly examined. One goes on in the sphere of Time, and consists in the accumulation from age to age of the strength, the knowledge, and the culture of mankind as a whole. The other goes on in Space as well as in Time, and may be described as the Contraction of the World, relatively to Man.

The accumulation of physical strength is most apparent in the increase of the human race. We have no trustworthy data for determining the population even of any one civilised country more than a century and a half ago; much less can we conjecture that of any country in primitive or prehistoric times. It is clear, however, that in prehistoric times, say six or seven thousand years ago, there were very few men on the earth's surface. The scarcity of food would alone be sufficient to prove that; and indeed all our data go to show it. Fifty years ago the world's population used to be roughly conjectured at from seven to nine hundred millions, two-thirds of them in China and India. It is now estimated at over fourteen hundred millions. That of Europe alone must have tripled within a century, and can hardly be less than three hundred and sixty millions. That of North America may have scarcely exceeded four or five millions in the time of Christopher Columbus or at the date of the first English settlements, though we have only the scantiest data for a guess. It may now exceed one hundred millions, for there are seventy-six millions in the United States alone, more than twelve in Mexico, and five in Canada, besides the inhabitants of Central America. The increase has been most swift in the civilised industrial countries, such as Britain, Germany, Russia, and the United States; but it has gone on in India also since India came under British rule (famines notwithstanding), and in the regions recently colonised by Europeans, such as Australia, Siberia, and Argentina, the disappearance of aborigines being far more than compensated by the prolific power of the white immigrants. Some regions, such as Asia Minor and parts of North Africa, are more thinly peopled now than they were under the Roman Empire, and both China and Peru may have no larger population than they had five or ten or fifteen centuries ago. But taking the world at large, the increase is enormous, and will apparently continue. Even after the vacant cultivable spaces which remain in the two Americas, Northern Asia, and Australasia have been filled, the discovery of new modes of enlarging the annually available stock of food may maintain the increase. It is most conspicuous among the European races, and is of course due to the greater production in some regions of food and in others of commodities wherewith food can be purchased. It means an immense addition to the physical force of mankind in the aggregate, and to the possibilities of intellectual force also, — a point to be considered later. And of course it also means an immense and growing preponderance of the civilised white nations, which are now probably one half of mankind, and may in another century, when they have risen from about five hundred to possibly one thousand or fifteen hundred millions, be nearly two thirds

As respects the strength of the average individual man, the inquiry is less simple. Palæolithic man and neolithic man were apparently (though here and there may have been exceptions) comparatively feeble creatures, as are the relics of the most backward tribes known to us, such as the Veddas of Ceylon, the Bushmen, the Fuegians. Some savages, as for instance the Patagonians, are men of great stature, and some of the North American Indians possess amazing powers of endurance. The Greeks of the fifth century B.C. and the Teutons of the time of Julius Cæsar had reached a high physical development. Pheidippides is said to have traversed one hundred and fifty miles on foot in forty-eight hours. But if we think of single feats of strength, feats have been performed in our own day, such as Captain Webb's swimming across the Straits of Dover, equal to anything recorded from ancient or mediæval times. To swim across the much narrower Hellespont was then deemed a surprising exploit. Nor do we know of any race more to be commended for physical power and vigour of constitution than the American backwoodsmen of Kentucky or Oregon to-day. The swords used by the knights of the fifteenth century have usually handles too small for many a modern English or German hand to grasp. Isolated feats do not prove very much, but there is good reason to believe that the average European is as strong as ever he was, and probably more healthy, at least if longevity is a test of health. One may fairly conclude that with better and more abundant food the average of stature and strength has improved over the world at large, so that in this respect also the force of mankind as a whole has advanced. Whether this advance will continue is more doubtful. In modern industrial communities the law of the survival of the fittest may turn out to be reversed, for it is the poorer and lower sections of the population that marry at an early age and have the largest families, while prudential considerations keep down the birth-rate among the upper middle class. In Transylvania, for instance, the Saxons are dying out, because very few children are born to each pair, while the less educated and cultured Rumans increase fast. In North America the old New England stock of comparatively pure British blood has begun to be swamped by the offspring of the recent immigrants, mostly Irish or French Canadians; and although the sons of New England who have gone west continue to be prolific, it is probable that the phenomena of New England will recur in the Mississippi Valley, and that the newcomers from Europe who form the less cultivated strata of the population — Irish, Germans, Italians, Czechs, Poles, Slovaks, Rumans — will contribute an increasing proportion of the inhabitants.[1] Now the poorer sections are in most countries, though of course not always to the same extent, somewhat inferior in physical as well as in mental quality, and more prone to suffer from that greatest hindrance to physical improvement, the abuse of alcoholic drinks.

We come next to another form of the increase of human resources, the Accumu-

---

[1] Some of these, and especially the Irish and the Germans and the Scandinavians, are among the best elements in the American population and have produced men of the highest distinction. But the average level among them of versatile aptitude and of intellectual culture is slightly below that of the native Americans.

lation of Knowledge and of what may be called intellectual Culture and Capacity, for it is convenient to distinguish these two latter from Knowledge.

In Knowledge there has been an advance, not merely a tolerably steady and constant advance, but one which has gone on with a sort of geometrical progression, moving the faster the nearer we come to our own time. Whatever may have befallen in the prehistoric darkness, History knows of only one notable arrest or setback in the onward march, — that which marks the seventh, eighth, and ninth centuries of the Christian era. Even this setback was practically confined to Southern and Western Europe, and affected only certain departments of knowledge. It did not, save perhaps as regards a few artistic processes, extinguish that extremely important part of the previously accumulated resources of mankind which consisted in the knowledge of Inventions. It is in respect of Inventions, especially mechanical and physical or chemical inventions, that the accumulation of knowledge has been most noteworthy and most easy to appreciate. A history of inventions is a history of the progress of mankind, of a progress to which every race may have contributed in primitive times, though all the later contributions have come from a few of the most civilised. Every great invention marks one onward step, as one may see by enumerating a few, such as the use of fire, cooking, metal working, the domestication of wild animals, the tillage of the ground, the use of plough and mattock and harrow and fan, the discovery of plants or trees useful for food or for medicine, the cart, the wheel, the watermill (overshot, undershot, and turbine), the windmill, the distaff (followed long, long after by the spinning-wheel), the loom, dye stuffs, the needle, the potter's wheel, the hydraulic press, the axe-handle, the spear, the bow, the shield, the war-chariot, the sling, the cross-bow, the boat, the paddle, the oar, the helm, the sail, the mariner's compass, the clock, picture-writing, the alphabet, parchment, paper, printing, photography, the sliding keel, the sounding-lead, the log, the brick, mortar, the column, the arch, the dome, till we come down to explosives, the microscope, the cantilever, and the Röntgen rays. The history of the successive discovery, commixture, and applications of the metals, from copper and bronze down to manganese, platinum, and aluminium, or of the successive discovery and utilisation of sources of power ; — the natural sources, such as water and wind, the artificially procured, such as steam, gas, and electricity, — or of the production and manufacture of materials available for clothing, wool, hair, linen, silk, cotton, would show how every step becomes the basis for another step, and how inventions in one department suggest or facilitate inventions in another. Recent discoveries in surgery and medicine, such as the use of antiseptics, tend to improve health and to prolong life ; and in doing so, they increase the chances of further discoveries being made. Who can tell what the world may have lost by the early death of many a man of genius? One peculiar line of discovery which at first seemed to have nothing to do with practice has proved to be of signal service, the working out of mathematical methods of calculation by means of which the mechanical and physical sciences have in recent times made a progress in their practical application undreamt of by those who laid the foundations of geometry and algebra many centuries ago. It may indeed be said that all the sciences need one another, and that none has been without its utilities for practice, since even that which deals with the heavenly bodies has been used for the computation of time, was used by the agriculturist before he had any calendars to guide him, and has been of supreme value to the navigator.[1]

Another kind of knowledge also grows by the joint efforts of many peoples, that which records the condition of men in the past and the present, including history, economics, statistics, and the other so-called social sciences. This kind also is useful for practice, and has led to improvements by which nearly all nations have profited, such as an undebased currency, banking and insurance, better systems of taxation, corporations and joint stock companies. With this we may couple the invention of improved political institutions, such as representative government, tribunals not controlled by the executive, and the union of a number of locally self-governed communities in a federation. Yet not all such inventions are to be deemed improvements. The machinery of party and that which is called in the United States the Boss system are also the result of the application of creative ingenuity to political phenomena.

The accumulation of knowledge, especially of scientific knowledge applied to the exploitation of the resources of Nature, means the accumulation of wealth, — that is to say, of all the things which men need or use. The total wealth of the world must have at least quadrupled or quintupled within the last hundred years. Nearly all of it is in the hands or under the control of the civilised nations of European stock, among whom the United States stands foremost, both in rate of economic growth and in the absolute quantity of values possessed.

Two further observations belong to this part of the subject. One is that this stock of useful knowledge, the accumulation of which is the central fact of the material progress as well as of the intellectual history of mankind, now belongs to (practically) all races and States alike. Some, as we shall note presently, are more able to use it than others, but all have access to it. This is a new fact. It is true that most races have contributed something to the common stock; and that even among the civilised peoples, no one or two or three (except possibly the Greeks as respects ancient times) can claim to have contributed much more than the others. But in earlier ages there were peoples or groups of peoples who were for a time the sole possessors of inventions which gave them great advantages, especially for war. Superior weapons as well as superior drill enabled Alexander the Great, and afterward the Romans, to conquer most of the civilised world. Horses and firearms with courage and discipline enabled two Spanish adventurers to seize two ancient American empires with very scanty forces, as they enabled a handful of Dutch Boers to overcome the hosts of Mosilikatze and Dingaan. So there were formerly industrial arts known to or practised by a few peoples only. But now all inventions, even those relating to war, are available even to the more backward races, if they can learn how to use them or can hire white men to do so for

---

[1] It has also been suggested that an observation of sun spots may enable the advent of specially hot seasons, involving droughts, to be predicted.

them. The facilities of communication are so great, the means of publicity so abundant, that everything becomes speedily known everywhere.

The other observation is that there is now no risk that any valuable piece of knowledge will be lost. Every public event that happens, as well as every fact of scientific consequence, is put on record, and that not on a single stone or in a few manuscripts, but in books of which so many copies exist that even the perishable nature of the material will not involve the loss of the contents, since, if these contents are valuable, they will be transferred to and issued in other books, and so on *ad infinitum*. Thus every process of manufacture is known to so many persons that while it continues to be serviceable it is sure to be familiar and transmitted from generation to generation by practice as well as by description. We must imagine a world totally different from the world we know in order to imagine the possibility of any diminution, indeed of any discontinuance of the increase, of this stock of knowledge which the world has been acquiring, and which is not only knowledge but potential Wealth.

When one passes from Knowledge considered as a body of facts ascertained and available for use to the thing we call Intellectual Aptitude or Culture, — namely, the power of turning knowledge to account and of producing results in spheres other than material, — and when we inquire whether mankind has made a parallel advance in this direction, it becomes necessary to distinguish three different kinds of intellectual capacity.

The first may be called the power of using scientific methods for the investigation of phenomena, whether physical or social.

The second is the power of speculation, applied to matters which have not hitherto been found capable of examination by the methods of science, whether observational, experimental, or mathematical.

The third is the power of intellectual creation, whether literary creation or artistic creation.

The methods of scientific inquiry may almost be classed with the ascertained facts of science or with inventions, as being parts of the stock of accumulated knowledge built up by the labour of many generations. They are known to everybody who cares to study them, and can be learnt and applied by everybody who will give due diligence. Just as every man can be taught to fire a gun, or steer a ship, or write a letter, though guns, helms, and letters are the result of discoveries made by exceptionally gifted men, so every graduate in science of a university can use the methods of induction, can observe and experiment with a correctness which a few centuries ago even the most vigorous minds could scarcely have reached. Because the methods have been so fully explained and illustrated as to have grown familiar, a vast host of investigators, very few of whom possess scientific genius, are at work to-day extending our scientific knowledge. So the methods of historical criticism, so the methods of using statistics, are to-day profitably applied by many men with no such original gift as would have made them competent critics or statisticians had not the paths been cut by a few great men and trodden since by hundreds of feet. All that is needed is Imitation, — intelligent and careful imitation. Nevertheless there remains this sharp contrast between knowledge of the facts of applied science and knowledge of the methods, that whereas there is no radical difference between the ability of one man and that of another to use a mechanical invention, such as a steam plough or an electric motor car, there is all the difference in the world between the power of one intellect and another to use a method for the purposes of fresh discovery. Knowledge fossilised in a concrete invention or even in a mathematical formula is a sort of tool, ready to every hand. But a method, though serviceable to everybody, becomes eminently fruitful only when wielded by the same kind of original genius as that which made discoveries by the less perfect methods of older days. This is apparent even in inquiries which seem to reside chiefly in collection and computation. Everybody tries nowadays to use statistics. Many people do use them profitably. But the people who by means of statistics can throw really fresh and brilliant light on a problem are as few as ever they were.

When we turn to the exercise of speculative thought on subjects not amenable to strictly scientific, that is to say to exact, methods, the gain which has come to mankind by the labour of past ages is of a different order. Metaphysics, ethics, and theology, to take the most obvious examples, are all of them the richer for the thoughts of philosophers in the past. A number of distinctions have been drawn, and a number of classifications made, a number of confusions, often verbal, have been cleared up, a number of fallacies detected, a number of technical terms invented, whereby the modern speculator enjoys a great advantage over his predecessor. His mind has been clarified, and many new aspects of the old problems have been presented, so that he is better able to see all round the old problems. None of the great thinkers, from Pythagoras down to Hegel, has left metaphysics where he found it. Yet none can be said to have built on the foundations of his predecessors in the same way as the mathematicians and physicists and chemists have added to the edifice they found. What the philosophers have done is to accumulate materials for the study of Man's faculties and modes of thinking, and of his ideas regarding his relations to the Universe, while also indicating various methods by which the study may be pursued. Each great product of speculative thought is itself a part of these materials, and for that reason never becomes obsolete, as the treatises of the old physicists and chemists have mostly become. Aristotle, for instance, has left us books on natural history, on metaphysics and ethics, and on politics. Those on natural history are mere curiosities, and no modern biologist or zoologist needs them. Those on metaphysics and ethics still deserve the attention of the student of philosophy, though he may in a certain sense be said to have got beyond them. The treatise on politics still keeps its place beside Montesquieu, Burke, and Tocqueville. Or, to take a thinker who seems further removed from us even than Aristotle, though fifteen hundred years later in date, St. Thomas of Aquinum discusses questions from most of which the modern world has moved away, and discusses them by methods which few would now use, starting from premises which few would now accept. But he marks a remarkable stage in the history of human thought, and as a part of that history, and as an example of extraordinary dialectical ingenuity and subtlety, he remains an object of interest to those least in agreement with his conclusions. Every great thinker affects other thinkers, and propagates the impulse he has received, though perhaps in a quite different direction. The teaching of Socrates was the starting-point for nearly all the subsequent schools of Greek philosophy. Hume became the point of departure for Kant, who desired to lay a deeper foundation for philosophy than that which Hume seemed to have overturned. All these great ones have not only enriched us, but are still capable of stimulating us. But they have not improved our capacity for original thinking. The accumulation of scientific knowledge has, as already observed, put all mankind in a better position for solving further physical problems and establishing a more complete dominion over nature. The accumulation of philosophic thought has had no similar effect. In the former case each man stands, so to speak, on the shoulders of his predecessors. In the latter he stands on his own feet. The value of future contributions to philosophy will depend on the original power of the minds that make them, and only to a small extent (except by way of stimulus) on what such minds may have drawn from those into whose labours they have entered.

When we come to the products of literary and artistic capacity, we find an ever vaster accumulation of intellectual treasure available for enjoyment, but a still more marked absence of connection between the amount of treasures possessed and the power of adding fresh treasures to them. Since writing came into use, and indeed even in the days when memory alone preserved lays and tales, every age and many races have contributed to the stock. There have been ebbs and flows both in quantity and quality. The centuries between A.D. 600 and A.D. 1100 have left us very little of high merit in literature, though something in architecture, and the best of that little in literature did not come from the seats of Roman civilisation in Italy, France, Spain, and the East Roman Empire. Some periods have seen an eclipse of poetry, others an eclipse of art or a sterility in music. Literature and the arts have not always flourished together, and musical genius in particular seems to have little to do with the contemporaneous development of other forms of intellectual power. The quantity of production bears no relation to the quality, not even an inverse relation; for the pessimistic notion, that the larger the output the smaller is the part which possesses brilliant excellence, has not been proved. Still less does the amount of good work produced in any given area depend upon the number of persons living in that area. Florence between A.D. 1250 and A.D. 1500 gave birth to more men of first-rate poetical and artistic genius than London has produced since 1250; yet Florence had in those two and a half centuries a population of probably only from forty to sixty thousand. And Florence herself has since A.D. 1500 given birth to scarcely any distinguished poets or artists, though her population has been larger than it was in the fifteenth century.

The increase in the world's stock of intellectual wealth is one of the most remarkable facts in history, for it represents a constant increase in the means of enjoyment. Such losses as there have been have nearly all occurred during the

Dark Ages; but there is now little risk that anything of high literary or musical value will perish, though, of course, works of art, and especially buildings and carvings, suffer or vanish.

The increase does not, however, tend to any strengthening of the creative faculty. There is a greater abundance of models of excellence, models which form the taste, afford a stimulus to sensitive minds, and establish a sort of technique with well-known rules. The principles of criticism are more fully investigated. The power of analysis grows, and the appreciation both of literature and of art is more widely diffused. Their influence on the whole community becomes greater; but the creative imagination which is needed for the production of original work becomes no more abundant and no more powerful. It may indeed be urged, though our data are probably insufficient for a final judgment, that the finer qualities of poetry and of pictorial and plastic art tend rather to decline under the more analytic habit of mind which belongs to the modern world. Simplicity, freshness, spontaneity come less naturally to those who have fallen under the pervasive influence of this habit.

There remains one other way in which the incessant play of thought may be said to have increased or improved the resources of mankind. Certain principles or ideas belonging to the moral and social sphere — to the moral sphere by their origin, to the social sphere by their results — make their way to a more or less general acceptance, and exert a potent influence upon human life and action. They are absent in the earliest communities of which we know, or are present only in germ. They emerge, sometimes in the form of customs gradually built up in one or more peoples, sometimes in the utterances of one gifted mind. Sometimes they spread impalpably; sometimes they become matter for controversy, and are made the battle-cries of parties. Sometimes they end by being universally received, though not necessarily put into practice. Sometimes, on the other hand, they continue to be rejected in one country, or by one set of persons in a country, as vehemently as they are asserted by another. As instances of these principles or ideas or doctrines, whatever one is to call them, the following may be taken: — the condemnation of piracy, of slavery, and of treaty-breaking, of outrages on the bodies of dead enemies, of cruelty to the lower animals, of the slaughter of prisoners in cold blood, of polygamy, of torture to witnesses or criminals; the recognition of the duty of citizens to obey the laws, and of the moral responsibility of rulers for the exercise of their power, of the right of each man to hold his own religious opinion and to worship accordingly, of the civil (though not necessarily of the political) equality of all citizens; the disapproval of intoxication, the value set upon female chastity, the acceptance of the social and civil (to which some would add the political) equality of women.

All these dogmas or ideas or opinions — some have become dogmas in all civilised peoples, others are rather to be described as opinions whose truth or worth is denied or only partially admitted — are the slow product of many generations. Most of them are due to what we may call the intelligence and sentiment of mankind at large, rather than to their advocacy by any prominent individual thinkers.

The teachings of such thinkers have of course done much to advance them. Everybody would name Socrates and Confucius as among the men who have contributed to their progress ; some would add such names as those of Mohammed and St. Francis of Assisi. Christianity has, of course, made the largest contributions. How much is due to moral feeling, how much to a sense of common utility, cannot be exactly estimated. Economic reasonings and practical experience would probably have in the long run destroyed slavery, but it was sentiment that did in fact destroy it in the civilised States where it had longest survived.

How much these doctrines, even in the partial and imperfect application which most of them have secured, have done for humanity may be perceived by any one who will imagine what the world would be if they were unknown. They form one of the most substantial additions made to what may be called the intellectual and moral capital with which Man has to work his planet and improve his own life upon it. And the most interesting and significant crises in history are those which have turned upon the recognition or application of principles of this kind. The Reformation of the sixteenth century, the French Revolution, the War of Secession in the United States, are familiar modern examples.

Putting all these forms of human achievement together, — the extension of the scientific knowledge of Nature with consequent mastery over her, the scientific knowledge of social phenomena in the past and the present, the records of philosophic speculation, the mass of literary and artistic products, the establishment, however partial and imperfect, of regulative moral and political principles, — it will be seen that the accumulation of this vast stock of intellectual wealth has been an even more important factor than the increase of population in giving Man strength and dignity over against Nature, and in opening up to him an endless variety of modes of enjoying life, that is to say, of making it yield to him the most which its shortness and his own physical infirmities permit. The process by which this accumulation has been carried along is the central thread of history. The main aim of a History of the World must be to show what and how each race or people has contributed to the general stock. To this aim political history, ecclesiastical history, economic history, the history of philosophy and the history of science, are each of them subordinate, though it is only through them that the process can be explained.

In these last few pages intellectual progress has been considered apart from the area in which it has gone on, and apart from the conditions imposed on it by the natural features of that area. A few words are, however, needed regarding its relation to the surface of the earth. The movement of civilisation must be considered from the side of Space as well as from that of Time.

Space is a material element in the enquiry because it has divided the families of mankind from one another. Some families, such as the Chinese and the Peruvians, have developed independently ; some, such as the South and West European peoples, in connection with, or perhaps in dependence on, the development of other races or peoples. Hence that which each achieved was in some cases achieved for itself only, in other cases for its neighbours as well. The contributions made by different races have, at any rate during the last four thousand years, and probably in earlier days also, been very unequal; yet none can have failed to contribute something if only by way of influencing the others. Inequality in progress would seem to have become more marked in the later than in the earlier periods. Indeed some races, such as those of Australia, appear during many centuries, possibly owing to their isolation, to have made no progress at all. They may even have receded.

When we regard the evolution and development of Man from the side of his relations to Space, three facts stand out, — the contraction of the world, the overflow of the more advanced races, and the consequent diffusion all over the world of what is called Civilisation.

By the Contraction of the World, I mean the greater swiftness, ease, and safety with which men can pass from one part of it to another, or communicate with one another across great intervening spaces. This has the effect of making the world smaller for most practical purposes, while the absolute distance in latitude and longitude remains the same. The progress of discovery is worth tracing, for it shows how much larger the small earth which was known to the early nations must have seemed to them than the whole earth which we know seems to us. The most ancient records we possess from Assyria, Egypt, Palestine, and from the Homeric poems, show how very limited was the range of geographical knowledge possessed by that small civilised world from which our own civilisation has descended. Speaking roughly, that knowledge seems in the tenth century B.C. to have extended about one thousand miles in each direction from the Isthmus of Suez. However, the best point of departure for the peoples of antiquity is the era of Herodotus, who travelled and wrote B.C. 460–440. The limits of the world as he knew it were Cadiz and the Straits of Gibraltar on the west, the Danube and the Caspian on the north, the deserts of eastern Persia on the east and the Sahara on the south, with vague tales regarding peoples who lived beyond, such as Indians far beyond Persia and Pygmies beyond the Sahara. He reports, however, not without hesitation, a circumnavigation of Africa by Phœnicians in the service of Pharaoh Necho. Discovery advanced very slowly for many centuries, though the march of Alexander opened up part of the East, while the Roman conquests brought the far Northwest, including Britain, within the range of civilisation; while occasional voyages, such as that of Hanno along the coast of West Africa, that of Nearchus through the Arabian Sea, and that of Pytheas to the Baltic added something to knowledge. Procopius in A.D. 540 can tell us little more regarding the regions beyond Roman influence than Strabo does five and a half centuries earlier. The journeys of Marco Polo and Rubruquis throw only a passing light on the Far East. It is with the Spanish occupation of the Canary Isles, beginning in 1602, and with the Portuguese voyages of the fifteenth century that the era of modern discovery opens. The rediscovery of America in 1492, for it had been already visited by the Northmen of Greenland and Iceland in the eleventh century, and the opening of the Cape route to India in 1497–1498, were hardly equal to the exploit of Magellan, whose circumnavigation of the globe in 1519–1520 marks the close of this striking period. Thereafter discovery proceeds more slowly. Some of the isles of the central and southern Pacific were not visited till the middle of the eighteenth century, and the northwest coast of America as well as the northeast coast of Asia remained little known till an even later date. Those explorations of the interior of North America, of the interior of Africa, of the interior of Australia and of East Central Asia which have completed our knowledge of the earth belong to the nineteenth century. The first crossing of the North American Continent north of latitude 40° was not effected till A.D. 1806.

The desire for new territory, for the propagation of religion, and above all for the precious metals, were the chief motives which prompted the voyages of the fifteenth and sixteenth centuries. These motives have remained operative; and to them has been added in more recent times the spirit of pure adventure and the interest in science, together with, in increasing measure, the effort to secure trade. But the extension of trade followed slowly in the wake of discovery. China and Japan remained almost closed. The policy of Spain sought to restrict her American waters to her own ships, and the commerce which they carried was scanty. Communications remained slow and dangerous across the oceans till the introduction of steam vessels (1825–1830). Land transport, though it had steadily increased in Europe, remained costly as well as slow till the era of railway construction began in 1829. The application of steam as a motive power and of electricity as a means of communicating thought has been by far the greatest factor in this long process of reducing the dimensions of the world which dates back as far as the domestication of beasts of burden and the invention first of paddles and oars and then of sails. The North American Continent can now be crossed in five days, the South American (from Valparaiso to Buenos Ayres) in six or seven, the projected Transandine tunnel being still unpierced. The Continent which stretches from the Baltic to the North Pacific will soon be traversed in fourteen days. When this Trans-Siberian line has been completed, and its terminus connected by steam with the ports of Japan, it will be possible, using the existing routes, to go round the globe in little more than fifty days. Nor is this acceleration of transit more remarkable than its practical immunity, as compared with earlier times, not only from the dangers for which Nature is answerable, but from those also which Man formerly interposed.

The increase of trade which has followed in the track first of discovery and latterly (with immensely larger volume) of the improvement of means of transport, has been accompanied not only by the seizure of transoceanic territories by the greater civilised States, but also by an outflow of population from those States into the more backward or more thinly peopled parts of the earth. Sometimes, as in the case of North America, Siberia, and Australia, the emigrants extinguish or absorb the aboriginal population. Sometimes, as in the case of India, Africa, and some parts of South America, they neither extinguish nor blend with the previous inhabitants, but rule them and spread what is called civilisation among them,—this civilisation consisting chiefly in a knowledge of the mechanical arts and of deathful weapons, accompanied by the destruction, more or less gradual, of their pre-existing beliefs and usages. Sometimes again, as in the case of China, and to some extent also of the Mussulman East, though political dominion is not established, the process of substituting a new civilisation for the old one goes on despite the occasional efforts of the backward people to resist this process. The broad result is everywhere similar. The modern European type of civilisation is being diffused over the whole earth, superseding, or essentially modifying, the older local types. Thus in a still more important sense than even that of communications, the world is contracted and becomes far more one than it had ever been before. The European who speaks three or four languages can travel over nearly all of it, and he can find on most of its habitable coasts, and in many parts even of the lately discovered interior, the appliances which are to him necessaries of life. The world is in fact becoming an enlarged Europe, so far as the externals of life and the material side of civilisation are concerned. The dissociative forces of Nature have been overcome.

Putting together the two processes, the process in Time and the process in Space, which we have been reviewing, it will be seen that the main line of the development of mankind may be described as the Transmission and the Expansion of Culture, that is to say, of knowledge and intellectual capacity. The stock of knowledge available for use and enjoyment has been steadily increased, and what each people accumulated has been made available for all. With this there has come Assimilation, the destruction of weaker types of civilisation, the modification by constant interaction of the stronger types, the creation of a common type tending to absorb all the rest. Assimilation has been most complete in the sphere ruled by Natural Science, that is to say, in the material sphere, less complete in that ruled by the human sciences (including the sphere of political and social institutions), still less complete in the sphere of religious, moral, and social ideas, and as respects the products of literature and art. Or, in other words, where certainty of knowledge is attainable and utility in practice is incontestable, the process of Assimilation has moved fastest and furthest.

The process has been a long one, for its beginnings reach back beyond our historical knowledge. So far as it lies within the range of history, it falls into two periods, the earlier of which supplies an instructive illustration of the later one which we know better. The effort which Nature, that is to say, the natural tendencies of Man as a social being, has been making toward the unification of mankind during the last few centuries, is her second great effort. The first was in progress from the time when the most ancient records begin down to the sixth and seventh centuries of the Christian era. Greek civilisation, which itself had drawn much from Egypt, as well as from Assyria, Phœnicia, and the peoples of Asia Minor, permeated the minds and institutions (except the legal institutions), of the Mediterranean and West European countries, and was propagated by the governing energy of the Romans. In its Romanised form it transformed or absorbed and superseded the less advanced civilisations of all those countries, creating one new type for the whole Roman world. With some local diversities, that type prevailed from the Northumbrian Wall of Hadrian to the Caucasus and the deserts of Arabia. The still independent races on the northern frontier of the Empire received a tincture of it, and would doubtless have been more deeply imbued had the Roman Empire stood longer. Christianity, becoming dominant at a time when the Empire was already tottering, gave a new sense of unity to all whom the Greco-Roman type had formed, extended the influence of that type still further, and enabled much that belonged to it (especially its religious, its legal, and its literary elements) to survive the political dominion of the Emperors and to perpetuate itself among practically independent States which were springing up. The authority of Papal Rome helped to carry this sense of unity among civilised men through a period of ignorance, confusion, and semi-barbarism which might otherwise have extinguished it. Nevertheless we may say, broadly speaking, that the first effort toward the establishment of a common type of civilisation was, if not closed, yet arrested by the dissolution of the Roman Empire in the West. Close thereupon came the rise of Islam, tearing away the Eastern provinces, and creating a rival type of civilisation — though a type largely influenced by the Greco-Roman — which held its ground for some centuries, and has only recently shown that it is destined to vanish.

The beginnings of the second effort toward the unification of civilised Mankind may be observed as far back as the eleventh and twelfth centuries. Its effective and decisive action may however be assigned to the fifteenth, when the spread of literary and philosophic culture and the swift extension of maritime discovery ushered in the modern phase wherein we have marked its irresistible advance. This phase differs from the earlier one both in its range, for it embraces the whole earth and not merely the Mediterranean lands, and in its basis, for it rests not so much upon Conquest and Religion as upon Scientific Knowledge, formative ideas, and commerce. Yet even here a parallelism may be noted between the ancient and the modern phase. Knowledge and ideas had brought about a marked assimilation of various parts of the ancient world to each other before Roman conquest completed the work, and what conquest did was done chiefly among the ruder races. So now while it is knowledge and ideas that have worked for the creation of a common type among the peoples of European stock, Conquest has been a potent means of spreading this type in the outlying countries and among the more backward races whose territories the European nations have seized.

The diffusion of a few forms of speech has played a great part in both phases. Greek was spoken over the eastern half of the Roman world in the second century A.D., though not to the extinction of such tongues as Syriac and Egyptian. Latin was similarly spoken over the western half, though not to the extinction of the tongues we now call Basque and Breton and Welsh; and Latin continued to be the language of religion, of law, of philosophy, and of serious prose literature in general till the sixteenth century. So now, several of the leading European tongues are spoken far beyond the limits of their birthplace, and their wide range has become a powerful influence in diffusing European culture. German, English, Russian, Spanish, and French are available for the purposes of commerce and for those who read books over nineteen-twentieths of the earth's surface. The languages of the smaller non-European peoples are disappearing, in those places where they have to compete with these greater European tongues, except in so far as they are a medium of domestic intercourse.  Arabic, Chinese, and in less degree Persian are the only non-European languages which retain a world importance.  English, German, and Spanish are pre-eminently the three leading commercial languages.  They gain ground on the rest, and it is English that gains ground most swiftly.  The German merchant is no doubt even more ubiquitous (if the expression be permitted) than is the English; but the German more frequently speaks English than the Englishman or American speaks German.

It has already been observed that assimilation has advanced least in the sphere of institutions, ideas, and literature.  The question might indeed be raised whether the types of thought, of national character, and of literary activity represented by the five or six leading nations are not rather tending to become more accentuated.  The self-consciousness of each nation, taking the form of pride or vanity, leads it to exalt its own type and to dwell with satisfaction on whatever differentiates it from other types.  Nevertheless there are influences at work in the domain of practice as well as of thought, which, in creating a common body of opinion and a sense of common interest among large classes belonging to these leading nations, tend to link the nations themselves together.  Religious sympathy, or a common attachment to certain doctrines, such as for instance those of Collectivism, works in this direction among the masses, as the love of science or of art does among sections of the more educated class.  As regards the peoples not of European stock, who are, broadly speaking, the more backward, it is not yet possible to say what will be the influence of the European type of culture upon their intellectual development.  The material side of their civilisation will after a time conform to the European type, though perhaps to forms that are not the most progressive; and even such faiths as Buddhism and Islam may lose their hold on those who come most into contact with Europeans.  But whether these peoples will produce any new types of thought or art under the stimulus of Europe, as the Teutons and Slavs did after they had been for some centuries in contact with the relics of Greco-Roman culture, or whether they will be overborne by and merely imitate and reproduce what Europeans teach them, — this is a question for conjecture only, since the data for prediction are wanting.  It is a question of special interest as regards the Japanese, the one non-European race which, having an old civilisation of its own, highly developed on the artistic side, has shown an amazing aptitude for appropriating European institutions and ideas.  Already a Japanese physiologist has taken high rank among men of science by being one of the discoverers of the bacillus of the Oriental plague.

One of the questions which both the writers and the readers of a History of the World must frequently ask themselves is whether the course of history establishes a general law of progress.  Some thinkers have gone so far as to say that this must be the moral of history regarded as a whole, and a few have even suggested that without the recognition of such a principle and of a sort of general guidance of human affairs toward this goal, history would be unintelligible and the doings of mankind would seem little better than the sport of chance.  Whatever may be thought of these propositions as matters of theory, the doctrine of a general and steady law of progress is one to which no historian ought to commit himself. His business is to set forth and explain the facts exactly as they are ; and if he writes in the light of a theory, he is pretty certain to be unconsciously seduced into giving undue prominence to those facts which make for it. Moreover the question is in itself a far more complex one than the simple word " Progress " at first sight conveys. What is the test of Progress ? In what form of human advance is it to be deemed to consist ? Which of these forms is of the highest value ? There can be no doubt of the advance made by Man in certain directions. There may be great doubt as to his advance in other directions. There may possibly be no advance, but even retrogression, or at least signs of an approaching retrogression, in some few directions. The view to be taken of the relative importance of these lines of movement is a matter not so much for the historian as for the philosopher, and its discussion would carry us away into fields of thought not fitted for a book like the present. Although therefore it is true that one chief interest of history resides in its capacity for throwing light on this question, all that need here be said may be expressed as follows :

There has been a marvellous advance in Man's knowledge of the laws of Nature and of his consequent mastery over Nature.

There has been therewith a great increase in the numbers of mankind, and, on the whole, in the physical vigour of the average individual man.

There has been as a further consequence an immense increase in the material comfort and well being of the bulk of mankind, so that to most men, taking the human race as a whole, necessaries have become easier of attainment and many things which were once luxuries have become necessaries.

Against this is to be set the fact that some of the natural resources of the world are being rapidly exhausted. This would at one time have excited alarm ; but scientific discoveries have so greatly extended Man's capacity to utilise other sources of natural energy that people are disposed to assume that the loss of the resources aforesaid will be compensated by further discoveries.

As respects Progress other than material, — that is to say, progress in intellectual capacity, in taste and the power of enjoyment, in virtue, and generally in what is called Happiness, — every man's view must depend on the ideal which he sets before himself of what constitutes happiness, and of the relative importance to happiness of the ethical and the non-ethical elements which enter into the conception. Until there is more agreement than now exists or has ever existed on these points, there is no use in trying to form conclusions regarding the progress Man has made. Moreover, it is admitted that nearly every gain Man makes is accompanied by some corresponding loss, — perhaps a slight loss, yet a loss. When we attempt to estimate the comparative importance of these gains and losses, questions of great difficulty, both ethical and non-ethical, emerge ; and in many cases our experience is not yet sufficient to determine the quantum of loss. There is room both for the optimist and for the pessimist, and in arguing such questions nearly everybody becomes an optimist or a pessimist. The historian has no business to be either.

There is another temptation, besides that of delivering his opinion on these high matters, of which the historian does well to beware,— I mean the temptation to prophesy. The study of history as a whole, more inevitably than that of the history of any particular country or people, suggests forecasts of the future, because the broader the field which we survey the more do we learn to appreciate the great and wide-working forces that are guiding mankind, and the more therefore are we led to speculate on the results which these forces, some of them likely to be permanent, will tend to bring about. This temptation can seldom have been stronger than it is now, when we see all mankind brought into closer relations than ever before, and more obviously dominated by forces which are essentially the same, though varying in their form. Yet it will appear, when the problem is closely examined, that the very novelty of the present situation of the world, the fact that our mastery of Nature has been so rapidly extended within this century, and that the phenomena of the subjugation of the earth by Europeans and of the ubiquitous contact of the advanced and the backward races are so unexampled in respect of the area they cover that all predictions must be uttered with the greatest caution, and due allowance made for elements which may disturb even the most careful calculations. It may indeed be doubted whether any predictions of a definitely positive kind — predictions that such and such things will happen — can be safely made, save the obvious ones which are based on the assumption that existing natural conditions will remain for some time operative.

Taking this assumption to be a legitimate one, it may be predicted that population will continue to increase, at least till the now waste but habitable parts of the earth have been turned to account; that races, except where there is a marked colour line, will continue to become intermingled; that the small and weak races, and especially the lower sort of savages, will be absorbed or die out; that fewer and fewer languages will be spoken; that communications will become even swifter, easier, and cheaper than they are at present, and that commerce and wealth will continue to grow, subject perhaps to occasional checks from political disturbance.

There are also some negative predictions on which one may venture, and with a little more confidence. No new race can appear, except possibly from a fusion of two or more existing races, or from the differentiation of a branch of an existing race under new conditions, as the Americans have been to some slight extent differentiated from the English and the Brazilians from the Portuguese (there having been in the latter case a certain admixture of negro blood), and as the Siberians of the future may be a different sort of Russians. Neither is any new language likely to appear, except mere trade jargons (like Chinook or pigeon English), because the existing languages of the great peoples are firmly established, and the process of change within each of these languages has, owing to the abundance of printed matter, become now extremely slow. Conditions can hardly be imagined under which such a phenomenon as the development of the Romance languages out of Latin, or of Danish and Swedish out of the common Northern tongue of the eleventh century, could recur.

It may seem natural to add the further prediction that the great States and the great religions will continue to grow and to absorb the small ones.  But when we touch topics into which human opinion or emotion enters, we touch a new kind of matter, where the influences now at work may be too much affected by new influences to permit of any forecast.  Conditions might conceivably come into action which would split up some or most of the present great States, and bring the world back to an age of small political communities.  So too, though the lower forms of paganism are fast vanishing and the four or five great religions are extending their sway, it is conceivable that new prophets may arise, founding new faiths, or that the existing religions may be split up into new sects widely diverse from one another.  Even the supremacy of the European races, well assured as it now appears, may be reduced by a variety of causes, physiological or moral, when some centuries have passed.  Whoever examines the predictions made by the most observant and profound thinkers of the past will see reason to distrust almost all the predictions, especially those of a positive order, which shape themselves in our minds to-day.

# HISTORY OF THE WORLD

## I

## THE IDEA, UNIVERSAL HISTORY

### By DR. HANS F. HELMOLT

## 1. THE SUBJECT-MATTER AND AIM OF A UNIVERSAL HISTORY

WHEN I acknowledge that I shall treat of things in a very different manner from that adopted by my predecessors, I do so, thanking them; for it is they who have opened up the roads which lead to the investigation of facts. — NICOLAUS COPERNICUS.

IT is an error, widespread among men, to consider that portion of the earth which is limited by our intellectual horizon the entire world. To Cato the elder, Rome was the consummation of all history;[1] and the Chinese call their native land the Middle Kingdom. The German chronicler of the thirteenth century made no mention of the Turks; and even in the seventeenth century there was scarcely an educated man of western Europe who recognised Russia as a nation possessed of equal rights and privileges with his own. Fortunately the standard for judging events in the world's history has become far more comprehensive than would have been considered possible a few years ago. Therefore the time has come for us to think of such a work. Universal history is the history of the development of mankind in the aggregate. Previous works bearing this or a similar title have fallen short of their promise; the relation of any one of them to a true universal history is that of the autobiography of a man to the history of his time.

It is objected that the foundations are not yet laid firmly enough; that the preliminary studies are not yet closed. This doubt, however, is not conclusive. The high ideal of writing a complete universal history will never be attained; for the more extensive our investigation, the more often shall we discover unexpected doors which open only to mysterious voids and obscurity. But there are ample materials for a work that only claims to be a preliminary study for a universal history; and the greatest joy of a conscientious worker lies in the thought of that which will be accomplished by his successors. Investigations limited to special fields have been made in abundance, and, in these, history, according to the true meaning of the term, has often enough been neglected. The criticism of the work of German historians, uttered by Christian Garve just one hundred years ago, is instructive. He mentioned two chief faults:

"The first is, that few large histories, embracing an appreciable space of time, undertaken by able thinkers and scholars, have come to completion. Some authors intentionally selected small, neglected corners of history, upon which they sought to throw light

---

[1] Throughout this and subsequent sections the word "history" (*Geschichte*) is frequently used in its objective sense, signifying "development."

and certainty, choosing narrow fields because at the very outset they despaired of their lives proving long enough, or their strength sufficient, for them to deal with the history of an entire people, or of an epoch, with the minuteness deemed by them absolutely necessary for a historian. Others who in their first draught planned the complete treatment of a main branch of history, like Horace's potter, have seen that which they intended for a jug grow into a pipkin upon the wheel, and, wearied by their ever-increasing burden, have come to a halt before having travelled half or perhaps the tenth part of the road."

It is well to avoid such faults as these, however much they may have thoroughness to thank for their existence. From conscientious self-limitation, a result of modern education, which narrows the field of view and busies itself with the painfully minute, arises a disinclination to become master of the threatening excess of facts. An attempt boldly to make use of the stored-up material arouses hostile criticism: it is claimed that the work is not historical. The history of the human race has long been considered by scholars to lie without their province. Universality is something unlawful to the present régime of specialists.

But there is no necessity for being discouraged by such opposition. The conviction that universality is the field for scholars is gradually winning its way; and the time has come for all books and all sciences to be judged according to a higher standard. In 1893 Robert Pöhlmann brought out a history of the communism and socialism of early times,[1] in which he departed widely from obsolete philological-antiquarian methods; and each one of his later works has been a triumph for his broader views and his versatility. In 1895 a section on China appeared for the first time in the sixteenth volume of the "Jahresberichte der Geschichtswissenschaft" (Annual of Historical Science); and the establishment of professorships in Sinology in German universities is only a question of time.

From this point of view — universality — the International Postal Union, the Berne Agreement for the Protection of Scientific Property, the Geneva Convention, and the International World-Survey deserve special notice. The world is small. One hundred years ago, Christian Meiners, with prophetic insight, following a general discourse on the conditions of life on earth and the distribution of mankind, wished to describe and compare with one another the anthropological differences in races, the extent of civilisations, the conceptions of family and of state, and the customs and intellectual capacities, particularly of savage and semi-civilised peoples. Karl Ernst von Baer, too, was convinced that unexpected treasures would be brought to light from a study of the social and intellectual conditions of the hitherto uninvestigated uncivilised races. All this can and may be the task of a single science, a history of civilisation in the widest sense. Francis Bacon made the same demand even in respect to a pragmatic history of literature.

Every profound historical examination of the lives of large social aggregates presupposes a knowledge of such methods of investigation as are pursued in psychology, physiology, and ethnology. A competent philosophical training spares the historian tedious preliminary searches as to whether, in individual cases, domestic economy shall give precedence to religion, or morals to mind. It would be useless to attempt to draw a sharp line of distinction between ethnology and history, excluding the former from the latter. The existence of historical traditions is no sure indication of the moment when a nation became "historic;"

---

[1] "Geschichte des antiken Communismus und Socialismus." München, 1893.

according to .this conception the Aryans would have to be reckoned among the unhistoric branches of mankind. Ernest Renan said truly: "There are dull days in history, but none are unfruitful." The statement that no great discovery, no great religion has gone out from Africa into other lands is yet to be proved; Alexander von Humboldt disputed the opinion that some races of men must be less capable of complete development than others.

Europeans are pleased to speak of negroes as bastards of humanity. To be sure, there is something very delightful in the fact that almost the whole earth is at present under the rule of the smallest continent; and again, that of all Europe the smallest island kingdom possesses the farthest-reaching power. It is thus conceivable that Karl Friedrich Burdach (Kant and Lotze held similar views) could say:

"The tree of mankind, from the roots and branches of which culture proceeds, must lift its topmost bough in Europe; and it is destined that the fruit of humanity shall come to maturity upon this bough; and its seed shall be scattered over the entire earth."

Karl Ernst von Baer went still farther in an oft-quoted address of 1834. According to his opinion the civilisation of Europe, which surpasses that of all other continents, shall attain to its highest level in the Teutonic folk. In the face of this, however, it is well to remember that a large number of clear-sighted men share the hopes which Adam Mickiewicz, a Pole, places in the future of the Slavonic races. Heinrich von Treitschke's enthusiastic utterance — "One can say to-day, with the greatest certainty, that, in the future, the chosen of the people of European nations and their descendants shall be the rulers of almost the entire earth" — is explicable, however boastful. Excepting the inhabitants of China, Japan, Western India, and Mohammedan Asia, there are no races in existence capable of withstanding for any length of time the vast superiority of European weapons and commerce.

All these prophets commit the blunder of assuming that which is temporary to be lasting, that which is particular to be universal. In a treatise on the geographical distribution of civilised institutions,[1] Alfred Vierkandt warns us against overrating absolute culture. Even if some nations are able to point to their superiority in spiritual development, history teaches that spiritual power may assist in earthly battles only when it is based upon sufficiently sure and extensive economic foundations, and has sufficiently large masses of men at its disposal. Hence the warning for European nations to be on their guard is fully justified. It is no matter whether the threatening danger is to be looked for in the East, or, in conformity with the laws of the progress of civilisation from east to west, in the West; Europe certainly has before her the example of the devastation of Asia. At the same time there is no necessity for judging European civilisation from the standpoint of the Turk, who absolutely denies its advantages.

On the other hand, there are men who consider the present and past struggles of European races to create and to maintain states, a retrograde movement, or a period of transition, and that a gradual obliteration of boundaries and merging of differences — already indicated here and there — must follow. Held maintains that the end will be the establishment of harmony and balance between the

---

[1] "Die Kulturformen und ihre geographische Verbreitung": Hettner's Geographische Zeitschrift. er Jahrgang. Leipzig, 1897.

various forms of progress; Schäffle looks upon agreement and concord as a higher
step, as a sign of true civilisation, compared with the barbarities of war, and as
the goal of the highest developed individuals. "Nation" will be superseded by
"International." Then we should have only the question to answer: Has Russian
or English the better prospect of becoming the future universal language? It is
scarcely possible for all men to accept such theories of a return to primitive unity
and dreary uniformity. Then those, too, would be wrong who consider the sum of
life of civilised Man to consist in labour and in war — who say, Remove all
antagonism and all must languish. At present, Truth mocks the endeavour for
a universal prosperity of peoples and harmony of nations. According to Ernst
von Lasaulx, every great advance in the history of the world is closely associated
with a conflict between European races and ideals, and Asiatic or African opponents; it is thus quite evident that he believes in the truth of the aphorism of
Heraclitus: "War is the father of all." Whichever of these views — each very
fine from its own standpoint, but bitterly opposed to the others — may be the
right one, every man must settle for himself: the duty of the historian is but to
supply firm foundations upon which other inquirers may base further arguments.

Polybius and Machiavelli have shown that a nation or a reigning house is certain to decline as soon as it has completely expanded within the limits assigned to
it. Thus, when a state is at the height of its prosperity, it is already approaching
exhaustion; for it has performed its office. We also have Plato's cycles of government, before which all human communities tremble — with the one exception of
the Roman Catholic Church, if we are willing to agree with Macaulay and Lasaulx.
But science must not occupy itself with the consideration of fanciful theories. The
faithful Christian and the despairing pessimist learn very different things from
history: In the year 47 B.C. the famous words, *Veni, vidi, vici*, were uttered; in
1547 A.D. Charles V. said, "I came, I saw, God conquered." While one man sighs
that he was ever born, another, convinced of the reasonableness of an existence with
which he stands in inseparable action and reaction, orders his thoughts according
to the current of life, and weaves the determinations of his own "free" will into
the harmony of the whole. Nevertheless each considers his own wisdom alone to
be authentic — a result of narrowness of view.

Only he who, free from prejudice, studies every branch of mankind, excluding
none because it "has no history," avoids this error. It is not always necessary for
a race to have played a brilliant part on the world's stage in order to awaken
the interest of the writer of universal history. Just as frequently as the saying
"Much ado about nothing" has proved itself to be true in the lives of men, do
great effects arise from small causes. Just as Quintilian stigmatised as useless the
rummaging through of old compilations for this or that man's sayings, so Vives,
the first historian of civilisation, cared to know but little about wars and battles,
of which the greater number were mere robberies, but very reasonably desired to
chronicle the events of peace, the acquisitions of the intellect, of wisdom and experience in life, which, together with forethought, understanding, and judgment,
accomplish deeds of universal, lasting value. Such great actions, however, do not
arise from nothing; they have their sources. For this reason, accounts of all occurrences that have taken place in past times must be incorporated, so far as they are
necessary to the knowledge of later happenings and are indispensable as links in
a chain of events. Often, where superficial examination suspects no connection,

there are, in reality, sequences of causes and effects which must be traced out and followed. There is not in the world a single people, unmixed, consisting of but one race.

To be sure, the law of conservation of energy is not to be applied to ethnological problems. Vico has already proved that our civilisation is not fundamentally Babylonian, as has been maintained. For culture is not passed on, like a deposit, from people to people; and what is of value in a nation's production is seldom transmitted to its heirs unimpaired.

"The jackal howls in Ephesus, where Heraclitus and Paul once preached; thorns flourish and a few starved barbarians cower in the marble halls of a hundred cities in Asia Minor; the sands of the desert are blown about the gardens of the gods of Cyrené."

Thus Ulrich von Wilamowitz-Möllendorf described the decay of a high civilisation in his spirited address on "Periods of the World's History."[1] Truly, only that which is material may be destroyed. The intellectual products of ageing nations are absorbed by younger states, only then to be handed on — purified or vitiated — to still later peoples. What we have inherited from our fathers we must earn, that we may possess it; upon this rests the coherence of universal history. The culture-producing labour of humanity, indeed the very life of society, consists in gaining possession of the old, and in appropriating it to self. Together with the new, much remains that is old: thus mankind increases according to the number, perhaps also according to the value, of its institutions and customs. Total existence becomes enriched by itself and through itself. Therefore Wilhelm von Humboldt speaks of the production of intellectual power, — in always newer and often higher forms, — of the varying manifestations of this spiritual power, and of the source of the continuity of phenomena in mankind, as the truly creative forces working in concealed channels of human development.

Knowledge of the coherence of universal history may therefore only be gathered from an acquaintance with the development of all races. However abundant the traditions of a people may be, its development is by no means necessarily typical of all. He alone values things according to their true worth who, in the words of Montaigne, "has before him the sublime picture of our mother Nature in her complete majesty." He then also contributes to the attainment of that end which, according to F. Max Müller, is the highest ideal of humanity on earth, — "to study Man, to know him, and to learn to love him with all his weaknesses and folly."

"With his weaknesses and folly." As for this, we reject every teleological view at the very beginning. It is not wise to force universal history into a system of philosophy; and forced it would be, to deduce universally valid laws from the course of historical events, and then to apply them back to history itself in turn. The philosophy of history and the discovery of laws of evolution are two distinct sciences; in reality, however, every philosophy of history finally takes up the task of searching for all that it may find conformable to law in the historic raw material. Yet it is not the duty of the historian to write a philosophy of history (sociology, according to Paul Barth); for, as was long ago recognised by Thomas Hobbes, philosophy, deduced from reason, and history, founded upon experience, have nothing to do with each other. The philosophy of history may be an indispen-

[1] "Rede zur Feier des Geburtstags seiner Majestat des Kaisers und Königs am 27 Januar 1897 ... Weltperioden." Göttingen [1897].

sable requirement, and the summit of all higher education; however, it is not for
the historian to discover the scheme of the universe.

Every philosophy of history is a product of the past, usually the most recent
past. For this reason each latest philosophy of history comes to maturity in a
somewhat different manner than did its predecessor; although almost all of them
make their appearances attended by pretentious broods of dogmas. Were the
philosophy of history really so justified as it asserts itself, then there must be an
all-embracing, binding system for the explanation of the universe. This would
incorporate truth; truth can only be one and indivisible. Humboldt said very
clearly and well that the end of history is the realisation of that principle, or idea,
which manifests itself through humanity; but what this principle, or idea, is, and
how it manifests itself, — that he did not say. Nevertheless it is here that the
greatest difficulty lies; for in answering this question each of us brings with him
his own personal conception. The philosophy of history disturbs and troubles
with its subjectivity the objective conception, the pure science, deduced from the
course of all past events. Knowledge of that which has been called the causal
nexus of history must suffice; what lies beyond stands on too slender supports.

Shortly after Alexander the Great captured Ecbatana, the Athenian philosopher Demetrius Phalereus wrote:

" If, fifty years ago, a god had foretold the future to the Persians and to the Persian
king, or to the Macedonians and to the king of Macedonia, would they have indeed believed
then that to-day scarcely more would remain of the Persians, to whom almost the entire
earth was once subject, than their name, and that the Macedonians would acquire the sovereignty of the world — the Macedonians of whom in former times hardly the name was
known? Truly fortune is unstable; it orders all things contrary to our expectations and
exhibits its power in most miraculous dispensations. Now it has given the glory of the
Persians to the Macedonians in order to show men that it has granted them but the usufruct of all these possessions, which they may enjoy until it is pleased to decree otherwise."

And when Cæsar beheld the Germans of the Rhine, he would scarcely have considered it possible that but a few centuries later the Roman Empire should be
destroyed or — it can also be looked upon in this way — have new life infused into
it by their descendants. Tacitus was more susceptible to presentiments in this
direction. " In order to know what a nation is going to become, first of all we
must know its past," said Gaston Boissier; "that is the service which history performs for us." Development is not an uninterruptedly progressive movement; it
is not a process to which the word " progress " may be applied — progress, indeed,
leaves a decidedly teleological after-taste behind it.

Not Vico's " Provvedenza," Lilienfeld's " Idea of God " as the highest integration of the emotions, Baer's " Moral Perfection," Herder's, Kolb's, or the Russian
N. Syrkin's " Humanity," Bluntschli's " World-State." embodying material, visible
Man, Ludwig Stein's " Peace of Nations" and " Social Culture-State," or Johann
Unold's " Moral Constitution of the World " brought about by the greatest capacity
of the greatest number — can satisfy the historian as the end of all events, in spite
of the noble sentiment that lies at the bottom of every conception of history as a
glorification of God's works. Leopold von Ranke separated progress into ideal and
material; the former, crystallised in great spiritual tendencies, must pursue its
own way, excluding from itself the growth of material development through the
mechanical arts, and, in any case, so far as morals are concerned, has ceased to

exist since the beginnings of Christianity. On the other hand, Karl Ernst von Baer is convinced that the progress which leads to the goal of all history tends to the perfecting of the whole of mankind in every direction, intellectually and, even more, morally, — a labour which would continue through eternity. Each one of the foregoing theories is a personal conviction; they are the articles of faith of more or less small communities. We certainly have no reason to condemn dogmas on their own account, but to annex an eleventh to ten formulas of belief is not right.

Knowledge based on experience is more valuable than all speculation. To be sure, Paul von Lilienfeld believed that he had discovered the way to a law of development in universal history in his "Thoughts on the Social Science of the Future;"[1] but even he must acknowledge that the world's history lacks congruity. Ulrich von Wilamowitz infers from a contemplation of the history of Greece, a progressive movement that rounds itself into a cycle; this he looks upon as typical, maintaining that universal history is composed of a limited number of such rotations. Plato, and Vico who permits his watch to run down and then winds it up again, were of the same opinion. Should they be given preference over others for that reason? He who like Karl Friedrich Burdach looks upon all fluctuations and disturbances in development as immaterial; who like Karl Ernst von Baer, or Herder, in the last part of his "Outlines of a Philosophy of History,"[2] sees even in religious intolerance and persecution, in slavery and various other atrocities, only a finally resultant blessing; or, like Ernst von Lasaulx, sees something divine in war, — may truly be convinced of the rightness of the theory of an uninterrupted progression. In this respect Jean Bodin calls Leibniz's smiling optimism vividly to mind. The intellectual opponents of these kindly philosophers are the pessimists — the Bayles and the Schopenhauers. There are serious men who consider it superficial to maintain that modern civilisation could have brought people nearer to one another through the inventions of printing and the steam-engine, thus conquering the civilisation of antiquity. Moreover a thought intrudes here that must be kept out of the field of history — the question as to the amount of felicity to be attained as evolution advances. Happiness is a conception that has nothing to do with historical investigations.

In the preface to his history of Wallenstein, Ranke hints that every man appears almost as the expression of a universal tendency, or spirit, which also exists apart from him. This thought, which recurs in almost all the later works of the great master of German historiography, and is called Ranke's Ideology (*Ideenlehre*), is also easily to be recognised as Lasaulx's Spirit of the Time (*Zeitgeist*), the involuntary, objective spiritual power which controls all contemporaries. Wilhelm Wundt turns it to philosophic account when he says that the single scientific task of a universal history is to point out the spiritual forces by which historical events are governed. It is from history restricted to a special subject that we may obtain material for historical criticism and interpretation; the peculiar service of universal history lies only in the philosophic treatment of the whole. Ranke's attempt to unify the histories of the old civilised peoples of the East in conformity with the religious ideas by which they were dominated, is a model for such an undertaking. Unfortunately, Wundt himself admits that the difficulties of a

[1] "Gedanken über die Socialwissenschaft der Zukunft." Rudolstadt, 1873-79.
[2] "Ideen zur Philosophie der Geschichte der Menschheit." Riga und Leipzig, 1784-91, et

universal historical representation of spiritual forces must increase as time goes on. But it is not sufficient even to say this; the task, according to the philosopher's idea, simply cannot be brought to completion. Henry Thomas Buckle, who experienced the shipwreck of such a plan, spoke the following moving words respecting it:

"And let him toil as he may, the sun and noontide of his life shall pass by, the evening of his days shall overtake him, and he himself have to quit the scene, leaving that unfinished which he had vainly hoped to complete." [1]

No one may master the whole of history; it will not yield to the power of one conqueror. Karl Lamprecht was fully justified when, in his polemical treatise on the old and the new tendencies of the science of history,[2] he said: "We must not fail to recognise that these doctrines [Ranke's Ideology] rest primarily on the standpoint of personal belief, and only secondarily on that of scientific investigation."

In order that a universal history be accepted as scientific, it must remain neutral.

The reader who is unable to do without dogmas may frame his own articles of belief by working over in his mind the raw material — the whole world is included in it. It is not every one who brings such a firm conviction with him as did Karl Ernst von Baer, who believed he had perceived that the idea of creation lay in the final perfection of the human race. A clever sketch after the manner of Bolingbroke's "Letters on the Study and Use of History" is of but little consequence; very different, however, the building of a sure foundation. Speculation as to the end of all events is not history. For all our searching and for all our knowledge, even were we to devote a lifetime to the former and to the attainment of the latter, we may never approach nearer to the ultimate cause. Therefore Karl Ernst von Baer is logical when he speaks of his anthropological confession of faith. His Pantheistic Destiny, that orders the course of history, is a sort of counterpart idea to that of Ranke; Von Baer knew "nothing more attractive than an investigation of the sublime powers that urge Man on in his development." Whoever maintains that progress from lower to higher activities of civilisation is necessary, because civilisation increases as the land is organised and opened up to the sea, and that development is more rapid in temperate climates, where there are a greater number of races sharing civilised institutions in common, — that man has, without doubt, intelligently followed the course of history; but in the final summing-up there remains, nevertheless, a large amount of original individual opinion.

Wilhelm Roscher infers that the development of man's intelligence arises from the natural sources of ever-changing history, thus calling Buckle to mind. Otto Gildemeister has discovered that public opinion on moral subjects has become more elevated. Paul von Lilienfeld perceives a "potentiation of forces, a higher differentiation and integration of the social nervous system and social inter-cell substance" in the course of the history of mankind. On the other hand, we find in Ferdinand Lassalle's sketch of national economy, which contains his views on the philosophy of history, that progress signifies the actual growth and expansion of the idea of liberty in human-kind. He perceives a silver thread that runs through history in the fact that the sphere of private possession of property is constantly

[1] "History of Civilisation in England." Ed. 1869, Vol. III. p. 188.
[2] "Alte und neue Richtungen in der Geschichtswissenschaft." Berlin, 1896.

becoming more limited, and that, conversely, the territory without this sphere is growing more and more extensive. This is certainly ingenious, perhaps even correct from the standpoint of a historian of justice; yet it remains one-sided in any case. Consequently this line of thought is quite as inadmissible as, for example, Werner Sombart's likening of the world's history to a struggle for food and for the possession of food-producing localities. In truth, a large part of the history of the world consists of battles and wars; but surely not all of it. Whoever denies this denies reality.

The attempt to obtain a knowledge of all phenomena, at the same time starting out from a certain fixed point of view, reminds one of the following satire by Friedrich Theodor Vischer, a disciple of Hegel:

> " Providence, in thy works
> We may perceive thy existence;
> Indeed, thou art often obscure, —
> Here, on the contrary, manifest."

In most cases a progressive investigation leads to the painful discovery that the original assumption has not possessed the significance at first attributed to it. On March 24, 1877, Du Bois-Reymond, in an address on the history of civilisation and natural science,[1] defended the proposition that the true history of mankind is contained in the history of the natural sciences. For the true history of Man is—

" that which, together with all his vicissitudes, abominations, and errors, presents to us his gradual uplifting from half-brutishness, his advance in the arts and sciences, his increasing dominion over nature, his daily improving welfare, his emancipation from the fetters of superstition, — in a word, his constant approach to that which makes men human."

This sounds very like the claim of Vives, already cited; and we may read something similar in Kapp's " Elements of a Philosophy of Technics ":[2] the whole history of mankind, when closely examined, finally resolves itself into a history of the invention of improved implements. Unfortunately, a still closer examination convinces us that this delightfully simple solution does not hold good because it is indebted for its being to a one-sided view of a portion of the life of to-day: it considers only the marvellous technical progress of the nineteenth century. Kapp apparently agrees with Pascal, Schopenhauer, Ranke, and many others in believing that the spiritual beauty of a work by Sophocles cannot by any possibility be surpassed, and that material culture only —that is, the world of outward appearances, modes of life and institutions, instruments and tools — may become richer and more manifold. According to this belief Man will not increase in wisdom, goodness, or in spiritual welfare. Such purely personal sentiments, utterances from the world of emotion, have no place in a universal history.

It is true that history may not be written from an entirely objective point of view. Objectivity is practically nothing more than the effort to cause subjective prejudices to retire in favour of impartiality, which ever floats before the mind's eye as an ideal. At all events it is never attained by any one who, intentionally and throughout, permits his personal opinion to intrude. Therefore, although it represents an active demand of the feelings, Wundt's proposition must be rejected.

---

[1] " Culturgeschichte und Naturwissenschaft, ein Vortrag," etc.  Leipzig, 1878.
[2] " Grundlinien einer Philosophie der Technik."  Braunschweig, 1877.

Thus the perils to which a philosophy of history would be exposed in the hands of a Schelling or a Bunsen will be avoided from the very beginning. Herder also, although he would not hear of "concealed designs of a higher power" or a "hidden scheme of Providence" in a history, was yet unable to break from the tentacles of a philosophic-unhistoric conception. The pleasures of an attempt to disentangle the threads are too seductive. He who, like Eduard Meyer, believes history — "in the restricted sense" — to be the struggle of the individual for freedom from tradition and uniformity, who, like Kant and Lord Acton, understands universal history to be the development of the conception of Freedom; or, with Alexander von Humboldt, apprehends the goal of mankind to be the free development of spiritual power, — drags philosophic ideas into history, has preconceived opinions, and falls back upon teleological notions. However, eighty years ago, Wilhelm von Humboldt declared that the teleological conception of history will never attain to the actual truth as to the destiny of the world.

"Ends, as men call them, do not exist; the destinies of the human race roll on as streams flow from a mountain to the sea; as grass and herbage spring up in the fields; as the larvæ of certain insects spin cocoons about themselves and become butterflies; as nations drive others before them and are themselves driven, destroy and are themselves swept away: . . . not the imputed designs of a strange, imperfectly felt, and yet more imperfectly known being, gathered from the defective knowledge of a few thousands of years, but the power of Nature and of Man is what we must recognise in history."

Nature and Man are the two chief makers of history; their mutual action and reciprocal influences bring to pass all that comes to pass.

And how has all come to pass? Upon this hinges the writing of history. Nor is it the task of the historiographer, but that of the philosopher, the essayist, the artist, to answer the captivating question, Why? Indeed, fear of teleology may be a weakness, and, as such, is not to be praised. But it is no less evident that the teleological conception will enslave all who call history an art for its own sake. It bears the brand of individual prejudice on its forehead. Diodorus Siculus, the first teleologist with whom we are acquainted, is a proof of this with his "utility." To maintain that the historian should set down the personal conception of the world which he has, with more or less difficulty, won for himself, is false; on the contrary, he must exert all his power to escape from his own ephemeral ideas, that must constantly change as time goes on. The historian should be independent in every respect; consequently he should be independent of his own self. It is true, as Lord Acton remarked in 1895, that —

"the strongest and most impressive personalities, like Macaulay, Thiers, and the two greatest of living writers Mommsen and Treitschke, project their own broad shadows upon their pages. This is a practice proper to great men, and a great man may be worth several immaculate historians. Otherwise there is virtue in the saying that a historian is seen at his best when he does not appear. [1]

And the more exclusively a historical work rests upon its sources, the more lasting and effective will it be.

In his "Discourses and Contemplations on Religion," [2] Moriz Carriere communicates "thoughts in prison" which had been given to him in confidence by a

[1] "A Lecture on the Study of History, delivered at Cambridge," etc. London, 1895, p. 30.
[2] "Religiose Reden und Betrachtungen für das deutsche Volk." Leipzig, 1850.

German republican, who had written them down during the spring of 1836. The following beautiful passage occurs in them:

" The world knows that it is guided by divine wisdom, and that its goal is humanity, or an all-embracing community in complete harmony with the will of God, a community that recognises and fulfils that law given by God in accordance with which each individual feels himself to be a member of the whole, and includes all his brother men in helpful love."

This is a magnificent belief; but unfortunately it cannot be looked upon as universally binding. A conception that is only valid in part must on no account be permitted to have a determining influence on the moulding of a work on universal history. This statement, moreover, is supported by a train of thought derived from Karl Lamprecht's " Old and New Tendencies in Historical Science." According to this, a world is represented, one part of which is comprehensible to our reason; the other part, however, must still be considered as extending beyond reason: yet all the while human thought imperatively requires knowledge of the unknown, even though this knowledge may, perhaps, not be attained until we reach a far distant or indefinitely distant hereafter. In that case, however, the maintenance or development of a supernatural system for the explanation of the continuity of history is either no longer conceivable or is only to be looked upon as a retrogression. If the premises were other than bare assumptions, the conclusion would be convincing. Thus, there is still no necessity for our relapsing into the sophistry lately become popular among those materialists who feel themselves obliged to write universal history without mentioning a name. A powerful counterpoise to such exaggeration is the work of a man to whom the world's history was nothing more than a series of biographies of great men — Carlyle. One could scarcely comprehend the Seven Years' War or the Hundred Days without their quotas of heroes.

However perfect a monistic conception of the world may appear in theory, it cannot be carried into practice. It will never be possible to establish throughout an uninterrupted continuity of cause and effect; therefore, in spite of Hobbes, there will be room enough left in which to include both human " freedom " and " will." Wilhelm von Humboldt said very honestly: " Universal history is incomprehensible unless there be a power that guides and rules the world." Whence may the historian derive the strength necessary in order that he may represent ideas which, according to their very nature, lie without the realm of the finite ? Even when the greatest conceivable success has been obtained from investigation, it includes a comparatively insignificant number of possibilities only, attaining to an approximation — the very thing that is hidden to the objective historian. Possibilities are not reality; and knowledge of the relationship of reality to possibility is granted to no mortal — not even to the natural scientist.

Wilhelm Ostwald, in his Lübeck address of September, 1895, openly confessed that the theory of motion alone is insufficient. This mechanical conception of the world, which had until then served as a dogma, finally reduced all phenomena to a movement of atoms, regulated according to the same laws that govern the motions of the heavenly bodies. Indeed, there is necessarily incongruity between the eternity of phenomena and the finiteness of our intelligence; for every scientific generalisation leaves something over unexplained. Reality denies the truth of conceptions deduced from laws. Together with that which is constant, exists that which is mutable, and reality arises from a double action — that of the mutable upon the constant, and that of the constant upon the mutable. To be sure, in physical experiments, we have succeeded in reducing to a function the possibilities of variation from mathematical certainty; and science may hope gradually to narrow this field of error. But to determine clearly the nature of the mutable itself will always be impossible. Typical phenomena are far more conclusive when they have to do with the natural sciences than when they are connected with the human mind; because in the latter case the latitude for individual variations and their combinations is extraordinarily wide. In order to make this clearer, we may say that before certain recurrent phenomena in the lives of nations may be considered typical, or adduced as "laws," binding in all cases, together with the constant factor, not only one, but a whole series of variable factors must be known. Certainly history has scarcely deduced one single proven and undisputed law of human development. What we call laws are in most cases facts, among which we must first investigate in order that the law be found. Whether, with the assistance of an accurate observation of aggregates, and a methodical, consistent series of statistics applicable to history, we shall some day succeed in deducing laws, is as yet unknown. Thus it is unscientific to maintain that this or that must happen in consequence of the fulfilment of one or another preliminary condition. "Necessity" is a theory that belongs to the past.

It is enough to recognise that Columbus and Linnæus had chiefly the world of their day — their contemporaries -- to thank for their discoveries, which were not epoch-making through either of them, but in spite of them, — in fact, became epoch-making after their times were past. "The handful of snow that loosens itself from the mountain top will not become an avalanche unless the whole snow-mass over which it glides is disposed to fall."[1] But to claim, or even to attempt to prove, as did Karl Ernst von Baer, that the conditions and affairs of the time accomplished all, and that Columbus and Linnæus did little more than lend their names to their discoveries, is to strain the facts of history. It is scientific to endeavour to recognise the causal connection of historical happenings; but all that is beyond belongs no longer to scientific history: it lies within the province of philosophical investigation. The historian has but to define the limits of individual freedom. These are to be found in the so-called practical affairs of life. Gustav Rümelin had very good reasons for doubting if — of the thousands of men who made it a question of life or death whether there were two natures in Christ or one, and whether his being was synonymous with that of the Father or only analogous to it — many had a more intimate acquaintance with the nature of the dispute than a practical understanding of the material gains or losses which the one solution or the other would have in store for them. Already, a half-century ago, Hans Christian Örsted was sensible of the bonds that oppress all men, when he said that the development of intellect to which every individual inhabitant of the world attains, results from a combination of his own activity and the influences which the entire contemporary world has had upon him, and that that part of his surroundings which is made up of his fellow beings has, according to the rule, had the largest share in supplying these influences. The conditions and circumstances of our environment are inexorable necessities for each one of us — even for a Luther or a Bismarck.

[1] Karl Friedrich Burdach.

Therefore the conception of history in the aggregate, represented by the views of Karl Lamprecht, requires that, before all, the sequence of social-psychic tendencies, the various "ages" of civilisation, be established. Were this accomplished for several nations, one might believe that, by drawing comparisons, knowledge of such phenomena as are isolated, and of such as are recurrent in the lives of peoples, might be discovered. From this it would follow that causes and effects are joined together according to certain laws; and starting out from a basis of such comparisons, increasing our knowledge step by step, we should succeed in writing the universal history of the future. This would involve the discovery of "upon what forces universal development (which arises from the sequence of nations in time, and their common geographical relations, as well as from the civilising influences peoples have had upon one another — the latter dependent both upon their respective times and localities) rests." However, the realisation of this lofty ideal is, unfortunately, practically impossible. It is too difficult a task for one man, and it cannot be the work of an academy or a union of societies. Moreover a comparison of the eras of civilisation of various nations would scarcely afford the parallel cases which are first necessary in order that "laws" may be established. Such high expectations are always confronted by our variable factor; if it is disregarded, and typical epochs — such as the alternating double periods of Saint-Simon, for example — are adduced, it only signifies a violence to truth. Lavisse and Rambaud's "Histoire Générale" may serve as an example: in this, historical life on earth since the end of the fourth century A.D. has proceeded in conformity with the history of the French people.

There must be no missing link in the chain of reciprocal influences. If lifeless, savage, or torpid races, that apparently have no history or have produced no results, are drawn within the circle of observation, it is rarely entirely due to general human interest — akin to the sentimental fancy of the eighteenth century — or to fear lest valuable traditions, if not collected now, may sooner or later completely disappear, or even to a childlike joy in gathering together all sorts of memoranda. Races have exerted influences upon neighbouring peoples, of which a superficial examination cannot form even a conjecture. It is true that the extent of such irradiations is not always so clearly to be grasped as it may be from an exposition of the nation-uniting activity of a Matthew Arnold or a Thomas Carlyle. In other cases we must be content to know that we have broken the roads to fuller knowledge.

It is quite conceivable that up to the present day but little information has been desired about South Sea Islanders and negroes — the parts they have played in the human drama not having been precisely the most brilliant; but it is inexcusable to exclude the inhabitants of India, or, indeed, all the races of eastern Asia, from a true universal history; or to reduce the history of America to a summary of events under such headings as "Discovery" and "War of Independence." These are only methods for escaping difficulties which arise from imperfect knowledge or from narrowness of view: truly remarkable phenomena when we consider that more than a hundred years ago Herder wrote his "Outlines." Even Ranke's "Universal History," apart from its having been left a fragment, can be looked upon only as retrogressive. Von Wilamowitz said in his already cited address:[1]

---

[1] *Ante*, p. 5.

"We cannot but greatly admire how this comprehensive intellect was able to pierce through the whole development of the Christian Era; and hardly will there be another to follow in his steps. Subjectively it was perfectly justifiable for him to precede the main part of his history, which he commenced when a very old man, with a sketch of ancient times; and it was completely in harmony with his views, which had been acquired two generations before, to call his work a universal history. But it would be a great mistake — and indolence, as well as our national banality, would put it to evil use — if, out of respect for a great man's name, the temple of history were to be raised upon the civilisations of the Roman and Germanic peoples, earlier times being permitted to serve only as a vestibule. By this an understanding of civilisation would simply be eradicated."

If the single correct conclusion in respect to universal history be drawn, no occurrence of the past is without interest for us. The sources of bygone events lie still farther back in time: therefore prehistoric ages should also be taken into consideration. Bolingbroke said: "However closely affairs are linked together in the progression of governments, and how much soever events that follow are dependent on those that precede, the whole connection diminishes to sight as the chain lengthens, till at last it seems to be broken."[1] But Bolingbroke did not say that we should anticipate time, and wilfully tear asunder the lengthening chain. Thus his evidence has only to do with the execution. The wish to penetrate to the very beginnings of all history is presumptuous; unstable speculations as to early conditions and affairs should not be given place in a history. It would be foolish always to infer common origin, derivation, or translation of civilisation, from the general similarity of remains belonging to the Stone Age. In many cases, merely the grades of culture, or the environments of those who produced the remains, were similar. It would, however, be profitable to investigate to how great an extent fundamental ideas, dissimilar in themselves, grow to resemble one another, owing to their origins being constituted alike; and, conversely, to what degree fundamental ideas lose likeness to one another owing to differences in their original underlying sources. To treat of the same general truth in its application to different groups can only sharpen the insight and broaden the view. As a result, relationships between races, which would not have been considered possible in past times, may be deduced. In this we are no longer as timorous as we were ten years ago. Only through such a course may that body of statistics desired by Adolf Bastian for the classification of the store of ideas and thoughts held by different peoples be obtained.

## 2. ARRANGEMENT OF MATERIAL

### An Ethnologist's View of History. — DANIEL G. BRINTON.

AN inquiry into the aim and subject-matter of universal history leads almost of itself to the one correct method of arrangement. The single consideration that it is wrong to call the civilisation of ancient Egypt the "dawn of humanity" forbids us to commence with the Egyptians or the Babylonians, as is usually done. Schemes based purely on chronology cannot avoid being superficial.

Jean Bodin was the first to make a breach in Daniel's closed and sealed series of four world-periods, which was still accepted by such men as Melanchthon,

---

[1] "Letters on the Study and Use of History," etc. Letter VI., p. 50, Ward, Lock, & Co.'s ed.

Sleidan, and Leibniz; yet the threefold division of the world's history for which Cellarius prepared the way in 1685 was, in reality, no advance. The division into Ancient, Mediæval, and Modern is, at the most, only an aid to an intelligent comprehension of the subject-matter of history; it is especially effective, however, if one submits to the beauty of its exposition by Leopold von Ranke, as shown in Theodor Wiedemann's selections from the works of his master. But even then this system gives an impression of artificiality; and, as time goes on, thoughts which were originally absolutely alien to it are added and squeezed in. A purely external classification that is plainly intended only for a makeshift may, it is true, be of practical use within proper limits; but it cannot withstand the attacks of science. Thus we are entirely indifferent to such questions as, Did the Middle Ages begin with Augustus or Constantine, or with the Huns or the Germans? and Did they end with Luther or Gutenberg, Copernicus or Columbus? In truth the world's history is indivisible. Just as the expedients of geographers — meridians, equator, tropics, and other circles and lines which do not exist at all in reality — are, indeed, found very useful in looking over a map, so may divisions in history serve in assisting us to a knowledge of the sequence of events. Yet this must be their sole office. Heinrich von Sybel opened a new epoch with Frederick the Great; Heinrich von Treitschke preferred to close one with him. Both were right; every bud contains within it the germ of a new structure. Humanity is One, and " there is a course of great events by which all nations are united and governed."

There is yet another representation of the world's historical development which is to be avoided, and for other reasons than those which militate against the idea of progress and awaken in us aversion to fixed " laws." Following the example of Kant and Vico, some of us have been pleased to figure humanity as passing through different hypothetical stages of development. This is a sin against Reality. Capricious though Reality may be, and embodying many activities, it is certainly unfavourable to all misrepresentation and perversion of facts. Indeed, life on earth, with its many aims and co-operating and reciprocal influences, is so endlessly varied in all its manifestations that any one of us at all skilled in classifying tries his own experiment, and then imagines that he has demonstrated all by means of a few groups and sections. Thus Nilsson assumes four periods of development through which every portion of humanity must pass sooner or later: from savagery to nomadism, then from nomadism to agriculture, finally attaining perfection on acquiring a written language, minted coins, and division of labour. Ernst von Lasaulx's scheme is fuller: peasant, merchant, warrior, priest, nobleman, and prince are the classes of society according to individual callings in life; mining, cattle-breeding and agriculture, navigation, commerce and manufacture, civil prosperity, arts and sciences, are indications of the degree of progress according to modes of existence. Both of these points of view may be accepted if one agrees with Bacon in asserting the period of war to be the youth, that of the arts and sciences to be the manhood, and that of commerce and industry, luxury and fashion, to be the old age of the human race. It is remarkable that even to the present day every philosopher who has compared the processes of Man's development to the several periods in the life of the individual, whether his name be Julius Florus, Jean Bodin, or Ernst von Lasaulx, has believed his own time to be the age of senility. Naturally a look back into the past calls forth melancholy thoughts; but in spite of the constantly regretted decay of the human race, mankind still continues to flourish. "A nation grows neither old nor wise; it remains always childish,"[1] are the words of Goethe in the mouth of the Duke of Alba.

The classifications of Gustav Klemm and other sociologists are certainly very well thought out, especially those of Albert Hermann Post, whose four gradations — community based on family relationship, community arising from an aggregate of individuals occupying the same territory, ruling kingship, and social democracy — belong to the most brilliant products of German thought. However, such constructions are purely speculative, even when they are less inadmissible than Lewis H. Morgan's seven stages of development. It is scarcely conceivable that a worn-out scheme could meet with so much approval as has been given to that of the American sociologist. Already in 1820 Wilhelm von Humboldt clearly recognised that to follow out such lines of thought exclusively would lead us directly away from knowledge of the actual creative powers that underlie all action connected with life, and would only result in withdrawing from our view the most important thing to be reckoned with; and that determinations apparently mechanical are nevertheless governed by primordial, freely acting motives. If we strip away the mysticism which abounds in Humboldt's philosophy of identity, and which seems to be displaced by Christian ideas in the foregoing explanation, we again strike against the finiteness of our knowledge.[2] In like manner much mischief has been done by the alleged cycles of government, in their normal as well as in their degenerate forms. It is said that, without exception, governments must change from monarchy, through a cycle of tyranny, to aristocracy; from aristocracy, through oligocracy or oligarchy, to democracy; and from the latter, through periods of ochlocracy and anarchy, it must again revolve back to despotism. To be sure, this *may* happen; it has occurred in many cases; but that is no reason for assuming that it *must* be so.

The reason for this mistaken line of thought is usually found to lie in the fact that too little attention is paid to one factor: the earth. Already we have arrived at the same conclusion in another connection.[3] History is entirely dependent on the co-operation of Nature and Man. As a rule, study of the external conditions to which mankind is subjected is neglected in favour of subordinate subjects; too little stress is laid upon the situations and the various characteristics and resources of different parts of the world. "One could imagine a universal history which passed over Linnæus or Cuvier; not one, however, that did not mention Columbus, Cook, or Barth." Ever since the time of Montesquieu — of Jean Bodin, even — and especially since the days of Karl Ritter, we have recognised the influence which the earth has had on the development of the characters of races. Rudolf von Ihering, in a posthumous work, "The Early History of the Indo-Europeans,"[4] mentions climate, conditions of the soil, nearness or distance of the ocean, relations of locality and of animal and plant worlds, and hostile and friendly influences of neighbours, as the only constant factors, in contrast to the mutability of the human soul. It is possible from the very character of the soil to deduce "laws" that influence and determine more or less the

1 "Egmont," Act IV. 2.          2 See *ante*, p. 11.          3 *Ante*, p. 10.

4 "Vorgeschichte der Indoeuropaer." Leipzig, 1894. **English translation by A. Drucker, "The Evolution of the Aryan." London, 1897.**

course of human development; although here, too, we must not undervalue the variations to which the earth is subject owing to physical conditions.

But the co-operation of natural conditions and human capacities alone cannot produce history; for the same soil operates differently according to the abilities of its cultivators, and, again, its action varies according to the state of civilisation reached by different communities. Not for all times nor for all peoples have deserts been agents promoting intercourse between distant countries. No people remains unchanged in character upon its own soil. Many years ago, Heeren, in his "Thoughts on Politics, Intercourse, and Trade"[1] rightly emphasised the liquid, the mutable principle. Among some peoples changes follow on in close sequence; among others they come about very slowly: for example, among the Samoyeds, the Finns of the marches, the Arabs of the interior of Arabia, and various tribes of the steppes. And as races become modified, so, too, does the earth change. All things flow; history is constant motion. There is not a country in the world still inhabited by the races that first dwelt in it; plants, animals, and men have constantly been metamorphosing themselves, one race assimilating with another; they have emigrated, found for themselves new countries and new conditions of life. "Thus the history of Man finally becomes a theatre of transformation scenes." But the stage is by no means an indifferent object, playing an insignificant part in the transformations: its position and that of the actors must be looked upon as of equal importance. In the dedication to his edition of Pomponius Mela, Johann Cochläus wrote: "Geography to the historian is as the sun to the earth," an assertion the truth of which has been verified in classic times by Aristotle, Ptolemy, Pliny, Strabo, and Solinus. Even if the Earth is not disposed precisely according to design, since its destiny, arising within itself, may only advance through the innate faculties of Man, it is, on the other hand, surely no inert mass, but a complete systematised organism. From the very beginning there has been quite as intimate a connection between the lives of peoples and the earth, their natural origin, as there is between the soul and the body of an individual. Thus nature and history, physics and ethics, are not to be separated from one another.

Geography is necessarily the foundation for a comprehensive knowledge of universal history. Its chief use is to show how impossible it is to lay bare the historical development of ever so small a group of human beings without at the same time coming into contact with adjacent groups. From this it follows that the grounds for two further methods of classification may be dismissed as useless. One of these is classification according to race. For this there is very little to be said; there is no universally valid classification according to race, and wilfully to favour one at the expense of another is a dubious proceeding at the best. The conception "race" is too vague; and this is a defect that can only increase as time goes on. A classification according to institutions of civilisation, such as has been recommended by Alfred Vierkandt from a geographical standpoint, is also unsuitable, for the reason that it would either sever internal ties of development or bring with it too many repetitions. The historian would have to travel from Australia, the principal seat of the wandering races, the Philippines, Sumatra, Ceylon, and the Andaman Islands to South Africa and South America; and then, for his second group, the true primitive races, the farthest north, the Caucasus and the

---

[1] "Ideen über die Politik, den Verkehr, und den Handel der vornehmsten Völker der alten Welt." Göttingen, 1793-1812, etc.

mountainous portions of India and Polynesia, would be centres of observation. Further, in order to include the nomadic semi-civilised peoples, it would be necessary to visit an extensive territory of exceptional historic uniformity, that lies in the zone of steppes and deserts. The stationary semi-civilised races, however, lead us into all imaginable regions; and we should have the same experience with the last two divisions — full civilisations and mixed civilisations. In addition, there is the painful uncertainty as to which of the six divisions are to be looked upon as exfoliations of humanity; and, in such a dilemma, simply to consult Baer's table (South Sea Negroes, African Negroes, American Indians, Mongolians, Australians, and Caucasians were a proceeding scarcely justified by science.

Consequently nothing remains but classification from a purely geographical point of view. If a series of nations were taken as a basis, gaps would inevitably result: all those inhabited regions in which as yet no nation — " the most complete form of social aggregate " — has arisen, would be pronounced unhistorical. To conceive of states in this connection would be even more mischievous; for the state betokens in itself a development of culture which would at the very outset exclude a still greater number of branches of humanity. But if a purely geographical division, which admits of no presupposition as to whether the condition of a race be one of civilisation or of savagery, is taken as a basis, a structure results in which there is room for all portions of the human race, from the small and ephemeral to the great and influential: it is the habitable world itself.

This structure must not be a labyrinth. A good means for the avoidance of a too superficial and too shallow classification of races according to the regions which they inhabit would be furnished by a study of Bastian's works on the psychology of peoples; the best means is that furnished by Friedrich Ratzel's zones of the distribution of races, arranged on purely geographical principles. If, under such guidance, we survey the entire inhabited world, we may gradually build up a number of half-completed coexistent divisions; a course that in reality conforms with the plans of the elder Humboldt, which were rescued from oblivion by Leitzmann in 1896. Although we may begin with America and end with Europe, we will not say that the origin of all historical development is to be sought for in the former, and to be traced out from thence toward the west — the "east" of past times. The historian does not feel called upon to decide claims respecting priority of birth. America's being treated first will neither support the opinion of certain ethnographers as to the great antiquity of American history, nor answer the question whether the United States will some day take up the part once played by Rome in the world's development. We may leave all this for the future to decide; facts, only, are conclusive. History was and still is a path leading from the unknown to the unknown. One does not arrive at this conclusion under the overpowering influence of obscure, mystical conceptions; the process is more nearly akin to the " Know thyself " of Socrates.

The second part of the work consists in a psychological rehandling of the material; that is, a building of the bridges that connect one structure or division with another. The history of the ascending life of humanity is something more than the sum of all monographs on single races. Since no one people has developed through itself alone, a large number of phenomena will appear which may be summed up under the heading " Encroachments from Without " — so long as " encroachment " is not always taken to signify anything hostile or occurring by fits and starts. By following up the connections of these phenomena one may encircle the world with an endless chain. Already, in 1531, Juan Luiz Vives laid down the following principles in his "De Disciplinis":

> "It is good to become acquainted with the continuity of universal history from the beginning of the world or from the beginning of a people. In this way only may we understand and retain all; it is better to do this than to search through single isolated portions. It is precisely so in respect to the description of the earth. A representation of the world and the disposition of its parts can be more easily pictured by surveying at one glance the totality of lands and seas. For this reason we should combine the divisions of history in such a manner that an undivided whole results, a single structure."

These subdivisions of history, the zones or regions of the distribution of races, are broadly enough constructed to allow the tendency of a group or the civilisation of an age to be clearly seen and demonstrated. Epochs, even, will make their appearance, entirely independently, within them; the endless stream of cause and effect has periods of interruption, acceleration, and flood. Spiritual influences are more or less strictly limited in their areas of influence. The Reformation, the guiding principle of the sixteenth century; the impulse toward political unity, that of the nineteenth,—are watchwords of very narrow acceptance. Neither Hellenism nor Christianity, neither Mohammedanism nor any other spiritual phenomenon of history which has displayed a tendency to spread abroad, has attained to the status of an idea that could have governed the entire habitable world at one and the same time. However, the previously mentioned bridges connecting one race with another may be constructed whenever thoughts or feelings are found to be common to two or more different peoples.

The joining together of the comparative psychology of races and the simple descriptive narration of events, each of which permeates the other, finally results in a history in which peoples know themselves as they are. The execution of this task is of extreme difficulty; we only offer the first essay toward a universal history. Even if a complete history of the world can never be written, to have struggled for an ideal is ever a reward in itself.

# II

## FIRST PRINCIPLES OF A HISTORY OF THE DEVELOPMENT OF MANKIND

### By PROF. J. KOHLER

THE opinion that our own circumstances and affairs are the only standard for judging universal history has long been obsolete. Our day, with its conceptions, beliefs, hopes, and endeavours, is but a tiny portion of the past; for thousands of years peoples have existed who have lived in other intellectual spheres than ours, who have pursued other ideals.

The study of history does not consist in an examination of the past projected, as it were, into the present; it is the study of the past considered as a part of the constant coming and going of men; and in order to become qualified as historians we must first of all attain a point of view from which we may, independently of time, behold history with all its great events file by, as though we were men who had ascended to some elevation in the universe from which they could look down upon the whole earth lying as a unity before them. This is rendered possible through the power of abstraction gained from a study of history; it enables us, on the one hand, to adapt ourselves to strange times and beliefs, and, on the other, to look upon our own day — all time to its contemporary men — objectively, as a mere hour of the ages of human development. We must learn to escape from the present, to withdraw ourselves from that which we may call the tyranny of our own time; for every period obtrudes itself upon those whose lives fall within it as an absolute and sole master, according to whose decree depend their thoughts and all their being. To a certain degree this is the case; it certainly is so as far as practical life is concerned; but it is not so for historical contemplation, to which every age appears only as a period of development, as a passing picture in an endless panorama.

### 1. DEVELOPMENT

THE fundamental principle of history, for the full expansion of which we have Hegel to thank, is development. It is true that our understanding of the manner of development is different from that of Hegel. To us the world is no longer thought, but deed; development is no longer a universal idea evolving according to a strict formula; to-day we recognise it as something endlessly rich and manifold, as something that shapes itself through all the various individual forms that go to make up the aggregate of the universe: a development that throughout fails to follow a straight path, but which, now in one direction, now in another, by devious turns and circuitous by-roads, gradually advances toward the goal.

Our conception of history differs from that of the Hegelian school in so far that we never draw inferences from *a priori* conclusions; we strive first to acquire full details of life, and not until we have an abundance of recorded observations at our command do we seek to deduce therefrom a knowledge of development.

We do not prophesy, nor do we set up types; we do not endeavour to ascertain the history of one people by means of the history of another, without further investigation; we do not look upon development as progressing at a fixed rate, with the regularity of the beats of a pendulum; we recognise that the evolution of humanity displays itself as an endless organic activity. Thus we arrive at the conception of development with this understanding: for however varied and manifold development may be, it always displays certain characteristics by which it may be distinguished from all other phenomena.

Development is not a simple change of self, a progression, a transformation of either external or internal conditions; it is a struggling forth from a germ, the increase of something that is inherent, a growth more or less influenced by external circumstances.[1]

Hence the idea of development presupposes a duality: in the first place something must exist that has the power of shaping the whole future result; but this something is not that which is attained in the final result: it is the potentiality of that which will actually come to be in the future.

The conception of development presupposes the possibility of the future result, not its necessity; for the unfolding of the germ depends upon the action of a thousand factors in its surroundings which are brought to bear on it, and which may turn the development aside from its course, may even destroy it.

## 2. THE DEVELOPMENT OF THE HUMAN RACE

FROM universal history we obtain a picture of the development of humanity; that is, the development of the various active germs or principles inherent in Man. By these are meant the active principles innate in mankind in the aggregate, in contradistinction to those which may exist in single individuals or in single races.

What, then, is Man's relation to the innate germs or principles of civilisation? What is there latent in humanity from the very beginning, and what are its relations to the progress of life? How does it happen that the life-principle contains within itself a longing, a striving for growth and development?

This question is not for history to answer, nor does it lie within the realm of experimental science in the restricted sense; it is a question of metaphysics, of the psychology of races. The problem is to abstract from the countless individuals of humanity their psychic unity; from the countless manifestations of the spirit of nations in history, the manifestations of the general striving toward growth and culture, and to recognise the invisible and intangible threads which connect this striving for development with the underlying, inciting principle. That such relationships exist there can be no doubt. Closer investigation — so far as closer investigation is possible to our intelligence — is especially nearly connected with the great problem of time and causality, and with the relation of the world to

[1] For further details see the author's article in the "Juristisches Litteraturblatt" Vol. VII.

intellect in respect to these ultimate conceptions: how the world of the senses is related to that which lies beneath appearances. It has also particularly to do with the question of the relation of the individual to the generality of mankind, and of the individual consciousness to the collective soul, or consciousness, of races, and of humanity in the aggregate.

Special stress, however, must be laid upon this: According to our present conception of the world we first think of mankind as separated into units; we apprehend the separate individuals, and not until later do we conceive of mankind as a combination of individuals. Proceeding from individuality we form the totality from a multitude of individualities, at the same time uniting the separate units by a spiritual bond. This is not the original method of contemplation. The barrier that separates individual from individual is unknown to Man in a state of nature; we are first enabled to recognise it by means of a continuous process of abstracting the parts from the whole, at the same time ascribing special rights, special efficiency, and special elements of responsibility to these separate parts. According to the primitive method of contemplation the individual was completely identified with and merged in the family, the tribe; to the latter belonged all rights and privileges and responsibility. The modes of activity of individuals did not differ from the modes of social activity. It was unthinkable that the individual could emerge from the common life and labour of the family and travel on new roads — at least, such as did were only abnormal types, individuals who, as "overmen," forsook the community, and were therefore no longer taken into consideration by it. However, the idea of transmigration of souls also existed, — the exchange of soul from individual to individual, union of souls, and the notion of transmission of soul from father to son, grandfather to grandson. Thus the individual was a soul-being in spiritual continuity with other souls; he was merely the special incarnation of the collective spirit of the race, and this, too, only relatively.

This idea of the collective soul, of the unity of tribe and race, accompanied the nations in their life wanderings, consolidated them, and increased their power of resistance. Later races only, when rendered robust enough through sufficient acquisition of culture, were able to develop the individual and to recognise, together with the activity of the community as a whole, a separate activity of its individual units, to the end that, through a coexistent freeing of the individual, the development of all the faculties of the nation might be furthered. But this unification of the individual did not supplant the conception of a natural collective unity; and the idea that the unity of individuals was paramount to the unity of society, or that only the activity of individuals was natural, and that collective activity was fictitious or artificial, is not only factitious, but contrary to nature and to the teaching of history.


## 3. THE DEVELOPMENT OF CIVILISATION

### A. MATERIAL CULTURE

THE result of development is called "civilisation," — the state of intellectual being, and of outward, material life, attained by a people through evolution. Although spiritual and material culture flow into each other, they may be separated to this extent: as a physical being endowed with senses, Man endeavours to obtain satisfaction of his needs, and strives for a position in relation to his environment corresponding with the efforts he has made to obtain welfare; as a feeling, inquiring, spiritual being he contains within him an ever-present desire to fuse the multitude of separate impressions he receives into unity, and to struggle forward until he arrives at a conception of the world and of life. "Material civilisation" is the mode of life through which the obstacles opposed to humanity may be overcome. By the surmounting of obstacles is meant the conquering of enemies, particularly of hostile animals, the obtaining of means for the preservation of existence, and the employing of these means for the increase of bodily welfare. In respect to material civilisation Man passes through stages that widely differ from one another, that vary according to the manner in which the necessities for existence are obtained, and according to the way in which enemies are withstood for the safeguarding of life, welfare, and acquisitions already gained. Races are spoken of as supporting themselves by the chase and fishing, or by cattle-breeding and farming, according to whether they are accustomed to derive subsistence directly from "nature unadorned," or by means of the cultivation and utilisation of natural products. No sharp line of distinction, however, may be drawn. It is inadmissible to speak of races as supporting themselves solely by hunting and fishing; for the very same peoples feed on products of the soil wherever they are found and recognised as a means for subsistence. They live, it is true, upon flesh and fish, but also upon roots and the fruit of wild trees. While in this state of civilisation Man avails himself only of that which nature places before him; he neither adapts nature to his desire, to his needs, or to his manner of living, nor understands how to do it. He can make no further use of nature than to acquire a knowledge of the sources of supply, of how to seize time and opportunity, and to overcome the obstacles to life in his own territory. He ascertains the haunts of game, discovers how to obtain fish, explores for wild honey or edible roots, learns to climb the tallest trees and to let himself down into the deepest caves; but he lacks the ability to cultivate nature, to cause her to produce according to his will. Gradually the one phase amalgamates with the other. It is not seldom that hunting tribes have small tracts of land on which they raise a few edible plants. Observation of nature teaches them that germs develop from fallen seeds, and leads of itself to the idea that it is not best to allow plants to grow up wild, and that it would be expedient to clear the surrounding ground for their better growth. And when this stage is reached, the next step — not to allow seeds to spring up by chance, but to place them in the soil one's self — is not very far off; and thus the mere acquisition of nature's raw vegetable products gives place to agriculture. Often enough we observe instances of the men of a group carrying on hunting operations, while the women not only are occupied with their domestic employments, but also till the soil: thus the men are hunters and fishers, and the women are agriculturists. Domestic work led the latter to take up the cultivation of plants, even as it led them to the other light feminine handicrafts; while the repairing of weapons and of contrivances used for the capture of animals lay within the province of the men.

The discovery how to produce fire by artificial means, independently effected in all parts of the world, — as was also the discovery of the art of navigation, - was of the greatest importance for the entire future. Fire was first a result of chance.

When lightning set a portion of the forest in flames, and caused a multitude of animals or fruits to be roasted, men put it to practical use. They recognised the advantages that fire gave them and sought to preserve it. The retention of the fire which had been sent down from heaven became one of the most weighty and significant of functions. Man learned how to keep wood-fibres smouldering, and how to blow them into flame at will; he also learned that it was possible to convey fire, or the potentiality of fire, along with him in his wanderings. But even then success was uncertain until a lucky chance led him to discover how to produce flames at will, by rubbing two sticks together or by twirling one against the other. These actions were originally performed for other purposes: to bore holes in a piece of wood, or to rub it into fibres; finally, one or the other was carried out with such vigour that a filament began to burn, and the discovery was made. For hundreds of years men were conscious of the importance of this achievement; and the myth in honour of the mortal who brought to mankind the fire of the gods is as well known to the South Sea Islanders as to the Greeks. Sparks from flint must have suggested a second method of kindling a fire; certainly the art of igniting soft filaments of wood by means of a spark — thus enabling the very smallest source of combustion to be used for human purposes — was known to Man in the earliest times. The obvious results of the use of fire are means of obtaining warmth and of cooking food, thereby rendering it more pleasing to the taste and fit for digestion.

Self-defence had already led to the use of weapons; and, at the same time, the contrivances for hunting and fishing must have become more and more perfect. A weapon is an instrument employed as a means for inflicting injury on enemies. Weapons were fashioned out of such materials as nature offered — wood, stone, and the bones of animals and of large fishes. The advantage that lies in the employment of heavy substances from which to shape weapons was recognised, and also the advantages of cutting-edges and sharp points. Teeth of animals, sharp ends of fish-bones and of antlers, and the edges of shells were natural models, in which experience enabled men to perceive certain peculiarities and their significance. Thus the invention of axes, swords, and knives followed; men learned to sharpen wooden stakes, to chip stone into a required form, to bind a pointed object to a wooden handle. Spears and arrows were made, and the latter were feathered in order to render their flight more accurate. The recognition of the elasticity of some materials, and of the fact that, the more force exerted, the more violent the rebound, led, on the one hand, to the short sling, and, on the other, to the bow in all its various forms. A very low degree of civilisation is that of races unacquainted with the bow and arrow, and familiar with club or boomerang only — thus realising how to make use of the weight of a substance alone, or, as in the case of the boomerang, of a peculiar means of imparting motion.

The time previous to the discovery of the art of working in metal was the Age of Stone. It was a natural transition period during which men began to learn to make use of the malleable metals, which could be hammered and beaten into various shapes and finally discovered how to work in iron. Iron, by being placed in the fire, brought to a white heat and smelted, was rendered capable of being put to such uses as were impossible in the case of brittle materials — bone or stone, for example. Many races never acquired the art of working in the softer metals even, and procured metallic implements from other peoples. The great importance of metal-working is borne out by the fact that the position of the smith, even in legendary times, has been of the utmost significance. The Ages of Stone and of Metal belong to the most important stages of civilisation.

Having made himself weapons, Man did not employ them in fights with animals only; he also used them on his fellow men, and at the same time arose the necessity for protective coverings, — that is, the need for a means of neutralising the effect of weapons on the body. Thus followed the invention of the shield as a portable shelter, of the coat of mail and of the helmet, and of armour in general in all its different forms and varieties.

Together with weapons, utensils are characteristic of material culture. Utensils are implements used in the arts of peace, domestic and industrial; they are instruments which enable us to increase our power over nature. Some utensils have undergone the same transformations as have weapons; others have their own independent history. Just as the edges of shells served as patterns for knife-blades, so did hollow stones, the shells of crustaceans or of tortoises, become models for dishes and basins. From the discovery of the imperviousness of dried earth, the potter's art developed: it became possible to mould clay into a desired shape while moist, and then, when dry, to employ it in its new form as a vessel for holding liquids; for that which has always been of the greatest importance in the making of utensils has been the taking advantage of two opposite characteristics displayed by a material during the different stages of its manufacture: plasticity, which admits of its first being moulded into various forms, and another quality, which causes it afterward to stiffen into solidity and strength. A further acquisition was the art of braiding and plaiting, the joining together of flexible materials in such a way that they hold together by force of friction alone. Thus coherent, durable fabrics may be produced, and by joining together small parts into an aggregate it is also possible to give a definite form to the whole and to adapt it to various uses. The quality of adaptability is especially developed in the products of plaiting; but the quality of imperviousness is lacking. Wickerwork was used not only in the form of baskets, but also in other shapes, as means for protection and shelter, as material for sails, as well as for tying and binding. The art of weaving arises from plaiting, and along with it come methods for spinning thread. It thus becomes possible to make an immense number of different useful articles out of shapeless vegetable material. Fibres are rendered more durable by being bound together; and textures formed from threads are adapted to the most various uses of life. This has an influence on the development of weapons also: bow-strings, slings, and lassos presuppose a rudimentary knowledge, at least, of the textile arts; and as knowledge increases, so are the products improved in turn.

Means for conveyance are also invented, that difficulties arising from distance may be overcome. At first men carry burdens upon their backs, heads or shoulders, or in the hand, placing whatever they wish to transport in a utensil (basket, or piece of cloth), thus producing a coherent whole: later, in order to render conveyance still more convenient handles are invented. Objects are dragged along the ground, and from an effort to save them from injury the use of sledges develops. Things that are round enough are rolled to their destinations; this leads to the invention of rollers and wheels, materials of required form being brought into combination with rudimentary agents of circular motion, and thus, through a rotary, a horizontal movement is obtained; and so the force of gravity is made use of, consistency of motion procured, and the hindering effect of friction overcome to the greatest possible degree.

Means for carrying inanimate objects once invented, it is not long before they are put to use for the conveyance of Man himself; thus methods for the transportation of human beings are discovered in the same manner as are the means for the carriage of goods.

In primitive times transportation is employed to a far greater extent by water than by land. Man learns how to swim in the same way as other animals do, by discovering how to repress his struggles, transforming them into definite, regular movements. The sight of objects afloat must, through unconscious analysis, — experience. — have taught men to make light, water-tight structures for the conveyance of goods upon water, and, later, for the use of Man himself. The pole by which the first raft was pushed along developed into the rudder. Kayaks and canoes were built of wood, of bark, and of hides. In this connection, moreover, an epoch-making invention was that of cloths in which to catch the wind — sails; and this, too, was a result of observation and experience. Man had known the effect of the wind upon fluttering cloth, to his loss, long enough before he hit upon the idea of employing it to his advantage. Finally he learned that by adjusting the sails he might make use of winds blowing from any direction.

Habitations are structures built in order to facilitate and assure the existence of man and the preservation of his goods. Indeed, the presence of caverns caused men to recognise the protective virtue of roof and wall, and the knowledge thus acquired gave rise in turn to the making of artificial caves. Holes beneath overhanging banks and precipices led to the building of houses with roofs extending beyond the rambling walls. Perhaps the protection afforded by leafy roofs, and the walls formed by the trunks of trees in primeval forests, may also have turned men's thoughts to the construction of dwellings. Houses of various forms were built, circular and rectangular; some with storerooms and hearths. Smoke was either endured, or allowed to escape by various methods. The use of dwellings presupposes a certain amount of consistency in the mode of living, the presence of local ties, and a general spirit favouring fixed and permanent residence. Nomadic races use movable or temporary shelters only — waggons, tents, or huts.

The houses of stationary peoples become more and more firm and stable. At first they are built of earth and wickerwork, later of stone, and finally of bricks — as among the Babylonians. Foundations are invented, dwellings are accurately designed as to line and angle; the curved line is introduced, bringing with it arches both round and pointed, as may be seen in the remains of Roman and Etruscan buildings. The structure is adorned, and it becomes a work of art.

But Man also dwelt over the water, sometimes erecting his habitations upon rafts and floats, often upon structures that rose from beneath the surface. Thus, dwelling in communities of various sizes, was he secure from the attacks of land enemies. Even to-day there are uncivilised peoples that live over the water, constructing their homes upon piles, as did the builders of the lake-dwellings once so numerous in south Germany and Switzerland, whose villages were as old as the Stone Age.

Clothing, however, was invented partly that in cold climates men might survive the winter, partly for the sake of ornament. In tropical regions man originally has no knowledge of the necessity for clothing: garments are masks, disguises; they bear with them a charm; they are the peculiar property of the medicine-men or of those who in the religious dance invoke the higher powers. Modesty is a derived feeling; it cannot exist until a high state of individualisation has been attained, until each man desires exclusive possession of his wife, and therefore wishes to shield her from the covetousness of other men. This leads to the performance of sexual intercourse in private, and gradually to the concealment of the organs of sex.

With the knowledge of dress, a desire for adornment, the effort to assist nature in producing certain definite æsthetic effects, arises. Less uniformity in the appearance of the body is wanted, and this brings tattooing and the use of ornament for head, ears, nose, neck, loins, etc, into vogue. Later there is a fusing of these several aims: clothing becomes protection, veil, and ornament in one, fulfilling all three functions at the same time.

Another epoch-making discovery, often arrived at while races are still in the state of subsistence by hunting, is the domestication of animals. This may have originated from the practice of provoking one beast to attack another in order to vanquish them both the more easily. Further development, bringing with it the idea of totemism and the notion that the soul of an animal dwells in Man, drew him nearer to his animal neighbours; and he sought them out as comrades and attendants. The taming of wild creatures arose from two sources: human egoism, and the innate feeling of unity and identification with nature common to all savages: on the one hand, the subjugation of animals, and, on the other, their domestication; neither of which employments rendered it by any means less possible for men to hold animals in reverence, or to attribute to them virtue as ancestral spirits.

Such acquisitions of external culture accompany Man during the transition from his subsistence by the pure products of nature to the cultivation of natural resources, cattle-breeding and agriculture — occupations necessitating the greatest unrest and mobility. The simple life in nature incites men to wander forth that they may discover land adapted for their support; they rove about in search of roots as well as of living prey. The breeding of domestic animals also causes them to travel in the hope of finding ground for pasture; nor does agriculture in its primitive form tend to establish permanence of residence, although it contains within itself latent possibilities of developing a settled life, one of the most important factors in the progress of mankind. Only fixed, domestic peoples are able to create great and lasting institutions, to store up the results of civilisation for distant later races, and to establish a developed, well-organised commercial and civil life. The transition from nomadism to life in permanent residences has therefore been one of the greatest steps in the development of humanity. At the time of the beginnings of agriculture, however, Man was still a periodic wanderer. According to the field-grass system of cultivation, seed is sown in hastily cleared ground, which becomes exhausted in about two years and is then abandoned. A migration follows and new land is cleared. This system continues until men learn to cultivate part of the land in a district, allowing the remainder to lie fallow for a time in order that the soil may recover; thus they remain fixed in their chosen district Various circumstances — for example, the danger of enemies from without, and the difficulties attending migration — must have led to this change, the transition to the system of alternation of crops. The wanderings are confined to less extensive regions, the same fields are returned to after a few years, until finally the relation of patches under cultivation to fallow land is reduced to a system, and the time of wandering is past

With fixed residence the forms of communities alter. The group settles in a certain district, homes are built close to one another, and the patriarchal organisation gives place to the village, which, with its definite boundaries, is from now on the nucleus of the social aggregate. Often several village communities have fields and forests in common, and a common ownership of dams and canals; nature takes care that they do not become isolated, but unite together in close contact for common defence and protection.

With agriculture is associated the working up of raw products. These are fashioned into materials for the support of life and for enjoyment; furniture for dwellings, clothing, tools, utensils, and weapons are made. For however much agriculture favours a life of peace, so rarely does Man live in friendship with his fellows that agricultural peoples also find it necessary to arm themselves for war. At first manufacture is not separated from farming; the agriculturist himself prepares the natural products, assisted by the members of his family. Later, it is easily seen that some individuals are more skilled than others; it is also recognised that skill may be developed by practice and that employments must be learned. Therefore it is requisite that special individuals of the community should prepare themselves for particular activities in the working up of raw products, and pursue these activities in consistency with the needs of the society — trade or craft. The craftsman at first labours for the community; in every village the tailor, cobbler, smith, barber, and schoolmaster is supported by society at large. The craftsman receives his appointed income — that is, his portion of the common supply of food; and, in addition, every one for whom he expends his labour gives him something in compensation, or finds him food while employed about his house, until, finally, a systematic method of exchange is established; and with this another advance — epoch-making for civilisation — is arrived at. This is the division of labour. It is found advantageous not only that the craftsman be employed as he is needed, but also that he produce a supply of products peculiar to his trade; for the times of labour do not in the least harmonise with the times of demand. Although during the first periods of industrial life men sought more or less to adjust these factors, in later times they become wholly separate from one another. There is always in addition, labour ready to be expended on casual needs; in more advanced phases of civilisation this condition of affairs is not avoided; but wherever labour can be disassociated from fortuitous necessity, the capacity for production is greatly increased. Commodities are manufactured during the best seasons for production and are preserved until the times of need; thus men become independent of the moment. Here also, as in other problems of civilisation, it is necessary to surmount the incongruities of chance, and to render all circumstances serviceable to our purposes.

Exchange and division of labour are the great factors of the progress of a civilisation based upon industrialism. Crafts and trades develop and improve; greater and greater skill is demanded, and consequently the time of preparation necessary for the master craftsman becomes longer and longer. The worker limits himself to a definite sphere of production and carries his trade forward to a certain perfection. His wares will then be more eagerly sought for than those made by another hand; they are better, yet cheaper; for his labour is lightened by his greater skill. His various fellow craftsmen, and the agriculturist also, must exchange their goods for his: for the more specialised the work of an individual, the more necessary the community is to him, in order that he may satisfy all his various requirements. Exchange is at first natural; that is, commodities are traded outright, each individual giving goods directly in return for the goods he receives. The production of the community as a whole has become far richer, far more perfect. The labour of the organised society produces more than the activity of separate individuals.

Here again is shown the impulse of Man to free himself from the exigencies of the moment, to lift himself above the fortuitous differences that arise between supply and demand. The more varied the production, the more difficult it becomes to find men who are able to offer the required commodity in exchange for what has been brought to them. An escape from this embarrassment lies in the discovery of a universal measure of exchange value and medium of exchange — money. Money is the means of adjustment which renders traffic between men independent of individual requirements.

Mediums of exchange, particularly necessary for the carrying on of traffic between different communities, chosen from certain objects or substances universally recognised as valuable, which exist in large quantities and can be divided up into parts, make their appearance in very early times. At first their values are more or less empirical, dependent upon the conditions of individual cases; until gradually a medium obtains general recognition and thus becomes money. The same need for surmounting the lack of uniformity in individual requirements has led the most different peoples in the world to the invention of money. Naturally, many different things have been employed as mediums of exchange; these vary according to geographical situations, conditions of civilisation, and the customs of races. Pastoral tribes at first employed cattle; but tobacco, cowries, strings of flat shells (wampum), bits of mother-of-pearl, rings, and hides are also used. At last it is found that metal is stable, durable, divisible, and of generally recognised value; and finally the precious metals take precedence of all others. At first, value is determined according to weight only; and this method is still employed by civilised peoples of considerable development. Many traces of the same system are also to be found in the ceremonial institutions and laws of various nations. In later times the metal is divided into portions of convenient size; and upon the pieces thus obtained values are marked; thus rendering it possible for payments to be received, without dispute, at any place and under all conditions. Finally this form of money is adopted by all civilised races. Great difficulties, not yet overcome, have arisen from the use of two precious metals as mediums of exchange at the same time, owing to the fact that their frequent fluctuations in value in respect to each other are causes of severe disturbances to trade. Avoidance of this drawback is sought partly through regulation by law of the ratio of value of the two metals, — bimetallism, — which necessitates an international agreement; partly through the adoption of a system according to which gold alone is the standard, silver becoming a subsidiary currency, adopted for convenience sake only.

But humanity has not yet attained the final goal in respect to money. Together with the real mediums of exchange appear ideal mediums — substitutes for money. During times of misfortune and need, orders drawn on government treasuries, convertible into metal in the future, are issued. Documents, promissory notes, etc., are endowed with fictitious values, and the power of the community or state forces their acceptance as currency. The power of the state to stamp coins and to institute laws for the regulation of commerce is thus employed in imposing an obligatory exchange value on a currency that is not justified by its intrinsic worth. Various substitutes for money — leather, paper, and subsidiary coinage, having fictitious values — are brought into existence; but after fluctuations in the markets and commercial crises have taken place, experience teaches that, so far as money is concerned, governmental power is not omnipotent, and that the use of inconvertible currency must be limited to narrow bounds unless the whole commercial life of a nation is to be destroyed.

In case the government seeks means for the lessening of debts through a debased currency, commerce, on the other hand, knows how to help itself. Instead of direct payments, balances of accounts and compensation are brought into use. These are assisted by the transference of claims, especially through the exchanges; also by meetings of merchants in which mutual claims are adjusted and extinguished — clearing-houses. Here, too, is seen the endeavour to escape individual incongruity — in other words, the effort to control fortuitous necessities. Although accounts in themselves presuppose claims and counter-claims, merchants are able artificially to produce a state of affairs in accordance with which natural conditions of commerce are both controlled and obeyed — a circumstance which has always been peculiar to the progress of civilisation.

Division of labour originates in the development of the handicrafts, in the distinction made between the labour of working up the raw material and that of its production. With the help of a currency it leads to a complete transformation, not only of economic relations, but also of the social conditions of men

Country becomes city; centres of population which rest upon an industrial basis arise; in many cases growth of the various manufacturing industries is furthered by unfavourable agricultural conditions. Such industrial centres require markets and market-places; it is necessary for the producers of raw materials to come to market from the country with their goods, in order that they may meet together with the craftsmen of the city and with other producers from the country who offer their wares in turn. The market town is the point of departure for further culture. Here, too, the endeavour to harmonise individual incongruities exists: fruit is sent to market; each man has his choice; an exchange value is determined by means of comparison, through analysis of the individual prices which themselves do not furnish any rational determination of worth, and therefore expose both buyer and seller to chance. Thus a market-price develops. The city is the living agency promoting industry and exchange; it brings its population into contact with the population of the country by means of the market, and prevents men from separating into isolated, unsympathetic, or even hostile groups.

Here industry flourishes — arts, crafts, and large manufactures. In the latter, division of labour is developed to a maximum degree, and production in factories derives a further impulse through the introduction of machinery. Machines, in contrast to implements and utensils, are inanimate but organised instruments for labour, requiring subordinate human activity only (attendance), in order that they may impart force and motion in a manner corresponding with the designs of the inventor. Machinery is originally of simple form, dependent on water or wind for motive power: rude mills, and contrivances for the guiding of water in canals or conduits belong to its primitive varieties. But Man's power of invention increases; and in the higher stages of industrial evolution the facilities for labour are enormous. We have but to think of steam and of electricity with all their tremendous developments of power. Finally the discovery of the unity of force leads men to look upon nature as a storehouse of energy and to devise means by which natural forces may be guided, one form of energy converted into another and transferred from place to place; and thus Man becomes almost all-powerful. He is not able to create, it is true, but he may at least mould and shape to his desire that which nature has already formed. Thus the discovery how to direct the forces of nature enables us again, according to the principle already cited, to escape the disabilities of human differentiation with its attendant incongruities.

As already stated, division of labour leads to exchange; exchange leads to commerce. Commerce is exchange on a large scale, organised into a system with special regard to the production of a store, or supply. The latter requires a certain knowledge of trade: the centres of demand must be sought out, and the goods transported to these centres in a suitable manner. In this way a fruitful reciprocal action develops; and, as production influences trade, so may trade influence production, governing it according to the fluctuations of demand, and leading to the creation of stores of commodities for which a future market is to be expected. Thus commerce presupposes special knowledge and special skill; it develops a special technique through which it is enabled to execute its complicated tasks. Men who live by trade become distinct from craftsmen; and the mercantile class results. Merchants are men whose task is to effect an organised exchange of natural and manufactured products. As in every kind of activity connected with material production, so in commerce, egoism plays the greatest part: trade always endeavours to reap the greatest profits through the discovery of advantageous sources of supply and of the best regions for distribution; it endeavours to take advantage of favourable times in respect to both supply and demand — speculation. But here, too, egoism may be looked upon from the standpoint of universal history as a most important factor in the furthering of human culture.

Commerce always displays an impulse to extend itself beyond the borders of single nations, not to remain inland only, but to become a foreign trade also; for the products of foreign countries and climates, however valuable they may be, would be inaccessible except for commerce. Thus trade becomes both import and export. The first step is for the tradesman or his representative to travel about peddling goods, or for an owner of wares or money to offer capital to an itinerant merchant with the object that the latter may divide the profits with him later on. This leads to the sending of merchandise to a middleman who places it on the market in a distant region — commission business. The establishment of a branch or agency in a foreign country, in order to trade there while in immediate connection with the main business house, follows; and finally merchants deal directly with foreign houses without the intervention of middlemen, thus entering into direct export trade. This, of course, presupposes a great familiarity with foreign affairs and confidence in their soundness; consequently it is possible only in a highly developed state of civilisation.

Foreign trade is carried on overland by means of caravans, and, in later times, by railways; over sea, through a merchant marine — sailing-vessels and steam-ships. The magnitude of commerce, its peculiar methods, and its manifold, varying phases, combine to produce new and surprising phenomena: traffic by sea leads to insurance and to different forms of commercial associations; intercourse by cara-van gives rise to the construction of halting-stations, establishments for refresh-ment and repair, that finally develop into taverns and inns. And that which first arose from necessity is subsequently turned to use for other purposes: insurance is one of the most fruitful ideas of the present day; hotels are an absolute necessity for the traveller, rendering possible residence in foreign lands which has become an important means for education and for the recovery of health.

Commerce is able to bring further contrivances and institutions into being, here again, overcoming individual incongruity by means of combination. Trade cannot always be carried on directly between the places of production and of con-sumption: one district requires more, another less: it would be difficult to supply all from one centre of distribution. Thus an intermediate carrying trade is devel-oped, which so arranges that merchandise is circulated by means of commercially independent stations until it finally reaches its destination. At first one merchant may mediate between producer and consumer, then a number of merchants; this apparently increases prices; in fact, however, if properly carried out, it lowers them, for such organised co-operation renders the surmounting of obstacles less difficult and increases the stability of the market. The demands of the middle-man are amply compensated for by these advantages.

Thus the world's commerce develops, and that which is accomplished by market traffic in lesser districts is brought about by the concentrative influence of bourses, or exchanges, in the broadest spheres. Here, as in the smaller markets, the tendency is for all prices to seek a level, to become as independent as possible of individual conditions; and so commerce between nations, and the possibility of ordering goods from the most distant lands, bring with them an adjustment: world prices are formed; and to establish these is the business of the exchanges. The exchange is an institution which has developed since the sixteenth century in Holland, England, Germany, — in all civilised nations in fact; it is a meeting together of merchants for the transaction of business by purchase or sale. It has acquired still more the character of a world institution since men have been able to interchange advices by means of telegraph and telephone; it is possible for the bourses of different countries to transact business with one another from moment to moment, so that the ruling prices of a great part of the world — indeed, of all portions of the globe which have a determining influence on the markets in gen-eral — can be immediately known.

It is true that the world's commerce is accompanied by serious dangers. It furthers the obtaining of commodities and enormously increases their use; but it also advances the possibility that a country whose conditions of production are unfavourable may be greatly injured, its industries impeded, and a great portion of its inhabitants thrown out of employment. Every step in the progress of civi-lisation brings with it isolated haltings and disturbances; but a halt can lead to a general crisis, and a disturbance to a complete destruction of the masses; and this would take place so rapidly that it would be impossible to guide production into another channel before the damage were done. In addition, it is not well, considering the separation of peoples into states and the possibilities of wars, that one nation should be completely dependent on another for the necessities of life. Hence the efforts to avoid or to impede certain effects of international commerce, such as protective tariffs, discriminating duties, subsidies, etc., which, rightly used, are beneficial enough, but, wrongly employed, are elements of destruction, as all remedies may be under such conditions.

It will be of the utmost significance if ever it become possible to manufacture not only single natural products — indigo for example — but also the most important of materials — foodstuffs. The artificial production of albumen would not only bring about vast transformations in all industrial affairs and in the economic relations of states, but would also effect far-reaching changes in the social positions of the different classes of society; a prospect which I will only indicate, for, indeed, we are not yet on the eve of this great acquisition.

It has already been stated that deliverance from the burden of individual dissimilitude, and the discovery of methods by which it may be brought to pass, have been some of the main factors in civilisation. As time goes on, these expedients play a more and more important part. One of them, which draws from concrete things their abstract value, transforming the intrinsic worth of fixed bodies into money power, thus rendering mobile, as it were, immovable property, such as real estate, is the institution of liens, securities, and mortgages, with all its developments. It is founded on the possibility of rendering the exchange value of fixed property independent, thus transforming immovable possessions into articles of commerce: one of the most ingenious discoveries of mankind. Like most inventions it has developed from small beginnings, from impulses arising from necessity; and it is supported by one of the deepest and most intelligent conceptions of human rights.

But mankind has not remained content with this alone. Further means of rendering property mobile and of putting it to active use have been discovered. The right to the value of property now appears as the right of association, — the right to form private corporations. The company as a unity is distinguished from the totality of its copartners: these are transformed from joint owners into shareholders, and the association is made into an independent individual. Thus are formed stock, shipping, and mining companies, the essence of which consists in this: that the usufruct of a property is transformed into free, negotiable assets, and that thus immovable possessions may be speculated in and handled in the same manner as the most mobile of commodities. Consequently the possibility of organising and collecting capital is essentially increased; also, it is true, the probability of wild speculations and of stock-jobbing — mere external participation without real interest — abuses which have sometimes dealt severe blows to modern society.

It has already been stated that commerce leads to a taking up of residence in foreign countries; it also leads to colonisation, to a settling of foreign lands, particularly those of a lower grade of civilisation, in which organised settlements must be established owing to the fact that our necessities of life are not to be found there, but must be produced by our own labour. Colonisation is almost invariably a cause of conflict with the natives, of war and subjugation: thus a single colony becomes a colonial state, remaining in more or less close connection with the mother country, forming a profitable market for many of the products of the latter, and possibly offering a home to its surplus population without becoming independent. This increases, on the one hand, the economic and national sphere of power of the mother country; but, on the other hand, owing to the lack of compactness of the whole, many more weak points are exposed to attack; and often centrifugal tendencies arise, strivings for separation and complete independence. Nevertheless it is to be recognised that it is chiefly owing to the influence of commerce that civilisation is introduced into foreign lands.

It follows that, as civilised life becomes more and more complex, a corresponding change must take place in the relative social conditions of people. The distribution of necessities of life and of means for enjoyment constantly becomes more varied; the possession of power to control labour, obtained through personality, speculation, inheritance, etc., often grants an overwhelming superiority to the individual. This leads to the distinction between the employers and the employed.

In earlier centuries the labour question was settled by means of the lawful subjection of certain classes of men, until complete injustice was reached in slavery — the establishment of a social class bound to labour in the interest of owners and employers. The system was rendered still more efficient by making slave-ownership hereditary. Slavery originated in wars and man-hunting, in times when there were but few domesticated animals and no machines, when utensils were very imperfect and a more or less developed mode of life could only be conducted by means of the manual labour of individuals. There was no free labour, or labour by contract, with its necessary concomitant, good faith. What could be given to the workman in compensation for his services when there was abundance of unoccupied land, but little movable capital, and a very limited acquaintance with luxuries? There was nothing to be offered that he would not be able to procure in a better form himself, through his own labour. Therefore, in order to obtain labourers, men resorted to force, — to slave-hunts and to subjection in war, — thus introducing a slave population of which the individuals were either divided among the various households or kept in special slave habitations or villages. Slaves were recruited from among the descendants of slaves; and men guilty of certain specified offences, insolvent debtors, etc., were also placed with them.

Slaveholding has not developed among all peoples; it presupposes a certain economic development, the need for division and organisation of labour. Hunting races — for example, the American Indians — have but little use for slaves; at most they offer them up only as sacrifices to the dead. Slaves are useful only to races that carry on agricultural and manufacturing industries. But not all agricultural or otherwise industrial peoples have developed slaveholding; many possessed slaves, but only in a low state of organisation. There are but few traces of an acquaintance with slaveholding in the laws of the Aztecs or in the older laws of China. Other nations, however, have established slavery of the most oppressive sort. The industry of the slave was often increased by the promise of definite privileges or private possessions (*peculium*); he was often granted a home and family life; and thus he became a bondman — burdened and taxed and bound to the soil, it is true, but otherwise looked upon as a man possessed of ordinary rights and privileges. Even during the days of slavery there were instances of emancipation, and, through such opportunities, the possibility was opened of rising to the social position of a slave-owner. Sudden grantings of liberty did not always lead to well-being. In many nations the masses of emancipated slaves, with their foreign blood and exotic conceptions of life, have brought great dangers to the state, as in the case of the Roman Empire. In other countries the holding of bondmen for centuries, and the formation of widely divergent classes have led to oppression of the inhabitants and to moral and intellectual stagnation. In many cases violent oppression has occasioned serious wars and ruinous disturbances.

The evolution of a free working class, with recompense for labour, is one of the most important chapters in the history of modern civilisation. The chief sphere of development is that of the crafts and trades: craftsmen not only require long years of apprenticeship, but also long periods of probation and preparation — journeymanship; and the journeyman who expects some day to become an adept must remain in service for many years in close association with a craftsmaster, upon whom he is entirely dependent as to labour, wages, food, and lodging. The association of craftsmen — the guild — with its code of law even extends power over the private life of the individual member, who is not merely in the employment of a master, but in addition, as an associate of the guild, is under its control and protection.

With the establishment of factories the position of the workman changes. He is no longer the producer; his function is to control and attend to the working of machines, and to perform service in the final finishing-off of products. He no longer works in company with the craftsmaster; for the mental labour of the latter has grown to be absolutely different from the manual work performed by the former. A great division in society is created; a basic difference arises between the head that guides and the hand that performs; and, as the guiding head very often becomes a capitalist, a distinction between capital and labour develops — a distinction that grows all the more striking as the increased power and efficiency of machinery tends to diminish the value of hand labour; so that, finally, conditions favourable to a combination of mental and manual labour in the same individual disappear.

The position of the employers is, as already indicated, either one of independence and isolation or of association. The latter has long preponderated; it arose of itself with the development of specialised labour, which, in turn, emanated from the general labour of the community. The guild is a joint association against which the individual is powerless — an offensive and defensive alliance, with the establishment of certain laws, especially of definite rules for the overcoming of obstacles.

Among many races the guild has amalgamated with the family, members of a clan and their descendants following the same profession. The impulse for such transmission of profession to offspring is known to have existed in primitive times; many callings — for example, that of medicine-man or sorcerer — are hereditary among savage peoples. The system of hereditary succession has come to complete perfection in India, where the castes have become to a large extent classes of calling or profession, and have dictatorial power over the vocations of the descendants of their members. In other lands the system has either developed into one according to which the son-in-law shall follow the calling of his wife's father, or has been abandoned entirely, the choice of guild and profession being left to the pleasure of the individual. This has helped to prevent stagnation in trades by not allowing them to become strictly exclusive, open to the sons of members only. To be sure, it was insisted upon that the future master should be eligible by birth; but men were far from requiring that the son must invariably follow in his father's footsteps.

The power of guilds often induces legislation in their favour; thus they become monopolies, and only such individuals as are members of an association may adopt its particular trade or craft as a profession. Sometimes the unity of a guild is broken, and the individual right to form judgments enters in place of the rules laid down by the corporation: from this results competition, which finally leads up to free competition. Through free competition the encumbering rigidity of the guilds is avoided; it leads to a high development of the individual, and is therefore a great source of progress; it discloses the secrets of the craft, freeing men from deeply rooted prejudices in regard to different vocations, and increases Man's capacity for invention, producing new methods for carrying on trades and new combinations and connections. Naturally the evil side of Man also appears in free competition. The endeavour to rise, not through excellence, but through deception and speculation on the weaknesses of others, may often be seen in all its ugliness. Both the discipline and the enforced order of the guilds are lacking; grievous shortcomings arise from the desire for speedy reward and from the insufficient training of workmen. Oftentimes the necessary guarantees of responsibility and soundness are wanting; oftentimes there is a lack of capacity properly to estimate the value of sterling work. Such faults may be contended against by judicial and social means: there are remedies against deception and impurity; new connections are sought out by the industrial classes; new varieties of guilds are formed; and in one way or another the abilities of a worker are tested and verified before his independent entry into business is permitted.

Very different are the centralising tendencies of great manufacturing industries, which, unlike the smaller companies, do not seek to control the trade of limited areas, but strive to draw great populous regions within their spheres of authority. Large firms, single houses, and stock companies form associations in order to control entire branches of trade, imposing certain conditions of sale to which every member must conform if he desire to continue an associate and not to expose himself to ruinous isolation. Thus "trusts," and their efforts to accomplish the destruction of independent houses through competition, arise; but they also bring with them the risk of neutralising all the advantages derived from free competition. The position to be adopted by legislation in respect to trusts and monopolies is one of the most acute problems of the present day.

The labouring classes also, as soon as they are set free by law, follow the tendency of association, conscious of the fact that union produces strength. Associations are formed for the improvement of the economic condition of individuals; trade unions also come into being, in order that the labourer may enter into conflicts with capital, — in other words, that the living labour, or latent capital embodied in the workman, may set itself in opposition to the actual capital, or the results of labour, accumulated by employers.

All this is characteristic of the economic life of the present day. Analogous phenomena are known to universal history, although never before has there been such a vast development of organised capital and labour. The Babylonians had an industrial and monetary system resembling in many ways that of our own time; the entire industrial organisation of the Chinese was controlled by guilds; a rich commercial life with an elaborate commission system flourished under the

Caliphate, although there was but little tendency toward the combination of individuals; and the sea traffic of the Malays long ago exhibited characteristics analogous to the peculiarities of the maritime trade of to-day.

The chief economic problems of the present day arise from the opposition of free competition to combinations and trusts; from the contradictions between free, uncoerced labour and the labour which is forced upon men by necessities arising from present economic conditions; from the contrast between the subordinate position of the labourer and the tremendous power of trade unions; and from the discrepancies between free international commerce and the need for protecting agriculture, between enormous factory industries and the necessity for saving the handicraft of the individual from extinction. Much has already been done toward relieving the situation since men have become convinced that it is not always best to follow the principle of *laissez faire*, and that our intelligence should bring itself independently to bear upon social conditions with a view to their improvement. The position of the workingman has been bettered, partly by private, partly by state means; the principle of insurance has been applied, and the labourer is insured against accident, sickness, old age, even against lack of employment. Efforts are being made to raise the standard for hand work through the development of the arts and crafts; there is also an endeavour to secure agriculture from the dangers of flooded markets by means of protective taxes; indeed, it has been proposed that the entire corn trade should be placed under state control. Everywhere the possibility of supporting the individual in the battle against destiny is making itself felt. The problem is very difficult; it is essential that the strength of the individual be not weakened by exaggerated collectivism; that under a too extensive state authority the powerful incentive to industry that lies in the private activity of every individual be not smothered; that, owing to too ready assistance, individuality with its conceptions of self-respect and of duty be not destroyed; and that through national measures connection with the world's civilisation and the progress of humanity as a whole be not lost. It is important that possession not only of means for enjoyment but also of means for production be secured to all men, that the great furtherance of civilisation which lies in the development of the individual may be retained. At all events, however complicated the situation may be, we are at least confident to-day that although the close of the eighteenth century saw the world shaken in mighty convulsions, despairing of her task, we are now on the way toward becoming master of our difficulties through a peaceful course of development.

## B. Spiritual Culture

Spiritual culture may develop in the directions of knowing and of feeling. These two forms of the manifestation of consciousness are originally not to be separated from each other; but, as time goes on, a preponderance of one or the other becomes noticeable. Language is the first result of spiritual culture; the communication of thoughts by means of words (sound pictures of ideas). Language arises from the necessities of life, from the need for communication among the members of a social aggregate; linguistic roots are created under pressure of the laws of the human intellect; and, by means of combination, amalgamation, and metaphoric transference, a structure is formed from them, capable — at least in general practice — of expressing thoughts and also feelings, so far as the latter are capable of being expressed by thoughts.

The methods by which sounds and words are combined are exceedingly varied, and are more characteristic even than the vocabularies of languages. It is important to know whether a speech owes its formation to the mere adding together of roots, or to their amalgamation, or ultimately to a system of suffixes, prefixes, and affixes (inflection) in order to render it possible for the primary words to be put to various uses. Thus languages may be isolating, agglutinative, or inflectional. The methods of indicating place, time, cause (active, passive), and the psychological functions (affirmation, desire, doubt — indicative, optative, subjunctive, etc.), are also exceedingly varied.

Speech stands in contradistinction to the primitive method of communication by gestures, that reached a very high state of development in early times, and in accordance with which not single ideas, but combinations of ideas, were conveyed by significant signs, especially by movements of the fingers.

Together with speech appeared the faculty to enumerate or count; that is, the power to place units or groups of units in juxtaposition with one another, following an analysis of their individual peculiarities. From enumeration with the assistance of hands, fingers, feet, toes, etc., according to the decimal or duodecimal systems, or to methods of counting based on twos or fives, a knowledge of numbers developed. This of itself led to an acquaintance with the common laws that govern natural phenomena and to a perception of the relations that exist between quantities in time, space, and intensity: in other words, to mathematics.

A knowledge of geometrical figures also developed: certain portions of clothing are triangular or rectangular in shape; practical construction leads to a consciousness of definite forms and laws of form; ornamentation displays a preference for geometrical basic figures.

A much later acquisition, the art of writing, or the fixation of language in a definite, permanent form, stands in close connection with speech. Writing develops according to two systems: the one based on the symbolling or picturing of ideas (picture-writing, hieroglyphics), and the other on the breaking up of the speech-sounds of a language into a notation of syllables or letters (syllabic or letter writing). According to the first method thoughts are directly pictured; according to the second, sounds, not ideas, are represented by symbols, — that is, the sounds which stand for the ideas are transformed into signs. The transition from sign to syllabic writing comes about in this manner: if, during its development, a language uses the same sound to express various conceptions, men represent this sound by one sign; and whenever a foreign word is reproduced in writing it is first separated into syllables, and the syllables are then pictured by the same signs as are employed to represent similar sounds (but different ideas) in the native speech. Thus symbols are employed more and more phonetically, and less and less meaning comes to be attached to them. This process must continue its development if the pronunciation changes as time goes on; the old writing, with its national symbol-method, may be retained; but with the changing of speech-sounds the new writing is altered: syllables are now represented by signs, and combinations of syllables are reproduced by means of a combination of their corresponding symbols. Thus phonetic writing was not an invention, but a gradual development. Together with the phonetic symbols, ideograms or hieroglyphs also exist, as in Babylonian. It is especially interesting, and indicative of the unity of the human mind, that the transition to syllabic writing has been arrived at independently by different races : the Aztecs, for example, exhibit a wholly independent development.

Further progress is shown in the transition from syllabic writing to writing by means of letters. This advance is furthered if the dialects of a language retain the consonants and change the vowels only ; thus, for example, *a* in the original speech may become *o* in one dialect, and *œ* or *e* in another; or *i* may be altered to *e*, or *e* to *i*, and so on. In order to reproduce the various pronunciations in writing, it is necessary to choose common symbols for representing syllables that contain the same consonant, sometimes in combination with one, sometimes in combination with another or other vowels (*ba, be, bo*), so that the symbol in reality only represents the consonant, the vowel or vowels being differently supplied in the different dialects. In this way syllabic writing becomes consonant writing, through which there is a great gain in simplicity, the multitude of symbols being reduced to a comparatively small number. After this integration has taken place, as time passes, the vowels are pointed, or are themselves represented by symbols, and thus writing by means of letters is developed.

Communication by writing may be either single and private, or general and public; in the latter case plurality is attained through such methods as the affixing of bills and placards, or by means of transcripts or reproductions of the original copy. At first the latter are made in accordance with the ordinary methods of writing; and in slaveholding communities — Rome, for example — slaves who wrote to dictation were employed as scribes. The discovery of a method by which to obtain a plurality of copies through a single mechanical process was epoch-making. The printing-press has performed a far greater service to humanity than have most inventions: for, with the possibility of producing thousands of copies of a communication, the thoughts embodied in it become forces; they may enter the minds of many individuals who are either convinced or actually guided by them. Ideas become active through their suggestion on the masses of the population. This may lead to a one-sided rule of public opinion; but a healthy race will travel intellectually in many directions, and various beliefs supplement one another, struggle together, conquer, and are conquered. In this manner thoughts awaken popular movements, rousing a people to a hitherto unknown degree, and forcing men to think and to join issues. Thus the press becomes a factor in civilisation of the very first importance. The necessity for periodic communication, together with curiosity that refuses to wait long for information, leads to the establishment of regularly recurrent publications; and thus, in addition to the book-press, the newspaper-press, that has learned how to hold great centres of population under its control, appears. Naturally this method of aiding the progress of civilisation has its disadvantages, as have all other methods: the conception of the world becomes superficial, individuality loses in character: not only a certain levelling of education, but also a levelling of views of life and of modes of thought, results. But, on the whole, knowledge is spread abroad as it never was before.

Man, as a thinking being, craves for a conception of life; and in his inmost thoughts he seeks for an explanation of the double relationship of Man to Nature and of Nature to Man, striving to bring all into harmony. This he finds in religion.

Religion is belief in God; that is, belief in spiritual forces inseparable from and interwoven through the universe, — forces that render all things discrete and separate, yet make all coalescent and firm, permeating all, and giving to every object its individuality. Man is impelled by nature to conceive of the universe as divine. This idea exhibits itself universally among primitive folk in the form of animism, — a belief that the entire internal and external world is animated, filled with supernatural beings that have originally no determinate nature, but which may appear in the most varied of forms, may vanish and may create themselves anew, as clouds arise from unseen vapour in the air. Spirits are not far removed from Man; families as well as individuals consider themselves to stand more or less in connection with them; and men, too, have a share in the invisible world when they have cast aside the garment of the body in dream or in death. Every man has his protecting spirit, his *manitou*, that reveals itself to him through signs and dreams. Special incarnations, objects in which supernatural beings are inherent or with which they are in some way connected, are called " fetiches ": thus arises fetichism, in regard to which the strangest ideas were held in previous centuries when the science of anthropology was unknown. Trees, rocks, rivers, bits of wood, images of one's own making, — any of these are capable of containing beings of divine nature. Naturally, the tree or the fragment of wood or of stone is not worshipped, as men formerly thought, but the spirit that is believed to have entered it. In many cases the belief approaches worship of nature, especially among agricultural peoples; divinity is recognised in the shape of factors essential to agriculture — sun, sky, lightning, thunder — these the beneficent deities, in contrast to whom are the earth-spirits who bring pestilences, earthquakes, and other evils to mankind. Thus the cult is refined; spirits are no longer attached to fetiches, but men worship the heavens, and the earth also.

Religion accompanies Man from birth to death. Spirits both for good and for evil hover about him at his very birth. The soul of some being — perhaps an animal, perhaps an ancestor — enters into the new-born child, and from this spirit he receives his name. During the years of youth great transformations take place; the period for consecration approaches. He walks into the enchanted wood; a new spirit enters into him; after fasting and mortification, he learns in a magic dream of his new nature and of his destiny; he returns from the wood with another name and as another man.

Oftentimes there is a new consecration at the time of marriage; often when an heir-apparent succeeds to the chieftainship. At his decease Man enters the realm of shadows. At first he hovers over the sea or river of death, and often only after having passed through many hardships does he arrive in the new kingdom where he either continues to live after the manner of his former existence, or, according to whether his life on earth has been good or evil, inhabits a higher or a lower supernatural sphere. To the dead are consecrated their personal possessions — horses, slaves, wives even — that they may make use of them during the new existence: men go head-hunting in order to send them new helpmates. On the other hand great care is often taken that the spirits of the departed, satisfied with their new existence, may no longer molest the world of the living: propitiative offerings are made ; men avoid mentioning the name of the departed, that he may not be tempted to visit them with his presence ; they seek to make themselves unrecognisable during the time immediately following his death, wear different clothes, and adopt other dwelling-places. Sometimes the light placed near the deceased for the purpose of guiding him back to his old home is moved further and further away, so that his ghost, unable to find the right path, shall never return.

Indeed, worship of the departed may develop into cannibalism. Certainly cannibalism has an earlier and less spiritual origin ; but men are also led to devour the dead in order to absorb their spirits or to annihilate them. For that reason such parts of the body as are supposed to be the particular residences of the soul are eaten. Thus it is self-explained why even developed peoples have retained cannibalism, and how it is that among many races the funeral repast is ordered in such a way that relatives of the deceased have first a choice of morsels.

Thus the belief in spirits encompasses primitive Man, following him step by step.

The affairs of life also appear in the light of religion. Whoever breaks ground or fells a tree dreams of spirits with whom — according to the dream — his relations may be either amicable or hostile. Whoever builds a hut wishes to receive the blessing of spirits ; the hunter is accompanied by them ; and he who slays an animal fears its soul and seeks to conciliate it or to divert its anger in another direction. From this belief is derived the common custom for men either not to eat the particular animal which they have themselves captured, or to eat certain portions only.

From animism develops worship of heroes and polytheism, with their attendant mythological narrations. The idea of the unity of the supernatural world is lost ; and the indefinite forms of spirit become separate, independent beings, that are developed more and more in the direction of the souls either of animals or of men. This splitting up of the deity, which destroys the tendency toward unity in religion, is followed by a reaction that comes about partly through a belief in creation by a father of the gods, partly through acceptance of a historical origin of the mythological world from a single source (theogonic myths), and partly through direct banishment of the plurality of gods and a new formation of the belief in a unity according either to theistic or to pantheistic ideas. The theistic tendencies lead to the various creation legends and cosmogonic fables in which the creation of man, the discovery of fire, and the invention of weapons and implements play an especially important part. The pantheistic cosmology leads to the belief in incarnation, from which ideas of occasional miraculous appearances of the god in history, of the unity of the world, and of the possibility that the godhead may appear as an individual in detached form, arise. In spite of the conception of a world permeated and pervaded by God alone, the belief that certain persons and places are more powerful in respect to the divinity than others is retained ; and the appearance from time to time of a Buddha who incarnates and manifests the Supreme Being directly and completely within himself (in a special manner apart from other natural phenomena) is also not looked upon as inconsistent.

Religion is a thing of the emotions, not merely in the sense of having its origin in fear, or in the remembrance of lasting sensations derived from visions or dreams, but emotional in so far that it satisfies the necessity felt by men for a consistent life-conception, — not an intellectual but an emotional conception. It is not the matter-of-fact desire for knowledge that finds its expression in religion, but the joy

of the heart in a supreme power, the call for help of the needy, and the consciousness of our own insignificance and our mortality.  Judgment is not yet abstracted
from the other psychic functions; indeed, it really retires behind the emotions.

When men thus believe in divinity, whether as polytheists, monotheists, or pan-
theists, — pantheism, too, has its gradations and nuances, — if the belief have an
active influence on the emotions, it follows that the individual must establish some
connection between himself and the object of his worship.  This is brought about
through certain actions, or through the creation of circumstances in which special
conditions of consecration are perceived, and therewith the possibility of a close
relationship with the Supreme Being.  The acts through which this relationship
may be brought about, taken collectively, are embraced in the word "cult" (worship), and if performed according to a strict system they are called "rites."  Sacrifice has an important place among the ceremonies observed in accordance with
ritual.  It is based on a conception of the wants and necessities of the higher
beings, and, in later times, is refined into a representation of Man's ethical feelings, —
unselfishness and gratitude, which give pleasure to the deity and thus contribute
to its happiness.  But sacrifice does not retain its unselfish character for any great
length of time.  Man thinks of himself first: he makes offerings to the good
spirits, but more particularly to the evil gods, in order to pacify their fury and
appease their evil desires.  Sacrifices are also offered to the dead, and from such
offerings and memorials is developed the idea of a "family" or "clan" which out-
lives the individual.

The customary rites are then performed by the head of the family; or the
religious office becomes the function of particular individuals or of a special profession — priesthood.  The priest class develops from the medicine-men and sor-
cerers, individuals of exceptionally emotional natures to whom are ascribed special
powers in respect to the spirit world.  Capacity in this direction may be peculiar
to individuals, or it may become a hereditary quality: in the profession of medicine-
man the ranks are filled by means of election or through hereditary succession.
Thus it is with the "shamans" and "ogangas," seers and soothsayers, who play the
part of both prophet and augur, and who in later times are called upon to decide
the quarrels of men, and also, as representatives of the national deity, to throw the
lance of war into the hostile territory ("fetiales"), or, as consecrated messengers
and mediators, to carry on international negotiations.

Thus emotion is the principal active agent; but intellectual power also must
gradually lay its hold on the system of belief.  The principles discovered are formulated into a science; and the cultivation of this science becomes the special
duty of the priesthood, often as a secret art — esoteric system — in which concealment is conducive to the maintenance of the exclusiveness and peculiar power
of the priest class.  The science becomes partly mythologic-historical, partly dogmatic, and partly rituali tic.

But secrets are discovered; doubts and questions arise; systems of belief become
at odds with one another; and controversies develop, along with the growth of the
human intellect.  Men seek to reconcile the numerous contradictions, to weed out
all that has become obsolete; above all, however, to separate that which is intellectual from that which is emotional in a belief.  Religion becomes science, and — in
so far as the science frees itself from the control of the emotions and at the same
time from the dominion of tradition — philosophy.  If once the intellectual life be

awakened, the standpoint discovered from which the world of idea may be distinguished from the world of feeling, and unrestrained investigation be pursued for its own sake, then, together with the philosophy, or universal science, separate sciences appear, ever becoming more and more specialised, — on the one hand, the spiritual life of mankind (moral science), and on the other, Nature (natural science). Both are observed and studied, at first rather because of a transmitted stock of ideas, later, on account of the ever-increasing and always more fruitful store of material for investigation. For a long time the deductive method prevails : a general truth is assumed, and all particular cases are, if possible, brought into connection and harmony with it. In this way a conception of the world is sought (Vedantic, Socratic philosophy, Scholasticism). Soon, however, the inductive method develops, according to which general principles are built up from separate observations. This method has been found to be especially effective in the natural sciences ; it has also been applied to moral science, and here, too, has led to new results.

The artistic instinct develops partly in connection with worship, partly in the direction of its practical application to life ; and although no very sharp line of distinction is drawn between the two tendencies, the germ at least of the difference between the fine and the industrial arts is thus in existence from the very earliest times.

Worship gives rise to images and pictures, at first of the very roughest form. They are not mere symbols ; they are the garments or habitations with which the spirit invests itself. The spirit may take up its abode anywhere according to the different beliefs of Man, as shown on page 40 : in a plant, an animal, a stone, above all, in a picture or effigy that symbolically reflects its peculiarities. Therefore the ghosts of ancestors are embodied in ancestral images. Just as skulls were reverenced in earlier times, in later days the images of the dead (*korwar*) are worshipped. Such images are the oldest examples of the art of portraiture : and the oldest dolls are the rude puppets that according to the rites of many races — the American Indians, for example — widows must wear about them as tokens, or as the husks or wrappers of their husbands' doubles. In like manner belief in the identity of the ghosts of the dead with animals leads to the making of animal effigies and tokens. It also causes men to tattoo the symbol of an animal on the human skin ; to mould or carve images in which expression for the conception of the spirit that is worshipped is sought through composite figures partaking of the nature both of man and of animal.

In like manner prayer leads to song, rite to verse, cult to dance. Rhythm obtrudes itself into the minds of men as an expression or representation of the infinite ; the regularly repeated movement arouses of itself an idea of the eternally recurrent.

The religion itself becomes poetry : the belief in the identity of spirits of the departed with animals, and the myths of metamorphosis, take the form of fables and fairy tales ; the cosmogonic and theogonic conceptions develop into mythologies ; hero sagas become epics : the myths of life in nature become a glorification of the external world, an expression of unity with nature, and thus a form of lyric poetry.

Everyday life, too, demands artistic expression. At first the childish passion for the changing pictures that correspond with different ideas of the imagination joins with the desire to impress others, and finery in dress and ornamentation result. This has developed in every clime. Tattooing arises not only from a religious motive, but also from the desire for ornament. The painting of men's bodies, the often grotesque ideas, such as artificial deformation of the head, knocking out and blackening of teeth, ear ornaments and mutilation of ears, pegs thrust through the lips, and various methods of dressing the hair, may be in part connected with religious conceptions, for here the most varied of motives co-operate to the same end. Yet on the other hand there is no doubt that they are also the outcome of a craving for variation in form and in colour. In the same way the dance is not only an act of worship; it is also a means of giving vent to latent animal spirits: thus dances are often expressions of the tempestuous sensual instincts of a people.

The dance exhibits a special tendency to represent the ordinary affairs of life in a symbolic manner: thus there are war and hunting dances, and especially animal dances in which each of the participants believes himself to be permeated by the spirit of some animal, that throughout the dance he endeavours to mimic. In this way dramatic representation, which is certainly based on the idea of personification, on the notion that a man for the time being may be possessed by the spirit of some other creature that speaks and acts through him, originates. Thus the primitive form of masques arose, in which men dressed themselves up to resemble various creatures, real or imaginary, as in the case of the animal masques of old time; for according to the popular idea the spirit dwells in the external, visible form, and through the imitation or adoption of its outward appearance we become identified with the spirit whose character we assume. Among many races not only masks proper were worn, but also the hides and hair or feathers of the creatures personated. Dramatic representation was furthered by the dream plays — especially popular among the American Indians — in which the events of dreams are adapted for acting and performed. Even as men seek illumination in dreams as to questions both divine and mundane, so do they anticipate through dreams the dramatic representations which shall be performed on holidays as expressions of life.

Play is a degeneration of the dance; and it arises less from the instinct for beauty than from a desire to realise whatever entertainment and excitement may be got from any incident or occurrence. From another special inclination originate those satirical songs of northern peoples, written in alternating verses, in which the national tribunal and the voice of the people are given expression at the same time. Thus they have a truly educative character. These are the preliminary steps to the free satire and humour that gleam through the lives of civilised peoples, now like the flicker of a candle, now like a purifying lightning flash, freeing men from life's monotony, and illuminating the night of unsolved questions.

Capacity for organised play is a characteristic that lifts Man above the lower animals. The expression of individuality without any particular object in view, the elevation of self above the troubles of life, and free activity, uncoerced by the necessities of existence, are characteristic both of play and of art. Thus play, as well as art, exhibits to a pre-eminent degree Man's consciousness of having escaped, if only temporarily, from the coercion of environing nature; being without definite object, it proves that he can find employment when released from the pressure of the outer world, — that is, when he is momentarily freed from his endeavour to establish a balance between himself and the necessities of life, with a view to overcoming the latter. Man stands in close connection with his environment and with the immutable laws of nature; but in play and in art he develops his own personality — a development that neither in direction nor in object is influenced by the outer world and its constraint.

### C. The Overcoming of Instinct through Liberty

THE foregoing stages of development are attained in aggregates of rational beings, communities in which actions do not succeed one another as if performed in unreasoning, instinctive fashion, but in adaptation to circumstances, in a manner which shows a capacity to advance from one condition into other conditions, either because of a conscious knowledge of the necessity for modification and change, or because of an innate feeling of the possibility and need for variation. The spiritual force that enables us to step forth from the circle and to adapt ourselves to new systems is human reason. Many animals possess a somewhat similar though far less perfect faculty which is never developed to such an extent that it may be historically treated as having evolved and grown spontaneously by virtue of its own power.

The natural impulse in Man crystallises itself in custom — the plexus, as it were, of successive actions accepted as obvious requirements in life, instinctively preserved, often when the necessity for such constraint is no longer felt, and even when the very opposite is recognised. It is plain that custom is an important social factor in so far as it subjects the individual to the order of the whole without exercise of external pressure. It is the same as among animals, by whom the social impulse is expressed in a self-evident succession of instinctive actions.

But the true advantage possessed by Man lies in the fact that it is possible for him to overcome the blind tendency of custom; he has in him the germs of a further development, — in other words, he has a history. And this is founded on the manifoldness of Man's social nature; on the human characteristic that in social aggregates, together with the general, the special is perceived; together with social activities the activity of the individual is recognised. This leads to conflicts, and conflicts lead to progress. Thus the germ of progress lies in Man's very nature, and history is the history of development.

The step that leads to the overcoming of custom is the recognition of right. "Right" is that which society strictly demands from every individual member. Not all that is customary is exacted by right; a multitude of the requirements of custom may be ignored without opposition from the community as a whole, although, of course, detached individuals may express their displeasure. The aggregate, however, grants immunity to all who do not choose to follow the custom. In other words, the separation of custom from right signifies the development of a sharper line of demarcation between that which is and that which ought to be. In primitive times "is" and "ought to be" are fairly consonant terms: but gradually a spirit of opposition is developed; cases arise in which custom is opposed, in which the actions of men run counter to a previous habit. Man is conscious of the possibility of raising himself above the unreasoning tendencies toward certain modes of conduct, and he takes pleasure in so doing, — the good man as well as the evil. Whoever oversteps the bounds of custom, even through sheer egotism, is also a furtherer of human development; without sin the world would never have evolved a civilisation: the Fall of Man was nothing more than the first step toward the historical development of the human race.

This leads to the necessity for extracting from custom such rules as must prove advantageous to mankind; and this collection of axioms — which "ought to be" — becomes law.

The distinction between right and custom was an important step. The relativity of custom was exposed with one stroke. Many, and by no means the worst members of communities, emancipate themselves from custom. It is the opening in the wall through which the progress of humanity may pass. Nor do the demands of right remain unalterable and unyielding. A change in custom brings with it a change in right; certain rules of conduct gradually become isolated owing to the recession of custom, and to such an extent that they lose their vitality and decay. And as new customs arise, so are new principles of right discovered. In this manner an alteration in the one is a cause of change in the other — naturally, in conformity with the degree of culture and contemporary social relations. Custom and right mutually further each other and render it possible for men to adapt themselves to newly acquired conditions of civilisation.

Together with right and custom a third factor appears, — morality. This is a comparatively late acquisition. It, too, contains something of the "ought to be," not because of the social, but by virtue of the divine authority or order based on philosophical conceptions. Morals vary, therefore, as laws vary according to peoples and to times. The rules of morality form a second code, set above the social law, and they embody a larger aggregate of duties. The reason for this is that men recognise that the social system of rules for conduct is not the only one, that it is only relative and cannot include all the duties of human beings, and that over and beyond the laws of society ethical principles exist.

Naturally conflicts arise between right and morals; and such struggles lead to further development and progress.

The differentiation of morality and right is an achievement of European civilisation; it was accomplished as soon as men began to abstract such laws as were enjoined by society from the laws of God, committing the latter to the security of divine justice; a division that continued even when men sought to trace the rise of morality back to earthly, humanitarian principles.

Also the late appearance of ideas of morality proves that ethical considerations were originally foreign to the god-conceptions. The spirits, fetiches, and world-creators of different beliefs are at first neutral so far as morals are concerned; myths and legends are invented partly from creation theories, partly from historic data, and partly through efforts of the imagination. In primitive beliefs there is no trace of an attempt to conceive of deities as being good in the highest — or even in a lower — sense; and it would not be in accordance with scientific ethnology to appraise, or to wish to pass judgment on religions according to the point of view of ethics. Even the once often expressed idea that deities conform to the characteristics and peculiarities of races is only partially correct. Anthropomorphism is only applicable in so far that, on the acceptance of a spirit world, certain analogies to Man's knowledge, desires, and actions must intrude of themselves; moreover, the savage must immediately recognise that neither his customs nor right, that curbs or conquers his passions, is directly connected with the spirit world. And so far as morality is concerned, resemblance between men and the gods whom they have created only exists to this extent: both are originally morally neutral, moral aspirations neither filling the breasts of men nor appearing in the myths of their deities. Not until the importance of morality in life is realised, and the profound value of a life of moral purity recognised, do men seek in their religious beliefs for higher beings of ethical significance, for morally perfect personalities among the gods. Therefore nothing is more unjust than to demand morality from the mythologies of primitive peoples or to affect horror at the abundance of violence and treachery to be found in the legends of the gods of early ages. In later times men endeavoured to escape these difficulties by differentiating good from evil spirits, and by putting in apposition to the deity a devil in whom all the iniquity which had been previously ascribed to the gods is incorporated — and even more added into the bargain.

There is yet one general remark to be made. Different elements of civilisation vary greatly in their development in different civilised districts; one race may have a greater tendency toward intellectual, another toward material culture. No race has approached the Hindoos in philosophic speculation, yet they are as children in their knowledge of natural science. One people may develop commerce to the highest extent, another poetry and music, a third the freedom of the individual. The language of the American Indians is in many respects richer and more elegant than English. Therefore nothing is farther from the truth than to say that, in case one institution of civilised life is found to exist in a hunting-people, another in an agricultural race, or the one in an otherwise higher, and the other in an otherwise lower nation or tribe, the institution in question must have reached a state of perfection corresponding with the general development of the people possessing it. According to this, the monogamic uncivilised races were further advanced than the polygamous Aryans of India and the Mohammedans; and the Polynesians, with their skill in the industrial arts and their dramatic dances, perhaps in a higher state of civilisation than Europeans!

## D. Social Institutions

Development fulfils itself in communities of men. Except in a human aggregate it cannot come to pass; for the germs of development which are brought forth by the potentiated activity of the many may exist only in a society of individuals.

It has therefore been a significant fact that from the very beginning men have joined together in social aggregates, partly on account of an instinctive impulse, partly because of the necessity for self-defence. Thus it came about that primitive men lived together in wandering, predatory hordes, or packs. The individuals were bound to one another very closely; there was no private life; and the sex-relationships were promiscuous. Men not only dwelt together in groups, but the groups themselves assimilated with one another, inasmuch as marriages were reciprocally entered into by them. So far as we are able to determine, one of the earliest of social institutions was that of group-marriage (*Gruppenehe*). Individuals did not first unite in pairs, and then join together in groups — such would soon have fallen asunder; on the contrary, group-marriage itself created the bond that held the community together: the most violent instinct of mankind not only united the few but the many, indeed, complete social aggregates.[1]

---

[1] A more detailed account of the origin and earliest forms of marriage may be found in the writer's book, " Zur Urgeschichte der Ehe," 1897.

Group-marriage is the form of union established by the association of two hordes, or packs, according to which the men of one group marry the women of the other; not a marriage of individual men with individual women, but a promiscuous relationship, each man of one group marrying all the women of the other group — at least in theory — and *vice versâ*; not a marriage of individuals, but of aggregates. Certainly, with such a sex-relationship established, sooner or later regulations develop from within the community, through which the marital relationships of individuals are adjusted in a consistent manner; but the principle first followed was, as community in property, so community in marriage; and this must of itself lead to kinships entirely different from those with which we are familiar. The system of so-called classificatory family names is employed, according to which all the members of an elder generation are called father and grandfather, mother and grandmother; all the children are known to the elder generations as sons and daughters, grandsons and granddaughters; and individuals of the same generation are all brothers and sisters to one another. Moreover, many variations are possible according to whether a greater or a lesser lapse of time divides generation from generation.

The existence of this form of marriage relationship in primitive times is certainly a much controverted point; at all events its presence among Australian natives and American Indians — races whose institutions are of an especially primitive character — may be demonstrated with far greater certainty than may the historical existence of phenomena of the past in general.

Group-marriage was closely bound up with religious conceptions; single hordes, or packs, considered themselves the embodiment of a single spirit. And since at that time spirits were only conceived of as things that existed in nature, the horde felt itself to be a single class of natural object, — some animal or plant, for example; and the union of one pack with another was analogous to the union of one animal with another. Each group believed itself to be permeated by the spirit of a certain species of animal, borrowed its name thence, and the animal species itself was looked upon as the protecting spirit. The ancestral spirit was worshipped in the animal, and the putting to death or injuring of an individual of the species was a serious offence.

Such a belief is called Totemism. "Totem" — a word borrowed from the language of the Massachusetts Indians — is the natural object or animal assumed as the emblem of the horde or tribe, and correspondingly the group symbolised by the ·class of animal or natural object is called a Totem-group.

This belief led to a close union of all who were partakers of the spirit of the same animal; it also strictly determined which groups could associate with one another. And as the totem-group mimicked the animal in its dances, and fancied itself to be possessed by its spirit, it also ordered the methods of partaking of food, and all marriage, birth, and death ceremonies in accordance with this conception. It is said that, the totem being exogamous, marriages were not possible within the totem, but only without it. Precisely so; for the original conception was not that individuals formed unions, but that the whole totem entered the marriage relationship; a single marriage would have been considered an impossibility.[1]

To which totem the children belonged — to the mother's, to the father's, or to a third totem — was a question that offered considerable difficulty. All three possi-

[1] See "Zur Urgeschichte der Ehe," p. 27.

bilities presented themselves; the last mentioned, however, only in case the child belonged to another group, a sub-totem, and in that event its descendants could return to the original totem.

Descent in the male or in the female line occasioned in later times the rise of important distinctions between nations. If a child follow the mother's totem, we speak of "maternal kinship;" conversely, of "paternal kinship" in case of heredity through the father. Which of these is the more primitive, or did tribes from the very first adopt either one or the other system, thus making them of equal antiquity, is a much-vexed question. There is reason to believe that maternal kinship is the more primitive form, and that races have either passed with more or less energy and rapidity to the system of descent through males, or have kept to the original institution of maternal succession. There are many peoples among whom both forms of kinship exist, and in such instances the maternal is undoubtedly the more primitive; from this it appears very probable that development has thus taken place, the more so since there are traces of maternal kinship to be found in races whose established form is paternal.[1]

As time passed, marriage of individuals developed from group-marriage or totemism. Such unions may be polygynous — one man having several wives — or polyandrous — one woman having several husbands. Both forms have been represented in mankind, and, indeed, polygyny (also called polygamy) is the general rule among all races, excepting occidental civilised peoples. The form of marriage toward which civilisation is advancing is certainly monogamy; through it a complete individual relationship is established between man and wife; and although both individualities may have independent expression, each is reconciled to the other through the loftier association of both.

Marriage may be either temporary or permanent; in the latter case unconditionally contracted for life or only permanent in principle, — a separation being permitted when desired. The temporary marriage is entered into from the very beginning with the idea that it is only to last a short time. The tendency of development is toward permanent marriage; and permanent marriage is a powerful incentive to the world's civilisation, not only on account of the domestic life and the superior care for children thus obtained, but also because it creates lasting tranquillity and reserves many otherwise occupied powers for the work of civilisation. Nearly associated with monogamy is the belief in union after death; it arises from the religious beliefs prevalent among many peoples. Among other races there is at least the custom of a year of mourning, sometimes for husband, sometimes for wife, often for both.

Marriage of individuals has developed in different ways from group or totem marriage: sometimes it was brought about through lack of subsistence occasioned by many men dwelling together; sometimes it arose from other causes. One factor was the practice of wife-capture: whoever carried off a wife freed her, as it were, from the authority of the community and established a separate marriage for himself. Marriage by purchase was an outcome of marriage by capture and of the paying of an indemnity to the relatives of the bride; men also learned to agree beforehand as to the equivalent to be paid. The practice of acquiring wives by purchase developed in various directions, especially in that of trading wives and in the earning of wives by years of service. Gradually the purchase became merely a

[1] See "Zur Urgeschichte der Ehe," pp. 53 *et seq.*

feigned transaction; and a union of individuals has evolved — now sacerdotal, now civil in form — from which every trace of traffic and of exchange has disappeared.

Thus already in early times marriage had become ennobled through religion. It is a widespread idea that through partaking of food in common, blood-brotherhood, or similar procedures, a mystic communion of soul may be established; and in case of marriages brought about by the mediation of a priesthood the priest invokes the divine consecration. Marriage is thereby raised above the bulk of profane actions of life; it receives a certain guarantee of permanency; indeed, in many cases, by reason of the mystic communion of souls, it is looked upon as absolutely indissoluble.

In contradistinction to marriage stands hetairism, a state of irregular sexual relationship. It has appeared in all climes; often, as in India, in connection with religious conceptions, constituting the peculiarity of certain castes, justified through a feigned marriage (with a plant, for example); or, as among the native Australians and American Indians, it appears from time to time in the shape of a wild orgy, or, among other peoples, as a right of defloration granted to definite individuals. But also among races having a fully developed marriage institution, the unmarried are often permitted to live in conditions of sexual freedom, so that marriage, by giving a woman to her husband, merely separates her from other men in so far as the husband will not consent to possess her in common with them. The institution of child-betrothals marked an important step in development; for in such cases the bride was from childhood destined for her husband and bound to chastity. This is the historical significance of betrothal.

On the other hand, even from primitive times there has been no lack of ascetic conceptions, and of laws that impose celibacy upon certain classes of men or upon individuals of certain ages, or, at least, sexual abstinence at definite times and under definite circumstances.

The ownership of property also was originally communistic, and the idea of individual possession has been a gradual development. The idea of the ownership of land, especially when developed by agricultural peoples, is of a communistic nature; and, from common possession, family and individual ownership gradually comes into being. It is brought about in various ways, chiefly through the division of land among separate families: at first only temporary, held only until the time for a succeeding division arrives; later, owned in perpetuity. Nor was it a rare method of procedure to grant land to any one who desired to cultivate it, — an estate that should be his so long as he remained upon it and cultivated the soil, but which reverted to the community on his leaving it. There gradually developed a constant relationship between land and cultivator as agriculture became more extended and lasting improvements were effected on the soil: land became the permanent property of the individual; it also became an article of commerce.

Ownership of movable property even was at first of communistic character. Clothing and weapons, enchantments effectual for the individual alone, such as medicine-bags or amulets, were, to be sure, assigned to individuals in very early times; but all property obtained by labour, the products of the chase or of fishing, originally belonged to the community, until in later days each family was allowed to claim the fruits of its own toil and was only pledged to share with the others under certain conditions. Finally, individuals were permitted to retain or to barter property which they had produced by labour; and exchange, especially exchange between individuals, attained special significance through the division of labour.[1]

The individualisation of the ownership of movable property was especially furthered by members of families performing other labour, outside the family, in addition to their work within the family circle. Although the fruit of all labour accomplished within the family was shared by the members in common, the results of work done outside became the property of the particular individual who had performed the labour. Consequent expansion of the conception of labour led men to one of the greatest triumphs of justice, to the idea of establishing individual rights in ideas and in combinations of ideas, — recognition of intellectual or immaterial property (right of author or inventor), one of the chief incentives to modern civilisation.

On the other hand, individual rights in transactions led to conceptions concerning obligations and debts. Exchange, either direct or on terms of credit, brought with it duties and liabilities for which originally the persons and lives of the individuals concerned were held in pledge, until custody of the body (which also included possession of the corpse of a debtor) was succeeded by public imprisonment for debt, and finally by the mere pledging of property, imprisonment for debt having been abolished, — a course of development through which the most various of races have passed.

The relation of the individual to his possessions led men at first to place movable property in graves, in order that it might be of service to the departed owner during the life beyond : hence the universal custom of burning in funeral pyres not only weapons and utensils, but animals, slaves, and even wives.[2] In later times men were satisfied with symbolic immolations; or possessions were released from the ban of death and put to further use. The property of the deceased reverted to his family, and thus the right of inheritance arose. There was no right of inheritance during the days of communism; on the death of a member of the family a mere general consolidation of property resulted; with individual property arose the reversion of possessions to the family from which they had been temporarily separated. Thus property either reverted to the family taken as a whole, or to single heirs, certain members of the family: hence a great variety of procedure arose. Up to the present day inheritance by all the children, or inheritance by one alone, exists in eastern Asia as in modern Europe (right of primogeniture, right of succession of youngest son, etc.). An intermediate system is that of several heirs with the right of preference.

In like manner criminal responsibility was originally collective: the family or clan was held responsible for the actions of all its individual members except those who were renounced and made outcast. Such methods of collective surety still exist among many exceedingly developed peoples; but the system is gradually dying away, the tendency being for the entire responsibility to rest upon the individual alone.

### E. POLITICAL INSTITUTIONS

THE state is a development of tribal, or patriarchal, society. The tribal group is a community of intermarried families, all claiming descent from a common ancestor. From tribal organisation the principle is developed that parti ......

---

[1] See *ante*, p. 28.    [2] See p. 40.

in the community is open only to such individuals as belong to one or other of the families of which it is composed; and the political body thus made up of individuals related either by blood or through marriage is called a patriarchal, or tribal, state. This form of community was enlarged even in very early times, advantage being taken of the possibility of adopting strangers into the circle of related families, and of amalgamating with them. Still, the fundamental idea that the community is composed of related families always remains uppermost in the minds of uncivilised peoples. The tribal state gradually develops into the territorial state. The connection of the community with a definite region becomes closer; strange tribes settle in the same district; they are permitted to remain provided tribute is paid and services are performed, and are gradually absorbed into the community: the strangers and the original inhabitants — plebeians and patricians — united together into one aggregate. Thus arises the conception of a state which any man may join without his being a member of any one of the original clans or families.

In this way the idea of a state becomes distinct from that of a people bound together by kinship, the latter being especially distinguished by a certain unity of external appearance, custom, character, and manner of thought. This is not intended to suggest that an amalgamation of different race elements in a state and an assimilation of different modes of thought and of feeling are not desirable, or that a spirit analogous to the sense of unity in members of the same family is not to be sought for: such a condition is most likely to be attained if a certain tribe or clan take precedence of the others, as the most progressive, to which the various elements of the people annex themselves.

The tribal state has a fixed form of government. The chiefs or patriarchs of the various families stand at the head of affairs, the position of chief being either hereditary or elective. In most cases, however, it is determined by a combination of both methods, a blood descendant being chosen provided he is able to give proof of his competence. In addition there is often the popular assembly. In later times many innovations are introduced. Passion for power united to a strong personality often leads to a chieftainship in which all rights and privileges are absorbed or united in the person of one individual: so that he appears as the possessor of all prerogatives and titles, those of other men being entirely secondary, and all being more or less dependent upon his will. Religious conceptions especially have had great influence in this connection. Nowhere is this so clearly shown as in "teknonymy," an institution formerly prevalent in the South Pacific islands, according to which the soul of a father is supposed to enter the body of his eldest son at the birth of the latter, and that therefore, immediately from his birth, the son becomes master, the father continuing the management of affairs merely as his proxy. Other peoples have avoided such consequences as these by supposing the child to be possessed by the soul of his grandfather, therefore naming first-born males after their grandfathers instead of after their fathers. Another outcome of the institution of chieftainship is the chaotic order of affairs which rules among many peoples on the death of the chieftain, continuing until a successor is seated on the throne, — a lawless interval of anarchy followed by a regency.

The power of a chieftain is, however, usually limited by class rights; that is, by the rights of sub-chieftains of especially distinguished families, and of

the popular assembly, among which elements the division of power and of jurisdiction is exceedingly varied. These primitive institutions are rude prototypes
of future varieties of coercive government, of kingship, either of aristocratic or
of republican form, in which the primitive idea of chieftainship as the absorption of all private privileges is given up, and in its place the various principles
of rights and duties of government enter.

Class-differentiation with attendant privileges and prerogatives is especially
developed in warlike races, and in nations which must be ever prepared to resist
the attacks of enemies, by the establishment of a militant class. The militant
class occupies an intermediate position between the governing, priest, and scholar
classes on the one hand, and the industrial class — agriculturists, craftsmen,
merchants — on the other. Employment in warfare, necessary discipline, near
association with the chieftain, and the holding of fiefs for material support
give to this class a unique position. Thus the warrior castes developed in India,
the feudal and military nobility in Japan, the nobility in Germany, with obligations and service to feudal superiors and to the court. This system survives for
many years, until at last feudal tenure gradually disappears, and its attendant
prerogatives are swallowed up by all classes through a universal subjection to
military service; although even yet a distinct class of professional soldiers
remains at the head of military affairs and operations, and will continue to do
so as long as there is a possibility of internal or external warfare. However,
here too the militant class is absorbed into a general body of officials. Officials
are citizens who not only occupy the usual position of members of the state, but
to whom in addition is appointed the execution of the life functions of the
nation, as its organs; in other words, such functions as are peculiar to the
civic organisation in contradistinction to the general functions exercised and actions
performed by individual citizens as independent units. Officialism includes to
a special degree duty to its calling and to the public trust, and there are also
special privileges granted to officials within the sphere appointed for them.

In a society governed by a chieftain, as well as in a monarchy, there is a
popular assembly or consultative body: either an unorganised meeting of individuals, or an organised convention of estates founded on class right. A modern
development, that certainly had its prototype in the patriarchal state, is the
representative assembly, an assembly of individuals chosen to represent the
people in place of the popular gathering. The English government, with its
representative legislative bodies, is a typical example in modern civilisation.

One of the chief problems encountered not only in a society ruled by a chieftain, but also in states of later development, whether governed by a potentate
or by an aristocracy, is the relation of temporal to spiritual power. Sometimes
both are united in the head of the state, as in the cases of the Incas of Peru
and of the Caliphate. Sometimes the spiritual head is distinct and separate
from the temporal; frequently the two forces are nearly associated, a member
of the imperial family being chosen for the office of high-priest, as among
the Aztecs. Often, however, the two functions are completely independent
of each other, as among many African races, the medicine-man occupying a
position entirely independent of the chieftain. Such separation may, of course,
lead to friction and civil war; it may also become an element furthering to
civilisation, a source of new ideas, opening the way to alliances between nations.

and setting bounds to the tyranny of individuals, as exemplified in the relation of the Papacy to the Holy Roman Empire.

The form of state in which the functions of government are exercised by a chieftain contributes greatly to state control and enforcement of justice. The realisation of right had been from the first a social function; but its enforcement was incumbent on the same groups of individuals (families or tribes bound together by friendship). The assumption by the state of the power to dispense justice and to make and enforce law is one of the greatest events of the world's history. The idea of all right being incorporated in the chieftain (and social classes) played an important part in bringing about this condition of affairs; for as soon as this conception receives general acceptance, the chieftain, and with him the state, become interested in the preservation and enforcement of justice, even in its lower forms in the common rights of the subjects. On the other hand, not only the interests of chieftainship, but also those of agriculture and commerce, are furthered by the preservation of internal peace; and internal peace calls for state control of justice and enforcement of law.

Moreover the religious element worked to the same end. Wickedness was held to be an injury to the deity, whose anger would be visited upon the entire land: a conception that lasted far into the Middle Ages, and according to which the fate of Sodom and Gomorrah was held to be typical of the effect of the curse of God. Already in primitive times religion led to a strange idea of justice: secret societies consecrated by the deity *(Dukduk, Egbo)* took upon themselves the function of enforcing right instituting reigns of terror in their districts, maintaining order in society, and claiming authorisation from the god with whose spirit they were permeated. Later, influenced by all these causes, the social aggregate took over the control of justice. It was already considered to be the upholder of right, the servant of the deity, the maintainer of public peace, the dispenser of atoning sacrifices etc.; and so the various elements conceived of as justice, which had previously been distributed among the single families, tribes, associations, and societies, were combined and placed under state control.

Certain forms for the dispensation of justice, judging of crimes, and determining of punishments were developed. Thus arose the different forms of judicial procedure, which for a long time bore a religious character. The deity was called upon to decide as to right and wrong — divinity in the form of natural forces. Hence the judgments of God through trial by water, fire, poison, serpents, scales, or — especially in Germany during the Middle Ages — combat, or decision by the divining eye, that was closely allied to the so-called trial by hazard. A peculiar variety of ordeal is that of the bier, according to which the body of a murdered man is called into requisition, the soul of the victim assisting in the discovery of the murderer. Ordeals are undergone sometimes by one individual, sometimes by two. An advance in progress is the curse, which takes the place of the ordeal, the curse of God being called down upon an individual and his family in case of wrong-doing or of perjury. The curse may be uttered by an individual in co-operation with the members of families; thus arise ordeals by invocation and by oath with compurgators. Originally a certain period of time was allowed to pass — a month, for example — for the fulfilment of the curse. In later times, whoever took the oath — oath of innocence — was held guiltless. Witnesses succeeded to conjurors; divining looks were replaced by circumstantial evidence, and, instead of a mystic, a rational method of obtaining testimony was adopted. The development was not attained without certain attendant abuses; and the abolition of ordeal by God was among many peoples — notably the inhabitants of eastern Asia, the American Indians, and the Germans of the Middle Ages — succeeded by the introduction of torture. In many lands torture stood in close connection with the judgment of God; in others it originated either directly or indirectly from slavery. According to the method of obtaining evidence by torture, the accused was forced through physical pain to disclosures concerning himself and his companions, and, in case he himself were considered guilty, to a confession. However barbarous and irrational, this system was employed in Latin and Germanic nations (excepting England) until the eighteenth century, in some instances even until the nineteenth.

Judgment was first pronounced in the name of God; in later times, in the name of the people or of the ruler who appeared as the representative of God. The principles of justice, the validity of which at first depends upon custom, are in later times proclaimed and fixed as commands of God. Thus systems of fixed right come into being first in the form of sacred justice, then as commands of God, and finally as law. Law is a conception of justice expressed in certain rules and principles. Originally there were no laws; the standard for justice was furnished to each individual by his own feelings; only isolated cases were recorded. As time advanced, and great men who strove to bring about an improvement in justice arose above the generality of mankind; when the ruling class became differentiated from the other classes; when it was found necessary to root out certain popular customs, — then, in addition to the original collection of precedents, there arose law of a higher form: law that stood above precedent, that altered custom, and opened up new roads to justice. Great codes of law have not been compilations only; they have led justice into new paths. Originally a law was looked upon as an inviolable command of God, as unalterable and eternal; its interpretation alone was earthly and transitory. As years passed, men learned to recognise that laws themselves were transitory; and it became a principle that later enactments could alter earlier rules. The relations of later statutes to already established law, and how the laws of different nations influence one another, are difficult, much-vexed questions for the solution of which special sciences have developed — transitory and international law.

Judgment and law are intimately concerned with justice; the conception of right (as stated on p. 45) has evolved from the double action of life and custom. To this development of justice is united an endeavour of the state or government not only to further welfare by means of the creation and administration of law, but also to take under its control civilising institutions of all sorts. This was originally a feature of justice itself; certain practices inimical to civilisation were interdicted and made punishable offences. Already in the Middle Ages systems of police played a great part among governmental institutions, especially in the smaller states. Subsequently the idea was developed that not only protection through the punishment of crime, but also superintendence of and promotion of the public weal, should be administered by law; and thus the modern state developed with its policy of national welfare. With this arose the necessity for a sharper distinction to be drawn between justice and the various actions of an administration; and thus in modern times men have come to the system — based on Montesquieu — of the separation of powers and independence of justice.

Development is fulfilled through the interaction of contrary principles. On the one hand, the idea of individual right arises from the social conception of justice; on the other hand, the upholding of justice gradually becomes a duty of the greatest and most powerful community, that is, a function of the state. On the one side, justice strives for individualisation, on the other, for the centralisation of state authority, state supervision, and state protection. These contrasting elements are comprehensible when one considers the historical unity from which they have emanated: they arise from the same germ, — the idea of social justice; for the true nature of social conditions is precisely the union of individual and aggregate. In former times, when these contradictions were not understood, the basis of the state was supposed to have been a contract or agreement between men, according to which they bound themselves together with co-renunciation of individual activities. This teaching of the natural-right school — a social compact as foundation of the state — is, as may be seen from the preceding, a perversion of history. To-day it is rightly numbered among things that are obsolete.

## 4. CIVILISATION IN RESPECT TO DIFFERENT TIMES AND DIFFERENT NATIONS. — THE WORLD'S CIVILISATION

WE have just spoken of the errors of the school of natural right. To these another may be added: the theory that justice is, in reality, one, though it is differently conceived of by different races, and that therefore it should be our endeavour to fetch this ideal right from Heaven, as it were, for then positive justice would for the most part be set aside, or at least rendered unnecessary in essence. In the same manner men looked forward to an ideal state and to ideal conditions of civilisation, upon attaining which, progress would cease for all time. This is a mistaken view. Justice varies according to the development of civilisation, and according to the function that it must perform in this development; in like manner every age creates its own material and spiritual culture. Every poet is a poet of his own time.

Nevertheless, the idea of natural right marked an important period of transition; for the conception of an ideal always includes an idea of the possibility of changes for the better. For this reason the notion of ideal right led to a criticism of positive justice, followed by improvements. It brought about a decrease in the power of inertia and led to the opening up of new ways to progress. On the other hand it often destroyed, revolutionary-wise, fruitful germs of development, permitting artificial, unseasonable, and immature formations and malformations to take their place.

The notion of natural right, however unhistorical it was in itself, characterised a period of transition in so far as it enabled men to form a historical conception, — a conception of what might be: for, by contrasting actual with ideal justice, we are enabled to escape the bonds of the opinions of a particular time, and to look upon such opinions and views objectively and independently. Yet it is certainly a foolish proceeding to consider an ideal, deduced principally from conceptions and opinions of the present, to be a standard by which to measure the value of historical events of all times, sitting in judgment over the great names of the past with the air of an inspector of morals. The office of the historian as judge of the dead — and here we return to our preface — is quite differently constituted. Every age must be judged in accordance with the relation which it bears to the totality of development; and every historical personage is to be looked upon as a bearer of the spirit of his day, as a servant of the ideas of his time. Thus it is quite as wrong to pronounce moral censures on the men of history, as it is wrong to judge an era merely according to its good or evil characteristics. A period must be estimated according to what it has either directly or indirectly accomplished for mankind.

If in one period a violent national agitation shakes off the yoke of foreign rule; if in another great philosophers and poets flourish; if the one leads to an era of vast progress in culture, and the other brings the fruits of civilisation to maturity, — then both periods are of importance to us and significant to historical contemplation. Thus it is absolutely unhistorical to condemn without reservation periods characterised by other ideals than ours, — periods, for example, in which a craving for unity of religious belief has led to the oppression of the intellectual activity of the individual — Inquisition, or times in which wild outbursts of emotion were given vent to that new centres of equilibrium might be found. Ages, too, during which a civilisation becomes extinct, exhibit an important phase to the historian of mankind, for the reason that in the midst of all the destruction he sees the germs of new life budding forth.

There is yet another error in the conception of natural right. While seeking for an abstract ideal, men fail to recognise that the conceptions of justice and the culture of every age vary according to the individuality of nations. Every civilisation is relative to other civilisations: it must have its own peculiarities rooted in its own nationality; it receives from the spirit of its own people certain features which would not be suitable for the inhabitants of other countries, and for which justification is to be found only in its own individual circumstances. In fact, all that is important or characteristic is so closely connected with the individual spirit of the nation that we are constrained to say that only a people that knows how to create its own models and institutions of civilisation will, in the long run, produce anything truly great. Therefore it is absurd, in respect to the culture of nations, to reject as of little worth traits in the character of a state merely because they are not adapted to one's own people or to the sentiment of one's native land.

Yet even such a course as this ought not to be carried to excess. The natural-right method of contemplation had, to this extent, a true basis: national individuality does not exclude a borrowing from foreign civilisations in so far as the race is capable of assimilating exotic characteristics and incorporating them in its own being. Again, increase of traffic in the native country alone will of necessity overcome a whole succession of natural obstacles, and remove a multitude of barriers that hitherto separated single districts from one another; just as a written language brings unity in place of a number of struggling dialects, so a uniform code of law and a uniform method of judicial procedure remove many inconsistencies in justice. But there are also common factors of civilisation shared by nations themselves, through which many contradictions disappear. The religious civilisations of Christianity, Mohammedanism, Brahmanism, Buddhism, and Confucianism have been the determining factors of the intellectual and emotional life, even influencing the course of events, in vast regions. And thus it is also comprehensible that in the judicial life of nations there is an endeavour for a closer approach, and also the existence of equalising tendencies. In spite of countless variations in detail, there is a certain unity of law in the entire Mohammedan world; and although the hope of establishing the unity of Roman canonistic law over the whole of Christendom has not been realised, none the less it was a tremendous idea: that of a universal empire founded on the Roman law of the imperators, and placed under the rule of the German emperor, thus ensuring the continuance of the law of the *populus Romanus*, — an idea that swayed the intellects of the Middle Ages up to the fourteenth, even to the fifteenth century, and according to which the emperor would have been the head of all Europe, the other sovereigns merely his vassals or fief-holders. This idea, once advocated by such a great spirit as that of Dante, has, like many others, passed into oblivion; and in its place has arisen the conception of independent laws of nations. Yet the original idea has had great influence: it has led to a close union of Christian peoples; it opened a way for Roman law to become universal law, although, to be sure, English law, completely independent of that of Rome, has grown to unparalleled proportions as a universal system, entirely by reason of the marvellous success of the English people as colonists. Likewise international commerce will of itself lead to a unification of mercantile, admiralty, copyright, and patent law.

Then the idea of an international league must develop, arising from the idea of the unity of Christian nations. We have advanced a great distance beyond the time when every foreigner was considered an enemy, and when all foreign phenomena were looked upon as strange or with antipathy. Rules for international commerce are developed: state alliances are entered into for the furtherance of common interests and for the preservation of peace. Many tasks which in former times should have been executed by the empire are now undertaken by international associations; and the time for the establishment of international courts of arbitration for the adjustment of differences between states is already approaching.

It also seems probable that states will unite to form political organisations, wholly or partially renouncing their separate positions. Thus nations will be replaced by a federal state, and a multitude of unifying ideas which would otherwise be accomplished with difficulty will come to easy realisation. It is also to be said in this connection that federal states were already in existence during the times of patriarchal communities: an especially striking example is that of the admirably constituted federation of the Iroquois nations.

## 5. OUTLOOK INTO THE FUTURE

THE vision of no man may pierce through to the ultimate end of the processes of history, and to advance hypotheses is a vain endeavour, — quite as vain as it would be to expect Plato to have foretold the life of modern civilisation or the imperial idea of mediaeval times, or Dante to have foreseen modern industrialism or the character of industrial peoples. To-day we are more certain than ever that no process of development, however simple it may have been, has ever taken place according to a fixed model: all developments have had their own individualities according to place and to time. Thus it is obvious that we must forego discussion of the future; for our reasoning may only be expressed in accordance with shadowy, empiric schemes. In like manner there is no answer to the question whether, after thousands of years have passed, our life will still be terrestrial, or whether we shall ever succeed in passing beyond the bounds of our earth. There is but one reply: Who knows? — although a consciousness of our resources urges us to hope. However, there is yet another point of view.

Development of nations as well as of individuals leads either to progress or to decay. No people may hope to live eternally; and how many acquisitions already gained will be lost in the future it is impossible to say. If a nation declines, it either becomes extinct or is annihilated by another state; it becomes identified with the newer nation, and disappears with its own character: thus its civilisation may also disappear. This is a serious possibility. It is the Medusa head of the world's history, which we must face — and without stiffening to stone.

There is one truth, however, the knowledge of which fills us with hope for the future: it is the fact that the results of development and civilisation are often transfused from one people to another, so that a given development need not commence again from the very beginning. This is owing to the capacity which races have for absorbing or borrowing civilisations.[1] Absorption of culture is by no means universal; it does not prevent the occasional disappearance of a civilisation, for every civilisation has before it at least the possibility of death. Nevertheless the transmission and assimilation of culture is constantly taking place. There are various ways in which it may be brought about. A conquering nation may bring its own civilisation with it to the conquered; culture is often forced upon the latter by coercive measures. The conquerors may acquire culture from the vanquished; or assimilation of culture may come about without the subjection of a people, through the unconscious adoption of external customs and internal modes of thought. Finally, culture may be borrowed consciously from one nation by another, the one state having become convinced of the outward advantages and inner significance of the foreign civilisation. In this way the problem of development becomes very complicated; many institutions of vanished races thus continue to live on. Certainly the race that acquires a foreign civilisation must, among other things, be so constituted in its motives and aspirations as to lose the very nerves of its being, its very stability, in order that, intoxicated with the joy of a new life, all traces of its past existence may be allowed to break up and disappear. On the other hand many a promising germ of culture possessed by a vigorous people may come to grief, owing to the influence of acquisitions from without. But, in return, a race that knows how to assimilate foreign culture may obtain a civilisation of such efficiency as it would never before have been capable of attaining, by reason of the fact that its power is established on a recently acquired basis, and because it has been spared a multitude of faltering experiments.

Civilisation may be mutually obtained from reciprocal action, nations both giving and taking. Such a relation naturally arises when states enter into intercourse with one another, when they have become acquainted with one another's various institutions and are able to recognise the great merits of foreign organisations and the defects of their own. Especially the world's commerce, in which every nation wishes to remain a competitor, compels toward mutual acceptance of custom and law; no nation desires to be left behind; and each discovers that it will fall to the rear unless it borrow certain things from the others. Such reciprocal action

---

[1] For a detailed account of this see the writer's essay in the "Aula," I. 1 and 2.

will be the more effective the more like nations are to one another, the better they understand each other, and the more often they succeed not only in adopting the outward forms, but also in absorbing the very principles of foreign institutions into their own beings.

Thus we may hope that even if the nations of to-day decay and disappear, the labour of the world's progress will not be lost; it will constantly reappear in new communities which may rejoice in that for which we have striven, and which we have acquired by the exertion of our own powers.

# III

# MAN AS A LIFE PHENOMENON ON THE EARTH

## By FRIEDRICH RATZEL

---

### 1. EARTH AND MAN

THIS much is certain: History does not stand at the side of Nature, but *within* Nature. — CARL RITTER.

IN the preface to his "Outlines of a Philosophy of the History of Man," Herder tells us how he sought after a philosophy of history, and how he found it in "the ways of God in nature, in the intentions which the Eternal has actually displayed to us in the chain of his works." He saw the destiny of mankind written in the book of creation, and therefore to him, the interpreter and expounder of this destiny, the way was pointed out, leading from the universe of stars to the earth, and from the earth to the different forms of life that, together with human-kind, enjoy the light of the sun. Thus, when he looked upon the earth as one of many heavenly bodies, upon its position and development in the planetary system, and then upon the changes in mountains and in seas which have given rise to islands and continents, it was not to him a question of a scientific introduction to a historical-philosophical work, but a description of the earth as a vast workshop for the construction of the most varied of beings, among which Man occupies his preordained position. This position is only possible on this earth and under these natural pre-conditions, and therefore the earth has a far deeper signification in the history of mankind than it would have merely as the ground upon which men walk and labour and in which their graves are finally dug. Man belongs to the earth as a portion of the earth. The moment arrived in the history of the world when all forces that had previously acted, and all matter that had been formed, yet appeared only as a preparation for the entrance of this being in whom organic life was to reach its highest level.

For us there are no greater epochs in the history of the world, no divisions of time that are more justified, than the pre-human and human eras of the world's history. Yet Man was not perfect on his appearance in the world. He is a son of the earth, not only because he is born of the earth, and therefore composed of earthy material, nor merely because of the deeper reason that the earth was pregnant with him from the very time she bore the first germ of organic life, so that all that had been previously created only pointed toward mankind: Man appeared upon earth as a child, capable of receiving education and of developing, and to whom education and development were necessities: the earth has brought him up through a struggle with all her powers and beings, and into his special history is woven the general history of the world. Periods of heat and ages of ice have now extended, now limited his sphere of existence; he has seen species of land and of animals become extinct, and new ones arise. This being so, he himself could not possibly have remained unaltered. Thus Man of to-day is not only the product of his own development, but also a product of the development of the world. Both are inseparably linked together, and inseparable they will remain. Just as mankind did not appear until the earth had already left a long history behind it, so will he, the highest of all creatures, indeed disappear long before the evening of the world has come. The then still-continuing post-human history of the world would signify an impoverishment for the universe, and, for the life of the earth, the beginning of retrogression.

The insufficiency of a mere external survey of that which is called "the earth in history" follows from our conception of the relation of Man to Nature. It is not enough for us to be content with a description of scenery as an introduction to the history of a country. Even though the description be as richly coloured as Johannes von Müller's preface to the history of leagues and confederations, or Ernst Curtius's introduction to the history of Greece, it will not attain its end unless, for example, the relation of the surface of the land in question to the surface of the whole earth, and the relation of its situation to the entire globe, are determined.


## 2. THE PRINCIPLES OF ANTHROPOGEOGRAPHY

### A. The Coherence of Countries

THERE are more things necessary to an understanding of the dependence of history on natural conditions than a mere knowledge of the land upon which the development has taken place, particularly a mere knowledge of the ground as it was when history found it. From the fact that Man appertains to the earth, we deduce the rule that Man must look out above and beyond this ground. A topographical feature, a height of land, in fact, any geographical phenomenon, is not an isolated structure; each is rather the result of a great, wide-spreading power, and thus they will be found occurring in groups, scattered over broad areas, or recurrent in neighbouring regions. Greek coasts with wide harbours, steep promontories, and rocky islands are also to be found in Istria, Italy, Spain, Asia Minor, and even on the shores of the Black Sea. Wherever the Greeks were borne by their ships, were it from Colchis to Baetis, they landed on coasts whose conformation was familiar to them. Many years ago Herder warned us against establishing our knowledge of the influence of the German soil on German history upon an acquaintance with German ground alone: for Germany, too, is but a continuation of Asia. Who can deny that the branches of a Eurafrican race may not once, in pre-Aryan times, have populated the Mediterranean countries, extended themselves far into Africa, and spread over the same central European region now occupied by Germany? Since there is a constant passing of movable masses of water, and of still more mobile masses of air, over the rigid earth, the connection of one region with its neighbouring regions, that lies in the similarity and continuity of strata, does not remain constant. The Danube bears grains of Black Forest granite to the Black Sea; and the climate of Germany is influenced by the rotary air currents that travel across the Atlantic Ocean after leaving the coasts of Virginia, Labrador, or Iceland behind them. Under the influence of these same currents of air, warm water of the South Atlantic flows to the western coast of Europe, affecting the climate to such an extent that the warmth may be detected far inland. When we realise that in the middle Atlantic yet another system of trade winds wafted Columbus's frail ships to the West Indies, we begin to comprehend the historical effect of inorganic motion. In the case of the Danube, Bismarck denied the political connection of German interests with eastern European complications. Nevertheless the vague thought that recognises in the stream — from its very nature an indivisible whole — a connecting influence also in a political sense is by no means mistaken. The connection was so slight as to be imperceptible when Bismarck denied its political actuality; but who would continue to deny it to-day in the face of the increased significance of all south-eastern European connections which follow the same trend as the Danube? The roads to the Orient will not crowd the river into the background; on the contrary they will only render it the more important.

Thus, although each country is in itself an independent whole, it is at the same time a link in a chain of actions. It is an organism in itself, and, in respect to a succession or a group of lands forming a whole, of which it is a member, it is also an organ. Sometimes it is more organism than organ; sometimes the opposite is true; and an eternal struggle goes on between organism and organ. If the latter be a subjected province, a tributary state, a daughter country, a colony, or member of a confederation, the striving for independence is always a struggle for existence. Such a battle for life need by no means presuppose a state of war. Not only war, but the outwardly peaceful economic development of the world's industries reduces organisms to organs. When the wholesale importation of bad but cheap products of European industries into Polynesia or Central Asia causes decay in the production of native arts and crafts, it is a loss to the life of the whole people; henceforth the race will be placed in the same category with tribes that must gather rubber, prepare palm-oil, or hunt elephants to supply European demand, and who in turn must purchase threadbare fabrics, spirits that contain sulphuric acid, worn-out muskets, and old clothes. — in a word, all the rubbish of civilisation. Their economic organisation dies; and in many cases this is also the beginning of the decline and extinction of a people. The weaker organism has succumbed to the more powerful. Is the case so different, — that of Athens, unable to live without the corn, wood, and hemp of the lands on the northern Mediterranean coast? — or of England, whose inhabitants would starve were it not for the importation of meat and grain from North America, eastern Europe, and Australia?

In vain have men sought for characteristics in the rocks of the earth and in the composition of the air by which one land might be distinguished from another. The idea of great, lasting, conclusive qualitative variations in different parts of the earth is mythical. Neither the Garden of Eden nor the land of Eldorado belongs to reality. There is no country whose soil bestows wondrous strength upon man or an exuberance of fruitfulness upon woman. In India precious stones are as little apt to grow out of the cliffs as silver and gold are likely to exude from fissures in the earth. Nor is there any basis for the slighter differences between the Old World and the New which the philosophers of history of the eighteenth century believed they had discovered. The opinion that the New World produces smaller plants, less powerful animals, and finally a feebler humanity, was not unconditionally rejected even by Alexander von Humboldt. The degeneration and wasting away of the American Indians would certainly be a less disgraceful phenomenon could it be attributed to some great natural law instead of to the injustice, greed, and vices of the white men. In the course of development of the European daughter-nations in America we cannot recognise any such great and universal distinction. The course of history in America, just as in corresponding periods of time in northern Asia, in Africa, and in Australia, only confirms the belief that lands, no matter how distant from one another they may be, whenever their climates are similar, are destined to be scenes of analogous historical developments. It is certain that, so far, one of the greatest results of the labour of Man has been the levelling and overcoming of natural differences. Steppes are made fertile through irrigation and manuring; the contrast between open and forest land becomes less and less, indeed the destruction of forests is being far too rapidly and widely carried out; the acclimatisation of men, animals, and plants causes variations to disappear more and more as time passes. We can look forward to a time when only such extremes as mountains and deserts will remain,—everywhere else the actions of the earth will be equalised. The process by which this is carried out may be described shortly as follows: Man, in spite of all racial and national differences, is fundamentally quite as much of a unity as the soil upon which he dwells; through his labour more and more of this character of unity is transmitted to the earth, which, as a result, also becomes more and more uniform.

One of the most powerful of the ties by which history is bound to nature is that of its dependence on the ground. At the first glance any given historical development is involved with the earth only,—the earth upon which the development takes place. But if we search deeper we shall find that the roots of the development extend even to the fundamental principles of the planetary system. By this it is not meant that every history must be founded on a cosmological basis, that it must commence with the creation, or at least with the destruction of Troy, as was once thought necessary; but it is certainly safe to say that Herder's requirement also applies for our time: that a philosophy of the history of the human race, worthy of its name, must begin with the heavens and then descend to the earth, filled with the conviction that all existence is fundamentally one,—an indivisible conception founded from beginning to end on an identical law.

### *B.* The Relation of Man to the Collective Life of the Earth

In order that the cosmic conception of the life of Man may be more than a mere isolated idea, incapable of being applied and developed, it is necessary to indicate the relation which human life bears to the collective life of the earth. Human existence is based upon the entire development of vegetable and animal life, or, as Alexander von Humboldt said, in reality the human race partakes of the entire life on earth. Just as plants and animals, vegetable and animal remains and products occupy an intermediate position between Man and the inanimate substance of the earth, almost without exception the life of Man depends not directly upon the earth, but upon the animals and plants, which in turn are immediately bound to the earth by the necessities of existence. It is the dependence of later and more evolved types upon the earlier and less evolved. In 1845 Robert Mayer published his epoch-making thesis on "The Relations of Organic Motion to Metabolism," [1]

---

[1] "Über die organischen Bewegungen in ihrem Zusammenhang mit dem Stoffwechsel."

in which he described the vegetable world as a reservoir wherein the rays of the sun are transformed into life-supporting material and are stored up for use. According to his view the physical existence of the human race is inseparably linked together with this "economic providence;" and he even went so far as to connect it with the instinctive pleasure felt by every eye at the sight of luxuriant vegetation.

The history of mankind shows how various are the elements contained in this reservoir, and how manifold their action. Originally plants and animals share the soil with Man, who must struggle with them for its possession. The plains favour and the forests obstruct historical movement; the inhabitant of the tropics is hardly able to overcome the growth of weeds that covers his field; for the Esquimaux the vegetable world exists but two months in the year, and then only in stunted, feeble species. The unequal distribution of edible plants has in a large measure been the cause of divergence in the developments of different races. Australia and the Arctic countries have received almost nothing; the Old World has had abundance of the richest gifts showered upon it, Asia receiving more than Africa or Europe. The most valuable of domestic animals are of Asiatic origin. America's pre-European history is incomparably more uniform than that of the Old World, and this is owing to her moderate endowment of useful plants and almost complete lack of domestic animals. The transplanting of vegetable species from one part of the earth to another, carried on by Man, is one of the greatest movements in the collective life of the world. Its possibilities of extension cannot be conjectured; for the successful diffusion of single cultivated plants — the banana, for example — over a number of widely separated countries is yet problematical. This process can never be considered to have come to an end so long as necessity forces Man to get a firmer and firmer hold on the store of earthly life.

## C. RACES AND STATES AS ORGANISMS

THE relations of Man to the earth are primarily the same as those of any other form of life. The universal laws of the diffusion of life include also the laws of the diffusion of the human species. Hence anthropogeography must be looked upon only as a branch of biogeography; and a succession of biogeographical conceptions may at once be applied in relation to the diffusion of the human race. To these conceptions belong the main area of distribution, the habitable world, and all its various parts: zones, continents, and other divisions of the earth's surface, especially seas, coasts, interiors of lands, bordering regions, divisions exhibiting continuity with others as links in a chain, and isolated divisions. Also relations as to area: the struggle for territory, variations in the life development in small or in extensive regions, in insular or in continental districts, on heights of land and plateaus, and, in addition, the hindrances and the aids to development presented by different conformations — thus, advanced development in small, densely populated districts — also the protection afforded by isolated situations. All must be included. Finally, properties of boundaries must be conceived of as analogous to phenomena occurring on the peripheries of living bodies.

As races are forms of organic life, it follows that the organism of the state must appear more real to us than it did to Schäffle, who merely designated it as "relatively the best of all figurative characterisations of the state." The state cannot be comprehended otherwise than as an organised being; objections to this conception arise only from a narrow interpretation of the word "organism." Every people, every state is organic, as a combination of organic units. Moreover there is something organic in the internal coherence of the groups and individuals from which a state is formed. However, in the case of a people and a state, this coherence is neither material nor structural. Only in animal and plant life is the most perfect organism that in which the independence of organs is sacrificed to the whole to the greatest degree. In nations and in states the members preserve an independence which varies directly with the extent of the development. Therefore are not peoples and states most imperfect organisms compared with plants and animals?

The superiority of the state organism, so great as to exclude all comparison, is based upon very different grounds. States are spiritual and moral organisms. The spiritual coherence fills up the gaps caused by a lack of material continuity. And this spiritual coherence certainly creates many resemblances between the life functions of a people or state and those of an animal organism; thus we may speak of assimilation, circulation, and so on, in respect to social aggregates, as well as in respect to animals or plants. Yet such expressions are only metaphors and symbols. Organs are spoken of in the same way; but it can only be in the sense that there is a division of labour between the different groups of individuals forming the state, these groups having become organised through localisation. In this way frontier provinces may be designated as peripheral organs, designed to afford protection and to effect interchange. Yet we cannot be too cautious in our use of the word "organ," for in vegetables and animals many members and parts are transformed and subordinated into organs, thus sacrificing their independence to the whole. Man, however, as a member of a race or state organism, is the most individualised product of creation; he does not sacrifice one fibre, one cell to the aggregate. He sacrifices his will only, now humbling it to the will of the whole, now employing it in the service of the society. As forms of life, races and states certainly stand upon the same basis as do plants and animals; but, however far the comparison be extended, they are not true organisms, but aggregate organisms, that, through the action of intellectual and moral forces, not only grow to resemble, but far to surpass the highest organisms proper in concentration of life and of capacities.

Together with the spiritual there is also a material coherence between the individual members of a race or a nation, which, strange to say, has heretofore been but little noticed in controversies over the state as an organism. This is the connection with the ground. The ground furnishes the only material tie that binds individuals together into a state; and it is primarily for this reason that all history exhibits a strong and ever-increasing tendency to associate the state with the soil, — to root it to the ground, as it were. The earth is not only the connecting principle, but it is also the single tangible and indestructible proof of the unity of the state. This connection does not decrease during the course of history, as might be supposed, owing to the progressive development of spiritual forces; on the contrary, it ever becomes closer, advancing from the loose association of a few individuals with a proportionately wide area in the primitive community, to the close connection of the dense population of a powerful state with its relatively small area, as in the case of a modern civilised nation. In spite of all disturbances, the economic and political end has ever been to associate a greater and greater number of individuals with the soil. Hence the law that every relation of a race or tribe to the ground strives to take a political form, and that every political structure seeks connection with the ground. Morgan's notion of an unterritorial and a territorial epoch in the history of Man is incorrect; ground is necessary to every form of state, and also to the germs of states, such as a few negroes' huts or a ranch in the far West. Development consists only in a constant increase in the occupation and use of land, and in the fact that, as populations grow, so do they become faster and faster rooted in their own soils.

At the same time the nature of the movements of peoples must change. Penetration and assimilation of one race by another occur instead of displacement of one by another; and with the rapid decrease of unoccupied territory the fate of the late-comers in history is irrevocably sealed. Since the state is an organism composed of independent individuals and households, its decay cannot be analogous to the death and corruption of a plant or an animal. When plants decay, the cells of which they are composed decay also. But in a decayed state the freed individuals live on and unite together into new political organisms; they increase, and the old necessity for growth continues in the midst of the ruin. The decay of nations is not destruction; it is a remodelling, a transformation. A great political institution dies out; smaller institutions arise in its place. Decay is a life necessity. Nothing could be more incorrect than the idea that the growth of nations would come to an end were one state to embrace the whole earth. If this were to happen, long before the great moment of union came, there would be a multitude of processes of growth already in operation, ready to rebuild in case of decadence, and to provide for a new organisation if needed. As yet the political expansion of the white races over the earth has not resulted in uniformity, but in manifoldness.

### D. HISTORICAL MOVEMENT

ALL conditions and relations of peoples and states that may be geographically described, delineated, surveyed, and, for the greater part, even measured, can be traced back to movements, — movements that are peculiar to all forms of life, and of which the origin is growth and development. However various these movements may be in other respects, they are always connected with the soil, and thus must be dependent upon the extent, situation, and conformation of the ground upon which they take place. Therefore in every organic movement we may perceive the activity of the internal motive forces which are peculiar to life, and the influences of the ground to which the life is attached. In the movements of peoples, the internal forces are the organic powers of motion common to all creatures, and the spiritual impulses of the intellect and will of Man. In many a view of history these forces alone appear; but it must not be forgotten that they are conditioned as follows: they cannot be active beyond the general limits of life, and they cannot disengage themselves from the soil to which life is bound. In order to understand historical movements it is first necessary to consider their purely mechanical side, which is shown clearly enough by an inquiry into the nature of the earth's surface. Neglect of this occasions a delay in the understanding of the true character of such movements. Men merely spoke of geography, and treated history as if it were an atmospheric phenomenon. It is owing to this neglect that Carl Ritter's conclusion respecting the connection of geography and history has not led to more fruitful results.

Nations are movable bodies whose units are held together by a common origin, language, customs, locality, and often — the strongest tie of all — necessity for defence. A people expands in one direction and contracts in another; in case of two adjacent nations, a movement in the one betokens a movement in the other. Active movements are responded to by passive, and *vice versâ*. Every movement in an area filled with life consists in a displacement of individuals. There are also currents and counter-currents: when slavery was abolished in the Southern States of America, an emigration of white men from the South was followed by an influx of ex-slaves from the North, thus causing an increase in the black majority of the South.

Such external movements of peoples assume most varied forms. History takes a too narrow view in considering only the migrations of nations (*Völkerwanderungen*), looking upon them as great and rare events, historical storms as it were, exceptional in the monotonous quiet of the life of Man. This conception of historical movements is very similar to the discarded cataclysmic theory in geology. In the history of nations, as in the history of the earth, a great effect does not always involve a presupposition of its being the immediate result of a mighty cause. The constant action of small forces that finally results in a large aggregate of effect must be taken into account in history as well as in geology. Every external movement is preceded by internal disturbance: a nation must grow from within in order to spread abroad. The increase of Arabs in Oman led to an emigration to east Africa along highways of traffic known to times of old. Merchants, craftsmen, adventurers, and slaves left their native land and drew together in Zanzibar, Pemba, and on the mainland. The process was repeated from the coast to the interior, and as a result of the aggregate labour of individuals as merchants, colonists, and missionaries, Arabian states grew up in the central regions of Africa. Instances of the occupation of vacant territories are of the greatest rarity in history as we are acquainted with it. The best example known to us is the settlement of Iceland by the Northmen. The rule is, a forcing in of the immigrating nation between other races already in possession; the opposition of the latter often compels the former to divide up into small groups which then insinuate themselves peacefully among the people already established in the land.

The movements of nations resemble those of fluids upon the earth: they proceed from higher altitudes to lower; and obstacles cause a change of course, a backward flow, or a division. Though at first there may be a series of streams running along side by side, there is a convergence at the goal, as shown by the migration of different peoples to a common territory; there is concentration when there are hindrances to be overcome, and a spreading out where the ground is level and secure. One race draws other races along with it; and, as a rule, a troop of wanderers come from a long distance will be found to have absorbed foreign elements on its way. But it would be wrong to look upon the movements of nations as passive onflowings, or even to deduce a natural law from the descent of tribes from the mountains to the river valleys and to the sea, — an idea that once led to the acceptance of the theory of the Ethiopian origin of Egyptian civilisation.

Either the wills of individuals unite to form a collective will, or the will of a single man imposes itself upon the aggregate. The human will knows no unsurmountable obstacle within the bounds of the habitable earth. As time goes on, all rivers and all seas are navigated, all mountains climbed, and all deserts traversed. But these have all acted as obstructions before which movements have either halted or turned aside, until finally they have burst the barriers. At least two thousand years passed from the time of the first journey of a Phœnician ship out through the Pillars of Hercules into the Atlantic until the arrival of the day when a voyage across was ventured from the same starting-point. The Romans turned the Alps both to the right and to the left seven hundred years after their city had been founded, but how many nooks in the interior of those mountains were unknown to them even centuries later! Yet to-day Europe feels the effect of this circumstance, the fact that the Romans did not advance straight through the central Alps into the heart of the Teutonic country. They followed a roundabout way through Gaul, and thus Mediterranean culture and Christianity were brought to central Europe from the west instead of from the south; hence the dependence of the civilisation of Germany upon that of France.

It is precisely the Romans who, contrasted with barbarians, show us that will or design in the movements of nations does not necessarily increase with growth of culture, even though culture constantly puts more means of action at its disposal, improved methods of transportation, by which the way may be lightened. The mounted bands of Celts and Germans crossed the Alps quite as easily as did the Roman legions; and in spreading about and penetrating to every corner of the Alps and the Pyrenees, the barbarians were always superior to the Romans. Wandering tribes of semi-civilised people are smaller, less pretentious, and less encumbered. In every war that has taken place in a mountain land, the greater mobility of untrained militia has often led to victories over regular troops. Races of inferior culture are invariably more mobile than those of a higher grade of civilisation; and they are able to equalise the advantages of the superior modes of locomotion with which culture has supplied the latter. Mobility also indicates a weaker hold upon the ground, and thus uncivilised peoples are more easily dislodged from their territories than are nations capable of becoming, as it were, more deeply rooted. In nomadic races, mobility bound up with the necessity for an extensive territory assumes a definite form, and, owing to a constant preparedness for wandering and to the possession of an organised marching system, such peoples have been one of the greatest forces in Old World history.

Movements of nations are often spoken of as if certain definite directions were forced upon them by some mysterious power. This view not only wraps itself in the garment of prophecy — for example, when announcing that the direction in which the sun travels must also be that of history — but it formally presupposes a necessary east-to-west progression of historical movements, endeavouring to substantiate its doctrine by citation of examples, from Julius Cæsar to the gold-seekers of California. But this necessity remains always in obscurity. Not only is it contradicted by frequently confirmed reflex movements in historical times, but it is also disproven still more by the great migrations which have taken place on the same continent in contrary directions. In Asia the Chinese have spread over the entire area of interior plain and desert, westward to the nation-dividing barriers of the Pamir Mountains; other Asiatic races have overflowed into Europe — also from east to west. Contrariwise, ever since the sixteenth century we have seen the Russians at work conquering the entire northern part of the continent, constantly pressing on toward the east. Even the sea proved no obstacle, for they both discovered and acquired Alaska during the course of this same movement. We shall not attach any universal significance to such fashionable terms employed in historical works, as political or historical attraction, elective affinity or balance; least of all shall we presume to discover occult, mysterious sources for them. It is obvious that a powerful nation will overflow in the direction of least resistance; and in the case of a strong power confronting one that is weak there is a constant movement toward the latter. Thus, from the earliest times, Egypt has pressed on toward the south; and everywhere in the Sudan we find traces of similar movements to the south as far as Adamawa, where they are still to-day in energetic continuance. The history of colonisation in America shows a turning of the streams of immigration, in the south as well as in the north, toward the more thinly settled regions; the more thickly populated are avoided. The migrations of nations, which took place during periods of history when a surplus of unoccupied land existed, were determined to a great extent by natural causes. The more numerous nations become, the greater the obstacles to migration; for most of these obstacles arise from the very nations themselves.

Nations increase with their populations; lands with enlargement of territory. So long as a country has sufficient area, the second form of growth need not of necessity follow the first: the race spreads out over the gaps which are open in the interior, and thus internal colonisation takes place. If there is need for emigration, occupiable districts may be found in the lands of another people: for centuries Germans have thus found accommodation in Austria, Hungary, Poland, and America. Of course, such colonists gradually become absorbed into the people among whom they have settled. This is simple emigration, which is therefore connected with the internal colonisation of a foreign land. External colonisation first comes into being when a state acquires territory under its control, into which territory, if it be suitable, a portion of the inhabitants of the state settle. Colonisation is not necessarily a state affair from the first. If a race inhabit a country so sparsely as the Indians did America in the sixteenth century, a foreign people, having the power of spreading out, may press into the gaps with such success that this initial internal colonisation may also be advantageous from a political standpoint. The state then intervenes and appropriates the territory over which groups of its inhabitants have previously acquired economic control. The emigrants formed a social aggregate in the new country, and from this aggregate a state, or the germ of a state, develops. Since such an economic-social preparatory growth greatly assists in the political acquirement of land, it is obvious that this form of colonisation is especially sound and effectual. The opposite method follows when a state first conquers a territory which it occupies later with its own forces; this is colonisation by conquest. It can only be capable of development when subsequent immigration permanently acquires the land as a dwelling-place. Conquest that neither can nor will take permanent possession of the soil is characteristic of a low stage of culture: thus the Zulu states in Africa, surrounded by broad strips of conquered yet uncontrolled territory, and the old "world-empires" of western Asia exhausted themselves in vain efforts to obtain lasting increase of area through aggressive expeditions. That the Roman Empire lasted a longer time than any of the preceding universal empires was due to the fact alone that agricultural colonisation invariably followed in the footsteps of its political conquests.

The enlargement of a nation's area is associated with soil and inhabitants. If the increase of territory — for example, through conquest — is much more rapid than the increase of population, an inorganic, loosely connected expansion results, which as a rule is soon lost again. If, on the contrary, population increases at a proportionately greater rate than area, a crowding together, checks to internal movements, and over-population follow. In consequence great discrepancies between growth of territory and increase of population lead to the most varied results. The conquering nation expands over extensive regions for which there are no inhabitants. Passive races in India and in China become so crowded together that it is impossible for their soil to support them any longer; hence a continuous degradation and recurrent periods of famine, which may bring with them a relatively feeble and unorganised emigration. There are nations with whom conquest and colonisation seem to follow in most profitable alternation: this appears to have been the case with all colonising countries of modern history that have followed the example of the Roman Empire. But there are great contrasts presented by these nations even. Germany, Austria, and Russia, in immediate connection with their conquered provinces, have colonised and expanded toward the east. In spite of a rapid increase of population, Germany has been backward in establishing transmarine colonies, while France, with a proportionately smaller increase of population, began by colonising in all directions, but occupied more land than she was able to master; for which reason colonisation in the history of France has taken more or less the character of conquest. England, on the contrary, with a vigorous emigration and an expansive movement in all directions, presents an example of the soundest and strongest method of founding colonies which has been seen since early times.

Through the entire course of history an ever-increasing value attached to land may be traced; and in the expansion of nations we may also see that mere conquest is growing less and less frequent, while the economic acquisition of territory, piece by piece, is becoming the rule. The getting of land assumes more and more the character of a peaceful insinuation. The taking possession of distant countries without consideration for the original inhabitants, who are either driven away, or murdered, — speedily with the aid of bullets, or slowly with the assistance of gin or contagious diseases or by being robbed of their best land, — is to-day no longer possible. Colonisation has become a well-ordered administration combined with instruction of the natives in useful employments. The old method has left scarcely a single pure-blooded Indian east of the Mississippi in the United States, and not one native in Tasmania; the new method has before it the problem how to share the land with negroes, — in the Transvaal with eighty-seven per cent and in Natal with eighty-four per cent. Climatic conditions are also to be taken into consideration: for Caucasians are able to develop all their powers in temperate regions only; a hot climate impels them to ensure the co-operation of black labour through coercion.

During the course of centuries a motley collection of countries has developed, all of which are called colonies, although they stand in most striking contrast with one another. Several are nations in embryo, to which only the outward form of independence is lacking; not a few have once been independent; and many give the impression that they will never be fit for self-government. There are some in which the native population has become entirely extinct, such as Tasmania, Cuba, and San Domingo; others in which the original inhabitants, still keeping to their old customs and institutions, are guided and exploited by a few white men only; and, finally, colonies in which the rulers and the natives have assimilated with one another, as in Siberia. Once upon a time such tokens of the youth of races as may be seen in rude but remunerative labour on unlimited territory were widespread in many colonies. But the new countries fill up visibly, and even they show that mankind as a whole ages the more rapidly the more the so-called progress of civilisation is hastened. However, an examination of the peoples of the present day shows that the differences in age between mother-countries and colonies will, indeed, continue for a long time yet. Such differences exist between west and east Germans as well as between New Englanders and Californians; they are even to be detected in Australia, between the inhabitants of Queensland and of New South Wales. Such differences are shown not only in the characteristics of individuals, but also in the division of land and in methods of labour.

Divergence and differentiation are the great factors of organic growth. They govern the increase of nations and states from their very beginnings. Since, however, these organisms are composed of independent units, differentiation does not consist in an amalgamation and transformation of individuals, but in their diffusion and grouping. Therefore the differentiation of nations becomes eminently an affair of geography. Never yet has a daughter-people left its mother-country to become an independent state without a previous disjunction having taken place. All growth is alteration in area, and, at the same time, change in position. The further growth extends away from the original situation, the sooner dismemberment follows. In Australia, New South Wales spreads out toward the north, and at the new central point, Brisbane, a new colony, Queensland, is formed, which already differs materially from New South Wales. And Queensland itself expands toward the north, beyond the tropic of Capricorn into the torrid zone; and a younger, tropical North Queensland develops.

The fact that nations hold fast to their natural conditions of existence, even when growth impels them toward expansion in various directions, is a great controlling force in historical movement. Russia expands in its northern zone to the Pacific Ocean; England continues its growth on American soil, across the Atlantic, in almost the very same latitude. The Phœnicians, as a coast-dwelling people, remained on the coasts and on the islands; the colonising Greeks ever sought out similar situations to those of their native land; the Netherlanders are found everywhere in northern Germany as colonists of the moors and marshes. All German colonies beyond the Alps and the Vosges have disappeared; and the few Germans that remain are Latinised. Nations that are accustomed to a limited territory, as were the Greeks, always search for a similar limited area; on the other hand, the Romans discovered a main factor of empire-building in their judicious agricultural colonisation of broad plains; and the Russians sought and found in Siberia the endless forests, steppes, and vast rivers of their native land. Every nation, in expanding, seeks to include within its area that which is of the greatest value to it. The victorious state acquires the best positions and drives the conquered race into the poorest districts. For this reason compeition between the colonising nations has become so keen: they all judge of the character of territory according to the same standard. Therefore, wherever England has colonised, only a gleaning remains for the rest of the northern and central European Powers.

Differentiation, arising from the valuation of land, is the cause of a constant creation of new political values and of a constant lapsing of old. Every portion of the world has its political value, which, however, may become dormant, and must then be either discovered or awakened. Such a discovery was the selection of the Piræus as the harbour for Athens from among a number of bights and bays. Who believed the great marshy cross-valleys between Havel and Bug to be valuable before the days of eastern German colonisation? Every settlement and every founding of a city is at bottom an awakening of dormant political value. Capacity for recognising this value is a part of the genius of a statesman, whose policy may be called far-seeing partly because he is able to discern the dormant value while yet on the most distant horizon. It is obvious that political values vary; each is determined by the point of view from which it is looked upon. The French and the German valuations of the Rhine borderland are very different. Every nation endeavours to realise the political value which it recognises; and, in respect to political growth, ends are set up in the shape of the portions of the earth to which that growth aspires. Peculiarities in the conformation of states may be traced back to an appreciation of the value of coasts, passes, estuaries, and the like. With the spreading out and the concentration of nations, such portions of the world as are important from a political point of view have marvellously increased both in number and in value. But for this very reason a choice or selection has become necessary, and this we see in the use of fewer Alpine passes during the age of railways than before, and in the concentration of a great commerce into fewer seaports, — into such as are capable of accommodating vessels of the deepest draught. Others must withdraw from competition. To-day there are hundreds of worthless harbours, passes, and fortresses in Europe, that were once situated on the highways of historical movement; now, however, they are avoided, deserted by the current of traffic.

## E. NATURAL REGIONS

UPON the earth, with its varied configuration and formation of land and sea, are many kinds of hindrances and limits to life. The most obvious effect of natural region and natural boundary lies in the counteracting forces opposed by the earth through them to a formless and unlimited diffusion of life. Isolated territory furthers political independence, which, indeed, is of itself isolation. The development of a nation upon a fixed territory consists in a striving to make use of all the natural advantages of that territory. The superiority of a naturally isolated region lies in the fact that seclusion itself brings with it the greatest of all advantages. Hence the precocious economic and political development of races that dwell on islands or on peninsulas, in mountain valleys and on island-like deltas. Often enough growth that originates under such favorable conditions leads to ruin. A young nation deems itself possessed of all so long as it has the isolation that ensures independence; it sees too late that the latter has been purchased at the price of a suffocating lack of space; and it dies of a hypertrophy of development — a death common to minor states. This was the cause of the swift rise and decline of

Athens and of Venice, and of all powers that restricted themselves to islands and to narrow strips of coast.

The more natural boundaries a state possesses, the more definite are the political questions raised by its development. The consolidation of England, Scotland, and Wales was simple and obvious, as patent as if it had been decreed beforehand, as was also the expansion of France over the region that lies between the Alps and the Pyrenees, the Mediterranean and the Atlantic Ocean. On the other hand, what a fumbling, groping development was that of Germany, with her lack of natural boundary in the east! Thus in the great geographical features of lands lie pre-ordained movements, constrained by the highest necessity, — a higher necessity in the case of some than of others. The frontier of the Pyrenees was more necessary to France than that of the Rhine; an advance to the Indian Ocean is more neces-sary to Russia than a movement into central Europe. Growth is soundest when a state expands so as to fill out a naturally bounded region, — as, for example, the United States, that symmetrically occupy the southern half of the continent of North America, or Switzerland, extending to the Rhine and Lake of Constance. There are often adjustments of frontiers which force the territory of a nation back into a nat-ural region, as shown in the case of Chili, that gave up the attempt to extend its boundaries beyond the Andes, in spite of its having authorisation to do so, founded on the right of discovery, the original Spanish division of provinces, and wars of independence. A favourable external form is often coincident with a favourable internal configuration which is quite as furthering to internal continuity as is the external form to isolated development. The Roman Empire, externally uniform as an empire of Mediterranean states, was particularly qualified for holding fast to its most distant provinces, by reason of the Mediterranean Sea that occupied its very centre. All that furthers traffic is also favourable to cohesion. Hence the signifi-cance of waterways for ancient states, and of canals and railways for modern nations. Egypt was the empire of the Nile, and the Rhine was at one time the life-vein of the empire of Charles the Great.

A state does not always remain fixed in the same natural region. However advantageous they may have been, on increasing, it must forsake the best of boun-daries. Since one region is exchanged for another, the law of increasing areas comes into force. Every land, sea, river region, or valley should always be conceived of as an area that must be discovered, inhabited, and politically realised before it may exert any influence beyond its limits. Thus the Mediterranean district had first to complete its internal development before it could produce any external effect. And this internal development first took possession of the small territories, and, mastering them, turned to the greater. Thus we may see history progress from clearings in forests, oases, islands, small peninsulas (Greece), and strips of coast, to great peninsulas (Italy), isthmian situations of continental size (Gaul), only to come to a halt in half continents (United States and the Dominion of Canada) and continents. Europe — next to the smallest continent — has had the richest history of all, but with the greatest breaking up of its area into small divisions; Australia — the smallest — will, it seems, be the earliest to unite its parts into a continental state. Development expends all its power in bringing the areas of the three great-est land-divisions into play, and in opposing their one hundred and eight million square kilometres to the seventeen million of the smaller divisions; their economic action is already felt to a considerable degree. Thus there arises an alternation of

solation and expansion, which was clearly shown in the history of Rome, whose
territory grew from the single city, out over the valley of the Tiber, into Apennine
Italy, into the peninsula, across the islands and peninsulas of the Mediterranean,
and finally into the two adjacent continents.

The boundaries of natural regions are always natural boundaries. Although
this delicate subject may be left to political geography, it is by no means to be
neglected by those who are interested in history, boundary questions being among
the most frequent causes of wars. In addition, boundaries are the necessary result
of historical movements. In case two states strike against each other in expanding, the motion of both is impeded, and the boundary lies where the movement
comes to a halt. It is in the nature of the earth that growing states are very
frequently contiguous to uninhabited regions, not to other states. This contiguity
is always a source of natural boundaries. The most natural of all arise from
adjacency to uninhabitable regions: first the uninhabitable lands, then the sea.
The boundary at the edge of the uninhabitable world is the safest; for there is
nothing beyond. The broad arctic frontiers of Russia are a great source of power.
A high mountain range, also, may separate inhabited regions — which are
always state territory — by an uninhabited strip of land. After all, the sea,
marshes, rivers even, are uninhabitable zones. But traffic brings connection with
it, and the Rhine, that to the Romans was a moat, especially well adapted as a
defence, is now, with its thirty railway bridges and thousands of vessels plying
up and down and across, far more of a highway and a means of communication
than a dividing line.

## F. CLIMATE AND LOCATION

THE position, form, and movements of the earth seem far enough removed from
the deeds and destinies of peoples, yet the more we contemplate the latter, the
more we are led to consider the earth's inclination to its axis, its approximately
spherical form, and its motion, which, combined, are the cause of the recurrence in
fixed order of day and night, of summer and winter. The effects of these great
earthly phenomena are differently felt in every country; for they vary according
to geographical location. Practically, that which most conforms to any given situation north or south of the equator is the climate of a land. Day and night are of
more even length at the equator than in our country; but beyond the polar circles
there are days that last for months, and nights equally long. Scarcely any annual
variation in temperature is known to the inhabitants of Java, while in eastern
Siberia Januarys of fifty degrees below the freezing-point, and Julys of twenty degrees above the zero of Centigrade, winters during which the mercury freezes, and
summers of most oppressive sultriness, are contrasted with one another. In our
temperate region there is rain as a rule during all months, but as far north as Italy
and Greece the year is divided into a dry and a wet season. Great effects are produced over the entire earth and upon all living creatures by the thus conditioned
climatic differences. They must be considered at the very beginning of every
investigation into history. Since we know that a fluctuating distribution of heat is
caused by the $23\frac{1}{2}°$ inclination of the earth's axis, investigation also leads us to a
knowledge of further phenomena, to a consideration of the dependence of the winds
and of the precipitation of heat upon this very same condition. And thus w come

into contact with the thousand connecting threads by which Man's economic activity, health, distribution over the earth, even his spiritual and his political life, are inseparably bound up with the climate. Hence the first question that should be asked concerning a country is: What is its geographical situation? A land may be interesting for many other reasons besides nearness or remoteness from the equator; but that which is of the greatest interest of all to the historian is a consideration of the manifold and far-reaching effects of climate.

Anthropogeography teaches us that climate affects mankind in two different ways: first, it produces a direct effect upon individuals, races, indeed the inhabitants of entire zones, influencing their bodily conditions, their characters, and their minds; in the second place, it produces an indirect effect by its influence on conditions necessary to life. This is due to the fact that the plants and animals with which Man stands in so varied a relationship, which supply him with nourishment, clothing, and shelter, and which, when domesticated and cultivated, enter his service, as it were, and become most valuable and influential assistants and instruments for his development and culture, are also dependent upon climate. Important properties of the soil, the existence of plains, deserts, and forests, also depend upon climate. Effects of climate, both direct and indirect, are united in political-geographical phenomena, and are especially manifest in the growth of states and in their permanence and strength.

There is no climate that cannot be borne by Man; of all organic beings he is one of the most capable of adapting himself to circumstances. Men dwell even in the very coldest regions: the place where the lowest temperatures have been measured, Werchoiansk, with a mean January temperature of −53° C., is the capital of a Siberian province; and a district where the temperature is of the very hottest, Massowah, is the most important town in the Italian colony of Eritrea. However, both heat and cold, when excessive, tend to lessen population, the size of settlements, and economic activity. The great issues of the world's history have been decided on ground situated between the tropic of Cancer and the polar circle. The question as to whether the northern half of North America should be English or French was decided between the parallels of 44° and 48° north latitude; and in the same manner the settlement as to whether Sweden or Russia should be supreme in northern Europe took place a little south of 60° north. Holland did not lose and regain her Indian possessions in the neighbourhood of the equator, but in Europe; and Spain fell from the high estate of sovereign over South and Central America because her power as a European nation had decayed. The coldest countries in the world are either entirely uninhabited — as Spitzbergen and Franz Josef's Land — or very thinly populated. Some are politically without a master, — the two territories just mentioned, for example; some are politically occupied, as is Greenland, but are of very little value. History teaches that traffic between such colonies and the mother country may cease entirely without the mother country suffering any loss thereby. The hottest regions in the world are for the most part colonies or dependencies of European Powers. This applies to the whole of tropical Africa, Asia, Australia, and Oceania, and partly to tropical America. The exclusion of European nations from grasping for possessions in America was not determined on in the compromised territory of tropic America, but in the United States, a short distance south of 39° north latitude. What a difference in the parts played in history by the two branches of the Tunguse race,

the one held in subjection in the cold latitude of Russia, and the other that conquered and is now the sovereign power in the more temperate climate of China;
or between the Turks that, as Jakuts, lead a nomadic life in the Lena Valley, and the
Turks that govern western Asia! Latham called the region extending from the
Elbe to the Amoor — within which dwell Germans, Sarmatians, Ugrian Finns,
Turks, Mongolians, and Manchurians, peoples who strike with a two-edged sword —
a "Zone of Conquest." Farther to the north nations are poor and weak;
toward the equator, luxurious and enervated. The inhabitants of this central zone
have overrun their neighbours both to the north and to the south, while never,
either from the north or from the south, have they themselves suffered any lasting
injury. The Germans have advanced from the Baltic Sea to the Mediterranean;
the Slavs inhabit a territory that extends from the Arctic Ocean to the Adriatic
Sea; the Turks and Mongolians have penetrated as far south as India; and there
have been times when Mongolians ruled from the Arctic Ocean to southern India.
Finally, the Manchurians have extended their sphere of influence over northern
Asia as far south as the tropic of Cancer.

These differences occur over again in more restricted areas, even within the
temperate zone itself. The inhabitants of the colder portions of a country have
often shown their superiority to the men who dwell in the warmer districts. The
causes of the contrast between the Northerners and the Southerners, which has
dominated in the development of the United States, may for the most part be
clearly traced: the South was weakened by the plantation method of cultivation,
and slavery; its white population increased slowly, and shared to a lesser degree
than did the Northerners in the strengthening, educating influences of agriculture
and manufacturing industries. Thus, after a long struggle that finally developed
into a war, the North won the place of authority. In Italy and in France the
superiority of the north over the south is partially comprehensible; and in
Germany the advantages possessed by Prussia, at least in area and in seacoast, are
obvious. But when in English history also the north is found to have been
victorious over the south, conditions other than climatic must have been the cause.
In this case elements have been present that are more deeply rooted than in sun-
beams and rainfall alone. We must call to mind the zone-like territories of early
times, occupied by peoples from which the nations of to-day are descended; the
boundary lines have disappeared, but the northern elements have remained in the
north, and the southern elements in the south. It is well known that Aristotle
adjudged political superiority and the sphere of world-empire to the Hellenes
because they surpassed the courageous tribes of the north in intelligence and in
mechanical instinct, and were superior to the both intelligent and skilful inhabitants of Asia in courage. "As the Hellenic race occupies a central geographical
position, so does it stand between both intellectually." The thought that this
union of extreme intellectuality and power in arms on Hellenic soil could be the
result of ethnical infiltration did not seem to have occurred to the philosopher
The fundamental idea of Aristotle, the aristocratic state, in which the talented
Hellene alone was to rule over bondmen of various origins, who were, above all,
to labour for him, could not have been possible had his views been otherwise.
And yet he had clearly seen that the two talents — for war and for industry —
were unequally distributed among the different Hellenic stocks, and that they were
also variable according to time.

Considering the influence even of slighter differences in climate, the locations of regions of similar mean annual temperature, and the distances which separate them from one another, cannot be otherwise than important. A map on which the isothermal lines are drawn is rich in historical instruction. Where the lines diverge we have regions of equal temperature; where they crowd together, districts of different mean annual temperatures lie close to one another. The crowding of climatic variations in any region enlivens and hastens the course of history in that region. If the variations occur only at long intervals, all parts of a large territory having approximately equal mean annual temperatures, then climatic contrasts which act as a ferment, as it were, are not present to any appreciable extent, and their effects lose in intensity and are dispelled. Where are greater combinations of contrasting climatic elements to be found than in Greece and in the Alps? The joining together of the natives of rich, fruitful Zürich with the poor shepherds of the forests and mountains was of the utmost importance to the development of the Swiss Confederation. It was also a union of regions of mild and cold temperatures. The possession of central European and Mediterranean climates, that shade into one another without any sharp line of demarcation, is a great advantage to France. If climatic differences approach one another in too great a contrast, clefts in development are likely to occur, such as the gap between the Northern and the Southern States in America, and that between North and South Queensland. If it be possible to adjust the political differences, then the union of areas of different temperatures has an invigorating effect, as shown by the history of the American Southern States since 1865.

Winds blowing in a constant direction for many months at a time were of great assistance to navigation during the days of sailing-vessels, which, indeed, have not yet been entirely supplanted by steamships. Before the time of steam vessels all traffic on the Indian Ocean was closely connected with the change of the monsoons; and important political expansions have followed in the track of the same winds, — for example, the diffusion of the Arabs along the east coast of Africa and in Madagascar. The influence of the trade winds on the Spanish and Portuguese discoveries along the Atlantic coast of America is well known. The southeastern trade winds have been a cause of both voluntary and involuntary emigrations of Polynesian races. It may be clearly seen from the history of Greece what advantage was obtained by the race that won the alliance of the coast of Thrace and the wind that blows south from it with great constancy during the entire fair season, often eight months long.

Where the wind is most variable, visiting entire countries with storms, to the great destruction of lives and property, the result is a stirring up of the survivors to exertions that cannot fail to be strengthening both to body and to mind, and of direct benefit to life in general. At the same time that the people of Holland were engaged in forcing back the ocean, they won their political liberty. In another part of the North Sea coast the Frisians receded farther and farther south, owing to the invasions of the sea and the attacks of the natives of Holstein. The tempest that scattered the armada of Philip II was one of the most important political events of the time; and it is not to be denied that the snowstorm in Prussian Eylau, at the beginning of the battle in which Napoleon suffered his first defeat, contributed not a little to the result.

Acclimatisation is one of the greatest of human problems. In order that a nation expand from one zone into another, it must be capable of adapting itself to new climates. The human race is, as a whole, of all animal species one of the most capable of adaptation to different conditions of life; for it is diffused through all zones and all altitudes up to about thirteen thousand feet above the level of the sea. But single nations are accustomed to fixed zones and portions of zones; and long residence in foreign climates leads to illness and loss of life. In some races the individuals are of a more rigid constitution than in others, and are thus less capable of adaptation. Chinamen and Jews adapt themselves to different climates far more easily than do Germans, upon whom residence in the southern part of Spain even, and to a still greater degree in northern Africa, is followed by injurious effects. The constant outbreaks of destructive disease before which the German troops withered away are to be counted among the greatest obstacles opposed to the absorption of Italy into the German Empire. During the Spanish discoveries and conquests in America in the sixteenth century, whole armies wasted away to mere handfuls. The greatest hindrances to German colonisation in Venezuela are climatic diseases. Medical science has, to be sure, pointed out such deleterious influences as may be traced to unsuitable dwelling-places, nutrition, clothing, etc.; and the losses to Europe of soldiers and officials in the tropics have been greatly reduced. But even to-day deaths, illnesses, and furloughs make up the chief items in the reports sent in from every colony in the tropics. British India can only be governed from the hills, where the officials dwell during the greater part of the year.

Climatic influence is not limited to bodily diseases. The proverb, *Mens sana in corpore sano*, is also dependent upon the effects of climate; and intellectual influences are more far-reaching than those of the body. ' One of the first effects of life in warm climates upon men accustomed to cold regions is relaxation of what is known as will-power. Even the Piedmontese soldier loses his erect carriage in a Neapolitan or Sicilian garrison. Englishmen in India count on an ability to perform only half the amount of work they would be capable of at home. Many inhabitants of northern countries escape the bodily diseases of the tropics; but scarcely one man of an entire nation is able to resist the more subtile alterations in spirit. Their historical influence extends only the deeper for it. The conquering nations that advance from north to south have invariably forfeited their power, determination, and activity. The original character of the Aryans who descended into the lowlands of India has been lost. A foreign spirit rings through the Vedic hymns. West Goths and Vandals alike lost their nationalities in northern Africa and Spain, as the Lombards lost theirs in Italy. In spite of all emigration, immigration, and wandering hither and thither, there always remains a certain fixed difference between the inhabitants of colder and those of warmer countries: it is the nature of the land, moulding the more ductile character of a people into its own form. There are differences also between the northern and the southern stocks of the same race, and thus climate exerts here greater and there lesser influence upon nations and their destinies.

Since it lies in the nature of climatic influences to produce homogeneity among those peoples who inhabit extensive regions of similar mean annual temperatures it follows that a unifying effect is also produced on political divisions that might otherwise be inclined to separate from one another. In the first place, a similar climate creates similar conditions of life, and thus the northern and the southern races of each hemisphere, with their temperate and their hot climates, differ widely. Climate is also the cause of similar conditions of production over large territories. Leroy-Beaulieu rightly mentioned climate — above all, the winter, during which almost every year the whole land from north to south is covered with snow — as next in importance to the configuration of the country in its unifying, cohesive effects on the Russian Empire. Winters are not rare during which it is possible to journey from Astrachan to Archangel in sledges; and both the Sea of Azov and the northern part of the Caspian Sea are frozen over during the cold months, as well as the Bay of Finland, the Dnieper as well as the Dwina.

### G. Geographical Situation

Situation determines the affinities and relations of peoples and states, and is for this reason the most important of all geographical considerations. Situation is always the first thing to be investigated; it is the frame by which all other characteristics are encircled. Of what use were descriptions of the influence of the geographical configuration of Greece on Grecian history, in which the decisive point that Greece occupies a medial position between Europe and Asia, and between Europe and Africa, was not insisted upon above all? Everything else is subordinate to the fact that Greece stands upon the threshold of the Orient. However varied and rich its development may have been, it must always have been determined by conditions arising from its contiguity with the lands of western Asia and northern Africa. Area in particular, often overvalued, must be subordinated to location. The site may be only a point, but from this point the most powerful effects may be radiated in all directions. Who thinks of area when Jerusalem, Athens, Guanahani, or Gibraltar is mentioned? When it is found that the Fanning Islands or Palmyra Island is indispensable to the carrying out of England's plans in respect to the telegraphic connection of all parts of the empire with one another, merely because these islands are adapted for cable stations on the line between Queensland and Vancouver, is it not owing to their location alone, without consideration as to area, configuration, or climate?

Every portion of the earth lends its own peculiar qualities to the nations and races that dwell upon it, and so does each of its subdivisions in turn. Germany, as a first-class Power, is thinkable only in Europe. There cannot be either a New York or a St. Petersburg in Africa. Our organic conception of nations and states renders it impossible for us to look upon situation as something lifeless and passive; far rather must it signify active relations of giving and receiving. Two states cannot exist side by side without influencing each other. It is much more likely that such close relationships result from their contiguity, — that, for example, we must conceive of China, Corea, and Japan as divisions of a single sphere of civilisation, their history consisting in a transference, transplanting, action, and reaction, leading to results of the greatest moment. Some situations are, indeed, more independent and isolated than others; but what would be the history of England, the most isolated country in Europe, if all relations with France, Germany, the Netherlands, and Scandinavia were omitted? It would be incomprehensible.

The more self-dependent a situation is, the more is it a natural location; the more dependent, the more artificial, and the more it is a part of a neighbourhood.

Connection with a hemisphere or grand division, identity with a peninsula or archipelago, location with respect to oceans, seas, rivers, deserts, and mountains, determine the histories of countries.   It is precisely in the natural locality that we must recognise the strongest bonds of dependence on nature.   Apart from all other features peculiar to Italy, her central position in the Mediterranean alone determines her existence as a Mediterranean Power.   However highly we may value the good qualities of the German people, the best of these qualities will never reach so high a development in the constrained, wedged-in, continental situation of their native land, as they would in an island nation : for Germany's location is more that of a state in a neighbourhood of states than a natural location, and for this reason more unfavourable than that of France.

Natural localities of the greatest importance result from the configuration and situation of divisions of the earth's surface.   The extremities of continents — such as the Cape of Good Hope, Cape Horn, Singapore, Ceylon, Tasmania, and Key West — are points from which sea power radiates ; and at the same time they are the summits of triangular territories that extend inland and are governed from the apex.   Gades, Sicily, Cythera, and Crete were similar localities in the Mediterranean world.   The deeply founded geological clefts between the northern and southern continents, occupied by the three great central seas, grant to the Suez Canal, the future interoceanic canal, and the archipelago between Asia and Australia the unifying functions of lines of interoceanic communication.   In similar wise all narrowings of parts of continents are of importance.   France occupies an isthmian position between ocean and sea ; Germany and Austria between the North Sea, the Baltic, and the Adriatic.   Some states are situated on the coast, occupying a bordering position ; others occupy an intermediate, central location.   And the more isolated situations are all fundamentally different, according to whether they are insular, peninsular, or continental.

Situations in respect to the oceans are even more various.   How different are Atlantic locations in Europe from those on the Mediterranean, the Baltic, or the Black Sea !   Only a few nations — Russia and the United States, for example — occupy a position fronting on two great oceans.   The ideal natural situation for a state may be said to be the embracing of a whole continent within one political system.   This is the deeper source of the Monroe Doctrine.

Similar locations give rise to similar political models.   Since there are several types of location, it follows that the histories of such locations assume typical characters.   The contrast between Rome and Carthage, their association with each other, exhibiting the reciprocal action of the characters of the northern and southern Mediterranean coasts, is repeated in similarly formed situations in Spain and Morocco, in Thrace and Asia Minor, and on a smaller scale in the Italian and Barbary ports.   In all these places events similar to those in Roman and Punic history have taken place.   Japan and England are unlike in many respects : yet not only the peoples but also the political systems of the two island nations have insular characteristics.   Germany and Bornu are as different from each other as central Europe is from the interior of Africa, but central location has produced the same peculiarity in each, — a source of power to the strong nation, of ruin to the weak.

Only the most important of the relationships arising from contiguity with neighbouring states, shown to us by history, may be mentioned.   The most striking examples of such contiguity are to be seen in nations that are cut off from the coast of their continent and completely surrounded by other countries. Owing to the constant reaching out for more territory, characteristic of the development of large states, which endeavour to embrace as many natural advantages as possible, such a situation in Europe, as well as in other continents, signifies unconditional loss of independence. Only connection with a great river — as in the case of Servia and of Paraguay — can prevent the dissolution of a nation so situated. The Orange Free State and the South African Republic have striven in vain for complete independence. The instinctive impulse to extend its boundaries to the sea, shown by all nations, arises from the desire to escape an insulated continental position. It is even more obvious when not only the state but also the people are enclosed in an insular location, as are the Magyars in Hungary. Only the very smallest of states, such as Andorra and Liechtenstein, — which moreover do not aspire to absolute independence, — could have existed for centuries in the positions that they occupy. A medial situation held by one country between two others is also, in point of risk, comparable to a completely encompassed position. France was so situated when Germany and Spain were under the same ruler. The alliance of two neighbouring lands may place a third state in a similar position: thus France first sought an alliance with Turkey, and later one with Russia, against Germany and Austria.

Whatever the individual locations of neighbouring states may be, their number is a matter of great importance. It is better to have a multitude of weak neighbours than a few strong ones. The position of France has been weakened by the alliance between Germany and Italy, yet France still possesses the advantage of having in Spain a weak neighbour. The development of the United States that gradually ousted France from the south, Mexico from the west, and Spain from both south and west, in order to be in touch with the sea on three sides, has, with the decrease in neighbouring Powers, resulted in an enviable simplification of political problems. A nation covering various dispersed and scattered situations is to be seen at the present day only in regions of active colonisation and in the interiors of federal states. Powerful nations are consolidated into a single territory. We may see everywhere that when the area of distribution of a form of life diminishes in extent, it does not simply shrink up, but transforms itself into a number of island-like sites and oases, from which process the appearance may easily be given that, instead of decreasing, the form of life is proceeding from a centre to the conquest of new territory. In what does the difference lie between islands and oases of progress and of recession? With nations and states progress is to be recognised in the occupation of the most advantageous sites; retrogression, in their loss and sacrifice. The Indians, who have been forced back from the oceans, the rivers, and the fertile regions, form detached insulated groups of retrogression; the Europeans who took these sites from them formed isles of progress as one after another they seized the islands, promontories, harbours, river-mouths, and passes.

### H. Area

It is not without reason that so much importance is attached to extent of surface in geography. Area and population represent to us the two chief characteristics of a state; and to know them is the simplest — often too simple — means for

btaining a conception of the size and power of a nation. We cannot conceive of
ny man, much less of a human community, without thinking of surface or ground
t the same time. Political science may, through a number of clever conclusions,
educe the area of a state to a mere national possession: but we all know that
erritory is too tightly bound up with the very life of a state for it to assume a
osition of so little importance. In a nation, people and soil are organically united
nto one, and area and population are the measure of this union. A state cannot
xchange or alter its area without suffering a complete transformation itself. What
vonder, then, that wars between nations are struggles for territory? Even in war
he object is to limit the opponent's sphere of action; how much more does the
vhole history of nations consist in a winning and losing of territory! The Poles
till exist as they did in former times; but the ground upon which they dwell has
eased to belong to them in a political sense, and thus their state has been
nnihilated.

During the course of history we constantly see great political areas emerging
rom the struggle for territory. We see nations from early times to the present
ay increasing in area: the Persian and Roman empires were small and mean com-
ared with those of the Russians, English, and Chinese. Also the states of
eoples of a lower grade of culture are insignificant compared with the states of
nore advanced races. The greatest empires of the present day are the youngest;
he smallest — Andorra, Liechtenstein, San Marino, Monaco — appear to us only
s venerable, strange petrifactions of an alien time.

The relation of surface to the growth of spheres of commerce and of means
f communication is obvious. Communication is a struggle with area; and the
esult of this struggle is the overcoming of the latter. The process is complicated,
ecause, as control is gained over area, one also acquires possession of its con-
ents: advantages of location, conformation, fertility, and, by no means least, the
nhabitants of the territory themselves. But the loss in value of all these things,
rought about by their being widely scattered throughout an extensive area, can be
vercome only by a complete control of the region over which they are spread.

The development of commerce is the preliminary history of political growth.
his applies to all races, from Phœnicians to North Americans, who point out
o us a post of the American Fur Company as the germ from which Nebraska
leveloped. Every colony is a result of traffic; even in the case of Siberia,
nerchants from European Russia travelled thither as far as the Obi about three
enturies before its conquest. The phrase "conquests of the world's commerce"
s perfectly legitimate. The building of roads is a part of the glory of the
ounders and rulers of nations. To-day, tariff unions and railway politics have
aken the place of road-making. It has always been so; both state and traffic
lave had the same interest in roads and thoroughfares. Traffic breaks the
vay, and the state improves and completes it. It seems to be certain that
he firmly organised state in ancient Peru opened the roads which were later
f service to traffic. In a lower phase of development we may see commerce
eading directly to the establishment of states; in a higher, to victory in war,
rising from commercial and railway communication. It would be impossible
or France to construct the Sahara Railway without first subjugating the Tuareg
nd seizing their country. Highways of traffic as weapons for hostile states, the
mportant part played by commercial nations and the culture of strictly industrial

and commercial peoples, the endeavour of traffic to be of service to the policies of states, and, finally, the powerful reactions caused by the removal and disuse of thoroughfares of commerce to races, nations, and to entire spheres of civilisation — can only be indicated here.

Every political movement, whether it be a warlike expedition or a peaceful emigration, is preceded by movements which are not political. Inquiries must be made and relations instituted; the object must be determined, and the road explored. All the while that knowledge of the world beyond the bounds of a country is being gained, there is also an imperceptible broadening of the geographical horizon; and this not only widens out, but becomes clearer. Fabulous tales are circulated as to the terrors of strange countries; but the fear gradually vanishes as our knowledge increases, and with the latter a spirit of political enterprise awakens. One can say that every trader who passes the bounds of his country bears his state with him in his load of merchandise. To be sure, there are both long preparations made and quick leaps taken in the processes of commerce. Roman merchants prepared the way to a knowledge of Gaul and its conquest. But how different the attitude of the Romans to Gaul before and after the time of Cæsar! What a difference in the Spanish estimate of the worth of American colonies before the days of Cortez and Pizarro, and afterward! The broader and clearer the geographical horizon grows, the greater become political schemes and standards of policy. And with a widening horizon states and peoples also increase. The nation that renders an extensive area fertile gains in strength, in breadth of view, and in freedom: in this lies the reward of a labour that is full of self-sacrifice.

The widening of the geographical horizon and the clearing up of mysteries beyond are invariably a result of the travels of individuals or of groups for peaceful purposes. The first of these purposes is commerce; the chase and fishing are also to be taken into consideration; and the involuntary wanderings of the lost and strayed are not to be excluded. Europe possessed a Pytheas and a Columbus who discovered new worlds; and every primitive community had its explorers too, who cleared paths from one forest glade to another. If such pioneers return, they also bring back with them contributions to the general stock of knowledge of the world without; and it becomes less difficult for others to follow in their footsteps: finally armies or fleets may advance, conquering in their tracks. Whenever traffic makes busy a multitude of men, and employs extensive means by which to carry on its operations, the truth of the saying, "The flag follows trade," is finally established in its broadest sense.

With all this struggling and labouring, territory does not fall to the state simply as a definite number of square miles. It is very easy to get this impression from a study of maps and tables of statistics representing the alterations and transformations of nations; but it is not true. Just as single individuals bring enlightenment to the state, pointing out roads, in the same manner the idea of area arises in the intelligence of the aggregate. A Greek sharing the views of Aristotle must consider that nation the best whose citizens could meet daily in the market for the discussion of public affairs; on the other hand, Emerson claims that the political conception of the inhabitants of the United States should be comparable in broadness to the area that lies between the two great oceans, the tropic, and the polar circle. The development of a conception of an extensive territory from that of a small one, during the course of years, is one of the most obvious results of history. A few advanced peoples possess the former, and many backward nations the latter. When we say that an area increases, we must remember that by this we mean that the intelligence which views it and the will that holds it together have increased, and naturally, also, that which is requisite for rendering intelligence and will capable for their work. In this lies one of the greatest differences that exist between nations, one of the greatest causes of success and failure in development. The two conceptions may contend together in the minds of the same people: the broad view triumphed in Rome, whose citizens at first hesitated to step forth beyond Italy, and established a world empire; the narrow conception won the day in Greece, and Greece fell. The Roman Empire at maturity and at the beginning of its decline favoured a denationalising, human tendency, as did also primitive Christendom. A disposition for expansion that advances boundaries to the farthest possible limit is a sign of the highest state of civilisation. It is a result of an increase both of population and of intellectual progress. In Germany the theory of geography is well studied out, but the chapter on area is forgotten; Germany neglects to realise the value of her own territory, and it falls to ruin. Englishmen, individually bad theoretical geographers, are nevertheless both the greatest rulers of territory and the greatest practical geographers; and, with a clear instinct for constantly increasing development into greater and greater areas in the future, they carry on a sort of political speculation in vast regions.

There is something very attractive in the small political models of early times: those city-states whose development had in definiteness and in precision a great deal of the lucidity and compactness of artistic compositions. Lübeck and Venice are more attractive than Russia. The concentration of the forces of a small community in a limited, beautifully situated, and protected location, as may be seen in the ancient city-states, is a source of a development that takes a deeper hold on all the vital powers of a people, employing them more extensively, and therefore ending in a more rapid and definite perfection of historical individuality. Thus small areas take the lead of large territories in historical development; and we may see many examples of a slow but sure transference of leadership from the small area to the large, and of the gradual diffusion of progress in the latter. Thus Italy followed Greece; Spain, Portugal; England, Holland. The opposite of this is precocity in growth: the earlier a state marks out its limits without consideration for later expansion, the sooner the completion of its development. The growth in area of Venice and the Low Countries stood still, while all about them territories increased in size. The development of small countries flags unless the increase of population within a limited area leads to that disquiet and emigration and expulsion of citizens especially characteristic of small nations: the horizon grows too narrow for the times; patriotism becomes local pride; and the most important life forces are impaired. Thus minor nations, through which races are separated into little groups, develop: the great national economic and religious cohesive forces are broken up; and even the political advantages of the ground are reduced in value through disintegration and fraying away. Thus came about the stagnation of the German national currents during the time of the disunited empire. "In great nations there are direct, characteristic emotions which nourish and employ our feelings; in small states our passions are turned toward small interests."[1]

Under such conditions the impulse for new growth must be brought in from without. The native who is acquainted with only one home is always inferior to the foreigner, who has a knowledge of two lands at least. It is remarkable how numerous are the traditions of the establishment of states by strangers. Sometimes these are mighty hunters, as in Africa; often they are superior bearers of civilisation, as in Peru; and an especially large number of them have descended to the earth from heaven. In the face of history which tells of the foundation of a Manchurian dynasty in China and a Turkish in Persia, of the establishment of the Russian Empire by wandering North Germans, and that of the great nations in the west Sudan by the shepherds of Fulba,—these mythical accounts, although they may appear decidedly incredible when taken singly, as a whole are probable enough. The foundation of the nation of Sarawak in Borneo, by Brooke, is reality, and corresponds, feature for feature, with many of the old legends of the formations of states.

The broad conception of a state, which acts as a ferment does on a disrupted mass, is introduced from one neighbouring nation into another, each sharing in its production. When such territories are adjacent, the state situated in the most powerful natural region overgrows the other. The more mobile race brings its influence to bear on the less mobile, and possibly draws the other along with it. The more compact, better organised and armed state intrudes on weaker nations, and forces its organisation upon them. A nation left to itself has a tendency to split up into small groups, each of which seeks to support its own life upon its own soil, heedless of the others; and as such groups increase, they always reproduce in their own images: families families, and tribes tribes. We find all sorts of measures taken by some nations to limit an increase in growth that would carry them beyond their old boundaries and place them under new conditions of life. Many an otherwise inexplicable custom of taking human life is a result of this tendency; perhaps, in some cases, even cannibalism itself. This impulse toward limitation would have rendered the growth of nations impossible had not the antithetical force of attraction of one to another led to growth and amalgamation. Truly, the advance from a condition of isolated, self-dependent communities to one of traffic between state organisms, which must of necessity lead to ebb and flow and union of one group with another, is one of the greatest turning-points in the history of Man.

Since the tendency has been for territory to become the exclusive reward of victory in the competition of nations, balance of territorial possessions has grown to be one of the chief ends of national policies. The phrase "balance of power," which has been so often heard since the sixteenth century, is no invention of diplomats, but a necessary result of the struggle for expansion. Hence we find an active principle of territorial adjustment and balance in all matters concerning international politics. It is not yet active in the small and simple states of semi-civilised peoples: such states are much more uniform; for they have all originated with a uniformly weak capacity for controlling territory. In addition, the principle of territorial isolation hinders the action of political competition. As soon,

[1] Barthold Georg Niebuhr.

however, as necessity for increased area leads to the contiguity of nations, the condition alters. The state that occupies but a small region strives to emulate its larger neighbour. It either gains so much land as is necessary to restore equality, or forces a decrease in the neighbour's territory. Both alternatives have been of frequent occurrence. Prussia expanded at the expense of Schleswig and Poland in order to become equal in territory to the other great Powers. The whole of Europe fought Napoleon until France had been forced back within such boundaries as were necessary to international balance. Austria lost provinces in Italy and replaced them with others in the Balkan Peninsula. This loss and gain appears to us, in looking over an easily epitomised history, such as that of France, as an alternation of violent waves and temporary periods of rest attained whenever a balance is reached. Therefore it is not owing to chance that the areas of Austria, Germany, France, and Spain may be respectively designated by 100, 86, 84, and 80, that the area of Holland is to that of Belgium as 100 is to 90, and that the United States stands to Canada as 100 to 96. In order to be effective, such balances must presuppose equal civilisations, corresponding to similar means for the acquirement of power. Rome was so superior to her neighbours in civilisation that she could not permit any territorial balance. Perhaps the adoption of the Halys as the imperial boundary between Media and Lydia was a first attempt to establish a national system on the principle of balance instead of "world" dominion.

All mutations in areas are restricted to the given surface dimensions of the world. The 506,000,000 square kilometres of the earth's surface is the first area with which history has to do. Within it all other surface dimensions are included; it is the standard for measurement of all other areas, and also comprehends the absolute limits of all bodily life. This area is fixed and immutable so far as the history of mankind is related to it, although in respect to the history of the world it is not to be looked upon as having been unalterable in the past, or as being likely to remain unchanged in the future. The earth's surface may be divided into three unlike constituent parts: 135,000,000 square kilometres of land, 352,000,000 of water, and 22,000,000 of ice-covered and for the greater part unexplored land and sea in the northern and southern polar regions. The land is the natural home of Man, and all his historical movements begin and end upon it. The size of states is computed according to the amount of land which they include; their growth has derived its nourishment from the 135,000,000 square kilometres of earth as from a widespread fundamental element. The sea is not to be looked upon as an empty space between the divisions of land, merely separating them one from another: for the 352,000,000 square kilometres of water are also of historical importance, and the area of every ocean and of every portion of an ocean has its historical significance. History has extended itself over the sea, from island to island, from coast to coast, at first crossing narrow bodies of water, later broad oceans; and states whose foundations arose from connections by sea remain dependent on the sea. The Mediterranean held together the different parts of the Roman Empire just as the oceans unite the colonies of the British Empire.

Our standards for measuring the areas of countries have constantly increased during the growth of historical territories. The history of Greece is to us but the history of a small state; and how many years shall pass before that of Germany, Austria, and France will be but the history of nations of medium size. England, Russia, China, and the United States include the better half of the land; the

world; and to-day a British Empire in the other half could not be conceivable. Development has ever seized on greater and greater areas, and has united more and more extensive regions into aggregates. Thus it has always remained an organic movement. The village-state repeats itself in the city-state, and the family-state in the race-state; the smaller ever being reproduced in greater forms. The smallest nations and the greatest alike retain the same peculiar organic characteristics that are more or less closely united to a portion of the soil. Only in cases where the area occupied itself forms part of the being of a state, as in the city-state that cannot expand beyond the narrow bounds of a town without being transformed into another kind of state — the territorial — does variation in size occasion at the very outset a variation in the constitution of the entire political life. Under all other conditions growth is at first the cause of the development of secondary differences, whose total is determined at first by the distance which separates the growing parts of a nation from one another, and later by the new conditions in conformity to which growth transposes them from place to place.

The standards for measuring political areas are constantly changing; and as time goes on they must be constantly adapted to larger relations. This task lies naturally within the province of political geography: the study of the political divisions of territory in every portion of history with a special view to present conditions. History looks back upon the past, and for that reason is less capable of knowing the correct standard of measure for the present day and for the immediate future. If the Germans are taught that the diffusion of their forefathers over the country beyond the Elbe is yet to be looked upon as the greatest territorial event in German history (not to be confused with the history of the German Empire), the expansion of the Anglo-Saxons in North America and in Australia must appear to them as a performance of incomprehensible magnitude

## *I.* Population

THE surface of a state bears a certain relation to the surface of the globe, and according to this standard is the land measured upon which the inhabitants of a nation live, move, and labour. Thus it may be said that the 540,500 square kilometres of the German Empire represent about $\frac{1}{910}$ of the entire surface of the earth; further, that the empire has a population of 52,000,000, from which the ratio of 1.03 hectares to each individual follows. Although it is true that wholly uninhabited or very thinly populated regions, high mountains, forests, deserts, etc., may be valuable from a political point of view, nevertheless the whole course of the world's history shows us that, as a general rule, the value of territory increases with the number of inhabitants that dwell upon it. Thus, to-day, Norway-Sweden, with an area of 772,878 square kilometres — two fifths greater than that of the German Empire — but with a population of 6,800,000, cannot be looked upon as a first-class Power; while Germany closely approaches the Russian Empire in strength: for although its area is but $\frac{1}{43}$ that of the latter, its population is only one half less. Thus area alone is never the deciding factor of political power.

In the non-recognition of this fact lies the source of the greatest errors which have been made by conquerors and statesmen. The powerful influence that small states, such as Athens, Palestine, and Venice, have exerted on the history of the world proves that a great expanse of territory is by no means indispensable to great historical actions. The unequal distribution of mankind over a definite area is a much more probable source of political and economic progress. In Athenian time the Mediterranean region contained but few human aggregates — and these were concentrated within limited areas — and few fertile provinces, such as Egypt These districts are the *foci* of history. So, in every province, thickly and sparsely populated districts are contrasted with one another, historical rifts opening everywhere between them, whether they are regions inhabited by fixed or nomadic races, dwellers on plains or on mountains, country or city, that stand thus in contrast to each other. Civilisation and political superiority have always attended the thickly populated districts. Thus the whole of development has been a progression from small populations dwelling in extensive regions to large populations concentrated in more limited areas. Progress first awoke when division of labour began to organise and differentiate among heaped-up aggregates, and to create discrepancies promoting to life and development. A simple increase of bodies and souls only strengthens that which is already in existence by augmenting the mass. In China, India, and Egypt, population has increased for a long time; but development of civilisation and of political power has been unable to keep pace with it.

### *J.* THE WATER — OCEANS, SEAS, AND RIVERS

SINCE Man is a creature capable only of life on land, bodies of water must at one time have been the greatest obstacles to his diffusion. Thus the original family of human beings could have inhabited only one portion of the earth, to which it was restricted by impassable barriers of water. We know that in early geological times the division of the earth's surface into land and water was subject to the same general laws as to-day; therefore such a portion of the earth could not have been more than a part of the total land in existence, — a larger or smaller world-island. The first step beyond the bounds of this island was the first step toward the conquest of the whole earth by Man. The first raft was therefore the most important contrivance that Man could have invented. It not only signified the commencement of the acquisition of all parts of the earth to their very farthest limits; but also — and this is far more important — the potentiality for all possibilities of divergence and temporary separation offered by our planet. It brought with it escape from the development that always turns back upon itself, travelling in a circle, and the progress that constantly consumes itself, — factors inseparable from life confined within a small area; it led to the creation of fruitful contrasts and differences, and to wholesome competition, — in short, to the beginning of the evolution of races and peoples. Looked at from this point of view, even the discovery of Prometheus has been of less moment to the progress of mankind than that of the inventor who first joined logs together into a raft and set out on a voyage of discovery to the nearest islet.

From the time of this first step onward, the development of the human race was so intimately connected with the uninhabitable water that one of its most powerful incentives lay in the struggle with the sea. And so little have we advanced from this condition that the stoutest race of the present day is one that from a narrow island commands the ocean. England's strength is a proof of the tremendous importance of the sea as a factor of political power and of civilisation. But not to exaggerate the significance of the ocean, we may at the same time remember that it consists in the fact that, by means of the sea, open highways are presented from land to land. Command of the sea is a source of greatness to nations, for it facilitates dominion over the land.

By reason of its consistency the water is an important agent of levelling and equalising effects. As we perceive this in nature, so do we also in history. A race familiar with the sea in one place is familiar with it in all regions. The Normans off the coast of Vinland, and the Spaniards in the Pacific, found the same green, surging element, moved by the same tides, subject to the same laws. The ocean has an equalising effect upon the coasts even: the dunes of Agadir and of the harbour at Vera Cruz awaken memories of home in the mind of the sailor from Hela. The diffusion of the sea over three quarters of the earth's surface must also be taken into account. Thus the influence of the ocean in rendering men familiar with different parts of the world is far greater than that of the land. From the ocean comes a constant unifying influence which ever tends to reduce the disuniting effect of the separation of land from land. As yet no attempt to extend boundaries beyond the land out over the sea has been followed by lasting success. No nation can or ever will possess the sea. Carthage and Tarentum wished to forbid Italian vessels the passage of the Lacinian capes by treaty; the Venetians desired dominion over the Adriatic to be granted them by the Pope; Denmark and Sweden strove for a *dominium maris Baltici:* but all this is against the very nature of the sea; it is one and indivisible. Only near by the coast, within the three miles' limit of international law, and in landlocked bays, may it be ruled as land is ruled. The claims of the Americans concerning the sovereignty of Bering Sea have never been recognised, and England can retain dominion over the Irish Sea only by means of her naval power. The ocean has a unifying influence on the land, even when this influence consists only in the same ends to be attained being placed before different nations. During a time of the greatest disunion, German cities that lay far enough from one another were united by Baltic interests. The union of scattered land-forces prepared the way for the opening up of wider horizons to England in the sixteenth century in the same manner as for Italy and Germany in the nineteenth.

Sea power is far more closely connected with traffic than is land power: in fact, the foundation of sea power is trade and commerce. It is, however, more than mere commercial power and monopoly of trade. In spite of all egoism, greed, and violence there remains one great characteristic peculiar to maritime powers, spared even by Punic faith and Venetian covetousness. Even the neighbourhood of the ocean is characterised by its vast natural features: rivers broaden as they approach the sea, great bays lie within the coasts, and, though the latter may be flat, the horizon lines of their low dune landscapes are broad. The horizons of maritime races are also broad. Whether it be the hope of profit from commerce, or of gain from piracy, that lures men forth, many a ship has returned to port bearing with it inestimable benefits to mankind; for the greatest maritime discoveries have not been mere explorations of new seas, but of new lands and peoples. Such discoveries as these have contributed most to the broadening of the historical horizon. Even political questions expand, assume a larger character, and often become less acute, when they emerge from the narrow limits of continental constraint upon the free and open coasts. This is true even of the Eastern question, to the solution of which definite steps were taken upon the Mediterranean when it seemed to have come to a deadlock in the Balkan Peninsula.

The ocean is no passive element to maritime races. By deriving power from the sea they become subject to the sea. The more strength they draw from the ocean, the less firm becomes their footing upon the land. Finally their power no longer remains rooted in the land, but it grows to resemble that of a fleet resting upon the waves: it may with but small expenditure of effort extend its influence over an enormously wide area, but it may also be swept away by the first storm. As yet all maritime nations have been short-lived; their rise has been swift, often surprisingly so; but they have never remained long at the zenith of prosperity, and as a rule their decay has been as rapid as their elevation to power. The cause of the fall of all maritime nations has been the smallness of their basis, their foreign possessions, widely separated from one another and difficult to defend, and their dependence upon these foreign possessions. In many cases the overbalancing of political by economic interests, the neglect of materials for defence, and effeminacy resulting from commercial prosperity, have also contributed to their destruction.

Special combinations of characteristics arising from the geographical positions of oceans, continents, and islands are connected with the broad features common to oceanic continuity. These characteristics are reflected from the sea back to the land, and there give rise to historical groups. The historical significance of such groups is expressed in their names even, — "Mediterranean World," "Baltic Nations," "Atlantic Powers," and "Pacific Sphere of Civilisation." They are primarily the results of commerce and exchange, and of the furthering, correlating influences of all coasts and islands. What Ernst Curtius said of the Ægean may be applied in a broader sense to all seas and oceans: "As waves rolled from the Ionian strand to Salamis, so popular movements never arose on one coast without spreading to the other." When they united all peninsulas, islands, and coasts of the Mediterranean into one state, the Romans merely set a political crown upon the civilised community that had developed round about, and by means of, this same sea. And if we wish rightly to estimate the significance of Roman expansion from a central European point of view, we may express our conception very shortly, — the diffusion of Mediterranean culture over western and central Europe. It was at the same time a widening of the horizon of a landlocked sea to that of the open ocean. The Atlantic Ocean succeeded to the Mediterranean Sea. The Americans and the Russians, and the Japanese, repeating their words, maintain that in the same manner the Pacific must succeed to the Atlantic; but they forget the peculiar features of the Mediterranean, especially its conditions of area. It is no more probable that such a compact, isolated development will occur again, than that the history of Athens will repeat itself on the Corean Peninsula or at Shantung. The greater the ocean, the farther is it removed from the isolated sea. It was not the Atlantic that succeeded to the Mediterranean, but the broad world-ocean that succeeded to the narrow basin called the Mediterranean Sea.

There have always been differences between the various divisions of the main sea; and these variations will ever continue to be prominent, although constantly tending to become less and less so. The Pacific Ocean will always remain by far the greatest, including, as it does, forty-five per cent of the total area of water. Owing to its great breadth, the Pacific routes are from three to four times as long as those of the Atlantic. The Pacific widens toward the south; and Australia and Oceania lie in the opening, thus furnishing the Pacific with its most striking peculiarity, — a third continent situated in the southern hemisphere, together with the richest series of island formations on earth. Whatever the Pacific may contribute to history, it will be a contribution to the annals of the southern hemisphere; and if a great independent history develop in the antipodes, it will have the southern Pacific, bounded by Australia, South America, New Zealand, and Oceania, for its sphere of action. The area of the Atlantic Ocean is but half that of the Pacific. Nor is it for this reason alone that in comparison with the latter it is an inland rather than a world sea; for, owing to its narrowness between the Old and the New Worlds, the branches it puts forth, and the islands and peninsulas that it touches, it shortens the routes from one coast to the other. In it there is more of a merging of land and sea than a separation; and to-day it is chiefly a European-American ocean. The Indian Ocean is both geographically and historically but half an ocean. Even though important parts of it may be situated north of the equator, it is too much enclosed to the north; it widens to the south, and thus belongs to the southern hemisphere.

The great oceans open up broad areas for historical movements, and through their instrumentality peoples are enabled to spread from coast to coast in all directions; the inland seas, on the contrary, cause the political life of the nations bordering upon them to be concentrated within a limited area. The Mediterranean will ever remain a focus toward which the interests of almost all European Powers concentrate. It has, moreover, become one of the world's highways since the completion of the Suez Canal. The Baltic somewhat resembles the Mediterranean; but it would be saying too much to look upon its position as other than subordinate to that of the greater sea. The area of the Baltic is but one seventh that of the Mediterranean; and it is lacking in the unique intercontinental situation of the latter. In many respects it resembles the Black Sea rather than the Mediterranean, especially by reason of its eastern relations.

Originally the coast was the threshold of the sea; but as soon as maritime races developed it became the threshold of the land. In addition it is a margin, a fringe in which the peculiarities of sea and land are combined; and for this very reason seacoasts have a historical value greatly disproportionate to their area, especially as they constitute the best of all boundaries for the nations that possess them. Here harbours are situated, fortresses, and the most densely populated of cities. Owing to their close connection with the sea, the inhabitants of coasts acquire characteristics which distinguish them from all other peoples. Even if of the same nationality as their inland neighbours, — as, for example, the Greeks of Thrace and of Asia Minor and the Malays of many of the East Indian Islands, — their foreign traffic nevertheless impresses certain traits and features upon them which in the case of the Low Countries led almost to political disruption. A coast is more favoured than an interior in all things relating to commerce and traffic; yet neither may enjoy permanent life alone without the other: the French departments of the Weser and of the Elbe were among the most ephemeral of the political results achieved by the short-lived Napoleonic era. With the sea at their backs it is easy for the inhabitants of a coast to become detached from their nation, and but a simple matter for them to spread over other coasts. Ever since the time of the Phœnicians there have been numerous colonists of coasts and founders of coast states. The Normans are most typical in European history. The expansion of coast colonies toward the interior is one of the most striking features of recent

African development. Thus coasts are to be looked at from within as well as from without. To many barbarous races — such as Hottentots and Australians — the coast is dead compared with the interior; for Germany the coast has been politically dead for centuries. A river-mouth is best suited for carrying the influences of the coast inland.

Since the time of Carl Ritter geography has laid great stress upon the influence which the natural divisions and contours of coasts have had upon civilisation. All ancient historians supposed that the Mediterranean Sea, with its many bays, peninsulas, and islands, schooled the Phœnicians in seamanship. This, however, is not so. Nautical skill is transmitted from one people to another, as may be seen from some of the most obvious cases in modern history. No maritime people has become great through its own coast alone. It is not the coast of Maine, with its numerous inlets and bays, that has produced the best seamen, but the for the most part naturally unfavourable coast of Massachusetts, for the reason that the inland districts bounded by the latter are far more productive and furthering to commerce than are the interior regions of Maine. Nature has forced races to take to the sea only in such countries as Norway and Greece, where the strips of coast are narrow and the inland territory poor. In order to have political influence it is sufficient to have one foot on the seacoast. Aigues-Mortes, with its swampy environment, was sufficient to extend France to the Mediterranean during the reign of St. Louis; Fiume sufficed for Hungary. Forbidding, desert coasts have had a peculiarly retarding effect on historical development. It was necessary to rediscover the Australian mainland, to touch at more favourable points, one hundred and thirty years after the time of Tasman; thus the history of the settlement of Australia by Europeans originated, not with him, but with Cook.

As portions of the general water area, rivers are branches or runners of the sea, extending into the land, — lymphatic vessels, as it were, bearing nourishment to the ocean from the higher regions of the earth. Therefore they form the natural routes followed by historical movements from the sea inland and *vice versâ*. A solid foundation of truth underlies those rivers of legendary geography that joined one sea with another. The connection of the Baltic and the Black Sea via Kieff is not that described by Adam of Bremen; but Russian canals have established a waterway, following out the plan indicated by nature, just as the Varangians also realised it in a ruder way by dragging their boats from the Dwina to the Dnieper. By uniting the Great Lakes to the Mississippi by means of the Illinois River, the French provided a waterway from the North Atlantic Ocean to the Gulf of Mexico, a line of power in the rear of the Atlantic colonies. The latter fell back on salt water, the former on fresh. The Nile, flowing parallel to the Red Sea from Tanasee in the Abyssinian highlands, shares with the Red Sea, even to-day, in the traffic between northeastern and east central Africa. A railway from Mombasa to Uganda would complete a western Mediterranean-Indian line of connection, as a road along the Euphrates to the Persian Gulf would an eastern, each following the direction of rivers running parallel to the Red Sea. We can clearly see the transition of the functions of oceans to fresh, shallow water to sounds and lagoons, in which sea traffic is furnished with smoother, quieter routes under the shelter of the coasts.

In truth, only portions of the lines of traffic follow rivers; for rivers flow from highland to lowland, watersheds breaking their course here and there. In comparison with the oceans, rivers are but shallow channels, the continuity of which may be broken by every rocky ledge. Thus different regions for traffic arise at various points in the same stream. Only that part of Egypt which is situated north of the first cataract is Egypt proper; the territory to the south was conquered from Nubia. The farther we travel up a stream the less water and the more rapids and falls we shall find; therefore traffic also decreases in the direction toward the river's source. It may be seen from this that there is but little probability of truth in the analogy drawn between the flowing of rivers from elevations to plains, and the migrations of nations and directions in which states expand. History shows that migration and development follow a contrary direction to that in which rivers flow. There are examples of this to be found in all parts of the world in colonies established over-sea, proofs of the preponderance of traffic by sea and of the general influence of the sea in history. The French certainly settled along the central Mississippi from the north, but they arrived there after having first dwelt on the lower St. Lawrence. There are rare examples of great migratory movements which have followed the course of rivers. The Aryans wandered down the valley of the Indus into India, and the Goths along the Danube to the Black Sea.

Maritime and terrestrial advantages are concentrated where a river joins the sea; especially characteristic of such districts are deltas, at an early date rendered more efficient for purposes of commerce through canals and dredging. The fertility of the alluvial soil, the lack of forest occasioned by frequent floods, and the protection afforded by the islands of the delta, may have had not a little influence on the choice of such regions as settlements for Man. At all events, estuaries and deltas, both small and great, were in the earliest times centres of civilisation. Egypt and Babylonia both testify to this; the colonising Greeks also showed a preference for river mouths. Miletus, Ephesus, and Rome were states situated at the mouths of rivers, and so were the ancient settlements on the Rhone, the Guadalquivir, and the Indus. It would not be possible, however, to deduce from this proofs of a potamic phase of civilisation and formation of nations preceding the Thalassic, or Mediterranean. Estuary and delta states are far more a result of the Mediterranean culture. The latter led to the settlement of favourable districts on various coasts, all of which were finally swallowed up into the Roman Empire during the period of its northern and eastern expansion.

Another much more evident process of development through the instrumentality of rivers was shown at the time when traffic began to extend itself over wide areas. Rivers are the natural highways in countries which abound in water, and are of so much the greater importance because in such lands other thoroughfares are frequently wanting. Taken collectively, rivers form a natural circulatory system. In America at the time of exploration and conquest, in Siberia, in Africa to-day, they are natural arteries by means of which exchange and political power may be extended. The more accessible a river is to commerce, the more rapidly political occupation increases about its basin, as has been shown by the Varangians in Russia and the Portuguese in Brazil. The best example of a country having developed through conformity with a natural river system and in connection with it is that of the Congo State with part of its boundaries drawn simply along the lines of watersheds. Mastery among rival colonies is determined by the results of the struggle for the possession of rivers; this has been as clearly shown by the

St. Lawrence and the Mississippi in America as by the Niger and the Benuwe in Africa. The influence of riverways in furthering the path of political development may be best seen in the contrast between South America and Africa: the colonising movement came to the latter more than three hundred years later than to the former continent.

Every river is a route followed by political power, and is therefore at the same time a point of attraction and line of direction. The Germans have pushed their way along the Elbe between the Danes and the Slavs, and along the Vistula between the Slavs and the Lithuanians or old Prussians. The river that supports an embryonic nation holds it together when developed. The influence of the Mississippi was directed against the outbreak of the Civil War in America. As pearls are strung along a cord, so the provinces of new and of old Egypt are connected by the Nile. Austria-Hungary is not the Danube nation only because the river was the life nerve of its development, but also because eighty-two per cent of Austro-Hungarian territory is included within the regions drained by it. When the natural connection of rivers is broken, then this power of cohesion ceases. Thus the political and economic disunion of the Rhine, the Main, and other German rivers preceded the dissolution of the German Empire.

Where two rivers join there is always a meeting of two lines of political tendencies, and the place of their junction is the point whence the political forces must be controlled and held together. This is the significance of the situations of Mainz, Lyons, Belgrade, St. Louis, and Khartoum. The course followed by flowing water is far less direct than that of historical movements: the latter take the shortest way, and do not continue along the stream where a loop is formed; or they may follow a tributary that runs on in the original direction of the main stream, as in the case of the very ancient highway along the Oder and the Neisse to Bohemia. The sides of sharp angles formed by a river in its course lead to a salient point, as at Regensburg and Orléans. A tributary meeting the main stream at this point forms the best route to a neighbouring river,—for example, the Altmühl, that leads from the Danube to the Main,—or the angle may become a peninsula, so bounded by a tributary stream at its base as almost to take the form of an island. The island of the Allobroges, that lies between the curves of the Rhone and the Isère, is an example.

Breaks in the continuity of the land occasioned by rivers are caused rather by the channel in which the water flows than by the river itself. Thus we often find that dry river-beds are effective agents of this dividing up of the land: the more effective the less calculable the exact course which water would take were it to flow in them. Permanent inequalities of the earth's surface are intensified by flowing water. Therefore a river system separates the land into natural divisions. These narrow clefts are ever willingly adopted as boundary lines, especially in cases where it is necessary to set general limits to an extensive territory. Thus Charles the Great bounded his empire by the Eider, Elbe, Raab, and Ebro. Smaller divisions of land are formed by the convergence of tributaries and main streams, and again yet smaller portions are created by the joining together of the lesser branches of tributaries, and these take an especially important place in the history of wars: for example, those formed by the Rhine, Weser, Elbe, and Oder, and on a lesser scale by the Moselle, Seille, and Saar. Fords are always important, in Africa they have even been points at which small states have begun to develop.

Rivers as highways in time of war no longer have the value once attributed to them by Frederick the Great, who called the Oder "the nurse of the army." Yet rivers were of such great moment in this respect in the roadless interior of America during the Civil War, that the getting of information as to water-levels was one of the most important tasks of the army intelligence department. Rivers will always remain superior to railways as lines of communication during time of war, at least in one respect; for they cannot be destroyed.

### *K.* CONFORMATION OF THE EARTH'S SURFACE

THE variations of the earth's form from that of a perfect oblate spheroid are so small that they may be entirely disregarded from the point of view of history. All portions of the earth's surface may be looked upon as of equal curvature; the pyriform swelling which Columbus believed to be a peculiarity of the tropic zones in the New World was merely an optical illusion. Thus all portions are practically similar, and uniformity obtains over the entire earth to such an extent that there is room left only for minor inequalities in configuration. To these belong the differences in level between lands and seas, highlands and lowlands, mountains and valleys. Such variations amount to very little when compared with the earth as a whole: for the height of the tallest of the Himalayas added to the earth's radius would increase its length by about $\frac{1}{800}$ only; and the same may be said of the greatest depressions beneath the level of the sea, — inequalities that cannot be represented on an ordinary globe. Their great historical significance is chiefly due to the fact that the oceans and seas occupy the depressions, from which the greatest elevations emerge as vast islands. The remaining irregularities of the earth's surface are not sufficient to produce any permanent variations in the diffusion of races or of states. Their influence is merely negative; they may only hinder or divert the course of Man in his wanderings. Even the Himalayas have been crossed, — by the Aryans in the west, and by the Thibetans in the east; and British India has extended its boundaries far beyond them to the Pamirs.

The historian is concerned with but two of the variable qualities of the land, — differences in level and differences in contour. Variations in constitution, development, elementary constituents, and the perpetual phenomena of transformation and dissolution which present a thousand problems to the geographer, scarcely exist for the historian. Nor are those great inequalities, the depressions in which the seas rest, of any interest to him. It is indifferent whether the greatest of such depressions be covered by five miles of water, or, as we now know, by almost six miles: the fact that the Mediterranean reaches its greatest depth in the eastern part of the Ionian Sea has nothing whatever to do with the history of Greece. To be sure, there is a general connection between the depth of the Mediterranean, shut up within the Straits of Gibraltar, and the climate of the neighbouring regions, which has a direct influence on the inhabitants of Mediterranean countries; but it is a very distant connection, and it is only mentioned here in order to remind the reader that there is not a single phenomenon in nature that is not brought home to mankind at last. Still, as a rule, history is concerned with the depths of the sea only in so far as they are the resting-places for submarine telegraph cables; and this is a fact of very recent times. It may be said that the formation of the earth's crust occurred at a period too remote to have had any influence on the history of Man; and that therefore all questions concerning it should be left to geology. The first statement may be admitted; but the latter does not follow by any means. For if the whole Mediterranean region from the Caucasus to the Atlas Mountains and from the Orontes to the Danube is a region of uniform conformation, it is purely by reason of a uniformity in development. In the same manner there is an extensive region of uniform conformation to the north, between the Atlantic Ocean and the Sudeten.

There are great features of the earth's conformation that are so extensive that groups of nations share them in common. Russia and Siberia occupy the same plain upon which the greater portions of Germany, Belgium, and Holland are situated. Germany and France share the central mountain system which extends from the Cévennes to the Sudeten. A mere participation in a common geological feature produces such affinity and relationship as may be seen in the Alpine states, in Sweden and Norway, and in the nations of the Andes. This reminds us of the groups of nations that surround seas; but that which separates the Baltic states binds them together; and the mountains that unite the Swiss cantons also separate them from one another. Lesser features of conformation divide countries and often exhibit gaps and breaches in development, for the reason that they divide a political whole into separate natural regions. The history of the lowlands of North Germany differs greatly from that of the mountainous districts of the same country; the lowlands of the Po and Italy of the Apennines are two different lands. The great contrast between the hilly manufacturing west of England and the low-lying agricultural east extends throughout English history; and in like manner the Highlands and the Lowlands are opposed to each other in Scotland.

Wherever various orographic features are included in a country, the question arises whether, in spite of all diversity, they unite to form a whole, or whether they exist as separate, independent neighbouring parts. The elements of the surface formation of the earth are not only historically important in themselves as units, but also on account of the way in which they are connected with one another. We have in Greece an example of an exceedingly intricate mountain system in which barren plateaus are interspersed with fertile valleys and bays. Owing to the sea, such bays as those of Attica, Argos, and Lamia are to a high degree self-dependent; they became little worlds in themselves, independent states, which could never have grown into a united whole had they not been subjected to external pressure. The reverse of this state of disunion, arising from the juxtaposition of a great number of different formations, is the division of North America into the three great regions of the Alleghanies, the Mississippi Valley, and the Rocky Mountain plateau, which gradually merge into one another and are bound into a whole by the vast central valley. Austria-Hungary includes within itself five different orographic elements, — the Alps, Carpathians, Sudeten, the Adriatic provinces, and the Pannonian Plains. Vienna is situated where the Danube, March, and Adria meet, and from this centre radiates all political unifying power. If a still closer-knit unity is coexistent with a diversified geological formation of insular or peninsular nature, as in Ireland or Italy, it follows that this unity binds the orographic divisions into an aggregate. The discrepancies between Apennine Italy, Italy of the Po Valley, and Alpine Italy, which have been evident in all periods of history, formed, in their rise and in their final state of subjugation to political force, an example of orographic dissimilarity existing within peninsular unity.

The great continental slopes are also important aids to the overcoming of orographic obstacles to political unity. In Germany there is a general inclination toward the north, crossed and re-crossed by a number of mountain chains and successions of valleys. It is not to be denied that the intersecting elevations have furthered political disunion; without doubt, a gradual slope from the southern part of Germany to the sea, with a consequent partition of the country by the rivers into strips extending from east to west, would have been attended by a greater political unity. Again, but in another way, the preponderance of any one orographic element has a unifying effect on all the other elements, as we have seen in North America, where the simple, even course of development has been in conformity with the existence of geological formations on a large scale.

There are internal differences in formation in every mountain range and in every plain, all of which have different influences on history. The steep fall of the Alps on the Italian side has rendered a descent into the plains of the Po far easier than a crossing in the opposite direction, where many obstacles in the shape of mountain steeps, elevated plateaus, and deep river valleys surround the outer border of the Alps. Again, penetration from the plains to the interior of the Alps is less difficult in the west, where there are no southern environing mountains, than in the east, where there is such a surrounding mountain chain. The compact formation of the Alps in the west crowds obstacles together into a small space, where they may be overcome with greater labour and in a lesser time than in the east, among the broadened-out chains of mountains, where there are numerous smaller hindrances to progression spread out over a wider territory. The route from Vienna to Trieste is twice as long as that from Constance to Como.

In mountain passes orographic differences are concentrated within very limited areas, and for this reason passes are of great importance in history. The value of gorges and defiles increases with their rarity, and their number varies greatly in different mountain chains. The Pindus range is broken but once, by the cleft of Castoreia, and an easy passage from northern to central Greece is only possible by way of Thermopylæ; the shortest overland route from Persia to India is that of the Khyber Pass alone. The Rhætian Alps are rich in defiles and gorges; but the mountain ridges are poor in crossing-places, and, as a rule, the elevation of the passes decreases toward the east. The possibility of journeying over the Himalayas increases as we travel westward. During the Seven Years' War the great difference between the accessible, sloping Erz-Gebirge of the Bohemian frontier and the precipitous, fissured, sandstone hills of the Elbe was very apparent. Mountain passes are always closely connected with valleys and rivers; the latter form the ways leading to and from the former. The valleys of the Reuss and the Tessin are the natural routes to the pass of St. Gotthard; and were it not for the gorges of the Inn and the Etsch in the northern and the southern Alps, the Brenner Pass would not possess anything like its present supreme importance. Wherever such entrances to passes meet together or cross one another, important rallying-points either for carrying on traffic or for warlike undertakings are formed: such places are Valais, Valtcline, and the upper valley of the Mur. Coire is a meeting-point of not less than five passes: the Julier, Septimer, Splügen, St. Bernardin, and Lukmanier. The value of passes varies according to whether they cross a mountain range completely from side to side, or extend through only a part of it. When the Augsburgers, on the way to Venice, had got through the Fern pass, or that of Leefeld, the Brenner still remained to be crossed; but when the Romans had surmounted the difficulties of Mont Genèvre, the ridges of the Alps were no longer before them; they were in Gaul.

There are also passes through cross ridges that connect mountain chains, such as the Arlberg, that pierces a ridge extending between the northern and the central Alps. Passes of this sort are of great importance to life in the mountains, for as a rule they lead from one longitudinal valley to another; such valleys extending between ridges being the most fertile and protected districts in mountainous regions. In this manner the Furka Pass connects Valais, the most prosperous country of the Alps during the time of the Romans, with the upper Rhine valley; and the Arlberg connects the Vorarlberg with the upper valley of the Inn. Mountain passes are not only highways for traffic, they are the arteries of the mountains themselves. Commerce along the mountain ways leads to settlements and to agriculture at heights where they would hardly have developed had it not been for the roads; and the highest permanent dwellings are situated in and about passes. The Romans established their military colonies in the neighbourhood of passes; and the German emperors rendered the Rhætian gorges secure through settlements. There are political territories that are practically founded on mountain passes. The kingdom of Cottius, tributary to the Romans, was the land of the defiles of the Cottian Alps; Uri may be designated as the country of the north Gotthard; and the Brenner Pass connects the food-producing districts of the Tyrol with one another.

The transition point from one geological formation to another is invariably the boundary line between two districts that have different histories. The movements in one region bring forces to bear on the movements in the other. Hence the remarkable phenomena which occur on mountain borderlands. The historical effects of mountainous regions are opposed by forces that thrust themselves in from without; external powers anchor themselves, as it were, in the mountains, seeking to obtain there both protection and frontier lines. Rome encroached more and more upon the Alps, first from the south, and then from the west and the north, by extending her provinces. Austria, Italy, Germany, and France have drawn up to the Alps from different sides: they merely fall back upon the mountains, however; their centres lie beyond. The same phenomenon is shown in the regions occupied by different races. Rhætians, Celts, Romans, Germans, and Slavs have penetrated into the Alps; but the bulk of their populations have never inhabited the mountainous districts. The question as to which nation shall possess a mountain chain or pass is always decided on the borders. Here are the battlefields; here, too, are the great centres of traffic whose locations put one in mind of harbours situated at points where two kinds of media of transmission come into contact with each other. This margin, like that of the sea, also has its promontories and bays.

Heights of land obstruct historical movements and lengthen their course. The Romans remained at the foot of the Alps for two centuries before they made their way into them, forced to it by the constant invasions of Alpine robbers who descended from the heights as if sallying forth from secure fortresses. Long before this the Romans had encircled the western side of the Alps and had begun to turn the eastern side. The colonies on the Atlantic coast of America, the predecessors of the United States, had been in existence for almost two hundred years before they passed the Alleghanies; and it is certain that this damming up of the powerful movement toward the west, which arose later, had a furthering influence on the economic and political development of the young States. These hindrances are not dependent on the absolute elevation of the land, but on the height of the passes, the nature of the valleys, the total breadth of the elevation, on forests and water, on the presence of glaciers or their effects, and on the bareness of the soil. The passes of the Pyrenees occur at about two thirds of the distance from the level ground to the summits of the mountains; in the Alps the elevation of the gorges is but one half or one third that of the mountain tops: hence, as a whole, the Alps are more easy of access than the Pyrenees. The Colorado plateau is a greater obstacle than the Sierra Nevada range in California, which, although of much greater elevation, slopes gently and is interspersed with broad valleys. It was due rather to the forests than to the moderate elevation of the central mountains of Germany that their settlement was delayed until the twelfth and thirteenth centuries. The influence of the broad, desert table-land of the great basin in separating the western from the Mississippi States is greater than that of the Rocky Mountains with peaks more than twelve thousand feet in height. The extensive glacial formations and the sterility of the mountains in Scandinavia have held Sweden and Norway asunder, and at the same time have permitted the Lapps and their herds of reindeer to force themselves in between like a wedge. The broad, elevated steppes of central Tienschan enabled the Khirghese to cross the mountains with their herds and to spread abroad in all directions.

In such cases the natives of table-lands and mountainous regions, who inhabit little worlds of their own on the heights, themselves contribute not a little toward rendering it difficult to pass through their countries. The most striking example of this is Central Asia with its nomadic races, whose influence in separating the great coast-nations of the east, west, and south from one another has been far more potent than that of the land itself. And these nomads are a direct product of the climate and the soil of this greatest plateau in the world. The dry table-lands of North America, from the Sierra Madre in Mexico to Atacama in the south, were in early times inhabited by closely related races, having more or less similar institutions and customs. A like effect of life on plateaus, shown in the Caucasus Mountains, that have preserved their character as a barrier against both Romans and Persians, and have been crossed by the Russians only in recent times, points to a further reason for the sundering influence of the wall-like position of mountains between the steppes and the sea.

Phenomena similar to those observed in Central Asia and in North America occur on a smaller scale in every mountainous country: extensive uninhabited table-lands in which Man and free nature come into direct contact with each other. Independent development is thus assured to the dwellers on mountains, and to their states a preponderance of territory over population. The Tyrol stands sixth among Austrian provinces according to population; but it is the third in area. The political importance of Switzerland is not owing to its three millions of inhabitants, but to the impossibility of occupying one fourth of the Alps. The position — almost that of a great Power — held by Switzerland during the fifteenth and sixteenth centuries was due to the union of this element of strength (and the fact that Switzerland, by reason of its situation, includes many of the most important commercial routes in Europe) with the mountain-bred spirit of liberty and independence of its people. In other respects, too, mountain states stand pre-eminent among nations: as the Tyrol outshone all other Austrian provinces in 1809, so the mountain tribes of the Caucasus were the only Asiatics able to offer any permanent resistance to the advance of the Russians. The broad, rough character of a highland country is an active force; in all mountain wars it has led to the spreading out of armies and to the lengthening of columns. The wars of mountain tribes have ever been striking, — their predatory expeditions into the neighbouring lowlands as well as their tenaciously fought, self-sacrificing fights for independence.

The support afforded by mountains to weak nations that without the protection of a great uninhabited region would not have been able to maintain their independence, can be likened only to the protection which, as we have seen, is given by the sea. Switzerland has often been compared to the Low Countries; and there is even a still greater resemblance between city cantons such as Basle and Geneva, and ports like Hamburg and Lübeck. It was owing to similar reasons that the strongholds of French Protestantism during the sixteenth century were the Cévennes, Berne, and La Rochelle. The protection given by mountains must not be looked upon as of an entirely passive nature, as may appear to us owing to the preservation of remnants of races (Ossetes, Rhæto-romans, Celts in Scotland and Wales), or of old customs, or of independent states in fortress-like isolation, as Montenegro: for the rugged nature of mountaineers, and their concentration within small areas where a development is possible, that renders them conscious of independence and assists them to preserve it, are also a result of life in the highlands.

In low-lying countries differences in level cannot exceed a thousand feet; and, as the variations in conformation are correspondingly small, the lowlands offer fewer hindrances to historical movements than do rivers, seas, and marshes: thus there is a greater opportunity for the development of such movements upon the plains. Consequently there is a rapid diffusion of races over extensive regions whose boundaries are determined by area rather than by conformation. Lowlands occur in great, continuous masses, and owe their existence to the vast tellurian physical processes. Thus the distribution of races in lowland countries is correspondingly wide: the states of such peoples are correspondingly extensive in area, and the connection of the history of one lowland country with that of another is correspondingly close. As Germany and the Low Countries are bound together by a common tie, each sharing in the plains, so are Russia and Siberia bound together. Just as the steppes of northern Europe merge into those of northern Asia, so the northern Slavonic races gradually merge into the Ural-Altai. Lowlands hasten historical movements. There is no trace of the retarding and protecting effects of the highlands in lands where, as Dahlmann said of Savoy, a nation dwells together with its enemies on the same boundless level. Nomadism is the form of civilisation characteristic of broad plains and extensive table-lands. But the Germanic races of history, a great part of which were no longer nomads, exhibited a hastening in their movement toward the west when they reached the lowlands: for they appeared on the lower Rhine at an earlier time than on the upper Rhine, delayed in their wanderings toward the latter by the mountainous, broken races. Long after the Celts had disappeared from the lowlands — then memory only was preserved in the names of hills and rivers — they still continued to exist in the protected mountain regions of Bohemia. In like manner in later times the Slavs maintained themselves in natural strongholds after they had vanished from the plains of northern Germany. Compare the conquest of Siberia, accomplished in a century, with the endless struggles in the Caucasus. And what lowland country can show remnants of peoples equivalent to those of the Caucasus? The lowlands are also regions of the most extensive mingling and mixing of races. We have but to think of Siberia or the Sudan.

In the development of states, lowlands take precedence over mountainous districts. Rome expanded from the seacoast to the Apennines, and from the valley of the Po to the Alps; the conquest of Iberia began in the one great plain of the peninsula, in Andalusia, and in the lowlands of the Ebro; and foreign control of Britain ended at the mountains of Scotland and Wales. In North America colonisation spread out in broad belts at the foot of the Alleghanies before it penetrated into the mountains. In southern China the mountains with their unsubdued tribes are like political islands in the midst of the Mongolised hills and plains.

The lesser the differences in level, and the smaller the conformations of the earth, the more important are those differences that remain within heights of less than a thousand feet above the sea. Elevations of a few dozen yards were of the greatest importance on the battlefields of Leipzig, Waterloo, and Metz. The significance of the little rise in the land at Gavre, near Ghent, lies in the fact that even at times of flood a foundation for a bridge will remain firm upon it. The slightest elevation in the lowland cities of Germany and Russia offers such a contrast in altitude to its surroundings, that a fortress, a cathedral, or a kremlin is erected upon it. The two ridges that extend through the plains of north Germany are not only very prominent in the landscape, but also in history. Owing to their thick forests, their lakes and marshes, and small populations, they are peculiarly like barriers; and the breaches in them are of importance to the geography both of war and of commerce. The battles fought against Sweden and Poland, round about the points where the Oder and the Vistula cross these regions, are to be counted among the most decisive struggles in the history of Prussia. Wherever there are no differences in level a substitute is sought in water. In such cases wide rivers or numerous lakes and marshes form the most effective obstacles, boundaries, and strongholds. Finally the plains approach the sea and are submerged by it; and here lowland countries find a support safer than that of the mountains, and richer in political results. North Germany is supported by the sea; south Germany by mountains. Which boundary is the more definite, the more capable of development, politically and economically? Political superiority is ever connected with the protection and support of the sea.

The influences of vegetation upon historical movements are often more important than those of the earth-formation itself. Wherever extensive lowland regions are overgrown with grass, we always find mobile nomadic races that with their large herds and warlike organisations are great causes of disturbance in the development of neighbouring lands. Since the form of vegetable growth which covers grass steppes and prairies is dependent on climate, it follows that nomadism is prevalent throughout the entire northern sub-temperate zone, where such grass is abundant, — from the western border of Sahara to Gobi. Nomadic races of historical significance are even to be seen in the New World: for example, the Gauchos of the Pampas and the Llaneros of Venezuela. In comparison with plains and prairies, forests are decided hindrances to historical movements. Different peoples are separated from one another by strips of woodland; the state and the civilisation of the Incas ceased at the fringe of primeval forest of the east Andes. Thickly wooded mountains present the most pronounced difficulties to historical movements. The appearance of the oldest large states and centres of culture on the borders of steppes, in the naturally thinly wooded districts at the mouths of rivers, and on diluvial plains, seems natural enough to us when we think of the difficulties presented by life in a forest glade to men who had only stone implements and fire at their command. A description of the difficulties encountered during Stanley's one hundred and fifty-seven days' journey through the primeval woods of central Africa gives us a very clear conception of what are termed "hindrances" to historical movements. The early history of Sweden has been characterised as a struggle with the forest; and this description is valid for every forest country. Great state-formations have originated in thinly wooded districts, and have then gradually spread out over the forest belts both to the north and to the south. This is the process which we still see in progress in Africa, where Fulbas, Kanuris, and Arabs who came from the deserts are now pushing their states forward to the forests. The forest divides nations from each other; it allows small tribes only to unite, and creates but small states, or, at the most, loosely bound confederations. It is only where a great river system forms natural roads, as in the regions of the Amazon and the Congo, that great forest districts may be rapidly united to form a state. In other cases settlements in forest clearings and road-breaking must precede political control. In this way the Chinese conquered the races of the western half of Formosa in two hundred years: in the eastern half the land is still under forest and the natives have also retained their independence. The existence of small states, with their many obstacles to political and economic growth, still continues in forest regions alone; and the roaming hordes of hunters inhabiting them belong to the simplest forms of human societies.

## 3. RETROSPECT

Looking back upon the history of Man, it appears to us as the history of the human race as a life phenomenon bound and confined to this planet alone. We are thus unable to form any conception of progress into the infinite, for every tellurian life-development is dependent upon the earth, and must always return to it again. New life must follow old roads. Cosmic influences may broaden or narrow the districts within which Man is able to exist. This was experienced by the human race during the glacial period, when the ice sheet first drove men toward the equator, and later, receding, enabled them once more to spread out to the north. The limits of world-life in general depend upon earthly influences; and thus, for mankind, progress limited by both time and space is alone possible.

Perhaps it would be well, for the elucidation of the question of development, were geography to designate as progress only that which from sufficient data may be established as such beyond all doubt. Thus, to begin with, we have learned to know of a progress in space (man's diffusion over the earth) which proceeds in two directions. The expansion of the human race signifies not only an extension of the boundaries of inhabited land far into the polar regions, but also the growth of an intellectual conception of the whole world.  Together with this progress there have been countless expansions of economic and political horizons, of commercial routes, of the territories of races and of nations,—an extraordinarily manifold growth that is continually advancing.  Increase of population and of the nearness of approach of peoples to one another goes hand in hand with progress in space. Mankind cannot become diffused uniformly over new areas without becoming more and more familiar with the old.  New qualities of the soil and new treasures have been discovered, and thus the human race has constantly been made richer. While these gifts enriched both intellect and will, new possibilities were all the while arising, enabling men to dwell together in communities: the population of the earth increased, and the densely inhabited regions, at first but small, constantly grew larger and larger.  With this increase in number, latent abilities came to life; races approached one another; competition was entered into; interpenetration and mingling of peoples followed.  Some races acted mutually in powerfully developing one another's characteristics; others receded and were lost, unless the earth offered them a possibility of diffusion over better protected regions.  Already we see in these struggles the fundamental motive of the battle for area; and at the same time, on surveying this progress, we may also see the limit set to it,—that increase of population is unfavourable to the progress of civilisation in any definite area, if the number of inhabitants become disproportionately large in respect to the territory occupied.  Many regions are already overpopulated; and the numbers of mankind will always be restricted by the limits of the habitable world.

Already in the differences in population of different regions lie motives for the internal progress of Man; but yet more powerful are those incentives to the development of internal differences in races furnished by the earth itself through the manifoldness of its conformation.  The entire history of the world has thus become an uninterrupted process of differentiation.  At first arose the difference between habitable and uninhabitable regions; and then within the habitable areas occurs the action brought about by variations in zones, divisions of land, seas, mountains, plains, steppes, deserts, forests,—the whole vast multitude of formations, taken both separately and in combination.  Through these influences arise the differences which must at first develop to a certain extent in isolation before it is possible for them to act upon one another, and to alter, either favourably or unfavourably, the original characteristics of men.  All the variations in race and in civilisation shown by different peoples of the world, and the differences in power shown by states, may be traced to the ultimate processes of differentiation occasioned by variations in situation, climate, and soil, and to which the constantly increasing mingling of races, that becomes more and more complex with the diffusion of mankind over the globe, has also contributed.  The birth of Roman daughter states and the rise of Hispano-Americans and Lusitano-Americans from some of these very daughter nations are evidences of a development that ever strives for separation, for diffusion over space, and which may be compared only to the trunk of a tree developing and putting forth branches and twigs.  But the bole that has sent forth so many branches and twigs was certainly a twig itself at one time; and thus the process of differentiation is repeated over and over again. Progress in respect to population and to occupied area is undoubted; but can these daughter nations be compared to Rome in other respects?  They have shown great powers of assimilation and great tenacity, for they have held their ground.  Nevertheless, their greatest achievement has been to have clung fast to the earth; in other words, to have persisted. Certainly this is far more important than the internal progress in which the branches could perhaps have been able to surpass the older nation.

It is an important principle that since all life is and must be closely attached to the soil, no superiority may exist permanently unless it be able to obtain and to maintain ground. In the long run, the decisive element of every historical force is its relation to the land. Thus great forces may be seen to weaken in the course of a long struggle with lesser forces whose sole advantage consists in their being more firmly rooted in the soil. The warlike, progressive, on-marching Mongols and Manchus conquered China, it is true, but they have been absorbed into the dense native population and have assumed the native customs. The same illustration applies to the founding of nations by all nomadic races, especially in the case of the southern European German states that arose at the time of the migration of Germanic peoples. The health and promise of the English colonies in Australia present a striking contrast to the gloom that reigns over India, of which the significance lies only in a weary governing, deserving, and exploiting of three hundred millions of human beings. In Australia the soil is acquired; in India only the people have been conquered. Will a time ever come when all fertile lands will be as densely populated as India and China? Then the most civilised, evolved nation will have no more space in which to develop, maintain, and root its better characteristics; and the success of a state will not result from the possession of active forces, but from vegetative endowments, — freedom from wants, longevity, and fertility.

Even though the future may bring with it a union of all nations in the world into the one great community already spoken of in the Gospel of John, growth may take place only through differentiation. And thus there is no necessity for our sharing Felix Dahn's fear that a world-state would swallow up all national and racial differences, and all variations in civilisation. Nor can we agree with Jhering, who sees in the world-state the termination of a development through which society advances until the state and human society are one. We return to our *hologaic*, world-embracing point of departure, remembering that world-wide changes in the development of life must constantly appear. However, tellurial limitation will turn mankind back upon itself at the moment of farthest diffusion, and will cause it to journey along the old roads in new forms and ways. The development of nations will be no more likely to cease with a world-state than the development of the human race came to an end with the diffusion of mankind over the entire earth, or the universal development of life cease when the simplest life-forms have succeeded in making their way over the whole world; more likely would it be the beginning of a subversive movement, of a return to self-discrimination from self, by which an internal advance of the evolution of life which has not yet ended is replaced. This advance is a fact in the bodily and spiritual life of Man; the ground is no longer immediately connected with it. Hence Whither? are questions that no science is able to answer.

From the fact that history is movement, it follows, therefore, that the geographer must recognise the necessity for progress in space, in the sense of a branching out of the historical ground, and a progressive increase in the occupation of this ground; further, a development toward the goal of higher ends, calling together

with an uninterrupted struggle for space between the older and newer life-forms:
yet, for all this, the definite bounds set to the scene of life by the limited area of
our planet always remain.    Finally, all development on earth is dependent on the
universe, in which our world is but a grain of sand, and to the time of which what
we call universal history is but a moment.    There must be other connections,
definite roads upon which to travel, and distant goals, far beyond.    We surmise an
eternal law of all things; but in order to know, as Lotze said, we should need to
be God himself.    To us only the belief in it is given.

# IV

## PREHISTORIC TIMES

### By PROF. JOHANNES RANKE

---

### 1. THE HISTORY OF THE EARLIEST OR PALÆOLITHIC CIVILISATION

#### *A.* THE DRIFT AND ITS ANIMAL WORLD

THE history of the world is the history of the human mind. The oldest documents affording us knowledge of it lie buried in those most mighty and comprehensive historical archives, the geological strata of our planet. Natural philosophy has learned to read these stained, crumpled, and much-torn pages that record the habitation of the earth by living beings. But, abundant as the historical material gained by palæontology may appear of itself, in reality only a fraction of this book of the universe has hitherto been perused, and those sections which have already been carefully studied still appear but fragmentary in comparison with the whole task. The passages that relate to the human race are small in number and often even ambiguous, and it is only the last pages that can give an account of it.

The oldest certain traces of the presence of Man on the earth that have hitherto been discovered are met with in the strata of the Drift epoch, and it is only during the last generation that the existence of "Drift Man" has been palæontologically proved beyond dispute.

Up to the middle of this century research appeared to have established as a positive fact that Man could not be traced back to the older geological strata; remains of Man were said to be found only in the newest stratum of the earth's formation, — in the alluvial or "recent" stratum. The bones of Man were accordingly claimed to be sure guides to the geological formations of the present time, as the bones of the mammoth and cave-bear were to the strata of the Drift. Where traces of Man were found it was considered as proved by natural science that the particular stratum in which they occurred was to be allotted to the most recent system, which we see forming and being transformed under our eyes at the present day.

While it was declared that Man belonged to the alluvial stratum, it was at the same time stated, according to the doctrine of Cuvier, which had the weight of a dogma, that Man could not have belonged to any older geological stratum i epoch, and therefore not even to the next older one, the Drift. The beginning and the end of geological epochs are marked by mighty transformations which have caused a local interruption in the formation of the strata of the earth's surface. In many cases we can point to volcanic eruptions as the chief causes, but more especially to a change in the distribution of land and water. Cuvier had conceived these changes involving the transformation to have been violent terrestrial revolutions, and the collapse of all existing things, in which the living beings belonging to the past epoch must have been annihilated. It appeared impossible that a living thing could have survived this hypothetical battle of the elements, and passed from an older epoch into the next one; and the new epoch was supposed to have received plants and animals by re-creation. All this had to be applied to Man also: he was supposed to have come into existence only in the alluvial period. Not without consideration for the Mosaic account of the Creation, which, like the creation legends of numerous peoples scattered far and wide over all the continents of the earth, tells of a great deluge at the beginning of the present age, the Pleistocene epoch of the earth's formation preceding the present period had been termed the Flood epoch, or Diluvium. In its stratifications it was thought that the effects of great deluges could largely be recognised; but the human eye could not have beheld these, for according to the catastrophe theory it appeared out of the question that Man could have been a "witness of the Flood" (*homo Diluvii testis*).

Here modern research in the primeval history or palæontology of mankind begins, starting from the complete transformation of the doctrine of the geological epochs brought about by Lyell and his school.

Proofs of terrestrial revolutions, as local phenomena and epoch-marks, are doubtless to be found, imposing enough to make the views of the older school appear intelligible; but, generally speaking, a complete interruption of the existing conditions did not take place between the periods. Everything tends to prove that even in the earlier epochs the transformation of the earth's surface went on in practically the same way as we see it going on before our eyes to-day in a degree that is slight only to appearance. The effects of volcanic action; the rising and sinking of continents and islands, and the alteration in the distribution of sea and land caused thereby; the inroads of the sea and its work in the destruction of coasts; the formation of deltas and the overflowing of rivers; the action of glaciers and torrents in the mountains, and so forth,— are constantly working, more or less, at the transformation of the earth's surface. As we see these newest alluvial deposits being formed, so in principle have the strata of the earlier epochs also been formed, and their miles of thickness prove, not the violence of extreme and sudden catastrophes, but only the length of time that was necessary to remove such mighty masses here and pile them up there. It was not sudden general revolutions of great violence, but the slowly working forces, small only to appearance, well known from our present-day surroundings, which destroy in one place and build up again in another with the material obtained from the destruction,— it was these which were the causes of the gradual transformation of the earth in all epochs of its history comparable to the present. According to this new conception of geological processes a general destruction of plants and animals at the end of epochs, and a new creation at the beginning of the following ones, was no longer a postulate of science as it had been. The living creatures of the earliest epochs could now be claimed as ancestors of those living to-day; the chain seems nowhere ompletely broken. The ancestors of the human race were also to be sought in he strata of the earlier geological periods.

Among the forces which we find attended by a transformation of the fauna nd flora of the earth's epochs, the influences of climatic changes in particular re clearly and surely shown. In that primeval period in which the coal group as formed the climate in the most different parts of the earth was comparatively quable, little divided into zones, and of a moist warmth; this is proved by he really gigantic masses of plant growth implied by the formation of many oal strata, in which the remains of a luxuriant cryptogamic flora are everywhere mbedded. In Greenland, in the strata belonging to the Chalk period, and ven in the deposits of the Tertiary period, which immediately precedes the )rift epoch, the remains of higher dicotyledonous plants of tropical character re found. The occurrence of palæozoic coral reefs in high latitudes also goes ɔ prove that the temperature of the sea water there was higher at that time: ı fact that a tropical climate existed in the farthest north, — an extreme con- rast to the present ice-sheet on its land and the icebergs of its seas. In central !urope the climatic conditions will have been little different. During the niddle Tertiary period palms grew in Switzerland; and even at the end of the 'ertiary period, as it was slowly passing into the Drift epoch, the climate in 2ntral Europe was still warmer than now, being about like that of northern taly and its protected west coast, the Riviera. There was also a rich flora, artly evergreen, and a fauna adapted to such mild surroundings. Even in the ldest (preglacial) strata, and again in the middle (interglacial) strata of the 2ntral European Drift, there was still an abundant plant-growth requiring a ?mperate climate, at any rate not more severe than central Europe possesses t the present day. Our chief forest trees grew even then: the pine, fir, larch, nd yew, and also the oak, maple, birch, hazel, etc.; on the other hand northern nd alpine forms are absent among the plants. The same holds good of the nimal world, which was certainly much farther removed than the plant world ·om the conditions prevailing now. The gigantic forms — the elephant, rhi- oceros, and hippopotamus — appear particularly strange to us, as also the large easts of prey, — the hyena, lion, etc. But besides these, and the giant-deer with s powerful antlers, and two large bovine species, — the bison and the urus, — 1ere were also the majority of the present wild animals of central and northern !urope that were originally native; as the horse, stag, roe, wild boar, and eaver, with the smaller rodents and insectivora, and the wolf, fox, lynx, and ears, of which latter the cave-bear was far larger than the present brown bear, nd even than the polar and grizzly bears.

We have sure proofs that through a decrease in the yearly temperature a lacial period set in over Europe, north Asia, and North America, burying vast reas under a sheet of ice, of the effect and extent of which northern Greenland, ·ith its ground-relief veiled in inland ice, can give us an idea.

The immediate consequence of this total climatic change was an essential hange in the fauna. Forms that were not suited to the deteriorated climate, that ould neither stand it nor adapt themselves to it, were first compelled to retire and hen were exterminated. This fate befell the hippopotamuses, and also one of the wo elephant species, *Elephas antiquus*, with its dwarf breeds in Sicily and Malta probably thus developed by this retreat); then the rhinoceros-like *Elasmoth rium*, a species of beaver, the *Trogontherium*, and the powerful cat *Machairodus* or *Trucifelis*, which still lived in England, France, and Liguria during the Drift period. Other animals, like the lion and hyena, withdrew to more southerly regions not affected by the increasing cold and more remote from its effects. On the other hand (according to Von Zittel's description in the fourth volume of his "Palæozoology," and in his "Outlines of Palæontology"), an immigration of cold-loving land animals took place, which at the present day live either in the far north, or on the wild Asiatic steppes, or in the high mountain-ranges. These new immigrants mixed with the surviving forms of the older Drift fauna. The latter lived, as we have seen, by no means in a warm climate, but only in a temperate "northerly" one, even in the warmer periods of the epoch. So we can understand that many of this older animal community were well able to adapt themselves to colder climatic conditions, and among them two of the large Drift pachydermata, the elephant and rhinoceros, whose kin we now find only in the warmest climes. But a thick woolly coat made these two Drift animals well fitted to defy a raw climate; namely, the woolly-haired mammoth, *Elephas primigenius*, one of the two Drift species of elephants of Europe, and the woolly-haired rhinoceros, *Rhinoceros antiquitatis = R. tichorhinus*. A second species of rhinoceros, *Rhinoceros Merckii*, was also preserved and maintained its region of distribution. The horse was now more largely distributed, and inhabited the plains in herds; but, above all, the reindeer immigrated along with other animals that now belong only to far northern and arctic regions, and pastured in large herds at the edges of the glaciers. With the reindeer, although less frequent, was the musk-ox of the far north, besides many other cold-loving species, such as the lemming, snow-mouse (*Arvicola nivalis* and *A. ratticeps*), glutton, ermine, and arctic fox. Many of the animal forms that were very frequent then, in the Drift period, appear now in central Europe only as alpine dwellers, living on the borders of eternal snow, — such are the ibex, chamois, marmot, and alpine hare.

Of special importance for our main question is the great invasion of Europe by central Asiatic animals; immigrants direct from the Asiatic steppes pushed westward "as in a migration of nations," among them the wild ass, saiga antelope, bobac, Asiatic porcupine, zizel, jumping mouse, whistling hare, and musk shrew-mouse.

According as the glaciers and inland ice grew or shrunk, the animals of the glacial period advanced more or less far to the north or retired more to the south, extending or reducing their range of distribution. The glacial period was no invariable climatic phenomenon. It is perfectly certain that a first glacial period with a low yearly temperature, under the influence of which the ice-masses, with their moraines, advanced a long way from the north and from the high mountains (so that in Germany, for instance, only a comparatively narrow strip remained free and habitable for higher forms of life between the two opposing rivers of ice), was succeeded by at least one period of warmer climate, and that certainly not a short one. The mean yearly temperature had increased so much that the ice-masses melted to a considerable extent, and had to retire far to the north and into the high valleys of the Alps. In this warmer interglacial period, as it is called, the Drift animals advanced far to the north, especially the mammoth, which, with the exception of the greater part of Scandinavia and Finland (districts which remained covered with ice during the interglacial period), is distributed throughout

he Drift strata of the whole of Europe and north Africa, and as far as Lake Baikal
and the Caspian Sea in northern Asia.  Even the older Drift fauna, so far as it had
not yet died out or retired, returned to its old habitats, so that the interglacial
fauna of central Europe appears very similar to the preglacial fauna.  A long-
sustained decrease of temperature, again setting in, led once more to the growth of
the ice, which in this second glacial period almost reconquered the territory it
had won at first.

In consequence of these oscillations in the climatic conditions of the Drift
epoch as a whole, we have to distinguish the preglacial epoch and the interglacial
epoch, as warmer sub-periods of the Drift, from the real glacial periods.  The latter
appear as a first or earlier and a second or later glacial period, as remains of which
the zone of the older moraines and the zone of the later ones clearly mark the
limits of the former glaciation.

It was this second deterioration of the climate, with the fresh advances made
by the glaciers and masses of inland ice, that definitely did away with the older
Drift fauna that was not equal to the sudden climatic change.  Nor did the woolly-
haired rhinoceros, the *Rhinoceros Merckii*, and the cave-bear survive the climax of
the new glacial period.  Even the woolly-haired mammoth succumbed.  It and
the woolly-haired rhinoceros, accompanied by the musk-ox and bison, had made
their way into the far north of Asia.  But while the last two species bore the
inclemencies of the climate, the rhinoceroses and elephants met their end here.
And yet they had long preserved their lives on the borders of eternal ice.  Whole
carcasses, both of the woolly-haired and Merckian rhinoceroses, and also of the
woolly-haired mammoth, the bison, and the musk-ox, with skin and hair and well-
preserved soft parts, have been discovered in the ice and frozen ground between the
Jenissei and Lena, and on the New Siberian Islands at the mouth of the Lena.
The carcasses of the mammoth and rhinoceros found imbedded in the ice were covered with a coat of thick woolly hair and reddish-brown bristles ten inches long ;
about thirty pounds of hair from such a mammoth [1] were placed in the St. Petersburg Natural History Museum.  A mane hung from the animal's neck almost to
its knees, and on its head was soft hair a yard long.  The animals were therefore
in this respect well equipped for enduring a cold climate.  As regards their food
they were also adapted to a cold climate, traces of coniferæ and willows — that
is, "northern plants" — having been found in the hollows of the molar teeth of
mammoths and rhinoceroses.  The mammoth proves to have had greater resisting
power, and to have been more fit for further migrations, than the rhinoceros.  The
latter's range of distribution extended over the whole of northern and temperate
Europe, China and central Asia, and northern Asia and Siberia.  But, as we have
seen, the mammoth penetrated not only into north Africa, but, what is of the
highest importance for the proper understanding of the settling of the New World,
even into North America.

The connection which in earlier geological epochs had united Europe, Asia,
Africa, and North America in the greatest homogeneous zoogeographical kingdom,
the Arctogæa, was broken during the Tertiary and Drift periods, so that several
zoogeographical provinces were formed.  The connection with North America was
the first to be broken, so that even in the last two divisions of the Tertiary

[1] See Fig. 1, Plate at p. 120.

period, the Miocene and Pliocene epochs, the Old and the New Worlds stood in the relation of neighbouring geographical provinces to one another. Now it is generally accepted to-day that during the Drift epoch North America was stocked out of the immigrants from the Old World, according to Von Zittel probably over Behring Sea. Consequently during the Drift epoch communication was kept up temporarily between Asia and North America in the region of Behring Sea, sufficient to allow the mammoth and some companions to pass from one continent to the other. In Kotzebue Sound mammoth bones occur in the "ground-ice formation," together with those of the horse, reindeer, musk-ox, and bison. Mammoth remains are also known to have existed in the Behring Islands, St. George in the Pribylov group, and Unalaska in the Aleutian Islands. In that period the mammoth arrived in the New World, a colonist driven from the Old. It spread widely over British North America, Alaska, and Canada; it has also been found in Kentucky. A relatively recent union of the circumpolar regions of the northern hemisphere — of Europe, Asia, and North America — is also proved by the occurrence of animals that we recognise as companions of the mammoth, but which, surviving the glacial period, are still distributed over the whole region, such as the reindeer, elk (*Alces*), and bison. The absence in Asia of several animals specially characteristic of the European Drift (the hippopotamus, ibex, chamois, fallow-deer, wildcat, and cave-bear) explains also their absence in the North American Drift fauna. It is particularly strange that the cave-bear did not reach northern Asia. It is otherwise the most frequent beast of prey of the Drift period, and hundreds of its carcasses often lie buried in the caves and clefts it once inhabited. In southern Russia numerous remains of it are found, whereas in the English caves it is rarer, the cave-hyena predominating here. Apart from the exceptions just mentioned, J. F. Brandt considers north Asia and the high northern latitudes to be the region in which the European, north Asiatic, and North American land-fauna had concentrated during the Tertiary and Drift periods, and whence their migrations and advances took place according as it grew colder. As the northern fauna spread over more southern latitudes during the Drift period, they took possession of the habitats of the species there belonging to the Tertiary period, drove them back into tropical and subtropical regions, and formed the real stock of the Drift fauna, as described by Von Zittel in the fourth volume of his "Palæozoology." One thing is certain; namely, that the northern borders of Siberia were not the real home of the mammoth and its companions; the original habitat of these animals points to the far interior of Asia, particularly to the wild table-lands, where they so far steeled themselves in enduring the climate that in the course of the glacial period half the world became accessible to them. As far as is known to-day, the mammoth arrived in Europe earlier than on the northern borders of Asia, where, protected by climatic conditions, its remains are most numerous and best preserved. The number of these gigantic animals must have been very considerable in this far northern region for a time, judging from the abundance of bones found there. In central Europe only a few places are known — such as Kannstatt, Predmost in Moravia, etc. — where the mammoth is found with similar frequency.

The mammoth attained its widest distribution in the interglacial period. In that period it crossed the Alps, and arrived on the other side, in north Asia, at the border of the "stone-ice" masses of inland ice that were still preserved from the first glacial period. The vegetation there was richer then than it is to-day; now only the vegetation of the tundra can exist. Animals found coniferæ, willows, and alders (*Alnus fructicosa*) in sufficient quantity to enable them to keep in herds. All the same, we have not to imagine the climate on the borders of the ice to have been "genial," for from that period originate the mammoth carcasses that are found frozen entire in crevasses of the ice-fields. When the new period of cold — the second glacial period — began, these far northern regions must have become unsuitable for the mammoth owing to the want of food. Von Toll, who has examined the fossil ice-beds and their relation to the mammoth carcasses, particularly on the New Siberian Islands, says:

"The mammoths and their contemporaries lived where their remains are found; they died out gradually in consequence of physical-geographical changes in the region they inhabited, and through no catastrophe; their carcasses were deposited during low temperatures, partly on the river-terraces, and partly on the banks of lakes or on glaciers (inland ice), and covered with mud; like the ice-masses that formed the foundation of their graves, their mummies were preserved to the present day, thanks to the persistent or increasing cold."

The woolly-haired mammoth did not survive the second glacial period anywhere; in the postglacial period its traces have disappeared.

The Drift series of strata are nowhere so clearly exemplified as in the New Siberian Islands, where the Drift stone-ice still forms very extensive, high "ice-cliffs," always covered with a layer of loam, sand, and peat, and having precipices often of great height, — in one place seventy-two feet. Imbedded in these cliffs of stone-ice have been found the mammoth carcasses, which formerly sank into crevices in the ice. These crevices are partly filled up with snow, which has turned into "firn" and finally into ice, but partly also with loam or sand, which are merged above immediately into the strata overlying the stone-ice. In the year 1860 Bojavski, the mammoth-hunter (*promyschlennik*), found a mammoth, with all its soft parts preserved, sticking upright in a crevice in the ice filled with loam: in 1863 it was thrown down, together with the coast-wall that sheltered it, and washed away by the sea. The Tunguse Schumachow had been more fortunate as early as 1799. During his boating expeditions along the coast, on the look-out for mammoth-tusks, he observed one day, between blocks of ice, a shapeless block which was not at all like the masses of driftwood that are generally found there. In the following year the block had melted a little, but it was only at the end of the third summer that the whole side and one of the tusks of a mammoth appeared plainly out of the ice; the animal, however, still remained sunk in the ice-masses. At last, toward the end of the fifth year, the ice between the ground and the mammoth melted more quickly than the rest, the base began to slope, and the enormous mass, impelled by its own weight, glided down onto the sand of the coast. Here Adams found the carcass in 1806, or as much as the dogs and wild animals had left of it. The whole skeleton, with a portion of the flesh, skin, and hair, has since formed one of the chief ornaments of the collection in the Academy at St. Petersburg. According to Von Toll, who personally visited the site of Bojavski's discovery, the following profile presented itself there: first the tundra stratum; then an alternation of thin strata of loam and ice; under these a peat-like layer of grass, leaves, etc., that had been washed together; then a fine lay r of sand with rema u . S ., etc., and finally stone-ice. At another place, in Gulf Anabar, in 7.. 1 th latitude, Von Toll also found the ground-moraine under a p st ic e s wh appears to prove his theory of a Drift region of inland i , wi h the on ice beds of New Siberia and Eschscholtz Bay ar r th. are

On the s at e d u . on l am deposits over the stone-ice, containing the willow and ch at r are doubt s interglacial. Some of the remains of the alder are in s rh v c ful preservation that there are still leaves and whole clusters of cat-kin on the branches.

The Land-mass to which the present New Siberian Islands belong was only dismembered at the end of the interglacial period, when colder sea-currents procured an entrance, and the accumulation of snow-masses diminished simultaneously with the sinking of the land, whereas the cold increased. The flora died off, says Von Toll, and the animal world was deprived of the possibility of roaming freely over vast areas. Only one representative of the great Drift fauna, the musk-ox, has been able to preserve its life to the present day on the larger remnants of its former vast home, such as Greenland and Grinnell Land.

As we have said, the geological and climatic conditions in all regions of the earth affected by the glacial period were highly similar to those just described. In other places the Drift stone-ice has long disappeared, but the ground-moraines of the former inland ice-masses and the surface-moraines (terminal and lateral) of the former gigantic glaciers constitute its unobliterated traces. On the moraines of the earlier glacial period we find the strata of the interglacial period deposited, and on the later moraines of the second (last) glacial period lie the remains of the postglacial period, in the course of which a continual increase in the yearly temperature — probably only a few degrees of the thermometer — caused the glaciers to melt and retreat, and opened the way for the return of plants and animals to what had been deserts of snow and ice. The place formerly occupied by the interglacial and glacial fauna is then taken by the postglacial fauna, which proves considerably different.

A number of the most characteristic species of the former sections of the Drift period are already absent in the earliest postglacial deposits; the fauna approaches nearer and nearer in its composition to that of the present day. The inland ice-masses and gigantic glaciers began to melt away, and gradually retired to the present limits of the glaciation that forms the remains of the glacial period of the Drift. The animal forms at the beginning of the postglacial period are still living, and the plants characterising this final stage of the Drift period are still growing on the borders of the ice at the present day. In the postglacial period a few northern forms such as the reindeer, lemming, ringed lemming, glutton, zizel, whistling hare, and jumping mouse still retained for a time their habitats in central Europe. Part of the Drift fauna — as the horse wild ass, saiga antelope, and Asiatic porcupine — concentrated again in the Asiatic steppes, from which they had formerly won their territory of the Drift period: the specific glacial forms — the reindeer and his above-mentioned companions — followed the retreating ice-masses into the far north, and even into polar regions; another part — the specially Alpine forms, such a h ib x hamois marmot, and alpine hare — migrated with the Alpine glaciers into the high valleys of the Alps, where they could continue the life they had led in the lowlands during the glacial period.

The mammoth, woolly-haired rhinoceros, and cave-bear are extinct.

The present-day mammalian fauna of Europe and north Asia accordingly bears a comparatively young character; during the Drift, and especially in consequence of the glacial period, it underwent the most considerable transformations.

It is in the middle of this great drama of a gigantic animal world struggling and fighting for its existence with the superior powers of nature, during the inter-glacial period of the Drift, that Man suddenly appears upon the scene in Europe like a *deus ex machina*.

Whence he came we do not know.

Did he make his entrance into Europe in company with the Drift fauna that immigrated from central Asia, or have we to seek his original home in the New World?

## B.  WHERE DRIFT MAN HAS BEEN FOUND

THE remains of the Drift fauna are usually found mixed up and washed together in caves and rock-crevices.  From the investigation of the caves in Thuringia, Franconia, and elsewhere practically proceeded the first knowledge of the Drift fauna of central Europe.  Here, right among the bones of primeval animals, were also found bones and skulls of Man.  The strata in which they were discovered appeared undisturbed; that they came into the old burial-places of the Drift fauna subsequently — perhaps by an intentional burial of relatively recent times — was thought to be out of the question.  The discovery that became most famous was Esper's, in one of the richest caves of " Franconian Switzerland," the Gaillenreuth cave.  There, in 1774, Esper found a man's lower jaw and shoulder-blade at a perfectly untouched spot protected by a stone projection in the cave wall, in the same loam as bones of the cave-bear and other Drift animals.  Later on, a human skull with some rude potsherds of clay came to light in another place. Esper argued thus:

> "As the human bones (lower jaw and shoulder-blade) lay among the skeletons of animals, of which the Gaillenreuth caves are full, and as they were found in what is in all probability the original stratum, I presume, and I think not without sufficient reason, that these human limbs are of equal age with the other animal fossils."

The Cuvier catastrophe theory could not allow this inference; according to that theory it was a "scientific postulate" that Man could not have appeared on the earth until the alluvial period, and therefore after the Drift fauna had become extinct.  Therefore, in spite of appearances, the human bones must have been more recent; and it was indeed absolutely proved that the skull that Esper had found in the cave with the rude clay pot-sherds originated from a burial in the floor of the cave.  As this was full of remains of Drift animals, the corpse, which had been covered with the earth that had been thrown up in digging the grave, was necessarily surrounded by these remains, and even appeared imbedded in them. It was ascertained that in very early times, but yet long after the Drift period, the dwellers near by had had a predilection for using the caves as burial-places, so that the fact of human bones coming together with bones of Drift animals in the floor of the same cave is easily explained.  Moreover it was found that from the earliest times down to the present day the caves had been used by hunters, herds-

man, and others as places of shelter in bad weather, as cooking-places, and sometimes even — especially in very early times — as regular dwelling-places for longer
periods, so that relics of all kinds, and often of all ages and forms of civilisation
that the land has seen from the Drift period down to modern times, must have got
into the floors of the caves. If these were damp and soft, the remains of every
century were trodden in and got to lie deeper and deeper, so that, for instance, the
fragments of a cast-iron saucepan were actually found right among the bones of
regular Drift animals in a cave in upper Franconia.

The discoveries of human remains in caves appeared discredited by this, and to
be of no value as proofs of the co-existence of Man with the Drift fauna. And
indeed this position must practically be still taken at the present day: all cave-
finds are to be judged with the greatest caution. They in themselves would never
have been sufficient to establish the existence of Drift Man, although, according to
the general change in scientific thought that led to the overthrow of Cuvier's
theory, Drift Man is now just as much a postulate of science as was formerly the
case for the opposite assumption.

The first sure proofs were adduced in France by Boucher de Perthes, in the Drift
beds of the Somme valley, near Abbeville, at the end of the third decade of the
century now expiring. Fully recognising the inadequacy of proof given by cave-
finds, he had sought for the relics of Man in the undisturbed Drift beds of gravel
and coarse sand that contained the bones of Drift animals, and which by their
covering and depth precluded all suspicion of having been subsequently dug over.
And he was successful. He had argued in exactly the same manner as Esper had
formerly done, but with better right. In the stratified Drift formations every
period is sharply defined by the layers of differently coloured and differently composed strata horizontally overlying one another. Here the proofs begin. They are
irrefutable if it is shown that the relics of Man have been there since the deposit.
Being no less immovable than this stratum in which they lie, as they came with it
they were likewise preserved with it; and as they have contributed to its formation, they existed before it. That is the line of thought according to which
Boucher de Perthes was able, in 1839, to lay before the leading experts in Paris —
at their head Cuvier himself — his discoveries proving the former existence of
Drift Man. But his demonstration was not then sufficient to break the old ban
of prejudices that were apparently founded on such good scientific bases; his
proofs of the presence of Man in the Somme valley at the time of the Drift,
contemporaneously with the extinct Drift animals, were ridiculed. It was
twenty years before these long-neglected discoveries in the Somme valley concerning the early history of Man were recognised by the scientific world.
This was only made possible by Lyell, whose authority as a geologist had risen
above Cuvier's, placing the whole weight of it on Boucher's side, after having
personally travelled over the Somme valley three times in the year 1859, and
having himself examined all the chief places where relics of Drift Man had been
discovered.

According to Lyell's description the Somme valley lies in a district of white
chalk, which forms elevations of several hundred feet in height. If we ascend to
this height we find ourselves on an extensive tableland, showing only moderate
elevations and depressions, and covered uninterruptedly for miles with loam and
brick earth about five feet thick and quite devoid of fossils. Here and there on the

chalk may be noticed outlying patches of Tertiary sand and clay, the remains of a once extensive formation, the denudation of which has chiefly furnished the Drift gravel material in which the relics of Man and the bones of extinct animals lie buried. The Drift alluvial deposit of the Somme valley exhibits nothing extraordinary in its stratification or outward appearance, nor in its composition or organic contents. The stratum in which the bones of the Drift fauna are found intermingled with the relics of Man is partly a marine and partly a fluviatile deposit. The human relics in particular are mostly buried deep in the gravel; almost everywhere one has to pass down through a mass of overlying loam with land shells, or a fine sand with fresh-water molluscs, before coming to beds of gravel, in which the relics of Drift Man are found.

Everything shows that the relics of Man are here in a secondary *situs*, deposited in the same way as the bones of extinct animals and the whole geological material in which everything is imbedded. That is the reason why the finds cannot be more exactly dated. They doubtless belong to the general Drift, but whether to the postglacial period or the warmer interglacial period cannot be decided. The fauna admits of no absolute limitation, owing to its being mixed from both periods. The mammalia most frequently found in the strata in question are the mammoth, Siberian rhinoceros, horse, reindeer, ure-ox, giant fallow-deer, cave-lion, and cave-hyena. In very similar Drift deposits of the Somme near Amiens traces of Man were found beside the bones of the hippopotamus and the elephant (*Elephas antiquus*). These animals were chiefly prevalent in France and Germany in the preglacial and interglacial periods of the Drift. Part of the animal remains found near Abbeville, particularly those of the cave-lion and cave-hyena, also point to the warmer interglacial period; on the other hand the mammoth, Siberian rhinoceros, and especially the reindeer, appear to indicate with all certainty the second glacial and postglacial periods. The bones of the older Drift animals may have been washed out of other primary *situs;* the reindeer had certainly already taken possession of those parts of France when the relics of Man were imbedded.

In spite of the most eager search for similar " relic-beds " affording sure evidence of Drift Man, only a very few have as yet been discovered that can be placed by the side of those in the Somme valley. Two are in Germany, and are at the same time the more valuable as a more exact date can be given to them within the Drift period. One of them is near Taubach (Weimar), the other at the source of the Schussen. The one at Taubach belongs to the interglacial period, that at the source of the Schussen to the postglacial period. The former lies on the moraines of the first glacial period, which was followed by the interglacial period; the latter on the moraines of the second glacial period, which slowly passed into the postglacial period.

The Drift relic-bed in the calc-tufa near Taubach lies, as we have said, over the remains of the first glacial period, and according to Penck, one of the best authorities on the Drift, belongs to the warmer intermediate epoch between the two great periods of glaciation. The proofs given by the plant and animal remains agree entirely with the proofs given by the conditions of stratification. In the rich fauna found there, animals indicating a cold climate are entirely absent, and a comparison of the whole of the finds proves that at the time when Man was present there no kind of arctic conditions can have prevailed. There is no reindeer, no lemming. The roe, stag, wolf, brown bear, beaver, wild boar, and aurochs were at that some inhabitants of these regions, and the only inference they allow is that of a temperate climate. The mollusc fauna, in which also all glacial forms are absent, leads to the same conclusion; all that occur are familiar to us from the earth present day in the same district. These fauna would really appear quite modern were it not that a very ancient stamp is imparted to them by several extinct types. With the modern animals enumerated are associated the cave-lion, cave-hyena, are-elephant and Merckian rhinoceros, characterising the whole deposit as a distinctly Drift one, which is still further proved stratigraphically by the covering of "loess." The Taubach relic-bed is a typical illustration of the climatic and biological conditions of the warmer interglacial period; the regions of central Europe, which had been covered with masses of ice in the first glacial period, had, after the ice melted, become once more accessible to the banished plants and animals of the preglacial period, until they were annihilated, or at least driven definitely from their old habitats, by the second glacial period.

The celebrated relic-bed at the source of the Schussen, near Schussenried, at a little distance from Ulm, brings us — in strong contrast to Taubach — into quite glacial surroundings. It was on the glacier-moraines of the last great glaciation, and belongs therefore to that period which must still be reckoned as part of the Drift, — the postglacial period, which gradually passed into the warmer present period. Under the tufa and peat at the source of the Schussen we find the type of a purely northern climate, with exclusively northern flora and fauna; everything corresponds to climatic conditions such as prevail nowadays on the borders of eternal snow and ice, or begin at 70° north latitude. Schimper, one of the best authorities on mosses at the present day, found among the plant-remains under the tufa at the source of the Schussen only mosses of northern or high alpine forms. Among them was *Hypnum sarmentosum*, which has been brought from Lapland by Wahlenberg, and, according to Schimper, occurs in Norway near the chalets on the Dovrefjeld, on the borders of eternal snow, and also in Greenland, Labrador, and Canada, and on the highest summits of the Tyrolese Alps and the Sudetic Mountains. It has a special preference for the pools in which the water of the snow and glaciers flows off with its fine sand. There were also found *Hypnum aduncum*, var. *groenlandicum*, and *Hypnum fluitans*, var. *tenuissimum*, both mosses which have now emigrated to cold regions, to Greenland and the Alps. The most numerous animals were the reindeer, and yellow and arctic foxes, as distinctly arctic forms; and there were also the brown bear and wolf, a small ox, the hare, the large-headed wild horse, — which always occurs in the Drift as the companion of the reindeer, — and lastly the whistling swan, which now breeds in Spitzbergen or Lapland. There is an absence of all the present animal forms of upper Swabia, as well as of the extinct Drift animals, either of which would indicate a warmer climate.

More decided climatic or biological contrasts than those afforded by the relic-beds at Taubach and the source of the Schussen could not be imagined; here we have with certainty two perfectly different periods before us, but both belonging to the general Drift epoch.

Although almost all the other places where Drift Man has been found exhibit peculiarities, Taubach and the source of the Schussen seem the best representatives of the two chief types in Europe; places giving better proof have not yet come to light anywhere in the Old World.

At first sight the palæontological strata of South America, in which the presence of Man has been proved by Ameghino, appear to give a very different picture. The animal forms occurring here contemporaneously with Man deviate to such an extent from those familiar to us in the Drift of the Old World that it required the keen eye, and the complete grasp of the whole palæontological material of the world, that characterise Von Zittel to recognise and establish the connections here, while the discoverer himself thought that he must date his discoveries of Man back to the Tertiary period.

The strata in which the earliest traces of Man as yet appear proved in South America are the extensive "loess-like" loam deposits of the so-called "pampas" formation in Argentina and Uruguay with their almost incomparable wealth of animal remains, particularly conspicuous among which are gigantic representatives of edentates that now occur only in small species in South America: Glyptodontia (with the gigantic *Glyptodon reticulatum*) and Dasypoda, and of the Gravigrada the giant sloth (*Megatherium americanum*). The Toxodontia were also large animals now extinct (ungulates). But besides the specifically South American forms numerous "North American immigrants" also appear in the pampas formation. It was only at the close of the Tertiary period that the southern and northern halves of America grew together into one continent, and the faunæ of North and South America, so characteristically different, then began to intermingle with one another. The South American autochthons migrate northward; on the other hand North American types — as the horse, deer, tapir, mastodon, *Felis*, *Canis*, etc. — use the newly opened passage to extend their range of distribution. The northern animal forms are very conspicuous among the animal world of South America, hitherto cut off from North America and characterised by the above-mentioned wonderful and, in part, gigantic edentates, marsupials, platyrhine apes, etc. Of the great elephantine animals of North America only the mastodon crossed over to South America. In the middle and latest Tertiary formations the genus mastodon is widely distributed over Europe, north Africa, and south Asia. In North America the oldest species of the mastodon appear in the middle Tertiary (Upper Miocene), but the most species are found in the latest Tertiary (Pliocene) and the Drift (Pleistocene); in South America the mastodon (*M. americanus*) is limited to the time of the pampas formation. Its tusks are long and straight, or slightly curved upward; its lower jaw also possesses two tusks — permanent in many species, but only in youth in the case of *Mastodon americanus* — which project in a straight direction, but are considerably less than the upper tusks in size. From the results of Ameghino's investigations Man appears (according to Von Zittel) to have come to South America with these northern immigrants, especially with the mastodon. In Ameghino's lists of the animals of the pampas formation Von Zittel describes Man, like the animal forms enumerated above, as an immigrant from North America, as a northern type.

According to Von Zittel's statements there is no longer any doubt that the pampas formation, and with it early Man of South America, is to be assigned to the Drift epoch; he sums up the case in these words:

"In south Asia and South America the Tertiary period is followed by Drift faunæ, which in the main are composed of species still existing at the present day, but yet show somewhat closer relations to their Tertiary predecessors."

## *C.* Human Relics in the Drift

*a, Find in the Stratified Drift.* — The oldest remains affording us knowledge of Man are not part of his body, — not the skeleton from which, in the case of primeval animals, we have learned to reconstruct their frame, — but evidences of the human mind.

Until the discoveries of Boucher de Perthes turned the scale, search had been made in vain among the bones of the fossil fauna for remains of the skeleton of fossil Man of undoubtedly the same age: it was not bones, but tools, by which the Abbeville antiquary proved that Man had been a "witness of the Flood" in Europe; tools which taught irrefutably that the mental power of fossil Man of the Drift corresponded exactly to the present mind of mankind. The Drift tools prove that even in that early epoch to which we have learned from Boucher to trace him back Man was a complete man. Every discovery made since that time in any part of the world — even those in South America, which show us Man amid perfectly strange animal surroundings — have only confirmed this point.

Boucher de Perthes was an expert archaeologist, and he knew that in Europe, in a very early period of civilisation, men had made their tools and weapons of stone, as many tribes and races in a backward state of civilisation — for example, in South America, the South Sea Islands, and many other places — do at the present day. These stone implements are practically indestructible, and from ancient times manifold superstitions have attached to the curious articles that the peasant turns up out of the earth in ploughing. Such stone weapons were called lightning-stones by the Romans, as they are by country-folk at the present day. Scientific archæology occupied itself with them at an early date. In 1778 Buffon declared the so-called lightning-stones, or thunder-stones, to be the oldest art-productions of primeval Man, and as early as 1734 Mahudel and Mercati had pronounced them to be the weapons of antediluvian Man. Such views determined the line of thought in Boucher's researches. From the very beginning he sought, in the undisturbed Drift beds of his home, not so much for the bones of Drift Man as for his tools, which he suspected to be of the form of the lightning-stones, although he knew that, so far as was hitherto known, these belonged to a very much later epoch, that is, specially to the alluvial or "recent" period.

His expectations were crowned with success. Deep below the mass of overlying loam and sand, right in the strata of gravel and coarse sand, he found stone tools, which without the slightest doubt had been worked by the hand of man for definite and easily recognisable purposes as implements and weapons. Although to a certain extent ruder, they are practically the same forms as the tools, weapons, and implements of stone that we see in use among so-called "savages" of the present day.

It is the tool artificially prepared for a certain purpose that raises Man above the animal world to-day, as it did in the time of the Drift.

Upon his first visit to the relic-beds near Abbeville in the spring of 1859, Lyell had obtained seventy specimens of these stone tools from the chief of them. The tools were all of flint which occurs in abundance in the chalk of the district, and is still obtained and worked for technical purposes at the present day. The worked stones that Boucher found were termed flint or silex tools according to the material of which they were made. They occurred in the particular beds, as Lyell

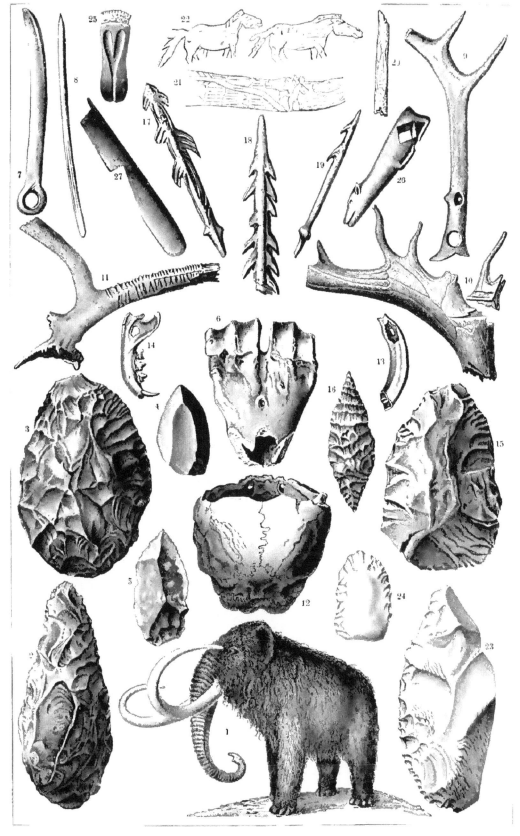

# EXPLANATION OF PLATE A

## (SEE OVER)

1. Mammoth.
2. Stone implement of spear-head form, from the Drift of St Acheul, near Amiens; side view. One-third real size.
3. Oval implement from the Drift of Abbeville; side view. One-third real size.
4. 5. Two stone knives from Taubach, near Weimar.
    4. Outer side.
    5. Inner side.
6. Broken bison's bone from the Drift débris of Taubach, near Weimar. In the centre below, the mark of the blow that broke it.
7. 8. Carvings from reindeer-horn, from the source of the Schussen.
    7. Dagger. One-fourth real size.
    8. Bolt. One-fourth real size.
9. Piece of horn of a young reindeer, doubly perforated, from the source of the Schussen. One-sixth real size.
10. Right crown-palm of an old reindeer with a neighbouring antler sawed off, from the source of the Schussen. One-twelfth real size.
11. Right branch of a reindeer's antlers with marks notched in, from the source of the Schussen. One-sixth real size.

12. Skull of a reindeer worked into a drinking-vessel, from the Hohlefels cave. One-third real size.
13, 14. Bones found in the Hohlefels cave.
    13. Horse's tooth perforated for suspension as an ornament or amulet. One-third real size.
    14. Wild cat's jaw-bone, perforated for same purpose. One-third real size.
15. Axe from St. Acheul, near Amiens; Broca's oldest type of Drift stone implements. Front view.
16. Spear-head from Solutré, chipped on both sides; Broca's latest type of Drift stone implements.
17, 18. Harpoons of reindeer-horn, from La Madelaine. One-fourth real size.
19. Arrow-head from Gorge d'Enfer. One-fourth real size.
20–22. Engravings on reindeer-bone, from the caves of the Dordogne.
    20. Fish.
    21. Man with horses.
    22. Wild horses.
23. 24. Flint implements of the Tasmanians.
25–27. Bone and stone implements of the Alaska Esquimaux.
    25. Scraper with handle.
    26. Arrow-stretcher.
    27. Bone needle for net-knitting.

---

(1 from Credner's "Elemente der Geologie;" 2–22, 25–27 from Ranke's "Mensch;" 23, 24 from the "Journal of the Anthropological Institute," XXXIII., 1893.)

expressed it, in wonderful quantities. The famous geologist distinguished three chief forms. The first is the spear-head form, and varies in length from six to eight inches. The second is the oval form,[1] not unlike many stone implements and weapons that are still used as axes and tomahawks at the present day, — for instance, by the aborigines of Australia. The only difference is that the edge of the Australian stone axes, like that of the European implements of later epochs of civilisation known as thunderbolts or lightning-stones, is mostly produced by grinding, whereas on the stone axes from the Drift of the Somme valley it has always been obtained by simply chipping the stone and by repeated, skilfully directed blows. According to Tylor the stone implements of the old Tasmanians were entirely of Drift (= palæolithic) form and make, all without traces of grinding, being simply angular stones whose cutting-edge had been sharpened by being worked with a second stone. Some of these stone implements of Drift Man may have been simply used in the hand when the natural form of the stone offered a convenient end, but the majority were certainly fastened in a handle in some way or other, to serve as weapons — spear-heads or daggers — both for war and the chase. Lyell's second chief form will have been used as an axe for such purposes as digging up roots, felling trees, and hollowing out canoes, or to cut holes in the ice for fishing and for getting drinking-water in the winter. In the hand of the hunter and warrior the stone axe also became a weapon. As the third form of stone implements Lyell distinguished knife-shaped flakes, some pointed, others more of an oval form or trimmed off evenly at one end, obviously intended to serve partly as knives and arrow-heads, and partly as scrapers for technical purposes.

Although there are many variations between the first two chief forms, yet the typical difference indicating the different purpose of their use is always easily recognised in well-finished examples. A large number of very rude specimens have also been found, of which many may have been thrown away as spoiled in the making, and others may have been only rubbish produced in the working. Evans has practically proved that it is possible to produce such stone implements in their remarkable agreement of form without the use of metal hammers. He made a stone hammer by fastening a flint in a wooden handle, and worked another piece of flint with this until it had assumed the shape of the axe form (second, oval form) of the Drift implements.

Lyell draws attention to the fact that, in spite of the relatively great frequency of stone implements, it would be a great mistake to rely on finding a single specimen, even if one occupied himself for weeks together in examining the Somme valley. Only a few lay on the surface, the rest not coming to light until after removing enormous masses of sand, loam, and gravel. As we may presume with Lyell that the larger number of the Drift stone implements of Abbeville and Amiens were brought into their present position by the action of the river, then this sufficiently explains why such a large portion of them were found at considerable depths below the surface, for they must naturally have been buried in the gravel with the other stones in places where the stream had still sufficient force or rapidity to wash stones away; they can therefore not be found in deposits from still water, in fine sediment and overflow mud.

Bones of Drift Man are absent from the deposits of the Somme valley, in spite of the wonderful abundance of stone implements; the "lower jaw from Moulin-

[1] See Figs. 2 and 3, Plate at p. 120.

Quignon, near Abbeville," had been fraudulently placed there by workmen. But in spite of this want the proof of the existence of Man — of complete Man — is undeniably assured by the objects, so unpretentious in themselves, that have been recognised as the work of his hands, as his own manufactures.

When once the recognition of Drift Man, founded on the authority of Lyell, was achieved, search for further relic-beds was made in England and France with the greatest zeal and with abundant success. Yet scarcely one of the newly discovered stations was to be compared to those of the Somme valley as regards purity of stratification and conditions of discovery; the relics of the "earliest Stone Age" or "palaeolithic period," as the period of Drift Man was called, frequently came from caves and grottos, whose primary conclusiveness Boucher had rightly doubted.

Under these circumstances it was of the greatest importance that in Germany Drift Man was discovered in two places, where not only was the geological stratification just as clear as at Abbeville and Amiens, but where also the relics of Drift Man were found, not in a secondary *situs*, as they were there, but in a primary one. In addition to this the two German relic-beds may be safely assigned to the last two great divisions of the Drift period, to the warmer interglacial period and to the cold glacial period proper with its postglacial period. They are the two already mentioned, — the one near Taubach, the other at the source of the Schussen, — and their climatic conditions were made perfectly clear to us from the remains of plants and animals found in them.

From the occurrence of reindeer in the deposits of the Somme that contain the stone implements of Drift Man we cannot, as we saw, exactly settle in what part of the Drift epoch Man lived there, whether in the interglacial period, to which numerous animal remains found there doubtless belong, or not until the "reindeer" period, as the last glacial and early postglacial periods were called, when the reindeer was most largely distributed over France and central Europe. One is inclined to date Man's habitation of the Somme valley back to the interglacial period; but this much is certain, that the relic-bed near Taubach is the first, and, as far as I can see, the only one hitherto, that has given sure proof of interglacial Man in Europe. There the oldest vestiges of Man in Europe were found that have yet been absolutely proved. We have not hitherto succeeded in Europe in tracing Man farther back than the interglacial period; relics of him are hitherto as absent in the older Drift as they are in the Tertiary.

The Taubach relic-bed also furnished no bones of Drift Man among all the parts of skeletons of Drift animals that we have mentioned above. Here, too, as in the Somme valley, the proof of the presence of Man is based on the works of his hand and mind. Here, too, stone implements and stone weapons are the chief things to be mentioned.[1] But whereas, in the chalk district of France, flints of every size were to be had in the greatest abundance for the preparation of weapons and tools, corresponding stones are not exactly wanting at the two standard German places, but they occur in limited number and size. It is due to this that the larger forms of flint implements, which are most in evidence in the Somme valley, are absent at Taubach. On the other hand smaller "knives and flakes" (Lyell's third form of Drift flint implements) occur here with comparative frequency and variety of form. Next to the usual lancet-shaped knife, worked flint flakes, of triangular prismatic

[1] See Figs. 4 and 5, Plate at p. 120.

form with sharp corners, are most numerous at Taubach, and scrapers, chisels, awls, and the chipping-stones with which the stone implements were produced, may also be distinguished among other things. The material for the implements was supplied by the older Drift débris of the valley, namely, flint, flinty slate, and quartz-porphyry.

Besides the stone implements, which alone were observed in the Somme valley, still further important relics were found here in their primary *situs*. Above all, numerous finds of charcoal and burnt bones prove that the Drift men of Taubach not only knew how to kindle fire, but were also accustomed to roast the flesh of animals they killed in the chase. Stones and pieces of shell-limestone also occur, which have become reddish and hard from the action of heat; these are to be regarded as the floors and side-walls of the fireplaces on which the food was then and there prepared. The animal bones, especially those that were taken up from around the fireplaces, appear in most cases to be remains of meals. This is shown at once by the fact that bones of young representatives of the large beasts of the chase — such as the rhinoceros (*Rhinoceros Merckii*), elephant (*Elephas antiquus*), and bear — are very frequent as compared with the rare occurrence of full-grown animals. It appears that in the hunting and capture of animals the young ones were most easily killed, and therefore served chiefly as food. Whenever a large animal was killed, it was probably cut up on the spot by the fortunate hunters, who consumed at once part of its flesh; the trunk was then left at the scene of the killing, while the head, neck, and fore and hind legs, on which was the most muscular flesh, and which were at the same time easier to carry away, were taken to the settlement. This may explain why, among the many large bones of the rhinoceros that have hitherto been found, the ribs and the dorsal and lumbar vertebræ are almost entirely absent. Some of the bones of the beasts of the chase bear the unmistakable traces of Man. They are broken in the manner characteristic of "savages" of all ages and climes, for the sake of the marrow, one of the greatest dainties of men living chiefly on animal fare. The broken-off heads of the metatarsal bones of the bison (*Bison priscus*) still show particularly clearly the method of breaking. They are broken off transversely exactly where the marrow canal ends, and on all these bones there is a roundish depression or hole at the same place, — namely, in the middle of their front or back surface, and just where the end of the marrow canal is, therefore about in the centre of the break of the broken-off piece. The hole is a "blow-mark" of one inch in diameter, evidently driven in by force from without, as several well-preserved specimens still show the edges and splinters of bone pressed inward.[1] These splinters and all the breaks are old, and have on the surface the same greasy coating, full of the sand in which they lay, as the bones themselves. The instrument that was used for breaking the bones in this way might very well have been the lower jaw of a bear with its large canine tooth, as Oscar Fraas has ascertained to have been the case in other places where Drift Man has been found. Such lower jaws were found at Taubach, and the nature and size of the hole and its edges agree with this assumption. The long bones of the elephant and rhinoceros were whole; Drift Man did not succeed in breaking these huge pieces, and where such bones are found broken they are accidental fractures. On the other hand almost all bones of the bear and bison are intentionally split, — in almost all cases transversely, and seldom lengthways.

[1] See Fig. 6, Plate at p. 120.

In the Somme valley we have only the flint implements — which, although rude, are very regularly and uniformly made for different recognisable purposes — to tell us of the life and state of Drift Man; but the finds at Taubach afford us a rather closer insight into the conditions of his life and culture. What we had suspected from the first finds is confirmed here. During the interglacial period we see here at Taubach, on the old watercourse of the Ilm, which had there at that time been dammed up into a kind of pond, a human settlement. This was occupied for a long period, as is proved by the large number of bones, which are evidently the remains of meals and by the quantity of charcoal. Immediately on the bank were the fireplaces, rude hearths built of the stones obtained without trouble in the neighbourhood. Here the flesh of the beasts of the chase, the bison and the boar, and also the elephant and rhinoceros, was broiled in a crude manner in the hot ashes, as is still done by savages on the level of the Fuegians and primitive tribes of central Brazil at the present day. For this no utensils are required, a sharpened rod or thin pointed stick being sufficient for turning and taking out the pieces of meat; the ashes that the gravy causes to adhere supply the place of salt and other seasoning. The meat was cut up with the stone knives, and many traces of cuts on the bones may also be attributable to these instruments. For cutting out larger portions a powerful and very suitable instrument was at hand in the lower jaw of the bear, with its strong canine tooth, which also served for breaking bones to obtain the marrow. In spite of the apparent meanness of the weapons, remains of which we have found, the Drift men of Taubach were yet able, as their kitchen refuse proves, not only to kill the bison and bear, but also the gigantic elephant and rhinoceros both young and full-grown. This shows Man to have been then, as he is to-day, master even of the gigantic animal forms which so far surpass him in mechanical strength. It is the mind of Man that shows itself superior to the most powerful brute force, even where we meet him for the first time. From the finds in the Somme valley it appears that Drift Man already possessed spear, dagger, and axe, besides the knife, as weapons. There the blades were of stone. The relatively small blades of the Taubach stone implements are, it is true, of the same character as the stone implements of Abbeville and Amiens, but they are chiefly, as we have said, merely knife-like articles, very suitable as blades for knives, scrapers, and daggers, and as arrow-heads, but not strong enough as hunting-weapons for such big game. The hunt will therefore have been more a matter of capture in pits and traps, as practised at the present day where similar large types of animals are hunted by tribes armed only with defective weapons. The kitchen refuse also proves that the settlement by the Ilm pond near Taubach was a permanent one, to which the hunters returned after their expeditions, bringing their game and trophies so far as they were easily transportable. But there is no trace of domestic animals. They could not have completely disappeared any more than remains of clay vessels, which are still less destructible than bones, and in this respect may be compared to stone implements; there was no trace of potsherds either.

The finds in the Somme valley and near Taubach are of incalculable importance as sure, indisputable proofs of Drift Man in Europe; but as regards the wealth of information to be derived from them respecting Man's psychical condition in that first period in which we can prove his existence, they are far and away surpassed by the find at the source of the Schussen, which Oscar Fraas, the celebrated geologist, has personally inventoried and described. Fraas has rightly given to his description of this find of glacial Man — the most important and best examined hitherto — the title "Contributions to the History of Civilisation during the Glacial Period." [1]

The geognostic stratification of the relic-bed on one of the farthest advanced moraines of the upper Swabian plateau proves that it belongs to the glacial period, and that this had already pushed its glacier-moraines to the farthest limit ever reached. In point of time the finds are therefore to be placed at the end of the glacial period, as it was passing into the postglacial period; everything still points to far-northern conditions of life. The finds at the source of the Schussen are therefore decidedly more recent geologically than those made at Taubach; they are a typical or, better, *the* typical example of the so-called "reindeer period" of the end of the Drift.

From Fraas's description there seems to be no doubt whatever that the relic-bed, with its remains of civilisation, was perfectly undisturbed, and its palæonto-logical contents plainly show its great geological age. It was perfectly protected by nature. On the top lies peat, the same that covers the lowlands of the whole neighbourhood for miles and forms the extensive moorlands of upper Swabia, on which no other formations are to be seen than the gravel drift-walls thrown up by glaciers of the Drift period. Under the peat lies a layer of calc-tufa four to five feet thick, a fresh-water formation from the watercourses that now unite with the source of the Schussen. Under this protecting cover of tufa were the remains of the glacial period and glacial Man. The tufa covered a bed of moss of a dark-brown colour inclining to green, the moss still splendidly preserved; under this bed of moss was the glacier-drift. The moss was drip-ping full of water, and intermingled with moist sand. In it were the relics of glacial Man — all lying in heaps as fresh and firm as if they had been only recently collected. A sticky dark-brown mud filled the moss and sand and the smallest hollow spaces of antlers and bones, and emitted a musty smell. Glacial Man had used the place as a refuse-pit. Among the bones and splinters of bone of animals that had been slaughtered and consumed by Man, among ashes and charred remains, among smoke-stained hearthstones and the traces of fire, there lay here, one upon the other, numerous knives, arrow-heads, and lance-heads of flint, and the most various kinds of hand-made articles of reindeer horn.[2] All this was in a shallow pit about seven hundred square yards in extent and only four to five feet deep in the purest glacier-drift, clearly showing that the excel-lent preservation of the bones and bone implements was solely due to the water having remained in the moss and sand. The bank of moss was like a saturated sponge; it closed up its contents hermetically from the air, and preserved in its ever-damp bosom what had been entrusted to it thousands of years before.

Under the peat and tufa at the source of the Schussen we find only the type of a purely northern climate, with only northern flora and northern fauna. There are no remains of domestic animals, — not even of the dog, nor any bones of the stag, roe, chamois, or ibex. Everything corresponds to a northern climate, such as begins to-day at 70° north latitude. We set upper

[1] "Beiträge zur Kulturgeschichte des Menschen während der Eiszeit."
[2] See Figs. 7-9, Plate at p. 120.

Swabia traversed by moraines and melting glaciers, whose waters wash the glacier-sand into moss-grown pools. We find a Greenland moss covering the wet sands in thick banks: between the moraines of the glaciers we have to imagine wide green pastures, rich enough to support herds of reindeer, which roved about there as they do in Greenland or on the forest borders of Norway and Siberia at the present day. Here also are the regions of the carnivora dangerous to the reindeer,—the glutton and the wolf, and, in the second rank, the bear and arctic fox.

According to Fraas it is on this scene that Man of the glacial period appears, in all probability a hunter invited by the presence of the reindeer to spend some time (probably only the better portion of the year) on the borders of ice and snow. It is true that the relic-bed that tells of his life and doings is only a refuse-pit which contains nothing good in the way of art productions, but only broken or spoiled articles and refuse from the manufacture of implements; the bulk of the material consists of kitchen refuse, such as, besides charcoal and ashes, opened marrow-bones and broken skulls of game. Not one of the bones found here shows a trace of any other instrument than a stone. It was on a stone that the bone was laid, and it was with a stone that the blow was struck. Such breaking-stones came to light in large numbers. They were merely field stones collected on the spot, particular preference being given to finely rolled quartz boulders of about the size of a man's fist. Others were rather rudely formed into the shape of a club, with a kind of handle such as is produced half accidentally and half intentionally in splitting large pieces. Larger stones were also found: gneiss slabs from one to two feet square, slaty Alpine limes, and rough blocks of one stone or another, which had probably represented slaughtering-blocks or done duty as hearthstones, as on many of them traces of fire were visible. Where these stones had stood near the fire they were scaled, and all were more or less blackened by charcoal. Smaller pieces of slate and slabs of sandstone blackened by fire may have supplied the place of clay pottery in many respects; for with all the blackened stones not a fragment of a clay vessel was found in the layers of charcoal and ashes of the relic-bed.

The flint implements are of the form familiar to us from Taubach and the Somme valley, being simply chipped, not ground or polished. At the source of the Schussen, also, only comparatively small pieces of the precious raw material were found for the manufacture of stone implements. So that here too, as at Taubach, Lyell's third form, the knife or flake, was practically the only one represented. They fall into two groups,—pointed lancet-shaped knives and blunt saw-shaped stones. The former served as knife-blades and dagger-blades, and lance-heads and arrow-heads; the latter represented the blades of the tools required for working reindeer horn. The larger implements are between $1\frac{1}{4}$ and $1\frac{1}{2}$ inches broad and 3 to $3\frac{1}{2}$ inches long; but the majority of them are far smaller, being about $1\frac{1}{2}$ inches long and only three eighths of an inch broad. The various flint blades appear to have been used in handles and hafts of reindeer horn; numerous pieces occur which can only be explained as such handles, either ready or in course of manufacture. Moreover, owing to the want of larger flints, numerous weapons, instruments, and implements were carved from reindeer horn and bone for use in the chase and in daily life. Fraas has ascertained most exactly the technical process employed in producing articles of reindeer horn, and we see with wonder how the glacial men of Swabia handled their defective carving-knives and saws on the very principle of modern technics. A glance at Figure 10 of the plate "Palæolithic Antiquities"[1] affords an illustration of the manner of procedure employed and of the various forms of articles produced. They are principally weapons,— for example, long pointed bone daggers, otherwise mostly punchers, awls, plaiting-needles (of wood), and arrow-heads with notched grooves. These may possibly be poison-grooves; other transverse grooves may have served partly for fastening the arrow-head by means of some thread-like binding material, probably twisted from reindeer sinews, as is done by the Reindeer Lapps at the present day; other scratches occur as ornaments. The forms of the bone implements show generally a decided sense of symmetry and a certain taste; for instance, a dagger with a perforated knob for suspension, and a large carefully carved fish-hook. Groove-like or hollow spoon-shaped pieces of horn were explained by Fraas to be cooking and eating utensils; probably they also served for certain technical purposes — as for dressing skins for clothing and tents, like the stone scrapers found in the Somme valley. A doubly perforated piece of a young reindeer's antler appears to be an arrow-stretching apparatus, like the ones, generally finely ornamented, used by the Esquimaux for the same purpose. A branch of a reindeer's antlers with deep notches filed in is declared by the discoverer to be a "tally;"[2] the notches are partly simple strokes filed in to the depth of a twelfth of an inch, and partly two main strokes connected by finer ones. "The strokes," says Fraas, "are plainly numeral signs, a kind of note, probably of reindeer or bears killed, or some other memento." Among the objects found were also pieces of red paint of the size of a nut, clearly fabrications of clayey ironstone ground and washed, and probably mixed with reindeer fat and kneaded into a paste. The paint crumbled between the fingers, felt greasy, and coloured the skin an intense red; it may have been used in the first instance for painting the body.

The glacial men at the source of the Schussen were, according to the results of these finds, fishermen and hunters, without dogs or domestic animals and without any knowledge of agriculture and pottery. But they understood how to kindle fire, which they used for cooking their food. They knew how to kill the wild reindeer, bear, and other animals of the district they hunted over; their arrows hit the swan, and their fish-hooks drew fish from the deep. They were artists in the chipping of flint into tools and weapons; with the former they worked reindeer horn in the most skilful manner. Traces of binding material indicate the use of threads, probably prepared from reindeer sinews; the plaiting-needle may have been employed for making fishing-lines. Threads and finely pointed pricking-instruments indicate the art of sewing; clothing probably consisted of the skins of the animals killed.

To this material, scientifically vouched for, concerning Drift Man, coming from Drift strata that have certainly never been disturbed, other countries have hitherto made no equal contributions really enlarging our view. Yet the numerous places where palæolithic — that is, only rudely chipped — implements of flint, such as were doubtless used by Drift Man, have been found must not remain unmentioned here; we know of them in northern, central, and southern France, in the south of England, in the "loess" at Thiede, near Brunswick, and in lower Austria, Moravia, Hungary, Italy, Greece, Spain, Portugal, north Africa, and Russia.

---

[1] See p. 120.   [2] See Fig. 11, Plate at p. 120.

It is of special importance to note that similar flint tools have also been found along with extinct land mammalia in the stratified Drift of the Nerbudda valley in south India, as the supposition more than suggests itself that Drift Man came to our continent with the Drift fauna that immigrated from Asia. The possibility that Man also got from north Asia to North America with the mammoth during the Drift period can no longer be dismissed after the results of palæontological research; it explains at once the close connection between the build of the American and the build of the great Asiatic (Mongolian) race.

Stone implements of palæolithic form have been found in Drift strata in North America, and the same applies also, as we have seen, to South America. The best finds there were those made by Ameghino in the Pampas formation of Argentina. Here marrow-bones, split, worked, and burnt, and jaws of the stag, glyptodon, mastodon, and toxodon have been repeatedly found along with flint tools of palæolithic stamp; and Santiago Roth, who took part in these researches, supposes that fossil Man in South America occasionally used the coats of mail of the gigantic armadillos as dwellings. But the civilisation of South American Man is doubtless identical with that of European fossil Man: tools and weapons of the stone types familiar in Europe, the working of bones, the use of fire for cooking, and animal food with the consequent special fondness for fat and marrow.

(b) *The Cave Finds.* — To the picture of Drift Man that has been drawn for us by the discoveries of human activity in deposits of uniform character and sharply defined age, the much richer but far less reliable finds in the bone caves add scarcely any entirely new touches. Von Zittel says:

"The evidence of the caves is unfortunately shaken by the uncertainty that, as a rule, prevails with regard to the manner in which their contents were washed into them or otherwise introduced, and also with regard to the beginning and duration of their occupation; moreover later inhabitants have frequently mixed up their relics with the heritage of previous occupants."

This doubt strikes us particularly forcibly as regards Man's co-existence with the extinct animals of the earlier periods of the Drift, the preglacial and interglacial periods. On the other hand the habitation of the caves by Man during the reindeer period appears in many cases to be perfectly established, and according to Von Zittel the oldest human dwellings in caves, rock-niches, and river-plains in Europe belong for the most part to the reindeer period, — that is, the second glacial and, in particular, the postglacial period. In many of the best-examined caves — for instance, in the caves and rock-niches of the Périgord and in the palæolithic strata of the caves near Schaffhausen — we even meet with quite pure, unmixed conditions for the reindeer period.

In the caves there is also no domestic animal, and no pottery or trace of potsherds, in the best-defined strata where Drift Man has been found. In the Hohlefels cave, in the Ach valley in Swabia, Oscar Fraas has clearly identified numbers of lower jaws of the cave-bear in the form of weapons and slaughter-axes; many bones bear unmistakable traces of them in round holes with the edges bent inward. A new utensil was found here in the form of a cup for drinking purposes or for drawing water, made out of the back part of a reindeer's skull.[1] Also a

---

[1] See Fig. 12, Plate at p. 120.

new tool in the form of a fine sewing-needle with eye, from the long bone of a swan, such as have also been found in the caves of the Périgord. Teeth of the wild horse and lower jaws of the wildcat, which are found in the caves, perforated for suspending either as ornaments or amulets, are also hitherto unknown, it appears, in the stratified Drift. As both animals are at a later period connected with the deity and with witchcraft, one could imagine that similar primitive religious ideas existed among the old cave-dwellers. In the stratum of the reindeer period at the Schweizerbild near Schaffhausen, Nüesch found a musical instrument — "a reindeer whistle " — and shells pierced for use as ornaments. The finds in the French cave districts prove that in the real flint districts — where a very suitable material was at Man's disposal in the flint that lay about everywhere or was easily dug up, and which was worked with comparative ease into much more perfect and efficient weapons and implements than those supplied by the far wilder stretches of moor and fen of Germany, with their scarcity of flint — Man was able to develop certain higher refinements of life, even during the Drift. If we compare the small, often tiny knives and flint flakes from the German places with the powerful axes and lance-heads of those regions, it is self-evident how much more laborious life must have been for the man who used the former. What labour he must have expended in carving weapons and implements out of bone and horn, while flint supplied the others with much better and more lasting ones with less expenditure of time and trouble! In this light a wealth of flint was a civilising factor of that period which is not to be underestimated. In the flint districts not only are the stone implements better worked, and answer in a higher degree the purpose of the weapon and the tool, but delight in ornament and decoration is also more prominent.

In the way of ornaments [1] we find perforated teeth of the horse and bear, and also of the wild ox, ibex, and reindeer. The finely coloured fluor-spars that have been found in the caves must also be mentioned here. Some of the bone implements are ornamented in a characteristic manner. Even the stone blades, like the famous ones of the Solutré type, — of which, moreover, a specimen has also occurred among other Drift finds in the Ofnet cave near Nördlingen, — show in the regularity with which they are chipped an attempt to arrange the surfaces of the breaks ornamentally, leading, in the later Stone Age, to the production of the neat herring-bone pattern on the finest specimens of flint daggers and lance-heads. The ornamental grooves on the many-toothed harpoon-heads may have partly had their origin in poison-grooves; other band ornaments crossing the shaft of the harpoon-head imitate the threads with which flint flakes were fastened on it as points and hooks, such as are familiar in later periods of civilisation. The harpoons of Drift Man correspond very closely to those of the Esquimaux and Fuegians.

Life in the caves and grottos and under the rock-shelters in the neighbourhood of rivers was by no means quite wretched. Lubbock and Boyd Dawkins speak with positive enthusiasm of the abundant accumulations of relics from the Drift in the caves on the banks of the Vézère. The remains left in the caves by their former inhabitants give almost as clear an idea of the life of Man in those primeval times as the buried cities of Herculaneum and Pompeii do of the manners and customs of the Italians in the first century of the Christian era. The floors of these caves in which men formerly lived appear to consist entirely of broken bones of

[1] See Figs. 13–19, Plate at p. 120.

animals killed in the chase, intermixed with rude implements and weapons of bone and unpolished stone, and also charcoal and large burnt stones indicating the position of fireplaces. Flints and chips without number, rough masses of stone, awls, lance-heads, hammers, and saws of flint and chert lie in motley confusion beside bone needles, carved reindeer antlers, arrow-heads and harpoons, and pointed pieces of horn and bone; in addition to which are also the broken bones of the animals that served as food, such as reindeer, bison, horse, ibex, saiga antelope, and musk-ox. In some cases the whole is cemented into a firm mass with calc-sinter. The reindeer supplied by far the greater part of the food, and must at that time have lived in central France in large herds and in a wild state, all trace of the dog being absent there as at the source of the Schussen.

Among these abundant remains of culture archæologists were surprised to find real objects of art from the hand of Drift Man, proving that thinking about his surroundings had developed into the ability to reproduce what he saw in drawing and modelling. The first objects of this kind were found in the caves of the Périgord.[1] They are, on the one hand, drawings scratched on stones, reindeer bones, or pieces of horn, mostly very naïve, but sometimes really lifelike, chiefly representing animals, but also men; on the other hand imitations plastically carved out of pieces of reindeer horn, bones, or teeth. Such engravings also occurred on pieces of ivory, and plastic representations in this material have been preserved. On a cylindrical piece of reindeer horn from the cave excavations in the Dordogne is the representation of a fish, and on the shovel-piece of a reindeer's horn are the head and breast of an animal resembling the ibex. Illustrations of horses give faithful reproductions of the flowing mane, unkempt tail, and disproportionately large head of the large-headed wild horse of the Drift. Of the plastic representations the first as regards beauty is the carved handle of a long, well-preserved dagger of reindeer horn, representing in a conventionalised and yet lifelike manner the death of a young reindeer, just collapsing; in form also it is perfectly adapted to the requirements of a handle. On another handle is the head of a musk-ox. A double representation has on one side a small roe's head, and on the other a small hare's head with the ears laid laterally. Engravings on stone, reindeer bones, and pieces of horn were also found—and in some cases were proved to be absolutely genuine—in the Kesslerloch and in the reindeer stratum at the Schweizerbild, both near Schaffhausen.

The most important among these representations are such as endeavour to reproduce an historical event. An illustration of this kind represents a group consisting of two horses' heads and an apparently naked male figure; the latter bears a long staff or spear in his right hand, and stands beside a tree, which is bent down almost in coils in order to accommodate itself to the limited space, and whose boughs, indicated by parallel lines, show it to be a pine or fir. Connected with the tree is a system of vertical and horizontal lines, apparently representing a kind of hurdlework. On the other side of the same cylindrical piece are two bisons' heads. Doubtless this picture tells a tale; it is picture-writing in exactly the same sense as that of the North American Indians. Our picture already shows the transition to abbreviated picture-writing, as, instead of the whole animals,—horses and bisons,—only the heads are given. The message-sticks of the

---

[1] See Figs. 20-27, Plate at p. 120.

Australians bear certain resemblances; Bastian has rightly described them as the beginnings of writing.

If we have interpreted them aright, the finds that have been made, with the tally from the source of the Schussen and the message-stick from the caves of the Dordogne, place the art of counting, the beginnings of writing, the first artistic impulses, and other elements of primitive culture right back in the Drift period.

"None of the animals whose remains lie in the Drift strata," says Oscar Fraas, "were tamed for the service of Man." On the contrary, Man stood in hostile relation to all of them, and only knew how to kill them, in order to support himself with their flesh and blood and the marrow of their bones. It was not so much his physical strength which helped Man in his fight for existence, for with few exceptions the animals he killed were infinitely superior to him in strength; indeed it is not easy, even with the help of powder and lead, to kill the elephant, rhinoceros, grizzly bear, and bison, or to hunt down the swift horse and reindeer. It was a question of finding out, with his mental superiority, the beast's unguarded moments, and of surprising it or bringing it down in pits and snares. All the more wonderful does the savage of the European Drift period appear to us, "for we see that he belongs to the first who exercised the human mind in the hard battle of life, and thereby laid the foundation of all later development in the sense of progress in culture." And yet, in the midst of this poor life, a sense of the little pleasures and refinements of existence already began to develop, as proved by the elegantly carved and decorated weapons and implements, and there were even growing a sense of the beauty of nature and the power of copying it.

The bone needles with eyes and the fine awls are evidences of the art of sewing, and the numerous scrapers of flint and bone teach us that Drift Man knew how to dress skins for clothing purposes, and did it according to the method still used among the Esquimaux and most northern Indians at the present day. Spinning does not seem to have been known. On the other hand Drift Man knew how to twist cords, impressions and indentations of which are conspicuous on the bone and horn implements; on which also thread-marks were imitated as a primitive ornament. Pottery was unknown to Drift Man. Indeed, even to-day the production of pottery is not a commonly felt want of mankind. The leather bottle, made of the skin of some small animal stripped off whole without a seam, turned inside out as it were, takes the place of the majority of the larger vessels; on the other hand liquids can also be kept for some time in a tightly made wicker basket. The art of plaiting was known to Drift Man. This is shown by the ornaments on weapons and implements, the plaiting-needle from the find at the source of the Schussen, and the hurdlework represented on the message-stick mentioned above, which may be either a hurdle made of boughs and branches or a summer dwelling-house. To these acquirements, based chiefly on an acquaintance with serviceable weapons and implements, is added the art of representing natural objects by drawing and carving. This results in the attempt to retain historical *momenta* in the form of abridged illustrations for the purpose of communicating them to others, — incipient picture-writing. The tally shows the method of representing numbers, — generally only one stroke each, but also two strokes connected by a line to form a higher unit. Of the art of building not a trace is left to us apart from the laying together of rough stones for fireplaces, nor have tombs of that period of ancient times been discovered.

(c) *Palæolithic Men of the Present.* — The civilisation of Drift Man and his whole manner of life do not confront the present human race as something strange, but fit perfectly into the picture exhibited by mankind at the present day. Drift Man nowhere steps out of this frame. If a European traveller were nowadays to come upon a body of Drift men on the borders of eternal ice, toward the north or south pole of our globe, nothing would appear extraordinary and without analogy to him; indeed it would be possible for him to come to an understanding with them by means of picture-writing, and to do business with them by means of the tally.

The manner of life led by Man beyond the borders of higher civilisation, especially under extreme climatic conditions, depends almost exclusively on his outward surroundings and the possibility of obtaining food. The Esquimaux, who, like Drift Man of central Europe in former times, live on the borders of eternal ice with the Drift animals that emigrated thither, — the reindeer, musk-ox, bear, arctic fox, etc., — are restricted, like him, to hunting and fishing, and to a diet consisting almost entirely of flesh and fat; corn-growing and the keeping of herds of domestic animals being self-prohibitive. Their kitchen refuse exactly resembles that from the Drift. Before their acquaintance with the advanced civilisation of modern Europe they used stone and bone besides driftwood for making their weapons and implements, as they still do to a certain extent at the present day, either from preference or from superstitious ideas. Their binding material consisted of threads twisted from reindeer sinews, with which they sewed their clothes and fastened their harpoons and arrows, the latter resembling in form those of Drift Man. They knew no more than he the arts of spinning and weaving, their clothes being made from the skins of the animals they hunted; pots were unknown and unnecessary to them. The celebrated Arctic explorer Kane gives an inventory of the furniture and arrangement of an Esquimau hut that he inspected:

"A vessel of sealskin for collecting and storing water; the shoulder-blade of a walrus serving as a lamp; a flat stone to support it; a second large, thin, smooth stone on which to lay snow to melt for drinking-water; a lance-head with a long band of walrus thong; a clothes-hanger and the skin clothes of the people, — these comprise all the earthly goods of this family."

But the walrus thong shows pretty ornamental plaiting, and the clothes are nicely worked, being both fine and serviceable after the fashion of Arctic people. The skins are dressed with the help of a stone scraper, whose exact counterpart every excavation in the strata of Drift Man supplies in numbers; the needles are likewise of bone. Moreover the Esquimaux show the same delight in representing things by figures and drawings, in carving and engraving; they do their engravings on blocks of every description, such as tablets of driftwood or bones, and these engravings, like those of Drift Man, not only represent single animals of the chase, but also historical scenes with Man, in the sense of picture-writing.

The Fuegians on the glaciers of the southern hemisphere live almost in the same manner, except that on the one hand they appear to be still poorer, and their artistic sense is apparently less developed, and that on the other hand they have the dog as a domestic animal. They, too, have no pottery; their weapons and implements correspond partly with those from the Drift strata of the French caves.

Even under other climatic conditions a very similar culture may be evolved. Edward Burnett Tylor undertook to prove that the state of civilisation of many primitive peoples at the present day faithfully reflects the conditions of life of the men of the Stone Age in general, and of palæolithic (Drift) Man in particular. He established the fact that the stone tools of the Tasmanians, of which a collection of about one hundred and fifty were at his disposal for comparison, are of a perfectly palæolithic character.[1] They are strong stone chips, on one side flat with the bulb of percussion, on the other having a raised middle edge, rudely worked into spear-head form (Broca's Moustier type). The material of which the Tasmanian stone implements are made consists partly of a clayish stone, comparatively not very hard, and partly of flint or quartzite. None of these tools show traces of grinding or polish; all are, like those from the Drift, simple angular stones, whose cutting edge is sharpened by chipping it with a second stone. These stone implements may have been set in handles as stone axes; it is known for certain that in use they were also simply held in the hand without a handle, — for instance, in flaying the kangaroo, between the thumb and forefinger. Even in the first half of the present century the Tasmanians represented a people that had not passed the palæolithic stage of civilisation. Further progress was first brought to them by immigrating Australians, who here play the part of bearers of civilisation.

The hope has often been expressed that some day the corpse of a man from the Drift — a contemporary of the mammoth with the woolly fur and of the woolly-haired rhinoceros — might be found frozen in the stone-ice of northern Siberia. We put the question: Should we identify such a corpse with certainty as that of a man of the glacial period? Even if it were found in the stone-ice beside the carcasses of extinct Drift animals, this of itself would prove nothing. We know that crevasses are formed in inland ice as well as in Alpine glaciers; new crevasses are formed before our eyes, as it were, and the number of ice-travellers who disappear for ever in such crevasses, and are preserved in them like those animals, is by no means small. Even in the Alps only a small proportion of those who fall into glacier crevasses are got out again dead or alive, and how rarely can one be saved from the crevasses of Arctic ice! If the corpse of an Arctic explorer, who had penetrated from civilised lands into the regions of eternal ice, were to be found buried in the ice, his fur clothing, which would be adapted to the Arctic climate, would not identify him as a civilised man, but possibly numerous small signs of civilisation — such as watch, pocket-knife, buckles, and buttons — would do so. On the other hand the body of an Esquimau, frozen in the ice there before acquaintance was made with modern civilisation, would show no definite characteristics distinguishing him from glacial Man; certainly not his stone implements, these belongings of primitive civilisation being as good as identical in both cases, as we pointed out with regard to the stone scrapers for preparing skins.

It has often been thought that we should have a definite criterion of the period if it could be proved that fresh mammoth ivory was employed at the particular time for making implements and weapons, or ornaments, carvings, and drawings. There can be no doubt that when Drift Man succeeded in killing a mammoth he used the tusks for his purposes. But on the borders of eternal ice, where alone we could now expect to find a frozen Drift Man, no conclusion could be drawn from objects of mammoth ivory being in the possession of a corpse to determine the great age of the latter. For the many mammoth tusks which have been found and used from time immemorial in north Siberia, on the New Siberian

---

[1] See Figs. 23 and 24, Plate at p. 120.

Islands, and in other places, are absolutely fresh, and are even employed in the arts of civilised countries in exactly the same way as fresh ivory. Under the name of "mammoth ivory" the fossil tusks dug up by ivory-seekers (mammoth-hunters) form an important article of commerce. According to Middendorf more than a hundred pairs of tusks yearly have been placed on the market from Siberia for the last two hundred years. The ground of the Bear and Liachow Islands is literally full of mammoth bones; as soon as the ice on the coasts is thawed by the sun they are found in abundance. A considerable number of our most modern ivories are made from such fossil mammoth ivory, and the eye of an expert could not prove, even from the piece of ivory used, whether it was carved immediately upon the death of the animal or from the tusks preserved in the ice many thousands of years after. Moreover the northern Asiatics are accustomed at the present day to use mammoth ivory for the handles of their stone implements and other things, particularly for small carvings and works of art, which are extraordinarily like those that have been found in the Drift caves. Jakobsen brought a rich haul of such articles of stone, mammoth ivory, and reindeer horn back with him from the Alaska Esquimaux,[1] and the Samoyedes have carved spoons and all kinds of utensils from mammoth ivory from the earliest times. Indeed they use the skin of the mammoth carcasses preserved in the frozen ground as leather for the harness of their dogs and reindeer, the fat for greasing purposes, and the flesh to feed their dogs with.

The same conditions as many parts of northern Siberia still exhibit at the present day prevailed over the whole of central Europe at the end of the glacial period and the beginning of the postglacial period; the find at the source of the Schussen bears unexceptionable testimony to such having been the character of the climate in central Europe at that time. Here Man lived on frozen ground on the borders of ice-fields with the reindeer and its companions, as he does to-day in northern Asia, and here, too, — as he does there to-day, — he must have found the woolly-haired mammoth preserved by the cold in the ice and frozen ground. The mammoth was, as we have just heard, scarcely less frequent in central Europe than in the celebrated Siberian districts: the number of mammoth tusks and whole mammoth carcasses that have been found at several places in central Europe, as at Kannstatt near Stuttgart, and in the "loess" near Predmost in Moravia, can compare favourably with the richest results of the mammoth hunt on the New Siberian Islands. The carvings and implements of mammoth ivory that have been found at Predmost and in the caves of the Dordogne, Belgium, Poland, and elsewhere, prove therefore only that the man who made these articles used the ivory in a fresh condition; but whether from the animal as soon as it was dead, or from its carcass preserved in the ice of the Drift period, no one can decide.

It will not occur to anyone who sees a present-day dandy with a stick ornamented with a carving of a naked woman in mammoth ivory to assign him — or at least the work of art he carries — to the mammoth period. Nor do these old articles and carvings of mammoth ivory prove anything more than that the latter was still fresh when it was worked. In France and the rest of central Europe this must have been the case, not only in the period in which the mammoth lived, but also in the early postglacial period, which we have come to know as the reindeer period. With critical acumen Steenstrup has assigned the

[1] See Figs. 25–27, Plate at p. 120.

" loess " accumulation of Predmost, with its abundant mammoth remains, — beside which remains not only of Man, but also of the wolf, bear, reindeer, musk-ox, and horse (the fauna of the reindeer period) are found, — not to the mammoth period, but to the postglacial reindeer period. The Drift reindeer-men of central Europe presumably searched for mammoth tusks just as much as the present reindeer-men in north Asia. The great field of mammoth carrion at Predmost was therefore a very powerful attraction, not only for the beasts of prey (chief among them wolves), but also for Man. This is corroborated by the bone and stone implements found, the numerous chipped flints, the large quantities of charcoal and ashes, the many charred splinters of bone, and the heaps of bones broken for eating purposes.

In France, especially, many primitive works of art of the " ivory epoch " have been found, and even the nude figure of woman is not wanting; but no proof is given that these carvings belong to the time when the mammoth still lived. Much sensation has been caused by an engraving on a piece of mammoth ivory representing a hairy mammoth with its mane and strongly curved tusks. This illustration has been taken as unexceptionable proof that the artist of the Drift period who did it saw and portrayed the mammoth alive. But could the mammoth-hunter Schumachow — the Tunguse who in 1799 discovered, in the ice of the peninsula of Tumys-Bykow at the mouth of the Lena, the mammoth now erected in the collection at the St. Petersburg Academy — have pictured the animal other-wise when it was freshly melted out of the ice? And the Madelaine cave in the Périgord, where the piece of ivory with the picture of the mammoth was found, certainly belongs to the reindeer period, as is confirmed by Von Zittel in the fourth volume of his " Palæozoölogy."

Had we not independent proofs that Drift Man lived in central Europe — for instance, at Taubach — with the great extinct pachydermata, neither the finds in the " loess " near Predmost, nor the articles of ivory, nor the illustration of the mammoth itself, could prove it. They furnish absolute proof of the existence of Drift Man only back to the reindeer period.

(d) *Bodily Remains of Drift Man.* — To decide whether a corpse frozen in the stone-ice belonged to a Drift man, the examination of the corpse itself, its skull, bones, and soft parts, would no more suffice than clothing, implements, and ornament. For at least so much is certain, that all the skulls and bones hitherto known to have been ascribed to Drift Man by the most eminent palæontologists geologists, and anthropologists cannot be distinguished from those of men of the present day. We know no characteristic by which remains of Man from the Drift would be surely indicated.

Von Zittel, in the fourth volume of his " Palæozoölogy," says:

" As compared with the great abundance of tools, remains of Drift Man himself belong to the greatest rarities. The age of the much-discussed skulls from the caves of Paviland, in Glamorganshire; of Engis, Engihoue, and Spy near Liège: of Gendron on the Lesse; from the Gaillenreuth cave; and from the caves of Aurignac, Cro-Magnon, Bruniquel, Lombrive, Cavillon near Mentone, and the Grotta dei Colombi on the island of Palmaria, is doubtful; the skull from Kannstatt and the skeletons from Grenelle and Clichy near Paris are certainly of a late period; the bones of extremities from the ' loess ' of Lahr are lost; the skeletons from the volcanic tufa of Denise, near Le Puy, and the skull from Brüx, in Bohemia, are of doubtful age; [the Drift age of the celebrated fragment of skull from the Neanderthal, with its strong superciliary ridges, is] not in the least proved. And the lower jaw from Moulin-Quignon, near Abbeville, was fraudulently placed there by workmen. The only remains of Drift Man of reliable age are a skull from Olmo, near Chiana, in Tuscany; a skull from Egisheim, in Alsace; a lower jaw from the Naulette cave near Furfooz, in Belgium; and a fragment of jaw from the Schipka cave in Moravia. This material is not sufficient for determining race, but all human remains of reliable age from the Drift of Europe, and all the skulls found in caves, agree in size, form, and capacity with *Homo sapiens*, and are well formed throughout. In no way do they fill the gap between Man and ape.

"In North America a skull from the Upper Pliocene auriferous gravel of Calaveras in California, described by Whitney, attracted great attention for some time; according to Mortillet this was the skull of a modern Indian buried in the ground by workmen.

"The finds in South America deserve more confidence. Lunel had discovered human skulls mingled with extinct and recent mammalia in Brazilian bone-caves, and flint implements and human skulls of dolichocephalic form occur likewise in the uppermost Drift (La Plata and Querandic stages) of Argentina. But split, worked, and burnt bones and jaws of the stag, glyptodon, mastodon, and toxodon have also repeatedly been found with flint implements of palæolithic stamp, as well as skulls and whole skeletons of men, in the Pampas formation of Argentina. Near Arrecifes a human skeleton lay under the coat-of-mail of a glyptodon. The fossil human skulls of South America have no uniform stamp; some are dolichocephalic and remind one of the Indians still living in South America, and others are of a brachycephalic form. One skeleton possessed eighteen instead of seventeen truncal vertebræ and had a perforation of the breastbone."

So far Von Zittel, the most celebrated scholar in the field of palæontology in Germany. My scientific results agree entirely with his, only I should like to put a mark of interrogation after some of the finds of human bones from the Drift that he takes for granted.


## 2. THE PALÆONTOLOGY OF NEOLITHIC MAN IN EUROPE

### A. THE STONE AGE OF THE RECENT PERIOD

IT is entirely in the sense of palæontological stratification that the Drift forms the lowest and oldest stratum for the occurrence of Man, attested chiefly by the remains of his primitive culture. This oldest "culture-stratum" hitherto known goes in practically the same manner far over the earth. There is no doubt that Asia, Europe, north Africa, and North America, so far as their ice-covering allowed of their being inhabited, form one continuous region for the distribution of palæolithic Man, in which all discoveries give similar results. In this vast region the lowest and oldest prehistoric stratum that serves as the basis of historical civilisation is the homogeneous palæolithic stratum. In the Drift period palæolithic Man penetrated into South America, as into a new region, with northern Drift animals. In central and south Africa and Australia palæolithic Man does not yet seem to be known. All the more important is it that in Tasmania palæolithic conditions of civilisation existed until almost the middle of the present century.

The palæontology of Man has hitherto obtained good geological information of the oldest, palæolithic culture-stratum of the Drift in only a few parts of the earth, and only in Tasmania does this oldest stratum appear to have cropped out free, and still uncovered by other culture-strata, down to our own times. Otherwise it is everywhere overlaid by a second, later culture-stratum of much greater thickness, which, although opened up in almost innumerable places, is scarcely less similarly spread over the whole earth than the palæolithic stratum. As opposed to the earliest Stone Age of the Drift, which we have come to know as the palæolithic period, this has been called the later Stone Age or neolithic period.

The neolithic period is also ignorant of the working of metals; for weapons and implements stone is the exclusive hard material of which the blades are made. But geologically and palæontologically the two culture-strata are widely and sharply separated. They are not drift, but alluvial strata in which the remains of neolithic civilisation are deposited. Moreover the stragglers of the Drift fauna, which with the reindeer were the companions of central European Man in the postglacial period, have disappeared; their remains are absent in the strata that supply us in abundance with remains of the culture and skeleton of neolithic Man. The fauna has also considerably altered in another way. To the beasts of the forest and the chase of the present day that already existed in the Drift, among which large forms like the bison, aurochs, and elk, with the bear and wolf, still frequently occur, are added large numbers of our breeding and domestic animals, — the dog, cow, horse, goat, sheep, and pig. The men of the neolithic period lived under practically the same climatic conditions as mankind of to-day, and surrounded by the same plants and animals; they practised agriculture, bred domestic animals, and made their weapons and implements of stone and of the bones, horns, and teeth of the animals they bred and hunted.

As regards Europe, and a large part of the other continents, this second stratum of the culture of the human race still lies at prehistoric depth. But in other extensive parts of the earth the stratum of neolithic culture was not covered by other culture-strata until far into the period of written history. Even a large part of Europe was still inhabited by history-less tribes of the later Stone Age at the time when the old civilised lands of Asia and of Africa, and the coasts of the Mediterranean, had everywhere — on the basis of the same neolithic elements, with the increasing use of metals — already risen to that higher stage of civilisation which, with the historical written records of Egypt and Babylonia, forms the basis of our present chronology.

When these civilised nations came into direct contact with the more remote nations of the Old World, they found them, as we have said, still, to a certain extent, at the neolithic stage of civilisation, just as, when Europeans settled in America, the great majority of the aborigines had not yet passed the neolithic stage, at which, indeed, the lowest primitive tribes of central Brazil still remain. Australia and a large part of the island world of the South Sea had not yet risen above the neolithic stage (Tasmania, probably, not even above the palæolithic) when they were discovered. There the Stone Age, to a certain extent, comes down to modern times; likewise in the far north of Asia, in Greenland, in the most northern parts of America, and at the south point of the New Continent among the Fuegians.

In those parts of the earth where, as in the oldest centres, civilisation developed into higher stages autochthonously, the neolithic stratum is overlaid by a regular series of strata in which the evolution of the human mind may be seen uninterrupted in its steady progress for long ages. Where, by means of external influences, the opening up of new intercourse with commerce and civilisation, wars and national migrations, etc., the native population in the neolithic stage of civilisation suddenly obtains the products of a higher civilisation, — like many Indians when America was discovered or many South Sea Islanders at the time of the great voyages round the world, — the connection with past ages appears catastrophically interrupted, as in so many geological stratifications; progress is made by leaps and bounds, and not in the natural steady advance from one stage to another.  But in this manner we can in many places ascertain with absolute certainty, from the more recent strata overlying the neolithic stratum, at what period the contact between the neolithic and the old civilisation took place there.  Thus a chronological link is obtained in the sense of confirmed history, by which the end of the prehistoric epoch, and therefore this itself, is joined to written history.

The strata of human culture form an uninterrupted series from the neolithic epoch up to the present day, and are in ideal connection over the whole earth. But nowhere in the world is the succession quite undisturbed, no point on the earth's surface shows all the strata of the development of civilisation following one upon the other uninterruptedly.  In lands of the oldest civilisation a continuous series of undisturbed strata is followed by a point of time from which the movement of civilisation is transferred to other places.

The men of the later Stone Age are the ancestors of the civilised men of to-day. Classical antiquity among Greeks and Romans had still a consciousness of this, at least partly; it was not entirely forgotten that the oldest weapons of men did not consist of metal, but of stone and even inferior material.  The worked stones which the people then, as now, designated as weapons of the deity, as lightning-stones or thunderbolts, were recognised by keener-sighted men as weapons of primeval inhabitants of the land.

### B. The Oldest Neolithic Stratum — The Danish Shell-Mounds

PALÆONTOLOGICALLY the neolithic culture-stratum, the stratum of the later Stone Age, is characterised all over the earth by the imbedding of bodily remains of Man, and weapons and implements of stone, in alluvial or "recent" formations together with the bones of domestic animals and the remains of cultivated plants.

The form and technique of the stone articles are not of themselves sufficient for a demarcation of the palæolithic and neolithic strata.  The stones worked by Man of the neolithic period are often scarcely less rude than those of the palæolithic period.  Many forms of flint implements — such as knives, scrapers, flakes, and the rudest axes and net-weights — are identical in form and technique in both periods, and to a certain extent have remained in use without any change whatever through all the prehistoric and historic epochs down to the present time: the flints which are still used as "strike-a-lights" by the peasants of northern Italy and the southern Tyrol at the present day cannot be distinguished from palæolithic ones.  The great test in determining what are neolithic finds is, next to the absence of remains of specifically Drift animals not belonging to the "recent" fauna, the presence of bones of domestic animals.  As a secondary point may be added that all ground and pierced stone articles belong to the later Stone Age, palæolithic Man not having known these arts.  So that, where we find such stone articles of finer workmanship, we are doubtless dealing with a find of the later Stone Age: but where such characteristic ones are absent it is impossible to arrive at any definite decision, and in caves — and especially in graves that have been made in the Drift floors of caves — both strata are, often enough, inseparably mixed. Such interments, by which the corpses with their otherwise characteristic adjuncts are imbedded in geologically older strata, are, as we have already pointed out, very frequent: in this way bones of Drift animals, etc., come to lie side by side with the bones and other relics of men of later periods. So that even the determination of the geological stratum in which the relics are found becomes, under certain circumstances, quite valueless as a means of determining their age, unless the conditions under which they were found have been noted with the greatest exactness, and above all the question is decided whether the imbedding of the particular relics took place primarily or at an evidently later date.

In spite of these difficulties, which are in the nature of things, the study of prehistoric times has geological and palæontological means of determining what are neolithic finds, which are no less reliable than the evidence on which it was possible to base the proof of palæolithic Man. It is especially due to Steenstrup that the geological and palæontological determination of the celebrated kitchen-middens on the coasts of Denmark does not fall short, as regards its certainty and the scientific use made of every circumstance, of the discoveries of glacial Man at the source of the Schussen by Oscar Fraas, and is thus one of the most reliable landmarks in the earliest history of mankind.

The Danish kitchen-middens belong to the earliest period of the neolithic culture-stratum, and here it was possible for geological-palæontological research to draw sharp lines between the neolithic and palæolithic stages. As early as 1840 Steenstrup was able to show, from the examination of clearly stratified bogs, that since the melting of the glaciers the vegetation and fauna of Denmark and south Sweden have undergone material and repeated changes. The bogs lie on glacial strata of loam and sand intermingled with boulders, in which strata mammoth remains have occasionally been found. In this clay under the bogs is found an arctic vegetation, likewise at the very bottom of the Zealand forest-bogs. Here are branches, leaves, and blossoms of far northern plants, especially of arctic species of willow (*Salix herbacea, S. polaris,* and *S. reticulata*) and the dwarf birch (*Betula nana*), besides dryas and saxifrage (*Saxifraga oppositifolia*). This stratum corresponds to the time when the glaciers melted in the postglacial period of the Drift, to which the relics of the palæolithic reindeer hunters at the source of the Schussen belong. In Scandinavia human relics are absent in this stratum. The bogs lying upon it show in their stratification the above-mentioned repeated change of vegetation, which proves an increasing mildness in the climate of Denmark. The next lowest stratum contains remains of the aspen; a little higher, forming the thickest stratum, follow pines. Still higher we find in the strata, first the remains of an oak vegetation, then alders, and only right on the surface beeches, which nowadays form the magnificent forests of Denmark. In the lowest stratum of these forest-bogs have been found remains of the reindeer and also the skeleton of an aurochs (*Bos primigenius*). But only in the pine stratum do the first traces of Man in Denmark appear, therefore undoubtedly in the "recent" period.

Corresponding to this change of vegetations there is also a change in the animal kingdom. The Greenland seal, which formerly lived much farther south, has been driven back to the north of Norway; the reindeer retired even earlier from the wooded regions, the great auk of the far north (*Alca impennis*) is now extinct even in Iceland, its last place of refuge; and the capercailzie, which was formerly very frequent in Denmark, has completely disappeared there. This disappearance of the capercailzie is explained by the fact that it is dependent for its food on the pine, on whose young shoots it principally lives in the spring. Accordingly the presence of the capercailzie in Denmark coincides with the period of the pine forest: with the disappearance of the pine its sojourn in those regions also became impossible.

The strata of the bogs relate the history of the country from the end of the Drift period like a chronicle, and form, in a geological sense, a chronology which informs us as to the time of Man's first appearance in Denmark.

As we have said, we meet with the first traces of Man in the "pine period," and these traces are those of neolithic Man. Pine trunks have been found worked with fire and stone instruments; but, more important still, the kitchen-middens have proved, through Steenstrup's careful examination of the animal bones occurring in them, that the men of the Stone Age who piled up these middens made their first appearance in Denmark in the pine period. Thus the time of their appearance is exactly fixed, on the one hand in relation to the Drift, whose last off-shoots had long disappeared, and on the other hand in relation to the later and latest strata of the "recent" period, in which proofs have been found of higher civilisations based on the knowledge of the working of metals.

The kitchen-middens on the Danish coasts mark places of more or less permanent settlement, consisting of more or less numerous individual dwellings. From these middens a rich inventory of finds has been made, affording a glimpse of the life and doings of those ancient times. The heaps consist principally of thousands upon thousands of opened shells of oysters, cockles, and other shellfish still eaten at the present day, mingled with the bones of the roe, stag, aurochs, wild boar, beaver, seal, etc. Bones of fishes and birds were also made out; among the latter being the bones of the wild swan and of the now extinct great auk, and, what is specially important in determining the geological age of these remains, large numbers of the bones of the capercailzie. Domestic animals are absent with the exception of the dog, whose bones, however, are broken, burnt, and gnawed in the same way as those of the beasts of the chase. Everything proves that on the sites of these middens there formerly lived a race of fishers and hunters, whose chief food consisted of shellfish, the shells of which accumulated in mounds around their dwellings. Proofs of agriculture and cattle-rearing there are none; the dog alone was frequently bred, not only as a companion in the chase, but also for its flesh. The numerous bones of the capercailzie prove that the middens were accumulated in the pine period.

The flint implements found in these Danish kitchen-middens are of a rude, antique character. They are simpler in form than those of the fully developed neolithic age, and are almost without exception unground,[1] although some of them are more finely worked by careful chipping of the surfaces and edges.

The state of civilisation of the old Danish shellfish-eaters was not quite a low one in spite of its primitive colouring, and in essential points was superior to that of palæolithic Man. Not only had they tamed a really domestic animal,

---

[1] See Fig. 1, Plate at p. 141.

the dog, but they made and used clay vessels for cooking and storing purposes. The cooking was done on fireplaces. They could work deer-horn and bone well. Of the former hammer-axes with round holes were made, and of animal bones arrow-heads, awls, and needles, with the points carefully smoothed. Small bone combs appear to have served not so much for toilet purposes as for dividing animal sinews for making threads, or for dressing the threads in weaving. In the way of ornaments there were perforated animal teeth. The fish remains found in the middens belong to the plaice, cod, herring, and eel. To catch these deep-sea fish the fishermen must have gone out to sea, which implies the possession of boats of some kind. Nor was only small game hunted, but also large game. Ninety per cent of the animal bones occurring in the shell-mounds consist of those of large animals, especially the deer, roe, and wild boar. Even such dangerous adversaries as the aurochs, bear, wolf, and lynx were killed, likewise the beaver, wildcat, seal, otter, marten, and fox. The very numerous fragments of clay vessels belong partly to large pot-like vessels without handles and with pointed [1] or flat bottoms, and partly to small oval bowls with round bottoms. All vessels were made with the free hand of coarse clay, into which small fragments of granitic stone were kneaded; as ornament they have in a few cases incisions or impressions, mostly made with the finger itself on the upper edge.

The great importance of the Danish middens in the general history of mankind is due to the fact that their age is geologically established, so that they can serve as a starting-point for chronology. It is to Japetus Steenstrup that the early history of our race owes this chronological fixing of an initial date. It is his investigations of the animal species occurring in the shell-mounds, compared with his researches into the strata of the bogs and of the whole " recent " formation, that have made it possible to establish the greater age of the shell-mounds as opposed to the fully developed northern Stone Age. The question is a purely palæontological one. In the shell-mounds are found remains of the capercailzie, which occurred in Denmark only in the pine period and has since disappeared there; the shell-mounds containing bones of the capercailzie belong therefore to that early part of the " recent " period in which the thick pine stratum was formed in the stratified bogs. Finds of the Stone Age in which bones of the capercailzie are absent are therefore evidently more recent than those in which they occur.

Every other attempt to determine real age has hitherto failed. Perhaps some day a locality will be found in which a regular, undisturbed series of the earth's strata will show older occurrences in the lower strata and more recent ones in the higher. As we have already indicated, differences in the form and working of the stone implements are not sufficient to determine the age of neolithic finds. It can be proved that the same forms as are found in the old kitchen-middens were used together with stone productions that have been very well and carefully worked and ground. If only the ruder forms are found at a place, it may be simply a coincidence, and does not of itself prove anything as to a greater age.

Even after the disappearance of the capercailzie, shellfish-eaters still lived on the Danish coasts who accumulated heaps of refuse around their dwellings

---

[1] See Fig. 2, Plate at p. 144.

very much like those of these earliest inhabitants of the northern countries. But now everything points to a higher state of civilisation. Among the bones of the beasts of the chase are found those of numerous domestic animals, and there are also clear proofs of a more advanced technique in the working of stone. In some shell-mounds stone implements of finer form, which we may accordingly claim to be more recent forms, have been found here and there. In a shell-mound near Svendborg on the island of Fünen, which in every other respect was exactly like the oldest ones, only more recent forms of antiquities have been found. Likewise near Kolinsund, in Jutland. Here ground stone axes, potsherds with the characteristic ornaments of the fully developed Stone Age of the North, and bones of domestic animals — pigs, sheep, and goats — were found.

It would therefore be quite a mistake if one, so to speak, were to pronounce a conformable geological stratum of the kitchen-middens to be the oldest stage of the northern neolithic period. In every single case the age of the middens must first be determined by other criteria. That we can do that is due to Steenstrup; it is his discoveries that have made it possible to divide the neo-lithic period of Denmark chronologically into an earlier epoch, corresponding to the oldest shell-mounds of the pine period, and a later epoch of the fully developed Stone Age. With the exception of the dog the domestic animals belong to the later epoch, likewise the ground and finely worked stone imple-ments, and the characteristically formed and tastefully ornamented clay pottery. To these may be added a number of other proofs of a more advanced civilisation. The middens allow us to trace this evolution of culture, and thereby become important material for comparing other and sometimes much richer finds of the Stone Age.

Mounds of shells and other food-refuse similar to the Danish ones just de-scribed have been found in England, on the coasts of France and Portugal, in Russia and Japan, and on the east and west coasts of America. At the south point of America the Fuegians, as modern shellfish-eaters, still accumulate such shell-mounds at the present day. The middens of different countries belong to different periods. Among the French ones, for instance, the middens near St. Valery, at the mouth of the Somme, yielded — besides shells, rude pottery frag-ments, and flint implements — bones of domestic animals, as the goat, horse, sheep, and a small species of ox. In an English "rubbish-heap" W. Boyd Dawkins found only bones of the dog, fox, badger, hog, roe, stag, goat, a short-horned ox, the horse, and other quadrupeds, and the eagle. In Spain, also, numer-ous bones of mammalia are found, at least in the upper strata of the middens; the lower strata consist of shells like the Danish ones.

It is to northern archæology, as we have seen, that primeval history owes the preliminaries most essential for geologically determining the "recent" epochs, which are marked by the occurrence of domestic animals. The far north of Europe offers the most favourable conditions for this classification. During the glacial period it lay deeply buried in ice, and was uninhabitable for glacial Man. Here, therefore, the palæolithic stratum of the glacial period is absent, and the occu-pation of the land did not take place until the "recent" period, a long time after the melting of the glaciers. This precludes all chance of confusing palæolithic and neolithic remains, which has elsewhere set innumerable obstacles in the way of research. It is to the northern archæologists that the honour is due of having recognised this circumstance and utilised it for the development of science.

## C. THE FULLY DEVELOPED NEOLITHIC EPOCH

THE earliest inhabitants of the north of Europe during the Stone Age, as recorded by the kitchen-middens of the Danish pine period, were scarcely superior to palæolithic Man in civilisation, judging from outward appearances. But a closer investigation taught us that, in spite of the poverty of their remains, a higher development of civilisation is unmistakable. And this superiority of the neolithic over the palæolithic epoch becomes far more evident if we take as our standard of comparison, not the poor fisher population, who probably first reached the Danish shores as pioneers, but the neolithic civilisation that had been fully developed in sunnier lands and followed closely upon these trappers or squatters.

Next to hunting and fishing, cattle-breeding and agriculture are noticeable as the first elements of neolithic civilisation, and in connection with them the preparation of flour and cooking; and as technical arts chiefly carving and the fine working of stone, of which weapons and the most various kinds of tools were made; with the latter wood, bone, deer-horn, etc., could be worked. The blades are no longer sharpened merely by chipping, but by grinding, and are made in various technically perfect forms. Special importance was attached to providing them with suitable handles, for fixing which the stone implement or weapon was either provided with a hole, or, as in America especially, with notches or grooves. In addition to these there are the primitive arts of Man,—the ceramic art, spinning, and weaving. In the former, especially, an appreciation of artistic form and of decoration by ornament is developed. The ornament becomes a kind of symbolical written language, the eventual deciphering of which appears possible in view of the latest discoveries concerning the ornamental symbolism of the primitive races of the present day. Discoveries of dwellings prove an advanced knowledge of primitive architecture; intrenchments and tumuli acquaint us with the principles of their earthworks; and the giants' chambers, built of colossal blocks of stone piled upon one another, prove that the builders of those times were not far behind the much-admired Egyptian builders in transporting and piling masses of stone. The burials whose ceremonies are revealed by opened graves afford a glimpse of the mental life of that period. From the skulls and skeletons that have been taken from the neolithic graves science has been able to reconstruct the physical frame of neolithic Man, which has in no way to fear comparison with that of modern Man.

(a) *The Neolithic Stone Implements.* — In this later period the progress of civilisation in the northern regions of Scandinavia and Germany was chiefly based on the working of flint into implements and weapons, as it was in the chalk districts of France during the Drift. Researches in these northern regions have acquainted us with a considerable number of different forms of flint implements, some not less rude than the palæolithic stone objects, but others finely worked, excellently chipped and ground, and adapted to definite technical purposes, — as axes, chisels and planes, saws and borers, knives and scrapers, lance-heads, arrows, and daggers, and many other things. Some of the ruder flint implements and weapons of the northern Stone Age, and even many of the more finely worked ones, are, in a certain sense like those in the palæolithic period found in the Somme valley and elsewhere, simply obtained by chipping from the lumps of flint which the ground of the chalk districts of northern Europe supplies in abundance and considerable size. Discoveries of workshops for stone implements of the later Stone Age, which furnished whole series from the very beginning of their manufacture, through all the stages of completion, down to the most finely ground, finished instrument, show that the raw material was first brought into the requisite shape by chipping, and only obtained its final finish by grinding.

Flint implements, as most important witnesses of the ancient presence of Man, have been found in thousands in the northern flint region. Most frequent are the quite rude types, which, however, in spite of their primitive simplicity and the easiness of their production, may not only be recognised with certainty as the work of Man, but have also remained longest in use — from the Drift, as we have mentioned, through all the subsequent progress of civilisation, even down to the present day among the civilised nations of Europe. These are the so-called flint flakes or knives. When the angle of an approximately prismatic piece of flint is broken off by pressure or a blow, the detached piece, according to the form and size of the core or nucleus,[1] forms a more or less long, double-edged stone blade, tapering to a point at both ends like a knife or lancet, — a so-called "stone knife."[2] The lower, or rather inner, side of the stone knife produced by striking it from the core appears even and smooth, whereas on the opposite, upper, or outer side the former angle of the core runs from one end to the other as a ridge-like elevation with either a simple or double edge. Flint is so elastic that at the spot where mechanical force was used on the core to strike off the flake, a conchoidal fracture is formed with a more or less protuberant surface. This is the bulb of percussion of the stone blade, a convex projection on its smooth inner side, from which its artificial production may be inferred with almost absolute certainty. The edges of such flint knives are as sharp and fine as that of a razor. If one of the edges is toothed like a saw, we have the saw of the Stone Age. Australians, Fuegians, Esquimaux, and others were able to make exactly similar knives of stone, flint, or similar material with a conchoidal fracture like obsidian, without metal tools, using the same methods as the prehistoric Europeans of the Stone Age.

A second very important instrument of the ancient Europeans of the northern Stone Age is the scraper, which is still known in just the same form as an instrument of the Esquimaux, the most northern tribes of American Indians, and others.[3] The scrapers are in principle just like the knives; they also are stone flakes detached from the core, but generally rather thicker. They have therefore, like the knives, a flat lower, inner side and a more or less angular, or roughly convex, side corresponding to the former angle of the core, generally an irregular one owing to the greater size of the piece. But whereas the knives were used in their original form, just as they were struck from the core, the scrapers are further worked. By systematic blows and pressure one end was generally formed into a rounded, bent, dull-sharp edge, which, in connection with the smooth under-side, seems well adapted for scraping, but not for cutting. The side-edges are also somewhat blunted by hammering, and likewise the end opposite to the scraping edge. This had to serve as a handle, either just as it was, but generally wrapped around or set in

---

[1] See Fig. 3 at p. 144.    [2] See Figs. 4 and 5 at p. 144.    [3] See p. 132.

# EXPLANATION OF PLATE B

## (SEE OVER)

1. Unground flint axe of the earlier Stone Age, from the kitchen-middens of Denmark.
2. Clay vessel of the earlier Stone Age. One-eighth real size.
3. Stone core or nucleus; right and left of the centre a concave hollow corresponding to the convex mark of percussion on the knives that have been chipped from it.
4, 5. Two flint knives of the northern Stone Age.
6. Stone axe of the northern later Stone Age.
7. Greenstone axe, from the graves of Rhosdigre, in England.
8. Stone dagger of the northern Stone Age.
9. Clay vessel with cut decoration, from Thuringia.
10. Drinking-cup with dot decoration, from Thuringia.
11. Drinking-cup without handle, from Brunswick.
12. Jug with handle, with band decoration, from Thuringia.
13. Clay vessel, from the cemetery of the Stone Age at the Hinkelstein near Monsheim.
14. Dab decoration, from Thuringia.
15. Remains of a pile hut of the Stone Age, at Schussenried.
    15 a. Transverse section of same.

16. Stone axe in deer-horn and wood
17, 18. Axe-hammers
19. Harpoon-point
20. Awl with handle
21–23. Ornaments
24. Spindle with whorl
25. Web
26. Mat
27. Basket-work
} from the Swiss lake-dwellings.
28. Hand-mill of sandstone: a larger, rather concave piece, and a smaller oval running-stone; from the cemetery of the Stone Age at the Hinkelstein near Monsheim.
29. Needle with eye
30. Fork
31. Bone chisel
32. Bone crochet-needle for net-knitting
33. Bone shuttle
} from the later Stone Age of Franconian Switzerland.
34. Carving in amber, from the Kurisches Haff, near Schwarzort.
35. Carving in stalactite, from the caves of the Jura range between Cracow and Tschenstochow.
36. Flint axe, from New Zealand.
37. Dolmen in southern Sweden.
38. Interior of a giant's chamber near Roskilde.
39. Stone circle of the later Stone Age in England.

---

(1, 3–37, 39 from Ranke's " Mensch ; " 2 and 38 from Sophus Muller's " Nordischer Altertumskunde.")

a holder; for this purpose the scrapers are often narrower toward the top. The Esquimaux and Indians use such or very similar scrapers; for instance, in Alaska, under the name of *ulus*, or women's knives, to dress the skins that they use as clothes or manufacture into tents and skin boats. Such scrapers serve also for planing the shafts of arrows and many other purposes.

Very similar to these scrapers, but still thicker and stronger, is a kind of small triangular or irregularly square flint hatchet, also produced simply by chipping, which found employment for a number of other than striking purposes; for instance, as net-weights. These three chief forms are also found in the oldest shell-mounds.

The more finely worked flint axes of the northern Stone Age are not knife-like stone flakes, but pieces of stone finely chipped on all sides, with their surface conchoidally fractured all over. The edge was generally first finely broken into shape from the two flat sides and then most carefully ground.[1] In the rough, unfinished state some of them approach to a certain extent in form and technique the above-mentioned small axes or net-weights. The majority of the ground flint axes have both sides converging to the edge convexly,[2] which makes them excellently adapted for rougher woodwork. In the evolution of the Stone Age the stone axes assume very varied forms, adapted to definite technical purposes. Some are of a long, narrow form, with the edge ground flat on one side, the other side being convex: these are chisels and planes; hollow-ground gouges have also been found. The flint axes were either used in the hand as they were, or set in a wooden handle. A number of these stone axes with handles have been preserved from that period; very often, as in the lake-dwellings of Alpine countries, the smaller stone axes were set in a holder of deer-horn, which in its turn was set in the handle proper. As stone axes were also employed for cutting leather and other purposes, many of the deer-horn holders that have been found are merely shorter or longer handles for using the instrument in the hand.

The finest products of the old flint art are, however, not ground, but conchoidally broken over the whole surface, some of them most ornamentally, so that, especially on the edges of the handles, the smaller breaks form, for instance, a fine herring-bone pattern. For this purpose also the stones were first chipped into shape roughly. Such rough stones are found especially in the so-called kitchen-middens of the Danish Stone Age, and appear to have served, even in this rough state, as lance-heads, daggers, scrapers, etc. In the finer working the edges and surfaces were most carefully flaked, not by blows, but by pressure, probably with a bone instrument, in the same way as the Fuegians, Esquimaux, and others proceed in making their flint lance-heads and arrow-heads at the present day. The chief forms of these finest conchoidal flint implements of the neolithic period are arrow-heads of great variety of form, daggers[3] and lance-heads, and semilunar knives and sickles proper.

Materially different from these forms are hammers and axe-hammers, perforated or provided with grooves for handles, which in a certain sense prepare the way for the forms which later periods of civilisation learned to make of metal.

The flint implements just described are the most important proofs of the neolithic Stone Age of the north European flint districts. Among the implements and weapons of flint, those of other kinds of stone are also found here in no small

---

[1] See Fig. 6 at p. 144.     [2] See Fig. 7.     [3] See Fig. 8.

numbers. But in districts where flint was scarce the larger articles were made almost exclusively of other sorts of stone; this is especially so in the case of hatchets, axes, hoes, and perforated hammers and axe-hammers. Scrapers and leather-cutting knives were also made of material that was inferior in itself, owing to its being generally less hard and tough. As a matter of fact the sorts of stone that were generally used were the hardest and toughest obtainable, such as are found among the boulders. Preference was given chiefly to black stones, such as flinty slate Lydian, and to basalt and green stones; of the latter, tough or flinty hornblende stones, amphibole, serpentine, gabbro, and eclogite are very frequently found. Tough dioritic stones, diorite proper, and diabase were also employed. In districts where these more suitable stones are scarce or quite absent among the boulders, gneiss, granite, porphyry, and even far inferior stones, such as trachyte, phonolithe, clay-slate (black or in light colours), sandstone, and jura-limestone are also found employed.

Special attention has been attracted by the small and large axes, generally of a very fine green colour, of nephrite, jadeite, and chloromelanite, the first stone being still held in high honour in China and Persia as an ornamental stone, ranking almost as a precious stone, and likewise in New Zealand; in South America also it was highly valued by the ancient civilised peoples, and is even still to a certain extent by their descendants of the present day. In central Europe only a few places are known where nephrite has been found, the best authenticated being in the Zobten Mountains, near Jordansmühle, in Silesia. Proof of jadeite and chloromelanite occurring in Europe is still entirely wanting, so that extensive commercial relations with Asia have been suggested as the means by which the men of the Stone Age came into the possession of these precious minerals. The chief district where nephrite is found is in the Kuenluen Mountains in eastern Turkestan; in Siberia some very large blocks have been found as boulders. The chief district where jadeite is known to be found is Burmah, in Further India, whence it is imported in large quantities into China. Chloromelanite is dark green and differs from jadeite, which it otherwise closely resembles, in containing a large percentage of iron; as yet nothing seems to be known as to its natural occurrence. Rough nephrite was doubtless worked at Lake Constance, as is shown by the large quantity of flakes and refuse, partly in the form of knives; it is supposed to have been found in the vicinity, but this has not yet been proved. The hardness and toughness of these stones are very considerable, so that we can understand that Man of the Stone Age must have spared no pains to procure them.

But by the side of larger implements of other stone material we find always and everywhere flint and chert implements, made in the characteristic forms of knives, flakes, scrapers, arrow-heads, and lance-heads. Occasionally flint is also replaced by quartz, quartzite, jasper, obsidian, etc. But as a general rule flint was quite indispensable for all the usual purposes of cutting, sawing, and carving. The flints are often — for instance, in the neolithic cave districts in northern Bavaria — strikingly small, and even tiny; but their careful working proves how valuable they were for the most various uses.

With their help and the application of sand and water the larger boulder-stones were sawn into pieces for finer work; with pointed flint, or flint borers, stones, amber, and so forth were often pierced, and the holes made with the flint borer are absolutely unmistakable. But the small flint instruments served chiefly for working deer-horn, bone, and wood, from which, in neolithic times, weapons and implements were often carved, their numbers being in proportion to the scarcity of flint and other suitable stones in the settlements of the Stone Age men.

In the above-mentioned cave districts of Bavaria the manufactures of deer-horn and bone so far outdo the stone articles in number, technical execution, variety of form, and possible uses, that the neolithic period of those districts might have been termed at once the bone and deer-horn period. The majority of the most important weapons are made of these two materials, and not only these, but also countless implements indicating a comparatively high development of technical requirements, namely, for spinning, weaving, plaiting, net-making, dressing animal skins, pottery-making, etc. The circumstances are very similar in the cave districts of Poland.

(b) *Neolithic Ornament.* — Of the ornaments of the Stone Age the most important and characteristic are perforated teeth of dogs, wolves, horses, oxen, bears, boars, and smaller beasts of prey. How much in favour such ornaments were is proved by the fact that imitations or counterfeits of them were even worn. Numerous articles of ornament, carved from bone and deer-horn, were universal: ornamental plates and spherical, basket-shaped, square, shuttle-like, or chisel-shaped beads were made of these materials and formed into chains. Other bead-like pieces may have served as buttons, or for other decorative or even technical purposes, particularly for spinning and weaving. Large black beads of burnt clay are also found, some of the typical form of the spinning-whorl. Besides the ornamental plates of bone and deer-horn there are also similar ones of stone, for instance, of slate and alabaster. These plates are of a variety of forms, often really elegant, and are sometimes also prettily ornamented on the surface with linear patterns, or even with engravings of animals, such as stags' heads. On round, flat ornamental buttons we find concentric depressed rings around the centre hole. Very elegant are the small rings and breloque-like beads, generally carved from diluvial shells and shining like mother-of-pearl, which were made into chains. Whole bracelets of such mother-of-pearl have been found; stone ones of that period, nicely polished, are also known. Other beads consist of hematite, jet, and, especially in the north, amber. Many of these ornaments, like the chains of tooth-shells, resemble those of the palæolithic period. Reddle, or fine-washed clayish hematite, was also used by the neolithic men, probably chiefly for painting the skin, but also for other colouring purposes.

In the Swiss lake-dwellings of the Stone Age have been found skilfully carved ear-drops, needles with eyes, neat little combs of boxwood, and hairpins, some with heads and others with pierced side protuberances. Remains of textile fabrics, even finely twilled tissue, and also leather, were yielded by the excavations of the lake-dwellings of that period, so that we have to imagine the inhabitants adorned with clothes of various kinds.

(c) *Cattle-Breeding of the Neolithic Period.* — What raises Man of the later Stone Age so far above palæolithic Man is the possession of domestic animals and the knowledge of agriculture. As domestic animals of the later Stone Age we have proof of the dog, cow, horse, sheep, goat, and pig.

Among the animals which have attached themselves to Man as domestic, the first and oldest is undoubtedly the dog. It is found distributed over the whole earth, being absent from only a few small islands. Among many races the dog was, and is still, the only domestic animal in the proper sense of the word. This applies to all Esquimaux tribes to the majority of the Indians of North and South America, and to the continent of Australia.

We have no certain proofs that palæolithic Man possessed the dog as a domestic animal. In the Somme valley, at Taubach, and at the source of the Schussen, bones of the domestic dog are absent. And yet, among Drift fauna in caves, remains of dogs have been repeatedly met with, which have been claimed to be the direct ancestors of the domestic dog. The dog's attachment to Man may have taken place at different times in different parts. Man and dog immigrate to South America with the foreign northern fauna simultaneously (in a geological sense) during the Drift. In Australia, Man and dog (dingo), as the most intimate animal beings, are opposed to an animal world that is otherwise anomalous and, to the Old World, quite antiquated; probably Man and dog also came to Australia together. We know of fossil remains of the dingo from the Drift, but no reliable finds have yet proved the presence of Man during that period.

In the later Stone Age the dog already occurs as the companion of Man wherever it occurs in historic times. In Europe its remains have been found in the Danish kitchen-middens, in the northern neolithic finds, in the lake-dwellings of Switzerland, in innumerable caves of the neolithic period, in the terramare of upper Italy, etc. It was partly a comparatively small breed, according to Rütimeyer similar to the "wachtelhund" (setter) in size and build. Rütimeyer calls this breed — after the lake-dwellings, one of the chief places where it has been found — *Canis familiaris palustris*, or lake-dwelling dog. Like all breeds of animals of primitive domestication, the dog at this period, according to Nehring, is small, — stunted as it were. With the progress of civilisation the dog also grows larger. In the later prehistoric epochs, beginning with the so-called "Bronze" period, we find throughout almost the whole of Europe a rather larger and more powerful breed with a more pointed snout — the Bronze dog — whose nearest relative seems to be the sheep-dog. At the present day the domestic dog is mostly employed for guarding settlements and herds and for hunting. In the Arctic regions the Esquimaux also use their dogs, which are like the sheep-dog, for personal protection and hunting; they do particularly good service against the musk-ox, while the wild reindeer is too fast for them. But the Esquimau dog is chiefly used for drawing the sledge, and, where this cannot be used, as a beast of burden, it being able to carry fairly heavy loads. In China and elsewhere, as formerly in the old civilised countries of South America, the dog is still fattened and killed for meat. So that the domestic dog serves every possible purpose to which domestic animals can be put, except, it seems, for milking, although this would not be out of the question either. The dog was also eaten by Man in the later Stone Age, as is proved by the finds in his kitchen refuse.

The reindeer is now restricted to the polar regions of the northern hemisphere — Scandinavia, north Asia, and North America, whereas in the palæolithic period it was very numerous throughout Russia, Siberia, and temperate Europe down to the Alps and Pyrenees. It does not seem ever to have been definitely proved that the reindeer existed in the neolithic period of central and northern Europe, although according to Von Zittel (in the fifth volume of his "Palæontology") it lived in Scotland down to the eleventh century and in the Hercynian forest until the time of Cæsar. The earliest definite information we appear to have of the tamed reindeer, which at the present day is a herd animal with the Lapps in Europe, and with the Samoyedes and Reindeer Tunguses in Asia, is found in Ælian, who speaks of the Scythians having tame deer.

Cattle of the genus *Bos* (ox) at present exist nowhere in the wild state, while the tame ox (*Bos taurus*) is distributed as a domestic animal over the whole earth, and has formed the most various breeds. In the European Drift a wild ox, the Urus (*Bos primigenius*), distinguished by its size and the size of its horns, was widely distributed, and it still lived during the later Stone Age with the domestic ox. In the later prehistoric epochs, and even in historic times, the urus still occurs as a beast of the forest, being mentioned in the "Nibelungenlied" among Siegfried's game. Cæsar describes its capture in pits by the Germans as "laborious hunting which hardens and exercises the young men;" he says that the largely developed horns of the urus were "in great demand among the Germans; they mount them at the edge with silver and use them at their great banquets as drinking-vessels." Cæsar relates that the Germans made attempts to tame ure-oxen caught quite young,—without success, as he was told. Proof of the possibility of taming them is given, however, by the breed of domestic oxen of the Stone Age that even then was largely distributed,—the *Primigenius* or *Trochoceros* breed, which has a decided resemblance to the fossil urus and evidently comes from it.

In later prehistoric epochs (Bronze Period) a younger breed, the *Frontosus*, was developed from the *Primigenius* breed. But even in the later Stone Age a second breed of oxen, the *Brachyceros*, occurs, with short, strongly curved, stemless horn-pegs, long, narrow skull, fine, short muzzle, and very prominent margins to its orbital cavities. This small breed is particularly frequent in the lake-dwellings, and, according to Von Zittel, probably comes from Asia. According to Nehring's studies of primitive domestication the diminutive, small-boned domestic animals of the later Stone Age appear to be certain species stunted by bad keeping, as we have already noticed in the case of the dog. This probably applies to a certain extent to those small oxen, which resemble the breed of so-called "moss-cows" that until recently were kept under unfavourable conditions on the extensive barren moors of south Germany.

In the later Stone Age the horse, too, is no longer merely a beast of the chase, but occurs also in the tame state. During the Drift the species *Equus caballus fossilis Cuv.* lived in herds all over Europe, north Asia, and north Africa. From this Drift horse comes the domestic horse that is now found all over the earth. Even the wild horses of the Drift exhibit such considerable differences from one another that, according to Nehring's studies, these are to be regarded as the beginning of the formation of local breeds. The taming and domestication of the wild horse of the Drift, which began in the Stone Age, led to the domestic horse being split up later into numerous breeds. The old wild horse was comparatively small, with a large head; a similar form is still found here and there on the above-mentioned moors of south Germany in the moss-horse, or, as the common people call it, the moss-cat. At the present day the genus of the domestic horse falls, like the ox, into two chief breeds,—a smaller and more graceful Oriental breed, and a more powerful and somewhat larger Western breed with the facial bones more strongly developed. The horse of the later Stone Age of Europe exhibits only comparatively slight differences from the wild horse; it is generally a small, half-pony-like form with a large head, evidently also a stunted product of primitive breeding under comparatively unfavourable conditions. The species *Equus hemionus Pallas* and *E. ónager Pall.* still live wild on the steppes of central Asia at the present day. The former also occurs as a fossil in the European Drift, although only rarely. That the ass (*Equus asinus L.*) occurred in the European Drift is probable, but not proved. It has not yet been found in the neolithic period of Europe.

The goats proper (*Capra L.*) inhabit in their wild state the mountainous parts of Asia, and were imported thence into Europe as domestic animals, where they occur as such very often in settlements of the later Stone Age. The existence of *Capra hircus L.* in the European Drift has not yet been definitely proved. The oldest fossil real goats (*Capra Sivalensis Lyd.* and others) appear in the later Tertiary strata, in the Pliocene of India, and are related to living Asiatic species.

A species or several species of sheep are found in the European Drift, the remains of large forms related to the argali being known in England and Moravia. Wild sheep live at the present day in mountains of Asia, southern Europe, north Africa, and North America. Bones of the sheep are found in numerous neolithic finds, but it is difficult, and very often impossible, to distinguish the skeletons of the sheep and goat. Of the origin of the domestic sheep we know nothing certain. The history of its breeds is comparatively very modern. Wild breeds of sheep have not a very curly fleece, but one often as smooth as goat's hair.

Our knowledge of the domestic pig is rather better. Formerly the European wild boar, *Sus scrofa ferus L.*, which is found very largely in the Drift of Europe and Asia, was regarded as the only original species of the European domestic pig. A comparatively small but long-legged species, the lake-dwelling or peat pig (*Sus palustris Rütim.*), was bred everywhere in the neolithic period, for instance by the lake-dwellers of Switzerland. But according to Nathusius and Rütimeyer the peat pig did not come from the European wild boar, but probably, like the present later breeds of our domestic pig, from an Indian (Indo-Chinese) species, which was related to the existing *Sus vittatus Müll.* of Java and Sumatra. Nehring shows that the south Asiatic and north Asiatic wild boars — the latter of which, as we have said, are identical with our wild boar — are probably only different breeds of one original species. Nehring considers the small peat pig to be a kind of stunted product of primitive domestication, like the early domestic horses and oxen.

Tame poultry does not yet exist in the Stone Age of Europe, nor does the domestic cat.

This survey of the palaeontology of the domestic animals shows that they come from wild Drift species, which (at any rate as regards the ox, horse, and dog) are now extinct, so that these most important domestic animals now exist only in the tame state. Some of the domestic animals came from Asia, and, according to Von Zittel, were imported into Europe from there: this applies to the peat-ox and the domestic goat and pig. The Asiatic origin of the domestic horse and sheep is probable, but not proved: the sheep is found wild in south Europe as well as in Asia. The tarpan, a breed of horse very similar to the wild horse, lives in herds independent of Man on the steppes of central Asia; this has been indicated as being probably the parent breed of the domestic horse, and the origin of the latter has accordingly also been traced to Asia.

One thing is certain, that a considerable number of animal forms that coexist with Man in Europe at the present day — for instance, almost all the forms of our poultry and the fine kinds of pigs and sheep — have originally come from Asia. Our compilation shows a similar state of things even in the neolithic period.

(d) *Agriculture of the Stone Age.* — In the north of Europe, which has furnished us with our standard information regarding the neolithic culture-stratum, the certain proofs that have hitherto been found of agriculture and the cultivation of useful plants having been practised at that time (to which civilisation owes no less than to the breeding of useful tame animals) consist not so much of plant remains themselves as of stone hand-mills and spinning and weaving implements, which indicate the cultivation of corn and flax.

Our chief knowledge of neolithic agriculture and plant culture has been furnished by the lake-dwellings, especially those of Switzerland, which have preserved the picture of the neolithic civilisation of central Europe, sketched for us, as it were, in the north, in its finest lines. So far we can prove the cultivation of the following useful plants in the later Stone Age; their remains were chiefly found, as we have said, well preserved in the Stone Age lake-dwellings of Switzerland, which have been described in classical manner by Oswald Heer. Of cereal grasses Heer determined, in the rich Stone Age lake-dwellings of Wangen, on Lake Constance, and Robenhausen, in Lake Pfäffikon, three sorts of wheat and two varieties of barley, — the six-rowed and two-rowed. Flax was also grown by neolithic Man. This was, it seems, a rather different variety from our present flax, being narrow-leaved, and still occurs wild, or probably merely uncultivated, in Macedonia and Thracia. Flax has also been found growing wild in northern India, on the Altai Mountains, and at the foot of the Caucasus. The common wheat occurring in the lake-dwellings of the Stone Age is a small-grained but mealy variety, which Heer has named *Triticum vulgare antiquorum*, to distinguish it from the better-nourished species grown at the present day; but the so-called Egyptian wheat with large grains also occurs. The cereals of the lake-dwellings correspond to the discoveries made in other prehistoric, neolithic finds. The plant remains that were taken from the celebrated find at Butmir, in Bosnia, by Radimsky, have been determined by E. Schröter, of Zürich. Of wheat he found the one-grained variety, *Triticum monococcum*, the same as is still grown in many parts of Europe at the present day. The one-grained wheat is hitherto known from the following neolithic prehistoric finds: from the lake-dwelling at Wangen, on Lake Constance; in Hungary, from the stalactite cave of Baradla, near Aggtelek, in the county of Gömör, near Toszeg and Felsö Dobsza, and in the prehistoric intrenchment at Lengyel. Of special importance is the discovery of the one-grained wheat in the citadel hill of Hissarlik by Heinrich Schliemann. The wild original species of one-grained wheat is indigenous to the East, — Asia Minor and Mesopotamia : it is also said to occur wild or uncultivated in the Crimea, Greece, and Servia. Of barley the species *Hordeum vulgare* was found, and of wheat also the species *Triticum vulgare var. compositum*, a dwarf wheat identical with small-grained wheats of the present day, and likewise probably with the small-grained lake-dwelling wheats of Heer and the wheat from the intrenchment near Lengyel. Of lentils a small-grained species, *Ervum Lens var. microspermum*, was found at But-mir; the find at Aggtelek, in Hungary, yielded the same variety. The lentils from Lengyel were larger, likewise those from St. Peter's Island in the Lake of Bienne (Bronze Age). Rye and oats are not found in the lake-dwellings or other finds of the Stone Age, but make their appearance only in the later lake-dwellings of the Bronze Age. Hemp is entirely absent. Of the remaining fruits of the field peas and millet were also found in the lake-dwellings of the Stone Age. Beans, lentils, and the white poppy do not appear until the Bronze Age, and no sign has yet been found of the turnip. Traces of regular gardening and vegetable culture are altogether wanting. Some finds, however, seem to indicate primitive arboriculture, apples and pears having been found dried in slices in the lake-dwellings of the Stone Age; there even appears to be an improved kind of apple besides the wild-growing crab. But although they are chiefly wild, un-improved fruit-trees of whose fruit remains have been found, we can imagine that these fruit-trees were planted near the settlements, and the great nutritious and health-giving properties of the fruit, as a supplement to a meat fare, must have been all the more appreciated owing to the lack of green vegetables. The various wild cherries, plums, and sloes were eaten, as also raspberries, blackberries, and strawberries. Beechnut and hazelnut appear as wild food-plants. Flax also was probably not grown merely for spinning purposes, but partly on account of the nutritious properties of its oily seed-capsules, or linseed. Even at the present day flax is used in India only for the preparation of oil, the plant itself not being worked. In Abyssinia also it is used only for eating purposes; in Greece and Italy the crushed linseed used to be eaten boiled down with honey. Victor Hehn refers to a passage in Pliny, who mentions this sweet dish as being eaten by the peasants in the district beyond the Po, probably as an old Celtic or old Ligurian custom; we may perhaps also attribute this custom to the lake-dwelling period.

The original home of the most important cereals — wheat, spelt, and barley — is not known with absolute certainty: probably they came from central Asia, where they are said to be found wild in the region of the Euphrates. The real millet, *Panicum miliaceum*, came from India; peas and the other primeval leguminous plants of Europe, such as lentils and beans, came likewise from the East, partly from India. So that, apart from flax, which probably has a more northern home, the regular cultivated plants of the Stone Age of central Europe — cereal grasses, millet, and lentils — indicate Asia as their original home. We have therefore a state of things similar to that observed in the case of the domestic animals.

(c) *Pottery.* — The potter's art was probably entirely unknown to palæolithic Man, for in none of the pure Drift finds have fragments of clay vessels been found. So where clay vessels or fragments of them occur, they appear as the proof of a post-Drift period.

On the other hand pottery was quite general in the neolithic age of Europe. Still the need of clay vessels is not general among all races of the earth even at the present day; up to modern times there were, and still are, races and tribes without pots. From their practices it is evident that the European Stone men of the Drift could also manage to prepare their food, chiefly meat, by fire without cooking-vessels. The Fuegians lay the piece of meat to be roasted on the glowing embers of a dying wood fire, and turn it with a pointed forked branch so as to keep it from burning. Meat thus prepared is very tasty, as it retains all the juices and only gets a rind on the top, and the ashes that adhere to it serve as seasoning in lieu of salt. On a coal fire not only can fish be grilled, stuck on wooden rods, but whole sheep can be roasted on wooden spits, precisely as people have the dainty of roast mutton in the East. To these may be added a large number of other methods of roasting, and even boiling, without earthen or metal vessels, which are partly vouched for by ethnography and partly by archæology, and some of which, like the so-called "stone-boiling," are still practised at the present day.

Although, according to this, pottery is not an absolute necessary of life for Man, yet it is certain that even those poorly equipped pioneers who first settled in Denmark in the pine period, in spite of their having an almost or quite exclusive meat fare, had clay pottery in general use for preparing their food, and probably also for storing their provisions. As we have already shown, the remains that have been preserved in the kitchen-middens are the oldest that have been found in Denmark. Simple and rude as the numerous potsherds that occur may appear, they are of the highest importance on account of the proof of their great age.

Unfortunately, as we have already mentioned, not a single perfect vessel has come to light. The fragments are very thick, of rough clay with bits of granite worked in, and are all made by hand without the use of the potter's wheel. The pieces partly indicate large vessels, some with flat bottoms, and others with the special characteristic of pointed bottoms, so that the vessel could not be stood up as it was. Smaller bowls, frequently of an oval form, also occurred with rounded bottoms, so that they also could not stand by themselves. It is very important to note that on these fragments of pottery we find only extraordinarily scanty and exceedingly simple ornamental decorations, consisting merely of incisions, or impressions made with the fingers, on the upper edge.

We shall see how far this oldest pottery of the Stone Age is distinguished by its want of decoration from that of the fully developed Stone Age. But it is very important to notice that this rudest mode of making clay vessels, which we here see forming the beginning of a whole series that rises to the highest pitch of artistic perfection, remained in vogue not only during the whole Stone Age, but even in much later epochs. These thick, rude, hand-made fragments of large pots, with the bits of stone baked in, and decorated by incisions or the imprints of finger-tips and finger-nails, are extraordinarily widely distributed in point of both time and space. It is with these rudest productions of the potter's art as with the simplest forms of stone implements, with knives and flakes and such-like relics: they have been preserved in their original form through all prehistoric and historic epochs. And as these forms of the simplest stone implements remain the same even beyond the borders of Europe, so is it also with the pottery; the rudest fragments of American pottery, for instance, are often only distinguished from those we have described by their having bits of shell worked in the clay instead of pieces of stone. This resemblance does not, however, extend to the form of the vessels, at least not to the pointed or rounded bottoms.

It is true that in the fully developed neolithic Stone Age of Europe the clay pottery is also all made by hand, without the potter's wheel, the oldest and rudest forms still occurring everywhere, as we have said; but besides these a great variety is exhibited in the size, form, and mode of production of the pottery. The clay is often finer, and even quite finely worked and smoothed, and the vessels have thin sides and are burnt right through. The thick fragments are generally only burnt outside, frequently only on one side, and so much that the clay has acquired a bright red colour, whereas the inside, although hard, has remained only a greyish black. We have numerous perfectly preserved vessels of the later neolithic age. They are frequently distinguished by an artistic finish and beauty of form, and on their surfaces we find ornaments incised or imprinted, but rarely moulded on them, which, although the style is only geometrical, cannot be denied a keen sense of beauty and symmetry. The clay vessels also show the beginning of coloured decoration. The incised strokes, dots, etc., are often filled out with white substance (chalk or plaster), which brings the patterns out into bold ornamental relief from the black or red ground of the surface. After that it is no wonder that pottery advanced to the real coloured painting of the vessels during the neolithic period, at least in some places.

On these vessels the handle now appears, in its simplest form as a wart-like or flatter projection from the side of the vessel, pierced either vertically or horizontally with a narrow opening just large enough to admit of a cord being passed through. Other handles, just like those in use at the present day, are bowed out broad, wide, and high for holding with the hand. These generally begin quite at the top, at the rim of the vessel, and are continued from there down to its belly, whereas the first-mentioned are placed lower, frequently around the greatest circumference of the vessel.

According to Klopfleisch and Götze we may distinguish as chief forms of vessels, especially in the later Stone Age of Thuringia, amphoræ and drinking-cups. The amphoræ are large vessels, wide in the middle, with a narrower neck and a flat bottom of about the same width, and having generally two or four narrow handles at the greatest width of the belly; their form often almost corresponds to two nearly equal truncated double cones meeting at the greatest circumference of the vessel.[1] The drinking-cup has a more or less spherical belly, generally flattened at the bottom, with a high but comparatively wide neck.[2] Generally the drinking-cups have no handles, but sometimes there are narrow handles for cords, of the form we have just indicated, at the neck. Many of the drinking-cups had a convex lid.[3] Between the drinking-cup and amphora comes the jug form.[4] Still further forms of vessels occur as cans and pots, and, more rarely, pails, bowls, dishes, jars, bottles, and square pans. Specially characteristic are also fairly high hemispherical bowls with wide mouths and round bottoms,[5] so that they could not stand alone, like the similar vessels of the kitchen-middens.

As ornaments the simple "dab" and "cut" decorations that the Danes of the pine period used for their primitive pottery also occur on the vessels of the fully developed neolithic period. Dab decoration consists in making impressions or dabs with the finger-tips at certain distances from one another on the surface of the vessel while soft. Frequently the finger-nail is also intentionally imprinted. Such dab impressions are sometimes made directly on the even parts of the sides of the vessel, but sometimes also on bands of clay, standing out in relief, put

---

[1] See Fig. 9, Plate at p. 144.     [2] Fig. 10.     [3] Fig. 11.     [4] Fig. 12.     [5] Fig. 13.     [6] Fig. 14.

on specially for the purpose of ornament. Instead of the tips of the fingers small smooth pieces of wood or bone, rounded underneath, were sometimes used to produce such dab-like impressions. Oblong indentations and crescent-shaped impressions also frequently occur.

The " cut " decorations are more or less deep incisions or scratches made with the edge of a flint knife or with the point of a bone awl, a sharpened piece of wood, or other instrument, arranged linearly. By the combination of such incisions herring-bone and feather patterns, or fir-branch and palm-leaf patterns, are formed ; and in these the direction of the oblique strokes often changes, they being made to run first to the right, then to the left or upward, then downward, so as to produce continuous rows or wreaths of such incised strokes, which in their repetition often show a certain parallelism. By deep longitudinal stripes, bands or rings, triangles, squares, etc., are formed. The triangles are generally more or less regularly hatched by scratches, likewise the squares ; the latter generally alternately blank and hatched, so as to form a draught-board pattern. In rare cases these bands are concentrically arranged ; more frequently we find a kind of festoon or spiral, a form to which even larger rows of triangles with slightly curved outlines incline. The " band " motives of decoration are usually distinguished by the terms " angle-band," " curve-band," and " circle-band."

Besides band decoration " cord " decoration also occurs, particularly on sepulchral vessels. It was produced — at least partly — by impressing a cord, of bast for instance, into the clay while still soft. In this way rings and systems of rings, consisting alternately of oblique elevations and depressions, could be produced, as also zigzag lines and other combinations of lines, so that cord ornament shows a fair variety of motives. Immediately connected with cord decoration is " dot " decoration, done with a finely pointed rod, with which rows of dots were produced, often closely resembling cord decoration ; it is then described as " false cord " decoration.

There is no doubt whatever that in the main these clay vessels were made on the spot where we find their remains at the present day. This easily explains the local peculiarity that we recognise in various finds, by which certain groups may be defined as more or less connected with one another. Different styles may be clearly distinguished by place and group. But, this notwithstanding, wherever we meet with neolithic ceramics, they cannot conceal their homogeneous character. In spite of all peculiarities this general uniform style of the ceramics of the Stone Age, which we can easily distinguish and determine even under its various disguises, goes over the whole of Europe. In finds that lie nearer to the old Asiatic centres of civilisation and to the coasts of the Mediterranean — as, for instance, at Butmir — the vessels are in part better worked, and the ornaments are richer and more elegant, and the spirals more frequent and more regular, and are sometimes moulded on, and sometimes even, as we have mentioned, painted in colour, etc. But the general character remains unmistakably neolithic, and may be found not only on the European coasts of the Mediterranean and the islands of the Ægean Sea, but in certain respects also in Mesopotamia and Egypt. The oldest Trojan pottery also exhibits unmistakable points of agreement with it. Such agreement consists in the vertical perforation and the peculiar form and placing of the small handles, and in the drawing of the ornaments ; the urn-lids, the handles pierced with groove-shaped holes, and particularly the white encrusted ornaments, also afford the most definite points of comparison. This conformity in the ceramics of the Stone Age may be traced even much farther; in Asia it extends as far as Japan, where the shell-mounds correspond largely to the Danish ones and also exhibit unmistakable conformity in their potsherds, although these have their local peculiarities. That the oldest pottery productions of America prove the same thing we have already pointed out.

Not only the stone weapons and implements, but, as far as we can see, even the remains of the oldest ceramics, show that uniform development of the culture of the neolithic period which proves a like course of mental development in mankind.

### D. Dwellings and Domestic Life

(*a*) *Sketch of the Civilisation of the Stone Age Lake-Dwellings.* — A picture, of unequalled clearness of delineation, of the general conditions of the life and culture of central European Man during the neolithic period was given, according to the results of the celebrated researches of Ferdinand Keller and his school of Swiss archæologists, by the lake-dwellings in the Alpine lowlands.

Whereas in cave districts the caves and grottos often served the men of the later Stone Age as temporary and even as permanent winter-dwellings, in the watery valleys of Switzerland the neolithic population built its huts on foundations of piles in lakes and bogs. In that period we have to imagine the Alpine lowlands still extensively covered with woods and full of wild beasts; at that time the huts standing on piles in the water must have afforded their inhabitants a security such as scarcely any other place could have given. The first founders and inhabitants of settlements of pile-dwellings in Switzerland belong to the pure Stone period. In spite of their lake-dwellings the old neolithic men of Switzerland appear to have possessed almost all the important domestic animals, but they also knew and practised agriculture. They lived by cattle-rearing, agriculture, hunting, and fishing, and on wild fruit and all that the plant world freely offered in the way of eatables. Their clothing consisted partly of skins, but partly also of stuffs, the majority of which seem to have been prepared from flax.

The endeavour of the settlers to live together in lasting homes protected from surprises, and in large numbers, is an unmistakable proof that they were aware of the advantages of a settled mode of life, and that we have not to imagine the inhabitants of the pile-dwellings as nomadic herdsmen, and still less as a regular race of hunters and fishermen. The permanent concentration of a large number of individuals at the same point, and of hundreds of families in neighbouring inlets of the lakes, could not have taken place if there had not been through all the seasons a regular supply of provisions derived principally from cattle-rearing and agriculture, and if there had not existed the elements of social order. Even the establishment of the lake-settlement itself is not possible for the individual man; a large community must have here worked with a common plan and purpose. Herodotus describes a pile-village in Lake Prosias, in Thracia, which was inhabited by Pæones, who defended it successfully against the Persian general Megabazos. The scaffold on which the huts were built stood on high piles in the middle of the lake; it was connected with the bank only by a single, easily removable bridge. Herodotus says:

" The piles on which the scaffolds rest were erected in olden times by the citizens in a body; the enlargement of the lake-settlement took place later, according as it was necessitated by the formation of new families."

According to the large number of lake-dwellings of the Stone Age in the Alpine lowlands, and according to the large quantity of products of primitive industry that have been found there, centuries must have elapsed between the moment when the first settlers rammed in the piles on which to build their dwellings and the end of the Stone period.

The huts of the settlements of the Stone Age were partly round and partly quadrangular, and, like the pile-hut discovered by Frank near Schussenried,[1] were divided into two compartments, — one for the cattle, and the other, with a hearth built of stones, for the dwelling of Man. The floor of the hut was made of round timber with a mud foundation, and perhaps also with a mud flooring; in Frank's hut the walls were formed of split tree-trunks, standing vertically with the split sides turned inward, firmly put together between corner-posts. The round huts had walls of roughly intertwined branches, covered with clay inside and out; of this clay-plaster numerous pieces have been preserved, hardened by fire, with the marks of the branches. The pile-huts of the lakes were connected with the water by block or rung ladders. Victor Gross found such a ladder in one of the oldest stations; it consisted of a long oak pole provided at fairly regular intervals with holes in which the rungs were inserted.

The most important finds illustrative of the earliest civilisation of the lake-dwellings are the stone implements and weapons, of the same forms and the same use and mode of production as have already been described. As the material for axes and celts the Swiss lake-dwellers generally employed boulders, such as were everywhere at hand, — for example, serpentine, diorite, or gabbro, — greenstones being preferred. But besides these the rare stones nephrite, jadeite, and chloromelanite were also used. The stone axes and celts were generally fastened into a handle; often they were first fixed into a holder of deer-horn, which was then in its turn inserted into the wooden handle. In rarer cases the axes were fastened into a club-shaped stick or into a handle consisting entirely of deer-horn.[2] In Switzerland it seems to have been only toward the end of the Stone Age that the idea came to Man of perforating the axe itself to receive the handle, thus producing the typical form of the axe-hammer.[3] Keller, Ford, and others have proved that with the assistance of water and sand any hollow bone is sufficient to pierce the hardest stone. Many instruments still show the round peg produced by the boring not completely ground out of the stone; loose pegs, small regularly ground cylinders of stone, have also been found. The stone to be pierced has, however, also been simply scraped through from both sides with a flint borer, and the form of the hole is accordingly not so regular. Here, too, we see the importance of the relatively small and insignificant-looking flint implements described above; " flint is the material," said Keller, " by which every tool directly or indirectly obtains its form."

The other stones served for a number of other purposes besides those we have mentioned. Of them were made, for instance, striking and hammering stones of every form, pestles and mortars, millstones, grindstones, smoothing-stones for the manufacture of pottery, spinning-whorls, and various ornaments. Among the

---

[1] See Fig. 15, Plate at p. 144.     [2] Fig. 16.     [3] Figs. 17 and 18.

flint weapons daggers are conspicuous, consisting of pointed flint blades set in handles. The handle is hollowed out at one end to receive the end of the blade; at the other it often has a knob-like protuberance. The flint blade was first fastened with resin, then the whole handle was wound round with hackled flax or bands of twisted rushes. The handle was often the brow-antler of a deer. Small axes for cutting purposes—made of nephrite, for instance—were also fastened in such handles. The flint arrow-heads and spear-heads were generally made with great care; the majority of the flint implements, however, appear in the well-known Drift forms of rude knives and scrapers. Countless refuse flakes prove that the flint was worked on the spot. Some large sickle-shaped blades, similar to the northern flint sickles, have also been discovered in the lake-dwellings of Switzerland. Large saw-shaped blades were sometimes made by fastening small sharp flint-flakes with resin in a groove of a piece of wood or deer-horn.

It has been asserted that even at that time flint was commercially imported into Switzerland,—for instance, from the flint districts of the north. What appears more certain is that toward the end of the Stone Age amber was brought in single lumps from the amber districts of the north.

The manufactures of deer-horn and bone exhibit an abundant variety. The quantity of deer-horn found in the lake-dwellings proves that in the Stone Age the woods were literally peopled with deer, and that the hunting of these animals, in spite of the apparently inadequate means at the disposal of the inhabitants of the lake-dwellings, offered no great difficulties. As the palæolithic men at the source of the Schussen carved all kinds of articles from the horns of the reindeer, so did the neolithic men in the Swiss lake-villages from the horns of the stag. From the thickest parts of the horns, particularly from the burr,[1] were made the above-mentioned sheath-like holders for axes and hammers that were set in the wooden handle. A branch with the brow-antler still on it represented a kind of pick; the many-pointed branch itself, transversely pierced, furnished a dangerous weapon and a kind of rake. Other implements remind one of shovels and hoes, and would probably in fact, like the pick, have served for agricultural purposes. In the way of fishing-implements hooks of deer-horn and excellently worked harpoons with barbs have been found.[2] In various lake-dwellings well-preserved remains of nets were discovered; also a number of stone net-weights still wound round with string, which were doubtless fastened to the meshes of the net to sink it to the bottom. Deer-horn was further used for making small cups, which were provided with holes for hanging up; also neck-beads and very skilfully carved ear-drops; large buttons, frequently decorated; needles with eyes; small combs, arrows, awls, and prickers; and larger and smaller pins or needles, some with heads, and others with added pieces pierced laterally, evidently for threading.

On account of its greater firmness, bone, chiefly of the deer and ox, was much used for making weapons and implements. The ribs of the cow or deer, pierced at the end and tied together in threes with string, formed combs for hackling flax. The majority of the daggers were also made of bone, and the handle was either formed by the natural joint-end, or the bone blade was fixed in a special horn handle. Arrow-heads and lance-heads of bone are far more frequent than those of flint; the bone lance-head was fastened to the wooden shaft by binding it round with thread, which was then enveloped with a coat of birch resin. A large number of

[1] Fig. 16, Plate at p. 144.          [2] Fig. 19.

awls and chisels of bone in all sizes are also found; one end is pointed and sharp, the other fixed in a handle of deer-horn.[1] Teeth of animals, chiefly of the wolf, bear, dog, and hog, were pierced for wearing as amulets or in necklaces.[2]

A good many wooden articles from the Stone Age of the lake-dwellings are also known. There is a yoke exactly like those that are used for leading cattle at the present day, and there are neat little combs made of boxwood. Boats worked from a single tree-trunk have also been preserved from that period; one was 31 feet long and 2 feet 3 inches to 3 feet broad. As supplementing the numerous arrows several bows have also been found; one of boxwood is 5 feet 3 inches long. A small bow of the same material was also discovered that evidently belonged to a bow-drill, either for piercing stone axes, or, more probably, for kindling fire. Other wooden things were flails, spear-sticks, bowls, and cups, — many provided with handles, — spoons, twirling-sticks, hammers, little ships as children's playthings, etc. In the Berne Museum there are even fragments of tables, benches, and doors from lake-dwellings of the Stone Age.

Of special importance in estimating the degree of civilisation attained by the lake-dwellers of the Stone Age are the remains of spinning and weaving implements and of webs[3] and textile fabrics, plaited work, etc. Flax has been found wound on the implements made of ribs, that we mentioned above as flax-combs; we have also mentioned the fixing of blades with flax, or threads made of it, and the numerous wide and narrow nets made of threads. For spinning the thread, spindles were used just like those of the present day, a spindle-stick of wood being fastened into a spinning-whorl made of stone, deer-horn, or clay.[4] The distaff was probably not yet known; a loom has not yet been found, either; but numerous weavers' weights, which served for spinning the thread, have been. Excellent webs, some of them twilled, were produced, of which we have many fragments. Remains of mats and baskets prove that these were manufactured from the materials still employed at the present day.[5]

Corn was baked into a kind of bread consisting of coarsely ground grains. The millstones that were used for grinding the corn are found in large numbers. They are rather worn, hollowed slabs of stone and smaller flat stones rounded on the top, with which the grains of corn were crushed on the larger slabs.[6] Some of the kitchen utensils we find already much improved. Large and small pots for storing purposes, earthen cooking-pots and dishes, and large wooden spoons and twirling-sticks, — the latter probably for churning, — have been preserved. Vessels like strainers served for making cheese; they are pots in whose sides and bottoms a number of small holes were made for pouring off the whey from the cheese.

Here in the fully developed neolithic period we find the early inhabitants of Switzerland to be a settled agricultural and farming population. Although hunting and fishing still furnished an important part of their food, so that in some places even more deer bones have been found among the cooking remains than bones of the ox, yet the milk, cheese, and butter of the cows, sheep, and goats, the flesh of these and of the hog, and bread and fruit already formed the basis of their subsistence.

*(b) The Neolithic Cave-Dwellings and Other Land Settlements.* — The results of cave research are almost as rich and varied as the results yielded by the study of

---

[1] Fig. 20, Plate at p. 144.    [2] Figs. 21–23.    [3] Fig. 25.    [4] Fig. 24.    [5] Figs. 26, 27.    [6] Fig. 28.

the lake-dwellings in their bearing on the neolithic stratum.  Where there is a
Drift stratum in the cave-earth the confusion of palæolithic and neolithic objects
can, as we have said,[1] scarcely be avoided.  But there are numerous grottoes and
small caves in which the neolithic stratum is the oldest, so that mistakes are out
of the question.  In a large number of such places in the cave-district of the
Franconian-Bavarian Jura the conditions under which finds have been made in
the neolithic stratum have proved almost as pure and unmixed as in the lake-
dwellings.

The cave-dwellers of the later Stone Age in the Franconian Jura were, like
the Swiss lake-dwellers of the Stone Age, mainly a pastoral race.  They possessed
all the important domestic animals that the latter possessed — dog, cow, horse, sheep,
goat, pig — and likewise practised agriculture, or, at any rate, flax-growing; at the
same time hunting and fishing formed a considerable part of their means of subsistence.  So that, not only on artificial pile-works on the shores of lakes, but
also on the banks of south German rivers, there formerly lived a race which,
although still mainly restricted to hunting and fishing, and using no metal, but
exclusively stone and bone tools, already practised cattle-breeding and primitive
agriculture, and was able to increase the means of existence afforded it by nature
by the first technical arts,— by the chipping and grinding of stone instruments,
bone-carving, and, above all, pottery-making, tanning, and the arts of sewing, weaving, and plaiting.  Real archæological treasures have been dug up from under the
protecting rock-shelters.  The majority of the articles are carvings from bone, teeth,
and deer-horn, weapons, implements, and ornaments of the most various kinds.
The firm antlers of the common stag served for making awls, needles, arrow-heads,
and larger tools.  Many of these latter are also carved from bones of the deer, these
having proved specially suited for this purpose owing to their firm structure and
the high polish that could be given them.  But, besides the deer, the ox in particular supplied hollow bones and ribs as material for making bone tools.  Besides the
tame ox, the bone material also shows signs of a wild ox, probably the bison
(*Bison europæus*), which has given its German name to the Wisent, the chief
river of those rocky districts.  A species of horse of medium breed is represented
among the finds by perforated teeth and by tools and weapons carved from its
bones.  The false ribs of the horse, which are almost square in section, furnished
handy bone daggers, rather curved and sharp-pointed, and large needles.[2]  Horses'
ribs, like the metatarsal bone of the horse elsewhere, also served as runners for
skates.  Boar tusks were ground into knives with sharp edges, and the canine
teeth of the dog, a large breed of hound, furnished perforated beads or amulets.

Among the stone implements knives, scrapers, and arrow-heads appear in large
numbers, and also refuse flakes of flint and chert, some of them tiny and most
insignificant.  The larger forms of stone implements — hatchets, axes, and
hammers — are similar to those of Switzerland, but their material, corresponding
to the local conditions, is in part much inferior, — jura-limestone and slate.  Stone
"leather-cutters" of the latter material were found which are almost exactly like
those that in Sweden are ascribed to the Stone Age of the Lapps; long, narrow,
sword-like blades of slate were also found.  Conspicuous among the perforated
stone implements are flat stone hoes, with the edge turned vertically to the length
of the handle; these probably served as instruments for tilling the ground.  Very

---

[1] *Ante*, p. 139.        [2] See Fig. 23, Plate at p. 144.

long, narrow stone implements of greenstone have also been declared to be a kind of ploughshare.

The characteristic forms of deer-horn and bone instruments are awls, daggers, styles, and bone knives, spoons, and forks,[1] bone chisels,[2] and bone hammers. The most frequent bone weapons are arrow-heads, lance-heads, and harpoons. The form of the arrow-heads is strikingly different in different places. The difference in form and fixing of the arrow-heads probably corresponded to the well-known owner's marks by which modern tribes of hunters generally distinguish their weapons. When a deer is shot, a hunter can thus claim that it was killed by his arrow. The bone harpoons with one or more points were adapted for spearing under water the larger salmon-trout, otters, and beavers, which at that time were native to the valley of the Wisent. Large bone hooks were also in use for fishing.

Of most importance, as showing the state of civilisation of the neolithic rock-dwellers, are the numerous articles carved from bone that must be looked upon as instruments for weaving and net-knitting. For the latter purpose there were large, finely smoothed bone crochet-needles, some of them carved from the rib of a large ruminant.[3] The handle-end is smoothed by use, and the end with the hook is rounded from the same cause. The end is frequently perforated, so that it might be hung up. Still more numerous were shuttles of various forms. Among the finds the form of shuttle that is still usual at the present day is frequently represented in various sizes.[4] Some are unperforated, but most of them have one or two round or oval openings in the centre of the flat sides for tying on the thread that is wound around them, besides an incision running around the breadth. But instead of the double-pointed shuttle we have very frequently a rather long, flat- or round plaiting or weaving needle, blunt-pointed at one end and rounded at the other, and perforated near the round end. There were also flat shuttles like arrow-heads, with a perforation of the flat end that was narrowed off shaftwise. A bone instrument toothed like a saw may have served for dressing the thread, and a long, flat bone blade, like a sword, for beating the thread in the loom. According to the numerous finds of perforated clay weaver's weights, the loom, like that of the lake-dwellers, must have been like the ancient implement that, according to Montelius, was in use on the Faröe Islands a comparatively short time ago. Spinning-whorls are very numerous, being partly flat, round disks of bone pierced in the centre, and partly thick bone rings or large beads of bone and deer-horn and flat burr-pieces of deer-antlers. The characteristic forms of the spinning-whorls of burnt clay, known only to the lake-dwellings, were also frequently found in the rock-dwellings of the Wisent valley. Sewing-needles of bone are frequent. They are much smaller and narrower than the plaiting-needles, and some of them are perfectly round and very well pointed and eyed, but for sewing skins the holes must first have been pierced with the small pointed flint awls often found.

Ornaments of bone and deer-horn are numerous: spherical or square, and shuttle-like or chisel-shaped beads; also perforated teeth of animals, chiefly of the dog, bear, boar, and horse. Some of the large black beads of slightly burnt clay are of the typical form of spinning-whorls. There were also decorative plates and pieces of bone, deer-horn, and a slate-like stone, occasionally of ornamental form. Some of them are ornamented with rows of lines or dots, and a few with engraved

[1] Fig. 30, Plate at p. 144.     [2] Fig. 31.     [3] Fig. 32.     [4] Fig. 33.

stags' heads; almost all are pierced for sewing on. Some are like ornamental buttons.

It was formerly thought that the neolithic Europeans did not possess the arts of engraving and carving animal and human figures which the palæolithic men had understood in such conspicuous manner. The progress of research has now produced more and more proof that in the later Stone Age the arts of carving and engraving had not died out. We have the celebrated amber carvings of the later Stone Age from the Kurisches Haff, near Schwarzort,[1] some of which probably served a religious purpose; those of ivory, bone, stalactite, etc., from the caves of France and the Polish Jura;[2] the figures from Butmir, etc.

As there is scarcely a lake in the whole Alpine lowlands, north and south, in which proofs of pile-dwellings have not been found, which correspond, down to the smallest detail, with those of Switzerland, and are doubtless contemporary with them, so there are in all the cave districts of Europe a large number of caves and grottoes in which, as in those just described, the existence of a neolithic culture-stratum, exhibiting everywhere the same type, has been proved with absolute certainty. Specially good investigations have been made of the neolithic caves in Austria-Hungary, England, France, northern Italy, Poland, European Russia, etc.

In Italy, in Lombardy and Emilia, another group of settlements of the Stone Age has been found, which again exhibit the civilisation and all other signs of the later Stone Age, and in many respects more closely resemble the lake-dwellings than do the cave-dwellings. These are the "terramare," whose inhabitants, however, had already to some extent advanced to the use of bronze. A sharp division of strata into habitation of the pure Stone Age and habitation of the Metal Age has not yet been made. The huts stood on pile-work on dry land, the piles being six to ten feet high; and the whole settlement was fortified with trench and rampart, generally with palisades, and was of an oblong or oval plan. Besides many natural and artificial caves in Italy the dwelling-pits (*fondi di campanne*), which may formerly have borne the superstructure of a hut, also belong to the pure Stone Age.

Such dwelling-pits of the Stone Age seem to have been distributed all over Europe. Burnt wall-plaster with impressions of interwoven twigs has frequently been found near or in the pits, doubtless indicating hut-building. In Mecklenburg, where the dwelling-pits were first carefully examined by Liesch, they have a circular outline of ten to fifteen yards and are five to six and a half feet deep. At the bottom of the pit lie burnt and blackened stones, hearthstones, charcoal, potsherds, broken bones of animals, and a few stone implements, the latter being mostly found in larger numbers in the vicinity of the dwellings. The same circular dwelling-pits of the Stone Age are found in France. Smaller hearth-pits were recently found in very large numbers in the Spessart, in Bavaria, with hundreds of stone hatchets and perforated axe-hammers; some of the former being very finely made of jadeite.

During the neolithic period dwellings were frequently made on heights, and it seems that even at that time they were to a certain extent walled round and fortified. Such settlements are numerous all over southern and central Germany, in Austria-Hungary, especially in the coast-country, and in Italy and France. Many of these stations belong purely to the Stone Age; indeed the majority were already inhabited during the Stone Age, and furnish the typical neolithic relics

---

[1] See Fig. 34, Plate at p. 144.          [2] Fig. 35.

familiar from the foregoing. On the other hand they continue to be inhabited even in the later metal epochs, and in some cases right down to modern times. The rock near Clausen, in the Eisack valley in the Tyrol, on which the large Saben monastery now stands, was a mediæval castle, and during the times of the Romans a fortified settlement called Sobona stood there; and when excavations were made several years ago (1895), for adding new buildings to the monastery, a well-ground stone hatchet of the later Stone Age came to light. On many hills in central Germany are found traces of the ancient presence of men who lived on them or assembled on them for sacrificial feasts; the earth is coloured black by charred remains and organic influences, and this "black earth on heights and hills" contains frequently, as we have said, the traces of neolithic men. In Italy many finds on such heights — for instance, those made on the small castle-hill near Imola — seem to exhibit that stage of the Stone Age that is missing in the terramare, and that precedes the beginning of the Metal Age of the terramare, but corresponds to it in every essential except in the possession of metal.

In north Africa, in Greece, on the coasts of the Black Sea, in Asia Minor; in the old Eastern centre of civilisation, the lands of the Euphrates; in China and Japan, — in the whole of the old civilised world are found the proofs of a former neolithic age; there, too, the strata of higher civilisation rest on this old stratum. In this vast region of lands man's state of civilisation during the developed later Stone Age was in the main similar: the latter is the general basis of the Old World civilisation.

The general outlines of the picture of civilisation are everywhere alike. But that does not exclude numerous local shadings, and we are probably not wrong in assuming that in the old civilised lands of the East and on the coasts of the Mediterranean, where cattle-rearing and plant-growing gave quite a different return, a higher stage of life could more quickly be reached than in the woods and marshes of central Europe, where hunting and fishing and the fight with inhospitable nature must have taxed the powers in much greater measure.

But the view that is opened up is still wider. The prehistoric times of the New World also exhibit a neolithic stage, corresponding to that of Europe, as the basis of the further development of the ancient civilised lands of America. And where a higher civilisation did not develop autochthonously in America, European discoverers found the neolithic civilisation still in active existence, as they did in the whole Australian world.[1] Accordingly in these vast regions, which have never risen above the Stone Age of themselves, the same stage of civilisation which in the old civilised lands belongs to a grey, immemorial, prehistoric period, here stands in the broad light of historic times. The study of modern tribes in an age of stone throws many a ray of light on the conditions of the prehistoric Stone Age; and this study, on the other hand, shows us that the primitive conditions of civilisation of those tribes stand for a general stage of transition in the development of all mankind.

(c) *Stone Structures and Graves.* — The lake-dwelling stations, and the land settlements resembling them, prove of themselves how far the culture of the early inhabitants of Europe was advanced, even in that ancient period which was formerly imagined to be scarcely raised above half-animal conditions. Such

---

[1] See Fig. 36, Plate at p. 144.

structures could not be erected without men combining into large social communities, which is indeed indicated by the very fact of the number of dwellings that were crowded into a comparatively small space. For the first ramming-in of the pile-works a large number of men working together on a common plan was absolutely necessary. The same applies to the construction of the artificial islands, produced by pile-works and partly resting on piles, termed "crannoges" by Irish archæologists, and to the Italian villages called "terramare," which likewise once rested on piles and were protected by ditches. From the extent of the pile-works we are able to estimate the number of the former inhabitants of the settlements supported by them. Quite as clear an idea of the number of the former inhabitants is also given by the early circumvallations on the tops of hills and shoulders of rock, which were likewise made and inhabited during the Stone Age.

The co-operation of a large number of men for a common purpose is also shown in the often huge stone structures to which, on account of the size of the stones employed in their construction, the name "megalithic" structures, or gigantic stone structures, has been given. In northern Europe they, too, belong to the Stone Age proper. The majority of these gigantic structures were originally tombs; the principle on which they are built is often repeated even in far less imposing tombs.

In northern Germany the megalithic structures are frequently termed "Hünenbetten," or "giants' graves;" in Scandinavia they are called "giants' chambers," as in their original construction they really imitate dwellings.

The stone blocks of which these gigantic structures are piled now often lie bare. Large stones placed crosswise, which represent as it were the side-walls of a room, support a roof of one or several "covering-stones" of occasionally colossal size.[1] For the erection of these in their present position without the technical resources at the disposal of modern builders, human strength appears inadequate; in popular opinion only giants could have made such structures. Some of the stones are really so large, and the covering-stones especially so enormous, that these buildings have defied destruction, for thousands of years, by their very weight.

In the time of their construction these giants' graves were mostly buried under mounds. They were the inner structures of large tumuli, in which the reverence of the men of the Stone Age once buried its heroes. One of the finest "giants' chambers" is probably that near Öm, in the neighbourhood of Roskilde, in Denmark.[2] The building material consists merely of erratic stone blocks of enormous size. The rough blocks were mostly set up by the side of one another, without any further working, so as to support one another as far as possible; at the same time all of them, as Sophus Müller observes, are slightly inclined inward, so that they are kept more firmly in position by their own weight. The stones thus erected, forming the parallel side-walls of the whole structure, stand so far apart that a huge erratic block, reaching from one wall to the other, could be placed on them as a roof. The distance between the side-walls of the giants' chambers attains a maximum of eight to nine feet; the covering-stones placed on them are some ten to eleven feet long. The pressure of the covering-stones from above helps considerably to hold the whole structure together. In

[1] See Fig. 37, Plate at p. 144.          [2] Fig. 38

order to distribute the pressure of the covering-stones regularly, smaller stones were carefully inserted under the wall-stones where they had to stand on the ground. How exactly these proportions of weight were judged is proved by the fact that these structures of heavy and irregular stones, resting on their natural, differently shaped sides and edges, have held together until the present day. The inner walls of the chambers were made as carefully as possible. Where, as on the outside, the rough and irregular form of the stone block projects, either the naturally smooth side was turned inward or the roughness was chipped off.

These are the beginnings of a real architecture; it is seen also in the regular wedging with small stones of the spaces left between the wall-stones and covering-stones and between the wall-stones themselves. These small stones were frequently built in, in regular wall-like layers. Sandstone was often used for the purpose, being more easily split into regular pieces, which gave this masonry a still more pleasing appearance. The number of stone blocks used for the wall-sides varies according to the size of the giants' chambers, as does also the number of covering-stones. For smaller chambers, with six to nine wall-stones, two or three covering-stones were required. But far larger stone chambers occur, as many as seventeen wall-stones having been counted. Such large chambers require a whole row of covering-stones beside one another. The door-opening often shows a special regard for architectonics. The two door-post stones are rather lower than the other wall-stones; on them a stone was laid horizontally, which kept them apart and distributed the pressure of the covering-stone equally on both posts. Very often there was also a stone as a threshold. Leading to the door is a low passage, made in similar manner to the chamber, but of far smaller stones. The passage is only high enough to allow one to creep through, whereas the chamber itself is about as high as a man, so that one could stand upright in most of them. Larger stone chambers are rarely without this passage, and from it such grave-structures have been named "passage-graves." Besides the building in of small stones, the holes still remaining between the stones were also coated over on the outside with mud to keep the rain-water from soaking in; mud was also frequently used for making a rough plaster floor for the chamber if the natural floor could not be made level enough. On the floor is frequently found a compact layer of small flints, or a regular pavement of flat stones, often rough-hewn, or roundish stones fitting one another as nearly as possible, which were then probably also covered with a thick layer of mud.

So that in these giants' chambers we have real buildings, which imply high technical accomplishments and have preserved for us the usual form of the dwellings of those early times. In what manner the huge covering-stones were placed on the side-walls of the giants' chambers is a problem still unsolved. Doubtless many hands were occupied on such structures; and the history of building teaches us that with the proper use of human strength — as, for instance, in ancient Egypt — great weights can be raised and placed in position with very simple tools, — round pieces of wood as rollers, ropes, and handspikes.

Some of these giants' chambers, which were originally enclosed in mounds or barrows, are still preserved at the present day, and splendidly too. Very often the chamber was quite covered with earth outside; it then formed the centre of what was generally a circular barrow, often regular small hills ten to fifteen feet high and frequently over ninety feet in circumference. On other giants' chambers the covering-stones lay quite bare, or at least their upper side was not covered by a layer of earth. Many of these chambers lie in an oblong barrow, with a rectangular wreath of large stones round the foot of the barrow: round barrows are often without this wreath, or it consists of very insignificant stones.

Besides these gigantic structures, smaller but similarly built stone graves of the Stone Age occur in the north. Others are "round graves," often surrounded with a wreath of large stones; otherwise the smaller stone grave, or several such, lies in a long enclosure of stones of rectangular outline. Graves represented by a quadrangular stone cist, square or oblong, are pronounced to be later forms. Still more simple are single graves set round with stones, or without anything of the kind, in the earth or in the floors of caves.

The corpses were buried, not cremated. They were frequently in a crouching attitude, or that of a sleeper lying sideways with the legs drawn up to the body. The smaller graves often represent single interments; the larger or largest ones are mostly family tombs, in which numerous corpses were interred one after the other at different times. But this repeated use of the graves is found also with smaller ones, and even with stone cists. Only the last corpse then lies in a normal position, while, through the repeated opening of the grave and the later interments, the skeletons belonging to previously interred corpses appear more or less disturbed or intentionally put aside.

The skulls of the corpses interred in the neolithic graves are well formed, their size indicating a very considerable brain development. The corpses were no bigger than the present inhabitants of the same districts, and the form of the head corresponds partly — for instance, in Franconia and Thuringia — to that of the present population of those countries. Nor do the skeletons otherwise differ from those of modern men.

The megalithic tombs of the northern countries of Scandinavia and Germany belong to the pure Stone Age. These structures may be found scattered far and wide over Europe; they, too, tell of the homogeneousness of primitive culture and thought. Stone graves are found in all three Scandinavian kingdoms, most rarely in Norway. In the west of Germany megalithic tombs occur in various forms, similar or closely allied to the northern ones, over the whole north German plain. In the east they extend to the Vistula, but are not found in Russia or in the interior of Europe; in Germany their offshoots go as far as Thuringia. Connected with the western north German group of stone graves are very large and numerous structures of a similar kind in Holland. Some of the megalithic structures in England exactly resemble the northern ones;[1] others differ considerably. They often consist of several chambers lying behind one another and connected by a short passage. Large covering-stones are generally absent: they are replaced by an arched superstructure of horizontal stones pushed forward over one another like steps. The mound covering these structures is of a long oval in shape. The Irish giants' chambers are similarly arched in, and some of them are of complicated form and particularly huge size. The numerous large chambers of Brittany are also related to the English ones. Besides these, imposing chambers occur in France, generally also with an arched covering, which traverse the tumulus in the form of long, high, regular passages. In Portugal passage-graves are found

---

[1] See Fig. 39, Plate at p. 144.

which closely resemble the northern ones. Some of the giants' chambers of Spain, which are scattered chiefly over Andalusia and Granada, are really huge art-structures; one of the most celebrated of these tombs lies near the village of Antequera, north of Malaga. Its interior measures eighty feet in length, twenty feet in breadth, and nine and a half feet in height, and a row of pillars support the covering-stones.

It has been pointed out, and certainly with reason, that the imposing and technically, far more perfect tombs of the countries and islands of the Mediterranean, although built of hewn stones, still breathe the same spirit as the megalithic tombs of unhewn stones, and may be placed on a parallel with them; for instance, the oblong tombs on the Balearic Islands, the chambers of the Maltese Islands, and the tower-like "nuraghs" in Sardinia. But the large forms of tombs of the old civilised lands of the East may also be mentioned, — their artificial tombs amid rocks, their stone chambers and domed sepulchres; indeed even the pyramids of Egypt afford bases of comparison. Everywhere it was the same line of thought which guided Man in the erection of colossal structures for the dead; everywhere it was the wish to protect them as carefully as possible and to preserve their bodies from desecration. This led to burial in natural or artificial caves, and in stone structures which were put together as firmly as possible and were meant to display a monumental character in honour of the deceased. Stone structures similar to the megalithic tombs have also been discovered in Algiers, Palestine, and India.

Besides the numerous covered stone structures there are others with the roof and side stones perfectly free. Many of these appear never to have been covered with a mound; others have doubtless been dug out, the story of treasures having been deposited in ancient graves having always attracted treasure-seekers. Such uncovered structures, which now as a rule consist of one or several colossal unhewn stones lying more or less irregularly as a cover on a number of upright blocks, were formerly termed pagan altars; in Brittany they are popularly called " dolmens," or " stone tables,"[1] a word which, like " cromlech " (" stone circle ") and "menhir" ("long" or "high stone"), has been adopted by the language of archæology. The menhirs are large, single, upright stones corresponding to rude obelisks; many are really gigantic. They are found in particularly large numbers in the Department of Morbihan; one of them is sixty-two feet high and sixteen and a half feet broad in the middle. In the celebrated field at Carnac there are eleven thousand menhirs erected in eleven rows.

Not only in the north of Europe, but also in Germany, the megalithic structures belong to the pure Stone Age, while in the south and west isolated metal objects and other things belonging to a later period of culture are often found in the stone chambers.

In America, also, gigantic structures were erected by the aborigines who lived in the Stone Age, to commemorate and to protect their dead. They consist partly of large mounds of stones and earth, which are likewise often regular small hills,[2] and partly of stone structures reminding one of the giants' chambers. Such ancient sepulchres are found in Peru and Bolivia under the name of "chulpas," and are built of huge stones covered with enormous stone slabs. Besides these rudest stone chambers there occur others of hewn stones, which partly

---

[1] See Fig. 37, Plate at p. 144.          [2] See Plate at p. 144.

represent domes, and in a certain sense remind one of the nuraghs of Sardinia. The majority of the mounds were doubtless mainly sepulchral; others may have served either sacred or profane purposes, such as temple-hills or sacrificial mounds, defensive works or observatories. Such mounds are extraordinarily numerous, especially in the Mississippi valley, but also in the valleys of the Ohio and its district, and in Wisconsin and Illinois. Some are geometrical in shape, truncated pyramids or terraces, circular, elliptical, semi-lunar, or cruciform; the outlines of others apparently imitate figures of animals, — often even of men, — and so forth. These animal mounds served, it is supposed, chiefly for religious purposes. In the real sepulchral mounds sepulchral chambers and cists are found, built partly of rough field-stones and partly of beams. The objects buried with the occupants belong mostly to the neolithic period, and consist chiefly of stone weapons and tools, some rude, but others finely worked and polished. Some are of pure natural copper, which was beaten into shape, cold with stone hammers. Besides these, and ornaments and pottery, an American specialty is found in the form of tobacco-pipes carved from stone, some of which give interesting representations of men and animals; this seems to prove that tobacco also played a part in the American funeral rites of those times.[1]

The graves of the neolithic period not only indicate that mankind generally was endowed with the same gifts as regards the first principles of the art of building, but they also afford us a glimpse of the mental life of that period of civilisation which at a more or less distant period was spread over the whole earth. What is so characteristic is the affectionate care for the corpse, for whose protection no amount of labour and trouble appeared too great. We can have no doubt that this reverence was based on a belief in the immortality of the soul, — a belief which we find also at the present day among the most backward and abandoned "savages." That the prehistoric men of the Stone Age held this belief is proved by the ornaments, weapons, implements, and food that were placed in the grave with the dead for their use in the next world. Their burial customs certainly express a kind of worship of the departed souls of their forefathers, which has played and still plays so important a part in the religious ideas of all primitive peoples, and is thus proved to be one of the oldest fundamental notions common to mankind.

## 3. THE PERIODS OF DAWNING HISTORY

The discovery of Drift Man, his distinction from Man of the later Stone Age, the investigation of the palaeolithic and neolithic strata of culture of Europe and of the whole earth, and the scientific reconstruction of the earliest forms of civilisation based on these, are due solely to the natural-science method of research. It was only when the exact methods of palaeontology and geology had been brought to bear with all their rigour on the study of ancient Man by savants schooled in natural science, that solid results were obtained. On this sure foundation the science of history now continues building, and uses, even for the later epochs, so far as recorded information is not available, and to supplement it, the same methods of palaeontology and natural science which were applied so successfully to the earliest stages of the evolution of mankind.

---

[1] For these and allied questions see post p. 208.

The first point is to collect the relics of the epochs of the evolution of culture which follow on the later Stone Age, and to separate them according to geological strata, uninfluenced by those older pseudo-historic fancies by which the deepening of our historical knowledge has so long been hindered. By carefully separating and tracing the earth's strata till we come to those that furnish remains of times recorded in history, it has been possible to establish first a relative chronology of the so-called later prehistoric periods of central Europe, whose offshoots pass immediately into recorded history. By digging, after the same method of palæontological science, through stratum after stratum in the oldest centres of culture, especially in the Mediterranean countries, and by arranging the products by strata — uninfluenced by historical hypotheses — after the same natural-science method of research which has produced such remarkable results in central Europe, the most surprising conformity in the evolution of culture in widely remote regions has been shown. It was found that in the Mediterranean countries, and also in Egypt and Babylonia, forms of culture already belong to the time of real history which were first recognised in central Europe as preliminary prehistoric stages of historical strata: so that it was possible also to establish an absolute historical chronology for those instead of the relative prehistoric one.

Thus times which, as regards central Europe, were hitherto wrapped in prehistoric night, are enlightened by history. Although, as regards central and northern Europe, we cannot name the peoples who were the bearers of those forms of culture, and although we disdain to give them a premature nomenclature of hypothetical names, yet their conditions of life and culture and the progressive development of these, in manifold contact and intercourse with neighbouring and even far remote historic peoples and periods, have risen from the darkness of thousands of years; and their relation in time to the latter has been recognised.

Thus prehistoric times have themselves become history. The historical account of every single region has henceforth to begin with the description of the oldest antiquities of the soil that tell of Man's habitation, in order thereby to obtain the chronological connection with the evolution of the history of mankind generally. That is the palæontological method of historical research.

The palæontology of Man has proved the Stone Age to be a general primary stage of culture for the whole human race. All further general progress in culture was affected by the discovery of the art of metal-working, — the extraction of the metals from their ores and the casting and forging of them. The later and latest epochs of culture are the Metal Ages, as opposed to the Stone Ages. It is not the use of metal in itself, but the above-mentioned metallurgical arts, that form the criterion of the advance of culture beyond the bounds of the Stone Age. Where, as in some parts of America, native copper was found in abundance, this red malleable mineral could probably be worked in the same way as stone, without any further progress necessarily developing therefrom. The same may apply to meteor-iron, which is said to have been used for arrows, together with stone points, by American tribes who were otherwise in the Age of Stone and but poorly civilised.

In civilised lands it is chiefly metal-casting and the forging of the heated metal which have made it possible to produce better weapons and tools and more valuable ornaments. The worked metals are first copper, then the alloy of copper and tin that bears the name of classical bronze, and to these are soon added gold and — especially in districts rich in the metal, as in Spain — silver.   Later on the extraction of iron from its ores and the forging of that metal are discovered.

According to this course of metallurgical progress the first metal period is distinguished as the Bronze Period, which is begun by a Copper Period lasting more or less long in different places.   The second or later metal period is the Iron Period, in which we are living at the present day.   In the course of time, by gradually displacing bronze and copper from the rank of metals worked for weapons and tools, this Iron Age has developed to its present stage.

In central Europe the pile-dwellings in the lakes of western Switzerland again present us with specially clear and uninterrupted series of illustrations of the progress of culture from the Stone Age to the Iron Age.   Ending the Stone Age we find first a period of transition, in which, while stone continued to be principally employed, a few ornaments, weapons, and tools of metal began to be used. This metal is at first almost exclusively copper, with only very little bronze; iron is quite absent.   Copper objects have been found in western Switzerland by Victor Gross, most extensively in Fenel's lake-dwelling station, which otherwise still belongs to the Stone Age.   The majority of these are small daggers, formed after the pattern of the flint daggers; some already possess rivetings for fastening the blade to a handle.   There are also chisels and small awls in bone handles, beads and small ornamental leaves, and hatchets of the form of the simplest stone hatchets, with the edge hammered out and broadened.   Much has proved the existence of a Copper Period corresponding to this description in the lake-dwelling in the Mond See in Austria, and in Hungary the remains of a Copper Period are particularly frequent.   Parallel cases also occur in many other parts of Europe, particularly, as Virchow has proved, in the Spanish Peninsula and in the Stone Age graves of Cujavia in Prussian Poland.   These are the more important as they are most closely related to the conditions of culture discovered in the ancient strata of Hissarlik-Troy.   Further unmistakable analogies occur with very ancient finds in Cyprus, and probably even with the oldest remains of Babylonian culture hitherto known.   Here, too, we may include the finds of copper in the Stone Age of America.

So that in the normal and complete evolution of culture there seems to be first a stratum of Copper as the connecting link between the Stone and Metal ages, and this must be missing in those regions in which progress from the Stone to the Metal culture was only brought about at a relatively later period by external influences.   This applies not only to all modern races in an Age of Stone, who obtained metal in recent times only through contact with European nations who had been living in the Iron Period for thousands of years, but, curiously enough, also to the greater part of Africa, where the use of iron was prevalent at a prehistoric period.   Just as the modern Stone races passed straight from the Stone Age into the most highly developed Iron Age of the most advanced culture, so also the Stone stratum of central and south Africa is immediately overlaid by a stratum of Iron culture, which was brought there in ancient times, probably direct from Egypt. As there is in Egypt and throughout north Africa a regular development from the Copper-Bronze period to the complete Iron culture, corresponding to the progress of the Metal cultures of Europe and Asia, the point of time is thus chronologically fixed at which this important element of culture was transmitted to the blacks of central and south Africa.

In western Switzerland the transition period of Copper is followed without a gap in the development by the Bronze Period proper. With the introduction of bronze all the conditions of life were more highly developed, in the sense of increased culture. With better tools the stations of the Bronze Age could be erected at a greater distance from the bank, often two hundred to three hundred yards; the space they take up is also much greater. The piles are not only better preserved according as the time of their being driven in more nearly approaches our own, but they are also better worked, are often square, and the points that are rammed into the lake-bottom are better cut. The settlements of the Bronze Age often cover an area of several hundred square yards, and are no longer comparatively mean villages, as in the Stone Age; the pile settlements of the Bronze Age are well-organised market-towns and even flourishing small cities, where a certain luxury already prevails. The products of their industry are graced by that beauty and elegance of form that only an advanced civilisation can create.

Stone, deer-horn, and bone have made way for bronze as working material, and are now only seldom used. Amber, which occurred only here and there in the lake-dwellings of the Stone Age, is now found in abundance, and glass and gold appear in the composition of artistically finished ornaments. Among these iron also sometimes occurs, although not yet as a working material, but only as a precious metal for embellishing fine work, such as show and fancy weapons. The pottery productions show a great advance on the often heavy and bulky vessels of the Stone Age; and although the home-made article cannot rival the ceramics of the classic period of Greece and Italy, yet the pots and vases of the Bronze Age of the Swiss lake-dwellings, in spite of their comparatively simple, hand-made forms, are none the less elegant and graceful. The housing, too, no longer consists of the modest mud huts of the Stone Age, but of wooden dwellings, large and solidly built. Their existence is proved by the number of pieces of wood and beams lying one on another between the piles, many of them as much as eleven yards in length. The dwellings had to be spacious, as they had to serve as shelter for both man and his domestic animals; this is proved by the numerous remains of cows, pigs, goats, horses, and dogs collected in the relic-beds. Around the dwellings, on the pile-work, extended a large open space, serving as a public place and for certain kinds of work which could not be done inside the dwellings — such as metal-casting — on account of the danger of fire. Metal work — casting, hardening, forging, etc. — was doubtless done on the pile-works themselves; numerous casting-moulds, melting-pots, molten remains of bronze, and broken articles intended for re-casting, have been collected on the site of the pile-dwelling itself. Victor Gross, celebrated for his researches on the pile-dwellings, was able to identify casting-places in several stations of the Bronze Age; here all the tools used in metal-casting were found lying together in a space of only a few square yards.

Generally speaking, the various lake-dwelling stations of western Switzerland belonging to the Bronze Age do not exhibit very characteristic peculiarities. The general types are mostly the same, the style little modified. But two stations, Mörigen and Corcelettes, stand out as more recent than the rest of the group, iron objects having been found in them.

An attempt has been made to distinguish a period of metal-casting and metal-forging in the lake-dwellings. Gross found, however, both hammered and cast articles without distinction in the lake-settlements of the Bronze Age that he examined, and in his opinion neither of these two kinds of metal-working represents a real advance on the other in the technical process. Certain ornaments, and, generally speaking, all light and fragile articles, were best produced by hammering, while the heavy and massive articles of use could be most easily obtained by casting. The two processes were even frequently combined, an article being first cast and then worked with the hammer, an edge or other finish being thus produced which casting could not give.

As in the Stone Age, so also in the Bronze Age of central and northern Europe, the most important working-implement, which was, however, also used as a weapon, was the axe or celt. The most primitive forms of axes, like the above-mentioned copper axes, still resemble the simple stone axes: like these, they have no special contrivance for fastening the handle. In more developed forms of axes such contrivances for fastening the handle appear first in the form of slight flanges, which become wider and wider; finally they develop into regular wings, which, by curving toward one another, develop into two almost closed, lateral semi-canals on the upper side of the celt. In the hollow celts a simple socket for the handle was cast in the making; an additional means of fastening the handle was provided in a loop, which also occurs on winged celts. Besides the celt, or axe-blade, broad and narrow chisels of bronze occur in various forms for working wood.

A second chief type of instrument is the one-edged bronze knife with elegantly curved back and a handle-tongue. There were further cutting-implements in the form of bronze sickles, and piercing-implements in the form of eyed needles, sewing-needles, borers, and awls; punches for ornamenting metal surfaces have also been found. The regular bronze weapons that were used were swords, daggers, lance-heads, and arrow-heads. The blades of the bronze swords are double-edged and generally imitate the shape of a willow leaf on a large scale; their ornamentation consists of raised lines or threads running parallel along the direction of the edge. The blades are generally cast by themselves, either with or without a handle-tongue, and then fastened on the handle with rivets: the handles and handle-tongues are of various forms, by which different types of sword are distinguished. On the hilt of a sword found in a lake-dwelling in western Switzerland was a row of circular grooves, skilfully inlaid with small iron plates, so that here iron appears as an ornamental metal. But the sword is also the first weapon for which iron as the material was employed in the lake-dwellings. One of the swords found by Gross has a blade of iron and a hilt of bronze, in which fine plates of iron are likewise inlaid. The shape of the sword is exactly the same as that of the bronze swords; the same raised thread-lines ornament the willow-leaf blade. Its material is steel, to which a good edge could be given; the thread-lines decorating the hilt were done with the graver after the smith's work was finished. The most important of the bronze ornaments are the large pins and the heavy bracelets and anklets. Fibulæ are absent.

The manner in which iron was found in the lake-dwellings, as mentioned above, shows the gradual development of a period of transition between a Bronze and an Iron Age. In spite of the difference in the material which the lake-dwellers used for making their weapons and tools in the periods of transition, they still imitated the old forms received from their forefathers. Just as the first metal axes of copper are copies of the stone axes, so also, when iron first became known, were weapons made of this metal which corresponded in form to the bronze weapons that had hitherto been used.

The lake-dwellings of western Switzerland give us, in a geographically small space, the picture of a steadily progressing development of culture from the most primitive Stone Age, which, with the celebrated lake-dwelling-like find of the matured Iron Age near La Tène, brings us down to the time of Cæsar's conquest of Gaul, or, as it is called, the La Tène Period. The period of transition from the Bronze to the Iron Age in the Swiss lake-dwellings, an excellent type of which is seen in the iron sword formed like the bronze swords, belongs to that great and widespread group of culture which in central Europe is termed the Hallstatt Period, after one of the earliest and best-known finds on Lake Hallstatt.

The Bronze Period was first proved to have been a complete form of culture in the north of Europe, — in north Germany and Scandinavia. We have now succeeded in establishing the fact that it was a preliminary stage of the Iron Age, in locally original development, in all ancient centres of culture. It is very remarkable that the civilised states of the New World also employed only copper and bronze as working metals. Thus the Peruvians did not know iron any more than the other American peoples until they came in contact with European influences. Besides copper and bronze they had tin and lead, gold and silver. The Peruvian bronzes contain silver to the extent of five to ten per cent. There are axes or celts of bronze similar to the rudest of the first European beginnings in metal, corresponding in form to the simple stone axes. Many of the other forms of weapons and implements familiar in the Bronze Age of the Old World were also made of bronze or copper in America: semilunar knives with a handle in the middle, lance-heads and arrow-heads, swords, war clubs like morning-stars, etc. At the same time weapons and implements of stone still remained in use. ·

In the Old World progress beyond bronze is everywhere due to iron.

Nearly the whole inventory of weapons, implements, etc., of the first Iron Age, or the period of transition from the exclusive use of bronze to that of iron as a working metal, has already been found in the celebrated cemetery near Hallstatt, on Lake Hallstatt, in the Salzkammergut, in Austria, in the thousand graves that have been opened there. It is after this find, as we have mentioned, that the corresponding group of culture in central Europe is termed the Hallstatt Period. The objects found are highly characteristic.

Only isolated stone implements occurred here. The weapons are partly of bronze and partly of iron, the iron ones already predominating in number. But at the same time they often exhibit — the swords especially — in the most marked manner the forms characteristic of the bronze weapons of earlier periods. The typical Hallstatt swords are distinguished by broad, heavy blades with their points cut off slantingly. The hilts terminate in large pommels, and on the blade, below the hilt-joint, lateral incisions may be noticed. Daggers are also frequent, the blade being almost always of iron and the handle of bronze. Some of the swords are in sheaths of chased bronze plate with characteristic wing-like chapes. One-edged daggers also occur, others are in the form of small swords. Further we notice small bronze axes, which can scarcely have served as weapons or tools, but probably only as symbols of such. Axes or celts are very numerous, especially a flat iron form, without flanges, but with two lateral stop-ridges where the blade rests on the handle; the chisels also are mostly of iron. The same applies to the lance-heads, which are of iron with few exceptions. Knives occurred in very large numbers; these were chiefly iron, but had still the curved blade common to bronze knives. Peculiar to Hallstatt culture are large iron chopping-knives with a thick, broad, rather curved, one-edged blade and generally with an iron handle; they are of considerable size and may be compared to small swords.

Among the ornaments, the splendid bronze girdle-plates, richly embellished with chasing or repoussé work, are chiefly conspicuous. These seem to have been fastened on leather or cloth. They were closed by means of a hook; strap-buckles not being known. Bronze plates with chased or embossed decoration, and representations of figures, seem indeed to play an important part among the ornaments of this period, as also do chains, etc., with rattle-plates. Bracelets are numerous; some are manufactured hollow by the bending together of bronze plate, others are cast solid. The underlying motive in the latter is often a string threaded with beads or balls. But the balls frequently become half-balls, often large, but occasionally so small and close together that they are converted into cross-ribs. Instead of the straight pins of various forms that were used in the Bronze Period for fastening garments, fibulæ or safety-pins now occur for this purpose and as ornaments, and are of two chief forms, — spectacle-spiral fibulæ and bow fibulæ. The latter especially exhibit a great variety of modifications; for example, simple bow fibulæ, boat fibulæ, snake fibulæ, drum fibulæ, crossbow fibulæ, etc. Large and small bronze vessels are numerous, some in bucket form (*situlæ*) with one or several handles, others cylindrical cross-ribbed cists; but there were also vases and bottles, cup-shaped vessels, bowls, flat dishes, etc. These vessels are all made of hammered bronze plate, not a single one being cast, as is so frequently the case with the fine bronze vessels of the northern Bronze Age. The Hallstatt bronze vessels consist of several sheets of metal, which are bent and riveted together with great skill. The clay vessels, — urns, vases, cups, bowls, — often very elegant in form and of fine smoothed clay, are still always worked with the free hand; some are blackened with graphite, and a few are painted in colour. The ornaments — lines, circles, and figures — are imprinted, or put on with colour.

The whole picture afforded us by the finds of the Hallstatt Period of central Europe shows a highly developed culture with a pronounced partiality for splendour and outward show, supported by technical skill and highly developed industry. There are also unmistakable signs of an extensive intercourse with peoples far and near. For instance, even the ivory occurring on sword-hilts in the Hallstatt cemetery points to the South, not to mention glass vessels and shells from the Mediterranean; and the fact of amber being so much in evidence betrays the North. Some of the representations of figures on embossed bronze plates come from the East; for instance, the finely drawn winged animals on the lid of a *situla*; on others — for instance, on a *situla* belonging to Hallstatt culture, found near Watsch, in Austria — processions, etc., of human figures are represented whose counterparts we find in Greece and Italy. The same is the case with the animal figures of bronze and clay, comprising oxen and cows with curved horns, horses and riders, and birds, some of which are unmistakably meant to represent doves, and others, from their broad beaks, ducks or swans.

Furtwängler's standard publications on the small bronzes yielded by the excavations at Olympia show us that the oldest votive offerings that can be found

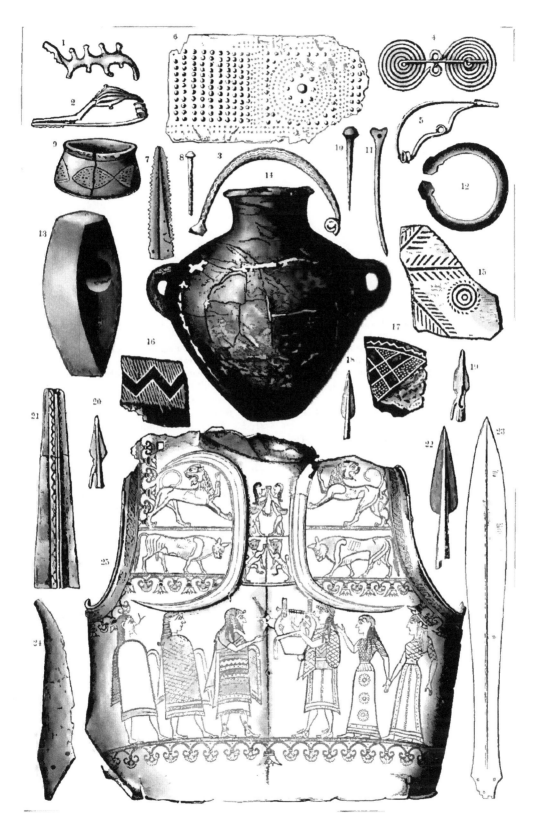

GREEK TOOLS, WEAPONS, AND IMPLEMENTS OF EARLY HISTORIC TIMES

# EXPLANATION OF PLATE C

## (SEE OVER)

1–5. Garment pins.

    1. Fibula. One-half real size.

    2. Garment pin. One-half real size.

    3. Garment pin. One-third real size.

    4. Fibula. Two-fifth real size.

    5. Snake fibula. One-third real size.

6. Portion of an ornamental girdle-plate. One-half real size.

7. Two-edged flint saw. One-half real size.

8. Copper stud. One-sixth real size.

9. Vessel with decoration scratched in. One-sixth real size.

10, 11. Pins.

    10. Ivory pin. One-third real size.

    11. Bone pin with perforated head. Three-eighths real size.

12. Child's copper bracelet. One-half real size.

13. Perforate polished axe. One-sixth real size.

14. Hand-made vase. One-ninth real size.

15–17. Fragments of clay pottery.

    15. Shiny red fragment with impressed ornament. Two-thirds real size.

    16 and 17. Fragments of clay pottery. One-third real size.

    The ornamentations are filled in with white chalk.

18–20. Arrow-heads from Olympia. One-half real size.

21, 22. Spear-heads from Olympia.

    21. Spear-head. Two-fifths real size.

    22. Spear-head. One-sixth real size.

23. Sword-blade from Olympia. One-sixth real size.

24. Copper knife. One-fifth real size.

    The two holes at the lower end were for the nails with which the knife was fastened in the handle.

25. Back of an ancient Greek cuirass, in a private collection in the island of Zante. One-fourth real size.

---

(1–6, 18–23, 25 from Furtwängler's " Broncen von Olympia; " 7–17, 24 from Schliemann's " Ilios.")

there belong to the sphere of culture of the early Iron Age, first known in central Europe,—the Hallstatt Period. The differences that occur are in the main only special local developments of the same general type. The weapons of the earliest times of Olympia furnished by the finds were, bronze swords with broad tangs,[1] lance-heads and arrow-heads[2] (some of the latter barbed[3]), poleaxes, double axes, and girdle-plates,[4] cuirasses, and greaves with lineal and figured ornament, both corresponding to the Hallstatt forms of central Europe. Some of the decorated plates are also diadems for the head and ornaments for other parts of the body. Hanging ornaments of various kinds, such as rattle-plates and wheel-like pendants, and pins, pincers, and combs, have also been found; nor are other articles of toilet wanting. There are innumerable rude animal figures (votive) of bronze, some cast, others cut from plate, and also some made of clay, such as correspond everywhere to the Hallstatt type. The same applies to the ring ornaments, which we find in the form of bracelets, necklets, etc. But the most characteristic are the fibulæ,[5] whose numbers and style most strongly characterise the Hallstatt sphere of culture. The form that occurs with special frequency at Olympia is the snake fibula in various modifications,[6] but there are also simple bow fibulæ, semicircular fibulæ, boat-fibulæ, leech-fibulæ, and the spectacle-spiral fibulæ so typical of the Hallstatt cemetery itself.[7] The bronze vessels correspond to those of the Hallstatt Period, not so much in form, which shows traces of local influences, as in technique and ornamentation.

The chief difference between Olympia and the Hallstatt finds of central Europe is visible in the Oriental influences, which, as was to be expected from the former's position, are far more extensive and pronounced here than at Hallstatt itself. There, too, we were able to trace Oriental influences, but at Olympia they appear in abundance, and form, besides the objects of European-Greek style,—as Furtwängler has called the Hallstatt style of Olympia,—a second large group of an Oriental-Greek character. The ornamentation in particular determines the Oriental nature of the style: winged griffins and other winged hybrids, some formed more like men, others more like animals; double creatures reminding one of the double beasts of heraldry; and lions, sphinxes, and bulls. Among the ornamental figures at Olympia there were, as in the Hallstatt finds of central Europe and northern Italy, representations from daily life, and hunting and battle scenes, with combats between men and beasts. On a bronze cuirass there is a figure-ornament representing Apollo with the Muses approached by three men in worship.[8] The whole of this kind of representation corresponds in a great degree to the groups of figures on the bronze plates and *situlæ* of the Hallstatt Period.

With these discoveries the Hallstatt Period is removed from pre-history and linked on to history. The same conditions of culture that we meet with in that early historic period in Greece appear widespread as a contemporary epoch in the lands of the Mediterranean and in central Europe. The civilised life of the barbarians proves to be built on the same elements as that of the Hellenes.

One place has also already been found and most completely investigated after the method of palæontological research, with all the help afforded by archæological and historical science, where, in overlying geological strata, the evidences have been found of a progressive development of culture from the end of the

---

[1] See Fig. 23, Plate at p. 174.  [3] Figs. 19, 20.  [5] Figs. 1–3.  [7] Fig. 4.
[2] Figs. 18, 21, 22.  [4] Fig. 6.  [6] Fig. 5.  [8] Fig. 25.

Stone Age down to the brilliant days of Græco-Roman history. There the chronological connection has been obtained, not only for the metal periods, but also for the end of the neolithic period. This most important place is Troy, the citadel-hill on Hissarlik, by the excavation of which Heinrich Schliemann has won immortal fame. Schliemann's excavations, supplemented and completed in decisive manner by Dörpfeld have brought about the most important advancement of the history of mankind that our century can show. Virchow's name is inseparably associated with Schliemann's. Furtwängler, in his account, based on personal observation of the results of the excavations at Troy, has accomplished the great service of exactly determining the chronological connections of the prehistoric with the historic epochs, and thereby linking the former to history. Says Furtwängler :

"On the spot on which tradition placed Homeric Troy, there really has stood a stately citadel, which was contemporaneous with the golden age of Mycenæ, the epoch of the Agamemnon of legend, and was intimately related to Mycenæan culture, and which at the same time corresponds most exactly to the idea of Troy underlying the old epic."

The citadel-hill of Troy (Hissarlik) terminates a ridge of heights which stretches westward from Mount Ida, almost parallel to the Hellespont, and slopes steeply into the Trojan plain or the valley of the Scamander. The natural hill itself is not very high, but it was overlaid by enormous layers of ruins of buildings and walls, whereby it has not only been considerably increased in height, but also in breadth. Stratum after stratum lies one upon the other like the leaves of a bud, so that the history of the habitation of this venerable place from the most ancient times can be read from these strata, which have been opened up by Schliemann and Dörpfeld, as from the leaves of a book. The original ground of the hill-plateau now lies some sixty feet above the plain, but the latter may have been raised something like sixteen to twenty feet by alluvial deposits since the Trojan War. The whole stratum of ruins lying on the original ground of the hill, which Schliemann opened up, amounts to about fifty-two and a half feet. Schliemann distinguished seven or eight different layers or strata, corresponding to as many towns which were successively built on this hill, one on the ruins of the other.

The lowest stratum, lying immediately on the original ground, belongs, accordingly, to the oldest or first town on the citadel-hill of Troy. Furtwängler says :

"By moderate computation this settlement must belong to the first half of the third millennium before Christ, but it may very well date back even to the fourth millennium. The inhabitants already used copper implements in addition to stone ones.[1] Their whole culture is most closely connected with that which prevailed in central Europe during the Copper Period. Clay vessels of the Copper Period from Lake Mond, in Austria, agree completely with those of the first Trojan town. Troy represents only an offshoot of central European culture, and its inhabitants were in all probability of European origin."

We have already learned that the Copper Period is the end of the neolithic period and the beginning of the Metal Age. In the first Trojan town there is still extraordinarily little metal used, the axes, hatchets, knives, and saws still being

---

[1] See Figs. 8, 12, 24, Plate at p. 174.

of stone, of the familiar central European types and of the same materials, among which nephrite is particularly frequent. Other materials are serpentine, diorite, porphyry, hematite, flint,[1] etc. The forms of these implements correspond entirely to those of the later Stone Age of Europe.[2] The character of the ceramics also[3] conforms in many respects, according to Virchow, to that of the European Stone Age; and the Stone Age finds at Butmir, in Bosnia, and similar ones in Transylvania, seem especially to offer close analogies. It would be a highly important step toward connecting history with the neolithic period if the first town could be even more closely investigated, and perhaps more sharply divided from that second stratum which lies between it and the stratum described by Schliemann as the second or burnt city, and which Schliemann afterward separated into two strata, corresponding to two towns. Perhaps the metal comes only from the second or higher stratum under the burnt city. In that case the oldest would belong purely to the Stone Age. The ceramics would not contradict this. Furtwängler continues:

"High above the first town, on a deep layer of débris, is the level surface of the second town, which must at least be dated back to the second half of the third millennium before Christ. It was the first period of Troy's glory. Mighty walls protected the citadel. Three different building periods may be distinguished. The walls were brought out a long way and strengthened, and magnificent new gates were built. During the third period of this second city a prince fond of splendour had the old narrow gateway replaced by magnificent propylæa and a large hall-erection with a vestibule. A great conflagration destroyed his citadel. A treasure was found by Schliemann — he called it Priam's treasure — in the upper part of the citadel-wall, which was made of straw-bricks. The tools of the second city are still partly of stone, but also partly of bronze, so that they already belong to the Bronze Age."

The general character of culture is, according to Furtwängler, still essentially central European. And yet many an individuality has developed, and the influence of the great Asiatic (Babylonian) culture is everywhere apparent, although it does not go very deep. To this influence our authority chiefly attributes the occurrence of a few pots turned on the wheel, especially flat dishes; for the potter's wheel was still quite unknown at that time in Europe, and even at a post so far advanced toward the East as Cyprus, while in Egypt and Babylonia it had been in use from the earliest times. In this period also Troy inclines more to central Europe as its centre of gravity, but remains far behind the peculiar development that bronze work attained there; in the metal tools no advance is made on the forms of the Copper Period. Into any close relation with Cyprus it does not come; only the basis of their culture is common to both. But this basis had a wide range, relics from German districts being often more closely related to the Trojan ones than are those from Cyprus.

"The brilliant period of the second city is followed by a long period of decline for Troy. Ruins are piled upon ruins, walls rise upon walls, but each poorer than the others; no new citadel-walls, no gates, no palaces belong to this period, in which three strata — the third, fourth, and fifth towns — are distinguished. The first half of the second millennium before Christ must at least be regarded as the time of this deposit. The inhabitants evidently remained the same, and their culture is that of the second city. But no progress was made; nothing but stagnation: the same forms of vessels continue to be made

---

[1] Fig. 7, Plate at p. 174.    [2] Fig. 13.    [3] Figs. 9 and 14.

the same decorated whorls. Naturally no active intercourse with abroad could develop in this period. And yet this was the time when an active civilised life began to develop on the islands of the Ægean Sea and on the east coast of Greece, which was to bloom in all its splendour in the following period. To this time the finds at Thera belong, where the pottery, all turned in the wheel, is already painted with a so-called varnish-colour which shines like metal, and in which plants, flowers, and animals are treated in quite a new and promising naturalistic style hitherto unheard of in Europe. In Cyprus, too, the decoration of pottery developed exceedingly in wealth and variety in this period of the Bronze Age. Troy, on the other hand, is poor and degenerate.

"But a new period of prosperity arrived for Troy too; this is the sixth town. Rich and powerful princes again ruled in this citadel. They enlarged it far beyond its former compass. They built strong new walls,—the old ones had long since sunk in ruins,— not of small stones and straw-bricks as before, but of large smooth blocks, and gates and turrets. They did not have the sloping mound of ruins levelled, as the lords of the second city had done; they let the new buildings rise in terraces on the ruins of the old: stately mansions with wide, deep halls covered the acropolis. Constant intercourse existed with the princes of Greece who at that time — the second half of the second millennium before Christ — built their citadels with cyclopean walls. The Trojans employed the same peculiar, constantly recurring small projections in their walls, that we find in a Mycenæan town on Lake Copaïs in Bœotia. And, above all, the Trojans now provided themselves with those beautiful vessels painted with shining colour that characterise Mycenæan culture in Greece, and whose natural style had so wonderfully developed there on the basis of the attempts that we found at Thera. In Troy these things caused some imitation,[1] but the results remained far behind the originals. The living, imaginative conception of the natural was closed to the Trojan; the home-made pottery kept, on the whole, to its unpainted vessels, although these were now almost entirely made on the wheel.

"Yet what chiefly interests us is the historical. The sixth town, too, was suddenly given up, destroyed, and burnt. What follows it are again only poor settlements. Its destruction must have taken place about the end of the Mycenæan epoch of culture. The seventh town, which is built immediately on the ruins of the sixth, shows, already, other and later culture. It had long been suspected that a historical kernel was concealed in the legend of Troy — now we have the monumental confirmation. There really was a Troy, which was strong and great at the same time as the rulers of Mycenæ, rich in gold and treasure, held sway in Greece. And that Troy was destroyed — we may now safely affirm, from this agreement between relics and legend — by Greek princes of the Mycenæan epoch, whom the legend calls Agamemnon and his men."

The seventh and eighth towns, built soon after the destruction of the sixth, show an interruption in the intercourse with Greece. There the Mycenæan period was broken by the displacement of peoples known as the Doric migration, and that rich civilised life was replaced by a relapse into the semi-barbaric conditions of the North. In Troy, too, we perceive a period of decline. "a relapse into a stage long since past; black hand-made vessels, which in their form and decoration are strikingly like the home-made pots usual in Italy, especially Etruria and Latium, in the first part of the first millennium before Christ." Finally, the seventh town also furnishes inferior imported Greek vases with painting, but not coming from Greece itself, but from the coast of Asia Minor, where Greeks had settled in connection with the Doric migration. "The Æolic colonisation of Troas brought Ilium no

---

[1] See Figs. 15–17, Plate at p. 174.

fresh prosperity. Other places rose, Troy remained a miserable village. In the Hellenistic period the sky clears over Troy. What Alexander intended, Lysimachus carried out; he restores Ilium to the place of a real city with new walls, and erects a magnificent temple to Athene on the top of the acropolis. . . . Yet artistic creation came to no real perfection. It was only when the great men of Rome, mindful of their Trojan ancestors, began to interest themselves in the place, that new life bloomed on Troy's ruins."

Thus the geological-archæological method relates history, merely relying upon the monuments of the soil, without requiring written evidences. Pre-history has here attained its end; it has become history.

# V

## AMERICA

### By PROF. KONRAD HAEBLER

---

### I. THE PRIMITIVE RACES OF AMERICA

#### *A.* GENERAL

THE problem how the first men may have come to America has always given much food for reflection to both learned and unlearned. Many could not imagine that a continent should exist with countless different races for whom no place could be found in the genealogy of Genesis, and for want of a better way out of the difficulty they assumed that the inhabitants of America were the descendants of the ten lost tribes of Israel. This naïve assumption did direct service to science itself, by offering occasion to some intelligent observers to go thoroughly into the manners and customs of the American Indians, in the hope of discovering analogies which might serve them as proofs.

A second hypothesis regarding the origin of the Americans has received a far more scientific colouring. The fabulous island-world of the western ocean, the oldest evidence of which is the mythical Atlantis of Plato's Timæus, exercised an indirect influence on the discovery of the New World, in so far as even Columbus was under the spell of belief in it. Whether it was based on any historic or prehistoric fact has not hitherto been proved. But men of science are not wanting who answer this question in the affirmative, and who see in a land-bridge over the Atlantic Ocean the way by which the first men came to the American continent. It is true that modern research no longer takes up so naïve a position on this question as the old Spaniard who therewith attributed to the Indians a Celtiberian origin. The sinking of a continent between Europe and America in an age when our part of the earth was inhabited by peoples whose traces are still to be found must in any case have left some signs which could not have escaped the advanced investigation of the earth's surface. The attempt to trace the outlines of this continent from the cliffs and shoals of the Atlantic Ocean is also worthless trifling. On the other hand geologists of note believe that they can prove that the northern part of the Atlantic Ocean was not always covered by water, and they think it was by this way that man came from the Old World to the New, in times when the climatic conditions of our part of the globe were still considerably different from those of history.

Finally, still a third hypothesis exists for the population of America. It would be the simplest of all, did not the same science which admits the possibility of a

North Atlantic land-bridge having existed, dispute the same possibility for this. Nowhere do the continents of the Old and New World approach nearer to one another than in the northwest of America, where Bering Strait separates them by only a narrow arm of water, and the Aleutian Islands also make it possible for a navigator provided with but the most primitive appliances to cross from one to the other. At all times vessels of the inhabitants of the Asiatic coasts have occasionally been tossed by wind and weather as far as the shores of Alaska, and that an immigration took place in this direction even in historic times is almost a certainty. The resemblance of the American aborigines to Mongolian peoples, and the similarity of certain ethnological peculiarities of races of the Pacific States of America to those of the civilised nations of Asia, have long brought this hypothesis many adherents. Some, indeed, would find direct proof of intercourse between the Chinese and America in the accounts of the land of Fu-schan, and on the strength of this would boldly claim the Aztec civilisation to have been an offshoot of the Chinese. It is true that such inferences have not been able to stand the test of strict examination. In the ages which we could connect with even the earliest Chinese epochs, America was certainly not populated by this means; and if the geologists are right who assert that the far Northwest did not rise from the waves of the Pacific Ocean (which once flowed with a boundless expanse to the North Pole) until after the glacial period, then the first inhabitants of America certainly did not get there in this way, for by this time the bones of many generations were already bleaching on the soil of the New World.

Since it has been proved that the human race on American soil can be traced back to the same periods of the earth's history as in the Old World, the question whence the first men came there has lost much of its importance. It is true that the cradle of the human race can hardly have been in America; to cite only one objection, the anthropoid apes, which are indispensable to the theory of evolution as the connecting link between the animal world and man, have at no time been native there, any more than they are to-day, as the fossil finds in all American excavations have proved. But if the first men came over during periods in which the distribution of land and water on the earth's surface was still quite different from that shown by history, then geology will one day, at least, be able to give an answer to our question. Yet even this negative result is of unqualified scientific importance, for it puts all those in the wrong who pretend to see in the customs of the savage and civilised races of America the influences of certain ethnographic units familiar to our ideas. If the first man made his home in America at the time when his fellow in the Old World still vied with the beasts in gnawing the bones of the game he had killed, and if a hollow in the hills was the only shelter he knew, the dispute as to whether the civilisations of America are to be traced to Aryan or Semitic influences may be given up as idle. For this much at least is irrefutably proved by the palæontology and history of the New World,—that its development from the times of the mammoth to its discovery by Christopher Columbus was continuous and was not influenced from without.

America is also highly interesting to the student of the early history of the human race, as well as to the geologist, in that it preserved the witnesses of a past of which we find in the Old World only scanty and often obliterated traces until a later time. This later time did not, it is true, possess such a developed method of research as the present day, but in its accounts, and in the memorials that it handed down to posterity it has consigned to us far richer material for research than has the Old World, and has given us information of events and conditions in the early history of Man which we should otherwise seek in vain. Even the most highly civilised races of America were only at the beginning of the Copper Age when they were discovered, while most of the inhabitants of the New World still lived entirely in the Age of Stone.

Americans once asserted that they had dug human bones out of strata of the Tertiary period; but, like those who had made similar assertions regarding finds in the Old World, they failed to give scientific proof. On the other hand human relics have come to light there, as they have here, that belong to the interglacial period; nor are such relics, although naturally not very numerous, limited to a small area, but are found both in the mountainous regions of California and in the vast plains of the Argentine pampas. In America, too, Man was the contemporary of the mammoth and other ancient gigantic species of animals, and at a later but still prehistoric period the New World even had a population which in places was fairly considerable. This is evident from the considerable number and unusual size of the refuse-accumulations of prehistoric Man that are known by the name of "kitchen-middens." These refuse-mounds exist in North and South America, on the shores of the ocean, on the inland seas, and on the banks of the great rivers, and, besides their scientific name, are called "shell-mounds" in the north and "sambaquis" in the south. They consist of accumulations of the inedible parts of fish and other aquatica, especially shell-fish, and naturally contain among this refuse fragments of objects that were used by the men who inhabited their sites. That these objects belong chiefly to the earliest human culture, the palæolithic, was to be anticipated, but it must not be forgotten that refuse-mounds are also met with, especially in South America, which belong not only to the neolithic period, beyond which the wild Indian of eastern South America has never advanced, but even with certainty to historic times.

What number of people and what time it may have taken to throw up these mounds, which are often hundreds of feet long and of considerable height, we have as yet no reliable means of determining. But it can scarcely be assumed that they were formed very slowly, for otherwise the action of the elements, especially on the seacoasts, would scarcely have ever allowed accumulations to be made which have stood the test of thousands of years. We are therefore undoubtedly justified in concluding, from the large extent and wide distribution of these mounds, that large areas of the continent were thickly populated even in prehistoric times. This fact must especially be kept in view, in order to estimate at their proper value the hypotheses regarding the civilising influences of the peoples of the Old World on those of the New; for if, in times when even Asia and Europe still possessed an exclusively uncivilised population, America was already inhabited by Man in exactly the same manner, then, considering the geographical conditions of the continent, foreign influences can only be called in to account for culture phenomena when the supposition of independent development is insufficiently strong.

If we now view the American continent in its entirety on its appearance in historic times, it affords us surprising confirmation of the extraordinary influence of geographical position on the development of human culture. The comparatively narrow strip of coast which accompanies the mountain-chain of the Cordilleras — the backbone of America, as it has been significantly called — at its western foot, with the terraces in which these mountains rapidly rise to considerable height, was almost in its whole extent, from Alaska down to Chili, the seat of civilised and half-civilised races; at any rate their degree of civilisation was far above the level of that of the population of the vast plains and extensive lowlands through which, east of the Cordilleras, the mightiest rivers of the earth roll their waters to the sea. Here lay the two great centres of civilisation of Peru and Mexico, the latter of which, it is true, spanned the American continent from ocean to ocean near its narrowest part. In the enormous regions east of the Cordilleras, which probably form three-fourths of the whole area of the continent, Man was still, at the beginning of the sixteenth century, in a primitive stage of civilisation. North America showed him then at best as beginning to rise from his state of "natural Man:" whereas in the Southern continent no traces of this are to be discovered. The clever paradox that hunger is the father of all progress, because it forces Man to fight with his surroundings, has probably nowhere been more strikingly confirmed than in South America. The Peruvian of the mountains, for example, on a soil from which he wrung his living by energetic toil, created one of the most ingeniously organised of bodies politic in the world's history, while his eastern neighbour, revelling in the luxuriant wealth of tropical nature, roved about in a condition which did not even bring before his mind the principal difference between man and beast. It is true that nature held the Indian back, keeping him at the lowest stage of civilisation, not only through its bounteous gifts, but also by reason of other and less beneficent influences. On the vast plains which accompany the great rivers far along their upper courses, nature denied to Man even a permanent abode, one of the most necessary conditions for the development of progress in culture. The floods which recurred periodically, placing areas of many square miles under water for weeks and months, compelled the Indian — who had to build his hut close to the banks of the rivers on account of the fish that gave him food — regularly to abandon his dwelling and leave it to destruction. It is no wonder that he became an indefatigable swimmer, an excellent boatman, and an expert fisherman; but his mind became as little associated as his body with the soil he lived on, and the water that washed away his light hut effaced also from his mind any remembrance of the past.

Historical research was for a long time helpless as regards these primitive races. Attempts were first made to pick out from the endless mass of races and tribes the groups that were more or less closely related to one another; but even these attempts encountered the greatest obstacles. The outward appearance of the aborigines, their complexion, and the form of their skulls and bodies, were first tried as distinctive marks. But it proved that races of different complexions exhibited undoubted signs of relationship, whereas the same complexion and figure were repeated in races that were not related at all; and the skull-measurements often gave every gradation from the dolichocephalic to the brachycephalic among the individuals of a single small tribe. Nor did ethnological peculiarities prove much more useful than anthropological characteristics. The wild Indian proved to be in a much greater degree the child of his surroundings than the child of his race; and the same tribe that had had its peculiar methods of clothing, arranging its houses, and burying its dead in the hill country, adopted under other conditions.

in another place, the more suitable manners and customs of its new neighbours. Thus these characteristics also, although in some cases of no little importance, were not sufficient for making a classification out of the chaos of tribes.

The only guide that has hitherto proved at all reliable is the linguistic one. On the basis that we obtain with its aid is founded, almost exclusively as regards South America, the little we know of the history of these races, or rather the little we know in the way of facts. The uncivilised Indian knows nothing of the history of his tribe. He rarely knows more than the names — and perhaps, in the country not subject to floods, the dwellings — of his father and grandfather. After a few generations the knowledge of long migrations fades away into a dim tradition, and in his legends the overgrowth of mythological fantasies completely stifles clear historical recollection. This also explains how the Indian's habits are easily changed under the influence of new surroundings. Language alone followed this process of transformation comparatively slowly, and contained elements of persistency which asserted themselves more lastingly amid all change. It, too, was not entirely spared. Otherwise it would be scarcely conceivable how the New World came to form for itself almost as many idioms as have all the other continents put together. There were two forces in particular which also exercised on it their transforming influence, — isolation and mixture. The Indian possesses in a curiously marked degree the sense of independence. Even the family ties are looser among most Indian tribes than elsewhere, and beyond kinship and the closest clan relationship the uncivilised Indians, with few exceptions, never attained any great degree of unity. This is partly the consequence of their mode of life: a nomadic existence supported on the bounty of nature allows of no large assemblage of people, and necessitates a continual search for new districts not yet visited by others. But if the races of one tongue were thus split up into small groups, each of which for generations kept to itself or had intercourse only with tribes speaking other tongues, the idioms must necessarily have become differentiated one from another.

But far more importance must be attached to the influence exercised by mixture on the languages of the Indians. It will seldom have resulted from peaceable intercourse. The Indian in his natural state, while looking on the beasts of the forest almost as his equals, considered every strange man, on the other hand, much as game, and every man was strange to him who was not of his clan. This explains that war of "all against all" that existed among most of the Indian tribes. Whether we have to regard this same conception as accounting for the anthropophagy which seems at times to have existed throughout the whole American continent, from one end to the other, may perhaps be disputed. In any case the Indian pursued his human enemy with the same unmercifulness as he pursued his worst enemies in the animal world, and his war was, as far as the male portion of the hostile tribe was concerned, a war of annihilation. But he behaved otherwise toward the women. In the restless life of the nomadic Indian a great share of the daily toil and care fell to the female sex, and the Indian knew well how to appreciate the faithful services of his women. So, when he succeeded in capturing the women of a hostile tribe in battle, it was only rarely that he wreaked his wrath on them; far oftener he saw in them a welcome addition to the hands that provided for his bodily well-being. It is clear that these strange women who were adopted into the tribe must also have exercised an influence for change upon it under certain circumstances, especially if such adoptions happened repeatedly. It must often have come to pass that a tribe whose outward circumstances were favourable rapidly increased, so that at last all its members could no longer find room within its circle. It was then naturally the youngest members — those in the first stage of manhood — whom the uneasy pressure first affected, and who must have first migrated. Only a few women, or none at all, would have followed them on their journey into the unknown, for their diligent hands could far less be spared at home than the surplus warriors. So that, in order to establish a home, these warriors would have to resort to the abduction of women. The nearest village that offered hope of a successful invasion would then be attacked; the men that could not escape would be slaughtered; but with the women the band of warriors would combine to form a new tribe, which must naturally show in every respect the mixture of different elements. This formation of new tribes is not only logically quite admissible, but is verified by historical instances among the races of South America.

## *B.* THE PRIMITIVE RACES OF SOUTH AMERICA

FROM the few historical facts that we are able to glean with the help of the sciences of language, ethnology, and anthropology, we are still only able to ascertain in rough outline the past of the chief races of South America. Of those that we can still recognise the Tapuyas are considered to be the oldest. "Tapuya" is really not a name at all, but the term in the Tupi language for all "strangers," or "enemies." Karl von den Steinen calls this group that of the Ges tribes; others follow the example of some of their Indian neighbours and call them the Crens, meaning the "old" or "ancient ones." They have become most popular under the name of Botocudos, from the lip-peg (*botoque*), which, however, is worn as an ornament of distinction not only by them, but also by most of the other primitive races of South America: even the warriors of the Chibchas, who must be unconditionally reckoned among the civilised races, stuck as many pegs through their lower lips as they had killed enemies in battle. The name "Tapuya" recommends itself most, because in history it has been specially applied to the Ges tribes, and did not at any rate, like all the other names, actually belong only to a small number of the tribes that are called by it. The age of these tribes is shown by the fact that their neighbours, who have driven them farther and farther from their former abodes, call them "the Ancients." The most decisive proof that they have lived in the regions of Brazil from the earliest times, long previous to history, is the circumstance that the palæozoic skulls from Lagoa Santa, which Lund brought to light in the caves there, exhibit all the characteristics peculiar to the Tapuya skull. On the other hand it is doubtful whether the "sambaquis," or refuse-mounds, of Brazil are also attributable to them, because the Tapuyas seem at all times to have been, as they are to-day, a nomadic race of hunters, and never a race of navigators and fishermen. Only such a race, and a comparatively sedentary race too, could have consumed such quantities of shell-fish as form the mounds of the sambaquis.

The Tapuyas have played an historical part only passively. They were probably once the sole masters of the whole of Brazil from the watershed of the Amazon down to the Parana; but probably even in prehistoric times they were hemmed in on all sides, so that at the time of the Spanish conquest they ruled practically only the hill-country of the interior of Brazil. Tribes of them were also drawn into the great racial migration which, several centuries before their discovery by the Spaniards, set out from the east to make an onset upon the more highly civilised races of the Andean highlands; but the Semigaes, who on this occasion penetrated into the region of the upper tributaries of the Amazon, became differentiated in character from their race, and so assimilated themselves with the surrounding Tupi and Carib tribes, that only their name and their language still show their old connection.

There have probably never been any races of the Tapuya stock on the north side of the Amazon. Here, until a few centuries before Columbus, one of the most extensive races of the New World, the Aruacs, held unlimited sway. They, too, belong indisputably to the oldest nations of America. Where their real original abodes may have been can be only approximately determined. The Aruacs also represent the type of an inland race. Although in later times many of their tribes were quite at home on the water as navigators and fishermen, their primitive culture points unconditionally to an inland home. And although they were subsequently the undisputed masters of the vast regions north of the Amazon from the Andes to the shores of the ocean, their original abodes cannot have been in the luxuriant, tropical lowlands of the great river territories of South America; on the contrary, the characteristics we find common to all their widespread branches, as the original elements of their culture, lead us to the conclusion that their home was situated above the region of periodical floods, and yet was still in tropical climes. Now, as we find them on the eastern slopes of the Cordilleras from the peninsula of Goajira in the north down to the borders of Chili, and in specially large numbers in eastern Bolivia, the original home of all these tribes is probably to be sought in this direction.

The tribes of the Aruac group, among which must also be counted those called the Nu tribes by Karl von den Steinen, ranked far higher in civilisation than the Tapuyas; and although Tupis and Caribs subsequently became fully their equals, the civilisation of the Aruacs was founded much earlier than theirs. There is abundant proof that the Aruacs were the teachers of their younger conquerors. When the Aruac group may have begun to spread from the hill-country of eastern Bolivia to the northeast, east, and southeast, and whether in its advance it found the basins of the Orinoco and Amazon and their tributaries still unpeopled or inhabited by other races, cannot be ascertained even approximately. It is probable that it found these new regions uninhabited, because Aruac races have formed a uniform substratum over large areas of northern South America, which substratum of race reappears everywhere that the later conquerors did not completely fill the area. But to judge from its extent, and from the great deviations in the language of its various branches, this group of races took not only hundreds but thousands of years for its migrations.

In spite of this the Aruacs were not a rude, savage race when this process began, for even the original race knew an agriculture that cannot be called quite primitive. In large parts of South America the agricultural Indians live not only on maize, which is grown all over America, but even to a greater extent on the tuberous root of a species of Euphorbiaceæ, the mandioc (Manihot Plum.) or cassava. In the raw state these roots are highly poisonous, owing to their containing prussic acid; otherwise they are rich in nutritious properties. Now in early times some unknown Indian tribe made the discovery that the mandioc is deprived of its poisonous properties by squeezing the sap out of the root and preparing the latter in a suitable manner: a discovery of far-reaching importance, considering that the mandioc afterward formed the almost sole means of subsistence of hundreds of thousands of Indians. As the mandioc shrub does not flourish in the tropical and flood-exposed lowlands, neither the Tupis nor the Caribs, both of whom probably were originally pure fish-eaters, can have been the inventors of this process; still less the Tapuyas, who did not practise agriculture at all. It does not naturally follow that the honour of this discovery is due to the Aruaes, whose probable original abodes certainly correspond to the special climatic conditions necessary for the mandioc; it is conceivable that they too were first instructed in the art of preparing the mandioc by a still more highly civilised race. But this certainly took place in the original home of the race, which with its gradual expansion spread the cultivation of the mandioc, so that finally the Indians of other stocks also learned the art from them.

The Aruac races are further distinguished by their skill in making earthen vessels. This is still so characteristic of them at the present day that of the races of central Brazil, Karl von den Steinen classes those of the Aruac stock under the name of "potter-tribes" (*Töpferstämme*). It is certainly not a coincidence that, the farther one goes from the east coast of the continent toward the mountains, the better and finer the pottery becomes. All the races that inhabit the eastern slopes of the Cordilleras were comparatively far advanced in the working of clay, and the products of their industry are distinguished by variety of form and purpose and by elegance of decoration — which ranges from simple lineal ornament to the plastic imitation of living things — from the products of the primitive races of the lowlands. This distinction is certainly not limited to the Aruac races. South of them, among the races of the Gran Chaco, which are still regarded as belonging to other stocks, the same thing is observed, and the pottery which has been dug up from the ruins of the old Indian settlements in Catamarca vies with that produced by many civilised nations. There can be scarcely any doubt that with the Aruaes it is not a case of independent development, but of an influence exercised by the ancient civilised races of the Peruvian highlands on their eastern neighbours. But this influence must also belong to an extraordinarily early period, for even the Aruac races who have never risen to a higher mode of life, and still live at the present day, hundreds of miles away from their ancestral home, in the state of almost pure savages, are the providers and teachers of their neighbours in the matter of pottery.

The Aruac races have acquired quite a special claim to a comparatively higher culture from the fact that anthropophagy had long been absent from their ranks, whereas round about them it still existed, even among races of an unquestionably higher civilisation, at least as a religious rite.[1] It is remarkable that the great mass of the Aruac races, in spite of the fact that some of their tribes lived for many generations in the closest contact with tribes of other stocks, among whom the enemies they killed or captured in war were regularly eaten, never relapsed into this barbarous custom.

This progress in culture also must have belonged to the period that preceded the migrations of the Aruac races, because it was common to every tribe. We were

[1] See *post*, p. 190.

we consider that this ancient race was already familiar with agriculture, skilled in
the preparation of earthen vessels, and disinclined to anthropophagy, we are
almost tempted to look for the ancestors of the Aruacs among the civilised
nations that peopled he high valleys of the Cordilleras long centuries before
the founding of the Inca dynasty. But an important circumstance stands in
the way of this hypothesis. The Aruacs, as we meet with them in history, never
developed a really higher civilisation than, as we have shown, probably belonged
to the original race; the latter must therefore have reached the limit of its
progress — that is, it must have passed the culminating point — before the
expansion of the nation over the whole north of the South American continent
began. Here we have a contradiction. A nation whose progressive development
is over can no longer generate an expansive force such as is seen in the spread
of the Aruac stock, and all that we know of the history of Indian migrations
shows that they have proceeded only from comparatively young and rising
races. We shall therefore have to explain the historical process thus. At a
period when their original stock on the plateaus of Bolivia began to develop
vigorously, the Aruacs were raised from the pure natural state by the cultural
influences of the more highly civilised races in the west, and were advanced in
a manner that indirectly served to strengthen the aspiring power of the race.
In the old home there was no scope for this abundant energy, and so the
emigration began. Whether this moved simultaneously in a southern and
northern direction cannot be ascertained. We meet with detached tribes of
this family south of their original abodes and likewise in the far east. But
they throw no light on the date and direction of their migrations. On the other
hand we can trace the northern current for a long time, and fairly clearly. As
the Aruacs had already begun to till the ground in their home, their migrations
will on the one hand have progressed much more slowly than those of races
that did not know any artificial means of procuring food; on the other hand
they must certainly have moved first in a direction that did not compel them
to accommodate themselves to other habits. This was only possible if they followed the spurs of the Cordilleras northward. We find them in the sixteenth
century in the mountains between Santa Marta and Venezuela, and at the
present day in the peninsula of Goajira, their most northern continuation. The
Carios in the neighbourhood of Coro also practised agriculture on Venezuelan
soil and lived in permanent abodes at the time of the discovery. At the Cabo
de la Vela nature checked their northern advance; but their migration was
continued in an easterly direction, and reached, still centuries before the discovery of America, the mouth of the Orinoco.

Meanwhile a change had taken place in respect to part of the race: Aruac
tribes had become used to the water, and had become navigators and fishermen.
Whether this change began among the coast tribes, or among those which had
penetrated from the old home into the flood-districts of the upper tributaries
of the Orinoco, is doubtful; the latter appears the more probable, as the sea
offers too many difficulties for elementary navigation. Moreover Aruac tribes
are repeatedly found scattered in the basin of the Orinoco. At any rate the
race must still have possessed a considerable power of expansion, for even the
ocean on the east coast set no limit to its migrations. The Aruac navigators
ventured out from the mouth of the Orinoco upon the open sea, and gradually

gave the whole island-world of the Caribbean Sea what is supposed to have been its first population. A little farther, and they would have reached the North American continent from the islands and made the connection between it and the southern continent, which does not seem ever to have been effected. Meanwhile their brother tribes on the mainland still followed the seacoast in their new change of direction. Through Guiana they turned again to the south, and even the Amazon did not prove an insuperable obstacle to them. Aruacs are found, with the sure signs of an immigration from the north, as far as the watershed between the tributaries of the Amazon and of the Paraguay.

The migrations of the Aruacs came to a standstill only when they were met by other races with the same desire for expansion. This probably took place comparatively early, the tribes that were advancing southeastward coming upon the Tupi races. At a later period they encountered the Caribs, to whom finally, in a struggle which lasted for centuries, the majority of the northern Aruacs fell victims.

Although the Tupis have had uninterrupted intercourse with the white man from the first discovery of Brazil down to the present day, the methodical investigation of this race is considerably behind that of others. The reason for this lies in the fate that awaited the race upon the occupation of the land by Europeans. At an early date the missionaries formed, from a dialect of the Tupi language, the so-called *lingua geral*, in which a series of grammars, translations, etc., have been written. It is due to this that the study of the wild Tupi languages, if they may be so termed as opposed to the *lingua geral* cultivated under European influence, has been improperly neglected, and thus one of the best means of ascertaining the ancient history of the Tupi stock has been withheld from us. The same circumstance — long familiarity with the race — has also kept ethnologists from giving their closer attention to the Tupis, whose characteristics have meanwhile been gradually succumbing to the influence of civilisation, so that for the ethnographical and historical study of the best-known stock of the South American Indians we are restricted to inadequate material.

The original home of the Tupis has also been said to have been in the highlands of the interior, but this is based on quite unreliable data and is in contradiction to what is shown by the characteristics of the race in historic times. The mother country of the Tupi races is presumably to be sought not very far from where Europeans first met them, although their expansion and migrations had then been going on in different directions for centuries. Their original home was, in any case, in the region of the northern affluents of the La Plata, but scarcely on the other side of the watershed from which the rivers run northward to the Amazon. In contrast to the Aruacs, the Tupis are a decided water-race. Although most of their tribes, but not all, also tilled the ground to a limited extent, in the sixteenth century they still lived almost exclusively by fishing and hunting. On the Paraguay and its tributaries, and on the rivers of the regions of which their wandering hordes further took possession, they boldly launched their canoes in peace and war. In early times they peopled the few islands that lie at inconsiderable distances from the coast, and they were evidently at home on the sea itself so far as their small craft permitted. Even the Tupi tribes who went far into the interior in their migrations still remained navigators and fishermen.

A map of the races of South America shows at once the direction in which the Tupi race expanded.[1] It first followed the affluents of the La Plata in a southerly direction to the ocean, but only slowly so long as it had no special need of expansion. On the other hand the migration of the Tupis along the coast of the Atlantic Ocean in a northerly direction seems to have proceeded, comparatively speaking, much more rapidly. Up to the mouth of the Amazon they never occupied a very broad area, but satisfied themselves with driving the old Tapuya races from a narrow strip of the coast-land, on which, always with an eye to the water, they settled. That their territory at the time of the conquest still formed an exceedingly narrow strip as compared with its length, but one which was nowhere broken by the return of the hostile nations they had displaced, goes to prove that its occupation took place quickly and at no very remote period.

The migrations of the Tupis must have been of a considerably different character from those of the Aruacs. Whereas the latter evidently proceeded slowly and without serious fighting (in the territory of the Aruacs we scarcely ever find clear traces of a strange population not merged in them by assimilation), the migrations of the Tupis bear throughout the stamp of having been warlike in their nature. Even the name Tapuya ("strangers" or "enemies"), which they gave to all races with which they came in contact, is historical evidence of this. In their intercourse with Europeans the Tupis by no means proved to be a particularly savage and cruel nation; they were the good friends of the first settlers, and subsequently became tractable material in the hands of the Jesuit missionaries. But in their relations with their Indian neighbours they seem to have been pre-eminently the aggressors, and with proud self-consciousness the southern Tupis called themselves Guaranis ("warriors").

Nor must we forget that with few exceptions, to be explained by special circumstances, the Tupi tribes were given to cannibalism. It was certainly no longer a scarcity of food that made them cannibals, nor was it a sacred ceremony springing from religious conceptions, such as we find among several civilised races of ancient America. The Guarani ate the prisoners he made in battle to celebrate his victory over his enemies. The custom observed in this connection is almost a characteristic of the Tupi tribes. The prisoners were not put to death immediately upon the captors' return from the warpath, but were first kept for some time in by no means severe imprisonment, which became lighter and lighter the nearer the time of their end approached, and terminated with most luxurious living, during which the prisoner was not only abundantly provided with the best of food and drink, but was even married to the daughters of the tribe. Meanwhile, without his being aware of it, preparations were made for the feast which was to be crowned by his death. In the middle of the ceremonial dances of his enemies he received the fatal blow; immediately thereupon followed the definitely prescribed dissection of the corpse, and the distribution of the portions among the members of the tribe. The women, and even the sick who were prevented from attending the feast, also received their share. In this form of cannibalism it is obvious that the characteristic features of different stages of culture come into contact. It still contains reminiscences of the time when the flesh of an enemy, like that of a wild beast, served to appease hunger. But it is already pre-eminently the

---

[1] See the map at p. 190.

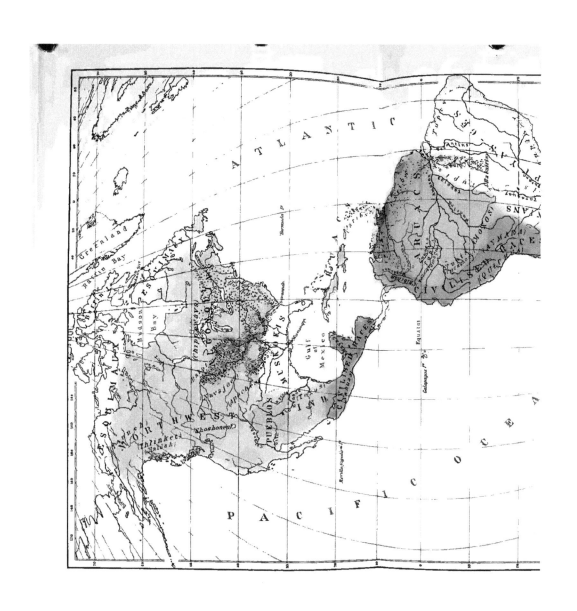

expression of proud triumph over the conquered enemy, for we have special testimony that the feast bore the character of the celebration of a victory. But finally ceremonial influences also begin to show themselves to such an extent that the transition from the cannibalism of the Tupis to the human sacrifices of the Aztecs appears near at hand.

As anthropophagy in this or in a similar form is a common trait of almost all Tupi tribes, it must have originated in the original home of the race. This is a further argument against the Tupis having come from the highlands of Bolivia. The Tupi tribes which live nearest to this region, and should accordingly present the most archaic forms, are the only ones which have entirely done away with cannibalism, and have generally reached the highest degree of civilisation of any members of the race: these are the Omaguas between the Putumayo and Caquetá, and the Cocamas at the confluence of the Marañon and Ucayali. How these tribes of the Tupi stock could be cut off so far from the others is by no means difficult to explain. The Aruacs coming from the north halted at the great waterway of the Amazon at about the same time as the Tupis from the south reached its other bank. So that, to the difficulties that nature set in the way of a farther advance, was here added the hostility of new and powerful tribes. It was probably this, even more than the river with its innumerable sluggish arms, — which is no grave obstacle to a race familiar with boats, — that was the chief reason why the main body of the Aruacs could not advance any more to the south bank than the main body of the Tupis could advance to the north bank. That attempts could not have been wanting on both sides is shown by the small detached tribes of each nationality that are met with in turn on the hostile bank. But on the whole the division is sudden and sharp. To the Aruacs it meant the end of their onward movement. They seem still to have possessed the power to offer the Tupis an invincible resistance, but not to continue their advance in a new direction.

But the Tupis continued to advance. Their traditions show that they followed the Amazon and its tributaries upward; and that the passage up the Amazon did not appear an impossibility to these Indians was proved in the year 1641, when some of them served the Portuguese as guides during the first expedition of the kind undertaken by the latter. Owing to the enormous extent of the Amazon, it no longer appears possible to follow the Tupi migration upward in its basin, but probably even the tribes of the Xingu and Tapajoz did not come down from the watershed to the Paraguay, but from the Amazon up its tributaries. For, in contrast to the Aruacs and Tapuyas, traces of Tupi tribes only occur where there was sufficient water to allow them to remain true to the characteristic of their race. Numerous hordes of Tupis may have been scattered and destroyed in the network of the Amazon, and we cannot now ascertain to what circumstance it was due that the ancestors of the Omaguas and Cocamas managed to break through the central mass of the Nu-Aruac tribes and penetrate almost to the foot of the Cordilleras. Probably the report of a rich cultivated land led them up the Amazon and its tributaries, as in later times the legend of the Omaguas and of the ever-vanishing *Dorado*[1] led the Spaniards down the same way. According to the traditions of the Spanish chroniclers the remembrance of an invasion by the hostile population of the lowlands had not quite died out even among the Indians of the civilised states.

---

[1] See *post*, p. 290.

Between the immigration of the Omaguas to their later abodes and the discovery of America there must in any case have been a considerable space of time. For the Omaguas not only rose far above the average degree of civilisation of the Tupi races under the influence of more highly civilised peoples, so that they renounced cannibalism, tilled the ground, and occupied permanent dwelling-places, — indeed even founded large towns, — but the knowledge of all these achievements had even had time to spread abroad among their less civilised neighbours, who reported the name of the Omaguas to the Spaniards as being a race of fabulous wealth and extraordinary power.

The youngest of the races of South America is that of the Caribs. It is partly due to this circumstance, and to good fortune in the field of ethnographic research, that we know its history somewhat better than that of the other groups. The original abodes of the Carib race probably lay near the original home of the Tupi race. As the latter peopled the upper affluents of the Paraguay, the Caribs peopled the upper basin of the Tapajoz and of the rivers flowing in the same direction to the lower Amazon. The degree of civilisation attained here by the Caribs must be described as extraordinarily low; their language could not count farther than three, really only to two, and we must imagine that their other conditions of life corresponded to this poverty of ideas. Even here mutual intercourse will have taken place between them and the Tupis, which may have had lasting influence on both races. Their development was so similar that one of the first investigators in this field, Karl Friedrich Philipp von Martius, even regarded the Tupis and Caribs as brother tribes and descendants of a common race. At present, however, one is more inclined to the view that the Tupis and Caribs came from different stocks, but were early and closely co-related.

The Caribs were likewise chiefly a race of fishermen, and their relations to the world of water were those which earliest reached a higher development. They too, like the Tupis, the more the old home became too small for them, followed the rivers of their native land downward, so that they gradually got to the Amazon itself and so to the open sea. The traces of their migration in this direction are much obliterated, and it is not impossible that their arrival at the mouth of the Amazon preceded the appearance of the Tupis. But in that case it was probably also the Caribs, and not the Tupis, who first checked the advance of the Aruac races; indeed the enmity between the Caribs and the Aruacs has left widespread traces, whereas between the latter and the Tupis contact took place at only comparatively few points.

What may have given the impulse to the migrations of the Caribs is no clearer than the causes of all the other great movements of the races of the American continent. On the other hand we are better informed as to the manner of their progress, owing to the fact that it was still fresh in the memory of the generation of aborigines found by the Spaniards when they discovered America. Of all Indian races the Caribs were by far the most feared. Even to the Europeans these dauntless sons of the wilderness offered a stubborn resistance, and indeed frequently came off victorious in their bloody battles with the first bands of discoverers, but only to fall, later on, before better equipped expeditions. The Caribs were ruthless in their warfare, not only with Europeans, but also with the Indian population, before the white men appeared. At what period they were transformed, from a comparatively harmless race of fishermen, as Karl von den Steinen found them recently in the original home of the race on the upper Xingu, into the nation of bold and savage water-pirates, spreading terror far around, as we find them in the fifteenth century, is of course a mystery. But the fact that the Caribs made their language prevail over almost the whole region north of the Amazon, including a large part of the Antilles, and that, so far as tradition leads us to infer, by violent methods alone, shows that the race must have possessed quite extraordinary power.

When the Caribs began their migrations they were still at the stage when the flesh of their enemies was welcome food; and they apparently never rose above this rather rude standpoint of anthropophagy. Eating their enemies was so characteristic of the Caribs, that among the Spaniards their name was identical with the term for man-eaters, and in its corruption to "cannibals" this term has become the common property of all civilised nations. This circumstance has fatally affected historical research, as of course races of other origin also adhered to the custom of anthropophagy, and it was generally sufficient for the discoverers of the sixteenth century to ascertain that a race was given to cannibalism to count it at once among the Caribs. It was only later and often most recent research that succeeded in bringing order into this confusion. In the cannibalism of the Caribs, as in that of the Tupis, there are no signs of the beginning of a refined conception. It is true that actual hunger will have but rarely driven them to it, for as fishermen and hunters they knew how to gain their livelihood from a bountiful nature; moreover, as soon as their expansion over Aruac territory began, their women probably continued the agriculture practised by these tribes, although on a more limited scale. But it is at any rate chiefly the expression of warlike triumph which serves to explain their cannibalism, and their wars with all hostile tribes were wars of extermination, in which no captives were made, but all the adult men were put to death. The shy and peaceable Aruacs could not have been dangerous opponents; they even met the Europeans upon their first appearance with respectful timidity, which was only changed to fearful flight after they had learned by years of suffering what bitter experiences were in store for them in intercourse with the white man. So that even weak parties of Carib warriors must often have succeeded in overcoming far superior bands of their opponents.

But if the Carib on the warpath behaved with ruthless ferocity toward the male portion of hostile tribes, he, too, spared the women. On the restless expeditions that he undertook, often for considerable distances, in his narrow canoe, women could not accompany the warrior; they would have been a far greater hindrance to him than on expeditions by land. But as at least the longer expeditions were not undertaken exclusively for the purpose of spoil and plunder (although the warlike expeditions of the Caribs are often decidedly distinguishable from migrations), but had for their object the founding of new settlements, the Caribs probably mixed extensively with the women of another race. And it is only due to the circumstance that the Carib expeditions were made almost exclusively on territory inhabited by Aruac races that the intermixture did not become more multiform.

The time of the Carib migrations can be somewhat more precisely judged than that of any other similar event. We have already indicated that the advance of the Caribs to the mouth of the Amazon seems to have preceded the arrival of the

Tupis at that river.[1] But the Tupi races must also have been pretty near the same goal at that time. Otherwise it can scarcely be explained why the Caribs should have extended their conquests exclusively in a direction in which they got farther and farther from the tribes they had left behind, so that finally they lost all touch with them. The discovery of these almost venerable remains of a people at the most primitive stage of development on the Xingu is really due to mere chance. From there to the Amazon the Tupi population forms a perfectly continuous mass in which sprinklings of the Carib stock are nowhere to be found. So that it must have been the advance of the Tupis that gave the Carib movement its northerly direction, and the weak resistance of the Aruacs must then have enticed the Caribs farther and farther, and allowed them to spread over the north of South America very much more quickly than we can assume to have been the case with the migrations of the Aruacs, or even with those of the Tupis. In spite of this it was of course centuries before the Caribs could make their race the prevailing one from the mouth of the Amazon to the lagoon of Maracaibo. Their extreme outposts broke through the belt of the Cordilleras, presumably at no great distance from the northern seacoast: even in the basin of the river Magdalena there is still a tribe of unmistakably Carib origin, although rather as a detached horde amid nations of other races. But, generally speaking, the higher civilisation of the races in the mountain regions of the Andes placed an insuperable obstacle in the way of their progress. In the basin of the Orinoco, whose tributaries they navigated in their canoes far into their upper courses, right to the foot of the mountains, spreading fear and terror among the dwellers on their banks, Carib tribes seem to have settled only to a limited extent; but at its mouth we find them numerously and almost exclusively represented. That here, too, they established their dominion on a stratum of Aruac races is unquestionable, although the direct proof of it is not so clear as in other parts.

The last conquest of the Caribs, which had not yet come to an end at the time of the discovery of America, was that of the Antilles. When the Cordilleras checked his advance westward, the Carib, whose continual roving into new lands for centuries had become to him a necessary of life, looked around for new objects. While some made their raids up the Orinoco, others made their aim the small islands lying off the Venezuelan coast, often within sight, of whose Aruac population they presumably had heard from the coast-tribes of the mainland. It was probably here that they made a further and — for American conditions — important advance in the art of navigation: they learned to use the sail, an art probably known by none of all the other aborigines of the New World except the Maya races, but by these more perfectly. The circumstance that the conquest of the islands took place in such recent times is of special importance in judging the nature of Indian migrations. On the large islands of the Antilles the first Spanish settlers found an almost unmixed population of the Aruac race, — a peaceable, friendly, good-natured people, living on the abundant produce of their agriculture, with a little hunting and fishing added. But even these Aruacs already lived in constant fear of the Caribs, who sprang up on the coasts in their fast-sailing canoes, sometimes here, sometimes there, and plundered and burned one settlement of the Aruacs after another, murdering the men and carrying off the

---

[1] Ante, p. 192.

women. The Aruacs knew, from the fate that had befallen the smaller islands in the course of the last generation, what the ultimate issue of this unequal struggle would be. When the continual raids had sufficiently weakened the male population of an island, the Caribs no longer appeared merely as flying robbers, but came in larger bands to crush the last resistance of the islanders. A war of extermination would then be waged upon the occupants of a permanent settlement on the island, and after the massacre or flight of the last of these the settlement furnished a new centre of expansion to the Caribs.

On the lesser Antilles the Spaniards found almost everywhere the remarkable phenomenon that the language of the women was different from that of the men. In early times this gave rise to every possible kind of incorrect conjecture, until a closer study of the linguistic elements revealed the fact that the language of the women was a dialect of Aruac, while that of the men was Carib. This discovery, in connection with the stories told by the islanders of the invasion of the Caribs, showed that the Antilles had been conquered during the existing generation, and that the women of the Caribs, with their different language, were none other than the female portion of the subdued Aruacs, who had become the wives and servants of the conquerors. To the historical student of Indian migrations this fact was of no ordinary significance, for it shows us, in the first place, how slowly the expansion of one race over the territory of another proceeded, it having taken generations to fill districts so small in extent as the islands of the Antilles. On the other hand it gives us the key to the explanation of the extraordinary multiplicity of the American languages, and to the bounds, effaced almost beyond recognition, between the races of one independent linguistic stock and those of another. For, though not in the conquering generation, in the offspring proceeding from the intermixture with strange women both the anthropological-physical and the ethnic and linguistic elements must naturally have blended in such a manner as, attaining a new fixity, to form a new race.

The question has been much discussed whether the excursions of the Caribs may not have extended to the mainland of North America, which is at no great distance from the Antilles, and thereby have brought the native populations of the northern and southern continents in contact with one another, of which there is no trace on the isthmus connecting the two parts. But what one was inclined to regard as Carib influence in the art productions of northern Indians has not stood the test of scientific investigation. It is certainly singular that the two parts of the American continent — on which for thousands of years Man had been making slow progress in the development of his faculties — not only remained uninfluenced and unknown by mankind of the other continents, but should also have remained just as strange and unknown to each other, in spite of isthmus and island-bridge. And yet it seems to have been so. The line dividing the northern and southern races on the land-bridge of Central America certainly does not come at the narrowest part: on the contrary the territory occupied by the nations of southern origin extends to the primitive sphere of culture of Central America. But the line is a sharp one: different races do not overlap one another here, as we so frequently find to be the case in the interior of every continent, nor can we trace any influences of any consequence having been exercised by the inhabitants of the one half on those of the other.[1]

---

[1] See *infra*, p. 222 *et seq.*

### C. The Primitive Races of North America

LIKE the southern half, North America also witnessed extensive migrations in prehistoric and even in historic times, but the investigator who seeks to trace them is in a much more unfavourable position on the soil of the northern than in the southern continent. The civilisation brought to the New World from Europe has already extended its victorious march over almost the whole of the United States; a triumph which has filled the mother civilisation with undivided admiration and the daughter with pride. But this victorious march has swept away with unusual inconsiderateness the traces left of the ancient civilisation of the aboriginal population. Whereas in South America we still find the Indian master of vast regions, under conditions of life that evidently form to a large extent analogies to the peculiar aboriginal civilisation found by the first Europeans, in North America the Indian has for centuries been continuously driven by the white man from the neighbourhood of his settlements; only in isolated cases have there been men in North America in earlier times who took a benevolent interest in the Indian, and attempted to reconcile him to the new civilisation and win him over to the new conditions. Naturally such attempts have borne far less fruit than in South America, which to-day possesses a far more numerous population of educated natives than North America.

It is only in the last few decades that the American people have also recognised that they were on the point of destroying their solitary and last opportunity of ascertaining the earlier history of their home, and, with that liberality which we so often find there, works have now been undertaken on a large scale, some of which have already been brought to a successful conclusion, with the object of ascertaining the historical meaning of the ethnographical relics in the territory of the United States. It is true that the Indians themselves no longer play any part in large portions of this territory. Where they have not already been quite exterminated or absorbed by civilisation, their traditions, although not generally quite so scanty as those of the Indians of South America, are still of very limited value; for, apart from the remembrance of their struggles for generations with the white man, their shadowy reminiscences of the time when the Indian was still sole lord of wood and prairie have been almost entirely effaced. Here, too, the most valuable part of our material is on the one hand language, and on the other hand what the oldest writers were able to ascertain from the Indians when they first met them. To this are added the results of excavations, which have certainly been undertaken on a larger scale than in South America. But down to the present day the American has had fantastic and erroneous ideas concerning the most important marks of the earlier history of his land, the famous artificial mounds of the pre-Columbian period. A far wider gap separates the history of recent from that of olden times in the northern than in the southern continent.

Both for geographical and for historical research North America falls into three groups, not always sharply defined, but clearly perceptible.

The first is formed by the lands in the extreme north of the continent, extending from Alaska to Greenland, which are broken up by numerous flowing and standing waters, though these are rigidly ice-bound for a considerable part of the year. It has been supposed that these lands did not always bear the inhospitable character with which the long-continued cold and gloom of the polar winter has stamped them in the present period of the earth's history. But if this supposition is at all correct, it refers at best to times that are not separated from us by historical, but by geological periods; and if, perchance, the first man came to America by way of these most northern lands, this event was certainly followed by thousands of years in which his passage was sunk in absolute oblivion. Not until times rather later than the decline of the Roman Empire did a new migration take place here, which is of very little importance in the general history of mankind, but has left some slight traces behind.

The Esquimaux — or, as they call themselves, the Innuits — have been taken by many for an American race, or for descendants of those Indians who had had a special development under the influence of polar nature. If certain resemblances in build and in mode of life between them and the most northern Indian tribes of the Pacific coast, the Haidahs and Thlinkits, are not to be traced to mutual influence, we are certainly driven to such a conclusion. But, considering the strikingly Mongolian character of the Innuits and the still closer relationship that connects them with the races of northern Asia, it is far more probable that their home is to be sought in Asia; as immigrants they have always been treated with hostility by the Indians. The custom of the Indians, by no means confined to South America, of annihilating the men in their tribal wars, but of incorporating the women in their own tribe, involved the formation of mixed peoples where the different races were in close contact for a very great length of time. In this case it was the northwest coast of Alaska, opposite the Asiatic continent, and in a more favoured climatic situation, which, at all events, afforded the first home to a large number of Innuit tribes which gradually came over, or else mutual influences have been at work which explain the analogous manners and customs of the Innuits and the Indians of northwest America.

In any case the Innuits found the American continent already peopled by Indians up to the latitude of Bering Strait; otherwise in their further migrations they would scarcely have turned to the inhospitable north, over whose vast area their traces extend in scanty relics of houses and implements. Whether they made other attempts at a southward advance elsewhere cannot be ascertained from these finds; but in any case they must have met with the same hostile reception from the races of Indian blood as met them in the northwest. Such a contact between the races can certainly not have been of long duration, as otherwise ethnographic proofs would have been found, as in the extreme west. Those who would regard the Innuits as an Indian tribe gradually driven toward the Pole would find proof of their view in the fact that the northern sagas that relate the voyages of Eric Rauda to Vinland ascribe the destruction of the settlements there to the Skraelings, a name given by the northern settlers in Greenland to the Esquimaux. Now, it is an undoubted historical fact that the Vikings undertook voyages to the northeast coast of America about the year 1000, but owing to the saga's poetic dress, in which alone the little information relating thereto is preserved, we do not know with certainty where these settlements were, nor the character of the population found there. The difference between the Skraeling, the Viking's enemy in Greenland, and the skin-clad North Indian, with whom he fought under similar conditions in Vinland, could easily make so little impression on the Viking's mind, used to the dress and manners of north European civilisation, that both would appear as one to the bard who recited Viking deeds in saga song.

In spite of this the sagas give us a clue to the date of the migrations of the Innuits. They doubtless made their way to Greenland from the American coast or from the islands lying north of it. As the Innuits were at war with the northerners of Greenland about 1200, and succeeded in driving them away during the course of the two following centuries, we may conclude with a fair amount of certainty that the expansion of the Innuits over the North American continent must have come to an end about the same time.

The migrations of the Esquimaux have no connection with the history of the rest of America, whereas, on the other hand, there was frequent contact between the Indian races of North America, as there was between the races of South America. For the northern as well as for the southern half of the continent the eastern chains of the Cordilleras formed an unmistakable boundary of culture. In the north as well as in the south the region of higher civilisation lies on the Pacific side of the mountains, not on the Atlantic side. But the further step in assuming a connection between northern and southern civilisation and between the northern and southern primitive races is not justified. If the Indian in the extensive basin of the Mississippi is more closely related, ethnographically, to the Indians in the basin of the Amazon or Orinoco than to his western neighbours on the other side of the Cordilleras, this fact is sufficiently explained by the similarity of their conditions of life. Man at a low stage of civilisation is everywhere, both in the Old and New Worlds, dependent in the highest degree on his natural surroundings, and where these produce similar conditions the development of Man will also tread similar paths.

On the whole the Indian population of North America east of the Cordilleras exhibits a far greater uniformity of race than is the case in South America, and, although with the aid of language a number of largely different stocks may be distinguished (which presuppose a separate development for hundreds if not thousands of years), the division of the North American races is more recent than that of the South American. This is shown by the mere fact that, of the thousand or so different languages and dialects of the New World named by Brinton in his "History of the American Race," about seven hundred and fifty belong to the part south of the Isthmus of Panama and only two hundred and fifty to Central and North America. But at the same time the multiplicity of the latter races is also so great as to have required an extraordinary length of time.

The most important problem of the pre-Columbian history of North America is formed by the question, Who were the builders of the so-called mounds?[1] These mounds of earth or, more rarely, stones, erected by the hand of man, often with a considerable expenditure of labour, are scattered more or less numerously over the greater part of the United States. We find them in the north near the Great Lakes and far into the territory of Canada. And although toward the south, from the confluence of the Mississippi and Arkansas, they become rarer, their traces may be found not only as far as the mouth of the Father of Waters, but even in the most southern regions of the peninsula of Florida. On the west side the southern limit of the mound region has not yet been ascertained with certainty,

---

[1] See *ante*, p. 167.

but even there it extends to Texas and Mexico, touching the region of civilisation of the Pueblo Indians and the races of Central America. Its bounds are scarcely narrower in an east-and-west direction, for while the artificial mounds almost reach the 70th degree of longitude in the State of Maine in the east, their most western outposts in the north are beyond the 101st parallel. Now the mounds in this vast area are certainly not numerous everywhere or equally distributed. On the other hand it seems as if the real home of the mound-builders lay in the basin of the central and upper Mississippi and its eastern affluents, especially the Ohio, while the groups of such erections lying outside this region are characterised more or less as radiations from this centre.

When more careful attention was first given to the earthworks in the States of Ohio, Illinois, and Wisconsin in the early part of this century, people were quite astonished at their large number, the considerable size attained by some of them, and the original forms, sometimes bordering on the regularity of mathematical figures, which they exhibited in many instances. Astonishment grew when the interest that was thus awakened led to earthworks of like or allied character being constantly discovered in new parts, and when the excavations, which were at first made at only a few places, yielded inexplicable results. Thus the conviction gradually dawned upon scientific and lay investigators that the mounds must be the relics of a long-vanished nation. Those whose conjectures were aided by a vivid imagination did not hesitate to connect the race of the mound-builders directly with the Toltecs, the race that for a long time was held to be the standard-bearer of every civilisation discovered on the soil of North and Central America. But even the more cautious were convinced that these erections proved the existence of a highly developed civilisation in an epoch thousands of years back. Unquestionably the artificial mounds were the work of a sedentary race, for the Indian who roved about in the state of a nomad could not possibly have had time, power, or inclination to erect even the most insignificant of these earthworks, not to speak of the structures — not very numerous, but of imposing dimensions — of Etowah, Cahokia, etc., the largest of which had a content of 3,000,000 to 4,000,000 cubic feet. To erect such structures required a population not only of far greater density than had ever been found anywhere on the North American continent, but one that must also have been excellently organised to be able to subject such labour as these gigantic works entailed to a common will. But what a race, what a state must that have been, which not only produced these structures, but protected the banks of the chief river-courses for many miles with extensive fortifications, such as would seem in early times to have accompanied the Mississippi in an almost uninterrupted chain from the mouth of the Arkansas up to the Illinois. And an almost incredible range of territory is given to this state, if, instead of merely taking into account the region most thickly covered with such earthworks, we extend its boundaries as far as the earthworks can be found.

A sedentary population of such density must naturally have been mainly dependent on a cultivated food supply, and that the mound-builders had been agriculturists was evident from all that was brought to light in the excavations made in the mound region. Not only were ears and grains of maize found, with the vessels and implements necessary for its preparation, but the excavations, or inferences from them, proved that other seeds and fruits were also possessed by the mound-builders. Indeed their agriculture must have been already highly developed, for careful investigation revealed not only irrigation-works and aqueducts, of considerable extent in places, but, in the valleys of the great rivers, even cultivated patches, on which the excess of moisture had been counteracted by a raising of the ground in beds. The mound-builders must also have possessed rich experience in handicraft. Their pottery exhibited not only a great variety of forms, adapted to the most different purposes, but in the better articles attained great technical perfection. Here, too, no trace could be found of the use of the potter's wheel, but some vessels seemed to have been given a glaze of very fair quality. The excavations could naturally not give a very definite idea of the people's accomplishments in weaving, on account of the greater perishability of all fabrics, but even of this art both coarse and fine specimens were by no means wanting. It was thought that special proof of a higher civilisation was given by the specimens of copper ornaments brought to light in the earthworks. The whole of America was in the Stone Age when Columbus discovered it, so that if worked copper was found here, although in no considerable quantity, it must necessarily have belonged to a race of higher civilisation, and long periods must have elapsed since the decay of this race for its progress in culture to have been entirely lost again to after-ages.

The race had certainly had a special knowledge of architecture. This was proved not only by the almost incredible number of earthworks erected by them, and the astounding massiveness of the large mounds, but above all by the variety of form that they had been able to give to their works. It is true that the structures were often merely accumulations of earth of truncated conical form, or oblong-oval or rectangular mounds or terraces, but in other places they exhibited the most surprising forms. The outlines of some of them were unmistakable representations of living creatures, — snakes, fishes, birds, and mammals, and even the human form. If this proved that this ancient race possessed an artistic eye, another kind of earthwork was still more calculated to inspire respect for its achievements in culture. Earthworks were discovered which reproduced the mathematical figures of the circle, rectangle, square, and polygon with an accuracy which their first investigators pronounced to be quite inconceivable without the use of instruments.

In its religious ideas such a race must certainly also have risen far above the naturalism and animism of uncivilised races, and of this too the remains seemed to offer proof. If a considerable part of the earthworks had served as fortifications, dwellings, and cultivated land, there were innumerable others which, from their position and form, would not have been suited for these purposes. Many of them proved to be graves, either of single persons or of whole families, and there were even graves for large numbers and burial-grounds like cemeteries. The manner in which the dead had almost always been interred with articles used in their earthly occupations left no room for doubt that the race of the mound-builders believed in a second existence. It even seemed as if religion played an extraordinarily important part among them in all the concerns of life. Almost everywhere that earthworks occurred with any frequency there were mounds of a certain kind which could not be explained at the first glance. These mounds, generally of conical form, had at their base, or even in their higher strata, a horizontal layer of firmly beaten clay or clayey earth, which, upon the removal of the overlying masses, in general proved to be a carefully levelled surface like a floor, rather inclined toward the middle, in the centre of which the traces of fire were often found.

The discoverers of this form of mound thought themselves justified in regarding these floors as sacred places, and the remains of fire as affording traces of sacrifices; and as human bones were also repeatedly found in the ashes, human sacrifices were supposed to have played an important part in the mound-builders' religious rites, as in many other parts of the New World. The discoverers therefore gave these earthworks the name of altar-mounds, and from their frequency they drew the conclusion that the old civilised state must have possessed a numerous and influential sacerdotal caste, to which presumably the most imposing of the great earthworks, the terraced pyramids for sanctuaries honoured by special worship, owed their origin.

Thus the picture of the race that erected the earthworks was no longer shadowy and indistinct; on the basis of these discoveries, and with the aid of the analogies of the civilisations found on American soil by the first Europeans, fairly definite ideas had been arrived at. But it was thought that quite an extraordinary age must be ascribed to this race, because at the time of the discovery of America all memory of these peoples had already vanished, and, from the high stage of civilisation they had occupied, it was thought that their gradual decline and the extinction of all their traditions must have taken a considerable space of time. On the other hand a particularly remarkable discovery had been made. One of the mounds representing living things was discovered in the neighbourhood of Bloomington, Wisconsin, and several of the older archæologists thought they recognised in it the form of an elephant, or some other animal with a trunk. Now, among the pipe-bowls in the form of animals that have been found in large numbers in excavations in the mound region, the representation of an animal provided with a real trunk (as distinguished from the trunk-like snout of the tapir, which in Chiapas is a sacred animal) also occasionally occurs; they were therefore convinced that the builders of that mound must at least have had a traditional recollection of the form of an elephant or mastodon. But as the proboscidians were extinct on American soil long before historic times, the tradition of the mound-builders must have gone back to the ages to which the mastodon skeletons of the Missouri valley belonged. From the arrow-heads that were found with those skeletons it was assumed that the animals had been killed by man.

Now, although the above view of the mound-builders was formerly the predominant one, for a long time scholars have not been wanting who, doubting the existence of a prehistoric civilised race on the soil of North America, are of opinion that the ancestors of the same Indians who inhabit the United States to-day erected these mounds in comparatively recent times. The more the ancient history of the New World was subjected to methodical investigation, the greater became the number of the mounds. In the course of the last few years the systematic examination of the earthworks in the most different parts of the Union, which has been undertaken on a very extensive scale by the North American Bureau of Ethnology at Washington, has proved irrefutably that the mounds really possess neither the age commonly attributed to them nor all the peculiarities demanded. On the contrary they are not the work of one race, but are probably the relics of the different Indian races which inhabited the territory of the United States before and after the discovery of America by Columbus.

The inferences as to the age of the mounds drawn from the "elephant mound" had not met the approval even of many who still did not doubt that the builders of this mound intended to represent an animal with a trunk. But after recent investigations this too seems by no means certain. The soil of the mound has undoubtedly been under cultivation for years, but its form, although not so clear, has remained quite recognisable. It now appears that the ground is very light sand, and the trunk has probably been formed at the head-end merely by the long-continued influence of the elements, especially of the wind. The mound was presumably meant originally to represent the bear, an animal frequently used as a totem. In a similar manner the most recent surveys have done away with other old erroneous ideas. There is no denying that a number of earthworks in the valley of the Ohio, especially those of the so-called Newark group, exhibit forms of almost mathematical regularity; but the circumstance that of all the circular circumvallations only one or two are almost perfectly round, while the great majority only imperfectly attain this evidently desired end, goes to prove that they were built experimentally rather than with the help of instruments of precision. It likewise proves to be quite erroneous to regard the artificial mounds over the whole extent of their range as uniform, and therefore as the relics of a single race. Closer investigation shows rather that a number of different groups of mounds can be so clearly distinguished by their form and contents that in certain districts we are even able to trace the settlements of two different mound-building populations at one and the same place. The hypothesis of a particular ancient civilised race being the mound-builders therefore collapsing, the mounds remain to us as a class of highly important monuments, from which we can derive information of the earlier history of the North American Indians that no other source can give.

Starting from the assumption that the state of Indian civilisation had remained practically the same since the discovery of America, if it had not advanced through intercourse with the white man, the Indians were considered to have been almost without exception nomadic races of hunters, whose unconquerable love of unrestrained freedom would never and nowhere have permitted them to form large communities and erect permanent dwellings. This conception is perfectly unhistorical. In extensive tracts of North America there were certainly, even in the sixteenth century, restless hordes of Indians who lived almost exclusively by hunting, of which they were passionately fond. But near to them or separating them, and probably throughout the greater part of the present United States, there were also Indian races which had made, compared with them, quite considerable progress in the path of their culture development. So far as there are still any descendants of these races in existence, the policy of the Anglo-American colonists toward the Indians, which has been guided merely by self-interested motives, has certainly reduced them again to a stage of civilisation little different from that of their nomadic and savage fellows. But the Indian mounds and graves have left us evidences of a civilisation that tell an undeniable tale; and an impartial examination of the oldest accounts of the first meeting of the white man and the red man on North American soil confirms in numerous particulars what the mound-finds lead us to suppose. Individual researches are certainly not yet far enough advanced for the valuable material of the discoveries to be used wholly and fully. We know too little of the ancient migrations of the pre-Columbian Indians to be able with certainty to connect the boundaries that archæology traces in certain districts with definite racial boundaries. But where this has become possible the antiquities serve materially to clear up historical hypotheses, and a combination of the different methods of research will further reduce the uninvestigated area year by year.

The whole basin of the Mississippi — a broad strip of land beginning at the Great Lakes in the north and extending to the lowlands of the lower Mississippi — was in earliest times peopled by tribes comprised under the common name of Algonquins. Of the better known Indian tribes belonging to them are the Chippewas in the north, the Delawares, Mohicans, and Ottawas in the northeast, and the Shawnees in the southeast. From their traditions it is supposed that their original home is to be sought in the northeast, beyond the Great Lakes, although they had been driven thence before the time of Columbus by the nations of the Iroquois race. Their migrations from the north seem to have proceeded by two separate branches. The one went in a southeasterly direction, mainly along the seacoast; not, like the Tupis in South America, peopling only a narrow strip, but spreading out widely, and following the rivers that flow into the sea far into the Alleghany Mountains. In spite of their being near the water the Algonquins were scarcely ever exclusively a race of fishermen. Whether they were already agriculturists when they moved down the east coast is doubtful. In any case even the eastern Algonquins practised agriculture in later times, but their fellows who moved along the Great Lakes on their way westward, and in earlier times inhabited their banks, certainly did so even at the time of the migration. As was always the case, the farther the tribes were led apart by their migrations, which continued slowly for centuries, the more differentiated they became in customs and mode of life. If it were not for the unmistakable sign of a kindred language, one would scarcely suppose that the Chippewas of the northwest and the Shawnees in the south were brothers of one and the same race.

A number of nations of the Algonquin race are distinguished from all other Indians of North America by their comparatively advanced civilisation. There is no doubt that even in early times they had taken to a settled mode of life and devoted themselves to agriculture. Nor is it a mere chance that in several points their religious ideas border on those of their neighbours in the extreme northwest. Indeed, from certain peculiarities in this respect, one might be inclined to seek their home in the northwest rather than in the east, for many of them remind us of the Tinnés on the one hand and the Pueblo tribes on the other. The Chippewas and Lenapés already possessed, in their painted wooden tablets or sticks, a system of interchange of ideas that had advanced beyond the purely pictorial character to a kind of hieroglyphic symbolism, which was specially employed for preserving the remembrance of sacred rites. Their religious system, with the worship of the sun and the four cardinal points, as the homes of the wind-gods, we shall find further developed among the Pueblo Indians.[1]

A further resemblance to the latter obtains in the cult of the totems, or clan tokens, which we meet with not only in the pueblos, but also among many other Indian tribes of the Pacific coast as far as the Thlinkits and Haidahs on the borders of Alaska. For this reason we may at all events regard races of this stock as the builders of the peculiar earthworks known as effigy mounds. It is an interesting fact that all the animals, — bear, snake, various birds, fishes, etc., — from which most of the designations and sacred objects of the clans (totems)[2] were

---

[1] See *post*, p. 221.          [2] See *ante*, p. 48.

derived are represented in these mounds. As these earthworks did not serve as burial-places, and were little adapted for fortifications, we may perhaps regard them, like the meeting-hall of the Iroquois or the "kiva" of the Pueblo Indians, as the centre of the cult of the clan. Whether Indians of the Algonquin race were also the builders of the mounds on the central Mississippi and on the Illinois we would rather doubt, especially as this district exhibits mounds of various types that are all different from those of Wisconsin. If a not very reliable tradition of the Lenapés or Delawares can be credited, the answer would have to be decidedly in the negative.

In spite of their great progress in the paths of civilised life the Algonquins did not manage to build durable dwellings. This is the more peculiar, as they might have seen those of the neighbouring Pueblo Indians, with whom commercial relations seem to have existed. But we may not place them lower in the scale of civilisation solely on this account. The erection of stone buildings — which are better able to defy the destructive influence of time than wooden huts at best only coated with lime, and even than mounds of loose earth — creates only too easily an erroneous idea of the degree of civilisation of a race. At the lower stages of civilisation Man is, however, primarily dependent on his natural surroundings, and if the limestone and sandstone plateaus of the west offered the Pueblo Indians the opportunity of easily becoming no mean builders, the wooded hill-regions of the Lake district denied to the Algonquins the opportunity of handing down to posterity similar impressive proofs of their civilisation. But the Algonquins achieved something that scarcely any other race of North Atlantic Indians did: they knew and worked copper. It certainly occurred in such purity in the hills between Lake Superior and Lake Michigan that in the best specimens it could even be shaped by hammering in the cold state. Probably, however, they also knew a primitive and not very efficient method of smelting and welding, with the help of which they formed beads and small plates of the metal, while they were able to emboss the latter with figures.

The bands of the Algonquins who were advancing southeastward, having crossed the Savannah River, came upon solid masses of strange Indians who rendered the continuation of their migration in the same direction impossible. This probably led first to a temporary halt, but, space eventually proving too limited for the gradually increasing numbers of the Algonquins, their migrations were resumed in a westerly direction. The Indians who marched up the Savannah, crossed the Alleghanies, and began to spread over the valleys of the Green River and Tennessee, were called after the Savannah by their neighbours, from their long sojourn on this river, and as "Savannees" — which with time has become "Shawnees" — have preserved the remembrance of this stage of their migrations down to historic times.

The Shawnees and related Delaware tribes are proved to have taken an important part in the erection of the earthworks that occur throughout Tennessee and the neighbouring States on the lower tributaries of the Ohio. A large number of such mounds in this district have been erected for burial purposes, sometimes singly, but generally in groups, and very often in connection with larger earthworks and circumvallations, and the manner of interment has so characteristic a stamp that in it we find undoubtedly a racial peculiarity. Whereas in other parts of the mound area the dead were frequently buried in a crouching position, like the mummies of South America, or in bone-heaps after removal of the flesh, the mode of interment practised here reminds one greatly of that usual in Europe. The bottom and four side-walls of a hole in the earth were lined with flat stone slabs, and the corpse was laid in it, lying full length on its back. Flat stones served to close the sarcophagus, and, if there was any fear of the earth falling through the spaces between them, these spaces were often covered by a second layer of smaller slabs. Such graves are repeatedly found, even without mounds over them, but they are especially numerous in the small conical mounds[1] on the southern tributaries of the lower Ohio, where the Shawnees and kindred Indian races lived down to historic times. We should expect these Shawnees to have been the builders of the graves and the earthworks connected with them, and we are able to prove it. We thus obtain an important argument in judging of the age of many groups of earthworks, in opposition to the fanciful theory of a past of thousands of years. The custom of interring the dead in stone receptacles, as above described, has been practised by Shawnee Indians not only in historic times, but, where there was suitable stone, down to the present century, and has been observed by numerous writers in different places independent of one another. In accounts of earlier times the erection of a mound a few feet in height and of conical form is repeatedly mentioned. Moreover, if excavations have revealed that burial-places of this particular kind have repeatedly contained articles of undoubted European origin among the things placed with the dead, the mounds of this type are certain proof that the particular localities were some time occupied by members of the Shawnee group of the Algonquin race, whose migrations have been going on in this region down to historic and even post-Columbian times.

The Indians who checked the advance of the Algonquins in a southerly direction belonged, presumably, to the group of the Muskokis, whose best-known representatives were the Creeks and Chickasaws. Although these Indian tribes were the first to come in contact with Europeans at the time of the discoveries, — the best part of De Soto's adventurous expedition from Florida to the Mississippi having been made through the territory of Indians of the Muskoki race, — they have hitherto been more neglected by research than the more northern tribes. As descendants of this race have been found only on the banks of the rivers flowing into the Gulf of Mexico parallel to the Mississippi, and as in this district they formed a compact body unmingled with foreign tribes down to the discovery of America, we must assume that they were less given to migration than most of the other Indians. The land occupied by them in the sixteenth century was presumably the ancient home of the race; we may perhaps behold in them descendants of the earliest inhabitants of eastern North America. In early times their abodes near the Mississippi undoubtedly extended much farther northward, and possibly even farther east; so that there may be some truth in the tradition of the Lenapés that they drove the Muskokis from their more northern settlements on the Mississippi.

The Muskokis were also by no means at the low level of civilisation that, judging by modern views, is usually attributed to the earlier Indian population of the continent. They tilled the ground on the most extensive scale, and their agricultural produce excited the admiration of De Soto's Spaniards. Their settle-

---

[1] See Fig. 1, Plate at p. 206.

ments were called "towns" by the Spaniards, and some of them contained a large number of inhabitants. They, too, took a large part in the erection of the artificial mounds, and the characteristics of their work are speaking witnesses to the progress they had made. In the district of the Muskokis are some of the largest mounds that the whole region of the mound-builders can boast. These earthworks — which probably bore at the same time the dwellings of the foremost members of the tribe, and formed a place of refuge for the whole tribe when attacked by enemies — are not, like the smaller mounds, round or conical in form, but remind one rather of the terraced erections on which rose the temples and palaces of the civilised races of Central America. The De Soto mound, although it is not absolutely proved that it was erected by the Muskokis, gives a fair idea of this type.[1] The most imposing erection of this kind is the Etowah mound in the south of Georgia, and we can prove with tolerable certainty that it was still inhabited by Muskoki tribes at the beginning of the sixteenth century, being used as a palace and fortress by their chiefs. As it is surrounded by a large number of smaller mounds, which are enclosed by a kind of fortification, partly rampart and partly moat, we can form from this an idea of old Indian towns which agrees in so many respects with Le Moyne's description[2] that a great degree of reliability may be accredited to the latter.

The Muskokis had acquired a degree of civilisation that leads us to infer that they had been a sedentary race for a very long time. Although the ground of the district they occupied did not afford them suitable material for massive buildings, yet they, almost alone among the Indians of the East, built stronger dwellings than could be erected of purely vegetable materials. The most recent investigations and excavations have proved that some of the mounds that, by reason of their floor-like layers of clay and the remains of bones and ashes found in and beneath these, were pronounced by their first discoverers to be altar-mounds, in reality bore the houses of the Muskoki Indians. The ruins of these houses, which appear here and there to have been round, but generally square, show that these Indians constructed their dwellings of a framework of wooden posts, between which the groundwork for a stucco-like wall-plaster was formed with cross-beams and interwoven twigs and branches. The plaster was left rather rough outside, but inside it was carefully smoothed and probably whitewashed, as in the archaic buildings of the Pueblo Indians.[3] It was applied only to the side-walls, on which it seems to have reached rather above the height of a man; above rose an arched roof borne by the thin ends of the posts and by pliant staves, and covered with vegetable matter, — a reminiscence of the leaf-hut that had been usual among most Indian races, and doubtless also in earlier times among the Muskokis. The bones and heaps of ashes in the mounds are explained by the custom, also recognisable from the illustration,[4] of consigning a man's house to the flames when he died. In Le Moyne's description the deceased seems certainly to have been buried outside the village circle, under a mound which, on account of its smallness, we may perhaps regard as only the nucleus and beginning of the one to be erected. But among the Muskokis the deceased was generally buried in the house itself, and, as soon as

[1] See Fig. 2, Plate at p. 206.
[2] See Fig. 3, Plate at p. 206.
[3] See post, p. 214.
[4] See Fig. 3, Plate at p. 206.

NORTH AMERICAN MOUNDS

1. The Avondale Mounds, Washington County, Mississippi.  2. De Soto Mound, Jefferson County, Arkansas.
3. Small Mound from Le Moyne's "Brevis Narratio." (XII. Annual Report of the Bureau of
Ethnology, 1890-91, Washington, D. C., 1894.)

the fire had so far consumed the walls that the building collapsed, the place was covered up with earth. This peculiar mode of burial, of which traces may likewise be found in historic times, characterises in its turn, like the stone graves of the Shawnees, an ethnographic district, and enables us to throw a ray of light into the darkness that almost completely veils the earlier history of the Indian races.

As in the south, so also in the north the territory of the Algonquins was bordered by foreign races of Indians. The land around the great North American lakes and their outlet to the sea, the river St. Lawrence, was the abode of the races of the Iroquois stock. Of all the Indians these were most distinguished by their fine physical development and — probably as its consequence — by bravery, love of fighting, and warlike virtues, which long made them the most dreaded enemies. The real Iroquois only became an important factor in the history of these districts in the last few centuries before the colonisation of North America. In far earlier times the race of the Cherokees had seceded from them, and played no less important a part in the earlier history of America than they did subsequently in the time of colonial rule. The original home of the common race of the Iroquois and Cherokees is supposed to have been in the farthest northeast of the territory they afterward occupied. It is true that in historic times the whole Lake region, including the districts bordering it on the south and west, was occupied by the Iroquois and the kindred race of the Hurons. But this removal cannot have occurred in very early times, for these races seem to have taken but little part in the erection of artificial mounds. We are therefore forced to ascribe the earthworks of Michigan and Wisconsin to an earlier occupation of this district by Algonquins. And as these northern works are but rarely of a defensive character, it seems as if they were erected earlier than the period of struggle which must have attended the expansion of the Iroquois. The races that erected the effigy-mounds were therefore probably past their prime, and had perhaps even settled in other parts, when the races of the Iroquois family received the impulse that helped them to expand over the greater part of northernmost America.

On the other hand the separation of the Cherokees from the main race belongs to a much earlier period. The direction of their migrations agrees admirably with the theory that the original home of the race was in the extreme northeast. The Cherokees would then have moved off as a first wave in a southerly direction, so that in course of time they came to the basin of the Ohio, where they are proved to have long had their abodes. Even they do not seem to have found these districts uninhabited; on the contrary it is certain that Algonquin tribes not only sojourned there temporarily before them, but, as they did farther south and west, built permanent settlements and tilled the ground. At least some of the mounds in the further course of the Ohio may owe their origin to the latter; and under Algonquin influence, but also in consequence of continual fighting, the Cherokees in turn proceeded to build artificial mounds, which once more form a special province, within the vast mound region, by their ethnographic peculiarities. Two things are characteristic of the Cherokee mounds: in the first place the dead are buried in a lying position, but only in a more or less perishable covering (bark or stuffs), and generally in mounds that served as burial-places for large numbers; in the second place pipes, ranging from the most archaic to almost modern forms, such as are peculiar to the Indians, occur in these graves.

Pipe-smoking is found in the mound region far beyond the borders of the Cherokee district, and we must assume that the cultivation of tobacco played an important part in the agriculture of the whole region.[1] But the upper valley of the Ohio furnishes not only the most numerous, but also, to judge from their forms, the oldest types of the Indian pipe, and shows the uninterrupted course of its further development so clearly that we must suppose it to have been the abode of a race particularly closely connected with the history of the tobacco-pipe, as the Cherokees were. The mounds of this district furnish the most remarkable instances of circumvallations of almost mathematical regularity. But as these are not exclusively limited to the upper course of the Ohio, it remains doubtful whether the greater number of them may not have been erected by the earlier inhabitants of the valley for protection against the advance of the Cherokees, but were restored by the latter, after the conquest, to serve the same purpose. Cherokee graves certainly occur in connection with many of these groups of mounds, and at least bear witness to the fact that the invaders adopted the manners and customs of the conquered as far as the earthworks were concerned; what part they may have taken themselves in developing this primitive architecture is of course difficult to ascertain. The migration of the Cherokees through the valley of the Ohio took place practically in pre-Columbian times, but it had not yet come to an end when the white man entered this district. And only a little farther south, in the valley of the small river Tennessee, the agreement between the still existing groups of mounds and the position of the so-called "overhill towns" of the Cherokees, as recorded by the earliest visitors, testifies that these Indians, having once adopted the custom of mound-building, remained true to it even on their further migrations.

Yet another large branch seems to have been detached from the Iroquois race in the Hurons, who expanded in a westerly direction along the south bank of the river St. Lawrence as far as the Lakes. Whether this took place at a time prior to the migrations of Iroquois tribes to the south cannot be proved, but is very probable; for whereas the "Five Nations" of the Iroquois and the Tuscaroras in the far south had so strong a consciousness of belonging to the same stock that at the beginning of the eighteenth century the latter returned to the north and were received into the League as a sixth nation, even in the time of the first settlers there existed between Iroquois and Hurons a bitter enmity which had lasted from time immemorial, and which had a decided influence on the settlement of the land by Europeans in colonial times.

. As regards civilisation these Iroquois races were doubtless behind the Cherokees in most respects. They also were agricultural and sedentary to a small extent. When the first colonists ascended the river St. Lawrence, Hochelaga was a decidedly town-like settlement of permanent character. Nor are earthworks entirely wanting, in this district, that mark the sites of old Indian settlements. But they do not bespeak the higher civilisation of the more southern districts. They are clearly defensive works, and therefore were probably not built until the real Iroquois undertook the forcible extension of their dominion over the ter-

---

[1] See *ante*, p. 168.

ritory of their neighbours. But this cannot have been long before the discovery of America, as these wars were still going on when the first white men began to penetrate from the coast into the interior.

By "Iroquois," in the narrower sense, are meant only the tribes that inhabited the most northern States of the Union and the neighbouring districts of Canada down to the time of early colonisation. These, too, seem to have occasionally erected earthworks,—a proof that even they did not lead an entirely unsettled life, although permanent dwellings and agriculture—these bases of progress in civilisation—play a smaller part with them than with most of the other nations. Of all the races that the first European settlers found on American soil the Iroquois best represent the type that has erroneously been regarded as characteristic of the whole Indian population of North America.

In the main the Iroquois were still a race of hunters, and one that pursued its human game with the same cruelty and ruthlessness as its animal game. As they were an inland race, navigation and fishing did not play the same part in their economy as it did with the Tupis and Caribs, although they constructed excellent canoes of the bark of trees, and possessed a skill in damming up streams, for the purpose of catching the fish, that told of long experience. But their element was hunting and war. In build the Iroquois were superior to most of their neighbours, and to their comparatively wild life they owe a development of all their physical powers such as was no longer possible even at the commencement of a civilised life. By their strength, and still more by their bloodthirstiness and savage cruelty, they had made themselves a terror to all their neighbours far and wide. That racial relationship did not prevent them from displaying their warlike propensities is proved by the struggles between them and the Hurons, in which the latter, despite their equality in numbers, on account of their more peaceable disposition were forced to retreat farther and farther before their enemies. But the warlike expeditions of the Iroquois extended by no means exclusively, perhaps not even mainly, westward. Their southern neighbours had also to suffer severely from their hostility, and in all probability their invasions were the cause of the last American migration, which we have still to mention, namely, that of the Sioux-Dakotas, which must probably have taken place only in the last few centuries before Columbus. It is a characteristic sign of the superiority of the Iroquois in war, that the only bands that pushed southward seem to have been small in numbers; at any rate they were able only to establish tribes of moderate size in the conquered districts, such as the Conestogas, and the Susquehannas on the banks of the river of the latter name.

What has made the Iroquois specially famous is the League in which the five tribes that remained in the old home combined with one another for attack and defence. This has been regarded as proof of a special talent for statesmanship, and as showing consequently a higher degree of intellectual development than the other Indians possessed. But very weighty reasons are opposed to such an interpretation. In the first place it is by no means certain that this League was the product of the uninfluenced mental development of the Indians. Hitherto it has been pretty generally assumed that the League of the Iroquois was concluded in the fifteenth century,—about 1430. But the farther the examination of Indian tradition with regard to underlying facts has been proceeded with, the more we have been convinced that all that seemed to appertain to the savage of an infinitely remote past, without history or record, in reality only applies to a few generations back. According to the latest calculation the League was probably not made until about 1560; this assumption is strengthened by the stories of dissensions between the various Iroquois nations, which can scarcely belong to so remote a past as would result if the League was created about 1430. But if the alliance came about only at so late a date, the earliest contact with the white man must have preceded it; whether this was of a hostile or amicable kind, it must certainly have exercised a very different influence on the origin of the idea of an alliance if the latter had grown out of purely Indian conditions.

Too much honour has likewise been done the chiefs who formed the League by the conception that has been spread of its purposes. The idea that the League was intended to do away generally with the state of war, and bring about perpetual peace among all Indians, is in such striking contradiction to the whole history of the Iroquois race before and after it was made, that this interpretation may unhesitatingly be pronounced an erroneous one. The exaggerated manner the Indians have of expressing themselves may certainly be credited with having formulated it in such grandiloquent terms, although certainly no more was intended by them than to put an end to the dissensions between the small Iroquois tribes, which had previously been only too frequent. Even so, there still remains sufficient in the League of the Five Nations to assure to the Onondaga chief Hiawatha (who is considered to have been the father of the idea) quite as prominent a place in history as has been prepared for him in literature by Longfellow's immortal poem. In the whole history of the American races, the civilised races by no means excepted, there is no second instance of the natives having had the insight to subordinate their sense of independence, which was carried almost to unruliness, for any length of time to higher considerations.[1] Among the Mexicans we also find alliances of kindred races; but these neither rested on so intelligent a basis as the League of the Iroquois, nor were they destined to last so long or to exercise a similar influence on the fortunes of the nation. In the case of the Iroquois the self-denying act of their chiefs had as its consequence the maintenance of their supremacy among their neighbours until the time when the latter, even earlier than they themselves, sank into insignificance before the invasion of the white man. And if the nations of the Iroquois League exhibit at the present day the highest percentage of natives who have not succumbed to European civilisation, but have been able to reconcile themselves to it and become good citizens of a modern state, they owe this mainly to the wise foresight of their forefathers, who, by forming the League, created the first basis of a political order, from which accrued to them power over their kind, and respect and consideration on the part of the new immigrants.

When the races of Iroquois stock began to expand southward,—a process which, as we have mentioned, belongs to the last few centuries before the discovery of America,—they not only became involved in hostilities with the Algonquins, but another race was also driven by them from its abodes and forced to seek new districts. This was the Sioux or Dakota race, which certainly does not seem to have possessed in those times the importance that it afterward acquired under the government of the United States. That the

---

[1] Cf. *post*, pp. 216 and 229.

original home of these Indians, noted for the resistance they offered to settlers in the far West in the course of the present century, was also east of the Alleghanies, — in Virginia and North Carolina, — is a discovery for which historical research has to thank linguistics. For in the language of the long-neglected Indians of the central States older forms of the same linguistic stock have been found, whose later dialects are spoken in the vast regions of the Sioux and Dakotas west of the Mississippi. Even in the East the nations of this group were almost exclusively restricted to hunting; it seems that they never seriously took to agriculture or possessed permanent dwelling-places. Therefore we cannot connect them, either, with any of the different provinces of mound-building Indians. Moreover, as the earthworks that occur in their later western abodes are only scanty and are on the borders of other races, we must assume that they took no part in the erection of these ancient monuments. A race that grew so little attached to the soil as these restless hunters must naturally have retired more quickly before the energetic advance of an enemy than the agricultural Algonquins and Cherokees. Whether they fought with the latter in the valley of the Ohio we cannot tell from the obscure tradition of the Sioux tribes regarding this migration from the East. The migration certainly belongs to a later period than the secession of the Cherokees from the main race of the Iroquois. But probably the courses of the two races came but little in contact, as the Sioux, coming down the Big Sandy, reached the Ohio at a point lying on the southwest border of the territory over which the Cherokees expanded. As soon as they were beyond reach of the hostility of the Iroquois, the migration of the Sioux would also have assumed a slower pace, names of places and rivers confirming the tradition that they settled for some time in different parts of the Ohio valley. But they never seem to have settled permanently; for Europeans who followed the Ohio downward came across no nations of this race on its banks. The names given by the Sioux themselves to the different groups reflect a long separation between the upper and lower part of the river. But when De Soto crossed the American continent he came upon nations of the Sioux race only on the other side of the Mississippi, — a proof that the whole migration of the races from the eastern States to the borders of the region they still occupied in this century took place in pre-Columbian times.

Probably many other races peopled these vast regions when the first white men set foot on American soil; but what we know of them is infinitely little. Even what has been brought to light, by laboriously following up scarcely perceptible traces, regarding the great races of the Algonquins, Muskokis, Iroquois, and Sioux, is so scanty that it can scarcely be called their history. The zealous researches that have only recently been commenced on American soil will bring to light many other memorials to which even historical attributes may be given; but more than a few main features in the pre-history of the American Indians science will scarcely ever be able to trace.

### D. THE INDIANS OF THE NORTHWEST

IF we cross the Rocky Mountains from the east, we enter the region of a development in culture of an evidently different kind. This difference is most striking if we cross by the upper Rio Grande and the affluents of the Colorado from the hunting-grounds of the buffalo-hunters into the territory of the Pueblo Indians. On closer examination, however, it appears that all the races of the Pacific coast, up to the borders of the Esquimau region in Alaska, exhibit close agreement in the evolution of their customs, so that in spite of linguistic differences they are more closely related to one another than to their eastern neighbours.

The inhabitants of the far Northwest — the Thlinkits, Haidahs, and Nootkas — are almost exclusively races of fishermen, — a not very frequent occurrence on North American soil. It is evident, moreover, that they were not driven to this mode of life by their natural surroundings, but developed thus from the very beginning. This we may infer from the fact that, in spite of their racial individuality being comparatively highly developed, they have no traditions indicating an earlier and different state of development. When they first came in contact with Europeans they had developed, independently of foreign influences, a number of institutions that told of a very long period of gradual progress in culture. That they were expert navigators and fishermen and skilled boat-builders was too natural under the prevailing conditions to justify us in basing general conclusions upon it. But two things are characteristic as showing the age of their civilisation and the progress they had made in it, — their social organisation and artistic inclinations.

Like some of the Indians of the East, the natives of the Northwest also attached chief importance, not to the family, but to the *gens*, or clan; accordingly they, too, did not occupy single houses, but built one house for all the families of a clan, in which each had only a compartment. The same community also ruled their life outside the house: common the work, common the benefit. A special feature with them was the system of totems,[1] or clan symbols derived from living things, for which a reverence similar to fetichism was shown by all the members of the clan, but only by them. These totems certainly also had their share in developing the artistic efforts of the race, for the representations of the clan fetiches (sometimes of huge dimensions, as on the wooden totem-posts of the Haidahs and Bellacoolas) are one of the most frequent proofs of their artistic sense, which exercised itself on the most diverse raw materials, such as wood, stone, and bone, but not clay. Now with time a more highly developed social system had grown out of the gentile system. Almost all the Indians of the Northwest were familiar with slavery, and that in its most pronounced form, according to which the slave is the chattel and therefore the saleable property of his master. This presupposes a higher development of the ideas of clan, family, and property than we find among many other Indian races, whose slaves were almost exclusively captives taken in war, who either met a painful death or were amalgamated with the tribe. The same development is shown by the fact that almost all these races carried on a more or less extensive trade (the Sahaptins journeyed from the upper Columbia to the Missouri), and even used shell-money as a standard medium of exchange, which seems to have been recognised throughout the greater part of the Pacific coast to the borders of the Mexican States. Finally, all the Pacific tribes, although agriculture was either entirely unknown to them in consequence of the climatic conditions, or only played a subordinate part, were sedentary, but with this peculiarity: they possessed permanent winter dwellings built of stone

---

[1] See *ante*, pp. 48 and 203.

and earth, but in the fishing-seasons they erected also temporary summer dwellings at different places. In all these peculiarities there prevails among the Indians of western North America (always excepting the sprinkling of tribes of much lower development in central California) a very general agreement, which is by no means limited to the coast tribes who live by fishing, but in many respects extends to the agricultural tribes living farther south and east. Closer connections must have existed here among them than the mere influence of living together as neighbours under similar conditions would bring about.

### *E.* THE PUEBLO RACES

SOUTH and southeast of the territory of the Northwest Indians, and separated from them by a number of small tribes, some of them still at a very low stage of development, is another large region of a similarly developed culture, which from the earliest times has interested scholars in no common degree, — the region of the Pueblo Indians. Remains of these races have been preserved through all the vicissitudes of colonial wars down to the present day, and under circumstances which make it still possible to study among them the traces of their early civilisation. The boldest historical conjectures have been made about these races. Like the mound-builders, they, too, were supposed to have formed in prehistoric times a mighty and extensive empire with a highly developed civilisation. Such theories connected them, far more directly than was possible in the valleys of the Ohio and Mississippi, with the Central American civilised States of the Toltecs and Aztecs. A peculiar tradition of the latter supported this in a remarkable manner.

When the Spaniards, after the conquest of Mexico, inquired of the Aztec priests and scribes the early history of their race, they gave the following account: At a remote period they had set out from a place called Aztlan, which lay on a great lake in the far north; had wandered for countless years, during which they had been split up into several tribes, and founded temporary settlements at the most various places; and had finally settled on the Lake of Mexico, to found the town of Tenochtitlan. This tradition has supplied food for the imagination for several centuries. In the great water on which Aztlan lay was seen a remembrance of the region of the great North American Lakes, and a clever American even gave a group of earthworks in Wisconsin the name of Fort Aztlan. All erections of an unexplained type that occurred north of the borders of the Mexican empire as far as the Lake district were considered to have been stations of the Aztecs. But whether any actual circumstances can be proved to underlie this tradition is very doubtful. As regards the direction in which a higher civilisation spread, we shall find in the history of the Central American races facts that are difficult to reconcile with the Aztec tradition.[1] But the idea that an indistinct knowledge of a prehistoric relationship between the civilised race of the Aztecs and their less civilised northern neighbours may be reflected in the legend must not be rejected offhand. It is thought that linguistic affinity with the races of the Nahua stock, of which the Aztecs of Mexico became most famous, can be traced into the heart of the Pueblo region, as far as the group of towns called by the Spaniards "Tusayan," but better known at the present day by the

---

[1] See *post*, p. 249.

name of the chief place, Moqui. Resemblances in customs, religious ideas, and old traditions are unmistakable in all these races. But quite as unquestionable, if not more important, are similarities of this character between the Pueblo Indians and their northern neighbours, so that we should finally arrive at the result that in the whole mass of races from Alaska nearly to the Isthmus we have the members of one great family, which, however, seeing that its linguistic disunion is so great as almost to deny all connection, must have been broken up into different branches in very early times.

Considering how firmly half-civilised races in particular cling to everything connected with their religious ideas, often even when the original conditions on which the traditional institutions were founded have long disappeared, it is certainly noteworthy that in this very respect remarkable points of agreement have been discovered between the Indians of the Northwest and the Pueblo races. In the whole region of the latter the sacred hall in which a great part of the religious ceremonies are held, and the others at least prepared for, is the "estufa," erroneously so called by the Spaniards from its peculiar structure. The Pueblo Indians call it kiva. In structure the kiva differs very considerably from all the other buildings of the Pueblo Indians in the most important points. It always lies more or less away from the rooms of which a pueblo (village) is composed, and which are built close to and over one another. It has the peculiarity that it is at least partly, and often entirely, sunk below the ground, and is only accessible by a ladder from an entrance built in the middle of the roof. The kiva is to the Indians of the pueblos what their meeting-house is to the eastern Indians: here the men assemble to discuss common affairs, but especially to prepare for and to perform their religious rites. Even at the present day there exist in the pueblos still inhabited by Indians a large number of such underground meeting-houses, which, so far as missionary activity has not yet done away with the remains of the original rites, serve the old purposes. If we compare these kivas with those that occur in the remains of old Indian towns that have long been in ruins, it appears that centuries of intercourse with the white man have made scarcely any change in the kiva.

In the inhabited pueblos, and even in many that in all probability have sunk into ruins without being trodden by European foot, the kiva is a rectangular hall; on the other hand, the older the ruins are, the more exclusively do we find kivas of circular form, although all the dwelling-rooms of the same ruins are rectangular, and circular buildings occur only rarely throughout the Pueblo region in the form of towers. The circular kivas undoubtedly represent an older type, for whereas the four-sided kivas are lined with stone, carefully coated with plaster, and neatly whitewashed up to the posts forming the roof, the stone wall of the round kivas reaches to only three-fourths of the whole height. This is then completed by horizontal beams fitting into one another, which approach roundness owing to the number of angles they form, and are constructed exactly like those of the log-house type of building, which the pioneers of the West learned from the Indians.[1] This form of the kiva is certainly a reminiscence of the time when the Pueblo Indians were not the skilled builders they afterward became. Its being sunk below the ground (a custom by which the Indians of various parts sought to give their dwellings greater height and better protection from the ele-

---

[1] See ante, p. 206.

ments) and its beam-work point unmistakably to other conditions of life; but we can well understand how it is that only in these halls that served for religious purposes, long unintelligible to the Indians themselves, the memory of conditions has been preserved of which almost all trace has been lost in their general life.

Now, it is undoubtedly very remarkable that round and square houses, partly dug in the ground, lined with stone slabs, and, at least in some cases, only accessible by an opening in the roof, occur as dwellings among various Indian races of California who are not particularly closely related to the Pueblo Indians either linguistically or ethnographically. Moreover these same Californian races, like the Pueblo Indians, make a great feature in their religious ceremonies of certain dances reminding one almost of theatrical performances, which in both cases, if not exclusively performed in the common dwelling-hall, were prepared in a part of it curtained off temporarily for the purpose. Now, as in these dances almost similar masks fashioned as snakes, skeletons, etc., occur in both cases, we are justified in assuming that these races have a common stock of traditional ideas that is not due to late adoption or transmission, but to an original relationship.

The region of the Pueblo Indians bears witness in its antiquities to a progressive movement from north to south, attended by a certain measure of development in culture. That the stone structures of the cliff-dwellers, in the almost inaccessible cañons of the rivers that cut their way through the central plateau, are to be regarded as dwellings of the same races whose last remnants now inhabit the pueblos of the regions of Cibola and Tusayan under the name of Zuñis and Moquis, is beyond all doubt. The transition between the architectural forms is unmistakable, and the connection between cliff-dwellings and houses, both on the plateau and in the river valleys, has also been clearly proved by excavations, as has also the chronological sequence. We must certainly not overlook the fact that the migrations of the Pueblo Indians also proceeded slowly, in consequence of their living almost exclusively by agriculture. Indeed at times events occurred which positively caused a retrograde movement, and to such an extent that the wanderers returned to parts they had left long ago and occupied anew their partly ruined dwellings. Such occurrences are even related in the traditions of the present Pueblo Indians of times certainly later than their first meeting with the Spaniards about the middle of the sixteenth century. But although the most northern evidences of the Pueblo civilisation, the cave-ruins, reveal an architectural development that is in no respect inferior to that displayed by the carefully built pueblos of the valleys of the Chaco and Chelley, yet the other antiquities show an earlier type in the north, and furnish evidence of a later development that continued down to the time of those degenerate Pueblo Indians whom we know to-day.

Pottery especially affords us a further glimpse of the early history of these races. It is not chance that the north Californian tribes, who could work wood and stone skilfully and otherwise occupied by no means the lowest rung of social culture, had no pottery. The potter's art develops only where nature is not bountiful with that necessary, water, and man has to procure and preserve a supply. For races that live by fishing, wickerwork, more easily produced, suffices, and for this nature had given these peoples a suitable material in the reed and other aquatic creeping plants. Of these they made baskets, which even served as vessels in which fish could be cooked in water heated by the primitive method of throwing red-hot stones into it. But water could not be kept in these receptacles for any length of time, and when these races migrated into drier districts their need of pottery led to its manufacture. The evolution of their pottery from spinning and basket-making is unmistakable from the manner, peculiar to the Indians of both north and south, of building their pots from an endless thread of clay.

If the far Northwest is the common home of the Californian and Pueblo Indians, the latter evidently did not develop into potters until after the separation of the groups. This stage has not yet been discovered from the antiquities. We find the Pueblo races, even in their earliest northern abodes, at a respectable stage of development, not only as architects, but also as potters. In the central Pueblo regions, on the Chaco and Chelley, we then perceive a further advance, while the culmination of their artistic activity was reached at Sikyatki (not far from Moqui), which was destroyed only shortly before the arrival of the Spaniards. We are not entirely without an explanation of this. As already mentioned, the races of the West in the latitude of the Californian peninsula are divided up by nations in the lowest stage of civilisation. Not only do the traces of a struggle with these occur in the south, in the cave-dwellings and the pueblos built on easily blockaded spurs of the plateaus, but dwelling-places agreeing remarkably with the pueblos also occur in the north as far as the Haidahs,—a proof that the Pueblo races sought to protect themselves from the aggression of hostile tribes. This first attack by Athabascan or Tinné tribes (for as such we must regard them in spite of the scanty proofs of linguistic affinity), although not the immediate cause, probably decided the direction and subsequent development of the tribes that were driven south, and which are first met with in history at the Mesa Verde and the river San Juan.

The theory that the whole region of the Pueblos, from the river Mancos in the north to the mouth of the Gila in the south, and from the Rio Pecos in the east to the Colorado in the west, ever constituted a united body politic, is quite as untenable as the similar hypothesis regarding the region of the mound-builders. The statesmanship of the American natives has scarcely anywhere been great enough to form, much less maintain, an extensive State.[1] In the territory of the Pueblos there prevailed probably during the whole period of their social prosperity the same system of small communities based on the *gens* that the Spaniards found existing there at the discovery; its remains may still be recognised without difficulty from the traditions of the Pueblo Indians, in spite of the mixtures caused by the fusion of the population. It has its root in the soil. Their primitive agriculture, which is certainly said to have supplied in a good year crops sufficient to last for two or three years, did not suffer any great number of people in one place, owing to the unfavourable climatic conditions. The Pueblo region was certainly more thickly populated in earlier times than it is now, but when the Spaniards first entered it its period of prosperity seems to have been past. For although the earliest accounts give the number of large and small towns of the Pueblo Indians at seventy or seventy-one, these lie exclusively in the southern and eastern part of the Pueblo region, the same as are still partly peopled by the descendants of the old natives, while the central and northern parts, in which the most architecturally perfect buildings have been found, seem to have been then, as they are to-day, forsaken and in ruins. Now, although it is probable that many of the southern pueblos may not have existed when the more northern ones were built

---

[1] Cf. *ante*, p. 210, and *post*, p. 229.

and inhabited, the circumstance that the latter are also technically the most perfect is a certain sign that the southern races already show the commencement of a decline which, as it is displayed in quality, must also be assumed in quantity. For the height of development in culture often comes after the first traces of decline in a nation, but it scarcely ever precedes the culmination of the material development.

The petty jealousies and feuds of the small communities with one another had a fateful influence on the history of the Pueblo Indians. Occasion for these was incessantly given by outward circumstances, — in the limited areas fit for cultivation, and the insufficient quantity of moisture, the most careful use of which could alone make the soil productive and the land inhabitable. These outward conditions had an influence on the development of the Pueblo civilisation similar to the influence they had on the inhabitants of Peru, who had to fight with the same climatic difficulties. We therefore not only find here, as we do there, surprisingly ingenious and extensive irrigation works, but, from the analogy to Peruvian conditions and from the existing customs of the present Pueblo races, we may also infer that a water-law was carefully made and enforced among the old Pueblo peoples. A continual struggle with drought is not solely indicated by the recollections of the present Indians or by the ruins of the old works, but dependence on the fertilising moisture plays so prominent a part in the whole pronounced religious system of these races, that we must suppose that the climatic conditions were little different then from what they are now. Excavations in the ruins have certainly often proved the existence of old sources of water in or near them, and it has often required only moderate labour in removing sand and rubbish to increase considerably the yield of these springs. But that a race whose whole existence depended on obtaining water would have spared no pains to increase it, is also testified beyond doubt by the discovery of artificial reservoirs and similar works.

In spite of this it would be wrong to see in variations of the sources of a water supply the only reason for the migrations of the Pueblo races, because these migrations were not from the dry districts to the more favoured ones, but exactly the reverse, — from the woodland farther and farther into the arid sand-steppe. If it were a mere hypothesis that the southward movement of the Pueblo Indians was brought about from an invasion of the central Californian savages, there can scarcely be any doubt that the aggression of similar hostile races decided the further course of these migrations. And if some of the magnificent ruins of the valleys of the Chaco and Chelley are not well adapted for a prolonged defence, it only proves that at the time of their erection the pressure of hostile races had not yet commenced. But this is easily accounted for by assuming that the buildings in these valleys, among which even cave-buildings are fairly numerous, were erected at a time when the more northern settlements (which almost entirely lay protected, especially the numerous and extensive cave-dwellings on the Rio Mancos and other northern affluents of the San Juan) were still inhabited and were adapted to form a barrier against marauding savages.

According to European ideas we are much inclined to think cave-dwellers men at the lowest stage of culture. But the cliff-dwellers of western North America were not this at all. Sedentary, living almost solely by agriculture, they had already reached the stage of keeping domestic animals, and as basket-makers, weavers, and potters they were superior to almost all their neighbours.  It was they who, like the Mexicans, produced those original feather-covered webs that excited the great astonishment of the Europeans.  Their pottery is quite equal, in purity and simplicity of form and decoration, to that of their neighbours.

But there was one art in which the Pueblo Indians were superior to all the other races of the northern continent, including the Aztecs (the Mayas, in part, excepted): namely, the art of building.  A race that was able to erect buildings in caves like the Cliff Palace discovered by Gustaf Nordenskiöld in a side valley of the Mancos[1] was no longer rude and primitive; it was a race which, if not to be numbered among civilised peoples, was at least well on the way to become one.  Nature herself had certainly gone a long way toward making the inhabitants of this district builders.  In the sandstone that encloses the narrow valleys of most of the waters of the northwestern plateau-land in layers of varying resistance, the natives were offered a material that can almost be shaped of itself.  This stone broke down to a considerable extent, under the influence of atmospheric forces, in pieces that required but little working to make them fit for house-building.  The rudest buildings, — sub-structures, — such as are also to be seen at the Cliff Palace, were therefore probably constructed merely by piling up stones selected for the purpose; but of these simplest beginnings only a few traces have been preserved.  The material is for the most part brought into the proper shape with great care, the layers secured by an almost invisible but sufficiently strong cement, and every joint so carefully faced with small stones that the outer surfaces of the buildings have not merely withstood the action of the weather for centuries, but even at the present day seem to be firm and smooth.

Moreover the Pueblo Indians had two other architectural accomplishments in which few races of the New World equalled them: layering the material in strips of equal size — an advance which they probably learned from the long layers in the stone of their native valleys — and mortising the joints, an art not even known by the Maya architects of Chichen-Itza.  Such skill naturally presupposes long practice in the art, but we cannot trace its development.  Besides the great assistance rendered by nature, the migrations of the Pueblo Indians undoubtedly furthered the development of their architectural knowledge to an extraordinary degree, by giving them occasion to use the experience gained in the course of a building period whenever they erected a new settlement.  But the migrations which we have had to assume as having been from north to south, in historic times, have not to be included in this respect.  On the contrary the buildings of the northern and central Pueblo regions, — for instance, the Cliff Palace, and the ruins of Kintiel, Pueblo Bonito, and Nutria in the Chaco valley, — while bearing traces of greater age, exhibit the highest development of Pueblo architecture, whereas the later settlements of the same regions and farther south are not nearly so well and carefully built, although this is by no means explained by a want of material.  Thus there is no alternative but to assume that the latter buildings were erected at a time when the conditions under which the Pueblo Indians lived had already changed for the worse.  But as even these buildings belong to a period prior to the discovery by the Spaniards, we come once more to the conclusion that the golden age of the Pueblo races was already past in the sixteenth century.

---

[1] See Plate opposite p. 218.

CLIFF PALACE IN CLIFF PALACE CAÑON, SOUTHWEST COLORADO

(From G. Nordenskiöld's "The Cliff Dwellers of Mesa Verde.")

Here again we are led to the further inference that the migrations of the Pueblo Indians cannot have been spontaneous. Ideas drawn from modern warfare have been applied too much to ancient times, and consequently the defensive strength of the Pueblo towns has been declared so inadequate that the purpose of defence has been positively denied them. But we have only to consider the offensive and defensive weapons of the Pueblo Indians, who were in any case considerably superior to their opponents in social culture, to see at once that very primitive means of defence must have sufficed. The war waged by the Indians upon one another has always consisted in surprises; the idea of a siege, if only of days, or of the artificial cutting off of indispensable resources, especially of water, which of course became a dangerous weapon as the art of war advanced, need scarcely be seriously considered in the wars to which the Pueblo Indians were exposed. The attacks of the enemy had for their object plunder that was of immediate use and easy to carry away, and, if possible, prisoners, especially women and young persons. The enemy would certainly also have tried to damage the crops of the Pueblo Indians in these wars; but to gather in the ripe fruit was a comparatively long business with the means at the disposal of these primitive races, and so the plundering Apache or Navajo would let the Pueblo Indian himself do this first; he much preferred to fetch the stored-up crop from the house than the ripe crop from the field. But even the pueblos that did not lie in the inaccessible caves of the cañons or on the easily blockaded spurs or ledges at the edges of the plateau, but on the level ground of the river valleys or in the plains at the foot of the table-land, afforded sufficient protection from a sudden attack. Owing to the massive style in which they were built, a larger number of inhabitants would be always threatened at the same time, and therefore could easily combine for common defence. Moreover the older pueblos are far more closely built even than those now inhabited, so that outside they show an unbroken wall several stories high, while inside the stories rise in terraces from a central court. The entrance to this court was in most cases easily defended; moreover, the ground floor had no entrances opening on to the court, access being obtained to the rooms of the occupants solely from the first platform, which could be reached only by ladders. Of course the enemy also were educated by the continual struggle, and if the danger of their attacks and their numbers increased in the same measure as the strength of the defenders diminished through unfavourable outward circumstances, the more civilised and physically weaker Pueblo Indians would have eventually to yield to the more robust and hardy sons of the desert. But this would take place through circumstances mainly independent of the strength of the settlements.

So at least we must imagine the war that gradually crushed out the civilisation of the Pueblo races over a considerable part of their ancient territory. They were surrounded north and east by Indian races that belonged to the most savage and brutal of the whole continent. The Apaches and Navajoes made themselves a terror even to the Anglo-Saxon pioneers of the West in the present century, and they were nations of the same stocks that surrounded the Pueblo region on various sides. Even when the Spaniards first entered this region they heard of the deadly enmity between the Pueblo Indians and their neighbours, and were themselves sympathetically drawn into the struggle. Just as the peaceable inhabitants of the pueblos were at continual war with the flying robbers of the prairie in historic times, so, too, did their forefathers certainly fight with their enemies' forefathers for their existence.

From the circumstance that a marked relationship exists in build and in various customs between the Navajoes and the northern Pueblo Indians at the present day, some would draw the conclusion that the former are to be regarded, not so much as a tribe hostile to the Pueblo Indians, but rather as a kindred tribe that once itself occupied settlements in the Pueblo region, and became a roving race of robbers only through hostile oppression. Although the fact remains that the Pueblo civilisation succumbed to the invasion of hostile neighbours, these must certainly have been other than the Navajoes. It is true that since the last century these Navajoes have been known as a tribe that practises agriculture, though to a limited extent; that possesses the largest numbers of horses and sheep of any Indians of the West; and whose squaws weave the finest coloured cloths of sheep's wool. But all these are acquirements that belong to times subsequent to contact with the white man. Moreover the social progress of the Navajoes rests chiefly in the hands of their women, whereas among the Pueblo Indians the main burden of tilling the ground falls to the men. This civilising influence of the female sex may be traced, however, in its ultimate origin, to the Pueblo Indians, whose women, captured in their raids, have been their teachers. This intermixture explains also the physical affinities of the races and resemblances in their languages.

One more point in the early history of the Pueblo races needs mention: their relations to their southern neighbours, the civilised races of Mexico. If in the foregoing we have assumed that the Pueblo civilisation progressed from north to south, we have left a whole group of Pueblo ruins — and that the most southern of all — unnoticed. The attention of the first Spaniards who entered the Pueblo region from Mexico was attracted by a number of ruins that met their eye in the basin of the Gila River, the most southern affluent of the Colorado. These were remains of important settlements which unmistakably bear the character of the pueblos, although they constitute a group of themselves. The Gila valley did not offer its inhabitants the suitable building material that had made the Pueblo Indians in the upper parts of the table-land such excellent builders. The ruins of this and the adjacent valleys are therefore distinguished by the material used, which is a kind of brick made of mud mixed with vegetable substances and air-dried; a material known in many parts by the Spanish name of "adobe," and frequently used in historic times and even to the present day. But otherwise these buildings are also distinctly the work of Pueblo tribes. Here, too, we have towns consisting mainly of a single solid mass of houses, or really only rooms; these rooms, built over one another in stories, enclose an inner court, from which they rise in terraces, while the outer walls are mostly perpendicular. This is therefore exactly the character of the more northern settlements of stone, such as we found from the cave-buildings on the San Juan to the open towns of the Moquis and Zuñis. These buildings must have been erected by the same races that built the more northern ones, or by races nearly related to them.

Now, as these towns were found forsaken and in ruins by the Spaniards at a time when the central pueblos were still largely inhabited, they must certainly belong to an earlier period than many of the stone pueblos. But no conclusions may be drawn from this antagonistic to the view that the Pueblo civilisation developed generally from north to south. The race that built the ruins of the Gila valley generally known as Casas Grandes certainly did not learn its architecture here. Generally speaking, the material, owing to its comparatively poor resistance to atmospheric influences, is by no means calculated to induce man to erect hollow buildings above ground.[1] In the ruins on the Rio Gila we can perceive only the endeavour to retain architectural forms that had gradually become a need of the race, even in districts in which the natural conditions were considerably less favourable. The race that erected them separated from the body of the Pueblo Indians only when the latter had fully developed its characteristic civilisation farther north, on the plateaus of the sandstone mountains, and as no traces of the same civilisation occur farther south, it appears that this race, whether it was harassed by hostile peoples, or induced by natural causes again to change its abodes, rejoined the more northern members of the race before historic times.

In the legends of the Indians who have settled in the vicinity of these ruins since the last century they are almost exclusively called houses, palaces, or fortresses of Montezuma, and we shall scarcely be far wrong if we regard this as the survival of an indistinct recollection of the deeds of Mocteuzoma I. Ilhuicamina. But such a tradition was certainly not developed until after the conquest of Mexico by the Spaniards. This is obvious, not only from the fact that the empire of Mexico-Tenochtitlan never extended to anywhere near these parts, but above all from the circumstance that there is absolutely no style of architecture like that of the ruins of the Gila within the sphere of civilisation of the Central American States, and that the resemblances to the architecture of the Central Americans are much less within the Pueblo region than, for instance, in the region of the mound-builders. It may be considered historically proved that the spheres of civilisation of the Pueblo Indians and of the Maya and Nahua races, at least during the time that their respective characteristic architectures were developing, were entirely exclusive of one another and had no connection whatever.

But in all probability this was not always so. Although the legends of an original home in the far Aztlan of the north, in the form in which they became known to the Spaniards, referred only to comparatively unimportant changes of abode made by the various nations of the Nahua race at no very remote period, this does not preclude the possibility that in the very earliest times races lived even as far down as the region of Mexico, who exhibited a racial relationship to all the other nations inhabiting the Pacific coast of North America. Besides widespread linguistic resemblances there is the striking recurrence of religious ideas and customs, which are too peculiar to have been the result of simultaneous independent development in different places.

The simultaneous worship of the sun and fire is certainly in itself an idea so familiar to the primitive races of all ages and all lands that from its occurrence in different tribes we could not infer that they were related, even if it were not practised in like manner in other neighbouring tribes. On the other hand it is very remarkable that both among the Pueblo Indians and among the civilised races of Central America all the fires throughout the tribe had to be extinguished at regular intervals; and that at one place only, amid elaborate religious ceremonies, priests appointed for the purpose, by rubbing two sticks, obtained the new fire, which was then spread from this one centre by speedy messengers. Another highly characteristic religious idea common to these same races is that of the

---

[1] See *post*, p. 233.

feathered snake. Apart from the fact that nature itself furnishes no creatures as patterns for such a form, the snake is often one of the most dangerous enemies of man in the legends of American races, while in the Central American sphere of culture the feathered snake constitutes the symbol of the gods from whom all beneficent institutions and all the blessings of civilisation proceed. Among the Pueblo Indians it is also most closely connected with the deities of fertilising moisture, which to them is the essence of all good. Besides these there are a whole number of other resemblances. We may mention a parallel of a non-religious character. Feathers, especially those of the gorgeously coloured tropical birds, or of the eagle as the symbol of power, have played an important part in the ornament of all primitive races. But only in very few parts of the earth has the attempt been made by primitive races to imitate, by weaving, the feather coat that adorns and protects the birds. Now the races of the Mexican empire brought this art to a perfection that has never since been attained, so that it is most singular that, of all the American races, only the Pueblo Indians practised a similar art, although considerably more primitive, and that not as a comparatively late acquirement, but where we first found them, on the northern borders of their territory, farthest from the Mexican borders, dwelling in the caves of the Mancos valley, and producing their characteristic archaic pottery.

Probably we have in such features the traces of very early connections between the individual groups, long effaced when they appear in history. For the ideas we have mentioned, although they are chiefly familiar to us as specific characteristics of the Mexican race, were not first developed by them, but belonged to the older civilised race from which the Nahua races generally received almost all the good on which the wide reputation of their high civilisation is founded. In this connection it is perhaps not without significance that a similar combination of fire-worship and many customs and ideas peculiar to the Pueblo Indians occurs also in a tribe of eastern North America, — the Muskoki tribe of the Creeks, whose migration, so far as can be traced, points to a western home.

With the Pueblo Indians the sphere of "historyless" primitive races is concluded.


## 2. THE CIVILISATIONS OF CENTRAL AMERICA

### A. THE CONFIGURATION OF CENTRAL AMERICA

AT the Isthmus of Panama, the Cordilleras, the backbone of the American continent, sink so far below the level of the sea that only their highest points rise above the waters to form a narrow range of inconsiderable height; but a few degrees farther north they begin again to tower mightily aloft. The district known to-day as northern Panama and Costa Rica is a mountainous country; its highest points even there rise nearly seven thousand feet above the sea-level. However, the range is again interrupted in its northward advance. The marshes of Nicaragua and the Isthmus of Tehuantepec form two more depressions of great depth, and here, rather than at the narrowest point of the continent, we should place the true line of demarcation between the peoples of North and of South America. Between these two points is the only place where Central America seems to have made the attempt at continental expansion, so characteristic of the eastern portions of the two great half-continents. But the Isthmus of Yucatan, a thickly wooded hilly country lying before the mountain plateau of Guatemala, has no developed river-system on any large scale; and to its position between the bay of Campeche and that of Honduras it chiefly owes the admirably favourable character of its climate, lying low as it does in the tropic latitudes.

Above the Isthmus of Tehuantepec the northern continent begins to expand, but for nearly ten degrees of latitude farther north it is formed by the Cordilleras, which spread wider and wider, leaving only a narrow strip of shore at their feet on the east and west, and filling up the main portion of the continent with their peaks. Hence the peculiar character of the Mexican climate. Although the district of ancient Mexico lies entirely within the tropics, yet only on the seaboard is the real tropic temperature encountered, which, if it brings the advantage of nature's fullest glory, involves also the disadvantage of a dangerous climate. This disadvantage is nullified by the nature of the country, which consists of a high plateau rising sufficiently high above the sea to be free from the dangers of malaria, and yet only so high as to enjoy an almost uninterrupted springtime and to provide for man's necessities with generous hand and reward his toil with richest bounty. The main mountain-range, however, rises boldly and majestically to the regions of the everlasting snow which shines down from the peaks of Popocatepetl and the summit of Orizaba upon the eternal springtide at their feet.

In the immediate neighbourhood of this highest point the Cordilleras divide into an eastern and a western range. Between these there stretches a highland studded with numerous lakes, of moderate size, but extraordinarily fruitful, — the Mexican highland. Here was played out to its close the drama of the ancient civilisation of America.

## *B.* The History of the Ancient Civilisation of Central America

THE country from the lake of Nicaragua to the northern parts of the valley of Mexico has been the home of one of the oldest civilisations of the New World. It is as yet wholly impossible to give any exact dates for its beginnings in the past, and impossible it will probably remain, even if success should crown the attempt, to interpret those undeciphered memorials which now look down upon our efforts to solve their riddle. But if anyone, starting with the conception of the "New" World, considers this civilisation as moderately young, he does it great injustice: nearly as great as do those who place its most flourishing period more than eleven thousand years in the past. The native authors who have written the history of the peoples of Central America, working in the first century after the conquest, and aided by the old traditions and the pictorial sculptures, occasionally place these ·beginnings as far back as the last century before the Christian era. There is, however, little congruity in their productions, which do not inspire us with confidence. The dynasties which have been successfully deciphered from the pictorial decorations previous to the time of Columbus agree with the Spanish and Nahuatlac sources of information, and go back in a great number of individual states from seven hundred to eight hundred years before the discovery of America. Only these testify to an almost invariable character of the civilisation, even in the earliest times, and certainly do not go back nearly as far as that primal starting-point at which we are entitled to place the beginnings of the history of these peoples.

We can probably get nearer to the truth with the help of the chronological indications which can now be gathered from the memorials of the Maya civilisation. The Maya were accustomed to reckon from an established point in the past, exactly as we reckon from the birth of Christ; and only not the year, but the actual day, which forms the starting-point of their chronology, has been satisfactorily made out. This was the 28th of June, according to our reckoning, of a certain year dating back more than 3750 years before the erection of the monument which forms the basis of these calculations. Even here, however, we unfortunately have no sure foundation for chronological limitations: for we do not know by our reckoning the time at which the inscription in question was set up, nor can we be certain whether that day marked a real event in the remote history of the people, or whether it represents a point on which to base calculation and inference, resembling in this respect the Jewish chronology, which goes back to the creation of the world. We must therefore attempt to gain a conception of the earliest history of these civilisations by other means; and their memorials, which have come safely down to us through the storms of centuries, afford richer and more copious information, although it be not entirely complete.

The highly painted pictorial work which the Spanish conquerors of Montezuma's kingdom have handed on to us has induced men for centuries to consider the civilisation of the peoples of Central America as Mexican. This is a great historical error. The Mexicans — or the Aztecs of Mexico-Tenochtitlan, to give them their proper ethnographic name — are neither the founders nor yet the most important representatives of this civilisation to which their name has been unfortunately attached by the sport of circumstance. Shortly before the Spanish invasion of the district they had obtained a leading position among the peoples of the country. A consciousness of the fact that their civilisation was not the result of their own efforts, but was inherited by them from others, was inherent in the Aztecs themselves, and appears in the chronicles of their native historians; yet so cloudy is it, so interwoven with error, that we could scarce have arrived at the truth with nothing but these indications to help us. That truth became plain only when the ruined monuments were discovered of another civilisation, older and more highly developed than the Aztec, and when something of its language had been learned. But progress in this direction did not begin before the close of the eighteenth century; and even to-day we have advanced only half-way toward the full understanding and appreciation of these highly important historical materials.

The chief obstacle to the progress of discovery has been the fact that historical investigation had taken a wrong direction until recent times. The errors thereby produced were further disseminated by two great visionaries, the Indo-Spanish historian, D. Fernando de Alba Ixtlilxochitl,[1] and the French missionary and author, the Abbé Brasseur, of Bourbourg. The first-named, during the last ten years of the sixteenth century, was the author of a large number of historical treatises concerning the countries of ancient Mexico, based upon extensive investigations into the several modes of writing current among the ancient Indians of the country, and also into the physical characteristics of the western peoples of his own time. In these works he gives an exhaustive account of the civilisation presumed

---

[1] Pronounced Ischtlilschotschitl.

to be the most ancient in Central America, that of the Toltecs; and he traces back to their civilising influence almost all the intellectual development of the ancient nations of Central America known to us. This theory obtained credence far and wide, and to an extraordinary extent. The rediscovery of the old ruined cities brought about the search for fresh material. It aroused intense enthusiasm in the youthful missionary Brasseur, whom chance had brought to the seat of these old civilisations. Eagerly, but without thorough historical and philological training, he collected Central-American antiquities and quickly published a series of works upon the subject. He was not content to pile all the culture of ancient America upon the Toltecs: he hinted also at vague connections with the civilisations of Egypt and India, and attributed to this race an extent of knowledge that the peoples of to-day could scarcely attain again.

American ethnology is a science still in its youth. But the methods of historical criticism have been brought to bear upon the ancient history of Central America; and one of the first results has been to clear away the wild speculations of the Abbé Brasseur and to shatter the tradition of the all-prevailing influence of Toltec civilisation. Two facts are now incontestably established. Among the numerous peoples and constitutions which rapidly followed one another, and which played an important part upon the table-land of Anahuac, there existed, probably toward the end of the first thousand years of the Christian era, a kingdom and a dynasty of rulers who were known as Toltecs, from the name of their capital, Tollan or Tula. They are mentioned in almost all the native historical documents. The particular historical facts handed down by these documents are extraordinarily scanty: we shall come back to them in treating of the history of Anahuac.[1] Neither the date at which they existed, nor their relations to the surrounding peoples, afford us the smallest justification for considering these transitory nationalities as the creators, or even as the chief exponents, of that great civilisation whose highly developed monumental art is rightly the admiration and astonishment of the latter-day world. The little principality of the Toltecs was situated at a considerable distance from the seat of that civilisation: moreover, the nationality to which it has given its name belonged to the great mass of Nahuatl-speaking races, to which also the Aztecs of Mexico-Tenochtitlan belonged. The oldest and most highly developed memorials of this civilisation bear unmistakable tokens of its being derived from another race.

This brings us to the second historical fact that has been indisputably established. The whole of Central America has undoubtedly passed through a uniform process of civilisation. Its foundations, and most of the development that has been built upon those foundations, belong to an epoch in the remote past; and that particular civilisation with which we meet in all Central America was already in existence, complete in all its details, before the peoples of Nahua origin came down from the north and invaded the district of Central American civilisation, or at any rate it was thus complete before the peoples of this civilisation and those of the Nahua race had so closely cohered as to make it possible to speak of them as exercising each an influence upon the other. But if this old civilisation did not originate in the Nahua race, then the Toltecs could not have originated there either. A Nahua race has been their origin: grant this, and the whole Toltec legend, which has so long played a great part in the more ancient history of America, collapses utterly.

[1] See post, p. 265.

(*a*) *The Maya*. — The peoples to whom Central America owes the peculiarly high development of its civilisation belong to the Maya race. The name Maya-Indian is now the usual designation of the natives of the Yucatan peninsula, and this limited application of the term has been in force since the time of the discovery of America. Consequently the Yucatan peninsula has been regarded as the cradle of this civilisation for a considerable period. This is, however, a mistake; in the scientific sense the name Maya-race included all the peoples speaking a language distinguished by marked differences from the Nahua tongue. The purest dialect of this is the true Maya, but its kindred dialects were spoken in the whole district between the Cordilleras and the Atlantic Ocean from the Isthmus of Tehuantepec to Nicaragua. In the luxuriant tropical districts which spread from the foot of the Cordilleras to the Bay of Tabasco and are watered by the rivers Usumacinta and Rio de la Pasion, in the modern province of Chiapas in the Mexican republic, and in the neighbouring portions of the small republics of Central America, — in these it is that we must locate, if not the birthplace, at any rate the habitation of the Maya peoples, who there brought the civilisation peculiar to their race to a high pitch of development.

Even to-day it is wholly impossible to write the history of the Maya peoples. Such of their old traditions as have come down to us through the medium of the Spaniards are quite insufficient and far scantier than what we learn of the history of their more northern neighbours, the Nahua peoples; even there, and in the few historical texts written in the Maya language, the traditions of the people are still distorted and warped. As in political life, the Nahua not only pressed upon and crowded the Maya, but to some extent scattered and absorbed them, so in their historical picture-designs much is due to the influence of the traditions of these more powerful neighbours. Moreover these designs, as far as history is concerned, go back only one or two hundred years; the more extensive chronological register of "ahaus" (epochs) unfortunately refers only to Yucatan; this province must, upon internal evidence, be considered as conquered comparatively late. Thus for the earlier history we are almost entirely thrown back on such information as we can gain from the monuments which have come down to us. These are, at any rate, of great richness and extraordinary importance.

On the conquest of the Mexican kingdom the Spaniards were so dazzled by this nationality, which confronted them, to all seeming, in full vigour, that they concentrated their attention exclusively upon it and hardly deigned to bestow a glance upon the States of Tlazcala and Tezcuco in the immediate neighbourhood. Hence we cannot be surprised that they give us no information of these monuments of the ancient Maya kingdom, hidden in the boundless forests, although they far surpassed in splendour all that Montezuma's kingdom could display. In the real Aztec district but one single building of monumental character has been preserved (the ruins of Xochicalco[1]), whereas the ancient Maya cities of Chiapas and the neighbouring district afford hundreds of temples and palaces for inspection.

Later again, when the Spaniards entered into closer relations with the Maya peoples on the peninsula of Yucatan, they became acquainted with some, at least, of the interesting buildings which served the early needs of these peoples, yet they did not fully grasp their importance. While the land of Mexico offered them its

---

[1] Pronounced Schotschikalko.

# A PAGE FROM THE DRESDEN MAYA MANUSCRIPT

THE thirty-sixth page of the Dresden Maya Manuscript shows, in its three divisions, a section of a so-called "tonalamatl," a sacred season of 260 days, which began on the preceding and ends on the following page. These "tonalamatl," so constantly met with in manuscripts, were certainly employed for prophetic purposes. To this end they were divided into specific periods of time, which were denoted by figures: a dot means one, and a stroke, five. The date — that is, particular days in the week of thirteen days — appear in red, the intermediate periods of time in black: we give the latter in Roman, and the former in Arabic numerals. Thus we see at the top: 17 V 5 X 1 XI
in the middle: 6 V 9 I 4 V
below: 10 XI 15 XIII 9 IX
In the lower division are added to the red numerals the special days of the period of twenty days in which they fall (the days *mon*, *oc*. and *cauac*).

To each of the nine dates belongs a mythological picture, and to each picture four hieroglyphs. We shall denote the pictures 1 2 3, and the hieroglyphs 1 2. Among the pictures is the great
4 5 6                                   3 4
7 8 9

god Kukulkan-Quetzalcoatl with the tapir-nose and serpent's tongue, whom Schellhas in his "Göttergestalten der Maya-Handschriften" (Dresden 1897) denotes as B. In picture 1 we see his head, with its snake body, in pouring rain ; in 3 he strides along, a burning torch in each hand ; in 5 he is carrying a woman over the water in a canoe from the East ; in 7 he is walking with an axe (the Indian machete); in 8 he is standing in the water and looking up to a cloud from which the rain is pouring ; in 9 he is sitting in retirement in the hermit's tabernacle, to gain strength by fasting for fresh exploits. In 2 the lightning animal is rushing down to earth amid flames from the sign denoting the heavens. In 4 we see a goddess, her head continued to the neck and head of a bird holding a fish in its beak ; rain streams down the picture. Picture 6 shows a vulture, the mythological *coz quauhtli* of the Aztecs, in the act of fighting with a snake, the ordinary symbol of time. It is, unfortunately, as yet impossible to put this picture in connection with any definite facts.

Similarly the hieroglyphs afford material for question rather than definite result. Moreover those to pictures 1 and 2 are partly destroyed. The most we can say is that we have here the well-known hieroglyph of Kukulkan : *e. g.*, picture 3, hieroglyph 3, pictures 7–9, hieroglyph 2 ; in greater detail, picture 5, hieroglyph 2. The goddess in picture 5 is indicated in hieroglyph 1 to that picture, and the vulture in picture 6 in hieroglyph 2.

The hieroglyphs of the divinities of the North and of the Night appear, according to Schellhas, in the fourth hieroglyph of the sixth picture. The frequent compound hieroglyph "kan-imix" is No. 4 of picture 1. Ernst Förstemann would interpret it as meaning "Feast." We see Day and Night ("kin-akbal"), picture 5, number 3, picture 8, number 4. The fourth hieroglyph to picture 3 appears (according to the same authority on the Maya question) to bear on the religious use of car-piercing. The number 8 in the fourth hieroglyph of the fourth picture is still unexplained ; so is the hieroglyph repeated in pictures 7, 8, 9, and many others.

London: Wm Heinemann.        Printed by the Bibliographisches Institut, Leipzi        New York: Dodd, Mead & Co.

A PAGE FROM THE DRESDEN MAYA MS.

Royal Free Library, Dresden.

boundless treasures, the temples of the Maya and the land which loving Maya toil had changed into a garden contained nothing which the greed of the conquerors could have reft away. Only when the destructive floods of the conquest and its confusion had passed by, and when the first friars came over, did it begin to dawn upon the Spaniards what important testimonies of the past lay hidden among this people, insignificant though they had become. Here it was that they found, what they never met with again on the whole of this recently discovered continent, a people that had learned to preserve its thoughts in written text. The Maya characters[1] still remain one of the most interesting problems in American antiquarian science. Although some of the early Spanish friars in Yucatan had been able to acquire a knowledge of them sufficiently extensive to enable them to read and, within limits, to write them, yet in the course of time this knowledge has been so entirely lost that the most skilled American antiquarians of to-day cannot agree upon the system to which the Maya writing should be ascribed. To some extent controversy upon the point is futile: the Spanish clergy who were able to learn the writing from the inhabitants have clearly confirmed its phonetic character. As a comparison of the two shows at a glance, the writing of the Nahua peoples, who probably derived the use of written characters from the Maya, is far in the rear of the Maya system.[2] As they also had already formed a system more or less phonetic for the writing of proper names, all attempts to reduce the Maya writings to the level of ideographic or purely hieroglyphic characters are pronounced erroneous once and for all. On the other hand it would apparently be just as erroneous to attempt to reduce this writing to an alphabet in the way that the Spanish clergy of the sixteenth century reduced it, selecting individual elements from the old Maya writing for use in instructing their catechumens.

Success has now rewarded the efforts to establish the Maya arithmetical system. Their system of figures employed only four signs altogether: the point for unity, a horizontal stroke for the number 5, and two conventional signs for 20 and 0. This arithmetical equipment is not particularly impressive, and the Maya might be thought far behind many older and newer nations whose systems can employ figures of greater value and in larger number. But the ingenious method has been discovered by which the Maya, with these simple aids (and no use is made of the 20 in this method), can write figures up to the equivalent of many millions, and we rightly feel a high respect for their intellectual penetration. In the Maya arithmetical notation, exactly as in ours, it is the position of the sign that gives it its value; but they placed their signs in a vertical line (whereas we write them horizontally) and employed one of them as a decimal multiplier. In fact the lowest figure of a column had the arithmetical value which it represented; the figures in the second, fourth, and each following place had twenty times the value of the preceding figure; while figures in the third place had, for reasons based upon the Maya calendar system, only eighteen times the value of those in the second place. With this notation, which is absolutely unlimited, the Maya were ahead of not only all the peoples of America, but even of the Greeks and Romans.

It is certainly to be expected that this people would have employed some ingenious method for writing words; and the delicate signs of their script, the firm execution of their inscriptions in lapidary style, confirm this conjecture, though

---

[1] See Plate at p. 226.  [2] See Plate at p. 226.

the inscriptions are unintelligible to us. In spite of this their script is a valuable help in investigation; for it affords the only criterion by which we can precisely separate the districts of Maya and Nahua civilisation, which are often with difficulty distinguished, owing to constant communication and their interacting influence one on another. For even though the Mexicans had also formed a hieroglyphic system capable at least of describing concrete objects intelligibly, yet it was so clumsy in comparison that a glance at a manuscript, and a complete examination of inscriptions carved in stone, inform us at once to which of those two civilisations the creators of any given monument belonged.

As we cannot understand the historical writings, and cannot rely upon the oral tradition handed down by the Spaniards, the Maya script is the only means of defining the extent of the district which was subject to the civilising influences of their culture in ancient times. In this connection the greatest importance attaches to the fact that the Maya peoples had an extraordinary fancy for adorning their buildings, their sculptures, and even their earthenware, not only with pictorial decorations of more or less richness, but also with inscriptions of considerable length. We owe it to this fact that we can ascribe buildings which show unmistakable affinities with Maya architecture to their real founders, and on the other hand can attribute many a monument to the Maya which lay outside of their known dominions.

The number of the sites of the Maya civilisation, the ruins of which lie hidden in the impenetrable forests of Chiapas, Honduras, Yucatan, etc., continues to increase year by year; more abundant opportunities are thereby afforded us for investigating the life of this forgotten people. Now and again an unexpected discovery extends the known area of the Maya civilisation beyond its previous limits in one or another direction; but, upon the whole, the boundaries of this area are tolerably well settled. In the first place the whole of the Yucatan peninsula belongs to it, with the numerous islands which lie along the coast and were taken over by the Maya, obviously with a view to civilisation. On the northwest of Yucatan their district has not spread so far, and at most reached to the Isthmus of Tehuantepec. However, in this district, in Chiapas, on the banks of the Usumacinta, and in the low-lying valleys of its numerous tributaries, we must place not only the highest development of the Maya civilisation, but also its original home. Here lay and here still lie the famous ruined cities of Palenque, of Ococingo, of Menché, and the recently discovered Piedras Negras group, all remarkable for the splendid richness of their artistic decorations and the extent of their inscriptions. Here too, on internal evidence, must be placed the home of that most important and most beautiful among the few Maya manuscripts that have been preserved for later generations, the Codex Dresdensis; the remaining two — the Codex Perezianus in Paris, and the Tro-Cortesianus in Madrid — are of later date and probably of Yucatan origin.

On the southwest of Yucatan the Maya district spreads up into the Cordilleras; and though we cannot follow the traces of this nationality on to the Pacific seaboard in any direction, yet it was only a narrow strip of coast which they failed to bring under their influence; for the mountain range shows traces of their settlements up to and beyond its watershed. The southern boundary of the Maya district is perhaps as yet the most uncertain. On the Atlantic coast two of the most famous Maya ruins, Quirigua and Copán, are hidden by the valley walls of the

Motagua in Guatemala and Honduras; and the whole of Guatemala up to the boundaries of the republic of San Salvador seems at one time to have been inhabited by people of the Maya race. On the north the characteristic memorials of the Nahua element make a sharp division of areas possible; but on the south the style of the neighbouring peoples was of no definite character, and so it has not yet been settled whether coincidences and similarities in this district are due to the neighbouring influence of the Maya or to a real ethnological connection with them. Within these boundaries the area of Maya civilisation embraces an extent of about seven thousand square miles (that is, rather more than the kingdom of Prussia); in more than half of this, traces of an unusually close population are apparent.

Was this district ever a united Maya kingdom? There is no difficulty in arriving at the assumption that it was. The half-mythological, half-historical traditions which have been transmitted to us in the dialects of Kakchiquel and the Maya of Yucatan mention a great kingdom on many occasions. Now it is the Nachan kingdom, the kingdom of the great snake, a mythological symbol which meets us over and over again in the whole district of Maya civilisation. In another legend it is the kingdom of Xibalbay, the kingdom of a mighty and powerful ruler from whom the heroes of the legend won their independence with toil and struggle. Historical coincidences have been observed in both these stories, and the capital of the Nachan kingdom has been identified with Palenque, that of the Xibalbay kingdom with the Zapotec Mitla. Even if these conjectures were justified — and they are still in dispute — it need not necessarily follow that these kingdoms had ever embraced the whole or even the greater part of the Maya district. In the disruption which is so prominent a feature in the ancient constitutional history of Central America, a power of very moderate dimensions according to modern ideas, proved a sufficient foundation for the legend of a mighty kingdom.[1] The historical circumstances of later times, at any rate, afford no evidence in favour of a previous political confederacy of the little Maya principalities. And the assumption is confirmed by many external proofs that the district of the general Maya civilisation was early divided into a number of little States independent of, and often at war with, one another.

The Maya language, moreover, not only in recent times, but at the period of the Spanish conquest, was divided into a set of dialects sharply differentiated each from the rest. When the monks began to study individual dialects for purposes of communication, they recognised in them that relationship to a common source which the natives themselves had totally forgotten. This fact obliges us to place the disruption of the Maya in a remote antiquity, and to suppose a long period of separate existence to the several communities wherein the different dialects were formed.

More careful examination of the Maya memorials has led to a similar result. The monuments of Copán in Honduras, of Palenque in Chiapas, of Chichen-Itza in north Yucatan, of Peten and Tical on the boundary of the Guatemala table-land, — in short, all the monuments that are scattered over the district of Maya civilisation, — bear the marks of a uniform development of that civilisation. Only a more particular study of their individualities has made it equally unmistakable that all these buildings do not belong to one and the same period, and that the coincidences

[1] See _post_, p. 251.

they display are not such as to enable us to ascribe their foundation to any one people or to any one constitutional unity. Under these circumstances the fact becomes all the more important that it was not merely one member or a few individual members of this nation that rose to the perfection manifested in their ingenious system of writing, of arithmetical notation, and of chronology. On the contrary, on the highlands of Guatemala, in Copán and Chamá, in the lowlands of the Usumacinta, in the valley of the Motagua, in the far east, in the island of Cozumel, all the peoples of Maya origin could record their traditions in the same script, and controlled the complicated calculation of their festivals by the same astronomical rules, — rules that presuppose observation over a great lapse of time. In a word, the astonishing achievements of the Maya peoples in civilisation — achievements unparalleled in the New World — must belong to an epoch previous to the period of disruption.

Only one branch of the Maya people had no share in these achievements, — the Huasteca, on the north coast of Mexico, who had been driven to the estuary of the Panuco River. This fact is important for the criticism of the legends of the Nahua migration. In historical times the Huasteca were divided from their southern kinsfolk by a wide district peopled generally by the Nahua, though these were divided into numerous small States. Whether the Huasteca had migrated into the Nahua district, or whether immigrations of the Nahua had cut them off from their parent stem, the fact remains that at one period the Maya and the Nahua must have found themselves in opposition, and this at a time when the Maya had not completed the most important part of their progress. Otherwise either the Huasteca would have shared in the Maya civilisation, or else, isolated in the midst of Nahua peoples, they would not have retained their national peculiarities undisturbed. Such a case of arrest upon the lower planes of civilisation is only possible when the neighbouring elements are in a state of mutual repulsion.

Until the key to the inscriptions has been found, we can draw conclusions as to the circumstances and conditions of life among the peoples of antiquity only from the general character of the Maya cities and from the pictorial decorations of their architecture. In no single district, with the exception of the Yucatan peninsula, has the attempt as yet been successful to trace a connection between the Maya States of the sixteenth century (the history of which can be retraced some ten generations, that is, two or three hundred years) and the States which centre round the great ruined sites. It is only during the last ten years that these have been carefully investigated. To-day nearly all these places lie far from the roads which the traffic of later times has opened up; they are hidden in the wild depths of the tropical forest, where vegetation springs up with such overpowering vigour that often a few years after an expedition has cut paths and made the ruins accessible the next expedition finds that the jungle has again reconquered the whole. Under these circumstances it is hopeless to try and infer the age of the ruins from that of the trees under which they are hidden: all the more so, as historical tradition tells of more than one ruined city that the Spaniards found hidden in tropical vegetation when they made their first discoveries in the sixteenth century. Even then the imposing erections with which the soil of Chiapas is thickly sown were for the natives, as well as for the Spaniards, merely the long-silent witnesses of a remote past to which there was attached neither the traditions of history nor the legends of romance. The very names of these places had long been completely forgotten:

the appellations that later times have accepted have no original authority, but rest upon Spanish tradition or have been transmitted to us by the wild Indian tribes of the neighbourhood.

A peculiar characteristic of the old Indian peoples has contributed not a little to this result. The names of their towns, of their persons, and even of their gods, were taken without exception from material objects; hence they could easily be represented by hieroglyphs of a conventional and universally intelligible nature. Of this we have countless instances in the manuscripts of Nahuatlac origin. This mode of writing was intelligible over the limited region where it persisted, but its phonetic interpretation was by no means everywhere the same. For instance, the Mexican read as "Cinacatan," in his language, "the Town of the Bat" (probably a totemistic denomination of a little Maya State that was still in existence in the time of Cortes); but the Maya vocalised the same concept as "Tzutuhil." Each of these names was equally employed and equally well understood in the one district as in the other,—a proof of the intimate association of the Maya and Nahua peoples. Now, at the time of the discovery of America, the area of the oldest Maya civilisation had been already abandoned by the Maya; the Spaniards undertook the colonisation of the land under the guidance and with the help of the Nahua. Consequently, in the case of a district that for hundreds of years was the home of the highest Maya civilisation, and had never entirely fallen into the hands of the Nahua, we find in our authorities only place-names of Nahua origin. Hence the ruined places of Chiapas are designated without exception by Spanish and Nahuatlac names; yet these places show indisputable signs of their Maya occupation in the style of their pictorial decorations, and, above all, in the numerous inscriptions in the Maya character.

To judge from extent, from beauty, and from technical perfection, an important, if not the central, point of the civilisation of this people must have been situated on the eastern slope of the Cordilleras, in Chiapas. Separated by no great distance, reaching from the foot of the mountain to the sea, the ruined sites remain of Ococingo, Palenque, Menché, and Piedras Negras. Each of these must once have formed a large town, a centre of religious and political life, round which a thick population clustered. To us there remains little save the sites of the temples and perhaps of one or two palaces. It is a characteristic peculiarity of all Central American civilisation to have practically no profane buildings to show, but a large number of religious erections of great extent and particular beauty. At once the conclusion offers itself that in the political life of the old Maya towns the religious element must have been of transcendent importance; so much so that to some, at least, of the old Maya cities a government by the priestly caste has been attributed. The analogy of neighbouring conditions and the scanty counter-statements of historical tradition do not confute the theory.

The migration legends of the Central American peoples are of great importance: for the settlements, even of those peoples that had made a considerable advance in civilisation, were only of relative duration. In the legends we constantly meet with the story that the peoples, under the guidance of their national god, wandered about until the god, speaking himself or through one of his servants, ordered the people to settle definitely on a certain spot and to build him a dwelling-place. This merely means that the priests were the ruling class, as being the servants and representatives of the godhead: the fact is confirmed by our own historical knowledge of peoples who were ruled by religious and not by warrior-leaders.[1] We consider the almost exclusive preponderance of religious buildings in Palenque, in Menché, and other ruined places; we observe the pictorial decorations remaining in these temples, which we find to be almost entirely composed of divinities and priests in nearly every case with the insignia of temporal dominion,—the sceptre and a peculiar head-dress of richest featherwork; and hence we conclude that the same conditions must have prevailed to an unlimited extent in these old Maya towns. Certainly centres of political power might have existed elsewhere and have left behind them fewer and less-enduring memorials. We might be led to this conclusion by the analogy of the neighbouring Nahua district, where Teotihuacan and Cholula were recognised centres of religious life and were adorned with greater buildings than many a royal capital, without being in any unusually close connection with the political life of those districts. But the old Maya towns, with the extensive precincts of their temples, are very numerous, and are not very widely separated; hence it is impossible to find room either near or between them for the existence of such independent political centres as would form the natural counterpoise to this high development of the priestly forces.

One, at least, of the ruined cities, Palenque, bears traces within and around itself which admit the possibility of other than sacred conceptions attaching to the ground. Within the limits of the ruins are to be found constructions for bringing water and serving it throughout the district, which are too extensive to have been connected with the temple buildings alone. The remains of an ancient Indian town are not great, even though the town was of considerable extent and population. The common folk were occupied by their agricultural labours at a distance from the town for most of the year. The monuments themselves show us how thorough and extensive ancient Maya agriculture was: many of the elements current in their hieroglyphic script were borrowed from agricultural implements; in their religion the divinities of fruitfulness played a most important part and are adorned with symbols relating to agriculture. The reports of the Spaniards further confirm the fact: in the districts inhabited at their time they found everywhere a dense population supporting itself by careful tilling of the soil. As winter caused but a short interruption of agricultural operations, the population had no permanent habitations in the immediate neighbourhood of the temples; their houses for their daily needs being placed in the middle of their fields. Their frail dwellings, built of wood and wattlework, straw and matting, offered no resistance to the march of time, and left no traces of their ruin which could have survived the lapse of centuries. On the environs of Palenque, in the depths of that forest which has covered the town more or less since historical times, there are, it is true, concealed memorials of antiquity, isolated and at a distance from the town: probably, therefore, when Palenque was a flourishing town, its neighbourhood was also inhabited by an industrious agricultural population. We know, from the figures which have been transmitted to us of the state of things in Mexico-Tenochtitlan, what large crowds of people were occupied in the temple services of the Central American peoples. So, as the temples in each of the old Maya cities are always numerous and often of considerable extent, we have in this fact an exact correspondence with

---

[1] The Spaniards gave these latter the somewhat incongruous titles of "king" and "emperor."

the traditions. At the same time the extent and importance of the temples are evidence for the strong powers of the ruling priestly castes.

The Maya buildings, which we must consider, without exception, as monumental buildings in our sense of the word, were almost always erected upon a foundation in the form of a hill, displaying many resemblances to the mounds of the North American Indians. Here and there, where the ground was favourable, natural hills were employed for this object, and cut down to the size of the designed erection. But generally the whole mound or terrace was artificially constructed of boulders, rubble, gravel, or earth, according to the nature of the material at hand. In countless cases these mounds, known as "ku" in the Maya tongue, are all that remain to tell of an ancient building. In such cases we must suppose that the mound was crowned by an open altar, or a construction of some perishable material, of which all traces have disappeared. "Kus" without buildings upon them are found in Chiapas only in connection with more permanent erections; but in Yucatan, where the Maya architecture can be traced in many other directions, there stand, or stood, unnumbered "kus" in complete isolation, and these in the later Spanish period often formed the only memorials of the ancient Indian settlements. All the larger temple sites of the Maya show a number of earth terraces: these were arranged in an exactly parallel order, and formed the four sides of a lower court in the midst. But in the case of such groups of mounds the sides are usually covered with flagstones or with smooth plaster spread over them; and the terraces almost invariably support buildings which may be of considerable size. At the eastern foot of the Cordilleras, both in Chiapas and on the boundaries of Honduras, nature provided the Maya with a moderately hard sandstone of an argillaceous kind. This was an ideal material for their purposes: it could be quarried in large blocks without trouble; being only moderately heavy, its transport offered no insurmountable difficulties, and it was capable of being worked even with their inadequate instruments. For the Maya, in spite of their artistic cleverness, apparently made no use of metal tools in their work, although they seem to have had some knowledge of copper work for decorative productions.

Their ignorance of the arch is a fact of importance for the Maya architecture. They overcame the difficulty by making each new course overhang the one beneath it until the opening became small enough to be closed by a single slab. However, this kind of arch could cover only a moderate breadth, could hardly be built firmly enough to support a second building, and obliged the construction of the roof to be extremely massive. The consequence was that the fore-wall of the building that composed the roof provided a surface often more than half the size of the story beneath it. The Maya architects were in the habit of using this surface for ornamental decoration, and it became so important an architectural feature that the monuments of the highest development often retain it without the massive roofing behind, merely as an isolated ornament to finish off the building. A façade of this kind, which really contained but one floor of rooms, often produced the appearance of a three-storied building. The Maya could only place one story upon another in tower-shaped buildings of considerable extent; on the other hand they have built many temples in another style of two or more stories. This was done in pyramidal form. The foundation upon which they were raised gave all the Maya buildings the appearance of a terraced pyramid.   The building did not stand exactly upon the edges of the artificial mound; an open space ran around every side of it.   If a second story was to be raised, it was only necessary to increase the height of the mound at the back of the building until it was upon a level with the roof.   This roof then formed an open space before the door, and in the centre of the mound thus raised a second story could be erected.   Entrance to this could be gained either from the sides of the mound which were not built upon, or by a stairway against one of the sides of the building.   The Maya architects were invariably obliged to construct buildings of considerable breadth, because bold and lofty erections were unattainable with the means at their disposal.   The heaviness of the broad and massive roof is dispelled only by the rich ornamental design of the sides and the façade.

The boldness of design and the scrupulous finish of detail are extraordinary. The Maya buildings entirely exclude the supposition that they were formed by merely putting together any material at hand.   They are, without exception, the result of uniform design, and their arrangement most certainly implies previous survey and full calculation.   The sculptures are even stronger evidence for this fact: they often rise a considerable height from the ground, and their design occupies many yards of wall space: this is especially the case with the stone carvings.   It is wholly inconceivable that these masses of stonework should have been begun only when the blocks had been placed in position; on the contrary it is plain from the manner of their insertion that they were previously worked apart. This implies a previous capability for planning and disposing ornamental designs which is possible only to the highest powers of the surveyor and calculator.

All these architectural peculiarities are to be found, though with certain local differences, among all those Maya races which have left buildings of any importance behind them.   They are to be found not only in the ruins of Chiapas, but also in Guatemala (Tikal), in Honduras (Copán), and in Yucatan (especially Uxmal and Chichen-Itza).   But the sculptured figures in each of these several districts have such strongly marked characteristics that they require separate description. In the ruined cities of Chiapas, the oldest district of Maya civilisation, the basrelief is the prevailing feature of their sculpture.   At one place it is a form of relief in clay or stucco, a development of the potter's art: instances are the altar slabs of Palenque and a long row of interesting examples.   Elsewhere it is relief in stone, requiring far greater artistic skill: for instance, the famous altarpieces of Palenque, and the splendid slab from Menché-Tenamit, reproduced on the plate facing this page, "A Victim before Kukulkan."   If we leave out of sight the fundamental peculiarities of style, the skill of the Maya in each of these materials must excite our highest admiration, both for the designs conceived and for the technical perfection of execution.   With them are to be ranked by right of birth the artists in the neighbouring district, forming the modern republic of Guatemala.

The true Guatemala highland need not be considered with reference to the most ancient Maya civilisation.   At the beginning of the sixteenth century in that district the Spaniards certainly met with the independent Maya States, Quiché, Kakchiquel, and Tzutuhil.   But there is hardly a doubt that these States first came into existence in later centuries.[1]   On the other hand the lowland on the east of Guatemala, on the borders of Yucatan, was in the occupation of the Maya at the

[1] See *post,* p. 245.

A VICTIM BEFORE THE MAYA GOD KUKULKAN

(After the bas-relief in stone from Menché-Tenamit in the British Museum at London.)

## EXPLANATION OF THE FOREGOING PICTURE

THE bas-relief from the British Museum is catalogued as "Victim before Kukulkan." The god is habited in the royal insignia, the sceptre and the rich feather-dress; before him kneels the high-priest in the act of sacrifice; the rich clothing and the feather head-dress denoting his office. The sacrifice consists in his tearing his tongue with the thorns of the rope he holds in his hands, and allowing the blood to drip into the sacrificial vessel standing before him. This was the only manner in which the ancient Maya offered human blood.

The twelve hieroglyphs on the two cartouches above and at the side of Kukulkan are composed, with the exception of the first on the left above, of two portions parallel to each other, so that they are to be considered as written in two columns, as is found upon the numerous memorial pillars of Maya. The first and second compose a calendar date; they consist of signs denoting a day and month, severally marked with a number. Unfortunately neither these signs nor the remaining hieroglyphs can be identified with any certainty.

height of their civilisation: the States of Tikal and Peten certainly belong to a far earlier period of development than do Utatlan, Iximché, and Cinacatan, the capitals of the three principalities previously named. The highly carved wood panels which have travelled from the ruins of Tikal to the museum of Basle, if allowance be made for difference of material, must certainly, by their design and execution, be placed in the same category as the Chiapas memorials. Unless we are to conceive entire independence for each separate Maya State, the towns of Chiapas and those of lower Guatemala must have been more closely connected with each other than they were with the rest of the Maya district. At any rate, in this district remains of old Maya roads can be traced here and there, whereas such roads are rarer toward the south and reappear in any number only around a central point in Yucatan.

The most southerly ruined sites, Quirigua and Copán on the Honduras boundary with their numerous characteristics, form another district of civilisation still wider in extent. Quirigua, on account of the stiffness and clumsiness of its artistic figures, is considered one of the oldest States of the Maya civilisation. It may perhaps be older than Copán, which was more advanced and which probably contained the germs of an early destruction; but it is certainly of later date than the northern Maya settlements, for its art is more advanced than the art of the north was, and has closer affinities with the art of Copán. With the exception of two efforts in Yucatan, Quirigua and Copán are the only States which rose to the full portrayal of the human form: real statues there are certainly none, but we find caryatids and memorial pillars of human shape. These unmistakably represented particular individual personalities, though trammelled by symbolical and stereotyped accessories. Each of these stele is covered with extensive inscriptions; but though these cannot be deciphered as a whole, their value is manifest from the fact that they have already made us acquainted with seven dates which are calculated from the fixed point of time before referred to, 3,750 years before the erection of the oldest of these pillars. The dates upon these seven monuments are important, inasmuch as the respective ages of the pillars give us a minimum length of time for the Copán civilisation which erected them. The difference between the earliest and the latest date amounts to 108 years: we may therefore conclude that the destruction and fall of Copán formed the conclusion of this period; for it is improbable, given the continuance of certain conditions and the absence of any counteracting cause, that the established custom of erecting portrait memorials should have been dropped. This train of argument certainly does not lead to much: the time and the circumstances which brought about the fall of Copán are as little known to us as are the same circumstances in the case of the other Maya States. When the Spaniards entered the continent, Copán was already in ruins, a mystery overgrown by the primeval forest. So entirely had it fallen into oblivion that Cortes with his band was able to march past it at the distance of but a few miles, while his Indian guides, who must have informed him of all the wonders of the country, never mentioned it even once.

As almost all the monumental buildings in the Maya district with which we are acquainted consist of temples, we see that religion must have played a most important part in the public life of the ancient Maya. The Maya possessed a large number of different divinities, without reckoning the little fetiches, or household gods, which every house possessed, and which were known here, as in the Antilles, by the name of "zemes." Their polytheism was, however, of a limited character compared with that of other peoples: this is the more likely owing to the probability that many of the different names of the gods which have come down to us were current among different Maya races to denote similar conceptions. Moreover the varied representations of the gods in the monuments and in manuscripts were certainly to some extent only different forms of one and the same divine power. The missionaries were able to describe this consciousness of an underlying unity in the case of the god Hunabku, who was invisible and supreme: naturally their zealous orthodoxy saw here some fragmentary knowledge of the one God

Hunabku does not appear very prominently in the Maya worship or mythology: of this the sun is undoubtedly the central point. Kukulkan and Gukumatz — probably in his essence Itzamna also — are only variant names, originating in difference of race, for the power of the sun that warms, lights, and pours blessings upon the earth. As the sun rises in the east out of the sea, so the corresponding divinity of the traditions comes over the water from the east[1] to the Maya, and is the bringer of all good things, of all blessings to body and soul, of fruitfulness and learning. In the last character the divinity is fully incarnated: he appears as an aged greybeard in white flowing robes: as Votan he divides the land among the peoples and gives the settlements their names: as Kabil, the "Red Hand," he discovers writing, teaches the art of building, and arranges the marvellous perfection of the calendar. This part of the myth has undoubtedly a historical connection with the sun-myth, the real centre of all these religious conceptions, and is further evidence of the powers of the priesthood and of the fact that their influence was exercised to advance the progress of civilisation.

Fully realistic is a conception of that particular deity which is represented in the Maya art by the widely prevailing symbol of the feathered snake.[2] This is also a branch of the sun worship. In the tropical districts for a great part of the year the sun each day, at noon, draws up the clouds around himself; hence, with lightning and thunder, the symbols of power, comes down the fruitful rain in thunderstorms upon the thirsty land. Thus the feathered snake, perhaps even a symbol of the thunder, appears among the Maya, on the highland of Central America, among the Pueblo Indians, and also among some Indian races of the North American lowland. It represents the warm, fruitful power of the heavens, which is invariably personified in the chief luminary, the sun. The symbols of the snake and of Quetzal, the sacred bird with highly coloured plumage, are attributes of more than one Maya divinity. Under different shapes in the Tzendal district, in Yucatan to a large extent, and particularly in Chichen-Itza, they have so coloured both the religious and the artistic conceptions of the Maya that we meet with traces of this symbolism in almost every monument and every decoration.

The dualism of the Maya Olympus also originates in a mythological interpretation of natural phenomena. The representatives of the sun — light and life — are opposed to those of the night — darkness and death: both have nearly equal powers and are in continual conflict for the lordship of the earth and of mankind. Moreover the good gods have been obliged to abandon man after expending all their benefits upon him, and have made him promise of a future return, to support him in the struggle, and to assure him of victory at the last.

---

[1] See Plate at p. 234.
[2] This is the meaning of the name "Kukulkan" or "Gukumatz."

Around these central mythological conceptions, which in different ??? are practically common property among most early peoples, are grouped, in ?? ? ? ?? of the Maya, a large number of individual characteristics, each diversely dev ? ? ? Not only was human life subject to the power of the gods in a large and ? ??? eral way, since the gods had created and formed it, but also religion — or, to be more exact, the Maya priesthood — had contrived a special system whereby man's life was ostensibly under the permanent influence of the gods, even in the most unimportant trifles. Upon this subject the quarters of the heavens and the constellations were of decisive importance; careful and keen observation, lasting apparently over a great period of time, had put the Maya priesthood in possession of an astronomical knowledge to which no other people upon a corresponding plane of civilisation has ever attained.

Their calendar still bears traces of its development; in earlier times it consisted of eighteen months of twenty days each, as with many other American peoples. At the time of the discovery of America the Maya knew how to correct the solar year by means of five intercalary days, a piece of knowledge which the Nahua peoples also possessed; but they were also aware that this did not correspond with the real length of the solar year, and corrected the error with greater accuracy than the Old World had done previous to Gregory's alteration of the Western calendar. Herein they were superior to the Spaniards, who destroyed their civilisation without suspecting this fact. This carefully corrected solar year was then considered in relation to all other possible annual calculations, and upon it the priestly caste established a number of astronomical laws more carefully worked out than in any other nation. Of nearly equal, if not of even greater, importance to the solar year was the ritual year of twenty weeks with thirteen days each; each division of it belonged to a particular divinity. Here the four quarters of the heavens played an important part, since to each of them a quarter of the ritual year belonged. But in all this diversity the consciousness of a higher unity clearly existed; evidence for this is the special symbol of the four quarters of the heaven, — the *cross*, — which the Spaniards were highly astonished to find everywhere in the Maya temples, as an object of particular veneration. Moreover an influence upon the motions of the earth was certainly attributed to the morning and evening stars and to the Pleiades. Perhaps also the periods of revolution for Venus, Mercury, and Mars were approximately known and employed in calculation.

The knowledge of these minute astronomical calculations was the exclusive possession of the highest priesthood, though at the same time they exercised a certain influence upon the whole national life. Upon these calculations the priests arranged the worship of the gods. The Maya worship is sharply divided from that of the Nahua, and in particular from the bloody idol-worship of the Aztecs, which has been erroneously considered as almost the typical form of Central American worship. However, human sacrifice does not seem to have been entirely excluded from the Maya religion. But in earlier times, before communication with the Nahua peoples and their lower forms of civilisation had exercised a deteriorating influence upon the Maya culture, human sacrifice was practised most rarely, and the Maya knew nothing of the cannibalism which, even among the Aztecs, accompanied these sacrifices. It was only on the high festival, when, at the close of a new year, the Maya kindled the fire anew to symbolise the commencement of a

period, that a human victim was offered to the gods. The Maya were certainly
fully aware of the high value of blood as a sacrifice; only the power of atonement
was not inherent in the blood of a slaughtered victim, but in that of a living man.
The blood was shed in honour of the god, with fasting and discipline, by tearing the
tongue [1] or some other sensitive portion of the body with thorns or other instruments of torture. Yet this happened only upon high occasions. The usual offerings were of a wholly inoffensive kind, and consisted of the first-fruits of the
huntsman's spoil or of the produce of the ground. The most widely spread of all
forms of offering was the censing with burning copal resin, a religious use which
continued to the time of Christianity, and, in individual cases, until recently: at
any rate, upon the discovery of outlying Maya ruins, traces of such incense offerings of quite recent time have been found.

Peacefully, with no shedding of blood, the life of this people passed by; under
the unlimited but mildly exercised administration of a priestly aristocracy they
passed a life that was laborious but free from care. Upon their memorials and in
their manuscripts the weapons of war appear only as attributes of the gods. Tales
of conquest and destruction, which occupy so much space in the Nahua works of
art, are entirely wanting here. Certainly amid the blessings of prosperity and
advancing civilisation they came to know the dark side of life. Long and careful
cultivation of the fruitful tropic soil had given them a kingdom which they
increased by an extensive trade. It may have been a merchant ship from a harbour in the Maya district that met with Columbus and his comrades upon their
fourth voyage over the Atlantic between Jamaica and the mainland; its sails, its
well-clothed crew, and its cargo may have pointed to the existence of a higher civilisation behind the district of the Antilles and the naked savages who inhabited it.
But prosperity was fatal to the nation. Phallic worship, reverence to a divinity of
unnatural lust, are signs of moral decay among the ruling classes of this people;
and so it is intelligible that they went down before an external shock, though it
was the shock of an enemy by no means of overpowering strength.

It was about the ninth century of our era — perhaps a century or two earlier —
that the peace of the Maya States of Chiapas and Tabasco was broken by the invasion of the Nahua peoples. A manuscript of Kuikatec origin informs us of a wave
of conquest which passed from the southwest of Central America to the Isthmus
of Tehuantepec, then turned toward the east, troubled some part of Guatemala, and
finally penetrated to the Acalan district, directly bordering on the Yucatan peninsula. The enemy was then situated in the rear of that group of States to which
Palenque, Menché, and other centres of Maya civilisation belonged. The reason
that we cannot recognise these ancient names in the lists of the Kuikatec conquest
is, perhaps, simply because the documents have not been deciphered. At any rate
invading hordes of the kind did not spare the Maya district, which was easy of
access and possessed all the allurements of a high civilisation. It is doubtful
whether hard fighting took place or not between the unwarlike Maya and the
fierce, invading Nahua. The ruins of Chiapas and Tabasco show scarce a trace of
wilful destruction such as is unmistakable in the case of Mayapan (Yucatan).
Moreover it was far less difficult for this people to give up their wonted habitations
than it would have been for a more civilised race: it was only for their gods that

---

[1] See the priest on Plate facing p. 234.

they built permanent edifices; they were themselves satisfied with frail thatched huts in which they slung their hammocks, almost their only furniture, for the night. It is just possible that Copán, with its one century of flourishing civilisation,[1] was only a temporary halting-place of the Maya peoples, who had abandoned their more northerly settlements in the Usumacinta lowland before the invasion of the advanced guard of the Nahuatlac migration. If this be the case, then there also they were left only a few generations in peace. The later devastation of this district by numerous and compact bodies of Nahua races would show that the conquerors followed later the tracks of their flying adversaries and there also put an end to their peaceful existence.

The final result, at any rate, of the struggle between these two different races, a struggle which apparently lasted a considerable time, was to shatter the old Maya civilisation and to divide the races belonging to it into two essentially distinct groups, the Maya peoples of Yucatan and those of the Guatemala branch. Upon their invasion the Maya found Yucatan still uninhabited, whether this invasion followed upon their flight before the Nahua peoples or was an event of earlier times. Probably Yucatan offered no great or immediate attractions to them. Thanks to its position between two seas, the climate of the peninsula was healthy enough; the sea-breezes also brought moisture sufficient for the needs of a luxuriant vegetation. But running water — that indispensable condition of a permanent settlement — is scarce to be found on the whole peninsula. A troublesome search for the precious liquid in subterranean caverns, the collecting of it in reservoirs, and the transport of it often to the height of three or four hundred feet up steps and ladders, is an undertaking not lightly entered upon by any people that can find more suitable ground at its disposition. Undoubtedly Yucatan was first settled by the Maya far later than Chiapas or Tabasco. All the remains that have been brought to light by the manifold excavations, even those from the lowest strata, point to the highly advanced civilisation of the inhabitants; traces of a gradual development of this civilisation there are none. The immigrating people must therefore have gained their culture elsewhere, as is demonstrable in the case of the Maya in the neighbouring districts farther west. In Yucatan, also, a considerable portion of the civilised districts was in ruins at the time of the Spanish invasion; but other towns and temples, which fully correspond in character with those destroyed, were then in full perfection. And tradition was certainly able to give a more or less connected account of the cities that had been abandoned and destroyed.

The Yucatan buildings display an art of an undoubtedly late period compared with the art of the more westerly States; the execution is not so careful, and there is a certain admixture of foreign elements. In place of the simple design of the old monumental buildings, where the sole decorations were the carved slabs and their accompanying inscriptions, we have here, partly resulting from the nature of the material employed, an excess of ornamental detail, a wilfully exaggerated symbolism, the existence of which is far more intelligible in the case of an older people than it is in a nation advancing by the strength of youth. The lavish employment of stereotyped forms leaves but meagre space for inscriptions, so that this valuable adjunct of the ancient Maya art is here almost entirely wanting. In the sculpture and wall paintings the influence of elements of Nahuatlac origin is quite unmis-

---

[1] See *ante*, p. 235.

takable: this brings the foundation of the Yucatan ruins nearer to the time when the two races came in contact. The calendar of the Yucatan Maya also shows traces of a later origin, and diverges in many points from that of the Maya race of Chiapas. These differences have a particular importance, as they show the Yucatan people in concord with the Nahua (who certainly developed their civilisation later) and in divergence from their own original race. Tradition also — though often, after the manner of tradition, returning upon the creation of all things — does give grounds for the supposition that the occupation of Yucatan was the result, in the first instance, of the collapse of the old Maya civilisation.

Yucatan appears to have been originally divided into a number of small individual States, each with their own separate traditions; consequently the history of the peninsula contains a large number of different traditions which cannot be traced to a common source and do not show sufficient points of contact among themselves to enable us to construct a general history of the Maya race. We may, however, conclude that the emigrations and the settlements in Yucatan were not the result of one uniform leadership, but that separate little bands, independent of one another, had fled beyond the thick woods that bound Yucatan. Individuals among these groups retained the old institutions under which they had seen happier times in their more western home. The god Itzamna was named as the founder and the first ruler of the sacred town Itzamal. Similarly Kukulkan, who was certainly only the incarnation of a similar group of ideas, is said to have been the first king of Mayapan to have carried on for many years a rule of peace and prosperity, and to have been the origin of the princely house of the Cocomes. This means that the bands of Maya who chose Itzamal and Mayapan for their new abode were still under the government of their old priestly caste. On the analogy of Mexico we may conclude that these priests had marched at the head of the emigrants with the holy images of the gods, and had finally given them commands, presumed to be from Heaven, for the colonisation and the building of the new towns. In Itzamal the priestly caste seems to have been pre-eminent until the town was absorbed in the neighbouring States which were rapidly extending under a secular rule. Mayapan in the course of time took a predominating position among these. The fact, however, that the race of kings in that town traced their origin from Kukulkan himself is a proof that this royal house either owed its origin to a secularisation of its priestly rulers, or, at any rate, was founded with the help and approval of the priesthood of their national god.

Circumstances seem to have been somewhat different, even from the beginning, with those bands of the Maya who were known as Itzaes, and who founded and gave its title to the town of Chichen-Itza. In this case, even at the outset of their emigrations, a secular government appeared in place of their priestly leadership; for although the Tutul Xius are occasionally mentioned as holy men, they appear everywhere as a family of warriors and princes. Their traditions most distinctly point to their origin from the Maya States of the west: the land Nonoual is particularly mentioned as a starting-point of their migrations, that is, the Nonohualco of the Nahua, the coast-line of Tabasco. Starting at that point, they arrived, after long wanderings, at Chacnouitan, the most southerly part of Yucatan, and they founded their first important town in Ziyan Caan on the lake which was afterward called Bacalar. In later times, as also appears in the annals of the Tutul Xius, the historical interests of Yucatan gravitated to the north of the peninsula; only on the lake Bacalar the Spaniards, under Montejo, met with a numerous Maya population in several extensive towns. For about sixty years the rulership of the Tutul Xius lasted in Ziyan Caan; then they also marched northward and chose Chichen-Itza for their residence.

Chichen-Itza is a town which has played a considerable part among the sacred places of Yucatan, a part resembling that of Teotihuacan in Anahuac; its fortunes had no lasting connection with the race of the Tutul Xius which had founded it. In the meantime the territorial principalities in the whole neighbourhood had been greatly strengthened, and their conflicting interests brought war and destruction upon the rising towns. It seems to have been the Cocomes, the rulers of Mayapan, who overthrew the throne of the Tutul Xius in Chichen-Itza after a government of a hundred and twenty years; the town itself they made loosely dependent upon their own State, but the governors and their followers were obliged to start upon a fresh emigration. According to these traditions Yucatan owes to this same race of princes another of its noblest towns and the rich artistic decorations with which it is adorned. At any rate the Tutul Xius fled in a slanting direction across the whole peninsula as far as the northern coast, and settled in Champoton, where they are said to have ruled for more than two hundred and fifty years. This fact is confirmed by the extensive burial-grounds of a Maya people which have been discovered on the little islands which lie opposite to the town of Champoton, or Potonchan, known later as a site of Nahuatlac population. Apparently it was here that the Maya people who were subjects of the Tutul Xius entered into relations with the Nahua people, who had gained considerable accessions of strength in the meantime. In the fourteenth century troops of Nahuatlac soldiers played an important part in the internal wars of Yucatan; and that it was not, as tradition relates, only the Cocomes of Mayapan who availed themselves of the services of these strangers, is proved by the artistic style of the productions with which we meet even in the territory of the enemies of the Cocomes, especially in Chichen-Itza; here chiefs and warriors are repeatedly immortalised in an art the style of which betrays its affinity to the pictorial art of the Aztec manuscripts at the very first glance.

Such confederations as these enabled the Tutul Xius to extend their rulership from Champoton toward the north and east. They entered into treaties of peace with the princes of Mayapan; and families of ruling princes again held the sceptre in Itzamal and Chichen-Itza. At this time the Tutul Xius changed their residence from Champoton to Uxmal.[1] Their splendid State buildings in that district are sure evidence of a long period of peace, which they utilised to advance further their civilisation. The different little States were under a rulership that was at least mild, but forced them to keep peace with one another; the artistic energy resulting from this peace expended itself in the countless monumental ruins with which we meet upon the soil of Yucatan. It was in this period, too, that the country was opened up, as was formerly the district between Palenque and its neighbouring towns, by the extensive and carefully made system of high-roads, remains of which have been found in the most widely separated places. Religious purposes were the chief object of this work. According to the traditions the roads led from the chief temple of Chichen-Itza and Itzamal out into the country in all directions, as far and wide as people prayed and made pil-

---

[1] Pronounced Uschmal.

grimages to Kukulkan, the feathered snake, unmistakably the chief among the Maya deities of later times. Chichen-Itza was specially connected with Cozumel, an island town not far from the eastern coast, which seems to have formed a wide circle of temples in the whole of its extent; it was here that the Spaniards first found the cross, the symbol of the god who ruled the four quarters of the heaven.[1]

The Indian summer of the Maya civilisation was not fated to last long in Yucatan. The yoke of the Cocomes was heavy upon land and people. At the beginning of their rule, in order the better to secure their position, they had created an aristocracy which was obliged to give personal service to the government; for this, however, they were recompensed by rich grants of land and people, which they ruled — or, more exactly, plundered — through their representatives. The result was that the Cocomes introduced, probably in imitation of Nahuatlac predecessors, the institution of slavery, which had hitherto been unknown to the Maya. They based their rights on the principle of conquest. The State of Mayapan owed a considerable portion of its extent to the sternness of this rule; in this way probably Chichen-Itza became tributary to the government of Mayapan.

The iron hand of government growing heavier and heavier may very well, in the course of time, have brought it about that the position of the common people, who were subject to the tributary caciques, degenerated into a kind of subjection not very different from slavery. Moreover the ruling classes abandoned themselves to the unlimited enjoyment of life; even the legends of the founding of their State speak of acts of dreadful immorality. The result was that the rulers did not feel their position secure, though they were situated in the midst of a nobility bound to themselves by common interests. After the manner of tyrants they thought they would find their surest protection in a foreign body-guard, and they took warriors of the Nahua race from the district of Tabasco into their service. Even with their help they were not entirely successful in suppressing all manifestations of dissatisfaction. One of the first to revolt against the tyranny of the Cocomes was the prince of Uxmal, but the fortune of war decided against him, and factions which broke out in Uxmal itself resulted in the abandonment of the royal town by its inhabitants, though not in its destruction. The remainder of the Tutul Xius were again obliged to retreat, and founded a new principality in Mani, which, however, never attained the splendour and importance of the imperial towns Chichen-Itza and Uxmal.

The rising of the Tutul Xius had, however, set the example of revolt, and soon found imitators among the petty kings who were hard pressed by the Cocomes, though not so hard as had been the aristocracy of Mayapan. The next to refuse the respect he owed to the tyrant of Mayapan was the prince of Chichen-Itza. But he also was brought to punishment. A man of extraordinary energy sat upon the throne of the Cocomes. Hunac Eel was certainly an even harsher tyrant than his predecessors had been, but he was also a far-seeing politician. He knew very well that he could not rely upon the fidelity and dependence of his subjects; therefore he sought protection for his rule outside of his kingdom. The chronicles speak of a treaty which Hunac Eel had made with the governors of the kings of Mexico in Tabasco and Xicalango; this is certainly

[1] See *ante*, p. 237.

an anachronism, for at the time when Hunac Eel was king of Mayapan, the Aztec rulers of Mexico-Tenochtitlan were fighting to win their own independence from the Tecpanec kings of Azcaputzalco. But the fact is certainly well attested that Hunac Eel entered into alliance with the warlike Nahua of the neighbouring principality. In spite of his great display of power (Hunac Eel entered upon his campaign against Chichen-Itza with thirteen tributary princes) the result of his expedition was far less decisive than had been his war against Uxmal, but Chichen-Itza succumbed to overpowering forces. The town, however, retained its own princes, who were to some extent dependent upon the Mayapan government.

For some time past the kingdom of Cocomes had been in a state of internal war. The uncertainty of the chronological calculations of Yucatan history does not make it plain how long these internal struggles in the kingdom of Mayapan had continued; apparently about a century passed by before the crash came. This was, however, brought about by continual revolts in Chichen-Itza. Religious motives may have been at the bottom of this invincible animosity, or may at least have stimulated it. Mayapan and the priestly town of Itzamal, which were in close alliance, reverenced Itzamna as their divine founder, while Chichen-Itza by degrees had become the central point of the whole district of Maya civilisation for the worship of Kukulkan, the feathered snake, representations of which are a predominating characteristic in Chichen art. The rivalry between Itzamal and Chichen-Itza gave occasion for complications resulting in hostilities between the States; it certainly gave considerable impulse to the animosity with which the people of Mayapan were accustomed to regard the rival they had never entirely subdued. But the Cocomes were also blind to their own real interests; they allowed the spirit of division to make further and further inroads into their kingdom, until at last even their foreign mercenaries could no longer cope with the power of the enemy. An alliance was concluded between the Tutul Xius, who had retreated to their highlands of central Yucatan, the rulers of Chichen-Itza, and the enemies in the immediate neighbourhood of the Cocomes, and neither the bands of Nahua warriors nor the fortifications with which Mayapan had long since been surrounded could make head against the united forces of so many opponents. The Cocomes kingdom collapsed, and with it disappeared the last trace of a Maya confederation. The proud capital which for nearly five hundred years had been the central point of the kingdom — a kingdom whose boundaries had embraced the greater part of the Yucatan peninsula — was utterly destroyed by its revengeful enemies. Though this is a most important occurrence in Yucatan history during the century which preceded the Spanish conquest, yet its date remains quite uncertain. Apparently the decisive battles took place about the year 1436, after a previous period of nearly twenty years had passed almost without any cessation of hostilities.

That this conflict must have consisted rather of a series of revolutionary combats than of a continuous war is certainly to be inferred from the change in circumstances which had taken place. Even the hated Nahua body-guards were not involved in the tyrant's fall, but were spared by the conquerors. They were even allowed to settle in the province Aculan, in the neighbourhood of Campeche, and there to form a little Nahua State. But this was apparently soon absorbed by the Maya who surrounded it on all sides; for a century later, at the time of the conquest, not a single Nahua-speaking inhabitant was to be found on the whole peninsula.   The conquerors left equally unmolested a last branch of the Cocomes race, which was in Ulua at the time of the revolution apparently attempting to enlist fresh Aztec reinforcements for the help of its mother State.   It may have collected around itself the last surviving dependents of the old dynasty, and have founded another small State with their help; by this means the name of Cocomes survived to future generations.   The province of Zotuta, with its capital Tibulon, situated deep in the forests of the central regions, was the scene of its rule until the Spaniards made their way there also.

It is not easy to explain the nature of the influence which the fall of the Cocomes power exerted upon the two rival priestly towns of Itzamal and Chichen-Itza.   Under its king Ulmil, Chichen-Itza had been for a long time the central point of the resistance offered to the kings of Mayapan, consequently the vials of the royal wrath had repeatedly been poured out upon town and land.   In spite of this, up to the time of the destruction of Mayapan, the king of Chichen-Itza invariably appears as a powerful ally of the revolted party.   One would have expected that the holy town of the feathered snake would now increase in strength and vigour; on the contrary its name entirely disappears from the traditions: upon the division of Yucatan into seven little kingdoms, a condition of things which the Spaniards found upon their conquest, Chichen-Itza appears no longer as an independent kingdom.   The abandoned ruins of the town, which were speedily covered by a luxuriant vegetation, were offered by the kings of Itzamal as a resting-place for the first small Spanish troop which made its way into Yucatan.   A possible explanation of this remarkable fact may be found in the legend that a prince of Chichen-Itza had abandoned the land, with the greatest part of his people, in one of the many revolutions which disturbed the last days of the Maya-pan dynasty.   He is said to have turned again to the original dwelling-places of the Maya in the far west, hoping thus to avoid these scenes of war and oppression. The little Maya State of Peten-Itza, on the lake of Peten, in Guatemala, is said to owe its origin to him.   On his expedition to Honduras, Ferdinand Cortes visited its capital, which was situated on the island of the Peten lake called by the Spaniards the Isla de Flores.   In this district, also, ruins of Maya towns have been recently discovered which would not disgrace the architects of Chichen-Itza, supposing them to have really been the founders of a second younger civilisation in this district which was, for the Maya, classic ground.

Another curious tradition is connected with the little kingdom of Peten-Itza. The favourite horse of Cortes is said to have been so ill in that place that it could go no farther.   It was therefore handed over to the Maya, with orders to look after it carefully, that it might be given over to the next Spaniards who should come that way.   But the Indians, whose reverential awe of the horse — an animal with which they were entirely unacquainted — is known to us from many episodes of the conquest, thought that the best way to look after the horse was to pay him the honours due to a god, to quarter him in a temple, and to feed him with sacrifices.   This worship continued until the noble charger was killed by this unusual food, and must then have been replaced by a fac-simile in clay.

The Maya State of Peten was the longest to maintain its independence against the Spaniards.   The remoteness and isolation of the district in which the last Itzaes had set up their habitation were their best protection.   Here, for more than a century after the visit of Cortes, the worship of the old gods, the practice of the ancient art, and the study of the old sacred books were maintained; more than one attempt on the part of missionaries and governors to destroy this last retreat of heathendom came to an inglorious end in the extensive jungles which spread their sure defences around the little kingdom of Peten on all sides. It was only in 1671 that a simultaneous attack upon different sides succeeded in uniting a sufficient force at the lake of Peten; even then the Maya, who had learned the arts of war in their century of battles, resisted with the courage of despair; but the Indians and their rude implements of destruction could not make head against protective armour and better weapons. And so destruction came upon the last town in which the most ancient civilisation of the New World had gained a respite for its independence.

Long before this time a similar fate had befallen all the other Maya kingdoms. Strangely enough that town had gained the most profit from the revolution against Mayapan which should have been most deeply involved in the fall of the Cocomes, as being their closest ally. The greatest part of the district which formed the old kingdom of Mayapan did not fall into the power of the Itzaes of Chichen, or the Tutul Xius of Mani, but to the old priestly town Itzamal; and the race of the Cheles, from which the high-priesthood of the kingdom of Mayapan had been drawn for many generations, also provided secular rulers for the newly rising principality. The Cheles did not probably attempt to revive the aggressive policy of the Cocomes. Nevertheless their State, next to the State of Zachi, was by far the most extensive which the Spaniards found in the peninsula, and embraced, with the exception of the little Nahua territory of Campeche, the whole of the north and east. The district of this principality, in which the Spaniards found a friendly reception from the outset, became later the germ of the Spanish province of Yucatan; Merida, the capital of this province, was built upon the site of the ancient Tiho, only a few miles from Itzamal. Chiefly in consequence of their foolish conduct, the Spaniards had many a hard battle to fight before they subjugated the whole Maya district of Yucatan; but when once peace and order had been firmly re-established in the country, the native population, which was even then numerous, displayed all the virtues peculiar to the ancient race. The docile, pliable, and frugal Maya-Indians tilled the soil for their Christian lords and priests with the same industry which they had displayed under their ancient masters, and the clever architects and sculptors now erected temples and palaces upon modern designs with all their ancient skill.

It is doubtful whether the Maya kingdom of Guatemala, and the later kingdoms of Quiché, of Kakchiquel, and of Tzutuhil, were first populated when the inroads of the Nahua race menaced the old civilisation of the Tzendal district. It is far more probable that the acquisition of these territories by Maya peoples belongs to an earlier period. The connection of kindred nations in their immediate neighbourhood in so momentous a fashion naturally could not fail to have an influence upon these kingdoms; at any rate the people of the western highland gained then a strong additional element which was more advanced than they in civilisation and consequently must have had a considerable influence upon these races.

The Maya people of Guatemala also had a full share in the important acquisitions which the civilisation of their race had gained. They were well acquainted with the art of writing in the hieroglyphic signs peculiar to the Maya civilisation

Their legendary traditions, which have come down to us in even greater number than have those of their most advanced kinsfolk on the east, show the same number of religious conceptions; the same gods, with now and then even the same names, are prominent here as there. The complicated astronomical calendar, which must count among the most important scientific achievements of the Maya peoples, was for them also the governing principle in religious and civic life. But the habits of their daily life, and the buildings thereby developed, were essentially different, and resulted in a sensible difference in the artistic character of the district. This is especially the case with their architecture, which cannot but surprise us, supposing it to have been exclusively derived from the architects of Palenque, Menché, etc. The highlands of Guatemala, in which the capital towns of Quiché and its related governments were situated, offered, for the expression of their artistic tendencies, a material of the same value and nature as the Maya had at their disposition in the lower districts. Nevertheless the architecture of the western races never even approximated to the rich decorations of the east, and the number of memorials in the plastic art, the highland origin of which is indisputable, is very small. However, from the numerous examples of pottery found in the highlands and in the western district of Guatemala, we observe that these Maya peoples did not break away, as did the Huastecs, from the specific Maya civilisation of the original race, but that they had shared in every form of its development. On pottery ware from Quiché and related towns inscriptions and calendars have been transmitted to us which we are accustomed to find carved in stone or moulded in stucco as architectural decorations among the other Maya races.

The number of sites in the western Maya district the ruins of which have been discovered is by no means small, and remains of massive stone buildings, though without the usual artistic decoration, are by no means lacking. But the preponderance of fortifications in the sites of the west distinguishes them in a marked way from those of the lowlands and the Yucatan peninsula. Among the buildings of the lowlands are to be found many the position of which was certainly chosen with a view to resisting hostile attacks. But consideration of strategical necessities is nowhere very conspicuous, and in many places entirely wanting. In Guatemala quite the contrary is the case. The choice of site here shows that strategical considerations were generally of the first importance. Walls, fortresses, and citadels, often of considerable extent, which could have been reduced only by the combined attacks of large forces of men, are the most remarkable remains in the district of Quiché. The Maya in the lowlands were of a distinctly peaceful character; possibly in the course of time an entire change in their national character was brought about by their continual wars with the warlike Nahua races, some of which can be demonstrated to have made their way even as far as Nicaragua. It is, however, more probable that from the outset differences existed between the peaceful races of the flourishing coast-land and the ruder peoples of the mountains, differences derived from the internal divisions of the district, which did not manifest themselves within the historical epoch.

The old town Tulan continually appears as a source of all emigrations, and must be sought for in the district of Tabasco if by Tulan we may understand an individual town. From this town Nima-Quiché — the great Quiché — emigrated with three brothers, and turned his steps westward to the mountains, as we learn from the traditions of the western peoples. The brothers are said to have then divided the land so that one obtained the district of Chiapas (Quelenes), the other obtained Verapaz (Tezulutlan), and the third the district of Mames and Pocomams (on the northwest of Guatemala), while he himself gained the land of Quiché, Kakchiquel, and Tzutuhil; the royal house of this kingdom traced its origin from him. In spite of its Nahua influences this tradition clearly shows the consciousness of a national unity, even among such Maya peoples as have played no further part in history; and it also refers their origin to a time when this national consciousness had not been so wholly deadened as it afterward was. Chiapas now appears as one of the four Maya kingdoms, and there is nothing to show that this district had already fallen into the hands of foreign conquerors; therefore this division of peoples must be regarded as belonging to a time long before the flight of the Maya from Chiapas.

The later history of the race is hopelessly confused. Continual internal wars, constant emigrations and change of place, revolts against tyrannical power, and confederations of peace are its chief constituents. The very dynasty of the Quiché race is by one historian given as consisting of eleven generations, by another as consisting of seventeen, and even sometimes as of twenty-three. However, the kings of Quiché certainly held an important position among the ruling races of Guatemala, and a chronicler declares that the Quiché kings date back to the era of the Aztec rulers of Mexico-Tenochtitlan, adding at the same time that the Quiché kingdom was not merely equal to the Aztec kingdom in extent, but was even far superior to it.

For the disruption of the small kingdoms of Kakchiquel and Tzutuhil, different reasons are suggested. The succession to King Acxopil, the successor of the Nima-Quiché, the real founder of the Quiché kingdom, may possibly have led to the disruption. The rulers of the smaller kingdoms remained, however, in honourable relations with the chief kingdom of Quiché, and were even interested in the maintenance of the supreme power in consequence of the mode of succession peculiar to these American kingdoms. Acxopil had during his lifetime handed over to his eldest son the government of the kingdom of Kakchiquel, and to the younger the government of Tzutuhil, with the stipulation that after his death the elder son should govern the whole kingdom, including Quiché, the second son should govern Kakchiquel, and a third should rule over Tzutuhil. The object of this arrangement was that each ruler, before obtaining the highest position in the State, should undergo a training for supremacy in positions of gradually increasing importance. It does not appear, however, that this regulation was strictly observed after his death. Icutemal, the elder of the sons of Acxopil, certainly got possession of the throne of Quiché; but he handed over the rulership of Kakchiquel to his own elder son, and not to his brother. This was a signal for the outbreak of protracted internal struggles which lasted uninterruptedly almost up to the Spanish conquest. In this case also the neighbouring Nahua races were enlisted as allies in the wars of these related Maya kingdoms. Their influence was here so strongly pronounced that the bloody human sacrifices and the cannibalism practised by the Nahua were also adopted by the Maya. At any rate all our information testifies that the Maya people in Guatemala were far more extensively commingled with Nahua elements than in Yucatan.

The three kingdoms continued mutually independent and in a state of constant internal struggle until the arrival of the Spaniards. In 1492 a number of the chiefs of Kakchiquel revolted against Cay Hunahpu, who had again attempted to extend his empire at the expense of his neighbours. He was defeated, and atoned for his aggression by his death. In this there is nothing extraordinary ; but the Kakchiquel attached such importance to this victory that they made it the starting-point of a new chronology. In true revolutionary style they abolished the whole of the old priestly calendar and created a year of four hundred days, divided into twenty months of twenty days each. They are the only race of Central America which abandoned the scientific astronomical calendar of the Maya. It requires no great penetration to see that their new year was no advance upon the old one, but was an act as futile as it was arbitrary.

In spite of numerous relations with the Nahua races there seems to have been no real connection between the Maya kingdom and the Aztec kingdom of Monte-zuma. The existence of each was known to the other, and embassies may have been exchanged between them even before the arrival of the Spaniards. The Aztec conquests certainly came extremely close to the boundaries of the Maya kingdom in the last ten years of Aztec dominion; this, however, did not conduce to any close connection between the two groups of States. The Quiché were so much occupied with warding off the attacks of hostile kinsfolk within the bounda-ries of their own kingdom that they could not turn their attention to foreign con-quest, which might have brought them into conflict with the Aztecs. When the Spaniards began to encroach upon the Aztec kingdom, Montezuma II is said to have sent a great embassy to the king of Kakchiquel : they do not, however, seem to have been able to come to an understanding. Before the Spaniards had under-taken the subjugation of the Maya kingdom of Guatemala, emissaries of the king of Kakchiquel appeared in Mexico, which was the first kingdom to fall before Cortes, and asked for his help against the Quiché. Naturally this help was gladly lent in view of future possibilities. In the year 1524 the Adelantado Pedro de Alvarado appeared in Iximché, and, in alliance with the Kakchiquel, began a war against the Quiché, and conquered them in several bloody conflicts. The Tzutuhil had remained neutral, trusting to the inaccessibility of their kingdom, and had refused their help, not only to the Quiché, but also to the Spaniards. This fact provided a pretext for Alvarado to turn his forces against them ; and neither the resources of nature nor those of art could avail to protect the Tzutuhil against the power of Spain. The Kakchiquel learned too late that they had gained a Spanish alliance at the price of their own freedom. When they tried to shake off the yoke which was imperceptibly laid upon them, the moment had long since passed when their resistance could have been attended with any hopes of success. The blood that they shed in vain could only expiate their criminal action in being the first to throw open their country to the foreign invader.

(b) *The Nahua.* — In the sixteenth century the Spaniards found a numerous population of Nahua people who had been settled for many hundreds of years in a territory which lies upon the north of the districts of Maya civilisation, and stretches to the borders of the Pueblo Indians, — that is, from the Isthmus of Tehuantepec up to the boundaries of Texas and New Mexico. These peoples did not, however, consider their country as their original home ; in fact there was there a remnant of a foreign population which had, in general, followed the steps of Nahua civilisation. The migration legends which were widely extant among the

Nahua give very consistent narratives, and point to the home of the race having been situated in the far north upon a great water. In this legend the place-names Aztlan ("The Town on the Water") and Chicomoztoc ("The Seven Caves") play a great part. This legend has evoked a whole literature. From the coast of the Pacific Ocean to the North American Lakes, from Bering Strait to the Plain of Mexico, scarcely a spot can be found which one or another inquirer has not connected with the emigrations of the Aztecs from Aztlan-Chicomoztoc to Mexico-Tenochtitlan.

The traces of emigration of the Nahua peoples in a northerly direction, other than those of a legendary nature, are extremely inadequate. The district which lay a little to the north of the later centre of Nahua civilisation—that is, the plateau of Anahuac—was populated in comparatively early times by the race of the Pueblo Indians. Their civilisation shows some points of resemblance to the Nahua culture; but the fundamental differences are so striking or extreme that it is impossible to suppose a Nahua migration through this region even in remote times. Traces of the Nahua language have certainly been found in proper names, or, as it were, fossilised in the dialects of the Pueblo peoples in Sinaloa, and as much farther north as the Hopi of Moqui or Tusayan. Even in the district of Maya civilisation we are surprised to find in the chronicles of the sixteenth century many names of places derived from the Nahua speech. But we are well assured that the reason for this is not that the Nahua district extended into this territory, but that the Spaniards were guided into this district by Indians who were only acquainted with Nahua power and with Nahua names for the places. These names have thus been stereotyped by tradition, and confirmed by the preponderance of the Nahua element in the midst of the Spanish colonisations. A similar state of things must undoubtedly have come to pass on the north also.

The historical traditions of the Nahua race invite the conclusion that their original home was certainly situated in the northern portion of the district in which the Spaniards found their race predominant. Not only the hieroglyphic designs, which were partially complete before the period of conquest, but also the Spanish chroniclers, who collected their information from the natives, point to the fact that the Nahua races had long lived as a wholly uncivilised fishing and hunting people within those boundaries where they were discovered in the sixteenth century. Even then there were individual related peoples who had not yet obtained a share in the civilisation of their more favoured brethren, and only a short time had elapsed, if we may believe tradition, since certain races who at the time of the Spanish conquest stood high in the scale of general civilisation had given up their wandering lives and turned to agriculture and the blessings of progress.

The desire for a settled life was certainly not prominent among the Nahua, and least of all among the Aztecs, and it is a tendency which we cannot consider to have been gained by imitating civilised predecessors, even in the case of the most civilised peoples of America. Like the Maya, the Indians of Central America made no difficulty about abandoning their habitations, where for generations they had been settled and had worked and built, supposing their political circumstances to have altered for the worse. The wanderings of the Aztecs are of themselves evidence that they were the last to leave their common home, Aztlan-Chicomoztoc. For at least ten years in historical times they wandered among the different nations of the Nahua race, which ages ago had obtained a secure settlement and made great advances in civilisation. That tradition should have remained pure in the case of such inequality of development, under the unfavourable circumstances which the nomad life of an uncivilised people involves, is wholly incredible: mythological and religious conceptions have much more probably formed the basis of the legends of the migration of the Nahua from Aztlan-Chicomoztoc.

Constantly and for all time the Nahua have been an inland race. Both on the Atlantic and also on the Pacific coasts at a late period, they drove out an older population which does not seem to have been akin to themselves. But even after some of their peoples had settled in the tropical climate of their coast-land, they still retained the objection of an inland race to the "great salt water." The Maya engaged in an extensive maritime commerce from their own harbours; the Nahua peoples engaged in commerce too, but their extensive traffic was carried on exclusively on the highroads, although many of the Nahua people were acquainted with the construction of fishing-boats. Yet in their history we find the Nahua, with all their objection to the sea, unmistakably associated with the water. A legend which places their birthplace on a great water is evidence of this, and in their history the lakes on the highlands of Anahuac play a most important part. Even without this lake district a number of centres of Nahua development were also situated on the shores of lakes,—as, for instance, Tezcuco, Chalco, and Tenochtitlan. Over and over again, in history and legend, we meet with the water and that which it brings forth.

The nature of their environment had made the Nahua a people of hunters and fishers; it had also created in them a further characteristic, a fierce warlike spirit. It is true that under the snowy peaks of the Cordilleras an everlasting spring reigned in the deep valleys of Mexico; the climate was far more suitable for a people of careless enjoyment than for a race of ferocious warriors. Hunting, moreover, could not have exercised a very hardening influence: in the whole kingdom there was no wild animal which could have been particularly dangerous to huntsmen, even when armed with the simplest of weapons. It was the ancient inhabitants of the land that made the Nahua a nation of warriors. Upon their immigration they did not find their future country uninhabited, as the Maya had done in Yucatan. That they found there a race of inhabitants foreign to themselves may be concluded from the traditions, although the inadequacy of our information makes it impossible to establish the ethnological character of this race. In the myths of the Nahua giants of superhuman size and unbounded strength appear, and though we cannot put a literal interpretation on this, as did the old Spanish chroniclers, who identified the bones of antediluvian animals with the skeletons of this giant race, we may none the less conclude that the Nahua had a long and bitter struggle with a powerful enemy, and that they must have exerted their utmost resources and carried on a war of unceasing destruction before they succeeded in winning a territory where their race might develop to its full strength. It was in this warfare that that fierce warrior spirit was implanted in this untutored people.

We find the Nahua everywhere a race of warriors alike fearful and feared, and we come across some of them outside their later district, as, for instance, in Yucatan and Guatemala; but the traditions within their own territories are of an equally warlike character. Battle and victory, conquest and destruction are the dominant features of their art; and in their case war was closely connected with religion,—religion in its most horrible and frightful form, as it appeared in the bloody worship of the Aztecs, for their national god Huitzilopochtli. In the strange horrors of this worship inquirers have attempted to trace the influence of peoples earlier than the Nahua; they have ascribed the cult to the temporary stay of the Aztecs in the district of Tarasca. But even leaving out of sight the fact that a remote branch of the Nahua race was possibly settled even in Tarasca, this cruel worship, with its numerous human sacrifices, is by no means peculiar to the Aztecs. It appears in a more or less horrible form among almost all the Nahua people, and it is no external accessory of divine worship; it is rather the typical form of that worship. Let us suppose that the majority of this race were not under the influence of similar conceptions; we have then to ask by what possibility that compact could have been brought about between Mexico, Tlazcala, and Huexotzinco, the provisions of which regulated wars for these three States, with a view to providing a sufficient number of captured enemies for sacrifice to their gods upon given occasions. War, human sacrifice, and ceremonial cannibalism are characteristic of the Nahua. The special influences that led the national character of the race in this direction must certainly be placed in a period long anterior to the disruption of the Nahua people into its separate branches, and still further anterior to the supposed stay of the Aztecs among the people of Tarasca.

At the time of the Spanish invasion the Nahua certainly were no longer that nation of fishermen, hunters, and fierce warriors which had begun to develop at the outset in the highlands of Anahuac. On the contrary a development lasting for centuries had resulted in a civilisation which in many districts could compete with the civilisation of the Maya, and the external splendours of which completely dazzled the Spaniards. This civilisation, however, as almost all our sources of information consistently assert, was not the result of slow development on the part of the people themselves, but was acquired and imported from without. The Nahua races of the valleys of Mexico, the traditions of which are known to us, were proud to consider themselves Chichimecs; and almost all the Chichimec races appear originally as half-wild, wandering, ill-clothed tribes of huntsmen, who received their first introduction into the ways of civilisation by communication with older nations who were already firmly settled in confederate towns and States and were occupied in agriculture. The different histories of the race which were not confused by an attempt to harmonise the Christian and old American chronologies go back some six or seven centuries into the past. Many a race which has later played an important part in the history of Central America must have given up its wild and wandering life and have gained its first impulse to civilisation within that short period; these traditions, which almost without exception avail themselves of long dynasties to serve their chronological necessities, imply the previous existence of several civilised States.

The Toltecs, as the chief exponents of Nahua civilisation, appear to some extent in the more ancient sculptures, and still more often in the later histories which were modelled upon European examples. According to the later legends which have come down to us, the Toltecs were a branch of the Nahua race, and also came from the north, from Chicomoztoc to the town Huehuetlapallan, about the fourth century of our era. At the beginning of the sixth century they are said to have been settled on a table-land of Mexico——Tula being the capital of their kingdom — and soon to have risen to a fabulous development of civilisation. Here all their esoteric knowledge is said to have been acquired, and it was also here that the scientific regulation of the calendar, which became an example for all other peoples, was carried out by the Toltec priests and kings. Moreover the Toltecs are also said to have compiled the history of the past and to have established an authentic text of it. But above all they are reputed to have been the teachers of all later nations in the sphere of art, especially in architecture and sculpture. The buildings which adorned their settlements displayed a splendour and a magnificence almost unrivalled by the famous palace towns of later times, such as Tezcuco and Tenochtitlan. After an existence of several centuries the Toltec kingdom is supposed to have collapsed, about the year 1055, as a result of internal struggle and external attacks. Its territory fell into the hands of the other neighbouring States. The Toltec nobles, however, who fled into every district of Anahuac upon the fall of the kingdom, were everywhere the missionaries of that advanced civilisation which was acquired by the other peoples of the Nahua as a direct result of the fall of this kingdom.

These are the general features of the legend; the details, however, are terribly confused. Even in the case of the Indian historian Ixtlilxóchitl, the author of the Toltec legend, who has depicted it in two different places, the chronology of the names and the details are anything but consistent in his two accounts. A great part of the Toltec stories is mere legend, in which we can unmistakably recognise a strong mythological element. For instance, there is said to have been a decree that the rule of each individual monarch should last neither more nor less than fifty-two years; if he lived longer, he was obliged, after a reign of fifty-two years, to abdicate in favour of his eldest son; supposing he died before that period, a council of the elders continued the government in his name until the legal term was fulfilled. Fifty-two years, however, was the period of the great Mexican cycle of years which was used to make the ritual calendar coincide with the solar year: at the beginning of this period the holy fire was again kindled with ceremonial festival, under the belief that by that means the existence of the world was again insured for a like period. The farther we retrace the story, however, the more doubtful do the facts become and the stronger is the mythological element. Excavations have certainly laid bare ancient ruins upon the site of the presumed settlement of the famous Toltec kingdom in the town of Tula, some miles north of Mexico, but these ruins are neither extensive nor imposing. The artistic value of the ruined buildings upon the soil of the old Nahua States sensibly diminishes as we advance from south to north, — a fact in opposition to the Toltec legend. Moreover, with the exception of the foundation and destruction of cities, almost everything that we know of the Toltecs centres round the personality of a king Quetzalcoatl. But this name, which denotes the feathered snake, like the Maya Kukulkan, is also the name of a divinity which in later times was worshipped far and wide throughout the Nahua kingdom also: his appearance makes us the more suspicious, as other names in the dynasty also coincide with the names of gods, and several kings have been deified by tradition. For these reasons the historical substratum of the Toltec legend becomes more and more hypothetical. Once, perhaps, there may have existed a Toltec principality, with Tula for its capital, which may have played a certain part in the racial feuds of the little Nahua kingdom; but the Toltecs have no right to the importance which has been ascribed to them as being the chief civilising influence of Anahuac.

The name "Tulan" also appears in the original legends of the Maya; it does not, however, denote any one particular place, but is a general designation for a large royal settlement richly adorned: the legend also alludes to no less than four Tulans existing at the same time. If we could venture to identify the Tula of Nahua tradition with the similarly named Maya towns, and could then consider the Maya people themselves as the Nahua Toltecs, this would be the easiest solution of the problem. Unfortunately there are great difficulties in the way of such an explanation. The Toltecs are invariably a people related to the Nahua, and therefore speaking their language; and their habitations upon the north of the later Nahua district — the plateau of Mexico — are in accordance with this fact: neither of these can be brought into connection with the Maya by any means. If, however, we cannot venture to identify the Maya with the Toltecs, we may consider the connection between Maya and Nahua civilisation as indisputable. We have now to ask in what manner the advance in civilisation which the Maya had gained also fell to the share of the Nahua peoples, and how these peoples advanced from the coast of Tabasco up into the northern heights of the Mexican table-land.

The political circumstances which the Spaniards found on the Mexican table-land at the conquest have brought it about that we possess reliable information concerning the history only of those people who lived in Anahuac, — that is, in the neighbourhood of the Mexican lakes. The numerous related nations that had settled on the north, and even more extensively on the south, of the table-land, were almost as much strangers to the Aztecs and their related nations of Anahuac as the Maya peoples were. In historical times the immediate neighbours of the Maya of Guatemala were the Zapotecs, the Mixtecs, and the Kuikatecs. Even if their habitations remained unchanged, as they apparently did, throughout the period that the Nahua settlements of Anahuac lasted, we can, however, suppose a long-existing connection between the Maya and this branch of the Nahua nation, and this all the more because the necessary indications which we have at our disposal for the reconstruction of the earlier history of this race point to a close connection.

An illuminated manuscript of Kuikatec origin that has only recently been discovered informs us that the Kuikatecs, under the guidance of their racial god, apparently entitled "Maollin," wandered and fought for six centuries in the district which formed the boundary between the Maya and Nahua peoples in ancient times. The localities mentioned in the manuscript cannot all be certainly identified, but they point to the districts of Guatemala and Chiapas. The migrations then continued in a southerly direction not far from the Pacific coast; there, however, the Kuikatecs finally met with an insurmountable obstacle, and therefore turned aside in an easterly direction, crossed the north of Guatemala, and finally arrived safely in Chiapas, in a territory of Acalan, a district immediately bordering upon Yucatan. Probably these and similar migrations of the Nahua races brought about the fall of the flourishing Maya towns of Chiapas and Tabasco.[1] The majority of the Maya peoples may have abandoned their old home to this enemy; but some of their members there certainly were who either became the subjects of the new arrivals, as their tributary vassals, or were prevented by force from

[1] See ante, p. 238.

escaping the new dominion.  It is in these causes that we must seek the inter-change of civilisation between the Maya and the Nahua races.

The well-known precedents of the Germanic migrations upon our own conti-nent make us familiar with the fact that a people in a high state of civilisation may collapse helplessly before the vigorous attacks of a less cultured race, but that in a short time their own higher culture leavens the mass of the conquerors and again brings the old civilisation to the front.  How far the Kuikatecs were influenced by Maya civilisation we cannot exactly define; but in the case of the Zapotecs this influence is very characteristic.  Their invasion into the district of Maya civilisation cannot be affirmed with the same certainty; but in later times we meet with them in the immediate neighbourhood of the Maya, and settled upon a portion of that district the antiquities of which indisputably point to a previous settlement of Maya peoples.  On the Zapotecs the influence of Maya civilisation was extremely powerful.  Even their language has undergone a strong admixture of Maya words and forms.  It would, however, be a mistake to dispute their con-nection with the Nahua race; for the Spanish chronicles regard the Zapotecs as a nation foreign to the Maya and connected with the peoples of Mexico.  Moreover even the scanty accounts which we learn from this people themselves show that they must be placed among the nations of the Nahua race.  Among these nations, however, they were at any rate one of those peoples who very early gave up the savage life of the old hunting races for a more civilised mode of existence; for centuries they have unmistakably taken a leading position in all the acquisitions of civilised progress among the Nahua peoples.  A considerable portion of the literary treasures which have come down to us from the time when the Nahua civilisation was developing independently belongs to the Zapotecs.  Their manuscripts [1] are not written in Maya script, but, with the exception of some small characteristic divergences, coincide with the mode of writing found in Aztec and other undoubt-edly Nahuatlac documents.  Probably the Zapotecs, or their kinsfolk, formed their mode of writing, which later became the property of all the Nahua peoples, under the influence and in imitation of that with which the Maya had made them acquainted.

A further relationship is visible between the Maya manuscripts and those of Zapotec origin in the extensive representations which are concerned with the re-ligious calendar, in which, as we know, the Maya have given proof of astonishing astronomical knowledge.  The peculiar sacred calendar system of the Maya shows the combination of the numbers 20 and 13, — a combination which appears nowhere else in the world.  This system was adopted in its main elements by the Zapotecs and four other Nahua peoples.  Moreover more careful examination has established the fact that the titles for each particular day, which are invariably taken from the objects of daily life, are essentially the same in the case of every language the calendar names of which are known to us.  So close is this coinci-dence that even the names of the days with which the sacred or ritual year might begin (a year composed of $13 \times 20 = 260$ days, in combination with the solar year) hang together, in the case of Maya and Nahua peoples respectively, in such a way that a more ancient group of names in combination among the Maya of Chi-apas and Tabasco, and the Zapotecs and related nations, can be distinguished from a more recent combination in use among the Maya of Yucatan and the Aztec-

[1] See Plate opposite p. 254.

# A PAGE FROM THE VIENNA NAHUA MANUSCRIPT OF ZAPOTEC ORIGIN

THE page reproduced belongs to the series of the Codex Viennensis, in which regular pictorial designs appear in connection with dates. Hence it is to be presumed that these hitherto inexplicable designs are of a historical nature. The dates are composed of combinations of the signs for day and year; a year is denoted by its first day, with the hieroglyph for year which resembles the Roman A. The dates with the better known Aztec denominations are as follows:

| | | | |
|---|---|---|---|
| 5 tecpatl i. J. 5 tecpatl (flint, zap : opa) | 6 ocelotl i. J. 1 tochtli (Tiger zag : ech.) | 4 nacate i. J. 4 . 1 p l. '. c tl ( c _ zag : cl.. \ | 1 p l. '. c .tl 7 d n i. '. li c in |
| 7 tochtli i. J. 5 calli (rabbit-house zag : lapa ela) | 13 cheatl i. J. 5 lli (Wind zag : laa) | 7 . t. i. [. 7 a tl | z . p |
| 1 tochtli i. J. 1 tochtli 1 cipactli i. J. 1 acatl (crocodile reed zag : chilla quij) | 7 checatl i. J. 7 atl | 2 a t i. J. 2 a tl | 1 qa tl i. J. 1 l |

Of the pictorial representations some are certainly to be understood ideographically: e. g. the second of the first column, representing a man in warrior's array, with shield, spear, and throwing-stick; perhaps also the designs at the bottom of the first three columns. Others prefer to give them a phonetic (proper name?) value: e. g., the first, with its components house, month, and outer garment; or the second of the second column, with the components tunic, shield, and mat. However, as we have said, the manuscript has not yet been successfully deciphered.

A PAGE FROM THE VIENNA MANUSCRIPT OF ZAPOTHEC ORIGIN.
Imperial Library, Vienna

Nahua. It is plain that these are no chance coincidences, and when we consider the remarkable development which astronomical science had reached among the Maya, it is equally plain in this case who it was that gave and who it was that received.

Finally, the Zapotees were instructed by the Maya in another department, — that of architecture. The old Zapotee district, which is to-day the Mexican province Oaxaca, contains ruins of ancient Indian buildings in different places; but most of these are so dilapidated that we can draw only the vaguest conclusions as to their original condition. The ruins of Mitla are an exception to this rule, chiefly because their stronger and bolder buildings made them more capable of resisting the attacks of time. Mitla is only the Mexican name for the town which the Zapotees themselves called Yopaa; both names mean "The Place of the Dead." Possibly the Xibalbay of the Maya, which also means "Town of the Dead," is the most ancient name of this town, and goes back to an epoch when this district was also in possession of the Maya peoples.[1] At any rate there is no particular proof of this in the paintings which exist in the rooms of the temple-building of Mitla and are still in good condition; they are undoubtedly of later origin and belong to the Nahua civilisation. On the contrary the architectural style of the building — partly below and partly above ground, with its decorated rooms and its roof of overhanging courses — resembles far more nearly the Maya architecture than that of the younger Nahua peoples. For instance, the temple buildings of the Aztecs consist almost entirely of high pyramids artistically faced, on which there are no buildings at all, or erections of only a temporary nature. In the tradition of the Indians Mitla continued to survive as the town of the dead, and it undoubtedly was for a long time the sacred burial-ground for the kings and the highest priests and dignitaries of the Zapotec kingdom. At any rate the place did not possess the gloomy character of a burial city during the flourishing period of the kingdom. Much more probably it was then not only the residence of the highest priests of the chief divinity, but also the royal capital, in which the king or one of the most important princes held the Zapotec court.

Our historical information about the Zapotec kingdom goes back only a few decades — certainly not a century — before the Spanish conquest. When the Aztec kingdom began to extend in a southwesterly direction, the Zapotees appear in the circle of the Aztec princes. About the year 1484 Ahuitzotl, the seventh king of Mexico-Tenochtitlan, made an invasion far into the Zapotec district in the direction of Tehuantepec, and in the fortress Huaxyacac he laid the basis of further conquest. At that time different Zapotec towns or principalities became either subject or tributary to the Aztecs; and on this occasion Mitla also, the sacred town of the Zapotees, was conquered and destroyed by the Mexicans. Traditions dealing with this point are confirmed by the fact that the last kings had taken up their residence in Teotzapotlan. It was then that the Aztecs erected the fortresses of Quauhtenanco, Teotitlan, and Huaxyacac, which formed a refuge, not only for the Aztec garrison that was left there, but also for the financial officials and the merchants who almost invariably undertook the duties of spies and scouts in the Aztec wars.

About ten years later the country of the Zapotees became the scene of a new war. The Mexicans had succeeded in making themselves so thoroughly hated

[1] See ante, p. 229.

within the whole of their fortified district that their opponents laid aside their own
mutual differences and formed a wide confederacy with a view to an attack in
common. Everything that fell into the hands of the invaders outside of the fortress
walls was mercilessly destroyed by the confederate Zapotecs, Mixtecs, and the
smaller neighbouring races, and a complete blockade of the fortresses was begun.
Ahuitzotl sent in vain one body of troops after another at the anxious summons of
the besieged. The confederates were skilful enough to avoid any conflict in the
open country; when they had succeeded in enticing the Mexicans deep into the
gorges of their mountain range they unexpectedly attacked their defenceless
opponents and left hardly a single messenger to announce the overthrow at headquarters. At the same time the Aztec forces were required elsewhere; Ahuitzotl
finally determined to end the war in the south by coming to an agreement. The
Mexicans had never been able to overpower their opponents by force of arms; their
political measures, however, were more successful. The chief of the confederates,
the Zapotec king, Cociyoeza, desired to secure the peace, independence, and extension of territory which they had gained from the Mexicans by marriage with a
Mexican princess. The Mexicans on their side utterly defeated the Mixtecs, and
thus succeeded in restoring their shattered prestige. Cociyoeza retained his independence against the later Mexican kings, and upon his death was able to hand
on his empire to his son Cociyopu. The hatred and dread of the Aztecs became
plain when the Spaniards entered the country; the Zapotecs, like the Tlazcalans,
offered the Spaniards alliance and help against their hated foe, and in the end
were themselves subjected to a yoke which was scarcely lighter than the Aztec
rule had been.

The Central American civilisation, with the changes which the Zapotecs had
imposed upon it, made its way northward, and finally became the common property
of almost all the Nahua peoples. The individual steps of this progress cannot be
recognised in the scanty remains which have come down to us from the Nahua
races which were settled between the Zapotecs and the highland of Anahuac. As
to the Mixtecs, we know that they also built terraced pyramids, on which were
raised the altars of their gods; they too had learned to hand down to posterity the
histories of their gods and princes in those written characters with which we first
meet among the Zapotecs. They measured the lapse of their days and the recurrence of their festivals by a calendar founded upon the same principles as that of
Central America. It is impossible, however, to give any more accurate description
of the position which this race held among the advancing civilisations. As we go
farther north, this civilisation assumes a more general character, and can be designated as the Aztec offshoot of Central American culture. It is a civilisation which
certainly has affinities with the ancient Maya, though it struck out a line of its
own in those centuries when its progress was free from external influence.

Once more in the northern districts we meet with traces which recall to our
minds the southern origin of the Mexican civilisation; these are in the town of
Cholula. The famous pyramid which has been named after this town, and which
excited the astonishment and amazement of the Spanish conquerors, has been for
a long time in such a ruined condition that it is impossible to assign its position in
American art from its artistic style. The old chroniclers, however, inform us that,
unlike the Aztec temple pyramids, which were usually crowned by an open altar
of the god, this pyramid bore a roofed-in building on its summit. This reminds us

of the architectural style of the more southern races, and the name of the god to whom the temple was dedicated points in the same direction; his name was Quetzalcoatl, — that is, the feathered snake. The religious conception on which the symbol of the feathered snake is based is so widely spread over American soil that we cannot at once assume it to have been borrowed from any similar neighbouring worship; the analogous development of the mythological conceptions of the American peoples would lead us to a complete explanation of this occurrence of identical symbols. However, in Cholula, and in the cult of the god Quetzalcoatl, we have to deal, not only with an observed similarity to the Kukulkan or Gukumatz of the Maya peoples, but we have also to consider the complete identity of the god, his mythology and his worship, which could not be established without some internal communication.

According to Mexican tradition, Quetzalcoatl came to the country in a boat, passing over the western ocean with a few companions;[1] he is said to have landed upon Mexican soil in the far north of the country, on the river Panuco. To the naked savages who then inhabited the land he was a marvellous apparition, a figure clothed in shining raiment, and wearing a beard, an appendage unusual among the natives. Quetzalcoatl soon taught them the arts of peace, in particular agriculture and weaving; he gave them writing to preserve his teaching, and the calendar to regulate his worship. After he had established a well-ordered State in the land where formerly only wandering huntsmen dwelt, he disappeared with the promise that he would again revisit his people. This legend in every particular coincides so exactly with the Maya legend of Kukulkan that we cannot doubt the one's being borrowed from the other. There is a further point to be considered. The custom of human sacrifice is a characteristic feature in Nahua worship; at the bottom of it was the religious belief that the offering to the god was sanctified by its sacrifice, and that to some extent transubstantiation into the divine essence took place. Consequently the sacrifice — often before its death — became an object of veneration. Thus, too, it was that the corpse was eaten, in order that everybody who tasted of it should assimilate a portion of the divine substance; and for this reason again the skin of the victim served as a sacred covering for the image of the god himself, or for his earthly representatives, the priests.

These ideas are entirely Nahuatlac, and are altogether wanting among the Maya of ancient times who had not been influenced by the Nahua; also among younger nations of the same origin, among whom the custom of human sacrifice was in restricted use, the particular Nahua adoptions of it are nowhere to be found. Quetzalcoatl, in Maya consciousness, has always been a divinity who not only objected to human sacrifice in his own worship, but entirely abhorred the characteristic Nahua use of the offering, and this at the time when it gained its highest importance and extent under the Aztec dominion. The worship of Quetzalcoatl was carried on in a closed temple-chamber with penance and discipline, but only with inoffensive victims: it formed a kind of secret worship in opposition to the bloody sacrifice openly made to Huitzilopochtli and Tezcatlipoca; and to it the last king of the Aztecs, Montezuma, resorted as soon as his own gods and their priests had proved helpless before the stranger who had come forth from the waters of the west, with his beard and his armour of gleaming brass.

[1] See section 5 of Plate opposite p. 226.

In one other place we find a wide district of Mexico thickly covered with the ruins of old buildings,—that is, on the eastern coast-line, north of Vera Cruz, in the district of the Totonacs. It is possible that these Nahua architects also had Maya neighbours upon their borders; these must have been the Huastecs, who had been driven northward far from the mass of the Maya people. But the ruins that have been found in their own district are very inadequate, and our knowledge of their history is extremely scanty; it would therefore be a bold conclusion to assign the existence of the numerous architectural remains in the district of the Totonacs to the influence of their civilisation. Moreover the position of the buildings is here of a different character from those in the Maya district. The terraced pyramid here, too, forms the foundation of that space which was consecrated to the worship of the gods, following the universal character of the pyramids in the Maya and Nahua territories. But the heavy flights of steps, and a wall running round the upper terrace, are a distinct divergence from the normal type; they excite particular attention, as they remind us of the strategical purposes so strongly marked in all the Totonac cities. Generally the Totonac pyramids do not seem to have been crowned with a massive temple of stone, and in this respect they have approached the Nahua type; but in the few cases where the upper platform is decorated with a stone temple, a coincidence with the style of the Central American architecture is apparent in the unusually heavy roof rising above a building which is low and narrow in comparison with the main mass of the erection; the impression of heaviness thus given is only dispelled by the prominent façade which crowns the whole.

We should be the better able to decide how far the Nahua peoples succeeded in independently developing their highest civilisation and their artistic style after the Spanish arrival, if more extensive ruins had been left of those great towns which the astonishment of the conquerors has painted for us in such brilliant colours, at the time when a systematic examination of them was at length undertaken. The few antiquities that have been found upon these ancient centres of progress are so little consonant with the glowing descriptions of the conquistadors, that we must either suppose their surprise led them into considerable exaggeration, or we must assume that a large portion of the ornamental buildings was constructed of far more perishable material than was the case elsewhere.

Of the ruined sites of pure Nahuatlac origin, only two are worth particular consideration; namely, Teotihuacan and Xochicalco. Teotihuacan is a striking example, showing us how short was the historical recollection of the different Nahua royal families in spite of all the long genealogies that have been put forward. This town had already become mythical to the generation with which the conquerors came into contact, and yet for centuries it had been the religious centre and the sacred town for the Nahua races of the table-land of Anahuac, even as Mecca is for the Mohammedans or Jerusalem for the Christians. Our historical sources give us no information as to whether it played any part in politics under the most ancient Chichimec dominion; but they ascribe its foundation to the remotest antiquity; they put it forward consistently and invariably as the holiest and most venerated of temples, with the most influential priesthood. The question may be left undecided as to whether the modern designations of the most important pyramids of Teotihuacan—as "the hill of the sun," "the hill of the moon," etc.—have been justified by archæological inquiry; at any rate the name "path of the dead" is correct for the long range of little hills which stretches out behind the larger pyramids. Teotihuacan was, like Mitla, not only a place of pilgrimage for the living, but also a sacred place, in which to be buried was to be sure of salvation. Even in the most recent times the neighbourhood of the ruins has been an inexhaustible hunting-ground for the little pots and clay figures which formed the offerings with which the dead were usually committed to the earth. Moreover the other names above mentioned are in entire accord with the ancient Nahua civilisation.

The Nahua religion was founded upon those startling manifestations of nature which have struck the imagination of men in every part of the world. Nature-worship, under later influences, was wholly changed to an anthropomorphic realisation of religious conceptions, and by degrees many accessory notions fastened themselves around individual divinities. Yet almost without exception the gods of the different Nahuatlac nations can be traced back to particular phenomena of nature. Even Huitzilopochtli, the fearful war-god of the Aztecs, whose worship was accompanied by a shedding of human blood that has never been equalled elsewhere, originally sprang from an entirely inoffensive conception of nature. He is the incarnation of the sun's beneficent power, which in the early spring begins a fruitful reign, and in the autumn fades away and dies before the burning heat and the drying winds. Legend tells of his miraculous procreation, of his battle with the hostile twins, and of his death, proceeding in exactly the same manner as among the most different peoples in the Old and New Worlds. The sacred symbol of Huitzilopochtli is the Colibri, the feathers of which decorated the god's left leg, according to the legend, to remind him of the fact that his mother Coatlicuë received him in the form of a bunch of feathers which she carried unwittingly in her bosom. To the Mexican highlands, however, the Colibri is what the swallow is to the temperate zones, — the messenger who announces that nature again awakes from her winter sleep. In autumn the image of the god was every year destroyed by a priest of another godhead by shooting at it with an arrow to the accompaniment of particular religious ceremonies; this was the end of the good part of the year, the return of which was celebrated in the spring as the return of Huitzilopochtli. Under the form of the Colibri he had also been the guide of the Aztecs on their migrations; he had continually called them on with his cry, "Tiui, tiui!" until they had come to the seat of their power. Here was the first impulse to anthropomorphism; for along with the bird, the image of the god and his representatives, the priests, had accompanied the people. These conceptions then became so confused that the belief finally arose that Huitzilopochtli was only a casual historical personality who had been exalted to a height of a racial god. Human sacrifices played an essential part in all Nahuatlac worship; but the great extent to which they were carried in the Aztec worship of Huitzilopochtli arose from the unusually ferocious disposition of the Nahua national character.

The real godhead of the Nahua people is Tezcatlipocá. He is much more easily recognisable as an incarnation of the sun, and this not in its beneficial character as the bringer of all good, of light and warmth and fruitfulness, but also in its dangerous and destructive power, as hot drought and devouring fire. In its first character Tezcatlipocá was no doubt originally to the Nahua that which Kukulkan-Quetzalcoatl had been to the Maya people, — the father of civilisation and culture. But when in the course of time the worship of the feathered snake as Quetzalcoatl made its way among the Nahua, then the legend began to be formed of the enmity between these two divinities; with a recollection of the previous power of Tezcatlipocá, the legend certainly ends with a victory of this god over the foreign intruder, but shows him more and more in the light of a hostile, cruel god, while all the ideas concerning beneficent kindly powers group themselves around Quetzalcoatl, notwithstanding his defeat.

The numerous gods of the beneficent powers of nature and of the fruitful soil are a peculiarity of the Nahua religion. On the one hand they show the important influence of animism on the conceptions of Nahua mythology; upon the other hand they make it evident how important was the part that agriculture played in the life of these peoples at the time when their conceptions of the gods were coming into existence. In this there is matter for surprise, inasmuch as in later historical times we meet with individual Nahua races upon a somewhat lower plane of civilisation. A confusion of the divinities of different races had unmistakably taken place in a large portion of their mythology as it existed at the time of the Spanish conquest and has come down to us. Every people that rose to an important position in this civilisation contributed its own national divinities to the common stock of conceptions; in worship and legend it created for them an important position, but side by side with their worship it worshipped and preserved all the more ancient deities. This is the simplest mode of explaining the extraordinary number of the gods in the Aztec Olympus which the ancient historians have also described with expressions of astonishment.

After the power of the sun, which warms the earth and makes it fruitful and flourishing, the most important element of the Mexican highland climate was the rain. The success of every crop depended entirely upon the opportuneness and the sufficiency of this heavenly gift. The old historical sculptures of the different Nahua races of the East often describe the pregnant effects upon the general life of the people consequent on years of drought. Hence we need not be surprised if the gods of water, of moisture, and of the clouds that pour forth rain, take an important place in the national worship. There are but few divinities of which we have so many and such extensive sculptures as of Tlaloc, the god of rain. He was depicted in a peculiar position, semi-recumbent, with the upper part of the body raised upon the elbows, and the knees half drawn up, perhaps with the intention of symbolising the fructifying influence of moisture upon the earth. By his side there was also a goddess with similar essential characteristics; as a symbol of fruitfulness she had presented him with numerous children.

In addition, the fruitfulness of the soil was represented by a large number of independent divinities, for the most part of the female sex. Coatlicue, who had brought up Huitzilopochtli, as being the mother of the Colibri, was the goddess of flowers and fruit. The legend of the Aztec goddess of the fruitful corn-land, Centeotl, was especially detailed. In the narrower sense she represents (and to a larger extent than Xilonen, who appears as her daughter) the maize, the staple food of the Americans, the yellow colour of which was sacred to her. The fact that the maize plays an important part in the hieroglyphic writing of both the Maya and the Nahua testifies to the importance of this grain in the domestic economy of ancient America. As the goddess of fruitfulness, Centeotl is also the protector of women in childbirth; in spite of this her worship was accompanied with far more human sacrifices than were customary for all the remaining Nahua divinities. The idea which runs throughout the Aztec sacrifice — namely that the victim, even before his death, by being dedicated to the god, becomes a part of the god and is one with him — is especially to be recognised in her worship; in this the numerous female victims received a share in the reverence paid to the goddess in a complicated ceremonial which took place before their death.

The god of death has already appeared among the Zapotecs; his sacred town, Yopaa (or Yapooh), became famous under its Mexican title, Mitla. Mitla is a popular reduction of the form Mictlan, and is at once the name both of the god of death and of his kingdom. He also is accompanied by a female goddess, easily to be recognised in the pictorial representations of Mitla by the invariable death-mask with its prominent row of teeth. As in the case of most peoples the conception of death is connected with the ideas of the north and of darkness. His kingdom is situated in everlasting darkness within the earth; his worship was carried on by the priests at night, clothed in black or in dark-coloured raiment.

According to Aztec ideas the kingdom of death was not the inevitable end of all life. The common herd — that is, everybody who had not been able during his life upon earth to make good his claim to a better lot — found their way to Mictlan sooner or later. It was not, however, as in the Christian hell, a life of endless torture which was there prepared for the departed. The journey was certainly long and surrounded with every kind of danger; for this reason they never forgot to bury food, drink, and all kinds of amulets — especially strips of aloe paper — together with the corpse; but of the final fate of the dead man, who passed after all his journeyings into the ninth division of the lower world, the Mexicans themselves could give no adequate account. Far different was the fate of those who, according to the conceptions of these peoples, had shown particular merits in life or death. All the offerings brought to the gods entered, as we know, into immediate and close connection with the godhead; this connection was naturally continued in the future life, where such victims shared in all the joys of heaven, in the service and the company of their gods. The nature of these pleasures has been fully detailed for us in the case of those who entered into connection with Tlaloc. They went up to the summits of the highest mountains the abode of the clouds, where a splendid garden awaited them, in which all the waters of the world had their source and cooled and refreshed the whole neighbourhood. There they lived among everlasting feasts and games, and could even descend again to the earth upon the most important festival of their gods in order to be witnesses of his honour. There came into the kingdom of Tlaloc not only those who were sacrificed to him, but also all those who were drowned or struck by lightning. The manner of their death was a sign that the god loved them and took them to himself. The 'highest heaven (for the heaven also rose in nine divisions above the earth) was that of the Sun and his incarnations Huitzilopochtli, Tezcatlipoca, and Quetzalcoatl. Hither came the souls of the kings and the mighty, of the priests and the nobles, who had been able during their earthly life to approach more nearly to the gods than common men. But above all, the souls of those went to the Sun who had fallen in battle, and by these means many were able to lay claim to the heaven from which they would have been naturally excluded. Hither, too, came all those who had been sacrificed to the sun-gods as prisoners of war or had fallen in religious struggles; and this conviction of the meritorious nature of death in battle certainly contributed not a little, as among the Mohammedans, to nourish and maintain the warlike spirit of these peoples. Finally there also came to the Sun the souls of all women who had died in childbirth. There they all carried on a life of unending pleasure; with song and dance they accompanied the Sun on his course; and when he sank in the west, in holy sleep they renewed their strength to begin their work anew upon the morrow.

As we see, the religion of the Nahua peoples was by no means without its mild and kindly side. Their peculiar conception of the consubstantiation of the victim with the divinity deprived human sacrifice of much of its native horror, and the desire to win a life of everlasting joy induced many to offer themselves as willing victims to the god. The continued practice of cannibalism rested upon a similar conception: by tasting the victim, which had become to some extent divine, the eater of it also shared in the godhead; similarly, with certain ceremonies, an image of the god which was not offered in sacrifice, but formed of eatable material, was broken and consumed by the worshippers. The greater refinement of manners which the advance of civilised development brought to many of the Nahua races may also have had a share in opposing the horrible human sacrifices. We hear of several rulers who were averse to these celebrations: and the wide extension of the bloodless worship of Quetzalcoatl among the Nahua shows also that religious development was moving in a direction unfavourable to the continuance of human sacrifice. The Spaniards at the conquest certainly found that these horrors prevailed to an appalling extent, but this is to be ascribed to the influence of the Aztecs, who exercised an undisputed dominion over Central America at the beginning of the sixteenth century.

When the Aztecs first invaded the particular district of the Nahua peoples, they had but little civilisation, but were a race of bold warriors of great physical development: in the district of the lakes of Chalco, Tezcuco, and Zumpango they found other races springing from the same stock, who had developed a highly cultured civilisation as a result of centuries of residence. Here, as everywhere, civilised progress had not made these races either stronger or more capable of resistance; and the attacking Aztecs, though of similar origin to the other nations, saw in their refinement a falling away from the old customs,—a degeneration. Their consciousness of their superiority, the success that invariably attended their efforts, were to them proofs of the good will of the gods, who preferred to be worshipped in the old fierce manner rather than with the modern milder cult; and by degrees this idea tended more and more to bring back the dreadful bloody form of worship. The Aztec power extended over countries containing the most different peoples, who had been more or less subjugated: from these their religious ideas led them to exact that awful tribute which made them hated by every nation that was dependent on them. These peculiar circumstances were neither of long historical duration nor very widely spread, but have none the less greatly contributed to throw back our knowledge of the preceding history of the Central American district, and to spread abroad false ideas concerning it. The chief task, at the moment, for Mexican archæology, is to distinguish what is transitory and isolated from what is characteristic and universal.

The name Teotihuacan, representing the company of the Nahua gods, leads us naturally to the consideration of their religious conceptions; similarly the name Xochicalco, the last of the ruined towns that we need mention, affords an excellent opportunity for some remarks upon Nahua art. In their general character the ruins of Xochicalco are very similar to those in the district of the Totonacs. Spurs running out into the plain from the main mountain range have been made defensible by stonework and trenches on every side; and these works of art are erected in terrace fashion over a considerable extent of the mountain side. In the immediate neighbourhood of these there seems to have been an ancient settlement, a village or a town; but the fortified space itself contained only temples and palaces and the dwellings of the garrison, and served as a refuge for the inhabitants of the place in time of danger. Within the fortifications, though not on the summit of the hill, stands the temple pyramid which certainly gave the name to the place; for Xochicalco means " in the house of flowers." There stood a house of flowers, the temple of the flower goddess, Xochiquetzal. In spite of the destruction to which it has been subjected in the course of centuries, this building is still one of the finest that has been discovered upon American soil. Ancient chronicles would have us believe that at the time of its completion the temple pyramid of Xochicalco had five or more stories; examinations of the position have proved that it never had more than one, and that the story which can now be seen. Upon this, following the sloping rise of the pyramid, a building without a roof, running round three sides of the pyramid, but open in front, contained a sacred temple space, but was not itself a properly enclosed temple. This particular form of building is certainly connected with the worship of the Nahua peoples, whose religious ceremonies were almost entirely carried on under the open heaven and in the full light of day.

The special importance of the building consists in the rich plastic decoration with which all the external walls both of the pyramid and the circular building were entirely covered. The bodies of great snakes, depicted in bas-relief, wind over the whole building; and among their coils pictures and hieroglyphs are carved in stone, the artistic execution of which is inferior to none of the monumental work known to us in Central America.[1] At any rate this is the only memorial of a district apparently inhabited by Nahua people which displays plastic decoration of a richness and uniformity of execution equalled only by the work which is found upon the temples of the Maya peoples. This fact and the important part which was played in the sculptures of Xochicalco by the well-known feathered snake of Maya buildings has led to the conclusion that it may belong to the style of the art of Palenque. But the temple pyramid bears the evidence of its Nahuatlac origin, with unmistakable clearness, in the numerous calendar dates carved between the sculptures, dates which belong to the Nahuatlac script and to none other. Unfortunately the different dates do not permit us accurately to fix any point of time for the erection of the pyramid. The high development of the sculptor's art, as shown in the reliefs, would be evidence against the remote antiquity of the monument. On the other hand particular forms of the calendar signs do not permit us to connect the ruins of Xochicalco with the last stage of Nahua history, — the Aztec dominion; moreover the place seems to have been destroyed by internal Mexican war, and not by the Spaniards.

---
[1] See Plate at p. 264.

It was within the boundaries of the civilisation above described that the history of the Nahua peoples was developed. If we would pass a right judgment upon this history, we must, above all things, keep one point in view,— the extreme narrowness of the conditions within which the early ancient history of Mexico was brought to a close. The limits of the older historical traditions nowhere overpass the mountain range which on almost every side surrounds the valley of Mexico proper; places like Tula and Tulancingo, only a few miles distant from the central point of Nahua history, the lake of Tezcuco, are lost in avenues of distance. The main portions of those peoples who spoke the Nahua language were entirely unknown to this tradition; in the last century, at the time when the Aztec warlike expeditions penetrated into more remote districts, one or two names of individual kings are mentioned. The district in which the ancient Mexican history ran its course according to tradition is little more than 10,000 square kilometres in area; that is, only two thirds as large as the kingdom of Saxony. Separated by a distance of but a few miles were here situated the capitals of all the States which succeeded to the empire of the district of Mexican civilisation during the last century of the ancient régime, and it is these towns which the Spanish historians describe as the seat of so many empires and dominions.

According to tradition the oldest inhabitants of Anahuac are the Olmecs (or Ulmecs) and the Xicalancs. These apparently were regarded as the giant people the conquest of whom cleared the way for the settlements of the Nahua race; more often, however, the Olmecs and Xicalancs are considered as the conquerors of the giants, and as the founders of the oldest sacred towns Teotihuacan and Cholula. That these names were invariably used to designate the Nahua peoples at large is proved by the fact that their names are always to be found in that district whither the seven races were led who left their common home, the seven caves of Chicomoztoc, in order to seek the promised land. The Olmecs are said to have been accompanied on their migrations by the Zapotecs and Mixtecs; to these are occasionally added the Totonacs, and even the Huastecs, who spoke a Maya dialect; by this we may understand that the settlement of the Olmecs in Anahuac was supposed to be contemporaneous with the settlement of the other people of the same race who did not form the focus of the Nahua interests; that is, the people with whom we meet as intruding upon and shattering the Maya civilisation. Beyond this, tradition has nothing to say of the Olmecs and Xicalancs; no royal name, no event, was preserved in their history. But the fact that they were closely connected with the seat of the highest and most ancient priestly knowledge shows that we must not think of them as a rude hunting tribe, but that their arrival marked an epoch of civilisation for the highland of Anahuac.

The next group of Nahua races that found their way into Anahuac and became of historical importance were the Chichimecs. The ancient historians employed this name in a double sense. In its general meaning it denotes the whole group of the later Nahua people; in this sense our historical sources speak of the Teo Chichimecs (the inhabitants of the district of Tlazcala), the Toltec Chichimecs, the Colhua Chichimecs, and the Aztec Chichimecs. In this case the name means neither more nor less than those peoples who were of true Nahuac origin and belonged to a great group of Nahua-speaking races; these

RUINS OF THE PYRAMID-STEPS OF XOCHICALCO IN THE DISTRICT OF
CHOLULA

(After Penafiel, "Monuments of Ancient Mexican Art")

# EXPLANATION OF THE FOREGOING PICTURE

THE ruins of Xochicalco (Xochicalli = House of Flowers), not far from Cuernavaca, in the district of Tlalhuica, are the remains of an extensive fortified position, the central point of which is marked by the temple-pyramid. The first discoverers gave it an original height of five stories; but complete investigation has shown that the pyramid consisted only of a foundation, and of a temple which rose thereon and was perhaps unroofed; its sloping outer walls giving the appearance of a second pyramid. The whole building was overlaid with large, highly sculptured plates of trachyte, while the space within was filled with rubble. On the western side a flight of steps, now largely ruined, led up to the temple entrance; moreover the entire exterior of the building was adorned with rich decorative work which covered the sloping walls of the two pyramidal erections, and also the horizontal frieze which lay between them. The bas-reliefs in the lower story depict feathered snakes symmetrically arranged; between their coils pictorial designs alternate with dates. The frieze was divided into single panels, in which can still be made out figures repeated one after another, with varied dates and symbols. Similar to these, but less sharply divided, were the bas-reliefs of the upper story, now much ruined. All the designs were covered with bright red colour. From the bas-reliefs and other discoveries in the neighbourhood it is concluded that the pyramids were a shrine of Xochiquetzal, the goddess of the flowering, fruitful earth.

races were called savages (this is the sense of the word) when other related races had already undergone the influence of civilisation and so had grown out of their ancient national characteristics. These changes took place under the influence of a foreign nationality (that of the Maya, as we already know): hence the name Chichimec gained the meaning of "unadulterated," "pure," and in this sense it was a term applied to all the Nahua peoples who could claim purity of origin. We learn that no individual Nahua race was originally called by this name, from the fact that the Teo Chichimecs, the Toltecs, the Colhua, the Aztecs, but never the Chichimecs are mentioned as having come among the seven races from the caves of Chicomoztoc. In spite of this, in the course of time, and as a result of long traditional transmission, the name Chichimec came to be the designation of a race, or, more properly, of a certain body politic. For a time this body must have played an important part among the peoples of Anahuac; we have mention of kings of the Toltecs, of the Colhuas, and of the Aztecs; but in the case of the Chichimecs an emperor is mentioned, and the title Chichimecatl Tecuhtli ("the lord of the Chichimecs' was the highest to which a governor of the different Nahua States could lay claim.

Eleven kings, including Chichimecatl, had apparently already reigned over this people when the Toltecs of Tula sent an embassy to the Chichimec court and offered the government of their country to the king's second son: there is here a vague recollection of some family connection between the Chichimecs and Toltecs. The first Chichimec prince who is said to have ruled after the fall of the Toltec kingdom — the king Xolotl — is said to have had a reign of nearly three hundred years. The artistically conceived system of ancient Mexican chronology has been traced far into the past by native writers who were influenced by Christianity, and for this reason they went back only far enough to make the chronologies of the Old and New Worlds coincide, and to connect their people with the confusion of tongues at the tower of Babel. The chronologies proposed for the history of the old kingdoms have no scientific value whatever. The tradition of numerous peoples of Anahuac preserved the legend of a long row of kings or princes who are said to have ruled the land; and in many cases these genealogies are connected with the gods, or include such gods in the genealogical tree. Certain authors like Ixtlilxochitl, and probably many before him of whose writings he availed himself, arranged a number of such dynasties in a vertical line instead of in parallel columns, however, by their means we have been able to trace back Mexican history to the beginning of the Christian era, or even farther.

The kingdom of Toltec civilisation is one of the unhistoric legends which originated in the manner we have described; its legendary source is betrayed by the fact that its kings constantly bear the names of gods, and that the town Tollan (Tula) from which the name Toltec is supposed to have been derived, can scarcely have been the capital of a Toltec kingdom. In the Toltec legend is reflected a recollection of the historical importance of a State the central point of which was Culhuacan. This, however, cannot be traced back into those remote times in which the Toltec kingdom has been placed, but belongs to a historical period: at that time a large number of other Chichimec States, together with Tezuco, had a flourishing existence, and then it was that the youngest branch of the Nahua race, the Aztec, began to attract attention to itself. Such knowledge as has come

down to us of the ancient kingdom — extending over a period from the sixth
century, in which tradition places its beginnings, up to the thirteenth century, in
which its historical period begins — is of importance in only this respect : it shows
us in abstract form, little influenced by the realities of the time, those conceptions
and ideas which the Nahua people themselves held concerning their common
civic life.    Thus far the legends throw light on the internal history of the race,
both in ancient and in more modern times.

The tradition of the oldest times, speaking, as it does, of numerous reigning
deities, would of itself show us the important influence of the priestly caste among
the older Nahua races, even if we had no examples from historical times of the
energy and tenacity with which the priests struggled against the inevitable inroads
of a secular power.    The gods, partly under their own sacred names, and sometimes appearing as princes who ruled for centuries and were canonised after their
death, are the constant guides of the Nahua races on their migrations, or laid the
foundation of particular prosperity and unusual growth during their periods of
settled existence : this fact proves that theocracy and a rule of priests under the
special protection of Heaven was a typical characteristic among the Nahua, and
also among the Maya peoples, for a long period of their development.    It was at
this time that most of the great temple pyramids were founded; and their foundation under such a government explains to us why tradition has considered them,
for the most part, anterior to the founding of a secular State, or has ascribed them
to some earlier people.    As long as nations of a common origin and similar religious conceptions were in exclusive contact with one another, so long were the
priests able to keep the peace without great difficulty.    There was certainly rivalry
among the priests of divinities belonging to different races, and this now and then
led to those animosities which the legend represents as the battles of the gods
among themselves; at the same time peace and prosperity were well-nigh universal and gave every necessary encouragement to a rapidly spreading civilisation.

But the spread of this civilisation threatened the priestly States with a twofold
danger.    Among their subjects there were to be found now and then certain
people outside of the sacerdotal caste, who realised the true state of affairs and
objected to a monopoly of profit on the part of the priests.    Moreover increasing
prosperity invited attacks from less civilised neighbours, with which the priestly
power alone could not cope.    Thus there grew up, side by side with the priests,
the class of " caciques," the military power.    The importance of this class increased
in proportion to the growth of danger from without, and to the value of their
services in repelling it, until at length the military leaders recognised that they
were indispensable and declined to surrender to the priests that power which they
had with difficulty acquired.    Civilisation thus enters upon a fresh struggle, — that
of the secular and religious powers. · At the outset the priestly caste often succeeded in frightening their superstitious people with threats of divine wrath;
every defeat in battle, every failure of the crops, every devastating plague, enabled
them for a time to keep the balance of power between the secular and the religious
forces.    Here we have the cause of those repeated long interregnums with which
we meet at the beginnings of almost every dynasty.    In many cases the secular
power attempted to win over the religious power and to reconcile it to the new
state of things by means of liberal concessions; but the natural result everywhere
came to pass.    The military class, when once they had gained the upper hand,

concentrated the power more and more in themselves, declined to resign it in times of peace, and by degrees created a military nobility which acted as a counterpoise to the priestly power and invariably led to the establishment of a dynasty in which succession was regulated either by election or by inheritance.

Among the related peoples these changes were accomplished in a gradual and uniform manner. The mere fact that one little race had shaken off the priestly yoke and chosen a king for itself demanded a similar development on the part of its neighbours, and at an early period the caciques became connected by a community of interest with the dynasty, both in their political and family relations. Only when their common enemy, the priestly caste, had finally been forced into a secondary position, did the desire for empire on the part of the secular rulers become obvious. This ambition led to the wars of conquest among the petty princes who from time to time rose from one or other of the nations of Anahuac to be a dominant power. The nations of Mexico were incompetent to organise a large empire, and, like almost all the peoples of the New World, remained thus divided up until the Spanish arrival. Even the greatest monarchs exercised direct lordship over only the immediate neighbourhood of their residences. The outlying districts, even when closely connected with the central State, were almost invariably ruled by feudal princes, whose fidelity was not proof against many external temptations. If the ruling monarch was strong enough to subdue his disobedient vassals, then his kingdom not only extended over his own territories, but included those lying without it; but, the larger the number of these subject kings, the greater became the danger that this loosely constructed political organisation might entirely collapse. As a matter of fact it is in this fashion that one empire after another, Chichimec, Colhua, and Tezcucan, came into existence and fell to pieces again; and if the Spaniards at the beginning of the sixteenth century had not brought the whole system to an end, the Aztec empire would undoubtedly have suffered a like fate.

Naturally under these circumstances the yoke of the central government was generally light. When a disobedient vassal was subdued, or when the king with his army passed through the subject provinces to make fresh conquests, then his hand was heavy upon the land, and the life and property of his people were at his absolute disposal. But the contributions which in time of peace were sent up to the seat of power in acknowledgment of subjection were in few cases more than nominal gifts, and were generally only a half-voluntary tribute, rather symbolic than real. So easy was this rule that the lords of neighbouring and also of more distant districts occasionally preferred to recognise the dominion of some other prince, and to pay him a voluntary tribute, in order to assure themselves against the possibility of his forces being turned against themselves. This is the explanation of those kingdoms, nominally of large extent, being so often overthrown by a mere handful of people in a very short space of time. For as soon as the prestige of the king, which was founded more or less upon the imagination of his people, had been shattered, then all who had paid him tribute immediately shook off his feeble yoke and declared themselves independent until a new potentate from another race succeeded in making himself a terror in the land.

Although numbers of princely houses imagined, as we have said, that they could trace their genealogy uninterruptedly through six or seven centuries, yet it is only at the beginning of the twelfth century that history begins. At that time a number of so-called kingdoms were already in existence in Anahuac; among these the Chichimec kingdom, with its capital Tenayocan, on the west side of the lake of Tezcuco, held the leading position. The next in importance was the kingdom of Acolhua, with its capital Culhuacan, lying to the north of the lake of Chalco; it had apparently inherited the Toltec civilisation and was the chief centre of the culture of the time. Its ruling dynasty traced its origin to Topiltzin, the last Toltec king. In the middle of the century this line of kings had to struggle again an unexpected attack from the Chichimec power, and to make way for a dynasty from that race, which paid a nominal allegiance to the lords of Tenayocan. Atzcaputzalco, Coatlichan, and Xaltocan are named as being other kingdoms under the protection of the one we have mentioned; all these places are to be found in the immediate neighbourhood of the central lakes. Moreover the States of Tlazatlan, Zacatlan, and Tenamitec are also named as being countries which were subject to the authority of the Chichimec dynasty, so that this Chichimec power seems to have extended nearly over the whole valley of Mexico. All these principalities had made long strides in civilisation, an advance generally attributed by the chroniclers to Toltec influences.

The invasion of fresh Nahua races still living in unreclaimed savagery threatened this civilisation with unmistakable dangers toward the end of the century. The Tecpanecs and Chalca obviously were sprung from Chicomoztoc,—"the seven caves"; the consciousness of their relationship with the Nahua races already settled in the valley of Mexico had never been lost, and consequently Tollan also appears as one of the resting-places of their migration. Then they appear in Anahuac proper, at Chapultepec, but in spite of their considerable numbers they do not seem to have pressed the Chichimecs either very long or very hardly. A short time later they formed a political community completely organised in the most southerly portion of the lake district, and here the Chalca States attained an importance in the next century before which the fame of the Chichimecs and of Acolhua began to pale.

At that time also the youngest of the Nahua races — the Aztecs — had appeared in the lake district; their own traditions relate that they had been the last to leave the "seven caves," and that their migrations had lasted longer and their wanderings been more extensive than those of the other races related to them. At that time they were entirely under the government of their priests, who carried the image of their national god, Huitzilopochtli, upon a litter before them, and issued their orders as commands from Heaven. The race cannot have been numerous when it first obtained permission from the Chichimec lords to make a settlement in Chapultepec, but the addition of numerous related tribes, and the acquisition of friendly contingents from neighbouring towns, increased their importance every year, and their warlike prowess began to make them famous — even notorious – in the unending wars of the different dynasties, in which they played a considerable part as allies of one or the other party. Up to this point they had remained true to their old institutions; in spite of all the chances of war, and the changes which it brought, the priests of Huitzilopochtli continued to hold the power. It was then, apparently, that this god began to undergo a metamorphosis from the character of sun-god to that of war-god. But finally even the Aztecs could not resist the influence exercised upon them by the exigencies of their position and the example of neighbouring races; and in spite of the vigorous objections of the priesthood they chose their first secular monarch, Huitzilihuitl, about the year 1250. Like the princes of the neighbouring States he had a king's title and exercised a king's power within his own race, but he was not successful in founding an Aztec dynasty. He had entered into an alliance with the cacique of Zumpanco against the Tecpanees of Xaltocan, had started upon a campaign, but had only succeeded in exciting the opposition of the other Tecpanec princes to his Aztecs. As he declined to pay tribute to the Tecpanecatl Tecuhtli, the ruling monarch of the race who resided in Atzcaputzalco, he was attacked on every side by the subjects and the allies of the Tecpanees, and after numerous losses and a vain attempt to summon to his aid the Chichimec king of Tezcuco, he was obliged to abdicate. The priestly caste again obtained the power, and succeeded in making peace with their neighbours, though at the sacrifice of that independence which Huitzilihuitl had defended.

The ruling powers of Anahuac had meanwhile become more or less weakened; the Chichimec ruler, Tlotzin Pochotl, and his successor, Quinantzin, did not succeed in keeping their territory intact. Their inclinations were rather toward arts of peace than feats of war. They had turned their attention chiefly toward the decoration of their capitals, and had neglected to protect their boundaries, so that the reins of power fell from their hands.

The ties which bound the subject kings of Atzcaputzalco, Xaltocan, and other States, to the central government, grew looser and looser. Owing to the circumstances under which the Aztecs appear among these States, scarcely any traces are left of a defensive alliance between the Tecpanec States and the kingdom of the Chichimees. The direction which their development took was largely influenced by the change of settlement from Tenayocan to Tezcuco under Quinantzin. Tezcuco, under the preceding government, had become a dangerous rival of the old capital, while the Chichimec princes were devoting their attention to the decoration and adornment of their palaces and gardens. The government of the important province of Tezcuco fell into the hands of the presumptive successor of the emperor, Chichimecatl Tecuhtli. As governor, Quinantzin had already held a royal court in Tezcuco; while still in Tenayocan he had established his position as emperor, and had then entrusted the government of his present capital to another's hands and gone back to his chosen Tezcuco. In consequence of this change of capital from the western to the eastern side of the lake the whole Chichimec kingdom naturally gravitated in that direction.

At that time the boundaries of the Chichimec kingdom stretched far away over the valley to the east. Tlazcala, Huexotzinco, and other States upon the eastern table-land, were then governed by princes of Chichimec race. But as the kingdom gained ground in the east it became enfeebled on the west and abandoned the field to the Tecpanec States. The change of residence to Tezcuco did not entirely commend itself to all the Chichimees, and as Quinantzin could not rely on the fidelity of his satraps a great confederacy was soon formed against him, which was secretly fostered by the Tecpanees and tended to the separation of the whole of the western portion of the kingdom of Tezcuco. Once again a Chichimec State was formed about the ancient capital Tenayocan, in which a relation of Quinantzin usurped the title of Chichimecatl Tecuhtli. The emperor himself seemed little disturbed at this occurrence; he made sure his power in the east, and on the west he allowed things to take their course, as he was not strong enough to control them. The rival State was, however, of no long duration; within a short time the opposition king was attacked by the Tecpanecs, who had succeeded in bringing the Aztecs to their help. After the fall of Tenayocan the Chichimec power was firmly established in the western districts. This state of affairs soon after received the sanction of an international confederacy which was formed between the Tecpanec king of Atzcaputzalco, as emperor of all the Tecpanec States, and Quinantzin. To Quinantzin the Tecpanec king yielded the predominant position of Chichimecatl Tecuhtli, but by thus cleverly renouncing the appearance of power he gained a signal advantage in reality, for Quinantzin in return admitted all his claims to the ancient territory of the Chichimecs and confirmed him in their undisputed possession.

These battles had so entirely broken up and confounded every element in the Nahuatlac nationality that the new kingdoms were founded on a territorial far more than on a national basis. Thus we find Tezcuco the capital of districts that had been named by the different Nahua races. Tecpanecs, Aztecs, Colhua contributed at least as much to their population as did the Chichimecs and the eastern races. The Aztecs were in the worst position; their habit of offering their services in war to the highest bidder, the wild ferocity with which they carried on their warfare, which had been the chief factor in forming their religion with its infamous sacrifices of human blood, made them the objects of universal hostility. The wars which ravaged the country on the north of the lake district at the end of the thirteenth or the beginning of the fourteenth century brought destruction upon their capital Chapultepec; and the Aztec race, like many another, was broken up and dispersed. Scattered companies of them entered again into the services of the neighbouring States as mercenaries, with the intention of gaining permission to form fresh settlements as a reward for their prowess in war. But only two races — the Mexica and the Tlatelulca — kept their lineage sufficiently pure in the following ages to have a clear remembrance of their origin, until their turn for rule also came in the course of time. They had, however, much ground for thankfulness to the prince of Colhuacan, who had offered a refuge for their wanderings in Tizaapan or in Iztacalco.

The Tecpanecs had gained the chief advantage from the troubles of these times. The western portion of the lake of Zumpango from the north, as far as Chalco on the south, had become their almost undisputed territory. The eastern portion belonged similarly to the kings of Tezcuco. But the weak point of all these American States — their inability to organise a government over a large extent of country — became apparent here also. Atzcaputzalco, as the early centre of the whole Tecpanec kingdom, for some time retained considerable importance, and for a number of years its kings bore the title of Tecpanecatl Tecuhtli. But imperceptibly, in the course of time, the centre of gravity of the political world shifted more and more toward the south. While the ancient Culhuacan again flourished next to Atzcaputzalco and Tenayocan, and quickly surpassed them both in importance, Chalco, Tenanco, and Amequemecan rose in the south as fresh centres of Tecpanec government. Circumstances threw the leadership into their hands when, a century later, a common enemy of all the States of the lake district appeared in the Mexica people. At the time of their greatest development the Tecpanec States are said to have been no fewer than twenty-five in number; many of these were closely bound together by ties of relationship. A feeling of close connection was certainly alive among them all, and this sentiment became the more vigorous when the very existence of the race was threatened. But in the meantime individual Tecpanec kings had been fighting as furiously among themselves as the princes of the Chichimec race under similar circumstances had fought and were continuing to fight with all other kings.

In the first half of his reign Quinantzin, the Chichimec emperor, was apparently indifferent to the loss of the western province of his kingdom; but he had not finally renounced his claims upon it. For the time being he had concentrated all his powers on strengthening the newly formed kingdom on the eastern table-land. When signs of insurrection became visible even there, he met them with an unusual display of energy, and was generally able to restore order. When this was done he again turned his attention to the province he had lost. His first attack was upon the prince of Xaltocan, whose kingdom, owing to its inaccessible situation, had never been made tributary to the Tecpanecs. The well-organised forces of the united kingdom of Tezcuco easily overcame all attempts at resistance on the part of the Xaltocans. After this rapid victory the Tecpanec emperor did not think it expedient to allow the possession of this loosely connected province to be entirely contingent upon the uncertain results of a war. With a view to strengthening this connection he offered peace and alliance to the Chichimecs, declared himself ready to recognise their claims to the dominion of the whole lake district, and to acknowledge their overlordship, which was in his case to be merely formal. Quinantzin was satisfied with this result. He allowed the Tecpanecs the possibility of pursuing their peaceful and statesmanlike projects while he exercised at least a nominal suzerainty over a district which was far wider than any that his forefathers had possessed. When he died, in the year 1305, no less than seventy subject kings were present at the magnificent ceremonies which attended his burial in Tezcuco; no less than seventy kings paid homage to Techotl, the youngest son of the deceased monarch, whom he had nominated as his successor, for the elder brothers had lost all claims to the throne by participation in an attempt at revolt.

The most remarkable feature of the government of Techotl is that he first in Central America attempted to introduce a general change in the organisation of the States which had hitherto been of a loose and wholly unstable character. Hitherto every subject king had reigned in his own province as free and unfettered as the Chichimecatl Tecuhtli himself had in his government of the central portion of the kingdom; so long as he paid the moderate tribute and in time of war offered no opposition to the passage of an army through his dominions, he might be sure that no heavier burdens would be laid upon him by his feudal lord. Quinantzin's reign had repeatedly displayed the serious dangers to the continuance of a united kingdom which were involved in such a state of affairs. The old king himself had, by sternly suppressing any attempt at insubordination, done much to increase the security of the political unity. Techotl energetically followed out these views. He contrived to gather most of the vassal kings together in Tezcuco, and to keep them in his immediate neighbourhood, under the honourable pretext of forming a council of state; their representatives, who ruled in their places, owed even greater allegiance to their feudal master. Moreover a new division of the country was arranged, the old racial boundaries were definitely abolished, the number of districts for the purposes of government was increased almost threefold, and thereby the danger that local insurrections might spread far and wide was largely diminished. Finally Techotl, by means of a number of ordinances that were binding throughout his realm, kindled a spirit of unity among his people.

All these arrangements could only have been valid for his dominions on the east of the lakes; the west, which was almost as closely united, though perhaps not so strictly organised, under the Tecpanec king Tezozomoc, was almost beyond the reach of any kind of aggression. The state of nominal vassalage which Quinantzin had established remained undisturbed under the rule of Techotl; but after an energetic and ambitious monarch in the person of Tezozomoc had ascended the Tecpanec throne the danger of rivalry between the Chichimec kingdom, now known as Acolhuacan, and the Tecpanec kingdom became gradually more threatening. It was under the son and successor of Techotl, the king Ixtlilxochitl that the storm broke. The satraps whose powers had been limited by Techotl's reforms, and who entertained for him an animosity not difficult to comprehend, made all kinds of excuses to avoid taking part in his funeral ceremonies. Their passive resistance was, on the whole, of little danger; more important, however, was the attitude of the Tecpanecatl Tecuhtli. Tezozomoc openly declined to recognise the suzerainty of the young Chichimec prince, and was unmistakably striving to throw off a yoke that had been sensibly relaxed. With the careless patience which for generations was a striking characteristic of the Chichimec rulers, Ixtlilxochitl bore with the equivocal behaviour of his most powerful vassal. On the other hand, however, he appeared to be firmly determined to settle his dubious relations with the Tecpanec king in the spirit of his father's reforms. Tezozomoc met this straightforward policy with craft and dissimulation of every kind. As soon as Ixtlilxochitl threatened to enforce his demands, Tezozomoc declared himself ready to fulfil all claims. But as soon as he had appeased him by a show of submission he again declined to fulfil the responsibilities he had accepted, under pretexts of the most trivial kind. It was a mistake fraught with most important consequences that Ixtlilxochitl permitted these intrigues to continue year by year. He shook the confidence of his own friends and allies, and gave his opponent time, not only to make proper preparations in every direction for a decisive conflict, but also to make allies of some of those vassals whose fidelity was weakening.

According to tradition, Tezozomoc, in three successive years, had sent a heavy tribute of raw cotton to Tezcuco, and had first requested, then required, and finally commanded that this tribute should be redelivered at Atzcaputzalco ready woven into stuff. Twice were his commands fulfilled; but the third time an embassy was returned to the effect that the Chichimec ruler had received the tribute with thanks, and would use it to arm his warriors, who were determined to punish their disobedient vassals. However, even then Ixtlilxochitl proceeded to wait for the attack of the Tecpanecs. Tezozomoc sent his army twice across the lake into the district of Tezcuco, but twice suffered a heavy defeat at the hands of adversaries whose numbers continually increased. In spite of all this he unconditionally rejected all the offers of the Tezcucan emperor to make peace on condition of recognising his superiority, and now openly advanced the claim that the title of Chichimecatl Tecuhtli belonged to him, in the first place, as being the direct successor of the founder of the Chichimec empire the king Xolotl. In spite of this he would undoubtedly have been defeated if Ixtlilxochitl could have made up his mind to follow up with vigour the advantages he had won. Repeated victories brought to his side many of the little kings who had hitherto remained neutral; and many of the allies of Tezozomoc were beginning to weaken in their fidelity. Thus when Ixtlilxochitl finally made his attack, he could easily collect a considerable army; and in the province of Tepotzotlan he won a brilliant victory against a hostile army of two hundred thousand men. It is difficult to understand how Ixtlilxochitl allowed himself to be again befooled by the cunning Tezozomoc. After a four months' siege the capital of Atzcaputzalco was incapable of offering further resistance. Tezozomoc agreed to an unconditional surrender and begged for pardon, appealing to the sentiment of kinship. Although he had been so many times deceived, Ixtlilxochitl was once again satisfied with mere promises. Without completing the work of conquest he withdrew his victorious army from the walls of his enemy's capital. This was a signal for a general collapse. Expectation of booty had brought certain waverers to his side to fight against the dreaded Tecpanecs; but they had no idea of exposing themselves to the revenge of Tezozomoc, who had been left in possession of his princely power, without themselves gaining any corresponding advantage.

An ominous stillness greeted the Chichimec emperor when he returned to his capital. Reports soon began to come in that Tezozomoc was making fresh preparations; and when he at last invited the king and his son, Nezahualcoyotl, to come to Chiuhnauhtlan to receive his oath of allegiance, the king no longer dared to trust himself in the traitor's hands. But his prudence came too late. When Tezozomoc perceived that his cunning plan had been laid bare, he hastened to Tezcuco by forced marches. While defending his capital, Ixtlilxochitl expiated the many mistakes of his life with his death. His son and heir, Nezahualcoyotl, with difficulty escaped the sentence of death which Tezozomoc, the newly crowned Chichimecatl Tecuhtli, passed upon him.

The fall of the Chichimec kingdom of Acolhuacan took place in the year 1419. We must, however, go back for a century to pick up the threads required for the understanding of its further development. We saw above[1] that the Mexica had been deprived of their refuge, Chapultepec, which they gained upon the change of the Chichimec capital to Tezcuco, and that it was with difficulty that they obtained from the Tecpanec ruler permission to settle elsewhere. The priests may have explained the preceding misfortunes as due to the wrath of the gods at the deposition of the theocracy and the choice of a king; at any rate they did not succeed in regaining the favour of Heaven for their people, though for a considerable time they had been in undisputed possession of power. While the Mexica were feared among all their neighbours for their plundering raids, they were constantly sought for as allies in times of war. But in times of peace the chief anxiety of their neighbours was to keep these restless strangers as far off as possible. They probably then paid the Tecpanec princes an unusually heavy tribute, and submitted to a certain measure of degradation, for their presence was barely tolerated, and they were sent about from one settlement to another.

Thereupon Tenoch, a priestly guide of the Mexica, once again exhorted them to migrate in the name of the god Huitzilopochtli, and led the scanty remnants of his people forth from their flourishing towns into the marshy coast-land on the west of the lake of Tezcuco. There, being warned by an omen from Heaven, he probably founded that town which in the course of time became the capital of

---

[1] *Ante*, p. 270.

the Aztec kingdom, Mexico-Tenochtitlan. Almost at the same time the related Tlatelulca withdrew from the tyrannical oppression of the Tecpanecs, and founded a second settlement in their immediate neighbourhood, Tlatelulco, which later on became a keen rival of Tenochtitlan, but was at last outstripped by and incorporated into the rival town. This migration to Tenochtitlan, which is placed in the year 1325, had not gained independence for the Mexicans. There, too, they found themselves within the dominion of a Tecpanec king, were obliged to obtain his permission to settle, and continued to owe him tribute. As they had fixed their capital at a distance and settled in an uncultivated district considered almost uninhabitable, they did, however by degrees, free themselves from his crushing tyranny.

In spite of its unfavourable situation the sister town developed with unexpected rapidity. The Mexicans were not the only people who were trying to escape from the dominion which had so long oppressed them. The reforms of the Tezcucan kings were felt to be as unsatisfactory as the tyranny of the Tecpanecs, and from both kingdoms numerous fugitives streamed into the barren wilderness and were readily received by the Aztecs of Tenochtitlan and Tlatelulco, eager to increase their strength. Thus these towns entirely lost their national character, and their population was composed of elements more and more diverse. The new arrivals, while they gladly fell in with the civilisation and the customs of the ancient inhabitants, exerted a refining influence upon the harshness of the Aztec customs, began to amalgamate the latter with their own institutions, and contributed in no small degree to soften the deep hatred with which the worshippers of Huitzilopochtli were regarded by all their neighbours.

From the outset Tlatelulco far outstripped the neighbouring Tenochtitlan. It was to Tlatelulco that the emigrants from the country of the Tecpanecs turned by preference, and we can easily understand that the relations of the ruling prince gained concessions more easily than outsiders. Thus it was a special mark of favour that the king of Atzcaputzalco agreed to set up a member of his family as a feudal prince in Tlatelulco, when the town was strong enough to demand a king of its own. On the other hand, numerous emigrants from Culhua turned their steps toward Tenochtitlan. The ancient Culhuacan capital had long ago obtained an almost independent position under the suzerainty of the Tecpanecs, and had repeatedly played an important part in the political history of the whole kingdom. Internal dissensions had broken out at last somewhere about the time when the Mexicans had founded their new capital. Numerous peoples of the Culhua who had been driven from their homes by that revolution made their way to Tenochtitlan, where within a short time their nationality was more strongly represented than was that of the Aztecs. The newly founded State owed to these circumstances its first important revolution. Mexico had been founded under the guidance of the priests; the name Tenochtitlan ("the town of Tenoch") was derived from the priestly guide who had led the people thither. But the traditions of centuries had made the Culhua accustomed to a monarchy; and though in religious matters they yielded to the custom of the country, in temporal affairs they declined to submit permanently to priestly government. Several members of the old royal family had come to Mexico among the fugitives. A compromise between the old inhabitants and the new colonists finally led to the choice of a king in the town of Tenoch, and the colonist element was sufficiently strong to bring about the election of Acamapichtli, the son of the king who bore the name of Culhuacan. After the fall of his father's dynasty he had fled to Tezcuco, and had there married a princess of Chichimec race, Ilancueitl. The connection of these dynasties has an extraordinarily strong influence upon all the later history of the Aztec kingdom of Tenochtitlan, and we have here the primary explanation of many facts that would be wholly unintelligible if we were to consider the town and the kingdom only from the Aztec point of view.

Mexico now remained, in spite of its friendly relations with Tezcuco, a Tecpanec vassal kingdom. Acamapichtli was obliged to obtain the confirmation of his election in Atzcaputzalco; it was in the service of Tezozomoc that the young king of Mexico made his early expeditions, which were so successful that he soon became highly respected among the vassal kings. The first campaign that he undertook in the Tecpanec service was in a southerly direction against the Chalca. These people, although related to the Tecpanees, had founded a kingdom on the southern shore of the lake Tezcuco, and on the lake which they called the lake of Chalco. This State had grown so large that it had split up into numerous vassal States. The Mexican chronicles of these wars describe them as the exploits of the Mexican kings only, but, until the fall of the Tecpanec kingdom, the kings of Mexico acted only as allies in these wars. Acamapichtli died in the year 1403, without having left any commands as to the succession; this fact probably marks the ascendancy of the priestly caste, which was once again making despairing efforts to restore the theocracy. But foreign elements, accustomed to a dynasty of monarchs, had already become too strong; though the priestly caste succeeded in making a succession dependent upon a new election, they could not prevent the choice from falling upon the son of Acamapichtli, Huitzilihuitl. We are particularly told of him, too, that he was obliged to obtain a confirmation of his election from the Tecpanec ruler. As subject to Tezozomoc he took part, in the following year, in the war which led to the overthrow of Ixtlilxochitl and of the Chichimec kingdom, although this king was closely connected with him by his marriage with his sister. Even allowing for the exaggerations of the chroniclers, we see very plainly that the kings of Mexico had become at that date most important vassals, from the fact that the king of Tlatelulco was commander-in-chief of Tezozomoc, and therefore also of the troops of Huitzilihuitl. These two kings did not live to the end of the wars. The ruler of Tlatelulco fell in one of the battles in which the Tezcucans were victorious; Huitzilihuitl died in 1417 in Tenochtitlan, the town which he had striven to extend without and to organise within. The result of his efforts was that his half-brother Chimalpopoca succeeded to the throne unopposed, representing his country upon the fall of Ixtlilxochitl.

We must suppose that it was only by force of circumstances that Huitzilihuitl and Chimalpopoca continued to fight on the side of Tezozomoc, for they had far greater advantages to expect from the success of Ixtlilxochitl, who was their friend and connection by marriage, than from the victory of their tyrannical emperor. They could not, however, have given the Tecpanec king the smallest grounds for suspicion. When this monarch proposed to increase and organise his kingdom by uniting with it the Tezcucan territories, the Mexican Chimalpopoca was regarded as one of the six subject kings, together with the rulers of Chalco Tlatelulco, Acolman, Coatlichan, and Huexotla. Tezozomoc's intention to make his kingdom more secure both within and without was only incompletely realised.

The conditions imposed upon the vassal kings were most oppressive; two thirds of the income from their provinces they were obliged to send to the king, retaining only a third for themselves; consequently they felt the unjust burden of this tribute far more than the honour of their promotion, and they expressed their dissatisfaction with no attempt at concealment. Moreover the newly crowned Chichimecatl Tecuhtli was not successful in obtaining recognition of his power throughout the kingdom of Ixtlilxochitl. The distant provinces on the north and east gladly seized the opportunity of refusing all payment of tribute and declaring their independence; and so strong was the hostility of the Tlazcalans against Tezozomoc that they received the exiled heir of Tezcuco, the prince Nezahualcoyotl, and offered him a secure refuge in their mountains until the intervention of the Mexican king of Chimalpopoca was successful in obtaining the repeal of the sentence of death that had been passed upon him. Tezozomoc was already advanced in years when he united the whole of Anahuac under his rule; he enjoyed the fruits of victory for eight more years before his death, and named his son Tejauh as his successor. But by this act he sowed the seeds of dissension in both his family and his kingdom.

Among all the sons of Tezozomoc, Maxtla, who had been appointed regent of Coyohuacan, was unquestionably the one who was most like his father, though he had not inherited his tenacity and his calmness in addition to his energy, bravery, and cunning. He took it as an insult that he should have to content himself with a second place in his father's kingdom, and the indifference of Tejauh enabled him, after a few months, to drive his brother from the throne, and to set himself up as Chichimecatl Tecuhtli, the king of the whole of Anahuac. This revolution was bloodless, but not so its results. The vassal kings had already borne the yoke of the aged Tezozomoc, the hero of a hundred fights, with the greatest impatience, and they considered it wholly intolerable to become the vassals of Maxtla, a young prince who in his own government in Coyohuacan had only succeeded in making himself thoroughly hated by his subjects and the neighbouring princes. Moreover it was by an act of violence against the legitimate ruler that he had thrust himself into his place. The kings of Mexico and Tlatelulco placed themselves at the head of the dissatisfied subjects; Tejauh had fled to Tenochtitlan, and so it was there arranged to surprise Maxtla at a festival, to overthrow him, and to reinstate Tejauh. But the conspiracy was betrayed, and the victim of it was not Maxtla, but Tejauh. Maxtla did not know with which of the Aztec kings he would have to deal first; without waiting, therefore, for further developments, he attacked with swift decision first the Mexicans and then Tlatelulco. So successful was he in each of these campaigns that both kings were overthrown and their cities and countries laid waste. They would perhaps have been destroyed for all time if revolt had not broken out in every part of Maxtla's kingdom against his rule of lawlessness and oppression.

The sympathies which a large portion of the eastern provinces felt for the ancient royal house were greatly strengthened by Maxtla's aggrandisement. As his hands were entirely tied by the wars we have previously mentioned, the Chichimec Nezahualcoyotl considered that the time had come to make some attempt to regain his father's kingdom. Tlazcala and Huexotzinco willingly placed their bands of warriors at his disposal. The feeble opposition with which he met in most of the provinces of his father's kingdom easily enabled him to reconquer a large part of it, but the capital, Tezcuco, offered an unconquerable resistance. Tezozomoc had here set up the prince of the old royal house as his represent.- tive. This prince knew very well that he had nothing to hope from the mercy of the lawful heir of the Chichimec kingdom if he was once defeated; he therefore made the most vigorous and ultimately successful efforts to maintain himself in the capital. But as long as he remained unsubdued the position of Neza- hualcoyotl was untenable, chiefly on account of the moral impression conveyed The campaigns that had been begun with such brilliant success ended in a manner not very far removed from defeat.

The first result of this half success was that a number of allies began to weaken in their fidelity, so that Nezahualcoyotl must have begun to fear that attack of Maxtla which he would certainly have to withstand. In this dangerous position the allies whose aid he most desired — the Aztecs — offered their help. After Maxtla had retired from Mexico they had at once re-established the empire. For a moment their choice had wavered between Itzcohuatl, the brother of Chimalpopoca, and his nephew Montezuma, who, though young, had already been crowned with the laurels of many victories. Fortunately their constitu- tion was wide enough for more than one vigorous man to make himself useful in it. The kingdom still bore unmistakable traces of its development from an aristocracy. Apart from the priesthood, still most influential, the king had by him two high temporal dignitaries, the Tlacatecatl ("lord of the armies") and the Tlacochcalcatl ("lord of the arrow"). Montezuma was called to the first of these two positions; he was able thereby to satisfy his ambition and also to expend his energy in acting with his royal uncle for the good of the realm. Recent events pointed sufficiently clearly to the direction his energies should take, for Maxtla unconditionally refused to recognise the choice that had been made, and was threatening a new attack. Thus a common enemy again brought the Mexicans and the Chichimecs together.

Montezuma went to Nezahualcoyotl and formed a confederacy with him against the Tecpanecs, which confederacy was at once joined by the newly chosen king of Tlatelulco. It was immediately agreed that they should carry the war as soon as possible into the enemy's country. Nezahualcoyotl openly announced his intention of re-establishing the old royal house in Tezcuco, thereby certainly estranging many friends who had hoped to gain their own independence if they stood by him in the hour of misfortune. But by entering into alliance with all the enemies of the Tecpanec tyrant he was fully compensated for the dangerous elements in his own situation. The campaign which he led in person along with the Mexicans was finally decisive after many victories on either side. With the support of the king of Tlacopan the allied Aztecs and Tezcucans gained a complete victory over the Tecpanecs. Atzcaputzalco was captured and de- stroyed, and Maxtla fell, either in battle or afterwards, beneath the blows of his opponents.

Those who had thought that with the fall of the Tecpanec tyranny freedom had come for Anahuac were cruelly undeceived. The more prudent of the dependents of Nezahualcoyotl had remained neutral in the decisive battles, and now they openly revolted. But the power of the allies increased no further: and the division of political power which had been arranged after the capture of Atzcaputzalco, at the festivities which took place in Tenochtitlan to celebrate the victory, was now immediately carried out. Anahuac was divided between the kings of Mexico and Tezcuco. Nezahualcoyotl, who had not even yet been able to effect an entrance into his ancient capital, obtained the whole of his father's kingdom, which had embraced the eastern half of Anahuac, and also the title of Chichimecatl Tecuhtli. The historical importance of this title still gave its recipient the right to claim the first place and the highest rank among the allies. The part played by the Mexicans had hitherto been of too little importance to enable them to dispute about this position; they had to thank their long friendship and relationship with the monarchs of Tezcuco for the fact that an important portion of the booty fell to their share. With the exception of the district of Tlacopan, which had been exempted from destruction to provide lands for those who had given their help against Maxtla, the whole kingdom of the Tecpanecs in which the Mexicans themselves, like the other kings, had hitherto been only vassals, now fell into their power, which at first they were obliged, no doubt, to enforce with arms. Their position in the councils of the allies became still more prominent; here they were considered as having equal rights with the Tezcucans, while the king of Tlacopan, the third member in this new triple alliance, remained independent, but was obliged to recognise the unconditional superiority of the two other members. In the future these conditions were to remain unchanged; it was arranged also that all future conquests should be divided between the allies, so that the king of Tlacopan should obtain a fifth part of the spoil and the rest should be divided in equal portions between the rulers of Tezcuco and Tenochtitlan. Such were the contents of the treaty between the leading nations of Anahuac.

These political relations continued to the time of the Spanish invasion; the confederation that would eventually have broken up remained undisturbed until the time of the conquest. The three allied kings carried on a number of wars, especially against their immediate neighbours on the south; no doubt the booty was then divided in accordance with the provisions of their compact. The Mexicans seem, however, to have gained greater accessions of territory even in these cases of common conquest. But each of the allied kings undertook isolated wars of conquest against adjoining territories. Consequently the division of the kingdom into eastern and western territories is not strictly adhered to: we meet with the Tezcucans on the west and on the coast of the Pacific Ocean, and similarly we find the Aztecs on the east as far as the shores of the Gulf of Mexico.

The most important change which the lapse of time brought about within the confederacy consisted in the fact that the kings of Tenochtitlan began more and more to take a leading part. Though keeping strictly to the legal conditions of the confederation, the kings of Tezcuco allowed themselves to be pushed into the background by the kings of Tenochtitlan; the reason lay solely in a national peculiarity of both peoples and their leaders. The kings of Tezcuco had always been more renowned for the care they expended upon the internal well-being of their kingdom than for their warlike expeditions. This reputation was supported by both of the kings who held the throne at the time of the confederation, Nezahualcoyotl and his son Nezahualpilli. It was not that they were lacking in warlike vigour; when it was a question of maintaining their authority or preserving the integrity of their kingdom, they were fully equal to the task; but they never undertook wars of conquest. War was never an end in itself to the kings of Colhuacan: it was invariably the means to higher ends.

During the first ten years Nezahualcoyotl concentrated his attention upon the reorganisation of his kingdom, which had been greatly shattered by revolutions following upon the death of Ixtlilxochitl. He kept in view that feudal system which his father, and his grandfather, Techotl, had introduced; and this in spite of the sad experience which both he and his predecessors had had of it. Similarly he followed the steps of his ancestors with regard to the organisation of a judicial system: his decrees were long respected by the Spaniards as being particularly valuable. Above all, he resembled the earlier kings in his love for the fine arts; temples and palaces, gardens and baths, streets and bridges, arose under his care, both in the capital and in the provinces. Wherever in the whole valley of Mexico more important artistic buildings were taken in hand, the finished art of Nezahualcoyotl and his architects became the guiding principle of their construction. He showed his thankfulness to the Mexicans for the support which they had given him in the hour of necessity, by his erection of the aqueduct which brought spring water in pipes of clay enclosed in stone from Chapultepec to the capital of the Aztecs situated among the marshes; and when in the year 1445 continuous rains had made the lake rise to a threatening height, and had almost flooded the whole of Tenochtitlan, he it was who built a wide mole of a semicircular form, and kept the low-lying water round the town from uniting with the lake which was threatening danger.

Nezahualcoyotl also devoted uninterrupted attention to intellectual progress. He was himself one of the foremost poets which the ancient American civilisation produced; his melancholy songs passed from mouth to mouth long after his race and his kingdom had disappeared from the face of the earth. The maturity of his intellect is to be seen in the traditions that we have of his religious ideas. His predecessors had been accustomed to exercise a wide tolerance toward the religious conceptions of their various subjects, which often differed materially from one another. But in this matter Nezahualcoyotl far surpassed the fame of his ancestors. In the very capital of his kingdom in the city of Tezcuco he allowed temples to be erected to the most different divinities, even a temple to Huitzilopochtli, although he was as averse to the blood-stained worship of this divinity as were his forefathers. Being thus convinced of the inadequacy and incompleteness of the worships of his people, he arrived at the conception of the one God who created and sustains the world. It would be a bold comparison to call the Tezcuco of Nezahualcoyotl the Athens of Central America; but in his time Tezcuco certainly was the centre of all the intellectual life, progress, and learning to be found in these kingdoms.

Although Nezahualcoyotl had a large number of sons by different women, it was only in the year 1463 that he entered upon lawful wedlock with the princess Azcaxochitl of Tlacopan. There was one son of their union, Nezahualpilli, who was eight years old upon the death of his father, which took place in 1472. Brought up under the care of the king Axayacatl, in Mexico, he remained none the less the true son of his great father in his intellectual capacities. He was not allowed to take the same important position in the triple alliance as his father had held, who was older than his Aztec confederates, and whose age and intellectual endowments had been a check on the encroachment of the neighbouring kingdom. His son was obliged to take the second place within the confederacy; for now not only might and splendour, but also the preponderance of age and experience, were on the side of the Mexicans.

The development of the kingdom of Tenochtitlan was different in many essential details. Its equality with Tezcuco in the confederation of 1431 had not been entirely deserved; immediately before the gates of the capital lay the sister State Tlatelulco, governed by its own independent monarch. And although the Mexicans were rather feared for their prowess in arms than respected over a wide district, they yet had first to subdue that kingdom before they could lay claim to suzerainty over the western Anahuac. A famous line of royal heroes, the sons and nephews of Huitzilihuitl, had devoted themselves successfully to this task. At first their expeditions were directed chiefly toward the south; after Xochimilco and Cuitlahua had been incorporated, the endless wars against the States of Chalca began. The Mexicans had already overcome the people of Chalca many times when they were in the service of the Tecpanecs; but these had not yet been entirely subdued, and at the time of the revolution they had again recovered their independence, as had many other portions of the Tecpanec kingdom. Even now the people of Chalca offered an invincible resistance to the Mexicans alone. But their provocations had also driven Nezahualcoyotl into the ranks of their enemies; and the numerous Chalca States were unable to offer any prolonged resistance to the united armies of the three allied kingdoms. For nearly twenty years (1446–1465) three successive kings of Mexico took the field yearly against the Chalca with varied success, until they succeeded in reducing their last fortress, the town of Chalco. From 1465 the Chalca were reckoned among the States tributary to Tenochtitlan.

In the year 1440 Itzcohuatl, who had helped to found the confederacy of 1431, died, and his nephew Montezuma[1] Ilhuicamina, succeeded him on the throne: this was the king who did most to extend the Aztec dominions. The war against Chalco, which was brought to a successful end in the last years of his reign, claimed most of his attention, but at the same time he extended the boundaries of his kingdom in other directions also. Moreover he made most important improvements in the internal organisation of the State. Even under the government of Itzcohuatl his high position enabled him to exercise great influence, for he had been at the same time commander-in-chief of the army and high-priest of Huitzilopochtli. Nor was it for nothing that he had been the intimate friend of Nezahualcoyotl. The capital owed to him the most important of those buildings which excited the astonishment of the conquerors: the dykes which connected the town with the mainland; the canals which served as its highroads; the temples, and in particular the temple of Huitzilopochtli, to which generations had made additions, and which was not even ended on Montezuma's death, although he brought out the final plans.

In religious matters Montezuma showed some sympathy with that toleration practised by the kings of Tezcuco. In Tenochtitlan there were already numerous temples to foreign divinities, and it speedily became the custom to celebrate every victory over another race by transplanting its gods and its worship to the capital.

[1] More correctly "Mocteuzoma."

As a matter of fact these importations exercised no material influence upon the peculiar character of the Aztec worship; on the contrary, the higher the power and the fame of the Mexicans rose, the more eagerly did they continue their horrible sacrifices of human blood. They seem to have been possessed with the idea that their successes, which became more brilliant year by year, were owing to the favour of Heaven which they had gained by their numerous sacrifices; and in order to retain this favour they increased their blood-stained hecatombs in proportion to the growth of their power. Every national festival, every victory, every recommencement of the cycle of years, every coronation, and every dedication of a temple was celebrated with bloody sacrifices; the greater the occasion, the more numerous the victims. Nor was it only a question of thankfulness to the gods whose favour they had won; by these means they attempted to make atonement to those whose anger they had incurred. When, in the year 1445, a famine which lasted several years came upon the whole of Anahuac, the Aztec desire for sacrifice rose almost to the pitch of frenzy. At first they were themselves sufficiently strong to make captives of their foes in border warfare; the brave hearts of these prisoners, which were torn still palpitating from the breast which the obsidian knife had cleft, were considered as the most welcome offering to the gods. But at length their necessities became greater, and their warriors thinned in number, and, exhausted by famine, were neither available for sacrifice nor equal to the fatigues of a campaign. The rulers of the State, trembling before the wrath of Heaven, then conceived an idea unparalleled in the history of the world. They concluded a formal contract with the warlike States of the East, the Tlascalans and the Huexotzincos, upon whom the famine had pressed less severely, to hold an annual sham fight in a particular place, between an equal number of warriors, apparently with the idea of providing the necessary victims for the services of the gods from the prisoners who should then be taken. As a matter of fact, during the years of famine such battles took place several times; but after that time had passed by the warlike disposition of the Aztecs provided a number of sufficient victims from real warfare, and mimic warfare became superfluous.

The greater the power and prestige of the Mexicans grew, the more oppressive they found it to have exactly in front of the gates of their capital an almost independent community ruled by its own kings, the sister town of Tlatelulco. The time when this State could have rivalled Mexico in glory and splendour had long passed away, but there remained a hostile disposition which was apparent in all kinds of little animosities. The Mexicans, naturally, only waited for a favourable opportunity to take their revenge for these; but, considering the number of enemies that they had both within and without their realm, it was a hazardous act to endanger peace at the gates of the capital by any show of aggression. It fell out exactly in accordance with their wishes that the king of Tlatelulco entered into a most traitorous compact with their enemies at a time when the wars against the Chalca claimed the undivided attention of the Mexicans. When Montezuma again returned to Tenochtitlan from the successful campaign in the south, he turned his overpowering forces on Tlatelulco; and, in the battles which followed, the allies, as usual, failed to come to the help of its short-sighted king, who lost his throne and his life. In spite of this the Mexicans were satisfied with setting up a vassal king of Tlatelulco in the person of a governor who was unconditionally subject to themselves. But although Moquihuix owed his elevation entirely to his uncle Montezuma, the deeply rooted aversion of the people of Tlatelulco to their more fortunate rivals won him over in the course of time. When Axayacatl, in the year 1468, ascended the throne of Tenochtitlan after the death of Montezuma, he made the attempt to win back the independence of his little State by force of arms. The struggle is said to have lasted full five years before the powerful Mexicans succeeded in definitely crushing the resistance of their neighbour. We see by this fact how the singularly loose organisation of the States allowed a little band of brave and determined warriors to threaten the existence even of a powerful kingdom, so long as they could rely upon the sympathies of its remaining subjects. After the subjection of Moquihuix the Mexicans did not again commit the folly of planting the seeds of disunion so close to the centre of their kingdom. Tlatelulco ceased to exist as an individual town; it was incorporated with Tenochtitlan, from which it had long been divided only by a canal, and all of its inhabitants who did not submit to the new order of things were banished.

Tenochtitlan, by its union with Tlatelulco, now acquired a considerable extension of territory, security against continually threatening danger, and an extraordinary increase of power. In the whole of Central America down to the Isthmus of Tehuantepec, and northward from that point, the Tlatelulca had been energetic traders, and nearly all the commerce between the north and the south had passed through their hands. Of all the States in and around Anahuac the Tlazcaltecs were almost their only rivals in this department, although their traffic was carried on rather among the States upon the Gulf than upon the Pacific coast. Hitherto the feeble character of their home policy had at times unfavourably influenced the commercial undertakings of the Tlatelulca; but after the Mexicans had gained possession of the town, the business interests of its inhabitants were also under Mexican protection. From this time onward the Mexican merchants play an important part as forming the reconnoitring and intelligence department of the Mexican armies, and as opening the way for acts of aggression in all their wars.

Under Axayacatl the kingdom of Tenochtitlan reached its widest extent. The Mexican power went at least as far northward as to overpass the mountain range which surrounds the high valleys of Anahuac. Here Tula and Tulancingo represent the extreme outposts, the connection of which with the Aztec kingdom was neither firm nor lasting. Moreover upon the west the Mexicans made conquests at a late period and of no great extent. Only the portions of Michuacan on their immediate boundaries were subject to their rule; with the Tarascos, who dwelt farther west and extended to the seaboard, they never really measured their strength. On the Pacific coast the influence of the central States spread first toward the south; but it was not exclusively the kings of Tenochtitlan who made towns and princes tributary to themselves in this district: the Tezcucans also had vassals here. We have observed in an earlier section [1] that the Mexican power was confined to a few fortified towns in the Zapotec country; but on the northwest and south, beyond the Isthmus of Tehuantepec, numerous vassal princes seem to have recognised their suzerainty. On the east, also, wide dis-

---

[1] *Ante*, p. 255.

tricts were subject to the central power. If originally the kings of Tezcuco held here overshadowed the Aztecs, yet the latter, in course of time, had the upper hand, owing to the peaceful inclinations of the princes of Tezcuco, by availing themselves of every opportunity which the Mexicans afforded. The king of Tenochtitlan undoubtedly may be reproached for having grievously employed his regency during the minority of Nezahualpilli to aggrandise himself at the expense of the allied kingdom; but in fact, even upon the coast the influence of the Aztecs was preponderant and overspread the States on the coast of the Mexican Gulf from Panuco in the north, through the district of the Huastecs and Totonacs, as far south as Xicalanco and Nonohualco to the borders of Yucatan.

However, in the immediate neighbourhood of these allied central powers there existed a point of continual disturbance which was a refuge for all those who wished to escape the ever-increasing tyranny of the Aztecs: this was the kingdom of Huexotzingo and the republic of Tlazcala. In earlier times both had belonged to the Chichimec kingdom of Tezcuco, and in the period of persecution had lent their support to the legal heir of that country, Nezahualcoyotl. But when he entered into alliance with the Aztecs, with a view to recovering his kingdom, his earlier allies broke away from him, and from that time forward created uninterrupted disturbances upon the boundaries of the kingdom. As a result of a whole series of campaigns, Huexotzinco seems to have been made tributary, at any rate for some time. But whenever the allied kings forced their way into the mountainous country of the Tlazcaltecs, and obtained some apparent result by devastating it with fire and sword, the lawless spirit of this brave little people invariably survived all the attacks of the motley vassal armies of the kings of Anahuac. Though shut in on every side, the Tlazcalans maintained their independence until the arrival of the Spaniards; and the ferocious hatred with which they regarded their neighbouring persecutors made them the firmest allies of Cortes against Tenochtitlan.

The organisation of the Aztec kingdom was essentially the same as that of the other Central American States. When they had firmly subjugated territories they made tributary vassal kingdoms of them, and attempted to secure the fidelity of their subject kings by setting up therein members of the royal family, or its connections by marriage. But the Mexicans attempted to secure their hold, not only upon the thrones of their conquered kingdoms, but also upon the land itself. Each successful campaign was followed by free gifts of land and people to all those whose warlike prowess had contributed to the success: at times we should be correct in speaking of an actual colonisation of the conquered district. Bravery in war was thus stimulated by the prospect of a brilliant reward which was within the reach of even the humblest warrior; and on the other hand this newly founded feudal aristocracy provided a protection and a counterpoise to any yearnings after independence that the vassal kings might have had. The colonisation and colonisation of conquests in this manner did not, however, extend beyond the country of Anahuac and the districts in the immediate vicinity of its southern border. Want of men chiefly prevented the extension of a similar form of government over the more distant provinces. But even there a victorious campaign was generally followed by the deposition of the reigning monarch and his own installation of a subject king. Provided a specified tribute were paid,

quered province remained in other respects almost as independent as before. Every year the messengers came from Tenochtitlan to collect a tribute, in cases where they were not permanently settled at the court of the vassal king; and, in order to insure obedience and respect to the king and to his land, particular points on the most important lines of communication were strongly fortified and power-fully garrisoned. These posts formed a meeting-place for the collectors, for other officials, and for merchants in times of peace, and a basis for resistance in case of revolt. We have particular notice of such garrisons in the outlying provinces of the Mixtec and Zapotec territory on the south, and in the district of the Huastecs and Totonacs on the east. With all these provisions the Mexicans did not succeed in preventing frequent insurrections, sometimes of a dangerous nature; but in spite of the burning hatred with which they were regarded by a great part of their subjects, on account of their bloody and tyrannical rule, during a whole century these subjects never succeeded in seriously endangering the existence of the empire by a general insurrection.

Axayacatl, who died in the year 1477 after a short but glorious reign, was followed by two monarchs who did not attain the fame of their forefathers. Tizocic and Ahuitzotl did indeed lead the armies of the Aztecs to victory in different directions beyond their borders; but they had neither the personal quali-ties nor the good fortune to confer any particular benefits upon the State, the extent of which made it more and more difficult to rule. But in the person of Montezuma II a monarch again ascended the throne of Tenochtitlan who seemed capable of reviving the great traditions of the past. Before he ascended the throne he had already covered himself with military glory, and he made it his particular object to justify the hopes which were set upon his rule; but fortune was not particularly favourable to him. In the last years of Ahuitzotl's reign belief in the invincible powers of the Mexican arms had begun to grow visibly weak; the Zapotecs had recovered their complete independence, and in Tlazcala the Mexicans had again received a defeat. A few isolated successes did not enable Montezuma, by means of a sensational victory, to remove the impression of the discomfitures they had suffered.

Prospects for the future within the realm were also threatening; the alliance between Mexico and Tezcuco, upon which the power of the central States had hitherto chiefly rested, began to grow weaker and weaker. Nezahualpilli, although his bravery had been proved upon many a field, had, like his predecessors, been no lover of war; and it was owing for the most part to the influence of the confedera-tion that he had supported the Mexicans in their restless desire for extension of territory, while at times he had stood aside and remained neutral. So it was no wonder if the kings of Tenochtitlan became more and more convinced that they were the sole repositories of strength and power, and that the other confederates had no right to equal prestige or to an equal share in the spoil. Their exaggerated opinion of themselves led to arrogance: and this produced distrust upon both sides, resulting in secret enmity. The Mexicans began to conceive the plan of attacking their previous confederates upon the first favourable opportunity, and reducing them to the position of vassal States. During an unsuccessful war against Tlazcala in the year 1512, which the Aztecs and Tezcucans undertook in common, Montezuma is said to have carried his faithlessness so far as to have left the confederates in the lurch during a battle, and to have even entered into treasonable correspondence with the Tlazcalans. Nezahualpilh had found courage to avenge this insult by an open declaration of war, but from the time the confederates regarded one another as enemies, and when Nezahualpilli died, four years later, hostilities broke out openly.

The king of Tezcuco had neglected to choose his successor during his lifetime, so Montezuma was able to obtain the election of a prince whom he hoped to use according to his desires. Cacama was Montezuma's own nephew, and if he were a man of strong character the fact had never yet been made manifest. Character, indeed, was far more apparent in his brother Ixtlilxochitl, who, though younger, had made a name for himself as a warrior during his father's lifetime. But all his attempts to prevent the election of Cacama were unsuccessful; and as he regarded his nephew merely as Montezuma's tool, Ixtlilxochitl might suppose himself fighting for the independence of his father's kingdom when he openly raised the standard of revolt. He did not succeed in maintaining himself any length of time in Tezcuco; but in the northern provinces he found numerous supporters. There he might reckon upon the help of all those who feared that the victory of Cacama would mean the establishment of an exclusively Mexican dominion; and so he succeeded not only in utterly defeating an army that Montezuma sent against him, but also in making progress slowly but steadily forward, until he so threatened Tezcuco that Cacama preferred to conclude peace with him on condition of dividing their father's kingdom. Sooner or later it would nevertheless have come to war again, if another enemy had not appeared upon the scene to threaten them all alike, – the Spaniards.

The kings of Anahuac must undoubtedly have heard long ago of the appearance of wonderful foreigners who had come over sea from the east into the neighbouring district. The extensive trade and the admirable organisation of traffic in the kingdom of Anahuac and the neighbouring provinces would certainly have brought them rumours, and perhaps particular information, concerning the first appearance and the further progress of these foreigners who for the last twenty-five years had been spreading over the islands and on the south. They could no longer conceal from themselves that this danger was beginning to threaten them when the expeditions of Hernandez and Grijalba, in the years 1516 and 1517, penetrated to their own coasts.

What superstitious ideas were excited by this occurrence can be understood from the important place given to discussions in the later historians, as to whether the appearance of the Spaniards had any connection with the old prophecies which spoke of an entire revolution of their conditions of life, which should come forth from the east. At any rate, as regards the Spaniards, the belief of the natives that their appearance was connected in some way with the promised return of Quetzalcoatl was to them a help no less important than was the universal enmity with which the nations of Central America regarded the Mexican dominion. This hatred brought to their side the large bands of native allies who helped them to overcome all the difficulties which confronted the passage of a few hundred men into the centre of these extensive States, while the religious awe in which they were held afforded them a friendly reception and a firm footing on the coast-land, and cleared the way for their entrance into Mexico, – an entrance which implied the fall of the old kingdoms.[1]

---

[1] See, on this point, *post*, p. 366.

### 3. THE ANCIENT CIVILISATION OF SOUTH AMERICA

#### A. THE CONFIGURATION OF SOUTH AMERICA

THE southern extremity of the Cordilleras of the Andes is formed of one mountain chain; but twenty-six degrees south of the equator they divide into two ranges which diverge more widely as they proceed northward. At first these enclose only a narrow table-land, on which one or two lake systems are to be found; afterward the mountain ranges become more complex. Between the main ridges and parallel with them long valleys form a river-bed, to which the streams on the heights at either hand contribute until the river is strong enough to force a passage through some outlet in these mountain walls. On the west the rivers, after a precipitous descent, rush wildly down across the narrow strip of barren coast-land to the ocean. On the east, after a fall quite as abrupt, they reach the wooded lowlands and feed the great river system of La Plata, the Amazon, and the Orinoco. Many of the valleys lie at very considerable heights: the level of Lake Titicaca is more than 12,600 feet above the sea; Quito has an elevation of 9,380 feet; and Bogotá, 8,750 feet. Yet it is not difficult to understand why it was only here that the native South American civilisation could take root and develop.

With the exception of occasional tracts, the narrow strip of coast-land lying between the mountains and the sea upon the west is not actually sterile, or at least is not wholly incapable of cultivation. But the almost entire absence of rainfall throughout the year, and the heat of a tropical sun whose rays are here nearly vertical, destroy all beginnings of vegetation before they have sufficiently established themselves to afford shade and protection to their own roots or to undergrowth. At intervals in the long stretch of coast-line, streams and rivers descend from the mountains, but the scanty limits of the level country afford them no space for development. So at the melting of the snows they rush down as devastating torrents to the sea, while in the dry seasons they are either dried up entirely or contain so little water that a narrow belt of vegetation in the immediate neighbourhood of their banks is all that can find a bare subsistence.

If on the western side it is the almost entire absence of rainfall which precludes human habitation and progress, upon the east the excessive rainfall is equally unfavourable to human industry. Here, too, for the most part, the mountain face descends abruptly to a considerable depth. But beneath it spreads a boundless expanse of lowland over which the rivers flow but gently. When the mountain streams are swollen by the melting snow, or the clouds that sweep over the wide lowlands strike upon the mountain walls and discharge their abundance upon the earth, these rivers rise high above their banks; districts of such extent are then inundated that the boundaries even between the most important river systems disappear, and a canoe can be borne from one river to the next. Here also primitive Man, with his rude implements, could gain no sufficient footing to enable him to wrest from Nature the means of life. Nor was any such struggle necessary; from the wealth of her tropical abundance Nature afforded him only too easily the means of satisfying his modest requirements, and he became a wanderer with no settled dwelling-place.

Thus there remained for men's habitation only that huge mountain mass which bears in its long folds the peaks and ranges of the Cordilleras, and forms low valleys between its mountain arms. It rises above the sea-level to a height of several thousand feet, almost to the snow-line of the Alps; but the temperature that prevails even at this height in tropical latitudes is by no means unfavourable to Man and to his requirements. Primitive Man here found that most indispensable of all requisites, water, — water in sufficient abundance to fertilise the soil, and yet not so abundant as to be an invincible enemy; water, too, that presented him with provision in the fish which were found in the greater and smaller lakes, into which brook or river swelled when its course was dammed; and these fish could be caught even with the primitive implements of early times. Here the forest offered him a refuge, and, in the next stage of his progress, material for his inventions. The rocks which the mountain torrents brought down to him were ready for him to build with. Finally, in the Cordilleras of South America he found two more precious gifts, which had the greatest influence upon the development of his civilisation: the potato, which grew even upon the heights where the maize could not flourish; and the llama, the household animal of the American continent, which bore Man's burdens, clothed him with its wool, and fed him with its meat.

All these conditions were perhaps not equally favourable over the whole of that great stretch of country which forms the region of the South American civilisation; yet it is plain from what has been said above that the natural conditions contributing to the development of a civilisation were at hand. At any rate, even in the remotest antiquity, these conditions raised culture to a higher plane than it attained at that time among the inhabitants of the rest of South America. In our sketch of Aruac,[1] we have observed that the knowledge of the proper mode of preparing the mandioc and skill in pottery ware seem to spring from those ancient civilised influences which proceeded from the peoples of the Cordilleras, apparently from the range of Bolivia, where they were more widely extended than elsewhere. It is in this region that we must seek for the early home, not only of many uncivilised peoples of South America, but also of all the civilised peoples; as is apparent from the fact that in South America all tradition points to the progress of civilisation from south to north, whereas in the districts of Central America the contrary was the case. The civilisation actually attained, though its development was by no means uniform, is, on the whole, of a higher standard as we penetrate southward. For this reason, and also because in the extreme north this civilisation existed undisturbed at the time of the Spanish invasion, while at the same time in the south numbers of older States had been absorbed by the Incas, we shall begin our narration of the ancient history of these civilisations from the north.

## B. The Ancient South American Civilisations

(a) *The Chibchas.* — The most northerly of the civilised districts of South America is that of the Chibchas. For philological reasons attempts have been made to show the relation of the Chibchas to other races, and in particular to those that inhabit the most southerly regions of Central America immediately on the north of the Isthmus of Panama; it has thus been inferred that the Chibchas emigrated to their later settlements from the north. Others, also, have attempted to identify scattered Chibcha bands in Costa Rica, which are said to have arrived there from the south. But even if their connection with races living outside their

---

[1] *Ante,* pp. 186, 187.

boundaries should be established, yet the peculiar nature of the Chibcha civilisation in Colombia justifies us in disregarding the historical importance of these, and confining our attention to the Chibchas themselves.

Their district lay upon the eastern bank of the central river of Magdalena, from which it was divided by a high range of mountains stretching from Rio Funza on the south as far as Carare and Sogamoso on the north and penetrated by no river of any importance. On the east it borders on the Cordilleras themselves. In a few places there were passes across those mountains, known to the Chibchas even then, and on the northeasterly corner in the later San Juan de los Llanos there seems to have been from early times communication between the inhabitants of the highland and those of the lowland upon the east. A high table-land, intersected by numerous rivers for the most part of small importance, covered with a great number of large or small lakes, and bounded by the two river systems above mentioned, — such is the district of the Chibchas. It has an area of about five hundred square miles, and was tolerably thickly populated at the time of the conquest.

In the Chibcha traditions there is nothing to lead us to conclude that their immigration into this district was of a late date. Their religious ideas invariably preserve the tradition of an early period of development; and so closely were their conceptions bound up with the localities in which the Spaniards met with them, that they seem to have considered themselves as autochthonous. This is their legend concerning the creation of Man. After Chiminigagua had created heaven and earth, and had sent out the birds that brought light into all countries, a lovely woman named Bachue or Furachogue is said to have risen from the lake of Iguaque on the northeast of Tunja, with a child three years old upon her arm, and to have built for herself a hut not far from there in a flowery valley, to have cultivated the ground, and to have carefully brought up the child. When the boy had become a man she is supposed to have married him, and to have presented him with a progeny so numerous that the surrounding country was occupied and peopled by it. When they grew old the couple wandered back to the lake of Iguaque, and there took leave of their posterity, and disappeared again, in the form of two giant snakes, into the lake from which they had first come forth.

In spite of this and similar legends it is doubtful whether the first home of the Chibchas is rightly to be placed in the river district of the Magdalena. It must be noticed that they were there surrounded by people with whom they were in a state of continual war, and whose language was in no way related to their own. Moreover the character of their civilisation was so entirely different that we can hardly believe the Chibchas to be a branch of the race surrounding them which had attained a higher cultivation under the influence of more favourable conditions. It is impossible, also, to establish any connection between the Chibchas and the other civilisations of the south. They were divided from their nearest civilised neighbours, the Quitus, by the deep depression which the valley of the Iça River and the lake of Coena makes in the Cordilleras at the sources of the Magdalena, and there are no coincidences in religion or civilisation to point to an earlier close connection between these peoples. Similarly upon the north there is absolutely no race or district which the Chibchas can be shown to have reached, carrying with them germs of the civilisation which brought forth a rich harvest in the river system of the Magdalena.

From the earliest times the Chibcha district must have been divided into a number of little communities about as numerous as the towns were later on; for over each of these settlements, with the districts surrounding them, a cacique continued to rule in later times. At first all of these towns were of an equal importance, were independent of each other, and perhaps were connected in groups merely by their common veneration of certain sacred shrines; but in the course of time some of these petty monarchs began to enrich themselves at the expense of their neighbours. Around each nucleus thus formed other families had gathered by degrees, under compulsion or persuasion, until at last five caciques divided the government of the district, almost all the other local caciques being dependent upon them. This distribution was not definitely settled once for all, but each of the five head caciques (the "kings" of the Spaniards) was continually attempting to aggrandise himself at the expense of the others. The period immediately preceding the Spanish arrival was one of furious struggle; its result would undoubtedly have been the closer incorporation of the political groups upon the highland of Bogotá if the Spaniards had not indiscriminately subjugated all the kings and extended their power over a district which reached far beyond the boundaries of the old Chibcha kingdom.

Of the five States which divided the district of Chibcha in the century immediately preceding the arrival of the Spaniards, the first was known as Zippá or Bogotá, after the name of its governor, which is said to mean the sun; the Spaniards gave this name to the capital of the country. The four others were as follows: the State of Zaque or Hunsa, with its capital Tunja; the State of Sogamoso, the priestly kings of which bore the title of Iracá; Guatabita, which lay on the lake of the same name; and lastly Tundama, to which belonged the extreme northeast of the district, from the line of the Cordilleras to the later San Juan de los Llanos. Although in later times the central point of political power was to be found in the States of Tunja and Bogotá, yet the tradition of the Chibchas recorded that this condition of affairs was of recent establishment. Between the States of Tundama, Sogamoso, and Guatabita, the traditions made no difference as regards the period of their foundation. But if their religious and mythological circumstances be considered, we may assert that Tundama was rather on the circumference of the Chibcha civilisation, of which Sogamoso formed the political centre, during that period which immediately preceded the rise of Zaque and Zippá; whereas Guatabita formed the oldest religious centre of the whole area of Chibcha population. Here, on the lake of Guatabita, tradition placed all those events of the past which served to explain the conditions of the present. Here in particular was placed the battle between the mythological hero of the Chibchas, Bochica, who was certainly an incarnation of the sun, and his wife Chia, an incarnation of the moon, who was as wicked as she was beautiful. According to tradition the Chibchas, at their first appearance, were mere savages living in the valley of the Funza River, which was then entirely surrounded by mountains upon the south. Bochica came to bring them the blessings of civilisation; he taught them how to cultivate the maize and potato, to make them garments by spinning yarn, and to live as an organised community. But Chia everywhere opposed his efforts toward civilisation, and when she saw that in spite of her energy the work of Bochica became more and more successful, she dammed up the outflow of the Funza until its waters filled up the whole valley, and only a few of the inhabitants succeeded in escaping to the highest peaks. Thereupon anger overcame Bochica. He banished Chia from the earth, and put her into the heaven as the moon; then with his lightning he split the enclosing valley wall, so that the waters rushed out in the mighty waterfall of Tequendama, and only the lake of Guatabita remained as a memorial of the universal flood.

The details of this legend reflect a high veneration for the powers of nature which is a characteristic feature in the religion of the Chibchas. Mountain and rock, tree and shrub, but especially water, brooks, and lakes, were considered by them as inhabited by divine beings and were objects of particular veneration. This veneration showed itself especially in pilgrimages, dances, and the burning of incense, and in the bringing of costly presents. The Chibchas offered these divinities objects peculiarly suitable for decoration and sacrifice, since their district provided them with many precious stones, especially emeralds, and also with gold. They had the greatest skill in beating out gold and then tastefully inlaying it with jewels. Hence their offerings were especially suitable for the service of the gods, and the habit of making these offerings turned their artistic tendencies into particular channels. This custom no doubt contributed not a little to the unusually high development of the goldsmiths' art among the Chibchas. The sites of their worship, — both of the gods and of the dead who were connected with them, — caves, lakes, and similar places, consequently provide a rich hunting-ground, and one only too easily attainable, for the costly antiquities of the Chibcha civilisation. From the Spanish conquest to the most recent times, treasures to a large amount have been gathered from such places, for the most part to be melted down and coined into money. It is only in more recent times that greater respect has begun to be shown to these remains of a remarkable civilisation. Fortunately a sufficient number of the inexhaustible and valuable antiquarian relics of the country has come down to us to enable us to form a judgment about them.

The lakes, and especially the lake of Guatabita, were localities much frequented for the purpose of making religious offerings. The festival sacrifices which the newly elected monarch offered in the lake of Guatabita even in later times gave rise to the fairy legend of the Dorado,[1] the golden man, who is said to have been thrown into the lake of Guatabita. The proceedings were as follows: In all the Chibcha States the accession of a new monarch was celebrated with prolonged religious ceremonies. His coronation was preceded by long and strict fasting; and at the end of this time of penance, sacrifices and festivals of unusual extravagance took place. But in Guatabita the following ceremony closed the festival. The inhabitants of the whole land came together in procession to the shores of the lake, and on the day of coronation the priests brought the young ruler from his place of penance to the lake, where a vessel awaited his arrival, richly loaded with the most expensive offerings of gold and emeralds. The four most important caciques, clothed in their richest and most brilliant robes, entered the vessel; on the shore of the lake, to the accompaniment of offerings of incense, which were continued throughout the whole crowd of people there gathered together, the new monarch was clothed in festival robes by the priests, smeared with a sticky kind of earth, and then powdered from head to foot with gold dust. Gleaming like the sun, — and in most of the Chibcha States the kings were considered as descended from the sun, — he, too, entered the vessel, took his place

[1] *Ante*, p. 191.

among his caciques, and was then rowed out upon the lake. In the middle of the lake the boat was stopped, and now the monarch offered to the gods, who were supposed to inhabit the lake, the rich store of offerings, while the people on shore celebrated the sacrifice by dancing to the accompaniment of their strange musical instruments until the monarch reached the land again and then for the first time began to take part in a festival continued for many days.

Though this mode of sacrifice was peculiar to Guatabita, yet the holy sacrificial spots were constantly visited by both the rulers and the subjects of the other Chibcha States. There were a large number of sacred lakes which were regarded as proper places for sacrifice, and were connected by highroads carefully kept in repair for the convenience of the pilgrims. Upon all extraordinary occasions — famines and epidemics, victorious battles, and at other times also — the kings of the different States ordained festival pilgrimages in which almost the whole people took part; for such pilgrimages were not only a duty that they owed to the gods, but were at the same time a festival for the people, who were then allowed free indulgence in all sensual pleasures. The main objective of all pilgrimages was Guatabita, the spot most highly and widely revered in the whole Chibcha district. Probably even now the lake contains immense riches, which were poured into it in the shape of offerings. Repeated attempts to drain it have twice been partially successful. Search upon the districts around the banks has brought to light gold to the value of thousands of dollars, although it was only the ordinary inhabitants who offered their gifts upon the shore. What boundless treasures must be hidden in that lake! For not only the rulers of Guatabita, but each "usaque," "guecha," and in fact everybody of any social position whatever, was rowed out a short distance upon the lake, and made his offering as nearly as possible at the central point of the sacred locality. When the Spaniards came into the Chibcha district, Guatabita had lost its independence, and formed a part of the kingdom of Zippá or Bogotá. But that the religious centre was situated originally in Guatabita, and not in the new seat of power, is proved by the fact that Bogotá is never mentioned in the mythological and legendary traditions, while the most extensive and most elaborate cycle of legends centres round Guatabita.

Side by side with Guatabita, Sogamoso (Sugamuxi) undoubtedly possessed some religious importance. The little State which bears this name lay on the eastern boundary of the Chibcha district, where two difficult passes over the eastern Cordilleras make communication possible with the lowland of Llanos. The development of many religious customs shows that the two States here came into contact, and that their communication was not without influence upon the Chibchas. The bloodless worship which the Chibchas offered to nature, natural objects, and especially water, held the first place in Guatabita. But their religion was by no means entirely composed of such harmless conceptions; human sacrifice formed an integral portion of their sun-worship. They certainly believed that the sun had been created by Chiminigagua. But this inexplicable creator seems never to have enjoyed divine honours, while the worship of the sun is everywhere to be found, as we saw in the case of the Dorado ceremonies at Guatabita. The especial servants of the sun were the priesthood, the "jeques," who were well organised and united by strict rules; as in the case of all early peoples, they exercised a wide influence upon the country and its inhabitants. The training which the jeques

were obliged to submit to reminds us of the manner in which the medicine-man
of the North American savages was forced to gain a reputation for holiness: but
in this case the process was more systematic. Not every man was at liberty to
proclaim himself as an intermediary between God and man. The priestly caste
was already one of the estates of the realm: the position passed from uncle to
nephew.[1] A period of penance and preparation extending over many years had to
be passed through, and the permission of the monarch obtained. Among the
Chibchas, also, every house had its own fetiches: these were little shapeless
human figures, in the case of the rich families made of gold, while those of the
poor were of clay or wood; they almost always contained an interior receptacle for
offerings. Besides these there were a large number of inferior divinities, to which
no especial priests were attached, but which special classes of the people worshipped,—a worship which might become universal on particular occasions. The
temples with their priests were employed for a very anthropomorphic form of sun-
worship, and all the celestial bodies were considered as the satellites of the sun.

Sacrifices of blood, and particularly human offerings, appear almost exclusively
in the sun-worship. The mode of sacrifice was peculiar. The chosen victim was
conveyed to a mountain-top upon which the rays of the rising sun smote. Here
he was killed at the moment when the sun rose above the horizon, and the rock
was smeared with his warm blood so that the sun could immediately derive nourishment therefrom. A similar conception lay at the bottom of another peculiarly
horrible form of sacrifice. In this case the victim was brought to the appointed
place, bound to the top of mastlike poles, and slowly done to death with arrows
and spears, while the priests caught the blood that streamed down and offered it
to the images in the temple. Greater refinement is apparent in another mode of
human sacrifice, where the idea[2] that the victim is identified with a divinity is
prominent. This idea is borrowed from Aztec customs. It is remarkable that
for this purpose there were chosen only boys who belonged to the races living
in Llanos, on the east. This circumstance is not only connected with the fact
that the sun rises in the east, but also points to the eastern origin of the primitive Chibchas. From the later San Juan de los Llanos there was carried on
a regular trade in small boys, whose navels were cut immediately after their
birth, as a mark that they were destined for sacrifice to the sun. When six or
eight years old they were brought into the towns by merchants, and the caciques purchased one or more of these sacred boys in proportion to their wealth.
Until fifteen years of age they were honoured almost like divinities. They lived
in the temples, where the priests were their servants; they acted as intermediaries
between God and man in the case of suppliants; and if they ever left the temple
buildings, which did not often happen, they were carried in litters, like kings and
nobles, in order that their holy feet might not touch profane ground. Thus they
lived until they became of age. If such a sacrificial youth found an opportunity to
commit an act of unchastity, he became unfit for sacrifice: he was driven out, and
sank to the level of an ordinary mortal, but otherwise his earthly career ended
with a great feast in which the Chibchas gave full rein to their passion for display
in processions, dances, and musical performances. The sacrificial youth was the
central point of the festival, and when it was at its height the heart and entrails

[1] This was the usual line of succession among the Chibchas. See *post*, p. 295.
[2] See *ante*, pp. 238, 251, 262.

were torn from the victim's body amid a deafening uproar from the mob, his head was struck off, and his blood and heart were carried to the feet of the gods as rapidly as possible. It was supposed, therefore, that the gods were supported by the flesh and blood of the victim. Both the Chibchas and their priests seem never to have practised cannibalism; the corpse was secretly buried by the latter, who gave out that the sun had eaten it.

One of the duties of the priests naturally consisted in the regulation of the calendar. All that has been said of the complicated chronology of the Chibchas, of their three different and concurrent methods of reckoning the year, is a figment of the imagination, and the pretended calendar signs of the Chibchas are a feeble attempt at deception. Writing was absolutely unknown to the Chibchas; even the mnemonic system of the Peruvians — the "quipus" — was never used by them. Their year consisted of twelve lunar months, which were divided into smaller divisions according to the phases of the moon. It is also entirely false that they devoted ten days to religious contemplation and retirement, ten to work, and ten to pleasure. A year of 360 days would soon naturally have brought them into obvious contradiction with the seasons; and as, for religious reasons, the priests carefully watched the sun, they were probably able to make the year coincide with the sun, though perhaps by arbitrary methods. The pillars found among people whose architecture has advanced very little have frequently been considered as dials or gnomons. It is certainly remarkable that in the Chibcha district, where stone architecture was entirely unknown up to the time of the conquest, numbers of stone pillars have been found, well set up and rounded, which apparently fulfilled no particular purpose; they lie there as if they had been casually left on the road. These may be considered as sun-dials; but the entire lack of information as to their use, and the fact that there are no traces of them in places well-known to have been thickly populated, make the theory very doubtful.

The oldest historical traditions of the Chibchas are connected with Sogamoso. A king, Nompanem, is said here to have immediately succeeded Bochica, and to have reduced the teaching of that hero to legal form. But the purity of the old teaching was lost among his successors. Idacansas, related by the legends to have been the most famous ruler of Sogamoso, is said to have kept his subjects in check far more by treachery and deceit than by virtue and valour. In later times we only hear of quarrels for the dominion of Iracá among the different caciques who were subject to the kingdom, and at the time of the conquest the political importance of Sogamoso was entirely overshadowed by Zaque and Zippá.

Side by side with Guatabita and Sogamoso, which may be considered as an older group of States, owing to the connection of their historical traditions with their religious ideas, the kingdoms of Zaque of Tunja, and the kingdom of Zippá or Bogotá, form a more recent group of States, founded on a purely political basis. Tradition intimates that they originated in a revolt against the ancient kingdoms. The first ruler of Tunja or Hunsa is said to have been set up there by a king of Sogamoso; according to some authorities the capital, Hunsa, was so called from his name Hunsahua, while others assign Ramiriqui as the ancient residence of the rulers of Tunja. At any rate these rulers, by means of their prowess in war, obtained in a short period not only considerable prestige, but also entire independence. When the kingdom began to extend its boundaries in all directions, its ruler was no longer satisfied with the title "Usaque," which he had hitherto borne, a title which belonged to most of the independent and tributary caciques; he therefore assumed the title of "Zaque," by which the rulers of Hunsa are better known than by their proper names. Of the successors of Hunsahua but little is told us, and that little is chiefly legendary. For instance, Tomagata is said to have been a kind of human monster with four ears and a long rat's tail, who by means of his piety acquired all kinds of magical powers which he did not employ for the benefit of his subjects. Another ruler, whose government lasted until the arrival of the Spaniards in South America, though not in the Chibcha district, has been equally shrouded in legend. He is said to have sprung directly from the sun, the rays of which made a daughter of the cacique of Guachetá pregnant. As a child of the sun he enjoyed great reputation for many years before he gained any temporal power. But when the ruling zaque made himself hated by his people for his tyranny, Garanchacha placed himself at the head of the revolt and easily gained a victory which at once gave him the position of a zaque. A change of residence from Ramiriqui to Tunja (Hunsa) has been ascribed to him, and the isolated stone pillars that we have spoken of above [1] have been connected with his rule. He is said to have proposed to build a magnificent temple to his father, the sun-god, in the neighbourhood of Hunsa, and for this reason he had those pillars brought from a distance; they were transported only by night, that the people might believe that the gods themselves created the material for their temples. But before the work was ended news came to the king of the arrival of the Spaniards on the lower Magdalena River and for this reason the temple building was suspended. To estimate the value of this tradition it is important to observe that a zaque named Garanchacha can find no place in the dynasty of the kings of Tunja, at any rate as their names have been transmitted to us in the histories of the battles with the Zippás.

The only kingdom in the Chibcha districts upon the history and civilisation of which we have any detailed information is that of Bogotá. Its kings played a part similar to that of the Aztecs in Mexico and the Incas in Peru, and, like them, so attracted the attention of the conquerors that other races and States were wholly disregarded. It is true that even in this case the traditions do not go back very far; and if we consider the entire lack of any aids to the memory we cannot be surprised at the fact. Originally the ruler of Bogotá (Bacatá) was merely a vassal (usaque) of the king of Guatabita. He was, however, obliged to protect the southwest boundaries of his kingdom from the constant incursions of the savage cannibal Muzos and Panches. The military power developed in these efforts soon gave him a considerable preponderance over the other usaques; he became, as it were, the generalissimo of the combined forces of Guatabita.

To protect their boundaries the Chibcha rulers in early times formed a special regiment of warriors, the guechas. This force was recruited from the whole dominion, underwent special training under the king's personal observation, and was then stationed on the borders. As the usaques (caciques) were taken exclusively from the warrior caste, the road to high position lay open to every man who could distinguish himself by especial bravery, although, as a rule, the usaque nobility stood aloof from the lower orders. A kind of military organisation existed in times of peace; the usaques upon the borders were the commanders of the portions

[1] *Ante*, p. 293.

of the warrior class there stationed and brought up their contingents if war broke out in another part of the district, however distant from the boundary entrusted to themselves. For this object the separate usaques carried different standards by which they could be recognised both in battle and in camp. The guechas also had a particular dress assigned to them. Like all members of the Chibcha races they never wore their head bare. They wore a head-dress not unlike a cap, the hair being close cropped; and it was a special privilege of their rank to pierce their ears, their nostrils, and their lips. For each enemy that a guecha killed in battle he was allowed to fasten a golden ornament in his under lip, a decoration which considerably increased his ferocious appearance. The guechas were armed with long spears, axes, slings, and throwing-sticks, from which they could sling short, sharply pointed arrows. A declaration of war, which was generally accompanied with particular formalities, was preceded by weeks of religious ceremonies; then the usaques and the guechas put on their most brilliant apparel, which consisted of waving feather garments, gold and precious stones; and they marched out followed by an endless company of women, who conveyed provisions and large quantities of the intoxicating chicha for their use. It was a peculiar custom to carry with them into battle the mummies of famous warriors; these were borne into the thickest part of the fight upon a richly covered litter surrounded by a chosen band of picked warriors. As in the case of their sacrifices and processions, singing, shouting, and the unpleasing din of their instruments played an important part in war. The victory was celebrated with weeks of festivals and dances, and rich thank-offerings to the gods; but a defeat, too, was the occasion for expiatory offerings to appease the divinities whose anger had presumably been aroused.

From the band of usaques to whom the protection of the southern boundary was entrusted arose, some two centuries before the Spanish arrival, the ruler of Muquetá, who is distinguished with the title of Zippá and Bogotá after his kingdom had become the most important in the Chibcha district. He is said to have won his independence from Guatabita by availing himself of a festival at the sacred lake to make an attack; he may have been invited to the festival from motives not wholly disinterested; at any rate it enabled him to win an easy victory over his master. He next proceeded to extend the boundaries of his kingdom at the expense of the hostile races on the south and west, and his rapid successes soon gave him the preponderance over the other members of the race. Partly by force of arms, partly by the voluntary help of such provinces as were not satisfied with their own rulers, the Zippá kingdom increased so rapidly that it was soon able to consider itself as uniting the whole Chibcha race under its sway.

The usual line of succession among the Chibchas, as among many American peoples, was from uncle to nephew on the sister's side. It was not, however, the royal race of Bogotá, but the race of usaques of Chia who appointed the Zippá, as appears from the following legend. The brother of a cacique of Chia had entered upon a *liaison* with one of the cacique's wives, and when this was discovered and he was threatened with death on the sacrificial mast, he fled to the court of the Zippá. Here he made himself so invaluable by his military capacity that he was appointed to the succession in default of any legal heir. When his brother attained this high position, the ruler of Chia began to fear for his personal safety. Thanks to the intervention of the mother and the sister of the two princes, a compact was made according to which the son of this sister should succeed the cacique of Chia, and should also succeed the Zippá in the event of his death; and this mode of inheritance is said to have endured for all future time. At the bottom of this peculiar custom, which is certainly also found among the Kakchikel, but with a different origin, lies the desire to give greater security to a kingdom composed of many little districts of doubtful fidelity. This could be done by appointing a mighty vassal, and especially a near relation, as the future successor, and by providing him with the means of seizing the power at the critical moment. Everyone who was destined to govern a district, small or large, had to pass through a long period of probation. The test of continence thereby involved had much in common with the probation of the priests; and the priests, too, superintended the ordeal. At the close of it the ornaments for the ears and nose were put upon the young warrior in token of his high position, and his accession then took place accompanied by the most licentious festivities. The power which a cacique exercised when once he was recognised was practically unlimited. Each usaque possessed in his own province powers similar to those of his master in his central dominion. To him the usaques owed unconditional obedience, but they had a power of appeal from their master, whereas the ordinary subject had none. The position passed from uncle to nephew, and though each succeeding ruler had to be confirmed in his position by the monarch, yet the latter could only nominate a prince of his own to the throne when a family of caciques became extinct or in case of treachery and rebellion.

The gifts and the tribute paid to the governor did not press heavily upon the people, and consisted chiefly of gold and woven cloth. Arrears, however, were rigorously exacted. In the kingdom of Zaque emeralds formed a costly portion of the tribute. The rich mines of Muzo, which were then in the power of hostile savages, were but little worked. These precious stones formed an important medium of exchange, commerce being carried on side by side with conflict, not only among the several Chibcha States, but also far beyond their boundaries. Almost every third day was a market day, and in particular places in the Chibcha district fairs were held at special times, to which merchants came in with their special wares from the most remote districts. Long measure and dry measure are said to have been in use; the medium of exchange consisted of a coinage made of fine beaten gold; and interest was paid upon trade debts from the day on which they were contracted. Although in this manner the most beautiful and costly precious stones came into the hands of the Chibchas, yet they themselves undertook mining operations in search of them. In Somondoco traces have been found showing that they knew how to lay bare those veins in the rock which contained the emeralds, and to pick out the veins with sharp instruments until they yielded the precious stones.

During the last half-century before the conquest, all the splendours of Chibcha art were concentrated at the courts of the Zaque in Tunja, and Zippá in Bogotá. It is true that the palaces of these rulers were constructed of only wood and straw, but the splendid proportions of their design impressed even the Spaniards. A double wall of palisades surrounded the palace quarters, which were of considerable extent, and, being covered with a roof of waterproof tapestry, formed a dry promenade. The outer stockade was interrupted at intervals with masts.[1] It was further decorated with little pieces of gold plate; these moved with every breath

---

[1] Cf. the description of the sacrificial customs, ante, p. 291 et s q.

of wind, glistened in the sunlight, and made a metallic noise as they clashed together. The interior of the court was kept scrupulously clean, and contained a large number of rooms wherein the ruler and his court resided and where his treasures were kept. The buildings in which the ruler received his subjects were naturally fitted up at the greatest expense. As in the case of the temples, so also in the palaces of the Zippá, the foundations of the main pillars were laid upon the corpses of victims who were apparently buried alive and crushed to death when the pillar was raised; the offering of their blood to the gods was supposed to preserve the house from ill fortune. The walls were constructed of wood, and the roofs of straw, but of these materials nothing was visible from within. The floor was thickly covered with clean mats; the walls and roof were hung with different-coloured tapestry decorated with golden ornaments and richly adorned with precious stones. The ruler sat upon a throne of wood which was richly overlaid with gold, surrounded by the highest priests and dignitaries. No subject dare approach him without bringing some gift, and then he was allowed to enter only with his head bowed and his eyes fixed on the floor. He was obliged either to maintain this posture or to turn away from the king as long as he remained in his presence; no one was considered sufficiently honourable to look him in the face, as to be placed face to face with the monarch was equivalent to a sentence of death. The ruler's feet were never allowed to touch the floor; if the necessities of religion or war obliged him to leave his palace, he changed his throne for an open litter, decorated no less richly with gold and precious stones, which was carried on the shoulders of four men. A numerous escort invariably accompanied the monarch. At the head of the procession were servants who swept the streets before him and laid down carpets; then followed a band of musicians and a numerous body-guard composed of priests and dignitaries. The common people, for whom each exit of the ruler was a festival, brought up the rear.

In the immediate neighbourhood of the palace, though not within its limits, were the dwellings of the king's wives; of these the last Zippá is said to have had as many as two hundred. Only one among these ranked as a legal wife, and her privileges were by no means insignificant: among others she is said to have had the right of enforcing a prescribed period of continence upon her husband at her death. It is related of the wives of the usaques, each of whom is said to have had a considerable number, that they were allowed to punish misconduct in their husbands with stripes, as they were not subject to the laws which governed the common people. Adultery among the women was visited with stern punishment upon both them and their paramours: upon mere suspicion, upon an incautious word, the outraged husband might kill his wife. That the position of the ruler, as well as of individual caciques, was inherited by nephews and not by sons, only the personal property of the dead man coming to the wife and children, has already been noticed.[1] Among the Chibchas, on the death of the king and the more important dignitaries, certain women and servants also followed them into the other world. The corpse was quickly embalmed and forced into a sitting posture, while the funeral ceremonies went on for days with singing and drinking; then the priests took the corpse by stealth to a secret place and buried it in a deep grave,—first the mummy, with its costly raiment and valuable offerings of gold and precious stones, and then, upon a thin covering of earth, were laid the women who were to

---

[1] *Ante*, pp. 292, 295.

accompany the dead man. These women were made almost unconscious by means of stupefying drugs, and upon them more earth was laid and then a number of slaves. The earth was often piled into a mound above the whole. After the burial the funeral lamentations lasted some days longer, being also renewed upon the anniversary; but the general interest was quickly concentrated on the new ruler, who had meanwhile been undergoing the ordeal previously mentioned.[1]

In the year 1470 Saguanmachica sat upon the throne of Bogotá. As the rules of the succession ordained, he had governed the district of Chia until his predecessor's death. Even at that time the kingdom of Zippá had attained important dimensions. Saguanmachica, however, contributed not a little by his conquests to gain for it that leading position among the Chibchas which it retained until the arrival of the Spaniards. His predecessors had already turned their arms against the foreign States around them, and had also subdued many of the kindred Chibcha peoples. Saguanmachica attacked the caciques of Fusagasuga on the farther side of the Pasca River and easily won a brilliant victory. But it led to important consequences; the king of Guatabita felt himself insecure and opened hostilities himself to anticipate a Zippá attack. Saguanmachica energetically repulsed him and penetrated into the land of Guatabita; but his victorious career was checked by the most powerful Chibcha king, the Zaque Michua, of Hunsa, who came to the help of Guatabita and threatened the boundaries of Bogotá. But neither of these warriors seems to have been wholly prepared for a decisive battle. Affairs relapsed to their former position, and the robber inroads of the neighbouring savage tribes gave the Zippá king so much to do that he was obliged to put off his campaign of revenge against the zaque from year to year. As soon as Saguanmachica had re-established peace upon his borders, he again overran the land of Guatabita and menaced the Hunsa boundaries from that point. But before he reached their country Michua marched against him with a powerful army, and both leaders perished in the furious battle which ensued. Success finally rested with the Bogotá, but, panic-stricken at the death of their king, they relinquished the fruits of victory and returned home.

The successor to the Zippá throne was Nemequene, the most important ruler that the land ever possessed. He, too, had previously been cacique of Chia, and his nephew, Tisquesusa, succeeded him in that position. The Fusagasugas, who had recently been subdued, considered this a favourable opportunity to regain their independence; at the same time the Zipaquira, the Nemza, and those hereditary enemies, the savage Panches, made an inroad into the country. But Nemequene showed himself equal to every danger; with one army he repulsed in person the external enemy while Tisquesusa subdued the rebels with another. After that he took up Saguanmachica's plans for conquest. Guatabita fell into his hands rather by treachery than by force. The people of Guatabita were the cleverest goldsmiths in the Chibcha district; they displayed the highest skill in covering stone figures with finely beaten gold, on which those artistic little engravings peculiar to the Chibcha art were produced, representing men and beasts individually and in groups.[2] Consequently every king, every usaque, every cacique, was anxious to have one or more of the Guatabita goldsmiths. But the monarch desired to turn the artistic skill of his subjects to his own advantage, and demanded that two

---

[1] *Ante*, p. 290.          [2] See Figs. 2 and 3, Plate opposite p. 302.

warriors should enter his service in return for every goldsmith that he sent abroad. This fact gave the Zippá his opening. He and his caciques suddenly expressed a desire for numerous goldsmiths; and the best warriors of Bogotá went to the ... of Guatabita in their place. There they not only formed a combination among themselves, but by means of persuasion and presents succeeded in winning over numerous allies among the other foreigners. By these means the Zippá got the border fortress of Guasca into his power, and when he one day suddenly appeared before the capital of Guatabita there was no one to oppose him. The king and his escort were killed in the palace, and his territory was incorporated with the kingdom of Bogotá and placed under the government of a brother of Nemequene.

The next object of Nemequene's attacks was the ruler of Ubaque. It was only after several months of fierce warfare that he made his submission to the Zippá and gave him his two daughters to wife; but the conclusion of peace brought a considerable accession of territory to the Zippá kingdom, although he left the ruler of Ubaque in possession of his dominions as a vassal prince. While Nemequene was thus rounding off the boundaries of his kingdom by these little conquests, a grave danger was threatening its internal peace. The brother of the monarch, who had been made governor of Guatabita, succeeded, partly by treachery and partly by force, in getting possession of the fortress where the prince of Ubaque kept his rich treasures. But before the robber could carry off his booty he was surrounded by the troops of the Ubaque, reduced to starvation, and finally killed in an attempt to break through the lines of the besiegers, after throwing the treasures into a neighbouring lake. Though his attack was entirely justified, the Ubaque was afraid of the anger of the Zippá, whose brother, the governor, had been killed. The rich presents which he sent to Nemequene were not received until he had appeared at court to plead his cause in person. But when he related to the monarch a full and truthful account of the circumstances, Nemequene recognised the injustice that his brother had committed and took no action against the Ubaque.

Nemequene's love of justice was equal to his reputation as a warrior; all the laws that were in force in the Chibcha district at the time of the Spanish conquest were ascribed to him. The number of these regulations was certainly limited, and the punishments assigned were severe. Death in different forms was the punishment for murder, desertion, rape, incest, and sodomy; a coward was clothed in woman's garments and given woman's work to do. The apparel and the ornaments of high rank were forbidden to the common people; only the caques were allowed to bore their ears and noses for the wearing of ornaments. To be carried in a litter was the exclusive privilege of the king and of those to whom he might grant permission. Among the regulations of the civil law which testify to greater progress in the idea of justice we have the following: the property of a man who died without heirs came to the monarch; if a wife died in childbed, and the child also, the husband was obliged to recompense his wife's family, though no such recompense was necessary if the child lived, he being then responsible only for its maintenance.

Throughout his rule Nemequene had never forgotten to prepare for a decisive battle with the Zaque. Quemuenchatocha, a boy aged eighteen years, had succeeded Michua in Tunja, and no doubt it was owing to his youth that war was not begun on his side first. But Nemequene could not resign the traditional claims of his predecessors to supremacy. He therefore, with a powerful army, began the subjugation of the vassals of the Zaque. After his first successes he sent a message to the Zaque advising him to recognise his supremacy if he did not wish to risk being driven from his kingdom. But the Zaque was not a man to be easily frightened. He knew that he might reckon upon the support of all those who, like himself, were threatened with the encroachments of the Zippá; a powerful army soon came to him from the Iracá of Sogamoso. The battle was hotly disputed and for a long time remained indecisive; both monarchs were visible far and wide as they were borne in their gleaming litters above the heads of the multitude, hurrying among the bands of warriors and exciting them to the highest displays of courage. Then the Zippá advanced too far to the front and received an enemy's arrow in the breast. In vain did he exhort his men to stand fast: the news spread rapidly through their ranks, and the troops of the Zaque attacked with redoubled vigour and won a complete victory. The army was obliged to return to Bogotá after abandoning all its previous conquests, the Zaque making only a show of pursuit.

Nemequene returned to his capital still alive, but five days afterward he succumbed to his wound. His successor, Tisquesusa, who had already won a high reputation as governor of Chia, immediately upon his accession resumed the war with the Zaque. His first campaign brought about the subjection of a number of usaques who had hitherto been the vassals of the king of Tunja. He was already preparing for a decisive conflict with his adversary when news came to him that an invasion had been made into the Chibcha district by a powerful foreign enemy, in the expedition of Queseda and his comrades. Here, as everywhere, the Spaniards won a brilliant victory at the first onset, and this they chiefly owed to the fear which their horses inspired in the natives. Tisquesusa fled into the woods; but his retreat was betrayed and he was crushed. His successor submitted to the foreign enemy. The Zaque awaited the Spaniards in haughty neutrality without offering resistance; for that reason he was not deprived of the throne, but died a natural death soon afterward. Many of the smaller rulers continued an obstinate resistance; but after the main kingdom had been subjugated to the foreign dominion, their efforts were useless, and only provoked that ferocity which so often stained the Spanish conquests in cases where the natives did not offer a ready submission. Upon the death of Tisquesusa the loosely organised kingdom of the Chibchas collapsed. The people never again were strong enough to attempt the recovery of their independence. In a few years the Spaniards obliterated the last traces of the native civilisation, with its peculiar characteristics, as much by their oppression of the natives as by the material improvements which they brought into the empire; their introduction of fresh blood rapidly modified the Chibcha race.

(b) *San Agustin.* — On the south of the Chibcha district, and only a few miles distant from it, on a little plateau on the right bank of the upper Magdalena River, are to be found remains of an ancient American civilisation presenting peculiar characteristics. The ruins are now named San Agustin, after a miserable village which was founded in the previous century by the natives who felled the quina-wood; but what its ancient name was, and who the people were who left such remarkable memorials behind them, are still wholly uncertain. The

Chibcha civilisation never extended so far, but with no other of the races with which the Spaniards came in contact can these antiquities be connected. At the time of the Spanish conquest, and also according to Chibcha traditions, though these do not go back very far, this district was inhabited by the wild hordes of the Paeces, a race of cannibals and restless hunters, upon the lowest planes of civilisation, and accounted the most dangerous neighbours of the Chibchas. The memorials of the San Agustin civilisation must therefore even then have been in ruins and have remained abandoned in the depths of the primeval forest, as they continued for another three centuries, until certain wood-cutters penetrated into this jungle in their search for quina-trees, and, in order to prove the truth of their marvellous accounts of numerous temples of human figures, brought forth from the darkness of the forest the monuments which to-day adorn the market-place of San Agustin.

Upon the wooded hills at the upper course of the stream which flows through San Agustin and takes its name from the town, the wood-cutters found a number of little temples the construction of which is without parallel upon American soil. The people who erected them were making their first attempts at architecture. They were unable to work or to build into walls the stones which the mountain streams brought down to the table-land which they inhabited; they therefore sunk their temples half in the ground. Great blocks of stone were set up side by side in the manner of dolmens, forming a four-cornered room small enough to be roofed in by a huge slab. One might be tempted to consider these cell-like constructions as burial-places. But nothing has been found to justify this theory; on the contrary the general character of their position shows undoubtedly that they were intended for temples. It also appears that they were never closed in upon every side; but the monuments clearly show sculptured pillars which formed the entrance, upon the back of which a large picture of a god was occasionally drawn. At the present time scarcely a temple remains in a sufficient state of preservation to enable us to get an accurate plan of it; but from the descriptions and drawings of the first discoverers we are forced to conclude that the numerous carved stones which are now lying about in the woods, and some of which have been brought down to San Agustin, were at one time united into a single area of temples consisting of little consecrated chambers; and the considerable number of these monuments points to a rich population.

The memorials of San Agustin fall into three classes: supports or pillars, which formed the temple entrance; altar-stones sculptured with pictures of the gods in human form; and monuments of various kinds to which no particular place in the temples can be assigned.

The temple pillars display the art of this unknown people at its highest development. Though their architectural capabilities were extremely limited, yet their plastic art had attained such a pitch of perfection as to imply a long previous period of development. In their representations of the gods, symbolical tendencies confined the makers to archaic types; on the other hand the pillars show a realism and a characterisation which tempt us to suppose that they were portraits of realities. But in this case the artists laid stress only upon the face and its expression; the rest of the body is never drawn with freedom, but for the most part is carved in relief upon the supports, the pillars, or the stones, and the figures are usually disproportioned. The clothed legs and the bare feet are often much reduced in size and occasionally disappear in the foundations. Their pictures of the human frame display a peculiar kind of clothing, now reminding us of flowing robes and now merely showing a waist-cloth. But the torso is nearly always conceived as clothed with a sleeved garment terminating in a band at the wrist. As in the case of nearly all South American civilisations, the sculptures of San Agustin never display the head bare: from the square helmet to the carefully wound turban we have before us almost all the head-coverings which appear in the gold-work of the Chibchas and the clay figures of the Peruvians.

The realistic character of these heads enables us to form some general conclusions upon the features of this unknown nation. The noses are strongly proportioned with broad cartilages, the cheek-bones are prominent, the lips remarkably protruding and giving an impression of sensuality where this is not the result of the artistic mode of representing the mouth. The eyes for the most part are large, with strongly accentuated pupils, of almond shape, covered by eyebrows often well marked. The most carefully carved pillars which formed corresponding pairs display above the head-dress the symbolic picture of an animal the head of which is broad and rather flat, the body thick, and the tail long and annulated. The representation has apparent resemblances to the chameleon or to a stumpy lizard; but as it displays many correspondences with memorials of a third race which have occasionally been considered as apes, but are more properly identified with the puma or American lion, this is probably the correct interpretation here. Lastly these "protectors of divinity" grasped weighty clubs in their hands; and when the figures of the gods are armed, they, too, carry only clubs and staves.

The figures of the gods are far less realistic; the living element in them is constantly overpowered by ornamental tendencies proceeding from symbolism. Only occasionally are nose and eyes depicted with any reality, and the contour of the face is constantly indicated merely by three small right angles; of this there are many examples in Chibcha gold-work. The most important feature of the gods is the mouth; this, too, is often drawn at right angles, but almost invariably displays a double row of powerful teeth from which the four eye-teeth in the upper and lower jaws protrude. This peculiar arrangement of teeth depicted in almost all their representations is an important indication for the solution of the riddle as to the origin of the monuments: it appears again in á large number of clay vessels with faces on them, of Peruvian origin, which have been found in the valleys on the coast-line from Chimu to Santa. If we retrace the conceptions upon which this facial representation was founded, a clay figure from Tiahuanaco leads us to the conclusion that the jaws of the puma were thus depicted. Thus we are here concerned with a divinity to whom the qualities of this bloodthirsty beast of prey were attributed. An excellent support for this theory is seen in the fact that occasionally even the images of San Agustin hold tiny figures of human victims in their hands, which for that reason must be children who had not yet been destined to sacrifice.

These results are also important for the identification of the monuments of the third race. Here the animal in one instance appears with its long annulated tail above a human victim of such small proportions that it holds it in its forearms. In this figure investigators have seen an ape in the act of copula-

1. *Poncho from Tomaval (Trujillo),*
   *Peru; ¹⁄₁₂ real size.*

2 and 3. *Gold figures from Columbia;*
   *½ real size.*

2. *from Boyacá.*

3. *from Sogamoso.*

4 and 5. *Jars; ¼ real size.*

4. *from M... ... (...zonga).*

5. *... m... ...*

... ...

... *... Cu... ..., Cund-na-*
*... ... Co...bia*

7. *A Cup from Manizales, Columbia;*
   *½ real size.*

8 and 9. *Jugs from Columbia; ½ real*
   *size.*

9. *from Manizales.*

10. *from Anserma vieja in Cauca*

11. *Mummy of a Peruvian woman;*
    *½ real size.*

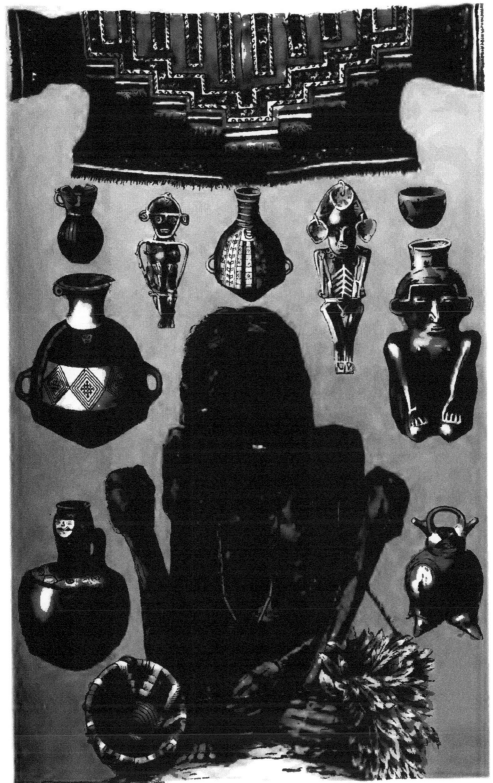

London: Wᵐ Heinemann.    Printed by the Bibliographisches Institut, Leipzig.    New York: Dodd, Mead & Cᵒ

SOUTH AMERICAN ANTIQUITIES.

tion; and, as at least two undoubtedly phallic representations have been found in a district of this unknown people, an attempt has been made to connect them with the powers of procreation. But in this case, too, we have to deal with the god incarnate in a sacred animal, the puma, which is devouring the victim that is brought to him. Among similar representations there exists a fish in the hand of a divine figure, and similarly a snake; and in another instance the snake is being devoured by a very realistic owl. The number of sculptured stones around the ruins of San Agustin is considerable; but in other directions similar stones are found in isolation between the Magdalena River and Popayan, and also in the neighbourhood of this town. In Quito we have no instances of stone sculptures of this character, but all the traditions concerning the worship of the bloodthirsty god Supay and his temples correspond so well with the ruins of San Agustin that earlier relations between these peoples can very well be presumed. The coincidences extend still farther southward. In the middle of Peru the Marañon and the Santa flow for a time northward in two parallel valleys, and finally take opposite directions, the one eastward and the other westward, until they pass through the Cordilleras; here we shall also meet with a civilisation[1] the monuments of which so constantly remind us of San Agustin as to lead us to the conclusion that in ancient times there was one single people of a uniform civilisation which inhabited the high valleys from ten degrees south latitude as far as several degrees north of the equator, and that it is the scattered remains of these that can be observed in the inhabitants of the Santa valley of Quito and of the upper Magdalena.

### *C.* THE CIVILISED DISTRICTS OF THE WEST COAST OF SOUTH AMERICA

AN intersecting system of mountains, where the Magdalena and the Cauca take their rise, is all that separates San Agustin from the most northerly province which belonged to the Inca kingdom at the time of the Spanish conquest. This range stretches uninterruptedly over thirty degrees of latitude, reaching almost everywhere from the coast of the Pacific Ocean to the eastern slope of the Cordilleras, whence numerous streams rush down into the great plains of South America. Here the Spaniards found for the second time a rich and well-organised civilisation in their newly discovered world.

The most mistaken ideas have prevailed until recently concerning the Inca kingdom of Tahuantinsuyu, and, as in Central America, mainly through the fault of the native chroniclers. In Mexico we saw that Don Fernando de Alba Ixtlilxochitl introduced an unhistoric factor into the ancient history of the country in his account of the Toltecs;[2] Garcilaso de la Vega has done the same for the South American provinces, by which we mean the different groups of States which were incorporated in the great Inca kingdom at the end of the fifteenth century; this historian is generally known as "el Inca," in order to distinguish him from other authors of the same name, and in reference to his descent from the royal house of Cuzco. During the sixteenth century he wrote a history of Peru in which such unbounded and unreasonable confidence has been placed, owing to the author's connection with the natives, that the accounts of other chroniclers of greater impartiality have, until recently, been entirely neglected. The work of Garcilaso is nothing more than an enthusiastic panegyric of the dominion of the ancient native

---

[1] See *post*, p. 311.      [2] See *ante*, pp. 223, 224.

rulers; it displays all their exploits in the clearest light, but sometimes fails to see, or entirely neglects, the shady side of their history. In particular the struggles which must have endured during thousands of years of previous development are dismissed as being the work of the Incas, although their dominion was only a few centuries old, and although their State was certainly the youngest among the different civilisations of South America.

The extensive district which was afterward subject to the Inca rule contained numerous centres of civilisation from the earliest times. It is as difficult here as in the case of the northern civilisation to decide whether the amount of culture which they all possessed, and which shows their connection with a particular civilisation, enables us to conclude the exact amount of culture that had been attained by the inhabitants before their disruption into separate races and peoples. In the history of human development the same phenomena continually occur under different circumstances; and care must be exercised in deciding whether coincidences and connections belong to a previous relationship or are rather results of earlier collateral influences. If such an early relationship existed at all, it must at any rate be referred to times earlier than the foundation of the kingdom of Peru, which is said to have taken place at the beginning of the Christian era. This tradition, at least, is due to the influence of that desire so remarkable among the Mexican chroniclers to make the history of their own country synchronise with the history of the Old World. The different civilisations within the Inca kingdom were situated in districts inhabited by at least three races which can be clearly distinguished on linguistic grounds. Geographical causes gave such a peculiar character to the development of each of these that the possibility of their common origin is counterbalanced by the difference in their monuments. Perhaps closer relations existed between special groups of these nations. The kingdoms of Quito, of Chanchan and the more southern provinces on the coast, seem to have been in closer connection with one another than with the Peruvians of the highland, the Quechua and Aymará. It can hardly be doubted that these latter were the originators of that civilisation which the Incas later made the common property of all their subjects.

In recent times the Aymará ran the risk of having a part ascribed to them in South America similar to that which was attributed to the Toltecs in Central America.[1] Early settlements on the most northern boundary of this civilised district have been ascribed to them, and to the influence of their migrations has been attributed all traces of unusual culture which have been discovered from Colombia as far south as Chili and beyond the eastern Cordilleras into the Argentine district of Catamarca. On the other hand we may consider it as proved that the Aymará were the authors of the remains of a particular civilisation, and one by no means despicable, existing upon the southeast of Tahuantinsuyu around the lake of Titicaca. We may also ascribe to the influence of this ancient civilisation the existence of the fine, artistically wrought pottery that has been brought to light upon the borders of Gran Chaco, now almost inaccessible to the white man, in a district that has been inhabited only by nomad Indians within human memory. This pottery displays ornamentation not only in colours, but also in modelling, of a kind that has been met with but rarely without the boundaries of the ancient civilised peoples. But the peculiarities of the Aymará civilisation are so distinct and so entirely consequent upon the geographical conditions of their

[1] See ante, p. 265.

early home that they do not justify us in attributing the origin of all civilisation exclusively to this people. That of the Aymará must rather be considered with the civilisation of the Quitu and of the Yunga as merely one of the factors which go to make up the general picture of South American civilisation.

Among those States which were incorporated with the Inca kingdom at the time of the Spanish conquest, but which could point to a long period of independent development, the most northerly was Quito. Its inhabitants were called Cara. They did not, however, consider their origin to have been in this district, but supposed themselves to have invaded between the ninth and tenth centuries of our era the territory which they possessed about the sixteenth century. Here they founded a new State. They were by no means certain of their original home. Migrating from a southerly district, they are said to have followed the coast to the Pacific Ocean; they then entered the province of Manta, somewhat inland, but continued their migrations along the coast-land, which offered but few attractions for settlement. Finally the Esmeralda River enabled them to gain the richer and healthier valleys of the mountains. The population in these was dense but un-civilised, and could offer no lasting resistance to the more highly developed mili-tary skill of the Cara, and about the year 1000 a king named Quitu firmly established their rule. He created the organisation of the country, one of those close oligarchical monarchies which are found almost everywhere among the early races of America. He introduced the worship of the sun and moon among all the peoples which he subjugated, and was the founder of a dynasty which ruled for several centuries over the Quito kingdom. His successors at first proceeded to extend the boundaries of the kingdom upon the north; the peoples in that direc-tion were as primitive as those which had been subjugated in the centre of the kingdom, and conquest in this direction was limited only by the difficulty of estab-lishing long lines of communication with their base of operations.

Matters were different toward the south. The later Scyris, the kings of Quito, soon began to turn their arms in that direction, but in the well-organised state of Puruha they soon met with a resistance which entirely barred their progress. After the two rulers had measured their strength, with indecisive results to either side, they concluded a treaty which was to do away with all possibility of hostilities for the future. Up till now the throne of Quito had descended eleven times from father to son, or, failing an immediate heir, from uncle to nephew, according to the customs of the land. Chance then brought it about that the Scyri possessed neither son nor nephew to take up the reins of government, but only a daughter. At such a conjuncture the princes and caciques of the realm had the right to elect a new Scyri; but the king was able to persuade them to alter these rules for the succession, and made a compact with the king of Puruha according to which his son was to marry the princess and ascend the throne of Quito, thereby fusing the two kingdoms into one. In this newly formed kingdom the town of Quito remained the capital, and all the more so as upon the southward the clouds of Peruvian conquest began to lower threateningly.

Quito was a kingdom not only extensive and rich, but also well organised and civilised,—a prize to excite the desires of any monarch anxious for conquest. Though the Cara did not understand, as the Peruvians did, the art of laying down highroads and building bridges in their country, they were by no means despi-cable architects. The king had laid out gardens and built palaces in Liribamba among a number of little lakes connected by canals; and these formed not only a royal palace worthy of a mighty prince, but also a strong fortress in which an army of thousands of warriors might offer a vigorous resistance to their opponents. The soldiers of the Cara and Puruha were armed only with spear and sling, but they used these weapons with most astonishing accuracy, as the Inca warriors were to learn when their turn came. Prowess in war had become somewhat impaired under the later Scyris; a generation of peace had produced much advance in wealth and material comforts, but had not called forth the fierce virtues of war. Consequently, when the Inca Tupak Yupanki first turned his arms against the Quitu he met with but little resistance. The outlying provinces, which were only loosely connected with the kingdom, were for the most part won over by the promises of peace which the Inca held out to them as he advanced threateningly at the head of his veteran army. When Tupak Yupanki invaded the kingdom of Puruha, every step of progress was bought at the price of blood; but when the Scyri general, trusting to superior numbers gave battle in the open, he suffered such a decisive defeat that the Inca gained possession of all Puruha almost without striking another blow. However, he did not at once invade the district of Quito; after establishing garrisons in the territory he had conquered he returned to Cuzco in 1460, as his attention was claimed elsewhere.

The Scyri died a few years after these events. His life had been peaceful, and he had grown old, before the attack of Tupak Yupanki had invested him with heavier responsibilities at a time when he was not strong enough to resist. But a year of battles had aroused those qualities in his son for which his ancestors had been distinguished. As soon as he had obtained possession of his father's kingdom he began a campaign against the invaders; and although he did not succeed in regaining the whole extent of his kingdom, yet he rapidly drove the Inca-Peruvians out of that district which had formed the nucleus of his father's realm. Many years passed before the Incas again turned their eyes northward. At last, in the year 1475, Huaina Capak appeared on the boundaries of Quito, but found them better guarded than they had been in the time of Tupak Yupanki. The Puruha had strongly fortified the bank of the Achupalla; and the unfailing accuracy of their slingers wrought terrible havoc in the ranks of the enemy and entirely neutralised their superiority in tactics and armament. But the Inca obtained by treachery what he could not win by force of arms; on this occasion, also, promises of peace made a great impression upon the subjects of the proud Scyri, and before the powerful Inca army many caciques began to waver. Treachery of this kind revealed an unfortified ford over the Achupalla; and when once the river had been crossed the Puruhas were obliged to evacuate their fortress and retreat. They again attempted to oppose the Peruvians, but so decisive was their defeat and so general the desertion of their vassals, that the Scyri was obliged to abandon almost the whole territory, with his capital, Quito, and his summer residence, Liribamba. He fled to Hatun Taqui, in the country of Otabalo, and, after unconditionally rejecting the propositions of peace which the Inca held out, he perished fighting for the last remains of his kingdom. Huaina Capak then considered that his conquests were complete. But immediately after the death of the Scyri resistance was renewed around the person of Paccha, the daughter and heiress of the king. She did not openly oppose the Inca's power, but she made it clearly understood that new dangers would be continually threatening him from her. In order to win her over without bloodshed, he added her to the number of his legal wives, though not without doing some violence to his own laws. As Quito and Puruha had formerly been united by this means he succeeded in completely incorporating the country with his own kingdom, and the histories of the two States are henceforward indissolubly united.

If the Cara of Quito had really migrated northward from another people on the coast of the Pacific Ocean, as their legend relates, this people must have been the Muchik, who are called Yunga by the Inca Peruvians, and Chimu by the Spaniards. From the Gulf of Guayaquil southward to the neighbourhood of the modern Callao the whole seaboard had long been in their power. Farther southward people speaking another language and with another political centre were situated on the borders of the provinces of the Chimu kingdom. Their civilisation, however, showed so many points of resemblance to that of their more northern neighbours that the Incas denoted all the peoples on the coast by the collective name of Yunga; moreover between the northern and the southern coast peoples political relations were so close that it is impossible accurately to divide the little that is known of their histories.

The very fact that an important group of States could be developed on the coast of Peru is evidence that this people had made considerable strides in their struggle for existence; for the country over which the Chimu kingdom extended was certainly unfavourable to a dense population. The ground of the narrow coast-line between the spurs of the Cordilleras and the sea is not wholly barren; but there is an almost entire lack of rainfall, and the burning rays of the tropical sun have made the country nearly a desert. Oases exist here and there, where the rapid torrents that flow down from the neighbouring range bring sufficient moisture with them to support some vegetable life. These rivers in their unchecked fury, are even dangerous to mankind. During the dry season the thirsty ground so entirely absorbs the moisture that often no single drop reaches the sea; but when a thunderstorm bursts with tropical fury above the spurs of the Cordilleras the rivers rise high above their banks in a few hours and in their resistless course sweep away every barrier to their power. The period must have been long before Man sought a refuge in this dangerous strip of country; but he succeeded in overcoming all difficulties and in wresting from nature the means to support a population far more numerous than that of to-day. For this the extensive remains of the ancient towns which are to be found at the mouth of almost every valley leading from the mountains to the sea are evidence.

The first requirement for a lasting settlement of the country was the power of controlling the water. The people that settled there may have had experience in their earlier home in the art of draining, an art widely diffused of old in the mountainous districts of Peru, and practised here at any rate with brilliant success. Where the river passed from the mountains to the plain it was divided or drawn off in great canals which followed the course of the river and led into a complication of smaller tributaries. By this means of irrigation a much larger extent of country could be cultivated for maize, sweet potatoes, yuccas, and cotton, and also the great danger of inundation was overcome. The labyrinth of water-courses broke the power of the flood and turned the extraordinary fury of the rivers into an extraordinary blessing for the land. A further evidence for the agricultural activities of the coast peoples is their knowledge of the excellent effects of guano. As guano was used for manure by the Inca-Peruvians, they must have learned its value from the coast races, who possessed inexhaustible supplies of this article : for they alone were sufficiently skilled in navigation to import it from the islands. It is certain that at the earliest times only individual valleys on the coast were populated, and as the long, wild stretches of sand which separate the belts of vegetation around the river courses from one another made communication by land almost impossible, these individual settlements lived for a long time in complete isolation. But the more the population increased in such an oasis the more urgent became the necessity of bringing new portions of land under cultivation. As differences of climate, and the hostility between the mountain and the coast peoples, confined these river settlements within narrow limits, the Yunga sought along the seacoast for fresh districts capable of cultivation, and gradually obtained possession of almost all the valleys which run down from the Cordilleras.

According to tradition their extensions of territory were made from the north southward. Against this there are archæological reasons. We have already noticed a tradition of migration from the south among the Cara of Quito ; it would be difficult to explain the relationship between their civilisation and that of San Agustin with the civilisation of central Peru if the centre from which these movements proceeded was situated in the neighbourhood of Guayaquil. And as the Chimu peoples extended their dominion no farther south than Lima, how is it possible that a similar civilisation down to the smallest details could have occurred in districts even farther south ? It is much more probable that the settlements on the coast proceeded from the south and drove the northern people more and more into their civilised districts, or pushed them northward away from the coast-line into the mountains. At any rate there was a uniform zone of civilisation in existence at an early period, which embraced the whole coast-land from Rio Maule as far as the Gulf of Guayaquil and contained certain highland races upon the northeast. This civilisation was ancient, and had long begun to fade before the Incas became important in the highland. Individual kingdoms and races broke away from the community ; no political unity ever existed. The unities of religion and language also disappeared under local influences, until a new centre of power was formed near the northern boundaries in the valley of Chimu. Here a number of powerful kings undertook to proceed in a contrary direction and extend their power southward, and again to unite in a political unity peoples already closely related. This course of events was in progress along the coast when the Incas began a similar career of conquest in the highland. Recollections of this, which were still fresh at the time of the Spanish conquest, are the cause of the mistaken idea that the civilisation of the coast-land proceeded in the same direction. In the sixteenth century it was perfectly well known that the kings of Chimu had extended their power southward and subdued a number of smaller States. Thus the valleys of Virú, Santa, Nepeña, Huarmey, Supe, and Huacho became incorporated in the Chimu kingdom partly individually and partly in groups which had enjoyed a uniform civilisation for a long time. On the south the priestly State of Pachacamak, which was tributary to the Cuismancu, and the group of valleys which was ruled by the Chupimancu, formed smaller States ; either they were obliged to offer an armed resistance to the Chimu conquest, or, like Pachacamak, they owed their further independence to the reverence paid to their temple towns. At any rate they display rich and carefully decorated ruins of that old civilisation which had attained a high and uniform pitch of development upon the north and south of the Chimu kingdom.

Both before and at the time of the Incas the coast district must have been extremely thickly populated. Chanchan, the capital of the Chimu kingdom, in the neighbourhood of the modern Trujillo, is by no means the only site which has an area of about two hundred and fifty acres. Ruined sites of equal size are situated in Pachacamak and in Huadea; and the cemetery of Ancon, near Lima, an inexhaustible hunting-ground for Peruvian antiquities, also points to a long-continued and dense population of the country. Almost all these sites are of similar appearance, since all the buildings in the extensive ruins are right-angled in construction and disposed at right angles to one another. As the coast does not provide sufficient stone or wood to be used as building-material, the coast peoples erected their buildings for the most part of little bricks made chiefly of pounded clay. The walls in consequence had to be made of considerable thickness; but the breadth decreased toward the top, so that the roofs and ceilings were wider than the floors. This was the case at any rate with the temples and palaces, the only buildings of which the walls display traces of decoration in the form of ornamental stucco-work. Concerning the mode of roofing we can only draw doubtful conclusions. The few roofs that remain are also composed of worked clay; but the great halls which exist among the ruins can hardly have been covered by such perishable means. Windows were entirely unknown; the rooms were generally built around a court, and air and light were admitted by the door, which often took up the whole of the front side. The most important ruins, however, are not dwelling-houses. These would be made of clay for the chief classes; the houses of the common people must have been made of reeds and canes, as wood was entirely lacking. The extensive ruins of walls, which can still be seen to have embraced the ancient cities, are partly the great walls of defence of which most towns possessed a double row with entrances at the angles, and are partly the weaker walls which divided the town into a number of districts like courts; these are supposed to have been inhabited in common by particular, clans or by officials.

The palaces and temples seem for the most part to have been erected around the circumference of the town; in the case of temples we constantly meet with terraces rising in steps, the walls of which were interrupted now and then by rooms and were built of brick, the interior being filled with rubble. Many of the temple pyramids also served as tombs, but only for the kings and the highest priests. Extensive cemeteries like that of Ancon are to be found in many places, particularly on the south of the Chimu kingdom. Here the mummies were placed fastened in a sitting position, sometimes alone, sometimes in groups, in vaulted graves or in enormous jars, occasionally with no protection at all, and often in tiers upon one another, but always decorated as well as possible and provided with the implements of their earthly profession. Often, however, a common man could not afford the expense of such a resting-place; he buried his dead in the floor of his dwelling, so that the city grounds are often honeycombed with such graves.

A people who showed such piety toward their dead must naturally have believed in a future life corresponding in some degree to their earthly existence:

beyond this we have no information concerning their religious ideas. We can hardly conceive that a people upon whose notice the destructive powers of the sun were so constantly forced as they were upon the inhabitants of the Peruvian coast should have made sun-worship the central point of their religion; it is intelligible that they should have regarded water as the chief object of their veneration, for their livelihood depended entirely upon its beneficent influences. The Chimu are certainly said to have reverenced the moon as their chief deity, and also the Pleiades and the three stars which form Orion's belt. But they also considered the sea to be a divine power, which helps to feed men with its fish, makes communication possible between nations, and moderates the sun's destructive glow with its refreshing breeze. A similar worship, either of the sea or of water of some kind, is spread over the whole coast-line. Fishes also obtained reverence, as being created by the water; the god of Pachacamak, the chief divinity of the whole coast district, was depicted with a fish's tail.

In Pachacamak we find a body of religious conceptions which proceed from different sources. In the highland of Peru we shall presently meet with a widely extended worship which displays much affinity with the Quetzalcoatl-Kukulkan of Central America. Originally perhaps a sun-god, he had become so entirely anthropomorphic in course of time, that the people thought of him only in his human form as a lawgiver and a civiliser and as in opposition to the sun-worship of the Incas. The Pachacamak of the coast peoples was originally a similar divinity; as the son of Con he is mythologically connected with the highland god and represents the same idea, the origin of all created things, including perhaps the idea of divinity, since all other deities are only emanations from him. On the coast the elements of the water-worship were brought into connection with him; thus he spreads his cloak upon the waves as a boat and passes out of sight over the sea, or in the roaring of the stream he delivers oracles as Rimak (the rushing one). Consequently he could be represented with a fish's tail, and the fish, as being his symbol, was regarded as a fetich.

Phallic worship has also been ascribed to the Chimu; figures of clay found in the coast provinces seem to confirm the theory. The peoples on the coast were also peoples of decaying civilisation, among whom such conceptions invariably recur. They had not only become rich, but so corrupted by excess of prosperity that their civilisation, although in many respects it was not only equal but superior to that of the highland people, collapsed before their onset.

The first inhabitants of Peru with whom the Spaniards met were Chimu Indians who had ventured a considerable distance from the coast in their rude vessels. As the stretches of land which divided the separate coast valleys from one another were incapable of cultivation, that communication between the towns which their size and prosperity would have led us to expect could not be carried on by land. The migration legends speak of the first inhabitants of almost all the coast-land as having come from the sea; and the conquests of the Chimu, to whom the llama of the mountains was unknown, can have taken place only by sea. Wood, however, was lacking just as much for shipbuilding as for architecture, and the canoe, so widely employed in other parts of America, was unknown on the Peruvian coast. The Chimu and Yunga used a kind of raft which rested on strong bundles of canes, the air contained in the canes giving it sufficient buoyancy. On the coast of Peru the Pacific Ocean fully justifies its name, and thus by these primitive means a constant communication, attended with little danger could be carried on. Those vessels, similar in construction, which the inhabitants on the lake of Titicaca used, were no doubt built for the first time by colonists from the coast district who had been transported thither after the Inca conquest; for nature there offered material far more suitable for shipbuilding in the mighty trees which were apparently employed by the exponents of the oldest civilisation, the builders of Tiahuanaco.

The races of the coast-line came under the Inca dominion at different times. Pachacutek had already subdued the valleys on the south without encountering any obstinate resistance. Similarly, in later times, Cuismancu and Chupimancu gave in their submission to the Inca-Peruvians at the first demand, hoping with their help to escape the oppressive dominion with which the Chimu kings threatened them. The sacred town of Pachacamak also submitted to the Inca without bloodshed; for the Inca had already learned to attract the adherence of other peoples by religious toleration. Near the temple of Pachacamak they erected a new and more splendid building for the sun, but they also made offerings to the god of the conquered people, and for this the priests expressed their thanks in favourable prophecies. From this point the Incas and the Chimu came into collision, but after long and bloody battles the fortune of war enabled the Inca Tupak Yupanki to advance after his first campaign against the Quitu toward the centre of the Chimu kingdom, the town of Chanchan in the valley of Otuzco. The ruler of the kingdom continued to offer a despairing resistance, but his satraps abandoned him one after the other, and bought the favour of the Inca by their submission, and when he threatened to interrupt the flow of water to the coast, the Chimu saw the uselessness of further resistance and surrendered himself and his kingdom on the field of Cajamarca.

In at least two places on the highlands of Peru before the times of the Incas a civilisation existed which had attained a considerable pitch of development. In the centre of Peru, where the Santa River runs for a long distance parallel with the Marañon River between the dark slopes and the snow-white peaks of the Cordilleras, until the former stream turns aside to the Pacific Ocean, a powerful, warlike people who were also acquainted with the arts of peace founded a great kingdom. Historical traditions give us practically no information about this; it must remain doubtful for the present whether the Cuismancu of Conchucos, already mentioned, is not the result of some apparent misunderstanding. Conchucos, which is situated on a little tributary of the Marañon, does at any rate belong to this civilisation; and the ruins of Sipa, which are not far distant, with its great tombs formed out of cubical stone blocks, is one of the most interesting points whence a conception can be gained of the manner in which this race developed. But the kingdom of the Cuismancu, which was subdued without opposition by the Inca Tupak Yupanki on his campaign against the Chimu, is placed by most chroniclers upon the coast; and the central point of the kingdom of which Conchucos formed a part did not lie on the Marañon, but in the Santa valley, the upper portion of which, notwithstanding the bleak aspect and the unfruitful nature of its highlands, contained the capital of the country, known by the Peruvians as Puna. Proceeding up stream the traveller arrives at Huaraz, Chavin de Huantar, and finally at the watershed at the sources of the Pasco: in Huanuco there are traces of ancient towns, fortresses, and temples which certainly have strong affinities with one another and with the ruins existing in the valley of the Marañon, but show strong points of difference from those in the neighbouring district.

The people of the Santa valley had attained considerable skill in architecture, no doubt partly through the influence of their geographical situation. The mountains afforded them admirable material of granite and sandstone, which the torrents brought down in blocks and slabs to the very gates of their town when the melting of the snows sent the streams roaring down to the lowland. Their art, however, had long passed the stage of merely employing material ready to hand; they understood how to work their stones carefully; they laid them upon beds of mortar which has endured for hundreds of years; and the enormous cubes of which their temple walls are partly built can have been laid in position only through long experience in the art of transporting heavy masses. The most important of their sites is Huanuco. But as the place was already populated with Inca-Peruvians we cannot decide so easily in this case as we can in others, which elements are of Peruvian origin and which belong to the ancient civilisation. On the other hand Chavin de Huantar, with its famous temple, was destroyed and abandoned by the Incas. The temple is said to have been built with no less than five stories of rooms and corridors; it stands so close to the mountain wall that it has been thought to be partly underground, although its foundations undoubtedly rested upon the surface of the valley. A characteristic feature is that its sanctuaries are all plunged in the deepest darkness, no sunbeam ever entering the sacred chamber; in these chambers we again find pictures of the gods with a double row of grinning teeth, which terminate at either extremity with the two overlapping fangs. We have already seen in the case of San Agustin[1] that this arrangement of the teeth originated from the puma. The theory is again confirmed by the fact that the puma continually recurs to an extraordinary extent among the sculptures of Chavin, Huaraz, and Huanuco, and is occasionally apparent in place-names, such as Pumacayan, Pumacancha. The sculptures of the Santa valley also remind us of those of San Agustin in so far as the proportions of the human frame are reduced and the head is sculptured in ornamental style. This can be no chance coincidence.

The kings of this territory pushed forward their boundaries to the coast at the point where the Santa River emerges from the Cordilleras, and a little before its entry into the coast plains remains are to be found of temples and fortifications built of granite blocks like those in the upper valley. The same remark applies to the valleys of Casma and Nepeña. The large number of fortifications invites the theory that there was a continual state of war between the rulers of the highland and the kings of Chimu, who were in possession of the coast. But the utter destruction which is unmistakably visible in the temple ruins of Mojeque in the Casma valley, and of Chavin in the Santa valley, must be ascribed, not to the Chimu, but to the Incas. After their conquests they took great pains to destroy the seats of the gloomy worship which the peoples of the Santa valley carried on, and to introduce in its place the worship of their sun-god.

The second district of highland civilisation before the time of the Incas has been more closely examined, and here tradition is not entirely silent. Its site is upon the southern and western shores of the lake of Titicaca, and its most splendid ruins are those of Tiahuanaco. The many questions which research in this district

---

[1] See *ante*, p. 302.

has raised will probably never be answered. It is pretty certain that a was an ancient nation of the Aymará race which erected these buildings. One portion of the ruins which bears the name Ak-Kapana was certainly a temple enclosure, consisting of a terrace in the form of a pyramid of moderate height, at the foot of which was a sacred enclosure of stone pillars. In the case of Ak-Kapana these pillars enclose a square room, while similar constructions in the neighbourhood of the lake of Umayo are circular; but we may consider them both essentially identical. Whether these erections have anything to do with stone-worship, which was widely spread in this district of the Peruvian highland, is very doubtful; the ruins of Tiahunaco are evidence against rather than for the theory. At any rate the gods that were worshipped here were certainly conceived as being of human form. Evidence of this fact exists in the remains of statues which are still to be found among the ruins; of these, according to the ancient chroniclers, there must have been a much greater number in earlier times. The statues of this ancient epoch, with their artistic stiffness, remind us of those of Chavin and San Agustin. Here also, as in the case of all peoples not fully developed, we find an excessive preponderance of the symbolic and a devotion to a particular style which entirely preclude any attempt at realism. But the gods of Tiahuanaco were other and milder than those of the afore-mentioned civilisation; their human forms are not the same, and moreover their worship was hidden from the light of day.

Tiahuanaco holds also an important position in the domain of architecture. Extensive as the ruins are, not a single closed building is to be seen. That the architects were able to erect such buildings of several stories is proved by a block upon which the façade of a two-storied building has been carved as a model. But the great blocks of stone lie about like those in Pumapungu, the other ruined town of Tiahuanaco, and certainly never formed a building. Many stones have undoubtedly been worked according to plan, and prepared for fitting in with other stones, but nothing can be constructed out of the whole. Certainly the monolith gates which have earlier attracted particular attention must not be considered as part of the building, but, like the Egyptian pylons, as boundary stones and entrances to the sacred enclosure, as we can see from their situation in Ak-Kapana. The most remarkable of these gateways also belongs to this enclosure. If it is not the most massive of the blocks scattered about Tiahuanaco, it is the largest and the heaviest of all the gates in existence, and at the same time is the only one which has been adorned with rich sculptured decorations.[1] Its sculptures are conceived in a style already known to us from other Peruvian patterns, — those, for instance, used in weaving, — and it shows a large picture of a god in its centre, apparently receiving adoration from side figures.

From certain appendages upon and near the figures it has been concluded that the picture has reference to the worship of Huiracocha; and as this or a similar worship was universal among the other peoples of Peru, on the highland as well as on the coast, we need not be surprised at finding traces of it in a memorial which must have belonged to the most ancient Peruvian civilisation. Huiracocha (or in the fuller form, which occurs at times, Con-Ticsi-Huiracocha) was also originally a sun-god, but in his capacity as the bringer of light and awakener of life he became in course of time the creator of mankind and the father of all civilisation. In this character he himself or his messengers passed through all

See **Plate** opposite p. 314.

the districts of Peru from Tiahuanaco onward, bringing the arts of peace and civilising the people, until at last he disappeared in the far north on the shores of the
sea that surrounds the world. No divinity, even under different names, enjoyed
so wide a worship as his. The Incas, who had at first been exclusively sun-
worshippers, became wholly devoted to the worship of Huiracocha, and he was
the only god among the divinities of the peoples they subdued that they worshipped. They admitted him to honour, not only in their sun-worship, but made
him an integral part of their mythological system. But his true origin is in the
southern district in which Tiahuanaco held the most important position.

In the immediate neighbourhood of the lake of Titicaca a number of other
sacred towns are situated. It is necessary to explain the closeness of their connection with the civilisation of Tiahuanaco, because in later times they were
converted to the Inca sun-worship. This is especially true of the islands of the
lake of Titicaca. Legends of the Inca period pretend that the sun-worship had its
origin in these islands, but that the sacred towns were none the less neglected
until the Inca Tupak Yupanki began to make pilgrimages to them and restored
them to their proper position. The fact from which this theory proceeds is that
Tupak Yupanki was one of the first Incas to visit the shrine of Huiracocha on
the lake of Titicaca and recognise his divinity. The southern shore of the lake,
with its islands, was up to that time obstinately defended against the Inca-Peruvians
by the Collas, one of the races peculiarly hostile to them; so there can be no
question here of an earlier possession and a later neglect of the shrine by the
Incas. In later times they erected numerous monumental buildings there; but
on the most sacred site, near the rock behind which the sun stood still until the
creator, Huiracocha, set it in motion again, appear remains of a character antecedent to Incan architecture. The sanctuary, moreover, is not a temple, but, like
Ak-Kapana and other most ancient homes of civilisation, an open enclosure
surrounded only by a palisade.

Another site in connection with the worship of Huiracocha was Cacha, situated
in the valley of Huilcanota half-way between Cuzco and the lake of Titicaca.
From their architectural peculiarities the ruins of the temples in that place do
not go back beyond the Inca period. Here there was a temple of Huiracocha,
erected, according to the legend, in memory of the fact that the god had sent
flame down from heaven and set the mountains on fire, in order to punish the
resistance which the Canao-Indians offered to his teaching until they recognised
his divinity.

The civilised districts of the south, previous to the Inca period, cover a still
wider area; but this did not exclusively belong to the civilised districts of
Tiahuanaco. Its destruction was not brought about by the Incas, but it had been
lying in ruins long forgotten, in its present condition, before the Peruvian Incas
pushed their conquests into the land of the Collas. The ancient kingdom of
Tiahuanaco has certainly suffered under the attacks of previous migrating hordes.
Even if the Collas themselves did not destroy it, yet they founded their kingdom
near and upon the soil of Tiahuanaco, and it reached a considerable pitch of
civilisation uninfluenced by the Incas. They were probably the builders of the
remarkable graves in the form of towers ("chulpas") on the lake of Umayo, in the
neighbourhood of Sillustani: the huge blocks of stone in these, which are well
smoothed and beautifully fitted to the curve of the surface, show little affinity

THE MONOLITHIC GATE OF AK-KAPANA IN PERU; EASTERN ASPECT

(After A. Stübel and M. Uhle, "Ruined Places of Tiahuanaco." C. T. Wiskott, Breslau.)

# EXPLANATION OF THE FOREGOING PICTURE

THE monolithic gate of Ak-Kapana is the most remarkable monument among the ruins of Tiahuanaco, which are situated not far from the southern shore of Lake Titicaca. It has not yet been fully explained. Whether the position of the stones, which is marked by the name Ak-Kapana, is connected with the similar arrangement at Stonehenge, is doubtful, for its present position is certainly not original. As the whole monument is only about ten feet high, the opening of the doorway scarce permits the passage of a grown man. The material is hard trachyte, which has been worked with the greatest skill. On both sides, in front and behind, the most careful symmetry has been observed. The sculptures behind appear to depict a two-storied building with window-like niches. The front part here shown is covered with sculptures in bas-relief; these, however, take up only the upper part of the gateway. The centre is occupied by the figure of a god, of great size and surrounded by a garland of feathers: his legs are cut off short. Probably the figure is Huiracocha. On either side, arranged opposite one another in three rows, are twenty-four winged figures bearing the sceptre, who do him homage, sinking on one knee. Nine of these figures on the outer edge have been copied later from the original fifteen by a less artistic hand. A frieze borders the sculptures on the under side; there, sharply characterised human heads are divided by Vitruvius scrollwork, which is embellished with the heads of condors (not snakes) and pumas. The style is pre-Inca; the artists probably belonged to the Aymará race.

with the masonry work of Tiahuanaco. The religion of the Collas was not the worship of Huiracocha, but was a stone-worship, which certainly had its influence. upon the holy places of the Titicaca islands when these came under their dominion; though the point of special sanctity was situated at the south of the lake, in Copacapana. Here two blue stones — the one representing a face and the other a figure in the coils of a snake — were objects of special reverence until the Incas finally forced their sun-worship upon the Collas.

Upon the ruins of these civilisations, and subject to the influences of each of them in a greater or lesser degree, rose the kingdom of the Incas. The history of this empire at its greatest extends over an extremely small period, scarcely two centuries of the time during which the various peoples that composed that empire were working out the particular civilisations they reached. But as, at the moment of the conquest, the Incas happened to be the leading power in South America, later generations have concentrated their attention entirely upon their history and upon that of peoples related to them. The Incas were not the exponents of a particular nationality or of a specially high civilisation, but they imposed their laws and customs upon a large area of country, and upon the basis of the ancient civilisations they made individual and extraordinary advances. In their kingdom, which was finally composed of a large number of peoples speaking different languages, they introduced the Quechua[1] language as the official dialect. However, this was not their mother tongue. The Incas were, on the contrary, a clan of the Aymará race, the ancient civilisation of which we have observed in Tiahuanaco. Upon the collapse of this kingdom they may have turned northward and settled in the valley of Huilcamayo, whence they entered upon their career of conquest toward the four quarters of the heavens.[2] As they could not reveal to the eyes of men the insignificance of their origin, they created a legend upon the subject, in which a common origin was pretended, both for their temporal power and their religious convictions, raising them above ordinary mortals to the level of the gods.

Before the arrival of the Incas — thus the legend runs — the peoples of the Peruvian highlands were living in complete savagery. They did not understand agriculture; they had no settled dwelling-places; and their only clothes were the skins of the beasts upon the raw flesh of which they fed. At last the sun-god, Inti, had pity on them; and so he put two of his children upon the islands of Lake Titicaca, which his sister and wife, Quilla, the moon-goddess, had borne to him, namely, the Manco Capak, with the latter's sister and wife, Mama Oello. He gave them a golden staff and ordered them to follow the valley northward until the golden staff disappeared in the earth at the point where it should touch it. There they were to settle, to convert the inhabitants to sun-worship, and to acquaint them with the blessings of civilisation; and he promised them his protection and support until their bountiful influence should be extended over all the peoples of the earth. Brother and sister, with this commission, started upon their wanderings down the valley of Huilcamayo. A few miles from Cuzco, near the mountain of Guanacauré, the golden staff suddenly disappeared. Here Manco Capak proceeded to build a house for himself and his sister wife. He then began to till the ground, which he planted with potatoes, quinoa, and other

---

[1] Pronounced Kétschua.

[2] It was from this that they named their kingdom Tahuantin-uyu - "the four quarters of the heavens."

plants; and Mama Ocllo worked within the house, cooking, spinning, weaving, and practising all the arts which her divine parents had taught her. After they had thus looked after their own comfort Manco began to fulfil his divine mission to the natives. The inhabitants of Cuzco were astounded at the sight of himself and his sister, who were clothed in bright garments and decorated with shining ornaments: they listened suspiciously to the message of the sun-god. When, under his guidance, they began to share in the blessings of civilisation; when the men had learned to till the ground and to build houses, and the women to spin and to weave,—then they recognised what benefits they owed to the mission of Manco Capak. They readily chose him to be their ruler, and the sun-god to be their god, and the little town which formed around the hut of this first child of the sun grew and increased visibly under the protection of his heavenly father.

This legend may be called the later official form of the legend of Indian origin. As to its connection with the lake of Titicaca we may conclude that this did not take place until the sun-worship of the Incas had become reconciled to the Huiracocha worship of the highlanders, who had their sacred temple upon the lake of Titicaca. As this religious compromise took place only under the Inca Huiracocha, the eighth in the Inca dynasty, this version of the legend was not more than a hundred years old when the Spaniards reached Peru.

The older form of the legend gives a different account of the circumstances preceding Manco's settlement. One day, from the heights of Paccaritambo, nine Spanish miles south of Cuzco, there appeared four sets of twins who were also called children of the sun: among these were Ayar Manco and Mama Ocllo. Now the biggest and strongest of these was Ayar Cachi, the husband of Mama Huaco; and his sister, being afraid of him, determined to get rid of him. They were certainly clothed in festal robes and richly adorned when they made their appearance; but they had left treasures far greater and more splendid behind them in the mountain cave. She now asked Ayar Cachi to fetch these out; but as soon as he had disappeared in the cave she rolled great blocks of stone to the mouth and entirely shut him in. His mad rage was terrible when he discovered the traitorous deception: he shattered in pieces the mountain which rose above the cave, and the earth trembled far and wide with the shock; but he could find no way out, and finally became changed to a mountain stone. The other twins now moved farther north and ultimately settled at the mountain Guanacaure, until they finally determined to move nearer to Cuzco. When they left Guanacaure, another brother, Ayar Utschu, voluntarily changed himself into stone, and the others promised to pray to him in the future. However, he put on mighty stone wings and flew up to their common father, the sun; whence he returned with the message that Ayar Manco was to take over the leadership of the twins, as Manco Capak, after which they moved down to Cuzco and there began their civilising mission; but Ayar Utschu remained on Guanacaure as a block of stone, in order to act as future intermediary between them and their father, the sun.

In this version of the legend two points are of importance. Upon the mountain Guanacaure there was, even at the time of the Spanish arrival, one of the most sacred temples of the whole kingdom of Tahuantinsuyu, the foundation of which was naturally connected with the legends of the race. In later times

his temple, like all the official sanctuaries of the Incas, was dedicated to the
sun; but the legends of its foundation undoubtedly point to the fact that in th
case, as in the case of the cave of Paccaritambo, we have to do with a sanctuar
belonging to the epoch of stone-worship. This worship was preponderant no
only among the Collas on the south and west of the lake of Titicaca, but als
n the district of Cuzco and still farther north, until the Incas spread the sun-
vorship. On this theory are to be explained the peculiar steps and platforms
hewn out of the rock of Monte Rodadero, in the immediate neighbourhood of
Cuzco, and other memorials of a like nature undoubtedly connected with stone-
vorship; such, for instance, as those at Concacha in the upper valley of the
Apurimac; the stone chair of Huillcas Huaman in the Pampas valley; and a
supposed throne of the Inca in Cajamarca in the far north. All these sites,
which were undoubtedly continual objects of veneration at the Inca period, make
t extremely probable that the Incas did not persecute stone-worship as assidu-
ously as they did that of other divinities; and when we remember the
tradition of the transformation of the two children of the sun into stone, and
the manner in which their worship was brought into connection with the sun-
worship, the inference becomes irresistible that the earliest Incas made a religious
and political compromise with the stone-worship which was flourishing around
them. For political reasons a compromise was made, a century later, with regard
to the cult of Huiracocha. While the opposition between stone-worship and sun-
worship died away, it is possible that the former has always been deeply ingrained
in the Peruvian natives from Inca times to the present day. And now every
native porter who travels over one of the numerous passes from valley to valley
in the country adds a new stone to the heap of those which his predecessors
have piled up as an offering to the Apacheta, "who gives him strength to bear his
burden."

The information that the legend gives us concerning the settling of the Incas
in Cuzco is equally important. Before their arrival the locality must have been
thickly populated, and the people must have long passed out of the state of
barbarism which the official traditions ascribe to all the Peruvians before the
Inca period, and have attained a settled mode of life; for the town of Cuzco
was the residence of the ruler, by name Alcaviza, who also ruled over the district
in the immediate neighbourhood of the town. It was from him that Manco
Capak and his little company asked permission to settle in the vicinity. When
this had been accorded to them, they soon made their proximity unpleasant.
Directly they had obtained a firm footing in one of the quarters of Cuzco they
set up an opposition to the ruler and to the priests of the worship that had
hitherto been carried on in the ancient Cuzco, and began to make proselytes
to their own worship, which was exclusively that of the sun. This separation
of parties soon degenerated into open war, the result of which was that Alcaviza
and his dependents were driven out. Thus the Inca-Peruvians got possession of
the town which was to become the centre of their extensive kingdom in the
course of centuries.

Peruvian tradition does not enable us to determine even approximately the
date at which the first rulers of the Inca race got possession of the power. The
"quipus," those bundles of different-coloured threads which the learned Peruvians
used as a *memoria technica*, seem to have been of no help for chronological pur-

poses; and all their permutations could in no way compensate for an ignorance of the art of writing. Oral tradition upon historical events certainly formed an important part of the education imparted to the young Inca nobles and the chosen nobility of the allied and subject races in the schools of the Amauta, the learned class. But all that remained of such knowledge in the Spanish period does not help us to a chronological record of the origin of the Inca kingdom. The number of rulers who held the throne of Cuzco from Manco Capak until Atahualpa is not even agreed upon. The estimates of the chroniclers variously give ten or thirteen rulers as predecessors of the hostile brothers Huascar and Atahualpa: there were at least eleven of them. It is remarkable that this uncertainty does not attach to the earliest period; the succession of the first five Inca kings has been made out with tolerable certainty. Discord then appears to have sprung up in the royal family and to have disturbed the legal order of succession. Efforts to hide this fact have produced two different accounts concerning the Inca rulers in the intermediate period, which contradict each other in many details and make it extremely difficult to discover the real state of affairs. Moreover the later Incas were much better known by their first names than by their proper names, which changed very little; but these lists of names are differently connected in the case of the three or four predecessors of Huaina Capak, so that the reign of this latter king is certainly the first of the events which can be regarded as possessing chronological and historical certainty. If an average reign of thirty years be ascribed to the eleven Inca kings (the legal succession was from father to son), their establishment in Cuzco would have taken place about the year 1200 of the Christian era. Upon its collapse the Inca kingdom would then have existed about three hundred and thirty years, — an estimate of time which is perhaps rather too long than too short, if we consider the instability of the institutions of ancient America.

Although Manco Capak is not really a proper name, yet the bearer of it must be considered as a historical personality. Perhaps the Amauta purposely allowed his proper name to be forgotten, in order to conceal the historical connection of the Inca rulers with the other States of ancient America, and to strengthen the popular idea of their direct origin from the sun-god. " Capak," in the Quechua language, the official dialect of the Inca State, means " kingdom " and " mighty," and is a royal title which other chiefs assumed before and at the time of the Incas. The same is true of the word " Manco." Its origin and proper meaning are not altogether so clear, but tradition speaks of a number of Mancos who were kings, in particular, of those districts which were situated in the westerly and northerly parts of the Inca kingdom. " Manco Capak " must consequently be translated " mighty king." — a name wholly suited to impress the people and to deceive them concerning the lowly origin of the Inca rulers in Peru. Of Manco Capak's rule, after his establishment in Cuzco, we have only the general tradition that he instructed his people in civilisation, introduced sun-worship, and increased his boundaries rather by the arts of peace than by force of arms. The legend attributes to him the foundation of all those institutions which left their impressions upon the later Inca kingdom, although a large number of the laws ascribed to him would have been useless and incapable of execution in the limited extent of the original realm. The Inca kingdom which roused the astonishment of the sixteenth-century conquerors, and to-day justly claims the greatest interest, was essentially the work of the four great rulers, Huiracocha, Yupanki (also called Pachacutek), Tupac Yupanki, and Huaina Capak.

These certainly built upon the foundations which their predecessors had laid, but they also entirely altered the general character of the kingdom. Consequently it is extremely difficult to gain a trustworthy idea of the condition of the Inca kingdom before the time of these monarchs.

The traditions give us as little definite information concerning the first three successors of Manco Capak as they do about himself. All our sources agree in naming them Sinchi Roca, Lloque Yupanki, and Maita Capak, and they are said to stand to one another in the relationship of father and son. But traditions are wholly at variance concerning the names and relationships of their wives and mothers. We have the official tradition that the marriage of Manco Capak with his sister, Mama Oello, was in fulfilment of a command of the sun-god, following the precedent of the marriage of the sun with his sister-planet, the moon; but this is most obviously derived from the ancient decree of the Inca kingdom, also well known in the later period, according to which that Inca son alone could legitimately ascend the throne whom the father has begotten of his own sister, or, failing a sister, on the next nearest relation of pure Inca blood. On the contrary another and apparently reliable tradition informs us that not only the immediate successors of Manco Capak, but also the majority of the Incas down to Yupanki Pachacutek, sprang from marriages which took place between the rulers of Cuzco with the daughters of neighbouring powers. The rulers until Maita Capak are consistently said to have extended the boundaries of their realm by peaceful methods. The official tradition also relates of one or two of the earlier Incas that they did not choose their "Coya" from the Inca family, but raised daughters of the neighbouring kings to the throne of the Inca kingdom. We cannot understand how Huaina Capak would have dared, after his conquest of Quito, to have included the princess who was heiress to the throne among the number of his own wives, if a religious decree had been in force from the foundation of the dynasty that marriage should be with the sister or with a mate of the closest relationship.

Moreover such a policy on the part of the Incas is easily intelligible. They had entered the valley of Huillcanota as a little band of foreign invaders, and their forcible expulsion of the Cuzco ruler was hardly likely to win over the sympathies of the neighbouring races, many of whom had apparently entered upon connections of friendship and marriage with Alcaviza. Moreover they remained foreigners by their continual opposition to the universal religion of the highland, stone-worship, and the worship of Huiracocha; and in the place of this they had introduced a worship which attracted less sympathy among the people as being less intelligible to them. For the first century of their rule the Incas were nothing else than little territorial princes among a crowd of others. They were totally incapable of imposing their political and religious customs upon their neighbours, and were probably thankful themselves to be left unmolested. In such circumstances that policy recommended itself which was likely to ensure their position by means of alliance; by setting up family relationships they attempted to destroy the recollection of their foreign and late invasion of the territory of the highland kings. We may believe the ancient traditions from the fact that they succeeded by these means in imposing their higher civilisation upon peoples who were less cultivated though not entirely savage, while the obvious advantages they attained by their careful tilling of the soil and their division of labour won over adherents to them who abandoned the neighbouring provinces and gladly settled under the Inca protection. In thankfulness for the material improvement in their position these last accepted a religion which they scarcely understood, and perhaps regarded the progress and prosperity of the Inca district as evidence of the higher powers of their god. But the extensions of the Cuzco kingdom under the first four Inca kings were very limited. At that time the Chancas were independent of the Inca kingdom; they possessed a district upon the immediate west of the valley of Cuzco, between Andahuailas and Ayacucho, which at that time was far more powerful than the Inca State. Independent also were the Quechua, whose language in later times became the official Inca idiom; they lived on the north of the Incas in the times of Maita Capak. The Cana and Canche also, who dwelt between Cuzco and the lake of Titicaca, were then wholly independent. Even in the immediate neighbourhood of their capital the Incas at that time possessed no real power. They were connected with all the little dynasties, lying over a radius of from twelve to twenty miles around Cuzco, who considered themselves of royal power, only by means of a compact concluded on a basis of equality of justice, which compact Huiracocha, the eighth ruler on the Inca throne, changed into a real dominion. Finally Maita Capak was at one time by no means securely settled in his capital; for the Alcaviza, the successors of the race who had exercised the chief power in Cuzco before the arrival of Manco Capak, looked enviously at that time upon their more fortunate rival. Under the fourth Inca king a bloody battle took place in order finally to banish from the town the restless dependents of the ancient dynasty.

The battle in which Maita Capak overcame the rebel Alcaviza is expressly noted as the first occasion upon which an Inca extended his power by the sword. Things were very different under the successors to the throne. The three following Incas, Capak Yupanki, Inca Roca, and Yahuar Huacac, whose collective reigns probably embraced about a century, were the founders of the greatness of the kingdom. With them begins the policy of conquest by which the Incas extended the boundaries of their power in every direction. In their immediate neighbourhood they seem to have preserved the confederation that had been set on foot, but they enlisted the youthful warriors of the allied kingdoms in their service and accustomed them to regard themselves as their leaders. By this means, and through the rich booty they took in war, they imperceptibly gained a preponderance over the other confederates which in course of time inevitably became a dominion.

Capak Yupanki began his rule by assuring his position at home. Maita Capak had left many sons whom he had set up in almost independent positions in the neighbouring districts. When Capak Yupanki gave them clearly to understand that he wanted their obedience, not their friendship, they made a conspiracy to depose him, and to set up a ruler in his place more in accordance with their own views. But their compact was betrayed: instead of the Inca, most of the conspirators fell by the sword; and in order to erase the impression of this tragedy, and to turn the energy of the youthful Incas into some useful direction, Capak Yupanki commenced that series of campaigns which led him speedily to the north (Condesuyu) and northeast (Andesuyu) along the course of the streams.

From that time the Incas became particularly aggressive and expansive. Hardly in the entire world has a power been seen which remained so moderate and humane in its warfare as the Incas, although generation upon generation grew up in the service of arms. Always ready to appeal to the sword, and gifted with heroic bravery, the Incas none the less invariably attempted peaceful methods before proceeding to attack. Their campaigns were not rapid surprises, like those of the wild and half-civilised peoples in the west of America, when the greatest possible number of the opponents were killed in order that they, laden with the enemy's spoil, might get home again as quickly as possible. Their warfare was systematic. The Incas never took an enemy by surprise: their armies invariably sent out ambassadors inviting a willing submission to their mild rule. They said that the Inca, the child of the sun-god, had come to them, not to do them harm, but to free them from all that was ancient and bad, and thereby to make them acquainted with the blessings of a more civilised mode of life and a higher religion. The more the Inca kingdom increased in power and extent, the wider spread the certainty, even among remote nations, that this message was no empty pretence, but that in reality the position of subjects in the Inca realm was far superior to the lot of those who opposed their rule in any district. Hardly ever did the Incas depose a ruler who voluntarily subjected himself to their government. Incorporation in the Inca kingdom certainly altered the position of the monarch, who became a vassal of the sun's child in Cuzco instead of an independent ruler. The relations of the king to his previous subjects were also largely remodelled upon the organisation of the leading power, but the Incas never appeared as fanatical doctrinaires. They invariably respected national peculiarities as far as these were consistent with their political necessities; but in course of time the influence of the ruling power threw such peculiarities into the background and tended to obliterate them entirely.

Upon religious questions the earliest Incas did not practise this conciliatory policy. The first races which they subdued were obliged to receive a common form of worship without exception. Maita Capak is said to have once ordered the subjects of the neighbouring regions to bring all their stone images to Cuzco, alleging as his motive the preparation of brilliant festivities to their common gods; but when all these stone gods had been collected he had them broken in pieces and built into the walls of the temple of the sun, in order to show the people the powerlessness of the gods which they worshipped. But even on this side their policy became far more diplomatic in the course of time, chiefly under the influence of political necessities.[1]

The Inca campaigns often ended without the shedding of a drop of blood, in spite of the great display of power they involved. They were, however, always ready to break down the most obstinate resistance. The difficulties of communication in that wide realm imposed a slow retreat upon the numerous Inca armies. Especially in later times, when the kingdom had become of considerable extent, it was not unusual for a campaign to last two or three years or even more. The army was furnished not only for the necessities of war, but also for its own maintenance. As in the case of those armed garrisons which were invariably established by the Incas in districts where obedience could only be enforced by arms, so the army, when marching out to attack, could till the soil with weapons at their sides if the campaign threatened to last long. But it was only in exceptional cases that an army was obliged to have recourse to these means. Not only the organisation of the troops for attack, but also the commissariat, the transport of reinforcements, and the withdrawal of troops, were marvellously well

---

[1] See *post*, p. 328.

arranged. The trades which were everywhere carried on in the Inca kingdom[1] enabled the rulers in times of peace to make important provision of food, clothing, and other necessary articles. These were collected in great magazines in every province, and in times of war, famine, or pestilence, these stores were opened. Such an organisation, together with that prestige which the Incas so rapidly acquired, enables us to understand that it was often unnecessary to appeal to arms in struggles with the less civilised races in the mountain valleys and on the inhospitable coast. The feeling of helplessness among their enemies was the best ally to the Incas.

Even in cases where their invitation to voluntary subjection was rejected, the Incas did not give up their policy of conciliation. An attack immediately followed from their side, and the superiority of their organisation and equipment almost invariably gave them the victory. But then the Inca ambassadors immediately renewed their peace proposals, and even then the native rulers were generally left in their positions, provided they had not continued their resistance to the last. Hardly any kingdom with which the Incas came in contact during their career of conquest was sufficiently closely organised to make the war one of extermination. Individual rulers who considered themselves equal to the Incas certainly thought it shameful to buy a continuation of their power by recognising the Inca superiority, and they at least felt the full weight of their anger. Yet even in those cases the Incas generally found certain vassals, loosely dependent upon their opponents, who were ready to listen to their enticing propositions and to give them their aid in bringing the war to a successful conclusion. But at the time of the Spanish conquest the soil of Peru showed unmistakable traces of the fact that the Incas were ready to wage unsparing war when necessary. In those cases they had no hesitation, with an army of extraordinary strength, in destroying fortresses like that of Mojeque, the gigantic blocks of which form a mighty field of ruins even to-day, or temples such as that of Chavin de Huantar, in spite of, or even on account of, the extensive reverence paid them; and here their object was not only to leave the enemy no opportunity for future rebellion, but also to make an impression upon him by their ruthless destruction of that which had cost so much trouble to build. And where a people persisted in revolting against the mild Inca rule they had a still more efficacious method at hand. They not only built numerous fortresses and kept them ready prepared in such conquered districts, but they also broke down the resistance of the peoples they had forcibly subdued by taking the most youthful warriors who would have been the most likely to revolt, and settling them in distant provinces among races of tried fidelity.

This picture of the warlike policy of the Incas was not realised to the fullest extent during the rule of Capak Yupanki. His armies were not so large, and his campaigns were not so distant, as to demand a highly organised military system. His successor, the Inca Roca, contributed perhaps no less to the later greatness of the kingdom of Cuzco than Capak Yupanki; but his efforts took another direction. We are certainly told of him and of Yahuar Huacac that they undertook occasional campaigns beyond the boundaries of their dominion, but they both seem to have been men of peace at bottom. On the other hand the beginnings of the extensions and improvements in the capital of Cuzco are ascribed to the Inca Roca. The work carried on under his government makes it quite certain that even in his time

---

[1] See *post*, p. 334.

the Incas were in a position to employ their subjects in the execution of immense designs. To him and to his Coya[1] is ascribed the installation of the ancient water-service, which brought to the town of Cuzco pure, fresh water at a time when it was growing more civilised in its necessities and of greater importance. This water-service is not to be confounded with the sluice-gates and irrigation works which were necessary for the soil of the Inca kingdom in most districts, to make that high cultivation of the land possible under its climatic conditions which the dense population of the empire demanded. With regard to this irrigation the Incas continued their long-sighted, careful policy by the erection of works which aroused the greatest astonishment. They are, however, by no means the first to have discovered the art of irrigation; this was practised to a considerable extent by almost all their subject peoples before they became members of the Inca kingdom. We see, then, that the legend is in no way worthy of credence which depicts Manco Capak as the discoverer and expounder of that mode of cultivation peculiar to the Inca realm.

The work which forms the chief memorial, and is in fact an imperishable monument of Inca Roca, is the palace which he began to erect in his capital. Architecture, before the Inca period, had attained considerable perfection uninfluenced by Inca models; and the Incas certainly do not merit any praise for having further developed an art which they found already at the highest stage of its earlier progress. In comparison with the technical perfection which the immense ruins of Tiahuanaco display, the art of the Inca architects of Cuzco was certainly something of a retrogression. Tiahuanaco is the work of architects who employed enormous blocks of stone, similar to those of the cyclopean buildings which are found in all parts of the world, and who were even then able to prepare every single detail with accurate measurements and plans. On the other hand the walls of the palace of the Inca Roca are cyclopean buildings in the ordinary sense of the term; the blocks are of the largest size which could be handled with the limited appliances of the time, and are often most wonderfully shaped to suit the necessities of the site on which they were erected; a particularly remarkable stone displays, for instance, no less than twelve corners. Moreover the fitting of these blocks thus carefully shaped, the outer surface of which was generally smoothed, is so exact, in spite of their irregular forms, that even to-day the blade of a knife can scarcely be driven into their joints, although no mortar or other cohesive material was employed. A later Inca once pulled down a portion of the town of Cuzco in order to rebuild it upon a uniform plan. But large numbers of buildings were exempted from this destruction, as is shown by the number of constructions built with irregular polygon blocks (which can be clearly distinguished from the architecture of the later Inca), standing at the present day. The most important monument in this style is the palace of Inca Roca, which was situated in a street of Cuzco now known as the Calle del Triunfo; its walls, artistically composed of many-cornered blocks, were used by the modern builders of later times as a welcome foundation.

The architectural perfection of the Inca-Peruvians advanced considerably in later times. Their preference for large blocks of stone invariably persisted, and this to such an extent that even where nature did not provide the ordinary

---

[1] Such was the title of the legal consort of the Inca king.

material of hard rock and obliged them to build with smaller stones, as their subject nations had done, their buildings can still be distinguished from those of
earlier times by the fact of their displaying individual stones of unusually large
dimensions. But at the chief period of the Inca power temples and palaces were
built with cubes of stone worked with extraordinary care, and laid with such
exactitude that the courses upon the front of the building present, upon a close
examination, the appearance of level bands. From a point of view at a moderate
distance the whole wall of the building appears as though it were made of one
stone. In spite of this marvellous technical perfection the Inca buildings were
never very beautiful; in their long, massive, heavy walls proportion is almost
entirely wanting; and as the Incas were never capable of constructing a vaulted
roof in the primitive mode of the Central Americans, the length of their buildings in comparison with their moderate height produces a disagreeable impression.

Moreover in the kingdom of Tahuantinsuyu sculpture was almost entirely forbidden. Very rarely in Inca buildings are to be seen any decorative carvings
whatever; the few gates above which a decoration of lions' heads appears are
probably only remains of buildings antecedent to the Incas, which they had pulled
down, and the material of which their architects had used for their own purposes.
The Inca worship forbade any kind of sculptural decoration, and in ancient times
waged a bitter war of extermination against the idols of the subject races; it thus
became a rule that living beings should under no circumstances be depicted in stone.
Their buildings display extraordinary skill in working even the hardest rock, and
their pottery ware shows equally clearly that they found no difficulty in depict-
ing real life with proportion and vigour; but every sculpture that has been found
on Peruvian soil is antecedent to the time of the Inca kingdom. The artistic
tendencies of the Incas have made it easy to distinguish their work from that of
their predecessors and successors. Generally an examination of the stone-work is
sufficient to settle any question as to the origin of an Inca building; for neither
before nor after them were blocks fitted together with an exactness that proclaims
most careful polishing.

Another characteristic feature in the Inca architecture is that all openings were
in trapezoidal form. Windows in their buildings are rather the exception than the
rule, a circumstance which increases the gloomy appearance of their houses.
However, upon the inside walls of their buildings are constantly to be found
niches which served them as cupboards, and these, as well as the doors, which
looked into an open court in a long row and admitted light and air to the rooms
grouped around it, display the peculiarity that the posts lean in toward one another,
so that the lintel is rather narrower than the threshold. The Inca architects clung
to this peculiarity, whatever the diversity of material and situation; from the lake
of Titicaca up to Quito, and from Cuzco to the shore of the Pacific Ocean, this
distinctive feature can be recognised without difficulty. Their mode of roofing
must have made the Inca buildings appear doubly strange and ugly. For that purpose they could not use stone, and trees were too scarce to provide sufficient
material for solid constructions of wood. Consequently the roofs of even their
most ornamental buildings were composed of canes and straw, which were supported by wooden posts of moderate strength. The exterior of the buildings was
apparently decorated by plates and artistically worked pieces of precious metal,
but this would be true only of the temples, and to a limited degree of the palaces;

for gold and silver were worthless to the common people, and served mainly as gifts to the gods, and to the kings, who were considered almost equal to them.

The foundation of the first schools in the kingdom was also ascribed to the Inca Roca. The Peruvians had their own learned class, the Amauta; but these formed only a subordinate division of the Inca caste. Far from desiring to spread education throughout the ranks of the people, the Incas were of the opinion that too much knowledge and power could produce only dissatisfaction and pride, and were consequently unsuitable for the common people. Hence only scholars of the Inca blood could be received into the classes of the Amauta; and besides the youths of the Inca race their schools in Cuzco were attended only by such children of the vassal princes as the special favour of the Incas allowed to come,— a favour which also served political purposes, as it made the young princes acquainted with those particular conceptions upon which the Inca power was founded. In these schools the young people obtained solid and valuable instruction; bodily exercises and intellectual training went on side by side; and the difficult problem of developing body and mind to an equal degree was thus solved sufficiently to meet the requirements of the time.

Languages formed an important department in their instruction. The Incas of the royal families are said to have spoken a language of their own; this was known to the Amauta, but upon the destruction of the Inca race, before and during the Spanish conquest, the knowledge of it was so entirely lost that at the time of the Inca Garcilaso there was no one living who knew it. This language cannot have been a wholly isolated dialect, as Garcilaso would have us believe, but was probably a dialect of the Aymará, which was spoken by Manco Capak and the race which was destroyed upon the migration of the Incas to Cuzco. It was an act of far-seeing policy that the Incas did not make these rude uncultivated dialects the official language of their realm, but used the Quechua, which was widely spread upon the north and west of Cuzco, and the sounds and forms of which were less harsh and more easily acquired. Under their rule this speech became native to all the subjects of their empire, so that it is even now spoken throughout the area of the former kingdom of Tahuantinsuyu, while only a few remains have survived of the national languages of the subject races and some dialects have become altogether extinct.

The higher learning was naturally exclusively reserved to the Amauta; it was pursued only in particular schools. Thus none but the Amauta understood the system of quipus, the different-coloured strings arranged in a row upon a cross-string, which served as the only existing help to the memory. This system may have been very well suited for that fixed condition of things which was the ideal of the Inca government, but it could not compensate for the lack of a proper handwriting as a real means of exchanging thoughts or of stereotyping expression. In the high schools of the Amauta the preservation of historical traditions was earnestly pursued. Epic and lyric poems are said to have been preserved by the Amauta during the Inca period; but these were undoubtedly transmitted entirely by word of mouth,— no use being made of the quipus, many examples of which are in existence, but none of which have been explained or translated. It has been indisputably established that the Ollanta drama, which was supposed for a long time to be a product of ancient Indian intellect, came into existence in the seventeenth century and is therefore owing to Spanish influence.

Finally the Amauta became the repositories of priestly knowledge, with which, as is usual to and characteristic of a kingdom of sun-worshippers, astronomical knowledge was closely connected. The Inca calendar seems to have been in a much earlier stage of development than that of many other American peoples; the Incas were probably too proud to borrow the discoveries of other nations, while their own civilisation was of too short a growth to have arrived at the discovery of an accurate calendar. Their chief festival, upon which their chronology was founded, the "Inti Raimi," was celebrated upon a date settled by observation of the sun; this was the day on which the shadow of the gnomon, known as "Inti huatana," showed that the northerly procession of the sun had ceased, — that is, that the winter solstice had begun, the day being about the 21st of June; consequently a difference between the actual year and the State year was impossible. The Peruvians do not seem to have gained these results by calculation; almost all their festivals were regulated by the position of the sun and the phases of the moon; they also knew and reverenced the Pleiades and the morning and evening star, under the name of "Chasca." Pachacutek, the Inca, was the first to divide the year into twelve months.

The institutions ascribed to the Inca Roca show that the Inca kingdom under his government had arrived at a high pitch of intellectual and material prosperity; but, as will be seen from the following occurrences, its organisation was still extremely loose and in no way corresponded with the political ideals which our sources show us to have prevailed at the time of the conquest. It was the immediate successors of Inca Roca who really founded and centralised the Inca kingdom. The government of the Inca Yahuar Huacac Yupanki was considered as a period of misfortune by the Peruvian Amauta; his name denotes "the man who weeps tears of blood." The history of the first six Inca rulers is related by all our sources with great consistency and but few discrepancies; but with regard to the kings between Inca Roca and Inca Yupanki Pachacutek there is such confusion in the ancient traditions that the number, names, and exploits ascribed to individual kings cannot be brought into any sort of harmony. It can only be asserted that during this period both the Inca dynasty and the Inca kingdom underwent heavy shocks and were subject to internal strife.

The dangers with which the Inca kingdom was threatened resulted from efforts to strengthen their rule over the races in their immediate neighbourhood who had hitherto been rather their allies than their subjects. Yahuar Huacac had made a step in this direction by demanding tribute from the races of the high valleys, who had been in the habit of making voluntary presents to the Incas; this was the signal for a revolt which brought the Inca kingdom to the verge of destruction for a second time. The Chanca, a warlike race widely spread upon the northwest of Cuzco between Andahuailas and Arequipa, marched against Cuzco, under the leadership of their king Uscovillca, with such overpowering force that Yahuar Huacac did not venture to await the enemy in his unfortified town, but fled southward.

The dangers which threatened the Inca State from without come at this point into connection with those which were originated by the internal conditions of the dynasty. The narratives make it tolerably plain that the legal line of succession was again interrupted. The official accounts, which always attempt to conceal any disturbance of the political law and order, represent matters as if the legal heir to the throne had, by his youthful haughtiness, excited the anger of his father to such an extent that he threatened to disinherit his son and reduced him to the humble position of shepherd to the sacred flocks in the mountains. There one of his ancestors, a prince of the royal house, by name Huiracocha, is said to have appeared to him one day in a dream and told him of the great dangers which threatened the kingdom, owing to the revolt of the Chanca. Thereupon the prince hastened to the capital, in spite of his father's prohibition. His father did not receive his explanation, but when he had fled before the approaching enemy the king's son is said to have inspired the timid citizens of the capital with fresh enthusiasm, and finally to have repulsed the attacks upon Cuzco. Moreover, with the help of the divine warriors whom Huiracocha sent to his assistance, he defeated the enemy in open battle and subjected them for ever to the Inca rule. The legend then continues to relate how the victorious prince declined the proposals of his thankful comrades to accept the crown, and proceeded to conciliate his royal father by submission until the latter voluntarily abdicated and announced himself as the first of his son's vassals.

However, the real course of events was probably as follows. The courage of the reigning king, and of the Incas around him, failed before the threatening advance of the Chanca. The State was so dislocated that he could not rely upon the greater portion of his subjects; and as the town of Cuzco and its environs offered no secure refuge, the Inca and his closest dependents determined to conceal themselves and their treasures in the mountains. But the supporters of the pre-Incan dynasty among the citizens who were now thus abandoned — that is, the worshippers of the old god Huiracocha — rose to power upon the cowardly flight of their ruler; even without the Chanca they would certainly have put an end to the rule of the foreigners if the long and prosperous government of the later dynasty had not formed a strong party among the people which was favourable to the Incas. Under these circumstances a youth of the Inca race appeared among the waverers; he had no legal right of succession to the throne, but was a man of Inca blood and Inca courage. The immediate necessity was to do away with the opposition between the remnant of the ancient inhabitants and the Inca dependents, which had broken out with greater vigour upon the flight of the ruler. For this purpose he invented the legend of the appearance of the god Huiracocha: he said that the god of the ancient people had chosen him, the Inca, as the saviour of his people. By this means he obtained numerous allies among the neighbouring highland races, who helped him to victory. This favourite of Huiracocha was naturally disinclined to lay the palms of victory at the feet of those Incas in whose absence he had won his success; but he was equally unable openly to usurp the power of the Inca king in the face of a strong party of allies who had materially contributed to his success. The consequence was that for many years the lawful ruler, who was greatly despised by his people for his cowardice, set up his court far from Cuzco, while his more fortunate rival held the reins of power in the capital without venturing to assume the royal title. Finally a compromise was brought about which enabled the aged king to spend his last years in peace and gave the real ruler the legal title he had won.

The Inca who took the name of the god Huiracocha had to thank his southern neighbours, the Canes and Cancha, for the salvation of Cuzco and for his victory over the Chanca. But there was collected beneath his standard, not a body of vassals, but a confederation which expected a rich recompense from the spoils of war. Here we have another proof of the fact that the Inca kingdom, both in extent and in internal compactness, was still far removed from its later perfection. But important strides were made under the rule of the far-seeing Huiracocha. In the first place the subjugation of the Chanca provided him with a numerous body of warriors immediately dependent upon him, whom he raised to honour and position. On the other hand there were many little dynasties in the neighbourhood of Cuzco loosely dependent upon the Inca State, who were disinclined to give in their allegiance to the new ruler and had regarded his predecessors upon the throne with displeasure. Huiracocha, with extraordinary cleverness, now changed the feeble suzerainty of the ruler of Cuzco into a virtual dominion. The dependents of the previous Inca did not find courage for an open display of hostility, and as the individual dynasties were unable to unite for common purposes they were reduced to the position of vassal States one after the other. The Canes and Cancha, when they refused to recognise the sovereignty of the Inca by sending him tribute, were attacked and subdued after a vigorous resistance. However, they later became the most faithful and reliable subjects of the Inca; to them was reserved the honourable duty of providing bearers for the king's litter; for the Inca, like the princes of the Chibchas and Quitus, was invariably carried on a litter when he went on a journey.

During a long rule the Inca Huiracocha carried his arms successfully against enemies in the most various directions; but his success was due quite as much to his political skill as to the bravery of his armies. We have a particular proof of this in his interference in the quarrels of the Colla. On the western and southern shores of the lake of Titicaca, two rulers, Cari of Chucuito, and Zapana of Hatun-Colla, were struggling for pre-eminence, and each was short-sighted enough to invite Huiracocha's help. That gave him the opportunity of being the first of the Inca race to press forward to the sacred islands of Titicaca and the ruined cities of Tiahuanaco. He took the side of the weaker and more remote Cari, who readily became a kind of vassal to the Inca, in order to repel his more powerful opponent; and thereby he adroitly prepared the incorporation of both districts in the Inca State, an incorporation which a rising in that district enabled his grandson, Tupac Yupanki, to complete.

A fundamental reason for the rapid and brilliant success of the new Inca lay in the alteration of his religious policy. The sun-worship which the Incas had set up as the religion for the State and the people could hardly appeal to the inhabitants of the highland. It was a mixture of reverence for the powers of nature and of ancestor-worship, which latter feature made it an important element in the Inca family life, strong emphasis being thereby laid upon the difference between the Inca race and the peoples subject to them, and so this cult became rather an opportunity for expressing disgust than an occasion for worship. The sun, with his beneficent influences of warmth and fruitfulness, was certainly an eminently suitable deity for the inhabitants of the bare, rough highland, and Huiracocha, as he was originally worshipped by the Quechua and other neighbouring peoples, was no doubt an offshoot from a sun divinity. Although the Incas must have conceived of the sun-god, Inti, as their forefather in a human form, they none the less banished from their worship every kind of anthropomorphism. When worship was not directly offered to the luminary, as it invariably was on great feast-days, the god was represented only by a bright golden shield. Pictorial representation was systematically objected to by the Incas, not only in their own worship, but also in that of all other gods. In their campaigns against hostile peoples the destruction of temples and images was considered an important duty. The peoples who reluctantly bowed to the yoke of the Inca dominion were not brought into any closer sympathy with their religion when they saw the hall of the sun-god in the temple at Cuzco changed into a hall of ancestors; along the walls stood the embalmed mummies of dead rulers, a band of solar children grouped around their father, the sun-god. There can be no question that this worship contributed to raise a barrier between the Incas and their subjects. The worship of Huiracocha now resolved upon by the new Inca, who borrowed his name from that of the god, implied a complete breach with the religious policy that had hitherto obtained. But this Inca, who was too cultivated to find any satisfaction for his own religious needs in sun-worship, could not afford to set up such a primitive idolatry as the ancient worship of the highland god must have been. The god whom the Amautas and Incas worshipped under the name of Huiracocha, as the almighty creator of all things, whom they honoured more than Inti, the sun-god, as being the source of all life, was no stone image; he defied all representation, as he worked and lived under no concrete form, existing as the mighty power which penetrates the whole world.

Upon the occurrence of one of those religious ceremonies with which the rising orb of day was greeted, and which were crowned by the presence of the king, the Inca Huiracocha is said to have asked the priests and Amautas collected around him whether it was conceivable that Inti was the highest god and the ruler of all things, as he invariably accomplished his course around the earth in a manner both regular and fatiguing. Supposing he were free and powerful, would he not at some time feel a desire to take a rest or to strike out another path than the one of which his daily routine must have made him thoroughly weary? Similar beginnings of scepticism and eclecticism not difficult to understand, are also related of his successors, and afforded an opportunity for the introduction of the ideas which the Incas attached to their worship of Huiracocha. In Cacha they erected a famous temple of Huiracocha for the benefit of the people; its ruins show strong divergences from the architectural style of the Incas, and also from that of all the other Peruvian peoples, and remain standing to-day as an unsolved problem. In Cuzco and other places altars were erected to the god, and his image was placed before them, generally in the form of an old man in flowing robes. Other national religions, which had been repressed hitherto, now celebrated their revival. In the version of the legend about the conquest of the Chanca, who are said to have been overcome with the help of the Pururauca, those stone statues of warriors which started into life and rushed into the ranks of the enemy at the Inca's call, we see at least a reminiscence of the revival of stone-worship. In the case of the succeeding Inca there is even better evidence of this, in the fact that after a visit to Tiahuanaco he ordered similar memorials to be set up in the neighbourhood of Cuzco; the results of this order were the peculiar steps, platforms, and sites hewn in the rock of Monte Rodadero near Cuzco. The worships of other subject peoples were also recognised later by the Incas, and transported to Cuzco; as, for instance, the worship of Pachacamak, the chief god of the peoples on the coast of the Pacific Ocean. At the time of the Spanish conquest Cuzco was a meeting-place, not only for princes and governors, but also for the gods and priests of every race which belonged to the Inca kingdom,— a regular arsenal of idols, differing widely in shape and meaning.

It was important for the Inca Huiracocha to find a successor to the throne who could continue and bring to perfection the work which he had begun. The rule of the Inca Yupanki, who was also called Pachacutek, was an open progress of almost uninterrupted triumph. On the east he extended the boundaries of his kingdom to the point where the mountain streams moderate their impetuous course in the boundless llanos. On the south he won several victories over the king of Hatun-Colla, and added the king of Chucuito to the number of his vassals. Upon the north he extended his dominion as far as Cajamarca and Conchucos; and as his father had left him no more room for conquest upon the west of the mountain valleys, he advanced to the shores of the Pacific Ocean and subdued the whole seaboard as far as the Rimak valley. His campaigns, which he sometimes led in person and sometimes entrusted to his brothers, and later to his successor, often lasted for years; under him was completed the military organisation of which we have spoken above.[1] The war upon the coast called for special precautions. Previous attempts to press forward in that direction had caused the Inca unusually heavy losses. His highland warriors could not endure the hot coast climate, and fevers were enemies against which they were almost powerless. But by relieving the armies fighting on the coast with fresh divisions at short intervals, and by removing the warriors to the highlands to recruit, he succeeded in extending his rule to the sea. When once this was accomplished, he found reliable soldiers in the races on the coast, and soldiers, too, who were inured to the climate. The principle of leaving an easy retreat open to the enemy against whom he marched was also followed by him. Numerous races and princes in the mountains and on the coast submitted to his display of power without obliging him to make them feel the sharpness of his sword. Among those which submitted voluntarily was the priestly State of Pachacamak in the valley of Lurin. The times when the Incas overthrew the temples had long since passed away. Pachacutek worshipped in person the gods who were honoured as far and wide upon the coastland as Huiracocha was in the mountains, and left the temples and their treasures undisturbed; to these latter he even sent costly presents. The only condition he laid upon the conquered people was that upon the heights which overlooked the town and temple of Pachacamak a new, greater, and more splendid temple should be erected to his own god Inti, the sun, and he ordered a similar temple to be built in Cuzco for Pachacamak.

The Inca power had not been so firmly established in these extensive and recently subdued districts that Pachacutek did not have to deal now and again with revolts. The Chanca reluctantly bore the Inca yoke. Neither permanent fortifications in their land, nor the fact that their ranks had been repeatedly weakened by the transportation of their warriors into more peaceful parts of the kingdom, served to break or to appease their haughty spirit. On the contrary they determined, when they were convinced of their weakness, to abandon their ancient home rather than give up their independence. The whole tribe started on a migration in a northeasterly direction, and founded a settlement in Chachapoyas, which was only again united with the kingdom under the last Inca ruler. Pacha-

[1] See ante, p. 321.

utek had also other battles to fight within his realm, but these did not seriously endanger it. Among the men of Inca blood there were still many remaining who knew to what change of succession the dynasty from which Pachacutek was sprung owed the throne of Cuzco. Thus an extensive conspiracy had been formed with the secret object of deposing the Inca Pachacutek and setting up in his place a descendant of the ancient royal family, the Inca Urco. But Pachacutek was informed in time of these treasonable designs, and before the conspirators had any suspicion that their plans were known the Inca Urco disappeared in the royal palace, from which he was never again to issue.

Pachacutek won great fame for himself by his victorious campaigns toward the four quarters of the heavens; and with just pride he named his territory Tahuantinsuyu, — the four cardinal points. But he left a still greater memorial of himself in the internal organisation of the Inca kingdom, an organisation that far surpassed anything else of the kind in existence upon American soil. To consider Peru under the Incas as a kingdom founded upon a basis of socialism is to misunderstand entirely the facts of the case. The Inca rule was an absolute theocracy, at the head of which was the Inca, who concentrated temporal and religious functions in his own person as being the child of the sun-god and the chief priest of that divinity. His power was absolute over body and soul, property and person, of his subjects; the only laws that were binding upon him were his own will and pleasure, and these he might change to any extent he pleased. A consequence of this powerful position was that the Inca alone possessed real property; the whole extent of the kingdom belonged to him, with every living creature in it; other men had only the usufruct of his property. It appears a hard ordinance that, as our historical sources inform us, a third of the produce of the country was appropriated for the support of the ruler, another third for the service of the sun, while only a third remained for the people. But the oppression of this law is only apparent; the Inca and the sun represented the financial department of modern times, and a large proportion of the people lived at their expense. Moreover those portions of the land assigned to the people lay in the neighbourhood of the villages and places of population; as such settlements had been purposely made on land that was capable of cultivation, the best third of the land was in the hands of the people. The extensive table-lands of the Puna, the high mountain ranges, were included in the land belonging to the sun and to the Inca, where the low temperature precluded agriculture. Here was the home of the great herds of llamas which belonged to the Inca or to the sun: the possession of these animals was forbidden to the common people.

The llama is the only large domestic animal which the American natives possessed. Different kinds of fowl, and in many districts little dogs, were tamed and bred; but they were of use to mankind only as food; their possession was a compensation for the increasing difficulty of gaining a living by hunting. The llama alone has the character of a domestic animal, in the full sense of the word, among the ancient Americans, for it alone was of use to man during its lifetime. In early times it was never used for riding or drawing vehicles. However, the Peruvians of the highlands (for the climate of the coast is fatal to the llama, and for that reason the animal was never used there in Inca times) made constant use of it as a beast of burden. The llama was equally valuable for its wool. Like the sheep, it can be shorn from time to time without injury to its health:

and in the Inca kingdom its wool was always woven into stuffs. The llamas, like all living animals, were the exclusive property of the Inca, — that is, of the State State servants performed the shearing, and officials divided the raw wool among the people according to their powers of working it and their necessities. The wool was not only woven for the clothing of the people, but a portion of it served in lieu of taxes. A kind of factory for wool-weaving went on in the abodes of the ladies of the sun, the Acllas; these were monastical retreats where hundreds of girls were constantly employed in spinning and weaving. Here was also worked the finer wool of the vicuña, a variety of the llama which ran wild and was driven into herds only at shearing-time. These fine stuffs were not intended for the common people, but were invariably worn by the Incas. For the royal families, and especially for the ruling Inca, the sun-maidens were obliged to provide large supplies of the finest stuffs; for state ceremonial exacted from the king that he should always be clothed in spotlessly new garments. In the provinces, also, the Acllas worked the coarser wool of the llama, and thereby contributed to supply the royal storehouses, in which large quantities of woollen garments were collected for the use of the army in time of war. Finally the llama was important as a food supply; game was neither plentiful nor varied, and the people could not have supported themselves thereby. Most of the inhabitants certainly kept and bred fowls in and near their houses. But beyond this there existed only the flesh of the llama, and a number of these animals were daily slaughtered for the Inca's table. But the herds were so numerous and increased so rapidly that now and again a large number of them were slaughtered and divided among the people, who were thus feasted by the monarch. The llama had descended from its wild forefathers, the guanaco and the vicuña, and had become a permanent species. Such a development must have required an extremely long period of time for its accomplishment, and consequently the llama must have been tamed long previous to the Inca rule. But although this acquisition of civilisation was not due to the Incas, yet they were the first to systematise the breeding and the use of the animal.

On one of his first campaigns of conquest the Inca Pachacutek subdued the district of Huilcabamba, and found that the veins of gold there situated were already being worked by the natives. Although they could work only the upper strata, and with their primitive implements could naturally extract the gold from only the richest lodes, yet the astonishing amount of gold and silver which the Spaniards found in the Inca kingdom shows that the work was profitable. The people were obliged to pay their tribute to the Inca from these mining operations. The work demanded of them was not hard; they were always allowed sufficient time to satisfy their own personal requirements. But the mountain peoples had as little claim to the precious metal which they brought forth to the light of day as had the owners of the corn in the lowland, or the shepherds of the llamas, to the possession of these goods; for real property belonged to the Inca alone. Gold and silver, the medium of exchange in the whole civilised world, brought neither power nor influence with them in the Inca kingdom, but were employed for the decoration of the gods and kings and were worthless in the hands of individuals.

A State which had no money and practically no property had also nothing wherewith to pay taxes. But the citizen himself was the property, the slave, of the

State, and consequently he owed a certain portion of his labour to the State. In the larger settlements a considerable number of the inhabitants paid their tribute in different kinds of manufacture, in which, in some cases, they had attained considerable skill. The ancient Peruvian weaving, both of woollen and cotton stuffs, though carried on with very simple implements, is of high quality in respect of both fineness and durability; and the weavers understood the employment of large and artistic patterns by the use of different-coloured threads. Still more remarkable is the Peruvian pottery ware, with its great variety of decoration, which is almost invariably tasteful, and with its rich and artistic colouring.[1] Their artistic powers were almost exclusively exercised upon this pottery; and ware that has been shaped into realistic but very fantastic forms has come down to us from almost all the provinces of the Inca kingdom.[2]

The country people were employed in herding the flocks of llama, or in cultivating the lands belonging to the Inca and the sun. The plough was unknown to the Peruvians; they turned up the soil with an implement like a spade, and, as they invariably worked in large numbers, digging in rows, their fields must have had a furrowed appearance. Agriculture was the foundation of the Inca kingdom; it was regarded as divine service, and every subject of the kingdom was entrusted with its accomplishment. When the season for tilling the soil had come round, the Inca himself, followed by all his court, proceeded in great pomp to a field that was dedicated to the sun in the neighbourhood of Cuzco, and began the agriculture in person with religious ceremonies. Each of his courtiers had to follow his example. The order was then transmitted by officials through the country that the subjects should begin the year's work upon the land. The head of every family was in annual possession of a particular plot of land proportioned to the needs of his household; if his family increased, so did his plot, a piece half the size of the original allotment being given him for each son, and a quarter of the original size for each daughter. But the land remained State property, and upon the death or migration of the occupant it reverted to the Crown. Cultivation was carried on in common and under the superintendence of overseers. First were tilled the lands of the sun; then those of individual citizens, including the allotments of the poor, the sick, and the officials; and finally the lands of the Inca were cultivated. In the milder districts of the kingdom a number of varieties of maize were raised. The mandioc, several kinds of pumpkins, beans, and some other vegetables, were grown more in the gardens around the houses than in the fields. But in many districts of the Inca kingdom the cold climate was unfavourable to these vegetables. In such cases potatoes formed the staple of agriculture.

The Inca-Peruvians carried on agriculture not only extensively, but also with great energy. The use of manure, for which purpose, after they had conquered the seacoast, they used guano, was as little a discovery of theirs as was the science of irrigation. In the narrow valleys of the highland they increased the ground available for agriculture by making terraces for miles, at a great expense of labour, in the precipitous mountain heights, which were then carefully irrigated by canals from the river running down the valley. Land that was in this way brought under cultivation naturally belonged only to the Incas; the amount of work necessary

---

[1] See Figs. 4–6, 8, Plate at p. 302.     [2] See Figs. 9, 10.

for its success was far more than individual sources could provide, and presupposed a strong and close organisation. A family of at least ten inhabitants formed the smallest administrative unity in the kingdom; an inferior official superintended this, whose business it was to care for and watch over it. Ten of such unities formed a "hundred;" here the superintendent was obliged to keep an eye upon the districts of his ten inferior officials, besides the care of his own office. The next political unity was formed of ten "hundreds," and a "ten thousand" was generally equivalent to a province of the kingdom. The highest power naturally lay in the hands of the Inca, who had a consultative council in Cuzco. But besides this council the governors of the provinces (who were generally chosen from the Inca class when political necessities had not left the rule in the hands of one of the old conquered princes), and also the officials of smaller districts, were obliged from time to time to appear personally before the central power, or to send in their reports with the help of the quipus. By this means the government was fully informed concerning the inhabitants of each province and their capabilities, and also concerning the supplies and provisions which every district was obliged to make, to meet its own necessities, and even to have a surplus in hand. Moreover the overseers were constantly inspected by officials of a higher class; in cases where faults were discovered, the guilty person was punished and so also were his superiors, who ought to have informed the subjects of their obligations and to have assured themselves that these were fulfilled.

As the common man, the "hatunruna," possessed no real property, he might also pay his taxes in military service. The Incas did not maintain a standing army, and any careful or extensive training in the use of arms seems to have been the privilege of the Incas alone, and of the sons of the nobles from the subject provinces. It is by no means clear in what manner the hatunruna obtained the training necessary to enable him to fulfil his part in the constant and distant campaigns of the Incas. There was, however, a system for regularly relieving the garrisons that were maintained in unsettled quarters, as well as for conveying reinforcements to the battle-fields; an arrangement must consequently have been on foot somewhat similar to the old Prussian system of relief, according to which the hatunruna returned to his agricultural pursuits after a short period of active service, until he was again called out in due course, though generally only for a limited space of time.

An important duty of the overseers of the "hundreds" was to see that the people performed their allotted portion of work; the women were included under this decree. Their essential duties in their households consisted in the care of the garden and of the poultry; but most important were the spinning and weaving, which they were obliged to practise beyond the mere satisfaction of their household necessities, as we have stated above.[1] Idleness was a punishable offence in the Inca kingdom; even when women made visits to their neighbours they took their work with them, unless the person visited was of higher rank than her visitor; in this case it was the duty of the visitor to ask for permission to take her work. It was the business of the local overseers to apportion as much land to each inhabitant as would suffice for the maintenance of himself and his wife. If, as happened in exceptional cases, the land belonging to the community did not suffice, the inhabitants had a claim upon the lands of the Inca; but when the population

---

[1] *Ante*, p. 332.

of a province rose to such an extent that the land was no longer capable of supporting them, colonists, known as "mitimaes," were sent out into less thickly populated or new provinces. The State undertook the duty of providing for the support of each individual, but avoided poverty, with its evil results of beggary and vagabondism, which was in fact entirely obviated by the necessity of labour and the prohibition which was laid upon an unauthorised change of residence. The State also recognised its duty of providing for its subjects in extraordinary cases; and, thanks to the general industry, the storehouses situated in every province were invariably sufficiently full of supplies to meet all necessities.

The conception of private property was not wholly unfamiliar to the inhabitants of the Inca State. Houses and land were, it is true, the property of the community, to which they reverted at the death of the holder. But so ample was the provision made for the support of the individual that he was able to put aside some savings, and to lay out these economies as he wished, even in the purchase of luxuries, as the State or community provided his necessities. The objects found in the Peruvian cemeteries show us that luxuries were not altogether unknown, even among the common people, and this personal property was almost invariably interred with its dead owner.

As new members were born into the family, the land allotted to it was increased. The young Inca citizens passed a long and tranquil childhood. It was incumbent on their parents to give them a practical education and to train them in domestic duties, but it was not till the completion of their twenty-fourth year that the State made any claim upon the young people. At twenty-five they were married. Marriage was also strictly controlled by the law, which denied to the Inca-Peruvian any opportunity of personal initiative from the cradle to the grave. The public officials were required to keep a register of persons of both sexes who every year attained a marriageable age in their districts. Each year a day was appointed for the celebration of marriages throughout the kingdom. The young men and maidens, clad in their best attire, appeared before the officers of their district, who publicly, but with little in the way of ceremony, assigned to each youth a young maiden. On the same day, at Cuzco, the Inca himself officiated for those of noble blood. The consent of the young people was superfluous in the eyes of the law, but, when possible, their inclinations were considered. No one, however, might marry outside of his own district. The usual allotment of land was now made to the young couple, and the community saw to the building of their simple and primitive dwelling. In this way they entered the ranks of the hatunrunas, accepting all the responsibilities involved, except that for the first year — the honeymoon of their married life — they remained exempt from public service. The duties of labour were obligatory up to the age of fifty; after that time the community, as also in cases of temporary or permanent disablement, became responsible for their support to the end of their lives.

While military service was demanded of the men, another tax was levied by the Inca upon the women. Every year the officials were required to select from the number of young maidens the best and most beautiful for the service of the ruler and of the sun. In each province the Inca had his palace and a house attached to it, in which these maidens led a privileged if a laborious existence. Whenever the Inca came into residence it was from their number that he chose the partner of his couch. If the connection resulted in pregnancy, the young

mother returned to her native home, where great respect was paid both to her and
to the child.   Very different was the lot of those selected for the service of the
sun.   Like the royal wives, they led a favoured but industrious life in religious
seclusion.   But in their case the law against incontinence was inviolable, and a
cruel death awaited the sun-maiden and her seducer if this statute was transgressed.
That the Incas should occasionally have taken children from their parents in
their tenderest years for sacrifice to the sun-god is hardly probable.   Such sacrifices
may in earlier times have been offered to the sun-god and to the deities of many
of the peoples afterward subdued.   But such a usage is wholly inconsistent with
the spirit of the national religion as it was practised under the later Incas.   In the
Inca State religion was much more a matter of politics than of dogma.   The late
Incas therefore imposed no restrictions upon the various races of their subjects as
to the number of gods they might desire to worship.   It was also from political
motives that they established at Cuzco the temples and priests of the various
religions; for thus they were in continual touch with the forces which they knew
to exercise a great influence upon the masses.   The introduction into every newly
acquired province of sun-worship as a supreme and universal form of religion
was also meant to serve their political ends.   Although there was at Cuzco a high
priest of the sun-god, who exercised a kind of control over priests of all denominations throughout the country, yet the real head of the church was the Inca.   As
descendant of the sun-god he stood nearer to the deity than his highest priest,
while as child of the sun he was himself entitled to divine honours after his
death, upon which he returned to his ancestor.   Dissensions between king and
priesthood, which recur so frequently in the communities of Central America,
were rendered impossible by the semi-divine character of the Inca.   For this reason
the decided revolution which the Inca Huiracocha brought about in the domain of
religious politics never at any place or time caused the slightest difficulty, although
it raised at once a host of formidable rivals to the priesthood of the sun.   The
privileged position, and the endowment of a third of the land, remained their
exclusive right; but even the Inca kings made numerous and extremely costly
offerings to the temples of Huiracocha and Pachacamak.

The laborious life of the masses was relieved only by the festivals which were
celebrated in honour of the sun-god; once at least in each month the inhabitants
of each locality were summoned by the officials to a feast.   Upon these occasions
the flesh of the llama, set apart by the Inca for the people, was certainly consumed;
at the same time large quantities of the maize beer called "aka" were drunk, and
dance and song contributed to the enjoyment.   Similar holidays followed the completion of all the more important tasks: the cultivation of the fields, the gathering
in of the harvest, or any exceptional undertaking,—housebuilding, roadmaking,
and the like.   Besides these, however, there were four high festivals common to
all the land: the Hatun Raimi, the Cusqui Raimi, the Situa Raimi, and the
Huaracuy.

The Hatun (or Inti) Raimi was celebrated at the time of the winter solstice
(the 21st of June[1]), and was the first and principal festival by which the year
was reckoned.   Lasting for nine days, it celebrated the return of the source of
life and heat, the sun having reached and passed its extreme northern declina-
tion.   The first three festival days were devoted to preparation: every inhabitant

---
[1] See ante, p. 326.

of the Inca kingdom was obliged to abstain from all food with the exception of a little uncooked maize and water, and, if married, from conjugal intercourse; all fires were extinguished. During these days it was the duty of the young unmarried women in each household, and of the sun-maidens for the use of the Inca and his court, to prepare the sacred bread, the first food that might be taken after the fast. The principal ceremony took place on the morning of the fourth day. At the approach of dawn the whole population poured out of their houses into the open space where the priests were awaiting the sunrise. Here the thronging multitude crouched barefooted in a wide circle around the priests, and, no one daring to rise, awaited the moment when the sun's orb should appear above the horizon, to greet it with solemn sacrifice.

Naturally it was at Cuzco that the feast was celebrated in its most magnificent form. Here, upon that day, the square of Haucaipata, around which stood the royal palaces, was thronged with the highest and noblest from every province of the kingdom. Clothed in festal attire, but barefooted and in the same attitude of humility, they, too, awaited the moment of sunrise. Thereupon the Inca king was the first to rise; upon this day, as being the child of the sun, he himself performed the office of high-priest. In either hand he held a cup inlaid with gold, filled to the brim with "aka." While he addressed a solemn greeting to the rising luminary, he emptied the cup in his right hand into a golden basin that stood before him, whence golden pipes conveyed the libation to the Temple of the Sun. The cup in his left hand he put to his own lips, and then invited his nearest relatives, and any on whom he wished to confer distinction, to take from this cup, with small golden chalices, a portion for themselves. Then, together with the higher priests and dignitaries, the Inca entered the temple in order to pay his adoration to the image of the god. The Temple of the Sun had undergone, at the hands of the Inca Pachacutek, a thorough restoration and extension; since which time, owing to its rich adornment with precious metals, it had been known by the name of Coricancha, "the Golden Precinct." It was an extensive group of buildings, encircled by walls of squared masonry, lying somewhat nearer the mountains than the market-place. In and around the great court were a number of edifices, the most sacred of which was the Hall of the Sun. Here, on the wall at the back of the temple, so placed as each morning to catch the rays of the rising sun, was the great golden disk, encircled with rays, which constituted the Holy of Holies. Walls and roof, as well as the altars before this and the other shrines of the temple, were richly overlaid with gold, while along the walls, seated in their litters and wrapped in the most costly fabrics, stood the perfectly preserved mummies of the dead Incas. Behind the Hall of the Sun a similar room contained the image of the moon and the mummies of the Coyas, the imperial wives who had given to the kingdom an heir to the throne. Here all ornamentation was in silver. Then followed smaller sanctuaries for the other heavenly bodies, the divine retinue of Inti, and for his earthly followers, the priests. After libations and incense had been offered at these shrines also, the Inca returned to the square, where the rest awaited him; for on this day the great sacrifices were performed, not in the enclosed court of the temple, but in the open market-place. The priests now led forth a young black llama. Black animals, as being more uniform in colour, were more highly prized than white ones, which as a rule showed darker patches; moreover black was the sacred colour and was specially favoured by the Inca. While the unbound victim was held by priests of lower grade, the high-priest cut open the body with an obsidian knife and tore out the heart and entrails. From these he foretold the events of the year that was just beginning. The body was now divided, and, in order to burn it as a sacrifice, the high-priest lighted with a burning-glass, which he wore on his right wrist, the new fire from which all the hearths in the city were kindled afresh. This concluded the more important ceremonies, which now gave place to general rejoicings. Numbers of the common llamas were slaughtered, but only the blood and entrails were offered to the god; the flesh was assigned to the people for food. The remaining days of the festival were spent in eating and drinking, dancing and singing, and revels of every description, the freedom of which often degenerated into license. For the people the feast closed on the ninth day, after six days of rejoicing. The Inca and his attendants seem, however, to have continued the celebrations for a whole month, and even then to have lamented their brief duration.

The second of the common festivals, the Cusqui Raimi, was connected with agriculture. It was celebrated before the beginning of harvest, and was a sort of procession in honour of the sun-god, who, after everything in mortal power had been done to secure the success of the crops, was implored with his divine favour to bless and increase the harvest. This feast also was followed by days of continuous and unrestrained revelry, meant, no doubt, to provide the people with recreation after the labours of the field.

Of a different character was the third feast, or Situa Raimi, which fell at the time of the spring equinox (in September). The assumption that every calamity or unexpected event which befell the individual or the community was due to some transgression was current in the Inca kingdom as elsewhere, and was reflected in the laws. But if the guilt of the individual might be expiated by atonement or punishment, it still adhered to the community, which had likewise to bear the weight of all the terrors which threatened it from the evil spirits with which earth and air were peopled. To appease or drive away these was the object of the feast. It was preceded, like the others, by a three-days fast and the preparation of sacred bread. In addition, however, to those intended for food, other loaves were baked, mixed with the blood of sacrifice. With this bread each man, on the fourth day at sunrise, rubbed his body, after bathing in running water, in order to purify himself. On the morning of the great day of the festival the crowning ceremony took place at the fortress of Sacsahuaman. This was a huge fortification built of enormous blocks of stone, which rose in five tiers on one of the heights commanding the city from the northeast. Its erection had been commenced by the Inca Huiracocha at the time when the Chanca invasion had threatened the as yet utterly defenceless city with extinction. The Inca Pachacutek had successfully completed the mighty structure. From the gate of the fortress, at the Situa Raimi, issued four youths of the Inca race, clad in complete armour. Brandishing their spears they ran at full speed through town and country in the direction of the four cardinal points. Everywhere the gaily clad multitudes flocked from their dwellings to meet them, and greeted them with loud shouts and waving of garments. At fixed distances others of the Inca race, similarly attired, waited to receive the lance in turn, and carried it farther and farther until the boundary of the district was passed. There the lance was driven deep into the earth, and it was supposed that the evil spirits had thus been expelled from the soil. During the night the Incas waved burning torches, which they extinguished on the farther side of the boundary in the streams that flowed out of the country. In this way the powers of darkness were also put to flight, and the following days were devoted to festivity.

While at the Situa Raimi the chief actors were the Inca youths, who symbolically delivered the people from the dangers that threatened it, the fourth great feast, the Huaracuy, was almost exclusively confined to the Inca class, and the people could participate only in the general rejoicings. This feast marked the conclusion of the probations which the children of Inca descent, as well as the sons of the noblest families in the provinces, had to undergo before they might be admitted to the privileges of manhood.

In spite of the efforts of the Incas to maintain the belief that the whole of the Inca class was descended from Manco Capak, and through him from the sun-god himself, they had not been able to banish from the memory of men the fact that a part of the caste could establish no blood-kinship with the founder of the dynasty. In the earliest times, in addition to the ruler of Cuzco, many other small dynasties of the Peruvian highlands had assumed the designation of Inca, which, like " Manco " and " Capak," was originally a mere title and not the name of a race. Whether these, on their incorporation into the empire of the son of the sun, maintained the name and privileges of the Inca, is doubtful. Thus arose a new class in the community, which, though unable to establish any blood-relationship with the Incas, shared all their privileges. When Manco Capak came to Cuzco, he was attended by a small band of dependents, with whose help he drove the Alcavizas from the city. In the infancy of the State these naturally formed a privileged class, and when, later, the constant extension of the empire brought to the capital a mixed population of every conceivable element, they and their posterity, the aristocracy of Cuzco, were admitted to all the essential privileges enjoyed by those of pure Inca blood.

On the other hand the Inca stock increased with great rapidity by the natural process of reproduction. Among the masses no man was permitted to marry more than one wife, but from this law the whole of the Inca caste was exempt, and the ruler might also grant dispensation to others. For himself, especially, it was not only a privilege to possess a number of wives, but also a duty to leave behind him as numerous a progeny as possible. Only one, however, of the ruler's wives shared his royal rank; she bore the name of Coya and took an important part in the public ceremonial that was incumbent upon the Inca. The Inca Pachacutek was the first to enact that the natural sister or the nearest female relation of the ruling Inca should always be chosen as the Coya, in order as far as possible to preserve the blood of the children of the sun from contamination. In addition to the Coya the Inca might take as many wives as he wished; if they belonged to the Inca class, they and their children were considered legitimate. The Inca also sought daughters in marriage from his vassal princes; this was considered a high honour, and no less so if the Inca married one of his illegitimate daughters to a dignitary or a vassal prince. Marriage between men and women of the Inca class was celebrated in the same way as that of the people, with the exception that the Inca ruler in person performed the ceremony in Cuzco. Youths of Inca blood might take only one wife of their own accord, though they might also have numerous concubines : but after the completion of an important task, or upon the occasion of a feast, the ruler often rewarded his kinsmen with one or more wives. Individual rulers are said to have left as many as a hundred children or even more; each of these became the founder of a family, the connection of which with the common stock was preserved in their name and insignia; such families united to worship the mummy of their ancestor in the Temple of the Sun. By law the Inca king was as completely master of the bodies and souls of the Incas as of his other subjects; but as a matter of fact the Inca class obtained special privileges in the kingdom of Tahuantinsuyu. The duty of labour, which was incumbent upon everybody in the Inca State, was not binding upon them. A memorial of the time when the Incas formed a small band in the middle of a foreign race was preserved in the right which they had of eating at the ruler's table; later this right became so extended that the Inca was obliged to support the whole of the Inca caste, and also all the officials of the kingdom who were not Incas, with the produce of that third of the land which belonged to him. The highest temporal and religious offices were filled with sons of the Inca race; and the man who could show his value in such a position was certain of the monarch's favour. To this many of the Inca sons owed large palaces and bands of attendants both in the capitals and in the provinces.

The education imparted to the Inca caste justified their special privileges. In the case of the young girls known as "ñusta," their education was a more refined type of that received by the daughters of the people and the sun-maidens. On the other hand the young men, the "auqui," not only received a careful intellectual training, as mentioned above,[1] but were also obliged to undergo a thorough course of physical exercise. This was concluded, when the auqui had reached his sixteenth year, with the ordeal which preceded the feast of Huaracuy, and gave him the right of assuming the name and the insignia of an Inca. These competitions consisted of a foot race, individual contests with weapons, similar contests between two bands, and finally a battle between two army corps, one of which had to defend a fortress while another attacked it. They also had to prove that they were able to bear pain and toil without complaining, and finally had to show their capability of making their own clothes and equipment. When these tests had been gone through successfully, the youthful band was led before the king by their masters, who were experienced Incas and Amautas. He invested them with the insignia of their new position, and henceforward they were no longer called auqui, but took the title of Inca. The king bored the lobe of each one's ear with a golden needle, and from that time he might wear gold and silver ear-ornaments. This habit was carried to such an extent that the Spaniards gave the Incas the name of Orejones, "large-eared," because the weight of their ornaments had drawn out the lobes to a remarkable extent. Up to this point the youths had been clothed simply and almost inadequately; but on their festival day their nearest relations put upon them fine sandals, as they were worn by grown-up Incas, fastened the "huara" of fine vicuña wool around their loins, and placed the head-covering, "llautu," upon their hair, that was now closely cropped. The marks of rank worn by the ruler coincided very nearly with these; only his llautu was bordered with a fine fringe of red wool (in the case of heirs to the throne, of full age, the colour was yellow), which descended to the eyebrows, and a thick tassel of similar colour, the "paicha," adorned his right temple.

---

[1] *Ante*, p. 325.

A juristic system can scarcely exist in a kingdom where the ruler is the source of all law and of every decree; the officials to whom the Inca deputed the rule of certain portions of the people decided what matters were punishable and what could be allowed. As there was no real property, there could be no pecuniary troubles and no fines. Any one who was guilty of an offence had outraged the laws of the Inca, the representative of the highest god, and was therefore almost invariably punished with death; that is to say, he was either strangled, knocked on the head, shot with arrows, or thrown from the rocks. The sun-maidens guilty of incontinence were walled up alive; but their seducers, and also the entire family which had brought up such an adept in wickedness, were put to death, and the place where its house had stood was sown with salt and left deserted for ever.

The greater became the extent of the Inca kingdom, the more important became the means of quick communication. In early times the Incas had confronted the question of crossing the high mountain ranges which divided one highland valley from another, and the watercourses which rushed furiously down the deeper valleys. When the Inca Pachacutek marched against Huilcabamba, his enemy broke down the bridges over the Urubamba, and thought thereby to oppose an impassable obstacle to the advance of the Inca army: but the Inca called up engineers and workmen from the capitals and from the whole country to his aid, and a new bridge was completed after a few weeks. The Inca Pachacutek, who here, as everywhere, showed his great faculty for organisation, had a highroad built from Cuzco as far as Cajamarca, a distance of nearly a hundred miles; it ran over passes and through valleys, over marshes and through rocks, and its remains are in existence to-day. Even in the time of the Spanish rule this highroad formed the main entry of the country, as also did a similar highroad built by the Inca Yupanki, running on the west of Pachacutek's road down to the coast, which it followed as far as Tumbez, the most northern settlement of the Inca kingdom on the sea, lying not far from the Gulf of Guayaquil. As the Peruvians were not acquainted with vehicles, the roads were intended only for the traffic of men, and at most for the llamas that were used as beasts of burden; consequently they were only eighteen to twenty-two feet broad, and were enclosed on either side by a parapet of some height. Upon deep precipices they became narrower, and flights of steps occasionally crossed the ranges which divided the several valleys. Where there were no fords, the rivers were crossed by bridges of stone, which in the mountain ranges gave place to suspension bridges constructed of hempen rope and of woven lianas; long boarded paths gave a footing across the marshes of the Paramos and the water-sheds. At regular intervals resting-places were built near the road, called "tambos;" they consisted of a walled-in courtyard intended for beasts of burden, to which adjoined two open rooms for the travellers themselves. Smaller refuges at shorter intervals on all the most important lines of communication were established for the public service. In them were stationed the foot-messengers, known as "chasquis," by whose help news of important events, even in the remotest provinces, could be brought to the capital in a short space of time. How highly swiftness of foot was valued can be seen from the fact that it was included in the tests which the sons of the Incas had to undergo.[1] Thus even among the common people the foot-messenger was a privileged person. Several runners were invariably stationed in the little post-houses; as often as a messenger

---

[1] See *ante*, pp. 325, 340.

came in, wearied by the rapidity with which he had passed over his section, one of those waiting took over his message, which was delivered either by word of mouth or by means of the quipus, to take it on to the next station at an equal rate. The service is said to have been so admirably organised that fresh sea-fish were by no means a rarity at the ruler's table.

It may be an injustice to the merits of the other Inca kings to ascribe nearly all valuable institutions to the Inca Pachacutek; but his name shows that he must have established the lion's share of these. "Pachacutek" means "world-organiser." He was succeeded upon the throne of Tahuantinsuyu by his eldest son, Tupak Yupanki, who, like his father, united military reputation to a capacity for keen and vigorous government at home. Under his rule the Inca kingdom was extended in nearly every direction until it recovered that territory which it possessed at the time of the conquest. He completed the subjugation of the kingdom of Chimu,[1] and pressed his conquest forward to Quito. On the other side he changed the confederation with the princes round the lake of Titicaca into a firm dominion over them, while he also extended his power into Chile as far as the Rio Maule. It was never the Inca policy to introduce the organisation of the ancient provinces, in all its carefully thought out details, into new districts immediately upon their subjugation. Where similar institutions already existed, as they did in the kingdom of Chimu, the process of assimilation was probably distinctly rapid. But other provinces, whose institutions showed marked differences, could only by slow degrees be incorporated in the social organism of the Inca State, as is proved by the frequent recurrence of revolts under the Inca régime. The Inca rulers found colonisation the best means of repressing these; Tupak Yupanki is said constantly to have practised it. At the time of the Spanish conquest the language of the Yunca had not entirely died out upon the lake of Titicaca, among the mitimaes whom Tupak Yupanki had settled there after the conquest of the Chimu kingdom. This Inca was a zealous worshipper of Huiracocha; after the conquest of Hatun-Colla he made a pilgrimage to his shrine on the lake of Titicaca, and adorned it with new buildings in his honour, though these included a sun-temple and a house for the sun-maidens. At the same time he prosecuted those unifying religious tendencies which the Incas had made their guiding principle since the time of the Inca Huiracocha.

When his son, Huaina Capak, ascended the throne, the Spaniards had already got a footing upon American soil; reports of their arrival can hardly have failed to reach Cuzco. The subjects of the Inca upon the coast-land carried on an extensive traffic upon the Pacific seaboard, exchanging their products for those of their northern neighbours, and such traffic must have been under the control and protection of the government. But the Incas were too entirely convinced of their own superiority to have had any suspicion that their period of prosperity was coming to a rapid end. The reign of Huaina Capak is full of those relations with the kingdom of Quito which were to exercise such influence upon the fate of his dynasty. The first act of his government was to take revenge upon the inhabitants of Quito for the blood of the Inca-Peruvians who had been slain upon the revolt of the provinces conquered by Tupak Yupanki. This business kept him far from the capital for many years. At that time the Inca developed

---

[1] See ante, p. 311.

a strong preference for the milder climate on the north of his kingdom; in Tumebamba, which he had fitted up as his headquarters during the campaign, he built palaces, temples, and gardens of a splendour almost equal to those of Cuzco. And when he eventually succeeded in completing the conquest of the kingdom of Quito he married the Princess Paccha, the only daughter of the last ruler, in order to unite the province more closely to his person and to his kingdom.

Huaina Capak was not very fortunate in his domestic life. While his father was alive he held the position of heir to the throne, according to the new laws of succession, and had therefore chosen his eldest sister to be his legal wife; but she bore him no children. Thereupon he took two other wives of the Inca race, a younger sister and a cousin, on the condition that the one who first bore him a son should receive the privileges of the Coya. Shortly afterward his sister presented him with a successor, Huascar. But while he was absent in Quito he began to forget the mother and child; and Paccha, whom he had made a legal wife in defiance of the law which governed his domestic affairs (for this princess was not of the Inca race), became doubly dear to him when she presented him with a boy whose lively spirit won his father's heart even in his childhood. Huaina Capak was naturally obliged to return at intervals to Cuzco, that being still the central point of the kingdom; but as soon as he had performed his State duties he again returned to his beloved Quito, and there he spent the greater portion of his life.

The Inca kingdom was at this time capable of extension only upon its northern boundary. On the west the ocean formed the boundary of the country for hundreds of miles In the south the kingdom extended into Chile, where the highlands, which became wilder and wilder at every step, seemed scarcely worth the trouble of conquest. On the east every inhabitant of the fruitful valleys of the Cordilleras was subject to his rule. The boundless primeval forest which bordered the lowland was inhabited only by wandering tribes of savages who avoided every attempt to subdue them by vanishing without a trace as soon as the Inca armies approached; and the unhealthy climate, and the impossibility of following their usual mode of life, induced the Incas to renounce all plans of conquest in this direction. Upon the north, however, they were enticed by a valuable territory where the conditions of life were very similar to those of their home. Huaina Capak turned his arms more than once in this direction; and Quito was an admirable base of operations for expeditions northward. It does not appear that Paccha ever accompanied her husband to Cuzco; the feeling among the Incas, who were so zealous to preserve the purity of their race, was anything but favourable toward her. It is equally unlikely that the mother of Huascar accompanied her husband to Quito; but the young prince was summoned there at least once, with many of his elder relations, to learn from his father's mouth the manner in which he desired the government to be conducted in the event of his death. He could not persuade himself entirely to exclude his favourite son from the succession. Atahualpa, who had grown up to the entire satisfaction of his father, accompanied him everywhere on his journeys and campaigns, and his lively manners had made him the favourite of the army. On the other hand Huascar developed but slowly: his character was serious and quiet; the court which the ruler had abandoned, the Coya who was scorned and rejected, and the danger that he himself might be disinherited, — all these facts tended to darken his early years. Huaina Capak did not venture upon the extreme step of changing the succession; but he stipulated that the kingdom of Quito should be held in independence by his favourite Atahualpa, and that Huascar should inherit the Inca kingdom, even as Huaina Capak had himself received it upon his accession. Huascar gladly agreed not to disturb his brother in his possessions, and to remain on terms of friendship with him; the arrangement was for him a relief from long anxiety. But Atahualpa had also reason for satisfaction: he was better provided for than an Inca's inferior son had ever been, and in his person was revived the royal house of Quito. It was only the legitimist party at the court of Cuzco who were dissatisfied; they thought it was a disgrace that the unity of the kingdom should be endangered by the caprice of Huaina Capak, that a province should be lost again to the Sun State which had been bought with the blood of its subjects under two kings, and all for the sake of a child who had neither position nor right. However, such objections were naturally not ventured in face of the unlimited powers of Huaina Capak, and when he died a few years later in the prime of life, in an epidemic of smallpox in Quito, he was able to close his eyes in the belief that he had secured the welfare of his kingdom and of his favourite.

Atahualpa had developed early, and, after sharing for years in all his father's business of war and peace, had become fully acquainted with the duties of a ruler. He immediately undertook the government of the State to which his father had destined him, and there remained at his side all those who had served Huaina Capak in his lifetime. In Cuzco, on the other hand, people clung obstinately to the old regulations. Huascar was not yet of age, and a council of the oldest relations of the dead monarch held the reins of power. In their eyes the capricious dispositions of Huaina Capak did not hold good, because they violated the succession of the house; they were willing to recognise Atahualpa only as the representative of the Inca for the province of Quito. The obligation of presenting himself in Cuzco to pay allegiance to the new king was as binding upon him as upon all the members of the royal family. The regents did not, however, venture to answer Atahualpa's contemptuous silence by an open attack. It was only when Huascar had been proclaimed monarch in Cuzco, after undergoing the customary period of preparation, and with all the usual brilliant festivities, that a different policy was begun. In order to make trial of the feeling entertained in Quito toward the claims of the legitimists, Huascar demanded of Atahualpa that he should send to Cuzco the wife and the treasures of the late monarch which were still in Quito. Atahualpa rejected this demand, appealing to the last wishes of Huaina Capak; yet he allowed it to be clearly understood that he was ready to continue negotiations. The embassy that Huascar had sent to Quito proposed to Atahualpa that he should put in an appearance as quickly as possible in Cuzco; he only asked to be allowed to make his entry with the ceremonial that befitted his rank, to be given a space of time for preparation, and to be permitted to bring a large company of retainers. These demands the Inca was foolish enough to concede. A period of feverish energy now began in Quito. All the old generals of Huaina Capak who had remained in Quito from inclination to the prince and respect to his father's will were now called up to Atahualpa and ordered to reorganise their contingents. It was not difficult, with the treasures of the old king, to provide the equipment of a powerful army; and small divisions of this force started toward Cuzco under pretext of forming the retinue of Atahualpa, who was coming to offer his allegiance.

When the Inca's eyes were at last opened, it was not difficult for him to call his subjects together in arms in great numbers; but these contingents did not form an army. A few miles from Cuzco, not far from the place where once the Inca Huiracocha had beaten the Chanca in a bloody conflict, the armies of the brothers met. The young troops of Huascar could not withstand the superior tactics of the enemy; Huascar himself fell into the hands of the conquerors as he was trying to cut his way through their ranks to Cuzco. Thereupon all resistance ceased throughout the kingdom, and the capital surrendered unconditionally to the victorious army. Atahualpa made a cowardly use of his victory. Under the pretence of settling the limits which should divide his power from that of Huascar, he summoned every member of the Inca blood to Cuzco; but every person who entered the town was arrested and slain by his generals, who held the town under martial law. Atahualpa had not been able to forget that the Incas were not willing to recognise his equality, as he was the son of a foreigner; those alone were spared who had favoured him from the outset. But Cuzco was no longer the heart of the kingdom. Atahualpa disliked visiting the scene of his dreadful vengeance; such departments of the government as had to be carried on in Cuzco were undertaken by his officials. He himself made a journey of inspection through the central provinces of the kingdom. But before he had returned from this expedition news reached him that strangers had landed in the extreme north of his kingdom. These were Pizarro and his following.

The Spaniards have often been reproached with their ruthless destruction in the New World of a civilisation which was but little inferior to their own, and afforded the best hopes for future prosperity. The romantic enthusiasm for the manners and customs of the past which possessed men in the first half of our century extended also to the New World. The organisation of the Aztec States, and still more that of the Inca kingdom, appeared to be the ideal of a polity in which king and people, in their mutual relations, had solved with complete success the great difficulty of all political science; namely, to make the freedom and prosperity of individuals exactly correspond with the general good. It is already sufficiently plain, from what we have said, that such a theory is entirely refuted by an examination of the actual conditions of the Inca kingdom. Undoubtedly the Inca State succeeded to a remarkable extent in solving the problem of an extensive State control for the good of each individual subject; but this success was attained only by means of an unparalleled system of surveillance which reduced individuals to the position of helpless instruments in the community and entirely destroyed all personal freedom.

Equally erroneous is the idea that anything remarkable was to be expected from a further development of the ancient American civilisation. Neither the Aztec nor the Inca kingdom represented the highest point of an uninterrupted development. The sites of civilisation in the new continent were the scene of the rise and fall of peoples, of their exodus, and of their immigration even as was the case in wide districts inhabited by uncivilised races, and the rise of a people implied a retrogression in civilisation no less in the New World than in the Old. Thus it was that the uncivilised Nahua overthrew the dominion of the Maya peoples, and the Inca Peruvians, or their predecessors, again destroyed the civilisation of the founders of Tiahuanaco. The progress which they themselves made, following the lines taken by the preceding civilisations, did not equal the general culture of their predecessors. And they would hardly have made any further advance of importance in this direction, even if the Spanish conquest had not blocked their way. Both the Aztec and the Inca kingdoms were in their decadence at the time of the Spanish invasion. In Central America the universal hatred of the Aztec power had already undermined the confederation of the three kingdoms situated upon the Lake, which were the sole support of the polity; and a revolt in the land of the Tezcucans would at once have caused a universal conflagration in which Montezuma's kingdom would have collapsed. The Inca kingdom had certainly passed through more than one internal dynastic revolution without receiving any important check to its development. But it would not so easily have survived the revolution which must have followed upon the fall of the Inca race, —a fall brought about by the passionate hatred of Atahualpa. Moreover, even here the size of the kingdom, in spite of the wonderful centralisation of the government, had almost reached the limits of what was possible at that period. The extraordinarily rapid successes of Cortes and Pizarro, who were able to shatter mighty kingdoms with a handful of hungry adventurers, can be explained only by the fact that both civilisations were in their decadence and bore the germs of destruction within themselves.

## 4. THE DISCOVERY AND CONQUEST

### A. CHRISTOPHER COLUMBUS

(a) *The Passage to the Indies.* — The ideas prevailing in the fifteenth century as to the formation of the earth's surface left no room for the existence of a new continent, although the learned had withdrawn their opposition to the theory of the earth's being round, yet this doctrine had hardly penetrated the minds of the public, and a number of other erroneous ideas still prevailed both in learned and in illiterate circles. Pierre d'Alliy's book[1] was still the textbook for the science of geography, and no more modern work on this subject could seriously claim precedence over it. The interest taken in the subject, moreover, remained for a long time very limited. The constructive method of the scholars of the day satisfied people so entirely that they did not consider it worth their while to acquaint themselves practically with that which lay outside their range of experience. Nor, indeed, was it eventually the science of the time from which proceeded that impulse which in its final consequences led to the knowledge, by mankind, of the habitable globe.

Even the Crusades, which were undoubtedly an important factor in the extension of Man's knowledge of the earth and of its inhabitants, affected that knowledge only within the limits of the world as it was already known through the traditions of antiquity. The Crusades might indeed serve to render such knowledge more real, and to reconnect those threads which had been severed by the events of the intermediate centuries; but they neither chiefly nor directly enlarged the stock of

---

[1] Petrus de Alliaco's "Imago Mundi."

eographical knowledge. Such a knowledge was, however, evolved by the more
itimate contact between the Christian and Mohammedan civilisations which t
rusades had brought about. The teaching of Mohammed had then already
ended beyond the limits of the world which had been disclosed to previous
he brisk intercourse between the holy city of Mecca and all the districts inhabited
y the followers of Mohammed, which was the natural consequence of the Prophet
recepts in the first instance, not only enriched the knowledge of the Arabs, but
lso, through them, became the means of its extension in the Old World, and thus
ave rise to the first voyages, undertaken by two enterprising Italian merchants,
iccolo de Conti and Marco Polo, into the remotest regions of the East. The news
f the immense wealth and splendour of the kingdom of the Great Khan, of the
wn of Cathay, and of the island of Zipangu (that is to say, in China and Japan)
hich these travellers had either seen personally or heard about from eyewit-
esses, gave a powerful stimulus in mercantile circles to the extension of the
nowledge, enterprise, and business of the time. This impulse was, moreover, not
onfined to those circles. The development of closer relations with the East led
o the knowledge that Christianity had advanced farther than had hitherto been
nagined. In place of the legendary tales of the journeys of the Apostle St.
homas, who was said to have preached the gospel to the heathen in the farthest
ast, came the story of the Christian realm of the priest John, which was said to
ave a remote but happy and brilliant existence on the other side of that great
esert which formed the boundary of the Old World of civilisation. The desire
o join hands with these distant fellow believers, and with their help to open up
ew regions for the spreading of the gospel, which mission in the Old World was
ontinually suffering reverses from Mohammedan rule, combined with the thirst
elt by adventurers and merchants for the fabulous treasures of the East. The
rst attempts to discover a route to the Indies sprang from these motives.

The Italians were the chief originators of such ideas, but the political disrup-
ons of their country proved a hindrance to the carrying out of any extensive en-
erprises on the part of Italy. It was rather the small kingdom of Portugal which
hrough accidental circumstances became the focus of these ideas. This kingdom,
hich on the land side was completely cut off by the Spanish States, was, both by
ature and by political necessity, dependent on the sea, and a large colony of for-
igners, among whom the Italians were numerously represented, quickened the
pirit of enterprise of its own people and brought them into contact with all that
ent on in the wider circles of the civilised world. It was therefore a peculiarly
ortunate circumstance that in the person of the Infante Henry — to whom pos-
erity has given the name of "the Navigator," although he had scarcely ever been
n board a ship — a man arose who brought energy and organising capacity to
ear on the efforts to procure for Christianity a wider extension, and for the Old
World a more direct connection with the legendary East.

When, at length, such voyages of discovery, originally undertaken entirely on
rince Henry's account, no longer merely involved sacrifices without returning any-
hing save purely theoretical gains, Portuguese vessels pushed farther and farther
long the coasts of Africa, at first, entirely at Henry's instigation, taking the
ourse indicated by him, with the definite object of discovering a way to the riche
f India and to the land of the priest John. They did not, it is true, attain their
oal until after the New World had arisen from the waters of the Atlantic Ocean

before the astonished eyes of Columbus and his companions; nevertheless it was their action as pioneers which alone rendered possible the feat of Columbus.

(*b*) *The Childhood of the Explorer.* — Cristoforo Colombo (or, as we will here call him by his more familiar name, Christopher Columbus), the son of a weaver and innkeeper, Domenico Colombo, by his wife, Susanna Fontanarossa, was born about the year 1447. As his father travelled backward and forward several times between Genoa and Savona, Christopher's birthplace cannot be fixed, for he appears to have looked on both towns as his home. All the pretensions of the numerous other towns are without justification. He was the eldest of Domenico's five children, three brothers and one sister being born after him. The weavers of Genoa had their own guild school, which, no doubt, Christopher attended. Naturally, the education which he received there was not very advanced, and the knowledge which he acquired in this period (and for those times it was not inconsiderable) was due to his bright intelligence and unusual energy. The boy had early to assist his father in his trade, although he seems to have had but slight inclination for the work, and even after he had succeeded in obtaining a berth on a merchant ship and had made some voyages, on his return home he was again obliged to resume his former occupation. It is certain that up to his twenty-fifth year he had not been able to free himself permanently. In 1474 he disappeared from Genoa, and some years later he reappeared at Lisbon as a sailor, making every endeavour to conceal the fact that he had ever been anything else.

Columbus was not one of those great geniuses who, in the certain consciousness of their own worth, look back upon their path with peace and satisfaction. Like many of his contemporary countrymen, he was an aspirer in whom a fair amount of self-complacency and boastfulness was joined to cleverness and energy, — a combination which in hundreds of cases produces a charlatan, and in rare instances a true man. He was ashamed of his low origin and of his humble trade; but if we were to rely only on his own words, we should assume that he had been of gentle birth and a sailor from his youth. As we can, however, prove this to have been untrue, we may also doubt his alleged naval achievements. It is quite possible that he sailed across the Mediterranean Sea as far as the Levant, and had seen the harbours on the coasts of the Atlantic, from England on the north to the coasts of Guinea on the south, — the southern limit of the Portuguese voyages. Evidently he did not always sail as a peaceful merchant, for he claims to have gone as a privateer in the service of King René, which must have been about the year 1472, when René supported the rebellious people of Barcelona; and in 1476 he is said to have been shipwrecked on the Portuguese coast, at the time when the Venetian gondoliers were engaged in severe battles with the dreaded French pirate Coullon. His naval activity can, however, have been neither of long duration nor very conspicuous, for the authentic accounts of his career give no time for the former, and the practical proofs of his nautical skill were inadequate to support the idea of long and profound training.

Columbus passed a number of uneventful years in Portugal, during which time he married Felipa Moniz, in whose veins the Italian blood of the renowned Perestrello flowed. This connection may possibly have had its influence on the formation of his life. In Portugal he evolved the plan for the western passage to India, and for this purpose the influence which he may have acquired through

CRISTOFORO COLOMBO

After a picture by an unknown painter, in the possession of an heir of the family of Giovio at Como.

his wife's relations possibly proved of some use to him. The story that he had received from a dying sailor the secret of the discovery of a whole western continent, as a Christmas legacy at the house of his mother-in-law in the Azores is so clumsy a fabrication that it is surprising that it has been so long credited. Truly such a gift was not needed to assist Columbus in his plan. The idea that the Indies might be reached by a short route by sailing around the globe in a straight westerly direction seemed more feasible to the Portuguese the more their discoveries led them to realise that the African continent stretched itself out in a southerly direction, necessitating a deviation from the eastern course. No doubt, in the first instance, the actual practicability of a western passage to the Indies was primarily taken into serious consideration by Portuguese circles; and as the opinions of Portuguese sailors were not considered sufficient evidence, the advice of foreign authorities on the cosmography of that region was also obtained.

(c) *Paolo Toscanelli.* Fernam Martin, the king's confessor, consulted the celebrated physician and cosmographer, Paolo dal Pozzo Toscanelli, concerning this question. Following up this inquiry, the great Florentine drew up a somewhat lengthy document on the practicability of a western passage to Asia. It was this pamphlet that, probably for the first time, gave a chart illustrative of that part of the unexplored world which was to be opened up by the western passage. By means of this letter and the accompanying chart, which later on — probably by illegal means — came into the hands of Columbus, Toscanelli became the actual originator of the discovery of America. He realised as little, of course, as did Columbus, to what results his instructions were destined to lead, but, taking into consideration the almost slavish dependence with which Columbus allowed himself to be guided in his voyage of discovery by the map and directions of Toscanelli, one cannot help crediting the latter with a very considerable share in the solution of the problem of the western passage. Stress must more especially be laid upon this point because Toscanelli's share did not consist of a combination of crude ideas and fatalism which, as in the case of Columbus, might lead an adventurer to sacrifice his life in the pursuit of a foolhardy idea, but was the result of well-founded and careful scientific research, which, though not proving to be absolutely correct, was nevertheless, in its principles, completely justified. Columbus's whole plan probably first originated through having received information of Toscanelli's statements, and then in giving out these views as his own.

Such an origin of the plan completely nullifies the statement that the account of the voyages of the Icelanders and Esquimaux to the North American continent had influenced the development of Columbus's ideas. Columbus certainly maintained that he had penetrated in a northerly direction a hundred miles beyond Thule; but, considering that Thule was by no means an established geographical fact during the fifteenth century, the whole bears the stamp of a swaggering invention. The Arctic archipelago no doubt forms a bridge between the old and the new continents in the extreme north, and we know for certain that a connection, apart from Columbus's achievement, has been established in both directions, from west to east and from east to west, between the inhabitants of both continents, the Esquimaux having penetrated as far as Greenland; the Icelanders, on the other hand, having been driven by east winds to the coasts of northern America. About 1000 A. D. Leif Eriksen — and some years after, his widow with Thorfinn Karlsevne

— founded colonies of northern Germanic vikings on American soil, which are mentioned in the Northern Sagas. Through unfavourable circumstances, however, these colonies after a few years died out. It is impossible that the northern Scandinavian bards had the slightest idea that Vinland and Huitramannaland — for so they called the newly discovered regions — were anything but a continuation of the chain of islands extending from Iceland and Faröe and beyond Greenland, and it is equally improbable that, even if it had reached the ears of Columbus, it would have proved of any significance to the furtherance of his plan for a western passage to the treasures of India.

The sailors' tales were of far greater value, not only to Columbus, but also to the council commissioned by the king to consider the possibility of a western passage. The Atlantic Ocean had cast up on many different parts of the Old World coasts specimens which showed that it also washed a completely different world; and the fact that these objects thrown up were often in good preservation strengthened the idea that the transatlantic distance of the east coast of Asia, which was regarded as the only possible home of these objects, could not be insurmountably great. The same inference was drawn from the reports of the few travellers who had penetrated as far as the Great Khan. These had purposely somewhat exaggerated the distances, and had unintentionally overrated the deviations from the direct course, so that people had been led to the conviction that the distance between Europe by land to Quinsay and Zaitun must greatly exceed the circumference of the globe, and accordingly the distance by sea, calculated in the western passage, would prove decidedly less. The great difficulty presenting itself, however, was that the greater part of the passage would have to be traversed without coming in sight of land, and as a matter of fact this really meant more than was then assumed. At that time people had indeed dared to attempt to cross the Mediterranean irrespective of the land, all its basins being well known in every direction, and the ships trading between the Mediterranean and Flanders, England and the Baltic countries, sometimes lost sight of land for days; but in general, in crossing the ocean from Guinea to England, the vessels always coasted, for the sailor kept within reach of land in case of threatening danger. There were numerous more or less extensive islands in the Atlantic Ocean, and that these were known is proved by the ancient maps. Among these were Antilia, the remnant of the continent whose destruction Plato describes in "Timæus," St. Brandan's Isle, and the Island of the Seven Cities, besides many others. Yet, although they appeared plainly on the maps, the sailors who had for days been driven out of their course on the ocean had never seen more than mere tracts of land on the farthest horizon, which invariably vanished from view on nearer approach. Columbus did not allow himself to be scared by such considerations; though conscious that he might go for weeks and months without discovering land, he was resolved to navigate the boundless ocean, and this was the one peculiarity of his plan and merits recognition and regard.

There are no means of ascertaining the truth of Columbus's claims that he urged his project for the western passage upon the king of Portugal during fourteen years. It is, however, quite certain that he stayed in Portugal for only eight and not for fourteen years, and that during his stay there he was often absent from court for long periods, occupied with other concerns. As a matter of fact, we begin to know more about him and his projects only from the time when he left

PAOLO TOSCANELLI

After Giorgio Vasari's copy of the picture by Alessio Baldovinetti: Palazzo della
Signoria in Florence.

Portugal. Columbus did not leave voluntarily, but because he had committed an offence for which he could expect only severe punishment. On account of this he deserted his wife and children, and, accompanied solely by his four-year-old son, Diego, fled the country. The nature of his offence is not recorded; doubtful financial affairs and disputes with the royal officials have been surmised; but probably his crime was more closely connected with his project, for which he had appropriated Toscanelli's letter and chart, the materials most essential to his plan. The commentators of the Toscanelli correspondence have always had to face great difficulties, because the only correct and comprehensible portion is that addressed to Fernam Martin, while the alleged postscript to Columbus, which, as well as the former portion, is known only through a copy by Columbus, is filled with impossibilities. Why should not the man who disowned his ancestors and his antecedents, and invented a coat of arms and a noble pedigree for himself, also have invented the postscript to a letter of which Toscanelli is said for years (if Columbus's representations be correct) to have preserved the rough draft, and even to have stupidly kept the address and signature? — a thing which Columbus did not even do in his forgery. This is also the simple explanation why King John was so willing to exempt Columbus from punishment and then assure his return when it became apparent that an attempt was to be made from Spain to carry out the project which John, with his seamen, had privately attempted.

(d) *The Plan for the Passage.* — Nor did the plans of Columbus meet with an immediate friendly reception in Spain. He had in this country also to strive with precarious circumstances for some years before he succeeded in gaining a small number of trustworthy followers who, allowing themselves to be convinced by him, assisted in his endeavour to gain a hearing from the king. During this time he made his living by the sale of books and maps, and no doubt, while carrying on this trade, he acquired that singular knowledge of books which, later on, is so prominent in all his writings. An attachment to a young lady of Cordova, Beatrice Enriquez, for a time bound him to the old city of the Caliph, but he proved as faithless to his mistress as he had been to his wife. During the whole of his life he retained an interest in the son whom he had had by her, Fernando Colon, who in course of time became celebrated for his writings and for his library, which to this day are preserved in Seville. Of his mistress he thought again, and then with remorse, only when, face to face with death, he was making his will. The children did not accompany him on his wanderings. Little Diego was in charge of a brother-in-law in Huelva, and Fernando remained for a time with his mother. It was not until after Columbus had attained his desire of gaining over the Spanish rulers in favour of his voyage of discovery, that his sons entered the royal service as pages, and from that time they shared their father's successes and failures.

The first assured partisans whom Columbus gained for his plans were the guardian of the Franciscan monastery, La Rabida, at Huelva, Fray Juan Perez de Marchena, and the doctor of the neighbouring little town of Palos, Garcia Fernandez. Both voluntarily occupied their leisure hours with cosmographical studies, and when Columbus, during his flight from Portugal, sought shelter in the monastery, a friendship founded on mutual interests soon sprang up between these men, which was to prove of extraordinary value to Columbus in later years. At that time he travelled on, after a brief sojourn, in order to make his own way independently, but it was many years before he again found anyone else to take so intelligent an interest in his plans, which were then still shrouded with many fantastic superfluities. Not until the year 1486 did Celi, Duke of Medina, espouse his cause, and he probably would have entrusted him with a ship for a trial voyage from his seaport town of Santa Maria, near Cadiz, had not Queen Isabella, in consequence of the Duke's reports, manifested her interest and summoned Columbus to the court. The position of Columbus at that time, with his imperfectly constructed and unscientifically formed ideas, was naturally a difficult one in the presence of the ecclesiastical and secular authorities whom Ferdinand and Isabella had assembled at their court. He was universally pronounced to be an Italian boaster, and the proofs which he gave were not considered convincing either in Cordova or in Salamanca, where he was also permitted to explain his plans before a learned assembly. It so happened that the final removal of the last remnants of Moorish power on the Iberian Peninsula formed the immediate aim of the Spanish ruler and demanded the consolidation of all the forces of the country hitherto so imperfectly developed. Columbus therefore had to remain satisfied; for although the further consideration of his plans was postponed to a more favourable time, the queen's interest, once aroused in his behalf, was the means of procuring him a yearly allowance.

It is true that in his impatience the time of waiting seemed long; and he had already formed the resolution to continue his journey and to offer his plans to other monarchs, when at last a combination of various circumstances brought about the fulfilment of his desire, which meanwhile had grown into a fixed idea. He returned to the monastery, La Rabida, with the intention of fetching his son Diego from Huelva and then travelling to France with him. His friends there were so impressed by his projects, which in the course of the negotiations had gained much in clearness and distinctness, that the warden invited him to remain while he made another and final attempt on his behalf. Brother Juan Perez de Marchena had in former years been father-confessor to the queen, and on the strength of this he undertook to press Columbus's enterprise most warmly upon her attention. The words of the priest fell upon fruitful soil. His message reached the queen while in the camp of Santa Fé before the Moorish capital of Granada, just at the time when the fall of the last hostile bastion and the final consummation of the great life-work of the Spanish nation was looked forward to with feelings of exultation. Columbus was once more summoned to the court, and received the assurance that after the fall of Granada he should be provided with means for his attempt. He arrived in time to witness the removal of the Crescent from the towers of the Alhambra, and the substitution of the Cross, which, shining from afar, was raised on the Moorish citadel.

In spite of all, the negotiations were, at the last moment, almost frustrated. Columbus's plans had seemed so sure to his own mind that he, penurious adventurer as he was, conducted himself as though he had kingdoms to give away, and made demands on his own behalf which, if he actually were to attain his object, would make him richer than the rulers from whom he was now obliged to beg a few thousand ducats. He not only desired a certain share for all time in all the material gain which might accrue through his discoveries, but he also claimed for himself and his descendants the hereditary dignity of a royal admiral over the entire ocean, besides the position of a vice-king in all lands which might be added to the kingdom through his discoveries.

King Ferdinand was particularly enraged by this presumption; all transactions were broken off, and Columbus left the camp; but in spite of this Queen Isabella prevailed upon her husband to agree to the conditions imposed by this extraordinary man. The treaty was drawn up to meet Columbus's demands, and the town of Palos, which was by chance under the obligation of providing certain ships for the royal service, received the order to place them at Columbus's disposal.

(*c*) *The Discovery of America.* — Nevertheless all difficulties were not yet overcome. Columbus had to bind himself, on his part, to share the cost, for which he at that time actually did not possess the means; and the manning of the three vessels caused considerable difficulties, as soon as their destination became known. By interesting the influential naval family of Pinzon, at Palos, in his plans, and gaining their material support for the undertaking by promising them a share of his chartered right, he succeeded in fitting out and manning the ships for the daring voyage. The little fleet — consisting of the "Santa Maria," piloted by Columbus himself; the "Pinta," under Martin Alonso Pinzon; and the "Niña," with Vincent Yanez Pinzon — was able to put to sea on the 3d of August, 1492. These caravels of Columbus were not large vessels; the "Santa Maria" had a tonnage of only 120, the "Pinta" 100, and the "Niña" 80; but they proved so exceptionally fitted for the special purpose of these voyages that they were soon after regarded as models when the much larger vessels which had been employed during the first delirium of success proved to give inferior results.

Columbus had taken Toscanelli's chart on board as part of his equipment, and treated it with the absolute and blind faith of a fanatic. After having lost almost three weeks on the Canary Islands while making necessary repairs, he sailed out into the unknown ocean on the 6th of September. Thence he took a decidedly westerly course, and he was so firmly convinced of its correctness that he would not permit himself to be diverted from this route even by apparent signs of the nearness of land, although he believed they coincided absolutely with Toscanelli's calculations on the chart. He kept a double record of the distance traversed, in order that the sailors should not become fully conscious of the adventurous nature of the voyage: in the public one he purposely minimised the distances; while in the private one, for his own use, his course followed the chart in order that he might ascertain the position of the land. In spite of all, he was not able to keep the courage of his ignorant sailors unshaken. He had reached the region of the monsoons, and the fact that a strong wind from the east swelled the sails day by day without bringing a sight of the daily promised land made the inexperienced men anxious about the possibility of their return. More than once their fear took the form of animosity against the unknown stranger, who proudly boasted of his authority and was by no means remarkably fitted for seafaring life. Probably his heart gradually grew heavy, as, morning after morning, the waste of water sparkled with unceasing monotony in the rays of the rising sun. But he did not lose courage or hope, and although the pilots of the other vessels began to lose faith in his ultimate success, they stood firmly by their admiral and assisted him in suppressing the attempts at insubordination, which were not infrequent among the crew of the "Santa Maria." At last, at the beginning of October, the signs which announced to the sailors the approach of land began to increase, and Columbus impressed on the lookout-man the necessity for special care, promising a reward to the one who should first sight the land. During the twilight on the 11th of October Columbus and several others believed they saw lights across the water in the distance; but night approached before a shot from the "Pinta" in the lead gave the sign that light had actually been sighted. The sails were hurriedly furled and the course altered, but a whole long night withheld from the expectant sailors the final certainty that the land which had so often been announced, only to vanish once more, was this time no phantom.

In the dawn of the 12th of October, 1492, Columbus and his companions saw a fairly large and well-wooded island rising from the sea; and before they had manned the boats and gained the island, they had been noticed from its shore. Brown, scantily clad men and women watched the approach of the strangers with unmistakable astonishment, and when the land was reached they proved to be good-natured and harmless people, though practically uncivilised, leading a miserable existence as fishermen and hunters. The land was the island of Guanahani[1] (the modern Watling Island), and its inhabitants, whom the Spaniards, in their conviction that the eastern end of Asia had been reached, had called "Indios," were the Aruac Indians, who had not yet been supplanted by the Caribs. Although the reality compared very unfavourably with the brilliant expectations which had been cherished, yet Columbus by the discovery of land had succeeded in his undertaking. Information which he obtained from the natives, in spite of imperfect means of intercourse, showed that this was not an isolated island in the ocean. With solemn public worship he took possession of the land, on behalf of the Catholic rulers of Castile and Aragon, and received the oath of allegiance as viceroy and governor from the crew, who from cowardice and hostility had veered round to the opposite extreme.

During the next few days almost every hour brought fresh surprises. After the ships had run up to a series of small islands, a larger expanse of land, the eastern end of Cuba, was sighted on the 28th of October, and was called by Columbus Isla Fernandina. After following up the coast in a westerly direction for some days without reaching its termination, he returned to the first anchorage, sailed round the eastern point, and, taking a southeasterly course, came upon a second expanse of land to which he gave the name of Española.[2] The novelty of the impressions received, and the tropical luxuriance of nature, easily tempted the discoverers to disregard the fact that they had not discovered the slightest trace of the great commercial towns of eastern Asia, Zaitun and Quinsay, which they had set out to find. When, in addition to this, the discovery of gold was made by the aid of the inhabitants of Española, Columbus was far more anxious to return to Spain, in order that he might bask in the sunshine of the triumph consequent upon success, than to prosecute his discoveries.

He was not to return, however, without tasting the first drop of bitterness in his cup of happiness. On the morning of the 22d of November the "Pinta" made no reply to the signal from the admiral's ship. Martin Alonzo Pinzon had deserted his superior officer, and had set out in search of adventures on his own responsibility, surmising, from the gestures of the natives, the proximity of a region rich in gold. It was the first instance of self-seeking treachery

[1] See the maps at page 5.        [2] See the accompanying plate.

De Infulis nuper in
mari Indico repertis

THE LANDING OF COLUMBUS ON ESPAÑOLA

(After one of the first contemporary pamphlets, printed at Basle, 1494.)

which, in the course of colonial explorations, was to be followed by many similar ones. This proved the more unfortunate as the "Santa Maria" ran aground and had to be abandoned, and thus the "Niña," the smallest of the vessels, alone remained to Columbus for the return voyage. Strange to say, while preparations were being made for the homeward voyage, the "Pinta" returned, and the admiral, more from prudence than from conviction, accepted Pinzon's excuses, and on the 14th of January, 1493, he set sail for home, leaving a small company of voluntary settlers behind.

Until they reached the Azores the weather proved extraordinarily favourable for the return, but on nearing their native shore the waves again threatened to engulf the secret of the newly discovered continent. The "Pinta" was driven far toward the north and finally entered Vigo harbour. Columbus, having escaped the dangers of the storm, arrived at Lisbon, and had the proud satisfaction of flying the colours of Castile on entering the royal harbour of that king whose belief in his now brilliantly vindicated plans he had failed to gain. His journey to the Spanish court, which was then at Barcelona, resembled a triumphal procession across the kingdom, and he stood in triumph before the rulers from whom he had previously departed as a beggar.

*(f) The Final Fortunes of the Discoverer.* — Preparations for a second voyage across the ocean, planned on a much larger scale, were begun almost at once after Columbus's landing. Whereas for the first voyage the great difficulty had been to raise a sufficient number of sailors, in this case it was to know how to select the right men from among the thousands who were anxious to go. The first regulations for the ordering of the colonisation date from the rules then drawn up. On the 25th of September a fleet consisting of seventeen large vessels, with more than fifteen hundred men on board, sailed from Seville for the newly discovered land, and was, as in the first instance, favoured by splendid weather. They first reached the island of Dominica by a slightly different course, and then, passing many new islands, they arrived at Española. Here, however, disenchantments began. The colonists who had remained behind had failed to maintain friendly relations with the natives, whose animosity they had aroused by their brutality, and through their recklessness they had succumbed to a man. Columbus, in order to lessen the impression that this news might make on the new arrivals, chose a different position for the founding of a permanent colony. The first town on the soil of the New World received the name of Isabella, and through the united exertions of the numerous colonists it rapidly rose above the ground. Not until after Bartholomew Colon had removed the colony and deserted the old town was the name of San Domingo given to the now existing capital. In spite of everything done, most of the settlers were filled with disappointment; they found neither treasures nor riches, and the reward of each man's work and duty seemed likely to be reaped only by future generations. The reports of those who returned home, therefore, sounded anything but encouraging. The value of the new discovery was doubted more and more, and the general feeling of enthusiasm among all classes of society that had preceded Columbus's second voyage was probably never again manifest during the entire history of Spanish colonial enterprise.

Having established a firm footing on Española, the admiral himself started out for fresh discoveries. As the coast of Cuba had been followed for weeks without its farthest point being reached, Columbus felt convinced that he had arrived at the Asiatic continent, and he thereupon drew up an authentic report which later on was frequently turned into ridicule. On his return to San Domingo he found that public opinion had quite changed. His authority among the disillusioned colonists was greatly shaken, and was still more weakened by the influence of the news of the failure of his latest expedition to discover any rich, populous, and civilised regions, such as were believed to exist in eastern Asia. Further reinforcements led by his brother Bartholomew also brought him the news from home that his reputation at court had suffered. When, in addition to all this, discord and rebellion broke out among the colonists, he deemed it advisable to retreat, and to return to Spain, in order to vindicate himself.

This time Columbus was able to leave his brother as his substitute at the head of the youthful colony; and as the latter, of all the brothers, possessed the greatest administrative talent, the admiral could cherish the hope that no such dire consequences would threaten the second colony as those that befell the first on his previous departure. When, without serious difficulty, he had succeeded, before the court of the Spanish rulers, in disproving the charges against him and had justified his actions, the government again placed three ships at his disposal, and he could not resist the desire to start once more with them on a voyage of discovery. On this third occasion he kept farther to the south than during his previous attempts, and, coming in touch with only a few islands, he reached the coast of the continent of South America just where it takes a decidedly western course. He followed it up for some distance, but at the highest point of the island Margarita he turned toward the north, more especially because he was himself ailing and in need of rest. After a more or less uneventful voyage around the islands of the Antilles he arrived safely at Española. A proof of how vague and unscientific Columbus's cosmological observations were, is his report of his discoveries. In this, led astray by the enormous quantity of pure water which the torrent of the Orinoco carries far into the Caribbean Sea, he gave himself up to the most fantastic speculations, believing that he had arrived at the environs of Paradise, and that his mission as the Bringer of Salvation appointed by God had been visibly established.

Bartholomew Colon had, during his brother's absence, held the reins of government with a firm hand, though he succeeded only in a measure in maintaining peace and order by banishing the most insubordinate members from the colony. Soon all those who for any reason whatever were dissatisfied with Colon's government had joined them, and Columbus actually found two hostile camps in place of his peaceful settlement. But the means which he employed to put an end to this state of affairs were the most unfortunate that he could have chosen. He drew up a covenant with the dissatisfied, and he certainly achieved the return of these doubtful factors to his dominion not merely by pardoning the leaders, but by re-establishing them in the positions which they had forfeited through their own fault. By doing this he irretrievably lost the confidence of those who desired the re-establishment of law and order. While, therefore, one party forced him to make concession after concession, and so led him farther from the paths of justice, the other party refused him their support and turned with complaints toward their native land.

Columbus, in the midst of this confusion, was at his wits' end, and finally joined his entreaties to the complaints of the colonists, requesting the Crown to send an official across the ocean with full powers to examine into the administration of the vice-regent and to re-establish law and order in the unsettled colony. Ferdinand entrusted Francesco de Bobadilla with this difficult mission, as he was a man experienced in native administrative affairs and one who had frequently distinguished himself in the Moorish wars; but he proved by no means the right person to deal with the abnormal circumstances in the colonies. Hatred of the specially favoured strangers, who possessed almost unlimited power in the colony, but did not always make a just use of it, inspired the malcontents, and no doubt Bobadilla participated in this feeling even before he reached Española. The full judiciary powers, also, over the vice-regent himself, with which he had been accredited by the Spanish ruler, without doubt gave him a formal right to deprive Columbus and his brothers of their office. The vice-regent not only submitted unconditionally to the royal decree, but also prevailed upon the less submissive Bartholomew to consent to a similar mode of action. Bobadilla, not content with putting the brothers in chains and transporting them to Spain, confiscated their joint property in the colony in the name of the Crown, and incurred at least the suspicion of party animus, from which he was wholly unable to free himself in spite of the fact of his having inflicted heavy punishments on numerous friends as well as on opponents of the admiral, among whom were many Spaniards.

It was a truly humiliating spectacle to behold the man who a few years previously had returned in triumph to lay a newly discovered world at the feet of his sovereigns, now land in chains to sue for the intervention of those rulers against the official whom they had endowed with their authority to act as vice-regent. The order which was sent immediately to Seville, that Columbus should instantly be set at liberty and despatched to the court with all the honours due to his rank, was as much instigated by gratitude as by justice; and of Bobadilla's recall there could be no doubt. In spite of this the rulers could not determine upon the simple reinstatement of Columbus, to the entire extent of his rights and possessions, which he himself demanded; for, although the inquiries which were instituted did not bring to light anything which seriously reflected on the discoverer, yet they undeniably proved that he was not in the smallest degree equal to the duties which presented themselves. He had therefore to rest content with the recognition of the validity of all his rights, and to see a new man (the choice of the rulers fell upon Nicolas de Ovando) appointed to conduct the inquiry into the grievances of the colonists while he himself was strictly forbidden, until further notice, to set foot in the colony.

Columbus was not the man to remain passive while a point of law was being decided which might be most unfavourably misconstrued by his inaction. The sovereigns had already given to others leave to undertake voyages of discovery, in spite of the wording of his contracts and without the knowledge and co-operation of Columbus. The best way in which most securely to preserve his rights of viceregal power over the whole region opened up by his discovery seemed to him to be to take as keen an interest as possible in the exploration of the land, which still presented many enigmas to him. The rulers placed no difficulties in his way, and for the fourth time he was entrusted with vessels fitted out for voyages of discovery (four in number), and in the event of necessity he received permission to run up to Española, but only on his return. How little attention Columbus paid to his duty is shown by the fact that he sailed almost straight to San Domingo and demanded permission to enter the harbour, — a demand which Ovando most justly refused, as it would most certainly only have tended to endanger the peace which had in a measure been restored. After he had weathered a severe storm in the shelter of the island, — a storm that to his satisfaction had engulfed a large number of ships just fitted out for a voyage home, and with them his enemy Bobadilla, because Ovando had not seen fit to pay any attention to his warnings regarding it, — he turned to the southwest, reached the Gulf of Honduras, and coasted for months toward the east, the south, and again to the east as far as the Gulf of Darien, where the Central American isthmus joins the southern continent. On this voyage he first heard rumours of another ocean in the west, and met with the first more highly civilised natives, people of Yucatan, in a trading-bark manned by twenty-five men; but as far as he personally was concerned Columbus only reaped bitter want and privation. These reached their culminating point when the last of the four vessels ran aground on the then uncolonised Jamaica, and he had to wait for months without resources until he succeeded in sending news by a fishing-boat to San Domingo, summoning help. When Columbus now actually again set foot in his viceregal residence, he was both mentally and physically too crushed to become a source of danger to the country. He returned to Spain after a short stay and found a fresh blow awaiting him there. Queen Isabella, to whom he owed the achievement of his first voyage, and who had always proved his kind patroness, was dead, and a dispute for the succession to the throne of Castile now arose between King Ferdinand and his son-in-law, Philip the Handsome, of Burgundy. Public attention was so exclusively taken up with this, that no one in the whole of Spain had time to spare for the concerns of the colony or for its discoverer. Though both had cost endless sums of money, so far the much sought after and often promised treasures had not been discovered.

Columbus had therefore to build his hopes on better times, but he was not to live to see their realisation. While on the point of paying court to the youthful Philip, to whom Castile deserted when he, contrary to Ferdinand's wish, took over the regency on behalf of his mentally afflicted wife, the heiress to the Castilian throne, Columbus became ill at Valladolid and died there, May 21, 1506, little noticed and mourned by few. His body in death was destined to be as unresting as he himself had been in life. His corpse, first buried in the Franciscan monastery at Valladolid, was, at the instigation of his natural son Fernando, conveyed to the small church of Santa Maria de las Cuevas in Seville, and thence, in 1537, when his heirs had again been restored to the viceregal administration, to San Domingo. In 1798, when the Spaniards had to abandon the island of Española, the discoverer's bones were taken to Havana, and until lately reposed in the cathedral there. When, however, in the war of 1898, Spain lost the remainder of her American colonies, Columbus's remains were brought back across the ocean and buried close to the Roman Catholic sovereigns at Granada, the city in which the explorer's hopes were first realised.

### B. The Voyages of Discovery of the First Twenty Years of the Sixteenth Century

COLUMBUS had died with the firm conviction that the country which he had discovered formed part of the continent of Asia. Even during his fourth voyage he intimated that there was another ocean on the western coast of the Isthmus of

Panama, and this prediction would only have been correct had he found himself on a peninsula of Farther India, whose other coast was washed by the wave of the Indian Ocean. The discoveries of other navigators had, however, already begun, even during his lifetime, to shake this conviction. While Columbus in 1492 was carrying on the negotiations with the Spanish sovereigns, and was almost despairing of a favourable termination, his brother Bartholomew was endeavouring to interest the king of England in the project, and had almost achieved a favourable settlement when he received the news of the success of the Spanish deliberations. He thereupon broke off the negotiations; but Henry VII, whose interest had been fully aroused, soon after empowered another Italian, Giovanni Gabotto, to set out in a westerly direction on a voyage of discovery under the protection of the English flag. In two voyages, which succeeded each other very rapidly, Gabotto discovered the part of northern America reaching from Newfoundland almost down to Florida.

After Columbus's third voyage, several Spanish sailors who had taken part in the admiral's voyages obtained leave to take an independent share in the extension of further discoveries. Among these were Hojeda, with the celebrated and oldest geographer of the New World, Juan de la Cosa, and the Florentine, Amerigo Vespucci, whose clear but unreliable descriptions of his experiences first popularised a knowledge of the New World and gave rise to the idea of calling the new continent by his name. Both Peralonso Niño and Cristobal Guerra had in the same year (1499) sailed as far as the northern coast of South America, beyond the borders which Columbus had himself reached. Vicente Yañez Pinzon, and after him Diego de Lepe, penetrated to the south as far as Cape St. Augustine, and were the first to discover the delta of the river Amazon.

Another accidental discovery, however, proved of greater importance to posterity. On March 19, 1500, Pedralvarez Cabral had sailed from Lisbon with thirteen ships, with the intention of going to the East Indies by way of the Cape of Good Hope, where the Portuguese, two years previously, had arrived during their voyages of discovery. In order to avoid the dangerous passage along the west coast of Africa he had turned aside in the open ocean far toward the west, and, being driven farther in that direction by easterly winds, he came in sight of the coast of Brazil on the 22d of April. After following the coast-line for a time he took possession of it in the name of his king.

This mode of procedure was based on the agreement regarding the settlement of a line of demarcation which had been signed between Spain and Portugal almost immediately after Columbus's discovery. That is to say, the rulers of Portugal had, in order to prevent any legal disputes, made Pope Nicholas V invest them, at the commencement of their era of active discovery, with all lands which they might discover during their voyages to the south and east. It so happened that Columbus's enterprise was directed toward the same India, which at the time of his first voyage had not yet been reached by the Portuguese; the Spanish sovereigns therefore hastened, after the return of Columbus, to have their claims also sanctioned by the Pope. This was done in the following manner: Pope Alexander VI awarded to the Spaniards all the land to the west of the degree of longitude which extended from pole to pole for one hundred miles on the other side of the islands of the Azores, and to the Portuguese all that which was situated to the east. Subsequent negotiations between the interested Powers led to an alteration, the line of division being removed three hundred and seventy Spanish miles to the west, on the farther side of the Cape Verd Islands. The Spaniards imagined, according to the position of the discoveries at that time, that they were surrendering to the Portuguese at the most some islands in the ocean, whereas they hoped to secure for themselves, by the displacement of the line, vast districts in the unknown eastern part of Asia. Not until the discovery of Cabral was it proved to what extent the South American continent jutted out toward the east compared with the latitudes reached by Columbus, so that a considerable portion of the newly discovered land belonged thereby to the Portuguese. Moreover the latter were at first so much occupied with the extension and security of their East Indian territory that they gave but little heed to their western colonial possessions. King Manuel, for State reasons, authorised two voyages in order to gain information about the domains which had devolved on him; but as they did not lead to the discovery of any treasures, either in precious stones or rare spices, he left all subsequent exploration of these countries to the spirit of enterprise in general. During several decades certain Portuguese merchants alone undertook occasional western voyages in order to bring to Europe colonial products, especially the highly valuable logwood, "brasil," from which the country in later times received its name.

One of those voyages led to the discovery of the river La Plata in the year 1514; but so trifling was the attention paid by Portugal to events there, that the claims of the discoverers were never seriously formulated or protected.

The last years of Columbus's life, as well as those following his death, were not taken up so much in new discoveries as with organising colonies in the land which had been acquired. Columbus had personally founded only the one town of San Domingo, on Española. He was averse to the division of the settlements over the entire island, because he feared that the colonists would thereby be removed from his control, and he deprecated any encroachment on his rights. During his last voyage Columbus had determined on a second settlement on the coast of Veragua; but it had to be relinquished almost before it had been decided upon, owing to the hostility of the natives. Nicolas de Ovando, who, not without design, in all questions of organisation advised exactly the opposite to that which Columbus ordered, as being the most serviceable to his own interests, first gave a certain impetus to the extension of the Spanish colonies in the New World. Not only do a number of new towns on Española owe their existence to him, but Puerto Rico was at least colonised by his order by Juan Ponce de Leon in 1510. No doubt he would have achieved much more in this direction had not the uncertainty of the colonial conditions of government had a deadening influence on him.

During his lifetime Columbus had proposed to King Ferdinand to renounce the enjoyment of his rights on condition that his son Diego should be permitted forthwith to possess them in their entirety. Diego urgently reiterated this demand on the death of his father, and as at first only a few financial concessions were granted to him, and the principal point at issue remained unsettled, he lodged a complaint against the government. Even so the settlement might have been long protracted had not Diego Colon, by forming ties of relationship with the ducal house of Alba, gained influential intercessors with King Ferdinand. At any rate Diego accomplished so much that in 1509 he was again permitted to take over the government of the newly discovered islands, with the title of Royal Governor and Admiral of the

Indies. When, in 1511, judgment was passed on his appeal by the Court of First Instance, he was awarded all the official positions, titles, honours, and privileges promised to his father in all the countries discovered by him. Diego Colon was however, in no wise satisfied with this; he and his descendants had, moreover, for many years been at law with the Crown in order to secure the extension of their claims, not only over all the land which had been discovered by Columbus himself, but also over that which had, in addition to his father's discoveries, been won for the Spaniards by others. This lawsuit however, was mixed up with every imaginable sort of unnecessary litigation, which rendered it practically interminable and anything but honourable for either side, so that it lost its actual significance soon after Diego Colon's death in 1526. His legal successor who was an utter scamp, surrendered the greater part of the prerogatives so that he might extricate himself from all manner of immoral transactions. After Diego Colon had again attained his viceregal rights, he, too, endeavoured to extend the province which had been secured by actual colonisation; and his first step in this direction was the founding of a Spanish settlement on the island of Cuba by Velasquez, Diego's friend of long standing, who was commissioned to carry it out. Diego, however, experienced the same fate with him as did his father with Martin Alonso Pinzon. Velasquez willingly undertook the management of the undertaking, for which the vice-regent paid the expenses; but no sooner had he established himself in Cuba than he sent reports of his successes direct to the court, representing his achievements in such glowing colours that his authorisation as governor of the island as well as vice-regent, for which he had sued, was not denied to him.

The first settlement on the continent also followed close upon the discoveries of Columbus. The eyes of the government, as well as of the lovers of adventure, had been turned to these regions by the gold which he had found in larger quantities on the coast of Veragua. Already in 1508 Alonso de Hojeda, a veteran explorer, and Diego de Nicuesa had received permission to found two new colonial provinces which were to extend from the Gulf of Urabá to the east, and from ocean to ocean in the west; but their undertakings had been followed by severe misfortune for many years. Not until both leaders had lost their lives through the vicissitudes incidental to their attempts at colonisation was the foundation of a modest settlement achieved on the coast of Darien, receiving the name of Santa Maria la Antigua.

This settlement also might have been ruined, owing to the lack of necessaries and the passive resistance of the natives, if Vasco Nuñez de Balboa had not made a specially suitable leader, who understood how to turn the undertaking into a success. Balboa wanted an accredited legal title for his influential position. While on the one hand he turned to Spain in order to have his leaderless companions' selection of himself confirmed, on the other hand he strove to commend himself to the government by some prominent deed. To him, as to Columbus, the Indians had given information about another ocean. The solution of this problem seemed particularly appropriate at a time when the necessity for a farther advance toward the west began to be felt. Partly through his personal ability in managing the Indians, and partly also by the extreme severity with which he met every attempt at insubordination, Nuñez de Balboa succeeded in confining the difficulties incidental to the crossing of the isthmus almost exclusively to bodily hardships and privations, which are unavoidable on a march through sparsely populated and tropically unhealthy forest-land. Even so he lost many of his followers before he, as the first European, caught sight of the Pacific Ocean from the last mountain range in the west, and was able some days later, on arriving at the coast, to take possession of it and all the islands situated within it. On account also of the treasures of gold and pearls which resulted from this expedition, his discovery proved to be highly important. He was not permitted to reap the fruits of his labours, for, before the news of his discovery reached Spain, Pedrarias Davila had sailed as governor of the province of Darien, and by his jealous distrust had prepared an inglorious end for Balboa. The country, however, — the Isthmus of Panama and the adjoining northern territories, — became the oldest continental province of the Spanish colonial kingdom, and on account of its treasures it received the name of Castilla del Oro, "Golden Castile." The question whether it was actually the eastern border of the Asiatic continent which Columbus had discovered received the first convincing answer through Balboa's discovery. Although people were soon certain that South America was separated from and different from the well-known regions of Asia, a considerable time elapsed before they were willing to concede the same with regard to the northern half of the American continent. On the whole, the knowledge of South America made far more rapid progress than that of North America. The mediæval superstition that the produce of the soil increased in value the nearer one got to the equator had in this case a distinct influence; and the rivalry between Spain and Portugal, though it was shortly given up, had its share in directing the expeditions of discovery in the direction of the equator. To it we are indebted for the voyages of Amerigo Vespucci (1502) and of Gonzalo Coelho (1503) on the part of Portugal, and for those of Juan Diaz de Solis (1515) on behalf of Spain, which opened up the coasts of South America far beyond the mouth of the La Plata. They also paved the way for the epoch-making achievement of Fernando de Magalhaēs, who, during his search for a southwestern passage to the east Asiatic Moluccas, or Spice Islands, which had in the meantime become better known to the Portuguese, sailed through the archipelago at the southern extremity of America.

By actually reaching the Asiatic islands Magalhaēs irrefutably exposed Columbus's error and first brought his project to complete realisation. When, after his death, his crew returned home by way of the Cape of Good Hope, the problem of the spherical form of the earth first received a practical solution. This voyage was without doubt infinitely more productive of scientific results than the achievement of Columbus, although of course the latter had served as a necessary hypothesis for it.

Up to that time the colonies of the western Indies had hardly fulfilled the hopes which had been centred on their discovery. Many profitable tropical products had been found, and their importation into Spain, as well as the maintenance of the colonists already scattered over extensive tracts of land, who yet depended almost exclusively on their native country for support, had led to tolerably brisk trade intercourse, in which, as the mother country was hardly equal to the whole task of colonisation, the traders of foreign nations — chief among them the Germans — took an active part. The colonies had, however, proved by no means profitable to the State. The equipment of so many expeditions, and the establishment of the necessary administrative apparatus at home and abroad, entailed considerable expense. In spite of the attempt which had been made to raise an adequate revenue by means of duties and taxes (among which the roy ltv of a twentieth part on all ore discovered ranked first), yet these had so far yielded but moderate profits. Auriferous sand had indeed been discovered on Español and Cuba and in several places on the continent, and washing for gold had commenced, but, owing to the poor quality of the sand, the labour was by no means combined with large profit. Moreover the colonies suffered through this discovery; for the natives, overburdened with hard work, diminished with astonishing rapidity, and already in the first third of the sixteenth century threatened, on the islands first inhabited, to become altogether extinct. The colonists, who sought only to enrich themselves by the gold washings as quickly as possible and at any cost, in order that they might lead an idle life of debauchery at home or in the settlements, were another dangerous element in the community.

The government must by no means be held entirely responsible for the fact that this state of affairs afterward assumed such proportions that the Spanish colonies could even with exaggeration have been described as "mining colonies." Ever since the second voyage of Columbus it had been made a universally binding rule that all vessels conveying emigrants to the new continent should carry with them an equal cargo, not only of indigenous cereals and seeds, but also of shrubs, trees, and useful plants for the colonies' experimentation in the various territories. The European domestic animals, the greater number of which throve in the New World, were first imported by the Spaniards. America possessed but few, and of these not many were productive. The horse not only became, in many districts of America, an almost indispensable possession, but it even propagated through wild breeding. Cattle also throve exceedingly well on American soil; not only did they, as livestock, form one of the most marketable articles for trade in the colonies, but their hides constituted one of the staple commodities for export to Europe. Sheep, too, acclimatised well. Nothing, however, increased as rapidly among the Indians as did poultry; after the middle of the century the pioneers of western civilisation were greeted by the crowing of a cock, even in districts where the foot of a European had never been before. Experiments with less simple cultivation had also early been made in the colonies. The planting of vines was subject to incessant, inevitable restrictions, it is true, since wine was an article which the mother country produced far in excess of its own requirements; besides which it formed one of the most suitable articles of trade for the freighting of the colonial fleets. The cultivation of sugar-cane, on the other hand, first made the settlers on Española independent of the varying results of the gold-washings; and it flourished considerably for the time being, when, from 1517, negroes were imported from the western coasts of Africa to replace the Indians, who were not equal to the exertions of agricultural and mining labour. The earliest attempt to transplant the mulberry-tree and the silkworm to American soil also dates back as far as the year 1526, although neither then nor subsequently had it remarkable results. In short, even if at an early date the considerable profit from precious metals so greatly absorbed the government's attention that many of the experiments in cultivation which had up to that time been made in the colonies were not continued with equal interest, it is wrong to assume that the search for gold, which had certainly even influenced the plans of discovery of Columbus, was, from the commencement and throughout, the guiding principle of Spanish colonial policy.

## *C.* THE CONQUEST OF MEXICO

THE fact that the interest of the government became more and more centred upon the quest for precious ores was chiefly due to the development of the discoveries during the thirteenth and fourteenth centuries. Columbus had ascribed but trifling importance to the encounter with the Yucatan trading-bark. He assumed that, because the traders had no ore on board, none was to be found in their native country or in the land of their destination. The comparative development of civilisation with which the explorers had here first come in touch thus remained unnoticed. Not until the superficially explored coasts of the Gulf of Mexico had been submitted to a closer examination was this half-forgotten trading nation again discovered, and while the new-comers were following in their track the first of the American fairy-lands was disclosed to the view of the astonished Europeans.

After Diego Velasquez had, during his personal attempts to colonise Cuba, achieved such important results, it is conceivable that he would show inclination and courage for further enterprise. Not many years after, in 1517, he sent a small fleet, in command of Francisco Fernandez de Cordoba, with orders to coast along the continent and barter with the natives. The ships reached the peninsula of Yucatan not far from its southeastern extremity; then followed it in a northerly and westerly direction, and only turned back on meeting with hostility from the natives. They gave astonishing accounts of massive temples in which the cross was adored side by side with stone idols; of towns in which thousands of people lived, following their respective trades. They also reported that the latter did not go about half naked, like most of the natives whom they had hitherto come across, but were completely clothed, many wearing rich and costly garments almost like Europeans. These accounts sounded so extremely tempting that Velasquez in the following year decided on sending a second and larger expedition to the same regions, placing his nephew, Juan de Grijalva, at the head. The new fleet sighted land off the island of Cozumel. When the Spaniards, however, found that the coast there extended toward the south as it did in the west, they were confirmed in their idea that Yucatan must be an island, and they sailed around in the wake of the previous expedition. Not until they had seen the rising land appear behind the coast, while following the yet undiscovered shores of Mexico farther to the north, did they believe they had reached the mainland. A vessel returned to Cuba with this intelligence. Grijalva himself, with the remainder of the crews, sailed along the entire coast of the Mexican realm, beyond Panuco in the north, trading and gathering information, without, however, venturing to attempt a settlement. For this, on his return, he had to bear the most serious reproaches from Diego Velasquez, although his mode of action had been in strict accordance with the terms of the instructions he had received. The possibility that some one else might precede and anticipate him in the discovery awakened in Diego Velasquez the most painful anxiety, when the rumours of the discoveries by Cordoba and Grijalva had begun to circulate in the colonies. The preparations for the fitting out of a fresh expedition commenced upon the arrival of the first ship, and when Grijalva returned they were carried on with increased energy.

Velasquez had already found a leader for this new expedition. His choice had fallen on Fernando Cortez, who, after spending fifteen years in the colonies, where

e had gained abundant experience and manifested singular fitness, was alcalde of
he capital, Santiago, and one of the most distinguished men of the island. Fer
ando Cortez is one of the most congenial of all the personalities who have taken
art in the extension of the Spanish dominion on American soil. He was descended
rom a distinguished family of Medellin, had the advantage of a superior education.
nd had even studied law for two years. Impelled by enthusiasm, he had, in 1504,
one to the newly discovered country, and had accompanied Velasquez during the
rst colonisation of Cuba, acting for a long time as his private secretary. The
rospect of taking part, from that time under better circumstances, in the discovery
f a new and promising tract of land, was suited both to his temperament and to
is desires; and he willingly agreed to share the cost of the expedition out of his
wn fortune. Velasquez, filled with jealousy, became suspicious of the enthusiasm
rhich Cortez manifested in the affair. Even before the preparations were con
luded he repented of his choice of Cortez, and foolishly enough allowed this to
ecome apparent; but Cortez was resolved not to be displaced. For this reason he
ailed to Trinidad, a western harbour on the island, without awaiting the equip
lent of his eleven ships. The order which he there received from Velasquez, not
ɔ leave until he had joined him for a further conference, served only to hasten
im in continuing his journey. He suggested that Cape San Antonio, the western
oint of Cuba, should be the meeting-place of the fleet. As the time for properly
quipping the vessels threatened to result in serious dangers for him, he took the
isky step of forcibly detaining two ships intended for the conveyance of provisions
ɔ Santiago and completed his equipment with their cargo, referring them for pay
lent to Velasquez, whose servant he still nominally was. Cortez was able to put
ɔ sea in the middle of February, 1519, with rather more than four hundred
Europeans on board his eleven ships, with about two hundred Indians, sixteen
iorses, and fourteen guns in addition. It was but a small troop considering all he
ccomplished with it, although, indeed, it was looked upon at that time as one of
he most imposing forces that had ever been sent forth to found a new colony.
'he voyage was at first along a well-known route to Cozumel, and around Yucatan
ɔ Tabasco. During the preceding expeditions the explorers had met chiefly with
nimosity from the natives at the latter place, so Cortez resolved to punish them.
Ɩ footing had, however, first to be gained by fighting; but with the help of the
luskets, and more especially of the guns and horses, the resistance of the people
f Tabasco was overcome. Having felt the edge of the Spanish sword, these
latives altered their previous demeanour, and, bringing presents, submitted them
elves to him.

Two further strokes of fortune succeeded this good beginning. A Spaniard on
he coast of Yucatan was rescued from Indian captivity, where he had been ship
vrecked years before with several companions, of whom he remained the only
urvivor. His knowledge of the dialects and customs of the country proved most
iseful to Cortez, more especially during the first part of his enterprise. He re
eived similar assistance at Tabasco. There happened to be an Aztec woman among
he twenty slaves whom, besides other things, the natives had presented to Cortez
is a peace-offering; and this woman, who received the name of Donna Marina in
)aptism, rendered most valuable service to Cortez as an interpreter. From her,
vith whom he had become closely connected as his mistress, he first heard of the
cingdom of the Aztecs and of the political conditions which then prevailed there.

This information enabled him to form the daring plans for their subjection which he carried into effect with almost inconceivable success. Cortez sailed from Tabasco along the coast as far as the small island of San Juan de Ulua, and founded not far distant from it the first Spanish colony on American soil, naming it Villarica de la Vera Cruz. He was accorded a friendly reception by the Aztec chiefs on landing. The news of the events in Tabasco had spread to Montezuma's capital, and opinions as to the reception to be accorded to the strangers had, at the king's council, been very much divided. But the dismay which the defeat of the people of Tabasco had created strengthened their superstitious ideas, according to which Quetzalcoatl was said to have prophesied his return to his people across the eastern ocean.[1] The Spaniards, who had as their attendants the lightning which flashed from the cloud, and the horse which sped along with lightning-like rapidity, seemed to give conclusive proof that they were the children of the God of Thunderclouds and of the Wind. The governor of the coast was therefore ordered to give the strangers a peaceful reception and to meet their demands as far as possible.

The ships, guns, and horses of the Spaniards astonished the natives; but the amazement of the court of Montezuma was still greater, owing to the skill of the Aztec scribe who made faithful sketches of the Spaniards for the illustration of the report sent to the capital. Cortez added a statement to the governor's message, saying that he was the envoy of a great king in the far east and the bearer of presents to the ruler of Mexico, as well as of a commission which could be delivered only by word of mouth. Montezuma's reply was not long delayed; it was accompanied by costly presents of gold and beautiful feathers; but it was to the effect that Cortez should be satisfied with these gifts and abstain from a personal visit to the capital. That, however, was not the intention of the Spaniards, nor did the costly gifts suffice to induce them to decide on a fruitless return. Cortez repeated his request to be permitted to appear before Montezuma, at the same time making preparations for accomplishing his visit to Mexico in spite of the ruler's desire. He looked around for confederates for such a contingency, more especially as the attitude of the Aztec governor at the coast began to assume unmistakable signs of unfriendliness. The Totonacs, who inhabited the neighbouring country along the shore more to the north, and who had but recently submitted reluctantly to the yoke of the Aztecs, had from the beginning been in touch with the Spaniards, and had repeatedly invited them to visit their capital, Cempoalla.[2] Cortez went there with part of his crew, and, returning to Vera Cruz, was satisfied that he could now, with this cover for his line of retreat, venture upon a march into the interior.

Before all things it was necessary to establish a feeling of unity in his small force. Cortez had no intention of allowing Diego Velasquez to reap the fruits of his labours after the evident signs of animosity which the latter had, at the last, shown toward him; and the majority of his followers were of the same opinion. Velasquez now himself experienced what he had brought on Diego Colon during the colonisation of Cuba. Cortez sent Montezuma's costly presents straight to Spain with detailed reports, and at the same time demanded for himself and for his followers the governorship of the country, which he intended to subjugate to the Spanish Crown. The pilot, Alaminos, who had directed all the voyages of discovery along this coast, was sent with the best ship, as the bearer of this mes-

---

[1] See *ante*, p. 285.　　　　[2] See the maps, p. 514.

sage, and, in order to prevent any attempt at desertion, the remainder of the fleet was declared to be no longer seaworthy and was therefore stranded and destroyed. As soon as this had been accomplished, the followers of Cortez declared themselves independent of Velasquez, and again chose Cortez as their commander-in-chief. The followers of Velasquez at least made some show of opposition, but they were defeated by the majority. After the leaders had been severely punished by way of example, the remainder submitted to the inevitable.

Cortez, having made sure of his men, started for the interior with a numerous retinue of native Indians. The farther, however, that he advanced, the more urgently Montezuma warned him against this visit to the capital; and as the Spaniards were repeatedly told by the Indians who accompanied them of the treacherous plans which had been laid by order of the Aztec ruler, the explorers advanced in continual anticipation of war. They first met with open hostility on entering Tlazcala's territory. These brave mountaineers, who had for centuries successfully repelled all the attacks of their neighbours, would not now submit to the new-comers. This meant a long and bitter struggle, entailing heavy losses for the Spaniards also, to convince the people of Tlazcala that even their fearless bravery could avail nothing in the face of firearms. They therefore sued for peace and became true and trusty friends of the Spaniards on hearing from the Totonacs that these strangers also entertained anything but friendly feelings for the Aztec ruler and that they were resolved to put an end to his tyranny in one way or another.

After the Spaniards had rested in Tlazcala's territory from the fatigues of the march and battles, and had reinforced their army with additional men from among the Tlazcalas, they resumed their march and first reached Cholula. Here they were again met by Montezuma's messengers, who challenged them to remain and advised their return. Cortez at the same time learned from his Indian confederates that the intention was to attack him and his followers on their departure. In order to anticipate this he seized the hostile ringleaders and gave up the town to his Indian allies to pillage. This they accomplished so thoroughly that even the great pyramid of the temple of Quetzalcoatl was thrown into a heap of ruins. Montezuma, intimidated, denied all knowledge of the outrage and did not again venture to oppose the Spaniards.

Unmolested they climbed over the mountain ridge of Popocatepetl down into the valley of Mexico, and through the highway leading from Iztapalapan they entered Tenochtitlan, which is washed by the sea. Thousands of the natives stared at them with scarcely less astonishment than they themselves felt at the advanced state of civilisation which they encountered at every step. Montezuma, attended by a numerous retinue, met them almost humbly, and assigned to them as their quarters the palace of his father, which, owing to the thick walls surrounding the whole building, was adapted equally for defence and for a dwelling-place. At first the intercourse between the king and the Spaniard was to all appearances quite friendly. Montezuma nevertheless, with quiet dignity, rejected all attempts at his conversion; on the other hand he declared his willingness to acknowledge the Emperor Charles V as his sovereign and to pay him a high tribute in ores and costly materials. Notwithstanding, his mode of dealing was not straightforward. An attack which had in the mean time been made by the Mexicans on the Spaniards remaining at Vera Cruz was proved to have been instigated by Montezuma, and this treachery served the Spaniards as a pretext for compelling the king to move out of his palace into the Spanish quarter, where he was treated more or less as a prisoner. He was forced to do homage to the emperor with solemn ceremony, and had actually to transfer the government to the Spaniards, who, after the suppression of one attempt to raise another descendant of the royal family to the throne as ruler, began to assume the government and administration of the country in an entirely peaceable manner. The transition would have been accomplished without bloodshed if disturbances from without had not intervened.

Although Alaminos had received orders to sail straight to Spain without touching at the colonial harbours, he could not refrain from stopping at Cuba, though but hurriedly and in secret, to circulate the news of Cortez' extraordinary success. The greater the prize, the keener became Velasquez' desire not to allow it to be wrested from him. For this reason he did not content himself with reporting the disloyal conduct of Cortez to Seville, but used every endeavour to fit out a second fleet for an expedition to deprive Cortez of the prize before he could gain a footing in the new country. Panfilo de Narvaez, to whom Velasquez intrusted the duty of humbling Cortez and bringing him back to a sense of obedience, headed a force which, though considerably superior to that of Cortez, yet lacked cohesion. The vice-regent, Diego Colon, had, without infringing the law, absolutely forbidden Velasquez to endanger Cortez' brilliant achievement by a forcible invasion, and the repeated protests of his envoy, who accompanied Narvaez' fleet to Vera Cruz, were not without influence on the crew, whose confidence Narvaez, who was even less popular as a man than Cortez, failed to gain by his personal qualities. To the challenge that the town Villarica should be surrendered to him, Cortez' representative replied by sending on the messengers to his commander in Mexico. Cortez, from his personal interviews, soon realised that there would not be much difficulty in drawing the men away from their allegiance to Narvaez. He therefore openly entered into negotiations with him for combined action, based upon a division of the administrative powers; but at the same time he collected all his available military forces and moved hurriedly foward to meet Narvaez, leaving a strong garrison, under Pedro de Alvarado, in the capital. As he had been exceedingly well informed by deserters, he was able to surprise Narvaez during a dark night, meeting with hardly any resistance. When the latter leader, who had lost an eye in the battle, had been taken prisoner, almost the whole force which he had brought with him joined Cortez; only a few, like Narvaez, taking advantage of a permission to return to Cuba.

This easy victory more than doubled Cortez' forces, for Narvaez had brought far more horsemen and riflemen than had Cortez himself. A threatening ferment had begun to show itself in Tenochtitlan immediately after the departure of Cortez, and when, during the celebration of a great festival, Alvarado was informed that the crowds were to be incited to attack the Spaniards and liberate Montezuma, he concluded that it would be highly advisable to anticipate such a stroke, and therefore he attacked the rejoicing multitude and dispersed it after a terrible massacre. The Mexicans now on their part changed to open hostility, and surrounded the Spaniards so closely that Alvarado had to summon Cortez to his aid as quickly as possible. Cortez hastened to Mexico as soon as he had again reorganised his forces. The Spaniards, of course, perceived everywhere a changed and unfriendly disposition toward them, but as they did not find their movements barred, they were able to join the besieged after a serious fight. Cortez recognised, when too late, that he had gained nothing thereby, but that instead he had made the Spaniards' supremacy, which had been won under such difficult dependent upon the issue of a single battle. As soon as he entered the town all paths were closed to him, and the reinforced host of Spaniards found themselves now as hopelessly menaced as Alvarez' division had previously been. At first the Spaniards attempted to gain the mastery over their adversaries by open fight and though they overthrew thousands of the badly armed natives, the latter seemed continually to increase. Cortez thereupon endeavoured to shelter himself under the authority of the imprisoned king, and the appearance of the latter on the battlements of the palace actually led to a short armistice. When, however, Montezuma asserted that he was not a prisoner, and commanded that the Spaniards were to be allowed to depart unmolested, then the rage of his subjects turned on him, and he was struck and wounded by so many stones that he died within a few days. With him also vanished the Mexicans' last remnant of consideration for their opponents.

It now became evident to Cortez that he would have to get out of the town, cost what it might. The investment by the enemy was so close that it was not even possible to make secret preparations. Each step of the retreat along the causeway over the lake, which was one and a quarter miles long, had to be gained by fighting. Cortez started, hoping thus to lessen the danger. The enemy, having long foreseen such a contingency, were at once prepared and pressed forward vigorously, fighting from boats on both sides of the causeway, which was broken through in various places, sending a shower of missiles after the retreating men. Cortez had thrown a portable bridge over the first of the three canals that intersected the causeway, which his men actually succeeded in crossing; but by the time the second canal was reached discipline had already been so weakened by the severity of the attack on all sides that the bridge was no longer available; in fact it had not even been carried forward. The crowd of fugitives now rushed on, over the bodies of those in advance, and when the mainland was at length reached, order was re-established to some extent. A cypress-tree marks the spot where the rout ended, and is preserved to this day as a monument of the "noche triste" ("sad night"). Two thirds of the Spaniards and an even greater proportion of their native allies had either been killed or taken prisoners there, and the latter were bled to death on the altars of the idols. All the artillery, most of the muskets, and forty-six out of the sixty-seven horses were destroyed. Cortez subsequently despatched only a fifth of the golden treasures as a royalty for the Spanish king, the remainder was handed over to the soldiers; but almost everything had been lost in the terrible fight. Those who had escaped and who were almost without exception wounded were in a highly critical position, for they were still hundreds of miles from the nearest friendly district.

Cortez, thinking that the enemy would have rendered the old road impracticable for him in various ways, marched around the lakes on the northern shore, and actually reached Otumba via Teotihuacan before fresh numbers were added to the pursuing enemy, who intended attacking him in front. There the Spaniards had once more to fight for their lives against an overwhelmingly superior force (Cortez estimated the number of his enemies at two hundred thousand), and the hardly won victory was no doubt due to the circumstance that they were able to kill the enemy's leader in the midst of his warriors. After the battle the Spaniards were at any rate able to continue the retreat under less pressure, but not until they entered the territory of Tlazcalan could they consider themselves safe, the Tlazcalans having remained faithful to the covenant which they had made with the Spaniards.

Months passed before the Spaniards had so far recovered from the terrible fatigues of the retreat and had been sufficiently reinforced by contingents from the islands that Cortez could once more think of taking the offensive. He left the hospitable Tlazcalas during the last weeks of the year 1520, and endeavoured, by the subjection of the neighbouring tribes, to restore the prestige of the Spanish arms. He then attacked Tezcuco, intending to make it the strategic basis from which to prepare for the conquest of the island town of Tenochtitlan. In consequence of the political situation which had been wisely computed by Anahuak, Cortez also found willing confederates at Tezcuco after the banishment of the Aztec governor. Cortez now proved himself to be as good an organiser as he had hitherto been a leader. While carrying on the war against the coast towns, chiefly with the aid of his allies, who were in command of small Spanish divisions, he made a canal from Tezcuco to the Gulf of Mexico, and in a practically unassailable position he built a fleet of thirteen ships, which, on the opening of the canal, put to sea, so that he was able to ward off the troublesome invasion of hostile vessels. Attacks on one coast town after another were now undertaken from both land and sea; those towns which commanded the entrance to the canal being the last to fall. As the fleet at the same time gained a decisive victory over the Mexican fleet of boats, which accordingly now no longer existed as a fighting sea force, the Spaniards were in a position to turn to the invasion of the capital itself.

Cuitlahuac, the king who had led the battles of the " noche triste," had died in the city after a reign of only four months. He was succeeded by Quauhtemoctzin (Guatemocin), who, as a brave ruler, proved in no wise inferior to him. After a few unsuccessful attacks the Spaniards had to acknowledge the impossibility of taking the town by storm, but the systematic siege which they had reluctantly resorted to proved both tedious and difficult. Every inch of the ground, as well as every house, was defended with the greatest courage by the natives, who were crowded together in overwhelming numbers in Tenochtitlan; and so long as the entrances to the town on the water side were not completely in the hands of the Spaniards, Cortez' ships were not in a position entirely to prevent provisions from reaching the besieged. In spite of this the Spaniards advanced slowly but surely, and, after a siege lasting almost ten weeks, succeeded in confining the enemy to a small portion of the town by pulling down the surrounding houses, so as to ensure the deployment, during the battle, of the artillery and cavalry which largely formed the Spanish strength. Quauhtemoctzin then, realising the impossibility of holding the starved-out town, attempted to escape by sea, but fell into the hands of the Spaniards. The besieged then also gave up all resistance, and on the 13th of August, 1521, the heroic defenders quitted the ruins of Tenochtitlan.

Immediately after this success Cortez resumed the activity which had been interrupted by the appearance of Narvaez on the coast. Montezuma's record of taxes enabling him to form as correct an idea as possible of the extent and constitution of the kingdom, he organised the territory and regulated the taxes on this basis. The news of a rich and highly civilised country which had at last been discovered on American soil, and was secured to the Spanish crown by his ?????, proved exceedingly useful to Cortez, for an impetus was thereby given to t?? ? for emigration such as had not existed since the second voyage of Colu.... ? The capital of Mexico, which, with his wonted energy, Corte? at on? e reb??? numbered, after a few years, thousands of inhabitants, and from then? a netw?rk of smaller European settlements spread over the whole of Montezuma's t?rritory.

During this period the return of the "Victoria," the only ship out of Magalhaes' fleet to complete the voyage around the world by the southern points of America and Africa, had directed attention to the Spice Islands. These were presumably situated within the Spanish sphere of authority; and the question of finding a shorter route than the one discovered by Magalhaes arising, two ships were immediately built at Zacatula, and shortly after began a systematic exploration of the Pacific Coast of Mexico.

Cortez for a time indulged in the hope of discovering a passage through Central America. This desire, and the wish to ascertain the southern boundaries of the country conquered by him as quickly as possible (for an invasion from the colonies of Darien might with certainty be expected, in consequence of the impression which his conquests had created), led him to equip two fresh expeditions as soon as circumstances in the interior of the province allowed of such a step. One, under the command of Pedro de Alvarado, advanced from the southern Pacific territories of Mexico into the province of the Maya tribes, who occupied the mountain districts to the north of the Isthmus, which is the Guatemala of to-day. Alvarado was able to take advantage of the same conditions which had proved of such assistance to Cortez in gaining the victory, and through the jealousies of the various chiefs he was able to incite one tribe against the other. Though occasionally encountering an obstinate resistance, he was obliged to concede that the bravery of the natives equalled the courage shown at the defence of Tenochtitlan; but they were not able, either here or elsewhere, to hold their own permanently against the Spaniards, and the campaign proved rich not merely in glory but also in material results.

The other expedition, which Cortez sent at the same time along the coasts of the Atlantic to the south, was less successful. The leader, Cristobal de Olid, from the beginning gave rise to the suspicion that he intended to serve Cortez in the same manner as the latter had served Velasquez. He had indeed, at Puerto de Caballos, after circumnavigating the peninsula of Yucatan, taken possession of the country in the name of Cortez, and founded a colony which he called Triunfo de la Cruz. Then, however, he evinced the unmistakable desire of securing for himself a small territory between Castilla del Oro, an organised province of Central America, and the Mexican territory belonging to Cortez. He began by attaching to himself all the restless and adventurous elements in both provinces, and with their help he either got rid of or intimidated the conscientious ones. It so happened that several contingents which Cortez had sent after Cristobal de Olid disappeared and never reached their destination, so that the commander-in-chief only heard rumours of his proposed defection. Cortez, however, foresaw no serious danger. His efforts to gain from the king his recognition as governor had not been crowned with entire success; therefore had Olid, in league with Velasquez, succeeded in establishing himself independently in the south it would certainly have cost Cortez the greater part, if not the whole, of his governorship.

Cortez, therefore, with the quick determination peculiar to him, quitted Mexico in October, 1724, and sailed along the Atlantic coast as far as Usumacinta. From thence traversing Yucatan where the peninsula joins the mainland, he crossed Lake Isabel and reached Olid's colony on the coast. The object of his journey had been attained before his arrival: Olid had been removed, and the colony had returned to obedience. During his march, passing through considerable regions of unexplored country, Cortez had become acquainted with the towns and countries of the Maya tribes of the east, establishing his claims on this country in such a way that all danger of foreign intervention was removed. The subjection of the peninsula of Yucatan, the seat of the last tribes who still adhered to the ancient, genuine Maya traditions, was not, it is true, seriously attempted until some years later by Francisco de Montejo, and it was carried through comparatively slowly and with varying success. After the peninsula had been explored on all sides, both by land and sea, its acquisition was but a question of time, as its principal secrets had been disclosed by Cortez. For a number of years, until new discoveries drew attention in other directions, the "flotas de Yucatan" sailed there from time to time from Seville, bringing back rich treasures.

But while Cortez advanced into the jungle to punish the insubordination of his subjects, they boldly held up their heads in the capital. Cortez was looked upon as dead, and his enemies — the energetic, unscrupulous conquistador possessed plenty of them in men who found that he had not been able to fulfil their exaggerated hopes — were so superior in force that they were able to annul the regency which he had instituted, and to seize the reins of government for themselves. This rival government, however, collapsed upon the approach to the town of the returning commander, who in the mean time had been constituted governor and commander-in-chief of the province of New Spain, by Charles V. But the germs of discontent which compelled him in 1527 to go over to Spain in order to lay his case personally before the court date from these circumstances. In spite of endless lawsuits he succeeded in acquitting himself well before the Council of the Indies, but, like Columbus, he, too, was not reinstated in his former position. When he returned to Mexico in 1530 he was forced to tolerate a new governor placed immediately over himself, and this weighed heavily on the proud and jealous conqueror. During this period he gave a fresh impetus to discoveries in a northwesterly direction. He repeatedly sent ships along the Pacific coast and also discovered the Bay of California. In the year 1535 he himself once more penetrated far up the coast of the Californian peninsula. Although he was not the discoverer of the desired northwestern passage any more than he had previously been the discoverer of Central America, he furthered a knowledge of the truth that North America was not connected with the continent of Asia, even in higher latitudes.

Long before the middle of the century the Spaniards had also pushed on far into the interior of the regions to the northwest of Mexico. Nuno de Guzman had, in addition to the subjection of the northern districts of the Aztec kingdom, advanced, in 1530, into the subsequent New Galicia (the provinces Durango and Sinaloa of to-day), with an army composed of Spanish and Indian warriors.[1] Rumours of towns rich in gold had enticed him to these districts. They received apparent confirmation when a few of the followers of Fernando de Soto, who had gone from Florida straight through the southern provinces of North America as far as

---

[1] See Plate opposite.

# THE BATTLES OF THE SPANIARDS IN MEXICO, AFTER THE DRAWINGS OF "LIENZO DE TLAZCALA"

The so-called Lienzo de Tlazcala was a canvas almost ... yards in length and two and a half yards in breadth, on which the events of the ... federates of the Spaniards were represented in ... originated in the sixteenth century, it was ... The original was lost during the revolution ... a faithful copy of the Lienzo exists. It is used in ... Columbina de Mexico in the work "Hom naj ... Junta Colombina de Mexico." (Mexico, 1892.)

The accompanying plate (No. 52) represents ... Guzman to Nueva Galicia in the year 1530. It was at the ... The Tlazcalans, led by one chief, who bears the bad ... Nuño de Guzman and his Spanish horsemen. Probably the ... Xi ... The identity of the second chief with the many feather ... accompanied by the dreaded war dogs. The cause of the war was the treachery of the ... which is typified by the man who has been hanged. In the upper right-hand ... glyphics for Michuacan, which is the land of fishermen. That to battle ends in the ... fied by the mutilated body of a champion, who is represented ... below.

guzmā. michvacá.

THE BATTLES OF CORTEZ IN MEXICO.
(After the Aztec drawings in "Lienzo de Tlaxcala")

Texas and Mexico, told of colonies where the houses were many stories high and where life was as gay and as luxurious as in Mexico. They called the largest of these towns Cibola. It became the goal of an expedition which Juan Vasquez de Coronado undertook in 1535 from Culiacan in a northwesterly direction. After he and his companions had, with many struggles and privations, wandered through the arid regions between the Great Colorado and the Rio Grande, they did in fact arrive at the towns of the Pueblo Indians, which had unmistakably given rise to the rumours;[1] but they failed to discover the reported treasures in possession of the homely husbandmen of Zuñi, Walpi, and Moqui, even as they had failed to find Nuño de Guzman. The reputed City of Gold now received a new name. Even after many long centuries the phantom of the treasures of Quivira still lured the Spaniards into the desert prairie land of the Llano Estacado. But the Spanish power in reaching the Pueblo towns had practically attained its northern boundary, beyond which it advanced only indirectly during the nineteenth century, when the opening of the Far West set in motion on all sides a stream of immigrants for California.

## D. The Conquest of Peru

New life had not only been infused into emigration by the achievements of Cortez, but they had also inspired the desire for fresh discoveries. The Council of the Indies had never previously been so occupied with requests for permission to make fresh attempts at colonisation as during the years subsequent to the conquest of Mexico. There was now no longer any need for the government officially to continue exploration in the new regions of the world; the enterprising spirit of its subjects competed for pre-eminence in the matter of discoveries. In little more than ten years hardly a foot of soil on the American continent remained which had not at one time or another been occupied by an explorer. Of course all the enterprises for which the Council of the Indies had granted concessions were not actually undertaken, while some, again, proved such absolute failures that the holders renounced their claims within a short time, and even colonies which, like Santa Marta, had subsisted for a number of years, had occasionally declined so rapidly that they had to be completely reconstituted. Even though vast tracts of land on the confines of the Spanish colonies remained for more than a century still unreclaimed, tracts over which the Spaniards were never in a position to exercise more than a formal claim, yet scarcely an unexplored region of larger dimensions was left in the southern half of the New World, with the exception of those lowlands to the south of the river Amazon which to this day are still almost unknown. In isolated instances the explorers pushed far forward into regions which up to now have not been identified with complete certainty because no white man who could give an account of his experiences has ever again advanced so far.

The Spaniards had presumably heard vague rumours from the Indians in Central America of the existence of rich and powerful States both in the north and also in the south, and when the expansion of the Central American province to the north was closed by the conquest of Mexico, their attention was naturally directed toward the south. The voyages along the Pacific coast had so far resulted only in the knowledge of various races who were in an unusually low state of civilisation,

---

[1] See Plate at p. 218.

and no doubt it was on that account that so long a time elapsed before the Spaniards guessed at the existence of the country of the Incas. Through a misunderstanding the name of Peru was again assigned to it. Biru was the name of a small kingdom on the bay of San Miguel, at the southwestern end of the Isthmus. Balboa had already touched there, and it had been the goal of an expedition which Pascual de Andagoya undertook in 1522. The direct result did not surpass what the expeditions into the regions of Darien had led one to expect. The natives, however, who had by that time become more intelligible, made it clearer than ever to the gold-seeking Spaniards that there existed great kingdoms in the south on the Pacific coast, where they would find the yellow ore in plenty. This news could apply only to the kingdom of the Incas.

The assertions of the Indians had made an indelible impression, especially on one of the followers of Andagoya. Francisco Pizarro was an adventurer of the ordinary type. He had tended the pigs at his home in Estremadura, but when still a youth he had, with Hojeda, crossed the ocean in 1508, and had also shared in all the dangers which preceded the founding of the Darien colony. After its annexation he was numbered among the constant participators in all voyages of discovery. In this way he had gained vast experience in all kinds of difficult positions, and manifested throughout quiet but almost inflexible perseverance which was highly appreciated by his superiors and comrades. While evolving the plan for the discovery of the golden land of the Indians, these same qualifications also proved of immense service to him. As his means were insufficient for the equipment of an expedition, in spite of fifteen years' service in the colonies, he turned to the colonists for assistance. Diego del Almagro, a man of the same type as Pizarro, brought him a host of resolute comrades, but, like Pizarro, he did not possess the necessary financial means. These, nevertheless, were also found. The vicar of the church of Panama, Fray Hernando de Luque, not only possessed a small fortune himself, which he was prepared to stake on the undertaking, but his relations with the governor, Pedrarias Davila, and with other notabilities of the colony, made it possible for him to smooth the way for the enterprise in every direction, so that Pizarro was able to make the first advance into the south in 1524.

The result of the expedition was by no means remunerative. Both Pizarro, who had sailed in advance, and Almagro, who followed him some months later, reconnoitred the coast from Panama about half-way up to the northern boundary of the kingdom of the Incas, and gained but little treasure as a reward for great hardships. Pizarro, however, again gave brilliant proofs of his imperturbable powers of endurance. Twice he sent his ship back to Panama, remaining behind on the totally strange coast with a little band of followers; and when he finally decided on a return, it was only with the object of attaining, through personal influence, the equipment for his expedition that seemed indispensable to him for such immense distances.

The conquest of Peru now became the object of a financial speculation for which a thoroughly businesslike agreement was drawn up. Luque and his sureties found the money, while Pizarro and Almagro staked their lives, and the division of the proceeds was regulated accordingly. Not many months after his return Pizarro was able once more to put to sea, this time accompanied by Almagro, in order again to resume the exploration of the coast on the southern spot which had been previously reached. This time, as a result of the better equipment and the more favourable time of year, more rapid progress was made; but in spite of all, their provisions ran short before they reached the more densely populated regions. Once again reinforcements and provisions had to be procured from Panama, and even thus the expedition threatened to become completely frustrated. Upon hearing the accounts of the disappointed men who returned, the governor decided that a continuation of the undertaking was only a useless waste of money and lives; he therefore sent to Pizarro and his followers on the Isla del Gallo and ordered their return. Pizarro remained immovable, and for seven months held out on the island with only twelve companions, until his partners were in a position to send him a ship and provisions. With these he energetically resumed his voyage to the south and finally reached the Inca kingdom. He got on friendly terms with the natives at Tumbez on the Gulf of Guayaquil, and was at length able, with his own eyes and ears, to investigate the truth of the rumours circulated by the Indians. The greatness of his discovery actually far exceeded all his hopes and necessitated another return home. This was no task which could be accomplished with the funds provided by his partners, and on this account a basis with extensive capital had to be established.

On his return with the news of his discoveries in Panama he had no difficulty in convincing his partners of the necessity of first acquiring in Spain the exploring rights for the conquest of the province, and it became evident to them that he would be the most suitable person to lay this proposition before the Council of the Indies. In the spring of 1528 he travelled over to Seville and presented himself at court. When he returned to Panama, two years later, he carried with him the nominations for himself as "adelantado," for Almagro as commandant, and for Luque the reversion of the first bishopric. Almagro, to be sure, felt that he had been slighted by the unequal division of the honours between him and his partners, but for the moment he was appeased. Apparently on the best of terms, they led a band of about two hundred Spaniards toward the south. Even before they reached Tumbez the expedition was strengthened by more than one reinforcement. Their reception by the natives there was again peaceful, the more so as Pizarro delivered them from their hostile neighbours, the inhabitants of the island Puno, whom, incited thereto by the people of Tumbez, he defeated completely. He there also heard of the war between the brothers Huascar and Atahualpa, which had just terminated, and of the seeds of discontent which the latter had sown.[1] This information made Pizarro hasten to the scene before the favourable opportunity for intervention had passed. When he had founded a colony (San Miguel) for the adjustment of the trade, he started for the interior, and made straight for the spot where, according to the accounts of the natives, he might expect to find the Inca Atahualpa.

To advance to meet a host of ostensibly forty thousand men, in quite an unknown country, with one hundred and sixty-eight Spaniards without any confederates, was most foolhardy. The smallness of the number may have been the means of his success, as the Inca-Peruvians did not consider it necessary to place hindrances in his way or to arm themselves for resistance. Atahualpa, on the contrary, seemed almost anxious to make the acquaintance of the Spaniards, to whom he repeatedly sent messengers with presents and an invitation to appear before the Inca. Unmolested, Pizarro climbed up into the mountains from the

---

[1] See *ante*, p. 344.

plains of the coast, and at last reached the town of Cajamarca, near which the army of the Inca was encamped. The town was deserted, — a circumstance which was not unwelcome to the Spaniards, enabling them, at any rate, to prepare unnoticed for defence, and also to make arrangements for their attacks. On the day after their arrival Pizarro sent to the camp a small division, composed entirely of horsemen under Hernando de Soto, and through them invited the Inca to honour the Spaniards with a visit. He had arrived at the conviction that it would be foolish to measure the strength of his own forces with those of the Inca in open battle. All his hopes were set on getting possession of the Inca's person, and then, as Cortez had done with such great success in Mexico, under cover of his authority, to get the country into his power. Atahualpa evinced unmistakable interest in the appearance of the horsemen, which were a novel sight for him, though he took scant notice of the message which Soto brought him ostensibly in the name of the Emperor Charles. He promised, however, to appear in Cajamarca on the following day, in order to make the acquaintance of the other Spaniards and of their commander-in-chief.

It became evident to Pizarro that the following day would decide the issue of his undertaking, and his suggestion that they should at once fall upon the Peruvians and take Atahualpa a prisoner at the earliest opportunity was received with universal satisfaction. All the preparations for the success of the daring plan were carefully made. With growing impatience the Spaniards watched the greater part of the next day pass without a single person coming within reasonable distance from the camp of the Incas, and they began to fear that, in spite of all the precautions which had been taken, their plan had been discovered. Late in the afternoon, however, a procession began to move toward Cajamarca, and in a moment every Spaniard was at his post. The town seemed deserted when the Inca entered ; he was able to proceed as far as the market-place without seeing a soul, and the market, too, was at first empty. When the Inca, carried in an uncovered litter, halted, he was met by a monk, Fray Pedro de Valverde, accompanied by two natives whom Pizarro had enrolled among his followers on his first voyages and had taken to Spain, where they were trained to be interpreters. The monk made the customary speech to the Inca which by command of Charles V had to be interpreted to the natives each time before force might be used toward them. Beginning with the creation of the world, he told of the vicariate of the Pope over the globe, and deduced from the papal deed the claim of the Spanish rulers to the obedience of his Indian subjects. Atahualpa listened to the address without change of countenance, and, as Valverde repeatedly referred to the Bible, which he carried open in his hand, the Inca desired to see the book. Not perceiving anything extraordinary in it, he threw it contemptuously on the ground, after turning over its leaves. It needed only the exclamation of indignation which this conduct evoked from the cleric to give the signal for the attack to the Spaniards, who had been following the proceedings with the keenest interest. The two small field culverins, which had been placed in such a position that they swept the market-place, were discharged ; the horsemen, standing near their saddled steeds at the back of the adjacent houses, mounted and dashed forward toward the market-place and the litter of the Inca, knocking down everything which happened to come in their way. The musketeers and unmounted warriors at the same time endeavoured to prevent the followers of the Inca, numbering several thousand men, from going to the assistance of the combatants in the market-place. The daring plan was carried out most satisfactorily during the confusion which followed upon the sudden and unexpected attack. As the bearers were thrown down, the Inca fell from the litter and was secured by the Spaniards without injury. His followers undoubtedly fought with great bravery in order to liberate him, but the large expanse of ground which had been most cunningly chosen gave them no opportunity. After a short but cruel battle the Peruvians, of whom about two thousand are said to have been killed, were forced to retire and leave the Inca to his fate.

By the success of this daring feat the conquest of the kingdom of the Inca had practically been accomplished. The tribe dispersed and left the country open to the Spaniards, who, secure under the authority of the Inca, obtained the realisation of all their desires. Atahualpa at once recognised that force could avail nothing. He was treated with every consideration, being waited on by his wives and household, but he was not permitted to leave Cajamarca, where he was lodged in one of the strongest buildings and carefully watched. He hoped to gain his liberation by means of negotiation. When he perceived with what greed the Spaniards fawned for gold and treasures, he offered to fill the room which he inhabited, as high as a man could reach, with gold and silver, on condition that he might be permitted to return to the throne of his ancestors. The Spaniards took good care not to reject so good an offer, and watched with delight and astonishment while, at the order of the Inca, the treasures actually poured into Cajamarca from all directions. The doubts which they had at first felt as to the possibility of such a promise ever being fulfilled vanished more and more. But this did not prevent them from continuing the attempt to conquer the country, which was their goal, by other means. Pizarro had, in the mean time, collected further information about the dispute concerning the succession, and found that Huascar, the rightful Inca, still lived. He was too valuable a tool not to be secured, but Atahualpa did not remain in ignorance of the design. In order to remove his dangerous rival he gave the secret order that Huascar should be executed. He little guessed that in so doing he had sealed his own fate.

As the collection of the ransom did not proceed fast enough to please either the Inca or the Spaniards, it was decided to send a contingent to the sanctuary at Pachacamac. Pizarro placed his brother Fernando at the head of this troop, which was the first to penetrate farther into the Inca kingdom. The real object of the expedition was not attained. Fernando Pizarro found the temple practically robbed of its treasures, and could do nothing but destroy the mud idol and replace it by the cross. On his return he again gave glowing accounts of the high state of civilisation and of the excellent administration of the kingdom. His reports were surpassed by those of two other Spaniards who had also pushed on as far as Cuzco with a safe-conduct from the Inca on account of the ransom. Nowhere was the slightest sign of resistance shown, and now, as before, gold flowed into the Inca's room. The sight of such treasures proved too much for the avaricious eyes of the adventurous troop, and even before the ransom was completed a division was decided on. The amount of gold and silver which had accumulated may be computed from the fact that the royalty for the Spanish king was worth almost one thousand ducats. From that time Atahualpa, who now claimed his liberty, was regarded only as an encumbrance. The strength of the Spaniards had been almost doubled by the addition of considerable reinforcements brought by Almagro.

Upon the advice of several of his followers Pizarro put Atahualpa on his trial as a usurper and matricide, and ordered his execution; he then nominated another member of the royal family as Inca, in order to secure the continued obedience of the natives. This object was however, only partially attained. After the death of both Inca kings the bond of obedience was severed in this realm also. The natives withdrew more and more from the Spaniards and at times even showed open hostility.

Pizarro then decided upon leaving Cajamarca. He led the main force toward the south in order to occupy the capital, Cuzco, and at the same time sent a smaller troop, under the command of Benalcazar, in a northerly direction to take possession of Atahualpa's capital and with it the kingdom of Quito. This was a very important step, as the report of the treasures of Peru had already aroused the envy of other Spaniards. Pedro de Alvarado, Cortez' confederate in the conquest of Mexico, and now governor of Guatemala, arrived in Peru some weeks later, accompanied by a host of adventurers, with the avowed intention of securing for himself in Quito a wealthier dominion than the one he had found in the north. The spectacle presented by Cortez and Narvaez in Mexico was almost repeated here, though Alvarado showed less consideration. He entered into negotiations with Pizarro and Almagro, and finally transferred the whole equipment to them in consideration of an indemnity, which agreement was gladly accepted by his confederates, for the kingdom of the Inca was large and rich enough to hold out the prospect of further spoils for them also.

Up till then the Spaniards had only once had to draw sword. Pizarro found, when pushing on to Cuzco, that the way was barred by a hostile force which only retreated after heavy fighting wherein the Spaniards suffered great losses. They were, however, again able to establish themselves without resistance and founded a Spanish colony in Cuzco, but Pizarro did not again constitute it the capital. Its position in the southeast of the realm and its distance from the coast precluded it from becoming a suitable spot for Spanish purposes. The arrival of Alvarado necessitated Pizarro's hasty return to the coast, and there the future seat of the provincial government was established, — the modern Lima, on the river Rimac, the Ciudad de los Reyes.

The continual reinforcements which Pizarro's forces received placed him in a position to continue his discoveries in every direction, and soon to push beyond the borders of the old Inca kingdom. Almagro commenced a series of expeditions, soon after the colonisation of Cuzco, by advancing toward the south between the two Cordilleras, through the present Bolivia. In doing so he subjugated without difficulty the provinces round the lake of Titicaca, and then marched on over the mountains toward the south, enduring untold hardships, cold and hunger finally necessitating the risk of crossing the icy crest of the western Cordillera in order to regain the less impracticable coast. He followed it beyond Coquimbo, in the region of Copiapo. On his return along the seashore he had once more to undergo the severest privations in the desert of Atacama. In spite of all this the only gain from his expedition was the exploration of a great part of modern Chile, and the conviction that there were no treasures there which could be carried away with ease.

Almagro returned just in time to rescue the Spaniards in Cuzco from a great danger. The Inca whom Pizarro had nominated in Cajamarca had soon after died, and Manco Inca had been made king in his place. The Spaniards, however, not meeting with resistance anywhere from the submissive natives, regarded him as superfluous. They paid so little attention to him that he was easily able to escape from Cuzco into the northeastern highlands, whence he planned a far-reaching conspiracy against the Spaniards. The weak garrison of Cuzco was surprised and fell into great straits, Fernando Pizarro's impetuous bravery alone saving them from complete destruction. After this failure Manco Inca also withdrew his forces, but turned the attack into so successful a blockade that the defenders of Cuzco were on the verge of death from starvation when Almagro's return at length dispersed the enemy and made the reprovisioning of the town possible. Almagro had made all the greater haste to relieve Cuzco, believing that thus he would be acting to his own advantage. While he had been suffering useless privations in Chile, Spain had at least done him justice, for Charles V. made him governor of a province to the south of the Peruvian kingdom, which extended from a westerly and easterly direction two hundred and seventy Spanish miles to the south from the river Santiago (in modern Ecuador), to undefined southern latitudes, and Almagro was of the opinion that Cuzco belonged to this province. Fernando Pizarro refused to acknowledge this, and as deliberations led to no decision Almagro finally forcibly entered Cuzco and took Fernando Pizarro and his brother Gonzalo prisoners, while Francisco Pizarro made the attempt to liberate the brothers by force. When, however, the contingent which had been sent was also beaten by Almagro, he agreed to negotiations which he immediately afterward annulled, as his attempts to liberate the brothers had been crowned with success.

A succession of civil wars now began in the Peruvian province which terminated only when all the leading members of the "conquista" had met a cruel end. First Fernando Pizarro engaged in battle with Almagro, and, beating him at Las Salinas, had him executed in a most summary manner.

When he returned to Spain, in order to lay his brother's case before the court, he was himself placed on his trial, and it was only because of his imprisonment for life that he survived his brothers. For the purpose of re-establishing justice and order the Council of the Indies sent the licentiate Vaca de Castro, with supreme authority, to undertake the government of the province. His arrival closed another scene in the cruel drama. Almagro's faction, led by his son, had fallen upon Francisco Pizarro and slain him, owing to his resistance. The younger Almagro had no wish to be nominated to the governorship of the whole of Peru, but he laid claim to at least the southern province which had been assigned to his father. Upon Vaca de Castro's refusal to grant this he rose against him, and a large number of the conquistadors were only too ready to follow his leading. Fate, however, did not treat him kindly, for his party suffered a severe defeat in the battle of the Chupas, not far from Huamango, in 1542, and he was himself treacherously delivered over to his opponents and paid the penalty of his mutiny by death.

Of the representatives of both conquerors only Pizarro's youngest brother Gonzalo, still remained at liberty. Since 1540 he had been governor of Quito, and in the battles of Vaca de Castro against Almagro he had remained in faithful allegiance to the former. When, however, in 1544, Blasco Nuñez Vela was entrusted with the regency, — chiefly in order to procure a happier lot for the natives, who during the period of the fierce party wars suffered most unjust oppression, — he also could not resist temptation. To the rough Peruvian settlers, forming the majority, the protection of the natives seemed synonymous with the loss of their own rights and privileges.   Therefore, as Blasco Nuñez showed a great want of tact in the discharge of his commission, even the judges of the Audiencia, the Supreme Court of Lima, joined against the government in the insurrectionary movement of which, at his own instigation, Gonzalo Pizarro was elected leader.   The more prudent among the colonists immediately returned to obedience when Blasco Nuñez was followed by Pedro de la Gasca, a priest who proved himself a discreet and energetic successor.   Gonzalo Pizarro became intoxicated by the consciousness of his power, and prolonged his resistance until, thanks to Gasca, his position became untenable and his case hopeless.   During the battle which ensued most of his false friends deserted him, and he was taken prisoner together with the ringleaders of his faction, and was put to death.   Gasca, who had reached Panama in 1544 without troops (it was then still subject to Pizarro), in less than six years established quiet and orderly conditions in Peru for the first time, then asked for a successor, and retired to a monk's cell, from which he had been summoned by the command of Charles V.

Francisco Pizarro had also turned his attention to the southern province which had been discovered by Almagro.   After the execution of his rival he considered it a constituent part of his own governorship, from which he sought to exclude all foreign intervention.   For this purpose he despatched an officer, Pedro de Valdivia, his faithful ally, with a commission to usurp governmental power by the establishment of a Spanish colony.   Valdivia chose the same road as Almagro, but during a more favourable time of year, so that though he had to contend less with natural difficulties he came more into contact with the enmity of the natives, who were anything but friendly after their experiences with the Spaniards.   The inhabitants of the newly founded town of Santiago led a wretched existence on that account during the first years, although reinforcements were frequently sent there from Peru, especially after rich mines had been discovered and started in the valley of Quillota.   Valdivia made use of the reinforcements more especially in order to continue the exploration of the country to the south.   Commissioned by him, the Genoese, Pastene, sailed along the coast in the year 1544 until he reached the western outlets of the Straits of Magellan (or Magalhães), which had been set as the southern boundary of the province.   When Pedro de la Gasca took over the governorship of Peru, he gave Valdivia his continued support, because, during the periods of unrest, the latter had rendered him valuable service.   He was then able to continue his advance by land into the more southern regions of the province   The foundation of the town of Concepcion, on the borders of the district inhabited by the warlike Arauca Indians, followed in 1550.   The battles with this tribe which for quite ten years fought with wonderful bravery for its independence have been celebrated in song by more than one poet.   But the heroic deeds which were performed on both sides during this period were, however, out of proportion to the reward gained by the Spaniards' victory.   This country, which Spain had won with such bloodshed, was certainly fruitful and possessed a good climate, yet the advantages which it offered did not equal those of many other parts of the Spanish colonial kingdom, so that its colonisation and usefulness promised to make but very slow progress.

The Spaniards had, in addition to the conquest of Peru, advanced beyond the borders of the Inca kingdom in two other directions.   There is no easier approach from the west coast of America to the vast lowlands of the east than the one to the south of Lake Titicaca, where the eastern Cordilleras extend into a series of moderately high mountain ranges which together surround and break into the highlands of modern Bolivia. Reference has been made in a previous division [1] to the great part which this country played as the cradle of the races of primitive times. By this road also the Incas seem to have carried their conquests beyond the sources of those rivers which flow, some through the Madeira to the Amazon, and some through the Pilcomayo to the La Plata. Almagro came into touch with those regions in 1535, during his expedition to Chile; but their exploration was systematically undertaken a few years afterward, when Blasco Nuñez Vela, during his short period of office, entrusted the governorship of the provinces of Charcas and Tucuman to Captain Francisco de Rojas. The first explorers passed the immense treasures of Potosi, not suspecting their existence, and pushed on far into the lowlands in a southeasterly direction, through the provinces of Jujuy, Calchaqui, and Catamarca, fighting not only with the natives, but quarrelling also among themselves, until at the river Tercero they came upon traces of the Spaniards who had advanced thus far from the east. This completed the transit of the continent.

After the Portuguese had, in 1514, discovered the mouth of the La Plata, and extended their exploration to the south far beyond it, without, however, attempting to found a settlement there, the Spaniards hastened to secure, by actual usurpation, their claims to these districts in the face of the adjoining kingdom. Diego de Solis was the first to explore a tract of the Paraguay in 1515, but after he had been killed in battle with the natives his followers returned to Spain. Then Sebastian Cabot and Diego Garcia, one after the other, quickly appeared on the river and carried on a lucrative trade with the natives, in consequence of which it received the name of Rio de la Plata (Silver River), but they also were not able to found a settlement. Owing to the reports which they brought back, Pedro de Mendoza undertook the colonisation of these regions in 1534. His fleet of fourteen ships is said to have had no less than two thousand men on board, who became the progenitors of the Spanish population of the Argentine provinces. After Mendoza had founded the first colony in Buenos Ayres, and had for months unsuccessfully endeavoured to secure the conditions essential to its continuance, he became discouraged and gave up the attempt. The men, however, whom he had left to carry on the undertaking, understood what was needed in order to vitalise the colony. Ayolas, the first of his deputies, resolutely forsook the low ground down stream, and founded the town of Asuncion, more than a hundred miles higher up, at the confluence of the Pilcomayo and the Paraguay, and it became the centre of the gradually developed province. He himself lost his life in the endeavour to extend his explorations farther to the west; but his worthy successor, Domingo de Irala, again took up his plans, and Francisco de Rojas' comrades found traces of his journeys near the Tercero. On a subsequent expedition he advanced from the upper Paraguay, through the territory of the Chiquitos, as far as the regions which had been colonised from Peru; and though he had again to return thence in obedience to an order from Gasca, the establishment of Santa Cruz de la Sierra as an intermediate station for trade communication between the Atlantic Ocean and Peru is the result of his achievements.

---

[1] See *ante*, pp. 304, 313.

Only one other incident in the earlier history of the colony of La Plata is of importance in connection with the exploration of the South American continent, and this was the arrival there of Alvar Nuñez Cabeza de Vaca, in 1540, to take up the governorship of the province in succession to Pedro de Mendoza. It seemed to him to be an unnecessarily circuitous route to sail first to the south as far as the mouth of the La Plata, and then again up the river; so he landed with most of his four hundred followers opposite the island Santa Caterina, and pushed on from there in a westerly direction through the wooded lowlands as far as Asunçion. It was only due to specially favourable circumstances that the march was accomplished at all, for both he and his followers had to pass through untold struggles and privations, and had, except for the opening up of the country, achieved no results. Some years later, when the colonists compelled him to resign his office in favour of Irala and return to Spain, he involuntarily discovered the easier approach by way of Buenos Ayres.

The colony of Asunçion — or Paraguay, as it is more familiarly called — occupied a special position among all the Spanish provinces, because there the Spaniards' relation to the natives developed most unusually. The Spaniards had, from the commencement, been accorded a friendly reception by the Guaranis about Asunçion, and as these terms continued in the future the consequence was that there, more than elsewhere, they married the daughters of the natives. The colonists everywhere made the Indian girls their concubines, especially before the influx of European women had increased. Actual marriages, also, often took place between the various races, more especially with the wives and daughters of the caciques, and resulted in an increase in the number of half-castes. In Paraguay the difficulty the Spaniards had in communicating with their native country, together with exceptionally friendly relations with the natives, combined to produce conditions especially favourable to the crossing of races. An endeavour has been made, even to this day, to trace the results of these conditions in the peculiar characteristics of the inhabitants of the province and subsequent republic of Paraguay. Just as the La Plata and the Paraguay had in the south suggested to the Spaniards the way from the coast to Peru, so, in like manner, another of the great rivers led them, almost against their will, farther to the north from Peru to the sea. During the few years of peace which succeeded the downfall of Francisco Pizarro, his younger brother, Gonzalo, to whom had fallen the governorship of Quito in the place of Benalcazar, undertook an expedition. The rumours of a wealthy kingdom in the depths of the continent decided its destination, and gave rise to a whole series of adventurous expeditions far into the interior, part of which has not even to this day again been thoroughly explored. If the crest of the Cordilleras through one of the passes from Quito is crossed in an easterly direction, it is quite evident that one must come upon one or other of the rivers which flow to the Rio Napo, and then with it to the Amazon. Later on, in the time when the missions instituted by various clerical orders in the regions of the upper Amazon called forth a noble spirit of emulation for the conversion and domiciliation of the natives, the road to Quito over the Embarcadero de Napo became a much-frequented highway. Almost a hundred years previously, when Gonzalo Pizarro led the first Spaniards by this road, they naturally, also, met with only the ordinary fate of all explorers, — weariness, hunger, and sickness; so that Gonzalo, in order to facilitate the departure of his band, decided on placing the sick and weak, with the baggage, on rafts, and, with the stronger, to follow along the banks of the river. Often, when the provisioning became more and more difficult, he sent the vessels far in advance, so that they might send or bring back food for those following by land. In doing this, however, the track was once lost just where the raft had been carried on especially far ahead, before known regions had been reached, and Gonzalo and his followers were obliged to turn back without being able to communicate with the others. Gonzalo had appointed Francisco de Orellana [1] pilot of the raft. When the latter realised that he had been abandoned, and saw the impossibility of taking his raft back against the current, he formed the daring resolve to drift along with it, knowing that it would finally bring him to the sea somewhere or other. Thus, with only fifty companions on rafts which they had had to construct themselves, he drifted down the Napo into the Amazon, and then not only on to the ocean, but also some distance along the coast to the north, until, after a water journey of seven months, he reached the first European settlement on the island of Cubagua. In spite of many battles he lost only a few of his followers, and not many other conquistadors have had to endure greater sufferings than they endured, or had to contend with such dangers as they overcame.

This same expedition from Peru was again undertaken in the sixteenth century. In the year 1559 the Marquis of Cañete, then vice-regent of Peru, after hearing the accounts of an Indian who had come from Brazil to Peru, out of the Marañon and Huallaga, and was supposed to have discovered inhabited and wealthy towns on the way, organised a voyage of exploration under the leadership of Pedro de Orsua. This expedition also gave him an opportunity of getting rid of numerous unruly spirits who, since the various risings, had threatened the security of the province. These malcontents, however, gave quite an unexpected turn to the undertaking. As soon as they had advanced far enough into the unknown district to be secure from pursuit, they murdered Orsua and completed the voyage up the river under the leadership of Lope de Aguirre, whom they had themselves chosen. Upon this they turned to Venezuela, and, after tyrannising over the province for months, they were at length overpowered in a battle near Barquisimeto, and the greater part of them were slain. The Amazon first became a permanent public road after the Portuguese had, in 1641, advanced with a great expedition from Para as far as Quito.[2] This was the beginning of the methodical exploration of the mighty river system in detail, which came to an end when the Indians became extinct and the missionary activity on their behalf had consequently terminated.

### *E.* THE ISSUES OF THE EXPLORATION PERIOD

THE northeastern portion of South America had at length become not quite an unknown region. Although Columbus had there first come in touch with the American continent, and almost the oldest attempts at colonisation on the continent itself had also been made on the northern coast, it had for a considerable time remained comparatively neglected, because it held out no prospect of unusual wealth and the natives were more warlike there than elsewhere. It was the tribes of the Caribbees belonging to this coast who had greeted the first Spaniards with poisoned arrows, and then vanished into the dense forests of the interior, in order

---

[1] See the maps, *post,* p. 514.  [2] See *ante,* p. 191.

to conquer by passive resistance the opponent whom they were not prepared to meet in open battle. Their name was so terrible to the Spaniards that it became the typical designation of all warlike and hostile races, and in its altered form, "cannibals," has become synonymous all over the world with "man-eater."[1] A considerable number of attempts at colonisation in the territory between the mouths of the Orinoco and of the river Magdalena were entirely frustrated before the Spaniards succeeded in gaining a footing in the region of the coast. However, this territory only played an important part in Spanish colonial affairs when, owing to the rapid decline of the population on the islands of the Antilles, it became, on a large scale, the hunting-ground for slaves, while the island of Cubagua, on the coast, served as the principal market-place for the spoil. Not until the first twenty years of the sixteenth century did Rodrigo de Bastidas succeed in founding a settlement in Santa Marta which promised to result in a permanent usurpation of the country. But it is possible that upon his violent death it, too, might again have been lost had it not received support from the neighbouring province, which the first Spaniards had already named Venezuela (Little Venice), after its native lake-dwellings on Lake Maracaibo.

The great German merchants had taken part in almost the first voyages of exploration to the West Indies as well as to the East Indies, and the accession of Charles V in Spain enabled them to secure for themselves an important and permanent share in colonial trade. Besides these mercantile agents, numbers of adventurous young Germans had also gone there, many of them passing through almost all the phases of discovery of the Conquista. It is small wonder, therefore, that two Germans once sued for and gained a concession for colonial discoveries. The Ehingers were closely connected with the House of Wels, whom many members of the family had served. When, therefore, they received from Charles V the right to colonise the interior from Cape Maracapana as far as the extreme end of the Guajiro peninsula, from one ocean to the other, they undoubtedly counted with certainty on the help of the Welses, and some years later they transferred their prerogative to them. The Germans did only the pioneer work in colonising Venezuela, and helped forward the development of this province by the Spaniards. This establishment of a colony was of peculiar importance in connection with the opening up of the unknown interior of South America, as it, in the first place, prevented the complete destruction of the colony founded by Bastidas in Santa Marta, and thereby formed the basis of the successful expedition of Gonzalo Jimenez de Quesada up the river Magdalena, besides becoming itself the starting-point of a succession of voyages of discovery. Almost simultaneously with Quesada and Benalcazar, Federmann led an expedition on to the plateau of Bogotá, while George Hohermuth and Philip von Hutten started along the eastern foot of the Andes; and, although they did not, as has often been asserted, advance as far as the river Amazon, they were the first Europeans who came upon its mighty northern tributaries, the Caquetá and probably also the Putumayo.

The rumour of the existence of another country rich in gold was still maintained after the conquest of Peru, and the accounts of the natives pointed to the northern regions beyond the Inca kingdom. Ambrosius Ehinger (whom the Spaniards called Dalfinger) had already explored the valley of Upare and along the Magdalena on the strength of these rumours, and had almost reached the boundary of the

---

[1] See *ante*, p. 193.

Chibcha kingdom when he decided to return. His successors, starting from the eastern Llanos, sought in vain for the entrance to the land of gold. George Hohermuth reached the entrance to the territory of the Chibchas while he was resting in San Juan de los Llanos, which region carried on a continuous trade with the Chibchas. Nicolas Federmann was the first to discover the pass from Llanos across the Cordilleras, but on setting foot in the country of the Bacatá he found the kingdom overthrown and in the possession of the Spanish victors.

The fortunate conqueror of this province, which, under the name of Nuevo Reino de Granada, became the pearl in the crown of Spanish colonial possessions, was Gonzalo Jiminez de Quesada. He had come to Santa Marta in the year 1536 with the governor, Pedro Fernandez de Lugo, and was by him immediately afterward deputed, with several hundred followers and three small vessels, to explore the river Magdalena up stream, and to advance upon the powerful ruler who, according to the stories of the natives, dwelt there. Near the river itself Quesada only met with the same fortunes as his predecessors, who, after many hardships, had discovered single Indian villages which were, no doubt, occasionally rich in spoils. The winter floods at length compelled him to leave the valley and ascend to the mountains. After he had with much toil advanced through the Sierra de Oppon, he came almost by chance upon the country of the Chibchas, in the neighbourhood of the subsequent Velez, for since he had quitted the river he could find no intelligible guide.

The resistance which the Spaniards met with from the rulers of the States and provinces of the Chibchas, who were divided among themselves by all kinds of rivalries, did not prove serious, and during three years Quesada gained almost fabulous treasures with comparatively small loss. He had just organised the newly acquired province and was on the eve of departure, when, within a few weeks of each other, Nicolas Federmann from the east, and Sebastian de Benalcazar from the south, appeared upon the scene. How the former arrived there has already been referred to.[1] Benalcazar had, as is well known, at first taken possession of the kingdom of Quito on behalf of Pizarro, and later on he was induced, by the same rumours which had guided the other two conquistadors, to undertake a voyage on his own account. His advance was slow and systematic; he had already founded a new Spanish settlement in Popayan and hoped to unite it with the territory of Chibcha; but he found it already in other hands and so well organised that he dared not make the attempt to take possession of it by force. However, neither he nor Federmann was prepared to resume the former conditions of dependence; consequently they were easily persuaded by Quesada to return with him to Spain, in order to leave to the Crown the decision as to the reward they should receive for their respective services. None of the three attained the object which they had mutually desired, — the regency of the rich province of Chibcha; Federmann brought up in prison, a fate he well merited owing to the perfidy which he had shown on all sides. Benalcazar had to be satisfied with the governorship of Popayan, to which was added the territory to the west of the Magdalena. Quesada did not reap the fruit of his conquests either, for he had to relinquish the governorship of Santa Marta and New Granada in favour of the unworthy son of Lugo, who in the meanwhile had died. After many years spent in legal proceedings he

[1] See ante, p. 378.

returned to the scene of his early conquests with the title of marshal, and died there, at a great age. after many adventures.

Although with the conquest of the Chibcha kingdom the land had come into the possession of the Spaniards, in whose " Institutions " the legend of the " Golden Man " (" El Dorado "[1]) originated, yet the voyages in search of the Dorado were never pursued with greater zeal than during the next following decades. Philip von Hutten. Hernan Perez de Quesada, brother of the conqueror of Chibcha, and finally the latter himself. sought for the Dorado in Llanos des Caquetá and Putumayo; but after an enormous loss of life they came in contact with only a few half-civilised Indian races. In consequence of this the kingdom of the Dorado was transferred to a lake of Manoa, which was sought for between the lower reaches of the Orinoco and the Marañon. On this occasion Quesada's son-in-law undoubtedly for the first time threw light on the river system of the Orinoco from New Granada as far as its estuary (during the sixteenth and seventeenth centuries the Guaviare was universally regarded as the river source of the Orinoco). In Trinidad he fell into the hands of Raleigh, who had recommenced his journey to the land of gold from the mouth of the Orinoco toward the Andes, and who, by his account of the expedition, has assisted more than his predecessors to spread abroad in Europe an idea of the geographical configuration of these regions. As a matter of fact, however, his whole expedition was only through a region which had long since been explored by the Spaniards. The hope of finding the Dorado was gradually abandoned, for in the vast colonial territory owned by the Spaniards there was no space left for it. Love of exploration could no longer find an outlet for its activity, and it was succeeded by the serious and difficult task of organising the extremely vast regions which had at least become known, if only superficially. The time of the " Conquista " was over, the period of the " Coloniaje," or colonial administration, had begun.

## 5. THE COLONIAL KINGDOM OF SPAIN

### A. The Casa de Contratacion

According to the interpretation which Columbus believed he might put upon his prerogatives, the whole of the vast colonial kingdom of Spain in America should have constituted a great empire over which he (and his descendants) should exercise almost unlimited authority as hereditary vice-regent, governor, and admiral, united in one person; while the Crown in the meanwhile should possess in the right of suzerainty only a limited influence in the appointment of officials and a certain share of the revenue. Not only was this view held by the explorer, but his descendants also, in a lawsuit against the Crown, upheld the claim that the documentary concessions extended not only to islands and lands which had become known through the personal activity of Columbus, but also to all land which, during subsequent transatlantic voyages of discovery undertaken by the first admiral, should become the possession of the Spanish Crown. The lawsuit terminated in a very simple manner, for the descendants of Columbus proved so utterly unfit for the duties imposed upon them by their claims,

---

[1] See *ante*, p. 290

that they finally themselves renounced their acknowledged documentary rights, because they had by vulgar debauchery incurred punishment at the hand of justice and had consequently fled. Apart from this, the point of law which was at issue proved by no means a simple one, for Columbus, on his part, had failed in more than one direction to fulfil the conditions of the treaty of Santa Fé. He had neither gained the object which had formed the aim of the entire undertaking, nor had he been able, or even shown a serious desire, to discharge the financial obligations which had been imposed upon him by the negotiations of 1492. Though he willingly left the equipment of the expeditions to the government, he would nevertheless not give up all claim to the share in the profits which had been assigned to him only as compensation for his proportionate share in the expenditure.

Within a very short time the question was transferred from the footing of a theoretical and legal debate to purely practical jurisdiction. The prospect which lay in store for the colonies under the government of Columbus, between the second and third voyages of the explorer, had already become evident. The colonial method which had been adopted by the Portuguese on the coast of Guinea appeared to the first admiral as the only feasible model: with this one exception, however, that he wished to be lessee of the general monopoly in the West Indies; that is to say, he desired to occupy the position which the Infante Henry had filled before his rights had receded to the Crown. But he was entirely wanting in that keen spirit of enthusiasm which induced the Infante, for many years, to make one sacrifice after another for the discovery of new countries and for the extension of Christendom; moreover his one object was, in a mean-spirited way, not to miss any possible gain for himself. For this reason he would not permit the settlers of San Domingo to spread themselves over the continent, and then, at their own risk, to undertake the search for precious ores and other trade commodities. He feared that by such means a portion of the spoil would escape his control and diminish his share in the profits. For the same reason, also, when sufficiently large quantities of other staple trade commodities were not procurable, he did not hesitate to freight his ships with stolen natives, in order to sell them to the mother country, after the example of the Portuguese. Not even the humane laws of the Spanish government had power to prevent the rapid extinction of the native population in the Antilles, and it is obvious that a similar result would have been the immediate and inevitable consequence of Columbus's ideas on colonisation. The first attempt at a slave trade with Spain had already been checked by the categorical inhibition of Ferdinand and Isabella, and as Columbus was incapable of maintaining order in his only settlement, this afforded the government an opportunity for a breach with his entire colonial system. He requested the assistance of an officer of the Crown to re-establish order,[1] and the subsequent investigation clearly showed how impossible it would have been to entrust the government of the entire territory to the explorer, although he claimed it as his prerogative.

The government of Ferdinand and Isabella had evidently originally planned a colonial undertaking according to the Portuguese model, and Columbus's expedition had given rise to the expectation that the discovery of flourishing and well-organised States would result in Spain's carrying on an extensive and

---

[1] See *ante*, p. 356.

successful trade with them. The real object of Columbus's expedition was not
so much to acquire territory as to divert the costly and much sought after products
of the Far East from the existing trade routes, and to establish the monopoly of
the Spanish harbours. The extension of Christianity in these far-off realms was
doubtless a second object. The Spaniard, who had for centuries carried on a
dreadful war upon the soil of his native land for the extension of Christianity
among unbelievers, without doubt did not shrink from pursuing the same object
by identical means in far-distant lands. If Columbus had really reached the
harbours of Zaitun and Quinsay, with their treasures, their trade, and their organisation, most probably Spanish rule would have been established there in the
same manner in which the Portuguese ruled in the East Indies. In this way
the first "Institution" established by the Spanish rulers for the benefit of colonial
affairs — the "Casa de Contratacion," or the "House for Commerce," intended
primarily for all commercial undertakings — was, in essentials, a copy of the
"Casa da India" at Lisbon.

The Casa de Contratacion was, on its foundation in 1503, intended to watch
over the interests of the Crown in colonial matters, more especially over commercial intercourse with the colonies. At that time the administrative powers
were, according to the contracts of 1492, almost exclusively in the hands of
Columbus, and the establishment of the "Casa de Contratacion" is sufficient
evidence that the government in no way aimed at disputing these prerogatives,
although Columbus had then already been suspended from the absolute power of
exercising them, and a governor had been nominated by the administration. But
the foundation of numerous settlements over the whole of Española and on the
neighbouring islands, and the subdivision of the land among the colonists, as
well as the advance into the interior of the island, portended a breach with
Columbus's colonial system, for his plan had been to draw the mercantile profits
of the land only from permanent ports on the coasts. The Crown's second decree
for the Casa de Contratacion already showed an altered face, though mercantile
interests still occupied the foreground. The realisation of the profits which the
government anticipated from direct participation in the colonial trade is therein
less prominently dealt with, and it now becomes more a question of the ordering
and control of navigation and mercantile intercourse between the mother country
and the colonies generally, whether carried on at the expense of the Crown or by
the private individual. As the Casa de Contratacion developed into a court of
administration, direct and judicial powers accrued to it. At least one lawyer is
referred to in the regulations of 1511, besides the manager, treasurer, and book-
keeper, as being in its employ. The control of the correspondence, which was
transferred to the Casa, formed the most important extension of power which
was accorded during that year, and laid the foundation for its future significance.
Not only all the letters which arrived for the government from the colonies had
to be opened and read, but all the government deeds intended for the colonies
had also to be registered in the books of the Institution, the officials even receiving orders to enter protests against such governmental instructions as seemed to
them injudicious or risky and to suspend their execution. By reason of these
powers the Casa de Contratacion became more and more a board of administration.
The qualifications necessary for such a board were in later years also specially
assigned to it: in less important matters the decision of the Casa was regarded

as final, whereas upon greater and more important questions the Consejo de Indias could be referred to as a superior court.

In spite of the far-reaching prerogatives which had, according to agreement, been assigned to Columbus as vice-regent, governor, and admiral of the Indies, colonial affairs, from the commencement, required extensive supervision and guidance on the part of the government. These increased considerably in importance from the moment when Columbus was suspended from the full enjoyment of his authoritative powers, and when a crown official was appointed in the interim to act for him provisionally. Ferdinand the Catholic, in order to secure the necessary uniformity and continuity of the colonial policy, had then already transferred the business connected with these powers to one distinct person. The Archbishop Fonseca was the authority on colonial affairs in the Privy Council; Secretary Gricio first acted as Under-Secretary, but after a short time he was succeeded by Lope de Conchillos, then already known for his unfortunate share in the quarrel about the succession between Ferdinand the Catholic and Philip the Handsome.

During the years 1509 to 1512 Don Diego Colon was reinstalled in the prerogatives of his father, but only to a limited extent.[1] The division of the continually expanding colonial kingdom was then already in prospect, by which division only those countries which had been won for Spain by the direct invasion of the first admiral were ceded to his descendants under the conditions of the treaty of Santa Fé. Even so these prerogatives were not granted without limitations, though the heirs were permitted to retain, as had been stipulated, the power to exercise jurisdiction, in the first instance, throughout the entire range of the country assigned to them. On the other hand, in 1511, by the establishment of the "Audiencia" of San Domingo, a court of appeal was instituted more especially for the entire colonial department, where appeals could be made against the decisions of the vice-regal courts of justice. The court was authorised to give judgment directly in the king's name, and it could eventually even summon the vice-regent himself before its bar. Owing to the fact that in all departments of national life, government and the administration of justice had not as yet become detached from each other, each magistrate not only pronouncing judgment but also executing it throughout the circuit of his authority, the Audiencia, in its capacity as a court of appeal for the legal settlement of all kinds of colonial affairs, became an important factor in colonial administration. This importance grew in proportion as the government recognised the necessity of creating a counterpoise to the vast prerogatives of the vice-regent and governor, and of constituting an authority in touch with the governor, by which to control him, and act under the immediate direction of the government in the colonial territories which were not administered according to the treaty of Santa Fé.

The government provided itself with another influence in the clergy. At first priests belonging to a religious order were almost exclusively sent to the islands to watch over religious interests and promote missionary work among the natives. Almost immediately upon their advent conflicts arose between them and the temporal authorities. Fray Bernal Boil, who had accompanied Columbus on his second voyage as Vicar-General, had, like the latter, soon to be recalled, because he became too argumentative in defending his own version of his official duties against

[1] See ante, p. 360.

the officials. As soon as the government had convinced itself of the vast extent of the newly acquired possessions it also became seriously concerned about the organisation of religious matters. At Ferdinand's suggestion Pope Alexander VI, in the year 1512, founded the first two bishoprics in San Domingo and La Vega on the island of Española. Almost immediately upon the definite settlement the erection of new dioceses ensued, and soon an extensive network of archbishoprics, bishoprics, and parochial dioceses was spread over the whole colonial territory. The possibility arising, however, that the church, not being a state within a state, might become dangerous to the power of the government, care was taken that the Crown should receive in 1508, from the Pope himself, the right of presentation to all benefices in the New World, in order to make the clergy of the colonies entirely dependent on the government, so that they even became a strong and influential support in all the vicissitudes of colonial events.

When, therefore, in the year 1516 Charles V inherited from his grandfather the extensive colonial possessions with the Spanish Crown lands, he found the colonial government under safe guidance; indeed one might almost say that the government had already begun to shape for itself a system for its colonial policy. As the discovery of America had been due exclusively to the initiative of Queen Isabella, the colonies, by political law, formed an integral and constituent part of the Crown of Castile. In the idea of a colony the sixteenth century held the conception of a country that was almost exclusively the private property of the Crown, at least so far as the possession of all privileges was concerned. The Spanish government, therefore, after the abolition of the prerogatives belonging to the Colons, regarded the colonies as a domain whose revenue should accrue exclusively to it and be employed at its discretion. One consequence of this idea was that the government issued strict regulations for admission to the colonies. In order seriously to control the execution of this decision, the entire intercourse between the mother country and the colonies was confined to the town of Seville, with the outer harbour of San Lucar de Barrameda. The disadvantages for trade which were the natural consequence of this monopoly by Seville soon became evident. During the first years of Charles V's reign an especially vigorous agitation arose, no doubt as a consequence of the union of the Spanish kingdom with the German and Dutch territories under one and the same sceptre; and this was the means of procuring a considerable mitigation of the system, if not an advance in the participation also of these nations in the transatlantic trade. For a time this counter-current was successful, and it probably gave rise to a hope for still greater success hereafter; but the fiscal interests finally conquered, and Seville's monopoly of the entire colonial trade was rigorously maintained for a considerable time.

### B. The Native Question

The fiscal and monopoly system, though characteristic, does not exclusively distinguish Spanish colonial policy, but it has, as in the case of the other States which have recognised it, left its special marks. But the most remarkable feature of the Spanish policy is its attitude toward the aborigines of the colonies. Columbus also considered the natives from the Portuguese point of view; that is to say, he regarded them either as a power with whom war could be waged and a treaty concluded; or as a commodity, like other colonial products, to be bought or sold, according to the requirements of commercial interests. In any case the natives were, from this point of view, either foreign persons or foreign things. As a result, Columbus, on his third voyage, endeavoured to cover his unsuccessful search for gold, spices, and other costly wares, by freighting the home-sailing vessel with a cargo of slaves, to be sold in Seville. But in this he met with opposition from the Spanish government, and more especially from Queen Isabella of Castile, as sovereign of the colonial kingdom. Immediately upon the news of the arrival of the living cargo, the officials in Seville received an order to stop the sale and to wait for a decision as to whether the slavery of the Indians was permissible according to the laws, humane and divine. It was followed by an order that the Indians should be taken back to their native country and set at liberty. This was a decision on the highest principles and of the widest scope, and it inaugurated a colonial policy such as had up to that time nowhere been attempted. It is extremely probable that King Ferdinand, a politician of temperate views, who by no means regarded the whole colonial enterprise of his consort and co-regent with favor, would have decided differently had his own view of the matter served as a standard. One is strengthened in this belief by the insistence with which Queen Isabella, in her will and its codicil, urges upon her husband the protection of the natives. This codicil is the next significant step in the legislation of the native question. Although short and concise, its statements regarding the natives are so far of great importance that the latter are therein recognised as subjects of equal birth, and their lives and property are under the protection of the Crown; and it is especially urged upon King Ferdinand, as executor, to repress and make compensation for any possible injustice which the natives might have to suffer. The practical treatment of this question did not, it is true, quite attain the high level of the theoretical decision. The declaration that the Indians were to enjoy the privileges of free subjects provoked opposition not only from the colonists, but also from the colonial officials and even from the clergy. It was impossible to form any conception of the revenues and produce of the colonies without having sufficient working material in the shape of native labour. Without a certain amount of compulsion, however, the native could not be induced, either to perform a sufficient amount of work to meet the requirements of the colonies, or to remain on a permanently friendly footing with the settler yet this was indispensable if the civilising influence and more especially the conversion of the natives to Christianity, which had from the commencement of the history of discoveries been so strongly emphasised, were to be carried on with success. For this reason both the temporal and spiritual authorities were unanimous in declaring that the granting of unlimited freedom to the natives would mean the ruin of the colonies, from both a spiritual and an economic point of view. The "Repartimientos" and "Encomiendas" were finally the result of the negotiations which were carried on with regard to these matters. The personal liberty of the native was therein specially recognised, but in order to promote their education by European methods of civilisation and to secure their conversion to the Christian doctrine, they were assigned ("repartir") to the charge of individual colonists and placed under their protection ("encomendar"). The latter thereby acquired a certain measure of patriarchal authority over their protégés which, according to the letter of the law, was most humanely designed, though in reality it created for the native almost

everywhere a sure state of bondage; and this bondage, along with the simultaneous existence of Indian slavery, often made the well-meaning designs of the
lawgivers entirely illusory for certain classes of the natives.

The law required certain moral guarantees from the holder of a Repartimiento,
and on the other hand quite definitely fixed the maximum of work to be done
by the natives. The governors of the various colonial districts, and, above all, of
those territories which had been newly discovered and had yet to be colonised,
could not, however, under the pressure of the actual circumstances, evade the
claims made upon them to reward (by the bestowal of the Repartimiento) the
services of the colonists who had first taken possession of the country. During
the voyages of discovery and conquest it was not generally men of specially high
morality who gained the highest honours for their comrades and their country.
As these expeditions made such great demands upon the participators, as to both
daring and powers of endurance, naturally these characteristics preponderated
among the recruits who had nothing to lose and everything to gain. It is only
natural that any one who had so schooled himself as to face famine and death at
the hand of the enemy for months should not be particularly disposed to treat with
lenience and consideration the lives of beings whom he was easily induced to
regard as creatures of an inferior order, creatures who could be brought to a peaceful state of subjection to the European yoke only after cruel and devastating wars.
Even with the best intentions of the favourably disposed governors, it was almost
impossible to carry through a conscientious administration of the laws of the
Encomiendas. In the districts which were but sparsely populated by Europeans
these rough settlers, who could hardly be dispensed with for the extension of the
Spanish power, in numerous instances mutinied against the officials when the
latter, in pursuance of the law, endeavoured to seize what the former looked on as
the well-earned wage of their own superhuman exertions and privations. More
than one governor was killed by his unruly followers, owing to his efforts to
enforce respect for the law concerning the Encomiendas.

That great evils existed in the treatment of the natives in the extensive regions
of the "Conquista" is certainly undeniable, although it is also incontestable that
the horrors of the Indian oppression have been extremely exaggerated by the
agitators for the rights of humanity, among whom Bishop Bartolomé de las Casas
occupies a prominent place. The Indians were undoubtedly often overburdened
by toil, and thousands of them succumbed; yet, from the point of view of self-
interest, it was of great importance to the colonists that those peoples under their
protection should be preserved, so that unscrupulous exploitation cannot therefore
be taken as the universal rule. The native population on the first discovered and
colonised Antilles diminished with extraordinary rapidity; but no doubt this was
brought about by many different causes. In the first instance their number had
been, on the whole, considerably overrated. Columbus made a point of doing this
in order to enhance the value of his discovery, and the vehement agitation for the
freedom of the Indians, which had already begun twenty years after the discovery,
did still more to falsify ideas as to the number of the natives. If one remembers
that the Antilles were only gradually populated by the Aruac race from the continent, and that this race of fishermen and hunters has nowhere else founded larger
or more densely populated settlements; and if one also bears in mind that this
race had for generations to suffer from a war of extermination with the dreaded

native pirates, the Caribs,[1] — a dense population on the Antilles at the time of their discovery would be an impossible assumption. The natives, however, soon realised that the newly arrived Spaniards would prove far more dangerous enemies than the Caribs had been. For this reason many of them fled from their villages into the jungle, where they suffered great loss among themselves and in war with the Christians. To these factors were further added those of unaccustomed kinds of labour, a change of food and manner of life, and finally maladies which had been imported by the Europeans and became epidemic among the natives, causing fearful devastation. The combination of all these influences must alone be held responsible for the depopulation of the Antilles.

This depopulation in one sense became of importance to the entire native question, as it led to a rupture with the general principle of the universal liberty of the Indians. In 1505 Ferdinand the Catholic had already allowed the natives who by arms might oppose civilisation and Christianity to be attacked and enslaved. Possibly this permission may in the first instance have been aimed at the Caribbean races, but the more apparent the retrogression of the native population became (when the larger islands grew to be more densely populated by Europeans), the more was this license employed as a cloak for the concealment of an extensive Indian slave-trade. Nothing was easier than by a defiant bearing to provoke the natives to take up arms so that without a violation of the law they could be dragged away as slaves. By these means the smaller Antilles, on which no Spanish settlements had been established, became within a short time entirely depopulated. But natives who had been exported to the larger islands as slaves, and there branded on the thighs with hot irons (a curious consequence of a law designed to be humanitarian) in order to prevent their exchange with peaceable Indians, were soon, also, no longer able to supply the ever-increasing demand for labourers and to replenish their own reduced numbers. The slave-hunts were then extended to the continent and more especially to the northern coast of South America, whose inhabitants, of kindred origin with the island population, showed an unusually violent and lasting opposition to the first attempts at colonisation.

At this stage the doings of the slave-hunters assumed such proportions that they gave rise to the first movements of opposition, and these soon became of great power, as points of view were brought to bear upon the question which had nothing actually to do with the matter itself. The clergy of the colonies, as has already been mentioned,[2] had at first not considered themselves in the least obliged to interfere on behalf of unlimited liberty for the Indians. Not only the secular priests, but also the Franciscans, who since the days of Columbus (when he also had belonged to the order as a lay brother) had played a prominent part in colonial administration, did not regard it as scandalous that the Indians were compelled by moderate pressure to join the Christians, or, in cases of resistance, were enslaved and treated as enemies. The Dominicans maintained a different attitude. The antithesis between the two points of view also aroused the opposition of the one order against the other, and thus, no doubt, contributed not a little to the aggravation of the question. The first to venture to stigmatise from the pulpit, as a disgrace and outrage, the hitherto existing treatment of the natives, was the Dominican brother Pedro de Cordoba, who thereby soon became distinguished far beyond his own diocese of San Domingo, where he preached.

---

[1] See *ante*, p. 192.     [2] *Ante*, p. 391.

Bartolomé de las Casas, who at that time was himself a keeper of slaves in Cuba, was won over to his views. His impetuous spirit took up the cause of the natives with such zeal that he became one of the best known among the champions of native liberty. Las Casas presented himself at the Spanish court, for the first time, shortly before the death of Ferdinand the Catholic. Though his vivid descriptions of the horrors practised in the treatment of the natives were met by the public with mixed feelings, he was the means of bringing about the decision that a special commission should be sent out to hold an inquiry into the actual circumstances. The native question had by that time become such an object of contention between the Franciscans and Dominicans that both orders were, on principle, excluded from election to the Commission; but as the question was intended to be treated as a matter of conscience, and had for this reason been placed in the hands of the clergy, it was finally agreed that three Hieronymite monks should be chosen and sent to the islands with discretionary powers.

Las Casas vehemently impugned the impartiality of the three fathers because they refused to take his point of view, but he certainly wronged them. As a universal remedy he proposed the formation of self-governed and self-administered communities of Indians, to which only the clergy from among the Spaniards should be admitted as leaders in religious matters, and this was also attempted by the Hieronymites. Las Casas, a few years later, failed to colonise, on the same plan, a tract of the Paria coast, far removed from intercourse with the white man; and the Hieronymites, contending against still more unfavourable conditions, were equally unsuccessful in their attempt to colonise San Domingo. No doubt, however, the fact of their being sent greatly increased the opposition of the religious orders among themselves, so that the government was forced at last to take the matter entirely out of the hands of the clergy and entrust it to a secular official. The licentiate Rodrigo de Figueroa kept quite aloof from all theoretical points of view and regulated the native question solely from the standpoint of the hitherto formulated laws on that point. These guaranteed a certain amount of liberty to the peaceable Indians, but permitted the enslavement of the hostile ones. In order to do this he first of all had to settle which Indians were to be regarded as hostile. As he was guided by entirely disinterested and well-intentioned ideas, he considerably circumscribed the territory remaining to the slave-hunters. The improvement in the treatment of the Indians as a whole, in the Repartimientos, and Encomiendas, was the necessary consequence of the increased attention which was paid to the regulations bearing upon it. An economic revolution was, in addition to this, carried out about the same time, at any rate in the island colonies. In spite of all efforts to the contrary on the part of the government, the Spanish settlements had for a long time been little more than permanent trade factories; all valuable objects which could be got from the natives by barter were collected, and with native help precious ores were dug and washed. But whenever the government sent seeds and plants across the ocean, their cultivation was not a success, because the natives did not understand their treatment, and the colonists considered it beneath them to have anything to do in the matter. As therefore only a limited amount of the valuable products of the soil could be found, the exchange trade soon also collapsed, and though the new discoveries revived the carrying trade of San Domingo, it at the same time continuously withdrew the labourers from the island, thus diminishing its individual importance. The settlements suffered much in consequence until, by the cultivation of the sugar-cane, new and profitable livelihood was found for the colonists. Labourers were also required for this, and though the necessary work was not as irksome as gold-washing, it entailed a settled mode of life and continuous work for the colonists, whereas the other implied only an uncertain search for fortune.

The cultivation of sugar-cane had an important share in maintaining the vitality of the Spanish colonies up to the time when, through the great exten-sion of these colonies, further opportunities for gaining a livelihood arose. Besides this, it was also of immense importance in their development, because it gave the impulse to the importation of negro slaves. These had in isolated instances been imported in the service of their Spanish masters from the time of the discovery of America. It was not long before it became evident in the colonies that the negroes became acclimatised exceedingly well there, and far surpassed the Indian natives in their capacity for work. The government, however, did not regard the importa-tion of negroes with favour. It was feared that they, being but recently baptised, would be only half-hearted adherents of Christianity and might have a bad influ-ence upon the conversion of the Indians, so that on that account the African negroes were entirely excluded from the colonies, and the immigration of black house slaves was also restricted as much as possible. The repeated petitions of the colonists for a plentiful supply of black labourers disclosed to the government the importance of this matter, so that it gradually came to be regarded in quite another light when Las Casas, from motives of philanthropy, urgently recom-mended the introduction of negro slaves in order to rescue the Indians from slavery. Although on this point the government still maintained the principle of inhibition for negro importation, it was now only on account of fiscal interests. It is a fact that since 1516 about four thousand negroes alone were almost an-nually transported, by the agents of the slave monopoly, from the coast of Guinea to the New World,—exclusive of the considerable number who reached the col-onies by special license, and in later times through smuggling. No doubt the negroes, and the half-castes who had already sprung from the union of whites with blacks and Indians, constituted in the middle of the sixteenth century a very im-portant element in the agricultural population, and, as such, demanded special attention. These negroes had received, even less than the Indians, the merest semblance of a civilising education from the colonists, and, as they were by nature far less submissive, they were more inclined to forsake their masters and revert to the manners and customs of their native life in the jungle. In 1550 the Spaniards had already to suppress dangerous insurrections of the negro population. These again recurred from time to time, until, after a successful insurrection in the year 1808, the negroes even succeeded in founding an independent State on the western half of the island of San Domingo in the republic of Haiti.

The mixing of races was of comparatively less importance in Spanish America. In most of the colonies during the first years savage marriages with the native women were no doubt the rule, so long as European women did not go there or could not, under the circumstances, be imported ; and wherever this continued, as was the case in Paraguay, it naturally resulted in a greater mixing of the races.[1] In Mexico and Peru, as well as also in Bogotá, the marriages of Spanish conquis-tadors with women of the native nobility were more often made from political

---

[1] See *ante*, p 382.

considerations, and the Spanish kings acknowledged this aristocracy by giving it an equal standing with the Spanish nobility. On the whole, however, the Spaniards in the colonies guard the purity of their blood with no less care than in the mother country, and the creoles unto this day regard it as the highest distinction to be the descendants of grandfathers and great-grandfathers of pure Spanish blood. Although the colonists of European descent, on the one hand, felt themselves the living antithesis of the native races, yet, owing to changed conditions of life, an altered climate and different social circumstances, in course of time an indistinctly recognised but later on fully appreciated variation on the Spanish type was developed, the pure-bred Spaniards remaining in the colonies only temporarily as merchants, soldiers, and officials, and never losing the feeling of being aliens.

On his accession Charles V found the native question at its height, and for a time he let it run its course. The bitter paper war between Las Casas and Sepulveda about the admissibility of native slavery belongs to the first years of his reign, as well as the unsuccessful attempt at colonisation by the Dominican who had been elected patron of the Indians. The institution of a special advocate for the native also became general, and in every colony a spiritual chief pastor was then charged with the protection of the natives. The laws, also, for the treatment of the Indians were permanently altered and developed in a more decided recognition of their interests, until the Edict of Granada, of November 17, 1526, included in six paragraphs all the regulations bearing upon their treatment. The edict, however, still distinguished between two classes of Indians, friendly and savage, and permitted the enslavement of the latter, while special officials were charged with the decision of each individual case. From that time this law became the standard for the treatment of the natives, not only in all the colonies, but also in all the agreements concerning discoveries. It was nevertheless followed, in rather rapid succession, by further regulations in favour of the Indians. In 1530 Indian slavery was definitely abolished, after many disputes both for and against it. Undoubtedly the carrying out of these rules in the various provinces often created difficulties and was extended over a number of years, but the law remained intact and was finally carried out in force, in spite of the opposition of the colonists.

In the same way the government made several attempts to abolish the Encomiendas, but this regulation was never carried through for two reasons: first, because it threatened to be prejudicial to the material advantage of the colonist, and, second, because it hindered the advancement of the civilisation of the Indian. The government, therefore, confined itself to freeing the system of the Encomiendas more and more from all the imperfections which adhered to it, and to watching more and more carefully over its conscientious execution. The principle of promoting the social advancement of the Indians by a closer union with the Spaniards, and of granting to the conquistadors and their descendants, as a reward and recognition, the supervision of Indian wards, was adhered to. All the Indians were, however, by no means divided into Encomiendas. From the beginning the Crown had always retained certain portions both of the land and of the population of every province and district, which were destined for the service of the crown and not for the use of the individual colonist. Beyond this, the more the misuse of the Encomiendas was attacked, the more its extension became limited and its attainment more difficult, so that finally only those Indians who were in the immediate neighbourhood of the places founded at the time of the conquest remained under the protection of the colonists. The vast territories which had not been so densely populated by Europeans remained, as before, the free land of the Indians, whose conversion and civilisation were almost exclusively transferred to the religious societies and to the missionaries sent out by them.

## C. THE MISSION

THE merits of the Spanish clergy on Spanish territory can hardly be rated too highly. The mysticism of the Renaissance united with the enthusiasm for the natural conditions of human society which had arisen from Romanticism in casting the reproach upon the Spanish missionaries that they, with blind fanaticism, had annihilated the last remnants of sacred antiquity in the New World and had brought to the people of America only spiritual servitude instead of spiritual salvation. It had been purely an act of necessity for the missionaries and clergy in the provinces, where they were confronted by a well-developed system of religion and an influential hierarchy, to interfere radically and energetically with the inhuman customs which they frequently found to exist among the natives; as, for example, in Mexico. It can certainly not be disputed that in so doing they had occasionally destroyed objects of heathen adoration, which destruction has been deplored by modern ethnographical science. On the other hand it was just these clergy, and in many provinces only they, who considered it worth their while to investigate, collect, and record the language, customs, and traditions of the natives, so that modern science is indebted to them for the most copious and valuable material for philological and ethnological research. No doubt few of them were fully conscious of the services they were rendering to latter-day research, as they were more engrossed by their immediate aim, the civilisation and conversion of the Indians.

Wherever the temporal and spiritual governments were in line in their treatment of the natives, one naturally hears less of the successful activity of the monks; although the fact of the appearance of the Dominicans and of Las Casas, besides the existence of numerous isolated notes in the official records and in the secular and clerical chronicles, prove that their activity extended in the same measure into territories other than those in which they were more especially active. They have raised for themselves an immortal monument, more especially in the history of these latter parts. After the whole of the new continent had been superficially explored during the period of the conquest, Spanish colonial activity was, toward the close of the sixteenth century, concentrated on those regions whose agricultural development promised immediate advantages from a European point of view. But wide tracts of land, where it was assumed that, owing either to climatic, political, or trade reasons, no remunerative cultivation was possible, remained almost entirely untouched. The greater part of the South American continent to the east of the Cordilleras and to the north of the mouth of the river La Plata belonged to this rejected territory. In this vast district, through which the mighty Amazon, with its tributaries, the Paraguay and other tributaries of the La Plata, flowed, the work of cultivation and of introducing and maintaining European standards of civilisation was almost exclusively the work of missionaries. At first it was chiefly the Franciscans and Augustinians who, from the monasteries and colleges of the Peruvian highlands, undertook the conversion of the Indians living farther down stream and along the numerous rivers flowing from the Cordilleras toward the east. These spiritual fathers, with incomparable self-sacrifice and self-forgetfulness, wandered among the savage natives, often only gaining, after months and years of activity, the means for the closer understanding which laid the foundation for their material and religious labour of civilisation. Recognising that the wandering life of the Indians was extremely fatal to all enduring spiritual influence, and that to gather them together in fixed settlements was an essential condition of their progress in civilisation, the missionaries invariably aimed, first of all, at finding and pointing out to the Indian tribes whose conversion was in contemplation likely dwelling-places which would suit not only their propensities but also the requirements of civilisation. In doing this they intentionally avoided the proximity of European settlements, in spite of the laws which prohibited a prolonged sojourn in the Indian villages to Europeans in general. Moreover in quite early times they covered the upper and middle valleys of the tributaries of the Marañon, and during the seventeenth century the valleys of this river also, as well as of other great rivers of South America, with an enormous network of Indian villages and hamlets. The greater number of these fell into ruin in course of time, owing either to the retrogression of the native population, which became evident there also, or to the persecution which was afterward stirred up against the activity of the spiritual fathers. But they had laid the actual foundation for the advance of European civilisation throughout the entire territory.

The sphere and the character of the missions to the Indians of South America became most familiar through the Jesuits, who, in the second half of the sixteenth and the beginning of the seventeenth centuries, extended their missionary activity, which had been inaugurated by the devout Francis Xavier in the east, to the New World in the west. One must not, however, overlook the fact that the peculiar constitution of the so-called "Reductions" and "Missions" was neither invented by the Jesuits nor ever exclusively maintained by them. Its conception has been more especially attributed to their order because the Jesuit missions of Brazil and Paraguay have influenced the political history of the South American continent as no other order has done. The Jesuits, in concurrence with other religious associations, early commenced their activity as missionaries, if anything, in a greater degree perhaps in the Portuguese than in the Spanish territory. But they only assumed an exceptional position when, in the year 1608, a special district in Paraguay was assigned to them, free from all civil authority, where they were able to carry out the attempts at the civilisation and conversion of the Indians on a larger scale. There was no special motive attached to the fact that the government, in so doing, endowed them with an unusual amount of independence.

The Bull of Alexander VI with reference to the line of demarcation[1] had in principle established the boundaries of the Spanish and Portuguese colonial sphere, but its general and indefinite wording was quite inadequate for a really political demarcation. Both governments soon recognised this when the mouth of the river La Plata was discovered simultaneously by rival explorers. Several attempts at a diplomatic understanding were made in consequence of this, but, in point of fact, both Powers still attached far too little importance to the unexplored and unpromising territory whose possibilities seemed doubtful. With time these

---

[1] See *ante*, p. 359.

circumstances, however, assumed real importance, chiefly through the dissimilar colonial policy pursued by the two Powers in these border districts. Asuncion, on the Paraguay, was the chief of all the Spanish colonies where from the beginning the relations between the natives and the colonists had been especially friendly, and where the best spirit of Spanish legislation for the Indians found expression regardless of outward circumstances. Bonds of friendship were formed between the brave and honest Guarani [1] and the confederates of Irala which during the course of centuries were scarcely ever seriously doubted. The covenant with this mighty and widely dispersed Tupi tribe soon brought out the underlying contrast between the Spanish colonists and their eastern neighbours, the Portuguese. The powers of little Portugal were so entirely engrossed by East Indian politics that the Brazilian colonial territory was, scarcely ten years after its discovery by Cabral, given over entirely to private enterprise. In this way a number of small settlements were founded in the Bahia de Todos os Santos, at Cape St. Vincent, and on the island of St. Caterina in the bay of Rio de Janeiro. These were at first regarded as Portuguese colonies, but, besides the few actual Portuguese and Portuguese Jews in the colony, there were a number of "shady" characters, the subjects of every realm, who carried on trade of a very questionable character, and whose products were sent, not only to Lisbon, but also, if they succeeded in evading the customs, to French, English, and even Hanseatic harbours. While the foreign merchants dealt principally in brazil-wood, sugar, and similar colonial products, the Portuguese chiefly carried on a brisk trade in Indian slaves, whom they did not take so much to Lisbon as to the colonial harbours, irrespective of whether these natives belonged to Portuguese or to Spanish territory. As was the case everywhere else, the consequence of the slave-hunts was that the natives retired farther and farther from the coast. The slave-hunters, however, followed their prey into the interior by the most accessible paths, — that is, by the water ways; and thus they soon also came in conflict with the Guarani, and through them, indirectly, with the Spanish colonists.

In order to put an end to these lawless conditions, and to draw greater advantages from this colonial possession, the Portuguese government decided on a change in its colonial system. In the year 1531 a great part of Brazil was divided into so-called "capitanries," — vast tracts of land for which the rights of feudal lords, as in the Old World, were granted to the owners in return for an insignificant royalty payable to the Crown. This colonial system was also tried by the English in a part of northern America. The thirty-five capitanries which arose under this system had this advantage that they brought about actual attempts at settlements in many places, and in this way the first sugar-plantations, with their refineries, and the first farms, were established. On the whole, however, the system did not work satisfactorily. Many of the capitanries were relinquished by the owners: others dragged on a weary existence. Above all, the illegalities in the trade with foreign countries and the sorties of the slave-hunters still continued, even when a central authority had been established for the separate districts, and a vice-regent had been sent over to occupy the residence at Bahia.

The attempt at colonisation by the French Protestants under Villegaignon proves how little real authority the Portuguese had over their Brazilian possession. The French expedition was the result of the trade which had for a considerable

See *ante*, p. 190.

time been carried on illegally, yet unhindered, between Dieppe and the coast of Brazil. Those lovers of adventure who were anxious to emigrate imagined they could easily found a new home there, and annex a valuable portion of colonial territory for their mother country without difficulty. As a matter of fact they were in possession of the bay of Rio de Janeiro for almost five years. If internal disputes and altered political conditions at home had not come fortuitously to the aid of the Portuguese, a long time might have elapsed before the future capital of Brazil had once more become Portuguese property. The French, retiring more and more toward the north, repeatedly attempted to gain a footing on Brazilian soil, and for this purpose made most clever use of the policy which they had so successfully carried through on a larger scale in their settlements on the St. Lawrence. They allied themselves with the natives, not only to gain peace with them, but also that they might incite them against their colonial rivals. This policy was easy in Brazil, because, in the eyes of the Portuguese, the native continued to be a commodity to be employed to the best advantage.

The union of Portugal with Spain in the year 1580 was not to be without influence on colonial legislation, although the government of Portugal and its colonies remained entirely separate, in spite of the conquest by Philip II. Many laws were formulated which in principle tended toward the personal liberty of the Indians. They were, nevertheless, almost entirely without influence on the actual circumstances, for the colonists always managed so that their property in Indian slaves should remain judicially unassailed. The conditions for the native were improved only farther toward the interior, where even to this day the views held are very divergent.

The Jesuits, of whom the first came to Brazil in 1549, found an extended field of labour there. That they were at first less harassed by the slave-hunters in the northern provinces may be due to the fact that the latter were principally kept in the south owing to long-standing custom, as well as from the insecurity of the political boundaries and other circumstances. There they soon developed into a perfect scourge, not only to the Indians, but also to the Spanish colonies. The remarkable State creation of the missions of Paraguay originated when the Jesuits inaugurated their efforts in favour of the natives in the south also; about which, then and to this day, opinions have been so divided.

The Jesuits' object was to save the Guarani from the persecution of the Europeans. As they had, however, made the discovery that the colonists and colonial officials of Asuncion and Buenos Ayres frequently made common cause secretly with the Portuguese slave-traders for their own advantage, they did not remain satisfied, as they had done elsewhere, with going into the jungle and gathering the natives around them there, but they induced Philip III, who was ruler of Spain and Portugal simultaneously, to transfer to them a tract of land to the east of Paraguay as far as to the Uruguay.. Here they were permitted to do as they liked, almost without interference from either temporal or spiritual authority. Their efforts to bring the Indians of the surrounding regions under their benevolent control were immediately crowned with extraordinary success, for the inhabitants of their Reductions soon numbered more than a hundred thousand souls. It was not exclusively Guaranis who gained admission there, but, as the tribes belonged almost without exception to the Tupi race, the Jesuits had no difficulty in making Guarani the general language. They attempted and achieved this also n the north Brazilian missions. The "Kunstdialekt" Guarani which they developed is actually the *Lingua geral* which still is the universal language of the civilised natives of Brazil.[1] The social order which the Jesuits instituted in the mission districts made a more marked impression both on contemporaries and on posterity. That they, in so doing, acted from philosophical standpoints, and that they attempted to realise Campanella's "City of the Sun," are probably only surmises which were introduced subsequently. The models by which the Jesuits were inspired were of considerably greater consequence to them. The extensive landed property of the religious communities was, on the one hand, managed, if not generally, at any rate in isolated instances, directly by the brotherhood. But the model of the Inca Peruvian social organisation, with its renunciation of private property and its universal labour obligation, had an even greater influence in the development of the most important characteristics of the Jesuit community. The conception of personal property was then but very little developed among most of the uncivilised Indian tribes, and labour in common was the rule. It is therefore not surprising that the missionaries experienced no difficulty in instituting the same arrangements, for they offered the Indian a number of things besides, which he coveted and prized, but which, under previous forms of association, he had but seldom enjoyed; these were regular and plentiful food and continued protection from his fellow-savage as well as from his white enemies. The clergy followed the only sensible plan for the mission to the heathen by making civilisation the first step to conversion. The mental capacity of the savage is unable to grasp the higher matters of Christian dogmas, and the civilised Indian must often enough have formed very extraordinary conceptions of them; and in order to be able to make him a Christian, even if only in seeming, a start had first to be made by civilising him. In consequence of the cruel slave-hunts of the Portuguese, and the often scarcely better treatment which the natives received from the Spanish colonists, the Jesuits succeeded, in a surprisingly short time, in collecting a considerable number of natives on the territory which had been assigned to them. They thus founded a number of districts, each of which contained at least two thousand inhabitants, but they all manifested a very typical conformity among themselves.

The church formed the centre of each Reduction. As the colony quickly acquired considerable agricultural wealth, which was allowed to be employed only for the benefit of the missions themselves, a number of almost monumental church buildings were raised in these Indian villages in the remote jungle.[2] In other respects these districts must have given a very monotonous impression. Next to the church there was a large open square surrounded by the most important buildings, — the dwelling of the padre and the store and meeting-houses. From it straight streets started rectangularly, and the prospect was in every instance formed by a chapel standing on the border of the common. The simple huts of the Indians were situated along these streets; and all the buildings were erected by the community and remained its property. The inhabitants had only the use of the dwellings, and of the small gardens situated near them they partly had personal possession. The garden was the only thing which the family supervised themselves, and, it is said, generally very badly. The extensive maize and cotton fields adjoining the common, and the considerable herds of oxen and sheep, which constituted the chief wealth of the Reduction, were cultivated and managed according to the directions of the missionaries for the benefit of the community. The entire produce found its way into the granaries, whence it was then distributed by the padres to each individual household. In the same way the regulation of the work depended upon them, each inhabitant being pledged to do some, according to his trade and capacity. With such labourers it was but a trifling matter for the missionaries to provide for the necessary requirements of shelter, clothing, and sustenance; they also introduced many cultured arts, such as carving, watch-making, and even printing. It is no doubt due to the steady method of their instruction, as well as to an actual mental deficiency, that the Indian, in all his training, never succeeded in getting beyond imitation, and never made any inventions or progress, in spite of the discipline of civilisation which had influenced him for more than one hundred years. The Jesuits defended themselves against the attacks of those who reproached them for having intentionally crushed the human liberty of their charges, with the assertion that it had been impossible to force the Indian from his condition of perpetual childishness, and that a greater degree of personal liberty would only have injured the individual and the general good. There may be much truth in this; at any rate it is certain that the natives were actually contented under the guidance of the missionaries, and that they not only rendered them almost unconditional obedience, but also took serious pains to retain their spiritual rulers when the government thought it advisable to recall them.

The authority of the missionaries was, it is true, directly as well as indirectly almost unlimited. There were in each Reduction only two Europeans, both regular priests, of whom one, the actual leader, supervised the spiritual, while the other managed the material concerns of the settlement. They were assisted by a kind of municipality founded upon the model of the Spanish colonial towns, which, though it depended upon the election of the community, was always absolutely subservient to the missionaries. The fact that there was hardly a temporal judicial authority proves how entirely the Jesuits had their charges under control. The inhabitants were governed almost exclusively by the power of the confessional, and the Jesuits have themselves shown that actual sins came to their knowledge but very rarely through the confessional. The Jesuits also naturally represented their communities abroad, for they had made them, as far as possible, independent of the outer world, both politically and economically. An outsider rarely found his way to the missions, and the twofold reason why the stranger became exclusively the guest of the padres was first in order to prevent his closer acquaintance with the natives, and secondly to preserve the latter from unfavourable outside influences. One of the missionaries left the settlement at long intervals, accompanied by one of the most reliable of the natives, for the purpose of exchanging, in the Spanish settlements, the surplus of their productions, consisting principally of cotton and hides, for anything which the Reductions did not themselves produce; but even then contact with the European was avoided as much as possible.

The Reductions increased rapidly in Paraguay and soon possessed a large population, and this circumstance in itself threatened to become fatal. All the settlements were unprotected, and the missionaries themselves considered it a decided advantage to calm the warlike tendencies of the Guaranis, who had once been

SAN JOSÉ, BOLIVIA, DURING ITS PRIME

(Drawn by Karl Oenike after D'Orbigny's Atlas and Hesenberg's "Missions of the Jesuits")

celebrated for their daring bravery; besides this, a law which was generally valid forbade the arming of the Indians. Thus the Portuguese slave-robbers, who in the seventeenth century already had at their disposal a well-organised and well-armed force, experienced no difficulty when the idea occurred to them, in the year 1637, of taking their Indian slaves from the missions instead of having to track them laboriously in the jungle. This development was indeed an eventful one for the Jesuits. Forthwith, in consideration of the prevailing circumstances, they secured for their native charges the suspension of the law against the carrying of firearms, and since then the friars have brought up the natives to be good and thorough soldiers. They not only easily repelled the attacks of other savage natives, but also beat the Paulists (so the Portuguese slave-hunters were called, after their native place, the Province São Paulo) so completely that they were forced to transfer the field of their activity farther into the northern continent. They also proved themselves reliable and well-drilled fighting-material whenever, through risings in the interior or hostilities on the borders, the Spanish settlements were threatened by other Europeans.

The Jesuits thus carried on the work of the conversion of the natives for more than a century without interruption, with the exception of the dissensions with the spiritual and temporal authorities of the neighbouring districts. In the meantime the tendency of the spirit of the age in the Old World had become more and more opposed to their order, and this attitude of things finally affected their settlements in the remote jungle also. The first impulse, it is true, arose from purely political motives. With the continuous opening up and development of the South American continent, Spain and Portugal at length in the same way felt the necessity for a more distinct demarcation of their colonial possessions. The personal union of the two kingdoms which had been established by Philip II was again annulled by the Portuguese protest of 1640, and in 1668, after long-standing animosities, Spain was forced to acknowledge the supremacy of the House of Braganza in Portugal, and of its colonies. Spain also changed its dynasty of rulers. When Ferdinand VI began from within to reorganise the State, which had been ruined by long mismanagement and by the prolonged war of succession, a newer, freer, and clearer impulse was also given to colonial progress.

The desire for the regulation of the Brazilian boundary was one of the issues. The Portuguese had repeatedly laid claim to the left shore of the mouth of the La Plata. They had founded a town, Colonia, opposite to Buenos Ayres, and had often attempted to extend their settlements in this region; and this became an especial thorn in the flesh to the government at Madrid, because these settlements were exclusively for the purpose of illegally breaking through the bounds by which Spain sought to secure her trade with the colonists.[1] As Portugal, however, possessed only a slight interest in these advanced coast towns, it readily agreed that Spain should exchange considerable plains of land in the interior, part of which formed the left bank of the Uruguay (on which were seven of the missions carried on by the Jesuits) for the left bank of the mouth of the La Plata.

The agreement provided that the natives should quit the territory under the guidance of their spiritual leaders, and should travel farther into the Spanish territory. When, however, the boundary commissioners at length began to carry out the agreement on this spot, they were not only met by the Jesuits with urgent

[1] See *post.* p. 409

remonstrances, but the natives by force of arms offered a resistance which was at first successful. The Jesuits soon again submitted to the order for obedience which had proceeded from Spain, and with the same spirit brought their influence to bear upon the natives. These could not, however, readily make up their minds to give up the loved home for whose defence they had taken up arms, and though it did not actually result in a serious battle, yet it required the approach of a considerable force, which had been collected by Spain and Portugal together, to convince them of the fruitlessness of their attempt.

The incident was in itself so simple and harmless that it scarcely offered a ground for complaint against the Jesuits; but in the hands of the all-powerful Portuguese minister, the Marquis de Pombal, who then already sought an occasion to attack the influential Jesuit orders, it assumed the guise of a heavy accusation. It was not difficult, by means of torture, to force from two captive Indians belonging to the mission the confession that the Jesuits had urged and goaded them on to armed resistance against the order of the allied monarchs. Then a baptised Guarani, whose name was Nicolas, gathered together the remaining Indians, who permanently disobeyed the order to leave, and formed them into a band of homeless and lawless creatures. With these he continued the war of robbery and plunder against the European settlements on both sides of the frontier. This gave rise to the fable of that independent kingdom which yielded obedience to no temporal power, and which the Jesuits, with the help of the natives, were supposed to have striven to establish in the interior of South America. This accusation was of great importance in connection with the expulsion of the Jesuits from Portugal, so much desired and finally accomplished by Pombal. It is also possible that it may have had some influence upon the deliberations of Charles III and his ministers, when it became a question of taking a stand against the Society of Jesus in the conflict which was waged throughout the whole world. Unquestionably neither Pombal nor any other far-seeing and intelligent statesman seriously believed in such an accusation; it was, at the most, brought up as an expedient in the agitation in order to conceal the purely worldly and political motives which, in the main, determined the expulsion of the Jesuits from Portugal and Spain.

Moreover the Jesuits have not left the slightest proof that the accusations brought against their missionary activity, where only their own personal interests were in question, were well merited. Both in Brazil and Paraguay they submitted with dumb resignation to the order which recalled them suddenly and without any preparation from the field of action where they had successfully laboured for a hundred years. Even the unworthy and revengeful manner in which the order was carried out by the officials appointed for this purpose did not in a single instance force them from their purely passive rôle of endurance. In obedience to the order they vanished from all places where either the welfare of their charges was threatened or where they foresaw that want and death would be inevitable for themselves. History has justified them in one respect. No matter how one may judge of their system with regard to the treatment of the natives, they at any rate perfectly understood how to take care of their individual well-being and to teach them to become absolutely submissive and useful subjects. Those who succeeded to their inheritance, in a few years again alienated the Indians from all the progress in civilisation which they had made under the Jesuits, and by a wrong treatment turned them once more into wandering savage tribes.

And thus they have remained wherever the bare jealousy of the more highly civilised European presumes to see, in the Indian who mentally has not yet grown out of the fetters of centuries of ancient prejudices, a creature of an inferior order.

The expulsion of the Jesuits is the last important phase in the native policy of latinised South America. From that time the care of the Indians in the sphere of missions was transferred to temporal authorities. While in the other provinces they had gradually been learning actually to carry into effect the well-intentioned aims of the native legislation, these first-mentioned provinces had once more to go through the entire range of experience with regard to the treatment of the natives, and their natural development, which had taught the others tolerance. With regard to the position of the Indians, scarcely any confirmed grounds of complaint existed in general during the last twenty years of Spanish colonial rule. Where there remained dependence and a certain lack of enterprise, this was rather the result of a natural propensity inculcated by the generations that had previously followed old customs than the effect of a perverted application of the law. The greater proportion of the Indians do not, even in the present day, completely understand the European's hypothesis of a progressive civilisation, or his attitude and mental outlook, even though for two generations past this development in progress has been maintained by free citizens of free republics with every imaginable guarantee of personal liberty. These are, however, conditions which have unavoidably manifested themselves, and will continue to do so as a necessity of nature, wherever two nations, holding entirely different theories concerning civilisation, and having such marked differences in the degree of culture, come into conflict. It is possible that certain specially gifted individuals might be able to raise themselves at length to a complete equality of culture, but the large proportion of less highly civilised people will always remain both mentally and physically dependent upon the more advanced race. All equalisation before the law will possess a far inferior actual value for the less civilised race than the practical conviction of men that it is a duty of honour for the higher civilisation to watch lovingly over the weaker.

## *D.* The Spanish Trade Policy

While it must be acknowledged that the policy of the Spanish government regarding the native question was the most enlightened and well intentioned of any which had been put into practice anywhere, this cannot be affirmed with reference to their trade policy. The fact that the entire trade communication with the colonies was monopolised by the one harbour of Seville was as much the result of the arrangements made with Columbus as an imitation of the Portuguese model. The explorer had, according to agreement, stipulated that he should receive, besides the right of participation in all subsequent colonial voyages, a share in the clear profit from the combined colonial undertakings. In order to fulfil this stipulation it became an unavoidable necessity that all colonial enterprises should be strictly controlled with reference to their cost and profit. This would naturally have been impossible if the ships destined for the colonies had been allowed to sail from every harbour of the Spanish peninsula, which was surrounded by the sea on three sides. As is well known, it was not until far into the sixteenth century that a definite understanding was arrived at, after long lawsuits and repeated agreements between the government and the heirs of Columbus. The fact, however, that the exclusive monopoly of the trade by Seville, and the strict regulations of the customs, were adhered to, was undoubtedly the consequence of the political views which on this subject prevailed with the government. The land which came to the Crown of Castile as an integral and permanent part through the discovery of Columbus was not regarded so much as a territorial accession of land as an increase of the Crown domains belonging to the kings of Castile. This acceptation was shared in the sixteenth and seventeenth centuries by all the Powers who carried on any colonial policy whatever, the remains of which can be traced almost everywhere. In Spain they have been maintained so strongly that modern Spain cannot quite free herself from them, in spite of three generations of progressive revolutions.

According to such an acceptation of the law it naturally depended upon the pleasure of the government, or of those to whom the government had transferred their rights, as to who should be admitted to the colonies, either with the object of settling there or for the purposes of trade. The restrictions were then also, from the commencement, very numerous, and they were, with the exception of several fundamental amplifications instituted during the first decades, maintained with, if anything, almost too great severity. As the colonies belonged to the Crown of Castile, the Castilians possessed in the first instance the natural right to trade therein, but this prerogative had also been conceded to the Aragonese since 1495. The privilege received yet further expansion after the accession of Charles V. Considerations of an agricultural nature were principally responsible for the resolution to permit all subjects of the many kingdoms ruled by the Spanish king to have access to the colonies. Spain was endowed with exceedingly extensive colonial possessions at a moment when such a national property could and did become extremely dangerous. Hardly had the political unity of the actual Spanish soil been established by the removal of the last Moorish kingdom, and scarcely had Ferdinand and Isabella taken the first steps to lead the country (whose agricultural development had been much impaired by the continued war against the Crescenta) to a greater expansion of its natural resources, when a new and dangerous enemy to its national industry arose. Thus the discovery of America removed thousands upon thousands of strong labourers from the national work of the by no means large population, and created serious competition between the life of hazardous colonial profits and the slow but certain and advancing field of labour in both agriculture and handicraft at home.

Although the agricultural development was successfully carried on upon the foundations laid by the Catholic rulers, yet the mother country could not, under such difficult conditions, carry on the exclusive maintenance of the colonial territory, which rapidly increased from century to century. From the time of the proclamation of the law in question, the exclusion of strangers had already been disregarded in favour of those who knew how to take care of the interests of the State and of the colonies while seeking their own gain. That Charles V, in opening up the New World to all his subjects, acted from the standpoint that the solution of the agricultural problems which had been imposed upon the colonies by the government lay in gaining new forces, is more especially evidenced by the fact that he called upon all the most powerful agricultural factors of his most distant Spanish dominions to co-operate in the colonial enterprises. From

Germany he summoned the Hanses and the Augsburgers, and from Italy, more especially, the great merchants.

The laws of the country concerning the trade with the colonies were, of course, also binding upon these. They, too, were obliged first to enter Seville with their ships and wares, pay the entrance duty, and also submit to the compulsory registration which was supervised by the Casa de Contratacion, according to which no person or trade commodity was permitted to enter the colony without satisfying the legal demands. Like the Spaniards, they were also bound to return to Seville and again go through the same formalities.

All costly articles from the colonies, more especially ores, also came under this prohibition, which forbade such articles being taken out of Spain. As Spain, with its colonies as well as through them, consumed considerably more trade commodities than it was able to supply to foreign countries, this regulation could not be enforced permanently, as in time became evident to the government, engrossed as it was in mercantile questions. However, it neither knew how to remedy the evil nor recognised the fact that, owing to the entirely altered conditions created by the production of ores in the New World, gold and silver had dropped in their exchange value to the trade level for wares the price of which no human laws can fix. Trade with the colonies was during the earlier years burdened by no customs duties, but as commercial intercourse increased, export and import duties were introduced, such as had been imposed between the several Spanish territories. As precious ores were not wares, they were not affected; but the State, by levying a royalty on the profits from their sale, secured a share for itself.

It was of the utmost importance, more especially at first, that the government should revive the trade with the colonies. For this purpose it readily granted, through the Casa de Contratacion, the necessary passes to every ship which proposed sailing across the ocean, and sold such charts as could be supplied. It also established its own court of pilots as a school for helmsmen and as a centre for examination. The rigour of the law was at first often suspended, and incidentally the number of ports of departure was considerably increased, the Canary Islands securing exemption from the enforced call at Seville. Forced registration, also, was not strictly maintained. It was a well-known fact that the returning vessels often secretly deposited a considerable portion of their costly freight on the shores of the Portuguese Azores, in order to escape the customs, and Philip II, during the first years of his reign, instructed his councillors not to interpose the full severity of the law against this practice, in so far as his own subjects were concerned. These restrictive regulations were naturally particularly burdensome to the colonies. By preventing free competition they, in combination with the comparative superabundance of gold and silver, caused the prices between the colonies and the mother country, at the end of the sixteenth century, to be in the ratio of five to one and even as three to one. The agitation for the removal of the trade restrictions was at that time particularly powerful there. But it was precisely the absolute impossibility of preventing in any way the misuse of measures intended to procure alleviation in a distant land, and over an endless extent of thinly populated coast, that caused the government to adhere with even greater severity to the system of enforced registration.

Before any harbour for imports in the New World, besides San Domingo, could become of importance for trade purposes, political circumstances in the mother country led to a fresh organisation of her commercial intercourse with the colonies. These proved of extraordinary service to the system of control pursued by the government, without tending to make the disadvantages connected with it perceptible to the colonists. The results which the Spaniards and Portuguese achieved with the aid of their transatlantic maritime power were not without reaction on the remaining European Powers. French and English sailors, often guided during their first voyages by Italian pilots, soon also ventured to cross the ocean; their discoveries in North America will be referred to subsequently.[1] As long as Spain remained at peace with the rest of the world, and its colonies yielded only moderate compensation in return for the disbursement made, this intermeddling of foreign Powers in the colonial sphere remained comparatively unimportant. When, however, under Charles V, the plans for the government of the world by Spain became more and more sharply defined, violent antagonism arose at first toward France under Philip II, and also against England. This gave rise to open enmity which led to repeated wars in Europe, daring privateering voyages on the ocean, and finally, also, to those buccaneering expeditions and attacks on the other side of the ocean from which the colonial ports had long to suffer, until at length the foreign Powers succeeded in securing portions of the ancient Spanish colonial possessions.

When this enmity first became apparent through the capture of single and unarmed ships sailing between Spain and the colonies, Charles V issued the decree, in the year 1526, that in times of war the ships should no longer set sail and return singly, but should, under the leadership of competent captains, be combined into fleets capable of resistance. This was the origin of the celebrated fleets ("flotas") and galleons ("galeones") which for two centuries carried on the trade exclusively between Spanish America and the remainder of the civilised world. This measure was at first introduced only with reference to the security of trans-oceanic commerce; that it rendered the most important services to the Crown's fiscal control was certainly soon proved and acknowledged by all the interested parties.

The diffusion of the Spanish race in the New World had not reached its termination when the fleets were introduced. Several phases in the development of this institution had to be passed through before it received its permanent establishment, after which it remained approximately as follows. The ships which intended sailing to the West Indies assembled annually in the months of March and September at Seville, or, when their draught did not allow of it, at San Lucar de Barrameda, or, later on, at Cadiz. They had to be at least ten in number, otherwise the fleet was not permitted to set sail. As a rule there were between thirty and forty, and in some cases a great many more ships. In the year 1589 no less than ninety-four vessels going from Panama to the South were required to transport all that the fleet had brought to Portobello. Ships of less than a hundred tons were, as a rule, excluded from participation in the voyage to the Indies, and all, even the heavily freighted merchantmen, were obliged to carry at least four heavy and sixteen light guns, and every man on board carried weapons. Two of the largest vessels were selected as "capitana" and "almiranta;" the first, carrying all the highest in command of the whole fleet, sailed in advance, while the admiral's ship formed the rear-guard with the special duty of keeping the fleet together. The "capitana" and "almiranta" were more strongly built than the other ships, and in order to increase their powers of action in battle they were not

---

[1] See *post*, pp. 427, 434.

allowed to be freighted to the same extent as the merchantmen. Besides these, the fleet was at first accompanied by at least one and, later on, by several larger ships,—the galleons,—whose chief duty it was to watch over the safety of the fleet. They had a tonnage of at least two hundred to three hundred, were powerfully equipped, and were allowed only light freight. They were at the same time intended to bring back in safety to Spain the gold and silver which were due to the Crown as taxes and duty. In times of war the Indian fleets, upon which the entire wealth of Spain depended, were not even thus considered sufficiently well guarded. A protecting fleet, consisting of galleys and galleons, was therefore also equipped out of the revenue from the additional tax which had been levied upon the Indian trade for this purpose, and these had to accompany the trading fleets on the high seas and escort the returning ones in the same way. Finally several lighter and smaller ships — despatch-vessels ("avisos") — were attached to each fleet, their duty being to go on in advance, so as to discover threatening dangers and to prepare the officials on either side for the arrival of the fleet.

The combined fleet sailed from Seville to San Domingo, where the official control to which they had been submitted at the port of sailing was renewed. The ships which were to sail via Porto Rico and Havana to Vera Cruz formed the so-called "Fleet of New Spain;" they then separated from those which first sailed through the Gulf of Mexico to Cartagena and thence to Portobello. The latter, called the "Continental Fleet," was by far the more important of the two, as it carried all the merchandise from the whole southern continent of America. All direct commercial intercourse with the mother country, except through these fleets, was not only forbidden to all the provinces, but was also so fettered by customs restrictions and trade rules that the colonies were at the most only permitted to exchange certain products of their own soil, but never European trade commodities. The Continental Fleet, in the first instance, supplied Peru and Chile, starting from Portobello, but soon after also Tucuman and Paraguay, the countries of the modern Argentina. The anomaly that the merchandise for the southeast of America had to traverse the watershed between the Atlantic and Pacific oceans twice before arriving at its place of destination arose from there being no noteworthy colony at the mouth of the La Plata. Buenos Ayres had, it is true, been founded in the year 1535, but it was almost immediately dissolved, its final colonisation taking place in 1562. It was, however, for the time being, of no importance, owing to its great distance from the centres of Spanish colonial government, and its exposed position on a coast which was difficult to defend, and also because of its immediate proximity to the Portuguese, who claimed the opposite shore of the bay as their territory. The Spanish government did not consider it advisable to recognise the town as a harbour in the trans-oceanic trade intercourse. This region was first organised in 1617 as a special colonial district, and remained for a long time the seat of an extensive but illegal trade with foreign nations before the government decided, in conjunction with the alteration in the trade with Chile and Peru by way of Cape Horn, to include Buenos Ayres also among the places to be affected by the trade of the fleets.

Up to that time the principal traffic was confined to the route via Portobello. As a settlement this town was of no importance, and it remained uninhabited during the greater part of the year, owing to its unhealthy climate. However, the greatest business transactions and the wildest speculations of the whole of South America were made there during the forty days' market, or fair, that followed the arrival of the fleet. A luxurious life of pleasure, incidental to easily won gains, reigned for a short time in the town, which consisted of hastily erected tents and huts. When, however, at the conclusion of the fair, preparations were made for the return, the population of Portobello vanished, not to come back again within another half or whole year, or even longer period, when the same scene was re-enacted. The regularity of the fleets left much to be desired; there never was a lack of adventurous vessels, but conditions of the weather and political complications often prevented the regular carrying out of the despatch of the fleets in sailing. More than once the fair of Portobello had to be postponed or stopped altogether, because the expected ships had been wrecked or had fallen into the hands of hostile privateers.

Thus it happened that though the optional sailings of the fleets had at first been joyfully welcomed as a sign of progress, the inconvenience caused by the ships arriving far too seldom to meet the colonists' requirements became a heavy burden, which was felt all the more when an extraordinary rise in the price of all trade commodities resulted. Nevertheless, owing to the ever-increasing insecurity on the ocean, the government strictly enforced the regulations which had been drawn up. It might have given way by allowing the departure of the fleets from Europe to take place at any time, and it did, as a matter of fact, make several concessions in this respect, but it had such a prominent interest in the safe return of the entire fleet that it never thought of the possibility of foregoing it. These fleets were actually the only means of communication between the two worlds, for the entire official and private correspondence was carried by them; but a still more important point was that only with their assistance could the whole of the colonial revenues, which were indispensable for the State budget, reach the government exchequer. All the colonial offices sent their reports and accounts to the respective ports for the custody of the fleets, where the letters and valuables were entrusted to the soundest and safest vessels. Three months after their arrival at San Domingo, the ships of the New Spain and continental fleets were instructed to reassemble once more at Havana. The galleons and the equipped convoys filled up the interval with occasional pirate expeditions, until they had once more to undertake the safe-conduct of the united fleets on their return, sailing under similar precautionary measures through the Bahama Channel into the open ocean. This part of the voyage was by far the most dangerous. Spain's political enemies, as well as the pirates, always turned their attention to catching the returning fleet, which, on account of its transport of precious metals, was called the "silver fleet." Occasionally the enemy succeeded completely in his design, but generally only in part.

The colonies, from the commencement, yielded the mother country all kinds of products. Besides the logwood which was much exported from all parts of America, various drugs, and, later on, large quantities of sugar and hides, formed the freight of the returning vessels. The most valuable portion of the cargo always consisted of gold, silver, pearls, and precious stones. Columbus had already found gold in moderate quantities with the natives. As soon as they had become convinced that it was of indigenous origin, the settlers began gold mining and washing. The gold-mines, in which, owing to the primitive manner of working, but comparatively little was achieved in spite of a great expenditure of labour, were the real places of torture for the Indians. At all times and in all places the flotsam and jetsam of human society have assembled among gold-diggers. In the presence of such elements all laws for the protection of the natives were powerless, because each official risked his own life in endeavouring to enforce respect for the law from such an assembly. But during the whole time of the Conquista the actual wealth was not derived from gold and silver mines, but through barter with the natives. Fully appreciating this fact, the government always willingly encouraged mining industry by granting an abatement of taxes and sending over experienced miners, mostly Germans; but, as always, it demanded and collected the fifth part of all gold gained by barter or on marauding expeditions.

The mining industry did not become remunerative until after the conquest of Mexico. The silver-mines of Sultepeque, and more especially of Guanajuato, yielded such rich ores that they were permanently worked. The Spaniards also found treasures of fabulous value in the possession of the natives of Peru; but there, as in all other provinces, the store of precious metals attainable by barter was exhausted comparatively early, and the prospects of the gold and silver mines were, for the moment, decidedly less favourable than in the north, until the silver-mines of Potosi were discovered, quite by chance, in the year 1545. This mining-district proved of untold wealth for a long period, and it is chiefly due to it, in combination with the Mexican silver-mines, that the production of precious metals in the New World has been maintained permanently on a comparatively high level.

The first primitive method of procedure made the working of only the richest ores remunerative. The discovery of a process of amalgamation, however, made it possible to gain more extensive profits from the rocks of Mexico and Peru. A German miner who, owing to a fire which burned out the quicksilver-mines of Almaden, had become penniless, was, according to the most recent research, the inventor of amalgam. He went into partnership with a Spaniard, Bartolomé de Medina, for the realisation of his discovery. However, as the Inquisition permitted only the latter, and not his German master, to go over to Mexico, the Spaniard so entirely assumed the credit of the discovery that not even the name of the German has become known. The process of extracting silver by means of quicksilver brought about a complete revolution in the mining industry of Mexico. The mine-proprietors promised to freight the ships of the New Spain fleet as high as the masts if they could only obtain sufficient quicksilver, and the price of it increased enormously. The monopoly of the profits from the pits of Almaden, which were the largest in the world, and, next to those of Idria, the only ones then worked, had already been acquired previously, and the Spanish government now also claimed the monopoly of the trade. It leased the pits to the Fuggers, who, by an intelligent process of working, under German direction, produced approximately one hundred per cent of profit during half a century. They were obliged to relinquish all the gains to the government, who sold the quicksilver in America to the mine-owners for three and four times as much as the purchase-money. Thenceforward the galleys, which on the return voyage brought the treasures of gold and silver from America, on the outward voyage carried from one hundred and fifty to two hundred and fifty tons of quicksilver. From 1563 to 1641 — that is to say, as long as the Fuggers were the leaseholders of the pits of Almaden — silver worth 253,000,000 ducats is said to have been gained from 12,658 tons of quicksilver which they had extracted. The royalty on this alone amounted to over 50,000,000 ducats.

## E. NEGRO SLAVERY

IN the whole export trade that Spain carried on with its colonies there was only one other article which equalled quicksilver in importance, and that was the negro slave. Reference has already been made[1] to the fact that access to the colonies had, in accordance with the oldest legislation, been closed to these slaves, but that the government was not strict in granting exceptions. The negroes did not begin to play an important part in the organisation of the colonies and in colonial trade until Las Casas, with his narrow philanthropic ideas, recommended the importation of negro slaves as a means of liberating the Indians from their state of servitude. If, as was evidently the clear intention of the Spanish government, the colonies were to be organised for other purposes than to serve as fulcrums for barter and trade, as had been established by the Portuguese in the Indies, then undoubtedly provision for labourers had to be made. It was quite evident that there were not enough Europeans for this purpose. On the one hand the climate enfeebled their working powers, and on the other hand the disproportion between the number of the European colonists and the expansion of the colonial possessions was such that to surmount the difficulties of colonisation by European forces alone was quite out of the question. Added to this, the conception which the Spanish government had of their duty to the colonies forbade Spain's deportation of criminals or doubtful subjects. Columbus wished to attempt the discovery of America with discharged convicts. Portugal, in the irregular method of her colonial policy, had made some experiments with convict settlements in Brazil, but the Spanish laws permitted only the nation's free men to emigrate, and the government, in single instances only, transported misdemeanants at the request of special colonial groups. Even with their help it would have been impossible to carry on mining, cattle-raising, and plantations in the colonies, simply for this reason, that many kinds — and more especially the higher kinds — of labour always remained to be done by the Europeans. If, therefore, the Indian (who, owing to his indolence and his spirit of independence, could scarcely be induced to do the work voluntarily, according to European standards) was to be exempt from all compulsion, then another supply of labour had to be imported into the colonies.

Las Casas' proposal, that negroes should be used for this purpose, in the same manner in which they were employed on the islands on the coasts of Africa, was favourably received by the government. For fiscal reasons the Crown nominally maintained the prohibition of negro importation, but, in consideration of the payment of certain fees, single individuals or companies were allowed to supply to the harbours of the colonies a fixed number of negroes annually. The colonial authorities had been called upon to give a report in respect to their annual requirements. In the beginning four thousand were named, but in the course of the long period during which the "Asiento" — the contract for the monopoly of the importation of slaves — lasted, the number was at various times

---

[1] Ante, p. 395.

increased or diminished. The colonists, however, always complained that the supply of negro slaves for the New World fell far short of the actual demand, and the trade in this valuable commodity was at all times the favourite business of the illegal smuggling-trade which was carried on by foreign shipowners. There is no doubt that this matter permanently engrossed the attention of the government.

The slave-ships enjoyed certain privileges, inasmuch as they were allowed, by the deposit of a security, to sail from the coast of Guinea, where they purchased their black merchandise from Portuguese dealers, straight to America, where a few ports were open to them for the landing of the negroes. The oldest Asientists already enjoyed certain privileges for the requirements of their trade, and in the return from Spain of their profits in the shape of colonial goods; but they remained bound by the obligation to return to Seville, as well as to be registered in the same manner as all other merchants. As control of them was far more difficult than of the voyages of the fleets and galleys, the Crown's toleration of the Asientists was soon taken advantage of for the general evasion of the oppressive colonial trade laws and for extensive smuggling.

Though the slave monopoly was at first in the hands of the Genoese and the Germans, it was comparatively little abused, and it was only slightly prejudicial to the legitimate trade in general; yet in time these conditions changed when other nations, with less friendly intentions, took the monopoly into their hands. The idea of leasing the sole rights in the traffic of slave importation to a Portuguese ("Consortium") was not bad in itself, as the Portuguese were in undisputed possession of the *materia prima* of the negroes themselves. The Portuguese merchants received the Asiento at the time when Portugal was bound to Spain by a personal union, and they retained it after the revolt of the Braganzas until the acknowledgment of Portuguese independence by the treaty of peace in 1668. Then the merchants of Seville temporarily obtained the Asiento for themselves. The Guinea Company, in which Louis XIV himself had a share, possessed the monopoly of the slave-trade after Spanish America, until political circumstances necessitated the retirement of France.

This was not advantageous to Spain, however, one of the conditions of the Treaty of Utrecht expressly stipulating the cession of the Asiento to the English, who undoubtedly profited most thoroughly by it. The English at the same time received a guarantee for the right to send annually to the colonies, which were closed to the trade of all the other colonies under privileged conditions, two vessels freighted with European trade commodities, of modest dimensions, in addition to the slave-ships. It has, however, been reported that these vessels, while they discharged their cargo openly and in sight of the harbour officials during the day, were again freighted by night from larger ships which did not disembark, but rode at anchor outside for no apparent reason. In this way three and four times the bulk of their actual merchandise was landed. These were serious evils, which finally induced Ferdinand VI to repurchase the Asiento contract from the English, even before its legal termination. The reason that the government was so long in deciding upon this step was not alone due to the fact that it was immediately interested in the profits of the English association, nor because the English alone had succeeded in transporting the prescribed number of slaves to the colonies; but it was chiefly owing to the large sums which accrued to the State exchequer by means of these transactions and played an important part in the revenue of the Indies. The original tax of two ducats per head, by means of which the first holders of the trade monopoly bought the license, was in time raised to from thirty to forty ducats. The importation of three thousand to four thousand slaves annually thus became also perceptible in the colonial budget of the eighteenth century, when the royalties from the gains of precious metals had diminished considerably. The question has often been discussed as to what amounts of gold, silver, and other valuables the Spanish State and country had derived from its transatlantic colonial possessions, but it has never been satisfactorily settled, owing to the utterly incomplete reports of the trade of Spain and its colonies which have hitherto been obtainable. While it has been asserted that the development of Spanish America was retarded for a hundred years by the colonial policy of Spain, an attempt has been made to attach the responsibility for Spain's economic downfall to the very abundance of precious metals, by the assertion that the gold from the New World corrupted and ruined Spain. That, like the previous statements, is an exaggeration. If Spain had been a sound economic State, there would have been as little likelihood of her corruption by the superfluity of gold and silver as there was of England's being injured by the treasures of India. That Spain did not allow her colonies a freer and more individual life, but regarded them as essentially an asylum for the mother country, and refused, until far into the eighteenth century, to make use of them in any other way, is a point of view which all the colonial Powers of that epoch had in common. Probably Spain's attitude would not have changed to this day if the powerful revolutionary agitations which in the New World led to the severance of the United States from England and of almost the whole of Latin America from Spain had not forced her to a different policy. The Spanish colonies fulfilled their object until the eighteenth century. They provided the mother country with such abundant means of gold (which was indispensable to her political position in the concert of Europe) that it aroused the envy of all other countries, and tempted them on the one hand to embark in colonial enterprises themselves, while on the other hand it made them take from the Spaniards as much of their colonial treasures as possible.

### *F.* The Historical Development of the Spanish Colonial Realm

From the position which the Spanish colonies held in relation to the mother country it naturally follows that they possessed no independent history. Their history comprised the change of officials, the incidental alterations in their administrative organisation, and the regulations for the furtherance of the economic interests instituted far more for the benefit of Spain than for that of the colonies. It was owing to Spain's dependence on them that they became involved in all the political complications of the mother country. The history of all that the colonies had to suffer, as part of the Spanish kingdom, at the hands of Spain's opponents, is the nearest approach to a general history of the colonial empire. When Spain came into warlike conflict with neighbouring European States, the latter did not fail to damage the trade and the naval power of their opponent, on her far-reaching seacoasts, by means of privateers. In the year 1512 ships were captured by the French, in consequence of such attacks, while struggling toward the harbour of Seville on their return from the colonies. A state of war — at times open and at other times latent — prevailed continuously against France during the reigns of Charles V and Philip II, and it spread the more on the sea because, by the opening up of Mexico and Peru, the colonial trading-vessels had become more desirable prey than they had been at the beginning of the century.

The Spanish regents were, however, not blind to this fact. The enemies' attacks upon the South American fleets helped in no small degree the development of that maritime supremacy which Spain maintained during the greater part of the sixteenth century. This ascendency might perhaps have been more firmly established if Charles V had not possessed such convenient sources of help in his great European dominions. The same thing happened here as with the colonial trade, for Spain was unable, during the first years of traffic, to satisfy her colonies' demands, so that she granted participation in maritime trade to all the allied nations, — the Italians, Dutch, and Germans. Owing to the abundance of treasure which the country drew from its colonies, this arrangement became permanent, and the fatal consequences which in such a state of affairs must arise from a defection of her allies were not taken into account. For the time being, at any rate, the Spaniards succeeded by these means in making themselves the ruling maritime Power. No nation could have dared, before 1580, to meet the Spanish fleet openly on the ocean. Even during the small naval war which the privateers — more especially the French privateers — carried on with the Spaniards, the latter were undoubtedly at first superior. It was only due to the exceptionally unfavourable position in which the country, with its colonies, found herself when face to face with the enemy, that the latter, in spite of many losses, reaped rich benefit and many advantages from the privateering wars.

The arrangements to safeguard the voyages of the trading-fleets, and for their convoy along the coast provinces by the naval ships, soon drove the corsairs away from the Andalusian coast and from Cape St. Vincent, where they might often have become dangerous to the ships returning to Seville. They were obliged to transfer their scene of action farther off, to regions where the home squadrons could not so readily come to the aid of the trading-fleets. But they were not able to remain on the Canary Islands, or on the Azores or the Cape Verd Islands, which they had chosen as their centre. The Spanish measures of defence finally even forced the enemy to seek for spoil in the very quarters where the Spaniard obtained his, — that is to say, in the colonies. The pirates did not long remain in ignorance of the sailing-routes appointed for the Spanish fleets, because they, too, depended on the ocean currents. In the same way they soon learned that many of the smaller Antilles, and even great tracts on the shores of the larger islands, had been entirely abandoned by the colonists and were therefore " no man's land." Thus the privateers had no difficulty in finding harbours of refuge, where they could equip themselves for their unexpected attacks, repair the damages incurred, and place the spoils gained in security.

Only a step remained between the capture of the Spanish ships in the transatlantic waters and the attack and plunder of the colonial settlements. The first stages of open hostility followed during the third Franco-Spanish war in the 'forties of the sixteenth century. The daring of the privateers (who, with the secret assistance of the French government, had been extremely well equipped) was so great that they not only plundered and laid under contribution the small and isolated colonial coast-places, but also attacked Santa Marta and Cartagena in 1542. In 1555 they seized the capital of Cuba, Havana, and occupied it for twenty-six days. In the face of such conditions all that the government could do was to order the coast-towns to be fortified as far as possible, and wherever this could not be done the settlements near the seacoast were to be abandoned and transferred farther into the interior.

New enemies then arose for the colonies. Up to that time it had been chiefly the French who had done their utmost to injure the colonial trade and the settlements of their traditional enemies. When Queen Elizabeth of England ascended the throne which Philip II had shared with her sister, the rupture between England and Spain increased year by year, and developed into open hostility, which became all the greater when Elizabeth firmly showed her Protestant tendencies. The English navy was then far inferior to the Spanish, and was not in a position to contend with it on the ocean, and moreover the English seamen did not then appear to be conducting active naval warfare against the Spaniards. They endeavoured, however, to break through the strict embargo laid on the Spanish colonies' direct trade with the Old World, and in so doing they did not scruple to attack the Spanish ships openly. Soon afterward they turned their attention to those settlements where their opponents were weak and where the colonial authorities had opposed their illegitimate trade. The tactics they generally employed were first to plunder a shipload of negro slaves of the Portuguese on the coast of Guinea, for which they were certain of securing a market in the colonies, often with the connivance of the Spanish authorities. At the same time they knew thoroughly how to seize any opportunity of striking a blow, and if it proved favourable they were at no loss to know how to provoke the Spaniards so that they themselves could always plead that they had taken up arms only in self-defence. Richard Hawkins had in 1530, as a slave-merchant, already laid the foundation for the wealth which in later years enabled his celebrated son, John Hawkins, to carry on privateering with his own flotilla. This mode of trading was, during the 'sixties, carried on by numerous English ships. If they reached unknown coasts, they exchanged wares with the natives. They forcibly extorted permission to trade in the Spanish settlements if it was not willingly granted. But such measures had seldom to be resorted to, except for the sake of appearance. When, however, the Spaniards once gained the upper hand, they naturally did not deal very leniently with them, as Hawkins and Drake experienced at Vera Cruz in 1568. The English did not scruple, when opportunity favoured them, to make an actual attack, such as Drake attempted without complete success on Nombre de Dios and Panama in 1572. This same Drake, a few years later, was the first enemy to advance through the Straits of Magellan into the Pacific Ocean, and to plunder the entirely defenceless coast districts of Chile and Peru, thus gaining an enormous amount of spoil. In order that these spoils should not be exposed to the risk of being seized by the Spaniards, who were on the lookout for him on the return voyage, he brought them safely to London by way of the southern point of Africa. There Queen Elizabeth, on account of his exploits, knighted him, in spite of the Spanish protests. Though the peace between England and Spain, which until then had not been officially declared, had imposed a certain amount of caution upon the English pirate, this was done away with when, in 1585, both countries were at open war. In this same year Drake went to sea with twenty-three ships and 2,500 men, and, apart from numerous privateering feats, plundered the towns of San Domingo and Cartagena, destroyed San Agustin in Florida, and brought back two hundred and forty guns from the conquered ships and from the subjugated coast-districts, besides rich treasures. From that time until the death of Queen Elizabeth scarcely a year passed in which more or less richly equipped fleets did not set sail, either to plunder the coasts of Spain or to ravage the colonies. It was because the English sailors had been thoroughly tried on their daring privateer voyages that they distinguished themselves in the battle against the Invincible Armada. After the halo which until then had surrounded the Spanish navy had been dispelled by this battle, the English came forward as serious rivals for the supremacy of the sea. This struggle, which began with Dunkirk, terminated at Trafalgar with their complete victory. The foundation of England's supremacy at sea was laid by the English seamen, who, like Hawkins and Drake, began as smugglers and pirates. They first convinced the government of the importance of the supremacy of the sea for the prosperity of England, who from her geographical position is dependent upon the sea. Then Walter Raleigh, by his privileged station as the acknowledged favourite of Queen Elizabeth, made the English aspirations for maritime supremacy acceptable at court. Raleigh himself made the first attempts at colonisation on American soil, though they had no immediate or permanent results. The expeditions to Guiana which he undertook in 1595, 1597, and 1616, were the first serious attempts by foreigners on the southern continent, not only to become possessed of the coast, but also to advance into the interior. As in the north, they gave the impulse to foreign Powers also to establish themselves within the Spanish-Portuguese colonial sphere.

Fresh competitors with Spain had appeared in the meanwhile, and these proved the more dangerous because their position, as subjects of the Spanish Crown, gave them full opportunity of becoming acquainted with all the conditions of colonial trade. When the first ships belonging to the Netherlands (which at that time had not yet revolted) brought their trade commodities to America, the colonists recognised the advantage gained, and made every kind of representation to the Spanish government, requesting it to concede to the Dutch, in the same way as to the inhabitants of the Canary Islands, the privilege of sailing straight to the colonies from Dutch ports, so making the call at Seville obligatory for only the return voyage. The Council of the Indies would never agree to this, but it often permitted the Dutch as well as the German and Italian ship-owners and merchants to participate in the colonial trade, even after the general permit of Charles V had ceased to exist, and the strong seaworthy Dutch hulks were often hired in the service of the king for the official voyages across the ocean. This commercial privilege was seriously endangered when the Protestant provinces rebelled against the Spanish yoke; but the attitude which Philip II assumed in connection with this insurrection was of advantage to the Dutch. He still desired that only his own, though rebellious, subjects should trade with the South American provinces, and so he continued to grant a share in the Spanish and colonial trade to those ship-owners and merchants of the northern provinces who had not been directly implicated in the rebellion. Thus the Dutch were able, as before, to carry on their business openly and under the Spanish flag, both at Seville and in the colonies, although it was notorious that in this way the money gained flowed into the money-chests of the rebels. Not until 1603 was this anomaly abolished, at any rate in part, when the Dutch trade was burdened with a special tax of thirty per cent ad valorem, until it, too, was again withdrawn during the twelve years' armistice (1609–1621). In spite of this, the Dutch, besides carrying on a legal trade, soon attempted to enrich themselves from the colonies by illegal means. Sometimes they captured Spanish ships, while at other times, by evading the forced registration, they traded directly with America, — partly with the Spanish-Portuguese settlements, but more frequently with the Indians in the then still uncolonised regions. The reason why they, like the English, turned chiefly toward the coast districts between the Orinoco and the Amazon, was probably because they still believed the legend of the Dorado, who was looked for between these rivers, though, with the practical disposition which is characteristic of their race, they did not forget to profit by an inferior but more certain gain while seeking for treasures.

The actual activity of the Dutch as colonists in America began only with the renewal of the war with Spain. Then, in the year 1621, a West India Company was formed upon the model of the East India Company. However, in the first instance, it made it its business to plunder and damage the Spanish-Portuguese colonies, establishing at the same time a number of small settlements on the Oyapok, the Berbice, and the Essequibo, which afterward developed into the colony of Dutch Guiana. The West India Company came more into prominence through the attacks upon Brazil, which was then still subject to the king of Spain. It succeeded, in a surprisingly short time, — during the first thirty years of the seventeenth century, — in gaining a firm footing in Olinda and Recife, and gradually the Portuguese were almost completely driven from the northern provinces of Brazil. By means of a clever policy of religious and international tolerance, the Company succeeded in making the greater part of the old settlers accept the new order of things unconditionally, while it retained their services for the new community, which soon flourished and experienced no difficulty in resisting the Spanish-Portuguese attacks. The colony was in its prime during the regency of Count Johann Moritz, of Nassau (1637–1644), who not only made his residence, Moritzstadt, the centre for commerce, but also a home for serious scientific studies, such as had hardly previously been carried on elsewhere on American soil. The altered political conditions first had a disturbing influence when Portugal, separating from Spain in 1640, made a treaty with the Netherlands. The West India Company at first maintained its claim to its Brazilian conquests and received the support of the States General. The eagerness for the retention of the disputed possession subsequently subsided, so that the Spanish colonial party, which had been considerably strengthened since 1640, succeeded in confining the Dutch more and more to the coast, finally even conquering the coast also, with the assistance of the Portuguese. The Dutch, in the treaty of peace in 1661, also officially renounced all their Brazilian pretensions for an indemnity. From that time attention was once more directed to the so-called savage coast of Guiana. The more ancient settlements of Berbice and Essequibo were ceded to England in 1814, but on the other hand the Netherlands possess up to the present day, in Surinam, a remnant of the land which had been colonised under the auspices of the West India Company.[1]

The example which the Netherlands had set by the foundation of State-aided trading-companies excited the attention of the rest of Europe, more especially on

[1] See the maps at p. 514.

account of the great results of their East India Company. The French also founded a privileged trading-company with the title of "The American Islands Company," almost simultaneously with the establishment of the West India Company. To this France owes its present West India colonies, Martinique, Guadeloupe, and its smaller dependencies, although its first possession was St. Christopher, which now belongs to England. Its fortunes were very variable before they finally came under the direct control of the State. The first company collapsed as early as 1650, and saved itself from complete bankruptcy only by disposing of its territorial rights to individual proprietors, who for a long time exercised an almost unlimited sovereignty, as had been the case in the Portuguese and North American capitanries. Colbert then supported the system of privileged companies with great zeal, repurchased the West India Islands, and handed them over, with other territories and rights, to the French West India Company, which also became ruined, during the first decades of the eighteenth century, in consequence of political complications. Denmark and Sweden also, for a short time, acquired their colonial possessions in the Caribbean Sea by means of privileged trading-companies, and in part endeavoured to retain them. Although, with the English, the impulse for colonial activity had been the result of personal and individual initiative, it was by the union of their forces into privileged trading-companies that they also first achieved greater results.

The inevitable consequence of the mighty expansion of the Spanish colonial kingdom was that the Lesser Antilles, which were but sparsely endowed with natural treasures, soon became entirely neglected, though they comprised the land which Columbus first discovered in the New World. In the beginning of the sixteenth century they had been occasionally visited by Spanish slave-hunters. When the latter, however, no longer reaped any benefit through these expeditions, most of the smaller islands remained entirely uninhabited, and at the most served as hiding-places for the freebooters of all nations who lay in wait for the Spanish ships. It was no wonder that at a time when, through the example of the Dutch, the desire for colonial conquests had been aroused, these uninhabited islands should have been regarded as suitable for the purpose. Some Englishmen had, in 1605, already taken possession of the completely deserted island of Barbados, without colonising it at the time. When St. Kitts (St. Christopher), however, had developed into a settlement in 1623, a speculator was also found for Barbados, and he induced the king to grant him the right of a "capitan" over the island and its trade. During the following years the English, French, and Dutch took possession of almost all the Lesser Antilles. England's colonial possessions attained a further expansion in the time of Cromwell. The Lord Protector, in the year 1655, attacked San Domingo with an important array of military forces, and though he was defeated there he was more successful in Jamaica, which became the permanent possession of the English. Until then Spain had regarded all other foreign settlements as a usurpation of her sphere of power, and it was not till 1670, when peace had been concluded with England, that she recognised the validity of England's colonial acquisitions. The same occurred in her relations with France during the subsequent conclusions of peace.

In spite of all, this was a period of outlawry for the Antilles. The English and French had adhered to the unusual custom of procuring labourers for the settlers by transporting convicts, on condition that they should do compulsory labour for the colonists for a specified number of years. Even though there were many among the number who had been convicted for political or religious offences, there was no lack of men of an infamous kind who made the worst possible use of their regained liberty. The renowned buccaneers and filibusters were recruited from their ranks, and, at the time when the European trading-companies were almost completely ruined, and when the English also were entirely occupied by wars at home, they became pirates and were the terror of the Caribbean Sea. Thus they once more revived the days of Hawkins and Drake by their daring attacks upon the Spanish colonial coasts as far as the Pacific Ocean. These homeless and lawless bands of robbers were composed of the subjects of all countries, Spain alone finding no place in their company; and while they were not in conflict with the other nations, they pursued everything that was Spanish with the most deadly hatred. For this reason the enemies of Spain often made use of and protected them, but, for the same reason also, the change in European politics consequent upon the accession of the Bourbons to the throne soon put an end to their doings. The filibusters then attached themselves to either the English or the French, according to the preponderance in force of either nation. Thus the best elements among them were assimilated by the colonial settlements, while the incorrigible ones gradually fell victims to their trade or at last received well-merited punishment.

Spain's change of dynasty, from the Hapsburgs to the Bourbons, which kindled in Europe a universal conflagration of more than ten years' duration, did not bring to the colonies any more serious shocks. The latter were content to take upon themselves unconditionally the consequences of the events in the mother country, as they had done previously at the union with Portugal, as well as at its revolt, which was a proof that they had not even then awakened to a life of their own. During the first decades the policy of the new dynasty was entirely occupied with European concerns. Not until various occurrences had led to the conviction that Spain was in need of reorganisation from within, if she was to occupy a place in the council of the Powers compatible with her great past, did the colonies also assume a higher value in the eyes of the government. Although, owing to the pressure of circumstances, she became nationalised in a surprisingly short time, yet much of the French spirit was infused into the country which till then had been kept in an extraordinary state of isolation. Without doubt the revolution which the system of colonial administration underwent under Ferdinand VI and Charles III is essentially the product of French ideas.

The altered conditions of trade and intercourse had in the meanwhile caused the mother country to suffer in as great a degree as the colonies from the restrictions which fettered the colonial trade. The first breach in the old system was still immaterial. Seville was not a suitable point of departure for an extensive transatlantic trade such as had been developed in the eighteenth century. In this matter it is of no consequence whether or not the navigable water of the lower Guadalquivir had really deteriorated from neglect. But the times when the caravels were considered the most suitable vessels for colonial trade were irrevocably past, and the enforced registration at Seville meant only delay and disadvantages for the larger ocean ships which had long since come into favour. The transference in 1715 of the staple Indian trade to Cadiz, whose bay and harbour were able to shelter the larger vessels and fleets, was at any rate an adaptation to the actual requirements, though it meant no real advance.

The monopoly of the trade with the Indies was soon seriously and generally taken in hand. The government felt keenly that it was an anachronism, that the trade between the mother country and the colonies was still essentially confined to the fleets which traded, at the most, twice in the year. A sense of the value of time also began to manifest itself in the political sphere, quite apart from the fact that the increase of the colonial commerce had proved the impossibility of meeting its requirements by the rare and uncertain arrival of the fleets and by having to encourage an illegal trade intercourse on an extensive scale, to meet the difficulty. For this reason it was regarded as a beneficial sign of progress on both sides, when monthly traffic from Corunna, by means of single fast-sailing vessels, was instituted between Spain and America under Ferdinand VI. Although these ships, in the first instance, were intended to meet the requirements of the government, they were also available for private trade as far as their cargo-space permitted. This measure had scarcely any appreciable influence on the fleets, which had lost considerably in importance, but it had the beneficial effect of making it possible to satisfy the needs of the colonies upon a more peaceful basis, and one which would frustrate the smuggling-trade of foreigners. The excellent results which were thereby gained finally inspired the enlightened government of Charles III courageously to break completely with all former systems. In 1774 the trade of the colonial provinces among themselves became enfranchised under certain limitations which aimed at the protection of Spanish produce, and thus a larger sphere of activity was opened up for the beginnings of a colonial industry. Four years later (1778) the transatlantic trade was also entirely reorganised. The trading of the fleets was suspended, and the Cadiz-Seville monopoly was annulled. In place of it, it was decided that the nine important harbours of the mother country should have the right to be starting-ports of the ships for the colonies, while on the other side of the ocean no less than twenty-two harbours were opened for direct traffic with Spain. A new table of rates, wisely adapted to the circumstances, was at the same time drawn up, so that, even though the smuggling of the English and the Portuguese could not be entirely suppressed, the essential part of the trading intercourse was once more placed on a legal footing.

The markets which had long since ceased to meet the requirements of Portobello therewith also came to an end, and the traffic which had once followed the road from Panama, via Peru and Chile, to Tucuman and Buenos Ayres was now completely revolutionised. Buenos Ayres, owing to its natural situation, became, with the new order of things, the specially favoured harbour for the trade of the southern colonies with Spain, as the ships intended for Chile and Peru, after running up to Buenos Ayres, now followed the route round Cape Horn, in order to reach the harbours of the Pacific Ocean. The province of Buenos Ayres had until then been the stepchild of the government, but under the new laws it was placed on an equal footing with the richest colonial province of Spain, because of the wealth of its plantations and sheep-farms.

The facilities offered to trade brought about an important revolution in commerce. The farmer and planter found it easier to procure a remunerative market for the product which could be drawn in unlimited abundance from the soil, owing to its luxuriant fruitfulness. The facilitated trade therefore reacted in a forcible manner upon agriculture and manufacture. The government under Charles III was, moreover, eager to make up in every way for the persistent neglect of the past. Scientific expeditions were sent out to make exact surveys, not only of the coasts, but also of the entire surface of the countries, and they were at the same time commissioned to examine carefully the mineralogical, botanical, and zoölogical peculiarities of the New World. This was the origin of the great collections of colonial products in Madrid, the precursors of our botanical gardens and natural-history museums. These researches have enriched science with many indispensable features, and we have to thank them for quinine, whose extraction has carried an industry far into those regions from which the European settler had not until then understood how to gain any advantage. How profoundly these events have influenced mankind, and what never to be forgotten achievements of science they have matured, may be sufficiently characterised under one name. By order of the Spanish government Alexander von Humboldt undertook his journeys of many years' duration through Central and South America. The scientific results of these travels inaugurated a new epoch in the history of geography and natural science, which he directed into those new channels where they have to this day remained.

The Spanish colonial policy was one of the most enlightened in this direction; but in matters of administration Spain could not brace herself for a severance from the old system, for she was still too much imbued with the ideas of posterity. She was avenged, however, all the more for this, when, during the second half of the eighteenth century, a powerful intellectual revolution, advancing with rapid strides, was brought about in the Old World also, which from day to day widened the gulf more and more between the conditions in the colonies and the demands of the spirit of the age. After a short time it seemed almost impossible to bridge these over by means of a normal continuation of culture, and it would even then have been impracticable if political circumstances had not, owing to a sudden catastrophe which brought disaster to both sides, torn asunder the bond of national association, thereby putting an end to the reciprocal influence of the mother country and the colonies, one upon the other.

## 6. THE ENGLISH COLONIAL EMPIRE

### A. The Discovery of the Northern Continent

THE North American continent during the sixteenth century, especially in those districts situated on the eastern seaboard, was a free field for discoverers of all nations; but during several generations no one of the rival Powers succeeded in rendering its possession effective by a permanent settlement. The reason for this was the unpromising appearance of the coasts, on which were to be found a pleasant climate, green meadows, and vast forests, but, in addition, powerful and warlike natives, who vigorously opposed the landing of strangers, and who, by their poverty and the simplicity of their customs, showed clearly the absence of treasure to be won without exertion. Thus it was that the various expeditions contented themselves, in pure platonic fashion, with taking possession of the land in the name of their sovereigns; but neither Spain nor Portugal took the trouble to make serious protest when districts within their respective spheres of discovery were for decades marked on the maps as French or English.

The first Europeans to set foot on North American soil were the Vikings under Leif Erikson and Thorfinn Karlsefne, who were driven thither while on a voyage from Iceland to Greenland about the year 1100. But their temporary settlements in Vinland, Markland, and Huitramannaland had been long forgotten when the discovery of Columbus unveiled a new world. It was the efforts to raise interest in his project, made by the discoverer at the various courts of western Europe years before the realisation of his hopes, that drew attention to his discovery and led to the opening up of the New World some years later.

The honour of having been the first among the discoverers of that day to reach the mainland of North America belongs to Giovanni Gabotto, or, as he was called in England, John Cabot. He was specially sent out in 1497, on a voyage to the West, to seek, after the manner of Columbus, the treasures of the Indies and to take possession, for England, of any unknown lands he might come across. It was in fulfilment of this commission that John Cabot in the years 1497–1498 made two voyages between England and America. The first time he landed in Labrador and followed the coast northward. On his second journey he reached the American coast at a point somewhat farther south, and, sailing southward, made, it is supposed, a rough exploration of the Atlantic seaboard till he reached the latitude of Florida.

Then for nearly a century the English paid no further attention to this land, in which their race was to have so great a future, except to send occasional ships to the inexhaustible fishing-grounds of the Newfoundland Banks; but even there they did less than most other nations.

The news of Cabot's landing showed the Portuguese that there were undiscovered lands in the north, similar to Brazil in the south, which, according to the delimitation of the spheres of discovery, belonged to them. This was, at any rate, the incentive for the voyages of the brothers Gaspar and Miguel Cortereal. To them King Manuel granted a charter giving them exclusive possession and trading-rights in whatever lands they might find to the north of the Spanish colonial sphere and beyond the line of demarcation agreed upon. These claims were recognised and remained in their or their heirs' possession till 1579, though no effective settlement of the newly discovered region was made by the Portuguese. On his first voyage, in 1500, Gaspar Cortereal discovered the island of Newfoundland, with its imposing forests and its bays teeming with fish. In his second journey, in the following year, he was led away by the phantom of a northwest passage to the treasures of India, and, following the coast of Labrador northward, he and his companions became the first victims of the Arctic ice. They perished, in all probability, in Hudson Strait. During a long period the Portuguese made occasional expeditions to the Newfoundland Banks. The first of these, undertaken by Miguel Cortereal to ascertain the fate of his brother, supplied a second party of victims for the ice-deserts of the North. Then these voyages were restricted more and more to the exploitation of the fisheries; and it was only occasionally that Portuguese sailors assisted the progress of discovery in North America. Among those who did so was João Alvarez Faguendez, who in 1521 sailed round the peninsula of Nova Scotia and into the Gulf of St. Lawrence.

The French followed the example of the Portuguese with especial zeal. From the year 1508, at least, the shipowners of Dieppe and Honfleur took a prominent part in the fishing on the Newfoundland Banks. These fishing-expeditions led to occasional visits to the neighbouring coasts, where supplies were taken in, repairs made, and the spoil of the sea dried and smoked for transport. From such settlements Cape Breton received the name it bears to-day, and "Tierra," "Bahia," and "Rio de Bretones" are names that frequently occur in old maps of Canada. Early in the third decade of the sixteenth century these transatlantic lands attracted the attention of the French government. Commissioned by it, Giovanni de Verazzano, in 1524, made an extended voyage of discovery, following the east coast from Florida nearly up to what is now the northern boundary of the United States. Perhaps this undertaking would not have been the only one had not the Portuguese made emphatic diplomatic protest.

But the Spaniards have done incomparably more for the opening up of North America, though their activity was confined principally to the southern part of it. Through slave-hunts among the Bahama islands the Spaniards made acquaintance with the southern extremity of Florida : but so uninviting did it seem that for years no one took the trouble to investigate whether this cape belonged to an island or to the mainland. It was not till 1512 that Juan Ponce de Leon, governor of Porto Rico, set out with three ships to investigate what truth there was in the fabulous reports that were current about the land in the north. On Whitsunday, "Pascua Florida," he reached an unknown coast and named it Florida. From there Ponce sailed along the east coast as far as what was later the site of St. Augustine. But, as the flat shore stretched ever before him in unending monotony, he turned, sailed round the southern extremity of the supposed island, and followed the west coast for a considerable distance ; but at last, finding neither a strait nor fertile land, but everywhere hostile Indians, he returned to Porto Rico, and let years pass before renewing the attempt to open up the lands he had discovered. That he did so at all was due only to the fact that districts which he included among those discovered by himself were touched at by other sailors whose competition he wished to exclude. In particular, Francisco Fernandez de Cordova, after completing his voyage of discovery along the coasts of Yucatan and Mexico as far north as Panuco, took, on his return journey, a course too nearly due east and reached a point, that we cannot fix, on the west coast of Florida. This discovery seemed so interesting that Francisco de Garay ordered his pilot, Pineda, who was then about to convey a number of colonists into the district of Panuco, newly claimed by him, to pay somewhat more attention to the north coast of the Gulf of Mexico. On this occasion Pineda not only came to the firm conclusion that the coast from Panuco to the peninsula of Florida was continuous, but he also discovered the mouth of the Mississippi, without inferring, however, the extraordinary extent of the "hinterland" from the volume of the stream, as Columbus had done in the case of the Orinoco.

Ponce de Leon considered his own claims as a discoverer endangered by these enterprises: he accordingly made application to the Spanish government, and was granted, in the usual manner, rights over the territory he had discovered, conditional upon his rendering his possession effective and actually colonising the land. In the year 1521 he made fresh preparations and shipped six hundred persons, besides cattle and supplies, to start a colony ; but his attempts to effect a landing on the west coast of Florida were all failures ; and at last, mortally wounded by the arrows of the enemy, he decided to return. The greater part of his company perished on the return journey, and he himself reached Cuba only to die.

The hostility of the Indians was just what kept Florida from being forgotten. Of the Indians of the islands, some had been pacified, and others had fled before the Spaniards, who had continually to go farther afield to obtain slaves. Two slave-ships belonging to the licentiates Matienzo and Ayllon met accidentally off one of the northern Bahamas, and made an agreement to venture on an expedition against the warlike Indians of Florida. They did, in fact, bring some booty back to San Domingo, and at the same time gave such favourable reports of the land that the licentiate Lucas Vasquez de Ayllon resolved to continue the exploration and eventually to proceed to colonisation. From the court he obtained without trouble exclusive rights over the territory left without a master by Ponce's death. After preparations lasting several years, during which his pilots explored the Atlantic coast as far as the Santee River, he set out from Española (San Domingo) in 1526 for his new province, with three ships and six hundred men. But he, too, was not favoured by fortune. Sea and shore alike were hostile to him: the largest of his ships was wrecked, and the Indians opposed his attempts at landing at Rio Jordan or San Mateo so vigorously that he was master only within the range of his muskets. The colonists had much to suffer in the swampy coast districts, and when Ayllon himself succumbed to fever the rest of his crew betook themselves to their ships and returned to Española.

After this the colonisation of the Atlantic coast was given up for years; but on the other hand the Gulf coast of Florida (a name then applied to the whole of the North American continent so far as it was known to the Spaniards) was the scene of further expeditions which were of great importance in opening up North America. As early as 1528 Panfilo de Narvaez, governor of the Gulf coast of Florida, the well-known rival of Cortez,[1] cruised from Cuba to Appalachee Bay, to explore, by land and water simultaneously, the territory promised to him in the west. But the land force and the fleet soon got out of touch. The latter returned to Cuba after waiting for months in the neighbourhood of the Mississippi for Narvaez and his company. When the expedition returned to the coast completely exhausted, nothing remained for them but to build the best vessels they could, and by means of these to make their way out of this inhospitable wilderness to more civilised parts. Imagining himself nearer to Panuco than to the Spanish islands, Narvaez steered his frail craft westward; but almost the whole expedition perished in the delta of the Mississippi. Only a few escaped; they continued their journey by land, and, being favoured by fortune, actually succeeded in reaching the Spanish settlements in New Mexico. It has been already mentioned how their exaggerated stories gave a new impulse to expeditions to the fabulous cities of Tusayan and Quivira.[2]

The adventurous expedition of Fernando de Soto took in still more of the interior of the continent. It is almost incredible how, despite repeated disasters, companies of considerable size assembled again and again to make the journey into the unknown with hearts as light as if it were a mere pleasure-trip. So strong was the attraction of the personality of De Soto, one of the richest conquistadors of Peru, that, despite the fact that he took only picked men for the expedition, his company on leaving Seville numbered a thousand men. After completing his preparations in Cuba, De Soto crossed over to Tampa Bay on the west coast of Florida,

---

[1] See *ante*, p. 368.  [2] See *ante*, p. 373.

where he had the rare good fortune to meet with a friendly reception from the natives and was able to prepare in peace for his journey into the interior. But it was not long that the Spaniards enjoyed the friendship of the natives. As soon as they began to press forward in a northerly direction they met with Indians who had sworn hostility to the Europeans from the time of Narvaez. During the whole course of their three years' wandering the Spaniards were able to gain the friendship of the natives only when they allied themselves with a tribe and helped it in war against its neighbours. The sum total of adventures, fights, and privations that reduced De Soto's splendid company to a band of little more than three hundred half-naked and wholly exhausted adventurers was indeed extraordinary.

But incidents of this kind are not what give the expedition its historic importance. What is most interesting for posterity about De Soto's expedition is the geographical and ethnographical aspect of the country traversed, which can be fixed, at least approximately, by the accounts that have come down to us. The Spaniards first made their way northward, at a fixed distance from the marshy coast, till they reached the head of Appalachee Bay. Then they turned their backs to the sea and pressed on toward the north and northeast through Georgia and South Carolina, till they reached the country where the rivers Altamaha and Savannah rise. Neither here nor farther south did they dare to cross the thickly wooded range of the Alleghanies, so terrible did its forest solitudes seem to them. Nor did the north attract them; they turned toward the west and southwest. Making their way through the present State of Alabama, they reached the river of that name, and, striking the sea at Pensacola, established temporary communication with the fleet that brought them supplies. In spite of the long, fruitless wandering De Soto could not be persuaded to give up the expedition. After a protracted rest at Mobile (then situated considerably more north than the modern town of the same name) he struck out again into the wilderness and reached the Mississippi not far from where Memphis stands to-day. The passage across the " Father of Waters " occasioned a long delay, but with the help of the Indians and by means of some improvised boats it was finally accomplished. Then the expedition continued its journey through the present Arkansas and southern Missouri as far as the upper reaches of the White River. Finding that as he advanced toward the northwest the land was less fertile and more sparsely settled, De Soto again changed his course and continued his journey southward and westward over the Washita to the Red River, only to learn that neither treasure nor civilised settlement was to be found in the forests and prairies. His decision to return to the Mississippi was a tacit abandonment of all his hopes. He reached that mighty watercourse just above its junction with the Red River, and, here, almost exactly three years after his departure from Cuba, he succumbed to fever and to depression at the failure of his plans. His companions imagined themselves so near to New Mexico that they at first attempted to make their way thither by land; but the lack of food supplies in the west compelled them once more to make for the Mississippi. Finally they were so fortunate as to be carried out to sea by the stream, in their frail improvised craft, before they had become too weak to resist the attacks of the ever-hostile Indians. The tedious journey along the Gulf coast had still to be accomplished before they could reach Panuco, the nearest Christian settlement, and there recuperate from their fatigue and privations. Of De Soto's thousand companions only three hundred and eleven reached the journey's end. So little had been gained by the sacrifice of life that the Spanish government issued a decree forbidding further exploring expeditions into this unfriendly land.

### B. French Efforts and Settlements

Though Florida had fallen into discredit with the Spaniards, it had not the same bad name among other nations. Religious discord in France had once before driven men to seek a land of peace and toleration beyond the ocean, when Villegaignon founded his colony in Brazil.[1] But while the object of this first attempt was to establish a colony where toleration should be extended to men of both creeds, the second, undertaken by Ribault and Laudonnière, in the years 1562–1565, aimed at establishing on the coast of Florida a settlement which, though not exclusively Protestant, was to be a place of refuge for those who in their own land were subjected to bitter persecution and oppression. There was, to begin with, not the least difficulty in finding a place on the deserted coast of Florida where the fleet could land its crews with their stores. For this purpose the leaders chose Charleston Bay, called by them May River and by the Spaniards Rio de San Mateo, and named their settlement, overlooked by a fortified hill, "Arx Carolina"[2] in honour of the French sovereign. If the settlers had had no other end in view than to live in peace and tolerance on this distant shore, tilling the land and seeking a peaceful livelihood, it is probable that they could have established themselves and founded a colony undisturbed, as did the English at this and at other points on the coast at a later date. But among the colonists workers were in a minority, and their favourite mode of earning a livelihood was to scour the seas around the Antilles in swift and lightly built craft, and, like pirates, to attack wherever there was a prospect of success.

By such proceedings they drew upon themselves the wrath of the Spaniards. Philip of Spain considered it a serious matter that a foreign nation, and especially Spain's hereditary enemy, should dare to establish itself so near to the Spanish colonial possessions and within the Spanish colonial sphere. Still more serious in his eyes was the circumstance that they were heretics who thus threatened the Christianising work which Spain regarded as her historic mission. Accordingly Menendez de Aviles, one of the best seamen then at Spain's disposal, received a commission to root out at all costs this foreign settlement on Spanish soil. He was specially instructed, as a matter of principle, to show no mercy to heretics. The accusation of treacherous cruelty raised by the French against the Spanish leader is scarcely justified. During their own religious struggles they showed themselves scarcely less fanatical than was Menendez toward them. But the latter's action was truly the cause of the transplantation of fanaticism in religious strife to the New World. Even before Menendez had reassembled his forces, which were scattered by a storm in crossing the ocean, he gained an important success. He succeeded in creeping in by night between the French fleet, anchored at San Mateo, and the land, and in driving it from the coast. He then, instead of attacking Fort Carolina from the sea, surprised it from the land side after a difficult march through the forest, and, meeting with scarcely any resistance, overmastered the garrison, suffering very slight loss himself. Meanwhile the French

---

[1] See *ante*, p. 399.　　　[2] See Plate at p. 428.

fleet had been wrecked during the storm, and the crews were thrown on the coast in so defenceless a condition that they had no alternative but to surrender unconditionally. Menendez showed no pity to them in their helplessness, and spared only those who professed the Catholic faith. This was barbarous severity; but he was only obeying his sovereign's orders, and he had never concealed the fact that every heretic he could lay hands on was doomed.

But Menendez's work was not one of destruction only: he was commissioned to colonise Florida for Spain. Accordingly, on the spot where he first landed, he founded the little town of St. Augustine, the oldest town in the United States, which, though several times shifted, has had an uninterrupted existence up to the present day. A second settlement that he founded on the site of Arx Carolina had a less happy fate. It was taken by assault some years later by French Protestants under De Gourgues, who, to avenge his fallen countrymen and co-religionists, mercilessly put to death all Spaniards who fell into his hands. But Charles IX disclaimed this deed as an act of unjustifiable piracy, and made complete and express renunciation of his claims to the coast of Florida, where the Spanish settlement of St. Augustine slowly developed and long resisted all foreign encroachments.

Here in the south France lightly gave up all her colonial aspirations; but on the other hand she had already begun to establish herself, commencing in the extreme northeast. These latter claims she persisted in much more tenaciously, and had indeed the idea of using the ground gained as a starting-point to bring the whole of the North American continent under her sway. As early as 1535 Jacques Cartier undertook a voyage of discovery along the coasts of Newfoundland and Labrador, and though those regions showed little wealth, he returned the following year to continue his exploration. On this second journey he went farther up the Gulf of St. Lawrence than before, and discovered the great river of the same name that flows into it. Cartier followed the river up stream and, with his ships, reached the site of Quebec; then he pushed on with smaller vessels as far as the Indian capital Hochelaga, the modern Montreal. The swiftness of the impetuous stream prevented him from continuing his exploration farther, so he returned to the fleet and spent a severe winter at its anchorage, suffering heavy losses. Next year he returned to France with the first cargo of Canadian furs. Two years passed before the attempt was made to render effective by colonisation the possession of the lands discovered by Cartier. It was in 1541 that Roberval was sent out by Francis I. Cartier was to accompany him as guide, and then to continue his own explorations. They crossed the ocean separately, and founded small settlements in the neighbourhood of Quebec, which served as centres for further exploration. But these settlements, like so many others, were of short duration. After enduring two long and dreary winters the settlers were taken back to France and the colonies abandoned.

A long time now passed before the attempts at settlement were renewed by the government; but there were always French vessels on the Newfoundland Banks, that traded also in furs on the St. Lawrence, and this trade turned out to be so profitable that early in the seventeenth century a number of Breton traders combined and succeeded in obtaining a monopoly for their company from the French king, Henry IV. The form of this Canadian colony was peculiar from the beginning. It was intermediate between a trading-company and a Crown colony. The

Ark Carolina, Built between the Rivers Ashley and Cooper, the Ancient
Fortified Settlement at Charleston, South Carolina

(From Dapper's "America." Amsterdam, 1673)

intention of the founders, Pontgravé, Chauvin, and De Monts, was only to carry on the fur-trade more vigorously and to organise it on a better footing. Their settlement, Tadoussac, at the junction of the Saguenay and the St. Lawrence, was intended to be nothing more than a trading-station. But when Samuel de Champlain entered the service of the company in 1603, not only were the aims of the undertaking widened, but its political status was gradually altered, the State gaining more influence and at the same time assuming more responsibility. In 1612 Count de Soissons was set at the head of the Canadian enterprise as viceroy; and the fact that a second prince of the royal family followed him in this position tended in no small degree to impress upon the colonial enterprise a more and more official character. But the economic conditions of the colony stood in strange contradiction to this. Till well into the eighteenth century the French Canadian settlements kept their character as trading-factories and mission-stations. Women, with the exception of nuns, were as rare as true settlers. The population was principally composed of soldiers, traders, and priests; and for many years the colonies remained dependent on their imports from Europe and on barter with the natives. The colonies were not in a position to feed themselves till they passed into the hands of the English, when their constitution underwent a radical change.

In spite of this a thoroughly characteristic feature of French colonial administration was the need for expansion, and that to an almost unlimited extent, out of all proportion to the strength of the colony. This was partly the consequence of the economic state of the colony. The receipts from the fur-trade had to cover the expenditure, which, in spite of the moderate number of the colonists, continually increased. This was possible only so long as a trade monopoly in an extensive region was assured; and, to accomplish this, effective possession became more and more necessary as the advance guard of Dutch and English colonies made its way over the Alleghanies and entered into competition with the French hunters and fur-traders. But in considering the disproportionate need for expansion we must not underestimate the influence of a number of individual discoverers, possessed of marked characteristics, who accidentally came together in this Canadian movement, and who, in spite of temporary failure, were continually giving a new impulse for advance. Thus the provinces of Canada and Louisiana developed into the colossus with feet of clay that the French colonial empire proved to be when put to the test.

The first of the discoverers who played so great a part in the expansion of New France was Samuel de Champlain. From 1603 to 1616 he was connected with the French colonial government, being either in its service or at its head. But the interests of the government or of the trading-company never tied his hands, even where his own interests were most intimately connected with them. The unfailing spell that drew him across the ocean into the solitudes of the west was an ardent desire to unravel the secrets of those remote tracts, and to claim as French all that might come to light in their primeval forests.

At the commencement of his enterprise he was convinced that the friendship of the Indians was absolutely necessary to him if he was to carry out his plans. The natives who came down the St. Lawrence to Quebec and Tadoussac to barter furs belonged chiefly to the Huron race and to some Algonquin tribes who lived near the Hurons and were allied with them against their common enemy the

Iroquois, who lived to the east and southeast.[1]  As the way to the unknown west belonged to them, Champlain did not hesitate to ally himself with them, and he even went so far as to buy their services by helping them against the Iroquois. The first campaign undertaken in the region where Lake Champlain still keeps alive the memory of the discoverer was so successful that it greatly increased the consideration in which the Europeans were held by their savage allies.  In this respect Champlain had completely carried out his intentions.  That he had drawn upon his fellow countrymen the undying hostility of the Iroquois did not appear a matter worthy of consideration to him or to anybody else; nor, considering the superiority of European weapons, would it have become so serious a matter as it did but for the fact that European enemies of France now naturally allied themselves with the Iroquois and provided them with weapons that placed them on equal terms with the whites in battle and rendered them very dangerous opponents to the scattered and sparsely populated French settlements.  Champlain could now, under the protection of the Hurons and their allies, explore the country about the St. Lawrence in all directions.  The limits to which he extended French influence were Lake Champlain in the southeast, the middle Saguenay in the north, and in the west Lake Huron, which he reached by way of the Ottawa and Nipissing, without, however, gaining any clear conception of the great system of North American lakes.

Champlain did even more to strengthen French influence; he summoned missionaries to Canada.  Those interested in the trading-company looked unfavourably upon the extra expense entailed by this, the more so because the endeavours of the missionaries to get the Indians to settle were prejudicial to the fur-trade; but the influence of the French government and Champlain's lofty views gained a complete victory over the narrower opinions of the traders.  Champlain first called the Franciscans into the colonies, and they built at Quebec the first permanent church in North America.  But although Protestant interests were strongly represented in the company, and hostility to the Jesuits was most pronounced, yet this order, which deserves all praise for its missionary work, could not be permanently kept out of the Canadian settlements.  From 1625 they worked side by side with the Franciscans.  How zealously they engaged in the conversion of the Indians of the north is shown by the extent of the literature which the brothers of the order have published on their work in Canada.  Favoured by political events at home (after the taking of La Rochelle, the last stronghold of the Protestants, the settlement of Protestants in the colonies was, through Richelieu's influence, forbidden), they became more and more the dominant element in the colony, and the stamp they impressed on it has not yet quite disappeared, in spite of years of English rule.

Even in these early times Canada had once been in danger of falling into the hands of the English.  In 1621 Sir William Alexander received from James I a charter to found a feudal colony under the name of Nova Scotia.  Its boundaries included the greater part of the French colony.  When war broke out between England and France on the religious question, Alexander attempted to enforce his claims.  His ships repeatedly forced a passage up the St. Lawrence, and, by capturing French ships, almost completely cut off communication between Quebec and the mother country.  In 1628 Alexander's ships appeared before Quebec and demanded its surrender; and it was only Champlain's ability that caused them

[1] See *ant*, p. 207.

to retreat with their object unattained. But they returned next year, and the colonists, exhausted by a severe winter, which was doubly hard on account of the absence of help from Europe, offered no resistance. Canada was at this moment in the hands of the English. But a treaty of peace had already been concluded in Europe, and by it the possessions of both parties were to remain unchanged. Quebec was given up by the British, and French Canada was thus enabled to prolong an honourable existence for more than a hundred years.

Champlain again returned to Quebec, and did much for the Canadian colony before he ended his life there in 1635. The English claims were practically nullified; the peace with the Hurons was again confirmed; and far up the St. Lawrence, at Three Rivers, a new settlement was founded. Still greater deeds were projected by him, but he received no news of their fulfilment before his death. Jean Nicolet, one of his most distinguished followers, had meanwhile revisited Lake Huron by the old route, and had then gone on through the Strait of Mackinac into Lake Michigan and far along its western shore. He failed, indeed, to discover the geological structure of the basin of these lakes and their peculiar connection; but in making alliances with the Indians as far as the Fox River he paved a way that became of great importance in the future.

The following years were, however, unfavourable to Canada. There was indeed a third French settlement founded at Montreal in 1643, but, like the older settlements, it suffered excessively from the hostility of the Iroquois, who made it almost impossible to go beyond the walls of the town. The consequences of Champlain's Indian policy made themselves felt in a most disagreeable way. The Iroquois would perhaps have made peace with the French, but only at the price of their abandonment of the Hurons. This price the French could not pay, as they valued their own existence; and though they were not able to ward off destruction from the Hurons, they at least kept the friendship of this tribe and of their neighbours by not actively supporting the Iroquois. The latter unmistakably maintained the upper hand, and, after long and disastrous contests, the Hurons, and with them some of the Algonquins, abandoned their dwellings on the St. Lawrence and the Ontario and turned to the Far West. After long wanderings they settled down between the Mississippi and Lake Superior. This was an additional inducement for the French fur-traders to penetrate farther west. The migration of the Hurons was directly favourable to the progress of discovery in this direction, and it had not the disastrous effects on the St. Lawrence settlements that were feared. Satisfied with their revenge, the Iroquois made a peace — though not a very stable one — with the French, and went so far as to receive French Jesuit missionaries. The Jesuits were the first to observe the especially favourable geographical position of the Iroquois, who were situated on the watershed from which rivers flow eastward to the ocean, northward to the St. Lawrence, and westward to the "Great Unknown Water;" and these observations did not a little toward the furthering of French exploration on the Mississippi and its final inclusion in the French colonial empire.

But on the whole Canada dragged on a languid existence till Colbert took up colonial affairs with his characteristic energy. He dissolved Richelieu's "Company of a Hundred," which had till then enjoyed a monopoly of trade with Canada, transferring the privilege to the great French West India Company, which by its activity did much to infuse new life into Canadian enterprise. The lake region was soon thoroughly explored in all directions, and the ascendency of French influence was assured by the establishment of mission-stations and trading-depots. Of these the most important were at Sault Sainte-Marie, between Lake Superior and Lake Huron; near Mackinac, between Lake Huron and Lake Michigan: and at Niagara Falls.

Hitherto the French explorers had been spurred on by the hope of finding by way of the Great Lakes a western passage to the seas of Cathay. But as travellers to the west found land ever before them, and rivers flowing east, more credit was given to the stories told by Indians about the "Father of Waters," whose name, Mississippi, was first learned by Europeans in 1670. Its exploration was then the problem before the adventurous French discoverers. With its solution the colonial power of France reached its highest point. The first Europeans to reach the Mississippi from the north were Joliet and Marquette. The former was, at Colbert's instigation, sent out by the new Canadian governor, Frontenac, in 1673, with express orders to fathom the mystery of the "Western Water." Marquette, a missionary in Mackinac, volunteered, to join him. The two followed the beaten track through Green Bay and up Fox River. There their Indian guides brought them to a place where they had only to carry their canoes two miles overland to reach a branch of the Wisconsin, and now they had but to trust themselves to the stream in order to reach the Mississippi itself in a few weeks. At the mouth of the Ohio they recognised the great waterway mentioned in the hazy reports of the Iroquois. When they reached the great confluence of the Missouri, the problem they were attempting was solved. A tributary of this magnitude implied extensive tracts of land and a large watershed in the north and northwest; and the Mississippi itself, flowing ever southward, could lead nowhere else than to the Gulf of Mexico. They followed the river as far as the mouth of the Arkansas, which was a further confirmation of their suppositions. Then, not wishing to run the risk of incurring Spanish hostility, which might render their discovery fruitless, they commenced the return journey and made their way along the Illinois and the Des Plaines to the site of Chicago.

In France the prospects which Joliet's discovery opened up for French colonial expansion were only gradually comprehended; but in Canada there were plenty of far-seeing men who were resolved to follow up these discoveries at once. Among these was the governor, Frontenac. It was through his interposition that René Robert Cavelier, Sieur de la Salle, the possessor of one of the small feudal domains of which a number were established round about Montreal, received letters patent from the Crown, granting him the monopoly of trade on the Illinois and the right to establish trading-factories there. It was thus that La Salle became the pioneer of western exploration and the discoverer of Louisiana, to the possession of which he attached great importance, believing that the future of French trade and of French colonisation depended on it. But he himself was not destined to profit by his discovery. He made his way over the lakes to the river St. John, and thence to the Illinois, where he built Fort Crèvecœur as a base for further advance. But misfortune dogged his footsteps. His boats were lost, and, while he himself returned to Canada to obtain means for pushing farther on, the garrison abandoned the fort. When La Salle returned some years later with a new expedition, he found the whole neighbourhood laid waste. The hostility of the Iroquois followed the French from New England even into this wilderness. But La Salle did not lose courage. He succeeded, with his party, in reaching the mouth of the Mississippi, and took possession of the land for the French king, Louis XIV, naming it Louisiana. This possession, it is true, existed only on paper. La Salle had neither the stores nor the colonists to found a settlement, so he returned once more across the Illinois. There he endeavoured to make sure of one point of support by erecting Fort Louis at Starved Rock. The object of his next undertaking, the erection of forts at the mouth of the Mississippi, was to render Louisiana safe against attacks by the Spaniards from the Gulf of Mexico, just as Fort Louis was to render it safe against English attacks from the Iroquois territory. His successes now aroused interest in France. No fewer than four ships set out to take him and his colonists to the mouth of the Mississippi, which unfortunately he failed to recognise from the sea. After sailing much too far west he landed in Texas at the mouth of the Colorado, which he took to be a branch of the Mississippi. When he recognised his error the ships were already beyond recall. He endeavoured to reach the Mississippi by land, but was killed by his own followers during the journey. The colonists on the Colorado succumbed to the climate and to the attacks of the natives. When Raphael de Tonty, La Salle's most faithful adherent, made his way from the Illinois to the Lower Mississippi to bring help to his leader, all he could learn was that the expedition had been a complete failure. Still La Salle's achievement had decided the future of Louisiana. Where Joliet and La Salle had shown the way, missionaries, fur-traders, hunters, and adventurers followed in their footsteps into that rich and extensive region to the west. Small settlements sprang up on the Illinois, on the Kaskaskia, and on the Arkansas. Here, just as at first in Canada, the French did not, indeed, take root as true settlers and tillers of the soil, but, by adapting themselves to the customs of the natives, they gained great influence over them and were able to keep them on the French side in the struggle which was becoming inevitable between the French colonies in Canada and the English on the Atlantic coast. The knowledge possessed by the Indians played no small part in disseminating information as to the extraordinary richness of the land. It is only by thinking of its subsequent development that one can fully realise the glamour which was connected for a short time with the name of Louisiana.

In 1699 Lemoine d'Iberville sailed from France to the Gulf of Mexico, to attempt once more to carry out the scheme for which La Salle had given his life. He met with better fortune, and, after experimenting and feeling his way for several years, founded the settlement of Rosalie, the first French town in the district about the mouth of the Mississippi. For years it remained nothing more than a starting-point for the expeditions of fur-traders, fortune-hunters, and others; but even their occasional successes were sufficient to attract renewed attention in France. The monopoly of trade in Louisiana was leased by the Crown to a merchant named Crozat for a term of two years. After this it passed into the hands of the India Company under the management of John Law; and under the régime of this financier, who for a time was all powerful at the Court of the regent, the wildest speculation was indulged in. The result, of course, was a financial collapse, — one of the greatest the world has ever seen. But during this period not a little was done for Louisiana. There were a large number of colonists sent out, though the majority of them were not of the most desirable class, and it was by these that New Orleans was founded. But the incapacity of the French for colonial enterprise, combined with Law's unscrupulous procedure, put an abrupt end to the great expectations entertained for Louisiana. As is always the case, the depression following the collapse was proportioned to the inflation before it, and the colony out of which, under sound management, much more might have been made than out of inhospitable Canada was left to itself for half a century. Before its development had been seriously taken up again, the blow was struck that put an end forever to La Salle's dream of a French colonial empire extending from the Atlantic Ocean to the Gulf of Mexico. After repeated contests, continually growing more bitter, France was hopelessly defeated in the struggle for the possession of the colonies; and at the Peace of Paris she surrendered all her possessions east of the Mississippi to England, and all west of that river to Spain.[1]

## C.  The English in North America

(*a*) *The Beginning of the English Colonial Empire.* — The father of English America is Sir Walter Raleigh. Inspired by the desire of snatching from Spain a portion of her enormous colonial empire, and of gaining for himself and his country a share in the treasure that Spain drew from her colonies, he formed, as early as 1584, the plan of founding an English settlement in Florida, — a name then applied to the whole Atlantic coast of North America. The first ships sent out with this object took possession of Roanoke and the adjacent mainland. They returned without attempting to found a settlement; but so inspiriting were the accounts they gave that Queen Elizabeth named the district Virginia — in allusion to her title, the Virgin Queen. Next year a fleet of seven ships set out to render the possession permanent. But the colonists of the Elizabethan period were not of the stock that rendered New England great. They had no intention of earning their bread by the sweat of their brows, but hoped to become rich without trouble and to lead a careless life of pleasure. But even in these blessed regions that was impossible. Raleigh's colony, in spite of the sacrifices made by its founder, did not enjoy a vigorous existence and was finally abandoned in 1590.

It was the example of the Dutch East India Company that led to the establishment of permanent settlements here. In 1606 James I granted charters to two English companies, one of which, the Virginia Company, was to settle the territory lying between 34 and 38° N. latitude; the other, the Plymouth Company, the territory between 41° and 45° N. It was agreed that the land between 38° and 41° should be free to both competing companies, with the condition that a distance of at least one hundred miles should be kept open between their settlements.

(*b*) *The Virginia Company.* — The Virginia Company began operations at once; the constitution that James I gave to the company was one of the most advanced ever formed. The company, which included many London merchants and persons of great influence (among others, Richard Hakluyt, known by his geographical publications), had sovereign rights in the colony. Virginia was thus not a Crown colony, but the manner in which the company was managed left free scope for government interference. Nay, more, it left the company completely in the power

[1] See the map facing p. 714.

of the king, who had the right of nominating both the directors of the company in London and the managers in America. The advantages possessed by the members of the company were that they had absolute possession of the land they had settled, that they remained English citizens, and that they had the right of unrestricted trade in colonial produce. This last privilege, which stood in strange contradiction to the usage of other nations, seemed to free the Virginia Company from the necessity of disposing of its products to the mother country or by its agency. The full effect of this privilege was certainly not foreseen by James I, and he made some efforts to render it ineffective. Later on, Cromwell's Navigation Act limited its application considerably; and the attempt to enforce more strictly in the English colonies the generally admitted principle of exclusive trade with the mother country was one of the many causes that led to the breaking away of the United States from England.

The colony had at first to struggle with the usual difficulties. The first settlers, who landed on the James River in 1607 and founded Jamestown were adventurers and men of fallen fortunes who had no idea of manfully overcoming their difficulties or of gaining a living by honest, hard work. Even the energy of Captain Smith, the real founder of the community, who by his efforts within and without it did everything possible for the welfare of the young colony, would have failed to save it had not the gold-seekers and idlers been followed, especially through Smith's efforts, by genuine colonists, — farmers and mechanics.

At first the colony was carried on on a communistic basis. Captain Smith introduced — for a time at least — compulsory labour of six hours daily. But the settlement did not begin to prosper till the land was divided among the colonists as private property. The discovery, in tobacco culture, of an industry that could be pursued on a large scale caused the settlements in Virginia to progress rapidly. Many of the colonists had been brought over at the cost of the company, and had to repay their debts before they could acquire property of their own; but, thanks to the high price of tobacco, especially in Holland, they were soon able to render themselves independent and to add, by purchase, new lands to what had already been granted them. The profitableness of the tobacco industry was the best advertisement for the colony, and enticed over many more emigrants, among them not only the shipwrecked and indigent, but also wealthy and enterprising men, who commenced tobacco culture on a larger scale and so brought it into better repute. The scarcity of women was soon remedied by the rapid industrial progress. In 1619 the company tried the experiment of sending to Virginia at its own expense a number of young women. Any one marrying one of these had to repay the passage-money to the company, tobacco being sometimes taken in payment. Very soon the young women were all married, and the company was enabled to repeat the experiment and even increase the charge for passage money. The system of transporting to the colonies criminals condemned to hard labour, which flourished to such an extent in the Antilles, was also tried in Virginia, which was at first occasionally used as a convict settlement. This might have gone on to a much greater extent had not the spirit of the colonists risen to such a degree that they most emphatically refused to allow such an element to be brought among them.

On the other hand they eagerly welcomed another undesirable addition to their population. In 1620 a Dutch vessel landed the first negro slaves at Jamestown. The demand for these was so great that not only were Dutch ships with richer freight attracted thither, but English and even Virginian traders undertook the sale of the blacks. Thus as early as the seventeenth century that plantation life grew up which was afterward characteristic of the southern States of the Union. Soon the whites in Virginia formed only the aristocracy; they lived as plantation owners on their extensive estates, or as mechanics in the not very numerous towns. But the bulk of the work, and especially of the work on the tobacco plantations, and on the cotton plantations that more than a century later surpassed them in importance, was, except where prison labour was employed, performed by negro slaves, whose number continually increased as the colony developed.

Political circumstances also played their part in the rapid development of the colony. But few years after the granting of the charter, James I renounced, in favour of the company, many of the rights stipulated for by the Crown. The choice of the directors was left to the members of the company. These nominated, in place of the colonial manager, a governor of the province, who had almost unlimited power on account of his great distance from his superiors at home. For this reason much depended on the choice of suitable persons for this position, and the company's selection was not always a happy one; but its directors were sensible enough to pay heed to the remonstrances of the colonists, whose influence on the management not only continually increased, but was soon afterward regulated by law. In 1612 the management of the company was transferred from the board of directors to the shareholders themselves, with the provision that four general meetings were to be held yearly, to settle matters connected with the management of the colony; and seven years later this general assembly granted to the colonists a share in the management of their internal affairs. Each of the eleven settlements then existing in Virginia was to send two deputies to Jamestown. These deputies were, in conference with the governor and the board of advice chosen to aid him, to discuss the affairs of the colony and to take action accordingly. As internal dissensions arose in the company, and as it was drawn more and more into the turmoil of home politics, this colonial assembly gained more and more importance; and when, in 1624, James I found it necessary to force the dissolution of the company and to place the colony directly under the management of the Crown, the spirit of independence had already appeared.

The native question had for a long time played no important part in Virginia politics. The first colonists, and especially Captain Smith, succeeded in gaining the friendship of the redskins, and friendly relations were strengthened when a much admired princess, Pocahontas, married an Englishman. When, in 1621, the Indians attempted to check the progress of the strangers, they were badly defeated. Then a long time passed before hostilities again broke out between the Indians and the colonists.

Materially the development of the colony was very rapid; but in other matters complete indifference prevailed. The economic conditions gave an aristocratic tone to the colony. Thus, during the struggle of Charles I against the rising democracy in the mother country, the sympathies of the colonists were entirely on the side of the monarch; and when the Roundheads' victory was complete, many a Royalist made his way to Virginia. But this did not prevent the colonial assembly from maintaining its own parliamentary privileges, nor from employing on the planta-tions the labour of the prisoners of war sent over by Cromwell. The Restoration, on the other hand, was followed by most disadvantageous consequences for Vir-ginia. Charles II enforced the provisions of the Navigation Act more strictly, and thus almost destroyed the freedom of trade enjoyed by Virginia and placed it in this respect in a position very similar to that of the Spanish colonies. This did not seriously affect the Virginians, who did not carry on a large trade; but other measures, that affected their interest more, roused their indignation. The unscru-pulous extravagance characteristic of Charles II led him to attempt to hand over all Virginia to two of his favourites for a period of thirty-one years, and though the colony maintained its constitutional rights it had to submit to be saddled with additional expenditure. The king's Virginia representatives were of as dull conscience as himself. An Indian rising that broke out after the two races had lived peaceably side by side for half a century was by some attributed to the shameless manner in which the governor, for his own personal profit, used his creatures to plunder and oppress the Indians. Matters went so far that a section of the colonists rose against the governor. During this civil war, which was put down with much bloodshed, the capital was burned. Still the greater part of the population remained apathetic as before. The typical Virginian sat, like a pasha, in the midst of his extensive estates, and kept himself apart from everything that did not bear upon his own well-being. His wealth enabled him to widen his intellectual horizon. Of all the colonists the Virginians had perhaps the most intellectual intercourse with the Old World. Among them it was the fashion to travel, and to show to guests from Europe a really princely hospitality. But the Virginians of that time took no further part in politics than the maintenance of their ancient constitutional liberties rendered necessary.

The material interests of the colony, the quibbles of the English government notwithstanding, suffered from the proximity of other colonial provinces that were springing up under similar geographical conditions. Carolina was not actually occu-pied till Charles II gave the district between Florida and Virginia to eight pro-prietors in perpetuity. What is most interesting about this colony is the history of its constitution. It was specially provided in the royal deed of gift that the colonists should have a share in the management of local affairs; further, the phi-losopher John Locke had drawn up for this province a constitution which was to unite a patriarchal aristocracy with parliamentary privileges. But Locke's scheme was so complicated and so impractical in detail that it was never fully carried out. Only two of the principles of Locke's constitution survived, — tolerance in religion, and slavery. As for the rest, the influence of her neighbour Virginia was of far more importance to North Carolina than the sovereign rights of its aristocratic possessors, which were revoked in 1729. Some settlers had migrated from Virginia to the northern districts of Carolina even before the royal letters patent had been granted; the Virginia plantation system also spread here. The governors of Vir-ginia repeatedly interfered in the management of North Carolina, and the northern part of Carolina was often involved in the internal struggles of Virginia. The principal difference between the two colonies was that in Carolina, during the first decades of its existence, no effective provincial government was established, and that a most undesirable class of immigrants were introduced, who made use of their rights of self-government only to perpetuate the unsettled state then existing. This was changed only when the province was constituted a Crown colony. As such Carolina advanced rapidly, developing on the same economic lines as her older sister Virginia, and becoming a dangerous rival to her in the tobacco markets.

The eight feudal lords of Carolina turned their attention chiefly to the south. Here, in 1670, the town of Charleston was founded[1] with settlers of whom the greater number came from Barbados Island. In accordance with the aristocratic and centralising tendency of Locke's proposals the rulers attached great importance to developing the strength of the colony in a town community, and to the avoidance of the scattering of the population characteristic of Virginia and North Carolina. For this reason Charleston sprang up more rapidly than Jamestown. Its better-regulated government and its religious toleration attracted to Carolina elements that were wanting in its northern neighbours, — Puritans from New York, Huguenots from France, Presbyterians from Scotland, — every element that desired to work its way upward by its own strength and was opposed to the development of the plantation system. Further, the proximity of the Spanish colony of St. Augustine caused the development of South Carolina to differ in many respects from that of the northern provinces. The contests occasionally engaged in by the neighbouring Spanish and English colonists were indeed, as a rule, of little importance, and both parties finally agreed to remain at peace even if war should break out between the home countries. Still the proximity of the Spanish colonies was a strong incentive to buccaneering, — an established institution among those of the colonists who came from the islands. Finally, Carolina followed the example of its Spanish neighbours in employing large numbers of Indians as slaves, generally such as had been captured on Spanish territory or dragged from Spanish ships. Owing to these Spanish influences a mode of treating the natives was established which differed considerably from that in vogue in the other provinces. The movement for revoking the rights of the eight feudal lords started in South Carolina. In the conflicts on the boundary Charleston was repeatedly ordered to abandon advantages gained over her Spanish neighbours, but on the other hand she had received no compensation when she suffered at their hands. Such guardianship, combined with misgovernment, led to repeated risings against the feudal lords, whose powers, in consequence, were suspended in 1719 and finally abolished in 1729, monetary compensation being given for their property rights.

About the same time another new province, under management of a quite different kind, was mapped out to the south of the English colonial possessions. The philanthropic movement made its appearance very early in England, and its influence, thanks to the example of the New England colonists and of William Penn, had been already felt several times in America. Pity for those languishing in the debtors' prisons of England induced Oglethorpe to start a movement in their favour. When public and private support had enabled him to collect the necessary funds, he secured from George I a charter giving the grantees exclusive rights of colonisation for twenty-one years in the territory that lay between the rivers Savannah and Altamaha, stretching from ocean to ocean. The colony received, as had her northern neighbours, the name of the reigning sovereign, and was called Georgia Augusta. To South Carolina the establishment of this colony, which lay between her and the Spaniards, was of great importance; for the new .

---

[1] See Plate at p. 428.

province undertook the defence of the southern boundary (Oglethorpe himself twice took the field against the Spaniards) and rendered possible to its northern neighbours a prosperous and undisturbed development. Alliances were made with the Indians, and few white settlers have been held in such esteem by their red-skinned neighbours as was the mild and worthy Oglethorpe. At first the province developed quite according to his ideas. It was a place of refuge for the oppressed and persecuted, and toleration, religious and political, was extended to all. But, as time went on, natural influences proved stronger than human will. It was impossible that the land, whose physical character specially fitted it for an agri-cultural development on the same lines as Virginia's, should remain forever in the possession of the poor and disinherited. In Georgia, as elsewhere, the planters got more and more of the land into their possession, brought their slaves thither, and thus crushed out the attempts of small holders to carry on a different system. By the middle of the eighteenth century Georgia had become a plantation State like Virginia and the Carolinas, and as such it continued its political development side by side with them.

The origin and development of the southern States of the North American Union differs widely from the picture usually regarded as typical of English colonisation in North America. Geographical conditions decisively influenced the course of development. Even in cases where it was the intention of the colonists to found settlements similar to those in New England, there was a gradual transi-tion to the system which developed first and in its most perfect form in Virginia. Most of the colonies were, for a time at least, under the influence of Old World feudal institutions. They did, indeed, very soon free themselves from these; but the aristocratic spirit characteristic of feudalism, with its classification of mankind according to their possessions and rank, came to life again in changed form. The place of the English feudal aristocracy was taken by the large landed proprietors, who kept not only their troops of slaves, but also the greater part of the free white population in a state of dependence. The doctrine of the equality of all did not prevail either in ethics or in law. The planters had practically unlimited power on their own estates, and, in combination, they made use of the parliamentary privileges granted to the landed interests to dominate almost without opposition the government of the province.

Thus the southern colonies, with their special views and special needs, were more closely related to the Spanish colonies than to the New England provinces in the north. Settlement often took place as in the Portuguese colonies; with this difference, that the latter had not the right, common to both English and French feudal colonies, of granting titles and dignities,—a right that did much to strengthen the aristocratic tendency of the southern States. The right of pos-session, as in the Spanish, Portuguese, and French colonies, was conferred by conquest. In the treatment of the natives in South Carolina the worst Spanish examples were followed : if hostile, they were made slaves, but even if they sub-mitted peacefully to the rule of the strangers, they were not, as in the Spanish colonies, granted the rights of subjects.

The North Americans make the claim for their forefathers that they treated the Indians better than others did. The Spaniards took possession, not only of the land, but also of the persons of the natives, compelling them to pay taxes and to labour in the fields. The French did not interfere with the personal liberty of the natives, but they took the land from them solely by right of conquest. The English, on the contrary (and with them must be classed the Dutch), neither interfered with the liberty of the natives nor contested their rights to the land, but often gained possession of it by purchase; yet a common view then, and the prevailing legal theory later, was that the Indian's rights were merely those of occupation.

The kings of Spain and Portugal, it is true, raised the claim that all this land, with its people, had become their property by virtue of the papal bull dividing the unknown half of the world between them; and when the natives contested these claims they were often very badly treated, especially at the time of the conquest and before the native question had been settled by law. In principle, however, Spain had, in accordance with the provisions of Queen Isabella's will, placed the natives in her colonial possessions on the same legal footing as her own subjects; and in return for the services they were bound to render the State they could claim justice and protection from it. The French did not go so far. The privilege of becoming French subjects was not granted to the Hurons, Illinois, etc., but from the days of Champlain France had regarded the Indians as allies and friends, and recognised that, as such, they had claims to the friendship and protection of their white allies. Times without number the French allowed these claims by taking the field, with or without Indian aid, against the Iroquois, the sworn enemies of all natives who were allied with the French. Besides this, the Spaniards and the French, by their missions, did more than words can express for the material and intellectual well-being of their protégés.

The activity of the Indian missions carried on by the English was, in comparison, extraordinarily small, and belonged in general to a period we need not consider; and as for the purchases of land, the great majority of these have been creditable neither to the people of the United States nor to their fathers before them. In former times a large tract of land could be purchased from the Indians, who scarcely understood the nature of the transaction, for a little spirits, gunpowder, or some European finery. But then there was room enough in the broad continent of North America, and it was not so very difficult for a tribe that had thus disinherited itself to find a new home farther west. As civilisation followed them westward, the space left to the Indians, whose mode of life required free expansion, was more and more limited. The unavoidable and by no means unrecognised consequence of the policy of dispossessing the Indians of their lands was that the tribes, now crowded together, carried on endless bloody feuds to preserve their very existence, except when opportunity offered of attacking their neighbours across the boundary of the district claimed by the State.

The fundamental distinction in the native question is that in law the Indian was to the Spaniard a brother, to the Frenchman a friend, to the Englishman a stranger.

(c) *The Plymouth Company.* — Contemporaneously with the Virginia Company, James I, in 1606, had recognised a second trading-company which was to colonise the territory lying between latitudes 41° and 45° N. This company was called the Plymouth Company,[1] since its most influential members belonged to Plymouth, England. Nothing was done, however, beyond making preliminary

---

[1] See *ante*, p. 434.

inquiries, even when James I, in 1620, organised a new company, the Council for New England, giving it all the land between latitudes 40° and 48 N. and granting it feudal privileges. In this district and at this same time the first English colonies were founded, but without any connection with, and rather in opposition to, Donatare's Company, which was dissolved in 1638, after having done little more than to make money by the sale of transatlantic titles. The first real colonists in this district were English religious refugees. Single groups and communities to whom the Reformation, as officially carried out in England, did not appear to go far enough, separated themselves very early from the English High Church. As their number increased they combined to form new sects, Puritans, Separatists, etc.; but in doing this they drew upon themselves the active persecution of the dominant Church. Before its power they fled, for the most part, to Holland. But when general attention was drawn to transatlantic colonial enterprises, there ripened among the Puritans a plan of seeking a place of refuge across the ocean where they could exercise their faith in freedom and security.

With the support of like-minded friends in England, their representative obtained from the Virginia Company the right to found settlements across the ocean. It was in the autumn of 1620 that the "Mayflower" carried to America the first colonists of the North, the founders of the town of New Plymouth. Despite Puritanic strictness and simplicity, this colony, too, had to pass through a time of severe struggle before it began to grow strong and make progress. Its agreement with the English company assured to the immigrants almost complete independence. From the beginning the Pilgrim Fathers were almost exclusively their own rulers. Though they had fled before English intolerance, this did not prevent them from establishing in their midst a régime at least as intolerant. Any deviation from their puritan orthodoxy was unrelentingly punished by expulsion from the settlement. At a time when every strong arm should have been welcome to help to build up the languishing colony, they more than once rejected capable settlers only because they would not submit to the religious and political severity of the colonial government. It was largely for this reason that they were unable to obtain a charter of their own from the mother country.

Political consolidation was attained only by combination with a later undertaking of the same kind which was more favoured by fortune in this respect. In 1629 Charles I granted to the Massachusetts Bay Company a charter which gave it the right to found colonial settlements. The form of a chartered company was chosen in accordance with current practice. What was really aimed at here was, as in New Plymouth, a place of refuge for the hard-persecuted dissenters. In the same year the charter was removed from England to Massachusetts, and the government of the colony was placed in the hands of those colonists who were members of the corporation. From that time the colonists chose their own governor and his councillors. There was, besides, an Assembly, in which every town was represented by two delegates elected by the freemen. The colony successfully defended its rights against the Plymouth Company. At a later date Charles I, aiming at centralisation, took steps to alter the constitution of the colony; but he fell before it had become necessary for the colonists to defend, by open opposition to the royal will, the privileges they had won for themselves. Under Cromwell a benevolent guardianship was extended to all the Puritan communities of the New World: Charles II failed to overcome the passive resistance of the colony, which, under James II, was forced to submit to the judicial revocation of its charter rights. William of Orange restored all its privileges; and when they had again to be defended against attacks by the government it was in alliance with all the other American colonies.

Religious intolerance, which had once driven the Puritans to New Plymouth and Boston, continued to thrive in their midst. In 1635 the Massachusetts Assembly banished a much-respected preacher, Roger Williams, only because he attacked the frequent amalgamation of Puritan orthodoxy with the political rights of the colony and stood up for perfect toleration. With the help of the Narragansett Indians he fled to Rhode Island. Many of like mind came to him from the neighbouring colonies and from England; and he founded new settlements which politically followed, in all respects, the model of Massachusetts, the popular vote being all powerful; but the principle was maintained that a man's religious beliefs are his own private concern, so that in law all faiths were actually equal. The struggle for an independent existence of the little colony of Rhode Island, situated among the intolerant Puritan colonies, was the more severe since the latter allowed it no place in the confederation established in 1643; but finally it succeeded in obtaining a charter from Charles II, thus securing its continued independent existence.

Meanwhile quite a number of little settlements had sprung up on the New England coast, founded, some from older colonies, some direct from England. New Hampshire, granted to English merchants under several patents, had drawn so close to the intolerant Massachusetts that it was united to it in 1642 temporarily. Connecticut, too, was largely a Puritan settlement constituted on more purely democratic principles than was Massachusetts. With the exception of New Plymouth these settlements progressed with surprising rapidity. They protected themselves against the Indians by their generally peaceful policy and by their confederation established in 1643. Against the home government they had at times scarcely any need of protection. The confusion of the civil war, and the changing fortunes of the two parties, gave the rulers in England so much to do that they were glad to leave the colonies to themselves. These same causes gave a great impetus to emigration; for not only did the conquered seek refuge under the freer rule of the colonies, but many others crossed the ocean only because the political disturbances which convulsed the mother country scarcely affected the progress of prosperous development in the colonies. The colonial policy of Cromwell, which found its complete expression in the Navigation Act, curtailed to a great extent the freedom of trade enjoyed by the colonies; but this measure was in agreement with the spirit of the age, and it was chiefly the trade with Holland that was affected. From France and Spain the colonies felt themselves separated by the same national and religious differences as the mother country, and the sense of their connection with England was still so strong that the idea seldom occurred of offering the Navigation Act that resistance which had successfully prevented all interference with the internal affairs of the colonies.

The internal constitution of all these colonies was similar. In general but secondary importance was attached to trade, the true basis of the community being found in labour. There was no search for the precious metals, no barter with the natives, no attempts at their subjugation. When it was impossible to come to a peaceful agreement with them, they were, it is true, driven back by force; but the colonists did not take more land than was necessary to secure their own livelihood by agriculture and the cultivation of a few staple products. Slavery and prison labour were no more excluded than in the southern English settlements; but the natural and economic conditions necessary for their extensive employment were absent. Agriculture here demanded harder work than was to be obtained by compulsory labour; further, the climate was unhealthy for blacks and unsuited for those products whose cultivation could be carried on on the large scale common in the south. Since every man lived, as a rule, on the returns of his own labour, the little communities required comparatively little space. They forced their way into the interior but slowly, and for a long time did not come into conflict with the inhabitants. On the other hand they rooted themselves to the soil more firmly than the colonists in any other part of America. The population was denser, and, owing to the smaller admixture of foreign elements, more compact than in the other colonies. Almost all of the settlers came with wife and child to the New World, with the settled purpose of remaining there and establishing a home for their descendants; thus there developed here the earliest and strongest manifestation of an American national spirit which was greatly furthered by the forms of local government which developed in the colonies.

(*d*) *The Dutch.* — The first against whom the awakening national spirit of the Americans turned were the Dutch. Their attention had been first drawn to the North American coast by English sailors, and it was under the Dutch flag that Henry Hudson, in 1609, discovered the river that bears his name. Though no actual settlement was yet made, Dutch vessels, during the next few years, paid frequent visits to the river and to the island of Manhattan lying at its mouth, considering that Hudson's voyage gave them claims over it. These were made good when the district about the Hudson was included in the sphere of action of the West India Company founded in 1621. Then arose on Manhattan Island permanent buildings in place of the temporary huts in which the Dutch traders had stored their wares for barter with the Indians; and when, in 1626, the whole island was bought from the Indians for sixty gulden, there stood among the houses of New Amsterdam the first stone church.

Still Dutch rule did not take firm root on the Hudson. There were several reasons for this: first, the West India Company, here as elsewhere, strove to promote trade rather than settlement; secondly, wishing to gain more profit from their possessions, the company allowed feudal baronies to be created, thus preventing the rise of a sturdy race of colonial citizens; finally, the company was not fortunate in the choice of its governors. It dismissed Peter Minuit, who had contributed so much to the prosperity of New Amsterdam, and drove him into the arms of the Swedes, whose colony on the Delaware lasted only as long as it was supported by Minuit's zeal and care. But even the inclusion of the Swedish colonial territory did not supply to the Dutch settlement that vigorous life which was wanting. Its New England neighbours contested with it the possession of the land, and even within the Dutch boundaries the English element became predominant. On the appearance of four English ships before New Amsterdam in 1664, the governor, left in the lurch by the West India Company, did not dare to make any resistance, and, before a drop of blood had been shed, he surrendered the town and all the Dutch territory to his opponents. In honour of the Duke of York (afterward James II) the capital was named New York.[1] Though the influence of the less favourable conditions due to the rule of the West India Company was felt for a long time, yet from the time of its conquest New York was intimately connected with the New England States. In 1673 and 1674 the Dutch succeeded in regaining temporary possession of it; but at the peace of Westminster they had finally to abandon their claims; and their possessions were absorbed in the English colonial empire.

(*c*) *William Penn.*—Another of the neighbouring States — Pennsylvania — owes its origin to the religious intolerance that was manifested against the Quakers not only in England, but, with even greater vehemence, in the New England provinces. As a religious sect, the Quakers, with their rejection of all ceremonies and their unbounded philanthropy, are rather a curiosity: their dogma is almost entirely negative; but from a social point of view the foundation of their State was an interesting if not a particularly successful experiment. What specially attracted the hostility of those who differed with them in belief was the interference of their doctrines in the region of politics, as manifested by their refusal to take oaths or to perform military service. In England the Quakers first came into notice in 1655. It goes without saying that the High Church party persecuted them with the same relentlessness with which it tried to drive out or subdue all who differed from it. It was from such persecution that the Quakers fled to New England; but there they made the disheartening discovery that, despite all their fine phrases about brotherhood and equality, the Puritans were even more intolerant toward them than the High Church. In England it was considered sufficient to imprison Quakers who refused to take the oath; in Boston they were beaten as disturbers of the public peace, and four of them were even executed.

It was therefore a deliverance for them when William Penn's action rendered it possible for them to found a colony of their own. The son of an English admiral, Penn had wealth as well as high connections. His father and many others considered it inexplicable eccentricity on his part that he should associate rather with the poor and persecuted Quakers than with the voluptuous court of Charles II; but it was as a Quaker that he attracted attention in the highest circles, without which it would have been very difficult for his sect to obtain the royal sanction for their projected settlement. With money partly supplied by himself and partly collected by his friends, he acquired a part of the territory which the English had taken from the Dutch, and which the Duke of York, with the extravagant liberality common under Charles II, had presented to two of his friends. For this colony, named New Jersey, Penn drew up a constitution on Quaker principles, and set about obtaining a charter from Charles II. Curiosity mixed with interest caused this to be granted him. Penn himself wished to call the colony Sylvania, the king added the name of the founder, making it Pennsylvania; for, according to the charter, Penn, like the former possessors, was to have the rights of a feudal lord over the new colony. Quaker emigration to America had much increased before Penn himself could go there; and when he appeared in person, in 1683, to found Philadelphia, "the City of Brotherly Love," some thousands of his co-religionists had already settled in New Jersey and in Pennsylvania proper. Penn made most honourable use of his power. The colony was organised on the same democratic basis as its New England neighbours; still Penn, despite the contradiction to the demo-

---

[1] See the maps *ante*, at p. 514.

cratic principles of Quakerdom, did not abandon his rights, and did his best to recover them when James II temporarily withdrew them. He died as possessor of Pennsylvania; but it must be added that the possession did not compensate him for the great expenditure he had made for its benefit.

Pennsylvania long preserved its Quaker characteristics, though the Quaker element formed a smaller and smaller proportion of the rapidly increasing population. This exerted a favourable influence on the development of the colony in two respects. True to the principles of his religion, Penn laid great stress on the establishment of friendly relations with the natives. The land was bought from them and cultivated in European fashion; but the colonists did not on that account drive out its old possessors with selfish harshness, but kept up friendly patriarchal relations with them. Thus it was that for a long time the colonists of Pennsylvania had nothing to fear from their red-skinned neighbours, even when the latter and the inhabitants of the neighbouring colonies were separated by fierce and bloody feuds. It was only when the prosperous development of Pennsylvania had attracted elements that did not admit the peaceful and brotherly doctrines of the Quakers that the good understanding between white and red men suffered. The immigration of those of different faiths early made itself felt. The love and toleration to all enjoined by the Quaker doctrines made it impossible for them to prevent the entrance to the colony of those of other beliefs. Elsewhere, even in the New World, religious toleration was a conception little understood, still less practised. Thus it was that sects of all kinds, persecuted in other colonies, sought refuge in Pennsylvania's Quaker toleration. Thus came, at Penn's own instigation, the first German immigrants, — Calvinists from the Palatinate, pietists and mystics; later came numerous Huguenots; all capable, hard-working people, who sought nothing but the opportunity of working at their callings in freedom from religious and political oppression. What they sought they found here in full measure; and in return they helped on, in no small degree, the development of Pennsylvania, which was more vigorous and more rapid than that of the other colonies; but by degrees they took away from the colony its exclusively Quaker character. All that remained of it, as common property of the whole province, was the friendly tolerance exercised there, and a certain political indifference caused, in some cases, by the colourlessness of the Quakers' beliefs and their renunciation of all worldly entanglements; in others by the tendency to put everything aside that could interfere with the pursuit of an exclusively material prosperity.

(f) *Maryland.* — There was another colony that rivalled, perhaps even surpassed, Pennsylvania in tolerance, — Maryland. The first charter for this settlement was granted to Lord Baltimore, a favourite of Charles I, whose Catholic inclinations he shared to such a degree that he actually went over to the Church of Rome. But he was far from adopting its intolerant views, and, learning from the persecution to which he himself had been subjected on account of his faith, he made absolute freedom in matters of religious belief a basic principle in the colony whose foundation was readily authorised by his royal friend. Maryland is the only one of the English colonies whose possessors were not Protestant, and even there the majority of the inhabitants belonged to one or other of the reformed sects. But while, in New England, fanatical Puritan intolerance prevailed, while even in the tolerant southern States Catholics were rigidly excluded, Maryland, on

principle, opened her doors to men of all creeds, and that without ever endangering her own liberties.   Here, as in most of the other colonies, the proprietary rights
of the founders were gradually relaxed before the self-reliance and self-government
of the colonists, who organised themselves on the democratic model of their neighbours.   The struggle to obtain recognition from the proprietors lasted perhaps a
little longer in Maryland; but here, as elsewhere, the goal was reached.   In consequence of its geographical position Maryland developed into a plantation State;
but large accessions of the humbler classes to its population saved it from the evils
of the plantation system as known in Virginia, while the kindly spirit that hovered
over its foundation saved it from the degeneracy that accompanies cultivation by
slave labour.   Moreover friendly relations with the natives were established, so
that in all respects Maryland afforded an example of wise moderation and good
government.

(*g*) *The Beginnings of National Spirit.* — Differences in origin, differences in
their political conditions, and finally the great distances separating the settlements,
made it for a long time impossible in North America, as it was in the Spanish
South, that the colonies should possess a common history.   In the early days of
settlement the different provinces were in almost every case confined to a narrow
strip on the coast, and, though not very far from one another, separated by dreary
forest-clad tracts.

Increase of population increased the opposition among the colonies instead of
abolishing it.   Contact with neighbours led to boundary disputes, and the several
colonies repeatedly carried on tedious lawsuits over the possession of certain boundary lands.   Even in North America the different settlements had no common history except when they came into contact with the subjects of other nations, who
were much more numerous here than in Spanish South America.   This circumstance may not have been without effect in causing the spirit of union to develop
much more strongly in the English colonies than in the Spanish.   From the beginning the supporters of the idea of union were the New England States, and they
have continued to play this part till most recent times.

It has been already mentioned [1] that as early as 1643 they combined to meet on
the one hand enemies at home, and on the other the threatened dangers arising from
the political complications in the mother country.   The following year they endeavoured to get the southern colonies to join their confederation; but differences in the
political and economic conditions of North and South prevented this; and for a
long time what may be called the common history of the English colonies is really
only the history of the New England States, the southern colonies having no part
in it.   The conquest of New Amsterdam and the expulsion of the Dutch were, it
is true, accomplished from England.   It led, not to the extension of the New England colonies, but to the establishment of a number of new communities, which,
however, as they developed, were drawn closer and closer to New England.   The
whole Atlantic coast, from Maine to Georgia, was now in English hands; not a
single foreign station remained on it.   This circumstance did not remain without influence on the feeling of union between the English colonies.   This time
it was the English government that tried to bring about its realisation.   Both
Charles II and James II made attempts to remedy the complexity of the English

---

[1] See *ante*, p. 442.

colonial relations, and to unite the colonies under a central government; but before the resistance of the colonists their efforts came to naught, and when the English Revolution of 1688 swept away the Stuarts with their centralising tendencies, William and Mary recognised the old colonial constitutions as established by charter.

(*h*) *The Struggles against the French Settlers.* At this time the rivalry between the French and English colonies made itself more and more noticeable. It was chiefly owing to the differences in their economic conditions that this had not happened before. The English settlements existed almost exclusively by agriculture; and their population was not so large but that the fertile district between the coast and the Alleghanies was amply sufficient for them. They had thus little inducement to penetrate farther into the interior, and did comparatively little to open it up. The French settlements, on the other hand, depending almost entirely on the fur-trade, required complete control of an extensive " hinterland:" and every step in the progress of the colonies, every increase in their commercial activity, increased the need for territorial expansion. This necessity had led them across the continent from the mouth of the St. Lawrence to the delta of the Mississippi.

The first to enter into competition with them were the Dutch of New Amsterdam. They, too, were traders rather than tillers of the soil, and the opposition between their interests and those of the French was the more accentuated in that their settlements were not far distant from one another and were separated by no natural barriers. As the fur-trade was to a large extent carried on by barter with Indian hunting tribes (" voyageurs " and trappers, though we often hear of them, were rare), competition in trade was naturally accompanied by rivalry for the good will of the Indians. As chance had made the French, under Champlain, the allies of the Hurons, the Dutch naturally allied themselves to the Hurons' enemies, the Iroquois. Unrestrained by political reasons, as the French had been, the Dutch, without thought as to the consequences, supplied their allies with arms more freely than ever the French had, and thus rendered them not only formidable opponents to all the Indians between the Lakes, the Alleghanies, and the Mississippi, but a permanent danger to all European settlements that did not enjoy the friendship of the Iroquois tribes. At the conquest of New Amsterdam the English inherited these friendships and enmities; the Dutch trading spirit remained a characteristic of the colony of New York. Thus we find it soon afterward as hostile to the French as ever the Dutch had been; and on the French side the feeling of hostility was now more strongly manifested than it had ever been against the unimportant Dutch colony. At first the contest was confined to commerce. But in 1670, at the instigation of two Frenchmen who, discontented with the Canadian government, had entered the service of the English, the Hudson's Bay Company was founded. This company, which extended its operations as far as the Saguenay, was for a time a dangerous competitor with the French in the fur-trade. But the boundary war, carried on for a long time on a small scale, became of greater importance when England and France, at war in Europe, tried to injure each other by attacks on the colonies.

These colonial wars, of which there were no fewer than five between 1688 and 763, had all much the same character. At the commencement the French with their Indian allies made their way through the marshy forests south of the St.

Lawrence to the English villages near the boundary, and there, fighting against the defenceless and scattered farmers, gained easy victories, disgraced, however, by the bloodthirsty cruelty of the Indians. The New England colonists sought to take revenge on the French mission and trading stations in the same manner; but they could not inflict the same amount of damage on the enemy because the posts attacked were not so valuable as the New England plantations, and not so helpless against attack. Besides, it was very difficult to win over to a common and energetic plan of action the many minds directing the affairs of the provinces, now united into the confederation of New England States. The colony of Massachusetts became a kind of leader, chiefly owing to the fact that its capital, Boston, was the seat of the federal Assembly. That, however, meant little more than that Massachusetts claimed the leadership and occasionally assumed it in cases where it was not sure of the agreement of the federated colonies and did not obtain their support; but it gained real authority neither for itself nor for the federal Assembly. Still Boston became more and more the point where the forces sent across the ocean from England to carry on the colonial struggle collected and prepared to take the offensive.

Naturally it was not to the interest of the English to split up their forces by small expeditions in the backwoods, for which their troops were not prepared, and which, even if successful, could have little effect on the result of the war. They had a decided preference for a point of attack where the fleet that had served to transport the troops could co-operate. Such a point presented itself in the peninsula which lay between the St. Lawrence and the northern boundary of the New England States, called by the French Acadia and by the English Nova Scotia. It had been settled by the French at the beginning of the seventeenth century; but some decades later it was included in the grant of land made to Sir William Alexander, and even taken possession of by the English. But the treaty of peace that restored to the French Quebec, which was taken at the same time, placed them once more in possession of Acadia, where, after a long period of unrest, a number of settlements began to flourish. The most important of these, Port Royal, was the capital of the province. But the New England colonists kept a watchful eye on this district, and did not let slip an opportunity of attempting its reconquest. An English fleet had come over to conquer New Amsterdam, but had been condemned to inaction by the rapidity with which peace had been concluded. This fleet, at the instigation of the New England colonies, made an expedition against Acadia and conquered it without difficulty. It was not restored to France until 1667, some time after Charles II's accession.

During the war of the Spanish succession Acadia was taken a third time, but was given up at the Peace of Utrecht. The French now withdrew to Cape Breton Island and erected there Fort Louisbourg, a fortress of such importance that it was known to the New England colonists as "the Northern Dunkirk." Like Dunkirk it was the starting-point of repeated piracies and raids, and its commanding position rendered it a perpetual menace to the unprotected New England coast. Upon the renewal of the war in 1743 the federal Assembly in Boston joyfully seized the opportunity offered for the conquest of Louisbourg. Escaped English prisoners announced that this important position was weakly garrisoned, badly provisioned, and, besides that, endangered by the presence of a considerable number of English prisoners who promised to aid the attacking party at the decisive moment. The

little army sent out in April, 1745, to conquer Louisbourg, was, from a military
point of view, scarcely a match for the French garrison despite its superiority in
numbers. But it was so aided by a succession of favourable circumstances that
the French, despairing of the possibility of holding out till relief arrived, began
negotiations and capitulated on being granted the right of withdrawal. When the
French attempted the reconquest next year, chance again favoured the English.
The French fleet sent out for this task fell into the hands of the English after
suffering severely from storm. Despite all this the war ended once again without
any advantage to the colonies. In the peace negotiations at Aix-la-Chapelle the
English government gave up this fortress, to win which the colonists had expended blood and treasure, in return for concessions which, though they might
appear important to it, were neither understood nor appreciated by the colonists.

Hitherto the war against the French, in so far as the colonies had directly
borne its burdens, had been carried on exclusively by the New England provinces.
The southern colonies looked on with complete indifference at the struggle of their
fellow countrymen in the north. No appeal to their national spirit could rouse them
from their apathetic tranquillity. Even the knowledge that the continued advance
of the French in the valleys of the Ohio and its tributaries threatened to cut them
off entirely from the "hinterland" beyond the Alleghanies would scarcely have
spurred them on to action had not the approach of French influence been brought
home to them by the increasing hostility and boldness of the neighbouring Indian
tribes. The English never understood how to keep on friendly terms with the
natives for any length of time. Even in the extreme north, where they took over
from the Dutch the valuable legacy of the friendship of the mighty Iroquois, they
did not succeed in keeping these redoubtable warriors permanently on their side.
The French proceeded from a truce with these their deadliest enemies to a temporary peace, and so successful was their policy that in the last decisive struggle
the Iroquois no longer gave the English their united support. This gradual progress in gaining the good will of the Indians failed, however, to save the French
from the final decisive defeat that put an end to their colonial empire; but till
long after the War of Independence the English suffered from the hostility of the
Indians stirred up so systematically by the French.

The Peace of Aix-la-Chapelle, in 1748, left matters in an even greater state of
ferment in the colonies than in Europe; and before hostilities had been recommenced in Europe the rival colonies had come into open conflict. In the district
about the source of the Ohio, English backwoodsmen had come into contact with
a French patrol. So serious did the danger appear to the English that they sent
their militia to help the squatters. In 1754 the Albany Congress interested itself
in the matter. As Pennsylvania and Virginia were now threatened as well as the
other provinces, they were invited to discuss how the threatened danger could best
be met. The English and French governments considered the situation that was
developing in America a critical one, and though they at first avoided diplomatic
communications on the subject, both quietly prepared to renew the struggle on the
colonial boundaries. As each watched the other suspiciously, the French did not
remain in ignorance of the despatch of English troops to Virginia, and the English
were quite aware that the French were strengthening the garrisons of their Canadian fortresses. A mere accident led to the outbreak of hostilities. On the
Newfoundland Banks English vessels seized two French transports that had been

separated from the fleet during a fog. The Canadians replied with threats and reprisals; thus the strife was renewed in America without formal declaration of war. From the beginning the English gained decisive advantages at sea ; but on land the French were more than a match for their opponents, though the English home government retained the management of the war and followed the definite plan of making combined attacks on the most important French posts, aiming not merely at limiting the French colonial empire, but at destroying and conquering it. But without means of communication, without depots for stores, and above all with incapable leaders, this was no easy task. A campaign in the forests of the Alleghanies or among the marshes and lakes about Lake Champlain was something quite different from war as seen on the battle-fields of the Old World ; and an English general trained in European warfare had to possess unusual capacity to enable him to accommodate himself to these completely altered conditions. Thus it came about that the first expeditions against the French forts in the valley of the Ohio and on Lake Champlain were either complete failures or brought only slight and temporary advantages.

In any case no decisive result was to be obtained by the war in the backwoods. In reality its only object was to prepare for an attack on points that were held as the keys of the French colonial empire, — Fort Niagara, which maintained the line of communication between Canada and Louisiana ; Montreal, which guarded the upper St. Lawrence and the way to Lake Huron; and Quebec, the heart of the French colony, and the gate through which went all communication with the mother country. After three years, which had brought the English little else but defeats, they succeeded in coming a little nearer to the realisation of their plan of campaign. Fort Louisbourg, which they had so lightly given back to the French in 1748, was captured a second time in 1758 by Amherst and Wolfe, after a siege lasting seven weeks. The key to the fortress of Montreal, Fort Frontenac, situated near the present city of Kingston, also fell into the hands of the English ; its capture seriously endangering communication with the fortresses in the valleys of the Ohio and Mississippi. But about the source of the Hudson, where the New England boundary was most vulnerable, the French arms still maintained a decided superiority. It was not until the following year that the English gained laurels in this field. At Ticonderoga, on Lake Champlain, Amherst gained a new victory that compelled the French to leave open the flank of Montreal. At the same time the region south of the Great Lakes was entirely cut off from Canada by the capture of Forts Niagara and Crèvecœur; thus the realisation of the concentrated attack from this side, planned for the following year by the English government, was rendered absolutely certain. When these successes had been gained, the year was so far advanced that it was considered impossible to do anything important toward the complete subjugation of Canada until the next spring; and yet it was the events of the few weeks remaining before the severe Canadian winter set in, that decided the fate of the land. Since the middle of July there had been stationed before Quebec an English force under Wolfe, which had set out, accompanied by a large fleet, to force its way up the St. Lawrence into the very centre of the French colonies, and, if possible, to conquer Quebec. But for weeks the contest went on in the immediate neighbourhood of the capital without either side gaining any decisive advantage. The English bombarded the lower parts of Quebec and rendered difficult the provisioning of the town and of Montcalm's defending army, which was concentrated in a fortified camp east of the town. But it was as impossible for the English to gain a firm footing on the northern bank of the river as it was for the French to contest the possession of the southern bank with them. The approach of winter filled the French with confidence that the time of dread and privation would soon be over; but it also convinced the English general that a decisive action must soon be fought unless the expedition was to end in a retreat the consequences of which would be the same as those of a severe defeat. As the French had still a few ships above Quebec, and as the northern bank of the river to the west of the town was almost inaccessible, attack and defence had been concentrated on the strip of land immediately below Quebec. But now the English formed a last plan, — that of effecting a landing above the capital and gaining possession of the plateau on the eastern extremity of which, between the rivers St. Lawrence and Charles, was situated the town of Quebec. This would give them a position overlooking the French army. The westward march of the troops on the south bank could not escape General Montcalm's observation. His anxiety was increased when a part of the English fleet forced the passage of the river under the fire of the cannon of Quebec and anchored some miles above the town. On account of this movement Montcalm sent part of his troops up stream. These took up a position at a considerable distance from Quebec, as the north bank was considered unscalable in the neighbourhood of the town, and the fleet had sailed far up stream. It was on this that Wolfe based his plan of attack. He had discovered, midway between the town and the western division of the French army, a spot where the ascent seemed practicable. On the night between the 12th and 13th of September his picked attacking force glided down the river in boats. As boats bringing provisions from Montreal were often passing down the stream by night, Wolfe succeeded in deceiving the first outposts, and when the French sentries discovered their mistake a body of men had already been landed strong enough to drive in the enemy's outposts and to wedge itself between the western division of the French army and the main body. Unfortunately, too, the commander of the former did not realise the significance of the English attack; he took it for one of the constantly recurring skirmishes and remained inactive.

Thus Wolfe was able to draw up his troops on the Heights of Abraham and to let them have several hours' rest before Montcalm came up from his camp, situated below the town, and commenced the attack. The position of the English, despite the surprise they had effected, was exceedingly dangerous. Though the French troops were not particularly well trained, and were somewhat disorganised by their continued privations, their numerical superiority was considerable, and in the event of defeat they could retreat under the walls of the town and bring up their other division. For the English a defeat meant not only the destruction of the picked force that had effected the landing, but also the loss of all the advantages won during the campaign, possibly also the loss of the fleet and the remainder of the troops. Wolfe knew how to impress this, not only on his officers, but on every single man in his force. He had given the order to await the enemy lying down, and to let him approach so near that every man was sure of his shot. Only when the attacking columns had been shaken by volleys at short range were the English to proceed to a bayonet attack. Montcalm had no choice: he had to attack, for every hour could bring the English fresh troops and turn the balance against him;

but his militia, supported by only a small number of regulars, could not face the destructive fire poured into their ranks at such short range by the English. The fight was over in a few minutes; the French took to flight, and reached their camp across the St. Charles River after having suffered great loss. General Montcalm and most of the principal French officers either fell or were severely wounded.

Quebec was left to its fate; the shattered remnants of the army retreated to Montreal; the western division also withdrew thither without having taken any part in the fight. Wolfe did not survive the victory; as he led the charge of one of his regiments against the wavering French columns, he was hit several times in quick succession and placed *hors de combat*. He died before the battle was over, the last he heard being his countrymen's shouts of triumph. Still the English could not follow up the victory: they were too weak, and their communities were not secure enough for them to be able to go very far from the fleet. But though the remainder of the French army escaped without hindrance to Montreal, the prize of victory fell into the hands of the English without further bloodshed. The town, half in ashes and reduced by hunger, surrendered some days later, and with the fall of the capital the fate of the land was sealed.

Quebec had, it is true, to withstand a French attack before winter set in, and next year it was subjected to a threatening though short siege. But the French did not succeed in taking it out of the hands of the English; on the contrary, the latter, as soon as winter was over, proceeded to the conquest of the last bulwark over which the French flag still waved. Cut off from all communication with France, and threatened by two superior English forces, which, operating on the St. Lawrence above and below the town, appeared before it almost simultaneously, Montreal could offer no serious resistance. To avoid useless bloodshed the governor surrendered the town without a struggle. He hoped, perhaps, that diplomacy or the events of the war in other parts would once again give back to France what her arms had failed to hold; but France had played her part in America. At the Peace of Paris Louis XV finally abandoned all claims on his Canadian possessions in favour of England, and recognised the Mississippi as the boundary between Louisiana and the English possessions.

Even Louisiana did not remain long in French hands. After Spain, in no very good humour, had looked on passively for years at the strife that involved all the European Powers, Charles III concluded with Louis XV the notorious Bourbon Family Compact, that completely deprived Spain, ever living on the memories of her splendid past, of her political position among European States. The hostilities between England and Spain, occasioned by the Compact, were confined principally to the Antilles. The British fleet took possession of Havana, and brought almost the whole island of Cuba under its power. On the Florida boundary no serious fighting took place; but with the conquest of Cuba the weakly garrisoned posts of St. Augustine and Pensacola became untenable even before a blow had been struck. In the peace negotiations that followed, England was prepared to give back Cuba to Spain, but demanded as compensation the evacuation and surrender of Florida. Charles III, left in the lurch by France, might consider himself fortunate in being indemnified for what he lost to England east of the Mississippi, by receiving from France Louisiana to the west of it. At the Peace of Paris French rule disappeared from North America, which was divided between

England and Spain. The Mississippi, "the Great Water," whose secrets had been revealed almost exclusively by France, now formed the boundary between the two nations that inherited her possessions

## 7. THE STRUGGLE FOR INDEPENDENCE IN THE NORTHERN CONTINENT

### *A.* EVENTS BEFORE THE REVOLT

THE revolt of the American colonies from England is intimately connected in many very different ways with the conclusion of the war that brought all North America as far as the Mississippi under English rule. The political relationship existing between the older colonies and the mother country was essentially the same as between Spain and her colonies. They were not so much part of the English empire as Crown lands. The consequence of this was that the important limitations which the English Parliament had in the course of time imposed on the absolute power of the king held only for the mother country and not for the colonies. Though the English Parliament had often attempted to interfere in colonial affairs, its functions had been strictly limited to the regulation of trade to and from the colonies and the representation of the colonies in foreign affairs. But in internal affairs each province claimed that its own legislative assembly took the place of a parliament between the king and his subjects; and before all it was maintained that these colonial assemblies, and they alone, had the right of taxation. In the case of the old provinces, settled for the most part by fugitives from religious intolerance, and developed almost without help from the home government, these rights were historic, and though they could not be altogether reconciled with the new ideas on the duties of government, it was not easy to set them aside.

The problem now was to organise the territory adjacent to the old provinces, and in parts exactly similar in natural conditions, placed by the Peace of Paris in English hands. It was not the king, but the English government — the ministry and the Parliament — that had carried on the war and conducted the advantageous peace negotiations. It is true that the colonies had taken part in the war, some of them, like Massachusetts, on their own initiative; but where their co-operation had been bespoken by the English government it was England, and not the colonies, that bore the expense, and at the conclusion of peace Massachusetts received from England considerable sums for its active participation in the struggle against the French, and was to receive still more.

It was indubitable that the subjection of the French provinces to English rule would bring very considerable advantages to the older English provinces, and it was understood, of course, that the mother country would not hand over these newly conquered lands directly to the colonies: nor had any one in the older colonies any objection to make to the English government's forming out of Canada and Florida a number of new colonial provinces controlled, not by the king, but by the state as constituted by ministry and Parliament. But the conflict of interests took a more serious form in respect to the district between the Alleghanies and the Mississippi. The colonies had never recognised the French claims to this region and had at times seriously contested them. By declaring the watershed formed by the Alleghany range the boundary of the old colonies, and at the same time reserving the land stretching westward to the Mississippi as Crown land, the English government created points of difference which did not at once make themselves felt only because neither the English government nor any one of the colonial governments was in a position to break up the French garrisons holding forts on the Alleghany boundary, and thus to take effective possession of the region in question.

The planters and squatters of Virginia and Pennsylvania took at first very little notice of this political limitation of their territory. The power that had hitherto opposed their advance into the fertile valley of the Ohio had abandoned all its claims in favour of England, whose subjects they could claim to be. They accordingly took possession with more or less legal formality of whatever land seemed desirable to them, and built new homes on the borders of civilisation, without stopping to inquire whether on this new soil they would be subject to the English Parliament or the colonial assembly of the province they had come from. After the conclusion of peace immigration set in strongly toward the west, the immediate consequence of which was a new Indian war.

In the altered political condition of North America, brought about by the Peace of Paris, none were worse off than the Indians. Under French rule the Indians were doubly favoured, because the French settlements, in which agriculture played a quite secondary part, had need of them in two ways: first, to obtain by barter articles of food and trade; secondly, to aid in resisting the overpowering competition of the English settlements. Thus the Indians were not only not driven out by the French, but were often encouraged to settle under the protection and in the immediate neighbourhood of the French boundary forts. The English back-woodsmen who now forced their way into this region brought with them an utter want of consideration for the Indians; and the conflict which soon broke out was occasioned rather by the colonists than by the natives. The latter were, it is true, not wholly free from blame. For generations the Indians had been accustomed to the idea of the unlimited power of their fatherly patron, the distant French king. There may have been, among the Canadian settlers and among the French fur-traders and rangers, who lived in the closest intimacy with the Indians, some who really believed that the present state of things was only transitory. At any rate the Indians were in many cases led to believe that the great king was only asleep, and that when he awoke he would certainly remember his children in the distant wilderness and free them once more from the heavy yoke of the stranger.

The general ferment caused by these circumstances threatened to become dangerous to the English. A determined Indian chief of clear judgment tried to take advantage of the situation to stir up a rising of his countrymen which should place him in a position of power and honour. A chief of the Ottawas named Pontiac had during the period of French rule played a considerable part as representative of a powerful tribe. After the defeat of the French, he too had made peace with the English; but when he was disappointed in his hopes of gaining honour and influence among them, he resolved to be revenged on them. He was able, by means of his messengers, to persuade the Indian tribes of the west, from the Lakes to the Mississippi, to join in a great conspiracy against the English. In May, 1763, he himself was to give the signal for a general rising by surprising Fort Detroit between Lake Huron and Lake Erie. A number of English forts were actually stormed, and land was ~ with the usual barbarities. But the failure of Pontiac's attack on Fort Detroit, which he besieged for months, paralysed the movement. It was completely checked when reinforcements, sent out from Pennsylvania to relieve Fort Pitt, which was also besieged, gained a decisive victory over the Indians at Bushy Run. Next year Pontiac went farther toward the southwest and tried to get the Indians on the Illinois and Mississippi to join in the struggle. How dangerous an opponent he was is shown by his endeavours to get the French garrisons which in many cases had not yet been broken up, to take his part against the English. But in this he failed, and as the English troops were at his heels, he gave up his warlike plans and submitted, as most of the chiefs allied to him had already done.

The Indian war had shown of what importance it was to render the west secure. But the force necessary for the defence of the North American colonies was estimated at 20,000 men. Was England always to make the sacrifice necessary to maintain this force, which, on the whole, benefited only the colonies? That the colonial assemblies took this for granted was not to be wondered at; but even in England there was a large party that gave utterance to this view. They maintained that in making a comparison between the sacrifices England made on behalf of the colonies and the advantages she derived from them, account should be taken, not only of the amount of the duties levied on trade between England and the colonies, but also of the present flourishing state of English industry, which was especially due to the colonies. The prohibitive measures which had prevented the growth of industries which could seriously compete with those of the mother country continually compelled the colonies to draw their supplies of clothing-material, hats, and machinery from England; though they could manufacture these articles just as well themselves, or get them at considerably lower prices, under free trade, were it permitted them. On the other hand this same compulsion to carry on trade exclusively with England forced the colonies to sell their staple products at prices far below those current in European markets; and it was the opportunity of obtaining raw material cheaply from the colonies that enabled English industry to compete so successfully and so profitably with the industries of other lands. It was urged that, taking into account this state of affairs, it was absolutely unjust to lay on the colonies, which had worked their way to prosperity without aid from England, and to which England's prosperity was largely due, burdens which the State had incurred through no fault of the colonies and which brought them no immediate advantage.

Speeches on these lines, uttered by prominent statesmen, were but too well calculated to confirm the colonists in their opinions. Though the Whig party more than once hurled at their opponents the taunt that their measures could only result in making the idea of separation from England popular in the colonies, it cannot be denied that it was just this agitation, by which the Whigs thought they were advancing the interests both of their own party and of the colonies, that contributed so largely to the result which they claimed their opposition would avoid. The manner in which the different ministries of George III carried on the struggle against the colonies would in any case have evoked their active resistance; but it can hardly be assumed that this resistance would have been so general and so persistent had not the parliamentary disputes shown the American that a powerful party in the mother country was in agreement with them and admitted their claims. It was thus a struggle for interest as well as a struggle for right that helped to bring about the Declaration of Independence on the part of the United States.

Differences between single colonies and the London government had already manifested themselves during the war against France, and had led the provinces most concerned to send special agents to the seat of government. Thus it was that Benjamin Franklin[1] came to London on behalf of the Assembly of Pennsylvania, to seek the protection of Parliament against the attacks of the Crown. There were also agents from Massachusetts and Connecticut at the court. They saw how the struggle between king and Parliament for the exercise of the executive power was developing, and how each party was only waiting for the conclusion of peace to introduce, each from its own standpoint, a stricter rule in the colonies. Laxity in the past, and the special conditions brought about by the intercolonial wars which followed one another in rapid succession, had almost nullified the laws dealing with navigation and trade with foreign countries. The colonies gained considerable advantages from the trade carried on with the Spanish settlements contrary to law, and the English revenue suffered not a little from it. This was the first point with which the new government was resolved to deal. The measures regulating trade to and from the colonies were again strictly enforced. Revenue vessels were stationed at all important points on the coast, and were given the right of stopping and searching any suspicious ship. Colonial officials were instructed to help the customs officers whenever the latter needed them; similar orders were given to the garrisons at different stations on the coast; and the warships were at the same time placed at the disposal of the customs authorities, the crews being incited to activity by promises of considerable rewards. Now of all the colonies the one most interested in trade was Massachusetts. There it was that opposition first raised its head to protest against the injury done to the interests of the province and the rights of its citizens. Hitherto the measures taken by the government had been oppressive and annoying, but not actually illegal; and the Boston merchants, who first made protest, would scarcely have found support in the other colonies had the government stopped here. But the government considered the reinforcement of the old prohibitory laws as but the prelude to its plan of action in the colonies.

The war with France had burdened England with a heavy load of debt. In spite of this there were still considerable sums to be paid to the colonies to reimburse them for their war expenditure, and besides this the government was to provide for the payment of an army there, which indeed seemed urgently necessary to the government to maintain its authority, but the avowed object of which was the protection of the colonies. The ministry was of the opinion that it was only right that the transatlantic provinces should help to bear these expenses. This could have been brought about in various ways. What would have been in any case most advisable was that the government should make use of the provinces of Canada, Louisiana, and Florida, gained by the war, to cover the expenditure incurred by their conquest. In these regions an administration had yet to be established, and there could be no question as to the competence of

---

[1] See portrait opposite.

BENJAMIN FRANKLIN

After an engraving by Willcox from a miniature by Duplessis.
(From Hale's " Franklin in France," Vol. II )

Parliament to interfere there. But to adopt such a course would have been to recognise a different political status in the case of the other colonies, and just this that the government was anxious. Besides agriculture had made little progress in the newly conquered territories that it would be years before the revenue derived from them was sufficient. Another course possible was for the government to settle with each province privately the amount it was to contribute. Every time the English government had approached a colonial assembly in this way it had received all that it asked for, and even more. But this mode of procedure did not fit in with the government's plan, inasmuch as it indirectly recognised the claim of the colonies that only such taxes could be levied on them as had been voted by their representative assemblies. The only remaining way was to provide for the new expenditure by increase of the customs duties, the assessment of which the colonies had always considered a matter for the mother country, or to sanction new taxation by a resolution in Parliament and then to levy it by force.

This last plan found most favour with the government, because its object was not merely to relieve itself of temporary financial difficulties by the aid of the colonies; its aim was rather to bring the colonies into more immediate dependence upon the mother country as a preliminary to the abolition of the provincial constitutions and the establishment of a common central government. The ministry in which Earl Grenville was premier and Richard Jackson chancellor of the exchequer, introduced a bill into the English Parliament in February, 1765, to provide the pay of the colonial army and the salaries of colonial government officials by the extension of the stamp tax to the colonies. This would relieve the mother country of the cost of maintaining the colonial army, and in addition render all government officials completely independent of the colonial assemblies which had hitherto paid them, and thus furnish the English government with an instrument for carrying out its vigorous policy. This plan had already been brought forward and discussed in 1754, but it had been dropped before the united opposition of the colonies. But now the bill was carried in the Lower House, after a short debate, by an overwhelming majority, and immediately afterward it was passed by the Lords without opposition. The stamp tax was to come into force in the colonies on November 1, 1765.

There, even before Parliament's decision was made known, preparation was made for future difficulties. The government had already instructed the commander of the English troops in Boston to claim maintenance for his force from the province; and it was this that gave the first impulse to revolutionary measures in Massachusetts, which was suffering severely from the restrictions placed on trade. The idea of a closer union among the colonies had already been discussed in detail at an assembly of delegates at Albany in 1754. Benjamin Franklin even came forward with the draft of a constitution for the North American colonies; but even with the centralising tendency of his plans he rendered little service to the cause of unity. But the idea of taking up a common position and agreeing upon a line of action in matters of general interest had slowly taken root in all the colonies. Thus the first step taken by Massachusetts when thus threatened, was to form the most prominent members of its assembly into a committee, whose task it was to enter into communication with the other colonies and to place clearly before all the world the subject of their three cen-

rights. The first result of its activity was a pamphlet upon the rights of the colonies, which attracted considerable attention even in England. The author, James Otis, energetically maintained that the colonies were bound to obey only such government measures as had been decided on and introduced with the consent of their representative assemblies. This pamphlet was directed against the Stamp Act, the introduction of which rendered general the resistance of the colonies.

The stricter collection of customs duties and the burden laid on trade had really affected only the merchants of the few trading-towns, most of which were situated in New England, and they were therefore viewed with indifference by the bulk of the colonists, who lived by agriculture. But the Stamp Act affected the whole population of the colonies, and led the aristocratic planters of Virginia to side with the democratic traders of Massachusetts. In the autumn of this same year, at the invitation of these two States, delegates from nine of the States met in congress at New York to decide on a common plan of action against the detested Act. The results were at first 'very small. Petitions to the king and Houses of Parliament were drawn up in conferences, protesting against the imposition of taxes by Parliament and the administration of the customs; but these petitions were approved of by the delegates of only six colonies, and even the president of the congress shrank from the responsibility of placing his signature to them. The only value of the congress was that it accustomed the colonies to settle their affairs in this manner.

The task of organising the opposition was left to single colonies. On the 1st of November stormy scenes were witnessed in Boston. The men who had consented to undertake the collection of the stamp tax, together with the unpopular members of the ministry, were burned in effigy. The house of the commissioner of taxes and a number of other government buildings were destroyed by the mob; but these excesses did not meet with the approval of the better class of colonists, nor did they in any way further the end in view. Moreover the colonial assembly had to agree, though with certain reservations, to make good the damage done. Much more serious and effective was the resolution which originated in New York, but was soon adopted throughout the colonies, not to import any English goods or to have any commercial intercourse with the mother country until the Stamp Act was repealed. This resolution was of special importance in that it gave the impulse to an enormous development of colonial industry which in the struggle just commencing swept away the barriers placed in its way by the laws of the mother country and began to deprive English factories of a market they were unable to regain, even when normal conditions had been re-established. The Stamp Act was rendered ineffective when not only the lawyers, but even the courts, did their best to avoid the use of stamped paper. There was a general return to verbal agreements; even in marriages the church ceremony had to suffice. At the same time all stamped paper on which hands could be laid was burned, and the validity of all stamped agreements was thus placed in doubt.

Of all these measures against the Stamp Act the only effective one was the interruption of commercial relations with England. The consequences of this made themselves felt at once; for the Americans not only gave no fresh orders to English manufacturers, but even refused to pay the debts they owed to their English creditors. The consequence was that that powerful class, the merchants, whose interests till recently had been the first consideration in the management of the colonies, used their influence to have the Stamp Act repealed. Their efforts in this direction were aided by a change of ministry. In February, 1767, two years after its enactment, Parliament repealed the Act after Pitt had made a remarkable speech in favour of the colonies, and Franklin had appeared as their representative at the bar of the House and given detailed information on the situation.

For a moment it seemed that the good understanding between the mother country and the colonies had been again established. The repeal of the Stamp Act was celebrated with almost as much noise in the city of London as in Boston or Philadelphia. But the germs of discontent were developing in secret. At the time of the repeal of the Stamp Act the government had succeeded in passing through both Houses a declaration expressly asserting the absolute right of the king to make, with the concurrence of Parliament, laws which were valid in the colonies. This was the answer to the Boston committee's petition, which the Parliament refused even to receive. In spite of this, the committee sent a second open letter to all the colonies, exhorting them to take common action against the dangers threatening them all. The English government, by means of the governors, declared this an act of rebellion in all the provinces, and called upon the Massachusetts Assembly, which had approved of the step taken by the committee, to rescind its vote immediately. But a number of unpleasant incidents had meanwhile caused the peaceful disposition of the colony to become once more hostile. In spite of the repeal of the Stamp Act the government did not abandon its intention of providing for the maintenance of the colonial army in the colonies themselves. This was to be done partly by again increasing the customs duties and by levying them more strictly, and partly by forced contributions for provisioning the troops of the various garrison towns. This last measure had already led to open resistance in New York; the government's answer had been to declare the town in a state of siege. The extortionate duties led soon afterward to disturbances at Boston. The custom-houses were broken into, and the officials driven out; and when the governor dissolved the colonial Assembly and called in troops, the colony summoned a General Assembly and elected a provisional committee. Hostilities would have broken out at once had not the political situation in Europe forced delay upon the government. The somewhat peremptory governor of Massachusetts was recalled, and a Boston citizen, Hutchinson, set in his place. The new governor did his best to reconcile opposing interests, but was unable to maintain his influence over discontented spirits.

Meanwhile the English commercial class had come to the aid of the colonies a second time. On the raising of the customs duties, and the use of force against the provincial authorities in New York and Boston, the colonies had replied once again by an agreement to break off commercial relations with the mother country. The marked decrease in exports prevented the attainment of the ends the government had in view in raising the duties, and did so much injury to British industries that the government carried the repeal of the new tariff through Parliament. But just as, in the case of the Stamp Act, the bill of declaration had been attached formally to maintain the authority of the government, so in the present case the higher duty on tea was maintained to make the colonies formally recognise that the government was justified in the course it had taken.

Under these circumstances the effect of the abolition of the customs duties was not so general nor so marked as that of the repeal of the Stamp Act had been. Relations were again strained when it became clear that the government had no intention of abandoning its plan of establishing order in the specially turbulent provinces, New York and Massachusetts. In 1770 the Provincial Assembly was removed from Boston to Cambridge; and the town citadel, which it had been agreed should be manned by the colonial militia, was occupied by English troops. For a time the Bostonians were dumbfounded by this energetic procedure, and two years passed before the scattered elements of resistance gathered themselves together for fresh action. But in the meantime the cause of colonial liberty had made great progress. During these two years opposition to the government measures had manifested itself in various quarters. In autumn, 1772, Boston recovered itself and chose a new committee to call for united action against the violent infringement of rights granted by charter, and this appeal found an echo in all the States.

Virginia was not, like Massachusetts and New York, among those provinces whose populace had indulged in riotous manifestations; consequently the Virginians had escaped the repressive measures employed by the government elsewhere. In spite of this, greater enthusiasm for the parliamentary rights of the provincial assemblies existed here than in any other of the southern States, and the Virginians perceived, in the action of the London government against Massachusetts and New York, a tendency hostile to the representative constitutions of all the colonies. They accordingly made the cause of Boston their own. They chose a so-called "committee of correspondence," declared that the programme put forward by Massachusetts had their complete approval, and suggested that all the colonies should appoint such committees to facilitate the exchange of opinions.

The tension was so great that the slightest impulse was sufficient to lead to open rupture. It was only natural that this impulse should come from Massachusetts, for here the hostile camps, ready for the struggle, had been facing each other for years. A Boston merchant, in spite of the non-importation agreement, wished to import a cargo of English tea which two ships had brought into the harbour. But when his intention became known the excited populace assembled before his house and so intimidated him that he abandoned his project. But the customs officials now demanded that the duty should be paid, whether the tea were landed or not, and refused to let the ships leave the harbour till it was paid. Then, on the night between the 28th and 29th of December, 1773, a mob disguised as Indians boarded one of the vessels and threw the whole cargo overboard. Otherwise there was no disturbance either in the town or in the province; but this act of rebellion furnished the government with a sufficient pretext for making a decisive stroke against Massachusetts, the focus of disturbance in North America. Four bills were passed by Parliament: one declared the port of Boston closed until the tea had been paid for; by the others the constitution of the colony was radically altered. General Gage was appointed commander-in-chief for all North America, and exercised in Massachusetts the powers both of a military dictator and of a civil governor. The government saw clearly that such a policy could be carried out only by the employment of force; but both king and Parliament had made up their minds to this. It was again decided to send reinforcements to the colonies;

and a resolution was passed by Parliament calling on the government to take energetic measures to have the laws obeyed in the colonies and to maintain the authority of the Crown. The conviction that this was equivalent to a declaration of war was so strong that diplomatic steps were taken to prevent the colonies obtaining war material from France and Holland.

In the colonies the number of those prepared to go to extremes and commence war was still very small; but the excitement increased rapidly in all the provinces when the repressive measures taken by the government against Massachusetts became known. General Gage entered on his duties as governor under no very encouraging circumstances, yet without meeting with any opposition. At his command the provincial Assembly met at Salem, which had been chosen as the new capital; but it immediately passed the memorable resolution to invite delegates from all the colonies to a congress at Philadelphia. The resolution was passed with closed doors, as Gage's secretary had already arrived with the writ for the dissolution of the Assembly. Thereupon the Assembly at Salem broke up, but met again at Concord and chose a government of its own; so that from that moment the province was divided into two hostile camps.

It was under circumstances such as these that the second American Congress met at Philadelphia, September 25, 1774. Here met for the first time the leading spirits of the American Revolution: George Washington and Patrick Henry from Virginia; Samuel Adams and John Adams from Massachusetts; John Jay from New York, the two Livingstones, the two Rutledges, and others. It is true that but few of the fifty-one delegates, representing twelve colonies, shared Massachusetts' eagerness for the struggle; but there was no danger of this second Congress having such a feeble termination as had the one at Albany. All the delegates rightly laid great stress on the importance of appearing unanimous in all their announcements. Then was established the standing order that excluded all debates from the records and made the strictest secrecy as to the proceedings of the Congress obligatory on the delegates. It was for this reason that the movers contented themselves with the comparatively tame resolutions with which the Congress ended. But it had strengthened the feeling, "each for all and all for each;" and that was what was most important. The Congress scorned another appeal to Parliament. It appealed to the English people, whether dwelling in the British Isles or between Hudson's Bay and Florida, and demanded that the rights the Americans possessed as men and citizens should be restored and not again interfered with. It turned to the king and in dignified and moderate terms begged him, as the loving father of his whole people, to intervene between his much harassed and long-suffering people and the oppressive measures of the ministry, and to give a gracious answer to their petition. But the Congress also considered the possibility of its representations being unheard, and was firmly resolved to meet force with force. Besides this the Congress resolved once again to break off all commercial relations with the mother country till its complaints were listened to, and finally adjourned with the resolution to meet again in May of the following year.

### *B.* THE STRUGGLE FOR SEPARATION FROM THE MOTHER COUNTRY

At the end of 1774 there was perhaps, with the exception of Samuel Adams, not a single delegate fully determined upon separation from England. But the state of affairs had completely changed before Congress met again. The armed peace between the governor and the provincial Congress of Massachusetts could not last forever. Each party felt that war was in the air, and tried to prepare for it and to hinder the preparations of its opponents. Gage collected much war-material in Boston from the province, and he secured the town from attack by fortifying the narrow neck of land connecting it with the mainland. But the provincial Congress had collected war-supplies at Concord and other places and was endeavouring to supplement them. Throughout the province the militia were secretly organised and were ready to take up arms at a minute's warning. On the evening of April 18, 1775, Gage sent out a reconnoitring party toward Concord, to capture, if possible, some patriots who had withdrawn from Boston, and to secure the province's war-material. But the militia immediately got wind of this, and when the English troops reached Lexington Common they found themselves face to face with a hostile force. Here the first shots were exchanged; here the war commenced. At first the militia retired, and the English entered Concord without resistance. But in a short time their position there became critical; a retreat was inevitable and it was not unaccompanied by danger. Once a shot had been fired, the colonists rose on all sides. The English troops were hard pressed, suffered severe losses, and continued their retreat to the trenches before Boston. In the next few days the investment of the town began, and continued almost a year, during which nothing more important occurred than an occasional skirmish between the opposing forces.

Such was the state of affairs when Congress renewed its sittings at Philadelphia. Its petition to the king had been contemptuously rejected; the English Parliament had given its consent to the employment of force to bring the colonies back to obedience, and had voted considerable sums for the strengthening of the fleet and the engagement of mercenaries, drawn chiefly from the smaller German principalities. Detachments of troops were continually arriving in America, and the fleet committed occasional acts of hostility on the American coast. The Congress, in which all the thirteen States were now represented, could no longer persist in the humble attitude of the preceding year. It took up the position, not as yet of fighting for independence, but of defending itself until England should give compensation for the damage done, re-establish the infringed rights of the colonies and recognise their constitutional demands.

The outbreak of war placed the Congress in an exceedingly difficult position. Though recognised by all the North American colonies, it possessed no real authority. It was a deliberative assembly devoid of all inherent power, and its resolutions could only be put into execution when the provincial Assemblies indirectly responsible for them had given their consent. In most respects each of the provincial Assemblies was supreme in its own district; and the petty jealousies between the provinces soon led them to keep watch most jealously over this local supremacy. It was only in taking action against England that the authority of Congress was fully recognised. Congress appointed George Washington[1] commander-in-chief of the forces of the thirteen colonies, and Montgomery and Schuyler leaders of the army which was to induce Canada to join the revolutionary movement. As money as well as men was necessary for an army, it established a war fund to which each State was to contribute proportionately. Congress went a step

[1] See portrait, facing p. 470, *post*.

farther in rejecting the English proposals for mediation and sending agents to several courts of Europe in order to dispose them favourably toward the cause of the colonies. A declaration of independence was as yet intentionally avoided; but in reality the Congress already claimed for itself the rights of an independent power.

Meanwhile the struggle was continued in the north. In 1774 Parliament had finally settled the form of government for Canada. The province was given a decidedly centralising organisation and was placed under a military governor. It was further decided to extend the southern boundary of the province as far as the Ohio. In resolving to make its first move in this direction the Congress had two objects in view: first, to reconquer the territory which the change in the boundary threatened to take from the New England States; and second, to induce Canada, if possible, to join the other thirteen provinces. Immediately after Lexington a bold stroke had placed the Americans in possession of Ticonderoga, Crown Point, and Lake Champlain, and opened up to them the way into central Canada. In August Montgomery and Schuyler took the offensive; but the movement was crippled by disagreements among the leaders of all ranks. Schuyler resigned his command. Montgomery besieged and took St. John's, and then pressed on toward Montreal. Before this town he made a long halt and thus prevented a third corps, which had marched against Quebec under Arnold, from accomplishing anything. When, in December, the two detachments at last united to make an attack on Quebec, it was repulsed with great loss, Montgomery himself falling. In so far as the campaign had in view the stirring up of revolution in Canada, it was a complete failure. It was only with difficulty that the position gained could be maintained.

Meanwhile another battle had been fought before Boston. Fifteen thousand men of the New England militia had gradually collected there, and so shut in the English garrison that its maintenance began to be a matter of difficulty. This induced Gage to push forward bodies of troops in various positions. The besiegers replied by an advance toward Charlestown. The opposing forces met at Bunker's Hill on June 17, 1775. The progress of the combat was typical of the war of independence. The militia fought bravely, but their leaders had so little capacity for their task that the battle ended with the abandonment of all the positions taken up. From a military point of view the English had gained a victory, but they reaped no advantage from it. The American losses were easily replaced, and both leaders and men burned with the desire to renew the struggle.

At the beginning of July Washington arrived in the camp before Boston, and took over the command of the army of the united provinces. This made no change in the progress of the siege. The evil results of the militia system were already making themselves felt among the Americans. The colonists were quite prepared to go through a short struggle, but the long inactivity involved in the reduction of a hostile position undermined their discipline and made them unwilling to remain under arms longer than the time of service agreed upon. It is true that some of the provinces were ready to send fresh men to take the places of those discharged; but, with these, training and exercise had to be begun all over again, and when they were proficient their term of service was nearly ended. Thus it was that the capabilities of the American army were by no means what was to be expected considering its numbers. The leaders must have possessed the highest ability, both as regards diplomacy and strategy, to attain with such material the results they did.

The English government gradually came to the conclusion that it was a mistake to keep its main force shut up in Boston. General Howe, who succeeded Gage in command, was ordered to evacuate the town. This he was able to do in good order and without loss. Nevertheless it was a triumph for the Americans to be able, after nine months' siege, to enter the town which had been first selected for punishment by the home government.

In May, 1776, Congress met at Philadelphia, for the fourth time, under most favourable auspices. The prevailing elation found expression in a proposal brought before Congress some weeks later, that the colonies should separate from the mother country and form an independent State. Congress was not elected by popular vote; each State legislature sent as many delegates as it thought fit. This peculiar composition of the deliberative body rendered it impossible to ascertain how far the proposal embodied the general desire of the inhabitants of the thirteen States. Public opinion, as known in England, did not exist at this time in the colonies. What appears to be the expression of the popular will was generally but the action of a small number of determined politicians who knew what they were aiming at, and who played a prominent part in the correspondence committees and in Congress. Under these circumstances it is specially significant that inquiries made led to the conclusion that the proposal to put forth a declaration of independence would not command a majority, even in Congress.

But the party for independence was in this case excellently led. Hitherto the leaders had not refused assent to the most conciliatory measures, convinced that every failure would bring those who hesitated nearer to their position, and now once more they found a diplomatic way of escape. To withdraw the proposal would be nearly as severe a check as to have it rejected; it was quite safe, however, to postpone discussion and voting for several weeks, as was done on the 10th of June. How little the leaders doubted that victory would ultimately be theirs was shown by their appointing a commission to discuss the steps which the declaration of independence would render necessary. They were justified by success; and when the proposal was again brought up a number of the opponents of separation from England withdrew from the Congress, so that on the 4th of July the Declaration of Independence, which the committee had meanwhile carefully prepared, was solemnly proclaimed as the unanimous decision of the Congress. Among the colonists the result of the struggle that had meanwhile broken out in different places was awaited with the greatest anxiety. Even those who from the outbreak of the war had looked on separation as its necessary consequence felt clearly that it was too early to give themselves up to rejoicing.

After the evacuation of Boston, Washington went, as early as April, 1776, to New York, in the expectation that this important port, whose population included a numerous royalist party, would be the next object of the English attack. At first it seemed that this expectation would not be justified. A part of the English fleet directed its course southward and tried to take possession of Charleston, in South Carolina. But on its being repulsed the English forces again united, and, under Sir William Howe, effected a landing on Long Island toward the end of August. This Washington with his militia was unable to prevent; nor could he offer serious opposition to their advance. He was fortunate in being able to lead his over-matched force across the East River back to New York without serious loss (it was useless for him to hope to hold New York), and thence continued his celebrated retreat, which, considering the difficulties he had to contend with, was a great achievement even for one so talented. Nevertheless, the retreat seemed a severe blow to the cause of American independence.

More dangerous to Washington than his English foe, that followed him from one position to another with deliberate slowness, was the condition of his own army. In each of the numerous letters in which he informs Congress of the course of events at the seat of war, Washington returns to the point that with the militia, badly disciplined and unwilling to serve a day more than their short term, he can gain no successes against Howe's army composed of well-trained professional soldiers. He repeatedly demands, at least for the period of the war, a standing army and a trained corps of officers.

The thirteen States had declared themselves independent; but Congress had still to draw up a scheme for their internal organisation. A considerable time must elapse before this could be approved of by the legislatures of the several States. At first each State turned to Congress with its own claims and appeals for help; but all left it to Congress to find help for their necessities and misfortunes. The separate States did not always recognise the paper money that Congress was forced to issue to cover the expenses of the war, and yet it was precisely money and soldiers that all demanded from that body. Though the army and its commander had often just ground to complain of the Congress, it must not be forgotten that the latter, though having the best of intentions, was often unable to give help.

Washington understood perfectly how to take advantage of Howe's slowness to protract his retreat as much as possible. The English took possession of New York on the 15th of September; but immediately thereafter were decisively checked by the Americans at Harlem Heights. A month later, after the English had moved by water to Westchester County and had thus swung toward the rear of the American position, the two armies met at White Plains. The result of battle there was to give to the English the control of a portion of the country between Long Island Sound and the Hudson, thus enabling their land forces to keep in touch with their naval forces on both bodies of water, and, on the other hand, to restrict further the lines of Americans and to separate them from their allies on the upper Hudson and in New Jersey. Finally, in November, the Americans at Fort Washington, being attacked from three directions, were forced to abandon the east side of the Hudson in its lower course, and to withdraw into New Jersey.

Washington had now to make a rapid retreat to the Delaware, and with forces disorganised by continued retreat he could no longer hold the enemy in check. At the beginning of December Congress believed the capital, Philadelphia, no longer secure, and fled to Baltimore[1] before the approach of the hostile army. But this time it was able to return without an enemy's having set foot in the American capital. The most serious thing was that with such ideas prevalent the cause of freedom was losing many adherents. Only after Washington, at the end of 1776, had surprised and defeated the enemy at Trenton, did the spirits of his men begin to rise a little.

Both armies now withdrew into winter quarters. But when Howe, in April, made preparations for a new campaign, he gave up the idea of continuing his

[1] See the map at p. 514.

march against Philadelphia by land, re-embarked his army, and sailed unexpectedly up Chesapeake Bay to attempt the conquest of Philadelphia from the south.   Enthusiasm for the war had now reached its lowest ebb in the colonies.   The news that arrived from England had not a little to do with this.   The amnesty which Howe had promised the New England States if they would submit was now assured by the English Parliament to all who returned to their allegiance.   The prospect was also held out of measures which would remedy the most oppressive evils complained of by the colonies.   Not only in a great part of America, but also in the European States which followed the progress of the War of Independence with strained attention, was a reconciliation between the mother country and the rebellious colonies believed to be impending.   Such expectations naturally drove all the lukewarm to the English side.   Even the presence of Congress, which had returned to Philadelphia, failed to keep public opinion unwavering in the Quaker City. Washington, by the resistance he offered during his skilfully conducted retreat, delayed the English advance; but in the middle of September he had to announce to Congress that he was no longer in a position to protect the way to Philadelphia. On September 26, 1777, the English army occupied the revolutionary capital.

But this apparently brilliant success soon appeared in another light.   A few days later Washington returned to the attack and succeeded in cutting off all Howe's communications with the interior.   The latter was now forced to attack the forts on the Delaware that were still in the hands of the Continental army and threatened his line of communication with the sea.   These forts were neither sufficiently fortified nor strongly enough garrisoned to be able to hold out long, but they withstood the English army and fleet for almost five weeks.   Even this was a decided advantage ; for the season was now so far advanced that both armies had to go into winter quarters.   The condition of the Continental army, which had to undergo privations of every kind, and in consequence suffered severely both in numbers and in *morale*, would have been serious, had not fortune in the meantime favoured the arms of the Americans in the north and thus brought about a decisive change in the entire situation.

After the Continental troops evacuated Montreal in June, 1776, every thought of inducing Canada to join the rebellion had to be given up.   On the contrary the old antipathy against their New England neighbours manifested itself so vigorously that the Canadian governors soon thought of taking the offensive.   In the autumn of the same year the English took the fortress of Crown Point, and, by means of a large flotilla of boats, kept control of Lake Champlain.   Early in the summer of the following year General Burgoyne advanced with an army of eight thousand well-trained English and German soldiers to establish a line of communication with New York, and thus cut off the northern provinces from the others.   The beginning of his campaign was an uninterrupted series of successes.   Ticonderoga, which the Americans considered the impregnable key of the North, fell into his hands almost without bloodshed.   The garrison that commenced its retreat partly by land and partly by water, was dispersed.   Until they reached the upper Hudson the English met with no serious opposition from the Continental troops ; General Schuyler had only time to destroy roads and bridges and to withdraw all supplies out of the reach of the English.   But in accomplishing so much he changed the whole course of events.   When Burgoyne reached the Hudson, his force was considerably reduced, as he had to leave garrisons behind him to keep open his lines of ommunication. Moreover the troops were exhausted by the excessive .. r ons hey had to make in the heat of the summer, to render passable the roads through he marshes between Lake George and the Hudson. To make matters worse, hey were quite destitute of supplies.

Misfortune suddenly broke on Burgoyne from all sides. Here in the north the var was much more popular than in the Quaker State Pennsylvania; and with he approach of danger the leaders of the Continental army received daily fresh ccessions of strength. It was the English right wing that received the first heck: it was ordered to take Fort Stanwix on the Mohawk; but after a fruit-ess siege of some weeks' duration it had to commence a retreat to Canada that uch resembled flight. A detachment that Burgoyne sent into Vermont to orage was almost annihilated in open combat; all its war-material fell into the ands of the Continentals. Finally Burgoyne himself had to advance, if only to btain provisions; he crossed the Hudson and met the main army commanded by eneral Gates at Freeman's Farm. The first indecisive encounter was equivalent o a severe defeat for Burgoyne; and when, a few days later, he made a second ttempt to gain breathing-space for his starving soldiers, he was so thoroughly eaten that his only course was to retreat. But even this was no longer open to im. Encouraged by their victory the Continental troops surrounded him on all des, and when Gates, with the main army, offered battle a third time before aratoga, Burgoyne and his army, seeing the uselessness of further bloodshed, laid own their arms, October 17, 1777. The armies that faced each other in this cam-aign were not very large according to modern ideas. But apart from the fact at England could not often replace an army of eight thousand men, the Ameri-ans gained great strategic advantages. Burgoyne's capitulation meant much ore than the failure of the plan to divide the American forces by occupying the ne of the Hudson; the Canada frontier was now secure for a time at least against nglish attack, and the English garrison in New York was isolated, having no eans of communication with the other English armies except by sea.

Its importance was perhaps fully appreciated only by those engaged in e struggle; still the capitulation of Saratoga attracted attention throughout the orld. Since the earliest signs of serious dissension between England and the lonies, France had watched events in America with the closest attention. Its ading statesmen waited longingly for the opportunity to take revenge for the sses and humiliation inflicted on them by the Peace of 1763. As early as 1767 a rench agent was sent to North America to obtain information, not only on the ate of public opinion there, but also upon the means the colonists had at their sposal in the event of war with England, and as to what kind of help they ould most urgently require. But French policy was then considerably in dvance of the claims put forward by the colonists. The reports which De Kalb nt from America did much to cool French eagerness to support the colonies. ie plan of taking revenge on England by promoting an American revolt had to abandoned for a time. But as soon as the first congresses were convinced that eir rights could be maintained against England only by force, they remembered e disposition displayed by France; and Paris was the first and most important int to which the Congress sent its agents, nor did it send them in vain.

Naturally the French government could not, in 1775, enter into open commu-cation with the agents of the still quite unorganised rebel provinces; but it nevertheless gave the Americans much secret support. As soon as war had openly commenced the Americans began hostilities at sea. It was quite in accord with the strongly developed business spirit of the northern provinces that they should be much more eager to do injury to English trade at sea by privateering than to carry on an honourable though less profitable war by land against the English army. Soon after the Declaration of Independence the first American privateers ventured across the ocean into British waters. The ship which in the autumn of 1776 brought Benjamin Franklin to France as accredited representative of the new republic brought into Havre, as prizes, two English vessels which it had captured on the way. This constituted on the part of France a breach of the peace then existing between her and England; but American privateers continued to take refuge secretly in French harbours. Though the American delegates were not officially recognised, it was an open secret, especially after Franklin's arrival, that they had the direct support of the French government in buying war-material fitting out ships, and enlisting officers and crews which were taken to America secretly or under a false flag.

Franklin, from the beginning, felt sure of the favourable issue of the negotiations for a treaty of trade and friendship with which the newly organised Foreign Office had entrusted him; but these sanguine expectations were not altogether realised. There can be no doubt that not only the French government, but the whole French people, sympathised with the cause of the United States. But this was not for any love they bore the Americans, but principally because they saw in a successful American rising a means of injuring the hated English, and they only too eagerly seized a chance of taking revenge on them. Thus Franklin was permitted to visit Paris, and in his private capacity could speak his mind freely to the leading French minister, De Vergennes. But a public reception was avoided; the more so because the campaign following the Declaration of Independence was unfortunate to such an extent that the final victory of the Americans was seriously doubted. France's attitude during the year 1777 was purely expectant. Even the amount of secret assistance given to the rebels was insignificant. The only event attracting attention was the departure for America of the youthful Marquis de Lafayette, who, with De Kalb and other Frenchmen, crossed over in a ship he had fitted out to join the enemy of his national foe.

France had at that time almost permitted England to gain the advantage of her. The American agents negotiated not only with France; they also sought to get into touch with other Powers, and even maintained relations with England. These threatened to take a peculiar turn immediately before and after the capitulation of Saratoga. After Howe's victory England had offered the colonies an amnesty and the removal of their principal grievances; after the capitulation of Saratoga she went a step farther and held out the prospect of the recognition of a certain degree of independence in return for a permanent and intimate union between the colonies and the mother country. The American agents were hardly empowered to make such an agreement with England. But the danger threatened by this combination, together with the improved prospects of the campaign, led France to take a decisive step. The treaty of friendship and commerce over which the Americans had been kept in suspense for more than a year was concluded in a few weeks (February 6, 1778). This amounted to an official recognition of the United States.

The immediate consequence was the retreat of the English from Philadelphia. England could not seriously hope to oppose on all fields the alliance of France and the United States which Spain, after much hesitation, joined in the following year (April 12, 1779). Holland, too, ranged herself among the enemies of England. Howe's position at Philadelphia kept the English forces idle in one place without seriously threatening the enemy. Accordingly a new general, Clinton, was placed at the head of the English army. He was ordered to evacuate the capital of the Union and to remove the war to a new field, where there were better prospects of success. American rejoicings over the retreat were increased by the fact that Washington succeeded in inflicting a defeat on his retreating opponents at Monmouth. But Clinton had only withdrawn his troops to New York, because the impending outbreak of war with France and Spain rendered it desirable to transfer operations against the colonies to the southern States, where it would be possible to keep in touch with the struggle that would probably be carried on among the Antilles.

In the winter of 1777–1778 France had not as yet declared war against England, and she made loud complaints in all the courts of Europe when the attack made by the English on a French ship, "La Belle Poule," enabled her to represent them as the aggressors. But in reality a fleet with its crews had been preparing, since February, to fight on the side of the Americans against England. At this time a considerable number of foreign officers had taken service in the United States. Lafayette and his friends had been fighting with the Americans since the preceding year, though originally received with such ill-concealed distrust that some of them returned to France bitterly disappointed. Lafayette's enthusiastic advocacy was not without effect in bringing the French government to consent to the despatch of an auxiliary corps under Rochambeau. In addition to these the Prussian colonel, Friedrich Wilhelm von Steuben, deserves special mention for his improvements in the internal organisation of the American army. After a long struggle Washington had gained his point that the nucleus, at least, of the army should be composed of permanent regiments. These owed their training to Von Steuben; and indeed the improvements introduced into the management of the whole army, in so far as the insufficient means available permitted, were the work of this officer of the school of Frederick II.

From the French alliance great wonders were expected, not only by Washington and the army, but to an even greater extent by the Congress, which had returned in triumph to Philadelphia. It was already so convinced that a decisive victory was impending, that it considered it superfluous to do anything more toward it. The disillusionment was the greater when a peculiar combination of unfavourable circumstances rendered the joint campaign of the Americans and the French almost fruitless. From the beginning there had been a party in Congress that did not look with favour on the French alliance. It found support in the New England States, which transferred their old antipathy to the Canadians to the French who were now about to fight as their allies for colonial independence. The repeated offers on the part of England to enter into negotiations with the rebels upon the removal of their grievances had caused the idea to take root that a reconciliation was imminent on the basis of the recognition of the United States by England. The politicians of the East were perhaps not far wrong in this: for in the face of the threatened interposition of her hereditary foe England was ready to make great sacrifices to put an end to the American war. The prospects of peace were seriously affected by the French alliance, for though the Americans interpreted the agreement in the sense that France would only secure their independence, and, this done, make no opposition to a direct understanding between the colonies and the mother country, yet the French government, in continuing negotiations at Paris with the delegates of Congress, especially with Franklin, and also, by means of its accredited representatives, with the Congress at Philadelphia, took care that the principle should be recognised that none of the contracting Powers should make peace with England without the concurrence of the others. This made the termination of the war no longer solely dependent on the recognition of the independence of the United States. These business politicians forgot how remote this had been before the French alliance, and tried to persuade the States that the continuance of the war was solely due to the French.

Though they undoubtedly overshot the mark in this, the Congress and an overwhelming majority of the American people were of the opinion that since France, as was natural, was seeking by this war to gain advantages for herself and her allies, especially for Spain, it was only right that she should bring the war to a conclusion with her own money and troops. The demands made on the French government by the leading statesmen of Congress were almost incredible. Their only excuse is the political and diplomatic inexperience of men suddenly transformed from lawyers and merchants into the responsible leaders of a mighty State.

There was, it is true, a small circle of really statesmanlike characters among the men who helped to found the United States. Foremost among these stood George Washington. The course of events suddenly placed this peaceful and ease-loving landowner at the head of the Union army; but in his case circumstances served only to develop great capacities and to bring to light splendid talents. At the outbreak of war Washington was in his forty-third year. He was not a professional soldier, and his only experience of war had been as an officer of the Virginia militia; but so successful was he in this capacity that he was appointed its commander-in-chief in 1755. He entered public life more from a sense of duty than from inclination, and he retired to his rich estates as soon as possible. He typified all that was noblest in the Virginia planters. His appearance was striking,—almost too aristocratic for a republican; but none was more enthusiastic than he for the cause of American liberty. His sound education and his knowledge of the world fitted him for a diplomat; his wide knowledge of national economies for a statesman. Nor was the limited experience gained in little wars his only qualification for the military position he held; for he possessed two distinguishing qualities that render him, in all respects, one of the most remarkable men America has ever seen. These qualities were, first, the power of taking a clear and unprejudiced view of the situation; this enabled him, even in the most trying circumstances, to calculate and consider with imperturbable composure, and to await the right moment with an iron patience; and second, an extraordinary energy that enabled him not only to accomplish much himself, but to move all around him to put forth their utmost strength. At the beginning his position was extremely difficult; even his rank as commander-in-chief, which the first impulse of national enthusiasm had given him, was not quite safe from the envy of jealous rivals or the eagerness of selfish place-hunters. He himself was perhaps the least concerned about his

GEORGE WASHINGTON

After an engraving by Cheesman from a picture by Trumbull.
The original engraving is now in the Royal Cabinet of Engravings at Dresden.

position; for he learned daily how many duties it imposed on him and how little real power he possessed. But he was even greater as a diplomat than as a strategist, and was thus enabled to solve the difficult problem before him, and to stand continually between the inexperienced politicians of Congress and the European diplomats schooled in the political etiquette of the Old World. From the time of the alliance with France he maintained, not only at the seat of war, but also in the field of politics, a kind of government independent of Congress; but in both spheres his characteristic reserve enabled him to avoid all dangers.

There was no other man of his nation who could be compared with him. Even Benjamin Franklin, with his homely honesty, stood far behind him in political far-sightedness. Despite this no one, perhaps, played a greater part than Franklin in bringing the Revolution to a successful issue. Born in humble circumstances, he had worked his way slowly and laboriously upward by his own efforts; and throughout his life he preserved something of the manners said to be characteristic of the inhabitants of Philadelphia, where he had spent his youth and middle age. He was not a man of great actions, but the long experience he had gained at the English court as agent for the colonies enabled him, more than all others, to win the sympathy of other nations for his struggling country; and the credit of having induced France to side openly with the United States belongs chiefly to him. But his attitude during the peace negotiations showed how much he was affected by the shrewdness that usually characterised the politicians of the youthful State. Many efforts have been made to clear him of the charge of having taken part in the negotiations with England which, though contrary to the agreement with France, were carried on in secret by the American diplomatists. But no amount of explanation can get rid of the fact that Franklin's characteristic appearance of confidential frankness and good-natured honesty served to screen the double-dealing of his fellow diplomatists, though he had perhaps no direct part in deceiving the allies he himself had gained. During the war he exerted little direct influence on affairs at home; but his sober and practical common sense and his business experience helped in no small degree to remove the formidable difficulties that lay in the way of diplomatic success.

Beside the two leaders stood a number of less important personages of similar political views; but among the influential politicians there were scarcely any others so clear-sighted or so unprejudiced. The significance of this soon appeared when, on the conclusion of the French alliance, weightier events took place in the field of diplomacy than on the field of battle.

In accordance with their plan of campaign the English transferred their operations to the South. In January, 1779, they conquered Savannah and defended it successfully against the French fleet. In February 1780, the English commander-in-chief, Clinton, landed in South Carolina and forced the American troops in Charleston to capitulate after a siege of five weeks. It appeared as if English supremacy would be re-established in the south; and for a time not a single detachment of organised American troops opposed the English. But the object aimed at soon showed itself unattainable. Except on the coast, the land was sparsely populated and but little cultivated. This rendered permanent military occupation impossible, and placed great difficulties in the way of all military operations. This was very well known at Washington's headquarters. Thus, instead of following the English to the south, the leader of the American army kept in view operations on the Hudson against New York as most likely to decide the issue of the campaign. Clinton was thus compelled to come north again, while in the South a partisan war went on with varying results. This was stirred up from both head-quarters by the despatch of regular troops under approved leaders, so that the Eng-lish were never in undisturbed possession and still could never be driven out. During these cross-expeditions a number of important battles were fought in North and South Carolina. At Camden the English gained a victory in which the brave De Kalb lost his life; at King's Mountain and at Cowpens the Americans were successful; other battles, such as that at Guilford, were claimed as victories by both sides. But the situation remained essentially unchanged: the English maintained their hold on the thickly populated coast districts; but in the interior bands of Americans carried on a guerilla warfare, making unexpected attacks on outposts and cutting off small detachments of British troops.

To change this state of affairs the English resolved to carry the war into Vir-ginia, which now provided almost entirely for the maintenance of the American army except in so far as this was done by France. But even this failed to draw Washington away from the Hudson; he merely sent down Lafayette with a part of the American troops. Lafayette showed himself quite worthy of the confidence placed in him. By his skilful movements he held the English general, Cornwallis, in check for weeks, until the latter was called back to the coast by the commander-in-chief. But in seeking to provide in Yorktown [1] a fortified point of support for the renewal, later on, of the campaign in the interior, Cornwallis fell into a danger-ous trap which was at once recognised by the American leaders. Lafayette hastened as quickly as possible to invest the place; Washington sent to his support the greater part of the French and American troops under Rochambeau; and a French fleet under De Grasse, which, though destined for the Antilles, offered its help to strike a blow against the English, completed the investment of the enemy. The hostile lines drew so closely about Yorktown that Cornwallis had to lay down his arms on October 19, 1781. Single points on the coast, notably Charleston and New York, still remained in the hands of the English; but the fate of their arms was sealed, even in the South, which could no longer be held against the American troops.

### C. THE NEGOTIATIONS AND CONCLUSION OF PEACE WITH ENGLAND

MUCH as the events of the war now served to excite those on the spot, they had comparatively little influence in determining its final result. The leading French statesmen soon came to the conviction that, instead of having gained an active ally in the struggle against England by their alliance with the United States, they had in reality only gained permission to carry on the war for the Americans with French money, French soldiers, and French ships. The Spanish government hesitated long before joining in the war against England; and though it took it for granted that it would receive Florida and the Mississippi in return for taking part in the war, it considered American affairs of quite secondary importance and wished Minorca and Gibraltar to be the main points of attack. Further, it let it be clearly seen that it wished to put an end to the war as soon as

[1] See map at p. 514.

possible, and merely wished to take advantage of England's critical position to obtain a revision of the Peace of 1763. The course of the war in America also led France to desire its speedy termination. Therefore it not only encouraged Spain in its endeavours for peace, but also prepared the American Congress for it, in order that the latter should decide upon the conditions it wished to impose upon England.

In the following years, up to the conclusion of peace, the negotiations in this connection occupied the attention of Congress much more than the concerns of the war had ever done. The debates were carried on with such vehemence that on more than one occasion the newly made Union of thirteen States threatened to fall asunder into groups with divided interests. What American politicians would naturally have preferred was that England should give up all its North American possessions and renounce all its claims in the northern continent in favour of the United States. In negotiations with the agents by whom England throughout the war strove to bring about an understanding, they based their claim on the state-ment that the proximity of the United States and a British Canada would be a perpetual cause of discord between the two nations of the same blood. Benjamin Franklin deserves the credit of having skilfully put forward this view during the negotiations he conducted with the British agent, Oswald; but in the final settle-ment the point was not again brought up, so that it was scarcely necessary for England to reject the demand.

In regard to their southern boundary the Americans were less greedy for terri-tory. They had become quite accustomed to the idea of giving back Florida to Spain as payment for her participation in the war, and especially for the subsidies which had been continually solicited, though without success, from the court of Charles III. But this point was not the true source of discord in the Congress. There were two other conditions, to one of which the representatives of the southern States clung with as much tenacity as those of the North did to the other. How far-sighted the politicians of the southern States were on points affecting their future interests is shown by the fact that they wished to have the cession of the "hinter-land," as far as the Mississippi, and the right of free navigation of this stream down to the Gulf of Mexico, regarded as indispensable preliminaries to the conclusion of peace with England. The English Colonial Office had organised the land west of the Alleghanies independently of the old provinces, and the settlement of this territory on any considerable scale had been but recently commenced from the southern provinces. Nevertheless the leaders in the southern States perceived per-fectly the importance for this district of the waterway to the Gulf of Mexico, and were resolved not to give up this security for the future.

The North put forward its claims in quite another manner. The business spirit characteristic of the northern States from the beginning made itself felt here. It was an open secret that the shipowners and traders of the New England States knew well how to take advantage of the existing state of war. The chase after British merchant ships was carried on by them so successfully that the profits from it must have been considerable. Besides, they carried on a more unpatriotic busi-ness in supplying provisions and other necessaries to the English in Halifax and even in New York. In spite of this the leaders of the Northern party, Samuel Adams, and other extremists, behaved as if their States had to bear the whole burden of the war, and demanded as compensation for this that the revolutionary government should not lay down its arms until England admitted the United States to a share in the fisheries on the Newfoundland Banks. Hitherto, as English subjects, they had had a profitable share in this fishery; and though it was a great exaggeration to assert that the northern States were dependent on these fishing-grounds for their food supply, it is true that a very considerable industry had been developed in connection with the Newfoundland fishery. The southern States would probably have been quite willing to act with their northern neighbours with a view to gaining this point in future peace negotiations; but the vigorous manner in which the northern party sought to enforce its claim could serve only to make the representatives of other States feel that the problem of the fisheries had been made a matter of sectional and not of national importance, and to justify them in treating the demand for an open Mississippi as vitally important to the local interests of the west.

For a long time these discussions upon the conditions of peace possessed a purely theoretical interest. The efforts of the leader of the army on the one hand, and of the representatives of France on the other, succeeded in restraining the embittered war of words and in obscuring those subjects on which utterly irreconcilable views were held. When, in March, 1782, by means of Franklin's personal relations with some of the members of the newly formed English cabinet, the general desire for peace was finally confirmed, strife broke out afresh in the Congress. The party of the northern States, that would have preferred that Franklin, the friend of the French, should be deprived of all share in the negotiations, were so far successful that they placed beside him two representatives of their own views, — John Adams and John Jay. The history of the peace negotiations shows once more the total absence of a real executive in the young State. The Congress had indeed established a department for foreign affairs; but its representatives, during the peace negotiations, never received definite instructions, and, once on French soil and removed from the immediate interference of Congress, they were really independent. That the negotiations were so quickly concluded, and that in a manner exceeding the expectations of the most sanguine American politicians, was due to the vacillation of the English politicians, who hoped to render many of the concessions less burdensome to their own country by securing in the United States a friend easy to control. Contrary to all diplomatic usage the American politicians did not even once inform the French government of the course of negotiations, though they could not be ignorant that peace negotiations were going on at the same time between France and England. It is true that no serious disadvantage accrued to France from this, and that the negotiations with England were soon brought to a successful issue.

The Peace which was ratified at Versailles September 3, 1783, recognised the thirteen United States of North America as an independent State. Almost all the demands of the American party politicians were conceded by England. Florida, which was restored to Spain, formed the southern boundary of the States; the Mississippi the western; and navigation on this river was to be free to Americans and to the English. The northern boundary ran from the St. Croix River across the watershed between the Hudson and the St. Lawrence, and then through the Great Lakes to the source of the Mississippi. The right of participating in the fisheries on the Newfoundland Banks was expressly conceded. As for the rest, a treaty of peace and commerce between England and the United States was to restore as far as possible the relations interrupted by the war. The recognition of the United States by the remaining European Powers was somewhat delayed, but this was a matter of comparatively little importance to the young States; it enjoyed not only the recognition but also the good will of the Powers which were of most importance to it. Thus, as far as the outside world was concerned, the republic of the United States was firmly established.

## *D.* THE CONSTITUTION

THE condition of the United States as regards internal affairs left much to be desired. The people in general were untrained for the political independence they had gained. Even some men who had for years been striving for these lofty ends and had played the rôle of party leaders in the provincial Assemblies showed themselves little fitted for the task of government. They had hitherto had experience only of the negative side of political life as members of an opposition that upheld the real and supposed rights of the provinces against the governors appointed by the Crown. A vehement and radical spirit often characterised the discussions in Congress, and it became the more pronounced in that it was not counteracted by the presence of a settled government maintaining an established course of procedure.

In the face of petty jealousies between the States, and the conflict of interests between the two groups of northern and southern States, it was no easy task to draw up a constitution for the thirteen United States. When the Congress first met in 1774, its authority was quite undefined. It was constituted, normally, by the revolutionary assemblies of the provinces, and thus lacked a strictly legal basis; and its object, its duration, and the scope of its authority were undetermined. If its course during the early years of the war, though calling into existence most stringent measures, met with no serious opposition, this was due less to its claims of authority than to the force of circumstances. The weakness of its organisation was felt by Congress itself, and even before the Declaration of Independence it appointed a committee to place the management of the common concerns of the colonies on a definite basis. The work of the committee, the Articles of Confederation, was approved by Congress in the autumn of 1777, and was submitted to the legislatures of the separate States for ratification. At the end of fifteen months twelve States had accepted the articles. Maryland withheld its assent for two years longer.[1] But Congress had gained nothing by this definition of its authority; rather the contrary. In the closing years of the war Congress sank lower and lower in the public estimation. It was to be feared that Congress, and with it the idea of unity, would fall into complete discredit as soon as the war was over, and the pressure from without, causing the States to hold together, was withdrawn. This was the feeling of all clear-sighted politicians, both those who wished well to the States and those who speculated on their breaking up. It was in the full consciousness of this that Washington, before giving up his position as leader of the army, the embodiment of the Union, and retiring into private life, wrote to the legislatures of the different States that celebrated letter in which he urged on them to hold firmly together, as this was the only basis for a great future; but for the time his warning was without appreciable effect.

[1] See *post*, p. 477.

The spirit of independence had been greatly strengthened in the various States during the war. Before the revolutionary steps of 1774 only two provinces, Rhode Island and Connecticut, had been completely republican. In all the others the representatives of the people had been controlled by a governor appointed by the Proprietor or by the Crown. The States under governors had during the war remodelled their constitutions on a republican basis; and they were far too proud of their newly won rights of self-government to be ready to give them up so soon for the common good. When peace and independence had been established, the important work of Congress, representing the States as a whole, was considered as ended. Each of the thirteen States began to adapt itself to the new situation in the way it considered most advantageous to its own particular interests. Common concerns were meanwhile most shamefully neglected. The Congress was not in a position to pay off the army, nor was it able to take over the military posts on the northern and western frontiers. The importance of the central government created an unfavourable impression abroad. American diplomacy often failed completely in its objects on account of the discredit into which the national government had fallen. Even at home Congress fell into discredit. Pennsylvania looked quietly on while the body representing the union of the States was driven from the capital by eighty mutinous reservists and forced to continue its sittings at Princeton. Each of the States was against all the others. New York set the example by erecting about itself a bulwark of protective duties, not only against foreign States, but, upon its own strict interpretation of the Articles of Confederation, against its immediate neighbours. These duties were strictly enforced with a total lack of consideration for the interests of neighbouring States. This gave rise to the question whether it would not be desirable to transfer to Congress the power of regulating commerce. It was solely because Congress did not possess this power that the desired treaty of commerce with Spain was not concluded; and England, which now enforced the Navigation Act against the United States, could not be combated because, while the New England States replied by bringing in a Navigation Act of their own, Connecticut willingly placed its harbours at the disposal of the English; and the southern States also declared against a Navigation Act because they feared that, when the New England ship-owners had crushed all competition, they would raise freights on the staple products of the South so high as to ruin Southern industry.

Old boundary disputes also cropped up again. From the commencement of the war the United States had laid claim to the territory beyond the Alleghanies; but they had not settled among themselves which State it should belong to. Massachusetts and Connecticut claimed a share on the ground that their colonial charters granted them the land from ocean to ocean. New York claimed all the land which had owed tribute to their allies, the Iroquois; and Virginia claimed all the land to the "west and northwest," as indefinitely granted in her charter. North Carolina had established government in Tennessee, as had Virginia and Kentucky. Now Virginia was at that time, apart from new acquisitions, the most populous and richest of the States, so that the small States whose geographical position precluded further expansion were little inclined to let the power of this one State increase indefinitely, as they had seen in the case of New York what dangers to its smaller and poorer neighbours would follow. The legislature sought to find a way out of this difficulty in 1777 by making a proposal to Congress that the latter should not decide upon the claims of the States to the territory between the Alleghanie and the Mississippi, but should treat the whole tract as national territory, out of which new States might later be formed. The proposal was quite unsupported and was rejected; but Maryland now made its ratification of the Articles of Confederation dependent on the acceptance of this proposal respecting the territory in the west. This was the real reason why this State, otherwise so faithful to the principle of union, delayed its assent to the Articles of Confederation till 1781. In the same year Virginia, following the example of New York and Connecticut, declared itself ready to abandon its claims, and was then followed by Massachusetts, North Carolina, and Georgia.

The settlement of the territorial dispute led to important constitutional consequences. Hitherto Congress, without power and without means, had had a precarious existence; but the abandonment by the single States of their claims to the "hinterland" handed over to it a region not only of great extent, but, as the flourishing settlements showed, of considerable wealth. In what form now was Congress to exercise its power over this region? The proposal put forward by the Virginian governor, Thomas Jefferson, to divide the territory into ten new States, was rejected; but already in Tennessee and Kentucky communities of such strength had sprung up that soon after the definite constitution of the United States they succeeded in getting themselves admitted as properly constituted States. On the other hand the land north of the Ohio was placed under the direct control of Congress, partly that it might have the means of paying the interest and capital of the war debt by the sale of land, and partly that it might be able to give the soldiers discharged at the close of the war an opportunity of establishing homes for themselves under favourable conditions. All that was laid down for the constitution of this region was that the rights of individuals, and the religious liberty common to the Constitutions of the thirteen States, should be maintained; and in other respects also Congress was free to arrange the provisional government as it saw fit, thus excluding slavery from the territory and making possible the gradual organisation of these new territories as commonwealths of the Union.

This procedure did little to increase the consideration in which Congress was held; but it was of much more importance in that it afforded an example of an extensive territory actually ruled by a central authority. The most enlightened politicians — and before all others Washington — were convinced that the only remedy for the unmistakable stagnation existing in the United States was complete unification. Government by Congress was a shadow. The future of America, as was even then recognised, lay in the development of its boundless resources. This was impossible as long as the petty jealousies of the States continually acted in opposition to the common interest, — to-day encouraging the English to cripple the American carrying-trade, to-morrow giving the Spaniards an opportunity of closing the mouth of the Mississippi against the southern States. A first attempt to entrust to Congress the supervision of the trade interests of all the States led to such a wonderful confusion of claims and admissions that nothing useful could be accomplished, and the attempt failed. But it was from this direction that the impulse came to which the Constitution of the United States owes its origin.

Washington took a lively interest in the economic development of the country,

as in all other political questions. Before giving up his post as commander of the
army he made a tour in the north to see for himself what communication there
was by water between the Hudson and the Great Lakes. After his retirement
into private life he took great interest in the project of making a waterway from
Chesapeake Bay, through the Potomac, to the Ohio; for, as he saw well, community
of interest was the best means of holding the States of the Union together. The
canal project rendered an understanding among the different States of the Union
necessary; and after a meeting of delegates from the four States especially concerned had been agreed to in principle, it was proposed to invite delegates from all
the States to this convention, and to consider, not merely the projected canal, but
the economic and especially the commercial needs of the United States. Thus
originated the Convention of Annapolis, which met in September, 1786. It produced no tangible results; but it passed a resolution, attended by the weightiest
consequences, that Congress be requested to summon a new convention to deal, not
merely with commerce, but with everything bearing on the national welfare and
particularly on the form of government of the United States.

Congress was not indisposed to comply with the request of the Convention of
Annapolis; but before it had done so the news was spread abroad that Virginia
had already chosen its delegates for the new convention, and that Washington had
consented to act in this capacity. The popularity of this name worked wonders;
in a short time four other States nominated their delegates, and Congress, at the
instigation of Massachusetts, hastened to send out invitations to a Convention that
was to meet at Philadelphia in May, 1787. The Convention, whose work was the
Constitution of the United States, comprised fifty-five delegates representing twelve
States (Rhode Island not being represented). At the first sitting Washington was
elected president. The proceedings were secret and were not binding on the
States represented. But it was exactly this knowledge, that their work could become law only after having been approved by Congress and by the States, that gave
the delegates the courage to put aside all timid compromise and bring forward a
thoroughly new Constitution on an essentially altered basis.

The majority of the delegates, though they did not openly express their conviction, knew well that the object of their assembling was to strengthen the union of
the thirteen States and place it on a firmer basis; but as the sittings proceeded, new
groupings were formed among the members, and the final resolutions of the Convention were the result of a long series of compromises. No dogmatic policy was
pursued; but by mutual concessions the interest of all groups in the work of
the Constitution was maintained, a circumstance that bears witness to the great
political wisdom displayed.

Virginia, which had largely given the impulse that led to the assembling of
the Convention, was now the first to bring forward a definite scheme. Governor
Edmund Randolph laid before the Convention a plan worked out in the main by
James Madison, to establish a more effective central government. Congress was
to be elected by a direct vote throughout the United States, in order that expression might be given to the sovereignty of the people. Following the example of
most of the States it was to consist of two Houses. The lower House was to be
directly elected; the members of the upper House were to be chosen by the lower
House from persons proposed by the State legislatures; in both cases the number
of delegates was to be proportioned to population and to the amount contributed

to the revenue. Further, in both Houses a motion was to be carried by a majority of members, not by a majority of States, as hitherto; and a bare majority now sufficient, whereas a two-thirds majority had often been required. Finally, Congress, in addition to its power of deciding all matters of concern, was to have the right of vetoing any resolution of a State held dangerous to the interests of the Union.

This scheme was, as a whole, too centralising to be acceptable to the Anti-federalists. But its essential feature, the formation of a bicameral legislature with a different basis of representation for each chamber, was saved for the future Constitution by one of those statesmanlike compromises. The Anti-federalist had urged a scheme called the New Jersey plan, according to which all the States, large and small, rich and poor, were to be represented by the same number of delegates in each House. By a third plan, suggested by a member from Connecticut, it was finally concluded, by way of compromise, to apply in the upper House the Anti-federalist theory of equal representation of the States, and to form the lower House according to the Federalist scheme of apportioning representatives among the States according to population. Equally significant was the agreement that in both Houses a vote should be allowed to each member, and not, as formerly, to each State delegation. The choice of delegates on a population basis led to further differences of opinion. What was to be taken as the population of a State? In deciding the number of delegates to be elected by each State, were Indians and negroes to be included in the population? This question at once renewed the dissension between North and South, and would perhaps have seriously hampered the Convention had not the parties agreed to a compromise based on the precedents of 1783; and now when the Southern representatives wished the negro population to be counted in full in settling the number of delegates for each State, the Northern opposition finally forced the South to be content with the system of counting five negroes as equivalent to three white men in the apportionment both of direct taxes and of representatives.

The principle that Congress should have complete control of all matters connected with foreign trade had been generally recognised as the chief reason for the meeting of the Convention. It was therefore considered right that the Convention should come to a final decision on the point. But the subject of slavery was involved in the matter, and the question was raised whether Congress should have the power of prohibiting the slave-trade. Many States were opposed to the continuation of the traffic; but in the face of the great division of interests in the Congress a compromise was once more agreed upon. The southern States agreed that Congress should, after a period of twenty years, have power to abolish the slave-trade, and the northern commercial States consented that Congress, acting by the vote of a majority instead of by the vote of two thirds, should have exclusive control of commerce between the States and with other nations.

After a series of far-reaching regulations had defined the authority of Congress and of the several States, the form of the Executive had still to be decided on. Despite the prevailing anti-monarchical spirit the idea rapidly gained ground among the members of the Convention that a single person should be placed at the head of the government. But the question as to how this person should be elected gave rise to endless discussions, during which the half-finished work was more than once endangered. It was finally settled that the President of the United States should hold office for four years, but was eligible for re-election; and that he should be chosen by colleges of electors specially constituted for the purpose. The composition of the colleges of electors was left to the separate States. It was not until 1868 that the practice of choosing the electors by the direct vote of the people became general.

The Convention of Philadelphia had done all its work with a feeling that it was binding on no one. This helped it, especially at first, over many difficulties. But though two delegates from New York ostentatiously retired in the course of the proceedings, and at the close three more (two from Virginia and one from Massachusetts) refused their signatures to what had been the result of months of discussion, the majority were quite well aware that the currents of public opinion in the young nation went with them. The subsequent treatment of their proposals showed that they were not mistaken.

On the 20th of September, 1787, Washington laid before Congress the work of the Convention.[1] The Anti-federalist party would have liked to neutralise by it the proposal to reconsider the Constitution in Congress, and, if need be, to alter it. But the Federalists by an overwhelming majority, carried their proposal that the work of the Convention should at once be submitted to the different States without change. The first State to decide in favour of the new Constitution was Delaware, whose convention accepted it unanimously on the 6th of December. Delaware was followed in the same month by Pennsylvania and New Jersey, by Georgia and Connecticut in January, and by Massachusetts, after heated debates, in February, 1788. According to the old Articles the consent of every State was necessary before a new form could be established. This constitutional requirement was ignored, and by procedure quite analogous to that of revolution it was provided that the new Constitution should be in force upon ratification by only nine States. Furthermore, efforts were made to qualify the several ratifications by conditions directed to securing more explicitly the civil rights of the individual; but Washington rightly pointed out that to impair what had just been accomplished was equivalent to rejecting it; that the Constitution itself afforded the means by which it could be supplemented and improved; and that the proper course for those States whose wishes the Constitution did not meet was to use these means to amend it. These arguments told in Massachusetts, and were not without effect on other conventions, and by June, before Virginia had come to a decision, nine States had agreed to the new Constitution. Arrangements were then made for the presidential election in which, on the 7th of January, 1789, all the States, with the exception of New York, North Carolina, and Rhode Island, took part. The sixty-nine electors unanimously chose Washington as first President of the Union.

### E. The Time of the Great Virginians

Without doubt the United States possessed no citizen other than George Washington in whose hands they could place their fortunes with equal confidence. He combined the tact of a man of the world with an unselfishness that had stood every test, and a firm faith in the future of his country, to whose service he devoted his intellectual talents and his wide practical experience. His unsought elevation to the position of president was but the just reward of his long public services.

---

[1] See Plate opposite.

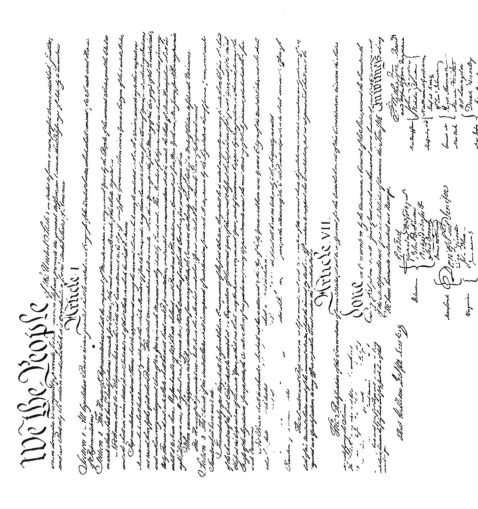

Throughout the Revolutionary War he had kept himself independent of party; and he wished to remain so now that he was the chosen ruler of the nation, and to unite all its forces around him in common activity. But experience soon taught him how impracticable this high ideal was. The struggles about the Constitution had led to the establishment of sharply defined party differences. These naturally manifested themselves among the men Washington had chosen as his fellow-workers. The most pressing task that lay before the new government was the re-establishment of the credit of the United States, and with it their repute both at home and abroad. In finance Washington had at his disposal a great force in Alexander Hamilton, a leading member of the Convention, and so keen an advocate of a strong central executive that he was the recognised head of the Federal party. His first measures, the funding of the debt of the United States, and the assumption of the debts of the separate States by the Union, were in accord with his expressed centralising tendencies. The objection his opponents made to these measures was that they gave an opportunity to the rich merchants of the North of carrying on a profitable if not particularly honourable business. The merchants bought up great quantities of the practically worthless bonds issued to cover the debts of the different States, and made great profit when these were taken over and redeemed by the central government. In order to provide the means of carrying out these financial operations Hamilton now proposed a tax which, he admitted, would remind every citizen of his connection with the Union by touching him in his most sensitive spot, his pocket; but in this he appeared so clearly as a party politician that the Anti-federalists at once declared themselves against him, and so bitter was the opposition that a revolt against the authority of the Union broke out in the West. This turn of affairs made it necessary for Washington to put an imposing force in the field to crush the rising; and also afforded an opportunity through which the power of the central government was early and forcibly demonstrated.

According to his political convictions Washington was a Federalist, but not in the party sense in which Hamilton was. Thus he was able to choose as one of his ministers the man who afterward became the leader of the Anti-federalists,—Thomas Jefferson. When the latter returned from his position as minister to France, Washington offered him the post of Secretary of State, which Jefferson accepted. He helped Hamilton with his plans for the assumption of the State debts by the national government. But just as Hamilton was a "Northerner," Jefferson had unconsciously become a "Southerner," and Hamilton had to buy his support by inducing his own party to agree that the future capital of the Union should be situated in the South, on the Potomac. The unfortunate thing about the party system was that the parties were based not on ideal principles and firm convictions, but were divided chiefly by conflict of interests. Thus it was that the Union was always geographically divided into two hostile camps, the interests of the commercial northern States being always different from those of the agricultural southern ones. The opposition between Federalists and Anti-federalists had justification and significance only during the struggles about the Constitution. After the Constitution had been completed and put into operation, these party names had less significance, for in reality the predominant party was always more or less Federalist, while the opposition made use of the decentralising tendencies of those who held out for the rights of single States, as a cloak to cover its own selfish aims.

Washington was very desirous of retiring to private life at the close of his four years' term of office; but at the request of all parties he consented to hold the presidency for another four years, and was once more unanimously elected. This was a piece of good fortune for the young nation; for these four years brought difficulties that were overcome only by Washington's tact and foresight. The friendship of France was still an important factor in United States politics; the more because the Revolution tended to establish political conditions in many respects analogous to those of the United States. But these conditions became critical when the abolition of the monarchy and the establishment of a republic involved France in war. The southern States which had been so eager for the French alliance in 1782, were now intoxicated by the high-sounding phrases of the French republicans, and were ready to stand shoulder to shoulder with them in their struggle against the despots. But this would have been bad policy for the United States; for their economic connection with France was slight, while the prosperity of the northern States was largely dependent on trade with England. For this reason Washington declared the strictest neutrality. The French republicans, it is true, took no notice of this, and their diplomatists showed the same bold assurance that those of the United States had formerly shown. The French plenipotentiary held himself justified in enlisting soldiers and fitting out privateers in American towns, as he was received with tumultuous applause by the people, not only in the South, but even in New York. But Washington did not deviate from the path he had chosen, and when he was forced, by the tactless behaviour of the French minister, to maintain the dignity of the American nation against him, the mass of the people was united in supporting the President.

The position of the government of the Union would have been much simpler had it not, at the same time, had to maintain certain claims against England. The English still held a number of posts in the West under circumstances which laid themselves open to criticism; and the regulations by which they endeavoured to check the trade of neutrals with France, and to monopolise all trade with their own land for themselves, injured the business of the United States in many very different respects. But it was difficult to remedy this completely as long as the war between France and England lasted. Washington succeeded in gaining partial relief by an agreement arranged by John Jay; but many sources of annoyance remained untouched, and succeeding presidents had for years to contend with these difficulties.

At the close of his second term of office Washington emphatically declined re-election, so that a new head of the state had to be chosen. In this matter the Federalist party began to dig its own grave. Hamilton indulged in electioneering tactics in order to keep John Adams, who was personally unacceptable to him, out of the presidency. He failed in this; but the factional controversy within the Federalist party made possible the election of an Anti-federalist President in 1800. The United States now seemed to be drifting, much against its inclinations, into war with France. The Directory, by its insolent proceedings, had forced the United States to discontinue diplomatic relations, and under the favourite pretext of searching for contraband it carried on a more vigorous war against American commerce than England had ever done. Then the Federalist party collected its strength, and demanded a resolution declaring war on France; but before war had been formally declared Adams took advantage of the first slight signs of concession on the part of France to effect a reconciliation. This was a severe defeat for the Federalists, and it was made worse by the fact that at the same time they took a disastrous step in home affairs. To guard against foreign agitation in the country, they introduced a severe law against this, and against insults to the government, and carried it in spite of vigorous opposition. The Anti-federalist party considered this the height of illegality, and the legislatures of Kentucky and Virginia held sittings to protest against it. During these sittings the famous resolutions were passed in which the champions of the rights of single States claimed the right of actively resisting illegal resolutions of Congress. The resolutions had no immediate significance, but later they served as a basis for the arguments of secessionists.

The new presidential election placed Jefferson at the head of the government. As the result of mismanaged electioneering tactics on the part of the Anti-federalists, Jefferson, and Burr who had been selected for the vice-presidency, received the same number of votes. The unscrupulous Burr would gladly have displaced Jefferson; but the Federalists who helped him in his attempt only succeeded in gaining contempt for themselves by their efforts. Jefferson emerged from the contest doubly victorious. His government gave additional proof that acting in opposition is a very different thing from leading a government.

The policy of the government was still determined by its relations to the belligerent Powers in Europe. Ever since the Declaration of Independence there had been differences between Spain and the United States about the free navigation of the Mississippi. This had been conceded by England to the United States at the Peace of Paris; but England had at the same time given up Florida to Spain. Thus the mouth of the Mississippi became exclusively Spanish, and the government at Madrid unconditionally refused to allow foreign ships to pass through its territory. It was only in 1795, after protracted negotiations, that New Orleans was declared a free port for American ships. Almost immediately after this negotiations were commenced which led to a further change at the mouth of the Mississippi, — the cession of Louisiana to France. The Union government had several times considered the best means of meeting the danger that the territories on its boundary, Louisiana and Florida, might pass from the weak hands of Spain into those of England or France; and Jefferson did not delay coming to an understanding with the new owner of Louisiana upon their neighbouring relations. In so doing he made the surprising discovery that the First Consul, Napoleon, was by no means disinclined to rid himself of this territory, which possessed but doubtful value for him. Now Jefferson had not the least doubt that the Constitution did not permit him to acquire new territory for the Union; but he had no thought of letting slip such an exceptional opportunity of extending and securing the boundaries of the Union. He therefore gave his unqualified approval to the act of his envoy, who purchased the territory in question from France for fifteen million dollars. Of course there was very considerable opposition, especially on the part of the northern States, which feared that their trade would suffer by the opening of the mouth of the Mississippi; but Jefferson's enemies were not so blind as to think seriously of annulling this profitable transaction.

In the autumn of 1804 Jefferson was elected to the presidency for a further term of four years. During his second term of office the political situation was graver. As Napoleon more and more revealed himself, the Old World became more and more plunged in war. The United States were affected by it, as each of the sea Powers, England and France, persistently harassed the commerce of the citizens of the Union with that of its enemies. In this the attitude of England may have been more unfriendly than that of France, though both nations captured American ships almost in their own harbours. But the old leaning of the southern States toward France, and Jefferson's enthusiasm for that country, were mainly responsible for the Union government's directing its anger chiefly against England. From the time of the War of Independence the idea had survived that the interruption of commercial relations was a specially effective weapon against England. As those on the American side who would suffer most from this were the commercial northern States, the party of the southern States, then predominant, immediately carried the proposal of an embargo of several months' duration. But in reality it was only American trade that suffered seriously from it; for even in American waters England was supreme, and so was able to protect an illicit trade which almost compensated for the loss of the regular commerce. The complaints of the North, continually becoming louder, were not without effect on Congress. Jefferson himself was considering the removal of the embargo; but toward the end of his term of office he had lost control over Congress to such an extent that his opponents carried its immediate repeal against his will.

The change in the presidency made no change in the situation either at home or abroad. Madison, like Jefferson, was one of the leaders of the Southern party, that championed the rights of the separate States; but, like his predecessor, he was forced more and more toward the Federalists by the duties of the office he had taken up. One thing was unmistakable, that his personal influence over the Southern party was appreciably less than that of his predecessor. On becoming President he had found relations with England and France unchanged. The former did not respond to the removal of the embargo by any serious attempt to remedy the grievances justly complained of by the Americans; on the contrary, the negotiations entered upon ended in England's rejecting all the American claims and refusing all concessions until the United States should take up a more decided attitude toward France. Now the latter deserved no consideration from America. Her attitude was quite as unfriendly as England's. But on account of the traditional friendship between France and the Union, ever kept alive by skilfully turned phrases, the government could not make up its mind to buy the friendship of England by a change of front toward France. Thus negotiations were continued with both Powers on the subject of the abolition of the regulations which crippled the trade of neutrals; but the Americans still had to put up with their ships' being treated as hostile by both sides, without daring to make reprisals. In this dilemma help came to the government from a quarter whence it was least expected.

In the South there had formed within the Anti-federalist party a new group that held more firmly to the one-sided policy of the party. The leaders of this group, Clay and Calhoun, were intoxicated with pan-American ideas, the first aim of which was the conquest of Canada. Accordingly they threatened to withdraw their support from Madison in the forthcoming presidential election if he did not adopt a more energetic policy against England. Now Madison's ambition was to serve two terms as President, like his predecessor; and to this desire he sacrificed his love of peace. On the 1st of April, 1812, he renewed the trade war by an embargo; but as the North was not inclined to a war policy, or willing to bear its expenses for the South, the embargo was laxly enforced and once again remained ineffective. The war party, however, was insistent, and Madison yielded.

As if in mockery of the American plans, the abolition of the decrees pressing hardly upon the trade of neutrals was consented to exactly at this time by both England and France; but before definite news of this could reach America the pliant majority in Congress had decided on war against England, and declared it on June 18, 1812. If the War of Independence, in spite of the community of interests then existing, had exhibited the military resources of the Union in a very unfavourable light, still more so did this war, which the northern States stigmatised as a party war of their opponents. It is probable that England for a time cherished the hope of breaking up the Union and forming the northern States in a separate Union friendly to England. This charge against the northern States has been founded chiefly on the proceedings of the Hartford Convention. But this assembly, in which, moreover, only Rhode Island, Connecticut, and Massachusetts were officially represented, did, in reality, no more than the southern States had done against Adams by the Kentucky and Virginia resolutions.[1] It claimed for the several States the right of refusing to recognise as binding unjust and pernicious resolutions of Congress, and maintained the principle of opposing such resolutions, if need be, by force. But it did not consider that such a necessity had already arisen, and, though refusing to take active part in the war, had no thought of entering into separate negotiations with England.

The course of the war showed how little preparation had been made for it, and how small was its popularity on the whole. Madison had announced that his plan of campaign was to maintain the defensive on the coast, but, by energetically taking the offensive in the North, to try to add Canada to the possessions of the United States. But he was quite unable to obtain the means of doing this. The recruiting and enlistment resolved on by Congress proved totally inadequate; even the militia avoided service as much as possible. Matters were made worse by the apparent incapacity of the generals, and the first campaign ended in most disgraceful losses which were only partially retrieved by the two following ones. The war of defence on the coast also brought to light a melancholy state of affairs. In privateering the ships and seamen of the northern States proved themselves no despicable opponents, as they had already done in the War of Independence, and it was owing to their bravery in many encounters between single ships that the Union government turned its attention more seriously to the creation of a navy. But where the English appeared with fleets and not with single ships, they scarcely ever met with serious resistance. This many coast towns found to their cost in the first two campaigns; and in 1814 the English landed on the shores of the Potomac and captured and partly burned the capital of the Union without once having to fight a serious engagement. The Union government was broken up and had almost ceased to exist.

In this state of affairs the Union received unexpected help from the South. Already in the War of Independence both English and Americans called in the Indians to their aid, but with very different results. Even when the Americans offered the greatest inducements the redskins did not forget the bad treatment they had received in the past, and still received from the English colonists; thus

---

[1] See *ante*, p. 483.

they were reluctant and untrustworthy allies. The English, on the other hand, stepped into the shoes of the French in Canada, and to some extent maintained their wise Indian policy. Besides this, even long after the War of Independence, the English held posts in the West, and thus kept in touch with the Indians, against whom Washington had already had to wage a war of several years' duration, in which, after repeated severe losses, success was attained only by the employment of overwhelming force. In the War of 1812 the Indians took the English side in large numbers. The warlike eloquence of Tecumseh, which spread from the northern lakes to Florida, gave rise to the scheme of a general Indian rising. In the north the project led to no very important results; but in the southern and southwestern States a rising of the Creeks threatened to become a serious danger to the Americans. It was here, in the south, that Andrew Jackson fought his first battle. He had decided military talents, and he was able, with the comparatively small means at his disposal, to combat the danger, in spite of the secret support the Indians received from Florida.

These struggles attracted the attention of the English to the southern and western boundaries. Knowing well the importance of the mouth of the Mississippi to the Americans, who were rapidly spreading westward, they resolved to try to gain a footing there. The boundary of the Spanish possessions in Florida had long been a subject of dispute between Spain and the Union. The Spaniards could not deny that New Orleans was a part of Louisiana; but otherwise they laid claim to the east bank of the Mississippi, while the United States strove to get possession of both banks and were not disinclined to purchase, if necessary, all west Florida. The English took advantage of this uncertainty of the boundary. They landed at Pensacola and used this Spanish town as a base for their attacks. But they found their match in Jackson, who held command on this boundary. He was as little restrained by international rights as the English. He took for his headquarters Mobile, which was also Spanish, and from this base attacked Pensacola so successfully that the English were forced to abandon it and withdraw to their fleet. New Orleans was the next object of the English attack; but Jackson fortified and defended it successfully, repulsing the English with heavy losses on the 8th of January, 1815. After this they had no desire to try conclusions with him a third time.

Before these successes became known, peace had been concluded at Ghent, December 24, 1814. The frivolous origin of the struggle, and its still more disgraceful course, gave the Americans little claim to favourable conditions of peace. But the political situation in Europe came to their aid once again, and they reaped where they had not sown. Negotiations were entered upon during the second year of the war, and anxiety on account of a menacing grouping of the European Powers caused England to drop the imperious tone with which she had at first repulsed every approach. As there were scarcely any real points of difference, peace was quickly concluded, and considering the situation the Americans could demand nothing better than the re-establishment of the *status quo*.

An immediate consequence of the conclusion of peace was the acquisition of Florida by the United States. Madison was not destined to accomplish this rounding off of United States territory. This was left to his successor, Monroe, who was especially fitted for the work, as, on account of his diplomatic missions to the courts of Europe, he knew all sides of the question better than any other. The war had shown that Spain was not able to defend the few localities from which its officials were supposed to rule Florida; it was the continual complaint of the Americans that Spain was quite powerless over the country, and that its province was the haunt of all criminals from the neighbouring States. Troops of filibusters had established themselves on some of the islands off the coast, and under the pretext of fighting for the freedom of the Spanish colonies, they made piratical attacks on both Spanish and American vessels. The Union government was forced to take action here, and, having once begun to establish order in Florida, found it difficult to determine how far it ought to go. On land the Seminoles were as great an annoyance to the neighbouring States as the pirates by sea. They had been furnished by England with money, powder, and officers during the war; and here the Peace of Ghent put no end to the strife. Finally Monroe entrusted the subjugation of the Seminoles to Jackson, and when the latter interpreted his task as the conquest of all Florida the government placed no hindrance in his way. On the contrary it tried to justify his action by diplomacy. This pressure sufficed to bring to the desired conclusion the negotiations with Spain which had been pending for years. In October, 1820, Spain ceded to the United States, for the sum of five million dollars, this territory which had really slipped from its grasp long before and had for long been of no real use to it. This removed from the path of the United States the last obstacle to the completion of its territorial development in that direction.[1]

After the acquisition of Florida nothing remained that was likely to involve the United States in diplomatic complications with foreign Powers. A long period followed during which its rulers had leisure to devote their whole attention to the development of the country, which made such progress as exceeded the wildest hopes of its founders. As early as 1806 Jefferson had been able to announce that the revenue of the government exceeded its expenditure, and the complications of the following years caused but a transitory interruption of this favourable state of affairs. By reason of the rapidly increasing immigration the population increased enormously and spread itself over a larger and larger area. By 1818 nine new States had been added to the thirteen original ones, and further admissions to the Union were impending. Besides this, in Monroe the nation had the rare good fortune to have at its head a President who was not merely a party politician. Monroe was the last of the great Virginians, and was elected as the candidate of the Anti-federalists upon a platform essentially Federalist; but the division between the old parties had completely disappeared, the all-powerful organisation of the Republican party had gained complete control of the political situation, and now within that party were gradually being formed those sectional and personal factions which were to become the nuclei of future parties. Monroe followed Washington's example in not limiting the choice of his advisers to one faction, but in seeking to enlist in the service of the State the most capable men of all groups. It is true that he could not crush out the dangerous germs of discord which had their origin in the great economic differences in the development of North and South; but it was a great advantage to the land that a serious attempt was once more made to further its general interests.

---

[1] See the historical maps at p. 514.

## 8. THE STRUGGLE FOR INDEPENDENCE IN THE SOUTHERN CONTINENT

ONE of the weightiest reasons why Spain could not support the energetic action of France in favour of the northern colonies struggling for independence was her consideration for her own colonies. The government of Charles III had abandoned the plan of completely preventing all intercourse between the colonies and the outside world, and for this reason it was doubly afraid of the influence which might be exerted on her own colonies by the spectacle of Spain's aiding the subjects of another State to oppose by force the introduction of institutions which Spain had always maintained in her own colonies and was by no means disposed to abolish. Thus, though in alliance with France, Spain commenced war against England only in Europe and in the West Indies, maintaining a most reserved attitude toward the United States. Spain had for long been convinced of the impossibility of excluding foreign influence from the Antilles, and had to a certain extent abandoned them to it. In comparison with Spain's extensive colonial empire on the mainland they were of small importance, and their value decreased from year to year. The greater number of these islands had already freed themselves from the Spanish dominion, and those remaining became of importance only when Spain had lost all her possessions on the mainland. To these earlier losses was added, in 1795, that of San Domingo. When the repeated changes introduced by French revolutionary governments had led to a general war in the west half of the island which belonged to France,[1] Spain did not disdain to pave the way to the recovery of a part of the island by an alliance with the insurgent blacks. On making peace with the re-established republican government in 1795, Spain was punished for this by having to cede the eastern half of the island to France. The Spanish government, which did not place a very great value on the Antilles, did not find the sacrifice very difficult and gave up the island. But the bones of the discoverer of the New World, which had till then lain in the cathedral of the capital, San Domingo were not left in possession of the foreigner. They were ceremoniously exhumed, placed on board the frigate "Descubridor," and taken to Havana. In the cathedral of that city they found a resting-place under the Spanish flag until 1898.[2]

But the peace with France, bought by the sacrifice of San Domingo, was destined to have more momentous consequences for the Spanish colonial possessions. Spain renewed the policy of friendship with France which the Bourbon Family Compact had rendered traditional, and even went so far as to enter into an alliance with Napoleon when all Europe combined to resist his growing power. The immediate consequence of this was the destruction of the Spanish fleet at the battle of Trafalgar, October 21, 1805. An English attack on the Spanish colonies in America followed immediately.

Through information supplied by General Miranda, of New Granada, who had served in the French revolutionary army but had afterward been exiled, the English were led to believe that the Spanish colonies desired nothing more earnestly than an opportunity to throw off the yoke of the mother country and to establish themselves as independent States. It cannot be denied that, under the influence

---

[1] See the maps at p. 514.     [2] See *ante*, p. 358.

of the North American War of Independence and the French Revolution, a few hot-headed individuals were carried away by an enthusiasm for political liberty for which they were as yet quite unprepared; and these, of course, held the same opinion as Miranda; but the mass of the Spanish-American population had no sympathy for such ideas, as the English learned to their cost when they acted on Miranda's suggestion and tried to kindle the flame of insurrection in Spanish America.

Of all the Spanish coast-towns none was more suitable for such an undertaking than Buenos Ayres. The mouth of the La Plata had always been the seat of an extensive illicit trade. The authorities had been able to limit this only by relaxing the old strict trade regulations in favour of this harbour. Thus Buenos Ayres, as the headquarters of the party of commercial revolution, made rapid progress, and there were perhaps within its walls more enlightened minds than in the other settlements. No harbour had profited more by the permission to trade unre-strictedly with all nations, which Spain temporarily granted to its colonies in 1797, in view of the permanent insecurity of the seas. But, in spite of this exceedingly promising situation, the English found no confirmation of Miranda's reports. After the conquest of the Cape of Good Hope in 1805, a part of the English fleet, with sixteen hundred men, was sent, under General Beresford, to make an attack on Buenos Ayres. The Spanish governor had been fearing an English attack since the spring; but he thought its object would be, not Buenos Ayres, but Montevideo. He had accordingly collected the scanty means of defence available at the latter place. Thus it came about that not only the governor, but the whole population, lost their heads when Beresford landed two miles south of Buenos Ayres, moved next day into the suburbs, and the third day into the capital itself. But there was not the least sign of enthusiasm for the English rule which Beresford forthwith proclaimed; on the contrary a decidedly hostile spirit per-vaded the community from the beginning. While the town apparently submitted to its new rules without resistance, crowds of determined patriots were assembling in secret in the suburbs and on the neighbouring haciendas; and when Captain Jacques de Liniers succeeded, under cover of a thick morning mist, in leading a small body of troops across the river, these formed the nucleus of an attacking force which in its swift onset drove the English from the streets of the town into the market-place and forced them first to take refuge in the fortress and then to capitulate. Thus Buenos Ayres was recovered by as rapid a blow as that by which it had been lost.

It is true that only a small portion of the English force had been destroyed; and the news of Beresford's initial successes had led to the despatch of consider-able reinforcements, which arrived in rapid succession. In order to secure a safe base for their operations the English now directed their attack against Montevideo. Though heroically defended, the town could not hold out against the enemy's superiority in numbers and weapons. After the whole east coast had fallen into their power, the English considered themselves strong enough to recover Buenos Ayres from the patriots. The latter, who had made Liniers, the saviour of the town, captain-general, were quite unable to face the English in open combat; but when the English general, Whitelock, forming his force into three divisions, attempted a concentrated attack through the streets on the market and the fortress, he was, after two days' fighting, so thoroughly defeated that in the capitulation which followed he had to agree to evacuate Montevideo and the east coast.   The captured English officers made fruitless attempts to awaken the spirit of independence among the colonists : even so enthusiastic a patriot as Belgrano had but one answer for such suggestions : "Either our old king or none."

The history of the South American revolution is usually considered from a false standpoint.   The simultaneous occurrence of revolutionary movements in almost all the Spanish colonies in the years 1809 and 1810 is generally supposed to indicate that the whole of South America was ripe for freedom ; that a longing for independence had everywhere taken possession of the minds of the people, and now, all at once, found expression throughout the continent.   But at the beginning of the nineteenth century, despite the influence of the colonial war in North America and of the French Revolution, the idea of an independent South America really existed only in the heads of a few men who had grown up in the centres where foreign influence was most felt, and who, during their travels abroad, had become enthusiastic for modern ideas without comprehending the presuppositions involved in them.   At any rate, up to the year 1808, all their attempts to loosen the bond between Spain and her colonies met with the same fate as the attack of the English on Buenos Ayres.   Such was Miranda's experience on two occasions, when, supported by the English, he landed on the coast of Venezuela, his native province.   The first time he failed to gain a footing ; the second time he succeeded in taking forcible possession of the town of Coro ; but, in the face of the indifference of the mass of the people and the hostility of the better classes, there was no prospect of success, and he was soon forced to give up the attempt at a rising.

The revolution that occurred in 1809 was not due to a change in the opinions of the Spanish Americans, but to the state of affairs in Spain.   When Napoleon, by the crafty comedy at Bayonne, had persuaded both Ferdinand VII and Charles IV to renounce their claims to the Spanish throne in order to create a kingdom for his brother Joseph, there arose in all the colonies, as well as in Spain itself, a hatred of their hereditary foe that neither the Bourbon succession nor the Family Compact could eradicate.   But the colonies maintained a quiet and expectant attitude.   Even Liniers — who, though a Frenchman by birth, had been made Spanish viceroy of the province in return for having twice saved Buenos Ayres — dared not listen to the enticing proposals which Napoleon made him in order to secure the recognition of Joseph, because he well perceived the impracticability of any such plan at that moment.   But had Napoleon succeeded in getting Joseph unanimously accepted as king in Spain, and in securing his recognition by the other European Powers, it is probable that the change of dynasty would have proceeded as smoothly in America at the beginning of the nineteenth century as it had at the beginning of the eighteenth.   It was only the political events conjured up by the "Dos de Mayo" (May 2, 1808) that aroused the spirit which led in Spain to the utopian constitution of 1812, and in the colonies to the separation from the mother country, — a step politically quite premature.

When Junot, in November, 1807, occupied Lisbon in order to force Napoleon's policy on Portugal, court and government crossed the ocean, protected by the all-powerful English fleet, chose Rio Janeiro as capital, and gave Brazil a constitution on similar lines to that of the mother country, in order to bind it more closely to its head.   These great events were much talked of in the neighbouring Spanish colonies, but exerted no immediate influence on their politics.   Still the colonies joined enthusiastically in the protest made by Spain against Napoleon's treachery and the attempt to force King Joseph on her. A spark of the national enthusiasm which accompanied the accession of Ferdinand VII at Madrid, March 19, 1808, extended to the colonies. The latter resolved, despite the French occupation of the mother country, to continue the government, as then constituted, on behalf of Ferdinand VII.

But the reports of the national rising, of the victory of Bailo, and of the capture of Madrid were soon followed by the crushing news of the flight of the regency to Seville, of the formation of the general Junta, and the subjugation of all Spain with the exception of Isla de Leon. A question here arose which was all-important for the future history of the colonies. The Regency and the Junta had proved themselves utterly incapable of defending the country against the national enemy, and their authority was unconditionally rejected by the few provinces that still were able to keep off the French yoke. Under these conditions were the Regency and the Junta to be looked upon as the representatives of Ferdinand VII, to which the colonies owed loyalty and obedience? The obligation itself was disputed neither by the Creoles nor by the Peninsulars (Spaniards who had immigrated). However, the latter, to a still greater extent than the former, took as a precedent the example set them in the mother country. There every successful partisan who succeeded in snatching a small district from the French, or in defending it against their attacks notwithstanding the breaking up of all established authority, formed a junta of his townsmen and adherents, declared the old officials incapable, and replaced them by his friends. Similarly in the colonies a feeling of discontent with the representatives of the old form of government spread among both Spaniards and Creoles. Led on by a desire for power, politicians who knew they had a large following rose against the viceroys and governors and compelled them to renounce the authority which had expired on account of the captivity of their prince. They then formed regencies and juntas of their own, everywhere considering themselves the representatives of Ferdinand VII, and in all respects the legal successors of the Spanish officials they had displaced. Such was the course of events in Quito, in Caracas, in Buenos Ayres, and in Mexico.

Now, as was inevitable, the governors and their followings soon came to the conclusion that it was by no means the will of the whole people by which they had allowed themselves to be intimidated. They accordingly commenced a struggle against the newly established rulers, and succeeded either in gaining a complete victory, as in Quito, or in regaining at least a part of their official authority, as in the case of the governor of Buenos Ayres who established himself in Montevideo. The abolition of the traditional legal authority brought with it the danger that all law would be disputed. The revolutionary movement had by no means always placed the best men of the people at the head of the various governments, and after an authority had once been set up by a tumultuous assembly, it was natural that every party which had any power whatever over the populace also had hopes of seeing its own ambitions fulfilled, if not immediately, at any rate during the course of further developments.

The revolution had led more and more to the predominance of such elements as had been working for the independence of the colonies, at first unconsciously, but ever with more definite aim. The risings of 1809 bore the stamp of loyalty; the colonists revolted in behalf of Ferdinand VII without understanding clearly who really represented his authority, and many a governor fell, as did Liniers, solely because he was suspected of being ready to recognise any established government, even were it that of Joseph Bonaparte. As time went on, American national influences made themselves unmistakably felt. The differences between the colonists born in America, the Creoles, and the "chapetones," or Spanish immigrants, had become more and more accentuated ever since the governments of Charles III and Charles IV — on account of some unimportant revolutionary attempts among the colonial-born population — had begun to maintain more strictly than before the principle of keeping all offices to which power and influence were attached, in the hands of men born in Spain. This exclusion from all important public positions was felt more keenly by the Creoles than were many other oppressive measures enforced by the mother country. Accordingly, when the regular course of government had once been interrupted, the Creoles saw no reason why they should not aspire to more profitable and important positions. Thus, for example, in Buenos Ayres, the first overthrow of established authority was soon followed by a second, which aimed at giving the government a more national, that is, a more Creole, character.

But still more happened in this initial stage of the revolution. The boundaries between the different Spanish colonies were not always justified by ethnographic and economic considerations, especially in the great provinces of Bogotá and Buenos Ayres. There were radical differences between the various districts. Though the governments that had sprung up so suddenly claimed the right of managing their own affairs, they were by no means disposed to allow the scope of their authority to be limited by the principles on which they based their rights to power. Where conflicting elements had been held together by the power of the law only, it was natural that, upon the dissolution of the legally established governments, they should demand consideration for their own interests. Thus civil war broke out in Buenos Ayres and in New Granada a few years later.

The chaos produced in the Spanish Cortes owing to the supremacy of doctrinaires could but create greater confusion in colonial relations. By the Spanish Constitution of 1812 the legal position of the colonies was completely altered. Though there was scarcely ever any close connection between the colonial delegates, crowded together in Cadiz and selected by party influence, and the districts they represented, nevertheless the doctrines concerning the rights of man proclaimed by the popular orators in Cadiz made dangerous progress among the colonial population, which was politically and economically less advanced than the people of Spain.

The revolutionary movement assumed the most serious character in Mexico. Here, too, the political changes in Spain had led to the overthrow of the government. But the movement among the Creoles was at its very beginning completely lost in a rising of the lower classes of the population, led by a fanatical priest. The latter threatened not only the Spanish authorities, but all who refused to submit unconditionally to the rule of the populace, composed principally of native Indians. This in itself rendered a permanent success impossible. With a rapidly assembled army of nearly 100,000 men, the priest, Dionysio Hidalgo, leader of the fanatical masses, was able to attack and plunder the towns of Guanajuato, Valladolid, and Guadalajara; but notwithstanding his great superiority in numbers he was unsuccessful in his assault on the capital, which Spaniards and Creoles united in defending. For his undisciplined army retreat was synonymous with dissolution. Though he received several severe checks while falling back, he was still able to rally a large force under his banner and again to take the offensive; but, as he was quite unable, with his horde of robbers and cut-throats, to establish any permanent government in place of the one he was opposing, his prestige rapidly decreased. During a second retreat he was betrayed to the Spaniards by his own officers, and shot. The movement was not yet completely suppressed; but none of the leaders who placed themselves at the head of the Indian population in the different provinces after Hidalgo's death succeeded in making the revolt as dangerous as it had been at its commencement. The movement had only served to unite all conservative forces for the common purpose of defence, and had placed the struggle for liberty in so unfavourable a light that for years afterward the province of New Spain was a stronghold of the royalists. It was only lost to them later on, when in blind self-confidence they allowed a conspiracy to be formed which merely borrowed the name of the liberty gained by the other provinces after a hard struggle, and in reality only replaced the country's lawful self-government by an illegal administration.

During the Napoleonic wars the revolutionary movement persisted in only two places in the South American continent. After temporary successes on the part of the republicans, Quito and Chile fell back completely into the power of the royalists; in New Granada and the neighbouring colony, Venezuela, the efforts to win freedom attained a certain importance; while in the La Plata States they led to permanent independence. But the forces producing the various movements differed widely from each other.

The members of the Junta of Creoles which forced the captain-general to resign at Caracas, April 19, 1810, considered themselves the loyal subjects of Ferdinand VII. They accordingly sent envoys, including Bolivar, the future hero of the South American war of independence, to England, the nation which was at that time giving the most valuable support to the adherents of the king in the peninsula. The object of this embassy was to agree with England upon a common course of action against the enemy of their country. The delegates returned with only conditional promises from the English government; but at La Guaira they were met by General Miranda. Under the influence of this veteran in the struggle for colonial freedom there was established at Caracas a republican government which preserved the rights of Ferdinand VII in theory only. This government, it is true, was supreme for a time in the capital and in the central provinces; but even there it did not find the least support in the people, while the east, the west, and still more the great plains of the south — the Llanos — were decidedly hostile to it. Thus it was that the royalists were soon able to proceed to the offensive. Their attack was so overpowering that Miranda was obliged to limit himself entirely to the defence. Misfortune produced dissension among the champions of liberty. Miranda was appointed dictator, but had no success; he was finally betrayed and handed over to the royalists by the very men who called themselves champions of freedom, — Bolivar also being entangled in the affair. Years afterward he died in prison at Cadiz.

The instigators of this heroic deed fled abroad, but did not abandon their plans. As the Junta of New Granada still remained independent, many Venezuelans · among them Bolivar — entered its service. Bolivar proposed anticipating the attack on New Granada which the Spaniards threatened to make from Venezuela, by carrying war into the latter province. In accordance with his wish, the Junta authorised him to wrest the border provinces Merida and Trujillo from the hands of the royalists. After succeeding in this in a surprisingly short time, he carried the war into the heart of the country, without authorisation, foolishly thinking that the possession of the capital, Caracas, would decide the issue of the contest.

With this step the war in the north assumed its special character. Simon Bolivar [1] is the type of those pronunciamento generals who until quite recently have played so great a part in the history of Spain, and a still greater in that of the Spanish-American republics. It may be granted that Bolivar was not quite so devoid of conscience as many of his imitators; but no one can fail to see that the idea for which he fought had no existence apart from his own personality. By his fiery, florid eloquence he may often have succeeded in deceiving himself as well as those he tried to convince. In any case he considered freedom, whose blessings he eulogised in the most extravagant terms, merely as a foundation on which to build up his own fame; and he held himself quite justified in ruthlessly persecuting and crushing all men who would not accept freedom as inaugurated by Bolivar.

With the exception of a small part of the town population, almost all Venezuela was royalist, or at least heartily sick of civil war. Thus, as he advanced, Bolivar met sometimes with secret opposition, sometimes with stolid apathy; and only where his arms were victorious was he able to excite a fictitious enthusiasm for the ideal blessings he professed to be fighting for. He entered Caracas with theatrical pomp as liberator; but the kind of freedom he brought to the Venezuelans betrayed its true character in his completely overlooking the civil authorities and assuming the powers of a dictator with the pompous title of " Libertador de la Patria " (" Liberator of the Fatherland "). But he failed to deceive even his immediate followers, chiefly persons whose interests were bound up in his own. He was not the only one, even in Venezuela itself, who was working on this plan. In the extreme east, on the boundary of Guiana, another liberator, Mariño, had arisen; but instead of combining against their common enemies, the Spaniards, each of these saviours of the people desired nothing more ardently than the defeat of his rival, that he might then appear as sole emancipator and obtain undisputed supremacy.

Yielding to the pressure of the half-breeds Bolivar had made the fatal mistake of declaring a war of extermination against the Spaniards; and all men were reckoned as Spaniards who did not willingly agree to all the demands of the so-called patriots. This savage warfare naturally led to reprisals on the part of the European population; but while they had on their side an excuse for retaliation, Bolivar, by his action, disgraced the principles he professed to be fighting for and did himself great injury, inasmuch as he had far less power at his disposal than that possessed by his enemies. Thus the war assumed an especially bloody character. Murder and robbery, the weapons employed by both parties, set free the lowest passions and brought to the fore the worst elements of the population. Bolivar meanwhile did not distinguish himself as a general; he had no plan of campaign, and he had drawn up no constitution. The Spanish flag still waved

---

[1] See the portrait opposite.

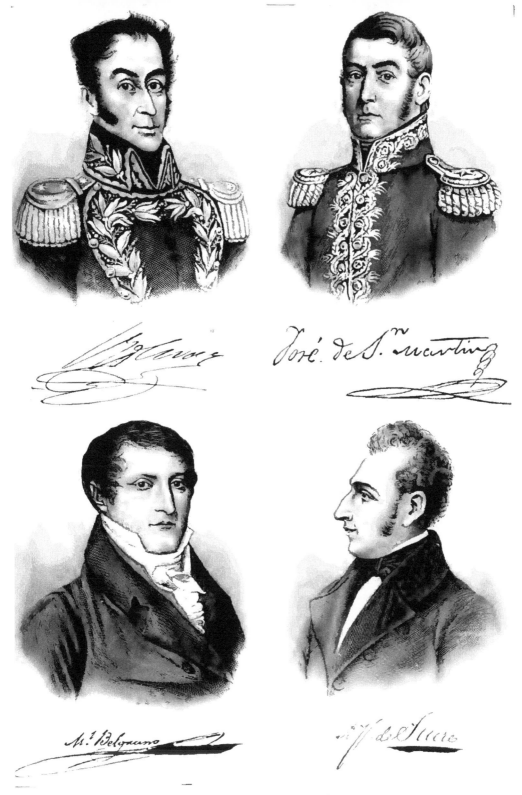

THE HEROES OF SOUTH AMERICAN INDEPENDENCE

(Simon Bolivar from the "Correspondencia General del Libertador"; Jose de San Martin and Manuel Belgrano from
Bartolome Mitres' Biographies; Antonio Jose de Sucre from his Biography by Villanueva.

history of the world.   facing p. 494.

over Puerto Cabello, the strongest point on the coast; battles were fought at Barquisimeto and on the Araure with varying results. Finally Bolivar himself had to fall back upon Caracas.

Here the hostility of the Llaneros completed his ruin. It was in vain that he sought to give his dictatorship a legal basis by calling together a congress at Caracas; it was in vain that he now concluded an alliance with the dictator of the eastern provinces, fully recognising his authority. Even their combined forces could only temporarily withstand the ever-increasing troops of horsemen which the fierce Boves brought from the southern plains in support of the Spaniards. Matters had gone so far that far-sighted persons assisted the latter, in anticipation of their speedy victory. First Mariño, then Bolivar himself, was repeatedly and so severely beaten that his retreat degenerated into flight. When he reached the coast at Cumaná, the Liberator had so little means of resistance at his disposal that he fled with the ships that contained his war-material. When his compatriots had again assembled, and he endeavoured to rejoin them, he was branded as a traitor and with difficulty escaped the fate which he himself, under similar circumstances, had prepared for General Miranda. The result of the campaign of 1813 was that the whole of Venezuela fell once more into the hands of the royalists. The latter were now free to bring about a similar state of affairs in the republic of New Granada, which was divided against itself, and from which Bolivar had withdrawn the greater part of its military resources for the purposes of his Venezuelan enterprise.

In the south, too, the revolutionary movement had by this time exhausted itself. The rising in the La Plata States was at its commencement conducted in a spirit which contrasted very favourably with that characteristic of the Venezuelan movement. The bulk of the people were, it is true, as indifferent to the revolution as in Venezuela; but there was a decidedly more progressive spirit among the middle and upper classes in Buenos Ayres than in Caracas. On the news of the dissolution of the government in Spain, the viceroy at Buenos Ayres was deposed. On the 25th of May, 1810, a junta declared the province independent of the Junta of Seville.[1] But it continued to rule, as did the governments that developed from it in the course of years, in the name of Ferdinand VII. There was even a party ready to invite to Buenos Ayres as regent Ferdinand's sister, the Infanta Carlota, who had married a Portuguese prince. The plan however, which led to long and complicated intrigues in Rio de Janeiro and Montevideo, came to nothing.

The newly formed government considered that its first task was to obtain the recognition of its authority throughout the La Plata province; but in this it met with serious resistance. The royalists had chosen Montevideo as their headquarters; and the arrival of support from the mother country not only rendered the city impregnable against the limited means of attack at the disposal of the Junta, but gave the royalists command of the bay and the mouth of the river flowing into it. But little by little the supremacy of the Spaniards was limited to the town itself; their naval schemes were brought to naught by the aid of the Brazilians and English, who were friendly to the Junta; and finally, when the Spanish ships had been defeated by the newly created rebel fleet, the fortress of Montevideo capitulated.

[1] See map at p. 514.

But meanwhile there had arisen in the province of Buenos Ayres the general confusion that in all the colonies followed the abolition of legally constituted authority; and the east bank of the La Plata also was only nominally under the rule of the various governments that rapidly succeeded one another in Buenos Ayres. In reality the division was springing up which finally led to the establishment of the "Republica Oriental del Uruguay."

A similar course of events had also occurred in another part of the old province. In December, 1810, the Junta of Buenos Ayres sent General Belgrano[1] to secure the recognition of the new government in the district of Paraguay; but the attempt ended in complete failure. Belgrano was enticed far into the deserted land before any enemy faced him; then at Paraguay he received a check that necessitated a dangerous retreat. It was only then that the liberal idea occurred to him of letting the province itself decide whom it would obey. Accordingly he concluded with the defenders of Paraguay a capitulation at Tacuary which allowed him to retire without further injury being done. The consequence was that progressive ideas were disseminated so rapidly in the province that it took its fate into its own hands, and in 1814 chose as executive Dr. José Gaspar Tomas Rodriguez da Francia. His was a rule of force, more ruthless and bloody than had ever been seen on American soil; but it was an enlightened despotism. By destroying the power and wealth of the priests, and promoting agriculture and industry in every possible way, he rendered the young State independent of the outside world. Thus the independence of Paraguay was rendered secure even after his death in 1840.[2]

The government of Buenos Ayres had now to contend with movements not unlike that to which it owed its existence. It was repeatedly occupied in combating efforts at decentralisation in various parts of its territory even after the Argentine Republic had actually secured its independence. But Buenos Ayres also played an important part in the struggle against the common enemies of all the provinces, the Spanish royalists. The authority of the Junta met with the most serious opposition in the district of Upper Peru, the modern Bolivia, which was then governed from Buenos Ayres. The first rising against Spanish dominion had taken place there in 1809, but had been easily put down by an expedition from Peru proper; and from that time the royalist influence was supreme. Accordingly the Junta sent out its first army against this dangerous opponent. By a brilliant victory at Suipacha General Balcarce forced the royalists back across the Desaguadero, the outlet of Lake Titicaca, which then formed a portion of the Peruvian frontier. But this advantage was not maintained. After receiving reinforcements, the Spaniards gained a decisive victory at Huaqui, drove the patriots out of the Bolivian highlands, and followed them into the Argentine Republic. But here Belgrano, who had been appointed general of the northern army, stopped the retreat, defeated the Spanish leader at Tucuman, and some weeks later, at Salta, compelled him and his whole force to lay down their arms. All these battles were fought with comparatively small armies; and this explains the transitory nature of the successes attained. Neither party could really dominate the sparsely settled land; and the inhabitants had no leaning toward either side, but always favoured the victors. Both royalists and republicans, even after a number of defeats, were soon able to

---

[1] See portrait facing p. 494.          [2] See *post*, p. 514.

collect an army of some thousands, and thus to renew the struggle: hence the manifold fluctuations of fortune in all the campaigns undertaken by the South American patriots against the Spanish royalists.

Belgrano, too, was not permanently favoured by fortune. On his advance into Bolivia he found the enemy reorganised at Huileapuyo; and both here and at Ayuma he was so severely defeated that he had again to retreat to Jujuy. He was then for a long time unable to act on the offensive, and although the royalists did not advance into the Argentine Republic itself, all Bolivia was again in their hands at the end of 1813. By reason of a contemporary royalist victory in Venezuela, the cause of Ferdinand VII never appeared more hopeful than when Napoleon opened the doors of his golden prison to the captive of Valençay and allowed him to return to the throne of his fathers.

During the war Spain had passed through many curious experiences; and the revolutionary trifling of the Cortes at Cadiz, which had introduced a parliamentary system of government, was not without influence on the movements in the American provinces. But in Spain the people were as little ripe for freedom as in the colonies; and as the conflict of interests in the mother country was of far less advantage to the new government of Spain than it was to the colonial strivings for independence, the artificial constitution collapsed even before Ferdinand VII had set foot on Castilian soil, and he lost no time in endeavouring to bring about a similar result in the colonies.

A great expedition, composed of twenty-five warships and sixty transports with 10,000 men, put to sea under General Morillo in March, 1815, to suppress the last efforts of the colonial rising. The original intention was to disembark the troops on the La Plata. But since the fall of Montevideo there was no safe landing-place there. Moreover Buenos Ayres recognised Ferdinand, at least nominally, as its rightful ruler, while in the most recent phase of the war in Venezuela and New Granada an independent republic had been declared. Accordingly Morillo received instructions to proceed to the subjugation of the northern provinces. If this was assured, the way to the La Plata region always lay open to him through Bolivia. His first steps gave every promise of success. The island of Margarita, ever the refuge and hiding-place of the patriots of Venezuela in misfortune, was quickly subdued. In the whole of Venezuela there was hardly a troop of patriots that deserved the name of an army; Morillo's march through the province was a military promenade.

In order to conquer New Granada Morillo chose Cartagena as his first point of attack, but here he received a foretaste of the difficulties that awaited him. He had already discovered, on endeavouring to embark the Venezuelan army in the fleet, replacing it by Spanish troops for the protection of the province, that the hitherto loyal Llaneros deserted in crowds. Still he had an overwhelmingly superior force when he invested Cartagena by land and water. But the town offered an heroic resistance. Morillo, who wished to avoid bloodshed as much as possible, tried to reduce it by hunger; but it held aloft the banner of independence for 108 days, although the Spanish general, losing patience, spared neither bombardment nor assault. Even when further resistance was impossible, the town did not capitulate; its defenders broke through the blockade during a storm, and the greater number of them escaped to San Domingo, to renew the struggle from there after a short rest. New Granada, indeed, did not defend itself with the courage of

Cartagena. From Quito a second Spanish army was working its way up to meet Morillo, and when it approached Santa Fé there was in this province too no patriot army to oppose it. But even Morillo, though victorious, felt that the ground he stood on was insecure. He therefore abandoned his original system of lenience and meted out severe treatment to the rebels. But notwithstanding hundreds of sacrifices he could not firmly establish Spanish rule.

Wherever the Spanish arms did not penetrate, rebellion broke out anew. The island of Margarita was the first to throw off the unaccustomed yoke; and on the Llanos of Casanare an army of horsemen from the plains under the half-breed, Paez, responded for the first time to the cry of freedom and gained its first victory over the royalists on the Apure. But the fierce warriors of the prairies spared the lives of their prisoners and thus induced most of these to join them. After a renewed disturbance in Cumaná, Morillo began to fear for the safety of Venezuela and removed his headquarters, then at the foot of the Cordilleras on the east side, to Varinas. But as yet there was no connection between the different risings. Finally there landed in Margarita the old leaders and the defenders of Cartagena who had prepared in Hayti for a fresh struggle with the aid of the English and of the president of the negro republic. But Bolivar was still no strategist. While troops of horsemen scoured the Llanos and kept the plains in a ferment, while his compatriots conquered in the east a district on both banks of the Orinoco where they enjoyed absolute security, Bolivar remained in the charmed circle of the capital, Caracas, and in the autumn of 1816 attempted to advance on it from Ocumare with an insufficient force. But, most disgraceful of all, on the false report of a defeat he took flight on board ship, abandoning his followers to destruction. His reputation had sunk so low that, banished a second time, he was compelled to seek refuge in Hayti. However he was recalled a few weeks later: for of the leaders of the numerous bands none was held in so high esteem as he; and, above all, no one else was possessed of a definite political and military plan of campaign.

In the year 1817 the revolution began to gain a firm footing in the north. The idea of creating a safe base for the champions of independence on the right bank of the Orinoco had not originated with Bolivar; but he immediately recognised the importance of the plan. While the investment by land of Angostura and Guayana Vieja, which commanded the river, was attended by only a moderate amount of success, he succeeded, with the help of English sailors, in overthrowing the Spanish supremacy by sea and in forcing the royalists to evacuate both places. The Orinoco, and farther west the Apure, now separated the independent territory from the Spanish. Morillo had meanwhile been wasting his time in a fruitless attempt to reconquer the island of Margarita. He brought the coast as far as the peninsula of Paria under his power, but this had no great importance.

At this time Bolivar had with difficulty succeeded in getting his authority recognised by the leaders of the different revolutionary parties; he now felt the need of establishing his position on a more legal basis. Accordingly in the autumn of 1817 he created a council of state and a supreme court of justice, and held out hopes of further political organisation. At the same time he declared his dictatorship a necessity, and, as before, exercised practically unlimited power. But the war still led to no definite result. Bolivar now advanced from the middle Apure against Caracas. He himself defeated Morillo at Calabozo, and Paez at the same time conquered San Fernando, the last bulwark of the royalists on the Apure: but these successes were counterbalanced by a series of unsuccessful undertakings which encouraged the opposition still secretly kept alive against the dictator. However he was once more able to blunt the edge of the opposition: he won over the discontented generals by the way in which he succeeded in providing them with troops, war-material, and money to renew the struggle; the politicians he disarmed by summoning a congress to form a constitution at Angostura. This congress was in reality a mere spectacular farce; but it gave his dictatorship an appearance of legality by unanimously electing him president of the Venezuelan Republic.

Of at least as great importance to Bolivar as this confirmation of his position was the arrival of a considerable number of trained English and German soldiers who had enlisted to fight for the cause of independence. They formed a nucleus about which the brave, but from a military point of view less valuable, troops of the South American provinces collected, and from which they could receive their military training. The English legion played a prominent part in all later campaigns, and enjoyed Bolivar's confidence to such a degree as repeatedly to call forth expressions of jealousy from the South American patriots. For the campaign of 1818 Bolivar settled on a plan calculated to decide the course of events. Once before he had carried the war from New Granada into the plains of Venezuela to fight for the freedom of the former in the territories of the latter; now he resolved to strive for the emancipation of his fatherland from beyond the Andes. This idea was perhaps suggested to him by the victories of José de San Martin;[1] but, be that as it may, his success proved the correctness of his calculations.

Even before the floods that during the rainy season render the Llanos impassable had entirely subsided, Bolivar moved southward from the Apure, which protected his flank from the royalists, and crossed the Andes by the route taken by the traders of the Chibchas[2] and the first conquerors of Bogota. He did indeed suffer considerable losses before he reached a settled district at Sogamoso; but his plan of surprising the enemy in the very centre of their sphere of power was completely successful. Everything now depended on his being able to gain a decisive victory before his opponents could summon their full strength. By rapid marches and countermarches he succeeded in so completely outwitting the hostile advance guard that he was able to seize the town of Tunja, and thus to cut off a large portion of his foes from the capital. But the Spaniards, trusting to their superiority in numbers, tried to force their way back to Santa Fé. A decisive battle was fought at the bridge of Boyacá: it ended in the annihilation of the royalist army. The viceroy evacuated the capital and retired to Cartagena with the remainder of the Spanish troops, while the patriots took possession of Santa Fé de Bogotá and re-established the independence of New Granada. Bolivar created here, as in Venezuela, a new civil government at the side of his military dictatorship, and paved the way for the union of the two sister provinces into one republic under the name Colombia.

The news of this victory reached Angostura, the temporary capital of Venezuela, just when Bolivar for the third time had been deposed as a deserter and banished as a traitor solely because there were others who were covetous of his

---

[1] See *post*, p. 501.      [2] See *ante*, p. 287.

power. But in the lustre of his recent victory he could treat such proceedings with contempt. The Congress, doubly compliant from the consciousness of its offence, adopted without debate the proposal of the Liberator that Venezuela, New Granada, and Quito should be combined into one republic named Colombia,[1] whose president would naturally be Bolivar, while in each of the three provinces there was to be a vice-president at the head of the civil administration. The constitution of the new State was to be framed in detail by a congress to meet at Cucuta for this purpose as soon as a truce could be declared.

This soon occurred. The news that reached South America in the summer of 1820 gave the situation a completely different aspect. The army which had been collected in the neighbourhood of Cadiz to give General Morillo the means of completely subduing the rebels had revolted; and as it felt compelled to find some pretext in justification of its action, it adopted as its watchword the restoration of the Constitution of 1812. With this, all who had fought for the restoration of the Spanish dominion since 1814 lost once more their legal basis. The immediate consequence was a cessation of hostilities, leading the way to a peaceful understanding between the mother country and the colonies. But the latter had already gone too far: too large a number of the colonists had with all their interests been compromised by the Revolution for an agreement to be possible under a constitution whose liberality, so far as the colonies were concerned, was known to be influenced by the desire of the whole Spanish nation for their continued dependence. The negotiations served rather to bring out the conviction that a return to the old state of affairs was impossible. Both parties took advantage of the truce to prepare for the inevitable renewal of hostilities, and the war broke out anew in the spring of 1821.

The supremacy of the patriots was so far assured in the highlands, that Bolivar had now better prospects of success in attacking the economic centres of Venezuela, Caracas and Valencia, so often fought for with varying fortune. As matters then stood, these districts were the last stronghold of the royalists: even the west of Venezuela, hitherto loyal, had been lost to them; and apart from the coast towns, all of which, from Cartagena to Cumaná, were in their hands, the Spaniards were masters only of the territory occupied by their forces. At Carabobo, where Bolivar had once before gained a victory, the Spaniards awaited him in a position deemed impregnable; but the natives were now on the side of the patriots, and led a part of their army by secret paths to the right flank of the enemy, whose position was easily carried from this side. The victory was complete. The Spanish were forced to evacuate the central part of the province and to take refuge under the walls of Puerto Cabello, while Bolivar once again made a triumphal entry into Caracas, whose freedom and independence from this time suffered no further attack.

The opening of the Congress at Cucuta was almost contemporaneous with the victory of Carabobo. Now met for the first time in the history of the northern provinces a legislative assembly really possessed of power; and it showed itself worthy of its calling by not submitting unconditionally to the dictator, as its predecessor had done. But it did not on this account undervalue the indisputable services Bolivar had rendered to the cause of freedom in the Republic of Colombia,

---

[1] See map at p. 514.

and was far from accepting the resignation of all his offices and titles which he handed in to it, as he had done to its predecessors. Neither did it place itself unconditionally in his hands, but, with the best intentions, drew up a constitution which gave free scope to the ambition of the Liberator without placing him above the constitution. His position as president of Colombia was confirmed by the Congress. But it was laid down by law that he could not exercise civil authority in this capacity while at the head of the army in the field. To provide for this eventuality, a vice-president for the whole republic was appointed; and it was only in such provinces as he should afterward free from the Spanish yoke that Bolivar was to exercise dictatorial power. In other respects, too, the new constitution differed widely from Bolivar's ideal. It rejected the scheme of an upper house, composed of life-members, which Bolivar had projected for Venezuela at Angostura; nor did it make the presidency hereditary or tenable for life, but followed the example of the United States in limiting the tenure of office of the head of the State to four years. Hitherto no constitution had had a fair test, since every successful partisan had considered himself competent to overthrow it; so, to secure a practical trial for its own work, the Congress passed a law forbidding any change in the constitution for the next ten years.

Bolivar submitted to the decisions of the Congress of Cucuta. The fortune of war also seemed to favour the new republic. After a siege of fourteen months one of Bolivar's generals had captured Cartagena, and the loss of this stronghold rendered the royalists in the district about the Isthmus powerless. Chagres and Portobello drove out their Spanish garrisons; and the Isthmus provinces not only made themselves independent of Spain, but even asked to be admitted to the Colombian republic. The last remnants of the army, with which Morillo once seemed to have brought all New Granada and Venezuela to absolute obedience, now held only Puerto Cabello and Cumaná. All danger had disappeared in the north.

In 1814 the cause of freedom in the southern theatre of war had stood on very slender supports. West of the Cordilleras the Spanish viceroy of Peru held sway over all the Pacific provinces from Cape Horn to the Gulf of Guayaquil and the tableland of Quito. The province of Buenos Ayres alone still held aloft the flag of freedom; and even it had suffered considerable losses of territory. While Bolivia had been brought back under the rule of the Spanish authorities, Paraguay in the north, and Uruguay in the east, had separated themselves from Buenos Ayres. The aimless policy of its leading men was quite calculated to keep alive the strife in the province itself; and the Spaniards had reason to hope that the colonies, exhausted by suicidal wars among themselves, would fall an easy prey to them. The prospects of such an issue would have been even more favourable had not there come to the aid of the patriots at this time of internal dissension a man who, by the influence of his personality, became the rescuer of the threatened independence to a greater degree than even Bolivar.

José de San Martin [1] did not return to his South American home in Buenos Ayres until the close of the Peninsular war, during which he had fought bravely on the side of the Spaniards. In Spain he had largely imbibed the liberal ideas then prevalent in the Peninsula, which found their embodiment in the Cortes at

---

[1] See portrait at p. 494.

Cadiz. He too was inspired by a lively ambition which expressed itself, not as in Bolivar's case by a morbid longing for the outward signs of power, but by an idealistic desire to distinguish himself in the service of his country and to secure for it a brighter future. San Martin, like most of the far-sighted politicians of the South, was not a republican in the sense that Bolivar was. He and others like him were convinced that Spanish South America was not sufficiently advanced either in politics or civilisation for a republican form of government like that of the United States. What he had learned of republican institutions in the sister colonies of the North, and in part in the provinces of his own country, had roused in him a strong aversion to an outward show of liberty instituted for the selfish ends of particular individuals, that at times stirred up civil war and at best only replaced Spanish tyranny by another as bad.

Even in Buenos Ayres San Martin found powerful influences which in his opinion worked against the true interests of the State. After he had had for a short time an opportunity of rendering his country valuable though modest services, partly on the banks of the La Plata, and partly in the provinces of the Bolivian highlands, the idea arose in his mind of placing himself in the service of freedom and of fighting not merely for the liberty of his country, but for that of all Spanish America. The plan he formed for the attainment of this object proves his capacity as a general. He recognised immediately that the fate of all the southern provinces depended on the expulsion of the Spaniards from their stronghold, the Peruvian highlands on both sides of the Cordilleras; for, secure in their command of the Pacific, the Spaniards could at any time use the ocean as a base for attacks on the patriots by land in three directions. The shortest way from Buenos Ayres to Lima lay through Upper Peru (Bolivia). But this route was the most difficult on account of the extraordinary breadth of the line of advance, and because the Spaniards could always obtain supplies by sea. For this reason San Martin chose another point of attack. In Chile, during the early years of the colonial rising, the cause of freedom had found numerous and enthusiastic adherents. The Spaniards had been compelled to employ a considerable force in order to bring back the province to its allegiance; and they would not have succeeded at all had not the despotic spirit of the pronunciamentos split the friends of independence into two parties. San Martin accordingly demanded from the government of Buenos Ayres means for collecting and arming the nucleus of a force to be employed first in liberating Chile and afterward to be used against the Spaniards throughout the southern part of the continent.

Internal dissensions had not yet so blinded the rulers of Buenos Ayres that they were unable to recognise the splendid prospects opened up by San Martin's plan for the cause of freedom; so, in accordance with his own desire, he was entrusted with the government of the district of Mendoza on the boundary of northern Chile, so that without unnecessarily attracting attention he might collect the means of carrying out his plan and proceed to its execution at what seemed to him the proper time. San Martin possessed what was wanting in almost all the other champions of independence, — a strictly methodical military training complete in all respects; a definite scheme harmonious from both a political and a military point of view, and conscientiously worked out in every detail; and an enthusiasm for the cause he served, which was exhibited by his personal readiness to make every sacrifice for it. He spent fully two years in collecting and training the troops for his campaign and in preparing the district in which he intended to begin operations; and when he gave the signal to march every detail had been foreseen and provided for so definitely that he was able to proceed step by step with mathematical precision, and saw his efforts crowned by complete success.

In the autumn of 1816 San Martin received authority from the government of Buenos Ayres to lead his army across the Cordilleras into Chile and from there to attempt to reconquer Bolivia. During the last months of the year extraordinary activity prevailed in the district of Mendoza, and the government did all that it could to furnish the expedition with the best possible equipment. On January 14, 1817, San Martin divided his force of 4,000 picked troops of all arms, with a train of 10,000 mules, into two sections, and set out from Mendoza to cross the Cordilleras by the passes of Aconcagua and Putaendo. The two divisions were to meet at Santa Rosa de los Andes, 210 miles from Mendoza; the greatest height to which they had to ascend was about 12,000 feet. On the 8th of February the divisions arrived at the rendezvous within such a short time of one another that the royalist outposts at the mouths of the passes did not know from which direction the real attack was to be expected. A short fight forced them to retreat. The first bold step of the plan of campaign had been successful.

But the army was still in the heart of the mountains, and it could neither adopt a proper formation nor gain support from a rising in the land until great distances had been traversed. San Martin knew that a rapid advance meant a victory half won, and that the shortest way to Santiago, the capital, was imposed on him by necessity. He allowed his exhausted troops to rest but a short time, and then advanced against the enemy, whose main force barred his way at Chacabuco. By a skilfully executed flank attack San Martin routed the hostile army in a few hours. Panic spread everywhere. The governor evacuated the capital, taking with him the remainder of the army, the treasury, the government officials, and many of the inhabitants of royalist leanings; and on the 14th of February the troops of the Liberator entered Santiago in triumph.

In the weeks following the victory San Martin's character was put to a severe test. He had come to give the people freedom, and indeed all northern Chile rose for the cause of independence as soon as the Spaniards had retreated. What had been done was now to be justified by a legislative body, and a congress was therefore called together at Santiago. But the new republicans could not conceive that a foreign general would fight for their cause for any other reason than to place himself at their head, and San Martin was almost unanimously elected president with dictatorial power. But he considered that he had taken only the first step on the road to fame, and refused the position unconditionally. He recommended the congress to appoint in his stead General O'Higgins, a Chilean who had fought under him at Chacabuco, and would accept for himself only the position of commander-in-chief of the army.

But the civil affairs of the republic had prevented the leader from following up the enemy with the rapidity necessary for complete victory. The royalist party had recovered from its first panic; the viceroy of Peru had sent reinforcements; and as the Spaniards had complete command of the sea they were able to land the latter without molestation in the fortress of Talcahuano, which commanded the bay of Concepcion. The cause of freedom was directly menaced when an attack on Talcahuano with an insufficient force failed, and on their retreat the patriots were completely defeated at Talca, not far from the Maule.[1] Fear and dismay spread even to the capital. The imminent danger finally roused San Martin from his inactivity. His force, continually kept in strict training, was undoubtedly superior to that of the enemy in military capacity, if not in numbers. This fact, combined with his ability as a leader, led, after a long and fierce struggle at Maipu, to a victory so complete that even the more southerly provinces took heart and threw off the Spanish yoke.

It was not San Martin's fault that he allowed a long time to pass after the victory of Maipu before again taking the offensive. Immediately after the battle he hastened back across the Andes to secure the approval of the government of Buenos Ayres for his plan of campaign against Peru. It was now time for the patriots to create a fleet in order to dispute the supremacy of the Spaniards on the Pacific, and thus to secure the possibility of attacking Peru by sea. The rulers of Buenos Ayres, like the new government of Chile, were quite ready to approve of San Martin's plans in theory; but neither government was in a position to give effective aid to their prosecution. In Buenos Ayres the federalistic loosening of old ties set in just at this time. The government had so much to do in providing for its own safety, which it saw or imagined it saw threatened from within and without, that for the time at least it could lend no aid to projects which were quite outside its sphere of action. All San Martin could obtain was a number of English ships that were being fitted out by the Chilean patriots to be used almost as much against the newly established government as against the Spaniards. But this laid the foundation of a sea power which, led with unprecedented boldness by an Englishman, Cochrane, did not a little to break the power of Spain at sea. For the army San Martin could do practically nothing in Buenos Ayres. He felt this the more keenly inasmuch as Chile at the same time placed considerable obstacles in his way.

It goes without saying that the troops which San Martin had led across the Cordilleras and from victory to victory in Chile were attached to their leader with unshaken loyalty; the Chilean regiments, too, that he had formed and trained before the battle of Maipu, followed him with blind obedience. President O'Higgins was also among the general's closest friends. But when once the danger from the royalists had been obviated, the majority of the Chilean patriots saw in the presence of the liberating army only an oppressive burden on the badly filled treasury of the young republic and a constant menace to republican freedom. These circumstances served only to spur San Martin to greater exertions for the realisation of his plan of campaign against Lima. But, as it was at that moment impossible to obtain the means for this, he had no alternative but to arrange for the return of the liberating army across the Andes. This measure, which apparently was only the result of the difficulty in provisioning and paying the army, had also great political significance. It was calculated to deceive the Spaniards in Peru as to the direction from which attack was to be expected; at the same time it deprived the Chileans of all grounds for complaint against their Argentine deliverers and also let them know how, in the absence of any effective protection, their existence as a State was threatened by the presence on their borders of the still numerous royalists. Finally the return of the troops to the Argentine Republic was calculated to convince the government of Buenos Ayres that the maintenance of the

[1] See the maps at p. 514.

army, even when condemned to inactivity, would prove almost as great a burden to the State as the moderate demands made by San Martin in order that he might be enabled to fight for the cause of independence in the enemy's territory.

These calculations were justified, at least in part, in all directions. The newly formed fleet of the patriots under Admiral Cochrane made a venturesome attack on the Spanish ships at Callao, and, though not in a position to do much damage to the enemy, it proved that the latter were so disturbed and weakened that a campaign undertaken from the coast in accordance with San Martin's plan would have every prospect of success. O'Higgins and other friends of the Liberator obtained a freer hand, despite the Chilean patriots, and proceeded to further his plans; they succeeded in procuring for him an invitation to lead his troops once more across the Andes into Chile, in order to prepare for an attack on Peru with the help of the fleet. Nor did San Martin's military policy remain without effect on the people of the Argentine Republic; he succeeded in winning approval for his schemes, and he was even assisted to some extent with money and war-material. Nevertheless it was from Buenos Ayres, and at the last moment, that the greatest danger threatened him; and the premonition that this must inevitably destroy every prospect of his plan being realised finally drove San Martin to take the risk of breaking the bridges behind him and plunging boldly into the unknown, though his equipment was defective and he had no security for the future.

The party of the patriots, which claimed that the authority of the government of Buenos Ayres extended over the whole of the region formerly included in the Spanish colonial province, had found itself compelled to resort to force almost from the beginning. In Paraguay, however, it had not attained its object; on the east bank of the La Plata, in Uruguay, it saw itself driven to hazardous concessions; and even in the northwest the victorious army had had to fight republican opponents as well as Spanish royalists. The opposition in this last quarter finally increased to such an extent that the government believed its rights could be maintained only by force. Thus it was that San Martin, after making preparations for his advance into Peru, suddenly received orders to return and protect the government from danger within the republic itself. San Martin was among the few patriots who saw clearly that a quarrel as to a greater or less degree of liberty meant the death-warrant of the new republics, if it were to degenerate into civil war before the Spaniards had been finally and completely driven from South American soil. He and others of like mind were undoubtedly republicans at heart; and if, notwithstanding, they repeatedly attempted, at different phases of the struggle for independence, to give the newly formed States a monarchical form of government, it was only because they had come to the conclusion that even among the leaders the great majority were as yet quite unfit for a true republican constitution. They saw that when once independence was secured the land would benefit more by a strong central power on a liberal basis — an enlightened despotism — than by unbridled freedom.

San Martin accordingly declared plainly to the government that even his own army, which under stricter discipline would yet be a still more powerful factor in the struggle against the enemy, would, if involved in the civil war, inevitably fall a prey to demoralisation, and in the long run would be no more a protection to the government than the troops and the population on which the republic had hitherto relied. He also entered into direct communication with different rebel leaders that he might induce them to use their forces in the service of their country, and to postpone the struggle over political opinions until their common enemy had been overcome. As this noble warning fell on deaf ears, and the government, shaken to its very foundations, kept repeating more insistently the order to return to Buenos Ayres to its support, San Martin finally decided to renounce his allegiance to it. In an address to the army he called on his soldiers to turn their backs on the civil war, and to seek glory and honour in the struggle against an enemy from whom they had already conquered a flourishing province. The appeal was enthusiastically received. A few days later the army assembled on the other side of the Cordilleras; the Chilean government took it under its protection; and in Valparaiso the Chilean-Argentine expedition, which was given the name " Exercito Libertador del Peru," embarked in Cochrane's fleet.

San Martin hoped that the population of Peru would revolt for the cause of independence, as the Chileans had done, as soon as the patriot army afforded it a point of support against the Spaniards. He had accordingly taken advantage of the last raid made by Cochrane's fleet, to distribute thousands of copies of a proclamation along the coast. But on landing at Pisco he discovered that the Peruvians maintained an attitude which, if not actually hostile, was as indifferent as that of the Venezuelans had been toward Miranda's proclamation. Besides this, immediately after his arrival, news was received from Spain that the rule of the Cortes had been restored, and that this body had strongly recommended the Spanish governors to enter into negotiations with the champions of liberty. These negotiations, which, on account of San Martin's well-known opinions, were begun with far better prospects of success than those between Morillo and Bolivar in the north, made very slow progress; but this did not displease either party. San Martin hoped that time would thus be gained for a movement to arise among the people in favour of the liberating army. The signs of any such movement had at first been surprisingly small, and it was against San Martin's principles to force upon the country the necessary change in its system of government. The royalists, on the other hand, considered that every day's delay was an advantage to them, and would weaken the little expedition, which was disproportionately small for the task it had undertaken.

The landing at Pisco had the double object of finding out the disposition of the people and of sending an expedition into the Peruvian highlands. When these objects had been attained, the troops were again embarked and landed at Huachi nearer the capital. The movement now began to make progress. The patriots came into touch with the enemy, even in the coast districts; and a Spanish regiment, in which the liberal tendencies then dominant in Spain had strongly developed, came over to them. Good news was also received from the highlands; the districts of Huaylas, Truxillo, Piura, and others, formed patriotic detachments to support San Martin's operations. Thus the Spaniards saw themselves shut in at Lima before they had once come into contact with San Martin's army. Since the threatened attacks from the coast and from the mountains rendered his position untenable, the viceroy finally resolved to abandon the capital. This was no very severe loss, as without the possession of the port of Callao, which the royalists still held, Lima possessed a moral rather than a strategic value.

San Martin did not display the activity in Peru that had been expected from him; but there were numerous and weighty reasons for this. He could not overcome his conviction that the mass of the people had no sympathy for the cause for which he was fighting. As long as he had to rely solely on his small command he could not risk a vigorous attack on the enemy, who outnumbered him many times. For him a defeat meant annihilation, and even a victory on the field of battle implied no real progress. Besides this, his little force was weakened by the unhealthy climate of the coast; and finally the negotiations, conducted with great diplomatic ability on the Spanish side, gave hopes that the object in view could be attained without bloodshed. None the less San Martin's waiting policy came in for much blame. Thus the evacuation of Lima occurred at the right time for impressing on his opponents the necessity for patience, though it was not, as soon became evident, accompanied by the important political and strategic consequences expected from it by the patriots.

The latter had hoped that the fall of the capital would be followed by a rising throughout the country, but in this they were once more deceived. They themselves could not actively follow up the Spaniards whom the Peruvians allowed to retreat to Cuzco unmolested. Here the connection with Bolivia permitted the royalist army to be reconstructed in a very short time; and it was even put in a condition for taking the offensive. San Martin had not dared to entrust the future of the country to a congress at Lima; for it was by no means certain that such an assembly, if it did not degenerate into a mere farce, would not reject the aid of the Liberators. Thus he had to content himself with declaring the independence of Peru without the sanction of the people, and with exercising an almost dictatorial power under the title of "Protector." But the new government received little support from the people, and found itself in a position of constant danger, threatened both by Callao, the bulwark of the royalists, and by the army advancing to the attack from Cuzco, which far outnumbered its own. The military situation became worse when the royalists gained a victory at Ica and for a short time menaced the safety of Lima. Politically this event was a deliverance. What success had failed to do, necessity accomplished: the population of Lima rose for the cause of freedom and willingly attached themselves to San Martin's forces. The fruits of this movement were immediate victories. Callao had long been invested both by land and water, and the advance of the royalists was for the special object of reprovisioning it. San Martin allowed the Spanish army to approach the immediate neighbourhood of the fortress; but there he surrounded it from all sides; and only a retreat, much resembling flight, saved it from the fate of being involved in the capitulation of Callao, which was now inevitable.

Nevertheless San Martin saw the impossibility, with the limited force at his disposal, of securing the province against renewed attacks of the Spaniards from the highlands. As the struggle for independence had always seemed to him a common cause of all the colonies, he lost no time in seeking to come to an understanding with Bolivar as to a mutual plan of campaign, since united action was more likely to lead to swift and sure success than the separate operations which had almost come to a standstill in both theatres of war. The two heroes of the war of independence had for some time been in communication with each other, but had not got beyond the exchange of expressions of reciprocal good will. The immediate occasion of this closer understanding was the circumstance that the harbour of Guayaquil, on the boundary between Peru and Quito, had risen for the cause of freedom, and had been placed by its junta under the joint protection of the two Liberators. The object of the patriots of Guayaquil in taking this step was to avoid all dispute as to what province their town belonged; for though it was politically a part of the province of Quito it was geographically situated in the viceroyalty of Peru, with which its administration had been closely connected. Cochrane's Pacific fleet had rendered the inhabitants of Guayaquil no little help in attaining their independence; and Bolivar, too, had sent a small force to their aid. No one could then foresee that, in spite of the joint protectorate, consequences by no means favourable to the cause of freedom were to follow.

The victory of Boyaca[1] had not led to the result Bolivar had expected from it. The Spanish flag still waved over Quito, and the fanatically royalist population of the provinces Popayan and Pasto placed insuperable obstacles in the way of the patriots' advance. It was this that caused Bolivar to agree to send a division of his army, under Antonio José de Sucre,[2] to Guayaquil, in the hope that an attack on Quito from the east would divert the attention of the royalists and facilitate his advance from the north. But Sucre's first campaign was a failure. After winning two battles, which caused him to underestimate the strength of the enemy, he suffered a severe defeat at Huachi, the consequences of which he avoided only by skilfully arranging an armistice. Bolivar's attack also failed in its object. He had hoped to slip by the royalist positions at Pasto without attracting attention, and to seize Quito from the northeast; but the enemy barred his way at Bombona and forced him to battle. He emerged victorious from the contest, but his plan became known to the enemy and was thus rendered impracticable. He was once more compelled to postpone the conquest of Quito, and retreated to the northwest.

The Liberators of the north were freed from this embarrassing situation by San Martin's help. The latter had repeatedly suggested that he and Bolivar should take common action against either Quito or Cuzco; since in this way only would it be possible for their armies, each too weak for its own task, to overthrow the Spaniards in one of their strongholds. But Bolivar, as usual, could not make up his mind to share the laurels he expected to win with an ally of equal rank, and constantly put off decisive action. Sucre, however, had little or nothing to risk in this respect, so he willingly accepted San Martin's unselfish offer to assist him in undertaking an offensive movement against Quito by handing over to him a part of his troops. With fifteen hundred Peruvian soldiers and about the same number of his own, Sucre, in February, 1822, made an incursion into the districts of Loja and Cuenca, which had hitherto been held by the royalists. When the latter gave him an opportunity of stopping their retreat at Riobamba, he gained a decisive advantage chiefly with the aid of his cavalry. Then, by a bold outflanking movement, he forced them to a decisive battle on the slopes of the volcano Pichincha. Here again the fortune of war favoured the combined patriots of the north and south, and Quito fell into their hands as the prize of victory. With this the back of the Spanish resistance in Ecuador was broken; and Bolivar could now hasten up to deck himself out with the laurels gained under the leadership of his subordinate.

In the hope that the victory in Quito would be followed by a second united campaign against Cuzco and Bolivia, San Martin arranged for a meeting with

---

[1] See ante, p. 490.  [2] See portrait at p. 494.

Bolivar at Guayaquil. But this was not the way in which Bolivar's unbounded ambition could be satisfied. There was some excuse for his immediately incorporating Quito in the Colombian republic, – though it had been conquered only by reason of the energetic support of the Peruvian-Chilean army — for Quito had always formed a part of New Granada. But the case of Guayaquil was not so simple; under the Spaniards there had been doubts as to which province it belonged to, and now it had set up an independent government. San Martin included this among the questions to be discussed at his meeting with Bolivar. But in Bolivar's mind the matter was already legally settled in favour of Colombia, and he actually put his idea in force. He did not wait for the appearance of his rival, but, to the surprise of all, suddenly appeared in Guayaquil and settled the matter with one word of command. While still on the way San Martin received the news that Bolivar would be glad to receive him, as his guest, on Colombian soil.

Such circumstances as these did not augur well for the meeting between the two Liberators in Guayaquil, and the fears entertained proved only too well grounded. The mystery surrounding their negotiations has never been fully cleared up; but so much is certain, that the two generals were unable to come to an understanding. To the astonishment of all concerned, San Martin suddenly departed from Guayaquil; nothing more was heard of a common plan of campaign; and San Martin now resolved on a step which he had not indeed contemplated for the first time at Guayaquil, but which was certainly hastened by the result of his interview with Bolivar.

After the victories of Callao and Quito, San Martin had arranged for the election of a congress to draw up a constitution for Peru. He had also the intention of resigning all his extraordinary powers in favour of this body. The latter step, however, was taken in accordance with certain concealed objects. San Martin did not believe in the possibility of establishing vigorous republics in the Spanish-American provinces. He saw the whole of the north in the hands of a dictator who, if enthusiastic for the cause of liberty, was nevertheless consumed by vanity and a thirst for fame. In the south he saw the attempt at a republican form of government in Chile and in Buenos Ayres on the verge of ruin, and the old provinces more or less involved in the general dissolution. On the other hand, the resistance of Peru had shown him how firmly monarchical sentiments were rooted in the hearts of the people; and the introduction of a constitutional monarchy into the neighbouring empire of Brazil, which was accomplished without any serious political disturbance, furnished an additional argument in favour of this form of government. San Martin was in complete agreement with those of his countrymen in the Argentine Republic who had aimed at setting up a Spanish-American empire with a younger prince of the royal house at its head, at first through the agency of the Infanta Carlota, but afterward through independent effort. He now worked, both in America and in Europe, by means of an ambassador sent across the ocean for this special purpose, at a scheme for establishing a great South American constitutional monarchy, in opposition to the South American republic planned by Bolivar; and he even hoped to see the republic of Colombia incorporated in it. The meeting with Bolivar dashed all his hopes to the ground. Though the European outlook seemed to point to the rapid fulfilment of his plan, he found the general opinion in Peru, as well as in the allied States, decidedly unfavourable to his monarchic proposals. His character as little fitted him to play the part of providence, after the manner of Bolivar, in the State he was at the time directing, as to take part in the inevitable civil war. Thus he came to the conclusion that the only course open to him was to retire from public life. He seized on this way of escape the more readily because he was firmly convinced that, after his retirement, Bolivar's ambition would leave no stone unturned to complete the work of liberation and to add Peru and Bolivia to his Colombian republic. Thus San Martin resigned all his offices and titles into the hands of the Congress that met September 20, 1822. Some of the delegates considered this a mere theatrical trick, such as Bolivar was wont to indulge in; others expected that he would at least continue to act as commander-in-chief; but he departed suddenly and secretly from Peru, and, disgusted with his experiences in Chile and the Argentine Republic, retired to Europe. Here he spent the remainder of his life in seclusion.

San Martin's prophecies were largely justified by the course of events. If Bolivar did not immediately take his place in Peru, it was because of the strong current of public opinion which regarded his devouring ambition with strongly marked distrust. But circumstances proved to be more powerful than the weak government which had undertaken the guidance of Peru. Their contemptuous rejection of Bolivar's proffered aid deprived the Peruvians of a great part of their trained troops, and the military expeditions they attempted on their own account led to two severe defeats at Torata and Moquegua. Finally they had no other resource than to beg humbly for the aid they had once refused to accept, and to appoint the president of the united republic of Colombia Dictator of Peru. But this step led to the outbreak of civil war in the latter country. Even a part of the army revolted against being handed over to Bolivar; Callao again raised the Spanish banner above its impregnable walls; and Lima was once more compelled to open its gates to the royalists. The immediate consequence of calling in Bolivar was that Peru was lost to the patriots.

Nevertheless the Spanish dominion was rotten and tottering to its fall. The abolition of the liberal government in Spain had led to discontent in the royalist army, part of which raised the cry "an absolute king" and renounced its allegiance to the viceroy. Meanwhile Bolivar had reorganised his army among the mountains of the north, and, after bringing up reinforcements from New Granada, renewed his campaign in August, 1824. His first operations were favoured by fortune. He moved toward the south, through the valleys between the two chains of the Cordilleras, screened by swarms of guerilla-warriors, who appeared from all sides on the approach of the patriots. South of Pasco, on the Lago de Reyes, he came into touch with the enemy, who had advanced to meet him. The battle of Junin was in fact a great cavalry engagement, in which the royalists were at first completely successful. But in their eagerness to pursue the retreating enemy they rushed by a body of Bolivar's cavalry without dispersing it. This body attacked them in the rear, riding down their scattered ranks; and the Spanish success was thus converted into a disastrous defeat. The royalist leader, who thought that victory was in his grasp, was forced to fall back into the neighbourhood of Cuzco, a distance of 466 miles. Bolivar was unable to move so rapidly, and when he again met with the enemy on the Apurimac the rainy season set in and put an end to all further operations. At this time Bolivar's dictatorial powers were considerably curtailed by the Congress of Colombia. He therefore resigned his position as commander-in-chief in favour of Sucre and returned to the north, provinces. From there he still directed military operations as long as communications could be maintained. At the end of November the Spaniards seized a position between Sucre and his base, so that he had no alternative but to fight. The royalists considered themselves sure of victory: Sucre was compelled to retreat by forced marches in order to avoid being cut off completely, and suffered considerable losses in the days preceding the battle. But neither he nor his army lost courage, however threatening the situation: they knew that the safety of more than one expedition depended on their fate. On December 9, 1824, the Spaniards — unfortunately for themselves — accepted the opportunity of joining battle, repeatedly offered to them. Sucre had chosen his position on the plain of Ayacucho with the greatest skill, and he directed the contest, which was almost entirely a hand-to-hand struggle, with extraordinary military talent. The victory was complete. The last royalist army was entirely dispersed, and fourteen Spanish generals, with the few troops remaining on the field, laid down their arms. The independence of South America, fought for at Chacabuco and Maipu, Carabobo and Boyacá, was rendered certain at Ayacucho.

The surrender at Ayacucho was accepted by almost all the military posts still in possession of the royalists. Sucre did not disgrace his victory by unnecessary bloodshed, and an honourable capitulation secured for the defenders of Spanish claims an unmolested withdrawal from the country. Owing to his clemency he secured more than he could ever have expected: not only the Peruvians but also the Bolivians laid down their arms. Only in Callao did the Spanish commander continue his opposition for almost a year longer, although hostilities had now become practically without object; for not only had the Spanish troops evacuated the land, but even the fleet had given up the hopeless contest in American waters. As a matter of fact, independence had been won at the beginning of the year 1825; the negative part of the war for freedom was over. Nothing further was necessary except to secure positive recognition for the new States and to constitute them into actual political structures.

## 9. THE INDEPENDENT SOUTH UP TO THE PRESENT TIME

As might have been expected, the Spanish colonies, even during an early stage of their revolt, had applied for the support of the United States of North America, whose example they considered themselves to be imitating in their struggle for liberty and independence. There, however, they met with a distinct refusal. The United States, whose own political status was as yet by no means firmly assured, declared themselves determined to hold aloof from any interference which might entangle them with other Powers. Various deputations, which in the course of the year made applications to England, met with a similar reply. There can be no question that both the United States and England were benevolently disposed toward the Spanish colonies, and they gave evidence of this feeling by not taking strict measures for preventing the despatch of private support from their harbours to the insurgent states. England, however, declared that the struggle of the colonies against the mother country was an internal matter in which, owing to its own close relations with Ferdinand VII, it was the less in a position to interfere. Thus the only open support given to the combatants came from the negro republic of Haiti, and was accorded the more readily owing to the fact that the revolted colonists had everywhere proclaimed the freedom of negro slaves in order to fill with them the thinned ranks of their own regiments, and had made slavery illegal. They did not suspect that by this action they were forfeiting the friendship of their nearest neighbours. After his great victories in New Granada and Quito, Bolivar summoned a Pan-American Congress at Panama, to which, besides the Spanish colonies, the North Americans also were invited. And indeed there was at the time a great party in the United States who were enthusiastic in their support of the idea of a Pan-American Federation. One of the principal reasons put forth by the United States for not participating in this Congress — which afterward proved a failure — was that, by being represented, they would be virtually sanctioning the abolition of negro slavery, and that their own representatives at the Congress would in all probability be placed on an equal footing with the delegates of the Haitian Republic.

The revolution in Spain first brought about a change in public opinion, more especially when Ferdinand VII was for a second time restored by the Holy Alliance to the throne of his fathers as absolute monarch. The revolutionary government was inclined, from principle, to make large allowances to the colonies, and when it saw that its power was becoming increasingly endangered it was willing to grant even the independence of a portion of the colonies in return for their support against France. The Argentine Republic might at that time, in fact, have obtained recognition by severing itself from the rest of the colonies; but it refused offhand every offer of separate treatment.

The interference of the Holy Alliance next had the effect of separating England from the other Powers. That country, actuated, of course, essentially by its own commercial interests, declared that it would have to regard any attempt at a restoration of the *status quo* in the colonies as an unfriendly act. Encouraged by this declaration, the President of the United States, James Monroe,[1] enunciated in his message to Congress the so-called Monroe Doctrine, — frequently reiterated since then in utterly different circumstances, — to the effect that the United States would view any attempt on the part of European Powers to conquer territories on American soil as an unfriendly act toward itself. This declaration had at first little significance, for as yet Spain had not officially recognised the independence of South America, nor had the South American republics met with such recognition on the part of the United States. It was, however, a long step toward it; for, Spain being forbidden to make any attempts at the restoration of its power over the seceded colonies, the full recognition of the independence of the latter could be a question only of time and expediency, subject to the one consideration as to what use the newly emancipated states would make of their liberty.

At the time when the victory of Ayacucho had destroyed the last vestige of the Spanish power in America not a single one of the old colonial provinces was organised on a firm basis. Buenos Ayres at first, without any real disturbances, gave signs of developing into a republic with the promise of vitality, though here, too, a rapid change took place in the form and *personnel* of the supreme Executive.

[1] See *ante*, p. 486.

After the independence of the Republic had been recognised in 1816, however, a Congress was elected by a free popular vote, and at times, too, the budget of this young State, which was still struggling for recognition, showed a balance. All these gains, however, were again entirely lost on the advent to power, in 1820, of the Federal party, which abolished the unity of the Constitution and not only acknowledged the independence of the seceded provinces of Bolivia, Paraguay, and Uruguay, but also dissolved all connection between the different provinces of the Argentine State *inter se* and with Buenos Ayres. The latter owed its endurance as the predominant power only to its geographical position, which brought it more in contact with foreign Powers than the inland provinces. And though historical tradition repeatedly led those in power for the time being at Buenos Ayres to assert the actual predominance of that province, yet for a considerable time its alliance with the neighbouring States rested on the basis of the complete sovereign independence of the contracting parties.

At that time the moral status of the government underwent a rapid decline. The Revolution had been effected by men destined for leadership by their surpassing culture. Belgrano, San Martin, Rivadavia undeniably towered above the majority of their fellow-citizens in abilities and talents. The collapse of all constitutional power was a powerful factor in the production of a class of less honourable politicians. The victory of the Federal idea was in reality the fruit of the ambition of local party leaders, whose principal aim, amid the general insecurity, was to obtain places for themselves and their supporters. To these aspirations the central party had no higher interests to oppose which might have sufficiently influenced the inexperienced masses. Hence resulted the collapse of this party and the degeneration of governments. It is in this way only that we can understand the dictatorship of a man like Don Juan Manuel de Rosas, who by cunning and an utter absence of principle rose from the office of steward in a *hacienda* to the presidency of Buenos Ayres; next succeeded, by more or less doubtful means, in restoring the predominancy of the latter State over the other provinces; and under difficult circumstances maintained his place as Dictator for more than twenty years. That during this régime every stir of an independent opinion was stifled in blood, that the security of life and property was reduced to a mere fancy, and that in spite of this the man was not overthrown, must be simply ascribed to the fact that even the better-minded among the people were as yet absolutely incapable of forming a real idea of the loudly praised blessings of republican liberty.

Nor was Rosas' final overthrow due to a reaction for the restoration of law and order; on the other hand he fell in a struggle with people who were no better than himself. The sore point with the Argentine Republic was its relations with the seceded provinces, especially Montevideo, to which, apart from the Independent party in that province, Brazil was repeatedly making claims. After a previous struggle for the possession of Uruguay, Brazil and Buenos Ayres agreed to consider that State as independent and jointly to guarantee its independence. There too, however, existed different parties, each fighting for the helm of the ship of state; and the support of a fallen President gave Rosas the welcome pretext of once more making his influence felt over Uruguay also. The war which resulted led, temporarily, even to the interference of France and England. It principally, however, served to bring into the field against Rosas a succession of ambitious party leaders, to whose attack his rule finally succumbed in 1852 on the battlefield of Monte Caceros. Under the guise of a convinced federalist, Rosas had managed, though by the most violent means, to maintain a government based on a fairly firm policy of union; his expulsion once more rendered the alliance of the Argentine Republic doubtful, and Buenos Ayres, for a considerable time, severed its connection with the latter. These contests, however, which were far less concerned with the federation of States or the formation of a Republican Union than with the acquisition of power by political parties, have hardly ceased at any time: revolutions in the Republic itself, or civil wars between its various provinces, have endured up to the present day.

The most important of these struggles was with Paraguay. In this country, which was a republic merely in name, the dictatorship of Dr. Francia[1] was followed by those of Carlos Antonio Lopez[2] and his son Francisco Solano Lopez. While Francia had sought salvation for his State by strictly excluding it from all intercourse with its neighbours, the two Lopez, by freely admitting foreigners of all sorts, considerably advanced its economic development. The younger Lopez, however, by interfering in the presidential conflicts of Uruguay, forfeited the friendship of the latter State, and in October, 1864, also that of Brazil; and while endeavouring to injure these opponents he also frivolously challenged the hostility of the Argentine Republic. In this manner arose the alliance of these three Powers against Paraguay, which in the course of a five years' war lost almost its entire wealth, a considerable portion of its territory, and its political importance. Since that time, too, Dictators appointed for a lifetime have been replaced in that country by republican Presidents. Nevertheless internal disturbances have been by no means infrequent, even in Paraguay; though revolutions have not in that country become a chronic condition to the same extent as in Uruguay, where the party wars between Colorados and Blanquillos, dating from Rosas' interference down to our own times, have brought matters to such a pitch that hardly a President has ever completed his legal term of office.

Nor did the last of the provinces once belonging to the viceregal province of Buenos Ayres experience a better fate than its sister States. Upper Peru, now known as Bolivia, did not acquire its liberty until Sucre's victory at Ayacucho. A congress summoned to Chuquisaca in August, 1825, declared the independence of the republic of Bolivia without a protest being lodged by either Peru or the Argentine Republic.[3] The young republic placed itself under the protection of Bolivar, and entrusted its future condition and development to his care. Nor did Bolivar allow the opportunity to escape of putting into substance his ideas of a constitutional government, but presented Bolivia with a Constitution in which, as in the case of Angostura, provision was made for a President elected for life, a hereditary Senate, and a lower House with limited powers. For himself Bolivar reserved the power of assuming, subject to a decree of Congress, dictatorial powers whenever he should enter Bolivian territory; but Sucre, the commander-in-chief at Ayacucho, was chosen as the constitutional President. The latter recognised much better than his master the dangers to which the Codice Boliviano exposed the young republic. He accepted the presidential office for only two years, but

---

[1] See *ante*, p. 496.    [2] Died 1862.    [3] See the maps herewith.

MAP of SOUTH AMERICA

MAP of AMERICA
Showing acquisition of different territories
and most important voyages of discovery

MAP of CENTRAL AMERICA
Showing the most important
voyages of discovery

resigned before the expiration of that period, when he perceived the opposition with which the republican patriotic party viewed the aristocratic tendencies of the Colombian Dictator.

Thus Bolivia, too, entered upon a period of successive military revolutions, which were interrupted only by the ten years' dictatorship of General Santa Cruz. The latter was of Indian descent, had fought in the wars of liberation, and so greatly distinguished himself at the Pichincha[1] as to merit his election to the highest office in the State. This, however, did not satisfy his ambition; for, like Bolivar, he had dreams of a federation of all the American republics under his leadership. The condition of Peru gave him an opportunity of seeing his plans realised. Though the dictatorship of Bolivar had ousted the National party, it had by no means extinguished it: and as soon as the Spanish power had received its final blow it at once revived. The province endured with but little relish the guardianship of the Colombian republic, and when the internal complications of the latter called the Dictator to the north, it shook off its yoke and in 1827 declared itself independent. This, however, was but the signal for the eruption of civil disturbances. Santa Cruz, delighted at having found his long-cherished wish for interference, contrived to bring about a closer connection of Peru with Bolivia, and, as chief of the alliance, wielded the highest power in both republics. In this capacity he rendered important services to the economic development of the States under his authority; but his foreign policy was not equal to the difficulties of the situation and brought about the fall of his government and the end of the Peru-Bolivian federation.

Chile was the rock upon which Santa Cruz was shipwrecked. In that State its first President, O'Higgins,[2] had fallen a victim to democratic aims at the moment when San Martin in Peru gave up the struggle for the establishment of a constitutional monarchy in South America. For Chile also, however, the rule of the so-called Liberals brought bad times: between 1823 and 1831 that State had no less than thirteen governments and seven times changed its constitution. It was not until the Presidency of Joaquin Prieto and the Conservative Constitution of 1833 that the development of Chile attained that stability which until recently has so favourably distinguished it from all the other Spanish-American republics. In the hope of attaching Chile to its confederacy of States, Santa Cruz had supported the attempt of the Chilean ex-President Freire, who by force of arms aspired to lead the Liberal party to victory against Prieto and the Conservatives. But not only did Freire himself fall before the constitutional government of Prieto, but he also involved Santa Cruz in his defeat, inasmuch as Chile declared war against the Peruvian-Bolivian alliance on account of the interference of the latter in Chilean affairs. The war, which was but feebly conducted on the part of Santa Cruz, culminated in the complete victory of the Chileans at Yungay in 1839, and was followed by the complete independence of all three republics and the resignation of the Bolivian Dictator.

Since that time a large number of Presidents have followed one another in Bolivia in rapid succession, almost all having been raised to power and hurled from office by military pronunciamentos. Outstripped by all its neighbours, that country has on only one other occasion since played a part in history, and that an essentially passive one; namely, in the war between Chile and Peru in 1879.

---

[1] See *ante*, p. 508.  [2] See above, p. 503.

The fall of Santa Cruz benefited Peru as little as it did Bolivia. Though more was done in this State for the economic development of the country than in the other republics, more especially through the efforts of President Ramon Castilla (1844–1854), the internal policy of most of the Presidents was nevertheless neither sufficiently prudent nor sufficiently unselfish to place the welfare of the State on a solid foundation. Its great natural resources were either unscrupulously squandered or were made the object of rash speculations which scarcely an old-established State could have survived. To the young republic they meant absolute ruin.

When the natural resources of the central states, which had been the first to be exploited, were exhausted, the southern districts began, toward the end of the seventies, to be regarded as specially valuable. The discovery of inexhaustible deposits of saltpetre and soda led to these barren deserts being looked to as a substitute for the guano deposits of the Chincha Islands, which had become unlicensed mining-grounds. Hitherto the borders of these somewhat dismal regions had received but little attention. Bolivia was, indeed, in possession of a narrow strip of territory extending to the Pacific Ocean and separating Peru from Chile, but had paid so little attention to it that it had almost resigned both its territorial claims and sovereign rights to Chile before the value of this possession was recognised. Thus it came about that not only in Atacama, the Bolivian coast province, but also in Tarapaca, the southernmost part of Peru, almost all industrial interests were in the hands of Chilean and other foreign subjects, who were here amassing riches, to the great envy of the real owners of the land. Having for a long time been in secret agreement, the opponents of Chile commenced hostilities; Bolivia in 1879 subjecting Chilean industries in Atacama to heavy tolls, and, on refusal of their payment, confiscating all Chilean property. Chile, however, was prepared for the struggle; its troops occupied, without serious resistance, the disputed strip of coast, and Bolivia during the whole war hardly made another attempt to recover its lost territory. The quarrel was really fought out between Peru and Chile, the former having stepped in on behalf of Bolivia in virtue of treaty obligations, and thereby given Chile the desired opportunity of declaring war. As long as the Peruvian fleet was successful in disputing with Chile its supremacy on the sea, the operations of the Chileans on land did not extend beyond investing the coast towns of the extreme south. But after the capture, October 8, 1879, of the "Huascar," the largest and swiftest of the Peruvian battle-ships, in an unequal fight against the Chilean fleet, both the fighting forces of the southern republic were able to act in concert and enter upon that succession of victories which culminated at Lima in January, 1881. Both in Peru and Bolivia the defeat was followed by the downfall of the existing government, and it was years before the relations of the conqueror to the conquered were accorded constitutional sanction. In the end, however, Chile was confirmed in the permanent possession of Atacama and Tarapaca, and in the temporary occupation of the provinces of Tacna and Arica; but the pledges given by Chile on that occasion, have not been redeemed up to the present day.[1]

This victory was a brilliant justification for the Chilean Constitution, which had been decried as an enemy to liberty. To it undoubtedly must be attributed the

---

[1] See the maps at p. 514.

fact that the government of Chile has since the Constitution of 1833 been firmer and more concentrated than that of any other of the Spanish-American republics. The reproach hurled at this government, of being an enemy to freedom, is, however, utterly unfounded. Even under Manuel Montt (1851–1861), the true founder of Chilean prosperity, the development of the Constitution on a liberal basis had been seriously begun, and his successors have not stood idle. Whether, however, the advances thus won by Chile have outweighed the disadvantages of subsequent party struggles more violent and embittered than those experienced under the Conservative Constitution of 1833 may well be left open to doubt. Upon them, at any rate, was based the conflict which, after a peace extending over decades, led in 1891 to a revolution and the violent downfall of the government. The experience that a war may be scarcely less dangerous to the conquering party in its industrial life than to the defeated one, once more proved itself true in the case of Chile. The extraordinary increase in the national wealth which had been the outcome of the war with Peru led to an extravagant activity in the industrial sphere. President José Manuel Balmacéda (1886–1891) especially had in this respect strained the resources of the country beyond their capacity. The financial crisis developed, however, into a political one when it was shown that these industrial speculations had been exploited from the public treasury for the personal advantage of the President and his creatures. This imparted to the Revolution, which was founded as much on political as on personal party considerations, an unexpected moral force, and in 1891, in a short time, procured for it a comparatively easy victory and one which was not exploited to excess. The fact remains, notwithstanding, that in Chile, too, the regular succession of constitutional governments was in this wise interrupted by a victorious military rising. The few years which have elapsed since then have sufficed to show that the civil power has not emerged from the struggle without having sustained a permanent shock. At the present time Chile has only a qualified claim to its former reputation of being the most trustworthy of the South American republics.

The Republic of Colombia, too, the creation of which had been Bolivar's special pride, did not enjoy a long lease of life. While the Liberator, reaping the fruits of Sucre's victory at Ayacucho, was holding his triumphal progress through Bolivia, his mind was already occupied with bold plans which again had for their object the expansion of his Colombian Republic. At one time he was offering his aid to the Chileans in driving out the last remnants of the Spanish army of occupation from the archipelago of Chiloë; at another he was planning with the Argentines an advance against Brazil, the last remaining division of the South American continent which was still under a monarchical constitution and which had not yet entirely severed its connection with the Old World. His dictatorial power, however, and the aristocratic Constitution which he had introduced in Peru and Bolivia, caused him to be looked upon with suspicion by republicans not only in foreign countries, but even in New Granada; and besides neither in Chile nor in La Plata was there a dearth of ambitious generals who were ready to follow his own example for their own benefit. In the end the growing distrust of the Colombian Congress recalled him from the south, and his unconditional obedience to their behest was perhaps the best defence he could offer.

In Venezuela a strong party, with Paez at its head, had ever since 1826 urged the separation of that country from the Colombian Republic. Indeed, the secession had almost become an accomplished fact when Bolivar yielded and by all kinds of concessions succeeded in inducing his old comrades in arms once more to recognise his authority and that of the Colombian Congress. In the meantime an exactly similar movement took place in Peru, where, as in Bolivia, the Colombians had, from the commencement, been extremely unpopular. As soon as the National party in that State saw itself freed from the menacing presence of the Dictator, it rose in revolt, abolished the government which Bolivar had established at Lima, and invited Bolivia to join it. The latter State responded to the invitation in a qualified manner by rising against Sucre and forcing him to resign.[1] The Peruvians, however, proceeded even farther; they caused pronunciamentos to be issued at Guayaquil and other places in Ecuador. Under the pretext of protecting the latter against oppression, the Peruvian Dictator Lamar declared war against Colombia. Here, however, Sucre again saved the honour of the Colombian arms, and by his victory at Tarqui brought about a revolution against Lamar in Peru. The new government, though insisting, like its predecessors, on the independence of Peru, nevertheless concluded peace on easy terms with its neighbour States.

Even at this time Bolivar had constantly to battle against a strong current of opposition which aimed at his deposition and the abolition of his dictatorship. After he had four times abdicated his government, in order only at the next moment to resume it with the most unlimited powers, his enemies determined to get rid of him by unconstitutional methods. After several unsuccessful attempts at revolution, a military rising took place on the 25th of September, 1828, at Bogotá, having for its object the assassination of Bolivar. His almost miraculous escape, however, so utterly threw into confusion the plans of the conspirators, that they were easily conquered, and once again Bolivar's cleverness induced him to seek for reconciliation with the vanquished rather than for vengeance upon his enemies. He was, however, unable completely to disarm the party which, in the constant renewal of the extraordinary powers of his régime, saw a serious danger to liberty. At last, having once more in the Congress of 1830 had recourse to the often-tried trick of a resignation, he had the painful experience of seeing it accepted, accompanied by all imaginable marks of esteem for his great exertions on behalf of liberty, while a successor was appointed in the person of Joaquin Mosquera. After somewhat prolonged hesitation Bolivar decided to submit to the decision of the Congress. Having for some time been in ill health, he at length left the country in which he considered himself to have been treated with ingratitude, and died at Santa Marta on the 17th of December in the same year.

The Colombian Republic had come to an end even before his death. Venezuela shortly afterward repeated the attempt to sever its connection with Colombia, and in 1830 these efforts assumed a new direction directly in opposition to the policy of Bolivar. Nor was the abdication of the latter able to stop the movement, for Paez and his following exercised unlimited control over the legislative assembly. All attempts to resist the new order of things were suppressed without much bloodshed, and before the close of the year Venezuela, within the range of the old general captaincy of Caracas, declared itself an independent republic. The same thing happened in Bolivia, with this difference, that that State upheld with gratitude the memory of its liberator and offered him an asylum when he laid

---

[1] See *ante*, p. 514.

down his offices in Colombia; an offer which he refused, as also the invitation to assume once more the government, sent to him after a successful revolution against the régime of Mosquera. In the following year (1831) the very name of Colombia disappeared; the provinces which still adhered to the government of Bogotá constituted themselves into the republic of New Granada, and, under a Conservative Constitution, handled vigorously by a series of energetic Presidents, enjoyed until 1857 a fairly undisturbed — indeed almost peaceful — development. Here also, however, the unfortunate civil war between the Central and Federal parties afterward broke out afresh, and the cause of the latter party, which was more than usually justified by the extraordinary differences in the geographical features of the separate provinces, was in the end successful. Under the name of the United States of Colombia they adopted, in 1861, a constitution planned on exactly the same lines as that of the United States of North America. Since then the country has, under more peaceful conditions, been able to devote itself to the development and opening up of its industrial resources.

Venezuela underwent a similar development. During the first twenty years José Antonio Paez, either in the capacity of President (1830–1838, 1839–1842), as Dictator (1846), or merely as adviser of the parties in power, virtually directed the destinies of the State for whose liberation he, next to Bolivar, had done the most. His vigorous government assured peaceful times to the Republic. Here too, however, a federal Constitution on the North American pattern gained an increasing number of supporters, although such a Constitution could hardly be said to have arisen out of natural conditions, but had become the watchword of the Liberal party more from a love of imitating North American political institutions. Venezuela belongs to those States of Spanish America which have been least able to establish themselves on a solid basis. After a civil war extending over several years, in which Paez also once more (1861–1863) took up arms in defence of the unity of the republic, the provinces, in 1864, formed themselves into the federal republic of "the United States of Venezuela." In spite of this, civil commotions broke out over and over again; and it was not until the almost dictatorial régime of Antonio Guzman Blanco (1870–1877, 1879–1884, and 1886–1887) that the republic enjoyed a temporary peace.

## 10. CENTRAL AMERICA AND BRAZIL

### A. MEXICO

DURING the whole period of the South American wars of liberation Mexico stood aside and pursued its own road. After the overthrow of Hidalgo and his adherents [1] Spanish rule seemed once more established, and even the introduction and re-abolition of the Democratic Constitution of 1812 passed off without incident. Naturally the events which were passing all around in States allied by race could not entirely fail to react upon the mind of the population; but the desire for freedom and independence was not strong enough to aim at the subversion of the existing order of things. The revolutionary impulse in this country took its start from an entirely different quarter.

---

[1] See *ante*, p. 492.

The viceroy had bestowed his confidence in a special degree upon the Principal Lieutenant, Iturbide, who, though a Mexican by birth, had distinguished himself by his energy and zeal, but also by his cruelty, in the struggle against the forces of Hidalgo. Iturbide, however, abused the trust reposed in him. He engaged in secret schemes with the Creole leaders and the scattered partisans of Hidalgo, and, though ostensibly he took the field against one of the latter, he caused the promulgation in the little town of Iguala of a military pronunciamento the point of which was directed against Spanish rule. In the programme of a Constitution which he drew up, Mexico was declared independent, and a constitutional assembly was held in prospect. The country, however, was declared a monarchy in anticipation, the throne of which was to be offered to Ferdinand VII and the other princes of his House. Iturbide's following increased with astonishing rapidity, so that the Viceroy and the Spanish party soon saw themselves confined to the capital. At that moment the arrival of a viceroy appointed by a Liberal Spanish government terminated the revolution without bloodshed. The new regent accepted Iturbide's plan almost in its entirety, and returned to Spain in person in order to exert himself in its behalf at the court of Ferdinand VII. Had one of the king's brothers decided at that time to go over to Mexico, that State would in all probability have been preserved to the Bourbon dynasty. The rejection of the Iguala plan, on the other hand, pushed its originators farther along on the road to revolution. Since the provisional arrangement threatened in the end to become dangerous to all parties, Iturbide allowed himself to be proclaimed Emperor of Mexico by his adherents in May, 1822, in order in this manner to save his constitutional edifice. His following, however, was neither large enough nor his past career sufficiently stainless to force the country to accept his rule. Hostile pronunciamentos were promulgated in the most widely different provinces, and as early as March, 1823, the Emperor was obliged to seek refuge on board an English ship.

Thereupon Mexico, too, was proclaimed a republic. It was, however, a republic merely in name, while a succession of more or less fortunate military pretenders were fighting for Iturbide's inheritance. The most prominent figure in this struggle was General Antonio Lopez de Santa Ana (Santana), who had already taken a conspicuous part in the overthrow of the Emperor, and afterward appointed and deposed presidents at his own will and pleasure until finally he himself accepted the chief office in the State, which he was destined more than once to lose and to recover. He is, however, undeniably entitled to the credit of having adhered in his internal administration to a strong policy of centralisation, as opposed to the federal doctrine which had sprung up out of a blind zeal for imitating the North American Constitution, and which was entirely unjustified from both geographical and historical considerations; while in his foreign policy he deserves recognition for having manfully and repeatedly, at the risk of his own personal safety, defended the honour and integrity of the country.

Mexico, however, was drawn into international complications to a greater extent than the other Spanish-American republics. As late as 1829 the Spaniards had made an attempt to reconquer the country, but had been defeated by Santa Ana and forced to capitulate. The rising which occurred in Texas in 1836 was, no doubt, primarily an internal matter, since at that time the borders of Mexico still embraced the Far West of North America. Santa Ana, however, in his attempt to bring the province back to its obedience, was defeated on the 20th of April, 1836.

and taken prisoner, as a result of which the Separatists gained the upper hand. Under the presidency of Houston, an American, Texas formed an independent republic which from its origin linked its fortunes closely with the United States, and in 1845 was, on its own application, actually received into the Union. Mexico was not prepared to accept this rebuff calmly; it declared war against the United States and entrusted Santa Ana with the chief command. The Mexican Republic, torn by internal factions and on the verge of financial ruin, was, however, no match for the North Americans. The invasion of the northern provinces by the United States troops met with no serious opposition, nor were the Mexicans able to prevent the landing of the enemy's forces at Vera Cruz. It is true that Santa Ana repeatedly opposed their advance, but he suffered one defeat after another, and finally fled to Jamaica at the very time when the troops of the Union were dictating the terms of peace to their opponents in their own capital. By this treaty Mexico surrendered its claims to Texas and all its northern Pacific provinces against an indemnity of fifteen million dollars.

In 1853 Santa Ana was once more summoned to undertake, as Dictator, the management and restoration to order of the exhausted State, — a task which he took in hand with his wonted energy; but he was hardly likely to restore internal order, seeing that since the 17th of December, 1853, he had openly been aiming at securing himself in a position of permanent authority. Accordingly, in 1855, his fall was brought about by fresh pronunciamentos. Thereupon Mexico was again plunged into a state of revolution which once more drew down upon the unfortunate country the interference of foreign powers. The prolonged condition of lawlessness had brought the State to the verge of bankruptcy, and, as may be easily conceived, during the period of financial stress the parties in power had not infrequently laid hands on the property of foreigners, in violation of treaty rights. As early as 1838 similar proceedings had led to a war with France, which had temporarily taken possession of the harbour of San Juan de Ulua. In 1861 President Carlo Benito Juarez, after long party struggles, had managed to secure for himself the supreme authority, though by no means without opposition. When, however, he once more began to make illegal encroachments upon the property of foreigners, Napoleon III, who by the glory of foreign exploits was endeavouring to make people forget the unconstitutional origin of his imperial rule, seized this opportunity and proposed to England and Spain to vindicate the rights of their subjects in Mexico by a common expedition against that country. The proposal was accepted in the first instance by both parties; and an army composed of contingents from all three states occupied Vera Cruz and advanced to Orizaba. But first England and afterward Spain withdrew from the enterprise as soon as the allies saw that France was by no means actuated merely by a desire for obtaining indemnification for suffered losses, but was in reality aiming at the overthrow of the existing government with the view of replacing it by a monarchy under its own protection.

Deceived by the whispered insinuations of Mexican fugitives, the French believed that the people would flock to them *en masse* and accompany them in triumph to their capital. Instead of this they received at Puebla so hot a reception that they were only too glad again to reach and hold their former quarters at Orizaba. Nor was the expeditionary force able to resume its advance until it had been reinforced to thirty thousand men. After a bitter struggle for the possession of Puebla, which ended with the capitulation of the Mexican garrison, Mexico also opened its gates to the conqueror. With this the object of the expedition seemed achieved. A Junta, rapidly summoned, appointed a provisional government which a few days afterward laid before the Congress the plan of a Constitution creating a monarchy under the name of an empire. The proposal was accepted by an overwhelming majority,—indeed almost unanimously. The candidate selected by Napoleon, of whose acceptance he had assured himself previous to taking any action, was the Archduke Maximilian of Austria. Hence, when a deputation of the provisional government proceeded to Miramare to offer the Prince the imperial crown of Mexico, the latter readily accepted the new dignity. In April, 1864, in the harbour of Trieste, he went on board the " Novara," which was to convey him to Vera Cruz. The voyage was quickly accomplished, and the people greeted their new sovereign with frank and open-hearted joy. On his entry into Mexico the party of opposition at whose head was ex-President Benito Juarez seemed practically vanquished.

Its importance, however, revived and increased with astonishing rapidity in consequence of the internal difficulties which the new imperial government was destined to encounter. From the very beginning Maximilian was not his own master. By his contracts with Napoleon III he was indeed assured of the assistance of the French troops; but in the person of their commander-in-chief, Marshal Bazaine, he was associated with a power over which he exercised only the most limited control. Bazaine was almost a sort of supplementary or accessory king in Mexico, and his powers in this capacity increased in proportion as the mutual confidence between the Emperor and the Marshal disappeared. The contracts, moreover, showed that the interference of the French in favour of Maximilian was by no means as unselfish as it had appeared to be. The financial demands made upon the country were extremely oppressive and unjustifiable in so far as, under the pressure of French policy, an unworthy speculation for the exploitation of Mexico was carried on with demands of a highly questionable nature. These in themselves were factors foreboding little good to Maximilian's authority. He himself fully recognised that the protection of a foreign power would alienate from him the sympathies of an important party in the country. He therefore not only endeavoured to withdraw himself as much as possible from French influence, but also made efforts to keep himself above the parties which divided the country into two hostile camps. The people, however, were not ripe for such a high-minded policy.

While the Conservative party, which had raised Maximilian to the throne, found itself deceived in its expectations, the Liberals looked upon his conciliatory attitude as a confession of weakness, and soon began to take fresh courage; the more so as they had found a support which promised a much surer protection than France was capable of offering to their opponents. French interference was confessedly directed against the United States, the enormous expansion and rapid rise of which had filled the monarchs of Europe with anxious apprehension. Napoleon thought he had seized upon a specially favourable moment for interfering at a time when the war of secession[1] kept the United States busily occupied with their own internal affairs. The rapid and complete victory of the Northern States,

[1] See post, p. 550 et seq.

however, left their hands free, and tended only to make them assume a more vigorous attitude in regard to the Mexican question. They indeed still looked upon Juarez as the sole legal authority in Mexico at a time when the latter, on his own absolute decision, had prolonged the term of his expired presidency and was actually wandering as an exile on the extreme confines of the country.

To Napoleon the prospect that the French support of Maximilian might give to the United States a pretext for invading northern Mexico seemed extremely annoying. Instead, however, of openly avowing the situation and endeavouring to the best of his power to bring about a solution in some other way, Napoleon made the non-fulfilment of its financial obligations by the Mexican government the miserable pretext for simply sacrificing Maximilian after leaving him for a long time faltering between hope and fear. Maximilian, it is true, had not shown himself equal to the task of controlling the extraordinarily difficult condition of Mexican affairs. His wavering attitude between the Mexican parties and his irresolute policy in regard to France had done much to impair the stability of his throne. To add to these troubles his health gave way, and he was further afflicted by the unfortunate condition of his wife, Charlotte, who had become insane while making vain efforts in Paris and Rome to further her husband's cause. At the time when the French troops began to be withdrawn from Mexico he seemed to have resolved on abdicating. All of a sudden, however, he returned and placed himself at the head of the feeble army which was making painful efforts to maintain his rule. But it was too late. Betrayed by his own generals at Queretaro about the middle of May, after a short informal trial he, in company with the last of his faithful adherents, was shot by the Republicans on the 19th of June, 1867.

Juarez had now an easy task. Once more in possession of power, he showed himself, as a politician, much better adapted for the work than his predecessors. Under the form of a republic, Mexico, since 1866, has been virtually subjected to the dictatorship of two men, — Benito Juarez (1867–1872) and Porfirio Diaz (1877–1881, and since 1884 without interruption). Pronunciamentos and revolutions have undoubtedly been as frequent among the orders of the day in that country as in the rest of Spanish America. Nevertheless, through the enlightened despotism of these two men, the country has recovered much that had been lost during the period of continuous revolutions. In alliance with its Spanish sister republics it has made slow but unmistakable progress on the road to true republican liberty.

### B. The Small Central American Republics

WHEN Iturbide, in 1821, brought the Spanish dominion in Mexico to a sudden end, the movement in favour of independence also spread to the general captaincy of Guatemala, which embraced the States north of the Isthmus of Panama as far as the boundaries of the kingdom of New Spain. Here, though the revolution, so far as separation from Spain was concerned, was accomplished without bloodshed, civil war at once broke out between the two parties of the Serviles and the Liberals. The former began, in opposition to the constitutional assembly, to carry through the union of Central America with the empire of Iturbide. This, however, involved them in the fall of the latter, which followed soon after and destroyed their influence in the country, the separate divisions of which now took

up the management of their own affairs under the guidance of the Liberals and
became the small republics of Central America. Even this, however, did not
entirely destroy the feeling of their kinship. Only Chiapa severed its connection
with its old allies and attached itself to the Mexican republic. Guatemala,
Honduras, San Salvador, Nicaragua, and Costa Rica, on the other hand, formed
themselves, April 1, 1823, into a federal union which in 1825 chose its first
President in the person of General Arce. This, however, was the signal for the
commencement of an incessant civil war which, while professedly defending the
cause of federal or central principles, was in reality merely a struggle of self-
seeking party-leaders for the possession of power.

Until the year 1839 the republic of the United States of Central America,
though shaken by many storms, nevertheless managed to maintain a constitutional
existence. In that year, however, the federal union of States was dissolved and
for a long time was not resuscitated. The five small States have indeed repeatedly come to the conviction that a closer union would be desirable, both as
a means of furthering their many common internal interests and of preserving
their independence against arrogant claims from without. Hence continuous
attempts have been made, either by diplomatic methods or by resort to arms, of
reviving a confederation of all or some of the old States of Central America.
While, however, these complications have in many cases seriously interrupted the
steady progress of the republics concerned, the advantages which their union was
to have produced have not been attained. It has never yet been possible to
discover a form of government providing safeguards against the subjection of the
weaker members of the Union by the stronger States. For this reason, hitherto,
every attempt at combination has shortly afterward been followed by a revolution tending toward decentralization. The last attempt in this direction, the
" Republica Mayor de Centro-America," created in 1896–97, although it left complete internal autonomy to the separate States, came to an end after a brief
existence in 1898.

### C. Brazil

THE collapse of the throne of Maximilian marked the triumph of republican principles over the whole of the American continent except Brazil. The
threat of a French invasion under Junot in 1808 had indeed induced the Portuguese royal family to transfer the seat of government to Rio de Janeiro; but this
was considered merely a temporary precautionary measure which was to make
no change in the political relations between the mother country and the colonies.
Circumstances, however, rendered the continuance of this state of affairs impossible. The revolutionary wave which passed over the Pyrenean State after the
expulsion of Napoleon, the struggle for freedom and independence which was
proceeding in the surrounding sister States, could not fail to exercise a strong
influence on Brazilian affairs. As early as 1815 Brazil was raised to the dignity
of a kingdom, an event which could not otherwise than considerably advance
the efforts which were directed toward a separation from Portugal. Again, however, the issue was brought about by the condition of affairs in Portugal and not
by the situation in Brazil.

The movement in favour of a parliamentary form of government, which was
set on foot in 1820 by Riego in Spain, spread also to the kingdom of Portugal and

thence across to Brazil. King John VI was completely taken by surprise : and as his successor to the throne, Dom Pedro, placed himself at the head of the Liberal party, the latter easily attained its object; namely, the promise of a separate parliamentary Constitution for Brazil. However, though the Liberals in the colony felt themselves conjointly responsible with those of Portugal, they were soon to learn that the Cortes of the mother country had ends in view quite different from those corresponding with their desires; for the latter asked for no less than the return of the court to Lisbon and the restoration of the Portuguese dominion in Brazil.

The first of these objects was actually attained; John VI returned to Lisbon, and Dom Pedro, who had renounced his succession in favour of his brothers and sisters, stayed behind in the first instance at Rio de Janeiro as Viceroy. The more manifest it became, however, that the Cortes was aiming at again reducing Brazil to the condition of a province, the looser became the tie which united the colony to the mother country. At last nothing was left to Dom Pedro himself but to tear the bond, and, on the 7th of September, 1822, to proclaim the complete independence of Brazil, which a month later was declared an empire. Up to this point Dom Pedro, carried along by the national movement, had remained in accord with the large majority of his people. In the disputes, however, which in the following years arose in regard to questions of internal and foreign policy, this agreement began to be more and more disturbed. Finally, when the populace endeavoured to intimidate him by raising commotions, as it had done successfully and with his co-operation under John VI, he resigned in 1831 in favour of his son, and a few days later ended his days at Lisbon.

Nor was Pedro II destined to die in his empire. Even during the time of his minority the adherents of a federal-republican party had attracted considerable notice amid the passionate struggles of party warfare. Their influence naturally fell again into the background during the time that Pedro II, who had been declared of full age before the proper time, was administering with great tact a remarkably liberal government. But even at that time the country did not enjoy a perfect or permanent peace. The province of Sao Paulo especially seemed to be an inextinguishable hearth of constantly renewed republican agitations. The victorious campaign against Paraguay, though it raised the prestige of the country abroad, on the other hand involved it in serious financial difficulties, which were still further increased by the expenses arising out of the abolition of slavery, which had been resolved upon in 1871. The discussions connected with the passing of this measure filled up the political life of Brazil for years and have also exercised a determining influence on the last remodelling of the Constitution of the country. After Dom Pedro had long endeavoured, with the aid of Conservative ministries, to solve the slavery question in such a way as to preserve all interests as far as possible, he found himself obliged, in 1888, to call in a Liberal ministry which, immediately after its accession to office, declared for the unconditional abolition of slavery and rejected all compensation to slave-owners. By this measure, however, it drove so large a portion of the population into the ranks of the Opposition that the latter was able, on the 15th of November, 1889, to organize a revolution to which the capital surrendered without an attempt at resistance. The combined Conservative and Federalist parties thereupon forced Dom Pedro to abdicate, and set up the republic of the

United States of Brazil, — a creation which up to the present time has not succeeded either in restoring peace in the country or in opening out prospects of a better future.

## 11. THE UNITED STATES OF AMERICA IN THE NINETEENTH CENTURY

IT has become customary to regard the recent history of the United States of America exclusively in the light of the struggle over slavery; but this process is not in this case so accurate as when applied to the last three decades of the history of Brazil. The ideal question whether slavery was admissible or justifiable had, indeed, been debated, and in some communities negatived, even at the time of the cessation of English rule in the American continental colonies, and was thereafter discussed quite continuously by individuals and corporate bodies. Nevertheless, the government of the United States, as such, had, far into the nineteenth century, regarded the enslavement of negroes as a perfectly legal institution wherever established by Commonwealth enactment; and thus the struggle between North and South could never turn upon the legality of slavery, but only upon the ethical status of the institution. It was not only a defensive struggle for the protection of certain purely economic interests, but it also by degrees assumed such a character that the preservation of slavery seemed to become a *sine qua non* to the South as clearly as did the destruction of the preponderance of the slaveholding southern States appear essential to the beneficial progress of the North. A government in which a man's vote upon national affairs was relatively influential in proportion to the number of slaves within his Commonwealth; which allowed to a slaveholder the unrestricted pursuit of his slaves even into States where the institution did not exist; a government, finally, which permitted slavery in the small federal district over which it exercised direct control, and in certain of the Territories governed by Congress, — such a government naturally entertained no doubts as to the legal status of slavery.

In the northern States, for reasons of climate, topography, and industrial development, slavery naturally was not very widely spread; in Massachusetts, in fact, soon after the adoption of its Constitution in 1780, slavery was made impossible by judicial decision. In New York, on the other hand, it was to be found for a half-century more, and similar conditions prevailed in other northern States. The slave-trade, which was more universally and less reservedly condemned than slavery itself, was carried on in full swing, not only legally during the twenty years fixed by the Constitution after the adoption of that instrument, but also, illegally, far beyond that period, and that, too, by the very merchants who were otherwise fully conscious of the industrial antagonism between North and South.

By the terms of the Constitution a measure became law if passed in the House of Representatives by a majority of the members, who were apportioned among the States on the basis of population,[1] and in the Senate by a majority of the members, who were apportioned equally among the States. As long as the conflict was undecided a serious danger to both parties lay hidden in this complex system of representation. In the House of Representatives the northern States, owing to their larger

[1] See *ante*, pp. 478, 479.

population, possessed from the beginning a small majority. Nor could this be affected by the constitutional concession to the Southerners by which, in computing population for purposes of representative apportionment, five slaves were made to count as three inhabitants. In spite of this the majority grew from year to year, for, notwithstanding the importation and the rearing of slaves, the southern States were unable to keep pace with the increase of population of the North. Thus the only protection of the South lay in the Senate, whose membership consisted of two Senators from each State, and not of State delegations varying in size according to the population of each State. The South, if industrially and politically it was not to be handed over to the North, was compelled to find means of maintaining a balance in the Senate. The New England States had, indeed, before this, in the most undisguised fashion, paraded their own sectional arguments and interests as a justification for possible separation. And even after the establishment of the Constitution and the later accession of Jefferson, a perverted federalism was for some years vainly used to further certain of their interests. But after the Hartford Convention the entire policy of the northeastern group, drawn together by similarity of interests, left no room to doubt what the South would have to expect when once it could no longer be able, of its own weight, to counterbalance the self-centred industrial policy of the northern States.

Thus the "planter" States had to guard their common life interests against the "industrial" States. These interests, indeed, were not exclusively bound up with the maintenance of slavery. Nevertheless this institution, so essential to their industry, furnished an outward, visible sign which became more and more a distinguishing mark of the section. Later the Northerners complacently made the alleged evils of an institution which they themselves had once by no means despised a pretext for attacking the South, while in reality they were seeking to protect their own political and industrial interests.

At the time when the thirteen North American provinces had joined together in a federal union, the industrial opposition of the planter States to the commercial and manufacturing States was by no means so marked as to enable one to speak of a majority of either of these groups. Later, however, the division assumed from year to year a more definite character. It was probably not a mere accident that in the nine new Territories received as States into the Union up to 1818,— as in the case of the thirteen original States, — the States with an essentially free, industrial, and agricultural population exactly balanced those in which plantation industry and slave labour were predominant. This balance seems to have been threatened for the first time when Missouri applied for admission into the Union, on which occasion it was proposed by certain Northerners to make the prohibition of slavery a preliminary condition of such admission. The question was indeed still an open one; for although, according to the Northwest Ordinance, slavery was to be prohibited in the Territories north of the Ohio, no definite limit in this respect had as yet been fixed on the other side of the Mississippi.[1] From its natural conditions and the manner in which it had been colonised Missouri was evidently marked out for another planter State; and accordingly the representatives of these States in both Houses protested energetically against the resolution, and, in conformity to the doctrine of public law which from the beginning had recognised

---

[1] See the maps at p. 514.

slavery as an institution exclusively within the jurisdiction of the States, demanded that the question of slavery should be left to the decision of the new State in its Constitution, and that under no pretence should Congress be allowed to reserve to itself the right of attaching to the admission of a new State such conditions as it might determine. On the other hand the North in reality was not concerned merely with the question whether there were to be slaves in Missouri or not,— a matter, indeed, of complete indifference to the great merchants; their real apprehension was whether, by surrendering this Territory to the Southern interests, the latter might not thereby acquire in the Senate such a decided preponderance as might possibly be used in a manner hostile and damaging to the North. Hence, as long as there was danger of such a majority, the North offered an obstinate and energetic resistance; but this at once disappeared when the Territory of Maine likewise applied for admission to the Union, whereby a check might be afforded to the North against the rising power of the South. In this connection what is known as the Missouri Compromise was effected in 1820 and 1821, which on the one hand admitted the two Territories into the Union without conditions and recognised the inability of Congress to impose such conditions, and on the other hand fixed the boundary between the slaveholding and non-slaveholding Territories west of the Mississippi at 36° 30' of latitude.

The acuteness with which this Missouri question was fought out by the two parties was in some measure due to another matter,— the development in the same years of another approaching conflict of interests between the North and the South. We have already stated[1] that New York, before its acceptance of the federal Constitution, had, for the purpose of supporting its young industry, surrounded itself with a system of protective tariffs. As this policy was gradually approved, and as industrial centres began to appear in all the States of the Northeast, the desire for protection by the laws of the Union became more general. This desire also found adherents in the States of the Northwest, in which the farmers were principally engaged in wheat-culture. To the South, on the other hand, free trade seemed a distinctly beneficial policy; for whereas the productions of the southern States were limited to a small number of commodities which were exported as raw products, they drew the whole of the manufactured articles they required from abroad, and could therefore view only with displeasure a protective tariff which rendered the competition of foreign countries in their markets more difficult, and which increased the cost of all articles which to them were indispensable. It was, moreover, doubly annoying to them, not only that they had to support, as they argued, by means of a protective tariff, the industry of the northern States, which formed the principal factor in their rapid increase of population, but also that, by the exclusion of foreign competition, they should render themselves directly dependent for all manufactured articles upon the States of the North. Nevertheless, in 1824 a bill was passed in both Houses of Congress, by a majority of a few votes, according to which a moderate protective tariff became a law of the Union. This, however, so far from terminating the struggle between free-traders and protectionists, did not even produce a temporary pause in the agitation; for while the North fought zealously for a further increase of tariffs, the South with equal energy contended for their abolition or modification.

---

[1] Ante, p. 476.

Monroe,[1] on retiring into private life in 1825, after the completion of his second term of office (1821–1825), was justified in reviewing his work with satisfaction. The reputation of the government had been strengthened at home and abroad, the industrial development of the country had been led into appropriate channels, and its financial condition had been placed on a satisfactory basis. These conditions remained virtually unchanged also under his successor, John Quincy Adams (1825–1829), during whose administration continued both the favourable external development and the unfortunate internal conflict.

John Quincy Adams, the candidate of the Northerners, was far from aiming to conduct his office in a sectional spirit; but the protectionists returned to each successive Congress with increased majorities, and the political situation seemed to them to be a justification of their efforts. England was still the principal purveyor to the United States, with an annual importation valued at twenty-five million dollars. Instead, however, of treating the commerce of so important a customer with consideration, England once more resorted to a strict application of the Navigation Acts, refused the conclusion of a commercial treaty, and endeavoured to exclude the Americans completely from the trade of its West Indian possessions. Hence a protective tariff against English manufactures became a measure as much of political as of industrial necessity. Signs of vigorous opposition, however, became more and more evident among the Southern minority and in various fields of political action. Indeed, on one occasion during Adams's presidency the authority of the national Executive was directly assailed. Georgia, in order to rid itself of the remnants of its Indian population, had concluded a treaty with certain Creek chiefs which turned out to be an undoubted violation of the law, the contracting parties having acted without any authority on behalf of their whole tribe, and moreover having unmistakably been bribed. In spite of this the governor and the State legislature not only upheld the treaty against the President, but also against the judgment of the United States Supreme Court; and they moreover expressed themselves in so defiant a manner against the national authorities that the Constitution was held up almost to contempt. Finally, they not only succeeded in their expulsion of the Indians, but also were countenanced and aided by President Jackson in his delinquent omission to enforce the decision of the federal Supreme Court.

In these proceedings, moreover, the doctrine of the sovereignty of the separate States had been much used; immediately afterward it was applied in a still more forcible manner by another of the southern States. Already in John Quincy Adams's time South Carolina had declared its unwillingness to submit to the policy of increased tariffs; it had, however, for the moment contented itself with a protest, since a presidential election was imminent and the choice was expected to fall on a man who, it was hoped, would consent to the abolition of the protective tariffs. Andrew Jackson, the hero of the war against the Seminoles and the victor of New Orleans,[2] having at the previous election obtained a plurality of votes, asserted that he had been defeated solely through an unworthy manœuvre concerted between Adams and Clay when the election of President was thrown into the House of Representatives. There was no doubt that he would be the favourite candidate at the coming election; for by his doctrinaire impartiality

---

[1] See *ante*, p. 486.　　　[2] See *ante*, p. 486.

Adams had managed to estrange even his friends. Jackson being a pronounced Southerner, the party of the South expected that the administration of a general so high in popular favour would not only abolish the protective tariffs, but would shape its general policy decisively in the interests of the southern States. Jackson's election, which followed with a crushing majority in 1828, did undoubtedly produce a radical change in the history of the United States; but in spite of this the champions of Southern rights did not, through him, realise the fulfilment of their ultimate expectations.

Jackson was a man of thoroughly honest and well-meaning character, and one who, as the South found to its cost, valued the welfare of the Union much higher than one might have expected after the eccentricities of his earlier career. It seemed true that his intellectual acquirements were not equal to the important task which the administration of the government imposed on him. The very fact that he entered the White House as the chosen of the masses was, in this sense, an omen of failure; for he was neither able to gauge the true motives of the bold demands made upon him by demagogic leaders, nor capable of holding himself aloof from them in a dignified manner. While showing himself too readily accessible to influences operating through irregular channels, he must also be blamed for having during his presidency given recognition to that fatal system under which a newly elected president might feel free to reward his faithful adherents with promotion to lucrative offices of state. But, on the whole, Jackson, in his administrative policy, allowed himself to be guided by that healthy common-sense which was so characteristically his own. The hatred with which he pursued the United States Bank, which he hampered in an autocratic fashion and finally overthrew, was undeniably short-sighted from the point of view of public finance, and led to a financial crisis in which business men sustained heavy losses. But the ideal which controlled him in this course of action was perfectly reasonable and justifiable in the views of Jackson and his associates; for, as then organised, the bank was charged with being little else than a support for some of the wild speculations and questionable enterprises which characterised the times.

In regard to the tariff question Jackson had cautiously refrained from interfering in any particularly incisive manner. Congress, in fact, continued the system of protective tariffs, in its main features, in the year 1832, although somewhat reducing certain especially unpopular duties in order to deprive the Opposition of its weapons of attack. Most of the southern States quietly accepted these facts, although they had without exception voted with the Opposition, or were satisfied with merely formal protests. In South Carolina, on the other hand, the anti-protectionist movement had begun to assume a more and more radical character. The constituent convention of the State finally declared explicitly that the tariff enactments of 1828 and 1832 were not binding within their territory, and fixed the 1st of February, 1833, as the date after which it would treat the tariff as abrogated unless Congress should before then remove the difficulty. Although Jackson, in the earlier stages of his career, had not taken too strict views as to the obedience due to the central authority, yet now, when placed at the head of the Union, he entertained no doubts as to the criminality of all resistance to its laws; and he, rough-and-ready soldier that he was, would have much preferred to overcome with the sword any such resistance. Nevertheless, in spite of the strength of his personal impulses, his course of action with reference to South Carolina proceeded in legal channels; for after that State had repeatedly rejected his advice and persisted in its illegal resolutions, his supporters introduced a bill into Congress by which the federal Executive was charged with the power and duty of providing, under certain circumstances, for carrying into effect the laws of the Union by force of arms.

It might, undoubtedly, have been fortunate for the future development of the United States if the conflict had at that time been thus decided. In spite of secret support in certain circles of Southerners, South Carolina at that time stood almost alone; and its cause was undoubtedly a bad one. No one could have been found more fitted for defending the national idea by force of arms than Jackson, who himself belonged to the party of the South and who enjoyed uncommon popularity. If South Carolina had at that time been forced into obedience, the conflict between National and State sovereignty might possibly have been decided as early as 1838, and the War of Secession would have been rendered less probable. But the National element and the Northerners had neither the courage nor the indiscretion to take up the gauntlet thrown down by South Carolina. The dispute was settled by an arrangement which left the real question at issue an open one, and therefore, though it secured an immediate victory, was considered by many as really a compromise of the authority of the Union. The basis on which an agreement was effected was a law in favour of a gradual, moderate reduction of the duties; this was first passed through Congress, so that South Carolina was enabled to withdraw its Nullification Ordinance, while the "Force Bill," which was passed nevertheless, was thus rendered aimless even before it became law.

Jackson, more conspicuously than the majority of his predecessors, during two terms of office (1829–1837), asserted his position at the head of affairs, though he was for a considerable time the last President who maintained himself as the really controlling force in national politics. Thus there appeared a marked tendency toward a presidential, as distinguished from a parliamentary, form of government. The regularly recurring change of the presidency, however, has operated to weaken the President and to harm the State, especially because almost all the Presidents, from Jackson's time, adopted his method of removing officials in order to appoint one's own adherents to the vacant posts. This system could not fail to exercise a most damaging effect upon the conscientiousness and honesty of civil servants; capacity for an office being measured, not by personal experience or fitness, but by the services which the individual might have rendered to his party or to the person of the President. Hence it tended to lead to the disappearance in official circles of the stable or conservative element. The commercial spirit, which from the beginning had attained considerable development in American life, seemed now about to invade also the governing classes; and thus by degrees large elements in the nation became habituated to have some regard for those principles according to which tangible success is the sole measure of all things.

In the eyes of professional politicians, however, these defects were amply balanced by the advantages which party organisation derived from general recognition of this political standard. The system had first been put into operation on an especially extensive scale in the State of New York, and under its influence not only had a distinct line of separation been drawn between different parties, but it had produced, always with a view to the immediate spoils accruing from a victory, a strict party discipline, in which every difference in the views of separate members or groups within the parties was made to give way unconditionally to the " platform " put up in the name of the whole party. Similar processes were next repeated on a far greater scale when this system of plunder and exploitation began to invade the administration of the federal government and produced that sharply marked party system by which the United States is still distinguished.

The great party in the country whose fame became historical was that of the Democrats. It embodied in the fullest sense the views of the founders of North American independence. The latter, indeed, had created the Constitution of 1787 merely as a preventive measure against the threatening tide of evils which had been the outcome of excessive decentralisation ; by its means they had endeavoured to solve the difficult problem of combining an effective central authority with the highest possible amount of unrestricted liberty. The Federalist party took its rise during the transactions connected with the drafting of the Constitution, and its importance, as a party, was largely temporary. Finding no support among the masses of the population, and being incapable of creating such support, it soon became disintegrated, its distinctive theory was adopted by its opponent, and after its apparently unpatriotic opposition to the War of 1812 it sank into insignificance. On the other hand the Republican party, later known as the Democratic-Republican and then as the Democratic party, arose by a quite natural process of evolution from the party of the Anti-federalists, whose principal demand — the unlimited sovereignty and the freest self-government of the separate States — it still recognised as a chief principle. The Democratic party was originally by no means the party representing the interests of the southern States, though men from the southern and central States certainly did, from the first, play a leading part in it. It was the abnormal preponderance of sectional influences, earlier discountenanced, which, in the second phase of the development of the Federalists, weakened permanently the power of that party, while the Democrats, representing a progressive, nationalist, and conservative policy, grew steadily in strength. It is true that, certainly as early as the insubordination of South Carolina,[1] that party, having completely overthrown its opponent, had become divided into two wings with quite widely divergent views. But the radical-democratic faction of extreme State-sovereignty principles, which gave the first proof of its strength during that conflict, formed at that time a minority of little importance. The vast majority of the Southern politicians repudiated its claims, not only from tactical reasons, because they believed that these claims endangered the continued adherence of the Northern section of their party, but also because they viewed them in the same light as did their Northern confederates, namely, as a departure from the genuine traditional dogma of their party.

In their capacity of champions of the interests of the separate States the Democrats were opposed to the high tariffs which, though largely in the interests of the commercial and industrial North, were cast upon the whole Union. They demonstrated, however, by the policy of their members who were elected to the

[1] See *ante*, p. 530.

presidency, that they were by no means unconditional free-traders, although free trade was as increasingly essential to the interests of the southern States as was protection to those of the North. They insisted only that the system of tariffs should remain subordinate to the administrative and fiscal needs of the Union. They demanded that whenever the surpluses derived from the duties began to accumulate (and this happened a number of times in the first half of the century), those duties which were essentially beneficial only to certain sections should be lowered to such a rate as would make their net return correspond to the actual needs of the United States.

The hostility of the Democrats to the United States Bank had its origin in a similar source. This bank, in the hands of their political opponents, was considered a dangerously demoralising force which was supposed by them to be operated solely in the interest of Northern speculators. It had actually only a short existence. The withdrawal of the government moneys from the national bank, and their distribution among a large number of local banking concerns organised under State laws, produced temporarily an unhealthy speculative fever which of necessity was followed by an extensive crash. Accordingly, under Jackson's successor, the bank was replaced by an independent treasury established as a branch of the federal government. By this significant measure the bank question was made a dead issue in party politics.

The opponents of the Democrats were at first thoroughly disorganised. All opposition disappeared in the collapse of the Federalist party,[1] and thereafter any possible opponents were long unable to form a platform which might have effected a reunion of the scattered elements. The interest in a strong central authority could no longer be used as a distinctive party programme, even in the North, and the question became so far immaterial that the new combination of politicians who appeared under the name of "Whigs" were willing, as had been the Democratic-Republicans earlier, to assign the furtherance of works of general public utility, such as canals and public roads, to the government of the Union and not to the separate States. In addition to this the protective tariff and contemporary financial questions formed points on which the new party was able to announce its attitude. It regarded as its principal task, however, merely the maintenance of an unconditional opposition to the Democrats, and it thus became substantially a party of negative opposition, with no positive programme. From this arose the introduction into electoral contests of vigorous discussions with reference to the personalities of candidates, and from it also arose a tendency to minimise the discussion and explanation of political principles. Such features of the political situation serve to make easily explicable the strong control secured and maintained by Jackson and his followers. Even at the end of his second term of office Jackson was still so high in the popular favour that his designation of a successor amounted almost to a nomination. By an overwhelming majority Martin Van Buren was elected to the presidency (1837–1841), — a northern Democrat from New York, where the organisation of the party and the comprehensive accomplishment of the policy of plunder were regarded as particularly his work; and he made good his assurance to continue in all respects the policy of his predecessor.

The inheritance which Van Buren now entered upon was by no means a wholly pleasant one. Jackson's financial policy had let loose a flood of wild specu-

---

[1] See *ante*, p. 482.

lation which directed its aims principally upon the still undeveloped treasures of the Far West. In the course of a few years many millions had been spent in the purchase of lands in the still unopened western Territories, and the value of these lands in a short time increased tenfold. In spite, however, of the marvellous expansion of the means of communication and the rapid growth of settlements,[1] years had to be spent upon the land before these imagined values could be realised by actual development, and these years had not entered into the calculations of those who were the last to find themselves loaded with mortgages. Accordingly, when the money scarcity from which Europe had been suffering affected sympathetically the United States also, these fictitious land values began to drop, and this, coupled with such administrative steps as the "Specie Circular," led to the general crash which dragged all enterprises, real and fictitious, down with it into the vortex of general financial confusion.

Now, although the government was almost, and Van Buren himself entirely, free from blame in these transactions, the popularity of the latter and the reputation of his party could not escape a decided shock. As early as 1837 there were signs that Van Buren would have little chance of securing a second period in the presidential office. Nor, indeed, did he secure this in spite of all the artifices of the administrative machine and the party organisation, both of which he, like no other, knew how to manipulate in his own interest. He did not, however, succumb because the platform of the Democratic party was rejected or because it was possible to bring out another giving promise of greater vitality. On the other hand it became at this time once more apparent how thoroughly the principles of the Democratic party coincided with those of almost the entire people; so that the election of 1840 was significant because of the conflict of personalities rather than because of any popular decision upon questions of public policy or political theory.

Even in the time of Jackson a small but active band of idealists had called into being a movement the final aim of which was the abolition of slavery. Its first steps on this road, to be sure, had been in no way precipitate. But the very appearance of a party which desired, even if from mere principle, to recognise the negro slaves as men and citizens with equal rights, aroused wide-spread regret and indignation, both in the South — where such chimæras were usually passed over with laughter — and in the North. The North, almost without exception at that time, shared in the aristocratic consciousness of the superiority of the white skin, — a consciousness which in the slave States caused even the most miserable to look down with contempt upon a black man. Among the rich merchants and shippers this feeling was stimulated by their personal and business relations with the large landed proprietors of the South, from whose industrial requirements the North to a large extent derived advantage. The central States were less bound by considerations of self-interest. There, too, slavery was legal according to the State laws, but the natural conditions were not especially favourable to slave labour. The population consisted mainly of small independent land-owners; and their neighbours, the adjoining "free" States, took care that this element should grow larger from year to year and exert a greater influence on the legislatures. But wherever slave labour was compelled to enter into direct competition with free

---

[1] See illustration opposite.

GROWTH OF SAN FRANCISCO: DEPICTED IN THREE STAGES

*Upper view:* As it appeared in November, 1848. *Middle view:* in 1858. *Lower view:* At the end of the nineteenth century. (The two upper views after old steel engravings, the lower drawn from a photograph by O. Schulz.)

labour, it was perceptible, even to the dullest comprehension, that it could not prevail against the latter for any length of time. Hence we find that only a small part of the population carried on the slave-trade in the true sense of the word. What the planters really engaged in more especially was the business of rearing negro slaves. Owing to hard labour and inconsiderate treatment, the naturally high rate of increase of the actual labouring population among the negro slaves had fallen very low. The general course of industrial development, however, was tending in such a direction as to make slave labour relatively less and less profitable, so that the slaveholders could acquire wealth and maintain their position only by constantly extending and enlarging their industries. For this purpose, however, they needed a constant supply of fresh slaves. The slave-trade with Africa having been almost suppressed by severe prohibitory laws, the idea arose of producing this urgently needed material in the country itself. Naturally the central States, in which slave labour did not yield sufficient profit, and which, moreover, were affected by the proximity of the industrial North, became the chief field of operations. Here an abolitionist movement at most could have effected only a change in the object of their commercial activity, but could not have destroyed the commerce itself. Hence, although the movement was watched with anxiety, no very serious fears about it were entertained.

But even in the North, amidst a population almost exclusively free, the movement met with nothing but bitter opposition. Here the advantages and disadvantages of the slave-trade were known only in name, but all the ire of true-born Americans was poured out upon those who proposed to make the despised negro, who was hardly considered a human being, a living member of a State whose Constitution all parties never tired of proclaiming as a sacred and inviolable possession. The mob, easily roused, made short work of those who dared to avow themselves Abolitionists; excesses occurred in different places, in which the lives and property of the opponents of slavery were threatened; but after a time the agitation of the extremists gradually subsided and its character became radically different.

In Congress affairs took a different turn, for there was in that body an overwhelming majority that would have nothing to do with the movement. It was by no means composed exclusively of parties having direct interests at stake, although the radical wing of this majority assumed, perhaps, the most uncompromising attitude toward the Abolitionists. The majority, moreover, was so large, and kept its ranks united for so long, partly because certain features of the Abolitionist movement were unquestionably opposed to the Constitution. In the latter, indeed, the word "slave" was not actually expressed, but by it all citizens of the Union were in clearly expressed terms guaranteed the enjoyment of the whole of their property, and that not only in the State in which such property might be situated, and where by the Constitution of such State it might be recognised, but unconditionally in all States of the Union. In so far, then, every State law which aimed at preventing a slave-owner from migrating with his slaves from one State to another was considered by the extremists as being in a strict sense a violation of the Constitution. This view found partial expression in the laws for the rendition of fugitive slaves which were established by the federal government and enforced upon the States. From this point of view, as well, the Abolitionist movement, however justified from a moral standpoint, was, in its opposition to the enforcement of the Fugitive Slave Law, directed against both the law and the Constitution.

Whatever help the Abolitionist movement received in Congress must be ascribed to John Quincy Adams, who was untiring in bringing before it petition after petition directed against slavery. On the other hand Congress endeavoured to resist this flood of petitions by measures which were branded with the name of "Gag Laws," and which brought their originators into moral discredit. Aside from the vital matter of the freedom of petition, the secondary cause for which Adams professed to be fighting was not ripe for solution, since it could be dealt with conclusively only by adding an amendment to the fundamental law of the land. The way in which Adams conducted his campaign served only to accentuate already existing differences instead of conciliating them, and to rob Congress of precious time which it required for other more urgent affairs.

Even before the middle of the century the entire development of the Union left no doubt that throughout the United States the days of slavery were numbered. In a large number of the States, without being proscribed by their Constitutions, the institution had nevertheless become quite extinct; in others, in spite of the extensive protection it enjoyed under the laws, it was undergoing a slow but steady decline; and even in those States whose whole industrial existence was dependent on it, it continued to occasion discussions which rendered even its most zealous defenders personally sensible of the shortcomings of the whole institution. Hence slavery seemed doomed in time to die out gradually and disappear. In the natural course of things the process of decay would, however, have been so slow that America would have groaned under the evils of slavery long after the rest of the world had shaken off its fetters. But the movement which in our century led to the abolition of slavery over the greater part of the earth's surface could not have failed, from the mere consideration of their own advantage, to influence the United States, even if the latter had not found the moral courage to rouse themselves for a decisive effort. From the manner, however, in which it was fought out, the struggle against slavery not only exemplifies the victory of a lofty ideal, but also affords a proof of how this ideal, through the admixture of political and material interests, had lost much of its original purity.

Throughout the whole struggle against slavery the southern States were acting on the defensive. They were in the position of defenders of a besieged fortress, who, however well provided for the moment with all the necessary material of war, were yet able to calculate with almost mathematical exactness the date on which they would have to surrender. Their natural shrewdness impelled them to make attacks and sorties in order to procure means for prolonging their resistance; but the ultimate defeat of their opponents lay entirely beyond their power. The northern States were able to carry on the struggle under the firm conviction that time, at all events, would finally bestow on them the victory. Meanwhile they not only steadily grew in strength internally, but they were constantly being joined by new allies, — the Territories, not yet admitted to the Union, which afterward grew into States. It was an open secret that even in the States and Territories in which slavery was still unrestricted it had found a dangerous competitor in free labour: the frontier farm life offered such ample opportunities for the development of the individual that slavery could hardly have achieved a complete victory in the newly constructed States. Sending settlers from the States which strictly protected slavery to the western Territories did not help matters, for there, under the favourable influence of the local conditions, a portion of them were led to adopt free labour; while it was beyond the powers of governments or magistracies to keep out free settlers. The matter, moreover, gained further importance from the fact that efforts continued to be generally made to maintain in the Senate an exact balance of the geographical divisions of the country, as a check upon the House of Representatives, in which the North retained a decided preponderance, by making the admission of a State belonging to one party always depend on the simultaneous inclusion of one belonging to the other side.

The slavery struggle acquired its peculiar complexion from the fact that during almost the whole time the agitation was carried on under the leadership of men who in some aspects were standing on the defensive. Those were not, however, always Southerners whom the Democratic party sent to Washington as Presidents. Nevertheless, northern Democrats could only hope to attain the highest office in the State by so adapting their democratic creed as to give no offence to the party of the South, which was possessed of a much stricter and more united organisation. First of all, indeed, Van Buren had managed affairs in a thoroughly sound manner. But toward the end of his term suggestion of irregularities was made so definite that the responsibility for such, coupled also with the administration's alleged responsibility for the financial collapse, made it impossible for the Democratic party to entertain any prospects of making one of its own men Van Buren's successor. The Whigs, however, were still far from being in a position to send to Washington anyone whom they could rightly reckon to belong to their party. Accordingly they put up for the presidency William Henry Harrison, an old general, politically almost unknown, and associated with him as Vice-President John Tyler, who, though no longer actually a member of the Democratic party, counted far more personal adherents and friends in that than among the Whigs. It was largely by this manoeuvre that the Whig party succeeded in getting its candidate elected by an overwhelming majority. But this apparent success was soon reduced to its true proportions. Harrison entered the White House only to succumb there to his last illness (April, 1841), whereupon Tyler apparently became reunited to those members of the Democratic party with whom he had all along remained in touch.

Under the pressure of financial conditions a majority both in the Senate and in the House of Representatives had in 1841 once more succeeded in passing a resolution in favour of the re-establishment of a United States Bank, which still formed an important item in the political programme of the Whig party. John Tyler, however, who was now President (1841–1845), vetoed both this proposal and a subsequent similar resolution of Congress; and by these acts effected what was looked upon as an open secession from the party which had raised him to office. On the whole, Tyler's presidency ran its course unattended by any special events. Diplomatic difficulties with England, financial measures intended to remove the evil consequences of the crash, and a gradual reconstruction of the *personnel* of the administration in favour of the Democrats, by whose aid Tyler had been elected to the presidency, filled up the time, while events of far greater importance were quietly but steadily approaching, though the time was not yet ripe for their appearance in energetic action.

When President Monroe sent his famous message to Congress, which until recently had been regarded as the guiding thread of the foreign policy of the

United States (though later a quite different interpretation was put upon it), the leading statesmen were of opinion that the territory of the United States had probably reached the extreme limits of its extension consistent with the republican form of government contemplated by the framers of the Federal Constitution. Two decades, however, sufficed completely to correct this view. It may have seemed justified as long as the vast basin of the Mississippi was still thinly peopled, and while the great roads and means of communication were still in their early development. Such doubts, however, as arose out of considerations of vast separation in space were soon set aside by the rapid utilisation — much furthered by the invention of the steamboat — of suitable waterways, such as the North American lake system furnishes in connection with the Hudson on the one side and the Ohio and the Missouri on the other; and toward the middle of the century by the construction of railways, which in America were taken up much sooner and more energetically than in the Old World. Even in the middle of the 'thirties the possession of a strip of coast on the Pacific was seen to be as indispensable to the prosperous development of the Union as the possession of the mouth of the Mississippi had once been considered. The wild speculation in the public lands of the West, which had conjured up such serious commercial dangers for the Union, had not only been far less fatal to the West, but at a time when it was a question of drawing some sort of profit from the less valuable titles to landed property, this speculation had actually had a stimulating and encouraging effect on the settlement of those sections. The far remote districts recovered rapidly from the effects of the crash, and their natural riches constantly attracted fresh emigrants to the borders of civilisation.

These events naturally reacted on the old States of the Union in such a manner as to make a further advancement of the western frontier desirable, and an extension of area came to be regarded as synonymous with national enrichment. The western frontier of the Union had never been definitely settled. In the Florida treaty[1] Spain had renounced her rights from ocean to ocean; this, however, was a paper claim to an indeterminate territory. The northwestern frontier was also under dispute with England, and at a time when no serious value was attached to the Far West the United States had by treaty agreed to a joint administration of Oregon by English and American officials. Hence the claims of the United States to the possession of an outlet toward the Pacific Ocean were up to that time still very questionable. For a long time, however, doubts had ceased to exist as to the manner in which they were to be improved.

The separation of the republic of Texas from Mexico[2] was to a large extent promoted by men from the United States, whose aim from the beginning had been the inclusion of these territories in the Union. The States of the Northeast were probably but little concerned about the matter, since they could not hope to derive any commercial advantages from this region. The South may have been influenced to some extent by the profit and political strength, unduly brought into the foreground, which might accrue from the acquisition of territories likely to become future slave States. But among the real influences toward this end were the populations of the young States of the West. Here, on soil reclaimed within the life of the Union, and which even in that brief space had undergone an astonishing

[1] See *ante*, p. 486.        [2] See *ante*, p. 520.

development, a party had come into existence under the watchword of "A Great America," which, though in the first instance confining its ambition to the mere acquisition of Texas, in the next place aimed at the possession of the whole country as far as the Pacific, and finally at the possible absorption of the whole of the decayed republic of Mexico even as far as Tehuantepec. From among the ranks of his party defenders had constantly arisen to protect the Texan government, completely powerless from constant want of money, against the attacks of the Mexicans; and their demands that the repeated applications of Texas for admission to the Union should at last be entertained, even at the risk of a war with Mexico, became the more urgent in proportion as the untenable conditions of this pseudo State threatened to make possible the interference of other Powers.

Texas, in its then unproductive condition, was not rich enough to furnish the means required by the government. At first the credit of the young State had been abused, and debts had been incurred recklessly in the hope that they would be covered by the reception of the country into the Union. This reception, however, was delayed, because Mexico refused either to acknowledge the independence of Texas or to sell the country. The Texans became tired of confining their petitions to the United States; they also applied to France and — so it is asserted, at least — to England. Thus there arose upon the political horizon of the Union the threatening spectre of a foreign power establishing itself in the Southwest and perhaps shutting them out from access to the Pacific. Even Tyler had made efforts to meet this danger by renewed negotiations with Mexico, which were conducted in a tone of so much provocation that the Young America party was daily hoping for an outbreak of hostilities. Tyler, however, could not summon either sufficient courage or the necessary rashness to attempt to force a declaration of war.

In the electoral contest of 1844 the Texas question was made one of the two great points at issue. To it, and to the plank in the platform on the Oregon question, James Knox Polk (1845–1849), a Democrat of little influence, owed his victory over Henry Clay, the Whig candidate, as well as over President Tyler. Clay had originally pronounced himself against the admission of Texas, but in the end offended the anti-annexationists by veering around, from electioneering motives, to a policy in favour of admission. Tyler, by his feeble policy on the Texas question, had completely forfeited his already slender chances of re-election. Nevertheless it was permitted him, during the last days of his term, virtually to carry into effect the admission of the neighbouring republic. Although the bill bearing on this matter had shortly before been rejected by the Senate, he now caused its reintroduction into Congress on the ground that the result of the presidential election of 1844 had shown that the majority of the people were in favour of annexation; a plea which so impressed the representatives that the bill was this time passed in both Houses. Tyler approved the joint resolution providing alternative methods of annexation during the last days of his official career, and in the following year Texas was received into the Union as the twenty-ninth State.[1]

This, however, settled only the relations between Texas and the United States. Mexico still considered the country as its own by right, and refused to enter into negotiations with the United States concerning it. But the federal government sent a division of troops to what was claimed as the western border of the new State,

---

[1] See the maps at page 514.

and thus attempted to solve the question whether the Rio Grande del Norte or the Nueces River formed the boundary by advancing its forces to the former. The first blood was shed in a surprise, by the Mexicans, of a troop of dragoons that had been cut off from the main body, and this was looked upon as tantamount to a declaration of war. Throughout the country few voices now ventured to protest against the general cry for vengeance against this provocation by the Mexicans.

At the seat of war in the north, General Zachary Taylor achieved a series of brilliant victories against the Mexicans in quick succession; and by the beginning of the year 1847 their resistance in the districts bordering on Texas was completely overcome. This was as yet, however, far from bringing matters to a decisive issue, for the American army was still some hundreds of miles away, and separated by immeasurable deserts from Mexico proper; and the losses suffered hitherto had made little impression. Polk was therefore obliged to determine on a more effectual move. It took the shape of an advance by General Winfield Scott from Vera Cruz upon the capital. Here, too, the Mexicans were unable to offer any serious resistance to the Americans. Vera Cruz capitulated in March, 1847, after a brief bombardment; and on each occasion that Santa Anna ventured to oppose the progress of the enemy's advance upon the city of Mexico he suffered heavy defeat. Nevertheless these very victories almost robbed the President of the possibility of gathering the harvest of his discredited policy. The vigorous onslaught of the American arms led to the collapse of Santa Anna's feebly supported dictatorship, and when the United States troops entered the capital they found no longer a government with which peace might be concluded. The victors, in fact, had to assist in establishing a government before they could attain their real object, the restoration of international relations between the United States and Mexico.

In the meanwhile, owing to circumstances, the prize to be won had been increased to an extraordinary degree. In addition to the army of Texas and the Vera Cruz division, a third army corps had been equipped for the purpose of invading California. This division had the most marvellous good fortune, for on entering the country it found its work half done. Captain John Charles Frémont had in 1844, during an exploring expedition, arrived on the borders of California; but he had so participated in politics that he had been expelled from Santa Fé. As soon, however, as war was declared, he returned, took possession of the town of Sonoma and there hoisted the flag of the Union. At the same time an American man-of-war touched at Monterey on the Bay of San Francisco, and there, too, met with so little serious resistance that its commander, with the assistance of the American residents, was able to take possession of this important place. The military occupation of California and New Mexico by the Union was thereupon announced, and in the face of this *fait accompli* the Mexican government had to strike its colours. In the treaty of peace the United States allowed the acquisition of the new provinces to take the form of a purchase; Mexico relinquishing these vast territories for an indemnity of fifteen million dollars, recognising Texas as belonging to the Union, and agreeing to acknowledge the Rio Grande as the western frontier of the United States.

In the meantime the Oregon question [1] had been settled by negotiation with England in an arrangement by which the forty-ninth degree of latitude was recog-

---

[1] See *ante*, p. 538.

ised as the boundary line between the possessions of the two countries. Thus the United States acquired in the Far West the frontiers which have remained ub tantially unchanged to the present day. The importance of this acquisition wa made at once apparent when, only a year afterward, the first discoveries of gold rere made in California.

In Congress the Mexican victories had a significant sequel. By what is nown as the Wilmot Proviso it was proposed that the grant of fifteen million ollars was to be made subject to the condition that slavery should be forbidden n all the newly acquired Territories. This proposal led to prolonged and em ittered discussions. Nor did its first defeat indicate the end of the struggle. It ras, in fact, the beginning of the struggle over congressional control of the Ter itories which was to become a conspicuous issue for the next decade. The nature f the soil of New Mexico and California almost excluded any industry in which lave labour would have yielded profitable results. Besides this, California apidly acquired a peculiar stamp of its own from the immigration, *en masse*, of he gold-diggers, who were almost without exception free labourers. Even in Texas, rhere slavery was considered as holding a legal status since the admission, it carcely managed to prolong its existence. The only significance attached to he proceedings in Congress lay in their affording evidence of the growing oppo ition to slavery, which was as much the outcome of the moral condemnation f the institution, aroused by the opponents of slavery, as of the recognition of ts disadvantages from an industrial standpoint. That in the end the majority, n this instance also, agreed to a decision apparently in favour of slavery, must gain be attributed to the feeling that repeated attacks on the institution itself night develop into broader and more serious controversy relative to the Constitu ion of the Union. From the course of the debates, however, the slaveholding ßouth could not fail to detect the remarkable growth of the dangers which threat ned its industrial particularism. Hence it is hardly to be wondered at that t this time there was revived in some quarters a discussion of the idea of a ecession from the Union in which the southern States considered themselves ustified according to extreme democratic principles, and of a closer union between hat group of States whose welfare was most intimately connected with the ontinued existence of slavery. For the time being, however, these ideas did not ead to actual results.

This state of affairs, moreover, was not without its effect on the presidential lection. Polk had paid too little respect to the Democrats to be able to enter ain hopes of re-election. The whole party was at the time in so disjointed a ondition that it had little hope of coming victorious out of the electoral cam aign; and its candidate, Cass, a Northerner, was not a sufficiently striking per onality to cover up the present weakness of the party. It was just in this espect, furthermore, that their opponents had been especially fortunate. Their can lidate, General Taylor, was of Southern origin, was himself a slave-owner, and had never taken a decided part as a politician, though he counted himself as belonging o the right wing of the Whig party. His campaign in Mexico,[1] moreover, had endered him popular; like Jackson and Harrison, he was a " people's " candidate. ßy their own exertions alone the Whigs would never have been able to procure

See *ante*, p. 540.

his election, for as a party they were weaker than ever. Their whole programme consisted in ranging on their side all those opponents of the Democrats who were unwilling either to throw in their lot with the enemies of slavery, who formed an insignificant minority, or to attach themselves to the so-called " Know-nothings," or American party. Both these groups were, in a sense, fragments of the dismembered Whig organisation; and the chief aim of the leaders was to devise a means of erecting a platform on which the discontented of all other parties might be able to fight by their side. It was necessary to put up a "ticket" which would also be conformable to such a collectivist policy after the election, and for this purpose the choice of Taylor and Fillmore was a decidedly skilful one.

The victory of these candidates signified the defeat of the Democrats without, however, implying a victory for the Whig principles. For the time being, politics were still exclusively centred upon the organisation of the newly acquired Territories, and the struggle carried on by slaveholders on behalf of their theory, even more than their real interests, was long and violent. Before it was brought to a close, President Taylor died (July 9, 1850). For the second time the place of a President chosen by the Whigs was occupied, before the completion of his official term, by a Vice-President who lacked even the small attachment which Harrison and Taylor had shown for the politicians who had prepared for them the road to the presidency. Millard Fillmore (1850–1853) did not, indeed, renounce the principles of the Whig party to the same extent as Tyler had done,[1] but in his advances toward the representatives of the South he went as far as he possibly could, in the hope of thereby rendering himself an acceptable candidate at the next election. Particularly did he co-operate, more or less directly, with Southerners, with Middle-State men like Clay, and with Northerners like Webster, in sanctioning the important Compromise of 1850, by which the principle of " squatter sovereignty " was applied to the Territories recently acquired, the slave trade in the District of Columbia was abolished, and the federal fugitive-slave law was re-enacted. By this arrangement it was supposed that slavery was made a dead issue, and this fiction was persistently maintained in the "finality" planks of the campaign of 1852. The effect of the Compromise, its relation to the Compromise of 1820, and the extent of the doctrine of "squatter sovereignty" were, however, to become the most engrossing problems of the decade, as soon as the introduction of the Kansas-Nebraska bill projected the whole subject of slavery once more into the sphere of congressional politics. Fillmore's term of office was almost entirely occupied by preparations for the approaching election; but his hopes were not realised. Some Whigs, indeed, entertained prospects of his re-election; but the nominating convention of the party gave preference to General Scott,[2] without succeeding, however, in making the latter a people's candidate. The Democrats, in imitating the electioneering tactics of the Whigs, were more fortunate, having nominated Franklin Pierce, a mere nonentity, and having tied him down to a platform which proposed nothing more than the dropping of all contested matters, to which so much time had been devoted during the last presidency, and which adhered to the Compromise of 1850 as an arrangement of the slavery question which was to be treated as a "finality." Such a programme was likely to find numerous adherents even outside the Democratic party. To the general wish of seeing these endless disputes

[1] See *ante*, p. 537.          [2] See *ante*, p. 540.

finally brought to an end, Pierce unquestionably owed a considerable part of the majority with which he achieved success in the electoral campaign of 1852.

It was by the very irony of fate that the first official acts of the President who had been especially chosen to settle internal strife happened to turn upon the very question which finally kindled the Civil War. By the admission of California as a non-slavery State the North had obtained a temporary preponderance. In order to balance this as speedily as possible, application was made for the creation of the two Territories, Kansas and Nebraska, in the hope of seeing at least one of them develop early into a slave State. The Territories in question, indeed, stretched northward far beyond the line of the Missouri Compromise (36° 30′), but the terms of the latter could no longer be legally maintained, it was now argued, inasmuch as, by the Compromise of 1850, it had been agreed to leave the question of slavery in certain Territories to be settled entirely by their own legislatures. Nevertheless, the Kansas-Nebraska question at one blow put an end to all peaceful sentiments. It aroused a cry of general indignation that in this wise slavery should be allowed to advance farther to the north. It was significant, too, that the movement in support of the Missouri Compromise was confined not only to Whigs and Abolitionists; a split became distinctly apparent in the very camp of the Democrats. A faction of Northern origin, opposed to slavery, began to develop, and a second larger one in which the Democrats of the slave States stood up as before for the "peculiar institution" of their section. The logical consequence implied in the national policy proved itself still stronger than the movement against slavery; the bill which provided for the organisation of Kansas and Nebraska became law, according to the spirit in which the Compromise of 1850 had been interpreted, without restrictions being made as to slavery. But the triumph of the slaveholders was only apparent. The bill inflicted a formidable blow to the cohesion of the Democratic party; and in the northern States it set on foot the movement which eliminated the feeble party of the Whigs from the ranks of political factors. Amid its ruins arose the Republican party. The latter now came forward with youthful vigour as the supporter of an idea which, owing to contemporary events, forcibly aroused the attention of all classes of the people. In the northern States several attempts had been made at infusing fresh vigour into the life of political parties; but neither the Abolitionists nor the American party[1] had succeeded in calling forth any deep or lasting emotion in party life. The impossibility of reconciling their aims with the fundamental principles of the Constitution made impossible for the Abolitionists a general political ascendency. The conviction as to the harmful nature of slavery and the desire to strive for its abolition were indeed steadily gaining ground in wider and wider circles of the American population; but they were not prepared to accept the platform of the Abolitionist party, which, owing to some obviously illegal proceedings, lost much in the general esteem.

The American party for a short time gained largely in numbers, owing especially to the attraction which the secret element in its organisation exercised upon the masses. Its platform, however, the most essential item of which consisted of a demand for rendering the acquisition of the rights of citizenship more difficult for new immigrants, met with a cold reception from the general public. It was especially directed against those immigrants who were coming to America as

[1] See *ante*, p. 542.

the forerunners of that large swarm of political malcontents who were seeking an asylum from administrative harshness, civil inequalities, and even famine. These, it is true, were by no means a wholly desirable addition to the population. They were, almost without exception, in a lower stage of educational training, and their moral and ethical development was deficient. The fact that these immigrants almost invariably attached themselves to the side of the Democrats did not cause them to be regarded with much favour by anti-Democratic politicians; and naturally, for the same reason, the Democratic majority was opposed to the enactment of such an immigration law as was desired by the American party. In this latter particular the Democrats were also supported by the Whigs, especially as the character of alien immigration had undergone considerable change in consequence of the revolutions which about the middle of the nineteenth century convulsed the Old World. The entrance of the foreigners into political life marks a point at which the development of party politics assumed fresh vigor. These men, especially those who came over after 1848, could under no conditions become adherents of the Democratic party. Those who in their old home had fought and suffered for the universal rights of men, as handed down in the formula of the French Revolution, could not possibly attach themselves to a party which through force of circumstances was compelled to give increasing prominence in its political programme to the maintenance of slavery. Though in theory they were thus largely Abolitionists, they were too little acquainted with the actual political conditions of the Union to join the Abolitionist party in large numbers. Still less, however, was there a place for them in the party of the " Know-nothings," which desired to close to their countrymen an asylum so much longed for and so much appreciated.

Amid such influences new life was infused into the ranks of those who once composed the Whig party. However much the foreigners may have imparted that leaven which by its fermentation produced the Republican party, they had nothing whatever to do with the formation of that party. The men who beheld with grief and anxiety the disintegration of the anti-Democratic organisation had already made several attempts to bring together all the vital tendencies of the day in such a manner as to engage the concerted efforts of a great and vigorous party. In its incipient stages the formation of the Republican organisation was nothing more than the renewed attempt of the more intelligent politicians of Whig leanings to found their platform upon an idea which might awaken their party, endow it with greater strength, and help it toward final victory.[1] In different places attempts of this kind were made simultaneously under different names; but even in the early day the name " Republicans " came into prominence. The basis of their platform was of course formed by the slavery question ; but they did not propose to seek for its solution in the radical manner of the Abolitionists. The new party adopted a thoroughly conservative view ; but while declaring that the rights of Man, as ideally expressed in the Declaration of Independence, should be placed above the letter and spirit of the federal Constitution, they demanded that the Union should no longer lend a hand in enacting laws, which were designed for the benefit of all, in the interests of a portion of the citizens. The greater part of the platform was devoted to the elaboration of this idea. The party, however, at the same time pro-

---

[1] See *ante*, p. 542.

claimed itself the inheritor of the Whig traditions by impressing upon the federal government the assumption of all internal improvements, more especially the construction of a transcontinental railway,—tasks similar to those which had been assigned to the federal government by the Whigs, and before that by the Federalists.[1]

At the presidential election which had resulted in the elevation of Pierce the Republican party, as such, had scarcely come into life, and it figured in no way as a national factor. It gained considerable strength, however, owing to the events which happened during the succeeding four years (1853–1857)[2] and more especially owing to the affairs of Kansas. The proposal to make the introduction or rejection of slavery in that Territory dependent on the decision of its inhabitants led to a contention between the friends and opponents of slavery, which, though at first conducted on constitutional lines, soon degenerated into an open struggle which set all law at defiance. Societies were formed in different States of the North for the purpose of organising methods for effecting the settlement of Kansas by free farmers, and their efforts had a decided success. Partly owing to the great immigration from Europe there was no lack of men who were quite prepared to undertake in the Far West their share of the struggle against wild nature and the Southern foe. Now it seemed beyond all doubt that in communities where free settlers had once opened up the soil, slaveholders would in vain attempt to gain a foothold. A settlement of this kind could not, however, be effected by leaps and bounds, nor could it occupy the whole Territory in one single rush. The journey to Kansas from the States of the East was long, troublesome, and expensive, and the means of the colonisation societies were as yet very limited.

For the slaveholders the position of affairs was much more favourable. The inhabited portion of the lands by which Kansas was bordered was almost entirely occupied by slaveholding States, and the people of Missouri who entered the Territory in especially large numbers were thus enabled to keep in continuous touch with their friends on the other side of the border, and could, if necessary, call in their help. Accordingly, when the governor of the Territory issued the writ for the election of a legislative assembly, the people from the adjacent southern districts poured in, and by participation in the voting, falsification of votes, and the use of violence against their opponents, brought about an election which every one knew did not in the least represent the real condition of affairs. The federal government, however, not only confirmed the election of the chosen candidates, but actually allowed the latter to draw up a Constitution for the Territory which was formed entirely in the interests of the slaveholders and with the object of suppressing their opponents. Indeed, the federal government actually went so far as to place federal troops at the service of the pro-slavery administration, although in the mean time the free settlers, too, had demonstrated, by means of a free popular vote, the presence of an anti-slavery population at least as strong as their opponents, and had organised by electing a legislative body and proclaiming a Constitution. Under such conditions a permanent peace became impossible. The first blood was shed probably by the slavery party; but their opponents also soon resorted to reckless violence. Thus, four years before Lincoln's election, a civil

---

[1] See *ante*, p. 533.　　　[2] See *ante*, p. 541.

war turning on the question of the permission or prohibition of slavery was raging in the heart of the Union.

The federal government seemed openly to sympathise with the slaveholders. The Democratic party, as such, was forced to do so according to its principles and its past history. Even the northern wing of the party, which, under the leadership of Douglas, did not indeed contend for the maintenance of slavery, but for the extreme consequences of the right of self-government of the separate States and Territories, was, nevertheless, by recognising the validity of the first elections in Kansas, logically bound to support the policy of the President. But even in the Democratic camp no one any longer failed to see that the discipline of the party in Congress could in future be maintained only with difficulty; that the reputation of the party among the people had been severely shaken; and that by its policy in the Kansas questions it had placed a formidable weapon in the hands of its opponents. This was made plain to all who could see, by the next presidential election. This, it is true, once more resulted in the victory of the Democratic candidate, James Buchanan (1857–1861), an old man of seventy-one years who had spent a long time as ambassador in England, completely removed from political struggles. But of the 4,000,000 votes returned, only 1,800,000 had been recorded for him; and he was elected only because it was still found impossible to gather all the anti-Democrats into one fold. The old Whigs and the Know-nothings had again nominated Fillmore; and though this name clearly enough proclaimed the feeble condition and want of principle of the party, his candidature nevertheless served to withdraw some hundreds of thousands of votes from the third party and thus to put it in a minority. In spite of this the election contest was of far-reaching importance to the Republicans, and through it they took a considerable step forward on the road to victory. Even during the negotiations for the nomination of a candidate an agreement had been effected between the old group of the Free-Soilers, the Abolitionist Know-nothings, and the true Republicans. The selection of Frémont, the discoverer of the Far West and the conqueror of California, as a candidate for the presidency, seemed a very fortunate move. He embodied the ideas of the Young American party, which would have nothing to do with the old struggle between the defenders of State rights and the nationalists, but which had inscribed on its banners the greatness of their common country in a free Republican development. The Republicans this time remained faithful to the old conservative spirit, not, however, in the sense of a retrogressive stagnation; but in that of a steadily progressive development advancing in definite legal channels toward the highest ends. With his 1,300,000 votes Frémont had so nearly approached the goal of victory that not only his adherents, but also his opponents, looked upon the success of the Republicans at the next election as certain.

This prospect loomed like a spectre upon the southern Democrats. Hitherto the only way in which their opponents had attained or had hoped to attain a victory had been by putting up a candidate to whom even a Democrat might still be able to give his vote. Now, however, for the first time, the Republicans had put up against them a man in whose programme not a spark of Democratic principle was to be discovered, and one who uncompromisingly placed the Union above the States, and the spirit of the Declaration of Independence on an equality with that of the Constitution. It was only by a mere chance that this programme had failed to secure the victory, and, even before the result of the election was known, the slave States recognised that this was the beginning of the end. As had happened earlier, a conference of the southern States was once more summoned, but it was poorly attended and insignificant in results. Nevertheless the slave States fully realised the seriousness of the situation. In the South the industrial contrast between free and slave States which rendered any community of interests impossible had been recognised much earlier and more distinctly than in the North. In times more remote it may not have been so easily perceived how the South, in such a struggle, was far less favourably placed than the North, but the events of the last few years and their thorough and business-like discussion had opened the eyes of the slaveholders on this point. They could not fail to notice what a difference was observable in the relative increase of population in the two sections of the Union, and how the wealth of the North was increasing in a proportion totally different from that of the South. Finally, they must have come to appreciate the reason why the value of land was so essentially different on the opposite sides of the border of a slave State. In Kansas and many other border districts they had learned from personal experience how much superior free labour was to the "peculiar institution" of the South; for of the settlers whom they sent to these districts at their common expense for the purpose of opposing free labour, not a few went over into the enemy's camp. If only at one and the same stroke they could have abolished slavery and possessed themselves of the industrial conditions of the North! As things were, however, the abolition of slavery meant nothing less than the ruin of the slaveholders and the bankruptcy of all the propertied classes of the South. It was not their haughtiness as slaveholders which so often, inside and outside of Congress, provoked the Southerners to words and acts unworthy of a highly civilised nation; it was rather the feeling of their own impotence, the certainty of being ruined men as soon as the federal government should be used to put the ban upon the system of slavery. It was such feelings which impelled the firebrands of the South to more and more exorbitant demands, and spurred them on to increasingly bitter struggles. In reality, the policy adopted by the government, which has often been criticised as displaying an unworthy desire to please the slaveholders, arose from a desire to mollify to some extent, by favourable enactments, the industrial disadvantages from which the southern half of the Union was suffering. It was the same desire which prompted so large a section of the Northern politicians to feel kindly disposed toward the Southerners.

On the other hand, if the majority of the people should renounce these sentiments (and the voting at the presidential election had shown that this was the case), and if they should succeed in filling the administration with men of similar opinions, the only natural result would be the commercial and political bankruptcy of the South. Its only choice then would be to break with its past, to secede from the Union, and to form a confederation of States whose interests rested on the common foundation of slave labour. Such a Confederacy, however, would have become rapidly impoverished, and must have succumbed in the competition with its neighbour States, unless, indeed, an internal revolution had forced it to change its system. For the moment, however, the slaveholders indulged the hope that by these means they might save their property and delay its inevitable overthrow. To the men of the South their method of proceeding did not appear revolutionary.   The doctrine of State rights had led many politicians, particularly in the South, to regard the Union merely as a compact between the States which the contracting parties were entitled to rescind.   South Carolina had already openly expressed a similar view in its conflict with Jackson;[1] but its procedure at that time had been considered by many as incorrect and illegal, even though the government on that occasion had preferred to attain its end by means of what some chose to call a compromise.   Of course in the meantime the feeling of an indissoluble connection had gained considerable strength among wide-spread classes of the population, and the secessionist longings of individual southern States only aroused in some sections a feeling in favour of Union.   Nevertheless there were those in the Northeast, where the contrast of interests with the South was sharpest, who began to regard the separation of industrially dissimilar groups as being as much of an advantage as did the Southerners themselves, and to draw conclusions from the doctrine of State rights, according to which a peaceful dissolution of the Union appeared the most desirable way out of the difficulty.

President Buchanan first of all made efforts to postpone this question, in the hope that such a course might bring counsel and deliverance.   From his predecessor he had received other problems the solution of which might be supposed to claim general interest, and he was in hopes that by taking such matters in hand he might turn the current of politics into another channel. For a long time past the island of Cuba had been one of those territories whose acquisition by the United States had been particularly desired by many.   Its geographical position of necessity brought it in many ways into contact with the United States, and the weakness of Spanish rule in the island made its eventual sale appear by no means impossible.   In such an event, however, it was of vital importance to the United States that the island should not fall into the hands of a Power which understood better how to utilise the industrial resources of the island in competition with their own products.   Whether Buchanan really did entertain higher expectations from the future must be left undecided; at any rate he now made use of this question for the purpose of diverting attention from internal affairs, and he attained his object,—in so far, at least, as his proposition to place thirty millions of dollars for this purpose at the disposal of the government for some time occupied the attention of the Senate and imparted a different character to the debates.   The Mormon difficulty was employed for a similar purpose.   Pierce had already called out the federal troops against the Mormons, in order to force the submission of Brigham Young's theocratic régime to the federal laws; and Buchanan had to carry through Congress the acceptance of the agreement by which matters were settled, at least apparently, in a satisfactory manner.   Nevertheless Buchanan did not succeed by these diversions in appeasing the internal feud.   The slavery question kept knocking louder and louder at the doors of Congress, which was neither able nor willing to refuse it admittance.

In Kansas parties were still facing each other for the fight.   The party of the slaveholders had once more, by means of the most shameless electoral frauds, pretended to be alone empowered to speak for the Territory, and at Lecompton had drawn up a Constitution on the basis of which Kansas applied for admission

---

[1] See ante, p. 529.

as a State. But although the Free State party discovered the fraud, and on their side, with the so-called Topeka Constitution, which prohibited slavery, made a similar application to Congress, Buchanan favoured the Lecompton Constitution and also got the Senate to accept it. But the House of Representatives could not be won over by straightforward means; a majority was, indeed, finally obtained by parliamentary manœuvres, but only after it had been agreed to submit once more the question of the Constitution to the vote of the people. On this occasion, however, the slaveholders' party was completely defeated. The consequence was that Kansas had to wait several years longer before it was admitted as a State; but it had already rendered an important service to the cause of liberty.

It had already been for some time a matter of considerable difficulty to hold to the policy of the majority those northern Democrats who at that time were led by Stephen Arnold Douglas. The question of the Constitution of Kansas served to effect their complete separation. The Democratic party defended in principle the right of self-government of the States. Douglas followed out the consequences of this policy in so far as he voted for submitting the Lecompton Constitution to the popular vote. It was, however, well known in Congress that Douglas's demand would seriously call in question the recognition of slavery in Kansas, and the Democrats of the South accordingly looked upon his action as a secession from the party and used every effort to make the split irremediable. They thus probably hoped merely to expel the unreliable elements from the party, and thereby consolidate it. But unfortunately, with the disruption of the Democratic party, the connection between North and South was again torn asunder, and the unavoidable conflict of interests was again recognised in a new sphere. Thus was typified the greater fact that the country, in entering upon the campaign of the next presidential election, was divided into two opposite and completely separated groups of States.

On this occasion the Democratic party, as already stated, was no longer united. Its first convention at Charleston adjourned without arriving at a nomination. Later, the Northern wing of the party nominated Douglas as its candidate, while the Southern delegates put up John C. Breckenridge. The Constitutional Union party nominated Bell. The Republicans held their convention in the Western city of Chicago, and here a Western candidate, Abraham Lincoln, was nominated for the presidency. Lincoln was a self-made man who had become known only in recent years through a contest which in 1858 he fought with Douglas for a seat in the United States Senate. His calm circumspection, his humour, and his readiness as a debater had already made him one of the foremost politicians of the young party. Moreover, his many qualities characteristic of a " man of the people " made him a candidate more desirable than the more dignified parliamentarians.

The voting was even less decisive than at Buchanan's election. Though Lincoln, on the 6th of November, 1860, received a majority of electoral votes, by which he was legally elected to the presidency, he fell short of a majority of popular votes by more than twice as many votes as did his predecessor. The significant feature of the election, however, was that its result was due entirely to the enormous numerical preponderance of the North. In the South Lincoln had not been presented as a candidate at all, and even in the border States he had obtained only a few thousand votes. He was therefore in reality nothing more than the chosen candidate of a section, and this was at once turned to account by the opposition.

South Carolina, then as much as ever the leader of the extremists, responded to the election with an ordinance of secession from the Union. At first she stood alone in taking this step. Soon afterward, however, a convention of several southern States was held at Montgomery, for the purpose of deciding upon some common course of action whereby the interests of the South might be safeguarded against a Northern President. It was in vain that Virginia summoned a convention for the purpose of bringing about a reconciliation; the most she could effect in that direction was to suggest a moderate course of action for the central States and to take measures for preventing a further spread of the secession movement. That it would be impossible to win back the southern States by negotiation was not only expressed emphatically by the latter, but was also clearly perceived by some in the North.

Buchanan considered it his duty, during the last months of his period of office, to preserve a passive attitude. He who, as a Democrat, had early defended the principle of State rights from conviction, found no difficulty in acknowledging the claim of the South to the right of secession. But he was destined, before leaving the scene, to execute another complete political *volte-face*. The February convention of the southern States at Montgomery had for its immediate consequence the formation of a separate confederacy which elected Jefferson Davis as its President and claimed the rights of an independent State. Buchanan felt disposed to acknowledge this claim. Indeed, the idea of allowing the apostate States to withdraw peacefully from the Union was so widespread among the Democrats of the northeastern States that the South was already led to entertain hopes of such an issue. The secession, however, had caused the retirement of some of the Ministers from Buchanan's Cabinet; and the men who stepped into their places were not only themselves resolved to maintain the integrity of the Union, but they also managed to convince the President of the necessity of such a policy. The latter, therefore, suddenly refused any further negotiations with the Confederacy, and though he could not be induced to adopt an active policy against the latter, his temporary advisers managed at least to prevent his yielding another step.

It was under such conditions that Lincoln entered upon office on the 4th of March, 1861. His inaugural address was entirely animated by that conservative spirit on which the Republican party had built up its platform; but he declared as his first principle the preservation of the Union and the enforcement of all its laws. He expressly guarded against giving utterance to abolitionist longings, which, indeed, then seemed contrary to his personal inclinations; but he held the southern States so much the more responsible if by their proceedings they should stir up a civil war. It soon became evident that these were not mere empty words. A deputation which desired to treat with the federal government in the name of the Confederate States was refused formal audience by the Secretary of State on the ground that the government did not recognise the existence of an independent republic of the Confederate States. In other respects, however, he preserved a temporising attitude until events forced him to adopt another policy.

The Secessionists had already demanded from Buchanan the delivery into their hands of all federal property in the Confederate States, but more especially the forts of Charleston; and though they had met with a formal refusal they had nevertheless practically succeeded in attaining their object. The Charleston forts were so feebly garrisoned that their commandant, Major Anderson, declared it impossible to defend them against even the slightest attack. But as the government did not promptly send him reinforcements he retired to Fort Sumter, built on an island and thus capable of being most easily defended, while the enemy occupied the other forts. Already in the beginning of January, 1861, shots had been exchanged here. On one occasion, when a Federal steamer endeavoured to convey supplies to Anderson, she had been obliged by the shore batteries to return without having effected her object, leaving Anderson to his fate. Nevertheless it was not until the 12th of April that the South Carolina troops found courage to direct their fire on Fort Sumter, which after a two days' bombardment was obliged to capitulate.

The South considered it a great victory when the Federal flag was hauled down from the last fort on its Atlantic coast line. But it was considerably mistaken in its calculations. As long as the Secessionists had sought severance from the Union by peaceful methods, the Federal government had to reckon with the fact that a powerful party in its northern dominion was disposed to agree with this demand, and was certainly not prepared to take up arms for the sake of upholding the Union. When, however, the South had shed the first blood, a storm of indignation arose in the whole North, and the people demanded that the sword should not be sheathed until the South had been brought back to obedience to the laws. This fighting ardour, turned to good account by the call for volunteers, placed in the hands of the government the means of extricating itself from the awkward position in which Lincoln's hesitation, as opposed to the resolute measures of the Southerners, had placed it.

Until now only eleven States had joined the Confederacy. Among the border States, however, several were undecided; the side they would finally take would depend, in all probability, on the issue of the first engagements. Virginia was at first among the waverers; but her importance to the southern States was so considerable that the Congress of the South used every effort to win her over to its cause. It was essentially on this account that Richmond, on the James River,[1] was chosen as the capital of the Confederacy, although it was situated not far from the border and was exposed to the attack of the enemy.

The situation of the national government at the beginning of the Civil War was somewhat critical. The Federal troops, in themselves inconsiderable, were in a state approaching disorganisation. The Secretary of War, before he resigned, had intentionally placed a portion of the war-material in the hands of the southerners, and the rest seemed to have been dissipated. A large number of the officers had left the Federal army and had taken service with the South. Even the numerical superiority of the North was at first of no weight. So completely had people in the free States mistaken the character of the impending struggle that some at first believed it would be settled by means of regular soldiers and the militia, while many citizens persisted in their national repugnance to everything military and went about their ordinary business.

The danger threatened most immediately the Federal capital. The neighbouring States of Maryland and Delaware were slave States and largely in sympathy with the South. Though the loss of Washington would have been of little military importance. its moral effect would have been more serious inasmuch as

---

[1] See maps at p. 514.

in the northern States the war party had, as a matter of fact, only an uncertain control. Fortunately it was possible to prevent such a catastrophe, for the militia regiments which had been rapidly summoned arrived in the capital in time. When Maryland prepared to offer armed resistance to the transportation of further reinforcements, its capital, Baltimore, was occupied by the Federal troops, and the pro-Secessionist government was replaced by one favourably disposed to the Union. This was the first blow received by the Secession, preventing once for all the attachment of the States of Maryland and Delaware to their cause.

In the West things were assuming a similar shape. Here, also, the Confederacy had reckoned on winning over to its side such slaveholding central States as Kentucky, Missouri, and Kansas. It was the more justified in this hope, since almost throughout the region the government was in the hands of Democratic majorities; but in spite of this they were nowhere successful. The western counties of Virginia adhered to the Union; and in Kentucky the firmness of the Federal officials prevented any false step on the part of the local government; and though Missouri could not, in its entirety, be preserved to the Union, it was nevertheless prevented from formally going over to the Secessionists. Beyond the Mississippi, in fact, even the Democrats were good Unionists, and with the exception of the Gulf States of Louisiana, Arkansas, and Texas, the whole of this division of the country remained faithful to the Union. Here indeed the conservative Unionist idea had become firmly rooted. The inhabitants of these regions had lived under the Union laws from the time of their first settling, and had always supported a Great-American policy, and were by no means inclined to allow the will of discontented citizens to determine whether the State was to continue a united whole, rich in future possibilities, or was to be divided into separate halves, each impeding and restraining the other's development. In the West the Union idea flourished; and from the Western territory began that succession of victories which, coupled with the parallel campaigns in the East, led to the final overthrow of the Confederacy.

The first attack by the North had a lamentable result. An army of 60,000 men under McDowell advanced into Virginia, and, falling in with the enemy at Bull Run, was disastrously defeated and retreated in a state of panic to Washington (July 21, 1861). In the East the struggle thereafter for years consisted in backward and forward movements of mighty armies between the two capitals of Richmond and Washington, which were only about a hundred miles distant from each other. Numerous battles were fought, lasting sometimes for days, in which the losses on both sides reached uncommonly high figures. And yet neither side was able to win any permanent success. The operations, as a rule, ended fatally to the attacking party, without, however, providing the defenders with an opportunity of pushing matters to a decisive issue. In generalship the South was undoubtedly superior. The leadership of a Joseph Eccleston Johnston and of a Robert Edward Lee, the wonderful expeditions of Thomas Jonathan (otherwise known as "Stonewall") Jackson and of his so-called "footcavalry," far exceeded the performances of the North. But even these leaders were unable to organise a plan of campaign laid out on an extensive scale and conducted with energy. No doubt they had to struggle with special difficulties. Inasmuch as the South, even during the first phase of the war, had been shut out from the sea, it was compelled to confine its operations exclusively to the land.

As long as the scene of these operations lay between Richmond and Washington, the Confederate troops enjoyed the advantage of having the population on their side. Nevertheless, for their commissariat, and in many cases, too, — owing to the almost entire absence of roads in the European sense of the word, — for their transport, the large army divisions were obliged to keep close to such few railway lines as were then in existence. This dependence naturally increased the difficulty of advancing for considerable distances, though indeed no advantage could have been derived from such movements in the conditions under which the war was being conducted. The events of the first year of the war had shown that Washington was secure from occupation by the South as long as the power of the Union remained permanently unshaken. But apart from the Federal capital the army of Richmond seemed to have no serious object of attack. The capture of the commercial and industrial towns of the Northeast would indeed have been a highly desirable prize; but to advance on them by land, with the centre of the enemy's force in the rear, was a task to which the armies of the South were not equal. True, they might succeed in temporarily subjecting to Southern sway some more or less extensive portions of the central States; or they might, by successful raids, ravage and alarm the neighbouring northern States of Pennsylvania or West Virginia; but neither of these moves could appreciably affect the result of the war. Indeed, General Lee twice made the attempt, but without any success whatever. Such operations could only have had a decisive effect if corresponding successes had been obtained simultaneously in the other theatres of war.

The principal obstacle to the success of the North was the want of good leaders. True, in the first two years of the war the troops themselves were so poor in quality that even better generals could not have achieved victories with them. This, however, no longer applied in the later years of the war, when bodies of tried and picked men and officers had become available among the volunteer regiments. But the hesitating tactics of such men as George Brinton McClellan and the dogged resolution and indomitable courage of Ulysses Simpson Grant fell far short of the skill and ability of their Southern antagonists. The North, however, enjoyed the advantage of free access to the sea, and McClellan endeavoured to make this the base of his campaign; but the attempt proved unsuccessful and was not repeated at the seat of war in Virginia.

In addition to this the power of the North, especially during the first years of the war, was weakened by political considerations. Lincoln refused to regard the rebels as other than fellow countrymen who had strayed from the right path. He was unwilling to fight with the Confederate States, whose existence he did not recognise, but was only endeavouring to bring those to submission who were in arms against the Union. In spite of this consideration, however, he was by no means successful in maintaining among his followers of the North that solid cohesion which on the side of the South was the natural outcome of events. In the East, in particular, and in a less degree also at the other theatres of war, the first two years of hostilities, while involving nothing but sacrifices, had produced no visible results. Instigated by Southern agents, the party of those who were in favour of allowing the South to secede peacefully from the Union now began to lift up its head in a manner which threatened danger. A time arrived when the Democrats in the East obtained ominous majorities and in some cases got possession of the State governments; and in New York the mob rose up against the "infamous" draft, and a resolution was actually brought forward in Congress calling on the President to commence negotiations with the government of the Confederate States for the purpose of putting an end to the quarrel. Lincoln's position was indeed one of the utmost difficulty. It would have been almost untenable had not the Middle West remained firm to the Unionist programme of the Republican party, and had not the governments of the western States, which at the outbreak of the war were still partially in the hands of the Democrats, been succeeded by others of Unionist principles.

In the East the danger would have been immeasurably greater had it not been that there, too, the war gained adherents. The South had obtained a temporary superiority owing to the fact that before Lincoln's accession to office it had acquired possession of very much of the war-material of the Union.[1] However, owing to the limited amount of human material it had at its disposal, it was incapable, at least during the years of the war, of establishing an industrial independence, and its position in consequence could not fail to become more and more unfavourable. This fact in itself served to stimulate the North toward exerting itself to the utmost of its powers, and provided the northeastern States with an opportunity of immensely improving their industries and of employing their activities in an exceedingly profitable manner. The factories engaged in the manufacture of ammunition, military outfits, articles of clothing, etc., were suddenly overwhelmed with orders, and naturally obtained most favourable contracts. The shipping industry, which had at all times given employment to thousands of hands on the North Atlantic coast, was especially benefited by these conditions. The few frigates and revenue-cutters which constituted the United States navy had before the war been ordered partly to Southern and partly to far-distant foreign ports, so that in this respect also the Union was rendered virtually powerless. The Unionists, however, fully realised that the only way of preventing constant accessions of fresh power to the South was by shutting it out from the sea.

In Washington it was well known what importance the Secessionists attached to this matter. They felt assured that, being unable to do without the cotton supplies of the South, the European Powers, and especially England, would, in the event of the North gaining the upper hand, at once hasten to their assistance. In the South cotton, as a matter of fact, was king. It formed the wealth of the large landowners; for its sake it was necessary to uphold slavery even at the risk of a serious war; with it the costs of that war were to be defrayed; and for its sake, too, the South hoped to obtain the recognition if not the support of Europe. Nor were they at all wrong in the last of these calculations. Napoleon III felt drawn to the side of the Confederates more from a feeling of selfish jealousy of the United States than from any other interests, but in the case of England a similar leaning was due largely to industrial conditions. Not only was that country annoyed at the interruption of its import trade and the consequent shutting down of mills and factories, but the fear that the industry of the North might appropriate the staple in such a manner as to drive English competition out of the field for ever helped to induce the British government to adopt an attitude toward the Confederacy which in the end obliged the United States ambassador practically to threaten the rupture of diplomatic relations, and thereby to cause the withdrawal of the protection which the privateers of the South had received from

---

[1] See *ante*, p. 550.

the English,—a feature brought conspicuously to light during the protracted dealings with reference to the "Alabama."

With an energy which compels our admiration the North set to work to organise a navy which should be equal to the great task before it; and by the end of 1862 the blockade of the southern ports began to have a telling effect. A few vessels, it is true, commanded by daring seamen, managed, even down to the end of the war, to run the blockade either undetected or without sustaining any serious damage. The lucky parties thereby earned large sums of money; but with a few shiploads they were able neither to exercise any appreciable influence on the European demand for cotton, nor, by their occasional and insufficient importations, to keep up the war supplies of the South. Thus, although the naval war exercised a direct influence on the struggle, it was not able of itself to determine the issue.

The decisive stroke came from the West. The formation of the Confederacy had once more placed the western States in a position similar to that which they held before the cession of Louisiana. Even at that time the free navigation of the Mississippi down to the Gulf of Mexico had been recognised as indispensable to the prosperity of the inland States of the continent. Still more was this now the case, when, in place of isolated forts and trading-stations, between which the Indian roamed, flourishing towns and villages had arisen, while sturdy farmers had converted thousands of square miles of virgin soil into rich arable land. As yet only a few railways connected the Father of Waters with the provinces of the East; and the project of a railway to the Pacific Ocean had not advanced beyond the preliminary stage. Thus the Mississippi formed the principal artery of traffic for the vast region which is watered by it and its tributaries; and even at that time a large fleet of steamers was employed in the exchange of the products of the inland States and of the East. The Secessionists threatened to close this road, both shores of the Mississippi from the mouth of the Ohio to the Gulf of Mexico being in their hands; and by a complete series of fortifications it was proposed to bar the stream against every foreign vessel. Owing to the fact that at the outset of the war Kentucky was preserved to the Union, the Ohio, at least nearly as far as its mouth, did not come into the possession of the Southerners. On the other hand the Confederates completely blocked the Cumberland and the Tennessee, at the place where these two rivers approach within a few miles of each other, by means of the two forts Henry and Donelson, and in this manner created for themselves a fortified camp of immense importance. This point formed the first object of attack for the Unionists.

It was here, even more than in the East, that the war acquired that character which so strikingly distinguishes it from all the wars of the Old World. With the high value which the Americans attach to all practical matters, and with their highly developed commercial instincts, the technical arts and sciences had in the United States attained a development such as one would have looked for in vain in the Old World. Even at that time railways and steamers played a part in the traffic of the United States which they did not acquire in Europe till many years later. In the War of Secession industry came to embrace a wide field, and Northern mechanics and artisans took up the new problems which presented themselves with an energy which attracted the attention of all foreign Powers. Technical inventions found greater application in this war than in any other, both by being employed for the first time on a much larger scale, and by actually owing their origin to the necessity of the moment. In a country without roads, railways acquired a high strategic importance. Not only their destruction, but above all their restoration, was among the important tasks of the contesting armies; and railways were applied even more directly to military purposes, as with armoured trains. The requirements of war had a still greater effect upon the shipbuilding industry, as was illustrated when the fleet conveying the northern army under McClellan[1] to the James River was met by a vessel of a strange and hitherto unknown type. The Southerners had, it appeared, cut down nearly to the water's edge a steam frigate belonging to the United States navy, and had then rendered her almost invulnerable to artillery — such as it was then — by means of armour plates, while the principal weapon of this ocean monster consisted of a tremendous ram. More than one ship of the Federal fleet succumbed to the " Merrimac" before she was met by a worthy opponent. The latter appeared under the name of "Monitor," and was built by a Swede named Ericsson. This vessel, likewise, had a low armoured deck, from the midst of which, however, rose a rotary armoured tower which carried two guns of the heaviest calibre. This period marks the beginning of that competition between heavy armour and guns in naval warfare which has assumed larger and larger proportions, and which appears only within recent years, owing to the tremendous effects of modern explosives, to have been decided in favour of guns.

In the western campaign also technical science was immediately called into requisition. The Unionists built a fleet of heavily armed and armour-plated gunboats which provided both a movable support for the land forces and a floating siege train for attacking the forts. To the performances of this river flotilla are in a large part ascribable the successes won by the Western forces on the Mississippi. While a force from the North, after the opening up of the Tennessee and the Cumberland, entered the Mississippi itself, another sent by sea from the East entered the mouth of the river and captured New Orleans as early as the beginning of 1862. The second half of this year and the beginning of 1863 were for the Union the most depressing period of the war. In the East the Confederates assumed the offensive; in the centre of the theatre of war they advanced far northward beyond the line of the Tennessee, which had been wrested from them in the previous year, and threatened the Union frontier; while on the Mississippi the Federal forces were for months vainly besieging the bastions of Vicksburg on the left bank of the river. By a happy chance Vicksburg fell on the same day (July 4, 1863) that Lee's army in front of Gettysburg was obliged to fall back into Virginia. The more decisive result, however, was that achieved in the West; it opened the Mississippi completely and thus separated the Southwest from the other Secession States. The importance of this success was fully recognised in the Northeast, and Grant,[2] the conqueror of Vicksburg, was placed in charge of those armies which, in the fall of the same year, engaged their opponents so decisively in the battles around Chattanooga. Early in the following year Grant was given the chief command of all the Federal armies, and then began, on a large scale, those two movements by which Lee and Johnston were to be overpowered and the Confederacy crushed.

Fortunately for the Union Grant found in William Tecumseh Sherman, also a Westerner, a worthy coadjutor. A succession of victories led him in September,

----

[1] See ante, p. 553.        [2] See ante, p. 553.

1864, to the city of Atlanta; and thence he marched straight across the enemy's country to the Atlantic coast. By the movement the war was carried through Georgia into the heart of the enemy's country the arrogant State of South Carolina, which now was to feel the sufferings of the war. With the progress of Sherman north from Savannah and the establishment of connection with the sea forces in December, 1864, and thus with the army in Virginia, the war entered upon its final stage. With simultaneous advances on the seat of the enemy's government by Grant from the north and by Sherman from the south, the armies of Lee and Johnston became more and more endangered. On the 9th of April, 1865, Grant compelled Lee to surrender at Appomattox Court House; and a few days later (the 26th of April) the last army of the South, under Johnston, which was opposed to Sherman, relinquished its useless resistance.

Thus the North had saved the existence of the Union. What, however, had become of the rest of its programme? Lincoln at first adhered to the view that the Union was not at war with the Confederate States, but was merely putting down an insurrection in its own territory, and that therefore the rights of the southern States and of loyal individuals would in no wise be affected. This opinion he repeated emphatically to the representatives of the central States who had remained faithful to the Union, when anxiety began to be expressed there in regard to the continuance of slavery. Nevertheless the course of the war had forced him to alter his position in regard to the slavery question, and also made possible such action as was necessary to make effective his final judgment.

On the 22d of September, 1862, Lincoln, in his capacity as commander-in-chief of the United States forces, issued a declaration announcing that on the 1st of January, 1863, all slaves within the portions of the revolted States occupied by Federal troops should be free. Under the prevailing circumstances a demand for the abolition of slavery could not fail to be raised in Congress also. Lincoln, however, still tried to make terms, as by the offer of money indemnities to the States affected by abolition, and by plans for aiding the emigration of liberated slaves to Liberia on an extensive scale; but none of his proposals met with immediate acceptance. Meanwhile the time for a new presidential election had arrived; and although Lincoln's re-election was contested both by opponents of slavery and by Democrats from opposite standpoints, he emerged victorious from the contest, with an overwhelming majority. In the meantime slavery had been abolished by law in the District of Columbia, while in Maryland it had virtually been abolished. At last the Administration proposed the Thirteenth Amendment to the Federal Constitution, which in terms abolished slavery throughout the whole of the United States. Its acceptance by Congress on the 31st of January, 1865, was followed by its ratification by the requisite number of States, and thus the victory of the Republicans, both military and political, seemed complete. It was dimmed, however, by the fact that almost at the same moment Lincoln, the man who had served them as a prudent, unimpassioned, but absolutely reliable leader, was, by the cowardly pistol of an assassin, deprived of the fruits of his well-earned victory (April 14, 1865).

Lincoln's death was a great misfortune for the whole Union, and to the Republican party it brought an unmistakable crisis. The platform on which Lincoln had been elected in 1860 had not only been fulfilled in all essentials during the few years of the war, but through the course of events had been carried far beyond its original limits. At the decisive moment, when, after an unexampled victory, all those meaner spirits were crowding in that always flock to the victorious side when the time comes for dividing the spoils, the party had neither a definite programme which set forth its higher aims, nor a leader with sufficient influence to keep it in the right path.

From Lincoln's just and fair-minded character it might have been expected that he would complete the restoration of the Union and the reconstruction of the southern States in the same spirit which had marked his policy during the whole course of the war. The man, however, who by Lincoln's death was called to the presidency, — Vice-President Andrew Johnson, — neither stood as high above the views of the party as his predecessor had done, nor did he possess enough power over it to keep in check its more radical elements. The Republican party now included such extremists as would strive, casting aside all ideal views, to take exemplary vengeance on the South for the five years' civil war and to render it incapable of ever again playing a part in the inner life of politics. Johnson himself by no means represented these aims, but he entirely failed to recognise the danger with which they threatened the Union, and therefore missed the right moment for averting it. He afterward proceeded manfully against it and battled with it strenuously to the end of his term of office, but unfortunately he did not succeed in conquering it. Like the Radical Republicans, Johnson had not considered it advisable forthwith to reinstate the rebel States in their former place in the Union; and the amnesty law proclaimed by him marked out such an extraordinarily large number of those who were to be excluded, by act of the Executive, from political privileges, that it acted as a direct encouragement to the Radicals. Johnson, however, made such a vigorous use of the measure and endeavoured so earnestly to control in the affairs of the South, that in connection with his amnesty policy the quarrel between him and the Radical majority broke out immediately on the meeting of Congress. The President had decided to readmit the southern States to their former relations, subject to the condition that they recognised the abolition of slavery and their obligations with reference to the Federal debt, while declaring the debt of the Confederate States void. A number of the southern States had actually been reconstructed on this basis and had sent their Representatives to Congress. The latter, however, were unconditionally sent back by Congress; and the moderate attitude of the President now began to be assailed by an embittered opposition the end of which, apparently, was to make the readmission of the southern States conditional on their agreeing to admit negroes to all the rights of white citizens. Johnson made vain efforts to frustrate the accomplishment of such a policy by means of his veto. His indiscretion, leading him so far as to malign Congress, gave some justification to the Radicals in impeaching him before the Senate, where he was finally acquitted by a single vote. One after another of the southern States was forced to accept the conditions imposed by the Radical party, and its complete victory was thus assured.

In this course of action Congress was actuated not exclusively by an ideal enthusiasm for the equality of all men. The elections which had been conducted on the basis of Johnson's plan of Reconstruction had shown that, in spite of their reverses in the war and the damage inflicted on their industry, the political influence of the South and of the Democratic party was by no means crushed, but would, under favorable conditions, rapidly reassume its normal position in the political life of the Union. It was this result, however, which the Republicans feared as likely to be speedily followed by their own defeat, and it was to prevent this that the Democratic South was to be rendered politically impotent. Hungry professional politicians now began to swarm to the South. With all kinds of demagogic tricks the party managed to appropriate all the different branches of government and administration, and, by the unscrupulous manner in which they dealt with State property, they succeeded in hastening the bankruptcy of some of the southern States.

Johnson did not see the victory of "carpet-bag" politics during his term of office; but the manœuvres of the Radicals succeeded in putting in his place a man entirely after their own heart. Hitherto parties had been fortunate in their choice of victorious generals for the presidency; and the services which Grant had rendered in the civil war were undoubtedly more potent than those of all the previous military candidates. As a statesman, and more especially as an administrator, however, Grant was certainly not less incapable than Jackson or any other of his predecessors. In 1869 he entered upon office as the chosen representative of the party which was determined upon gathering in for itself the fruits of victory, and during his career he seemed unable to prevent widespread corruption, not only in the southern States, but also in other parts of the Union. Almost the sole guiding principle of the Republican party now seemed to be that the government was to be used for the purpose of enriching the party in power. A system of high protective tariffs was introduced, ostensibly for the purpose of meeting the financial needs of the country, which had been greatly increased by the war; but it was abused for the purpose of providing certain industrial and commercial rings and companies with an opportunity for exploitation and speculation, by which even officials were supposed to have enriched themselves in the most open manner.

Even during Grant's first term of office these proceedings had increased to such an extent as to call forth in many places a vigorous opposition; but the coherence of the party, aided by those unprincipled followers who held the mastery in the South, was still so powerful that Grant's re-election in 1872 was accomplished without special exertions. During his second term of office, however (1873–1877), the Republican party was split asunder. A faction, the so-called Liberal Republicans, formulated as their primary demand the establishment of an honest administration. This section was composed to a considerable extent of that German-American element which had already played an important part in the early development of the Republican party. The influence of the Liberal Republicans was indeed not sufficiently important to hold out hopes of victory to a candidate of their own; but neither the old Republicans nor the Democrats, who now were once more energetically coming to the front, could do without these independent votes, and they both were accordingly obliged to propose candidates capable of effecting a thorough moral cleansing of the administration.

It was not until the advent to office of President Rutherford Birchard Hayes (1877–1881) that the insurrectionary epoch of the United States came to an end. From a material point of view the Union undoubtedly began to flourish very rapidly after the war, as was shown in a conspicuous way by the financial measures of the Administration. In consequence of high protective tariffs and an increase of internal taxation during the war the Treasury found itself face to face with a steadily increasing surplus. The federal debt, which after the war had reached the amount of $2,800,000,000, was reduced by half in the course of twenty years, the interest thereon, moreover, being reduced from six to three per cent. Thus a reduction in internal taxation and a lowering of the import duties were rendered possible, though political prejudices rather than financial needs as yet prevented a repeal of the protective tariffs. Hayes was succeeded in 1881 by James Abram Garfield, a President who gave every promise of leading the country farther on the road to moral regeneration, when once again the bullet of the assassin, July 2, 1881, proved the means of retarding this forward movement, for Garfield's successor, Chester Alan Arthur, once again permitted a return to the policy of exploitation; and though under his administration things did not become as bad as under Grant, the policy of regeneration suffered a serious check. It was on this account largely that the Republican party completely lost its hold over men's minds. In 1884, for the first time since the civil war, the Democrats succeeded in obtaining a majority for their candidate for the presidency, Grover Cleveland, with a platform which demanded a tariff for revenue only, an honest and trustworthy financial administration, and the restriction of the spoils system in the appointment of officials.

Since 1884 Republican and Democratic presidents have succeeded one another almost in regular alternation. The maintenance of this balance between the great parties has contributed considerably toward rendering impossible such conditions as had existed earlier. The Union then entered upon a new stage of its development. The strengthening of the central authority which resulted from the defeat of the supporters of State rights in the war of secession did not remain without its effect upon the spirit of American politics. The attention of the government still continued, it is true, to be occupied primarily with the internal conditions of the Union, which, indeed, are so varied and peculiar as to justify such a policy. Under a Republican system of protection carried to an extreme development the industry of the United States has reached dimensions which place it almost at the head of the productive nations of the earth. In no country as in America are the technical advances of modern times put to such immediate and comprehensive use. Steam and electricity are the dominating factors, not only in all branches of industry, but also in agriculture. The inexhaustible wealth of the country is exploited with iron energy; and nowhere is the struggle for advancement keener than in the United States. Undoubtedly the more ideal elements in human life have had to suffer somewhat thereby, for the fine arts have not long enjoyed a home in the United States; nor has the much-vaunted advancement of the sciences tended to the improvement of any of the branches of science, other than those devoted to practical purposes, on the same scale as in the Old World.

Woman in America has enjoyed a more really independent position than in any other country, and, in the nature of things feeling herself equal if not superior to man, has striven also to share in the activities and the rights of the male sex. Thus in America, more than elsewhere, she early created for herself the possibility of a freer movement in both social and municipal life. Not resting content with this, the more she actually employed herself as a fellow-labourer with man on equal terms, the more she aimed at being placed on an equality with him in other spheres. Social conditions in which material factors gained increasing prominence led in many cases to a restriction of marriages, or to marriages of such a kind as made the wife less a guardian of the home than a co-operating partner of the hus-

band. Many professions were opened to her; in consequence of her higher culture she finally developed the ability of filling at first a few and then an increasing number of minor public offices of the clerical and administrative classes.
Thus there arose a class of wage-earning women some of whom, not without
reason, claimed to have an equal voice with men in public affairs. The peculiarity of the American Constitution, which leaves the conditions attached to
the franchise entirely to the control of the separate States, considerably facilitated the movement toward political rights for women. They early obtained
in several States the right of voting merely upon school matters; and upon
this foundation there has been a marked development. At the present day,
however, women in only four States of the Union enjoy, in regard to the
exercise of the suffrage, the same political rights as do men; and it is hardly
open to doubt that in America as in Australia the emancipation movement will
gradually decline. American conditions will be hardly likely to alter the fact
that in the end the female sex will have nothing to gain, but everything to
lose, by stepping upon the same footing with man into all the different branches
of industrial life.

Whether or not the United States will always maintain their industrial affairs
in a sound and healthy condition is difficult to foretell. The Socialist danger, which
has caused so much anxiety to the governments of the Old World, has not been
present in America on the same scale. It has there been counteracted by the overthrow of all social barriers, the republican equality of all citizens, and the fact that
up to the most recent times it has been possible for individuals in the humblest
ranks, by skill and energy, to work their way up into the circles of the all-powerful
aristocracy of wealth. Naturally, with the increasing density of the population,[1]
this possibility is growing less. Though by no means overpopulated in proportion to
area, the United States has even at the present day a considerable proletariat of
unemployed.

For some time these conditions have exercised a considerable effect upon the
question of immigration. The period from 1830 to 1880, during which America
encouraged by all the means in its power the influx of immigrants, has been succeeded by another in which the country is beginning to close its doors to improperly
qualified foreigners. This movement at first was directed against the Chinese. In
the negroes and Indians the Union already had in its midst two foreign elements
of population whose improvement and absorption presented difficult and expensive problems. It was therefore justified in refusing to burden itself with
another foreign element, and one, moreover, which from its peculiarity seemed
unlikely to become assimilated to the rest of the population. The Union, however, is beginning to close its doors to European immigration also. It is not,
of course, trying to effect this indirectly in the manner once aimed at by the
Know-nothings,[2] — by rendering more difficult the acquisition of the rights of
citizenship. But on the other hand, now that its social conditions are no longer
such that physical powers alone are sufficient for obtaining a livelihood, it more
particularly refuses to receive those whose bodily and mental constitution would
lead one to expect that, so far from benefiting the country, they would become a
burden to it.

---

[1] See illustration at p. 534.     [2] See *ante*, p. 542.

The republican equality of all citizens is in the United States, even more than in other republics, modified by the power of wealth. In no country is the influence of capital so great as in the United States. Its "trusts" and "rings" have succeeded more than once not only in wresting to themselves monopolies for the New World, but also in threatening the Old World with them. Nor is either the tariff or the financial policy of the United States free from the reproach of having been abused for the business purposes of large commercial associations.

We cannot, however, deny the enormous capacity for development in the vast natural resources of the country. It is the growing recognition of this fact which has helped to induce the United States to adopt an entirely new foreign policy at the end of the nineteenth century. It is of course pretended that the policy first laid down and followed out by Monroe[1] is still, as in 1823, the guiding thread of American statesmanship, but a wholly new interpretation is nowadays placed upon Monroe's original declarations. Monroe, in those days, laid stress on the fact that the guiding principle of the foreign policy of the United States should be non-interference in American affairs by other nations. The declaration that they would consider the interference of foreign Powers for the restoration of the Spanish dominion in Central and South America as an unfriendly act against the United States was directed, as was the policy of England, more especially against the Holy Alliance, which was ready to support Ferdinand VII by the aid of an international force. The Union beheld with indifference more than one attempt of the Spaniards to reconquer their colonial empire, without regarding it as other than an internal affair of the provinces affected. The Monroe Doctrine was first introduced into diplomacy at the time of the Panama canal enterprise. The North Americans had for a long time made efforts to subject the industrial conditions of the Isthmus to their control, and became uneasy when there seemed a probability of the enterprise being carried out without their participation. They also have made continuous efforts for the construction of a Nicaragua canal, and at present it seems as if one of these projects would be realised, under the protection of the American government.

Still in another way did the United States attempt to obtain a firm footing in the neighbouring provinces of the South. In 1848 Yucatan, having once more severed its connection with the Mexican Republic, and being unable to settle a revolt of its disaffected Indian subjects, applied to the United States for help, offering in return to acknowledge their sovereignty. The offer, however, met with a refusal. Next, in the middle of the 'fifties, a plan for the incorporation of Nicaragua was under consideration. The interests of North American commercial companies had repeatedly provoked lively diplomatic discussions, and finally an adventurer from Tennessee, named William Walker, had raised himself to the presidency of Nicaragua. Regarded with suspicion by almost the whole of the native population, Walker was obliged to look for support to his own country; and his compatriots in the West repeatedly supported him, in the hope that his adventure would end in the admission of Nicaragua into the Union. In this case too, however, the object desired failed to be carried into effect. For another time, under Grant, in 1870, the expansion of the Union was brought under discussion. In the republic of San Domingo, which forms the eastern part of the island of the same name, a large

---

[1] See pp. 486, 487, 512.

party in whose hands was the presidential authority asked for admission into the United States. Ever since 1868 deputations in regard to this matter had been going backward and forward between the two countries; but it was not until Grant began to evince a lively interest in the matter that a treaty of annexation was arranged. While, however, in San Domingo, the treaty was passed by a vote of a majority of the people, Congress assumed a hostile attitude. Three times Grant introduced the scheme into the Senate, and as many times was he obliged to withdraw it before the opposition of that body.

All these failures were due to the same cause. The view prevailed quite generally in the United States that the territorial area of the Union had reached an extent large enough for its development, and that the acquisition of territories situated outside the present well-drawn boundaries could only prove a source of danger to the State. It was not until the last decade of the nineteenth century that their industrial development tended to force the United States to modify this conception of the original Monroe Doctrine. The extension of its industry is such that the Union at present not only amply supplies its own requirements, but produces far in excess of these, and hence is obliged to seek other markets. It is natural that its attention should be primarily directed toward those other States of the American continent which, owing to their inferior economic development, are still dependent on Europe for their industrial needs. In this connection a new and considerably amplified expression of the Monroe Doctrine has been called into existence. It was now proposed to restrict the activity of the European Powers upon the American continent even in the industrial sphere, as it had formerly been checked in the political, and to conquer "America for the Americans."

To this end the United States endeavoured to bring about a closer union of the independent American States. The centennial anniversary of the Declaration of Independence (July 4, 1876) first caused a revival of the idea of a Pan-American Federation; and in connection with the celebration of the four-hundredth anniversary of the discovery of America (October 12, 1892) a limited Pan-American arrangement was called into existence in the Bureau of American Republics.

The fruits of such a connection could not, however, be reaped immediately in such a manner as to satisfy the existing conditions of the labour market. Hence the United States, like the countries of the Old World, was forced to adhere to the policy of protection for their national industry. A protective tariff had of course been in force for a long time before this in the United States. But hitherto it had been used partly as a means of maintaining good order in the financial economy of the State as a whole, and partly for the purpose of supporting growing industries. The tariff of 1890, on the other hand, which is specially connected with the name of President McKinley, betokened a complete change in the tariff policy of the Union. Its object was to remove foreign competition from home markets and also to render home industries capable of competing in foreign markets. This policy was approved by the majority of the citizens of the United States, and at the election of 1896 William McKinley was chosen President (1897–1901).

The first year of McKinley's presidency, however, sufficed to show that the change in United States politics was not limited to the industrial sphere. The repeated risings against Spanish dominion in Cuba have more than once rendered

certain Americans desirous of acquiring an island so valuable to them from its
geographical situation.   In their relations to the disaffected population American
citizens have sometimes approached as nearly as possible to the limits of international law.   Spain, moreover, had tolerated a shameless misgovernment in the
remnants of its once opulent colonial empire.   The most justifiable demands of
its colonies were either disregarded or were appeased by empty promises, while
the Spanish government, allowing its governors to enrich themselves by extor-
tions, in the meanwhile derived only insignificant profits from its colonies.
The Cubans had already, in 1868, risen against this state of things, and it was
only after a ten years' struggle, accompanied by the expenditure of much blood
and treasure, that Spain succeeded, by the promise of reforms, in bringing the
island to obedience.   When this promise, too, was left unfulfilled, Cuba revolted
anew in 1896.   It was thereafter that occasion was given for the United States to
intervene in the quarrel.   Thus pressed, Spain renewed her promises of autonomous
government, and, as earlier, with no result of accomplishment.   The American
government demanded, in the interests of humanity, that the state of war in Cuba
should cease.   The American goverment also took the position that the independence of Cuba ought to be recognised ; diplomatic relations were severed ; and war
against Spain was declared to exist in April, 1898.

On the one hand, the United States possessed both a fleet and an army superior
to those of the Spaniards ; they excelled the latter in their facilities for procuring
material resources ; and the natural theatre of the war lay at their very doors.
On the other hand, the misgovernment of Spain weakened the administration both
in the mother country and in the colonies, and rendered quite impossible a vigorous or even adequate conduct of such a campaign.   When, finally, her fleets were
forced to engage in the contest, they suffered complete and speedy defeat.   After
the destruction of the Spanish fleet before Santiago, the islands of both Cuba and
Puerto Rico were occupied and controlled by the military force of the Americans.
Spain, as a result, was compelled to recognise the independence of Cuba, while
Puerto Rico was ceded directly to the United States, as were also, for an indemnity,
the Philippines.

For years past the United States had had their eyes set on the Farthest West ;
and, owing to the position of the latter region opposite to their own Pacific coast,
the Americans had become better acquainted with the methods of its development
than had some of the countries of the Old World.   At Samoa they had, it is true,
earlier yielded to the combination of European colonial Powers, although the
check, even there, was only temporary.   The manner, furthermore, in which in
1897 they succeeded in accomplishing the annexation of Hawaii showed how
obstinately the United States were determined to obtain a position in the Pacific
Ocean.   Here again the unforeseen results of the Spanish war semed to coincide
with the development of American policy ; for by the treaty of peace of December
10, 1898, America took title to the Philippine Islands.

It is at present impossible to foretell how these astonishing changes will affect
the future of the United States.   Their new acquisitions serve in a marked degree
to satisfy the need for industrial expansion, and in the changes which the Japano-
Chinese war of 1894 initiated in eastern Asia, America for the first time shows
herself prepared to enter into competition with European exporting countries.   In
view of the results of the Spanish war she is enabled to do so under exceptionally

favourable conditions.   But the colonies will, on the other hand, in all probability be a source of many future difficulties, both administrative and diplomatic, to the Union; and whether or not all these difficulties can be solved without shaking the foundations or altering the structure of the Constitution we must leave for the future to determine.

## VI

# THE HISTORICAL IMPORTANCE OF THE PACIFIC OCEAN

### By COUNT EDWARD WILCZEK

#### REVISED BY PROF. CHARLES WEALE

## 1. THE SCENE OF ACTION

IN considering the importance of the great world-ocean from the standpoint of universal history, nothing at the present day more forcibly arrests our attention than the phenomenon of the manifold relations which, through the intermediary of its various parts, are established between the inhabitants of different continents. From north to south, from east to west, the paths in which the political, intellectual, and commercial life of humanity rolls majestically onward stretch in a dense network from continent to continent. What an immense expanse is presented here as compared with the ancient sphere of civilisation, or even with that of the days before Columbus, confined as this was to the countries around the Mediterranean and the seas which encircle Europe! And yet every other division of the great ocean has in those far distant times contributed its share to the world's history; every sea has, in its own fashion, helped to promote the mutual relations of the peoples inhabiting its shores, relations which it has been left for the present age to gather within the domain of universal history.

The Pacific Ocean, too, has played a noticeable part in the course of human history. That this part cannot be compared, either in depth or grandeur, with that sustained by the Mediterranean, appears evident, if we merely consider the position of the latter as an ocean basin between three continents whose shore-dwelling peoples must have been driven almost irresistibly out to sea; in fact, the Pacific and the Mediterranean must be regarded from the point of view of history as incommensurable areas. Neither does the Pacific, from a historical stand-point, compare favourably, either in its situation or configuration, with the other great oceans. True, neither the Atlantic nor the Indian Ocean is entirely without its disadvantages in this respect; for in the southern half of the Atlantic we have the African continent, which, though sufficiently astir within, is outwardly dead; and also South America, the eastern part of which was once likewise a country "without a history." In the Indian Ocean, again, we have the Australian continent, a great mass of land, the history of which really does not commence until its rediscovery by James Cook. On the other hand the Atlantic is compensated for these drawbacks by its narrow, channel-like shape, and more

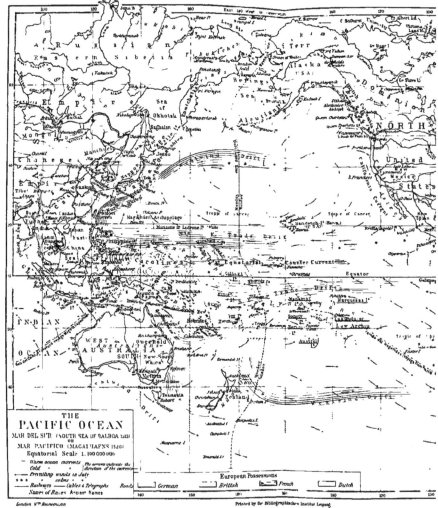

THE
PACIFIC OCEAN
MAR DEL SUR (SOUTH SEA OF BALBOA 1513)
OR
MAR PACIFICO (MAGALHAENS 1520)
Equatorial Scale 1:100 000 000.

especially by the immeasurable advantage of its proximity to Europe, the great spreader of civilisation, whose capacity for expansion has been sufficient to encompass the globe. The Indian Ocean, again, enjoys the advantage of possessing in its densely crowded East Indian Archipelago a continuous bridge of peoples, as well as the peninsulas of southern Asia, with their decided trend toward eastern Africa.

The Pacific Ocean possesses none of these features. It cannot be compared, in size, shape, or position, with either of the above-named oceans; the only point in which in certain parts it resembles its western neighbour is its richness in islands. Its most prominent feature, however, is its size. Of the three-quarters of the earth's surface which is covered by the ocean, it forms very nearly half. In conformity with its vast extent and its other natural and geographical features we find that the history of the Pacific Ocean bears the mark of grandeur, while at the same time, owing to its distribution over such an enormous area, this history is lacking in intensity.[1]

Friedrich Ratzel has aptly described the shape of the Pacific Ocean by calling attention to its widely sundered margins; a distance of three or four times the length of the Atlantic separating its Asiatic from its American shores. Its wide opening on the south is occupied by Australia and Oceania, whereby the Pacific acquires its most peculiar features; namely, the presence of a third island continent in the southern hemisphere, and the richest island formation to be found anywhere on the earth. Both the narrowing in of the ocean toward the north, and the bridge of islands in the south, besides imparting a special character to its shape and surface, also form, in a primary degree, the paths along which the history of the Pacific pursues its course; they represent the connecting elements, while the seas between them and the watery desert of the southern Pacific form the separating factors of the great world-ocean.

In its situation, too, the Pacific displays the same peculiarity as in its shape. The Atlantic Ocean throughout its whole extent preserves the character of an elongated channel interposed between the Old and New World; the Indian Ocean is like an enormous bay, which from the south cuts into the unyielding mass of the Old World. The Pacific Ocean, on the other hand, represents an enormous wedge directed toward the north, which, with a margin of the most varied shape, irresistibly drives asunder the two great continental masses of the globe, America and Asia. Accordingly the dominant features of this ocean appear to be of a separating nature; and to a certain degree this is correct. Yet there are few points on the earth's surface which more strongly argue in favour of a connection between continent and continent than the point where the two margins of the Pacific most closely approach each other, the narrow Bering Strait. What, therefore, have we to show in the way of proving the historical importance of this strait, which in the future, as heretofore, will remain of the utmost interest in the solution of the question of the aboriginal population of America, although it is hardly likely that that problem will ever be adequately solved?

So far as our experience goes backward, we cannot discover that Bering Strait has ever been of greater importance historically than any other Arctic channel bordered by two inhabited shores. Leaving out of consideration the long but

---

[1] See the map herewith.

still time-limited occupation of Alaska by the Russians, Bering Sea has as a means of commercial intercourse never attained more than an insignificant importance. Farther south, between Kamchatka, Alaska, and the Aleutian Islands, Bering Strait opens out into a wide inland sea which by its shape is in no way inferior to any other inland or intercontinental sea as a suitable means of intercommunication or ingress; and yet we can find no trace of any part played in history by this portion of the Pacific.

There is, in fact, in these icy regions of the north, an entire absence of all those preliminary conditions such as have occurred abundantly in the course of history in other parts of the earth's surface, much less favoured in regard to shape, but possessed of a happier climate. These desolate northern shores are far too inhospitable to favour the expansion of mankind in these regions; the high north, with its fields of ice and snow, its poverty in vegetable and animal life, provides but a poor home for Man, interferes with his powers of multiplication, and throws obstacles in the way of his expansion. And if the impulse for moving has once been aroused, he is driven by an innate inner force toward the south, to easier conditions of life, to those distant, happier realms of which he has conceived a dim idea. Thus, in spite of its convenience, our beautiful bridge is left unused, for the masses for whose crossing it might serve are wanting. On the other hand, as we pass southward toward temperate and tropical climes and more habitable coasts, the dividing expanse of water widens out in measureless breadth, and the opposite shore recedes farther and farther from both the real and the ideal horizon.

Nor is the conformation of the coast of the two great continents bordering the Pacific everywhere of such a kind as to attract their populations to the sea. This especially applies to America. From its farthest north to its southern extremity that continent throughout its whole length is traversed close to the Pacific coast by a steep and rugged mountain chain forming an almost insurmountable barrier between the coast and the interior, interrupted by only a few rivers in the northern continent but entirely unbroken in the southern portion. The Pacific side, in fact, represents the backward side of America from the historical standpoint; the face of the continent is turned toward the Atlantic.

The western shore of the Pacific Ocean has a much more favourable aspect. Numerous large and powerful streams hasten toward it from the interior of Asia, thus intimately connecting the latter with the ocean. The surface of contact is still further increased by the series of island groups which, like a band, fringe the eastern shore of Asia and provide the first halting-place to its inland population on venturing forth upon the sea. Thus, while on the one side these island groups invite the inland dwellers out to sea, on the other they intercept the migrating populations on their outward course and retain them for prolonged periods. We shall understand this better when we reflect that during their early migrations, when navigation was still in a primitive condition, only inconsiderable numbers of travellers can have crossed the littoral seas, and then only by degrees. Hence, while the exodus to the ocean is increased in intensity by the presence of the littoral islands, it is delayed and impeded in its extent, for it is necessary that each new territory should first absorb the slowly infiltrating new population before a fresh wave of population can cross the ocean. What vast periods of time, therefore, must have been required to saturate the rich island world of eastern Asia with this slow and gradual influx of peoples proceeding as it were by drops, and to impart to them the stimulus for continuing their advance over the immeasurable expanse of water! We know that on the mainland the impulse for the migration of large masses of the population arises from a pressing need, when the native soil is no longer capable of sustaining the increased numbers of the tribe. This applies in a still higher degree to seacoasts and island areas; and if it is difficult for migrating individuals or groups to surmount the obstacles of the water, this becomes impossible in the case of migrations *en masse*. Only the direst stress will induce Man in a lower stage of culture to leave the solid, firm sod which formed his home, and venture, without a definite goal in view, upon the vast waste of waters that threatens him with destruction. It is certain that on the islands of eastern Asia long periods of time must have elapsed before such a stress began to make itself felt.

This view is supported by another argument. According to the views of Darwin, which deserve the fullest consideration, the islands of Polynesia were not populated until a few centuries before their discovery by Europeans; on the other hand the traditional, mythical history of Japan traces back the existence of the population of that country to periods so immeasurably remote as to surpass the boldest flights of our imagination. Now, though the millions of years to which the son of the distant island empire proudly ventures to look back may not be able to stand the test of modern criticism, there is nevertheless usually a small grain of truth buried among the chaff of national vanity. At any rate this contradiction furnishes a kind of scale or measure for estimating the age of the history of the Pacific Ocean.

## 2. THE PERIOD PREVIOUS TO MAGELLAN'S VOYAGES

HISTORIANS have as yet failed to answer the question as to when Man first came to occupy the coasts of the Pacific, and in all probability this important event occurred in prehistoric times. Perhaps at some future time the geologist, the anthropologist, and the palæontologist may be able to throw some light on the question; but the present state of our science is not yet in a position to offer a solution. It is equally impossible to determine what race of men, still less what particular people, first arose on the coasts of this ocean. From palæontological reasons there is some ground for assuming that America was originally peopled by immigration from without; such an immigration would most easily take place from northern Asia, owing to the close proximity of that part of the Old World, and its effect would be the spreading of the Mongol type of population over America.[1] By this migration the prehistoric importance of the Pacific Ocean is brought into clear view. The Pacific facilitates the gradual efflux of the surplus of the population of eastern Asia into America, first of all, at its narrowest, northernmost portion. As the wanderers advance farther to the south, the ocean, gradually widening, prevents the reflux of the wave of population toward the point of exit; it retains it on the newly occupied continent, which in the course of long periods of time begins to exercise its modifying influence on the type of its immigrant population.

---

[1] See *ante*, pp. 180, 181.

Whatever views may be entertained as to the usual division of the races of mankind, whether we recognise three or five or even more separate races, no one will any longer deny that the answer given to the question as to the origin of the human race is inclining more and more to the view of a primary unity of type from which an apparent plurality of type has arisen by differentiation. In this fashion from a Mongoloid ancestral type common to the old Asiatic and the new American branches the red American race may have been developed; while a remnant of the same primitive type may, under the specific influences of Asia, have produced the Mongol race. In the light of this conception the influence of the Pacific Ocean, by operating first as a connecting and afterward as a separating agent, forms the primary determinant factor in the development of the human race as expressed in the division of the primary Mongoloid type and the separate development of the yellow and red races. In a similar manner we may ascribe to the Indian Ocean the formation of the Malay race, although the Pacific Ocean also may have had a share in this, at least so far as the peculiar racial variety of the Polynesians is concerned. Finally both oceans conjointly conveyed to the Australian continent, which was originally peopled by a Negroid race, immigrants of Malay and Polynesian descent, from the intermixture of which with the primitive inhabitants we get a new sharply demarcated type, — that of the Australian race. The latter next continues to spread eastward over a portion of the island world of the Pacific Ocean, or Melanesia.

Whether the Mongoloid type of the north-temperate or the Negroid type of the equatorial zone was the first to make its appearance on the shores of the Pacific Ocean must be left undecided. We know, at any rate, that in prehistoric times the margins of the Pacific, as well as its immeasurable island world, were still peopled by four distinct races, yellow, red, brown, and black. Only the white race is absent. Through indefinite periods the destinies of these four principal types of the human race pursue their course side by side without definitely crossing with or influencing each other. Each of them more or less pursues a separate, independent course of development within the limits of its own domain; for mutual contact is prevented by the immense expanse of the separating tracts of water. Their entrance, too, into the sphere of historic apprehension is marked by the widest differences. While the densely crowded populations of the Pacific coasts of Asia, pushing and being pushed onward in a continuous stream, have early arrived at a high state of culture and are therefore among the first to acquire historic importance, the isolated continent of America forms a world by itself, which for a long time appears wrapped in darkness and presents problems no less difficult to the historian than to the anthropologist. Even the key for the comprehension of undoubtedly historic characters has been irrecoverably lost. Hence America forms a very late addition, and one very difficult of comprehension, in the scheme of universal history. This remark applies still more forcibly to Australia, which, though less isolated, is still less favourable to human development, owing to its physical and climatic peculiarities. Its scanty population remains, up to the time when it comes in contact with the white man, in the condition of the Stone Age, and therefore by thousands of years behind the continents of the Old World. In spite of the fact that the sea renders them close neighbours to the progressive Malays, the Australian aborigines are content with playing a passive, merely receptive part. Thus, from a historical standpoint, the Australian forms a somewhat unproductive member of the human race; and he must therefore yield precedence to others, even if we may concede to him the right of racial seniority.

Of all the inhabitants of the Pacific Ocean, those in general primarily claim our attention who first, whether voluntarily or under compulsion, had recourse to the sea in their migrations, in other words, the seafaring peoples. The first beginnings of navigation are shrouded in darkness, and it would be a fruitless task to investigate in which part of the earth navigation was first practised. In any case, however, it is highly probable that the Pacific coasts of Asia are among those where navigation had its earliest home. It is there we meet with densely populated coasts, easily accessible by mighty river systems from the interior of the country, and therefore constantly exposed to the tide of an onward-pressing population, while seaward a fringe of islands, not too remote, likewise invites colonisation. Added to this, the littoral seas are not of so vast an extent that the idea of navigating them would of itself inspire fear. Again, since in its main length the Asiatic continent stretches from west to east, the continued forward movement of migrating populations in this direction must finally conduct them to the shores of the ocean.

For exactly opposite reasons the inhabitants of America could not have become a seafaring people, at least none of those dwelling on the Pacific Ocean. Here the longitudinal extension of the continent is in a direction from north to south. Moreover, it is of such enormous length that the forward movement of onward-pressing masses would not compel those in front to deviate toward the coasts; besides, these migrating hosts were by no means so numerous as those of the Asiatic continent. Further, the exit to the Pacific Ocean is barred by the mighty mountain rampart of the Cordilleras, which presents but few suitable breaks; and finally the Pacific Ocean, for enormous distances from the American coast, is almost entirely devoid of islands, so that the inhabitants of these shores would hardly conceive the idea of a country lying farther out to sea. Of course the two great Pacific currents, — the northern and southern equatorial currents, — as well as the trade winds, would have assisted the passage from east to west — from America toward Asia — to the same extent then as they do under the advanced conditions of present-day intercourse. Nevertheless, owing to the poorly developed state of American navigation in those early days, the conditions previously mentioned maintained the upper hand and impeded any outward movement toward the sea.

How different is the picture presented by the Western Ocean! Here, starting from the luxuriant shores of eastern Asia and the reef-fringed coast of Australia, a dense crowd of islands stretches outward to sea, beyond Melanesia and Micronesia, to the farthermost Polynesian isles, forming the most magnificent " bridge of populations " in the world. A road such as this could hardly offer obstacles to even less able seamen than the brown-skinned sons of the southern ocean. Thus, quite apart from anthropological and ethnographical reasons, we are more and more led to adopt the view according to which the gradual occupation of the island world of the Pacific Ocean by the human race could only have proceeded originally from the west. Thus, the sea first made its civilising influence felt in a direction from west to east.

In subsequent times, however, after the white race, with its remarkable capacity for expansion, had gained the ascendency in America, this condition of things was changed. Those peculiarities of the Pacific Ocean which favour navigation in an opposite direction to that mentioned above were now brought into action, so that, since then, the influence of the Pacific as a promoter of civilisation has proceeded in a direction from east to west. This reversion of the stream of ethnographical and cultural expansion, and the conflict between two movements in diametrically opposite directions which must have preceded it, constitute an additional unique and important factor in the historical significance of the Pacific Ocean. It forms the final link in that chain of predominance of the white race which is cast around the whole globe, — a race which, consciously and unconsciously, is working out in the most impressive and productive manner that federation of the whole human race which forms the last and probably the highest aim of the evolution of mankind.

### A. The West

WHILE the effect of the sea upon anthropology and history becomes patent and comprehensible exclusively by means of navigation, it is quite natural to recognise navigation itself as the principal factor in this influence. With many races and nations, familiarity with the sea seems an innate faculty, while in others, living in other respects under similar conditions, it is entirely wanting. Of this fact, too, the Pacific coast of eastern Asia supplies abundant proofs; and simultaneously with the consideration of this coast we enter upon the historic period.

On Yeso, Sakhalien, and the Kurile Islands we meet with feeble remnants of the Ainu, an originally dark-coloured people, who are at the present becoming more and more encroached upon by the surrounding nations and are undoubtedly doomed to a speedy extinction. Formerly the Ainu were much more densely spread over a long stretch of coast south of the estuary of the Amoor River; but by the powerful onward push of the advancing Mongol hosts, they were driven over the littoral seas to the islands, and finally took possession of the island empire of Japan. For a migration of this kind, seamanship of a much more than rudimentary development was required. And indeed the capacity for civilisation of the Ainu race seems to have been rigidly limited to this faculty; they appear, indeed, to have been born sailors. Although this originally numerous people has managed to drag out its existence for some thousands of years, it has always remained in a state of complete or semi barbarism, in which its superiority in the shipbuilding art forms, as it were, the sole redeeming feature. Now, if we except the modern Japanese, the idea of progress is not one with which other more highly civilised races of eastern Asia have shown themselves specially familiar; whence the past conditions of the Ainu, a people in a much lower stage of civilisation, open out a perspective in which even at this early age we behold their boat in the same technically and nautically perfect condition in which it has come down to us at the present day.

The same natural, innate capacity for seamanship is met with in another race, which, though originally belonging to the coast region of the Indian Ocean, also at an early period made its appearance on the Pacific coast of Asia, and which has exercised a considerable influence on the ethnography and history of the Pacific Ocean, — the Malay race. Being physically and mentally superior to the Ainu, the influence of the Malays must have been deeper and more lasting, inasmuch as the conditions under which they were brought in contact with the sea rest, in their case, on a much more favourable historic foundation. Undoubtedly continental in origin, like every other division of the human race, and likewise pushed out to sea by the irresistible expansion of the Mongol race, the Malays, on leaving their conjectural ancestral home in Farther India, saw before them three convenient and inviting island-bridges, each of which would finally conduct them to the Pacific Ocean. These three bridges radiate outward in the three eastern quadrants: the pillars of the northeastern of these bridges are formed by the Philippine Islands, Formosa, and the Loochoo Islands; those of the southeastern bridge, which leads to Australia, by Sumatra, Java, and Timor: the third, running true east, passes across Borneo and the Moluccas to New Guinea, whence it stretches far out into the ocean and is finally lost in the immeasurable island world of Micronesia and Polynesia.

All these bridges have been traversed by the Malays, who, by thus populating the richest and most fertile archipelagoes on the earth's surface, became a true insular people, and, what proved still more important from a historical point of view, a race of born seamen. This applies more especially to that portion of the brown-coloured race which took up the central of these three roads, and by pursuing it arrived on what was entirely virgin soil. The retentive and conservative force peculiar to islands could in their case operate to its fullest extent; here, too, owing to the difficulties placed in the way of any foreign admixture, the peculiar race characters of the population could be preserved perfectly intact. Here the further development of the race, proceeding entirely from within itself, and subject only to the influences of a purely oceanic environment and mode of life, was forced to assume a direction which led to the formation of a racial type exclusively confined to the Pacific Ocean. It is the Polynesian race which thus, as it were, took its origin from the ocean. Yielding originally to the press of onward-pushing masses, it afterward, through an innate and natural propensity for the sea, penetrated to the innermost parts of the far-stretching southern ocean and developed into a race of a perfectly distinct type.

Essentially different was the lot of those divisions of the Malay race that pursued their migration along the other two roads. On the southeastern road the Sunda Islands were the first to be occupied; and these, owing to their spacious extent, retained considerable numbers of the immigrants, who were thus enabled to preserve their original Malay character. Those, on the other hand, who penetrated to the Australian continent found there, as well as in Melanesia, an already existing aboriginal population belonging to the black race, by commingling with which they produced the type of the Australian and Papuan races, — a type which also displays a great natural propensity for the sea, but which in other respects occupies almost the lowest stage of human development.

In regard to the third migratory movement, — that along the northeastern road, — we are especially attracted by what is conjectured to have been its terminus, the island realm of Japan. Basil Hall Chamberlain's testimony to the survival of old Ainu local designations in the south of that empire shows that Japan was once peopled entirely by that dark-coloured and very hairy race. But the matter did not end there. The immeasurable expansion of the populations of the Mongol race inhabiting the whole interior of Asia had at all times resulted in a pressure exercised in all directions, which accounts for almost all the great migrations of peoples in the Old World; of these migrations those directed to the east probably belong to an earlier period than those which proceeded in a westerly direction. The displacement of the Ainu across the Sea of Japan to the islands[1] had not yet created sufficient room on the Pacific coast for the new arrivals, among whom the Tunguse and Chinese begin to make their appearance. This new population in its turn soon began to yield to the pressure of fresh migrations from behind, and, following in the wake of those they had themselves crowded out, they poured across the littoral sea and established themselves on the Japanese islands. It is highly probable that they were here joined by the outermost elements or vanguard of the Malay migration, who by still continuing on their northeastern course had advanced across the Loochoo Islands to Japan. Three distinct factors thus placed in juxtaposition could not fail to be subjected to the powerful influence of a process in which, as in a chemical combination, dissimilar elements are united into a harmonious whole; and though the Ainu element, being in a lower state of development, was in part separated mechanically,—that is, exterminated or pushed farther northward,—there nevertheless remained a residuum large enough to make its influence felt in the fusion of the more advanced Mongol and Malay factors. The final result of this process is the highly interesting and peculiar nation of the Japanese. That the origin of this people dates back to a prehistoric age is proved by the ancient tradition of the Japanese, who entirely repudiate the idea of their descent from the Chinese, but look upon themselves as an autochthonous people and as the direct descendants of their national gods. Now, although tradition cannot be admitted to have any value in a purely scientific investigation, it must nevertheless be pointed out that it can at no time and in no place arise entirely out of deliberate invention or from wilful imposture, but rather that it requires for its origin a long period of what may be called historical semi-darkness. In the present instance both the venerable age of the accredited history of the Japanese empire, as well as the manner of origin of its people as proved by anthropological investigation, afford ample evidence of the great antiquity of the Japanese nation.

Of the separate constituents which took part in the national growth of the Japanese people, it is natural that that one which excelled the rest in cultural development, namely, the Mongol element, should prove the determinant factor; and the yellow race does in fact seem to be the only one besides the white race which is capable by its own efforts of attaining higher planes of civilisation, and, what is more, of maintaining the place thus freshly acquired. At the same time the admixture of the other elements was sufficiently powerful to impart to the Japanese people a character quite distinct from that of the Mongols of the continent, and to preserve within them that capacity for seamanship which is innate in all the Malay race. Hence Japan assumes one of the first and foremost places in the history of the Pacific Ocean, and the more so since it represents the earliest well-ordered State organisation within the domain of that ocean. Further, till the arrival of the white race, Japan is the only country within the Pacific area which, as the researches of Kusonoki have shown, has had any relations with the remote opposite coast of America, and that not only with its northern coasts, but, according to tradition, even with Mexico and Peru. Whatever views we may hold on this subject, even if we relegate a former sea domination of such extent to the

---

[1] See *ante*, p. 572.

domain of fable, and limit Japan's maritime influence to the eastern shores of Asia, there can be no question that Japan was at all times more intimately connected with the Pacific Ocean than any other portion of the north Pacific coast.

This fact stands out in uncommonly sharp relief from the background of history when we come to consider the position of the continent which adjoins Japan in relation to the Pacific Ocean. From the point of view of antiquity the permanent settlement of the Mongols on the Pacific coasts of eastern Asia certainly dates back further than the first appearance of Japan as a State and a nation; yet, though the Mongol race forms an exceedingly important division of mankind in the general history of the world, how insignificant is its history as a sea Power compared with that of the population of the island empire! Undoubtedly this final occupation of the seacoast is of older date, inasmuch as it is the cause to which Japan owes its existence as a State; but its importance from the standpoint of universal history is secondary, since the yellow race as such — that is, in its pure unmixed state — for long ages found in the ocean an insurmountable obstacle to its further expansion. While, however, even at an early period, the yellow race developed a capacity for settling on the soil as well as for agriculture and fixed social and political forms, which in their turn produced a high civilisation, it is a characteristic fact that it displayed but little taste and capacity for maritime affairs, although the natural conditions of its abode could never have stood in the way of its acquiring this faculty. The absence of this faculty strikes us as all the more strange, since seamanship was in a high degree a peculiar characteristic of all other races descended from the common Mongoloid stock, though these, with the exception of a few branches of the red-skinned American race, advanced in other respects but little above the stage of natural races. The yellow race, on the other hand, embodies the continental character in its most marked form. Although, even at the present day, it still numbers about two-fifths of the whole human race, it appears up to modern times to have remained chained, as it were, to the Asiatic continent and firmly bound to its native sod. Only within the last few decades has it succeeded in advancing its range over the adjacent island groups, and even there it is already losing its characteristic features. But wherever it retains its hold upon the firm and familiar soil of the continent, it assumes types of unexampled solidity and tenacity, — types which serve as irremovable landmarks in the confused and inconstant movement of the world-embracing human race.

The most characteristic and — from the point of view of numbers — the most significant among these phenomena is the Chinese people. This people also has been unable to evade the great general law according to which the maintenance of the purity of the race excludes the admixture of foreign blood. Nevertheless the appearance on the Pacific coast of a people like the pure Chinese, which claims attention by reason of its numbers and has exercised a determining influence in respect to civilisation, must be regarded as an event of momentous import; the more so as by it the fluctuating phases of national life fermenting in these regions were definitely fixed and cast into political shape. Of course a considerable space of time had to elapse before the original divisions and "petty States" of the Chinese political system were consolidated into the mighty "Middle Kingdom."

The national and political appearance of the continental State of China and the island empire of Japan within the domain of the Pacific Ocean marks an important turning-point in history; for now the influence of the ocean, exercised in prehistoric times and concerned mainly with the shaping of mankind in the formation of races, gives place to the influence of history in general or to that of the history of particular peoples, who have now assumed a distinct individuality: a turning-point where the outer framework of the history of nations — that is the chronological determination of events — begins to assume a comprehensible shape. Although the organisation of the two above-named nations presents many fundamental differences, it also offers many points of agreement in other directions, and more especially in respect to their relations to the sea. The Chinese empire, before it began to be a sea Power of the Pacific Ocean, could look back toward a venerable past of many centuries; indeed it was not until the time of Shi-Hoang, who reunited the empire at the end of the third century before Christ, that China reached the Pacific Ocean. It has not, however, succeeded in obtaining the sovereignty of the sea, partly owing to the absence of a love and capacity for maritime affairs in the people, and partly owing to the policy of its rulers, whose main aim, from times immemorial, was to shut off the empire as much as possible from the outer world. Even in those early days China was already of such vast extent, and counted a population so immense, that it formed as it were a world of its own and could dispense with foreign intercourse. Moreover, being of a timid and effeminate disposition, the Chinese were lacking in that warlike spirit which might have inspired them to seek adventures and to make conquests; and the abundance and variety of their own home products rendered the introduction of foreign merchandise unnecessary, and thus one of the principal incentives to active foreign commerce was lacking. On the other hand their home trade flourished from a very early period; being supported by an extensive network of natural waterways which were farther extended, in very early times, by artificial channels. Even in the coast districts these internal waterways were used to a much greater extent than the sea. Hence the national shipping industry of the Chinese was much more developed in connection with river and canal traffic than with marine navigation, and to that end was supported by the government. In conclusion we must not overlook the fact that the coasts of China are not washed by the ocean, but by landlocked seas, the navigation of which, on account of frequent terrible storms, makes much larger demands in the way of seamanship than the navigation of the open sea. Another physical factor to be considered is the direction of the great ocean currents which trend from north to south, but toward the Sunda Strait instead of to the ocean. Thus neither the physical, ethnographical, nor political conditions were especially favourable to the development of a vigorous shipping trade; but it is the latter which originates the sea Power of a nation and remains indissolubly connected with it. "China's efforts, however," in the words of Friedrich Ratzel, "have at all times been directed toward spreading her dominion over the continent of Asia rather than toward extending it to the sea and to distant shores."

At the same time we must guard against denying that the Chinese carried on any marine intercourse whatever, or even undervaluing it. After the investigations of Gustav Schlegel we can of course no longer maintain the identity of Fusang with America in general, and with Central America in particular; and accordingly the stately bridge which bold orientalists have designed to connect the shores of the Yellow Sea with the Gulf of Tehuantepec collapses in ruins.

Nevertheless the fact remains that the Chinese for a long time — indeed almost for a thousand years — and with few interruptions held a leading position in the trade and commercial intercourse of southeastern Asia. This is not the place for discussing their important activity in the western part of this area, — the Indian Ocean, — which has been reserved for fuller consideration in the second volume of this work. But in the Pacific also the Chinese advanced far down to the south. Magelhães found Chinese goods in the Philippine Islands; and in the Mariana Islands, too, signs of Chinese intercourse were discovered. On the Sunda Islands the Chinese were found established on the arrival of the Europeans; nay, the influence of their civilisation seems even to extend to northern Australia.

Japan has used her oceanic position to greater advantage than China; and indeed she is naturally more favoured in this respect than her continental neighbour. The shores of her four principal islands are turned directly toward the Pacific, while the western island is only at an inconsiderable distance from the Asiatic continent. From its eastern shore, the oceanic current, never at rest, sweeps onward in a gigantic circle which, starting from Japan as the broad and mighty Kuro Siwo, passes across to the northwest coast of America, whence, reversing its course, it returns as the North Equatorial Current to the east coast of Asia and to the sea which gave it birth. These currents traverse the wide ocean like rivers, forming natural navigation routes, and were indeed recognised as such by accident or practice long before they were theoretically determined. When we consider its insular character, the great indentation and extent of its coast, the abundance of good harbours, and the innate racial bent of its people for the sea, it seems as if Japan has been almost forced from early times to turn its attention to the ocean. Its alleged intercourse with America has also, like the Chinese Fusang, been frequently made the subject of close but fruitless investigation. Further, seeing that the natural conditions of the country are such as would actually promote maritime intercourse, we may regard it as almost certain that relations of a similar kind also existed in historic times; in this case, as before, however, all evidence of a convincing nature is wanting as to whether these relations ever went beyond mere involuntary deviations from the proper course, such as are recorded in considerable numbers even in modern times. On the other hand the relations of Japan with the coast regions of the neighbouring continent have been for a long time very intimate, and certainly much more important than those of the Chinese. Japan has carried on trade with China and Cochin China, the Philippines, Java, and Cambodia; and when the Dutch entered Farther India they actually found a Japanese settlement in Annam.

That Japan should encroach on that portion of the Asiatic continent situated nearest to its own shores — Corea — was even more natural than that it should extend its influence to more outlying regions. Indeed this intercourse with far-distant countries afterward — especially when China under the Mongol and Ming dynasties forbade its subjects to engage in long sea voyages for commercial purposes — degenerated into a system of piracy, aptly compared by Friedrich Ratzel with the Norman robber-baron system of the early Middle Ages; and it had the effect of driving the Japanese pirates and smugglers far up into the navigable rivers of China. On the other hand Japan's intercourse with Corea developed more and more into a civilising factor of the first importance. It brought the inhabitants of the island empire into a closer acquaintance with a whole series of forms of pure Chinese civilisation, which in succeeding ages have exercised a powerful intellectual and material influence on Japan, and indeed have moulded that country into a sort of abridged edition of the Middle Kingdom. In respect to both civilisation and politics Corea forms the gate of entry of Japan to the continent. As was the case in 1894, when the Japanese war was first begun in Corea, so it happened more than fifteen hundred years ago, when this much-contested peninsula was for several hundreds of years subject to the island empire; and its loss and acquisition by China were not among the least of the causes which induced Japan to shut its doors to foreign intercourse. Alarmed by the failure of its attack on its powerful continental neighbour, and apprehensive of further losses of territory, Japan more and more withdrew itself within its insular position, closed its harbours to foreigners, and began to exercise the most careful watch over its intercourse with foreign countries. This nervous apprehensiveness reached such a height that, with the view of checking the shipbuilding industry, which had hitherto been in a flourishing condition, laws were enacted for rendering vessels unfit for long sea voyages, with the intention of weaning the population from their love of the sea.

In this way the idea of separation and isolation, so much in vogue in China, began to assert itself also in Japan, and to cast the enlightened and energetic population of that country under the spell of that rigid and narrow one-sidedness, so deadening to all progress, which forms the special characteristic of eastern Asia. It is the historical effect of this one-sidedness which "has caused this portion of the earth to look with rigidly set features at and across the Pacific Ocean, and has introduced the Buddhist idea of self-abnegation into the domain of politics."[1] Japan, in consequence of her insular position and her tendency toward expansion, was already on the fair road toward throwing off that spell and of exercising a dominion over the sea which would have secured for her a preponderating influence in the Pacific, when this sudden voluntary isolation once more caused her to drift back very nearly into the condition of a continental State. The natural result of this exclusiveness was that for a considerable period Japan ceased to play any part in the history of mankind, and indeed may be said to have fallen into a state of historical hibernation. It was the white race, that powerful leavening element upon the habitable globe, which first forcibly reawakened Japan from her stupor, with results which became only too evident in the second half of the nineteenth century.

### B. Oceania

While the attempts of China and Japan to turn to account the maritime advantages of their geographical position met with an early and almost insurmountable barrier in consequence of physical, ethnographical, and political conditions; while both States, pushing to its utmost limits the system of political isolation, withdrew more and more into themselves, and for a long time of their own accord resigned all active co-operation at the loom of history, another member of the human family was gradually spreading itself over all the island world of the central Pacific and was advancing its outposts to the outermost habitable spots of

[1] Friedrich Ratzel.

this ocean. This great realm of oceanic islands was now taken possession of by that branch of the Malay race from which, in consequence of repeated division and subdivision, arose the Polynesian (and Micronesian) races. This event — or rather the sum total of an innumerable series of such events distributed over long periods — is of a nature so entirely peculiar that it cannot be ranged side by side and on a par with the historical phenomena of the coast region of the Pacific; for, however important this event may be from an anthropological and historical standpoint, it is still very far removed from any connection with the interlacing texture of the general history of mankind. We are here dealing with a separated link which has been lost to the whole, and which, without knowledge of the rest of the world and unknown to the latter, drags out a separate existence and is finally lost in a life of pure nature; a link which only through its later insertion into the chain of humanity has come to acquire a retrospective historical interest. The fact that the range of distribution of the Polynesian race embraces an area of immense extent, forming, in fact, a considerable fraction of the earth's surface, has no bearing on this matter; it does not alter the fact that disintegration and insular isolation has reduced the gifted and receptive Malays to the aboriginal condition of the degenerate Polynesian, and has thus marked out the whole of this immense area, in the traditional sense, as the scene of retrogression.

We must grant that in regard to seamanship these Polynesians have developed a remarkable talent which indeed appears to absorb and exhaust their total capacity for civilisation. This, however, is in accord with the view[1] which regards seamanship as a kind of natural condition in man, or, in other words, looks upon certain races or nations as being endowed with an almost amphibious nature. Apart from this, the seafaring activities of the Polynesians, in their own peculiar condition, have never extended beyond their own geographical limits (except to the Australian continent), and have therefore remained without influence from the point of view of general history; while we cannot discern any reacting influence upon the general course of history any more than on the comparatively near civilised nations of eastern Asia. It was only through their association with the white races, at a much later period, that this capacity for seamanship received due recognition.

As regards the time when this gradual settlement of the Pacific island world had its beginning, Friedrich Müller assumes it to date back to about the year 1000 B. C. According to the views of later anthropologists this colonisation was not completed until a few centuries before the discovery of Polynesia by the white races, by whom the inhabitants of these islands were regarded as a race sharply distinct from the Malays. According to this view the relatively short period of a good two thousand years was sufficient to call into existence a new racial type, — a phenomenon which, so far as it can be accepted as true, is capable, more than any other, of throwing light upon the extremely important position which must be assigned to the Pacific Ocean in the history of the world.

We must further call special attention to the fact that however much the Polynesians, from the community of many characteristic features, may lay claim to a common ethnological origin, they display considerable differences from an anthropological standpoint. There is a sharp line of demarcation between the dark-skinned,

---

[1] See above, p. 572.

frizzly or woolly haired Melanesian, and the lighter-coloured, yellowish-brown, sleek or curly-haired Polynesian or Micronesian. The only feature common to all is that, in spite of many intellectual endowments, they for the most part remained a people in a state of nature, who probably never dreamed of regarding themselves as one people, or conceived the notion of forming a State. The almost interminable subdivision and insular isolation of their separate racial divisions; the wholly tropical situation of their homes, in which the presence of the cocoa-palm, the breadfruit-tree, and an abundance of fish and shellfish entirely relieved them from the necessity of labouring for a living; a climate which makes little or no demand for houses or clothing, — all these conditions could not do otherwise than generate a certain ease of living and absence of care which are impediments to the development of a higher civilisation in the sense in which we conceive it in the case of a firmly settled continental people. In spite of this, the Polynesians, though they knew nothing of iron and were only slightly acquainted with other metals, display a remarkable ability, combined with artistic skill, in the manufacture of different implements, which capacity reaches its culminating point in the shipbuilding art. To this advanced condition of their seamanship we must finally trace back the expansion of the race over the whole immense breadth of the ocean. On the other hand we must not deny that a certain indeterminable, but on that account by no means inessential, share in this expansion must be ascribed to the incapacity of the Polynesians to resist successfully all the dangers of the open ocean.

It is, in fact, in the form of these involuntary migrations of its inhabitants that the Pacific Ocean plays so important a part in this remote domain of the history of mankind. In opposition to the view which traces back the Polynesian race to the island world of southeastern Asia, William Ellis asserts with conviction that America was the point of departure of the population of the Pacific island world. He denies that it is possible for the Polynesians to have originated from the west, since the prevailing winds and currents tend in this direction, and, apart from this, because common ethnographic features between the Polynesians and the aboriginal inhabitants of America are by no means wanting. Now it is true that within a small area winds and currents often exercise a considerable influence; on the wide expanse of the Pacific Ocean, however, they have long since ceased permanently to determine the distribution of mankind. On the contrary, we have actually a series of observations extending over several hundreds of years which lead to the conclusion that extended migrations, whether voluntary or otherwise, have on a large scale taken place in a direction contrary to that of the prevailing winds and currents. At the same time we must constantly bear in mind that sudden unexpected storms are at least as efficacious in driving the most expert sailor out of his course as the constant regular currents of air and water which the skill of the sailor is capable of conquering. Thus these involuntary voyages are by no means the exception, but rather the rule in the Pacific Ocean, traversing it in all directions and even leading beyond its boundaries, and thereby forming a means of connection between the islands themselves and the neighbouring continents.

Important to the ethnologist as is this phenomenon, — which in the course of thousands of years has extended a dense network from land to land, — it is equally so to the history of Polynesia, which is entirely taken up by the mutual relations of different groups and the fusion of races which has resulted therefrom. In the majority of cases, probably these unpremeditated voyages were the precursors of planned-out migrations which on the one hand led to the permanent settlement of new islands, and on the other were followed by the establishment of colonies in districts long previously occupied. This series of later migrations and colonisations forms, as Ratzel justly points out, the sole fact which indicates the stage of civilisation reached by the Stone Age. On this account it cannot be easily understood, since it is impossible to compare it with other achievements of a similar character. The area which was thus brought within the sphere of colonisation many times exceeds the empire of Alexander the Great or of the Roman Emperors. In the sphere of territorial domination it represents the greatest achievement before the discovery of America.

Intimately connected with the abundant intercourse of which the Pacific has been the scene from times immemorial stands the fact that nowhere has it supplied time or space for the development of an independent civilisation. Neither the immense island of New Guinea, with its thinly scattered, idle population, nor the still more remote New Zealand, has been capable of becoming the centre of a new civilisation; to say nothing of the other innumerable smaller islands. Only a few isolated elements within the domain of civilisation have under specially favourable circumstances been able to undergo an independent development. Apart from this the Pacific Ocean presents merely variations of one and the same fundamental theme. In this the absence of a real political formation or State structure is constantly repeated; it was only in the Hawaiian islands that, at the time of their discovery by Europeans, three States existed. which afterward, under the native king Kamehameha, united into a single State. In all other cases the community or society, even when under monarchical sway, was limited to a single island, and hence remained quite insignificant in extent and influence. In all the larger islands, such as New Guinea and New Zealand, we fail to find even the slightest trace of a centralised political organisation.

Hence there can scarcely be a question of a real history of Oceania before its discovery. Nevertheless we ought not on that account to speak of the Polynesians as a people without a history; for tradition plays no small part in their social life. They have also an idea of chronology, in which the Creation forms the basis or starting-point; in the absence of written signs they make use of notched sticks, the so-called "history-rods," as aids for remembering names and periods of time. As one might expect, these traditions sometimes go back to a very remote past. At Nukahiwa, in the Marquesas Archipelago, eighty-eight generations are said to have been established, which would mean a period of about twenty-five hundred years; at Rarotonga the more modest number of thirty generations is claimed; and the Maori of New Zealand limit themselves to twenty. On the other hand the Hawaian king Kamehameha claimed a descent in direct line from a series of sixty-six generations of ancestors. Of course no real historical value can be attached to legends of this kind; but they nevertheless give evidence of a strongly rooted feeling of autochthonous descent, which must have originated in a fairly long period of residence on the soil, and accordingly been preceded by a certain degree of civilisation. Apart from this, according to generally accepted views, the civilisation of Polynesia had, at the time of its discovery, sunk to a very low level as compared with the development it had reached in earlier times.

### C. AMERICA

To the question whether the conditions of national life in the Pacific were affected by influences emanating from the eastern shores of the American continent, it is difficult to give a decisive answer either in the negative or in the affirmative. In the dissemination of the Mongoloid race over the continents of the northern hemisphere, America, according to the prevalent view, seems to have played the part of receiver, — that is, the movement took place in a direction from Asia to America; while the view of a reflux current in the opposite direction can with difficulty be accepted. On the other hand some of the island groups of the Pacific display so much analogy with the northwest of America in their flora and fauna, as well as in the ethnological characters of their population, that the idea of a causal connection between the two regions easily suggests itself; while on the contrary there is no lack of theories according to which the Polynesian population of the Pacific must be traced back to North America, nor of others which, instead of a single former movement in one direction, assume several movements in either direction, and which, in Ratzel's words, "would substitute for the artificial theory of a former single migration and of a simple descent, the idea of a diffusion and stratification of the different races *inter se*." However, no such influence on the part of America is discernible in historic times, and hence, from our standpoint, we are justified in regarding America as the passively receptive, not as the actively radiating or disseminating element.

We have already pointed out [1] the obstacles which stand in the way of the existence of any mutual relations between the west coast of America and the Pacific Ocean. Even if America was originally populated from the latter, the gate of entrance was afterward closed for a long time, or may be, indeed, for ever; for the voyages of the Chinese and Japanese to the opposite coast are based on mere conjecture. Native American civilisation, however, took a decidedly continental course, and did not take at all kindly to the sea, even in places where — as in that great Mediterranean Sea of America, the Gulf of Mexico and the Caribbean Sea — the natural conditions were most favourable to a seafaring life. It is only the American aboriginal peoples of the extreme north and south who have formed an exception to this rule; they, however, were too much subjected to the numbing influences of the Arctic and Antarctic zones to be able to acquire a historical importance. The oldest American semi-civilised aborigines — who, though they have left to posterity magnificent monuments,[2] have not handed down even the knowledge of their names — dwelt in the interior of the northern continent; the highly civilised Maya, of Yucatan, who were even acquainted with writing, scarcely spread beyond the neighbouring Antilles;[3] the later civilised races, whose appearance may be to some extent determined chronologically, such as the Toltecs [4] since the sixth and the Aztecs [5] since the thirteenth century before Christ, were almost exclusively restricted to the elevated plains of Mexico and Central America. Even the later Inca empire of Peru, though washed for some part of its extent by the waves of the Pacific Ocean, preserved its continental character;[6] for, although Peru-

---

[1] See *ante*, p. 571.
[2] See Plate at p. 218.
[3] *Ante*, pp. 226, 228-231, 234, 255, 238-241, 248.

[4] *Ante*, pp. 225, 251-253, 265, 268.
[5] *Ant.*, pp. 224, 225, 268-270, 276-279.
[6] See *ante*, p. 343.

vian annals record voyages along the coast [1] and even more extended sea voyages for purposes of conquest [2] or discovery, and though Pizarro fell in with ships of merchandise, we have no historical evidence to show that these voyages ever extended to the vast watery desert which in this region is entirely void of islands. The American race was in fact wanting in that mysterious innate impulse which urged the Malays onward of their own accord toward unknown horizons, and which regarded the ocean, not as the natural limit or the insuperable obstacle, but rather as the inviting road to unlimited expansion.

## D. General Survey

A COMPREHENSIVE historical glance at the immense border-regions of the Pacific Ocean enables us to recognise the commencement of a period in which its historical formative influence has for its basis, as it were, the human race itself; a period which may be described as the typically continental period. Both the border regions and the island areas are now occupied. All the energies of their inhabitants, however, are centred upon their own internal organisation and development, and there is an almost complete absence of mutual relations; even the knowledge of their existence in the case of widely separated areas vanishes completely from the memory of men. The various populations have now for the most part come to occupy their final dwelling-places, and their chief aim is to maintain themselves in the possession of them. At the same time, in the case of the coast-dwelling peoples, the impulse toward further expansion becomes extinct; while in the case of ocean-dwelling tribes expansion becomes restricted to small areas, and hence ceases to have any influence on the course of historical events. From the moment when the fleets of China and Japan disappear from the Pacific Ocean, the latter once more becomes a mere watery waste, and though a certain amount of national life is developed within its midst, this remains centred entirely within itself, and, being unable to radiate outward in any direction, ends by collapsing upon itself. On the other hand the great eastern edge of the ocean remains in a condition of dumb, inactive quiescence, forming a frontier wall between two different worlds without concerning itself about either: a world existing entirely for itself, in which "continentalism" attains such grand proportions that it consumes its own creations before they have reached maturity.

Thus we see how the civilised nations of eastern Asia gradually succumb politically, socially, and intellectually to a rigid paralysing formalism; how the States of America, soon discarding the sea, consume and early exhaust their energies in the struggle with a somewhat chary nature; how finally they and the natural populations of Polynesia and Australia lose touch with the rest of mankind and relapse into the condition of isolated, degenerating units. During all this time the centre of gravity of the real evolution of mankind has gradually shifted westward to the sea around which the continents of the Old World are grouped, — the Mediterranean. The further elucidation of the important part which this sea has played in history has been reserved for another portion of this work; [3] it has formed, if not the cradle, at any rate the playground of that portion of the human race which afterward came to excel all others, if not in numbers, at any rate in its

---

[1] *Ante*, pp. 303, 307, 341, 342.   [2] See *ante*, p. 330.   [3] Vol. IV. p. 1 et *seq.*

imperishable creative force.   From it too has emanated, in the shape of the white
race, the force which roused the Pacific Ocean to a new life from its state of historic oblivion.   That ocean, forming as it does an immense world in itself, has
never attempted to become acquainted with its neighbours; to its seafaring peoples
Bering Strait, Cape Horn, and the South Cape of Tasmania have always been the
uttermost limits, rarely reached and never exceeded.   Hence its introduction into
the general intercourse of the world had to proceed from without.   This task was
reserved to the white race, which even in ancient times and in the Middle Ages
had sought a road to it with slowness and hesitation, but toward the advent of
modern times with swifter and bolder strides.


## 3.  MODERN TIMES

THE first impulse to the enormous expansion of the white race through navigation undoubtedly originated from the Mediterranean.   The prosperity which its
seafaring nations derived from the profitable commerce of the East impelled the
western Europeans of the Atlantic coast to emulate their example and to seek
unknown sea roads to the far East; for it was only by such roads that that region
was accessible to Europeans.   The idea of an overland route across the gigantic
continent of Asia seems to have been allowed to drop; that it was not feasible
had been amply demonstrated by many fruitless attempts dating from the time
of Alexander the Great down to that of Frederic Barbarossa and Louis the Saint.
Moreover Asia was still, at irregular intervals, pouring forth its devastating hordes
toward the West, as in the Great Mongol invasion which as recently as the
eighteenth century inundated eastern Europe.   Of course a small continent like
Europe, with its comparatively small populations, could not cope by land with the
enormous populations of Asia.   Hence, since a road to the East had to be found
somehow or other, it could only be by sea.


### A.  OPENING UP OF THE PACIFIC BY THE ROMANCE NATIONS

THE history of geographical discoveries does not fall within the scope of this
work; it will therefore suffice to mention that the immediate object in the search
for a direct sea-route from western Europe to India was the rediscovery of the two
countries Cathay and Zipangu, which had vanished from the intellectual horizon,
but which were thought to be, as it were, neighbours of India, and whose existence
had been proved by Marco Polo.   The later and wider aims were merely the
gradual outcome of the enormous and quite unexpected extent of the original discoveries.   In the natural order of things the first attempts, undertaken chiefly by
the Portuguese, were made in an easterly direction ; their most important result
was the circumnavigation of the Cape of Good Hope, accomplished in 1486 by
Bartolomeo Diaz.   Almost about the same time, however, the conception of the
spherical shape of the earth, which was rapidly gaining ground, led to similar enterprises being undertaken in a westerly direction also.   It was in the pursuit
of such attempts that Christopher Columbus discovered the Bahamas and Antilles
for Spain in 1492, and John Cabot the North American continent for England in
1494.   Both discoverers imagined themselves to have really found the east

coast of Asia, a belief in which they persisted to the end of their lives.[1] Nor did Pedralvarez Cabral, who in 1500, while attempting to reach India by an eastern route, was driven by a western drift current to the coast of Brazil, recognise the importance of this discovery. He in fact believed it to be an island of no special attraction, and, altering his course, made haste to return with all speed to the coast of Africa. For shortly before 1497–1498 Vasco da Gama had succeeded, by rounding the Cape of Good Hope, in reaching India, being the first European navigator who had done so, and in forming there connections of the utmost advantage to his native country, Portugal. Inspired by this success, so important in a practical sense, the Portuguese now exclusively turned their attention to the route discovered by Vasco da Gama.

On the other hand the Spaniards, who on their side pursued farther the road first mapped out by Columbus, soon became convinced that the countries discovered in the west could not be part of Asia. Driven by a passionate longing for the gold which had been found during the early explorations, they followed the westward-pointing track of the yellow metal, and soon obtained from the natives of Central America the knowledge of the existence of that "other sea" on the coasts of which gold was to be found in superabundance. In the search for the precious metal, Nuñez de Balboa crossed the Cordilleras of the Isthmus of Panama and was the first European who from their heights set eyes on the Pacific Ocean, September 25, 1513. He applied to it the name of the "South Sea" and took possession of its coasts in the name of the king of Spain. This event forms an important landmark in history. Henceforth the newly discovered continental area was recognised as a portion of a large and independent continent. Further, the existence of the greatest ocean of the earth was made known and turned to advantage. The still existing civilised States of the New World were annihilated and extinguished almost at one blow, and the development of the human populations of the western hemisphere was thus turned into an entirely new channel. Finally, this discovery also led to a fundamental change in the political structure of the civilised States of the western hemisphere.

The discovery of the Pacific Ocean by Europeans had, in the first place, a double effect. First, it led to a definite general knowledge of the true shape and size of the earth; a knowledge which has had immense results in the domains of civilisation, commerce, and politics. In the next place it led up directly to the incredibly rapid conquest of the Pacific coasts by Spain. The lamentable helplessness with which the densely populated and civilised native States of Central and South America fell to pieces before the onslaught of a few hundreds of European adventurers, like the Aztec Empire of Mexico before the small band of Cortes, and the Empire of the Incas in Peru before Pizarro, remains one of the most remarkable phenomena in history.[2]

The discovery of an unexplored ocean separated from the Atlantic by the whole length of the American continent led to a series of zealous endeavours to find the connection between these two great masses of water. It was of importance to the Spaniards, first of all, who had been anticipated by the Portuguese in reaching India by the eastern route, not to be misled by the obstacle which had unexpectedly barred their course to the west. It was soon recognised that Central America,

---

[1] *Ante*, p. 358.         [2] See *ante*, p. 345.

which had been the first portion of the continent they had become acquainted with, possessed no strait connecting the two oceans; hence the problem for solution was to find one elsewhere. In the hope of discovering such a passage farther south, voyages of exploration were made along the eastern coast of Brazil, and in 1515 Diaz de Solis advanced as far as the mouth of the La Plata, where, however, he met with his death.

In 1520 Ferdinand Magalhães (or Magellan), a Portuguese in the Spanish service,[1] succeeded in discovering the strait called after his name, between the South American continent and Tierra del Fuego. Through this strait he entered the Pacific Ocean, in which he at once vigorously pursued his course. After a voyage of more than three months Magellan reached the Ladrones, and, later on, the Philippine Islands; and though he was not fated to enjoy the triumph of a successful return, he at all events is incontestably entitled to the distinction of being the first navigator and the first European who traversed the Pacific along its entire breadth. Magellan's companions continued the voyage after the death of their leader, and reached the Moluccas. Here, on the island of Tidor, they fell in with Portuguese who had previously arrived there by the opposite route, and who were not a little astonished to see white men arriving from the east. Here, then, two advance columns, which had set out from opposite directions, for the first time joined hands. It was here that the great girdle of knowledge which had been laid round the earth was made complete, and thus European energy and intelligence achieved in the course of some decades a result which the aboriginal inhabitants of the Pacific Ocean had never attained for as many thousands of years. Within a short time the whole Pacific and the Pacific coasts of America were discovered. California was reached even before the middle of the sixteenth century, and as early as 1527 a regular navigation route was established between the coasts of Mexico and the far distant Moluccas.

In the meantime the Portuguese also had advanced farther eastward from the Indian Ocean. This advance, however, was of a quite different character from the conquest of America by the Spaniards. The Portuguese did not make their appearance in India as "Conquistadores;" in fact, such would have scarcely been possible when we take into account the much more ancient and advanced civilisation of that country, its well-established political system, and the greater density and numbers of its population. They accordingly did not indulge the ambition of subjecting the newly discovered territories and adding them as provinces to their own small and remote empire, but contented themselves with establishing trading-stations on the coasts and with acquiring and fortifying for the protection of the latter several points on the coast as well as maintaining in constant readiness a capable fleet of warships. In other respects the sphere of Portuguese colonisation falls chiefly within the region of the Indian Ocean. The latter, however, served, after all, merely as a first step toward its greater neighbour, inasmuch as the Portuguese extended their explorations from the Indian Ocean more and more toward the east as far as the coasts of China, where they founded settlements, and to Japan, which they reached by accident in 1543.

For exactly one hundred years Japan was opened up to the outer world: a period forming but a small fraction in the history of the island empire, but one

[1] See *ante*, p. 362.

which was fraught with important consequences in the grouping and position of the European sea Powers. About the middle of the sixteenth century Japan began eagerly and zealously to open its gates to western civilisation and the teaching of Christianity; for three generations, however, it was the unwilling spectator of a jealous rivalry between Portugal and the Dutch, who had arrived in the country in the year 1600,—a contest rendered the more discreditable by the unscrupulous choice of the weapons with which it was carried on. This state of things the Japanese finally decided to terminate by what seemed to them the only possible solution, namely, by simply shutting their door in the face of the unruly strangers. By this step, which indeed is quite at variance with the character of its people, Japan for more than two centuries disappears completely from history, and ceases to exercise any influence whatever on the development of affairs on and upon the Pacific Ocean. This settled matters so far as the empire of the Mikado was concerned; but for Europeans they assumed an entirely different aspect.

## B. OPENING UP OF THE PACIFIC BY THE TEUTONIC RACES

IT is a remarkable phenomenon that the immense increase in power and wealth which the era of geographical discovery brought to Europeans fell much less to the share of the real discoverers than to others. The discoveries made between 1486 and the middle of the sixteenth century, with the sole exception of those of the two Cabots, were placed entirely to the political account of Spain and Portugal. Both these kingdoms suddenly came into possession of immense territories from which they drew undreamed-of wealth and treasure. The populations of these territories — at least of those in America — became the pliant and feeble tools of their conquerors. In spite of this none of these acquisitions brought any blessings with them, not even in the shape of an increase of political power. Thus Portugal, which during the sixteenth century had exhausted her national strength in distant India, fell a prey in 1580, with all her possessions, to her Spanish neighbour, and by the time she had shaken off the Spanish yoke in 1640 and had regained her national independence her most important possessions in the East were lost, and she fell back once more into the insignificant position of one of the small Powers. True, she still retained possession of the immense colony of Brazil, but even this did not render her capable of maintaining her former greatness. Spain, on her part, did not benefit by the opportunity. By an outrageous internal misgovernment, by a senseless exploitation of her colonies from without, she hampered all real progress and sowed the seeds of her own destruction. Colonies whose native populations are kept in a state of subjection are valued, in the strict sense of the word, merely as gold-mines; they withdraw from the mother country a number of its subjects who rush thither from lust of gain or love of adventure and are subsequently lost in the immense area of their new home; and finally they merely serve to multiply the number of vulnerable points in case of attack, without partaking in the defence of the mother country's possessions. It is, moreover, a curious and incomprehensible phenomenon that just at the time when the flag of Spain was waving over every ocean, her sea power was steadily on the decline.

The real fruits of geographical discovery, however, were to fall into the hands of those who had participated in the competition not with precipitate haste and with the sole object of enriching themselves suddenly and without effort, but with far-seeing deliberation and with silent but untiring efforts, — the Dutch and the English. The Dutch, a small people, subject to the powerful monarchy of Spain, had boldly risen against their political and religious oppressors, and, in spite of the enormous disproportion between their own resources and those of the suzerain Power, and chiefly on account of their excellence in seamanship, had carried out a successful resistance. They in part transferred the seat of war across the Indian Ocean, established themselves in the Hispano-Portuguese possessions, destroyed Portuguese influence in important localities, as they had done since 1600 in Japan, and gradually succeeded in getting the trade of India almost entirely into their own hands. But the activity of the English assumed still grander proportions.

At the time of the discovery of America, England had lost all her continental dominions with the exception of Calais, and found herself restricted to her island possessions; even her dominion over Ireland had at that time almost slipped from her grasp, and Scotland formed an independent kingdom. England possessed no territories outside of Europe, and she had fallen from her high rank as a great European Power, while outside of Europe her influence was virtually nil. It was at this time that the discoveries of the sea route to India and of America first turned the attention of this healthy and energetic people toward lands far distant; and the prudent sovereigns of the then reigning House of Tudor kept the eyes of their subjects fixed in this direction. The inborn love of this island nation for maritime adventure then, as if by magic, suddenly blossomed forth in luxurious growth and drove its people with irresistible force across the sea. It was not, however, merely for the quest of gold, as had been the case with Spain, that England entered upon the career of territorial exploration and colonisation, nor, like the Portuguese, with the object of making the profitable trade in spices a monopoly in their own hands, but with a nobler, more far-seeing purpose in which the overthrow of the newly found native populations and civilisations formed no part. Thus, from the moment when the existence of the Pacific Ocean was ascertained, it engaged the attention of the English. They quietly allowed the Spaniards and Portuguese to push forward their discoveries and conquests in the East and West Indies without, for the time being, entering into competition with them. On the other hand they concentrated their efforts upon finding a route into the Pacific Ocean unknown to the Spaniards and Portuguese, but available for themselves, toward establishing themselves in this route, and in this way spreading and developing their rule in, as it were, the opposite direction.

### C.   New Routes

The efforts of the English found a visible expression in the search for the Northwest Passage, which was pursued with an iron persistency and has proved of the utmost importance in history. That the newly discovered continent in the north was bounded by the sea, like that in the south, appeared beyond question; accordingly it was thought that there must exist a northern route leading from the Atlantic into the Pacific Ocean. Such a passage being situated nearer to England than any other, the problem was to find it. Though the attempts made in this direction did not at once lead to the expected result (nor indeed did it produce any result of practical value later on), they were nevertheless accompanied by effects of extraordinary significance. They acquired importance not only in a geographical sense, by leading to a true comprehension of the nature of the earth, but also in a political direction; for as a result of numerous enterprises the northern part of the American continent passed into the possession of England, which made much better use of it than the Spaniards had done of its central and southern portions.

The first reports of the success of Columbus had, as early as 1494, instigated John Cabot, a Portuguese in the English service, as well as his son Sebastian, to undertake a voyage by which even at that time they hoped to reach the land of Cathay, or China and the Spice Islands, by the shortest route, — that is, by a northwest passage. In the course of this voyage, however, they discovered the northern coast of the North American continent and took possession of it in the name of England. In a second voyage, undertaken in 1497, they enlarged the discoveries of their first expedition, and the same result was attained by a third voyage made by Sebastian Cabot alone in 1498. The actual search for the much-longed-for Northwest Passage was not, however, commenced until the year 1517, when the younger Cabot discovered Hudson Bay and very probably penetrated into Davis Strait to within the Arctic Circle.

The first attempt toward the solution of the problem was, however, soon forgotten in the beginning of the Reformation, which absorbed the entire attention of the English people. It was not until after the death, in 1547, of the royal theologian, Henry VIII, that the transmaritime movement was once more revived and attracted a much more general and lively interest than on the first occasion. Its special feature lay in the fact that the movement proceeded not so much from the State as from individuals and corporations, and that although it was favoured and supported by the government, it was neither initiated nor directed thereby; indeed up to the time of Queen Elizabeth (1558–1603) not even a royal navy existed. A few wealthy and influential and private individuals and merchant guilds fitted out, at their own cost, whole fleets which, according to circumstances, engaged in commerce or made voyages of exploration, or, on their own responsibility, sailed in quest of warlike adventures which in many instances had a strong savour of piracy.

At the beginning of this new period an expedition left England mainly for purposes of exploration; but with an object diametrically the opposite of the voyages which had been set on foot at the beginning of the century for the discovery of the Northwest Passage; for it was now proposed to discover the nearest route to China in an easterly direction and along the north coasts of Europe, or, in other words, to find a northeast passage which it was hoped by the English commercial world of that time would lead to a fresh development of their trade, then in a very depressed condition. On the 10th of May, 1553, Sir Hugh Willoughby sailed from London with this object; but neither his expedition nor those of later English navigators were successful in this sphere of exploration, in which they had to yield the palm to the more fortunate Dutch and Russians. Hence English explorers once more turned their attention to the Northwest Passage. Frobisher's voyage of discovery in 1576 was followed by a large number of others, those of Sir Walter Raleigh, Davis, Hudson, Bylot, Baffin, and others. Although from natural causes these expeditions did not attain the desired object, they nevertheless proved of infinite importance in considerably advancing the colonisation of North America, which had been begun by Sir Walter Raleigh in 1581. This was not a colonisation after the fashion of Spanish conquistadores or Portuguese spice-merchants, but a slow, gradual, tranquil, and thoughtful immigration of industrious, energetic, northern Europeans who did not go with the sole aim of rapidly gaining treasures, but in order to find a livelihood founded on enduring and arduous labour; who, while wresting the virgin soil from its native hunting population and bringing it under cultivation, became intimately attached to it, and thus laid the firm foundation of a political system which grew with surprising rapidity and was full of the hardiest energy.

Simultaneously with the bold explorers of North America a number of naval heroes left England in search of adventures, whose main object, however, was to inflict the greatest possible damage on the Spaniards, who were detested on account of political and religious antagonism, and thereby also to enrich themselves. Besides such names as Raleigh, Hawkins, Cavendish, and Howard, that of Francis Drake shines forth with special lustre. Drake combined the hero with the explorer. So great was his boldness that he was no longer satisfied with attacking the Atlantic possessions of Spain; indeed the West India islands and the coasts of the Gulf of Mexico had been already so much harassed by the English corsairs that the Spaniards in these possessions now kept a good lookout. On the coasts of Chile and Peru, on the other hand, they considered themselves perfectly secure and unassailable. Relying on their sense of security and consequent unguardedness, Drake, who was morally and materially supported by the Queen, at the end of 1577 left England with five ships, well equipped by himself, sailed through the Straits of Magellan, and, without encountering any resistance, commenced a private war with the Spaniards in the Pacific Ocean. He was entirely successful, and set out on his homeward voyage richly laden with spoil. He tried to turn the voyage to account by searching for the Northwest Passage from the Pacific Ocean, that is, in the reverse direction. However, after sailing along the west coast of America up to the forty-eighth degree of north latitude without finding a sign of the desired passage, he decided on the voyage across the ocean, and returned to England after having touched at the Moluccas and sailed around the Cape of Good Hope.

Drake's circumnavigation of the world, which had more or less the character of a warlike expedition, marks the first conscious and deliberate step on the part of England toward a policy of universal expansion and the sovereignty of the seas; a policy the surprising results of which not only produced a great change in the distribution of power in Europe, but also subsequently, and in a manner entirely unpremeditated, brought into the foreground a new and important factor in international life, — America. In this way, moreover, was laid the foundation of the predominancy of the white race over the whole globe. For the Pacific Ocean and its place in history generally, Drake's voyage had a special significance; for by it, at one stroke as it were, that ocean became the centre of public interest and the scene of the struggle for the sovereignty of the seas. Here was displayed for the first time in a striking manner the internal hollowness and weakness of the apparently gigantic strength of Spanish dominion; for, as seems only natural, numerous other piratical enterprises, not only English, but also Dutch, followed in Drake's successful track, and all of them with more or less impunity managed to harass and plunder the Spanish possessions and Spanish ships in the Pacific Ocean. True, the maritime war between England and Spain was not finally decided in European waters until 1588 (the destruction of the Armada), but we may safely assert that the issue was prepared by the events which took place in the Pacific Ocean, and that it was here that England found the key to her maritime supremacy.

## D. THE OPENING UP OF AUSTRALIA

ABOUT the year 1600 the third continent washed by the Pacific Ocean — Australia — also begins to rise from the mist which had hitherto enveloped it. Its discovery, however, at first attracted but little notice and had no immediate practical results. This was due to several causes: the natural features of the country were not very inviting, the climate was not favourable, and its native population was scanty and in a low grade of development. There was further a dearth of all desirable productions, and the coasts of the continent were difficult of access owing to the presence of barrier reefs. Meanwhile England had lost her American colonies, which now enter upon the stage of history as an independent political entity under the name of the United States of America; and besides this she was under the necessity of maintaining the deportation of criminals, who had formerly been sent to the American continent. She was thus obliged in the year 1788, nearly two hundred years after its discovery, to take possession of the Australian continent in earnest. This enforced settlement had, however, to yield to one of a voluntary character as soon as the real value of the formerly despised country became known. Immigrants now poured into the country and furnished ample proof that in Australia England had obtained an acquisition of extraordinary value. Owing to the fact that the new immigrants were almost exclusively of English nationality, the continent acquired a very homogeneous population, and England a colony which kept up very close ties with the mother country. Especially were those elements wanting which had driven the Americans into a political — indeed almost national — opposition to England. Accordingly the population of Australia has made this youngest of continents into a second antipodean edition of "Old England," a daughter land which furthers the policy of "Rule Britannia" on the Pacific Ocean with no less pride than her great prototype at home. In the colonisation of Australia its native aboriginal population is even of less import than the Indians in North America; politically it is of no account whatever, its scanty remnants having been forced back into the inhospitable interior parts of the continent.

Under the modest designation of "Colonies" five self-governing and mutually independent English States have come into existence on the Australian continent since its first settlement, — New South Wales, Victoria, Queensland, South Australia, and Western Australia, to which must be added the two island States of Tasmania and New Zealand. All these States possess their own administrations, their own parliaments, and all the other characteristics of self-government; to the mother country, apart from recognising the authority of the sovereign, they are united merely by the ties of a common nationality and common interests, but on that very account they form its strongest support. The most flourishing of these States, New South Wales and Victoria, are on the Pacific Ocean; together with the island States of Tasmania and New Zealand, and the numerous island groups of Polynesia, they provide for Britain's sea power so many safe points of support, such excellent stations for English commerce, and such sure markets for her exports, that in Great Britain's present position as a world Power they occupy a prominent place.   In addition to this, the inland States of Australia have developed into rich exporting countries, partly owing to the discovery of rich gold-fields in 1851, and still more through the immense development of the sheep, cattle, and horse-rearing industries, the presence of coal, and, at the end of the nineteenth century, the culture and exportation of wheat.   Being, moreover, self-governing States, they involve no expense to the mother country.   Thus they form a veritable sovereign State of England's empire of the sea in the western hemisphere, and by their geographical connection with the island world of the Pacific they bring the largest, most extensive, and, so to speak, cosmopolitan ocean of the earth within England's sphere of influence.   Their importance has been further enhanced since they have formed themselves into a federation of States, the "Commonwealth of Australia," which for the present has no higher aim than to foster with increased energy the British "Imperial idea."   For the acquisition of the Pacific Ocean by England, which was begun since Cook's discoveries, has not stopped at the Australian continent, but has been extended to numerous parts of Melanesia, Micronesia, and Polynesia.

## E. Partition of Territory

It is a remarkable fact that in their numerous voyages from the Mexican harbours to the Moluccas and Philippines, and, since 1565, in the opposite direction also, the Spaniards discovered so very few of the innumerable island groups which stud the intervening seas.   Even the few of the Archipelagoes they did discover — the Marshall, Bonin, Solomon, and Paumotu islands, and others — were not considered by them worth acquisition or colonisation; only the Mariana, Caroline, and Pelew groups were in course of time taken possession of or laid claim to in order to serve as points of support for their colonies in the Philippines.   The Portuguese and Dutch took still less interest in the acquisition of territory in the Pacific; they left that ocean entirely out of the sphere of their commercial policy, and in fact formed no settlements in it at all.   Thus it came about that during the voyages of the English and French in the latter third of the eighteenth century — those of Cook, Bougainville, La Pérouse, D'Entrecasteaux, and others — numerous island groups were discovered which were not yet occupied by Europeans and were therefore ownerless or unclaimed territory.   Of course the crews of the ships composing these expeditions were not sufficiently numerous to spare any of their men for the permanent occupation of these islands; but they were soon followed by compatriots in the shape of adventurers, explorers, merchants, and missionaries. Rapidly the islands of the South Sea, about whose inhabitants, products, and climate the most favourable reports were spread abroad, became centres of attraction for immigrants.   In this manner the white race, represented chiefly by Englishmen and Frenchmen, later also by North Americans and Germans, spread over the island world of the Pacific Ocean.   The English especially, who had just obtained a footing on the Australian continent, were in the vanguard of this movement. Besides settling in Tasmania and New Zealand, they also established themselves in Polynesia and Melanesia, and in the course of the present century have succeeded in acquiring a considerable portion of the Pacific island area.   The French, too, have secured for themselves a considerable portion, more especially in the

Polynesian groups, as well as New Caledonia. Later on, the North Americans also entered into the competition, and since 1885 the German empire, by the adoption of a vigorous colonial policy, has also acquired possessions in Melanesia and Micronesia.

Nor must we omit to mention here another European Power which, although it did not participate in the division of the Pacific island area, nevertheless, by a vigorous advance toward the ocean, early entered upon a path by which it gradually developed into one of the most powerful and determinant factors in modern history, namely, Russia. Recognising that its strength existed in its continental character, the mighty Slav empire by degrees withdrew from the ocean; it sold Alaska and the Aleutian islands to America, and exchanged the Kuriles for the pseudo-island of Sachalin; but on the other hand it has cleverly managed to extend its zone of contact with the ocean by a series of brilliant moves, vitally important to its own interests, toward the south. The ice-bound fields of the Sea of Okhotsk and Bering Sea may be possessions not to be despised, but what is their value when compared with a stretch of coast like that of the shore of the "coast province," and of Leao-Tong, with a position which dominates the sea, — possessions that render the empire of the Czar the uncontested sovereign of eastern Asia?

### *F*. Destiny of the Polynesian Races and the Problems Confronting the Immigrant Population

THE occupation of the whole expanse of the Pacific by the white race requires, like the advance of Russia to the shores of that ocean, to be regarded from a higher vantage-ground. It is, in fact, more than a political event; it is a fact of the utmost importance in universal history, an energetic step forward on the road which seems to have for its final goal the reunification of the divided human race, an issue not to be controlled by and scarcely patent to human consciousness, but one which is regarded by many as inevitable. Nowhere on the earth has this levelling influence of the white race operated more energetically than in Oceania, but of course always at the expense of the aboriginal population.

The Polynesian race, which was already in every sense on the downward grade before it came in contact with the white race, has displayed very little power of resistance to the latter. The distinct racial types of the native population did not in this case, as probably in North America, succumb to forcible expulsion or suppression, but rather to a subtle kind of decay. In general, the Polynesians showed themselves very accessible to "white" influences; they approached the white immigrants sympathetically, adopted with ease their manners and customs and their modes of life and thought; but in the acquisition of these foreign elements their own original structure became undermined. Wherever the influx of white elements is strong enough, mixed races are produced with great rapidity, and in these the white influence is always the determinative factor. Thus in New Zealand the pure native Maoris are fast approaching extinction; and the Sandwich Islands are nothing more than an appendage of the North American Union. On the other hand, where this influx is not sufficient to produce a rapid anthropological transformation, the native element is injured by a mere superficial contact with European culture or by what we may rather call its shady side. Men who as naked savages have led a true amphibious life, half on land, half on sea, die off prematurely when turned into civilised Christians.   The racial gaps thus formed, however, by the mixed breeding of races are being filled more and more determinately by the influx of white races, and here again, by their introduction of a higher civilisation, the course of events appears to tend toward the ultimate unification of the human race.   To be sure, the prospect is not an altogether pleasing one; nevertheless it has this advantage over the earlier condition, that it causes new life to sprout forth from the ruins of a decrepit world.

The white race, though it forms the determinative factor, does not, however, stand alone in this filling up of the gaps of defunct Pacific populations.   Side by side with it the yellow race is engaged in a similar task.   Of course, the motives from which the Chinese set out in this process are fundamentally different from those of Europeans and North Americans, and consequently their effect, too, is widely different; nevertheless, to a certain extent at least, the latter has a similar tendency in both cases.

It is neither love of adventure, lust for gain, nor political or scientific interests which drive the Chinaman to seek a home in foreign countries, but mainly the difficulty of obtaining a living in his own over-populated empire.   According to natural laws the efflux of this surplus population takes place in the direction of least resistance; but since Japan, till very recently, was closed to foreigners, while both divisions of India were themselves suffering from over-population, and the large islands of the Indian Ocean were very soon satiated with Chinese, the stream of Chinese emigration overflowed to Australia, America, and the island world which stretches between these two continents.   These latter, owing to the great disproportion between their extent and population, seemed specially adapted for receiving it.

Nevertheless, even there, the "yellow" invasion did not meet with a very welcome reception.   Nor is this a matter for surprise.   First, we have to deal with the apparently unbridgeable gulf which exists between the white and yellow races.   Neither the white man nor the Chinaman considers himself as the one the absolute superior of the other, — in the way, that is, that both look on themselves in relation to all other native races; but they recognise and fear each other as formidable rivals, without being able (owing to a total difference in mental outlook) to find some common ground of agreement.   Fear without respect is the character of their mutual relations, combined with a repugnance reaching almost to disgust of the one nature toward the other which prevents any direct intermixture of the two races, and consequently removes the most effectual means toward the levelling of racial differences.   In addition to this the Chinaman is a dangerous industrial opponent to the white man, whom he excels as an indefatigable, unpretentious, and at the same time intelligent workman, thereby lowering the value of white labour and depreciating wages.   Accordingly the policy of Australia and America is directed toward the prevention of Chinese immigration by all possible means, as much from the subjective standpoint of justifiable self-defence as from an inborn instinct.   We must not, however, shut our eyes to the fact that the Chinaman might put forward the same claims on his side — if he had the power.   It is therefore with the white race a simple question of self-help in the hard struggle for existence.   When we consider the profound differences of the forces brought into play in the contact of the spheres of expansion of the yellow and white races on and upon the Pacific Ocean, a final solution of this difficult problem must appear still very remote.

On the other hand it becomes more and more evident that the part which the island world shut in by the Pacific Ocean has played in the shaping of the history of the world is not yet concluded, but on the contrary, is destined to produce even greater effects in the future. The island groups of Polynesia, Micronesia, and Melanesia, in which new half-caste populations are being developed from the intermixture of white men and Polynesians, seem adapted for intercepting such part of the Chinese stream of emigration as is not mainly directed to the gold-fields of Australia and North America; and it is probable that, owing to the extensive subdivision which of necessity goes on in these localities, this portion may become absorbed in the other racial elements. Undoubtedly in these islands the Chinese element will find means of directly influencing the ethnographical transformation which is already in progress, by infusing into the mixed race now in process of formation some portion or other of its own physical and mental characteristics. In this way a link may and will be created fitted for bringing these sharply contrasted masses closer together and likely by degrees to smooth down their sharp angles; a nucleus, so to speak, which will gather around itself, at first sparsely and scantily, but later in increasing numbers and density, anthropological strata of yellow, white, brown, and black, which will subsequently, in various ways, become interfused. Transitional forms of this kind are, it is true, of only questionable value, especially during the period of their development; but they have nevertheless a great significance in ethnography and history, inasmuch as they present a natural counterpoise to the decay of similar large masses of population. Moreover, in new formations of this kind, one or other of the constituent elements usually comes to the front as a determinant factor, and finally tends to bring about a certain amount of enlightenment. The means and conditions of intercourse of the present time especially tend to further this process much more than the actual migrations of the past or the inrush of invading warrior hordes. Finally, modern oceanic intercourse may be looked upon as specially promoting this tendency toward race-amalgamation; for by means of a frequent and regular navigation from which the element of danger is almost eliminated, it brings the various ethnographical members in their most subdivided condition permanently into contact, and within numerous small areas provides them with the opportunity for becoming intimately fused with each other.

## G. The Part Played by America

THE eastern margin of the Pacific — the American continent — seems specially designed for co-operating in this gradual work of unification. This view will probably meet with as little favor in the United States as will the suggestion that that country, still exuberant in its youthful strength, can expect to exercise its influence for ever. It looks, in fact, as if America were the continent which, after being for a long time inhabited by a single race, is suddenly about to collect all races upon its soil. We have no more striking proof of the force of oceanic influence and the historical importance of navigation.

The mutual relations of the different races of America toward each other are very variable. The Indians of Central and South America, who led a settled, agricultural, and (according to their lights) civilised kind of life in States of their own formation, were naturally unable to withdraw themselves from the influences of the white man to the same extent as the nomad hunting populations of North America and the wild tribes of the South. The civilised Indians suffered the consequences of subjection, and hence furnished rich material for the formation of mixed races. The hunting and primitive races, on the other hand, avoided all contact with the white man except in a hostile sense; they have accordingly suffered annihilation in the unequal combat, and have had to leave their settlements in the hands of those who have supplanted them. The whites in their turn, especially in the tropical zone, have shown themselves neither willing nor able to bear the heavy burden of bodily labour on their own shoulders, and have therefore fastened it upon those of the subjected races. Where the latter were not present in sufficient abundance, or where their physical strength was not equal to the performance of the hard tasks demanded of them, other means of obtaining the necessary relief were resorted to. The institution of negro slavery in America forms one of the saddest chapters in the otherwise brilliant history of the white race; and though the nineteenth century may rest with the consciousness of having removed this shameful institution from the New World, and of having thus — at least partially — atoned for the sins of its fathers, this does not furnish any justification for letting pride at this act of civilisation banish our feeling of shame for the old moral wrong.

As things are to-day, America forms the centre whither stream the surplus populations of all the continents. It cannot resist this tide of immigration, inasmuch as there is still plenty of space for its reception. "In this crucible," says Friedrich Ratzel, "all the different races of mankind will become intermingled; there will, of course, be cases of retrogression or 'throwing back' in this process, but bastard races, when they are preponderant, have a considerable advantage over pure races." At the time of its discovery by Europeans, America was inhabited by a single race about whose numbers we have no information; but they certainly cannot have been very great. The densely populated Indian States of Central and South America formed mere oases within unpopulated deserts. At the present day, of its 100,000,000 inhabitants, 60,000,000 belong to the white race, 10,000,000 to the black, 9,000,000 to the red, 200,000 to the yellow, and some 20,000,000 to different mixed races. In this calculation are comprised the negro half-castes, to whom the pure negroes, however, are as one to four. Since this considerably increases the total of the mixed races, we may assume that about a fourth of the total population of America consists of mixed races. Now every pure race can furnish the material for the formation of a mixed race, while the reverse is impossible; farther, every mixed race, in the gradual crumbling away of neighbouring races, grows at their expense by absorbing the fragments. From these considerations it would appear that America is likely, in the near future, to be the scene of a great and general fusion of races.

## *H.* Part Played by the Civilised Nations of Eastern Asia

WHILE the eastern margin of the Pacific basin appears in a state of active fermentation pregnant with events, its western margin also is being aroused into fresh activity. We have already remarked on the appearance on the Pacific coasts of Asia of the greatest continental Power in the world; we have seen how Australia has become an excellent point of support to the greatest naval Power; we are daily watching the interesting efforts at colonisation made by France, the United States, and, above all, by the German Empire. It is therefore of special importance to consider the peculiar attitude assumed by the ancient civilised nations, the hereditary possessors of eastern Asia, toward the successful invasion of the Pacific by the white race, which has now become a matter of history. In Japan, about the middle of the nineteenth century, a complete revolution was effected with surprising suddenness. The throwing open of the country — effected, it is true, by compulsion from without — and the fall of the ancient feudal system, which reached its summit in the Shogun dignity, led to a complete and rapidly executed *volte-face* among the Japanese, who now proved themselves even more accessible to the influence of the white race than they did three hundred years before; though on the present occasion this influence did not operate in the domain of ethics, but concerned itself with material progress and the remodelling of the government. Since that time the Japanese — or at least the influential classes among them — have been seized with a veritable passion for adopting all the institutions and customs of the white nations, even to the extent of imitating their external appearance in dress. That they have been apt pupils was shown in 1894, in the war with China, when, by their energetic attack on land and sea, they thoroughly conquered a State infinitely superior to themselves in both size and population. This war at one stroke placed Japan in the ranks of the naval Powers, and, indeed, of the great Powers; and it has thereby afforded to Europe and America a very notable proof of being possessed of a very efficient fighting-machine and of knowing how to give effective force to its political claims.

The conditions are different in China. There, in spite of the multiplication of points of contact, we meet as yet with little comprehension of, and response to, European methods. Its people is still too strongly imbued with the consciousness of its own superiority; it clings too much to the unchangeable ideas and customs of thousands of years ago; and these have become so thoroughly ingrained that it could not possibly, without further ado, adopt a new course, like the more versatile Japanese. On the contrary, it opposes to the invasion of the white race the mechanical obstacles of its immense superiority in number and density of population; and, more than this, it meets this invasion by an expansion on its own side, which, in spite of its apparently pacific character, forms, for the very reason of its being unavoidable, an extremely menacing factor. The waves of Chinese emigration radiate in all directions, but farthest to the side of least resistance, that is, across the Pacific Ocean. Here will of necessity be performed the first act of the inevitable struggle between the white and yellow races, — a struggle viewed with much dread and fraught with much danger from the standpoint of ethnological history.

The beginnings of Chinese expansion thus coincide with the moment when the white race is closing up the net which it has stretched over the whole earth, partly in the form of its geographical distribution, partly in the form of a political and intellectual leadership. But it must not, therefore, be assumed that there is any internal connection between these two phenomena. The result of their coincidence, at all events, remains the same; it means, in fact, that the centre of gravity of human interest, and accordingly of universal history, is visibly shifting from the hemisphere which has hitherto enjoyed the preference to the opposite hemisphere. However great a part in the history of States and nations may yet be reserved for the continents of the Old World, he who regards the unification of the human race as the highest problem of universal history must seek for the solution now in its birth-throes on the shores of the Pacific Ocean. In the perception of this fact lies the key to a true comprehension of the importance of that ocean in the history of mankind.

## 4. RETROSPECT

THUS, if we cast a final backward glance over the Pacific, it appears at first as an element of separation and differentiation, assigning local limits to the various divisions or branches of the human race and providing them with the opportunity of accentuating and perpetuating peculiarities of type. Since this task has been completed, the ocean, slowly and gradually reversing its purpose, is destroying its own work, and tends in the opposite direction as an element of union, thus presenting us with a true image of the eternal circulating stream of Nature. The same glance reveals to us yellow, red, brown, and black races settling upon the coasts and islands of the ocean, stretching their limbs and extending themselves, supplanting or tolerating one another; soon, however, arriving at a certain pause from which only the yellow races emerge, owing to their great numbers and multiplying powers, while the rest degenerate in every direction. Finally, after many centuries of rest, — a period of historical somnolence, so to speak, — we behold the white races breaking in upon the ocean simultaneously from two directions, and in their impetuous manner, like a whirlwind, throwing all obstacles into a heap. Within the space of a few centuries — a short period in the whole span of history — the native Polynesian, the American Indian, and the aboriginal Australian have either been driven into an insignificant corner, where they are rapidly approaching extinction, or their individuality of type has been dissolved; that is, by constant intermixture of blood, they have developed into bastard or mongrel races in which — at least intellectually — the white element preponderates. It is only the yellow race, which, unassailable in its closed ranks, successfully resists the general subversion, asserts its old possessions, and even aims at making acquisitions of its own in the domain of ethnography.

Accordingly at the present day we see only two important elements as natural antagonists upon the shores of the Pacific, each prepared and ready for the fray: they are the ancient indigenous yellow race and the newly arrived white race. Both are ably and well represented: the yellow by the Japanese and Chinese, the white by the English and North American, with whom are associated, as aggressors from the seaward side, the French and Germans; while Russia, from the continent, is both ready and willing to attack on the flank. After several decades spent in skirmishing manœuvres, the struggle at the close of the nineteenth century entered upon a more serious stage. As has so often happened in history, a quarrel between brothers has provided an opportunity for the interference of a third party; and though Japan, after emerging victoriously from the fratricidal struggle, appears for the immediate future to have strengthened and ensured her position, we must not forget that the fruits of the victory have fallen, not to the conqueror, but to the European Powers, and in particular to Russia. Thereby the front of attack in the great racial struggle is still further enlarged: by the side of China, passive and exposed to every attack, we now have Japan roused to increased alacrity and energy and more than ever ready for the contest. And the contest on this occasion will not be directed against its kindred, nor, in its innermost essence, will it be one of a political nature, nay, rather, it will have to decide whether, by the permanent occupation of the northern Pacific, the white race shall accomplish its world-embracing destiny, or whether, with the goal already in sight, and for the first time in its history, it will have to make way for a stronger. True, as political ally in this struggle, China is undoubtedly not to be reckoned on; but as a fellow combatant in the sphere of industry and ethnography her assistance to Japan will be of inestimable value. For, indifferent to the fate of its native land, the Chinese stream of migration, uncontrollable and irresistible, will pour into the countries bordering on the coasts of the Pacific and into its islands, until the population becomes one of yellow blood. Then will take place that mighty damming up of the racial tide in which the various elements of population most easily and intimately permeate one another.

# INDEX

# INDEX

Lightning Source UK Ltd.
Milton Keynes UK
UKHW030638030521
383048UK00009B/767